Publications
Of
The Colonial Society of Massachusetts

Volume LXIX

The Eighteenth-Century Records of the Boston Overseers of the Poor

The Eighteenth-Century Records of the Boston Overseers of the Poor

EDITORS

Eric Nellis
The University of British Columbia

Anne Decker Cecere

BOSTON   THE COLONIAL SOCIETY OF MASSACHUSETTS   2007
Distributed by the University of Virginia Press

CONTENTS

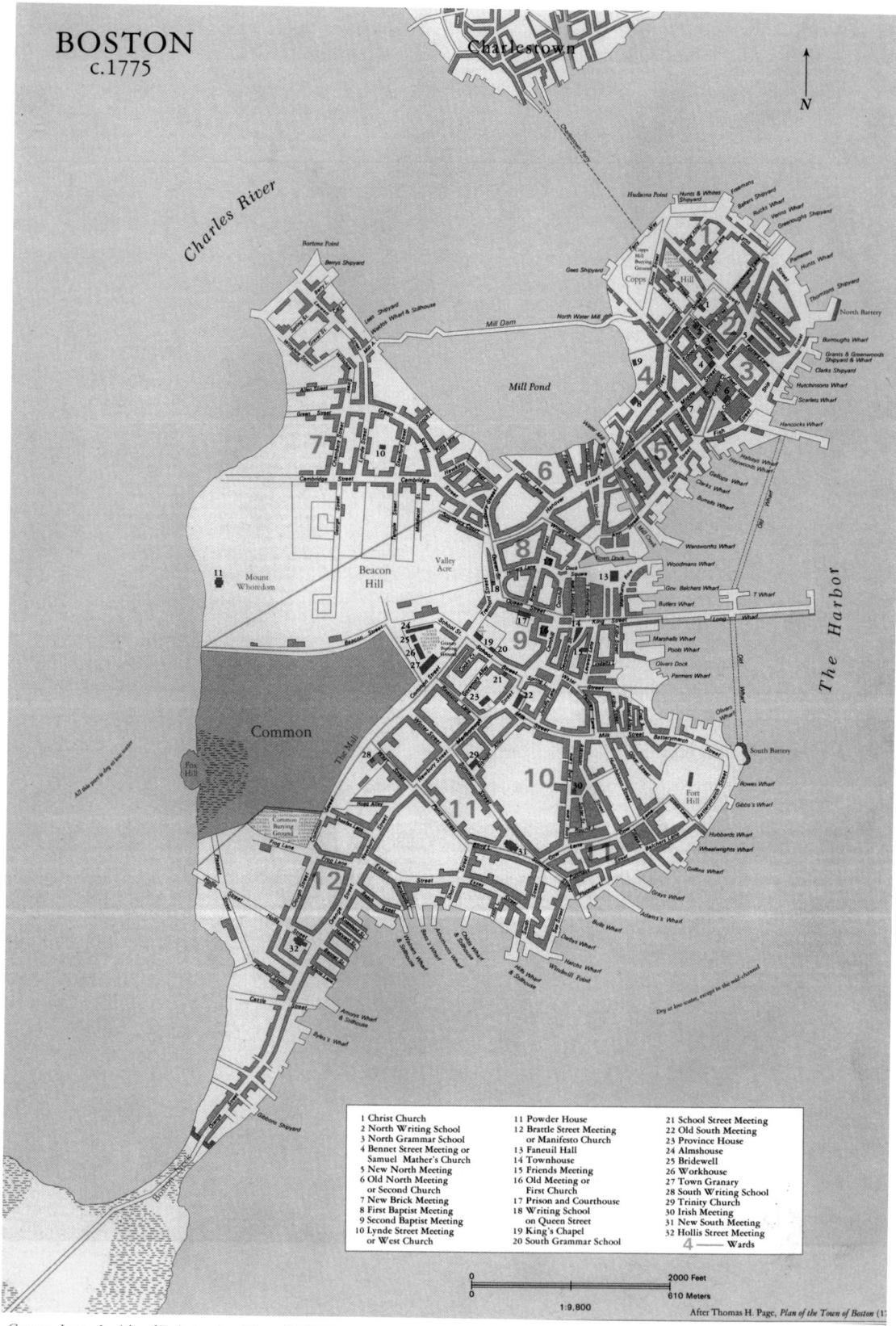

BOSTON
c.1775

Charlestown

N

Charles River

The Harbor

Mill Pond

Mill Dam

Beacon Hill

Mount Whoredom

Valley Acre

Common

The Mall

Fox Hill

Fort Hill

Copps Hill

1 Christ Church
2 North Writing School
3 North Grammar School
4 Bennet Street Meeting or
  Samuel Mather's Church
5 New North Meeting
6 Old North Meeting
  or Second Church
7 New Brick Meeting
8 First Baptist Meeting
9 Second Baptist Meeting
10 Lynde Street Meeting
   or West Church

11 Powder House
12 Brattle Street Meeting
   or Manifesto Church
13 Faneuil Hall
14 Townhouse
15 Friends Meeting
16 Old Meeting or
   First Church
17 Prison and Courthouse
18 Writing School
   on Queen Street
19 King's Chapel
20 South Grammar School

21 School Street Meeting
22 Old South Meeting
23 Province House
24 Almshouse
25 Bridewell
26 Workhouse
27 Town Granary
28 South Writing School
29 Trinity Church
30 Irish Meeting
31 New South Meeting
32 Hollis Street Meeting
4 —— Wards

0   2000 Feet
0   610 Meters
1:9,800

After Thomas H. Page, *Plan of the Town of Boston* (1

Cappon, Lester J.; *Atlas of Early American History* ©1976 Princeton University Press, 2004 renewed PUP. Reprinted by permission of Princeton University Press.

8

ACKNOWLEDGEMENT

This long and complex project benefited from the support of many agencies and individuals. The Professional Development Fund and Grants in Aid Fund at Okanagan University College (now the University of British Columbia-Okanagan) provided travel and other expenses, and the Arts Colloquium at Okanagan ran two seminars on the material. The encouragement and friendship of my colleagues in the History Department at Okanagan made the delays in the completion of the manuscript less problematic than they might have been. Special thanks are due to the members of the Pacific Northwest Early Americanists Workshop for their advice on the Introduction. The staff of the Massachusetts Historical Society helped with the detailed work on this project at every turn and my connection with that institution is one my professional pleasures. My wife, Vicky McAulay, was with the project from its inception and read every version of the text, notes, appendices and chapter headings and helped make the text clearer. Anne Cecere's superb collations of the transcribed documents clearly add luster to the volume. The Colonial Society of Massachusetts is to be applauded for funding this important project and for seeing it through. Finally, we are all especially indebted to Editor of Publications John Tyler for his industry, expertise and good will. His patience with this project and his commitment to scholarship are the reasons this volume is in print.

ERIC NELLIS
Boston and Vancouver, 2005

FOREWORD

When Frederick S. Allis became editor of publications of the Colonial Society following the death of Walter Muir Whitehill in 1978, there were eleven different manuscripts (in varying states of readiness) awaiting publication. Some had already been set in galleys, some were found in the back of desk drawers, and some were little more than an idea that had received Whitehill's magisterial blessing. Fritz Allis spent a good part of his twelve years as editor working down this backlog; of the fourteen titles published by Allis, only three were projects he had been able to approve at their inception: *Law in Colonial Massachusetts, 1630–1800, Seventeenth Century New England,* and *The Glorious Revolution in Massachusetts, 1689–1692.*

By contrast, in 1990 when ill health made it necessary for Fritz Allis to retire, I inherited only two projects already underway: *Shays's Rebellion: the Bicentennial of an Agrarian Revolution* and the Society's Centennial Hand Book, eventually published in 1992. This left the Publications Committee (at that time, William M. Fowler Jr., chairman; Frederick D. Ballou, the Society's peerless Treasurer; Malcolm Freiberg; Harley Peirce Holden; and Conrad Edick Wright) the very pleasant task of casting about for things to do. In a paper given at a recent conference at the Massachusetts Historical Society, fellow member Thomas O'Connor had called attention to the institutional records of the Boston Overseers of the Poor as a rich resource for the city's nineteenth-century social history. What more appropriate project for the Colonial Society could there be than to make the *eighteenth*-century records of this group more widely available to scholars? There was a particular aptness to the project, since Stephen T. Riley, a longtime vice-president of the Colonial Society, had, while serving as director of the Massachusetts Historical Society, retrieved these records from Boston's City Hall just shortly before they were thrown in the trash.

All that remained to be resolved was the not insignificant question of who would do the work? Who would transcribe the records from the original eighteenth-century handwriting and who could set these invaluable records in their appropriate historical context? At that point, I recalled Eric Nellis, whom I met long ago working at a nearby table at the Massachusetts Historical Society reading room when I was doing research for my dissertation on Boston merchants in the Revolutionary period. It was Nellis who explained to me William Molineux's efforts to revive the town Linen Manufactory during the political turmoil of the non-importation movement. No one understood eighteenth-century Boston's efforts at public charity better. In the intervening years, Nellis had written a number of well-regarded articles on poverty and labor in colonial New England. He was a natural choice.

Once the invitation was extended, Eric accepted with alacrity, although I think it safe to say that none of us at the time understood just how extensive the project would be or how long it would take. We came close to publishing the work in 1997, even going so far as to assign it a volume number and listing it in the University of Virginia Press fall catalogue, but then we became leery of the accuracy of our transcription. Robert Dunkle, who had done much similar work for the New England Historic Genealogical Society, was brought in to help with a new transcription, and Anne Decker Cecere came on board as Assistant Editor of the Colonial Society. During her time as Assistant Editor, nearly all of Anne's attention was devoted to this manuscript. Those who have not seen the original documents will have difficulty understanding how painstaking a process it was to collate the transcription with the originals. Different clerks working for the Overseers had different ways of recording information, as well as different ways of spelling the same names. The financial records imposed a need for special care to make sure the long lists of pounds, shillings and pence were all accurately transcribed and added up. Only someone with Anne's diligence, care, and attention to detail could have brought the project successfully through to its conclusion.

The manuscript records of the Boston Overseers of the Poor, which the Massachusetts Historical Society obtained from the City of Boston in 1957, cover the period 1735–1925 and run to eighty-five volumes. Most of the original boards were lost along with the titles and descriptions of most of the contents. The manuscripts were subsequently microfilmed in 15 reels as part of the MHS program of document preservation. In 1988 the MHS produced a Guide to the microfilmed and catalogued manuscripts. The eighteenth-century records represent approximately ten per cent of the entire collection, or at least ten per cent of what survives. The only parts of the eighteenth-century records not transcribed are the Warning Out Lists (which would have nearly doubled the size of this volume) and the Workhouse pay lists, which are both summarized in the Introduction; the Lists of Overseers, which appears as an appendix, was independently produced for this volume. Two documents that are not part of the collection are included as significant parts of the Overseers records: the 1756 Almshouse Census (in the Boston Public Library), and Samuel Whitwell's Accounts (in the MHS). Every effort has been made to retain the integrity of the originals and to present them in a logical order. The introduction, notes, appendices, and commentary are by Eric Nellis. Eric Nellis and Anne Decker Cecere edited the material for presentation in its final form.

JOHN W. TYLER
Editor of Publications

Abbreviations

The following abbreviations have been used throughout to identify the most frequently used references.

Acts and Resolves — *The Acts and Resolves, Public and Private of the Province of the Massachusetts Bay. . . .* 21 vols. (Boston, 1869–1922).

Boston Records — *Reports of the Record Commissioners of the City of Boston.* 39 vols. (Boston, 1876–1909).

Boston Town Papers — Manuscript records at Boston Public Library, Special Collections.

"Guide" — "Boston Overseers of the Poor Records, 1735–1925: Guide to the Manuscript Collection." (Boston: Massachusetts Historical Society, 1988).

MHS — Massachusetts Historical Society, Boston.

NEQ — *New England Quarterly.*

Overseers — The manuscript records of the Boston Overseers of the Poor. See "Guide" above.

Quincy Report — Josiah Quincy Jr. *Report of the Committee on the Pauper Laws of This Commonwealth.* (Boston, 1821).

Shattuck — Lemuel Shattuck. *Report to the Committee of the City Council to Obtain the Census for the year 1845.* (Boston, 1846).

Towner — Lawrence Towner. "The Indentures of Boston's Poor Apprentices, 1734–1805," Colonial Society of Massachusetts, *Publications* (1956–63): 417–68.

Wiberley — Stephen E. Wiberley Jr. "Four Cities: Public Poor Relief in Urban America, 1700–1775." (PhD diss., Yale University, 1975).

WMQ — *William and Mary Quarterly*, Third Series.

Chronology

⌣

1632	Space was assigned to a "beadle" for a prison in Boston.
1639	Legal provisions were established for care of the deserving poor, correction of the idle poor, and warning out of nonresidents.
1660	A major private bequest was given to build Boston's first free-standing public Almshouse.
1662	Boston's first Almshouse was in operation.
1682	That Almshouse was destroyed by fire.
1686	A new brick Almshouse was built at the northwest corner of the Common.
1690/91	The Boston Town Meeting selected its first Overseers of the Poor (four were chosen).
1692	The General Court of Massachusetts established the legal status of the office.
1704	The General Court defined "the poor" as those on alms and those not rated for taxes.
1713	The Boston Town Meeting approved a ward system based on earlier militia and fire-watch precincts.
1723	A freestanding prison (Bridewell) was opened near the Almshouse.
1735/36	The ward system was fixed at 12 with one Overseer assigned to each ward.
1738/39	The first freestanding Workhouse (separate from the Almshouse) was occupied.
1739	New warning out law. Transients could claim residency if not ordered out within three months.
1742	Renovation and expansion of the 1686 Almshouse.
1772	The Overseers were incorporated as an exclusive public arbiter of private bequests.
1793 and 1794	The Overseers' 1692 authority was renewed with modifications. The same laws effectively ended the practice of warning out.
1795	Almshouse, Bridewell and Workhouse properties were sold for redevelopment.
1801	The new Bulfinch-built Almshouse opened at Barton's Point. It doubled the capacity of the older Almshouse.
1821	Josiah Quincy Jr's *Report…on the Pauper Laws…* called for the reform of public poor relief, including an end to "outdoor" (that is, at home) relief.
1822	Boston received a city charter that required elected councilors and an elected mayor in place of selectmen. This meant an effective end

to the Town Meeting as the local authority. The House of Industry was built to replace the 1801 Almshouse, and combine Almshouse and Workhouse functions. The Overseers were excluded from its management by 1825.

1823   Josiah Quincy was elected Boston's second mayor and waged a campaign to end outdoor relief and curtail the Overseers' authority. As a result, the city government authorized a different system of the management of public poor relief that began to reduce the Overseers' roles to clerical functions.

INTRODUCTION

DURING THE EIGHTEENTH CENTURY the Boston Overseers of the Poor comprised a panel of private citizens appointed by the Boston Town Meeting to supervise public aid to the needy. By helping to define the policies and conduct of poor relief, the Overseers became a major force in public affairs in eighteenth-century Boston. The Overseers' historical significance lies in their legacy as shapers of a public institutional approach to poor relief. Their records, which open a window on the social history of pre-industrial Boston, chronicle an extraordinary example of institutional continuity through several generations of social and political change. They allow us to observe the influence of English institutional traditions and practices on the settlement of Massachusetts, as well as the way those practices were adapted to Boston's particular conditions and development. These pages reveal the formal yet intimate relations that existed between the guardians of civil order and public charity and the thousands of poor and needy people who came under their purview.

The Overseers were an institutional force whose persistence was a mirror of the overall stability of public authority. Their records suggest a broader reexamination of cultural, economic, and social change in eighteenth-century Boston and of the short-term consequences of the Revolution. Moreover, the Overseers stand as a useful example of the cultural intentions of earlier Puritan communal and civic values and the blending over time of Puritan charitable intentions and the eventual public responsibility for and management of the poor of Boston. This introduction summarizes the context, richness, and meaning of the documentary record.

The Historical Setting: the Boston Poor and the Records of the Overseers

The poor always ye have with you.

JOHN 12:8

EVEN AS THEY DEPLORED THE PRESENCE of the poor in their midst, the founders of Puritan Massachusetts and their successors accepted the inevitability of material as well as spiritual poverty even in their own godly and idealized communities. John Winthrop's ringing 1630 manifesto for the New England Zion and its "modell of Christian Charity" found it axiomatic that "God almightie in his most holy and wise providence hath soe disposed of the Condition of Mankinde, as in all times some must be rich some poore, some highe and eminent in power and dignitie; others meane and in subjeccion."[1] Poverty thus was ordained by the higher power, and that explained its inevitability even in the most dedicated Christian communities.

And just as the poor are always with us, so too must there be efforts to ease their condition, rehabilitate them, and even punish them. Poverty was accepted as part of the corporate polity because, as Winthrop noted, all classes were bound together in the Puritan mission, and "Mankinde" was "knitt together ... as one man" in the making of a reformed Christian community in New England. The community in that case had a mandate to regulate good order, including the care and correction of the poor. Winthrop and the founders knew that to appeal simply to individual responsibility would not prevent poverty, nor would appeals for private relief of the "meane" and "poore" succeed in expunging poverty, even in the most prosperous of times. Christian charity, whether it came from individual moral obligation, or on behalf of the community's collective self-interest, could at best only ease the burden of poverty on the poor for the sake of a more general order. Still, Winthrop's "Christian Charity" was largely a reflection of the civic culture he had just left and so dovetailed with the objectives and administration of the Elizabethan poor laws.[2]

The Massachusetts Bay Company adopted an institutional approach to the treatment of the poor that corresponded to Tudor ideas and models of local government. While Winthrop insisted that his fellow Congregationalists translate their Christian sentiments into a personal obligation to care for the poor, he also saw the need for a set of largely secular offices to administer those intentions. Those original models came to determine the philosophy and administration of relief and control of the poor from the founding of Boston in 1630 until at least the early decades of the nineteenth-century. It also meant that even in the most "Christian Commonwealth," Massachusetts, civil law would be made by civil authority and administered by elected lay officials.[3] Indeed, one of the earliest manifestations of civil control was the establishment of a prison and a "beadle" in 1632 in Boston.[4] As to the question of who was therefore responsible for the relief of the poor, the answer then was the poor themselves if they were able-bodied and the community or the state if they were not. That question has lingered into the twenty-first century in America, and for the most part has solicited similar answers to the problem of poverty.[5]

For Winthrop's generation, though, the community had first to specify in law what constituted poverty itself, and then determine who were poor and how they had come to be so. There was certainly a colloquial understanding of poverty and an empirical definition of the poor as those who were conspicuously needy and dependent. But a formal definition in law and by government was necessary so the community could fit its collective material means to its social and moral objectives. In Massachusetts any method of poor relief, care, and correction had to suit the colony's circumstances while drawing on the traditional Tudor experience and concepts of legal poor relief. But there was an immediate modification, because the scale of poverty in New England was negligible by Old World standards. If "the poor comprised the majority of the population in the late seventeenth century" in old England, that was certainly not the case in contemporaneous New England.[6]

One of the most cited, reliable, and respected sources of statistical evidence of poverty in early modern England is Gregory King's 1688 census. His simple division of economic society into two large groups, those "increasing" and those "decreasing the wealth of the kingdom," has logic as a model when applied to England in the late seventeenth century and, by extension, the rest of Great Britain by the eighteenth century. The 51 percent of Gregory King's census who decreased the wealth of the nation were the "poor," so defined because they drew on some portion of the nation's wealth through alms for some or all of their lives. There is no statistical comparison for that level of poor relief in New England, nor is there a useful socioeconomic basis for comparison. Yet while Massachusetts' lawmakers borrowed or extended familiar patterns of government from England they could not and did not replicate the conditions for their application.[7]

As New England's founders routinely adopted English statute law and imitated local custom where they could, they created a great many regulatory offices. These were as much a reflection of English standards of civil administration as they were of Puritan moral principle and were, in fact, a product of a general modernization and wider rationalization of public authority and its approaches to poor relief. The General Court's legal creation of the Boston Overseers of the Poor in 1692 was meant to specify functions that had been done earlier by Selectmen, and the new Massachusetts Charter of 1692, the local authority responsible for control of the poor and poor relief generally, was not significantly different in intent from the older Bay Colony laws. But Massachusetts had adopted the main mechanisms of Tudor-Stuart poor law at a time when the regulation of poor relief, and notions of public responsibility for and authority over the poor were, in fact, evolving in England itself through major changes in economic values and conditions and in government. As the general institutional apparatus was being entrenched by the Massachusetts Bay Company in the seventeenth century, it was in flux in England and as the Massachusetts poor law maintained much of its original principle, it became less English and more American over time.[8]

Meanwhile, in England, as Gertrude Himmelfarb writes, "the rise of Puritanism… coincided with the introduction of a national, legal, compulsory public system of relief, the first such in modern history." In fact, since the beginning of the Reformation, and especially under Elizabeth, the development of statute poor law in England had led to a shift away from voluntary help, including the older ecclesiastical determination of who was deserving and who was not, to a more formal and even secular definition and the compulsory funding of the needs of the deserving poor. Indeed, when it came to sorting out the deserving from the undeserving poor (the latter were often lumped by the law simply among the "rogues, beggars and vagabonds"), the use of statute law was indispensable throughout much of Western Europe, especially in England and Scotland. The origins of public poor relief in New England were consistent with that development; that much is certain. But then, as Himmelfarb goes on to say, the ethic of poor relief in England was not immune to profound changes in the English economy. By the end of the eighteenth century the poor laws of England had been influenced not only by industrialization and the laws of the market but also by the successive and sometimes successively revisionist theories of William Petty, John Locke, Daniel Defoe, Bernard Mandeville, Adam Smith, Thomas Malthus, and others. Himmelfarb's larger point is that the effects of economic change on the poor, and on the way the poor became central to how society saw itself after about 1750, influenced subsequent and significant changes in the poor laws of England.[9]

So, as much as English precedents and experience were vital to the underlying views of poverty everywhere in seventeenth-century English America, the somewhat divergent social and economic paths of colonial development led to different histories of public poor relief. Because New England did not develop as Himmelfarb's old England did, the way the dependent poor were treated in Boston in the seventeenth and especially the eighteenth centuries tells us a great deal about that society as it describes the distinctiveness of public charity and public welfare in preindustrial Massachusetts. In Boston, to the end of the eighteenth century, the Overseers of the Poor managed their office through a series of political and economic crises with scant change in their basic understanding of what poor relief meant—so scant, in fact, that the powers granted the Overseers in the Poor Relief Act of 1794 strongly resembled those granted in the act that had established the office in 1692 (see appendixes 1 and 2).

As early as 1639 the General Court had bestowed on local magistrates the responsibility to care for the deserving poor, and the arbitrary power to warn out transients and force the idle to work. As with similar kinds of legislation, the act was more an attempted replication of English statute than Calvinist orthodoxy. Even the name "Overseers of the Poor" derives from the English Poor Law of 1598. In at least one New England colony, Rhode Island, an office of Overseers of the Poor had been established as early as 1647 by simply adopting the Elizabethan codes intact. The English precedents that had provided broad guidelines for the orderly settlement of New England had included the famous Elizabethan Poor Laws of 1572 and 1601. Those statutes remained in force on paper in England until the reforms of 1834, but had been greatly modified in practice and had been effectively rescinded in 1795 by the Speenhamland system, which effectively subsidized the wages of the working or deserving poor and diminished the institutional approach to almsgiving, as opposed to workhouse or poorhouse correction for the idle poor. In the two centuries between Elizabeth and Speenhamland there had likely been more change in England's poor law administration than in New England's. Moreover, the continuous role of the Church of England in poor relief, at the Parliamentary as well as at the parish level, has no parallel in New England. The main influences of the Tudor laws on New England practices had been the move from voluntary to compulsory support of the poor and the assumption of local civic responsibility for financial and administrative control.[10] In Massachusetts the Overseers emerged from an act of the General Court in 1692 (see appendix 1) under the terms of the new charter on what appears to have been the advice of the Town Meeting of Boston, which had elected its first such Overseers in 1690/91. The General Court legislation covered all "town offices," but it specified separate authority for the Overseers and granted that office considerable executive authority.[11]

The Historical Setting

What follows, then, is a review of the documentary record of the most comprehensive public approach to the relief of poverty in colonial and revolutionary America. It is drawn largely from the several hundred pages of manuscript records generated by the Boston Overseers of the Poor during the period 1735–1800. Although the Overseers had operated from 1692, the 1735 date marks the earliest surviving manuscript of their record keeping (a manuscript copy of the "The Boston Workhouse Act" which had been authorized to be built), and any history of the Overseers prior to 1735 has to be drawn from town, legislative, and court records.[12] A major legislative reaffirmation of the Overseers' authority in 1793–94 serves as evidence of a consistent system of bureaucracy that began in the Puritan Commonwealth and ran through the inclusion of Massachusets in the new republic without major substantive change to the office (see appendixes 1 and 2). The transcriptions take the documentary record to 1800 to complete the eighteenth-century setting for this volume.

As Boston matured, so did its public welfare bureaucracy. Its organization was streamlined and its authority expanded and tightened. The original board of Overseers had consisted of only four members. In 1713 Boston had developed a system of eight wards, based on militia divisions and placed under the control of the Overseers and constables. In 1735/6 (old style calendar) the town was divided into twelve wards, with one Overseer assigned to each ward. This change was part of an overhaul of the Overseers' charter that specified rules for their own and their charges' behavior and fixed their number at twelve.[13] The Overseers were more than simply a part of a growing civic bureaucracy, however, for with the exception of the Selectmen, they were from the start the most powerful of civic officials. Although they were drawn mostly from Boston's merchant class, the best explanation for the Overseers' effectiveness, social status, and sense of civic duty notwithstanding, was that they possessed a legislated authority that matched their responsibilities. The legislation of 1692 and 1735, in particular, had conferred something akin to unilateral power, and that power was confirmed by the Commonwealth of Massachusets in 1794 with a mandate that would survive into the first decades of the nineteenth century. As punctilious as they were energetic, the Overseers met monthly as a group and as often as weekly in committee to discuss budgetary requisitions and disbursements. They also dealt with problems of transiency, health, and crime and with the status of the standing institutions under their control, including the employment of clerks and keepers. They petitioned the Town Meeting with requests and advice and contributed to town planning issues in concert with the Selectmen and in the full forum of the Town Meeting. No social history of Boston is complete without a serious consideration of them.[14]

But it was at the individual and neighborhood level, as virtual ward supervisors, that the Overseers' role was most conspicuous and influential. Each Overseer personally distributed in-home relief to residents in his ward, and with the collaboration of a Selectman, each Overseer had the direct authority to "send in" to the Almshouse or the Workhouse anyone who was deemed to require institutional relief or correction. They regularly patrolled their wards and removed children from homes where the standard of living or behavior appeared to them to threaten the child's potential as a stable and worthy citizen. They instructed constables to identify newcomers and beggars and could warn out "strangers" at will, although in the end, the actual removal of persons without settlement rights had to be ordered by a county court at the request of the Overseers (see appendix 3). In a manner that required some pomp, they conducted annual perambulations through their respective wards with Selectmen and other dignitaries in train as a demonstration of civic authority.[15]

By the end of the eighteenth century the Overseers had become a public agency of remarkable authority and influence. They had become sovereign in the private as well as public management of poor relief in Boston, to the point where a 1772 General Court "Act of Incorporation" had given them primary control over the distribution of all individual charitable donations for relief of the poor (see appendix 5). Even after its heyday, that is, after Boston's incorporation as a city in 1822, and as an increasingly marginalized branch of the new Boston city government, the office of the Overseers survived to the 1920s, by which time its role had been reduced to being executors of trusts of various charitable organizations.

The entire Overseers manuscript record is vast, and the transcriptions included in the present volume constitute only about 10 percent of the total volume of the documentation. But the eighteenth-century records are notable among surviving early American public welfare records because they identify several thousand individuals by name, and many by age and condition. The otherwise statistical poor of preindustrial Boston are thereby personalized in a way that enlivens the relationship between the poor and their public supervisors. The former included entire families, those who were entitled to "settlement" in Boston and those who appear to have been from "abroad," and orphans, single mothers, petty criminals, vagrants, transients, and the infirm. They all came under the purview of the Overseers.

Although the Overseers distributed public and some private funds and materials to "outdoor" relief, the bulk of their records are concerned with the administration of "indoor" relief, usually in the Boston Almshouse, or punishment or "correction" for the "undeserving" poor in the Boston Workhouse. The terminology here is ironic, in that "outdoor" meant "in home," and "indoor" relief referred to that given usually in a public facility such as the Almshouse. The records also note the warning out of thousands of transients and the relocation of orphans and illegitimate children. The Overseers moved into the community's affairs at almost every level as a conspicuous feature of daily life in the intimate world of the eighteenth-century seaport. Their records allow us the only means to measure the numerical extent of indoor poor relief in the second half of the eighteenth century. The scale of institutional poverty is succinctly noted in the number of Almshouse admissions, which ranged between 125 and 250 persons a year, with considerable variation at different times because of economic conditions and the disruptions of wars, including the Revolutionary War. Another 30 to 50 were admitted annually to the Workhouse. On average another 300 a year were wholly or partially supported by outdoor relief. The total of number of admissions to the Almshouse was always higher than the actual number of individuals. There were repeaters, and some persons were admitted and discharged several times in the course of a year as their circumstances fluctuated. The same was true of outdoor relief recipients whose fortunes might seesaw from month to month. Still, given that Boston's population for most of this period ranged from 13,000 to 17,000 people, the publicly supported poor amounted usually to about 4 percent of the total population.[16]

The way poverty was dealt with mirrored the corporate ethic of Boston. From 1630 to 1692 poor relief had been the direct responsibility of the Town Meeting in concert with the Selectmen. As noted, after 1692 the Overseers of the Poor became the official authority for poor relief. Neither the ecclesiastical authorities, during their period of unalloyed civic supremacy, nor the General Court, even in its superior legislative role, interfered much in the management of poor relief. Also, not only was the responsibility for the dependent poor of Boston a mostly public affair, but any privately volunteered charity prior to the Revolution was very narrowly applied. Its object was more the augmentation of means for the temporarily poor than it was to relieve the most persistent, disruptive, or aggravated kinds of poverty. In fact, it is clear that what we now consider private and voluntary charity did not have a significant role in poor relief until shortly after the Revolution, when for a brief period its incidence increased in scale and scope throughout New England.[17] Also, private charity was extended only to the "deserving poor." Care for the habitually idle, the "undeserving" poor, was openly and lawfully corrective or punitive in its end in a way that private charity could not be. The original Winthrop imperative meant that all the poor, everywhere in Massachusetts, were entitled to public support, but if the impotent poor were to be "relieved" of their distresses, then the indigent poor were to be ordered, persuaded, and even forced to be "brought up in some honest calling, profitable unto themselves and the publick" (see appendixes 1 and 4).

In the village atmosphere of Boston in its first few decades, all poor relief had been "outdoor" relief until the latter third of the seventeenth century. And not only were the deserving and "settled" poor cared for, but cultural norms forbade the community to stand by and allow even the most unsavory in their midst, even "strangers," to suffer or perish from want. During Boston's first generation even "worthy beggars" were supervised and nourished by volunteer families at public expense, or if absolutely necessary, were kept in the small prison that had existed in Boston from as early as 1637. A freestanding Almshouse for "indoor" relief of the "aged and infirm poor" had been proposed at various times, but there appeared to be no need for one until after midcentury. When private bequests were used to build one in 1662, a pattern of expectation was laid down: private funds could be solicited for capital funding for poor relief, but the funds for annual maintenance of the poor would come from public finances. The major contributors to the construction costs of that Almshouse included Robert Keayne, a successful merchant whose conscience had been so pricked by the smear of usury that he sought spiritual relief by writing a confessional and willing his assets to the public weal, including the relief of the poor.[18]

When the 1662 Almshouse was finally occupied in 1665, its occupants were kept at public charge. Then, in 1682, like so many Boston buildings in the seventeenth and eighteenth centuries, it was destroyed by fire. By then, moreover, there was a compelling need for a permanent and more commodious structure, and a large two-story brick "house" was completed and occupied in 1686. It would stand for over a century. When the Overseers of the Poor were organized in 1691/2, the Almshouse also served as the Workhouse, and it would do so until 1739, when a separate facility was opened. At least to that time, Boston's Almshouse served as the single shelter for the orphans, widows, solitary aged, feeble-minded, and infirm of the town who required indoor relief, as well as for other destitutes, vagrants, misfits, petty thieves, and runaway servants. Convicted criminals, who were technically the charge of the county justice system, had been housed in the Almshouse until Bridewell, the town prison, was built between 1721 and 1723. Even then some criminals would be housed in the Workhouse from time to time because of overcrowding in Bridewell. The truly criminal were subject to a different regimen from those in care in the Almshouse or committed to corrective industry in the Workhouse. For example, in Bridewell "beside the master, there was to be a whipper constantly in attendance." Also, of the 50' by 20' by 14' building, a "little part of the house was given up for the insane."[19]

There was then a strict observance of the traditional distinction, defined by law, between the involuntary, and therefore deserving, and the voluntary, and therefore undeserving, poor, as well as a conscious separation of the criminal from the idler. A potential third type, what might be called the "working poor," was only occasionally referred to in Boston. In eighteenth-century England, on the other hand, the intent of legislation and the routine administration of the poor laws considered the entire laboring population as "the poor." Also, English typologies indicated that "rogues" and "vagabonds" were sufficiently numerous and sinister so as to be a direct threat to public order in ways that even the most wayward of "worthy beggars" in Boston did not. The need to police the poor in England, and the sheer potential for riot when a majority of the population strained at the limits of social order, extended the range and complexity of the English agencies, both public and private, that were authorized to supervise and relieve the poor.[20]

In Boston, by contrast, the sole administration of the poor law codes remained with the office of the Overseers of the Poor, even as the numbers of poor increased in the late seventeenth and early eighteenth centuries, as family and neighborly assistance declined in a more socially pluralistic Boston. At the point when relief and correction were fused administratively, all of New England diverged somewhat from most English practices. Poverty in Massachusetts was largely an "urban" phenomenon in any behavioral or statistical sense, and Boston's distinction was that one agency, a public one, supervised the deserving and undeserving poor, both in and out of doors.

There was considerable logic in Boston's approach. Of the major North American seaports—the only approximately "urban" Anglo-American societies in the eighteenth century—Boston's civic administration was the most centralized. In contrast to the patchwork of local authorities that existed in other colonies, local government in Massachusetts was concentrated in the town, which retained nominal legislative authority over all local government. In fact, the counties of Massachusetts were little more than a mechanism for organizing a tax assessment system and a centralized judicial process.[21] In Massachusetts, everything from assembly representation to rights of "settlement" residency was determined by the original Winthropian model of corporation. Everyone who had a right to be in Massachusetts also needed to "belong" to a town.[22]

The distinctive character of civic government in Massachusetts is important in the evolution of the Overseers as keepers of the poor and administrators of the poor laws. The Town Meeting and Selectmen system had developed so early in Boston's history that by the end of the first charter it was a consolidated public bureaucracy that regulated all civic affairs, originally on behalf of the first charter proprietors, the company, the governor, and the magistrates, but over time and especially after 1692, in the common public interest. While there had never been any pretense of natural egalitarianism in Puritan society, each individual was held in equal measure to be ultimately responsible for personal maintenance. In the early days of the company, much of the supervision of personal responsibility and poor relief had been assumed as an obligation by the "freemen," who then guided the colony's "servants" in their behavior. But as that class distinction melted away with the decline of direct church authority and the broadening of the terms of citizenship in the late seventeenth-century, not only civic status but also civic authority became more democratic.[23]

For the vast majority of towns in Massachusetts the supervision of the idle poor and other deviants would continue to be done by constables and courts under the advice of the Selectmen and often directly by the Selectmen themselves. Also, the clearly stated purpose of the agency in Boston was less charitable than administrative, and just as corrective as it was caring. The preemptive powers given to the Overseers were considerable, and the act enjoined them "to take effectual care that [the poor] not live idly" (appendix 1). A 1704 General Court act defined the poor arbitrarily and quite broadly as those on alms and those not rated for taxes.[24] The latter, in that case, cannot be seen as a permanent or even regular class of paupers, and the definition is clearly intended to assist the supervisory role of the Overseers as guardians of neighborhood harmony. There is no doubt that increasing population created a parallel growth in the numbers of paupers in Boston. But given the Town Meeting's historical penchant for creating offices, growth as much as anything else, along with a desire to relieve the Selectmen of increased work, had spurred the need for a special agency for supervising the poor and also tending to their needs and gradually to the needs of the old, the sick, and the infirm. The Overseers of the Poor were designed primarily to cope with the consequences of population concentration, and it was not until the late eighteenth-century that Overseers of the Poor appeared formally in the other large towns of Massachusetts.[25]

Also, levels of poverty did rise in Boston after the middle of the eighteenth-century, largely as a consequence of regional and imperial events. After every colonial war the town's economy slumped, and so each peace brought at least a short-term decline in the aggregate income of the town's working poor. King George's War, the

French and Indian War, and the War for Independence created considerable residential dislocation, especially in coastal New England. The Overseers responded to each crisis by stepping up enforcement of the residency qualifications as their primary instrument of control. Since 1700 the Overseers had secured increased funding from the General Court for the support of those who could not be warned out in the short term or who, once warned, could not be immediately removed. The Overseers' records indicate that the great majority of those migrants who were warned out, because they were both poor and unsponsored, were kept on the "province charge," or after 1780 on the "state charge," and were not simply punished by being placed in the Workhouse. The Overseers were keen to keep the costs of Almshouse care under control. In concert with the Selectmen and the Town Meeting they kept precise accounts of the jurisdictions that were responsible for the care of the poor in the Almshouse. This was a crucial part of their administration because in the 1760s and again in the early 1780s for example, transients made up some two-thirds of the Almshouse population and had to be charged to the province or state.[26]

As bureaucrats, the Overseers produced prodigious records of their proceedings and accounts, of their appeals for funds, and their routine reports to the Selectmen and the Town Meeting. While the eighteenth-century records kept exclusively by the Overseers are incomplete, they do contain rich statistical detail for certain periods, such as the early 1760s and the 1780s and 1790s, and for certain kinds of entries, such as Almshouse admissions. As a composite, the body of records can be broken down into six major components that parallel the Overseers' major responsibilities and activities. The first component comprises the annual lists of elected Overseers that are summarized in this volume as an appendix. The second, the Overseers' accounts, contains financial records for the Almshouse and Workhouse, and here and there for outdoor grants of money or materials; most of these records appear to have been kept by the Overseers themselves, or the Almshouse keepers, or by professional scriveners and accounting clerks. A third category consists of the records of orphans and the many other poor children who were taken from their parents and bound out by indenture; these records complement the full-indenture manuscripts that Lawrence Towner classified and published over forty years ago in his essay "The Indentures of Boston's Poor Apprentices, 1734–1805." A fourth category is a miscellany of fragmentary Almshouse births, deaths, and residents' inventories. The fifth category, the Almshouse admissions and discharges lists, is the largest and in many respects the most important component of the records. Finally, the manuscript collection includes the warning-out lists, which identify the names, origins, and ultimate destinations of the huge numbers of migrants who ended up in Boston. The size of the so-called warned lists demonstrates the rising levels of transiency in late eighteenth-century New England and in the wider interrelated Anglo-American Atlantic world. There may be as many as eight thousand names in the lists of "warned" in the Overseers collection, and the sheer volume of the record is too great for inclusion here. Also, warning out was not a formal responsibility of the Overseers, and of those who were warned out of Boston not all were in fact poor. The practice of warning out derived from the very complex laws governing rights of residency. Even solvent migrants with sponsors who could not satisfy a battery of conditions could not simply take up residency as they pleased. Medieval custom, written into law, land availability, and ethnic, religious, and personality issues could be used as reasons for warning out.[27]

The records are characterized by the idiosyncratic habits of a succession of Almshouse keepers, assistants, and clerks. Some recorded the ages of all who were admitted to the Almshouse but not their discharge dates. Others included not only the discharge dates but also the obituaries of those who died in the Almshouse. Any clerk might indicate the ages of the Almshouse charges for several weeks' entries and then abandon that form of notation. There are sequences of entries that were obviously written after the fact in categorical and even alphabetical order by trained scriveners or perhaps by Overseers themselves. One or two constants are worth noting, however, and those include the apparent recording of the names of all Almshouse inhabitants, as they were admitted, and the names of the Overseers who ordered them in or who otherwise consented to a Selectman's order. This offers a glimpse into the ward or neighborhood distribution of poor relief during some decades of the eighteenth century. And while inconsistencies in the recording of data might make effective statistical analysis difficult, they do not preclude it; consequently, the records as a whole allow us to make accurate generalizations about the nature of poor relief in the eighteenth century.[28]

The notes made by clerks and other assistants were almost always marginal and brief and often cryptic. But occasionally a sense of the Almshouse culture can be inferred by noting the mix of young and old and the marital status, ethnicity, and domicile of the inhabitants. In the course of hundreds of pages, a few references to foundlings, or unruly or deranged residents, or neglected pregnant single women all add a palpable human energy to the lists, as do the notices of visits by physicians or clergy, or the accidental death of a child who "drown'd in ye well," or the runaways who "jump't the fence" to avoid being sent to the Workhouse. The two-story L-shaped brick building normally "entertained" about 150 people in thirty-three rooms. It was wholly residential, and apart from household chores, no "productive" work was performed; days were spent in rest, recovery, prayer, education, and child rearing. The mix of occupants was also more varied than simply the infirm, the abandoned, and the old. From time to time foreign sailors or other transients added a cosmopolitan flavor to the "family" of the "house." Older people from higher on the economic scale often ended up in the Almshouse simply for the care that was available there. Hardship or need could strike the young and the old, especially, regardless of status. On the face of it, some of those who were admitted to the Almshouse appear to be the unlikeliest of inmates, and included occasional middle-class persons with servants and furniture. The population in the house was not only diverse but fluid, but while there was a considerable turnover of the inmate population—about 40 percent stayed in fewer than three months, and 60 percent were gone within six months—there was always a core of residents who had been there for a year or more. That core group added continuity and familiarity to the environment so that newcomers entered into an existing domesticity.[29]

The Historical Setting

One striking anomaly in the Overseers records is that they provide extensive lists of the dates and names of Almshouse admissions and discharges, but offer no clearly defined set of rules or conditions for the residents who are identified. Conversely, the Workhouse records contain complete information on the rules and regulations of that institution, but only a few references to the actual inmates exist (see appendix 4). It can be supposed that some of the organizational requirements of the Almshouse, such as eating times, religious observances, behavioral etiquette, and a curfew schedule, would match the Workhouse codes; but there likely would be less threat of and occasion for punishment. Importantly, the Almshouse was not intended for productive employment.[30]

Not only were several thousand separate manuscript entries made by the Overseers' clerks, but several thousand separate references to and by the Overseers were published in the *Boston Records* as well. For example, each Overseer who served after 1742 is identified in the extant Overseers records, and all those who served before 1742 can be identified from other sources. The biographical profile that emerges from the lists of Overseers' names is instructive. All but a few were drawn from the wealthiest ten percent of Boston's population, and there are good reasons why that should be so. The position was a sensitive one that required reputation, status, and the opportunity and desire to serve. Overseers needed a good deal of free time to conduct the regular and frequent ad hoc requirements of supervision. In the case of outdoor relief, Overseers had to be wealthy enough to aid the poor out of their own funds, sometimes extemporaneously, to be recompensed later.[31]

Most of the Overseers were merchants who worked very hard at their businesses, to be sure; nevertheless, the tempo of merchant life allowed them to organize their activities and affairs so that the heavy demands of their public trust and obligation were not compromised. Also, the power of deference was necessary for effective face-to-face dealings with the majority of the poor. But perhaps the most significant cultural aspect of the Overseers of the Poor was that the combination of status, means, and opportunity was joined to a vigorous commitment to the position that resulted in a typical tenure of some ten years during most of the eighteenth century. There was no tangible material advantage to holding the office, but like Selectmen, the Overseers seem to have shared the sense of civic duty that obliged Boston's elite to spend their mature years in public service. That sense of duty was driven at least in part by paternalism, if not mostly by enlightened self-interest. If the poor could be kept moving, or made able or productive, then their demands on public funds would be reduced. The merchants of Boston, and others of the "better sort," were its major taxpayers. They not only supported the bureaucracy that tended to their public interests, but in fact were the bureaucracy where it counted.[32]

At the other end of the Overseer-pauper relationship, it becomes necessary to infer the status and interests of the poor, because the information on each admitted pauper is so limited. Still, the identification of several thousand Almshouse residents is a rare eighteenth-century documentary record for any American jurisdiction. The ability to identify the comings and goings of the "deserving" poor adds human force to the data of poverty in this age. The volume and rate of the Almshouse admissions in themselves underline the time and cost-consuming work of the Overseers.

When the Overseers records are combined with the extensive secondary references, they add range to the tax and probate records, the account books, the admonitory and jeremiad sermons, and the town and General Court records that have long been used to measure poverty in eighteenth-century Boston.[33] A generation of social and economic historians has focused attention on the impact of poverty on pre-revolutionary Boston, sometimes projecting their findings into the post-revolutionary era. Yet even as the Overseers records have long been known to historians and have been referred to in passing in some of the historiography, not enough consideration has been paid to the central role of the Overseers as a great urban innovation that shaped as much as it reacted to the rhythms of Boston's social history in the eighteenth century.[34]

Much of the most recent historiography of Boston acknowledges its relative size and growth, role, and development as a major seaport in the Atlantic world, as a fount first of Puritan and then of provincial and revolutionary politics and culture, and often as a setting for modern social fragmentation and decay. What the historiography hints at but has not adequately examined is the deeper consequences of Boston's eighteenth-century development in relation to the predominantly rural history of Massachusetts. The socioeconomic and cultural gap between Boston and the rest of Massachusetts increased during the eighteenth century. Part of Boston's significance to the social history of New England is that it can be studied and understood in something very close to isolation from the general history of the rest of Massachusetts prior to the early nineteenth century. The two societies that coexisted in New England—one urban and maritime, the other agrarian—can be more clearly defined by a close study of the records and activities of the Boston Overseers of the Poor. In all of rural Massachusetts there was nothing comparable to the culture of poor relief that was shaped by the Overseers and their mandate in Boston.[35]

Also, Boston's own history in the eighteenth century was marked by two contrasting problems. One was the continuation of the town's steady historical growth to 1740. That expansion had, in fact, made specialized control of the poor necessary because the Town Meeting and the Selectmen could no longer manage all of the town's social problems. The second problem resulted from a reversal of the first. After 1740, for the first time since its founding, Boston's population growth ceased, and a long period of stability—or stagnation—ensued, not to be reversed until the 1790s.[36] The latter has been seen as decline, in that the size and value of Boston's economy deteriorated. The poverty and social fragmentation that is observed from the latter part of the provincial period to the early national period in Boston has been accurately set in the context of urban scarcity rather than urban growth. By the middle of the eighteenth-century Boston had reached its optimum urban size as a pre-industrial seaport on the fringe of the British Empire and in a Massachusetts that was persistently agrarian.[37]

In that case, after about 1740 the activities of the Overseers were adjustments to limited economic development and population equilibrium. The Overseers had evolved from an agency designed to cope with growth and complexity to one that administered to the poor in a limited or declining economy, still distinguishing between the deserving and undeserving poor, and the transient and resident poor. They had coordinated the few private efforts to deal with poverty, such as Andrew Oliver's Spinning School in the 1720s or the grandiose John Hancock-led Society for Encouraging Industry and Employing the Poor of the 1750s. But those "charitable" private enterprises were not ultimately philanthropic, nor did they pretend to be; they were devised chiefly to relieve the tax burden on the town's merchants and capitalists.[38] For most of the eighteenth century there was some organized private, voluntary charity for some of the deserving poor. Most of that charity came directly from special fund-raising programs in Boston's churches.

Yet the growth in the number, membership, and sectarian diversity of churches did not translate into a significant rise in the role of churches as givers of alms. In fact, the contrary was often the case. From the founding of the first church in 1630 to 1792, at least nineteen churches were established in Boston, and thirteen of those congregations were founded after 1692, the year in which the Overseers of the Poor office was created. The proportion of poor relief that came from public money appears to have risen even as the numbers of churches increased.[39] The Quarterly Charity Lecture (QCL), inspired and led for a time by Cotton Mather, was an inter-congregational charity that raised monies to distribute private "alms" to up to a dozen families a month in the town. The Scottish, Scotch-Irish, and Anglican communities in Boston were served throughout this period by "charitable societies" who helped the poor with their own direct funding. But here, as with the QCL, the amount of money and materials distributed was less than ten percent of what the Overseers expended in public funds for "outdoor" relief. In fact, Samuel Whitwell, the Overseer for Ward 10 in the 1760s and 1770s, sometimes gave out nearly as much public funds for outdoor relief in his single ward as did the QCL for all of Boston.[40] In any case, by 1772 the Overseers were incorporated by an act of the General Court that specifically granted them the right to administer most privately donated poor relief funds. After 1772 the General Court authorized the Overseers to act as sole agent for the distribution of any private donations to the poor, whether or not the recipients of the gifts, usually in the form of bequests, had been specified (see appendix 5). Moreover, it is not clear how poor were the recipients of private charity, or even outdoor public relief. The neediest of Boston's poor would inevitably find themselves in the Almshouse if they deserved aid or in the Workhouse if they did not. The Overseers also solicited private funds for the deserving poor, usually by appealing directly to church congregations. Joseph Bennett comments favorably on the Overseers' cooperation with the town's churches in the 1740s: "the churches provide … good [outdoor] relief in so private a manner, that it is seldom known to any of the neighbors." But then Bennett makes a telling distinction in describing the dependent poor as "the meaner sort" (that is, the needy, not the dangerous) who are "kept in a decent manner" in the Almshouse. The work of the Overseers was no doubt responsible for isolating the "meaner sort," and for ensuring that there was "no such thing to be seen … as a strolling beggar."[41] It is worth noting that the Selectmen in 1744 organized a musical concert in Faneuil Hall to raise additional monies for the Overseers for the poor "out of doors."[42]

In the absence of significant private charity, it was tax abatement that inspired the Town Meeting to develop a policy of granting tavern licenses to poor widows, and the Overseers advised on which widows were deserving.[43] Here it would be extremely difficult to see the Overseers, most of whom were merchants, as being directed simply by a desire to "do good" as we might understand that meaning of benevolence. They were intended not simply to "do good" on behalf of the community's conscience, although they did, but also to keep the streets clear of vagrants and deviants, and to attempt to reduce or eliminate the poor relief portion of the town and province tax rates.[44]

The Overseers' workloads increased steadily along with their growing authority and the size of their constituency. For example, before 1739 the Almshouse had served also as the Workhouse. While it had long been felt to be cheaper and more efficient to support a fully dependent pauper in the Almshouse than in a private surrogate home, by the 1730s the mingling of the deserving poor with the "scum" of the town, the idle poor, was untenable for moral as well as space reasons. The general inadequacies of the old Almshouse prompted the building of a separate facility for the correction of the sturdy but idle poor between 1735 and 1739. The rules for the administration of the Workhouse (reproduced in appendix 4) were written by a committee of Overseers and were clearly more complex than any regulations that existed for supervision of the Almshouse, even when it had contained a Workhouse component. The new Workhouse was, in fact, an attempt at factory production and was designed not simply to better succor the deserving poor in the now roomier Almshouse but chiefly to sequester the idle poor to economize the use of public alms.[45]

The Workhouse was to be a profit-yielding enterprise based on oakum picking (part of the recycling of old rope). It would, it was hoped, simultaneously correct the idle poor and instill in them a habit of industry by obliging them to work to earn their keep, and a little more to boot, under strict codes of industrial discipline. Any revenues produced by the "house" were expected to cover the costs of materials, sustenance, and supervision. They did not. Still, even if the operation of the Workhouse continued to be subsidized by taxes, it functioned effectively as a minimum security prison of sorts, if not for convicted felons then at least for the potentially criminal. The same logic of fiscal and supervisory efficiency applies to the erection and operation of the Manufactory House of 1754, which attempted to fuse Almshouse and Workhouse functions in an innovative experiment in manufacturing for essentially private ends. Built by a combination of private and public funds, it was supervised by a committee of the Society for Encouraging Industry and Employing the Poor. But the conduit from the society to the town's poor ran through a committee of the Overseers, which provided the needy of Boston as the labor force for the society. In the Manufactory, as in the Workhouse, it was hoped that the poor would be gainfully employed, acquire rudimentary industrial skills, and be made to be self-sufficient and virtuous, always with a view to reducing taxes. Attempts to defray workhouse costs by fusing work-house function with the objectives of profit-making "manufactories" were made in other American cities, and Alexander Hamilton in New York, and Benjamin Franklin in Philadelphia can be seen as sharing John Hancock's failed vision in Boston.[46]

After the scheme failed, in the 1760s, the building was being used occasionally by the Overseers for the employment of the few "vagrant, idle and dissolute persons" who overflowed from the Workhouse. A controversial and amusing episode in the Manufactory's history concerned Lord Hillsborough's order that the vacant building be used to house British troops in 1768. Charges were made by Governor Bernard against the Overseers for trying to obstruct the quartering of the troops. It was claimed that the Overseers had allowed the "workhouse itself [to be] opened and the people confined there were permitted to go into the Manufactory House [which was then] kept filled with the outcast of the Workhouse & the Scum of the Town to prevent its being used for the accommodation of the King's troops." Although the Overseers blandly denied this, there can be little doubt that they used their not insignificant means to interfere with an unwelcome royal command. The Manufactory's fate was left in the end to a variety of private uses. The location of the building, at the edge of the Common, was close enough to the Workhouse, Almshouse, and Bridewell to form a large public welfare and security nexus that survived in that location to the very end of the eighteenth century. There the insane as well as the destitute were supervised by the Overseers and their appointees, the keepers' own internal bureaucracy. They identified, arbitrated, and executed all the laws governing poverty and poverty-related problems, so that constables and prison keepers, in addition to their own appointees, were subject to their authority.[47]

It did not matter, in the end, whether the causes of poverty were providential or sociological, because the dependent and especially the idle poor were impediments to social harmony and order. The organic model of community held that no one should be a charge to the aggregate or collective whole except in the rarest cases.[48] Yet even "deserving" transients, who were the object of much of the Overseers' work, could be treated with leniency, as when in 1741 "one of the Overseers … sent … George Berry who came from the Bay, to the Almshouse on the Province Charge and desire[d] … a certificate of his being a proper object of public charity." But a year earlier, in another case, the Overseers had demanded and received payment for their "charity": "the Overseers … received for the use of the Workhouse … firewood … amounting to thirty-one pounds ten shillings … of Thomas Fisher who became bound to indemnify the town on account of John Lashley, whom he imported into this town and who died in the Almshouse."[49] As always, families, testators, and even friends were initially obliged to provide for their poor relatives, one way or another. And that obligation extended to residents who had given verbal bond for transients (see appendix 1, section 9). That principle had long informed Puritan attitudes toward the poor and clearly influenced the Overseers in their work. They assumed that where possible the price for being poor would be borne by the poor themselves or their kin.

If John Winthrop's utopian vision had ever had a hope of realization, that hope was certainly gone by the age of the Overseers. But some of the communal ideal nevertheless survived to shape and guide eighteenth-century Boston's public administration. In fact, the purpose of poor relief meant a bit more than a cool measuring of costs and public order, at least into the early decades of the eighteenth century. For example, Cotton Mather had advocated a missionary approach to the deserving poor in the first quarter of the eighteenth century that was reminiscent of Winthrop's appeal to Christian duty. In *Bonifacius* in 1710 he urged Bostonians, not as taxpayers but as Christians and neighbors, to form "societies" to "relieve the widow, the orphan and the afflicted." He urged each Christian to do "extensive service for the Kingdom of our great Saviour in the world" to redress "the ... distresses of his poor, mean, miserable neighbors." Mather's approach, like his role in the Quarterly Charity Lectures, is instructive in that it was not only as rational as any in its time but was also underscored by the residue of Puritan moral imperative. Another great civic activist of the age, Samuel Sewall, has become a model and even a caricature of the neighborly Christian provincial. Yet he served as an Overseer in the first decade of the eighteenth century. He was intellectually tied to Calvin's *Institutes* and to the conviction that while supervision of the poor was a civic responsibility, its effective amelioration required the warmth of private Christian compassion.[50]

The "charitable" social spirit of Sewall and Mather was less apparent in the discourse of the clergy and lay moralists of mid-century Boston. Then, leading clergymen such as Thomas Barnard, Charles Chauncy, and Samuel Cooper and the economic moralist John Hancock urged make-work schemes to reduce taxes, without much appeal to the souls of the employers of destitute labor. Indeed, the language of those who attacked all poverty as "idleness" suggests that they little bothered about the fate of their own souls in the matter of "charity." At least a century earlier, Hancock's merchant predecessors had committed themselves less conditionally to assisting the poor. But the 121 subscribers to the 1735–39 public Workhouse construction fund and the more than 200 subscribers to the 1752–54 private Manufactory fund were unabashedly concerned with tax reduction. Their motives for "investing" in the poor are in sharp contrast to Robert Keayne's 1660 bequest, which was an exercise in atonement. The mid-eighteenth-century clerics used their pulpits to thunder forth on matters of public policy and to exhort the idle poor to save their souls with hard work. There is something quite practical, as well as ironic, in the Virgilian agricultural motto for the "Rules of the Workhouse" of 1739 which informs the keepers and the kept that *labor improbus omnia vincit* ("ceaseless labor always triumphs").[51] In the end, the great secular corollary to Winthrop's spiritual objectives remained and the chief legacy of Winthrop's experiment in social conformity and moral responsibility, the town, was the locus of social stability and security. The town could be cosmopolitan Boston or a rural or frontier hamlet of fifty families.

The Overseers records are more than an illustration of how a senior civic bureaucracy functioned. Even in their fragments and broken sequences the equally striking impression of the manuscript record is to identify the many thousands who failed in a variety of ways in the eighteenth-century economy. Especially in the lists of more than eight thousand transients whom the public officials of Boston warned out between 1745 and 1792, the records reveal a system of civil authority that was emphatically parochial in its concerns even as the world around it was increasingly mobile and cosmopolitan.[52] But the human face of the statistics is portrayed in the names and destinies of hundreds of identified children and youths who passed through the Overseers' hands. For example, in the second half of the century the Overseers bound more than 1,000 children to apprenticeships and domestic and agricultural service. An average of between 15 and 20 children a year were indentured between 1740 and 1800, with over 220 being bound out by the Overseers in the economically troubled decade of the 1760s. Lawrence Towner has produced an exhaustive and touching portrait of the indentures of hundreds of boys and girls who were taken from poor families, under the provisions of the 1704, 1722, and 1735 laws in particular, and put into service. Over 60 percent were sent out of Boston, and over two-thirds of those went into farm labor.[53]

The records show that poverty fell hardest on women and children, and hundreds of single women and their children were cared for in the Almshouse in the second half of the eighteenth century. Significant numbers of pregnant transient women and their families, along with other women with illegitimate pregnancies, were supported by the Overseers. For the entire transcribed record, estimates from the Overseers' clerks' entry books show that about 40 percent of the more than seven thousand names in the nearly six thousand Almshouse admission entries between 1757 and 1800 were of white adult women. Another 37 percent were adult males. These ratios varied over time and according to circumstances and by the end of the eighteenth-century the proportion of children in the Almshouse fell while the numbers and percentages of single white males rose. Overall, children made up an astonishing 21 percent of admissions; most unaccompanied children were in the Almshouse for very brief periods, however, usually a matter of days, before being bound out by the Overseers to service or apprenticeship. Some two-thirds of all children who went through the Almshouse were unaccompanied or arrived with one or more siblings and no adult company.[54] These children were the principal source of the indentures that Towner has identified and studied, but there was nothing to prevent the Overseers from removing a child from his or her parents in the Workhouse if, for example, the conditions of the 1735 law were not met by the parents. And many children were indentured directly from their homes by the Overseers without ever going into either the Almshouse or Workhouse. White women with one or more children accounted for slightly over 5 percent of total admissions, and "families," that is a husband and wife with or without children, made up about 2.5 percent of admissions. Workhouse admissions ran at a rate of between 20 percent and 30 percent of the Almshouse numbers. The evidence is strong that women and children predominated in the Workhouse at even higher ratios than they did in the Almshouse.[55]

As noted, the Overseers supported many widows in their applications for business licenses, usually to sell strong drink "out of doors" (that is, outside their residences). While there is no doubt that Boston's widow population was large and therefore a major problem for the Overseers, the figure of twelve hundred widows noted in the Boston Records at mid-century included a great number of "grass widows": abandoned women or the wives of mariners. As late as 1765 the adult white female population of Boston was thirty-six hundred, which would then suppose a widowed rate of 33 percent. That is an unlikely ratio of bereaved women. Still, many hundreds of women needed outdoor relief, and women were overrepresented at all levels of poor relief. Many hundreds of underemployed laborers and unskilled workers were kept off the poor rolls by being given preference in public works projects such as street, dam, and wharf construction and maintenance, on the advice of the Overseers.[56]

Another important function of the Overseers was their role in the inevitable smallpox epidemics that ravaged Boston every decade or so. In the great infections of 1721, 1730, and 1752, and in the last major eighteenth-century outbreak, in 1792, the Overseers played a crucial part in dealing with the emotional and logistical needs of a population that suffered as much as a 50 percent infection rate. The 1721 epidemic killed 850 persons, about 7.7 percent of the total population, and over 80 percent of the total deaths in Boston that year, 1,100. The numbers of deaths in Boston in 1721 and 1752 were the highest recorded in the town in any year after its founding. In addition to poor relief, the Overseers' had a central role in public health that included the running of a "well house," first on Spectacle Island and after 1737 on Rainsford Island, where smallpox victims could be quarantined and restored. Also, any smallpox victims in the Workhouse were removed to the Almshouse for care and convalescence, indicating an absence of medical care in the Workhouse. Occasional eruptions of smallpox in the town caused alarm for the Overseers, at least down to the 1790s. By then the great epidemics were in the past.[57]

In 1752 the Overseers not only assisted in inoculating the population but also tended to the sick, organized the burial of the dead, and made sure that the great exodus from the town was orderly. Also, in addition to their political actions during the 1768 billeting imbroglio, the Overseers' authority and skill was invaluable during the great military evacuation of Boston in 1776. Although the principal role of the Overseers was clearly in the administration of poor relief, their central role in the maintenance of public order allowed them the scope to act in a variety of ways in a variety of circumstances.[58]

The Overseers adapted themselves to fluctuating economic and demographic conditions and to the concomitant levels of poverty and dependency during the eighteenth century against a backdrop of political change. There were at least four distinct phases of jurisdictional order in Boston in the eighteenth century: the crown authority established by the provincial charter of 1692, the extra-legal patriot governments of the 1768-1776 period, the independent constitutional state of Massachusetts of the 1780s, and finally, the inclusion of the state into the republic. One might note an additional early phase in terms of the Overseers. Coming into being at the very end of an interlude between the original Puritan charter and the representative crown charter, they inherited much of the earlier administrative ethic. Each of these political phases coincided with social and economic disruption. For example, the numbers of paupers charged to the province and later the state increased in relation to town-supported paupers as levels of transiency increased with the wars of 1756 and 1775.

Also, during and after the War for Independence, the emergence of a "patriotic" and later a "national" identity was manifest in the way the Overseers began to discriminate in their treatment of transients. African-Americans appear in greater numbers after 1780, when emancipation made instant paupers of many of them. Poor African-Americans had not appeared in any conspicuous way in the Almshouse before the War for Independence but their numbers in the Almshouse doubled in the 1780s and doubled again by 1800.[59]

Yet as one of the most thorough studies of Massachusetts poverty after 1750 notes, independence and the new national ethos did not immediately change the way the poor were treated and did not ease the residency requirements of the waves of transient families who swept through Boston in the 1780s and 1790s. Indeed, despite the rapidly expanding criteria for settlement rights between 1750 and the liberal legislation of 1793, the frequency of warning out remained high and in fact surged in the 1790s. The "settlement" laws that governed the rights of residency in Massachusetts began to bend only in the second and third decades of the nineteenth-century; nonetheless, some residency criteria survived, and warning out was available to local authorities in residual form even in the late nineteenth century.[60] What is important here though, is that throughout the course of these changes, the role and activity of the Boston Overseers of the Poor was constant. Indeed, up to the moment when the Overseers' authority was shoved to the margins of poor relief after 1823, they functioned as they had throughout the eighteenth century, retaining not only legal cachet but the fiscal means to enforce their mandate as it had been first defined in 1692.

Questions remain about the extent and nature of poverty in eighteenth-century Boston, and the issue will continue to attract students of early American society just as poverty attracts headlines today. The questions that historians have asked recently of social conditions in eighteenth-century American port cities seem to be as pertinent to twenty-first century America as to the eighteenth century: Were there growing economic disparity and disrupted employment patterns? Was poverty expanding because of social dislocation and transience? Did rising levels of poverty echo a rising wave of public disaffection? Was there an upper-class backlash against the poor? Were the poor demanding more and more of the common wealth? Were the poor feared? Does the extent of eighteenth-century poverty blemish the roseate picture of liberal democracy that might have accompanied the Revolution? These questions remain contentious but the answer to at least the last question is yes, according to some historians who paint nightmarish images of a Boston on the eve of the Revolution in which close to 10 percent of the town's population was either in the Almshouse or on relief, and up to 25 percent of the adult population was too poor to be rated for tax.[61]

Contemporaries too painted grim images of a growing mass of dependent poor. The seventeenth- and eighteenth-century minutes of the Selectmen and of the Town Meeting are thick with reports and laments of economic distress, moral decline, and social fragmentation, and much can be gleaned from those sources. The cry of economic doom is repeated so often in the records that it cannot be taken at face value unless it is matched to other kinds of evidence of economic calamity and social disorder. It is tempting, in fact, to think of the spiritual jeremiads of the seventeenth-century evolving into the economic laments of the eighteenth-century. Even during the best of economic times there was private and public verbal hand-wringing about inevitable economic failure and anticipation of social and moral degeneration.[62]

While phrases such as "a growing number of poor" sprinkled the town records throughout the colonial period, events after the end of King George's War in 1748 clearly alarmed authorities. Their cries became more frequent and shrill during the postwar decline of the Boston distilling and shipbuilding economies in the early 1750s, when the town lost about a third of its taxpayers, unemployment among the unskilled and in the "maritime trades" created a great "number of thoughtless, idle and sottish persons," and the "charge of the poor [rose] from … fifteen hundred pounds to ten thousand." Yet for all that, and with little evidence of neighborly charity to offset the demands on a shrinking tax base, the Overseers, while their records reflect an increase in poverty generally and in the numbers of transients and dependent poor specifically, managed their responsibilities in a remarkably efficient way that hardly suggests a collapsing social order, blighted by roving bands of beggars and the spread of destitution.[63]

By and large, the Overseers records do add another measure to our understanding of eighteenth-century Boston by demonstrating the constant presence of poverty and the consistency of the poor relief model. What the records also indicate, as much as anything else, is an absence of significant private charity in Boston in the eighteenth-century, at least until its last decade. The domination of poor relief by a modern bureaucracy of considerable discipline and power in at least one early American urban society does not mean that the poor were treated wholly as faceless ciphers. The Overseers dealt with the poor, the sick, and the aged in a way that indicated a personal connection with them, even if their first responsibility was to public order and fiscal efficiency. John Hancock's version of economic "liberalism" in the second half of the eighteenth century required a view of the dependent poor as self-made failures. That would not change until all the poor could be seen as victims of social circumstances, and when their condition could be viewed as neither providential nor self-inflicted. That would have to wait until the giving of private charity could be seen as a civic virtue as well as a civic necessity. What is of particular note here is that Chauncy, Hancock and their supporters on the one hand, and the Overseers as a group on the other, belonged to the same eighteenth-century economic and social class, yet each group projected quite different attitudes or sentiments when it came to the application of public welfare.

In another usage, "liberalism" as a reform value began in the nineteenth century to shift the explanations of the causes of poverty away from the poor as authors of their own condition toward the idea that they were the victims of misfortune, of external social and economic forces. In the early nineteenth century, in fact, the giving of charity became a measure of citizenship and republican virtue. Private philanthropic associations flourished in the early republic, and there is persuasive evidence that what

Conrad Wright has described as a wave of genuine humanitarianism impulse was fueled by evangelical zeal.[64]

But the eighteenth-century model of poor relief would eventually be reconfirmed as a public and legislative responsibility whose end was as much the sequestering and control of the poor as it was beneficence. And even if providence gave way to circumstance as an explanation for the root cause of dependency, that too would be challenged by other explanations, including the idea that public alms could cause poverty to expand; as Josiah Quincy argued in 1821, the "poor … begin to consider [alms] as a right" if they are given unconditionally. Quincy was insistent that all public poor relief be conditional, that outdoor relief be stopped and public Almshouses as refuges of indoor care for the deserving poor be converted to "Houses of Industry" (Workhouses), and that even relief for the so-called deserving or "impotent" poor should not be encouraged because of "the difficulty of discriminating between the able poor and the impotent poor [in the] degree of actual impotency."[65]

It may be useful to look to the later nineteenth century to trace the conjunction of voluntary and involuntary dependence as simply reverse sides of the same coin. Even though the early burst of nineteenth-century philanthropy and private charity left a minimal legacy for treatment of the urban poor in Boston later in the century, it had indicated some measure of benevolence toward the poor in what turned out to be a brief era of private, voluntary support. The records of the nineteenth-century Overseers, albeit in their reduced role, agree with that era's hope that private philanthropy could remedy the problem of dependency.[66] In contrast, the eighteenth-century Overseers had much less optimism about human nature and the prospects for eliminating need, even if they did humanize the contact between the public givers and the individual receivers of alms. They understood that some of the poor were helpless and blameless in their condition, and if they were not as cynical as Quincy, they understood that some others of the poor should pay, in some way, for their support.

The history of poor law and poor relief in Massachusetts in the two centuries after the English arrival began with John Winthrop's acknowledgment of the presence of the poor and the need for a corporate approach to their needs. The arc runs through Cotton Mather's moral imperative of good works to Josiah Quincy's view that simply relieving the poor made sinners of the poor. The office of the Overseers of the Poor was the chief agency for the administration of the policies, theories, and law governing the poor for over a hundred years of that history. At no time did the Overseers shape policy in isolation from the larger public authority, but neither were they mere custodians. No other small group in Boston's history has had such a consistent relationship with the poor.[67] In their actions, and as representatives of what might be called the common interest, the Overseers made a clear distinction between the poverty that came from voluntary idleness and the poverty of incapacity. Despite Quincy's single-minded solution of the workhouse, the Overseers' model of deserved charity might have served as a moral legacy for poor relief in Boston after the Revolution. It did not, because as the Revolution assumed to liberate it also removed most of the vestiges of older communal charity, especially the notion of "deserving poor" and the practice of outdoor relief in the same way it removed political "toryism." In other words, as America in general and Boston in particular adopted a republican approach to social and civic matters, the older paternalistic patterns of *noblesse oblige* were removed slowly from the imperatives of poor relief.[68]

The Overseers retained their original mandate as the single dominant authority in the supervision of the dependent poor in Boston for a very long time—in fact, all the way to 1823, when reforms in civic government began to eclipse their authority. The first major challenge to the Overseers' monopoly immediately followed the incorporation of the City of Boston in 1822 and the election of Josiah Quincy Jr. as Boston's second mayor in 1823. In the course of his highly publicized 1821 report on the poor laws in Massachusetts, Quincy had included an attack on the "abuse of public charities" by the poor and, by extension, the Overseers' abuse of the system because of their preference for in-home relief as an alternative to institutionalized care or forced work programs. Quincy, reflecting the more disciplinary and punitive workhouse approach of his era, succeeded in usurping the power of the Overseers in a political struggle that ended a century and a half of hegemony. He would later explain his 1821–23 attack on the Overseers in his self-indulgent *A Municipal History of ... Boston* (1852). The Overseers ultimately lost their local sovereignty in part because the city administration derived its legislative power from the new city charter rather than from the administrative arm of the state legislature. After 1822 the long era of the Town Meeting, which despite its enormous administrative authority had always been subject to the executive supervision of the General Court, was over.[69]

The original Puritan neighborly mandate to care for the poor had survived with institutional modification down to the Revolution. It had derived from a highly personalized system of outrelief that evolved, out of necessity and opportunity, into a version of institutionalized charity. That mandate was destroyed in the wake of the Revolution as civic opportunists such as Josiah Quincy made civic paternalism a sin and statistical rationalism a virtue. The poor in the new republic would be treated as a drag on civic enterprise, rather than a civic obligation. According to Quincy, to succor the poor, even the "deserving" poor, would cause the poor to multiply (as Malthus predicted). Quincy's ostensibly democratic reform of civic government was predicated on the principle that the older paternalism was contradictory to liberal democracy because it favored an undeserving plurality, the poor, without the consent of other pluralities.[70]

This process, repeated throughout the former colonies, is more easily traced in the port cities of America than in the rural communities, since each colony became a state and then a part of the new nation. The example here of Boston, the "public city" of colonial and early national America and its experience with poor relief, is one of the paradoxes of the American Revolution. As crime became a more compelling concern of local government and as the blame for poverty and crime became associated more with groups and individuals and less with social conditions and circumstances, the treatment of the poor became harsher and depersonalized in the early national period. The imitation of British poverty control mechanisms by Boston authorities, who were elected rather than appointed under the new democratic city charter of 1822, contrasted vividly and ironically with the moral, intimate, and humane dicta of Winthrop and a legacy of his vision, the Overseers of the Poor.

The Overseers and Their Functions.

IT HAS BECOME A COMMONPLACE to describe the dependent poor and the working poor of eighteenth-century America as "inarticulate." Historians have for some time attempted to make the inarticulate speak, as it were, by interpreting vital statistics and other kinds of nonliterary evidence to recreate some image of the lives of those who left behind no verbal account of their perceptions, opinions, or actions.[71] In fact, much of the population of all classes have left no records of their activities, let alone their views, and in the case of eighteenth-century Boston, the poor are not alone in their silence. Those who cared for the poor and who controlled their lives on behalf of the "articulate" minority left no personalized accounts of their perceptions or explanations for their actions as Overseers, and appear to have made no comments for posterity on what it was like to be an Overseer of the Poor in eighteenth-century Boston.

The Overseers could hardly have been wholly inarticulate as historians think of the term, because as merchants most had to keep at least some personalized records of their businesses and accounts. But most of those written records have not survived. Perhaps the most famous Overseer, Samuel Sewall, was also the most open of diarists. But he did not keep a diary because he wanted to describe the means and ends of his public office, and he is effectively mute on his experience as an Overseer.[72] Is the reason simply that for the most part, unlike Sewall the Overseers were more concerned with the hard data of business and the straightforward recording of simple figures or names, in the case of their finances, and repeated that habit in their guardianship of the poor? Or might we suppose that even in the case of Sewall, a man of contemplation and academic curiosity, the office of Overseer did not warrant any further comment than the simple collection of human and fiscal statistics (usually recorded by a clerk or Almshouse keeper) and a few written depositions and memoranda?

Whatever the case, the way the Overseers of the Poor approached their duties, the importance they placed on the office itself, and their personal roles in the history of poor relief in eighteenth-century Boston have to be inferred from sources other than self-conscious reflection. It is no surprise, therefore, that the only personal Overseer's document of any size that survives, Samuel Whitwell's twenty-year account book, contains no annotation at all, but rather page after page of dense line entries of the names of outdoor relief recipients in his ward, the amounts they received, and little more.[73] For all that, some quite important characteristics of the Overseers, as individuals, as a class, and as bureaucrats, can be inferred.[74]

First, the Overseers have no reputation in the historical literature as a group because even those historians who have recently studied the civic officialdom of eighteenth-century Massachusetts have tended to ignore them.[75] Here and there, a comment surfaces to acknowledge the Overseers' existence, but apart from the excellent but unpublished work of Stephen Wiberley, there has been no attempt at serious interpretation of the men and the office, and certainly no other serious attempt than his to give any historical significance to the office.

In the most accessible and important social and institutional historical literature, the Overseers are mentioned only in passing, if at all.[76] Where they are mentioned it is not always with accuracy. In *Sibley's Harvard Graduates,* Clifford Shipton claims that "the Honorable Benjamin Austin had been very much a town father, and had labored particularly as an Overseer of the Poor and the Work House, an unpleasant office which Jonathan [his son] held from 1784 to 1802."[77] The fact is that Benjamin Austin had never been an Overseer but a Selectman, who in line with the legal requirements of his office had, with the consent of an Overseer, committed dozens of nonresidents into either the Almshouse or Workhouse on behalf of the Province of Massachusetts. The statute that instructed Selectmen to commit out-of-town paupers and others to the Almshouse required the consent of an Overseer, because at the point of admission, while the support was the responsibilty of the province, the responsibility for the inmate was the Overseers'. For Boston residents, the only official who could commit a person was an Overseer. Certainly, an Overseer's duties involved, from time to time, unpleasant tasks. The Overseer dealt daily with the emotional distress of orphaned, abandoned, or neglected children, and with the physical distress of the old, the ill, the infirm, and the dying. Because many of the inmates were sick when admitted, approximately 25 percent of those committed to the Almshouse would die there.[79] But without the intercession of the Overseers of the Poor, there surely would have been a great deal more "unpleasantness" in the alleys, streets, wharves, and tenements of Boston.[80]

Jonathan Loring Austin did not send the numbers into the Almshouse as did Royall Tyler in the 1760s or Edward Proctor in the 1780s or Stephen Gorham in the 1790s. He did not deal with as many outdoor poor as did Samuel Whitwell in the 1770s, because his wards, 8 and 9, were historically less needful than most of the others. But he was as dutiful as any other Overseer and stayed for nearly twenty years in a position that clearly suited his temperament and values. He surely did not force himself to stay on for so long. A sense of civic duty alone could not have kept him in the office for so long, and it might reasonably be inferred that he stayed on in part because of a personal rather than functional sense of responsibility, and a personal rapport with the needy in his ambit, in a way that cannot be documented. We can be sure that he cared for the unfortunate and helped correct the wayward not for pay nor profit nor professional gratification (certainly he was no "social worker"). Even from the distance of two centuries we can at least imagine that he did it out of compassion for the needy and a cultivated pride in the standards of duty and self-interest of his class and background. By keeping the streets clear of the idle poor and caring for the needy, Austin fulfilled a moral as well as a practical obligation. He might have done his civic duty in another way, but he chose to be an Overseer.[81]

The Austins were members of Boston's economic and social upper rank, a transgenerational class that dominated the merchant world, Harvard, and the political culture at the local and provincial (and later state) level. The 1771 Massachusetts Valuation lists twenty-four past and present Overseers. Of those, twenty-one were among Boston's wealthiest 10 percent, and the other three were in the top 20 percent.[82] It is worth remembering too that offices such as the Selectmen's and Overseers' were both political and bureaucratic; the former more political than the latter, perhaps, but every bit as clerical. During the Revolution, Boston's civic officials, including the Overseers, were overwhelmingly patriotic, in a way that reflects the intersection of mercantile interest and town politics. Indeed, on August 19, 1775 after the outbreak of war in Massachusetts, the Overseers offered a safe refuge to 16 people "Received…not as Subjects of the House but with the Poor of the House." On December 4 of that year 21 refugees "from Point Shirley" were admitted as a single group. Other large groups were housed by the Overseers as the military crisis in Massachusetts deepened. While the Overseers were manifesting their support for the cause, so too, it seems, were some Almshouse inmates. In a clear display of revolutionary sentiment, "Mary Vose & her Six Children three of them at Birth named Hancock Washington & Lee" were admitted on April 30, 1777.

While there is no accurate way to measure the amount of time in a week or a month that a Selectman or an Overseer might spend in the position, the records indicate that Overseers were always "on call." Contrary to Shipton's remark on the office being unpleasant, Daniel Oliver, who served as an Overseer for 16 years in the early eighteenth-century was said to have found "no Employment in which he took more pleasure than in being Overseer of the Poor.…The meanest was not beneath his Notice [and he] doubtless bestowed numberless Charities of his own upon them, which God and his Angels have only seen." Even if we look past this paean to Oliver to see his self interest, there was very likely genuine care in his approach to the office, and the eulogist's lyricism does suggest that, as much as it hints at exaggeration. Oliver had attempted to relieve some of the problems of tax relief with a for-profit spinning school, which he later bequeathed to the town poor, but he had become an Overseer late in life after having served as a Selectman earlier in the century. His progeny maintained the obligations of his class, and his son Andrew spent 17 years as an Overseer. Andrew later became Lieutenant Governor of Massachusetts and died at the height of the imperial crisis in 1774. Peter, his brother, was Chief Justice of Massachusetts and became a Loyalist refugee in 1776.[83]

Although all Overseers, as a class, did not fit the Oliver example precisely, a certain amount of personal financial security was necessary for anyone considering the office; for some Overseers, several hours a week were required simply to deliver outdoor relief.[84] For some Overseers, at certain times, that might expand into a near daily chore. In addition, over short periods Overseers "sent in" or "discharged" as many as one person a day, attended all Town Meetings, met regularly with constables, Selectmen, and the Town Treasurer, patrolled their wards, attended to the supervision of the Almshouse, Workhouse, and Pesthouse, and met together as often as weekly to deal with their collective affairs. As noted earlier, it was customary for the major part of the town government, including all the Selectmen, all the Justices of the Peace, the constables, and many others, to spend a day at least once a year "inspecting the town" by ward. As many as one hundred officials were divided into twelve groups and took part in this ceremonial but also practical display of management. Each party was led by the respective Overseer for the ward.[85]

Overseers were in their time the very antithesis of the ward "bosses" of the Gilded Age. Yet they wielded considerable authority simply by being responsible for public health and social order, even if they were not necessarily resident in their assigned wards. As assiduous as they were in their routine service to the town and to their constituents, perhaps the most striking characteristic of the Overseers was the length of time they spent in service. Jonathan Austin's eighteen years of service was not at all unusual. Between 1690/1, when the first Overseers were chosen, and 1805, a total of 141 serving Overseers are identified in the records. For several years in the 1690s no record exists to show how, or if, Overseers were chosen, and either the town did without them or, more likely, the incumbents were simply continued without notice of reelection by the Town Meeting. After 1700 the records are complete.[86]

Given that twelve Overseers were "chosen" each year after 1734/35, and that earlier as few as four and as many as twelve had served annually, the fact that only 141 Overseers served over the course of a century is a remarkable testament to individual continuity. For the entire period the average length of service was slightly more than eight years. But the average jumps to eleven and a half years for Overseers whose first appointment occurred after the twelve-ward system was introduced in 1735/36, when Overseers were assigned to a specific ward for the duration of their appointments.[87] From that point forward, the normal length of service grows, and of the forty-eight Overseers chosen for the first time after 1736 and before 1785, nearly half (twenty-three) served for at least ten years, and of those, thirteen served for at least twenty years. The longest-serving Overseer on record in this period was Edward Proctor with thirty-five years of service after 1775. William Phillips Jr., chosen for the first time in 1788, served for thirty-four years, and William Smith (1788) and Redford Webster (1796) each served for twenty-eight years. Jonathan Mason was an Overseer for seven years after 1760 and then returned in 1775 for another twenty-one years. John Sweetser (1776) was another long-term Overseer through a very fluid period and served twenty-six terms. Only two Overseers from the first half of the century matched those records: John Ruck, for twenty-eight years after 1706/7, and Jacob Wendell, first chosen in 1728/9, for twenty-seven years. Another remarkable feature of the Overseers as a trans-generational group was the number of families who provided multiple members to the office (see appendix 6). In the first few decades after 1690 the turnover each year was quite large. Many who were "chosen" simply refused to take the office. Those rates of turnover do not appear again until the 1820s when it is clear that the Overseers became more like clerks, as they had been in the 1690s, than managers. It appears that the Overseers were chosen by the Selectmen up to 1708 but were thereafter chosen by the Town Meeting. This had the effect of elevating the status of the office in that the Overseers were elected in much the same way as were the Selectmen themselves. Before 1708, the Selectmen had chosen the Overseers but had also hired the Almshouse "keeper" or "master." After 1708 the Overseers hired, or "appointed" as they put it, the keepers, clerks, doctors and ministers for the Almshouse. What is of further note here is the way in which the merchant-dominated Selectmen and Overseers offices represent a civic dimension of a class identity or role that included charity as well as economic and social success.[88]

The Overseers' durability corresponds to the long service of other officials such as Selectmen, Town Clerks, and Town Treasurers. Among the latter, David Jeffries served for twenty years and in effect managed the finances of the town through some of the most dynamic events in Boston's history and during the most economically strained decades of the eighteenth century. Every Overseer in the period between the Treaty of Paris of 1763 and the Treaty of Paris of 1783 was under the intense scrutiny of Jeffries, who was at times the most influential public official in town government. Jeffries, in some ways, was the quintessential custodian of public welfare as well as being in charge of the town's total finances. As tough as he was on financial matters, Jeffries shared the Overseers' concerns for the poor. When he died, in 1785, he was hardly well off, but he made the following allowance in his will: he left the Town of Boston two hundred acres of land in Maine and marked the proceeds of the land to be used "annually and for ever" as Shipton says, quoting from the will, "to purchase Tea, Coffee, Chocolate and Sugar for the refreshment of those Persons who in the providence of God are or shall be reduced and obliged to take Shelter in the Alms House after having lived reputably, the Overseers of the Poor to be Judges as to the Persons, but always giving preference to the pious Poor."[89]

Jeffries's thirty-one years of contact with the Overseers as Town Treasurer was matched by long-serving Selectmen such as John Scollay and Ezekiel Price, who shared a continuous relationship with the Overseers that underlines the closed and paternalistic nature of Boston's civic politics before the advent of municipal and electoral reform in 1822.[90] By the middle of the eighteenth century, of an eligible voting population of more than two thousand, the Boston Town Meeting could accommodate perhaps three hundred male polls. The "choosing" or "appointing" of officials to positions of power was the prerogative of the Town Meeting under provincial and later state authority and allowed for the most intimate and personalized "selection" of officials. In a way, the Boston Overseers of the Poor as well as the Selectmen chose themselves. What this meant for the poor and needy, and the criminal and infirm, was that they were supervised and relieved by a continuing body of Overseers who were not so much interested in political office for aggrandizement as they were committed to peace, order, and charity, on the basis of their familiarity with need and their conservative approach to relief.[91]

There are at least two reasons why Overseers' tenures became longer after midcentury. In the first place, profound changes marked the larger political, social, and economic world of Boston and its public welfare system. In 1735, when the Workhouse was proposed to remove the undeserving poor from the Almshouse, Boston was a thriving colonial administrative outpost in the empire, a major port in the Atlantic trading world, and the region's cultural and political hub. It was a tight-knit community of long-resident leading families whose world, for all its enterprise and assumptions, was "provincial" in the fullest sense of the word.[92] By the 1790s Massachusetts had endured three major wars in the eighteenth century, including one that reached into Boston itself, and had ridden an economic roller coaster that had begun in the 1740s and had resulted in a stagnant or shrinking and always uncertain tax base and no population growth for half a century. Of course, by the 1790s Massachusetts was a constitutionally different place from what it could have imagined itself becoming in 1735. For all that, and perhaps because of it, the Overseers tended to stay longer in their positions and represented a thread of tradition and civic intimacy through a period of turmoil, depression, and reconstruction. War was accompanied or followed by pestilence, too, in the shape of three serious smallpox epidemics, as well as military evacuations and a flux of refugees. Transiency itself certainly increased as a matter of routine, as the Massachusetts population rose faster than its small local economies could handle.[93] In fact, after the 1760s, the majority of the Overseers' subjects were regional rather than local (that is, Bostonian) in a way that brought Overseers and Selectmen together more often than ever in the past. The increased tenure of Overseers mirrored an increase in responsibility. By contrast, the Overseers of the Poor in Philadelphia served on average for only a year, at least into the Revolutionary period. The term "overseer of the poor" clearly had different meanings in different places and at different times. The authority and independence of the Overseers in Philadelphia for example were limited by a variety of private committees who controlled monies and policy. It is therefore a bit difficult to compare the institutional approaches to poverty of communities as diverse in history and social composition as Boston, Philadelphia and New York. The cultural and demographic homogeneity of the former certainly was not present in either New York or Philadelphia in the eighteenth century.[94]

At the same time and in the same way, the expansion of the ward system in 1735, from eight to twelve, and the fixed appointment of an Overseer to each ward roughly coincided with the important opening of the freestanding Workhouse in 1738/39. Both events expanded the role of the Overseers and required more commitment and more of their time and out-of-pocket expense. Now they began to deal with residents and transients in neighborhood settings and had added to their mandate the management and operation of a brand-new and separate facility for the dissolute idle. The era of extended Overseers' service had begun, and men such as Andrew Oliver, Samuel Whitwell, Edward Proctor, and others began to serve routinely for decades at a time, in increasingly personalized ways. Edward Proctor illustrates the potential scale of the Overseers' personal neighborhood interventions. Between March 1786 and March 1787, Proctor sent over sixty people into the Almshouse. That number constituted some 43 percent of all persons sent by all the Overseers to the Almshouse that year and cannot be seen as typical. Nor would all of those admissions be from his North End waterfront Ward 2. He likely attached his name to admissions from other wards. In other years, other Overseers' orders from other wards would dominate the statistics. But the point is that Proctor personally knew a substantial number of those sixty people he sent in because they were residents of his ward. He would also have been required to at least meet those people who did not reside in his ward. A formality did exist in admissions, as Overseers were required to attest to the individual circumstances of each Almshouse admission before they signed the orders for admission. All Overseers knew or came to know their "charges." Proctor left no account of the recipients of his outdoor relief disbursements, but his claims on the treasury suggest that he dealt with substantial numbers.[95]

The surviving official records of the Overseers do not show either the frequency of outdoor relief or the names or even numbers of recipients, and it is unlikely that they were ever kept. Any estimates are based on random sources, mostly incomplete financial records that cover only a part of the eighteenth century. But outdoor relief was central to the Overseers' roles, and a major bone of contention, along with indoor charity (the Almshouse), for the early nineteenth-century critics.[96] Overseers distributed mostly small sums of cash and varying amounts of wood for household fuel in their neighborhoods. Occasionally, funerals were paid for and some education for the poor was supported by payment to teachers by the Overseers. Each year Overseers submitted their out-of-pocket expenses for outdoor relief to the Town Treasurer. It is not always clear from the records that the Overseers always received full compensation, and evidence suggests some imbalance between submissions and repayment; we can infer that at least some Overseers were always out of pocket. In any case, although financial records exist only for the 1738 to 1769 period, we can be sure that the Overseers made records of every financial transaction within their mandate.[97] It would be useful, at the least, to know how they handled the wartime economy of the 1770s, and especially at the end of the war in 1782, when the Boston treasury became empty, David Jeffries resigned, and the Overseers fed and clothed the poor in the Almshouse, Workhouse, and "out of doors."[98] In an earlier example of the Overseers' close relationship to the poor, a private petition in 1753 requested that the Town Meeting post for public view all the recipients of relief. The petition was initially approved but the Overseers succeeded in having the vote rescinded. While the names of those getting relief in or out of doors were in the record, they would not be published in newspapers or elsewhere.[99] Even the financial records that exist can be read in a variety of ways; at times the Overseers' aggregate accounts do not match figures found in the *Boston Records*, for example, and precise budgets are difficult to establish. Still, the figures do suggest that in the 1760s costs for relief averaged in the range of some two thousand to twenty-five hundred pounds per year. That included some Almshouse expenditures for ill, infirm, and disturbed public charges in the Workhouse; the shortfall in debits and credits in the Workhouse; and all Almshouse and outdoor disbursements. Of the total, some 15 percent was charged to the province for the non-Boston residents under the Overseers' care.[100] Costs rose dramatically during and after the Revolutionary War as the numbers of state (province) poor and their lengths of stay increased as a percentage of the whole. Of the remainder of the budget, which was the responsibility of the town treasury, some 15 to 20 percent was claimed by individual Overseers for out-of-pocket expenses that ran as high as eighty and ninety pounds in some wards in some years. While there were as many as three hundred recipients of outdoor relief in some years, their impact on the poor relief budget was not great because most were on short-term and partial relief. It was the Almshouse that used up the poor relief budget. There were never more than a few outdoor poor on full-time support, in contrast to the 120 to 200 or more persons who were in the Almshouse at any given time during most of the period. The existing financial figures are quite emphatic in that regard and are supported by the Overseers' personal financial accounts, such as exist.[101]

Samuel Whitwell, an Overseer from 1769 to 1790, spent all but two of those years in charge of Ward 10, which was south of Long Wharf in the area of Fort Hill, with extensive waterfront habitation. The wards that Whitwell served (2, 10, and 12) each had populations somewhat larger than the average, which was about twelve hundred, in perhaps two hundred families, in the early 1770s.[102] Even if his account contains no commentary or observation, it nevertheless affords us a sketchy idea of the process of poor relief away from the Almshouse. His numbers are quite astonishing in what they reveal of the tireless work of a ward Overseer. In the fiscal year following March 1769, for example, Whitwell disbursed £64-12–8 1/2 out of his own funds, for which he sought repayment with interest from the Town Treasurer. In that same year Whitwell recorded 322 transactions for 59 separate individuals. Some 203 of the payments were made in cash, usually in sums ranging from two to six shillings each; the other 119 disbursements were for wood for fuel. In fact, the vast majority of grants in the winter months were for wood. In the warmer months grants were usually for small sums of cash, likely for food. Here and there the cash was assigned to specific purposes such as "paid John Cades for Mrs Flemmings funerall"; "schooling 4 poor Children 3 mo[nths] @ 2/– [two shillings] per week" (in May 1770); "digging Wells at Workhouse"; "to buy a spinning wheel"; support for "a free negro"; "for keeping a bastard child." He even paid someone three shillings "for crying that the Workhouse Windows were broke." Although Whitwell spent more money in 1771 and again in 1778, he tended to more people in 1769. In all there are 1,750 entries regarding more than 230 separate claims (names) in Whitwell's book—truly remarkable figures, when the sequence of those entries are considered. Most of them occurred prior to 1778, and over half of them, indeed, were made before the end of 1775, which is another reminder of the impact of the wartime evacuation of Boston.[103]

When much of Boston's population emigrated to safety in that period and only slowly returned by the early 1780s, outdoor relief declined rapidly and deeply. Contrast, for example, the 322 entries of 1769 with the 8 in 1780 and the 9 in 1781 (as many as 60 recipients to as few as 4).[104] That does not indicate an amelioration of poverty or need, however, but rather reflects that Boston's population had reached its eighteenth-century nadir then, and with no public funds available, the poor of Boston either went elsewhere or in some cases simply fended for themselves. Overseers continued to send large numbers of needy into the Almshouse in this period and were likely more concerned with feeding the completely dependent inmates than with trying to relieve a few outdoor claimants. What Whitwell's accounts tell us, above all, is that the ward system engaged the individual Overseers in dozens of personalized transactions of something very much like public charity under the patronage of the town's economic and social elite. It was very much a complement to the Almshouse in that help was given in a spirit of charity.

In some respects the most intimate of the Overseers' human relations was the binding out of orphans and neglected or abandoned children and youth. Children were "bound out" by formal indenture into apprenticeships, farm labor, or domestic service. The latter was clearly the fate of just about all the female children who ended up as indentures. The role of the Overseers in these cases was as surrogate parents. While English common law and Massachusetts statute did not require bound servants to be educated, parents and in many cases the Overseers, did require training (education) in the indenture, so that domestic service might have been formalized as "housewifery," a skilled status. The majority of bound children were indentured from the Almshouse rather than directly from home, often after they had been removed from unsuitable homes under laws that made Overseers the guardians of children who were abused or neglected or abandoned. Overseers were in fact obliged to act on their own to protect children under the various amendments to the 1692 act. They could remove children from homes or conditions when they judged the atmosphere to be immoral or indecent. Moreover, the residue of Puritan communalism insisted on the proper "citizenship" rituals of youth, which included scriptural and secular literacy and an understanding of what might be called civics. Overseers, in the wards, could make the proper legal recommendation for the removal of a child on any number of grounds.[105] Also, parents who wanted their children brought up or taught or trained outside the home volunteered their children for indentures. In a minority of cases, children came into the Almshouse, usually with a single woman, and were then indentured.

While the Overseers had great latitude under the law to make subjective decisions regarding the binding out of minors, they were under an equal or greater restraint to nurture. Overseers went to great lengths to ensure the security and prospects of their charges. In a procedure that occurred many hundreds of times in the second half of the eighteenth century, Boston's Overseers of the Poor reviewed the suitability of masters and mistresses in taking indentures for up to fifteen years in some cases. Normally, any person to whom any child was being bound was required to provide character references witnessed by the most senior local officials. An example from Bridgewater from 1739 gives a good sense of procedure for an out-of-town application to have a Boston child indentured:

Bridgewater November the 2d 1739

To the Honorable the Selectmen or overseers of the Town of Boston, these are to recommend Samuel Donbar and his wife as persons capable to bring up a child or children to any coman learning necessary to qualify them if naturally capable thereof to get a comfortable living in the world as witness our hand

Josiah Edson
Ephraim Toby   } *Selectmen of Bridgewater*
Recompense Cary

The records indicate that the applicant, Donbar, was accepted as a suitable master by the Boston Overseers in 1739.[106]

At the other end of the period there is a sharp example of how well the procedures were being followed. In a letter to the Selectmen of Eden, Maine, the Boston Overseer Jonathan Austin wrote, on April 18, 1797:

> *Sir*
>
> *It is unusual to bind children from the Almshouse without a certificate from the Selectmen of the Town recommending the Person to whom they are to be bound, but if Mr Smallige will obligate himself to bring such a certificate within three Weeks, & the Parents of the Child consent to the Boys going with him; upon these conditions I have no objection to have the Indenture [filled?] up and signed by him, the indenture on the part of the Overseers to be delivered when ever he sends the Certificate from the Selectmen [of Edem].*
>
>

Your hum[ble] Serv't
J. L. Austin, Overseer

The records confirm this indenture for Henry P. Clark, to learn "husbandry" on a Maine farm. It is clear that although the boy was in the Almshouse at the time of the indenture, his mother's permission was still required.[107]

The Overseers maintained that authority into the nineteenth century and retained an interest, and indeed a stake, in the welfare and fate of anyone they had indentured. The following letter was found attached to the original indenture of December 26, 1797, of Sophia Ridgeway.

> *Messers Gentlemen Overseers of the Town of Boston in the County of Suffolk,*
>
> *We the Subscribers Selectmen of the Town of Walpole would inform you that one Sophia Ridgway [sic] a Molato Garle was placed to Doc[tor] Jonathan Wild of said Walpole as an apprentice* [most likely a house servant] *till she showd arive to the age of Eighteen years which term was completed the Sixth day of December last, we would further inform you that for about Seven years past She has been in a great degree deprived of her Sight and hearing, the cause we know not, the medical assistance has been administered as much as was thought proper, and by information and our own observation it has not been in the power of humane wisdom to quallifier her with Such learning as your Indentures mention. We would Query whether it would be best under her circumstances and age to let her loose among the Tawny tribe, but we trust that you in your wisdom will be able to determine that matter—*
>
>

We are with all proper respect
your most Obedient Serv'ts
Ichabod Clap
Daniel Kingsbury
Sam'l Hartshorn

Selectmen of Walpole

The Overseers and Their Functions

The reference to casting out the "garle" to join the "Tawny tribe" or returning her to the Overseers' care is of particular note here. Neither Sophia Ridgeway's master nor the town officials of Walpole felt much obligation to care for this nearly blind and deaf "molatto" girl who, most likely, was barely literate if at all. It is unlikely that Doctor Wild had taken her in as a charity case in the first place, and he probably felt that her infirmities were the responsibility of the Boston Overseers, who retained ultimate responsibility for her health and comfort.[108]

These kinds of communications were repeated many hundreds of times in the eighteenth century. The manuscript indentures for about 1,100 children and youth in public care have survived, and their editor Lawrence Towner estimates that another 300 or so have been lost for the 1734 to 1800 period. There is no way of estimating how many children were indentured in that way by the Overseers of the Poor between the 1690s and the middle decades of the eighteenth century, but certainly the numbers should conform closely to the ratios of the 1740s and 1750s. During the period from 1756 to 1773 the Overseers kept precise lists and recorded the names, lengths of service, destinations, and masters or mistresses of 470 indentures in simple entry form. For the same period, Towner found only 397 indentures that match the Overseers' lists. He also found about 25 indentures not recorded by the Overseers. These figures confirm Towner's estimate that about 25 percent more orphans were indentured than the surviving records show. The indentures themselves ended up as part of the Town Records, and it appears that most of the lists kept by the Overseers have been lost. On a related matter, it might be noted that very few "private" indentures survive. It is likely that at the end of most private service indentures or apprenticeships the indenture forms were destroyed or discarded. The fact that so many Overseers indentures do survive reflects the official need to retain records. The Overseers indentures were similar to the many thousands of private and presumed lost Massachusetts indentures in terms of occupation, age, gender or length of service or contract.[109]

Perhaps the best way to think of the "binding out" to service or labor, in the social structure of Massachusetts, is to view it as an integral part of the regional labor economy on the one hand and as a form of social and moral communalism on the other. Formal apprenticeship indentures were also part of that socio-economic system. The rich practicality of the system is perhaps best illustrated by the experience of the Overseers' most famous indentured poor law apprentice, Isaiah Thomas, the son of a poor widow. Thomas was bound out for thirteen years as an apprentice printer to Zachariah Fowle of Boston and afterward became the greatest New England publisher of the age and America's leading historian of printing.[110] What is less familiar in Thomas's history is that he went back into the system that had nurtured him and in 1771 took Anthony Haswell for six years as an indentured apprentice from the Overseers. There is very likely no coincidence here, and certainly no irony. Isaiah Thomas fully understood the obligations of his station, his debt to the community, and the practicality of nurturing the needy.

The system of binding out was a complex one in strictly bureaucratic and legal terms, involving as it did Overseers, Selectmen, and Justices of the Peace in addition to the child, his or her parents, and the master or mistress in the indenture agreement. But the principal public officials involved in the process were the Overseers. In another way, however, the system was simply a deeply held cultural remnant from an earlier Massachusetts, and an even earlier English idea that children were the wards of the whole community and were valuable assets, in the present and for the future. We do well to remember that there was no "orphanage," and the notion of sequestering children in a specialized asylum would have been alien to the values of eighteenth-century Overseers, who knew the children they indentured and sought to expose them to the experience of the wider community and culture as much as maintain them within a conventional family setting. They were closer to them than any other public authority, and while Almshouse keepers, inmates, and ultimately a master or a mistress served *in loco parentis*, it was the Overseers who vouchsafed the child's welfare.[111]

The old Settlement Laws of Massachusetts were revised a bit in 1793 but essentially retained their original intent. They remained the most effective means of keeping order in the towns of Massachusetts.[112] The history of residency rights is one of the great seams that runs through Massachusetts's institutional history from its English precedents and the apogee of the Puritan commonwealth to the public commonwealth of the nineteenth century. The origins of "warning out" in Massachusetts are found in the original land distribution patterns that tied occupation of land and congregational membership to a "right" to residency in the towns of the colony. The practice evolved into more ad hoc settlement criteria that were based mostly on fears that allowing "strangers" to settle who might be or become a public welfare liability. The prospects of having to "entertain" at public expense the infirm and poor led in the seventeenth century to a custom of first warning out those who could not satisfy the Selectmen by guaranteeing their own solvency or by securing a notable sponsor. This form of transient and immigration control was finally formalized in Massachusetts by the sweeping act of 1692 that among other things created the office of the Overseers of the Poor and defined its functions. That act secularized the remnants of the congregational specifications for residency and remained the mechanism for removal of "warned" migrants into the nineteenth century. There is some debate as to when "warning out" formally ended, but it appears that the practice began to diminish if not cease after the 1793 act[113] even while the right to remove unwanted migrants remained under the modified residency requirements of the 1793 act. The residual "vagrancy" laws of twentieth-century American communities hark back to a notion of "legal residence."

In fact, warning out was only the second stage of a three-stage procedure for removing nonresidents (those without the right of "settlement") from Boston or any other town in Massachusetts. The first stage required the host of any stranger to notify the town. The second involved a formal warning, issued by an appointed agent of the Town Meeting and responsible to the Selectmen. The third stage was the physical removal of any warned persons who had not departed after the warning. That part of the process required the application of the Selectmen and the legal writ of two justices. In a strictly legal and clerical sense, warning out was not normally a concern of the Overseers. As the following excerpt from the published Selectmen's minutes of 1765 shows, the actual warning out of "strangers" was not even done by the Overseers, but by contracted individuals who were paid a bounty for each person warned out.

> The Selectmen this Day agreed with Messrs John Sweetser, Robert Love and Cornelius Thayer, the three Persons appointed to warn Strangers to depart this Town that there shall be paid to them the Sum of Fifty three Pounds six shillings and eight pence lawful Money, for a Years service which is to commence from the date hereof; said Sum to be shared and divided in proportion to the Number of Persons each have warned, for which Caution shall have been entered by them, and a Copy of their Return to the Clerk of the Sessions given in to the Selectmen every Month—their pay to be drawn for quarterly if desired.[114]

The Robert Love mentioned in the foregoing appointment kept a very good record of his activities. His account book at the MHS illustrates the scale of transiency in Boston. For example, over a nineteen-month period in 1765 and 1766 over 400 people were warned out, at an average rate of 20 a month. Love does not explain the precise reasons for his warnings but does offer a clear example of procedure. From October 14, 1765:

> John Rankin Last from providance By Land his Wifes name is Margret Came to Town the Last Day of Last August Lodged first att Mr Mortons At the Sign of the White Horse att present in a Chamber att the South End Warned in his Majestys Name to Depart this Town of Boston in 14 Days.[115]

If John Rankin's status was determined ultimately because of his financial condition, the Overseer who provided him with relief might have informed Love, or the Selectmen. As the senior civic officials in the dense but compact wards of Boston the Overseers often identified "strangers," and it was the Overseers who appear to have kept the lists of the names of the "warned," so that if an appeal for alms or outdoor relief was made by a person or family that had been warned out, the Overseers would have a record of that warning and would apply a charge to the senior Massachusetts government or to the original settlement location of the warned person. In short, warning out had a serious budgetary rationale; it allowed Overseers to identify those poor and needy who were entitled to relief as Bostonians because of birth, marriage, contract, or permission to settle. Several partial lists exist for various periods between 1745 and 1792, but the record is incomplete. Moreover, the lists of names, which also give original domiciles, indicate the fate of only a handful of those warned, and it is not at all evident in the lists who actually left or were removed from Boston after being warned. Occasionally the entry for a warned person or family notes that those warned had been "carried" to another town, indicating some forcible removals.

Strangers were likely warned out for minor criminal behavior, drunkenness, prostitution, Sabbath-breaking, public cursing or disorder.[116] What is more important is that only a few of those who were warned out were identified as poor or otherwise proper subjects of the Overseers' mandate. Indeed, what is one to make of the warning out of Sir John Anthony of Mt. Royal (Montreal?) and of a fifth-generation John Winthrop Esquire of Cambridge and five of his family in 1792? Still, there were poor and sick persons among the throngs who moved through Boston after mid-century. Those are indicated in the numbers of Almshouse admissions charged to the province or state, which ran as high as 140 a year in the early 1790s, in mostly short-term stays, and as low as 15 a year in the late 1770s. But the number of those identified as poor or lame or widowed or ill and then warned out is very low indeed and amounted to fewer than 5 percent of the total. There is some evidence that some transient poor or ill were warned but were cared for under the Overseers' mandate. Or it might be that the poor and infirm did not move into Boston in large numbers in the first place. The Selectmen who had initial contact with out-of-town applicants for poor relief dealt with between fifteen and twenty appeals each year in the 1760s from needy transients. Perhaps the identification of transient poor in the pre-1770 warning out lists was entered only sporadically or whimsically. There are few economic or health distinctions made in the surviving lists beyond 1770, and it might be supposed from the absence of comment that no poor or sick people were warned out after that date.[117]

In any case, the authority to warn out lay with the Selectmen under Massachusetts provincial and later state law, and the authority to remove lay with the court. The Overseers' role was to correlate the names of poor relief claimants with the lists of warned migrants to determine financial responsibility. A summary of the document lists in the Overseers records indicates by extrapolation the scale of migration into Boston for most of the second half of the eighteenth century. Also, the summaries speak volumes about the social and geographical range of the migrants; perhaps the most striking statistic is the overwhelming preponderance of Massachusetts migrants among those who were warned out of Boston in the eighteenth century. There is nothing really surprising in that fact, but it serves to underline the appeal of Boston, despite its economic hardships, prior to the 1790s, to the restless thousands in the region around the town.[118] The fifty-mile arc around Boston was the source of the majority of all the persons warned out. Any consideration of warning out practices in New England must be careful to see the practice as variable from place to place and over time. A recent history of Rhode Island's experiences and standards in the second half of the eighteenth-century focuses on poverty as a dominant characteristic of migrants and notes a rise and then a decline in transiency in the 1780s and 1790s. Neither of those features would fit the warning out statistics for Boston. Moreover, the volume of warnings out of the Boston magnet shows a concentration and scale of transience that is absent in the Rhode Island figures.[119]

The Boston Overseers records include only three sets of surviving records. The first covers over two decades from 1745 to 1770 inclusive. The other two deal with very short periods, from 1771–1772 and 1791–1792 respectively.[120] The 1745–1770 list is organized alphabetically and was clearly compiled some time after 1770. As it is, the list is misleading in its chronology, and nearly 90 percent of its entries are from the 1756 to 1770 period, with the majority occurring in the 1760s.[121] In addition, while regional transience increased in the wake of King George's War and the French and Indian War, the most plausible reason for the upsurge in recorded cases is the bonus system of reporting that was announced in 1765. The incentive of being paid for every person warned out would inspire alacrity and volume.[122] The figures for the later part of the 1745–70 lists represent a trend in residency and migration patterns that corresponds to other evidence of transiency in the middle of the century. As many as six thousand persons may have been warned out of Boston between 1750 and 1770.

The first impression made by the statistics from 1771–1772 and 1791–1792 is the enormous leap in numbers of warnings between those decades. The numbers increased more than two and a half times. The only way to compare the gross figures of 1771 and 1791 with the figures from the late 1760s is to guess, because part of the 1771 record is missing. The figures before 1770 indicate that the numbers of warnings issued in the period from 1765 to 1770 were about three hundred a year, close to the numbers we have and can estimate for 1771 and 1772. But in terms of volume, the figures for 1791–92 are impressive. There are several possible reasons for the huge volumes of the 1790s. One is that Boston was once more an attractive economic destination for migrants, and population had begun to increase rapidly. The broad economic changes occurring in New England agriculture had led to increases in regional relocation for many, and the numbers of New Englanders warned out of Boston in the 1790s reached nearly 73 percent of the total (in fact, Massachusetts migrants accounted for nearly 70 percent of the total, making the immediate Boston area the source for over two-thirds of all migrants). Thus the pressures on poor relief facilities and budgets made the Selectmen less sympathetic to out-of-town supplicants.

But here is where the warnings reveal an interesting characteristic of migration: very few of those warned out of Boston throughout the range of the data were identified as "poor" or in other ways infirm or impotent. In fact, the few entries that refer to condition suggest conscious attempts by the clerks to identify the needy. Another feature of the lists is the appearance throughout of very large families. It was not uncommon for families of five or more to be warned, and there are several examples of families of between eight and eleven members.[123] Still, about two-thirds of all warnings were issued to individuals, in a rough balance between the sexes. The Overseers' lists record the fact that there were generally very few deserving poor among the migrants, and no children alone.

As noted, the Overseers have left no personal written accounts or impressions of their activities, either individually or as an agency of government. There is scattered material in their remaining records for the eighteenth century that resembles minutes or reviews and reports to the Selectmen or the Town Meeting. The monthly meeting minutes of the Overseers from 1789 to the 1820s in the Boston Public Library are useful for confirming what we can infer from the rest of the record, but those minutes are essentially straightforward bureaucratic notes and reveal nothing of the Overseers' sentiments, or philosophies. While the Town Records have hundreds of references to the Overseers, these are notes in the recorded minutes of and by the Town Meeting and the Selectmen. In the end we are left with mostly line entries in a number of collected record books that nevertheless reveal the ends of the Overseers' work, the care of the needy and the correction of the idle poor. By reading into their records we can at least breathe a little life into the otherwise silent custodians of public welfare in eighteenth-century Boston to let them say something about the way one privileged class cared for a less fortunate or less competent class. At the end of the day, perhaps the clearest statement of the eighteenth-century manuscripts of the Overseers is couched in a simple number: ten thousand. That is a conservative estimate of the number of needy who received relief from the Overseers, indoors and out of doors, in the period from the mid-1750s to the beginning of the nineteenth century.[124]

The Almshouse and Workhouse

OF THE ESTIMATED TEN THOUSAND INDIVIDUALS assisted by the Overseers in the second half of the eighteenth century a substantial number, perhaps as much as half, were assisted "out of doors," that is, at home, mostly as occasional recipients of temporary and partial relief. Those who received outdoor relief experienced a personal and often repeated contact with the Overseers, one that helped define the ethos of poor relief in the eighteenth century.[125] But regardless of the numbers involved, the amount of public funds dispensed in the neighborhoods of Boston was overshadowed by the amounts spent for Almshouse costs. More important, the hardships of those on outdoor relief paled in comparison to the needs and suffering of those whose circumstances drove them to the Almshouse. The Almshouse, it should be remembered, was a refuge for the truly homeless, the ill, and the involuntarily idle.

Between late 1758 and 1800 some seventy-two hundred admissions were ordered into the Boston Almshouse by the Overseers of the Poor, for residencies of as little as a day to as much as several years. Between 70 and 80 percent of admissions were individual men, women or children, while the remaining admissions were nuclear or single-parent families. Of particular note are the numbers of repeat admissions. The same names sometimes appear as much as several times in a year or over the span of a few years. A dramatic example of this pattern was the case of Nathaniel Fowles, his wife and four children who were in and out of the Almshouse three times in one 10-day stretch in late 1793. So, the numbers of admissions is always greater than the actual number of individual recipients of Almshouse relief. The admission entries of those people have survived. Over half of them stayed for more than three months in the Almshouse, and a substantial number, as much as 10 percent of those who entered, lived in the house for more than a year. Between 20 and 25 percent of all who entered the Almshouse died there.[126] Unlike those who received outdoor relief, the Almshouse poor were wholly dependent. Yet they were considered to be fit subjects of public support. The naming of the institution was appropriate both in 1686, when it opened, and thereafter as it became the conventional seat of institutional charity. "Alms" is a "gift" given out of "pity," aid given gratuitously to relieve the poor.[127] It is the "freely given" aid that best defines the philosophy and objectives of eighteenth-century Almshouse welfare.

The surviving Almshouse admissions and discharges documents in the Overseers collection represent the most extensive record of identified poor and dependent people in Boston in the eighteenth century, and while not as fully detailed as the manuscript documents of the early nineteenth century, the amount of information yielded by the eighteenth-century lists is far from spare.[128] The hundreds of manuscript pages listing thousands of Almshouse admissions reveal an extraordinary aggregate picture of institutional poverty and want, and while the Revolution appears to have created increased demand for institutional relief, the means and ends of poor relief were not affected by the Revolution in the short term. It would take a revolution in thinking about poor relief to bring substantial change to the means and ends of public charity in Massachusetts generally and in Boston in particular.[129]

Even then, there were some changes in the characteristics of the poor as they were entered into the control of the Overseers. The records show a more cosmopolitan Almshouse constituency, with clerks self-consciously referring to foreigners, and after the war to "Brittanors." Following the Massachusetts emancipation of slaves, the period after 1780 shows many more African Americans entering the Almshouse as their freedom simultaneously made many of them instant paupers. Although they represented only 6 to 7 percent of all Almshouse admissions, their proportion of the Boston population was only 4 to 5 percent. After 1780 the rate of African-American admissions was about double the rate of the 1770s and nearly three times greater than the 1760s rates.[130]

Moreover, the volume of all admissions tripled after Boston's recovery in the early 1780s. Boston's population had shrunk dramatically in the mid-1770s because of the war, partial depopulation, and the devastation of the area's economy. And here the major trend in poor relief in the post-independence era is most clearly revealed in the Almshouse records. In the period from 1774 to 1779 only about one-third of admissions were on the "province charge," while for the five-year period after 1783 the figure jumped to 63 percent and then to 68 percent in the early 1790s. The figures were reliably reported because of the budgetary advantages to the Overseers of distinguishing town charges from province charges. Also, because the law required Selectmen as well as an Overseer to admit out-of-town persons to the Almshouse, the out-of-town charges are more easily recognized in the record, as town admissions show only the Overseer's name.[131] Before 1774 the records do not always indicate the residential status of the inmate and cite only Overseers for all entries, and estimates of town to province admissions ratios are difficult to establish. The following estimates indicate the trend in admissions from a predominantly Boston cast to a broader regional, national and international one:

Total entries charged to	Town	Province ("State" after 1782)
8/29/1774 to 8/28/1779	233	80 (34%) Percentages rounded off.
1/2/1783 to 8/30/1787	194	327 (63%)
1/1/1789 to 12/31/93	354	741 (68%)
1/1/1794 to end of 1800	1,152	1,141 (50%)

Foreigners, which now included Britons, were charged to the state, and in the 1790s the proportion of Almshouse admissions identified as foreigners rose significantly. A random sample of the recorded origins ("towns they belong to") from the 1795–1800 period shows that 43 percent of all Almshouse admissions were from outside the United States. Boston and Massachusetts combined for 47 percent, and the remaining 10 percent came from elsewhere in the United States. Of those on the 1791–1792 Warning Out lists, approximately 25 percent were identified as foreigners, a much higher ratio than the pre-Revolutionary warning out statistics. Moreover, as noted, the new Act of Settlement of 1793, which modified the existing regulations for warning out, represented an important shift in the administration of transience in Massachusetts. While it was still technically required that persons demonstrate residency rights, the new laws offered twelve ways to acquire settlement, and warning out became more difficult, even if Overseers continued to "charge" other towns for the care of their poor.[132]

There was a rise too in the 1790s of the proportion of single persons in the admissions lists; in the two decades up to 1800 single men outnumbered single women in the Almshouse population. The wider meaning of that statistic awaits further study of the social history of post-Revolutionary New England. There can be no doubt that the shifts in the composition of the Almshouse constituency in the Federalist age have implications for many other social changes in New England. In any case, the general rise in demand for public welfare derived in part from rising population in eastern Massachusetts and from significant changes in the impact of economics on the demographics of the region and Boston in particular. The increased pressure on the Almshouse in the 1790s led to a movement for new facilities. By that time the original Almshouse was over one hundred years old, having been built to serve a town with a population of about forty-five hundred. It had been enlarged by an addition of about 50 percent more space in 1742, and even if that and the 1738–39 Workhouse had eased the pressure at midcentury, by the 1790s it was once again discommodious, and because of its age, decrepit.[133] The Workhouse of 1738–39, when the town's population was about thirteen thousand, had been inspired first by a rapidly growing population and then by the overcrowding in the Almshouse brought on by the mingling of two kinds of poor: the deserving, and the indigent. Before 1739 the town records used the terms almshouse and workhouse to describe the dual functions of the Almshouse building, and there were clear attempts to keep the indigent poor away from the deserving poor (there would have been separate entrances to the building), but some mingling was inevitable. After the completion of the Workhouse the distinction between the inmates, and the supervisory roles of the keepers was made clear in the records. That timely institutional separation and the fact that Boston's population did not grow between 1742 and 1784 meant that, as taxed as the buildings' capacities became during times of rising demand, they were not continuously overflowing. After 1790, however, rapid population growth and the pull of economic opportunity in Boston put increased pressure on the overall civic infrastructure of Boston. The complex of Almshouse, Bridewell, and Workhouse at the northeast edge of the Common was by then clearly overwhelmed.

The following charts summarize the surviving recorded admissions to the Almshouse from the end of 1758 to early 1800. The figures presented here are estimates only, and were compiled by simply counting entries. There were difficulties in sorting out duplicated entries, and given the often unclear definitions used by the original clerks, many of the gender, age and family designations cited here have been determined by the author.

Admissions: November 9, 1758 to December 31, 1774

Individual men	538
Individual women	592
Men with children	2
Women with children	205
Men and women with children	38 (19 families)
Men and women with no children	70 (35 families)
Total white males	**608**
Total white females	**677**
Individual children	306
Children with parents	208
Total children	**514**
Indians	3
African American males	21
African American females	13
Total African American	**34**
Total admitted (persons)	**1,836**
Discharged, ran away, or bound out	891
Dead	424

The differences between the dead and discharged and the total admissions is about eight hundred, and indicate underreporting.[134]

Admissions: January 1, 1775 to September 30, 1788

Individual men	563
Individual women	624
Men with children	9
Women with children	122
Men and women with children	34 (17 families)
Men and women with no children	76 (38 families)
Total white males	**627**
Total white females	**801**
Individual children	177
Children with parents	203
Total white children	**380**
African American males	36
African American females (includes 3 couples)	44
African American children (includes 9 with women)	19

Total African American	**99**
Total admitted (persons)	**1,909**
Discharged	249
Ran away	164

Again there is a considerable discrepancy in the numbers recorded as admitted and those who were discharged or ran away. Even allowing for a 25 percent death rate, there is a clear underreporting of those leaving the Almshouse.

Admissions: October 1, 1788 to August 30, 1795

Individual men	601
Individual women	475
Men with children	8
Women with children	66
Men and women with children	36 (18 families)
Men and women with no children	50 (25 families)
Total white males	**652**
Total white females	**584**
Single children	118
Children with parents	151
Total children	**269**
Indian	1
African American males	48
African American females	36
African American children	8
Total African American	**102**
Total admissions (persons)	**1,603**
Discharged, ran away, bound out, died	1,097

Here too the numbers who are reported to have left the Almshouse are clearly too low, even if we allow for about 500 deaths in this period.

Admissions: September 1, 1795 to early 1801.

Individual men	766
Individual women	665
Men with children	no evidence of any

Women with children	60
Males and females with children	24 (12 families)
Men and women with no children	30 (15 families)
Total white males	**799**
Total white females	**752**
Individual children	107
Children with parents	118
Total children	**225**
Indians	9
Lascars (East Indian sailors)	7
African American males	65
African American females	49
African American children	21
Total African American	**140**
Total Admissions (persons)	**1,926**

These charts show changes in the composition of the Almshouse population that reflect some change in Boston's social and economic conditions over nearly a half a century. From the outbreak of war in 1775 to the early nineteenth century Boston society was subject to a succession of disruptions that redefined it. While the infrastructure of civic government survived, as did its political and economic ruling classes, a great part of the earlier population had been replaced. The evacuation of Boston in the 1770s and the town's eighteenth-century nadir was followed by a population boom in the 1780s and especially in the 1790s that had created a more fluid and less settled working-class population. In the Almshouse there was a decline in the ratio of families to general population and a clear and steady increase in the numbers of single adults, from about 60 percent of the whole of admissions in the 1760s to 75 percent by 1800. As noted, men outnumbered women in the Almshouse by the end of the eighteenth century. Children, either alone or with parents, declined as a percentage of the whole, from 28 percent in the first chart to 12 percent in the 1795 to 1800 lists.

As for the out-of-town admissions, these should be understood in relation to Boston population figures, especially those of the 1780 to 1800 period, as should the rapid increase in African Americans in the Almshouse, who were admitted at a rate considerably larger than their proportion of the general population. Boston's population in the eighteenth century showed the following boom, static, bust and boom cycle:

1700	6,700
1710	9,000
1720	11,000
1730	13,000
1740	16,382 (in 1742)

1750	15,731
1760	15,631 (in 1765)
1770	15,520
1780	10,000
1790	18,038
1800	24,937

In 1742 there were 1,374 (8.4% of the total population) African Americans in Boston; in 1750, 1,541 (10%); in 1760, 1,241 (8.0%); in 1765, 848 (5.5%); in 1790, 766 (4.2%) and in 1800, 1,174 (4.7%). In the 1795 to 1800 period, African Americans constituted some 7 percent of Almshouse admissions. Before the Revolution, their percentage of the Almshouse population had been only about 2 percent, in large part because slaves were normally cared for directly by their owners and would be admitted only in extraordinary circumstances.[135] As for Boston's demographics in relation to its hinterland, it is of note that during the eighteenth century the Massachusetts population grew from 56,000 in 1700 to 188,000 in 1750, to 235,000 in 1765, to 379,000 in 1790, and to 423,000 in 1800. The near doubling of the Massachusetts population from the end of the Seven Years War to the turn of the nineteenth-century taxed the public welfare systems of all towns in all regions and put additional pressure on Boston's poor relief physical and financial capacities as Boston attracted more and more migrants by the end of the century. As the admissions summaries show, the average annual admissions rates doubled between the late 1750s and the mid-1790s. As this trend continued, it inspired serious calls for reform of the poor relief system in the early nineteenth century.[136]

Boston, with a static or deteriorated tax base, remained the principal magnet for Massachusetts's increasingly mobile population, yet its Overseers were stuck with a dilapidated century-old Almshouse, its half-century old annex, and a crowded Workhouse. By the 1790s, as the Almshouse admissions swelled, the system in Boston was strained to the breaking point and would eventually become untenable. By then the new State House and a gentrified residential community had encroached upon the old site. And after 1790 Boston's population doubled every twenty-five years or so well into the nineteenth century, passing the 100,000 mark during the 1840s. By the age of Jackson, indeed, the scale and nature of poverty, and the "science" of applying numerical analysis to social problems, would change the meaning of poor relief beyond the imaginations of the eighteenth-century Overseers of the Poor. But at least to the turn of the nineteenth century the Almshouse retained its character as a haven for the needy and still reflected the philosophy of an earlier standard of paternalistic charity. Its routines, dietary regimen, and resident mix of men, women, and children of all ages, in families or alone, created a small intimate society. There was discipline, to be sure, but it had no clear intention to correct or even rehabilitate, and certainly no mandate to force the inmates to labor or to punish them.[137] In 1795 the buildings and land containing the Almshouse, Workhouse, and Bridewell were put up for sale and a new set of facilities was proposed for land obtained at Barton's Point. The days of the hundred-year old Almshouse were numbered, but the land at the corner of present-day Beacon and Park Streets on which the public welfare nexus had sat for decades, was not cleared until 1801, when a new Bulfinch-designed Almshouse was opened in Leverett Street at Barton's Point, near present-day Causeway Street. That building was about twice the size of the old Almshouse and while it had not been intended to be a catchall for Almshouse and Workhouse admissions and some prison functions, it served those purposes for most of its twenty-five year existence. It must have been impressive as public buildings go, and has been seen as the next most important, after the State House, of the many Bulfinch buildings in Boston.[138]

Any attempt to describe the daily routine of the old Almshouse with precision would be futile. But some assumptions can be made on the basis of the dense if silent statistics and the infrequent brief comments of the record keepers, and through the one known census of the Almshouse and inventory of its stock, taken in 1756. In the census of 1756, according to the clerk, 133 persons shared the thirty-three rooms of the house. Some 73 of the total population were women, including 17 with children. Twelve of the occupants were children without parents, but only four of those are named, in contrast to all the adults. Of the children who are named, all but one show up in the indentured lists for the period, along with four of the children who were in with their mothers. Altogether there were 44 children in the house in August 1756, including 32 who were lodged with their mothers. One woman inmate had five of her children with her, and another had four. Those figures are in keeping with the proportion of children who show up in the admissions lists for the late 1750s and early 1760s. The number of single men and women in the house, 24 and 48 respectively, also conforms roughly to the admissions ratios of the period. Five deaths were noted, probably reflecting changes from a previous census. There were three husbands and wives in residence, including one with a child. From newborn children to a ninety-two-year-old woman, and from a room with nine people in it to one with a lone woman occupant, the house resembled both a familial commune and a transient hostel. There were two "negro women" lodged with three other women and a child. There was a strict separation of the sexes, except when the married couples were lodged with single women. The tenure of this list of occupants is unknown because it cannot be matched to anything else. The admissions lists for 1756 have been lost, as have all those prior to 1758.[139] But slightly later figures, including the estimates of Stephen Wiberley, indicate that more than half the adults had been in the Almshouse for up to three months, and perhaps as much as a quarter of the adults for six months. A fragmentary list from September 1765 indicates that of the 37 inmates then in the Almshouse on the "province charge," 13 had been there for six or more months. That ratio fits the earlier and later estimates for residential continuity.[140] Not only would this little community be on familiar if subordinate terms with Samuel Proctor, the Almshouse keeper in the 1750s and 1760s, but each would have personal contact from time to time with an Overseer. The inmates ate together, prayed together, and attended lectures together. There was some freedom to leave the Almshouse during the day, for some, but most were confined to the premises. The simple daily routines of laundry, cleaning, schooling, cooking, and chopping wood were shared.[141]

Criticisms of the Almshouse were made by inmates and contemporary observers, and historians too have decided that the Almshouse was neither safe nor healthy. Towner claims that children were happy to be bound out because the Almshouse was less pleasant, apparently, than any destination they might have. He cites an observation of Cotton Mather, from 1697, who reported that one Abigail Day "had complained bitterly about the food at the almshouse, saying that 'she would thank neither God nor Man for such Victuals' and about the master of the house, who, she said, 'had several Times made Attempts upon her Chastity.'" And even the Bulfinch Almshouse of the early nineteenth century after only a few years of operation was considered unhealthy. Towner quotes a pungent 1819 Overseers report on construction at the site, which complained that the old "vaults" for the Almshouse "privies" had been directly connected to the water drain from the kitchen pump and cast a stench, according to rising tides and east winds, "not only...through the yard … but … into … the body of the house." Towner concludes: "Whether or not these pictures indicate the true nature of the food, the morals, and the smells of the almshouse, they suggest that getting out was a good thing [for children at least]."[142] Perhaps it was, but getting into it was also a good thing for thousands of others. As to the indictment of the keepers, it seems that the Overseers kept a tight rein on their assistants in both the Almshouse and the Workhouse.

There is very little documentary evidence on the Almshouse keepers, but what there is indicates that what Mather reported would not have been tolerated for long by the Overseers. They constantly supervised the keepers and scrutinized their accounts and behavior. When they got a good one, they kept him or her. When Henry Dyer died in 1742, his widow, Hannah, took over the position only after a two-year review. Samuel Proctor held the position for nearly twelve years because he could be trusted to look after the inmates as well as the finances. A handful of marriages were recorded as having taken place in the Almshouse, and it is tempting to think of them as compelled by the keepers or Overseers because of a pregnancy incurred there. In eighteenth-century terms, accommodations, diet, hygiene, and regimen of the Almshouse, even if it was unpleasant for some, would have been preferable to the conditions that prevailed in either the hovels or homelessness that were the alternatives for most of the poor. For others, who were sick or handicapped or aged, care was provided by doctors and possibly in some cases by attending relatives. From the earliest surviving Overseers financial records, from the 1740s, there is ample evidence of a sustained medical budget that was used to engage doctors for the Almshouse and Workhouse and "poor of the Town." The Overseers appointed at least one doctor a year to work on contract for the care of the poor, as follows in this example from 1744:

> Doctor William Rand was unanimously chosen Physician for the almshouse and for the poor of the Town—on the following Terms:
> Five Shillings old Tenor per day for visiting the Poor of the Almshouse and work house—

Five Shillings for the first visit of the Poor out of the House[;] 2/6 for after visits—

Medicine to be charged at [?] price[;] for amputation and salvation Ten pounds Old Tenor.

That function was sustained throughout, as is evidenced by the following note from an Overseers meeting in 1789:

Noted that Docter Aaron Dexter be physician to the Almshouse & Workhouse for the year ensuing. That the Docter's sallery be thirty pounds per annum for Medicines & Attendance, Sallivations in extraordinary Cases in the Almshouse & Workhouse. That the Physician be oblig'd to attend personally at both Houses at least once a Day & that he practice Physic, Surgery & Midwifery in both Houses & attend when call'd upon by any overseers to visit the sick in any of the wards. I agree to take the care of the poor of the Town on the above terms also to receive One hundred & twenty pounds [?] of the State for the same attendance on their poor. Commencing the 15th May 1789. [Signed] Aaron Dexter.[143]

The Almshouse, for many, was the only place to go to be treated for illnesses as varied as gonorrhea ("ye French P[ox]) or the "itch" or to be "salavated for ye [smallpox]."[144]

It is worth noting the 133-year span of Mather's remarks and the Towner quote from 1819 and the fact that anyone at any time could find a reason to criticize the poor relief system from any side of the issue of public welfare. Still, by the 1790s criticisms of the crowding and hygiene of the old Almshouse were not only being made by the Overseers, who were perennially appealing for more space and more protection for the deserving poor, but by others in the community, some of whom simply wanted the Almshouse removed from its site near Boston's grand new landmark, the State House. After 1801, according to a late nineteenth-century reflection by Nathaniel Shurtleff, one could now walk in the Common or in Beacon Street and not be

interrupted by the diminutive hands thrust through the holes in the almshouse fences, or stretched beneath the decaying gates, and by the small and forlorn voices of the children of the destitute inmates entreating for money…nor will the cries of the wretched poor in those miserable habitations [the old 1686 Almshouse] be heard calling for bread.[145]

The poignancy of Shurtleff's description reflects more his high Victorian sentiments and literary habits than it does the reality of even the worst conditions in the old Almshouse and Workhouse setting. But it indicates the lingering and persistent reputation of the old Almshouse as a decrepit refuge for the town's needy.

As for diet, there is no way of knowing whether or not what Almshouse residents were supposed to have is what they received. Cooking, brewing and eating areas were clearly laid out in the Almshouse of 1686 and its replacement in 1801, as were rules for assembly, meal times and proposed diets. No dietary chart exists for either the Boston Almshouse or the Workhouse before 1819. We can assume that a New York

Almshouse menu for 1736 discovered by Stephen Wiberley corresponded roughly with what the Boston poor would be offered. The foods listed below do also correspond with dietary evidence from Boston in the first half of the eighteenth century.

Weekly menu for the New York Almshouse, 1736:

Breakfast:		Dinner	Supper
Sun.	bread and beer	beef or mutton, with broth and herbs in season	sappan and milk
Mon.	milk porridge	pork and pease porridge	bread and beer
Tues.	sappan and milk	As Sunday	bread and cheese
Wed.	beef broth and milk	fish or pork and pease	sappan and milk Porridge
Thurs.	milk porridge	beef and cabbage	beef broth and bread
Fri.	sappan and milk	as Sunday	bread and cheese
Sat.	bread and beer	pork and pease porridge	sappan and milk or sugar[146]

This regimen is marked by at least two prominent characteristics: first, the amounts per serving are not shown but in the case of bread, porridge and sappan (most likely a boiled cornmeal mush) there was probably enough for the diners to fill themselves with caloric and carbohydrate bulk and there appears to be adequate protein in the diet. Second, the repetitions in the diet reflect inventory availability and control, and preparation efficiency. Feeding upwards of 150 persons required some careful organization.

The following Boston Almshouse menu from 1819 shows some changes in the varieties of foods on offer but also some persistent items such as broth (given here as "soup") and porridge. But there is some emphasis on "Plenty of Vegetables" and the diners are encouraged, it seems, to eat their fill. It is worth noting the strict orders regarding behavior.

Bill of Fare for Boston Almshouse

1 Quart of Milk Porage for Each grown Person in Proportion for Children- Each Morning in the week for Breakfast-

Mondays Wednesday & Friday
Boiled Rice and Mollasses for Dinner Each Day

Sabbath day Tuesday and Thursday
Beef or Mutton Soups with Plenty of Vegetables Each of those days

Saturday Salt Fish Potatoes Carrotts & Beats with Butter or Dip-when out of Fish-Baked Pork and Beans-or Beefs head Soup

For Supper Each day in the week
1 Quart of Bohea Tea Sweetened with Molases with Sufficient Milk for the Same with Bread—no Butter, nor Chease allowed the paupers in the alms-house—that are in health-no Rum or any other kind of spirit used in the Almshouse but for medicine—4 Hhds [hogsheads, about 85 imperial gallons] of Beer Brewed Weekly for the use of the Paupers—3 pounds of hoops [hops] & 3 galls of molasses to each Hhds-as all the Paupers Breakfast Dine & sup together except the Sick—they have Liberty to eat as much as their appetite Craves—but are not allowed to Carry any food from the victualing room.
Notification on the Door of the Dining Room
Notice
Any Subject of this house who may be found Bringing in any kind of Spirits Shall be put under Confinement –any Person who goe out of this House to Return the Same day and do not Return –shall be confined until released by the Overseers of the week.[147]

The Boston Records tend to bear out the adequacy of the Almshouse and Work-house diets, and while there were times when food was scarce, those are rare, and occurred during crises such as smallpox or wartime evacuation or disorder.[148]

The Almshouse population of 133 in 1756 was close to the capacity of the old building's design, with variations allowed for various types of residents and the rate of turnover. There were several ways of being released from the Almshouse. People were discharged to their original places of residence if they were not legally resident in Boston. Bostonians were released into the town when they found work or when they had recovered from illness; children were bound out to service, as were some adults; death took many of the very old, who in some cases had been admitted to the Almshouse for comfort and company in their final days, and death took some of the very young too; some inmates "ran," as it was recorded, which meant simply that they left of their own volition without formal release, in some cases under threat of being transferred to the Workhouse; some were, in fact, sent to the Workhouse if their behavior threatened the order or security or the morality of the Almshouse.[149] It could likely accommodate up to about 200 individuals with some effort (six to a room) and 160 in relative comfort if families were mixed into the population. Various sources have suggested Almshouse populations as low as 110 in the 1740s, and even lower in the first few decades of the smaller 1686 Almshouse, and as high as 250 in the 1760s, and even higher in the 1790s. While the crowding suggested by the higher figures could not be sustained for long, and was quite likely the result of temporary surges in demand, it is certain that by the 1790s, the Almshouse was persistently overcrowded.[150]

By the end of the century the days of the old Almshouse building as a refuge for the deserving poor were clearly numbered. Overcrowding and a subsequent deterio-ration of rudimentary sanitation alarmed Overseers and private philanthropists alike, and groups such as the Humane Society supported the Overseers in their attempts to replace the Almshouse. The Reverend Mr. Clarke's "Discourse to the Humane Society" of June 11, 1793, bubbles with indignation, and his invocation of John Howard, the late English prison reformer, is of particular note. Mr. Clarke's observations not only echoed an Overseers' report of 1790 but also added a measure of moral urgency to the matter:

> [The 1686 Almshouse] is wholly inadequate to the purpose. It wants every requisite to a place of refuge for age, sickness, and poverty. The benevolent Howard would say it is rather a dungeon than a hospital. It can neither be ventilated nor properly cleansed. And it is altogether disproportioned to the number of those, whom necessity drives to the melancholy retreat. The evils unavoidably resulting from bad air and filth, are notorious. These evils, neither the physician nor the overseer can prevent. As long as our poor are so ill accommodated, poverty and dependence will be the smallest of their calamities. How powerfully then, does humanity plead in behalf of these sufferers? Of what importance is it, that they should be provided with a better habitation! How much are the publick honour and character concerned in such a measure![151]

An Almshouse committee report to the Town Meeting in 1790 states: "the building now occupied for the Almshouse is too near the Center of the Town, and not sufficiently Large to accommodate the Number of the poor at present in the House—previous to the War—the number did not exceed. 150 … or 180 … in the Winter season. nor 100 … or 120 … in Summer—There are in the present month of August between 270 … & 280 … in the ensuing Winter it is Probable that there will be between … 300 and 400 —."[152] The report goes on to describe the house and the yard as "foul," "disease-ridden," with an increasingly noisy and "profligate" component who were a constant threat to the manners, morals, and health of the deserving inmates. While the Almshouse had become unsanitary and had far exceeded its population capacity by the Federal age, the Workhouse, on the other hand, even into the 1790s, was less subject to overcrowding because it had a very limited residential capacity and a far more specific type of inmate.

The Workhouse was only half the age of the 1686 Almshouse, and was a very substantial structure by the standards of the day even though it was over a half-century old. The design of the Workhouse building is known from a 1737 report that confirms its location next to the Almshouse. It was contiguous with the prison and at least one of its rooms was assigned to the institutionalized insane.

> As to the Model of the House, the Committee Propose, that it be One Hundred and forty feet long, Twenty feet Wide, Sixteen feet high, from the lower Floor of the House to the upper or Garret floor, To be Built of Brick, to be upon a line and face to the South West, the Chimnies all on the North eastern or Backside, A Common Hall of Thirty two feet long, Five Other Rooms, All

these below; Nine Chambers, the Roof pitch'd whole, A Well A Convenient Separate House for Washing, Brewing, and Baking; And a House of Office.[15]

Clearly, this building was not primarily residential. The structure was as large as the Almshouse, which contained thirty-three sleeping rooms ("chambers") in contrast to the nine allowed in the Workhouse. The majority of the indoor area was given over to working space, for the employment of the "able" poor and the belligerent.[154]

Apart from the financial references to Joseph Lasenby, a long-serving Workhouse keeper of the 1750s to the 1770s, the Overseers' accounts and the admissions and discharges of Workhouse inmates noted in the Almshouse admissions make only scattered notes on the Workhouse throughout the eighteenth-century documentary record. The only sustained records of Workhouse inmates for the eighteenth century are the names of several dozen women at work picking oakum for several months in the 1790s. As late as 1794 efforts continued to break even on the Workhouse operations, but as early as 1741, the committee that audited the Overseers' accounts had found that the overhead costs for the Workhouse exceeded the value of the product of the inmates' labor:

> By which it Appears the Neat Charge of the Workhouse for Nineteen Months past is Five Hundred Fifty three Pounds Fifteen Shillings Due on the Maintenance of said House, during which Term taking One time with another, We find there has been Upward of Forty People provided for, and that there is now in said House Fifty-five Persons, Vizt. Ten Men, Thirty Eight Women and Seven Children. We also find that the Furniture of said House Amounts to Two Hundred Twenty three Pounds Eight Shillings and Six pence, that there has been laid out for Clapboarding the Backside and other Repairs of the House Two Hundred Fifty four Pounds Seventeen Shillings and Seven pence, and for Tools and Utensils Eighteen Pounds, Twelve Shillings and Two pence, which, three Several Sums Amounts to Four Hundred Ninety Six Pounds Eighteen Shillings and three pence.[155]

Given that there were costs incurred in putting people to "useful labor," it seems certain that the public was willing to support that cost if it kept the idle and intemperate off the streets. What is interesting here too is the preponderance of women to men (thirty-eight to ten) and the presence of seven children in the Workhouse, indicating another, perhaps biased, objective of corrective labor that focused on females. While the ratio in this report seems skewed a bit in light of later estimates, it is the case that women were usually the majority of the Workhouse population. This corresponds to the official preoccupation at times with illegitimacy. The ongoing fear by officials, especially by Selectmen, of idle strangers adding to the town's relief budget was hardly greater than the additional expense of an illegitimate child, to say nothing of the moral disapproval of that kind of pauperism.[156]

Thus there were logical, separate ends to each of the Overseers' two indoor facilities. The Workhouse ethic represented a broad societal disdain for idleness and forced the able poor to work for their keep, in contrast to the Almshouse. While the "Rules of the Workhouse" have survived, along with an account of its original funding by private subscription, there are few ways of catching a glimpse of life inside the building and its grounds.[157] The Workhouse was separated from the Almshouse by the Bridewell Prison in physical alignment, just as Boston's institutional management of poor relief and deviance was clearly subdivided in a system that distinguished care of the deserving poor to correction of the idle poor to penal incarceration for criminals including the criminal poor. Overseers committed the idle poor or troublemakers among the deserving poor to the Workhouse directly from the streets or from the Almshouse by transfer. There inmates were reformed, or at least punished or corrected, and put to work at any number of trades, including spinning and leatherwork. The majority of inmates were women and they usually ended up with the menial task of "picking oakum" from old rope, that is, separating loose fibers to be sold for caulking, with an end to supporting their own rehabilitation.

While inmates of the Workhouse technically were not criminals, they were in fact kept at the pleasure of the Overseers and subject to severe corporal punishment for indiscipline. In 1748 the original 1735 rules were revised to allow for more "oversight" and correction. In addition to the earlier practice of thrice weekly sermons to the inmates, a practice repeated in the Almshouse, Overseers were obliged to take a turn in the physical management of the Workhouse, each for a week in sequence, "to Visit the House as often as may be, at least three times in each Week for inspecting the management of it & the behaviour of the persons in it." This same Town Meeting revision also recommended "That the Overseers at their Monthly meeting or the Committee of Overseers be further Impowered to Punish such Persons as shall be legally Committed to the House and who shall threaten or attempt to make their Escape therefrom, or such as having Escaped shall be again so committed by fixing a Wooden Clog with an Iron Chain to one of the Legs of such Offenders."[158] That kind of supervision was not necessary in the Almshouse, of course, but the supervisory authority of the Overseers in the Workhouse was an interesting example of their "penal" duties, sanctioned by the town under the sovereignty of the General Court.

The Workhouse never paid its way; it was maintained by necessity to reflect the eighteenth-century distinction between alms and relief on the one hand and idleness as moral failure on the other. That distinction was marked by the attempts by Boston clergymen and merchants just before the Revolution to collaborate with civic officials to fund private variations of the public Workhouse.[159] Meanwhile, the steady stream of people coming and going between the two institutions under the signature of the Overseers was an example of an ongoing effort to determine the status of some cases as "deserving poor" and others not. In all of 1759, for example, some thirteen persons were sent from the Almshouse to the Workhouse, not an unusual figure in the administration of the poor. By the 1790s, however, these kinds of transfers had increased in frequency and volume. In one case in 1794, for example, thirteen men were sent as a group to the Workhouse to make room in the Almshouse for the transfer of eight women from the Workhouse. It seems that the Overseers could find no room in the Almshouse for some deserving poor women and culled some disruptive males from the Almshouse to make room for them. As for the reputation of the Workhouse in the 1790s, it is tempting to see the six women who ran away together from the Almshouse in September 1790 as doing so to avoid the Workhouse regimen. It seems that the Workhouse was much more difficult to run away from than was the Almshouse.[160] In 1741 there had been fifty-five persons, including thirty-eight women, in the Workhouse. Half a century later, two surviving manuscript lists of female oakum pickers in the Workhouse in 1794 and 1796 indicate a similar population in the building, including twenty-five women who were assigned each day to pick oakum. Of those, as few as four and as many as twelve would be missing each day because of sickness or because they were baking, cleaning, or caring for the sick or the young. Many were simply marked "absent." If thirty-eight women is a reasonable number to expect in the Workhouse in the 1790s, then about twelve were usually spared from having to pick oakum. Pregnant and elderly women would likely have been excused from the oakum tables on a full-time basis, but in that case it is difficult to see why such women would be sent to or kept in the Workhouse if not to work, unless, of course, these women were deemed unfit for moral or behavioral reasons to be kept in the Almshouse. We may account for the discrepancy between the potential for thirty-eight residents and the twenty to twenty-eight who show up on the lists by supposing that those not assigned to pick oakum had other tasks assigned to them. A considerable amount of batch cooking had to be done, according to the fixed dietary orders, and that is one task that was not routinely assigned to oakum pickers. There were spinning wheels in the Workhouse where inmates could spin for commercial sale, as had happened from time to time before the Revolution; and while there is no documentary evidence of women in the Workhouse being assigned to either full-time cooking or spinning, it is likely that a few of the inmates were, in fact occupied full-time in either the spinning room or the kitchen. Oakum pickers, on the other hand, were assigned from time to time to cleaning and baking and to tailoring, mending, and washing clothes. They were also allowed "out on liberty" or to attend "lectures" and were thus temporarily spared from productive labor. Moreover, once a week the majority of workers was assigned to a "general washing of clothes."

It is possible that only twenty-five or thirty women were in the Workhouse at any time during 1794, and in fact, during a seven-month period in that year only a little over fifty separate names appear on the oakum-picking lists. That suggests a steady turnover of inmates, although twelve of the twenty-four women who were listed in the oakum works on May 27, 1794, were there on December 23, 1794.[161] Oakum recycling was the only apparent source of outside income for the women of the Workhouse, because chores such as "cleaning of Bull's Heads" and "making soap," routinely assigned domestic work, were effectively in-house functions. Certainly those jobs can be considered a preferred alternative to the dirty tedium of twelve hours a day, sitting at a table, picking at old rope. While the object of Workhouse incarceration was correction and supervised labor for profit, other daily occupations contributed to the self-sufficiency in food preparation and household maintenance that would be part of the Workhouse ethic. In addition, work such as "cleaning the men's room" or the "hospital room," in addition to the stairwells, kitchen, and "copper" indicates gender-specific labor, to the extent that women were assigned occasionally to wash some of the men's clothes and always to care for the sick. The women who were ordered to do this by the female keeper of the Workhouse were also oakum pickers, and any work, in any case, was deliberately combined with discipline. Comments in the records such as "at play" denoted idleness rather than sanctioned leisure, and Eunice Edey, for example, who was noted "at play" several times was eventually "confined to Bridewell" for a day "for her wickedness."[162]

We can only guess at the possible uses for the few cents a day that were earned by female inmates. In the 1790s the daily average aggregate income for those who worked with the oakum was about $1.30 a day, or less than ten cents a day per capita. Whether or not any of this was taken back for food or other costs is not known, but if it was kept entirely for the inmate's release, it would not have gone very far. Thus one way of seeing the piecework values is as a measure of rehabilitation, with the Workhouse in all likelihood keeping all the income from the recycled oakum. But the range of earnings and productivity was great, and the benefits for hard work cannot be inferred from the record. Elizabeth Cornish, for example, earned a total of just over eight dollars for the entire seven-month period covered by the 1794 record. Cornish was a below-average earner who was absent or sick about 25 percent of the time and was reported for idleness three times and punished once. The same Eunice Edey who was punished in Bridewell seldom earned more than four cents a day picking oakum. By contrast, workers such as Fanny Swift and Mary Haines often made more than twenty cents a day and earned on average two to four times what Cornish or Edey did. Elizabeth Farrier was capable of earning fifteen to twenty cents a day, but picked oakum on only about 60 of the 172 days she appeared in the record. Otherwise, she baked bread regularly, sometimes twice a week, and did more washing than any other woman on the list; but if any of that counted as earnings it was not recorded. Elizabeth Leach was reported three times as "taking off to take care of Negroes in Bridewell."[163] Clearly, she was ordered to do so, but if she was compensated for being absent from the oakum crew it was not noted. In any case, there is no clear evidence that the harder-working women were released from the Workhouse earlier than the loafers.

Illness and disability were common, and up to six women reported sick each day. Some were chronically ill, such as Sally Stone, who was "subject to fits" and worked only a few days during several weeks on the list. Her name was nevertheless kept active. Similarly, Ann Cox seldom picked oakum, "being lame in one of her feet," but she too was kept on the list. Like sickness, death was never far away in this institution, and several deaths are mentioned or alluded to in the Workhouse lists for 1794. None of the women workers appears to have died in this period, but two children of inmates did, and Sally Kemp and her daughter, both inmates, lost their husband and father respectively in the Workhouse.[164] The death of Mr. Kemp and the oblique references in the Workhouse records to other male inmates reminds us of the frustrating gap in our knowledge of what the few men in the Workhouse did for a living or for occupational punishment or reform or subsistence. Whatever it was, shoemaking, tailoring, or laboring, there is no doubt that women did all or most of the routine and heavy domestic chores, in addition to the dirty and tedious job of picking oakum.

The Workhouse inmates rested on Sundays, of course, and it may be that they were preached to in the house, as they were from time to time in the Almshouse. Work was suspended also for militia training days, for reasons that are unclear, and on public election days. Indeed, it appears that there were also elections among the inmates, possibly for various supervisory positions, or for specific functions such as child care, and those too resulted in rest days. Thanksgiving Day was observed on the third Thursday of November 1794, and on July 4 of that year the Workhouse was reported as "Vacant, by reason of the North American Independency," on what had become, by then, a formal American holiday, suggesting that the inmates were allowed out en masse, under supervision, to celebrate with the general population.[165] For all that, discipline was the primary function of the Workhouse regime, and there are examples of corporal punishment and removal to the town prison. While there is no way of making precise comparisons of the disciplinary methods and punishments of 1738 and those of 1794, it seems that the regulations of 1738 were not significantly softened over time. In fact, it appears from the 1790s evidence, as scant as it is, that the original supervisory orders were still being enforced.

The amount of absenteeism that appears to have been tolerated, and the varied work assignments and incomes, indicate some flexibility or pragmatism in the management of the Workhouse and are faint suggestions of incentives. But in the end the Workhouse was intended to mark off the undeserving poor from other kinds of needy people. As sparse as the Workhouse records are for this period, they make clear the distinction between the coerced labor that served as reform for Workhouse inmates and the care and communalism offered in the Almshouse.

Some people clearly fell into disorder in the Almshouse, or conversely were reformed by the Workhouse. But it is the image of the Workhouse and not the Almshouse that has endured and that the modern mind imagines when it thinks of the "poorhouse." That may result in no small measure from the influence of British Victorian sentimentalists and from the fiction of Charles Dickens and others, and in a practical way from the actual American imitation of the English models depicted in the literature. In the United States the public poorhouse was invented in the age of Jackson, but the model was taking shape before then. The model for Josiah Quincy's beloved House of Industry in the 1820s is not the Almshouse but the Workhouse.

Indeed, by 1813 the Overseers were becoming more aware of that possibility and were having great difficulty in maintaining the Almshouse for alms alone. Rising levels of crime, transiency, idleness and social flux in a fast-rising population put enormous strains on Boston's public infrastructure. In 1813 the Overseers approached the Town Meeting with a desperate plea to build a new separate Workhouse, "which may also serve as a house of Correction" in order to maintain the integrity of the Almshouse as a refuge rather than the sequestered catchall that it had become for a medley of criminals, drunks, misfits and the mentally disturbed. The Overseers remarked on a

"Catalogue of wretchedness" where "debauched and profligate persons" might mingle with the deserving poor and needy, and where resident idle criminals "vitiating and debasing each other by their language and example" were threatening to overwhelm the Almshouse. That same 1813 report notes that in the Almshouse there were "403 persons of which 283 are old people, invalids, children &c—50 sick persons in the hospital rooms, 20 insane persons, affected in various degrees, some go at large, others are in close confinement, 50 persons employed at work, some well disposed & able of body, but above ten of them are subject for a bridewell or house of correction and are locked up."[166] As the nineteenth century progressed the various subdivisions of need would indeed find specialized institutions, from orphanages to insane asylums, but there would be no communal refuge like the Almshouse, and certainly there would be little or no public outdoor relief.[167]

As for the old Almshouse, its communal nature lay in sharp contrast to what the Overseers of 1813 described and that becomes evident in the way some of the records report births, deaths, and even a few marriages in the house itself. In the records, the only period of the eighteenth century in which births, deaths, and the ages of those admitted were systematically recorded was in the 1760s. For the rest of the record vital statistics are recorded sporadically if at all. But between 1756 and 1771 the Overseers listed 120 births in the Almshouse: as few as 3 and as many as 17 births a year, though in ten of the years the number was steady between 6 and 10 births. Between 1758 and 1774 they reported 424 deaths. A sample of 554 names in the 1758 to 1774 record gives us a rough idea of the age distribution of the inmates.[168]

Ages (years)	number	percentage
0–5	39	7%
6–15	50	9%
16–30	108	19%
31–59	208	38%
60–69	82	15%
70 and over	67	12%

Births and deaths were not merely incidental to Almshouse management but were integral to its *raison d'etre*. Needy women went into the Almshouse to have children because it was a safe place to do so and had been established in part for that purpose. The admission of four pregnant "camp women" in 1758 has to be seen against the backdrop of the Seven Years War and may identify women who were part of the camp life of a militarized community. Thirty years later, several years after the Revolutionary War had ended "a soldiers drap [likely drab]" that is, a prostitute was admitted during a week that saw several other women, an "Irish" male and two children entering the Almshouse. Eight children on average were born each year in the Almshouse and it is difficult to estimate how many of those were illegitimate, but some were identified as such. Chistian Isbister, for example, was admitted as a town charge five times to the Almshouse between 1760 and 1771 and four times gave birth. Little more is known about her, but none of her children appear to have been bound out, indicating that her children were perhaps legitimate and that she had some home or family in town where she could care for them when she was discharged. Mary McGowan (or McGown), on the other hand, gave birth to three children in the Almshouse, and all three were bound out to service by the Overseers. The Edward McGown who was with Mary in the 1756 Almshouse census can be assumed to be her husband, and she named her third Almshouse birth Edward in 1761. Being married, however, did not stop Mary McGowan from binding out her children. The other side of those births is the death rate for infants in the Almshouse. Ten of the 120 children born in the Almshouse according to the record are reported to have died, some clearly stillborn or shortly after birth, and one identified as two years old. But the Almshouse was likely safer than some of the options open to pregnant needy women. Those mortality rates are within the range of the larger population for this period.[169]

For the entire period under review the women admitted to the Almshouse with children but no accompanying male constituted 13 percent of all adult females, declining from an average of 18 percent in the early period to about 8 percent by 1800. That corresponds to the steep decline in the overall numbers of children who went into the Almshouse. There are cases of women running away or being discharged and leaving their children behind to be indentured. In a few cases children were bound out while their mothers remained resident, but most women who came in with children or who bore children in the Almshouse left with them. In the case of children who were admitted without parents (some 15 percent of all admissions in the 1760s, declining to about 8 percent in the 1790s), almost all were bound out. It was often the case that those children, a substantial part of the Almshouse population at any time, were in the house in the first place to await an indenture, but there were also abandoned children to care for, and several cases of foundlings are recorded in the admissions lists. In the period 1775–78 there was a noticeable increase in the numbers of children admitted to the Almshouse without a corresponding increase in the numbers of indentures. It might have been the case that the disruptions of the Revolutionary War created the need for temporary or short-term care for children whose parents were split up by either military service or evacuation.[170]

The great disruptions of 1775–76 in Boston resulted in the movement of large numbers of people, of all classes, including the poor and the aged, as well as ill or infirm persons of all ages. As noted, in the 1770s there are entries in the records of groups of sixteen and seventeen and twenty-one people being admitted, and one group of thirty-two persons being discharged, all without much comment, although the impact of the war made refugees of large numbers of people.[171] Children were especially vulnerable to the vicissitudes of eighteenth-century life, and those in the Almshouse were not exempt from physical or emotional injury, illness, or loss. There were constant examples of children dying from smallpox, and the several recorded cases of children being orphaned while in the Almshouse are reminders of the fragile health and circumstances of some families. An Almshouse clerk's dispassionate note of November 12, 1759, on the virtual collapse of a family speaks volumes on the misfortune of some: The father, Richard Bill, had been sent to the Workhouse on

October 30, one of two children "was drowned in the yard well" on February 20, 1762, and Polly Bill, either the remaining child or the mother, "dyed of the smallpox" on April 13, 1764.[172]

Smallpox was the great scourge of the eighteenth century. Between 1702 and 1792 Boston saw eight major epidemics (there had been four in the seventeenth century). There were many other smaller, limited outbreaks, and occasional infections throughout. The disease was reported and recorded with dread from the earliest recorded epidemic, in 1649, until far into the nineteenth century—so much so that there was better statistical reporting of smallpox in the period prior to 1790 than there was for any other population statistic.[173] The Overseers' role in smallpox treatment and control merged most acutely with the responsibilities of the Selectmen. The Overseers had control of the great quarantine hospital, also known as the Well House or Pesthouse, first on Spectacle Island in Boston Harbor in 1717 and after 1737 on Rainsford's Island. Although there was a town hospital and at least one private hospital in Boston in the second half of the eighteenth century, any sign of smallpox in the Almshouse led quickly to a transfer to Rainsford's Island.[174]

Throughout its history the Almshouse was as much a hospital as it was a home for the poor. It was certainly a hospice for the old and dying and was perhaps the only designated common maternity hospital in Boston in an era when all births were at home. As noted, in the Almshouse, and Workhouse too, there was always an attending doctor, appointed and funded by the Overseers. The frequent references to people who were "sick and poor" or "old and poor" or "old and sick" amplify the caring and medical concerns of the Almshouse keepers. Unlike the systematic segregation of "Colored" in the 1801 Almshouse, the 1756 census suggests that the old Almshouse's rooms were racially integrated, and there is some evidence that the Overseers were colorblind in their administration of the town poor and sick: "a blind negro" or a "negro woman old & infirm" were as likely to be admitted on their own recognizance as was the aged slave of a local family, in the case of "Jane [aged seventy-five] a negro of Mrs Tyfield" being received in all likelihood to be cared for after becoming too infirm to perform as a houseservant. She died six months later. Those entries are found among admissions for white poor admitted in the same year (1775) as "blind" or "aged" or "Deaf & Dumb" or "an old Woman." All were admitted by order of a single Overseer.[175]

Selectmen too were integral to the administration of poor relief in Boston. Their role, however, was most clearly a senior administrative one in the hierarchy of civic politics, and their most crucial authority was in the primary determination of civic budgets, including poor relief. While taxes were nominally the purview of the Town Meeting as a whole, the influence of Selectmen, and through them the Overseers, was great when it came to setting rates. In a more tangible way, Selectmen were most responsible for the poor and needy who were not legal residents of Boston. As noted, the law required that two Selectmen had to authorize the admission of "strangers" to the Almshouse, with the consent and approval of an Overseer. In the period 1764–68 the Selectmen recorded seventy-five requests for relief including the following, which are typical of the hundreds of examples that occur throughout the Selectmen's minutes for the eighteenth century:

> Mr Greenleaf one of the Overseers acquainted the Selectmen that he had sent into the Almshouse one Michael Carney, who fell into a Cistern and is distracted, and cannot tell whence he came. Mr Greenleaf further informs that George Crist, John Henry Rainghee & Christopher Perver, supposed to have come from Broad Bay are sick & in necessitous Circumstances, and require relief…. Mr Farmer [the Almshouse keeper] was directed to receive into Alms house by Mr Sewall & Hancock one Richard Barrett a Stranger disordered in Mind & destitute of the means of subsistance.[176]

Examples of compassion by the Selectmen also occur in the Almshouse admissions lists. "A Molatto Child Picked up In ye Common street, we have Called it Clarica," was sent in at state expense by the Selectmen although the "we" who named the child were probably the Almshouse keepers (usually a married couple). Another state charge, Jane Sigourey, "A Molatto Garl about 11 years old And no Covenant Servant As she sais," was ordered into the Almshouse by the Selectmen in 1788 and later bound out by the Overseers.[177]

Displays of compassion extended beyond age, race, and domicile. Even former enemies were offered alms, and several former British soldiers and their dependents could be found in the Almshouse in the 1780s. Workhouse inmates who needed constant medical attention or pregnant women were usually transferred in the short term at least to the Almshouse. Some clearly "distracted" Workhouse occupants were sent over to the Almshouse, for either their own protection or because they were no longer considered "idle poor." Conversely, the Overseers were notably intolerant of unruly Almshouse inmates, and there are many examples of "distracted" persons being sent over to the Workhouse. The truly disruptive were simply cast out of the Almshouse, as in the case of Patrick Shanley in 1789. The Almshouse keeper, in a fit of phonetic indignation, remarked: "I think [Shanley] ye most troublisom Man that Ever has ben in ye hous since I have ben hear[;] a drunken Quarrelson fiteinging decriped Rech As I Know of." It is not clear how long Shanley had been upsetting the Almshouse peace, but this rare marginal comment by the keeper indicates how little tolerance there was for drinking and fighting in the Almshouse. Yet even Shanley, in need, was readmitted in April 1790.[178]

Finally, the Almshouse of the later eighteenth century, while it can be seen as a relic of institutional poor relief soon to be swept away by nineteenth-century reform, also reflects what later seemed to be quaint attitudes in a rapidly changing social environment. The remnants of the Puritans' paternalistic ethic would later come to be attacked as repressive. Also, the "amateurs" of poor relief administration, the Overseers, tolerated and even encouraged the coexistence in one openly communal building of vagrant African Americans, Italians, Spaniards and Native Americans, ninety-two-year-old homeless and destitute people, illegitimate and abandoned children, nuclear families, unemployed craftsmen, and solvent geriatrics. The question of why is perhaps best answered by first thinking of "alms" as a cultural value with long roots rather than as a sociological definition. The Overseers practiced a formal almsgiving, while the churches of Boston often ranted against the moral corruption of supporting idleness with public funds. Some sermon literature of the 1750s and 1760s reads like an attack on all the poor, and not just the "idle" poor.[179] The Almshouse population, as a mix of the destitute and the solvent, demonstrated a remarkable example of institutional as well as social tolerance. Its diverse sets of inmates appear to have cohabited without a great deal of strain. Classes and races mixed freely, it seems. The Almshouse, then, was emphatically not a "poorhouse" in the nineteenth-century American sense of only paupers in a workhouse facility, when needy children were isolated in orphanages and pregnant single women, the elderly, and the infirm were each kept in specialized institutions.[180]

A vivid example of the diverse social composition of the Almshouse contrasts the lists of indentured children and references to blind, lame, and destitute "negroes" with four elderly and ill but apparently solvent Bostonians who entered the Almshouse in the 1760s for care and who died there, three of them after a few months and the other after a year and a half of residence. The inventories of George Skinner, Mary Crawford, Thomas Eastwick, and Mary Pilsberry have survived in the Overseers records. Their possessions indicate a socioeconomic range within the group and invite the speculation that inmates did make themselves at home in the Almshouse. The most middle-class of the four was clearly George Skinner, whose substantial inventory shows some refinement as well as a little affluence. Skinner came into the Almshouse on April 27, 1762 and died there in November 1763. His inventory of furnishings, clothing, and accessories included a feather bed, chairs, rugs, a coffee pot, delft bowls, silver spoons and buckles, a quarto bible, and a few books. He also brought in two wigs, two cloaks, two jackets, two coats, a walking cane, and a good deal more. Not only would Mr. Skinner's possessions fill one of the Almshouse rooms, it represented some material quality.[181]

Another entry stated that "Mary Pilsberry came into the house Wednesday May 5, 1762 and brought with her Only The Cloaths on her Back the rest of her things as Household Stuff, Bed & Bedding being in the possession of Benj'a Austin Esqr [an Overseer]--since setled." Mary Pilsberry died on May 8, 1762. A third entry for a Mrs. Crawford states that she came into the house on February 14, 1763 and brought with her the following "Things or Household Stuff &c" including two tables, a bedstead, and two trunks of clothes. Her belongings were far less extensive and considerably inferior in value to those of Skinner but she did have means. Mary Crawford died on April 26, 1763, two months after being admitted. Finally: "Thomas Eastwick came into the House March 26, 1763 and Brot with him: A Feather Bed, Pillow, Two Blankets, And a Chest & Box containing Wearing Apparel Bedstead left behind at the desire of Mr Childs who he hired his Room of---." Mr. Eastwick died on June 25, 1763. Even Mrs. Crawford's and Mr. Eastwick's meager belongings, and certainly the relative opulence of Skinner's, are not what one might expect in what we might think of as a poorhouse. Yet they were all at home in the Almshouse. Also, as well as inmates with material means, the Almshouse was home in the eighteenth century to Bostonians with status. Doctor Jasper York in 1764 and Doctor Patrick Larey in 1770 were admitted in need. Benjamin Smith, a jeweler, was admitted in April 1765 "to be cured of the itch." A genealogist might probe the backgrounds of inmates with names such as Dolbeare, Scollay, Palfrey, Bangs, Greenleaf, Proctor, and Bulfinch to see if they have family connections to the middle- and upper-class Boston Selectmen, Overseers and merchants with those names. Coincidence or imitation was clearly the reason for inmates with names such as John Adams and George Washington to appear in the records.[182]

Thus a clear consistency of purpose and administrative practices emerges from the Almshouse admissions records into the early nineteenth century, but trends in the social composition of the Almshouse population do occur toward the end of the period. Then, higher rates of internal migration and the increase in the proportion of state to town charges indicate a clear shift in the demographics of Massachusetts. The warning-out lists bear that out. Another significant trend emerges in the increase in single-person admissions to the Almshouse in the late 1780s and early 1790s. A more modest trend, quantitatively, is the increasing numbers of African Americans in the Almshouse following the constitutional end of slavery in Massachusetts. In the 1790s there appear to be more examples of destitution than of middle-class elderly seeking rest and care. In 1795 and 1796, for example, four "molatto" children were admitted having been "Found at ye door" or "in ye Street" or "in ye shed."[183]

The admissions records of the Overseers from late 1758 to 1800 are included here in their entirety because they are nearly complete in volume and sequence and represent the longest sustained record in the eighteenth-century Overseers manuscript collection. The thousands of names that appear in this record must be viewed against the backdrop of fundamental transformations in the political, social, and economic history of Massachusetts, and especially as they illuminate the twilight era of the Almshouse. The urban face of Boston was redrawn after the 1790s more rapidly than it had ever been in the past. As this record closes in the early nineteenth-century the slow diminution of the authority of the Overseers of the Poor and their most significant instrument, the Almshouse, had begun. The Overseers' pleas of 1813 reveal, as well as any other index, the great changes to Boston's public welfare system that were now underway. Even though the statute of 1692 had been confirmed in the acts of 1793 and 1794, the Overseers' days as arbiters of relief were numbered. More important, the age of institutional alms would soon be over.[184]

Notes

1   John Winthrop, "A Modell of Christian Charity" in *Winthrop Papers*, Massachusetts Historical Society [hereafter cited as MHS], (Boston: 1929–47), 2:282.

2   *Ibid.*, 295. See the discussion of the interplay of clerical and lay authority and the realistic expectations of the first generation of Massachusetts clergy in Stephen Foster, *The Long Argument: English Puritanism and the Shaping of New England Culture* (Chapel Hill, N.C., 1991), 138–75: Timothy H. Breen and Stephen Foster, "The Puritans Greatest Achievement: A Study in Social Cohesion in 17th Century Massachusetts," *Journal of American History*, 60 (1973); 5–22. *The Colonial Laws of Massachusetts, Reprinted from the Edition of 1672, With the Supplements through 1686* (Boston, 1887), esp. 37, 44.

3   On the Tudor origins of early seventeenth-century American poor relief, see Paul Slack, *Poverty and Policy in Tudor and Stuart England* (London, 1988), especially 113–37. See also the superb bibliographical material in Slack, *From Reformation to Improvement: Public Welfare in Early Modern England* (Oxford, 1999). On the transfer and adaption of English law to the American colonies see the brief but comprehensive treatment in Peter Charles Hoffer, *Law and People in Colonial America* (Baltimore, 1992), especially Chapter 1. For a specific reference to Massachusetts, see David Grayson Allen, *In English Ways: The Movement of Societies and the Transferal of English Local Law and Custom to Massachusetts in the Seventeenth Century* (Boston, 1981). Another treatment of this ongoing question can be found in Darrett B. Rutman, *Winthrop's Boston: Portrait of a Puritan Town, 1630–1649* (Chapel Hill, N.C., 1965), 51–67 and 202–40. The same author's views on "adaptation" can be found in the reissue of some of his earlier work in *Small Worlds, Large Questions: Explorations in Early American Social History, 1600–1850* (Charlottesville, Va., 1994), especially chapters 4 and 5. See also appendix I.

4   On the 1632 prison, see Nathaniel B. Shurtleff, *Records of the Governor and Company of the Massachusetts Bay in New England* (Boston, 1853–54) I, 100. What is clear from this literature, and from Massachusetts Bay Company statutes such as the 1641 Body of Liberties, is the sanctity of civil authority in relation to the religious ends of Puritan settlement. See also Rutman, *Winthrop's Boston*, 159–60. The Massachusetts settlement was not a "theocracy" as we think of that term, but a well-ordered civic enterprise.

5   When Josiah Quincy Jr. recommended a major reform of Boston's poor relief system in 1821, he based his attack on what he saw as misguided public policy compounded by the manipulation of the system by "contented" recipients of poor relief. On the issue of what he called the "abuse of public charities" he quotes approvingly from an English report that "establishes the principle … that the existence of any permanent fund for the support of the poor, the appropriation of any revenue … has, upon the whole, a direct tendency to increase their numbers [in a way that is] directly productive of paupers." Josiah Quincy Jr., *Report of the Committee on the Pauper Laws of this Commonwealth* [Boston, 1821], 6; hereafter cited as *Quincy Report*. See also Quincy's *Municipal History of the town and city of Boston … 1630–1830* (Boston, 1852), 24–38, 47–53, 170–75. This great review of Quincy's career masquerading as history contains 41 pages on the first 192 years of Boston's history, and 401 pages on Quincy's revolutionary role in its history between 1822 and 1830. A very good study of Quincy's role in the popular politics of the early nineteenth-century is Matthew H. Crocker, *The Magic of the Many: Josiah Quincy and the Rise of Mass Politics in Boston, 1800–1830* (Boston, 1999), especially pages 132–48. Robert A. McCaughey, *Josiah Quincy, 1772–1864: The*

Last Federalist (Cambridge, Mass., 1974) is not only a useful personal portrait of Quincy but a very astute political biography and its chapters on Quincy's role as mayor are balanced and insightful.

Quincy's caveats in some way anticipate the entire debate on poor relief in the nineteenth and especially the twentieth centuries. The massive public attacks on poverty in the twentieth century, beginning with the Progressives' reforms but most notably in the New Deal and Great Society programs, have served mostly to confirm poverty's permanence and the constant opposition to taxes for poor relief. John Kenneth Galbraith succinctly notes the reasons why the majority in postindustrial America can tolerate permanent classes of poor in *The Culture of Contentment* (Boston, 1993), 13. The best treatment of poverty and poor relief in the twentieth century is James T. Patterson, *America's Struggle against Poverty, 1900–1994*, 3d ed., (Cambridge, Mass., 1994). A very accessible review of the subject for the nineteenth century is Robert H. Bremner, *From the Depths: The Discovery of Poverty in the United States* (New York, 1965). There is no comparable book-length survey of poverty and public relief for the seventeenth and eighteenth centuries. Of the article literature see especially Billy G. Smith, "Poverty and Economic Marginality in Eighteenth Century America," *Proceedings of the American Philosophical Society* 132 (1988); 85–115. Smith has some very useful observations and analyses on some of the issues and material dealt with in this introduction.

6   Geoffrey Taylor, *The Problem of Poverty, 1660–1834* (London, 1969), 3.

7   The Gregory King tables are reprinted in a great number of modern studies, but see the full essay in Gregory King, *Naturall and Political Observations, upon the State and Condition of England,* [1696], ed. G. Barnett (Baltimore, 1936). There is a useful comment on the seventeenth- and eighteenth-century context of this debate, with special significance for colonial America, in Stephen E. Wiberley Jr., "Four Cities: Public Poor Relief in Urban America, 1700–1775" (Ph.D. diss., Yale University, 1975), 57–60, 220–21. This thesis deserves to be more widely known for its treatment of the Overseers of the Poor in the cities it covers.

8   Paul Slack, *The English Poor Law, 1531–1782* (London, 1990), 9–10, and Slack, *Policy and Poverty*, 113ff. Allen, *In English Ways*, passim; *The Acts and Resolves, Public and Private, of the Province of Massachusetts,* I: 64–68; *Colonial Laws of Massachusetts*, passim.

9   Gertrude Himmelfarb, *The Idea of Poverty* (London, 1984), 3–31. The quote is from 24–25. Slack, *From Reformation to Improvement*, pp. 5–28, 150ff, makes a strong case for the steady secularization of charity in England after the seventeenth century. See also Slack, *English Poor Law*, 35–58; and Allen, *In English Ways*.

10   See *Colonial Laws of Massachusetts,* 66 (1633 and 1668) for idleness, and pp. 44, 123 (1639) for "poor." The 1639 law (p. 44) states: "It is ordered by this Court and Authoritie therof; that any Shire court, or any two magistrates out of court shall have power to determin all differences about lawfull setling, and providing for poor persons: and shall have power to dispose of all unstled persons into such towns as they shall judge to be most fit for the maintainance, imployment of such persons and families for the ease of the countrie." The 1639 act was included in *The Laws and Liberties of Massachusetts, 1648 edition* (reprint; Cambridge, Mass., 1929). See also Josiah Benton, *Warning Out in New England, 1656–1817* (Boston, 1911). On Rhode Island, see Bridenbaugh, *Cities in the Wilderness: The First Century of Urban Life in America, 1625–1742* (1938; reprint London, 1971), 80–81. On English law see Slack, *Poverty and Policy*, chapter 4; Jutte, *Poverty and Deviance,* 120–24; and D. M. Palliser, *The Age of Elizabeth: England under the Later Tudors, 1547–1603* (New York, 1983), 123–29. I am grateful to Professor William Rorabaugh of the University of Washington for his comments on the Elizabethan Statutes and their influence on American colonial apprenticeship and servitude. See also Lawrence William Towner, "A Good Master Well Served: A Social History of Servitude in Massachusetts, 1620–1750" (Ph.D. diss., Northwestern, 1955), chapters 1-3, and appendices.

11   *Reports of the Record Commissioners for the City of Boston*, 39 volumes (Boston, 1876–1909), (hereafter cited as Boston Records) 7:206, for March 9, 1690/1: "The 4 ouersers together with the Town Treasurer are desired and apoynted a Committee to drawe up & present unto the Generall Court such proposalls as they shall aprehend needfull for the orderinge and improving of them, to imploy and set the poore a worke." See also Robert Seybolt, *The Town Officials of Colonial Boston, 1634–1775* (Cambridge, Mass., 1939), 81.

12   Manuscript records of the Overseers of the Poor, 1733–1925, 14 boxes, microfilmed, indexed, and dated, MHS, Boston (hereafter *Overseers*). The entire manuscript collection has been catalogued, with a very good commentary on content, as "Boston Overseers of the Poor Records, 1733–1925: Guide to the Manuscript Collection" (Massachusetts Historical Society, 27 September 1988; hereafter cited as "Guide"). Most of the eighteenth-century manuscripts are in boxes 1 and 9 (microfilms 1 and 8). While these records are known to scholars and have been consulted, the only full treatment of them so far is Wiberley, 160–97. Wiberley has produced suberb analyses from part of the Boston Overseers collection, up to 1775, and is the only scholar so far to have examined the eighteenth-century manuscripts extensively. Gary Nash, *The Urban Crucible: Social Change, Political Consciousness, and the Origins of the American Revolution* (Cambridge, Mass., 1979), and Smith, "Poverty and Economic Marginality" both refer to the Wiberley dissertation.

13   *Boston Records* 1:15–19; 11:104, 114; 15:274–76; 20:198–200. Samuel Whitwell, "Overseer of the Poor Account Book, 1769–1791," MHS, (hereafter Whitwell, "Account Book") indicates some three hundred ward disbursements a year. His own disbursements were over fifty in some years; see Wiberley, 167. Boston's wards are illustrated very well in Page's 1777 map, which is published in Lester J. Cappon, ed., *Atlas of Early American History: The Revolutionary Era, 1760–1790* (Princeton, N.J., 1976). Under the direction of the tough-minded town treasurer of the 1750s, David Jeffries, the terms were greatly clarified for charging the Town of Boston for the care of its poor by others. For example, a pro forma of the 1750s looked liked the following: "Whereas Mr A.B. of C has received into his House D.E. a poore Wooman belonging to the Town of Boston, We the Subscribers Overseers of the Poor of sd Town hereby oblige oure selves … at all Times to save Harmless the sd Town of Woburn from any charge that may aris by sd D.E. being their, and will receive her again at any time when desired by sd A.B." (*Overseers*, box 1, folder 2).

       Where split dates appear in the manuscripts they have been retained throughout the transcription record and the commentary. Bostonians customarily followed English practice, and until 1752 the Anglo-American calendar year ended on March 25. Thus a date between January 1 and March 24 would be given either as 1735/36 (Old Style) or 1736 (New Style). After 1752, the Old Style calendar year was abandoned and the Anglo-American year, which was then eleven days longer than the rest of Europe, was fixed at 365 days with the year starting on January 1.

14   Most of the 39 volumes of the *Boston Records* contain indexed examples of this relationship. Volume 12 records a great many examples of the close relations between the Town Meeting and the Overseers. The Selectmen's minutes in volumes 11, 17, and 21 are indexed for Overseers matters. See also appendix 1 of this collection.

15   See, for example, *Boston Records*, 20:198–201.

16   On population figures, see Lemuel Shattuck, *Report to the Committee of the City Council Appointed to Obtain the Census of Boston for the year 1845* (Boston, 1846), 2–6. On the Almshouse and Workhouse populations see *Boston Records,* 15:369. The figures used here are averages drawn from Overseers, boxes 1, 9, 13, and from the Whitwell "Account Book" for 1770 and 1771.

17   The thesis that voluntary private charity is a postrevolutionary phenomenon is argued with considerable effectiveness in Conrad Wright, *The Transformation of Charity in Postrevolutionary New England* (Boston, 1992). "Pauperism" in the mid-nineteenth century is discussed by the significant

contemporaneous researches of Lemuel Shattuck, 100–112. Shattuck's figures support Wright's thesis that a substantial amount of poor relief in the first half of the nineteenth century was private. There was not necessarily a major change in attitudes toward the poor, or in the simple traditional dual distinction between the worthy and unworthy poor. More of the poor were treated "indoors," in institutions, even though more of the poor were subject to private and increasingly evangelical relief. On that development see Sheila Anne Culbert, "Sturdy Beggars and the Worthy Poor: Poverty in Massachusetts, 1750–1820" (Ph.D. diss., Indiana University, 1985). In a way that both complements and advances the chronology of Wiberley, this study is by far the most comprehensive treatment of the subject of public poor relief in Massachusetts in this period and concludes that definitions of the various kinds of poor relief recipients, and the laws that governed the process, were constant over the course of the century after 1750. Culbert's broader social context means that she deals in less depth with Boston than does Wiberley, but she fashions a very useful rural-urban comparison. Her extended time frame allows her to discuss, in her chapter 4, the context of the *Quincy Report*, which should be read in addition to Thomas O'Connor, "To be Poor and Homeless in Olde Boston," paper read at the New England and the Early Republic Conference, Boston, May 18, 1990. McCaughey, *Josiah Quincy*, Chapter 7 has useful comments on the contemporary perceptions of the specter of rapidly rising pauperism in Massachusetts in the 1820s. It is well documented by now that the 1790s was a crucial decade in the urban transformation of Boston that culminated in the 1822 city charter. The decade was marked by serious social issues that resulted from an economic boom. That boom put great pressure on Boston's infrastructure. See Jacqueline Barbara Carr, "A Change 'As Remarkable As the Revolution': Boston's demographics, 1780–1800," *NEQ* 73 (2000) 583–602, and the references to Boston in Carole Shammas, "The Space Problem in United States Cities," *WMQ* 57 (2000): 505–42.

18 Carl Bridenbaugh, *Cities in the Wilderness:* 81; *Boston Records* 7: 157–58; on Keayne's charitable motives see Bernard Bailyn, "The Apologia of Robert Keayne," *WMQ*, 7 (1950): 568–87.

19 *Boston Records* 1:78. Rutman, *Winthrop's Boston*, 202–40. Bridenbaugh, *Cities in the Wilderness*, 74–75. On the way that the poor were cared for out of doors in the seventeenth century, see Charles Richard Lee, "This Poor People': Poverty, Relief, and Correction in Massachusetts, 1620–1715" (Ph.D. diss., SUNY Buffalo, 1978). Lee traces the evolution away from redemptive charity and casual poor relief to a more institutional approach, with less rehabilitative expectation. His chapter 7 is instructive. Wiberley, 67–68, has some succinct comments on the term "poorhouse" in the eighteenth-century. On Bridewell, see *Boston Records* 8:174–75. The Bridewell was included in Bonner's 1722 map of "The Town of Boston." The term "Bridewell" was a generic term for free-standing prisons (gaols) and survived in usage in some parts of the English-speaking world into the nineteenth-century. The original Bridewell had been a building for training Tudor apprentices that evolved into a house of correction and was named for the district in London where it was located. The quotes are from Annie Thwing, *The Crooked and Narrow Streets of Boston, 1630–1822* (Boston, 1920), 222–3.

20 Robert Jutte, *Poverty and Deviance in Early Modern Europe* (Cambridge, England, 1994), 100–104. Stuart Woolf, *The Poor in Western Europe in the Eighteenth and Nineteenth Centuries* (London, 1986), 17–28. On the diversity of English population in relation to geography and poor relief see Slack, *English Poor Law*.

21 Edward M. Cook Jr., *The Fathers of the Towns: Leadership and Community Structure in Eighteenth-Century New England* (Baltimore, 1976). Two important studies are relevant here: Wiberley's unpublished dissertation, and Jon Christian Teaford, *The Municipal Revolution in America: Origins of Modern Urban Government, 1650–1825* (Chicago, 1975). See also the essays in Bruce Daniels, ed., *Town and County: Essays on the Structure of Local Government in the American Colonies* (Middletown, Conn., 1978).

Notes

❧

22   *Colonial Laws of Massachusetts*, 37. *The Overseers Guide …* (Brookfield, Mass., 1815), 1–33, offers a comprehensive review of settlement criteria from 1639 to 1795. See also appendix 2.

23   In what might be called the post-Perry Miller revision, historians continue to debate both the substance and the relevance of the Winthrop experiment and its alleged debt to or distinction from Calvinism and the English Puritan experience. Compare, for example, Stephen Foster, *The Long Argument: English Puritanism and the Shaping of New England Culture, 1570–1700* (Chapel Hill: University of North Carolina Press, 1991), with Miller's major works *Errand into the Wilderness, From Colony to Province,* and *Orthodoxy in Massachusetts.* The value of social history in interpreting the founders' purposes and legacies is argued with conviction by Rutman in *Small Worlds*, xii–xiii and passim. For a recent discussion of the issue see Mark A. Peterson, "From Founding Fathers to Old-Boy Networks: The Declension of Perry Miller's Puritans," *Reviews in American History* 23 (1995): 13–19. For a sometimes refreshing alternative to the Miller school and its derivatives see the sociological E. Digby Baltzell, *Puritan Boston and Quaker Philadelphia* (New Brunswick, N.J., 1996, originally published in 1979).

24   There is little evidence of boards of Overseers being constituted elsewhere in Massachusetts prior to the middle of the eighteenth century. Thereafter, Overseers appeared in the larger towns of the state, and in towns adjacent to Boston such as Charlestown, Roxbury, and Dorchester; see Culbert, "Sturdy Beggars," chapters 3 and 4. See also Louis J. Piccarello, "Social Structure and Public Welfare Policy in Danvers, Massachusetts, 1750–1850," *Essex Institute Historical Collections* 118 (1982): 248–63. On the 1704 act see *The Acts and Resolves, Public and Private, of the Province of Massachusetts* 1:538–39.

25   Meanwhile, in the vast majority of Massachusetts towns, the supervision of the idle poor and other "deviants" would continue to be done by the constables on the advice of the Selectmen, and by the latter themselves; see Culbert, "Sturdy Beggars," chapter 3. Even into the 1820s most Massachusetts towns were without freestanding "poorhouses." In addition to Culbert see David J. Rothman, *The Discovery of the Asylum: Social Order and Disorder in the New Republic* (Boston, 1971), 31, and *Quincy Report.*

26   *Overseers*, box 1, folders 1–3, and box 8, folder 3. For an example of earlier concerns about transiency see *Boston Records* 7:241, Town Meeting minutes for March 11, 1700. The record is instructive. It states: "Upon the Consideration of the great Charges this Town is at Yearly, from the Growing Numbr of Poore Amonge us & the great Number Come in amonge ous wch has been Occasioned by the Eastern warr wth the Indians, and other poor and vild persons yt has Come in amonge us from Other Towns, Our Town being so Populous and they shifting from place to place, so long before they be Descouered that the law makes them Inhabitants. Now these things do presage great Poverty to be hastening upon this Town if some sutable methods be not timely Taken to prevent the same. Upon Consideration of the things for mentioned, It was Voted that there be 500ld [500 pounds] raised upon the Inhabitants of the Town of Boston, To be Layed out and improved by the Overseers of the poor & such others wch shall by the Town be added to them, as a stock to be imployed for the procuring materials and Tools, To Sett and keep the poor people and Ill persons at work as the Law Directs."

27   Love, Robert, *Received, by order of the selectmen of Boston, Jan. 25, 1765…* MHS. Benton, *Warning Out,* chapter 1. *Acts and Resolves,* I, 64–68. See also Lawrence Towner, "The Indentures of Boston's Poor Apprentices, 1734–1805," Colonial Society of Massachusetts, *Publications* (1956–63): 417–68.

28   Compare, for example, the style of entry in *Overseers*, box 1, folders 1–3, and in box 9, folders 1–2 and 4, and box 13, folder 1. For an example of one Overseer's trained hand see Whitwell, "Account Book." I am assuming that Whitwell made his own entries, but his ledgers may in fact have been compiled by a clerk-scrivener. On the way Boston's merchant or legal class learned their

handwriting techniques, see "William Palfrey's Legal and Financial Papers," Houghton Library Manuscripts, Harvard University.

29   Town charges tended to stay a bit longer than province or state charges. There does not appear to be a significant change in the average or typical duration of residence between the 1760s and the 1790s. While some 60 percent of the sample were gone from the Almshouse within a year that still leaves large numbers of long-term indoor poor relief recipients. See *Overseers*, box 1, folder 3 and box 8, folder 3. See also Wiberley, 33, for a sample and chart of lengths of stays prior to 1775. The L shape of the building was likely a result of the 1742 addition, which stipulated a "Brick Building … Ninety feet long and the same Wedth of the Old House." See *Boston Records*, 12:281.

30   Wiberley, chapter 2, attempts to compare the regimen of the Almshouse with the Workhouse. *Boston Records*, vol. 12, passim, contains specific references to the separate functions.

31   Seybolt, *Town Officials; Wiberley,* Chapter 6. *Overseers*, box 1, folder 2. Whitwell "Account Book," passim. See the accounts in *Overseers*, box 1, folder 1.

32   Whitwell, "Account Book," contains no annotation but is a superb example of the personal involvement of an Overseer in day-to-day transactions with the poor "out of doors." See also Wiberley, 160–67, for a discussion of the Overseers' status and conduct.

33   The Overseers' own manuscript records are in the hands of the Massachusetts Historical Society (MHS), but vast external references to the Overseers can be found in the published *Provincial Acts and Resolves, the Records of the House of Representatives*, the unpublished "Boston Town Papers," at the Boston Public Library Rare Books and Manuscripts and scattered among the manuscripts in the Massachusetts Archives. The multiple volumes of the *Boston Records* print the Town Meeting and Selectmen's minutes and deliberations for the entire colonial, revolutionary and federal period. There are dozens of entries on the Overseers in each volume. These are mostly direct references such as reports by the Overseers to the Selectmen or the Town Meeting, but there are many incidental entries too. The *Boston Records* volumes are a mine of valuable material on all aspects of Boston's history before the 1820s and are clearly indexed. For the Overseers see "Poor," "Paupers," "Almshouse," "Workhouse," "Overseers of the Poor," or "Poor, Overseers of." Much of the original eighteenth-century records of the Overseers themselves have been lost, as the "Guide" indicates. In fact, in the monumental Justin Winsor, editor, *Memorial History of Boston*, 4 volumes (Boston, 1881) there are occasional references to Overseers records that apparently no longer exist.

34   *Boston Records.* See especially the entries in Overseers, box 1, folders 1–4. The exception to the comment here about an absence of a serious consideration of the Overseers as historically important actors is Wiberley, and to a lesser extent, Culbert, "Sturdy Beggars." But these two studies are unpublished. Otherwise, there is now an extensive and excellent recent historiography on poverty and social structure in eighteenth-century Boston that has grown out of the "new social history" and "New Left" or "Neoprogressive" theories of a generation ago. The subject and approaches may be gauged by reference to the following samples from the 1965–89 period: James Henretta, "Economic Development and Social Structure in Colonial Boston," *WMQ* 22 (1965): 75–92; Alan Kulikoff "The Progress of Inequality in Revolutionary Boston," *WMQ* 28 (1971): 375–412; Gary B. Nash," Urban Wealth and Poverty in Pre-Revolutionary America," *Journal of Interdisciplinary History* (hereafter cited as *JIH*) 6 (1975–76): 547–76; "The Failure of Female Factory Labor in Colonial Boston," *Labor History* 20 (1979): 165–88, and *The Urban Crucible: Social Change, Political Consciousness and the Origins of the American Revolution* (Cambridge, Mass., 1979); G. B. Warden, "Inequality and Instability in Eighteenth-Century Boston, A Reappraisal," *JIH*, 6 (1976): 585–620; and Eric G. Nellis, "Misreading the Signs: Industrial Imitation, Poverty, and The Social Order in Colonial Boston," *NEQ*, 59 (1986): 486–507, and "The Working Poor of Pre-Revolutionary Boston," *Historical Journal of Massachusetts*, 17 (1989): 137–59. Smith, "Poverty

and Economic Marginality" summarizes the general theme of these studies, which is, that America was becoming more economically stratified and inegalitarian in the second half of the eighteenth century. Warden's article is an attempt to soften the general gloom of these theses, but there can be no doubt that the need for poor relief increased in America's port cities after mid century. Any study of the evolution of poor relief in the eighteenth century must first address the questions raised in that literature. It may well be that the wheel of historiography has revolved to the flip side of poverty, which is wealth and capitalism. For example, James Henretta has incorporated his 1965 study into his recent book *The Origins of American Capitalism, Collected Essays* (Boston, 1991).

35 Lee, "This Poor People," and Culbert, "Sturdy Beggars," make this quite clear for their respective time periods.

36 In 1690 there were 7,000 residents of Boston and 50,000 in all of Massachusetts. In 1770, the ratio was 15,520 to 235,000. Thus Boston's percentage of the province's population fell from about 14 percent to 7 percent. Boston's prerevolutionary population peaked at about 17,000 in the early 1740s, then declined and leveled out at about 15,500. It did not recover to its 1740 levels until the 1780s. See Shattuck, 2–6; E. B. Greene and Virginia D. Harrington, *American Population before the Federal Census of 1790* (New York, 1932); J. H. Benton, "Early Census Making in Massachusetts, 1643–1765: With a reproduction of the lost census of 1765," *Massachusetts Historical Society Proceedings*, 2d ser., 4:136–39. While there was some "urban" growth outside Boston, in towns such as Salem, Marblehead, Ipswich, Newburyport, and Gloucester, Boston remained the only fully developed "urban" society in the period. See the extended discussion of "the typology of towns" in Cook, *Fathers of the Towns*, chapter 7. For rural Massachusetts see Bettye Hobbs Pruitt, "Self Sufficiency and the Agricultural Economy of Eighteenth Century Massachusetts," *WMQ* 41 (1984): 333–64. The best source for town populations is Jacob Felt, "Statistics of Population in Massachusetts," *Collections of the American Statistical Association*, 1 (1847): 148–57.

37 See Felt, 148–57 and Nash, *Urban Crucible*, 102–28, 312–38.

38 Nellis, "Misreading the Signs."

39 On the number of churches in Boston see *Boston Records* 1:6.

40 Whitwell, "Account Book." On the 1772 act see, "An Act for incorporating the Overseers," *Overseers*, box 13, folder 1. On voluntary charity and the background to prerevolutionary philanthropy in Boston see Peter R. Virgadamo, "Colonial Charity and the National Character: Boston, 1630–1775" (Ph.D. diss., University of Southern California, 1982). I am grateful to him for the use of two unpublished essays of his: "'To Give Alms and Do Justice': Charles Chauncy and Early American Philanthropy," and "Sermons and Alms: Boston's Quarterly Charity Lecture, 1720–1776." I agree with Dr. Virgadamo that Chauncy can be seen as philanthropic so long as the recipients of alms were not the chronic poor or the idle poor. On the rather short list of private charities see Winsor, IV:658.

41 Bridenbaugh, *Cities in the Wilderness*, 391–94.

42 *Boston Records*, 15:369.

43 *Ibid.*

44 For an example of the link between the Overseers' policies and the authority of the church see Charles Chauncy, *The Idle Poor Secluded from the Bread of Charity by the Christian Law: A Sermon Preached in Boston before the Society* (Boston, 1752).

45   Wiberley, 88–109; Nash, *Urban Crucible,* 188–90; Culbert, "Sturdy Beggars," 125–26, 153n; the rules of the Workhouse are in *Boston Records,* 12: 235–41, and are reprinted from the manuscripts of the Overseers in appendix 4. *Boston Records* 1:78 locates the Almshouse and Workhouse sites. The term "scum" was used by Governor Bernard. See *Overseers,* Box 12, folder 1. Even if there were some racial, class, gender and age segregation, the inmates were treated as a group and were close enough to each other, that the term "mingling" is appropriate. The Almshouse census of 1756 indicates strict gender separation of single persons in the room assignments.

46   *Rules of Incorporation for the Society for Encouraging Industry and Employing the Poor* (Boston, 1754 ed.), 2–12; Nellis, "Misreading the Signs"; Nash, "Female Labor" and *Urban Crucible,* 190ff.; Wiberley, 100–9.

47   "Rules and orders for the management of the Workhouse," May 28, 1735, *Overseers,* box 13, folder 1; the quote is from an exchange between Governor Bernard and the Overseers in manuscript form in <u>Overseers</u>, box 12, folder 1. On examples of the prison population and conditions in the middle of the eighteenth century see miscellaneous bound manuscripts for 1734, 1740, 1742, and 1752, MHS. The linen manufactory building was used for a time to quarter British troops in 1768. It failed to attract a permanent textile producer and was sold by the state in 1784 to the Massachusetts Bank. It was later converted to residences in 1792 and pulled down in 1806. See the Ezekiel Price Papers in the MHS.

48   Lee, "This Poor People," chapter 3, and Culbert, "Sturdy Beggars," chapter 1, have some very thoughtful views on this.

49   *Boston Records* 15:235, 16:144.

50   See Cotton Mather, *Bonifacius: An Essay upon the Good* (Boston, 1710; reprint, ed. David Levin, Cambridge, Mass., 1966), 57–59, 74, 110, 121, and 132–37 for "reforming societies." On Samuel Sewall see Milton H. Thomas, ed., *The Diary of Samuel Sewall, 1674–1729* (2 volumes, New York, 1973 edition), and Seybolt, *Town Officials,* 100, 105 for Sewall's Overseers service. See also Foster, *Long Argument,* 284.

51   Wiberley, 217–19. On Chauncy and Cooper see Nellis, "Misreading the Signs," 492–93. On the rest of the cream of Boston's merchant class who joined Hancock in his efforts to put the poor to work see *Rules of Incorporation.* For the subscribers to the 1735 fund for the workhouse see *Boston Records* 12:180–83.

52   "Warning Book from January 1745 to 1770," *Overseers,* box 1, folder 1. Lawrence Towner, "The Indentures of Boston's Poor Apprentices, 1734–1805," *Colonial Society of Massachusetts Transactions,* 42 (1956–63): 417–68. Along with Wiberley's dissertation and a 1958 MA thesis noted by Towner, this is the most detailed use of eighteenth-century overseers records to date. It should be noted that the indentures that were authorized by the Overseers were not retained by them but were kept as town records. The original Indentures have been preserved and are in six volumes in the Boston Public Library Rare Books and Manuscripts. According to Towner these manuscripts were microfilmed, likely in the late 1950s or early 1960s, by the Institute of Early American History and Culture in Williamsburg, Virginia. See Towner, 434. Many of the indentured children went from their homes to the Almshouse and thence to service; see Overseers, box 9, folder 1. Age and education were among the important determinants in the occupational fate of children. W. J. Rorabaugh, *The Craft Apprentice: From Franklin to the Machine Age in America* (New York, 1986), Preface, Prologue, and chapter 1.

53   *Overseers,* box 9, folders 1–4. Towner, 430. The pro forma used by the Overseers to bind out children to formal indentures is worth quoting: "We the Subscribers of the Town of [blank] do

hereby recommend Mr. [blank] as a person of sober life & conversation & in good Circumstances & further Certify that both he & his wife are suitable persons to be intrusted with the education of any Child which may be bound to them as an apprentice."

54   *Overseers*, box 1, folder 1–2. There is a need for a more specific study of women as paupers and as the major focus of institutionalized poor relief. Gary Nash in "Female Labor" and *Urban Crucible*, esp. 189–96, has offered some guidance for the pursuit of a full study of preindustrial female poverty. But evidence is hard to come by and can be misleading. For example, Wiberley, 94–95, cautions against reading too much from limited sources and notes a four-to-one female-male ratio in the Workhouse. Nash accepts Wiberley's ratios without asking why the three-to-two ratio in the Almshouse was not transferred approximately to the Workhouse ratios. Were men more difficult to keep inside? Were women in the Almshouse more difficult to release into the town than were men, and more likely to be sent from the Almshouse to the Workhouse?

55   *Ibid.*

56   Whitwell "Account Book," suggests that at certain times widows made up 25 percent of the Ward 10 outdoor relief recipients. The 1200 figure comes from *Boston Records*, 15:369.

57   *Boston Records* 1:11–13; *Shattuck,* 142–44. A very good history of smallpox in colonial Boston is Ola Elizabeth Winslow, *A Destroying Angel: The Conquest of Smallpox in Colonial Boston* (Boston, 1974). See also the scores of references in *Boston Records*, passim, for a sense of the constant presence and threat of smallpox.

58   Miscellaneous bound manuscripts for July 24, 1752, MHS. See also Ezekiel Price Papers, sheets 299ff., MHS, and Massachusetts Archives 59:566ff, for examples of the range of contact the Overseers had with the various public and private affairs of Boston.

59   *Overseers*, box 9, folder 4. "State" charges rose in relation to "town" charges for the poor after the mid–1780s, from about 40 percent to 60 percent of the total who were identified. On African-Americans see *Overseers*, box 9, folders 1–4, and box 11, folder 1, and the Almshouse Admissions charts in this introduction. See also Joanne Pope Melish, *Disowning Slavery: Gradual Emancipation and Race in New England, 1780–1860* (Ithaca, N.Y., 1998), 240–41 and Emily Blanck, "Seventeen Eighty Three: The Turning Point in the Law of Slavery in Massachusetts," *NEQ* 75 (2002), 24–51.

60   Culbert, "Sturdy Beggars"; O'Connor, "To be Poor"; Shattuck, 106–13; Benton, *Warning Out*, 40–62. Benton, 63, claims that as strict as were the settlement laws of Massachusetts, the Connecticut laws were even more "carefully guarded."

61   Nash, "Urban Wealth."

62   A good example of the language that was repeated over and over in any comment on either the decline of trade or the increase of the numbers of poor can be found in appendix 3, which is taken from *Acts and Resolves* 2:757. For the volume of repetitions of these laments see *Boston Records*, vols. 7–14, indexes, under "Trade" and "Poor."

63   Douglas Lamar Jones, "The Strolling Poor: Transiency in Eighteenth-Century Massachusetts," *Journal of Social History* 5 (1975): 28–54, suggests that not only Boston but also rural Massachusetts was being overrun by numbers of wandering beggars who were being shunted from town to town. While his case is overstated, Jones is right to identify what was a growing problem for local authorities, especially after midcentury. The problem, as always, was greater in Boston than in rural Massachusetts.

Notes

64 Wright, *Transformation of Charity,* and Culbert, "Sturdy Beggars.

65 The quotes are from *Quincy Report,* 4. See McCaughey, *Josiah Quincy,* 119–20 for an elaboration of Quincy's view of the "vicious poor" and other hopeless categories of pauperism, and on the model of the House of Industry.

66 In fact, in 1794 the Overseers were once again, as in 1772, made a corporation under legal definition that included civic authority and private philanthropic organization. See *Overseers,* box 13. After 1823 they became mostly concerned with private sources of charity and by the 1840s were responsible only for private charity. See Shattuck, 106.

67 Rothman, *Discovery of the Asylum,* 25, 30–42, is right to emphasize that in the eighteenth century the fixed "institution" was a "minor theme" in Boston's "pragmatic" approach to poor relief. His point that both the Almshouse and the Workhouse were modeled on the principles of family organization, in contrast to the post-Jacksonian denaturing of the "asylum" generally, is valid. But Rothman perhaps misses the most compelling legacy of the Overseers, that the office itself became an institution that would serve as the first formalized agency of poor relief in Massachusetts. The essay by Katherine Lloyd and Cindy Burgoyne, "The Evolution of a Transatlantic Debate on Penal Reform, 1780–1830" in Hugh Cunningham and Joanna Innes, editors, *Charity, Philanthropy, and Reform from the 1690s to 1850* (New York, 1998) is a welcome note on the transatlantic nature of early nineteenth-century theories of reform.

68 The best place to see a Boston example of this is in the *Quincy Report* and Rothman, *Discovery of the Asylum.* Conrad Wright in *The Transformation of Charity* has useful things to say about the rise in private charities in the early republic.

69 *Quincy Report,* 5–7; see also O'Connor, "To Be Poor." Crocker, *The Magic of the Many,* is now the fullest study of the issue, while McCaughey, *Josiah Quincy,* Chapters 6 and 7, offers a brisk and informative analysis of the great civic "revolution" of 1822. Still the best study of the nineteenth-century development of the "institution" is Rothman, *Discovery of the Asylum.* Rothman's claim that the sequestering and correction of "deviants" became a tenet of public welfare in the nineteenth century is sound, but his reading of the eighteenth-century institutional treatment of the poor is not always accurate, in the case of Boston at least. For example, his remark that "the colonial community typically cared for its dependents without disrupting their lives" is not as appropriate to Boston as to rural Massachusetts. The latter, though, is closer to the "typical" social environment of the time. A very exotic treatment of almshouse history is Charles Lawrence, comp., *History of the Philadelphia Almshouse and Hospitals from the Beginning of the Eighteenth to the Ending of the Nineteenth Centuries* (Philadelphia, 1905). There is no comparable review of Boston's almshouse. A recent and useful study of poor relief in Mexico City in the late eighteenth and the nineteenth centuries reveals a sharp cultural difference in the ways the Massachusetts authorities viewed the treatment of poverty compared to a Catholic New World society. See the early chapters in Sylvia Marina Arrom, *Containing the Poor: The Mexico City Poorhouse, 1774–1871* (Durham, N.C., 2000).

70 Although Quincy is seen by a variety of historians as a conservative Federalist and as anti-republican, his autocracy was scarcely the paternalism of his eighteenth-century civic predecessors. See Baltzell, *Puritan Boston,* 200–201; McCaughey, *Josiah Quincy,* Chapter 7. McCaughey notes Quincy's links with the earlier "Puritan–Federalist" culture and class but also acknowledges the end of "Boston's ... deferential pattern of politics." By 1820 the Boston Town meeting had 8,000 eligible voters. Quincy may have believed in his rights to deferential authority but he was obliged to appeal to a broad and assertive electorate. See Vernon Parrington, *Main Currents in American Thought, Volume Two: Romantic Revolution in America, 1800–1860* (New York, 1954. First published in 1927), 267–287, for characteristically dismissive comments on Quincy and his class, "The Passing of the Tie-Wig School." Parrington makes the mistake of seeing Quincy and his ilk being

marginalized by popular democracy, when, in fact, Quincy adapted rather well to the new forces in politics and thought.

71 The genre of quantitative history, which appeared in earnest in early American historiography in the 1960s, has produced a huge corpus of titles. There is no single methodological text, or even a comprehensive summary available, but the collected essays in Henretta, *The Origins of American Capitalism,* and Rutman, *Small Worlds,* have useful examples of the approach as does Smith, "Poverty and Economic Marginality." For an early and very useful example and overview see Jesse Lemisch, "The American Revolution Seen from the Bottom Up" in Barton J. Bernstein, ed., *Towards a New Past: Dissenting Essays in American History* (New York, 1967), 3–45.

72 Thomas, ed., *The Diary of Samuel Sewall,* passim. Ezekiel Price, a long-serving Selectman with a long record of collaboration with the Overseers and an advocate of private and public make-work schemes, has little to say in his extensive papers (MHS) about the Overseers and the Almshouse. Sewall does make passing reference to the Overseers in his diary, as does William Tudor, another early eighteenth century Overseer, but these references are not at all revealing. See Wiberley, 225.

73 Whitwell "Account Book." It is unlikely that Whitwell was the only Overseer to keep such a ledger, and the absence of any other is unusual in a society that routinely preserved and passed on personal papers. None of the persons listed in Whitwell's January 1771 accounts were on his July 1774 list and only four of the July 1774 recipients were getting relief in January 1775. It is not surprising that the number of those on relief doubled between July and January. In the summer months, Whitwell gave out cash, but in the winter most of the relief was in the form of firewood. Males dominate the lists, likely as heads of households. In July 1774 Whitwell made 29 disbursements in total and 15 of those went to three males, John Hobbs, Hugh Smith, and Jonathan Maker, who appear five times each. These are clearly "pensioned" poor relief recipients who might otherwise have been in the Almshouse.

74 For examples of extrapolation from sparse commentary see the imaginative job of reconstruction in Daniel Vickers, *Farmers and Fisherman: Two Centuries of Work in Essex County, Massachusetts, 1630–1850* (Charlottesville, V.A., 1994), and Winifred Rothenberg, *From Market Places to a Market Economy: The Transformation of Rural Massachusetts, 1750–1850* (Chicago, 1992).

75 Cook, *Fathers of the Towns,* is the most recent (as long ago as 1976) and comprehensive study we have of town officials in eighteenth–century Massachusetts. But while Cook talks about poor relief, he does not mention the Overseers as important officeholders, and "Overseers" does not appear in his index. Perhaps the omission is reasonable in that the bulk of his study mostly concerns towns outside Boston, but his interests in the Boston civic "fathers" might have made more of the important status that the Overseers enjoyed. Conrad Wright, *Transformation of Charity,* has some comment on the Overseers, but his study is mostly outside the subject of public poor relief. Josiah Quincy Jr., in his 1852 polemic *A Municipal History of ... Boston* discusses the Overseers with more contempt than scholarly detachment. Historians' priorities shift over time, of course, but a recent and very useful set of essays on class in early America does not specify topics for the analysis of the public institutional manifestations of inequality. See Carla Pestana and Sharon Salinger, eds., *Inequality in Early America* (Hanover, N.H., 1999).

76 Culbert, "Sturdy Beggars," deals with them only insofar as her study touches on Boston. Her focus is more legal than social. Nash, *Urban Crucible* and "Urban Wealth and Poverty," and Kulikoff, "Progress of Inequality," acknowledge the importance of the Overseers but cast them too easily in minor clerical roles. Smith, "Poverty and Economic Marginality," has much to say about the administration of public poor relief but he sets the Overseers somewhat in the background because his focus is on the poor themselves and not the class relationships between the keepers and the kept.

Notes

〜

77   Clifford K. Shipton (and John L. Sibley), *Biographical Sketches of Those Who Attended Harvard College* (Boston, 1873–) (hereafter cited as *Sibley's Harvard Graduates*), 16:303–8.

78   See *Acts and Resolves*, 1:538–39, 654–55; 2:242, 756–58; and appendix 1 of this collection. The Town Meeting was subject to the legislative oversight of the General Court, and while it exercised a de facto form of municipal sovereignty at times, it could not pass laws that did not conform to the presumptive sovereignty of the General Court. Most of the laws and amendments affecting local poor relief were in fact colonial, provincial, and ultimately state acts at least down to 1822 in the case of Boston. See also T. Metcalf, ed., *The General Laws of Massachusetts from the Adoption of the Constitution to February, 1822* (Boston, 1823).

79   On death rates generally, see Daniel Scott Smith, "The Demographic History of Colonial New England," *Journal of Economic History* 32 (1972): 165–83. For an example of Almshouse rates see the Admissions chart for 1758 to 1774 in this introduction.

80   The personal interventions of Selectmen and Overseers were crucial to the process of poor relief, and those public officials took their responsibilities seriously, of course, but according to *Sibley's Harvard Graduates*, 11:314, Royall Tyler padded his figures so as to appear more industrious than he was. Shipton quotes an anonymous critic: "So sure as any person in his [Tyler's] brethren's ward was to be committed to the w----k h----se, he would by some means or other, hear of it before they could … commit them; and by this means he committed a great many more than they… and this he got trumpeted about, that he has done more than all of them." Shipton quotes Ebenezer Parkman that "the paupers complained about him, but since they could not vote this did him no harm." Tyler appears, then, not to have been popular with either his colleagues or the poor; nevertheless, he is the only Overseer, of the few who are mentioned in Shipton, whose hard work and long service are seen as self-serving and not altruistic.

81   It is difficult to know from the entries in the *Boston Records* whether there was a formal nomination procedure. But there are very few cases of a "chosen" Overseer turning down the post ("refused"). It is my belief that most of the Overseers who served first volunteered their names to the Town Meeting.

82   Wiberley, 163; *Overseers*, box 1, folder 1; Massachusetts Archives 132:92–147 (Boston lists). The entire province valuation for 1771 has been edited and published by Bettye Hobbs Pruitt as *The Massachusetts Tax Valuation List of 1771* (Boston, 1978). Wiberley's list of names is arranged alphabetically: Samuel Abbot, John Barrett, Melatiah Bourne, John Bradford, Benjamin Dolbeare, Joseph Gardner, John Gore, William Greenleaf, Nathaniel Greenwood, John Hill, John Leverett, Jonathan Mason, Andrew Oliver, Samuel Partridge, William Phillips, James Pitts, Edward Proctor, Joseph Sherburn, Isaac Smith, Ebenezer Storer, John White, William White, William Whitwell, Jonathan Williams.

On the distribution of wealth and the estimating of decentiles, see Henretta, "Economic Development." To compare tax data, say, from the 1771 valuation, with any body of officials, see Seybolt, *Town Officials*, and compare with W. H. Whitmore, ed., *Massachusetts Civil List for the Colonial and Provincial Periods, 1630–1774* (Albany, N.Y., 1870). At least 15 of the pre-1776 Overseers were Harvard graduates, including Thomas Hubbard, a tireless supervisor of the Workhouse who was later Treasurer of Harvard, as well as Andrew Oliver, Samuel Sewall and William Hutchinson, a distant relative of Thomas Hutchinson. The great Boston Treasurer David Jeffries was a 1732 graduate. See *Sibley's Harvard Graduates*, passim.

83   See John W. Tyler, *Smugglers and Patriots: Boston Merchants and the Advent of the American Revolution* (Boston, 1986), appendix. Tyler lists over four hundred merchants who were involved in various ways with the Revolution in Boston. Thirty-one of his merchants were or had been or would be Overseers, and all of them who were alive in 1776 were patriots. On the 1775 refugees and the 1777 Vose reference, see *Overseers*, box 9, folder 3. The comments on Daniel Oliver are from

Thomas Prince, *The Faithful Servant Approv'd At Death* (Boston, 1732), 32, quoted by *Wiberley*, 185–86, who does not acknowledge the fact that Prince was a beneficiary of Oliver's will. Still, even if Prince's remarks are consistent with a memorial oration by a favored friend, and even if they do hint at paternalism, Oliver's many years as an Overseer in old age is a measure of a genuine commitment to the welfare of the lower classes. On the Olivers as a Boston "dynasty" see Annie Haven Thwing, *Inhabitants and Estates of the Town of Boston*, 1630–1800 (CD ROM, New England Historic Genealogical Society and MHS, Boston, 2001).

84 Whitwell's weekly outlays amounted to about twenty shillings in busy periods to several individual recipients, see Whitwell "Account Book."

85 *Boston Records* 20:198–99. Phyllis Whitman Hunter, *Purchasing Identity in the Atlantic World: Massachusetts Merchants, 1670–1780* (Ithaca, N.Y., 2001), endnote on page 204, sets this ritual in a very imaginative context, by suggesting that all of Boston's merchants used civic "duty" as a measure of their class identity.

86 *Overseers*, box 1, folder 1; Seybolt, *Town Officials*. There has long been a false assumption about when the Overseers' office was established by law. Towner and O'Connor, "To be Poor," cite the date as 1735, over forty years after the first Overseers were appointed under the new laws of the new Massachusetts Charter.

87 Even in 1735 wards were not new to Boston. Militia wards had existed from 1713.

88 Seybolt, *Town Officials*, 111. Phyllis Hunter, *Purchasing Identity in the Atlantic World*, Chapter 4, 129–30, has some very sensible things to say about the self-conscious gentility, style, and civic duty exhibited by senior town officials. As noted, these were mostly merchants, and Hunter supposes that by serving the community in public office, and by demonstrating care for the needy, Boston's merchant class filled out their roles as respectable citizens of the Empire. There would be a redefinition of civic responsibility in the Republic, as the truncated role of the Overseers after 1823 shows.

89 David Jeffries resigned as Town Treasurer in March 1782 when the Boston treasury finally went empty. Soldiers patrolled the streets, and public security and public welfare was left largely to voluntary acts and contributions. *Sibley's Harvard Graduates* 9:177–79 also notes sympathetically that Jeffries was owed "some hundreds of pounds" by the town when he left his office, "overcome by the problem" of civic insolvency. Jeffries's own extensive papers are at the Massachusetts Historical Society. Shipton makes the wry observation that the "treasurership of Deacon Jeffries still haunts the City of Boston, for his notes, repudiated in the settlement after his resignation, are occasionally presented for payment."

90 Seybolt, *Town Officials*; *Overseers*, box 9, folders 3–4.

91 Royall Tyler's "self aggrandizement" (*Sibley's Harvard Graduates*) is a conspicuous exception but an exception nonetheless. By "conservative" is meant an insistence on separate facilities for different classes of need or "deviance."

92 See Thwing, *Inhabitants and Estates*, Seybolt, *Town Officials* and Whitmore, *Massachustts Civil List*.

93 Rothenberg, *From Market Places*, 1–55, contains the best new analysis of that phenomenon and offers a rich historiographical summary of the issue.

94   The stated general economic and demographic crises that appear in the *Boston Records*, vols. 12–20, and later in the sheer volume of transients seeking relief (*Overseers*, box 9, folder 3) attest to the need for more oversight. Wiberley, 76–78, makes the interesting observation that a new "breed" of Overseers began serving in the 1760s. He implies that they were tougher on paupers and more discriminating in fiscal terms. Perhaps, but they also appear to have been more committed to the welfare of the needy as their numbers increased and their conditions deteriorated. On Philadelphia see Wiberley, chapter 6 and Smith, "Poverty and Economic Marginality." Smith notes committees with titles such as "the Guardians of the Poor." Gary Nash, *First City and the Forging of Historical Memory* (Philadelphia, 2002), 70, mentions a "Committee to Alleviate the Miseries of the Poor." Nash also notes that the Philadelphia almshouse built in the 1760s was the largest building in America at the time. It was aptly named the "Bettering House" and unlike Boston's Almshouse was intended to combine the functions of alms and corrective work for the idle poor. On the differences in the public administrative culture of eighteenth-century American ports the older secondary literature is still useful. See, for example, Bridenbaugh, *Cities in the Wilderness* (1938) and *Cities in Revolt* (1955); Sam Bass Warner Jr., *The Private City: Philadelphia in Three Periods of its Growth* (Philadelphia, 1968); G. B. Warden, *Boston, 1687–1776*; Nash, *The Urban Crucible*: Wiberley finds structural differences in his four sample cities, but similar class identities among the overseers. See also Robert E. Cray Jr., *Paupers and Poor Relief in New York City and its Rural Environs* (Philadelphia, 1988); Simon P. Newman, *Embodied History: The Lives of the Poor in Early Philadelphia* (Philadelphia, 2003).

95   For Proctor, see *Overseers*, box 9, folder 3. Samuel Whitwell spent sixty–nine pounds on fifty–nine persons in 1769. The cost of providing indoor relief to the stream of inmates that Proctor sent in would have been three to four times that. See Wiberley, 76, 142, 178, for estimates of costs. In some years the Almshouse accommodated more out-of-town admissions than local ones. See *Overseers*, box 9, folder 4.

96   Quincy, *A Municipal History*, 34–38, 47–53; *Quincy Report*, passim.

97   Scattered financial data can be found in the *Boston Records*. See also Wiberley's estimates.

98   *Sibley's Harvard Graduates*, 9:177. Whitwell, "Account Book." The Overseers resorted to threat during the acute crisis of 1780–83. In 1781 they informed the Town Meeting that "unless they are furnished with some [money] they must open the Almshouse Doors to let the Poor out." *Boston Records*, 26:189, 205. See also *Boston Records* 26:242, which quotes the Overseers as reporting that "the Poor in the Almshouse … have been without Bread ever since Last Tuesday, untill Saturday when only two hundred [weight] of hard Bread was procured for them … and nothing but Water for them to drink."

99   *Boston Records*, 15:245–46.

100   *Overseers*, box 1, folder 2. A summary of the total poor relief expenditures claimed by the Overseers for the 30 years up to 1768 is offered here with some confidence in light of the complete financial statements in *Overseers*, box 1, folder 2. A caution is advised on the percentage assigned to outdoor relief. I have used Stephen Wiberley's estimates, but like my own, which are about the same, they are subject to some guesswork. See Wiberley, 76.

Year	Total expenditure (% outdoor) (in Pounds)	Year	Total expenditure (% outdoor) (in Pounds)
1738	3,165 (49% outdoor)		
1739	3,021 (44%)	1754	1,287 (35%)
1740	3,155 (50%)	1755	1,376 (44%)
1741	3,981 (48%)	1756	1,454 (48%)

1742	7,801 (28%)		1757	1,555 (33%)
1743	4,640 (42%)		1758	1,123 (39%)
1744	4,248 (48%)		1759	1,403 (26%)
1745	5,553 (40%)		1760	1,602 (26%)
1746	5,058 (43%)		1761	1,607 (29%)
1747	10,028 (43%)		1762	1,556 (29%)
1748	10,866 (45%)		1763	1,723 (23%)
1749	9,496 (45%)		1764	1,837 (27%)
1750	1,455 (43%)		1765	2,102 (29%)
1751	1,276 (52%)		1766	2,521 (31%)
1752	1,517 (35%)		1767	3,127 (30%)
1753	1,165 (30%)		1768	2,597 (31%)

The huge increase in expenditures in 1742 is an aberration. In 1741 the Town Meeting agreed to expand the size of the Almshouse. It was completed in 1742 and the costs of the expansion were charged to the town treasury along with the normal poor relief budget. As much as three thousand pounds of the 1742 expenditure is therefore construction cost. The percentage of outdoor relief expenses did not drop, as they appear to in the chart, because those expenses were factored into the gross amount for the year. My estimate of the outdoor expense percentage is 45 to 48 percent for 1742. See *Overseers*, box 1, folder 2, for June 2, 1742. See also *Boston Records* 12:281; 15:292. As for the numerical fluctuations, and in particular the 1746 to 1747 and 1749 to 1750 amounts, it should be noted that between 1730 and 1750 the value of Massachusetts currency, "Old Tenor," was eroded steadily to about one-third its sterling value. Not only do the figures look high, there is little consistency in their relation to other economic values. The return to a silver-based currency by the General Court in 1750 (*Acts and Resolves*, 3:430–41) led to "twenty-five years of . . . stability in the course of exchange [against sterling] in Massachusetts. Par was set … at 133.33 ['lawful money' to sterling]." The conversion rate of lawful money to Old Tenor was initially set at 1:7.5. See John J. McCusker, *Money and Exchange in Europe and America: A Handbook* (Chapel Hill, N.C., 1978), 133, 141.

Only a few random separate figures survive for Workhouse expenses. They are clearly only partial expenditues and are for direct out-of-pocket expenses by Overseers specifically for the Workhouse. Figures are given for every year up to 1753 and for only four times after that. The largest number of separate accounts, including payments to tradesmen, suppliers, the Overseers themselves, and the keeper, is twenty-six, compared to over one hundred annually for the Almshouse. In most years only a handful of claims appear. The most consistent charge is for the keeper, usually Joseph Lasenby, who served for more than twenty years after 1751.

Old Tenor			Lawful Money	
1740	926–1–0		1750	53–6–8
1741	643–15–9		1751	206–1–8
1742	1,439–19–9		1752	238–16–5
1743	968–3–9		1753	141–4–11
1744	406–7–9		1755	99–1–8
1745	1,094–11–4		1757	50–10–4 3/4
1746	209–14–5		1758	70–10–11
1747	300–0–0		1760	100–0–0
1748	700–0–0			
1749	1,304–8–4			

Given the exchange values between Old Tenor and lawful money, the aggregate sums for the 1740s and 1750s are very close. It is not likely that these figures were duplicated by the Overseers in their general annual charges to the Town Treasurer. These accounts were found with the manuscript version of the "Rules of the Workhouse" (*Overseers*, box 13, folder 1) that are transcribed in appendix 4.

101 Whitwell "Account Book" indicates that he had only 19 full time "pensioners" (that is, recipients of a monthly support stipend) between 1768 and 1775. Wiberley, 141–42, estimates that only 39 claimants received full and continuous (month-to-month) pensions outside the Almshouse between 1750 and 1775.

102 *Boston Records*, 15:369.

103 Whitwell "Account Book."

104 *Ibid.*

105 See appendix 1. Towner, 424, notes that those paying taxes did not have to give up their children, even if the Overseers wanted to bind them out.

106 Boston Indentures, 6 vols., Boston Public Library, 1:n. p.

107 Boston Indentures; Towner, "Table of Indentures."

108 Boston Indentures, 6:97.

109 As noted the original manuscript contracts (indentures) are in the Rare Books and Manuscripts division of the Boston Public Library. When Towner used them they were in the possession of the Boston City Clerk. The lists that have survived in the Overseers collection are in *Overseers*, box 9, folder 1.

110 Towner, "Table of Indentures."

111 This assumption is based largely on the 1756 Almshouse census where children without parents are shown to be lodged with other adults.

112 *Overseers Guide*, 26–29; *General Laws of Massachusetts From the Adoption of the Constitution to February 1822* (Boston, 1875); Benton, *Warning Out*, chapters 2, 3, 7; Culbert, "Sturdy Beggars," chapter 3.

113 *Ibid.*; Benton, *Warning Out*, 52.

114 *Boston Records* 20:130, 139. The Sweetser mentioned here, or more likely his son, became an Overseer of the Poor in 1776. See also Robert Love, "Received by Order of the selectmen," MHS.

115 Love, "Received by Order."

116 *Overseers*, box 1, folder 2. Those warned were given precise instructions on how they were to leave. A note in the Boston Town Papers manuscripts in the Boston Public Library, 7:73, shows that 205 persons were warned to depart "by land" and 67 "by water" between January 29 and September 1, 1765.

117 *Overseers*, box 1, folders 3–4. There are references throughout the *Boston Records* and the Boston Town Papers to the care that the Overseers provided to sick transients. The extensive minutes held by the Boston Public Library Rare Books and Manuscripts Collection identify many cases of this kind of care. See Boston Overseers of the Poor Vote Book, 1788–1809 (catalog number Ms q. Bos. W1, and a second volume for 1809–1820, catalog number Ms. q. Am 2322). There is no record of

how these Overseers documents, and many others at the Boston Public Library, were separated from the main collection now at the MHS.

118   See Nash, "Urban Wealth and Poverty," and Jones, "The Strolling Poor." See also *Boston Records*, 20: passim.

119   See Ruth Wallis Herndon, *Unwelcome Americans: Living on the Margin in Early New England* (Philadelphia, 2001). This is a welcome study of warning out and of New England transiency in general, and is much more analytical than Benton's older study. But its emphasis on case studies and its use of New England in the title, when it is concerned exclusively with eighteenth-century Rhode Island, limits its application to the Boston Overseers Warning Out Lists.

120   *Overseers*, box 1, folders 3, 4; box 9, folder 4. My counts differ slightly from those in Wiberley, 47, and Alan Kulikoff, "The Progress of Inequality," 400, but the differences do not affect the similar frequencies of warnings that we find. (The surnames beginning with A and part of B are missing from the 1771–3 lists). The counts here are approximate and were done by hand from the manuscripts.

Table 1. 1745–1770

Total Warnings (includes groups and individuals)	3,409
Origins New England	2,313 (68 percent)
Group (including families) warnings (approximately 3,200 persons)	700
Individual warnings	2,598
Total number of persons warned out (including)	5,798
"Blacks," "Negroes," "Molattoes"	74
"Indian"	56
"Widow"	26
"Poor" (including "very poor," "and wicked," "a stroller")	13
"Crazy," "Distracted" (including "a noted thief")	7
"Sick", "Lame"	2
"Soldiers" with families	8
"Soldiers' Wives"	9
"With Servants" (including one family with four servants)	6

Table 2. 1771–73 (part of the record is missing)

Total warnings	429
Origins New England	273 (64 percent)
Other American (13 colonies)	74
Other	82

(including North America)

"Negroes"	10
"Molattoes"	3
"Indians"	5
<u>Total persons warned out</u>	800

(Males: 309)
(Females: 272)
(Children: 229)
(identified as such)

<u>Table 3. 1791–92</u> (two full years)

<u>Total warnings</u>	2,113
Origins	
Massachusetts	1,482
Other New England	51
Other United States	79
Foreign	501
<u>Total number of persons warned out</u>	2,528

(Males: 1,242)
(Females:1,091)
(Children:195)
(identified as such)

121 *Ibid.*, and under the 1739 act, a person not warned out within three months of arrival could legally claim residence in the town.

122 It appears that before the bonus system was introduced the job of warning out was ill defined; the responsibility was with the Selectmen. (*Boston Records* 15:50.)

123 *Overseers*, box 9, folder 4.

124 As for indoor relief, there is no question that at least 5,000 persons were admitted into the Almshouse in this period, some of them several times; see *Overseers*, boxes 1 and 9, passim. The estimates for outdoor relief are based on projections made on the basis of Overseers' claims on the town treasury (*Overseers*, box 1, folder 2), and estimates of numbers of outdoor relief constituents for all Overseers drawn from Whitwell "Account Book." Whitwell alone, as one of twelve Overseers, assisted about 250 different people in the 1770s.

125 The figures for the numbers of people getting outdoor relief are quite speculative. They are extrapolated from the hundreds of names entered in the only surviving list of outdoor poor, Samuel Whitwell's, matched with his submitted costs, and then applied in a rough per capita estimate to the known costs of outdoor relief for all twelve Overseers in certain years. Nash, "Urban Wealth and Poverty," 463, makes a somewhat higher estimate of recipients than I do. Wiberley, 166ff., suggests the same kind of frequency for outdoor relief as does Nash.

126 On Fowles, see *Overseers*, box 9, folder 4. After 1795 the Almshouse entries contain more personalized information on inmates, and regular censuses begin to appear in the records by 1810. The insane and sick are specifically identified in the later documents. See "Guide."

127 Alms comes from the Greek *eleos* ("pity"). The term eleemosynary ("charitable") is from the same root. In fact, the appearance of the word alms in the English Middle Ages gives the word a deep root in the history of Anglo-American poor relief. But it was a much wider concept, as Robert Jutte, *Poverty and Deviance*, has noted in his references to European poor relief. A very sound review of the English tradition, and a very useful chronology is in Slack, *English Poor Law*.

128 See *Overseers*, box 9, folder 6. As noted, the early nineteenth-century Almshouse lists are more detailed than the earlier records and include much more data on inmates' ages, residence status, medical condition and so on.

129 *Quincy Report*.

130 *Overseers*, box 1, folder 4; box 9, folders 1–4. As noted, as their numbers rose in the Almshouse, the number of African Americans in the Boston population fell, as did the ratio to whites. See Shattuck, 5, and Felt, "Statistics," 208–14. Carr, "A Change," 598–601, does not discuss the upsurge in Almshouse admissions for African Americans in her study of demographic change. See the interesting comment in J. Melish, *Disowning Slavery:* 240–41.

131 The entry for a province or state charge was accompanied by the names of two Selectmen and one Overseer. For town charges, only the Overseer's name was entered, because only the Overseer's authority was required for Bostonians' admissions.

132 Culbert, 90–92.

133 For the original Almshouse see *Boston Records* 1:78 and 7:174 and passim. For the 1742 addition, see *Boston Records* 12:281, 15:292. While there is no final declaration in the record that this proposed addition was completed there is enough circumstantial evidence in the *Boston Records* and in the Overseers financial records to indicate that a leg of the 'L' was added then. The history of Boston's late eighteenth-century alternative "workhouses" is dealt with in detail by Nash, *Urban Crucible*, 190–96; Nellis, "Misreading the Signs"; and Wiberley, 97–109.

134 Wiberley, 33, finds 249 deaths. I cannot find the reason for the discrepancy in our counts.

135 The 1742 census figures may in fact be conservative. See the census and comments in *Boston Records*, 15:369–70 and in Shattuck, 3. On most of the population estimates see Shattuck, 5, 26, 46. There may be no more variable sets of numbers for Boston than those that are used for its pre-1790 population. See the figures in Nash, "Urban Wealth and Poverty," for example. Shattuck, who combed all the old censuses, is reliable, but he sometimes omits the "colored" from his tabulations. Alfred Young, *The Shoemaker and the Tea Party: Memory and the American Revolution* (Boston, 1999), Part II, chapter 4, has some very useful points to make about the substantive changes in Boston's population during and after the revolution. See also Carr, "A Change."

136 Culbert, "Sturdy Beggars," 82–117, 160ff. The *Quincy Report* of 1821 both reflects reforms underway and calls for more radical reforms.

137 Perhaps it is better to think of Almshouse "punishments" in terms of restricted privileges for bad behavior. Inmates could be sent to the Workhouse for breaches of the conduct rules. There is no allowance that I can find for corporal punishment. Discipline was maintained, in part, by the threat of expulsion to the Workhouse. See *Overseers*, box 9, passim.

138 Walter Muir Whitehill, *A Topographical History of Boston,* 2d ed. [Boston, 1968], 64; *Boston Records* 31:399–400; Harold and James Kirker, *Bulfinch's Boston, 1787–1817* (New York, 1964), 97. The site was in the West End in 1800, but that area is now considered to be part of the North End. In

Notes

❧

1800 the old North End was in general decline as new buildings in "Bulfinch's Boston" eclipsed the quality of the town's older architecture, and when the commercial, governmental and prime residential areas were redefined. See *Bulfinch's Boston*, 11–13, and the maps on the inside of the front and back covers, and Young, *The Shoemaker*, II:126–27, for examples. Bulfinch had been a long-serving Selectman in Boston and according to Kirker and Kirker his involvement in the 1799–1801 Almshouse resulted from an abiding interest in the poor. This seems to be a bit of a stretch, because Bulfinch took any civic architectural job that he could. The Kirkers also conflate the roles of the Selectmen and the Overseers.

139   The Almshouse manuscript census of 1756 appeared in the most unexpected of places, in volume 1 of the Indentures collection in the Boston Public Library (the collection was formerly at Boston City Hall), stuck to the back of page 1. The only other reference I have seen to the document is in Nash, "Urban Wealth and Poverty," 559. Nash counted 148 people in the house, while I can find as few as 121 and as many as 141, depending on how I decipher the clerk's notations. The clerk states that 133 was the total.

140   "Samuel Proctor Account," MHS Miscellaneous Bound Manuscripts, September 1, 1765.

141   *Ibid.*

142   Towner, 428–29.

143   The 1789 quote is from Boston Overseers of the Poor Vote Book, 1788–1809, Boston Public Library. For the 1740s see *Overseers*, box 1, folder 2. See also J. B. Blake, *Public Health in the Town of Boston, 1630–1822* (Cambridge, Mass., 1959).

144   For frequencies see *Overseers*, box 9, folders 1–4. The examples here are from the 1760s.

145   Quoted in Kirker and Kirker, *Bulfinch's Boston*, 97.

146   Wiberley, 149.

147   "Bill of Fare, Boston Almshouse, 1819," MHS (not part of the Overseers Records).

148   *Boston Records*, Volume 26, contains some references to wartime victualing.

149   For frequencies see *Overseers*, box 1, folders 1–4.

150   *Boston Records*, 35:351–54. On the 1760s, see *Overseers*, box 9, folders 1, 2, 3.

151   The quote is from T. Pemberton, "A Topographical and Historical Description of Boston, 1794," in MHS *Collections* 3:251–52.

152   *Boston Records*, 31:239.

153   *Boston Records*, 1:78; 12:159–60.

154   By the 1790s the absence of sleeping space in the Workhouse was clearly adding to the space problems in the Almshouse.

155   *Boston Records*, 12:273.

156 *Boston Records*, 15:4, 6, 33, will serve as examples. Once again it is regretted that there are no surviving records of Overseers' meetings minutes until the 1790s, and those are not part of the Overseers collection at MHS. For the 1790s there are numerous sets of minutes of Overseers meetings at the Boston Public Library (Department of Rare Books and Manuscripts, see catalog number Ms.q. Bos w1). These manuscripts contain a regular accounting of budgets for burials, medical care, repairs to the buildings, salaries of keepers, clerks, watchmen and the various indoor and outdoor expenses of poor relief. But for the rest of the period under review, and in regard to the transcribed documents in this volume, details have to be gleaned from the published Selectmen's and Town Meeting minutes in the *Boston Records*.

157 The original list of subscribers is in *Boston Records*, 12:180–83.

158 *Boston Records*, 14:150.

159 The linen manufacturing scheme of the 1750s and 1760s is the most ambitious attempt to implement the model. As with all similar schemes in colonial America, it failed. See Nellis, "Misreading the Signs."

160 *Overseers*, box 9, folders 1 and 4.

161 *Boston Records*, 12:273 for 1741; *Overseers*, box 13, folder 2, for the 1790s.

162 *Overseers*, box 13, folder 2.

163 *Ibid*.

164 *Ibid*. The deaths appear to have been among the elderly, for the most part. What is not known is the number who went into the Almshouse deliberately to spend their last days there.

165 *Overseers*, Box 13, folder 2.

166 *Boston Records* 35:351–4.

167 Rothman, *Discovery*, passim; *Quincy Report*; and the dense polemic *The Overseers of the Poor … to their Constituents* (Boston, 1832), 32 pages. Copy at MHS. The quotes are from *Boston Records*, 35:351–54.

168 *Overseers*, box 9, folder 1.

169 *Ibid*.

170 Carr, "A Change," and Young, *The Shoemaker*, Part I, for the depopulation and repopulation of Boston.

171 *Overseers*, box 9, folder 3. The thirty–two who were evacuated were reported to have "gone over on the ferry," but which ferry is not clear.

172 *Overseers*, box 9, folder 1.

173 Shattuck, 142–44; Winslow, *A Destroying Angel*.

174 *Boston Records*, passim (indexed) can be consulted for many examples of this.

Notes

175 Winslow, *A Destroying Angel* and *Overseers*, box 9, folder 3.

176 *Boston Records* 20:246, 261.

177 *Overseers*, box, 9, folder 4; Towner.

178 *Overseers*, box, 9, folder 4.

179 Chauncy, *The Idle Poor*, and Cooper, *A Sermon Preached in Boston*.

180 Shattuck, passim, refers to a blind asylum, house of industry, house of correction, state jail, house of reformation (for wayward children), and a lunatic hospital. There appears to be no mention of a separate facility for unmarried mothers or pregnant girls.

181 *Overseers*, box 9, folder 2.

182 *Ibid*; Thwing, *Inhabitants and Estates*, is a useful starting point for a review of family associations.

183 *Overseers*, box 11, folder 2.

184 In a clear demonstration of that change, Lemuel Shattuck's magisterial *Report* of 1846, as humane as it and its author were, is a celebration of a statistical determinism. It offers no homage, not even a sentimental one, to eighteenth-century public welfare ideas or practices.

EDITORIAL METHOD

Materials Included and Their Arrangement

ΤHE RECORDS PRINTED IN THE PRESENT VOLUME are from the collections of the Massachusetts Historical Society, with the exception of the 1756 Almshouse Census and Inventory found among the Boston City Records in the special collections at the Boston Public Library. The eighteenth-century documents printed below are only a fraction of the Massachusetts Historical Society's voluminous collection of Boston Overseers of the Poor, Records, 1733–1925, comprising 19 boxes of manuscripts and 15 corresponding reels of microfilm. The boards were removed from the volumes before they were purchased by the Society, thus titles and descriptive material were lost. Wear and tear along the edge of the manuscripts has resulted occasionally in the loss of some text. The disbound volumes were arranged by the Society. The editors have assigned names to the volumes, as designated below.

A complementary volume catalogued elsewhere within the collections of the Massachusetts Historical Society and chosen by the editors to be printed here is a thin volume of accounts kept by Overseer Samuel Whitwell for twenty-one years.

MHi: Boston Overseers of the Poor, Records, 1733–1925

Financial Register

One disbound volume, recording the monthly financial disbursements by the overseers, 4 March 1738 – 1 March 1769. The payments include both charitable disbursements and business accounts. The volume also contains several lists of overseers, blank forms and certificates, and miscellaneous documents on its opening and closing pages. The entries were made by various writers. The volume measures 7 $^{7}/_{8}$" x 12 $^{1}/_{2}$" and consists of 188 unnumbered pages. Located on Reel No. 1 of the microfilm.

Admissions Register 1

One bound volume, incomplete; 8" x 13" in size. Numbered pages 11–57 record admissions into and discharges from the almshouse, 9 Nov. 1758 – 27 April 1774. An alphabetical index of almshouse residents includes entries for the ten missing pages (see [*Admissions to the Almshouse, ante 9 November 1758*], p. 122, below). The index has been compared to the extant entries and any variations in spelling or additional information are recorded in a footnote to the admissions record.

Although Register 1, which is laid out in table form, contains the earliest dated admissions records in the Historical Society's collection, it apparently was compiled by a clerk who examined older admissions registers. For this reason only those entries in Register 1 that are not duplicated in Registers 2 and 3 are printed below. Duplicate entries have been compared and any differences or additional information are recorded in a footnote.

Register 1 also contains a list of children bound out of the almshouse, 21 April 1756 – 3 Nov. 1773, 2 April 1785 – 2 Feb. 1790, on 16 numbered pages. Pages 14–16 are by a different writer than the rest of the volume. An index corresponding only to pages 1–13 follows. While the index is not printed below, its entries have been compared to the list of indentures and any variations in spelling or additional information are recorded in a footnote.

Record of births in the almshouse, 17 Aug. 1756 – 1 May 1768, 3 unnumbered pages. As with the admissions records, a portion of the list of children born in the almshouse in Register 1 duplicates similar entries in Register 2. Duplicate entries have been compared and any differences or additions are included by the editors in a footnote to the entry in Register 2.

Located on Reel No. 8 of the microfilm.

Admissions Register 2

One disbound volume, 7 $\frac{1}{4}$" x 9 $\frac{1}{4}$" in size, consisting of 118 unnumbered pages. The entries consist of almshouse admissions and discharges, 14 Feb. 1763 – 28 June 1768, 81 pages; "Record of Children born in the Alms house," 29 Nov. 1763 – 21 April 1767, 3 pages; "Account of People Deceas'd In the Alms house," 25 March 1763 – 10 May 1771, 20 pages; "Account of Children Born in the Alms House," 6 Sept. 1767 – 5 Nov. 1771, 22 Oct. 1771, 4 June 1767, 3 pages; "Account of Deaths in the House Brot forward," 17 May 1771 – 13 Nov. 1771, 1 page; almshouse admissions and discharges, 2 July 1768 – 27 Dec. 1768, 8 pages; inventories of personal belongings brought into the almshouse by several residents, 2 pages; and almshouse admissions and discharges, 4–30 Jan. 1769, 1 page. The entries in the volume are written by several individuals.

Located on Reel No. 8 of the microfilm.

Admissions Register 3

One disbound volume, inscribed "Register from 12th. Decr. 1768 to 30 Sept. 1788" on the titlepage. This is a record of almshouse admissions and discharges over 266 unnumbered pages, measuring 7 $\frac{7}{8}$" x 12 $\frac{1}{2}$", written by various individuals. Located on Reel. No. 8 of the microfilm.

Admissions Register 4

One disbound volume, 8" x 12 $\frac{3}{8}$" in size. Numbered pages 41–197 record almshouse admissions and discharges 1 Oct. 1788 – 31 Aug. 1795. The entries are all by the same writer. Beginning with the entry dated 7 Feb. 1791 on p. 97 the format of the entries change from brief notations to a table. A 13-page index compiled by another writer follows. The index, not printed below, has been compared to the main entries and any variations in spelling or additional information are recorded in a footnote.

Bound with a list of persons warned out of Boston, 16 June 1770 – 31 Aug. 1773, located on numbered pages 1–39. A true copy attested by Ezekiel Goldthwait, Boston, 20 Sept. 1773. Not printed below.

Located on Reel No. 8 of the microfilm.

Admissions Register 5

One disbound volume, 9 $^1/_2$" x 14 $^1/_2$", 364 unnumbered pages. A record of almshouse admissions and discharges arranged alphabetically, 4 June 1795 – 29 Aug. 1817, all by the same writer. Also includes a 4-page list of "Notifications," identifying persons belonging to Massachusetts towns other than Boston who were admitted to the almshouse and a list of expenses charged to the various towns for their keep. Located on Reel No. 10 of the microfilm.

Boston Asylum Ledger

Accounts with the state and various towns for the support of inmates, 1 Oct. 1795 – 3 May 1806. Also includes accounts for supplies and service. One disbound volume, with 127 numbered page openings, measuring 6 $^1/_4$" x 7 $^3/_4$". Debit and credit columns for the accounts are written on facing pages that are each assigned the same page number. Only the eighteenth-century accounts (1795–1800), pages 1–41, are printed below. The entries were all made by the same writer. Located on Reel No. 13 of the microfilm.

MHi: Boston Poor. Accounts of Samuel Whitwell, 1769–1792

One bound volume, 6 $^3/_4$" x 8 $^3/_4$", the cover of which is inscribed: "Town Treasurer's / Accots. in this Book / & State Treasrs. / Disburstments / For the poor of the Town / Boston / 17[69]." Compiled by Overseer Samuel Whitwell (1717–1801), the volume contains his accounts of disbursements made to the poor in Boston's Wards 2 (1769-1770), 12 (1770–1771), and 10 (1771–1790), pages numbered 1–74; "Memorandums," [*ante* 21] June – 6 Oct. 1790, 2 unnumbered pages; and miscellaneous accounts and drafts upon the treasurer of Boston (1790–1792), 11 unnumbered pages.

MB: Almshouse Census and Inventory, 1756

Both the Almshouse Census ("A List of Persons, Beds &c. in the alms House Augt. 1756") and Inventory ("a List of Sundrys in the Alms House taken Augt. 1756") are interleaved in the first of six volumes of Boston Overseers of the Poor, Indentures, 1734–1805. The Census is interleaved before page 1 and the Inventory is interleaved before page 2.

Textual Policy

THE PRIMARY GOAL OF THE TEXTUAL POLICY is to provide a readable text while striving faithfully to retain the spelling, capitalization, and punctuation of the original manuscripts. The character of the documents, many of which are tables, the many writers who kept the records, and the nature of the material itself (dominated by proper names) requires that the manuscripts be followed faithfully, with minimal expansion or insertion by the editor.

Spelling. The unnamed individuals who recorded the activities of the almshouse residents and the overseers possessed drastically varying degrees of spelling ability. Regardless of the level of standardization or consistency displayed by the writer, spelling is retained as written.

Capitalization. Capitalization is preserved as found in the original manuscripts. When the intent of the writer is unclear, modern practice is employed.

Punctuation. Punctuation is retained as written, except for the following conventionalizations. Superfluous dashes and suspension points at the end of lines have not been transcribed. The obvious omission of opening or closing parenthesis is silently corrected by supplying the missing partner. Commas employed as apostrophes have been modernized. Punctuation within monetary amounts is regularized by supplying a decimal point after pound, shilling, and dollar figures (£2. 5. 10). The virgule symbolizing shillings (15/) is retained; punctuation following the virgule has not been transcribed.

Abbreviations and contractions. Abbreviations and contractions along with their terminal punctuation are preserved as written. Superscript and subscript letters used to indicate contractions are brought to the line; if no terminal punctuation is employed in the manuscript a period is supplied. The macron or tilde (Hañah) used in on-the-line abbreviations is retained. The ampersand (&) and the tailed ℘ are preserved. The thorn (yt, ye) is always printed as "th."

Interlineations. Interlined words or passages are silently brought to the line where indicated by the writer. A note is appended if clarification is necessary.

Missing and illegible matter. Missing and illegible matter is indicated by square brackets enclosing the conjectural reading (with a question mark appended if the reading is doubtful), or by suspension points if no reading can be given. If only a portion of a word is missing, it may be silently supplied when there is no doubt about the reading. When the missing or illegible matter amounts to more than one or two words, a footnote estimating its amount is attached.

Canceled matter. Words and phrases struck out by the writer are generally omitted unless the change is deemed significant. False starts, slips of the pen, and obvious repetitions of text are eliminated. Substantive cancellations are italicized and enclosed in angle brackets.

❧

Editorial insertions. Editorial insertions are italicized and enclosed in square brackets.

Format. Financial Register. Ruled lines separating the monthly entries have not been transcribed. The placement of the dateline and heading for each monthly entry has been regularized by placing the dateline flush right on the first line of the entry and the heading flush left on the following line. Each entry within the month is set flush left, if the entry extends beyond one typeset line, succeeding lines are indented.

Admissions Registers. The admissions records are presented in tables and brief notations. In both formats, ruled lines separating the entries have not been transcribed. Table headings are preserved as written at the start of the table in the original manuscripts. Unless the format of the table is changed (column order rearranged, or a new column of information added to the table) the headings at the top of each succeeding page in the original manuscripts have not been transcribed.

Almshouse admissions and discharges recorded in brief notations are irregularly spaced over the page in the original manuscripts. The format for these entries has been regularized as follows: 1. The date is placed on the first line, flush with the left margin. 2. Information on the individual is indented following the date and, if necessary, run into the next line of the entry. 3. If noted separately, the entity being charged for the admission (town or state) is placed flush with the right margin following the description of the admitee. 4. Overseers information is set flush left on one line. 5. Selectmen's information is set flush left on one line. 6. Commas are inserted to separate proper names. 7. Braces grouping two or more lines of text in the original manuscript are placed at the end of line. Thus, an entry in the original manuscript that is written:

Jany. 24th.   Recd. into the Almshous Sarah Ford with her⎫   (state)
                Two Children   ⎭
Approved of by ⎱one of the oversears   Pr. Ordor of Jno. Andrews⎱
Jonathon Mason⎰   Moses Grant ⎰ Selectmen

is rendered as:

Jany. 24th.   Recd. into the Almshous Sarah Ford with her Two Children}   (state)
Approved of by Jonathon Mason} one of the oversears
Pr. Ordor of Jno. Andrews, Moses Grant} Selectmen

Annotation. Annotation of the original manuscripts is limited to textual notes commenting on the appearance and physical description of the manuscript (for example, clarifying interlineations, identifying tears, or noting marginalia) and comparing variant copies of the text.

❧

Guide to Editorial Apparatus

Textual Devices

<italic> Matter canceled in the manuscript but restored in the text.

[…] Words(s) missing or illegible and not conjecturable.

[roman] Conjectural reading for missing or illegible matter. A question mark is inserted before the closing bracket if the conjectural reading is seriously doubtful.

[*italic*] Matter editorially inserted.

Location Symbols

MB   Boston Public Library

MHi   Massachusetts Historical Society

THE DOCUMENTS

THE ALMSHOUSE CENSUS
AND INVENTORY
1756

The Almshouse census and inventory manuscripts are not part of the Over-seers collection at the MHS though they were most certainly produced by or for the Overseers in 1756. The two transcribed documents that are here presented together are identified as "A List of Persons … in the alms House" and "A List of Sundrys in the Alms House." The documents are dated August 1756 and were likely drawn up then, and annotated later. While they may have been part of the vast Overseers Records held for decades by the City of Boston they became separated and appeared glued to the front leaf of volume one of the six volumes of children's indentures that were the basis of Lawrence Towner's study. When Towner did his research, the indenture records were in the City Clerk's office at the Boston City Hall. Those records, and the attached Almshouse census and inventory, are now in the Manuscripts and Special Collections at the Boston Public Library. So far as we can determine, this is the only manuscript of its kind for the eighteenth-century Almshouse. Other eighteenth-century references to the Almshouse and Workhouse populations can be found in scattered references, mostly in the Boston Records, *but the manuscript transcribed here is rare because of its identification of people, living arrangements, and inventory. There are no extant Almshouse admissions and discharge records for 1756 and so it is impossible to measure the lengths of stay of the occupants in this list. While there are comparable censuses for nineteenth-century Boston institutions, and for eighteenth-century institutions elsewhere in America, it is likely that this is the only glimpse we have into the eighteenth-century Boston Almshouse.*

A List of Persons, Beds &c. in the alms House Augt. 1756

Room No. 1 vizt.	Beds	Ruggs & Blanketts	Prs. of Sheets	Shirts & shifts
1 Mary Odlin 2 Sarah Battells 3 Sarah Boleson	3	6	3	6
No. 2 4 Mary Whitehead 5 Maratha Kingstone 6 Sarah Bumstead	3	6	3	6

No. 3
7 Penelope George
8 Eliza. Coombs
9 Ester Warden
  <John Cushing> gone to servis
10 Thos. Field   Children of 6 & 7 years
  Margaret Blake 2 Children
	3	6	3	10

No. 4 11 *<Martha Colton>* Ann Tyley *<Mary Blake>* gone to Workhous 14 Mary Fleet & 2 Children 16 Martha Colton & Daughter	2	4	2	8
No. 5 17 James Mellins 18 David Osborne Dead Ebenzr. Grater	3	6	3	4

No. 6
19 William Morto
  <John Dewen> gone Phillip More
20 Thos. Bickford
  <Robert Feathergill> Dead
21 John Finley
	5	10	5	8

Room No. 7
22 Sarah Mead
23 *<Sarah Green>* Dead   7 in all
24 Sarah Peirce   4   8   4   12
   <Susanna Newcomb>   *<gone to Servis>* Return'd again
27 2 Children Sarah Wincot & Child

   No. 8
28 Hepsibeth Griffith
   <Mary Davis> Dead
29 Sarah Richards child   4 womn. [&] 3 Childn.
   <Anna Mason>   gone to Servis   4   8   4   14
32 3 Children
34 Mrs Townsend / Sarah Boyles

   No. 9
35 Susanna Lynde &
36 Daugr. 11 Years Old
37 Mary Brisco   4   8   4   12
38 Sarah Stover
40 Sarah Harding & Child
43 3 Children

   10
44 Eliza Skinner   Mary Gullion
45 Kathn. Legg & Child
46 *<Sarah Rhoads>*   Buckleys & child 4   8   4   12
47 *<Sarah Flyng>* Dead

   11
Furniture of [J?] Davis

   12
Mrs Garns
48 Rebecca Reed   1   2   1   2

   13
Movd. *<Saml. Edy>*
49 Benja. Phillips   3   6   3   6
50 Saml. Marion
Thos. Odel Lodges in the house only
Ebenzr. Grater

No. 14
51 Hannah [Crehose?] & Sarah Roads
52 Mary Crumpton No. 15 &
53 Mary Crumpton   Susana Dix
54 Eliza. Mccurde   Eddy Child 3   6   3   10
Eddy Joanna <*Savage*> & child
55 <*Margaret Buckly*>

No. 15
Dead <*Owen Cunningham & Thos. Odell*> 4   8   4   4

No. 16
56 Sarah Rice
57 Mary Mortgaridge   4   8   4   16
58 Abigail Lynch & 5 Children

No. 17
64 Sarah <*Livingston*> Livett   3   6   3   6
65 Sarah Jones 92 yrs. old
66 Mercy Ryland Margaret Clefton
   young man

No. 18
67 Mary Ann Anderson
68 Jane Champion   4   8   4   12
70 Margaret FitchGerald & Child
72 2 Negro Women Hagar & Rachel

No. 19
73 Rebecca Burnet
74 Ann Ashley   Edward McGowen
75 <*Eliza. Garnes*>   Mary McGowen 4 8   4   10
76 Eliza. Copp   & Child
78 <*Jane Thompson*> a Child
gone

No. 20
79 Nathl. Gordon
80 John Hughes
81 <*Delve a Dutchman*> Christopher Delve 5   10   5   10
82 Tho. Plaisted
<*Wm. Saymore*> gone away Mrs. Dyer

21
85 Mary Wyat & 2 Children
86 Eliza. Gray   2   4   2   2

22
87 Content Gordon
88 Mary Water<*house*>man & 2 Children } 2   4   2   6
Sepr. 4 Layd. 3 weeks

No. 23
91 Hannah Ivory
92 Eliza. Lewis
93 Mary Harr all   5   10   5   12
95 Mary ann Sack & 2 Children
97 Phebe Randal

No. 24
98 Ann Hogg
99 Mary Higgens   4   8   4   10
100 Jane Young
104 Mary Linnington & 3 Children

No. 25. & <*26*>
Eddy & wife   1   2   1   2
106 Macks Room the Hall & Chairs

No. 27
107 John Warrick
108 Thos. Dilla
109 John Dinsdell   4   8   4   8
110 Thos. Frazier

No. 28
111 Mary Monk
112 Susanna Jackson   3   6   3   8
113 Mary Heath & 1 Child

No. 29
115 Benja. Storrer & susana his Wife   2   4   2   8
116 Eliza. Bill
117 Abigail Dawson

No. 30
118 Thos. Mason   4   8   4   8
119 <*John Mccollam*>
121 John Preston and Danl. Mondon

No. 31
123 Eliza. Peirce and Mary Thorn   2   4   2   4

No. 32
124 Desire Hawes
125 Sands Gibbon   3   6   3   6
126 Christophr. Thornton

No. 33
127 Jane Taylor
128 Mary <*Freeman*> Shaw   3   6   3   12
133 Eliza. Barger & 4 Children

❧

a List of Sundrys in the Alms House
taken Augt. 1756

In the Garrett vizt.
A Large Parcell Old Cloths
19 Trunks Some wth. herbs &c.
8 Qts. fish
3 Bushell Beans
a Desk wheel & Table
some Old Chairs & Cask
2 Case Drawers
4 Old Ditto
7 Tables
abt. 40 [Hopps l?]
a Clothiers Frame & Tools
2 New Beds
8 Old Ditto
13 New Duffell Blanketts
2 New Pillows
1 Do. Old &c. &c.

_____

In the Meal Room viz
a pr. steel yards
a pr. Scale Beams & Weights
a Meal Troth shovels &c.
abt [1/2 ll.] Brown Sugar

_____

In the Yard
about 200 Cord Wood
1 Cross cut Saw
2 hand Saws
1 Wood Ax
Betel & Wedges
4 Live Hogs
6 Beds wth. Covering for Four

In the Grainery &c.
abt. 150 Bushell Rye
350 Bushell Corn

_____

In the Kitchen vizt.
1 Large Copper
1 Brass Kettle
1 Brass Ladle
2 Do. Skimmers
5 Wood Trays
2 Platters
4 Large Earthen Pans
5 Do. Dishes
7 Milk Potts
2 Pitchers
1 Bell Meltle Mortar
Pewter unweighd
3 dishes
3 plates
1 Bason
1 porringer
2 Table
1 Large Iron Slice
7 Trammells
2 pr. Dog / 1 pr. hand Irons
3 Iron Candle Sticks
1 Looking Glass

_____

In the Cellar vizt.
about 90 Gall. Mollasses
4 Barrells Pork wantg. 2 or 3 pieces
1 Large Chest
3 Smaller Do.
part 2 Cask Pork
2 Brs. Hogs Fatt
a parcell Empty Cask
2 Chests
1 Grindstone
1 hhd. Soap

The Almshouse Admissions

THESE TRANSCRIPTIONS OF THE ALMSHOUSE ADMISSIONS AND DISCHARGES constitute the greater part of the surviving eighteenth-century manuscripts of the records of the Boston Overseers. They are also important for the way they identify the thousands of people who passed through the institutional authority of the Overseers of the Poor. The Almshouse was a rest home for the elderly, a refuge for the "deserving poor," individually or as families who might be homeless, a "lying in" hospital for single pregnant women, an orphanage, and a haven for the infirm and mentally ill.

The manuscripts reflect the work of a variety of clerks, whose handwriting and editorial habits resulted in shifting standards of recorded information and style presentation. Some of the entries were collected and listed after the fact and some were ordered by column and others by line entry. There are clear omissions of births, deaths, runaways and discharges, and these data are underreported in the records. But the admissions appear to be complete or nearly complete for the period, judging from the sequential dates and given the Almshouse's residential capacity. The transcriptions have been organized into four chronological sections to reflect the historical context of Almshouse life. The subdivision of the record in this way will allow for the matching of Almshouse admissions to events and change.

Almshouse Admissions 1758–1774: The period from the French and Indian War to the Coercive Acts and the military occupation.

Almshouse Admissions 1775–1788: The War for Independence, and the debate over the Constitution dominated this period.

Almshouse Admissions 1788–1795: From the creation of the national government to the second Federalist administration.

Almshouse Admissions 1795–1800: The rise of the Republican Party and the election of Thomas Jefferson as President in 1800 are important national developments, and improved economic conditions, population growth and rising transiency in Boston put pressure on the Overseers and the Almshouse facilities as the number of poor appears to increase.

These transcriptions are from the registers located in Box 9, folders 1, 2, 3, 4 and Box 11, folder 1 in Overseers Records at MHS. Please consult the "Guide" to Editorial Apparatus, as well as the descriptions of the Admissions Registers, pp. 105–107. The notes are recorded as endnotes at the end of each of the four Admissions sections.

ALMSHOUSE ADMISSIONS

November 9, 1758 – December 31, 1774

There are three distinct entry formats here. The first is an alphabetical list of inmates who were in the Almshouse shortly before the 1758 admissions. The second is a column entry format and the third, which is dominant, is the line entry method.

[*Admissions to the Almshouse, ante 9 November 1758*]

A[1]

Anderson Mary Ann	4
Ashley Ann	4
Adams Joanna	5
Arthur Mary	9
Arnault Ann	9
Alford Abigail	10

B

Bickford Thomas	1
Beard Thomas	2
Bish John	2
Beetle Sarah	2
Borlandson Sarah	2
Bumstead Sarah	2
Blake Mary	2
Blake Mary	2
Blake Wm.	2
Byles Sarah	3
Briscoe Mary	3
Buckless Mary <*Margtt:*>	3
Burnet Rebecca	4
Bill Eliza.	5
Barjer Eliza.	5
Bickford Abigl.	5
Brown Mary	5
Banister Jane	6
Brailsford Hercules	6
Bennet John	7
Burden Mary	7
Blair Hannah	7
Bailey Deliverance	7
Bennet Prudence	8
Ballard Esther	9
Bates Margt.	9
Bridges Mary	9
Beck Mary	9
Bensy Abigl.	10
Bodge Mary	10
Banks Moses	10

C

Cunningham Owen	1
Colley James	2
Combes Eliza.	2
Coulton Martha	2
Carnes Eliza.	3
Crehore Hannah	3
Crompton Mary	3
Crompton Mary jur.	3
Curdie Eliza.	3
Clifton Margt.	4
Champion Jane	4
Copp Eliza.	4
Croutch Mary	5
Clark Sarah	7
Croge Hannah	7
Colbert Richard	8
Cox Eliza.	8
Cave Rebecca	8
Cole Mary	8
Carrell Elizabeth	9
Compton Frances	10
Calder Jannet	10

D

Dowen John	1
Delbe Christo.	1
Dilley Thomas	1
Dinsdell John	1
Davis Thomas	2
Davis Mary	3
Dix Susanna	3
Dawson Abigail	5
Doyle Jane	5
Davis Eliza.	5
Davis Eliza.	6
Dumphy James	6
Dantree Ann	6
Dawson James	6
Dollison Arthur	6
Devereux Kata.	6
Dorothy Mary	7
Davidson Martha	7
Davis Mary	8
Dry Mary	8
Darrington George	9
Dowdell Elear.	10
Dorr Mary	10
Dring Eliza.	10

E
Eddy Saml. 1
Eddy Joanna 3
Ellis Mary 9

F
Finley John 1
Frazier Thos. 1
Field Thomas 2
Fleet Mary 2
Fling Sarah 3
Fitzgerald Margt. 4
Fairservice John 4
Fuller Rebecca 5
Finley Eliza. 5
Fadre Eliza. 6
Fosdick Margt. 6
Fosdick John 7
Ferrill John 8
Fost Mary 8
Fullerton Susanna 8
Fitzgerald Garrit 8
Florence Susanna 9
Fee Wineforth 9
Fisher Ann 9
Frith Eliza. 10

G
Grater Ebenr. 1
Gordon Nathl. 1
Goggin Ephraim 1
Gibbons Sands 1
Greenwood Saml. 2
Gordon James 2
Gilbert Benja. 2
George Penelope 2
Green Sarah 2
Griffiths Hepzibah 3
Goggin Mary 3
Gullion Mary 3
Gordon Content 4
Gallop Sarah 5
Gritt Margt. 5
Gray Elizabeth 5
Green Ann 6
Green John Child 6
Greenough Mary 6

Galt Mary 7
Gyles Abigail 7
Griffin James 7
Galley Mary 9
Griffiths Thos. 9
Guy Bridget 9
Gardner Winnes 9
Grisget Margt. 10

H
Hughes John 1
Hawes Desire 1
Harding Sarah 3
Hagar Negro 4
Harrell Mary 4
Hog Ann 4
Heath Mary 5
Harwood Martha 5
Hilliard Sarah 5
Hemgly Margt. 5
Harris Alice 6
Hart Robert 6
Henderson Hannah 6
Hendly Charles 7
Halsey Abigail 7
Hubbard Lazarus 7
Hubbard Mary 7
Howlett Patrick 7
Holles Agnes 8
Holmes Susanna 9
Hoggins Ann 10

I [J]
Jones Sarah 4
Ivory Hannah 4
Jackson Susanna 4
James Mary Indian 5
Jeffries Margt. 5
Jarvis John 7
Johnson John 7
Innys Francis 8
Innys Margt. 8
Jeffries Frances 9
Inglish Eliza. 10

K
Kingston Martha 2

Kelton Mary		5	McPherson Mary		10
Kellon Lydia		6	McGregere Mary		10
Keeves Barnabas		6	McDaniel Mary		10
Kilby Robt.	Child	7	McCre Hendre		10
Knowles Judith		10	McIntosh Martha		10
			McIntosh Margt.		10
L			Morris Eliza.		10
Lucas John		2	Marshall Martha		10
Lynes Susanna		3			
Lynes Susanna junr.		3	**N**		
Legg Katha.		3	Newcomb Susanna		3
Legg John	Child	3	Nuttage Eliza.		5
Lynch Abigail		4			
Leavit Sarah		4	**O**		
Lewis Elizabeth		4	Osborn David		1
Linnington Mary		4	Odle Thomas		1
Lucas Mary		5	Odlin Mary		2
Lewis George		6	Ogilby Alexr.		6
Lackey William		6	Ogden David		8
Layman Robert		8	**P**		
			Phillips Benja.		1
M			Plaisted Thomas		1
Mellens James		1	Pressman John		1
Morto Willm.		1	Pierce Sarah		2
More Phillip		1	Phillips Nathl.	Child	4
Marion Saml.		1	Pressman Mary		4
McGowen Edwd.		1	Perry Esther		5
Mason Thomas		1	Pimm Rebecca		6
Mundon Daniel		1	Peterson John		6
Marett Martha		2	Poor Robert		7
Meads Sarah		2	Pratt Thomas		7
Mason Anna		3	Procter Mary		8
Muggridge Mary		4	Perkins Jane		8
McGowen Mary		4	Passman Nichola		8
Monk Mary		4	Peers Dorothy		9
Moodey Eliza.⎫ Childn.		5	Plant Alice		9
Moodey Mary⎭			Parker Jane		10
McCurdie Eliza.		6			
Morgan Eliza.		7	**Q**		
Murphey Mary		7			
Murphey Mary	Child	7	**R**		
Miller William		8	Ross Alexanr.		2
Marrow Anna		8	Richards Sarah		3
McAfee Margt.		8	Rhodes Sarah		3
Moade Eliza.		9	Rice Sarah		3
McLane Archd.		9	Ryland Mercy		4
Marshall Mary		9	Randall Phæbe		4

Rumbow Peter		6
Rachel	Negro	4
Robinson Lydia		7
Ryal John		7
Rolston Eliza.		7
Rawson Rachel		7
Ryan Patrick		7
Rusher Mary		10

S

Seymour William		1
Storer Benja.		1
Stevens James		2
Stover Sarah		3
Skinner Eliza.		3
Saxe Mary Ann		4
Storer Susanna		5
Shaw Mary		5
Street Mercy		5
Stone Eliza.		5
Sweetland Margt.		5
Simpson Ann		6
Spear Thankful		7
Salter Susanna		7
Stokey Robt.	Child	9
Saunders Martha		9
Stanton Katha.		9
Stanley Rachel		10
Stainer Roger		10

T

Thornton Christo.	2
Tyley Samuel	2
Tyley Ann	2
Townsend	3
Thompson Jane	4
Thorn Mary	5
Tailer Jane	5
Thomas Nathl.	6
Tarbox John	6
Tatness Sarah	7
Tapper John	7
Thompson Maria	8
Thompson Kata.	9
Tunks Kata.	10
Teal Kata.	10

U V

W

Warwick John		1
Windsor Thomas		2
Williams Saml.		2
Whitehead Mary		2
Warden Esther		2
Winkley Sarah		3
Wyat Jere	Child	3
Walker John	Do.	4
Waterman Mary		4
Waters Eliza.		6
Whittaker Eliza.		6
Wilkinson Neal		6
Whitehouse Charity		6
Wesson Mary		6
Woods Eliza.		7
Wallet William		7
Willicutt Eliza.		8
Whittaker Mary		8
Whitney Daniel ⎫ Childn.		8
Whitney Sarah ⎭		
Ware Jannet		8
Walker Mary		8
Ward Nancy		10
Woodward Joseph		10
Williams Susanna		10
Whittaker Martha		10

X

Y

Young Jane	4
Young Mary	10

Z

Almshouse Admissions, 1758–1774

Names	By whom sent in	when receiv'd into the House	Age	Discharge	Death
Rebecca Pimm[2] 2 Childn.	Royal Tyler Esqr.	Novr. 9th 1758	30		
Barbary[3] Brason	Ditto	16th.	30		
Mary Morgan	Mr. Isaac Smith	21st.	44		
Jona. Hambleton	Mr. John Barrett	27th.	61	Janua. 23. 1759	
Robert Pritchet	Thos. Flucker Esqr.	28th.		Decr. 26th. 1758	
Elear.[4] Higgins 1 Child	Ebenr. Storer Esqr.	Do.	21	gone away	
Isaac Orr	Royal Tyler Esqr.	Decemr. 2d.	57	Mar. 27th. 1761	
John Taylor & 4 Childn.	Melatiah Bourn Esqr.	5th.	42	Childn. bound out	
John Dollerson	Ditto	Do.	45	gone away	
Mary Curtis	Mr. John Barrett	Decr. 2d.		Decr. 8th. 1758	
Eliza. Jones	Royal Tyler Esqr.	20th.		went to Hallifax	
Ann Perry	Ditto	19th.		Workhouse	
James Smith	Mr. John Tudor	Janua. 3. 1759	50	Janua. 15th. 1759	
Katha. Stevens	Ditto	4th.		gone away	
Margt. Haveley	Ditto	ditto		Do.	
Margt. Kitchen	Mr. Wm. Phillips	5th.		Do.	
Thos. Thompson	Thos. Flucker Esqr.	8th.	21	went to Hallifax	Mar. 1759
Mary Thompson	Do.	do.	20	Do.	
Christo. Monks[5]	Do.	do.	26	went to Hallifax	Mar. 1759

Names	By whom sent in	when receiv'd into the House	Age	Discharge	Death
Margt. Monks[6]	Do.	do.	26	Do.	
2 Children	Do.	do.		Do.	
Robert Cooper	Royal Tyler Esqr.	9th.	63	went to N.York	
John Jordan	Mr. William Phillips	18th.	40	went to <*Ha*>	New York 1759
Barby[7] Jordan	Ditto	do.	37	Do.	
1 Child	Do.	do.	1	Do.	
Rebecca Pierce	Royal Tyler Esqr.	19th.	34	April 1759	
David McDaniel	Thos. Flucker Esqr.	20th.	45	March 12th. 1759	
Ann McDaniel	Ditto	do.	34	Ditto	
1 Child	Ditto	do. 17 mos.		Ditto	
Elizabeth Campbell	John Phillips Esqr.	Janua. 10. 1759	30		
John Pilsberry	Ditto	Ditto	50	Septr. 22d. 1764	
James Sinclair	Royal Tyler Esqr.	Janua. 27th. 1759	55	June 23 1759	
Benja. Davis	Royal Tyler Esqr.	Janua. 27th. 1759		Feby. 4th. 1759	
John Bradley	Mr. John Tudor	31st.	35		

127

Names	By whom sent in	when receiv'd into the House	Age	Discharge	Death
Katharine McGennis 2. Children Eliza. Dauphin 1. Child Susanna Bayard 1. Child Feby. 16th. 1759 Eliza. Badkee 1. Child Margarett Lidie 1. Child	Melatiah Bourn Esqr.			went to Hallifax Feby. 7th. 1759	
Eliza Bulman	Mr. Isaac Walker	Feby. 14th. 1759	50		
Ann Joy & 1 Child	Thomas Flucker Esqr.	18th.	45	April 1759	
John Kenney	Mr. Benja. Dolbeare	March 9th	55	Workhouse	
Mary Procter junr.	Royal Tyler Esqr.	22d.	25	sent to the Work House	
Alexr. Ross	Royal Tyler Esqr.	20th.	40	Mar. 24th. 1759	
Nathl. Vial	Melatiah Bourn Esqr.	28th. 2 ½ year			
Clara Harley	Mr. Benja. Dolbeare	April 9th.	22	April 22d.	
John Taylor	Mr. Isaac Walker	10th.	45	Workhouse	
Mary Dunton	Ditto	do.	35	gone away	
William Curtain } Children Eleanor Curtain }	Mr. John Barrett	April 13th.	6 8	<Nelly> Wm. bound out	
Susanna Cain[8]	Mr. Isaac Smith	14th.	19	gone away	
John Brown a Child	Ebenr. Storer Esqr.	24th.10 Mos.			
Peter Labradore	Mr. Benja. Dolbeare	25th.			Dead

Names	By whom sent in	when receiv'd into the House	Age	Discharge	Death
John Fling	Mr. Isaac Smith	May 1st.	65		May 3d:
Mary Wise & 2. Children	Melatiah Bourne Esqr.	2d.	30	June 1759	
Mary Nichols / Rebecca Nichols } 2. Childn.	Mr. John Barrett	3d. / 3 years	6	Bound out / Bound out	July 16th. 1759
Robert Lasele[9]	John Phillips Esqr.	18th.	22	July	
Esther Townsend	Mr. Isaac Smith	Do.	76		Octo. 18 1760
Mary Capron	Ditto	28th.	55		May 6 1761
Jane Bowman	Royal Tyler Esqr.	29	40		July 4th. 1759
Eliza. Garrick	Ditto	31	60		
Grace Gibson	Deacon John Barrett	June 11th.	80		Mar. 9th. 1760
Mary Durham	Mr. Isaac Smith	Do.	28	gone away	
Patience Lillie	Melatiah Bourn Esqr.	14th.	31	Do.	
3 Children / Mary Mills	Do. / Royall Tyler Esqr.	Do. / 22d.	37		1759 Augt. 2d.
1 Child—a Boy	Do.	Do.	7		
Sarah Winkley	Ebenr. Storer Esqr.	27th.	27	Workhouse	
1 Child		Do.	3		
Elizabeth Glover	Mr. Willm. Phillips	July 3d. 1759	38		1768. Janua. 10th.
William Thornton / Hannah Thornton }	Melath. Bourn Esqr.	4th.	61 / 65		Mar 5th. 1761 / 1765. April 7th.

Names	By whom sent in	when receiv'd into the House	Age	Discharge	Death
Ann Warwick	John Phillips Esqr.	5th.	30		1759 Augt. 4th.
Eliza. Clough 2. Children	Ebenr. Storer Esqr. Ditto	7th.	28	Bound out	
Hannah Burk	Mr. William Phillips	11th.	40	gone away	deceased Janua. 23. 1770
Martha Davidson	Royall Tyler Esqr.	14th.	36		
Grace Niles	Mr. Isaac Walker	24th.	72		Septr. 4th. 1766
Andrew Flood	Mr. Benja. Dolbeare	Do.	21	Workhouse	
William Gaskin	Mr. John Tudor	Do.	9	Bound out	
Thomas McDonald	John Phillips Esqr.	Augt. 22		gone away	
Daniel Sullivan John Turner	Mr. Wm. Phillips Royall Tyler Esqr.	23 Septr. 1	75 73	Octo. 6. 1759	Septr. 26 1759
Willm. Vallicott & his Wife	Mr. Isaac Smith	Do.			
Hannah Jenkins	Mr. Benja. Dolbeare	4th.	38	Married to John Anslem } May 1761	
James Butler	Mr. Willm. Phillips	6		gone away	
Glocester Negro	Melatiah Bourn Esqr.	Do.	70		May 8th. 1761
Mary Kellon & 2. Children	Royall Tyler Esqr.	7			
Hannah Perraway	Deacon Jno. Barrett	24	55		Jany. 8. 1771
John Patterson & his wife	James Pitts Esqr.	26			Decr. 29 1761 Septr. 3 1763

Names	By whom sent in	when receiv'd into the House	Age	Discharge	Death
Susanna Morey	Mr. Isaac Smith	Octo. 3	70		May 14th. 1761
Eliza. Skinner	Ebenr. Storer Esqr.	9	25	Workhouse	Se
Abigail Reed	Thoms. Flucker Esqr.	11	55		June 11th. 1761
Andrew Muckutow	Ebenr. Storer Esqr.	19	25	Decr. 26. 1759	
Sarah Odle	Mr. Isaac Walker	Do.			Mar 20th. 1760
Joanna Flood	Thos. Flucker Esqr.	24	59		Novr. 28 1759
Kiah Bailey	Mr. Wm. Phillips	Novr. 12	22	gone away	
Richard Bill & his Wife & 6 Childn.	James Pitts Esqr. his Child Rd. was drowned in the yard Well Feby. 20th. 1762 polly Bill dyed of the Small pox aged 4. yrs. April 13. 1764	Do.		Workhouse	Octo. 30 1761
Eliza. McDowell & Child	John Phillips Esqr.	21		gone away	
Mary McDaniel	Mr. Isaac Walker	16th.	40		Decr. 4th. 1759
John O'Bryan	John Phillips Esqr.	27			May 3 1760
Hannah Dicks	James Pitts Esqr.	28		gone away	
Sarah Moore[10]	Melath. Bourn Esqr.	Do.	70		Feby. 28. 1764
Moses McConnor	Mr. Benja. Dolbeare	Decr. 4. 1759		gone away	
Jane an Indian	John Phillips Esqr.	7th.			
George Pringle	Thos. Flucker Esqr.	8th.		gone to Engld.	

Names	By whom sent in	when receiv'd into the House	Age	Discharge	Death
William Shirley John Shirley Nancey Shirley (Childn.)	Mr. John Tudor & James Pitts Esqr.	Do.			dyed Decr. 21 1762, in Boston
John Anselm	Mr. Isaac Walker	18	50	Halifax Nova scotia	
Mary Barrett (Child)	Melatiah Bourn Esqr.	19th.	3 years	Bound out	Jany. 10th. 176[...][11]
Susanna Youngman	Mr. Isaac Smith	25		gone away	
Margarett Allman[12] & 4. Children	Melatiah Bourn Esqr.	26		gone away	
Susanna Bodge	Melatiah Bourn Esqr.	29		gone away	
John Kercawtau (Span'd.)	John Phillips Esqr.	Jany. 2d. 1760		July	
Sarah <Nathan?> Fessenden	James Pitts Esqr.	18th.	50		May 5. 1764
Ann Perry	Thos. Flucker Esqr.	19		Workhouse	
Eleanor Lyon & 2. Children Lucretia Spalding & 1. Child	John Phillips Esqr.	21		gone away	
Sarah (Negro woman)	Mela. Bourn Esqr.	Feby. 8th.			Septr. 7th. 1762
Margtt. White	Royal Tyler Esqr.	11th.	47		March 20th. 1760
Sarah Richards Sarah her Girl (Daur.)	Mr. Isaac Smith	18	42 8		
Mary Kneeland	Mr. Willm. Phillips	March 7	50		March 23d. 1760
Anna Allen	Mr. Willm. Phillips	do.	56		July 20th.
Christiana Isbester	Overseers sitting day		23	July 2d. 1760	

Names	By whom sent in	when receiv'd into the House	Age	Discharge	Death
Eliza. Harris	Mr. Willm. Phillips	22	50	<75> Work house	July 14 1770
Sarah Manson	Mr. Willm. Phillips	24	22	gone away	
Sarah Allen	Royall Tyler Esqr.	Do.		gone away	
Hannah Barrett } her Child	Mela. Bourn Esqr.	27			
Peggy & John Miller	Mr. Benja. Dolbeare	31	{6 {4	Bound out	
Hannah Hoare	Thos. Flucker Esqr.	April 8			Deceas'd Janua. 14th. 1765 (59 yrs.)
Abigail Greenleaffe & Mary Greenleaffe {	Mela. Bourn Esqr.	11th.	65 / 15		Ab Greenleaf Novr. 28 1761 / deced Octo. 11. 1772
Mary Dyer / James Dyer } 3 Childn. / Willm. Dyer }	Royall Tyler Esqr.	11th.		gone away	
Mary Webb[13]	John Phillips Esqr.	April 27th. 1760	45		Decemr. 7th. 1766
Willm. Daniels	Mr. Isaac Smith	28	60		deceased June 25. 1770
Alexr. Martin	Do.	30	73		Novr. 20th. 1764
Eliza. Nicholson	Thos. Flucker Esqr.	May 2			
Stephen Harris / John Harris }	Deacon John Barrett	{3	6 / 5	Bound out / gone away	
Hannah Williams	Royall Tyler Esqr.	12	28	July 1760	
Isaac Orr	Mr. Benja. Dolbeare	10th.	50	June 23d. 1760	
Benja. Bridge Prov.	John Phillips Esqr.	June 7	55	gone away	

Names	By whom sent in	when receiv'd into the House	Age	Discharge	Death
Thomas & William Carle } Prov.	Deacon Jno. Tudor	do.	6} 8}	Bound out	
Mary & Jane } Childn. McKeal	Mr. Saml. Dexter				
Dorcas How[14]	Mr. Isaac Smith	14	67		Augt. 2d. 1760
James Melvin	Mr. Jona. Mason	11	7	Bound out	
Eliza. Ray	Overseers Sitting Day	June 4			Septr. 27th. 1761
Agnis Lemone	Royall Tyler Esqr.	14th.	65		Septr. 21st. 1760
William & John O'Brian[15] }	Mr. Benja. Dolbeare	July 9		Bound out	
Hugh Gilmore alias David Miller }	Deacon Jno. Tudor	26		gone away	
Rachel Scribner	Mr. Isaac Smith	do.	63	Workhouse	Decr. 18th. 1768
Sarah Mary Kenney (Childn.) Eliza. }	Mr. Benja. Dolbeare	August 15th.		Bound out Do.	
John McMurphy	Mr. Dolbeare & Jno. Scollay	do.			Novr. 10th. 1760
Eliza. Lambert	Mr. Isaac Walker	28th.		at Service 1765	
Ann Harris Susanna Merrick }	Overseers Sitting day Do.	Septr. 3d	70 yrs.		Octo. 8th. 1760
John Burk Child	Mr. Isaac Walker	12	7 yrs.	Bound out	
William Brown Do.	Mr. Isaac Smith	18	7 yrs.	Do.	

Names	By whom sent in	when receiv'd into the House	Age	Discharge	Death
Eliza. Heath	Thos. Flucker Esqr.	25		Workhouse	
Mary Hamilton	Mr. Isaac Smith	30		gone to Ireland	
John Townsend	Overseers Sitting day	Octo. 2d.			Octo. 15th. 1760
Ann Griffins[16] Child	Mr. Isaac Smith	do.			
Kiah Stevens	Mr. Isaac Walker	do.		gone away	
Hannah Banks Child	Do.	8	4 yrs.		April 25 1762
Frances Sparrow	John Phillips Esqr.	Octo. 18th.	79		Feby. 13th. 1761
Elias Cox Child	Mr. John Barrett	20th.	3	Bound out	
Mary Bartlet	Thos. Flucker Esqr.	28th.	22		
John Hewett	Mr. Jona. Mason	Novr. 15th.	74		Dead
Eliza. Edmunds	Royall Tyler Esqr.	18th.	26	Workhouse	Sepr. 22d. 1762
John Banks / Mary Banks / Thos. Banks	Mr. Isaac Walker	do.		gone away / Bound out	
Benja. Tarbox	Royall Tyler Esqr.	28			Novr. 28 1760
John Lewis	John Phillips Esqr.	do.			29th.
Isabella Iago	Royall Tyler Esqr.	Decemr. 1st.		April 18th. 1761	
William Manning	Royall Tyler Esqr.	10		gone away	
John O'Bryan	John Phillips Esqr.	15			Jany 20 1761

Names	By whom sent in	when receiv'd into the House	Age	Discharge	Death
Judith Norman	Thos. Flucker Esqr.	do.	70		Jany. 16. 1766
Mary Tuttle	Do.	23		gone to Eastwd.	
Henry Moreton					
John Tuttle	John Phillips Esqr.	Feby 25. 1761	47		Jany. 19th. 1761
Jeremh. Rhodes	Mr. Benja. Dolbeare	30	74		1763 Apl. 5
Sarah Norton, Saml. & John Dollison } Grandchildn.		Jany. 8th. 1761 / do.	61	Bound out	Jany. 23 1762
John Tyrrell	John Phillips Esqr.	do.	29	June 18th. 1761	
Anna Smith	Do.	10th.	23	gone away	
Mary Smith a Child	Do.	do.	4		
John Larkin a small Boy	Mr. Isaac Smith	8th.		Bound out	
William Loveless Do.	Do.	14	5	Bound out	
Rose Negrowoman	Thos. Flucker Esqr.	20	80	Bound out	Feby. 19th. 1761
Ann Wise a Girl	Mela. Bourn Esqr.	21	6	Bound out	
Lettuce Molatto	Mr. Jona. Mason	24	4	Ditto	
Mary Blanch	Mr. Isaac Smith	30	21	gone away	
Eliza. Blanch a Child		6 weeks			
Jona. Edmunds	Royall Tyler Esqr.	Mar. 10	73		Augt. 2[4][17] 1764
Robert Barry	Do.	12	33	gone away Jany. 1762	

Names	By whom sent in	when receiv'd into the House	Age	Discharge	Death
Willm. Pratt	Mr. Saml. Dexter	24	65		May 8th. 1761
Mary Jones	Mela. Bourn Esqr.	April 3	43	gone away	
Hannah Williams	Mr. Henry Bromfield	Mar. 28	30		Apl. 3d. 1761
John & Hannah[19] {Prest} Childn.	Mr. Saml. Dexter	April 7th.	5 / 7	Hannah Bound	May 2[...][18] 1762
Jane Price	Mr. Isaac Smith	April 16 1761	25	August 1765	
Willm. Clear	Mela. Bourn Esqr.	do.			Octo. 15th. 1761
Mary Kellon & 2 Childn.	Mr. Saml. Dexter	28		gone away	
Mary Pimm a Girl	Do.	do.		Bound out	
George Mills a Boy	Royall Tyler Esqr.	29		gone away	
John Kenney	Do.	May 7th.	60	Workhouse	
Sarah Freeman	Mr. Benja. Dolbeare	22d.	22	gone away	
John Pue	John Phillips Esqr.	25th.	20	gone away	
Widow Nowell	Mr. Isaac Walker	do.	60		Decr. 14th. 1762
Eleanor Desain alias Street		Do.	30		April 30. 1764
John Seahouse[20]	John Phillips Esqr.	June 4	36	June 17th. 1761	
Jona. Jones[21]	Do.	15	30	Discharg'd	
Ann Stone & Daugr. wife of Benja. Stone	Royall Tyler Esqr.	16			
Lydia Negro (free)	Deacon Jno. Barrett	29			July 21. 1761

Names	By whom sent in	when receiv'd into the House	Age	Discharge	Death
Meheta. Lewis	From the Workhouse	July 20		gone away	
Francis Wood & his Wife	John Phillips Esqr.	Augt. 6			
John Jackson[22]	Do.	do.	25	Halifax	
Eliza. Cook	Mr. Henry Bromfield	7	70		Novr. 14
Mary McLane	Mr. Jona. Mason	do.	75		deceased June 2[4] 1769
Susa. Fullerton	Mr. Isaac Smith	15	35	gone	
Kata. Legg[23]	Mr. Willm. Phillips	17	30	run	
Mary McNeal	Royall Tyler Esqr.	20			Septr. 16. 1761
Saml. Burnal	Mr. Benja. Dolbeare	do.	85		1764. Feby. 26.
John Wall[24] / Richard Check	Royall Tyler Esqr. / Mr. Isaac Smith	25			1764 Augt. 26.
Thomas Roberts	Deacon Barrett	28	50	gone away	
Eliza. Gould[25]	Mr. Jona. Mason	Septr. 2d.			Septr. 15th. 1761
Mary York	John Phillips Esqr.	3d.		gone away	
Arthur Keeve a Child	Mela. Bourn Esqr.	16			June 8th. 1763
Jane Butler do.	Mr. Jona. Mason	do.			
Thomas Cox / Mary Cox / Sarah Gouge	Mr. Jona. Mason	19		Bound out / Bound out	

Names	By whom sent in	when receiv'd into the House	Age	Discharge	Death
Mary Treboo	Mr. Saml. Dexter	21		Bound out	
Martha Orne[26]	Mr. Isaac Walker	30			Feby. 28 1762
Rd. Dunham	Royall Tyler Esqr.	Octo. 1		Octo. 15th. 1761	
Hannah Chadwick	Mr. Isaac Smith	6			June 5th. 1765
Isaac Walden	Mr. Benja. Dolbeare	Octo. 11th. 1761		Octo. 20th. 1761	
Archd. McLane[27]	Royall Tyler Esqr.	29	60		
Susa. Dix	ditto	31	65		Mar. 6 1771
Mary Sloper	ditto	Novr. 2		gone	
Sarah Collins	Mr. Isaac Walker	do.			Decr. 8 1761
Stephen Rollo		3	63	Work house	dyed Decr. 4. 1769
Eliza. Williamson a Child	Mr. Benja. Dolbeare	3			
Mary Linten	Mr. Jona. Mason	11			
Ann Gorge	Mr. Jos. Gardner	14	75		deceased June 8 1771 } Dyed of Small Pox
Eliza. Ruddocks	Royall Tyler Esqr.	18			May 9th. 1761
Sarah Buck	John Phillips Esqr.	do.			Decr. 8th. 1761
Wm. Warner a Child	Mr. Isaac Smith	do.		Bound out	
Eliza. Langdon	ditto	20			Decr. 1. 1761
Eliza. Carnes	Mela. Bourn Esqr.	25	65		dece'd May 6 1771

Names	By whom sent in	when receiv'd into the House	Age	Discharge	Death
Josiah Snelling Wife & Child	Mr. Saml. Dexter	26	58 & 37	Child Bound out June 29 1764	May 28 1764 June 29th. [1764]
Mary Mullins	Mela. Bourn Esqr.	Decr. 1		gone away	
John Welden James McMackin	John Phillips Esqr.	do.		went to Phila Jany. 6. 1762	
Wm. Valecutt & wife[28]	Royall Tyler Esqr.	7	70. & 60.		
John Taylor	Mr. Henry Bromfield	8	60	In the Workhos.	
John Forbus	John Phillips Esqr.	9		gone away	
Saml. Nicholson	ditto	31		ditto	
Isaac Orr	Mr. Benja. Dolbeare	Jany. 1. 1762	70		deceased Octo. 22 1771
Eliza. Bartlet	Mr. Jona. Mason	do.			April 21. 1762
Ann Tyrrell (alias Dantry)	Mela. Bourn Esqr.	15th:		gone to Ireland	
Margt. Cunningham	Saml. Dexter Esqr.	do.		gone	
Moses & Nichs. Mangent	John Barrett Esqr.	25		Bound out	
Susanna Knott	Mr. Henry Bromfield	28	75		Novr. 5th. 1763
Thos. Taylor & wife	Mr. Isaac Smith	Feby. 2			
Ebenr. Bowman a Child	Do.	9			
Abigl. Elson & Child	Do.	10			Child deceased Septr. 1 1764. æt. 2 yrs.
Anna Smith & Child[29]	John Phillips Esqr.	15			
Abigail Peaks	Mr. Isaac Smith	do.			

Names	By whom sent in	when receiv'd into the House	Age	Discharge	Death
Lablong & Wife French Neutrals	Joseph Gardner Esqr.				Deceased
John Clear	Mela. Bourn Esqr.	March 5th.	60		Mar. 5th. 1762
John Rice	Do.	6	75	82	June 16th. 1766
Mary Hair a Child	John Barrett Esqr.	March 12th. 1762			
Mary Turner	Mr. Benja. Dolbeare	15			Mar. 20th. 1762
David Gregory / Lydia Gregory Childn.	Do.	29		Bound out	
James Negro	Wm. Phillips Esqr.	30			June 18. 1762
John Beltsworthy	Joseph Gardner Esqr.	April 5		Workhouse	Septr. 3d. 1764
Eliza. Blair	Mr. Henry Bromfield	16			May 29. 1762
John Hoar	Royall Tyler Esqr.	19		gone away	
Abigl. Thomas	Do.	26			May 3 1762
Geo. Skinner	Do.	27			Novr. 27. 1763
Mary Pilsberry	Mr. Jona. Mason	May 5	62 Years		May 8th: 1763
Sarah Bailey	John Barrett Esqr.	6	84		Mar. 8. 1764
Silvester Taylor	Mr. Isaac Smith	Do.			
John Harker[30]	Do.			May 27th. 1762	
Ann Middleton[31]	John Phillips Esqr.	10		gone away	
Mary Jones & Child	Isaac Smith Esqr.	18			

Names	By whom sent in	when receiv'd into the House	Age	Discharge	Death
Bristol (old Negro)	Mr. Henry Bromfield	do.	70		Augt. 2d. 1762
Abigl. Hicks & Child[32]	John Phillips Esqr.	June 9th.		July 8th. 1767	
Magnis Erving[33] (Boy)	John Barrett Esqr.	24		Bound out	
Kata. Orr & Child	Joseph Gardner Esqr.	July 8		gone away	
Mary Brooks—do.	Royall Tyler Esqr.	16		do.	
Susa. Fullerton	John Phillips Esqr.	17			Dead
Henry Coningen[34]	Royall Tyler Esqr.	22			
John Robinson	Mr. Henry Bromfield	Augt. 6			Augt. 22d. 1762
Sarah Parsons	Royall Tyler Esqr.	11			
James Gregory a Child	Mr. Benja. Dolbeare	18			Octo. 16th. [1762]
Hannah Marshall	Mr. Henry Bromfield	Septr. 6	75		Dyed Apl. 26. 1764
Rebecca Poor	Royall Tyler Esqr.	do.			Jany. 26th. 1763
Edmund Cahill	Isaac Smith Esqr.	15			Octo. 7th. 176
Sarah Pibbitts (Tibbitts)	Joseph Gardner Esqr.	23	84		May. 8. 1767
Patrick Barrett	Royall Tyler Esqr.	Octo. 4		Gone to Nfoundld	
Mary Lintee / Saml. Lintee / Ann Lintee / Lydia Quiner	Mr. Benja. Dolbeare	12		Bound out & Dead	Apl. 21. 1764

Names	By whom sent in	when receiv'd into the House	Age	Discharge	Death
Mary Burk	Mela. Bourn Esqr.	14		Bound out	
Danforth Champney	Mr. Benja. Dolbeare	15			
Margery Forrest & Child	John Barrett Esqr.	do.		since married	
John Forbetty	Royall Tyler Esqr.	19		Octo. 20th. 1762	
Mary Brister & Child	John Barrett Esqr.	do.		gone away	Child Bound
Simon Andrahan	Mr. Wm. Whitwell	Octo. 22 1762		gone away	
Wm. Hudson	Isaac Smith Esqr.	23d.			
John Childs & Wife	Royall Tyler Esqr.		74	John Childs dischgd. Sarah Childs dec'd. June 14. 1763	
Lawrence Clemmens	John Phillips Esqr.	Novr. 8th.		gone away	
Mary O'Brian	Mr. Benja. Dolbeare	do.	60	April 2d. 1765	
Sarah Burk	Isaac Smith Esqr.	12	15	Bound out	
Anna Pool	Royall Tyler Esqr.	16			Dyed May 19th. 1763
Mary Durham	Mr. Henry Bromfield	23			Novr. 26 1762
John Budd	Mela. Bourn Esqr.	24		gone away	
John Tyrrell	John Phillips Esqr.	do.		gone to Ireld.	
Joseph Milton Thos. Milton } Childn.	Mr. Benja. Dolbeare	25th.		Thos. Milton deced Novr. 15. 1764	June 1st. 1763

143

Names	By whom sent in	when receiv'd into the House	Age	Discharge	Death
John Anslem [35] Hannah Anslem	Mr. Benja. Dolbeare	29th.		Deceased	Decr. 21 1762 Augt. 1. 1771
Ann Killeren	The Overseers Sittg. day	Decemr. 1st.		Augt. 1768	
Mary Hammond & 1. Child	Royall Tyler Esqr.	2d.		gone away	
Hannah Kelley	Mela. Bourn Esqr.	4			Decr. 26th. 1762
Mary Wakefield	Mela. Bourn Esqr.	28th.		gone away	
Mary Colman [36]	Joseph Gardner Esqr.	29th.	60		Septr. 17. 1768
Robert Lassley [37]	Mr. Jona. Mason	Janua. 8th. 1763		gone away	
Mary Pimer	Mr. Henry Bromfield	12th.			Feby. 22. 1763
Mary Long	Joseph Gardner Esqr.	do.	60		Jany. 17th. 1763
Isaac Orr	Mr. Benja. Dolbeare	18th.		gone away	
Mary Marshall	Mr. Wm. Whitwell	28th.			Deceased
Mrs. Rebecca Hall	Mr. Henry Bromfield	22d.			Mar. 25 1763
Thos. Manson (Child)	Mela. Bourn Esqr.	29th.	5		June 4. 1765
John Smith	Royall Tyler Esqr.	Feby. 1st.			April 29. 1765
Mrs. Ann Twing & Child		Ditto	5th.		Feby. 24 1763
Mrs. Mary Evans	Mela. Bourn Esqr.	8th.			Deced May 9th. 1764

〜

1763 Febr. 14[38]   Receiv'd. Into the house James Adlington
pr. ordr. Mr. Henry Bromfield Overseer of the poor
Decd. 16th. Instant

Do.   Receivd. Into the house Mary Croxford
pr. ordr. John Barrett Esqr. Overseer of the poor

Do. 22d.   Received Into the house Eliza. Marshall A young Woman very bad with
P[ox]
pr. ordr. Joseph Gardner Esqr. Overseer of the poor

March 3d.   Receivd. Into the house on Province Account John Heskew and his
wife

pr. Ordr. Mesrs. John Scollay Esqr., Saml. Sewall} Select Men
and Mr. Henry Bromfield Overseer of the poor

Do.   Receivd. Into the house from the work house Abigail Waddle[39] also
Mary Champny a Molata Child 17 Months Old
pr. Ordr. Overseers Sitting Day

4th.   Receivd. Into the house Saml. Bradley a Child Abt. 18 Moths. old Son
of Eliza. Lewis
pr. ordr. Mr. Jona. Mason overseer of the poor

11   Receivd. Into the house Hannah Collis
pr. ordr. Mr. Henry Bromfield Overseer of the poor

[11][40]   Receivd. A Child abt 2 years old / Into the House Namd Anna Paine
Pr. ordr. Mr. Jona. Mason overseer of the poor

[176]3 March 15   Receivd. Into the house Mary Ozment Very Bad P[ox]
pr. ordr. Joseph Gardner Esqr. overseer of the poor

29   Received Into the house On the Province Account James Bowes &
Elinor his Wife & their Child Charles[41]
pr. ordr. Messrs. {Thos. Cushing, Saml. Hewes} Esqrs. Select Men
and Mr. Jona. Mason Overseer of the poor

26   Receivd. Into the house Thomas Eastwick
pr. ordr. Mr. Henderson Inches Overseer of the poor

31   Receivd. Into the house Freelove Bass with three of her Children[42]
pr. ordr. Mr. Wm. Whitwell Overseer of the poor

April 26   Receivd. Into the house Hannah Burrell[43]
pr. Ordr. Joseph Gardner Esqr. Overseer of the poor

May 5   Receivd. Into the house Baxter Granger
pr. ordr. Mr. Jona. Mason Overseer of the poor

[M]ay 17   Receivd. Into the house Mary Craige[44] a Young Woman from Mr. Wm.
Hunts / With a bad broken brest
pr. ordr. Isaac Smith Esqr. Overseer of the poor

May 30th. 1763   Receivd. Into the house Hanah Burk A Young Woman / Sick[45]
pr. ordr. Mr. Henry Bromfield Overseer of the poor

June 4 1763   Receivd. Into the house On the Province Account James Perrin a poor
Strainger
pr. ordr. Messrs. {John Scollay, Ezekiel Lewis} Esqrs. Select Men
℘ Royall Tyler Esqr. Overseer of the poor

June 6   Receivd Into the house William Daniels from the Work house
pr. ordr. Royall Tyler Esqr. overseer of poor

June 21   Receivd. Into the house Susannah Fullerton
pr. ordr. Royall Tyler Esqr. Overseer of the poor

June 30   Receivd. Into the house John Bradley, his Wife & Child
pr. ordr. Mr. Benja. Dolbeare Overseer of the poor

July 1st.   Receivd. Into the house Rose a Negrow Woman
pr. ordr. Mr. Benja. Dolbeare Overseer of the poor

July 5th.   Receivd. Into the house On the Province Account Moses Larkin A
Blind Man
pr. ordr. Messrs. {Saml. Hewes, Benja. Austin} Esqrs. Select Men
Capt. Benja. Hammat Overseer of the poor

1763 June 23d.   Received Into the house John Warrick[46]   Ommit'd.
pr. ordr. Melatiah Bourn Esqr. Overseer of the poor

July 11th.   Received Into the house Deborah Wood[47]
pr. ordr. Mr. Henderson Inches Overseer of the poor

July 27   Receivd. Into the house Henry Stanney A poor Man[48]
pr. ordr. Mr. Benja. Dolbeare Overseer of the poor

Do. 29   Receivd. Robert Ingolls a poor Sick Man Into the House[49]
pr. ordr. Mr. Benja. Dolbeare Overseer of the poor

Augst. 1st.   Receivd. Into the House Patrick Burk & his Wife[50]
pr. ordr. Melatiah Bourn Esqr. Overseer of the poor

Do. 2d.   Receivd. Into the House Jude Cox A poor Woman[51]
pr. ordr. Mr. Henderson Inches Overseer of the poor

Do. 8th.   Receivd. Into the house Moses Mangent (a poor Child)[52]
pr. ordr. John Barrett Esqr. overseer of the poor

Do. 8   Receivd. Into the house Mary Sparrow a poor Woman
pr. ordr. Mr. Henderson Inches overseer of the poor

Do. 13   Received Into the house Mary Ricks[53]
pr. ordr. Mr. Ebenzr. Storer Overseer of the poor

1763 Augst. 18   Received Into the house Eliza. Southerland[54] A poor woman
pr. ordr. Mr. Henry Bromfield Overseer of the poor

Sepr. 7   Receivd. Into the house Hannah Rust A poor Woman
pr. ordr. Mr. Henry Bromfield overseer of the poor

Ditto   Receivd. Into the house Wm. McKim & his Wife from the Work house[55]
pr. ordr. Isaac Smith Esqr. overseer of the poor

Ditto 23[56]   Receivd. Into the house on the Province Account Hannah Kelton a
poor woman
pr. ordr. Messrs.} Benja. Austin Esqr. Select Man
and Royall Tyler Esqr. Overseer of the poor
left the house in two Days Cash pd. her £4. 10 pr. ordr. Ezel. Lewis Esqr.

Octr. 6   Receivd. Into the house Eliza. Addlinton[57] from the work house
pr. ordr. Royall Tyler Esqr. overseer of the poor

Do.   Receivd. Into the house Mary Chadwell Abt. 12 Years Old
pr. ordr. Joseph Gardner Esqr. overseer of the poor

Do. 27   Receivd. Into the House On Province Account James Green A poor
Soldier
pr. ordr. Messrs. {John Scollay, Ezekl. Lewis} Esqrs. Select Men
and Royall Tyler Esqr. Overseer of the poor

Do.   Receivd. Into the house A Child Abt. 2 Years old Named Samuel Young
pr. ordr. Mr. Henry Bromfield Overseer of the poor verbal

1763 Octr. 28   Received Into the house Eliza. Fadre a poor woman
pr. ordr. Mr. Wm. Whitwell Overseer of the poor

Do. 31   Received Into the house Willm. Waters
pr. ordr. Capt. Benja. Hammatt overseer of the poor
Deceas'd Novr. 4th. following

Do.   Receivd. Into the house James Bassett A Negrow Man
pr. ordr. Joseph Gardner Esqr. Overseer of the poor

Novr. 5   Receivd. Into the house Cornelius Campbell & his Wife[58]
pr. ordr. Mr. Henderson Inches Overseer of the poor

Do. 11   Receivd. Into the house Margarett Forbush & 3 Children woman neare
her time[59]
pr. ordr. Isaac Smith Esqr. Overseer of the poor

14   Receivd. Into the house On the Province Account Moses Larkin & his
Wife and John Fabre and his Wife
pr. ordr. Messrs. {John Scollay, Saml. Hews} Esqrs. Select Men
and Royall Tyler Esqr. Overseer of the poor

Do. 15   Receivd. Into the house Rebekah Pim / brot. to bed with A Daughter Abt.
4 hours after She Came in to the house[60]
pr. ordr. Mr. Benja. Dolbeare Overseer of the poor

1763 Novr. 16th.   Received Into the house on the Province Account David McClane a
poor Soldier[61]
pr. ordr. Messrs. {Ezekiel Lewis, John Scollay} Esqrs. Select Men
and Royall Tyler Esqr. Overseer of the poor

Novr. 23   Receivd. Into the house Martha Daverson[62]
pr. ordr. Royall Tyler Esqr. Overseer of the poor

Do. 30   Receivd. Into the house A Girl Namd. Abigal Weston[63] 7 years old
pr. ordr. Mr. Henry Bromfield Overseer of the poor

1763 Decr. 13th.   Received Into the house Michel Cavenu[64] A Sick Man
pr. ordr. Mr. Benja. Dolbeare Overseer of the poor
Decsd. 15th. 2 Days after Came in

Ditto 16   Receivd. Into the house On Province Account Isaac Orr With A
broken Leg
pr. ordr. Joseph Gardner Esqr. Overseer of the poor

Do. 20.   Received Into the house Michael Butler and his Wife
pr. ordr. Mr. Ebenzr. Storer Overseer of the poor

Do. 21   Received Into the house Susannah Berry big With Child
pr. ordr. Mr. Ebenzr. Storer Overseer of the poor

1763 Decr. 26   Received Into the house On the Province Account John Cahill With the
french P
pr. ordr. Messrs. {John Scollay, Benja. Austin} Esqrs. Select Men

and Joseph Gardner Esqr. Overseer of the poor

Decr. 28   Received Into the house On the Province Account Abraham Mathews a poor Stranger
pr. ordr. Messrs. {John Scollay, Ezekiel Lewis} Esqrs. Select Men
and Mr. William Whitwell Overseer of the poor

1764 Janr. 4   Receivd. Into the house On the Province Account John Mortagh a poor Stranger[65]
pr. ordr. Messrs. {John Scollay, Ezekl. Lewis} Esqrs. Select Men
Mr. Wm. Whitwell Overseer of the poor

Janr. 7   Receivd. Into the house On the Province Account Thos. Murphy a poor Man[66]
pr. ordr. Messrs. {John Scollay, Saml. Sewall} Select Men
and Joseph Gardner Esqr. Overseer of the poor

1764 Janr. 9th.   Receivd. Into the house On the Province Account Jacob Sweler[67] a poor Stranger
pr. ordr. Messrs. {Thos. Cushing, Saml. Sewall} Select Men
and Mr. Henderson Inches overseer of the poor

Ditto 6   Receivd. Into the house Margarett Lawrence A young woman big with Child
pr. ordr. Capt. Benja. Hammett Overseer of the poor

Ditto 10   Receivd. Into the house Luke Ryan blind, Wife & Child
pr. ordr. Capt. Benja. Hammat overseer of the poor
the woman Deceasd. Same Night abt. 11 Clock

11   Received Into the house A little Boy Namd. Ebenzr. abt. 3 years old / Son to Mrs. Killcup
pr. ordr. Mr. Willm. Whitwell Overseer of the poor

11   Received Into the house Eliza. Boston A Young Woman
pr. ordr. Mr. Benja. Dolbeare overseer of the poor

5   Receivd. Into the house Tabitha Akley And 4 Children[68]
pr. ordr. Mr. Benja. Dolbeare Overseer of the poor

12   Receivd. Into the house David Tweed & his Wife
pr. ordr. Mr. Henry Bromfield Overseer of the poor

18   Received Into the house on the Province acct. Patrick Kenaly[69]
pr. ordr. {Messrs. John Scollay, Benja. Austin} Esqrs. Select Men
and Royall Tyler Esqr. overseer of the poor

1764 Janr. 28   Receivd. Into the house Nathl. Simson[70] / April 23 1764 Went Away from the house
pr. ordr. Mr. Benja. Dolbeare Overseer of the poor

31   Receivd Into the house Jannet Sayword[71]
pr. ordr. Joseph Gardner Esqr. Overseer of the poor

Febr. 11   Receivd. Into the house Mary Long
pr. ordr. Joseph Gardner Esqr. Overseer of the poor

14   Receivd. Into the house A Child Named Eliza. Brewer[72]
pr. ordr. Isaac Smith Esqr. Overseer of the poor

15   Receivd. Into the house Elizabeth Garrick[73]
pr. ordr. Mr. Henry Bromfield Overseer of the poor

14   Received Into the house A Child Namd. Rebeckah Richardson also a little boy Namd. Georg Richardson
pr. ordr. Mr. Henry Bromfield Overseer of the poor

17   Receivd. Into the house Susannah Fullinton[74]
pr. ordr. Mr. Benja. Dolbeare Overseer of the poor

21   Receivd. Into the house A Negrow Woman blind Namd. Cober[75]
pr. ordr. Isaac Smith Esqr. Overseer of the poor

Do.   Received Into the house A Child Namd. Robert Wharfe[76]
pr. ordr. Mr. Henry Bromfield Overseer of the poor

1764 Febr. 22   Receivd. Into the house from the Work house Mary Berry[77]
pr. ordr. Mr. Benja. Dolbeare overseer of the poor

Do. 22   Receivd. Into the house John Blake a young Man Very Sick with P[ox][78]
pr. ordr. Messrs. John Barrett, Royall Tyler, Joseph Gardner Esqrs. Mr. Wm. Whitwell} overseers of the poor

do. 23   Receivd. Into the house Judith Cox from the Work house
pr. ordr. Mr. Wm. Whitwell overseer of the poor

Febr. 24   Received Into the house Hannah Meaney A Girl abt. 10 years old
pr. ordr. Melatiah Bourn Esqr. Overseer of the poor

March 12   Receivd. Into the house Nickolas Mangee a litle boy[79]
pr. ordr. John Barrett Esqr. Overseer of the poor

17   Receivd. Into the house two Children of Eliza. Melvills Namd. Lucretia & Hannah[80]
pr. ordr. Mr. Ebenzr. Storrer Overseer of the poor

20   Receivd. Into the house On the Province Account Ralph Curtis a poor Stranger[81]
pr. ordr. Messrs. {John Scollay, Joseph Jackson} Esqrs. Select Men
Royall Tyler Esqr. Overseer of the poor

1764 April 5th.   Received Into the house Eliza. Rollston[82] A poor Woman
pr. ordr. Mr. Benja. Dolbeare Overseer of the poor

Ditto   Received Into the house   Tincom[83]
pr. ordr. Mr. Henry Bromfield Overseer of the poor

[do.][84]   Receivd. Into the house Ann Fosdick Sick with the Small Pox In the Natural Way[85]
pr. ordr. John Barrett Esqr. Overseer of the poor

7th.   Received Into the house On Province Account James Perrin a poor Starnger
pr. ordr. Messrs. {John Scollay, Joseph Jackson} Esqrs. Selectt Men
and Royall Tyler Esqr. Overseer of the poor

13   Receivd. Into the house Eliza. Fretoo With Small pox in the Natural Way
pr. ordr. Mr. Benja. Dolbeare Overseer of the poor

Do.   Received Into the house Hannah Roberts Widow
pr. ordr. Royall Tyler Esqr. Overseer of the poor

Do.   Received Into the house a litle Girle abt. 4 Years Old Named. Hannah Hawskins In a Suffering Condition with Small pox[86]
pr. ordr. Messrs. Tyler & Gardner Esqrs. & Mr. Whitwell Overseers of the poor
the mother of the Child Sd. to Mr. Boxs Daughter

1764 April 18   Received Into the house George Darrinton[87] Sick With the Small pox In the Natural Way
pr. ordr. Mr. Ebenzr. Storer Overseer of the poor

Do. 20   Received Into the house Mary Tufts, Eliza. Melvil[88] and Patrick Burk[89]
pr. ordr. Royall Tyler Esqr. Overseer of the poor

20   Received Into the house Mary Jones, bad with P[ox]
pr. ordr. Mr. Henderson Inches Overseer of poor

Do.   Received Into the house Eliza. Kelleham,[90] A Young Woman
pr. ordr. Mr. Jonathan Mason Overseer of the poor

[do.][91]   Received Into the house a Child Namd. Eliza. Mullin abt. 2 years old Inoculated
pr. ordr. Mr. Henry Bromfield overseer of the poor

23   Received Into the house Patrick Welch abt. 10 years old
pr. ordr. Mr. Benja. Dolbeare overseer of the poor

Do.   Received Into the house A Child Namd. Joseph Gray 8 Months Old
pr. ordr. Royall Tyler Esqr. overseer of the poor

24   Received Into the house a Negrow Man Sick With the Small pox
Namd. Sipeo Bolton
pr. ordr. Royall Tyler Esqr. overseer of the poor

26   Received Into the house two Children of David Scudder[92]
pr. Ordr. Royall Tyler Esqr. overseer of the poor

1764 April 23 Received Into the house John Dunn A boy Abt. 9 Years old
pr. ordr. Isaac Smith Esqr. overseer of the poor

26   Received Into the house Sarah Seegraves big with Child / June 24th
brot. to bed with a Daughter
pr. ordr. Mr. William Whitwell Overseer of the poor

27   Received Into the house Peggy Cavernex big with Child / brot. to bed
with a Son June 10th.[93]
pr. ordr. John Barrett Esqr. Overseer of the poor

28   Received Into the house James Butler a poor Man[94]
pr. ordr. Joseph Gardner Esqr. Overseer of the poor

May 5   Received Into the house Margarett Lawrance[95] Sick with Small pox In
the Natural way Verry bad
pr. ordr. Capt. Benja. Hammatt overseer of the poor

[do.][96]   Received Into the house Ann Hobbs from the Work house
pr. ordr. Royall Tyler Esqr. overseer of the poor

18   Received Into the house Eliza. Jones abt. 12 years old Enoculated for
the Small pox
pr. ordr. John Barrett Esqr. overseer of the poor

Do.   Received Into the house Jo Bill A Negrow Man[97]
pr. ordr. Mr. Henderson Inches overseer of the poor

1764 [*May*] 17[98] Receivd. Into the house Charles Patrick[99] a Molatah Man Sick With
Small pox in the Natural Way belongs to Cituate as he sayes
pr. ordr. Mr. William Whitwell Overseer of the poor

Do.   Received Into the house Mary Richardson[100] A Girl abt. 12 Yeares old
(with the Small pox In the Natural way)
pr. ordr. Mr. Ebenzr. Storer Overseer of the poor

⟨Do.   *Received Into the house Eliza. Utenox 4 years Old*
pr. ordr. Mr. Jonathan Mason Overseer of the poor⟩

18   Received Into the house A Negrow Girl Namd. Phillis with Small pox, almost well[101]
pr. ordr. Mr. Benja. Dolbeare overseer of the poor

June 9th.   Received Into the House On the Province Account Eliza. Utinock With two of her Children
pr. ordr. Messrs. {Joshua Henshaw, Saml. Sewall} Esqrs. Select Men
and Mr. Jonathan Mason Overseer of the poor

Ditto 14   Received Into the house on the Province Account Simon Colingow a poor Stranger
pr. ordr. {Joseph Jackson, John Scollay} Esqrs. Select Men
and Mr. William Whitwell Overseer of the poor
went away from the house Same Day
July 9th. Returnd. again to the house

1764 June 19   Received Into the house Mehetable Hickes[102] a poor aged woman
pr. ordr. Mr. Ebenzr. Storer Overseer of the poor

June 22   Received Into the house Eliza. McElroy,[103] big With Child
pr. ordr. Joseph Gardner Esqr. Overseer of the poor

[do.][104]   Received Into the house Olive Slooper[105] with her Infant Child
pr. ordr. Isaac Smith Esqr. Overseer of the poor

                     Received Into the house Frances Salter, from the Work house

June 28   Received Into the house James Stuart a poor Cripple[106]
pr. ordr. Mr. Henderson Inches Overseer of the poor
put on the Province Acct. pr. ordr. Messrs. {John Scollay, Benja: Austin} Esqrs. Select men

June 28   Received Into the house Susannah Thomas
pr. ordr. Mr. Benja. Dolbeare Overseer of the poor

July 5   Went Away from the house Margaret McKimm
pr. ordr. overseers Sitting Day

July 11   Received Into the house Eleonar Cahale,[107] to be Cured of the pox
pr. ordr. Royall Tyler Esqr. Overseer of the poor

Ditto   Received Into the house Jona. Kilby a Child 15 Months Old
pr. ordr. Royall Tyler Esqr. Overseer of the poor

1764 July 10th.   Jumpt. the fence & went of from the house Mary Tufts

Ditto 11　　　　　A Child of Mr. Akely taken Away from the house by Her Mother
pr. ordr. Royall Tyler Esqr.

Do.　　　　　A Child of Scudder's Delivd. to it's Grandmother
pr. ordr. Royall Tyler Esqr.

Ditto 17　　　　　Received Into the house 3 Children Mary, Sarah & John Follins[108]
pr. ordr. Mr. Benja. Dolbeare overseer of the poor

20th.　　　　　Went Away from the house John Dunn Capt. Dunn son

Do.　　　　　Went Away from the house Eliza. McElroy

24　　　　　Received Into the house Mary Goggin[109]
pr. ordr. Royall Tyler Esqr. overseer of the poor

Do.　　　　　Received Into the house Eliza. Freetoo[110]
pr. ordr. Mr. Benja. Dolbeare overseer of the poor

Do. 31st.　　　　　Received Into the house On Province Account Ishmael Bomfort & his
Wife poor Straingers[111]
pr. ordr. {Joseph Jackson, Saml. Sewall} Esqrs. Select Men
and Royall Tyler Esqr. Overseer of the poor

Augt. 7　　　　　Dischargd. from the house Widdow Tweed
pr. ordr. Overseers

Do.　　　　　Ran Away from the house Archibald McLane

Do.　　　　　Received Into the house Captn. Isaac Doubt[112]
pr. ord Mr. Wm. Whitwell Overseer of the poor

1764 Augst. 7　　　　　Received Into the house Ann Gooch's Child[113]
pr. ordr. Mr. Ebenzr. Storer Overseer of the poor

Do.　　　　　Received Into the house Eliza. Wharf & her Child[114]
pr. ordr. Mr. Henry Bromfield Overseer of the poor

Do.　　　　　Received Into the house On Province Account John Bourk[115] A
Stranger
pr. ordr. Messrs. {John Scollay, Saml. Sewall} Esqrs. Select Men
and Isaac Smith Esqr. Overseer of the poor
14 Instant left the house Sent Away to Hallifax

9　　　　　Received Into the house Sarah Norton a poor Woman[116]
pr. ordr. Mr. Ebenzr. Storer Overseer of the poor

11 Received Into the house Hannah Turpine & 2 of her Children[117]
pr. ordr. Mr. Wm. Whitwell Overseer of the poor

14 Received Into the house Cristian Isbester[118] big With Child
pr. Ordr. Mr. Henry Bromfield Overseer of the poor

14 Went Away from the house James Stuart, for Hallifax

Also the Eldest Daughter of George Follins DD[119] her Father

Do. Received Into the house Mary Evens[120] Abt. 5 Years Old
pr. ordr. Mr. Benja. Dolbeare Overseer of the poor

17 Receivd. Into the house Mary Fulker[121]
pr. ordr. Mr. Wm. Whitwell Overseer of the poor

27 Receivd. Into the house On Province Account John Fabre and his Wife
pr. ordr. Messrs. {Joshua Henshaw, John Scollay} Esqrs. Select Men
and Royall Tyler Esqr. Overseer of the poor

Do. 31 Received Into the house Willm. Bright A lad 12 Years Old
pr. ordr. Mr. Benja. Dolbeare Overseer of the poor

Sepr. 3 Received Into the house Eliza. Dring a poor Woman[122]
pr. ordr. Mr. Henderson Inches Overseer of the poor

5 Received Into the house Ann Goffe a poor Woman[123]
pr. ordr. Mr. Ebenzr. Storer Overseer of the poor

Do. Received Into the house Mehettable Lewis from the Work house big
With Child[124]
pr. ordr. Overseers of the poor on Sitting Day

7 Received Into the house Sarah Freeman A poor Woman
pr. ordr. Joseph Gardner Esqr. Overseer of the poor

Do. Received Into the house Sarah Bright a poor Woman[125]
pr. ordr. Joseph Gardner Esqr. Overseer of the poor

1764 Sepr. 8 Received Into the house Danl. North & his Wife[126]
pr. Ordr. Mr. Ebenzr. Storer Overseer of the poor

Do. 11 Discharg'd from the house A Child of Ann Gooch's
pr. ordr. Mr. Ebenzr. Storer Overseer of the poor

Sepr. 9 Born In the house A Male Child, the Mothr. Hannah Bomfort

Do. 13   Receiv'd Into the house Eliza. Kelley & her Child
pr. ordr. Royall Tyler Esqr. Overseer of the poor

15   Received Into the house three Children of Mary Buffets[127]
pr. ordr. Capt. Benja. Hammatt Overseer of the poor

17   Discharg'd from the house Wm. Bright A Boy abt. 12 Years Old bound
Out

Do   Received Into the house On the Province Account Mary Robinson &
her Child
pr. Ordr. Messrs. {John Scollay, Joseph Jackson} Esqrs. Select Men
And Royall Tyler Esqr. Overseer of the poor

Do. 21st.   Simon Colingo left the house
pr. ordr. Select Men

Do. 23   Mary Jones Went Away from the house

Do.   Eliza. Utinock left the house Gone to Doct. Church to Nurse his Child

1764 Sepr. 27   Received Into house Isaac Herault A poor Man[128]
pr. ordr. Mr. Ebenzr. Storer Overseer of the poor

Octr. 2   Received Into the house Rebeckah Bradley & her Child[129]
pr. ordr. Mr. Benja. Dolbeare Overseer of the poor

Do. 3   Received Into the house On the Province Account Moses Larkin &
Katharine his Wife
pr. ordr. Messrs. {Joshua Henshaw, Benja. Austin} Esqrs. Select Men
and Mr. Wm. Whitwell Overseer of the poor

Do.   Received Into the house from the work house Eleonor Higgens & her
Child[130]
pr. ordr. Overseers Sitting Day
       Also Nathl. Bristow A Child abt. 3 Years Old, the Mother In the work
house

Do.   Received Into the house Mary Taylor With P[ox] & her Child Also John
Taylor a poor lame Man[131]
pr. ordr. Overseers Sitting Day

Do.   Received Into the house On the Province Account Alce Mollogen & 2
Children She Also big With Child[132]
pr. Ordr. Messrs. {Joseph Jackson, Benja. Austin} Esqrs. Select Men
and John Barrett Esqr. Overseer of the poor

〜

1764 Octr. 4th.   Charles Buffard a litle boy put out to Prentice

8   Received Into the house Mary Turner from the work house[133]
pr. ordr. Isaac Smith Esqr. Overseer of the poor

12   John Akely and Sarah Forbes put to Prentice

                        Deliver'd to John Gray his Child Joseph Gray

[12][134]   Received Into the house On the Province Account William Hudson a
poor Young Man[135]
pr. ordr. Messrs. {Joseph Jackson   }
& Royall Tyler Esqr. Overseer of the poor

Octor. 16   Receiv'd Into the house Mary Bufford[136]
pr. ordr. John Barrett Esqr. Overseer of the poor

Octr. 25   Dischar'd from the house Abraham Mathews
Sent Away by the Select Men to the West indes

Do.   Received Into the house John Hewitt
pr. ordr. Mr. Jona. Mason Overseer of the poor

Do.   Received Into the house Doctr. Gasper York from the Work house[137]
pr. ordr. Mr. Benja. Dolbeare Overseer of the poor

Do.   Went away from the house Mrs. Melvin

Do. 30   Received Into the house William Daniels[138]
pr. ordr. Royall Tyler Esqr. Overseer of the poor

Novr. 1st.   Went Away from the house James Buttler for Hallifax
                        Went Away from the house Margarett Cavernox to Servis

Novr. 2   Received Into the house Mehittable Clough[139]
pr. ordr. Joseph Gardner Esqr. Overseer of the poor

Do.   Received Into the house Hannah Phillips
pr. ordr. Mr. Benja. Hammatt Overseer of the poor

9th.   Jo Bill Dischargd. from the house
pr. ordr. Overseers Sitting Day

Novr. 10th.   Received Into the house On the Province Account John Davis a poor
Sick Man
pr. ordr. Messrs. {John Scollay, Saml. Sewal} Esqrs. Select Men
and Royall Tyler Esqr. Overseer of the poor

12   Received Into the house Thos. Jones & his Wife to be Cur'd of the P[o]x
pr. ordr. Mr. Henderson Inches Overseer of the poor

13   Received Into the house Margarett Dorrinton[140]
pr. ordr. Mr. Ebenzr. Storer Overseer of the poor

16   Received Into the house Joseph Ayers from the Work house
pr. ordr. Mr. William Whitwell Overseer of the poor

19   John Blake left the house to Goe a Voyage to Sea

20   Receiv'd Into the house from the Work house Saml. Holland[141]
pr. ordr. Mr. Willm. Whitwell Overseer of the poor

1764 Novr. 22   Eliza. Freeto Went away from the house

Ditto   Receiv'd Into the house On Province Account Ann Dubois a poor
Stranger from Pensilvania
pr. ordr. {Messrs. Joseph Jackson, John Scollay} Esqrs. Select Men
and Royall Tyler Esqr. Overseer of the poor
Janr. 5th. 1765 above Dubois left the house

Do. 23d.   Received Into the house Sarah Gent[142] a poor Woman
pr. ordr. Joseph Gardner Esqr. Overseer of the poor

Do. 27   Received Into the house On the Province Account Phillip Ryley a
poor Sick Man
pr. Ordr. Messrs. {Joshua Henshaw, Joseph Jackson} Esqrs. Select Men
and Joseph Gardner Esqr. Overseer of the poor

Do.   Received Into the house John Pikes A Child abt. 2 & 1/2 years Old
pr. ordr. Mr. William Whitwell Overseer of the poor

Decr. 3d.   Received Into the House Patrick Burk[143]
pr. ordr. Melatiah Bourn Esqr. Overseer of the poor

Decr. 4   Received Into the house Hannah Prest & her Child
pr. ordr. John Barrett Esqr. Overseer of the poor

1764 Decr. 6th.   Received Into the house James Canaday A poor Boy
pr. ordr. Mr. Henry Bromfield Overseer of the poor
left the house the Next Day

Do. 10   Received Into the house On Province Account Daniel Digby a poor
Indigent Man
pr. ordr. Messrs. {John Scollay, Samuel Sewall} Esqrs. Select Men
and Royall Tyler Esqr. Overseer of the poor

Hannah Phillips went away from the house

Ditto 12   Received Into the house on Province Account Bartholamew Andras a poor Man
pr. ordr. Messrs. {Joseph Jackson, John Scollay} Esqrs. Select Men
and John Barrett Esqr. Overseer of the poor

13   Received Into the house Susannah Fullerton
pr. ordr. Royall Tyler Esqr. Overseer of the poor

17   John Davis on Prov Acct. left the house, taken A Voyage

Mrs. Mollogens. little boy put to Prentice

22   Received Into the house Redman Burk A Sick Man
pr. ordr. Mr. Henderson Inches overseer of the poor

22d.   Received Into the House Mathew Wheeland[144] A Sick Man
pr. ordr. Royall Tyler Esqr. overseer of the poor

1764 Decmr. 27   Received Into the house On the Province Account David McLane a poor Indigent Man[145]
pr. ordr. Messrs. {Joseph Jackson, John Scollay} Esqrs. Select Men
and Royall Tyler Esqr. Overseer of the poor

Ditto   Received Into the house a Child Calld. Pelatiah Martin A molatto
pr. ordr. John Barrett Esqr. Overseer of the poor

1765 Janr. 1st.   Mrs. Scilby's Child Deliv'd to his Mother out of the house}
pr. ord. Royall Tyler Esqr.

Janr. 4th.   Received Into the house On the Province Account William Davison a poor Stranger
pr. ordr. {John Scollay, Joseph Jackson} Esqrs. Select Men
and Royall Tyler Esqr. Overseer of the poor

1765 Janr. 5th.   Ann Dubois Went Away from the house
Do. 15th.   Mrs. Utinock had her Child away from the house
Joseph Ayers Went Away
Peggy Darrinton Went Away
Pikes Child takeen away by his Mother
Daniel Digby left the house

1765 23d. Janr.   Received Into the house John Triskall from Mr. Bromfield's[146]
pr. ordr. Melatiah Bourn Esqr. overseer of the poor

Febr. 6   Received Into the [*house*] Charles Brooks a poor Boy[147]
pr. ordr. Capt. Benja. Hammett Overseer of the poor

Febr. 7   Redman Burk Dismisd. from the house
pr. ordr. Overseers Sitting Day

Do. 8   Phillip Ryley Dismisd. from the house

14   Mrs. Robinson & her Child left the house

Do. 8   Receiv'd Into the house Eliza. Freeto A Young Woman[148]
pr. ordr. Mr. William Whitwell Overseer of the poor

Do. 9   Received Into the house Martha Sartley a poor Woman[149]
pr. ordr. Capt. Benja. Hammatt Overseer of the poor

                           Abigail Elson Left the house Jumpt the fence

Do. 11   Received Into the house from the Work house Margaret Hasley[150]
pr. ordr. Capt. Benja. Hammat Overseer of the poor

Do.   Received Into the house on the Province Account Christopher Stovel
A poor Boy[151]
pr. ordr. Messrs. {Joseph Jackson, Saml. Sewall} Esqrs. Select Men
and Joseph Gardner Esqr. Overseer of the poor

                           Sent Away from the house Polly Clough A Child bound Out

                           <Redman Burk lef the house
pr. ordr. Overseers Sitting Day>

[11][152]   Mrs. Prest Went Away from the house With her Child

1765 Febr. 18   Received Into the house A litle Boy Abt. 3 Years Old Nam'd John
Fulton Love
pr. ordr. Mr. Henderson Inches Overseer of the poor

                           Sent Away from the house Hannah Melvin A Child bound Out

                           Dismis'd from the house Eleonar Higgins & her Child
pr. ordr. Mr. Whitwell

March 4   Receiv'd Into the house Susannah Dix[153]
pr. ordr. Royall Tyler Esqr. overseer of the poor

Do.   Receiv'd Into the house from the Work house Jeane Carter[154]
pr. ordr. Mr. Ebenzr. Storer Overseer of the poor

Do.   *<Recd. Into the house a poor Boy Namd. Wm. Smith*
pr. ord. Mr. Whitwell>

March 7   Isaac Orr Was Gone from the house

19   Went Away Mr. Bomfort & Wife and Child
                 Also Sarah Seargreaves & her Child
                 Also Christian Isbusters and her Child
                 Christopher Stovel A Boy put to Servis

March 20   Received Into the house On the Province Account Richard Leodur[155] a
poor Stranger
pr. ordr. Messrs. {Joshua Henchaw, Joseph Jackson} Esqrs. Select Men
And Royall Tyler Esqr. Overseer of the poor

March 20   Received Into the house Mary Stanley[156] Mary Goggin A poor Woman
pr. ordr. Mr. Willm. Whitwell Overseer of the poor

1765 March 12   Receiv'd Into the house Margarett Ware
pr. ordr. Capt. Benja. Hammatt Overseer of the poor

25   Receiv'd Into the house Dorcas Ballard[157] Also three Children Eliza.
Barger one from the Work house & two of Kellons
pr. ordr. Isaac Smith Esqr. Overseer of the poor

                 Received into the house William Smith aged about 6 years, his Mother
Mary Swan in the Workhouse
℘ Order Mr. Willm. Whitwell Overseer of the poor

                 Received into the house Charles Buffard aged about 8 years
℘ Order of the Overseers who took him from his Master &c[158]

Apl. 1.   Received into the house Benjamin Smith (Jeweller) to be cured of the
Itch[159]
pr. Order of Mr. Benjamin Dolbeare Overseer of the Poor
said Smith to pay the Charge

do.   Received into the House Jane Price[160]
pr. Order of John Avery Esqr. Overseer of the Poor
Order dated 30th. March

2d.   Went Away from the house Mary Briant

                 Elizabeth Kelly & Child left the House

5   Received Into the house John Burgis Abt. 8 years Old & Stephen
Burgis Born May 5th. 1760
pr. ordr. Overseers Sitting Day

[do.][161]   Received Into the house Sarah Haden And her Child
pr. ordr. Mr. William Whitwell Overseer of the poor

1765 April 5   Received Into the house a Negrow Girl Nam'd Margtt. Hammond[162]
pr. ordr. Mr. Willm. Whitwell Overseer of the poor

Do.   Received Into the house Joseph Moffatt A poor Man[163]
pr. ordr. John Avery Esqr. Overseer of the poor

Do   Received Into the house Joseph Fothergill from the work house[164]

Jones & his wife gone away from the House

Do. 7   Went Away from the house Moses Larkin & his Wife
14   Went Away from the house John Fabre & his Wife
          Went Away from the house Thos. Daniels

10   Received Into the house On Province Account Robert Lassley a poor
Blind Man[165]
pr. Ordr. Messrs. {Joseph Jackson, Saml. Sewall} Esqr. Select Men
and John Barrett Esqr. Overseer of the poor

13   Received Into the house Mary Linte[166] & her Child
pr. ordr. Mr. Ebenzr. Storer Overseer of the poor

Sarah Haden gone away

22d.   Went away from the House John Heskew & his Wife

23   Received Into the house Mary Truman[167]
pr. ordr. Royall Tyler Esqr. Overseer of the poor

1765 April 29   Went away from the House Hannah Burrell & Mary McGoun
          —— also John Smith

Sent away Peggy Forbus to Mr. Bently 22d. April

Thomas More (alias Pimm) Bound out to James Flagg <*Son of* G[…]
Flagg>

30   Received into the House Thankful Spear from Hingham
℘ Order of John Barrett Esqr.

Do.   Received into the House Joseph Simpson a Lad about 12 yrs. old
℘ pr. Order of John Barrett Esqr.

Received into the House Rebecca Bradley about 26th. April
℘ Verbal Order of Mr. Benjamin Dolbeare

May 5   Receiv'd Into the house Willm. Rownand[168]
pr. ordr. Joseph Gardner Esqr. Overseer of the poor

May 14   Received Into the house Joanna Delotte
pr. Ordr. Mr. Ebenzr. Storer Overseer of the poor

15   Received into the House on Province Account William Dicks[169]
℘ Order Messrs. {John Ruddock, John Hancock} Esqrs: Selectmen
And Melatiah Bourn Esqr. Overseer of the poor

27   Received Into the house Eliza. Carrell[170]
pr. ordr. John Avery Esqr. Overseer of the poor

1765 May 28   Received Into the house Mary Berry & her Child
pr. ordr. Mr. Ebenzr. Storer Overseer of the poor

30   Received into the House Cadet Perew[171] & her Son on province
Account:
℘ Order Joseph Jackson Esqr. Select Man
and Melatiah Bourn Esqr.—Overseer of the Poor

June 7   Received Into the house Mary Hutter a poor Girle P[o]x[172]
pr. ordr. Joseph Gardner Esqr. overseer of the poor

Do.   Received Into the House Mary Hammons Child
pr. ordr. Mr. Benja. Dolbeare overseer of the poor

June 10   Received Into the house Margarett Dorrinton P[o]x[173]
pr. ordr. Mr. Ebenzr. Storer Overseer of the poor

Ditto 13   Received Into the house Nathaniel Bird
pr. ordr. Isaac Smith Esqr. overseer of the poor

Do.   Discharg'd from the house to the Work house Mary Turner
pr. ordr. Isaac Smith Esqr. Overseer of the poor

17   Received Into the house Katharin Murffe[174] a poor Girl of Capt.
Reighly
pr. ordr. Mr. Jona. Mason Overseer of the poor

21   Received Into house John Gray A poor Sick Man P[o]x
pr. ordr. Mr. Henderson Inches Overseer of the poor

1765 June 8   Received into the House Lucretia Severs on province Account[175]
℘ Order   Selectmen
Joseph Gardner Esqr. Overseer of the Poor

22   Received into the House Martha Soring P[o]x
℘ Order The Honble. Royall Tyler Esqr.

July 3d.   Received Into the house On the Province Account John Fabre and Wife the Man is Blind
pr. ordr. Messrs. {Benja. Austin, John Hancock} Esqrs. Select Men
and Royall Tyler Esqr. Overseer of the poor

July 1   James Perrin & his Wife & Child Went Away from the house

Do. 3d.   Bartholomew Andras Went away from the house

July 5   Received Into the house Mary Mugford[176] with the P[o]x & her Child
pr. ordr. John Barrett Esqr. Overseer of the poor

July 9   Received Into the house Alexdr. Stuart[177]
pr. ordr. Royall Tyler Esqr. Overseer of the poor
Went Away from the house 24 Instant July

10   Received Into the house on the Province Account Eliza. Utinock a little Girle[178]
pr. ordr. Messrs. {Joseph Jackson, Saml. Sewall} Esqrs. Select Men
and Mr. Jonathan Mason overseer of the poor

1765. July 17   Received Into the house Holms Simpson[179]
pr. ordr. Melatiah Bourn Esqr. Overseer of the poor

July 18   Received Into the house On Province Account Moses Larkin a poor Blind Man & his Wife
pr. ordr. {Messrs. Joshua Henchaw, Benja. Austin} Esqrs. Select Men
and Royall Tyler Esqr. Overseer of the poor

Do.   Receiv'd Into the house Mary Hartley a poor Child[180]
pr. ordr. Mr. Jona. Mason Overseer of the poor

July 25   Received Into the house Mary Tuttle A Young Woman big with Child[181]
pr. ordr. Joseph Gardner Esqr. Overseer of the poor

1765 Augst. 2   Received Into the house from the Work house Robert Lassley & his Wife on the Province Account
pr. ordr. Royall Tyler Esqr. overseer of the poor
As also the Select Mens. ordr.

Do. 5   Received Into the house Elizabeth Eustis[182]
pr. ordr. Mr. Jonathan Mason Overseer of the poor

Do. 9   Received Into the house Eliza. Whealer
pr. ordr. Captn. Benjamin Hammatt Overseer of the poor

1765 Augt. 12th: Received into the House Edward McGowen a Child
℘ Order   overseer of the poor

13 to 15}[183]   Received into the House from the Workhouse Katha. Crane, Dorcas Ballard, Mary Davidson, Lenne Lewis}
℘ Order of   overseer of the poor

Augt. 12. to 15.   Discharged from the House John Bradley to Workhouse—William
Hudson

             Alice Mullikens Child put to Nurse—Kata. Murphy to the Eastward
William Dix—Augst. 20 Alice Mulliken the Woman left the house

Augt. 16.   Patte[184] Sorin went to the Workhouse

Do. 19th.   Received Into the house On the Province Account Miles Henley
pr. ordr.   } Select Men

Royall Tyler Esqr. overseer of the poor
Deceas'd Next Day after Came in

Do. 21   Received Into the house On the Province Account A Child Nam'd John
Higgins abt. 2 years Old
pr. ordr. Messrs. {Joshua Henshaw, Saml. Sewall} Esqrs. Select Men
and Mr. Wm. Whitwell Overseer of the poor

26.   Went away from the House without leave Mary Lintee & her Child

27.   Rebecca Pimm & Child discharged ℘ Order John Barrett Esqr.

28   Cadet Perew & her Child Went Away—for Quebeck

1765. Augt. 10.   Robert Lassley & his Wife discharg'd from the House in order to proceed
for England &c

29   Received Into the house Thos. Wilkinson a poor Man[185]
pr. ordr. Mr. Benja. Dolbeare Overseer of the poor

Sepr. 5th.   Received Into the house On Province Account Lawrence Cooper a poor
Sick Man
pr. ordr. Messrs. {Joshua Henshaw, John Hancock} Esqrs. Select Men
and Mr. Henderson Inches Overseer of the poor
Dec'd octor. 21 1765

Ditto 12   Received Into the house On the Province Account James Perrin his Wife
And A Child
pr. ordr. {Joshua Henchaw, Benja. Austin} Esqrs: Select Men
and Royall Tyler Esqr. Overseer of the poor

Ditto 13   Received Into the house on Province Account Wm. Hudson[186]
pr. ordr. Messrs. {Saml. Sewall, John Hancock} Select Men
and Royall Tyler Esqr. overseer of the poor

Ditto 17   Received Into the house Sarah Burk & her Grand Child Sarah Cowley[187]
pr. ordr. Joseph Gardner Esqr. Overseer of the poor

1765 Sepr. 16   Received Into the house Ann Johns a poor Woman
pr. ordr. Mr. Jonathan Mason Overseer of the poor

Do. 20   Received Into the house Edward Tavenu[188] a litle Boy
pr. ordr. Royall Tyler Esqr. Overseer of the poor
his young man Comeing with him

23d.   Received Into the house Mr. George Glean[189] a poor Man
pr. ordr. Isaac Smith Esqr. Overseer of the poor

23d.   Received Into the house Lydia Richardson big With Child
pr. ordr. Mr. William Whitwell Overseer of the poor

27   Received Into the house Mary McGouin[190]
pr. ordr. Mr. William Whitwell Overseer of the poor

28   Received Into the house On the Province Account John Newnon a poor
Sick Man
pr. ordr. Messrs. {Joseph Jackson, Benja. Austin} Esqrs. Select Men
& Royall Tyler Esqr: Overseer of the poor

         Margaret Forbes has left the house.

30.[191]   Richard Leodore left the House

         Elizabeth Eustis went away about the beginning of the Month[192]

ommit'd Augst. 21st.   Anna Murrey alias Taylor A Negrow Woman, Recd. into the house
pr. ordr. Royall Tyler Esqr. Overseer of the poor

1765 Sepr. 30   Out of the house put On the Province Account Joseph Mazaroan a poor
French Man
pr. ordr. Messrs. {Benja. Austin, Saml. Sewall} Esqrs. Select Men
And John Avery Esqr. overseer of the poor
his Care

1765 Octor. 4   Received Into the house Ann Richardson from the work house[193]
pr. ordr. Mr. William Whitwell Overseer of the poor

Octr. 4   Dischargd. from the house Anna Murrey alias Taylor A Negrow Woman
had 1 pr. Shoos 35/ & 2 1/2 yds. homspun [9]7/6

Do. 7   Received Into the house On Province Account Isaac Orr a poor Man
pr. ordr. Messrs. {Benja. Austin, Saml. Sewall} Select Men
Mr. Benja. Dolbeare Overseer of the poor

Do. 8   Received Into the house Deborah Lambert
pr. ordr. Mr. Willm. Whitwell Overseer of the poor

9   Received Into the house Sarah a Child of Sarah Youngs[194]
pr. ordr. Melatiah Bourn Esqr. Overseer of the poor

10   Received Into the house Thomison Charleton A Young Woman big
With Child[195]
pr. ordr. Royall Tyler Esqr. overseer of the poor

       Received Into the house from the work house Dorothy Lewis big with
Child, Katharain Crane, Mary Brooks & Eliza. Cotney

12   Received Into the house Benja. Bodge
pr. ordr. Mr. Henderson Inches Overseer of the poor

12   Receivd. Into the house on Province Account Peter Grines[196] a poor
Man
pr. ordr. {Messrs. Joseph Jackson, Benja. Austin} Esqrs. Select Men
and Royall Tyler Esqr. Overseer of the poor
went away November 16th. 1765

16   Received Into the house Joseph Boucher
pr. ordr. Mr. Wm. Whitwell Overseer of the poor

1765 Octr. 16   Received Into the house Eliza. Nickerson[197] big With Child
pr. ordr. Mr. Ebenzr. Storer Overseer of the poor

17   Received Into the house Mary Liddle With her Child[198]
pr. ordr. John Avery Esqr. Overseer of the poor

18   Received Into the house John Smith
pr. ordr. Mr. Ebenzr. Storer Overseer of the poor

28   Received Into the house On the Province Account John Wheeland[199] A
poor Man
pr ordr. Messrs. {Saml. Sewall, John Ruddock} Esqrs. Select Men
and Mr. Wm. Whitwell Overseer of the poor

29   Received Into the house John Child a poor Man
pr. ordr. Joseph Gardner Esqr. overseer of the poor

30   Received Into the house Sarah Woart A Child of Christian Isbuster's
pr. ordr. Mr. Jona. Mason Overseer of the poor

1765 Novr. 1   Received Into the house On the Province Account Mary Montgomery
& her Child
pr. ordr. Messrs. {Joseph Jackson, Saml. Sewall} Esqrs. Select Men
and Joseph Gardner Esqr. Overseer of the poor

<Joseph Burjear a French Man received into the House somtime in October>

                      Discharg'd Nicholas Mangent
5th.   Eliza. Wheeler ditto

6   Receiv'd Into the house from the Work house John Brew & his Wife
pr. ordr. Mr. Jona. Mason Overseer of the poor

8   Received Into the hous On the Province Account Jane McCloud a
poor woman a Stranger
pr. ordr. Messrs. {Joshua Henchan, Benja. Austin} Esqrs. Select Men
and Royall Tyler Esqr. Overseer of the poor

9   Received Into the house Margarett Johnson big With Child[200]
pr. ordr. Royall Tyler Esqr. overseer of the poor

1765 Novr. 9   Received Into the house Eliza. Pim, Daughtr. of Rebekah Pim
pr. ordr. Royall Tyler Esqr. Overseer of the poor

Do. 11   Received Into the house Hannah Phillips
pr. Ordr. Royall Tyler Esqr. Overseer of the poor

Do. 16   Received Into the house two Children one Boy Nam'd John
McDaniell, the other A Girle Nam'd Catharine Neal
pr. ordr. John Avery Esqr. Overseer of the poor

Do. 20   Received Into the house On the Province Account John Lewis a poor
Stranger
pr. ordr. Messrs. {Joshua Henchaw, Saml. Sewall} Esqrs. Select Men
and Royall Tyler Esqr. Overseer of the poor

Do. 26   Dischargd. Mary Heartly A litle Girl gone to Servis Deliver'd the Child
to Mr. Mackintire
pr. ordr. Royall Tyler Esqr.

Decr. 11   Receivd. Into the house On the Province Account Peter Murry[201] a
poor Man
pr. ordr. {Messrs. Joshua Henchaw, John Hancock} Esqrs. Select Men
and Mr. Wm. Whitwell Overseer of the poor

1765 Dec. 14   Received Into the house On the Province Account George Briant A
poor Sick Man

pr. ordr. {Joseph Jackson   } Esqrs. Select Men
and Royall Tyler Esqr. Overseer of the poor

Decr. 17   Received Into the house Hugh OBriant
pr. ordr. Wm. Whitwell Overseer of the poor

Decmr. 18   Received Into the house Edward Lack a poor Man
pr. ordr. John Barrett Esqr. Overseer of the poor

Do. 21   Received Into the house Margarett Riddle A poor Woman
pr. ordr. Mr. Wm. Whitwell Overseer of the poor

Decmr. 20   Went Away from the house John Lewis on Prov. Acct.

Ditto 30   Received into the house Susanna Austin a poor Woman
pr. ordr. John Barrett Esqr. overseer of the poor

Do. 31   Received Into the house Ann Brazier
pr. ordr. Capt. Benja. Hammatt overseer of the poor

1765 Decmr. 31   Received Into the house from the work house Mary Rook a young woman
pr. ordr. Mr. Wm. Whitwell Overseer of the poor

1766 Janr. 4   Received Into the house Margarett OBriant
pr. ordr. Mr. Wm. Whitwell Overseer of the poor

Ditto 4th.   Received Into the house Ann Warren & 3 of her Children
pr. ordr. Captn. Benja. Hammatt Overseer of the poor

Janr. 8   Received Into the house Francis Jewsear[202] a litle Boy 5 years Old
pr. ordr. Mr. Henderson Inches Overseer of the poor

Do.   Received Into the house Eliza. Robinson & her Child 2 Years Old
pr. ordr. Mr. Henderson Inches Overseer of the poor

Do.   Received Also Mary Blake Into the house from the Work house
pr. ordr. Mr. Henderson Inches Overseer of the poor

Do. 10   Received Into the house On the Province Account John Domineca a poor Sick Man & a Strainger
pr. ordr. {Joshua Henchaw, Joseph Jackson} Esqrs. Select Men
And Isaac Smith Esqr. Overseer of the poor
the Charge of the above pd. by Wm. Muluinox & Not Carried to the Prov. Account

1766 Janr. 10   Received Into the house Margarett Ridle[203]
pr. ordr. Capt. Benja. Hammatt Overseer of the poor

Janr. 11　　　　　　Received Into the house Bant Bronsdon
pr. ordr. Deacon Ebenzr. Storer Overseer of the poor

Do.　　　　　　　Received Into the house Esther Burgoin a Child
pr. ordr. Mr. Henderson Inches Overseer of the poor

Do. 20　　　　　　Received Into the house A Boy 5 Years Old Named Willm. Porfery[204]
belonging to Eliza. Sunderland her Son
pr. ordr. John Avery Esqr. Overseer of the poor

Do.　　　　　　　Received Into the house Margarett Smith
pr. ordr. Joseph Gardner Esqr. Overseer of the poor

Do.　　　　　　　Received Into the house from the Work house Mary Brooks Also
Merea[205] a Negrow Woman
pr. ordr. Deacon Ebenzr. Storer Overseer of the poor

[20][206]　　　　　　Went Away from the house Peter Murrey On Pro. Acct.

Janr. 28　　　　　　Mary Rook and Dorcas Ballard both Jumpt. the Fence & Went of

27　　　　　　　　Received Into the house Silvester Smith & his Wife
pr. ordr. Captn. Benja. Hammatt Overseer of the poor

1766 Janr. 29　　　　Received Into the house Lydia Calder A litle Girl abt. 3 Years Old
pr. ordr. Melatiah Bourn Esqr. Overseer of the poor

Febr. 1　　　　　　Received Into the house Joseph Snelling
pr. ordr. Capt. Benja. Hammatt Overseer of the poor

3　　　　　　　　Mary McGraw & 3 Children Rec'd Into the house
℘ Order Melatiah Bourn Esqr. Overseer of the poor

11　　　　　　　　Received Into the house Eliza. George & Grand Son
pr. Ordr. Capt. Benja. Hammatt Overseer of the poor

13　　　　　　　　Received Into the house Robert Lenox An Old Man bad With P[o]x
pr. ordr. Mr. Ebenzr. Storer Overseer of the poor

13　　　　　　　　Went Away from the house John Newnon

24　　　　　　　　Received Into the house from the Work house Juda Simmons A Young
Woman big With Child
pr. ordr. Melatiah Bourn Esqr. Overseer of the poor

17 Febr.　　　　　Received Into the house On the Province Account John Adams a poor
Sick Man[207]

pr. ordr. Messrs. {Saml. Sewall, John Ruddock} Esqrs. Select Men
and Mr. Wm. Whitwell Overseer of the poor

1766 [*Feb.*] 23   Received Into the house Abigail Glover[208]
pr. ordr. Royall Tyler Esqr. Overseer of the poor
27   Received Into the house Christian Isbuster big With Child[209]
pr. ordr. Mr. Benja. Dolbeare Overseer of the poor

March 1   Received Into the house Thomas Wilkinson
pr. ordr. Messrs. Royall [*Tyler*] & Joseph Gardner Esqrs.
& Mr. William Whitwell Overseers of the poor

7   Received Into the house On the Province Account Thomas Martin a
poor Sick Man
pr. ordr. Messrs. {Benja. Austin, Saml. Sewall} Esqrs. Select Men
and Mr. Willm. Whitwell Overseer of the poor

10   Received Into the house Mary Gardner an Inhabitant of Roxberry
pr. ordr. Melatiah Bourn Esqr. Overseer of the poor
22d. Instant Sent away to Roxberry by Constable Salmon

18   Received Into the house Mary Linty[210] big With Child
pr. ordr. Joseph Gardner Esqr. Overseer of the poor

1766 March 18   Received Into the house from the Work house Benja. Chubb,[211]
Katharain Legg, & Jane McCloud
pr. ordr. Mr. Henderson Inches Overseer of the poor

March 22d.   Received Into the house Patrick Keily
pr. ordr. Joseph Gardner Esqr. Overseer of the poor

Do. 24.   Received Into the house Nathl. Vial A litle Boy
pr. ordr. Mr. Wm. Whitwell Overseer of the poor

Do.   Received Into the house Rebeckah Weston
pr. ordr. Isaac Smith Esqr. Overseer of the poor

March 31.   Received into the House on the Province Account Edward Ryan a
poor sick Man
℘ Order Messrs. {Joseph Jackson   } Esqr. Select Men
and Royall Tyler Esqr. Overseer of the poor

do.   Received into the House on the Province Account Robert Sandford a
poor sick Man
℘ Order Messrs. {John Ruddock, John Hancock} Esqrs. Select Men
And Royall Tyler Esqr. Overseer of the poor

1766 April 4   Received Into the house James Martin a poor Sick Man[212]
pr. ordr. Joseph Gardner Esqr. Overseer of the poor

Do. 5   Received Into the house Eliza. Cleverly a poor Child 1 year old[213]
pr. ordr. Mr. William Greenleaf Overseer of the poor
7 Day after Date being 2 days / above Child Dd.[214] to Eliza. Banks

[5][215]   gone Away from the house Patrick Keiley, Edward Ryan, Robert Sandford

April 17   Received Into the house Anna Lenox big With Child[216]
pr. ordr. Isaac Smith Esqr. Overseer of the poor

18   Received Into the house Mary Atwood a Sick Woman
pr. ordr. of Joseph Gardner Esqr. Overseer of the poor

Omitted   Received Into the house Rebeca Choat a widow from Roxberry
December 31: 1763 Went Away to Roxberry During the time of Small pox being in town gone Abt. 4 Months

May 2d.   Received Into the house On the Province Account Owing[217] Neal a poor Sick Man
pr. ordr. Messrs. {Joseph Jackson, Saml. Sewall} Esqrs. Select men

1766. April   Discharg'd Hannah Phillips, (Natl. Vial, John Forbus, Richard Warren Children)

May 6th.   Received into the House Willm. Trout
℘ Order Mr. William Whitwell Overseer of the Poor
May 13 1766 Went Away from the house

7   Received into the house On the Province Account John Clark A Child
Abt. 6 Months old, son of John & Mary Clark
pr. ordr. Messrs. {Joseph Jackson, John Hancock} Esqrs. Select Men
and Isaac Smith Esqr. Overseer of the poor

May 12th.   Received Into the house Ruth Lee
pr. ordr. Isaac Smith Esqr. Overseer of the poor

Do. 14   Received Into the house Joseph & Thomas Osborn 2 Boys
pr. ordr. Mr. Benja. Dolbeare Overseer of the poor

Do.   Received Into the house James Morris A poor Boy
pr. ordr. Royall Tyler Esqr. Overseer of the poor
Deliverd. above Boy to his Mother the Next Day pr. ordr. R. Tyler Esqr.

Do. 19   Received Into the house Eliza. Bradshaw A Child 5 years old the 18th.
Day of October 1765
pr. Ordr. Royall Tyler Esqr. Overseer of the poor

1766 May 21st.   Received Into the house Mary March A Young Woman big With Child
pr. Ordr. Mr. Henderson Inches Overseer of the poor

Do. 26   Received Into the house Susannah Sloper a Young Woman big With
Child
pr. Ordr. Mr. Henderson Inches Overseer of the poor

June 2   Received Into the house Margery Williams[218]
pr. ordr. Mr. Ebenzr. Storer Overseer of the poor

4.   Received into the House Alexander Steward on the Province
Account[219]
℘ Order Joseph Jackson, Timo. Newell} Selectmen
And William Greenleaff Overseer of the Poor

7   Received Into the house Mary Greenleaf
pr. ordr. Joseph Gardner Esqr. Overseer of the poor

10   Receiv'd Into the house Sarah Seargrave[220] & Child
pr. ordr. Joseph Gardner Esqr. Overseer of the poor

18   Received Into the house Abigial Nations
pr. Ordr. Mr. Willm. Whitwell Overseer of the poor
Discharged September 14th. 1767

1766. June 28.   Received into the House Deborah Harley & 4 Children
℘ Order Captn. Benjamin Hammatt Overseer of the Poor
NB. The Childrens Names Benjamin Aged 6. years April 9th. 1766, Solomon Aged 4. years
Decemr. 19th. 1765, Rebecca & Mary

Do. 28   Received Into the house Hannah Williams
pr. ordr. Capt. Benja. Hammatt Overseer of the poor

July 16   Received Into the house Kate A Negrow Woman A Servant of Capt.
James Day
pr. ordr. Royall Tyler Esqr. Overseer of the poor

July 19   Received Into the house On the Province Account William Caten a
poor Sick Man[221]
pr. Ordr. Messrs. {Joseph Jackson   } Esqrs. Select Men
Consented Mr. Wm. Greenleafe Overseer of the poor

Augst. 1　　　　Received Into the house On Province Account Willm. Lee & Peter Brown two invalids from Castle William[222]
pr. ordr. {Messrs. Joseph Jackson, Saml. Sewall} Esqrs. Select Men
Consented to Willm. Greenleaf Overseer of the poor

1766 Augst. 5　　　Received Into the house from the Work house Old Mr. Brew[223] & Moll Turner Big with Child

pr. ordr. Overseers Sitting Day

Do. 6　　　　Received Into the house Mary Turner from the Work house big With Child[224]
pr. ordr. Joseph Gardner Esqr. overseer of the poor

Do.　　　　Received also from the work [house] into the house Eliza. Davis An old woman[225]
pr. ordr. Joseph Gardner Esqr. overseer of the poor

Do.　　　　Received Into the house Joseph Harley[226]
pr. ordr. Capt. Benja. Hammatt overseer of the poor

Do. 14　　　　Received Into the house Nancy Storey big With Child[227]
pr. ordr. Mr. Will Greenleafe Overseer of the poor

14[228] Ditto　　　Received Into the house On Province Account Francis Wheland[229] a poor Sick Man
pr. ordr. Messrs. {Joseph Jackson, Timothy Newell} Esqrs. Select Men
and Mr. Benja. Dolbeare Overseer of the poor

1766 Augst. 10[230]　Received Into the house John Plant a lad Who was bound to the Rev'd Mr. Wheeler Returnd by ordr. Overseers[231]
pr. ordr. Mr. William Greenleafe Overseer of the poor

Ditto 21　　　Received Into the house On the Province Account Dennis Gleason a poor Man helpless[232]
pr. ordr. Messrs. {Joseph Jackson, Saml. Sewall} Esqrs. Select Men
& Royall Tyler Esqr. Overseer of the poor

Ditto　　　　Received Into the house Eliza. Jones & her Daughter
pr. ordr. Mr. William Whitwell Overseer of the poor

25　　　　Received Into the house A Child Nam'd Mary Hicks
pr. ordr. John Barrett Esqr. Overseer of the poor

27　　　　Received Into the house 3 Children of Mrs. Lemoins[233]
pr. ordr. John Barrett Esqr. Overseer of the poor

Septr. 2d.   Received into the House a Child named Eliza. Trumble about 7.
Months Old
℘ Order Capt. Benja. Hammatt Overseer

1766. Septr. 2.   Received into the House Eliza. Frothingham Ætat. 88
℘ Order Mr. William Whitwell Overseer of the Poor

Sepr. 6   Received Into the house Dorcas Simpson
pr. ordr. Mr. Henderson Inches Overseer of the poor

9th.   Gone Away from the house Mrs. McGraw & 3 Children

11th.   Received Into the house Christian Tregaay A Child two years old July last
pr. ordr. Melatiah Bourn Esqr. overseer of the poor

Do. 15   Received Into the house On the Province Account Moses Larkin and
his wife
pr. ordr. {Saml. Sewall, Will Phillips} Esqrs. Select Men
Mr. Jonathan Mason Overseer of the poor

Do. 16   Received Into the house Eliza. Sherwin[234] or Mason
pr. ordr. Joseph Gardner Esqr. overseer of the poor

Do.   Received Into the house the wife of David Poor and their Daughter
Bridgett Nevel
pr. ordr. Mr. William Whitwell overseer of the poor

1766 Sepr. 27   Received Into the house On the Province Account Katherine Legg.
Stay'd a day or two & went away again

30.   Received into the House Mary Phips[235]
℘ Order Mr. William Greenleaff Overseer of the Poor

do.   Received into the House Joseph Roberts
℘ Order Mr. William Whitwell Overseer of the Poor

Do.   Received Into the house On the Province Account Abigail Branch A
poor woman[236]
pr. ordr. Messrs. {Joseph Jackson, Timothy Newell} Select Men &
The Honble. Royall Tyler Esqr. Overseer of the Poor

Do.   Received into the House Elizabeth Smith
℘ Order Mr. Henderson Inches Overseer of the Poor

Octr. 2   Francis Wheeland Went Away from the house

4.   Received into the House on Province Account Edward Robertson a poor Man returned from Captivity a Native of England[237]
℘ Order Messrs. {Joseph Jackson, Timo. Newell} Select Men &
The Honble. Royall Tyler Esqr. Overseer of the Poor

1766 Octor. 8   Received Into the house from the Work house Margaret McKim &
Mary Tuttle
pr. ordr. Mr. Willm. Greenleaf overseer of the poor

Do. 11   Received Into the house John Sarjant[238]
pr. ordr. Mr. Willm. Whitwell Overseer of the poor

14   Went Away from the house Dennis Gleason Pro Man

                 Also Sent to the Work house Alexdr. Steward a Pro Man

Do. 16   Received Into the house On Province Account Joel Rollings a poor
Sick Stranger
pr. ordr. Messrs. {Joseph Jackson, Timothy Newell} Select Men
& Royall Tyler Esqr. Overseer of the poor

Do. 18th.   Received into the house on Province Account James Perrin his wife &
her Child
pr. ordr. Messrs. {Joseph Jackson   } Select Men
& John Barrett Esqr. Overseer of the poor

1766 Octor. 22d.   Received Into the house On the Province Account Thomas Marston a
Stranger[239]
pr. ordr. {Joseph Jackson, John Ruddock} Esqrs. Select-Men
and Royall Tyler Esqr. Overseer of the poor

Octor. 20   Received Into the house John Plant a poor Boy on the Province
Account
pr. ordr. Messrs. {Saml. Sewall, John Ruddock} Esqrs. Select Men
and Mr. Willm. Greenleaf Overseer of the poor

25 Ditto   Received Into the house On Province Account Nickolas Moyce & his
wife poor Strangers
pr. ordr. Messrs. {Joseph Jackson, Timothy Newell} Select Men
and Royall Tyler Esqr. overseer of the poor
1766 Novr. 20 Went Away for Ireland

27   Received Into the house Mehetable Clough[240]
pr. ordr. Joseph Gardner Esqr. Overseer of the poor

Do. 31   Received Into the house On the Province Account Giles Lane a poor
Sick Stranger[241]
pr. ordr. Messrs. {Joseph Jackson, Timothy Newell} Select Men
and Royall Tyler Esqr. overseer of the poor

1766 Octor. 31   Received Into the house Mrs. Cottench
℘ Order Joseph Gardner Esqr. Overseer of the Poor

Octr. 31   Received Into the house Asher[242] A Negrow Man
pr. ordr. Mr. Henderson Inches Overseer of the poor
Novr. 1st. Sent Away to Plymoth to his Master

Novr. 4   Received Into the house David Dennie[243]
pr. ordr. Mr. Jonathan Mason Overseer of the poor

Ditto 5   Received into the house from the work house Alexander Stewart
pr. ordr. Mr. Wm. Greenleaf Overseer of the poor

Do.   Received Into the house Jo Bill a Negrow Man

Do.   Received Into the house Ephraim Coneway a Negrow Man
pr. ordr. Mr. William Greenleaf Overseer of the poor

Novr. 7   Received Into the house On the Province Account Ann Callahon[244]
With her two Children
pr. ord Messrs. {Wm. Phillips, Timothy Newell} Select Men
and Mr. Ebenzr. Storer Overseer of the poor

Do. 10   Received Into the house Sarah Larnard[245]
pr. ordr. John Barrett Esqr. Overseer of the poor

1766 Novr. 12   Received Into the house On the Province Account Willm. Smith a
poor Stranger
pr. ordr. Messrs. {Saml. Sewall, Wm. Phillips} Select Men
& Mr. Wm. Whitwell Overseer of the poor

Do.   Received Into the house On Province Account John Anderson a poor
Stranger
pr. ordr. Messrs. {Saml. Sewall, Wm. Phillips} Select Men
Mr. Wm. Whitwell Overseer of the poor
Decr. 17 Went Away from the house

Do.   Received Into the house On Province Account Michael Foremon[246] a
poor Stranger
pr. ordr. Messrs. {Saml. Sewall, Wm. Phillips} Select Men
Mr. Wm. Whitwell Overseer of the poor

Do. 13   Received Into the house On Province Account Roger Slegg a poor
Stranger
pr. ordr. Messrs. {Joseph Jackson, Timo. Newell} Select Men
Mr. Benja. Dolbeare Overseer of the poor

1766 Nov 20   Nickolis Moyce & wife went away to Ireland

21   Alexdr. Steward, Edward Robinson & Wm. Smith Sent Away to England

Novr. 24   Received Into the house Elizabeth Eustice
pr. ordr. Mr. Wm. Greenleaf Overseer of the poor

26   Received Into the house Mary Marrow[247] and Mercy Miller[248] two Young Women to be Salavated for the P[ox]
pr. ordr. Mr. Ebenzr. Storer Overseer of the poor

Decr. 2   Received Into the house Mary McGraw[249] & 3 Children
pr. ordr. John Barrett Esqr. Overseer of the poor

Ditto 4   Received Into the house on the Province Account Phillip Reily a poor Sick Man
pr. ordr. Messrs. {Joseph Jackson, Timothy Newell} Select Men
and Mr. Wm. Whitwell Overseer of the poor

Ditto 5.   Received Into the house Margarett Smith
pr. ordr. Melatiah Bourn Esqr. Overseer of the poor

Ditto   Received Into the house Eliza. Hayes
pr. ordr. Mr. Wm. Whitwell Overseer of the poor

[6][250]   Went away from the house Lydia Richardson & her Child

1766 Decemr. 12   Received Into the house Peter A Negrow Man and his Wife
pr. ordr. Joseph Gardner Esqr. overseer of the poor

Decemr. 16   Received Into the house Patrick Burk
pr. ordr. Melatiah Bourn Esqr. Overseer of the poor

18   Received Into the house Mary Harley[251] & Child
pr. ordr. Melatiah Bourn Esqr. Overseer of the poor

Ditto 17   John Anderson Went Away from the house.

Ditto 29   Received Into the house On the Prov Account Lawrance Bride A poor Sick man (Briant)[252]
pr. ordr. Messrs. {Joseph Jackson, Timothy Newell} Select Men
and Royall Tyler Esqr. overseer of the poor

Ditto 29   Received Into the house Mary Haynes big with Child
pr. ordr. Melatiah Bourn Esqr. Overseer of the poor

1767. Janua. 9th.　　Received into the House Jacob Bartlet[253] & his Wife
℘ Order Mr. Benja. Dolbeare Overseer of the Poor

1767. Janua. 3.　　Received into the House John Burges's[254] Child
℘ Order Mr. Ebenr. Storer Overseer of the Poor

Decmr. 25. 1766　　ommited　Received Into the house On the Province Account Thos.
Fling a poor Man
pr. ordr. Messrs. {Joseph Jackson, Saml. Sewall} Select Men
Joseph Gardner Esqr. Overseer of the poor

1767 Janr. 19　　Received Into the house on the Prov Account James Clark a poor Man
pr. ordr. Messrs. {Joseph Jackson, Timothy Newell} Select Men
Isaac Smith Esqr. Overseer of the poor

Do. 18　　Received Into the house Amy Colesworthy
pr. ordr. Joseph Gardner Esqr. Overseer of the poor

Do. 20　　Received Into the house from the work house Eliza. Waters[255]
pr. ordr. Mr. Wm. Whitwell Overseer of the poor

Do. 28　　Received Into the house Cornelius Coffin
pr. ordr. John Barrett Esqr. Overseer of the poor

Do.　　Received Into the house Joseph Osborn
pr. ordr. Mr. Wm. Greenleaf Overseer of the poor

1767 Janr. 29　　Received Into the house Henry Connel
pr. ordr. Mr. Wm. Whitwell Overseer of the poor

Februa. 4th.　　Received into the House Eliza. & Mary Lemoine Children of Widow
Mary Lemoine
℘ Order The Honble. Royall Tyler Esqr. Overseer &c

10th.　　Received into the House Samuel Cleverly with the Itch
℘ Order Mr. Willm. Whitwell Overseer of the Poor

11　　Received Into the house Daniel Brachenberry[256] A Child
pr. ordr. Mr. Benja. Dolbeare Overseer of the poor

Janr. 23d.　　Receivd. Into the house On the Province Account Robert Rogers a
poor Man
pr. ordr. Messrs {Joseph Jackson, Timothy Newell} Select Men
ommitted

<Febr.>　　In the Work house On the Province Account Abraham Fairbanks a poor
Man

pr. ordr. Messrs. {Saml. Sewall, John Hancock} Select Men
Royall Tyler Overseer of the poor

Febr. 23d.   Received Into the house On the Province Account Willm Landaragir[257]
a poor Man
pr. ord. Messrs. {Joseph Jackson, Timo Newell} Select Men
Royall Tyler Esqr. overseer of the poor

1767 March 13   Receivd Into the house Hannah Steward
pr. ordr. Mr. Jonathan Mason Overseer of the poor

March 30   Received Into the house from the work house Margaret Reed
pr. ordr. Mr. Joseph Waldo Overseer of the poor

Do. 31   Receiv'd Into the house James Butler A poor Man
pr. ordr. Mr. Wm. Whitwell Overseer of the poor
put on the Prov Acct. pr. ordr. Jos. Jackson, & Saml. Sewall Esqrs. Select Men

April 5   Received Into the house On the Province Account Mary Clark A poor
woman brot. to bed the Same Day
pr. ordr. Messrs. {Joseph Jackson, Timothy Newell} Select Men
and Royall Tyler Esqr. Overseer of the poor

Do. 7   Received Into the house Margaret Grainger Servant Maid to Stephen
Greenleaf Esqr.[258]
pr. ordr. Mr. Joseph Waldo overseer of the poor

Do. 10   Received Into the house Benja. Hunt a poor Boy Eleven years old Last
August[259]
pr. ordr. Royall Tyler Esqr. Overseer of the poor

16   Received Into the house Christian Isbuster big with Child
pr. ordr. Royall Tyler Esqr. Overseer of the poor

1767 April 14   Received Into the house from the Work house A Child of Margaret
Johnson 13 Months Old
pr. ordr. Mr. Benja. Dolbeare Overseer of the poor

Ditto 27   Receiv'd Into the house Ann Hains
pr. ordr. Mr. Willm. Whitwell Overseer of the poor

Do 30   Receiv'd Into the house Martha Eggleston[260]
pr. ordr. Royall Tyler Esqr. Overseer of the poor

May 2   Received Into the house John Evens
pr. ordr. Royall Tyler Esqr. Overseer of the poor

Ditto 4   Received Into the house Sarah Smallage[261]
pr. ordr. Mr. Benja. Dolbeare Overseer of the poor

Ditto 18   Received Into the house On the Province Account Dennis Dunnavan[262]
a poor Strainger
pr. ordr. Messrs. {Joseph Jackson, Timothy Newell} Select Men
Royall Tyler Esqr. Overseer of the poor

1767   Received Into the house On the Prov Account Jane Bailey & her four
Children Nam'd Nancy, Nelley, James & Thomas
pr. ordr. Messrs. {Joseph Jackson, Timo. Newell} Select Men
Mr. Wm. Whitwell Overseer of the poor

1767 June 2   Received Into the house Richard Wiggens a poor Soldier not
Inhabitant of any Town within this Province upon the Province Accot.[263]
Joseph Jackson, Wm: Phillips} Select men
order Thos: Tyler} one of the overseers of the poor

June 5th.   Received into the House James Lenox[264]
℘ Order John Barrett Esqr. Overseer

June 6   Received into the House on Province Account George Guthridge a
poor Stranger[265]
℘ Order {Joseph Jackson, Timo. Newell} Select Men
Mr. Benjamin Dolbeare Overseer of the Poor

1767. June 6   Sarah Cotton discharged
By order Thos. Tyler Esqr.

9   John Richardson & Wife sent to the Workhouse

June 8   Received into the House on Province Account John Askew a poor
Stranger[266]
℘ Order Joseph Jackson, Samuel Sewall} Select Men
Honble. Royall Tyler Esqr. Overseer of the Poor

9th.   Received into the House Catharine Fitzgerald a poor Girl[267]
℘ Order William White Esqr. Overseer of the Poor

do.   Received into the Alms House Mrs.   Sampson[268]
℘ Order John Gore Esqr. Overseer of the Poor

15th.   Discharg'd John Evans

16.   Received into the House Judith Clear[269] wife of James Clear & her
Child Mary
℘ Order Mr. Benjamin Dolbeare Overseer Poor

19.   Received Susanna Sloper[270] & her Child into the House
℘ Order William Whitwell Overseer of the Poor
Dischargd. the next Day

[do.][271]   Received into the House Ann Moloy[272]
℘ Order Capt. Saml. Partridge One of the Overseers of the Poor

1767. June 23.   Received into the House Hannah Nelson[273]
℘ Order The Honble. Royall Tyler Esqr. Overseer of the Poor}

23.   George Guthridge Prov. Charge went away—also Richard Wiggins

do.   Discharg'd Mr. Greenleaffes Maid Margtt. Grainger
℘ Order Mr. Wm. Whitwell

do.   Received into the Alms House Margtt. Rogers[274]
℘ Order Capt. Saml. Partridge Overseer of the Poor

24th.   Discharged Jacob Skweller Prov. Charge
℘ Order Selectmen June 24th. 1767.

30.   Received into the House Francis Treboo[275] a poor Infirm man
℘ Order Thomas Tyler Esqr. Overseer of the Poor

July 1st.   Received into the House Dinah a Negro Woman[276]
℘ Order Thomas Tyler Esqr. Overseer of the Poor

6   Received into the House Edward Whittemore[277]
℘ Order John Gore Esqr. Overseer of the Poor
afterwards sent to the W House (Mr. Lasenbys Work House sent home since)

July 1.   Dischargd Eliza. Utinock (Prov. Charge) upon Trial at Mr. Goldthwaits
Sons

7   Received into the House Rachel Crage[278]
℘ Order Jonathan Williams Esqr. Overseer of the Poor

1767. July 8.   Discharged Abigail Hicks & her Child

July 13.   Received into the House Abigail Young[279]
℘ Order John Barrett Esqr. Overseer of the Poor

July 22d.   Dischargd Black Pegg
by order Capt. Partridge
gone to Lacks

July 20.   Received into the Alms House Richard Barrett Province Charge
℘ Order The Honble. Royall Tyler Esqr. Overseer &c
Deceas'd 7th. Jany. 1768. Funeral Charges 12/

27.   Thomas Marston discharged
by Order Select Men

29.   Received into the House Thomas Roach[280]
℘ Order John Leverett Esqr. Overseer of the Poor

Augt. 5th.   Dischargd James Butler Province Charge

13.   Received into the House Jonas Webber & his Wife[281]
℘ Order John Leverett Esqr. One of the Overseers

16.   Received into the House on Province Account Mary Woodburn a poor
distressed Woman[282]
℘ Order Joseph Jackson, Saml. Sewall} Esqrs. Selectmen
Mr. Joseph Waldo One of the Overseers of the Poor

18.   Received into the House Mary Jebute a poor Woman[283]
℘ Order John Barrett Esqr. overseer &c

July 30th.   Larkin & Wife Jumpt. the Fence

1767. August 19th.}   Received into the House on Province Account Thomas Marston a
poor Stranger[284]
℘ Order Joseph Jackson, Saml. Sewall} Esqrs. Selectmen
Mr. William Greenleaffe Overseer of the Poor

               Discharg'd John Askew Province Charge Augt. 17th. 1767

20th.   Discharg'd Judith Symmons

27th.   Discharged Ann Lenox   (29th.) Discharged Mary Haynes

29th.   Dennis Donavan Province Charge saild for Ireland

31.   Received into the House on Province Account Dudea Benway[285] Wife
& Child
℘ Order Joseph Jackson, Saml. Sewall} Esqrs. Selectmen
Mr. William Whitwell Overseer of the Poor

Septemr. 1st.   Received into the Alms House Eliza. Maker[286] and her Child
℘ Order Mr. William Whitwell & Jonathn. Williams Esqrs. Overseers of the Poor}

7th.   Received into the House from Work House John Mitchell[287]
℘ Order Thomas Tyler Esqr. Overseer

do.   <*Mary Perrin run away*>

Septr. 2d.   Mary McGraw went away with her Child & left one behind

Septr. 17.   Received into the Alms House William Grigg
℘ Order Captn. Saml. Partridge Overseer of the Poor

25.   Received into the Alms House Benjamin Chubb[288]
℘ Order Jonathan Williams Esqr. Overseer of the Poor

28.   Received into the House John Miers a sick Man[289]
℘ Order John Gore Esqr. Overseer of the Poor

Octo. 3.   Received into the House Moses Larkin & Wife on Prov. Account
℘ Order Samuel Sewall, Timo. Newell} Selectmen
Mr. William Greenleaffe Overseer of the Poor

                        Discharged 4 Children vizt. William Warren, Polly Goggin, Jacob
Winslow, Eliza. Williams

3.   Received into the Alms House Susanna Jarden[290]
℘ Order Capt. Samuel Partridge overseer of the Poor

6.   Received into the House James Hinks[291]
℘ Order John Gore Esqr. Overseer of the Poor

7.   Received into the House Thomas Rainsford[292]
℘ Order Jona. Williams Esqr. Overseer of the Poor

8.   Received into the House Joan Dukes[293] & Child
℘ Order Jona. Williams Esqr. Overseer of the Poor

1767. Octo. 15th.   Received into the House Widow Brown[294]
℘ Order John Gore Esqr. Overseer of the Poor

16.   Received into the House Widow Milward[295]
℘ Order John Gore Esqr. Overseer of the Poor

Novr. 2   Received into the House John Lovelace a poor Child[296]
℘ Order The Honble. Royall Tyler Esqr. Overseer of the Poor

3.   Received into the House James Miller a poor Sick Stranger on Province Account[297]
℘ Order Joseph Jackson, Timo. Newell} Esqrs. Selectmen
The Honble. Royall Tyler Esqr. Overseer of the poor
deceasd. Novr. 9th. 1767.

4.   Received into the House Cuffey a Negro Man[298]
℘ Order William White Esqr. Overseer of the poor

5.   Received into the House Sarah Brown a sick Woman[299]
℘ Order John Gore Esqr. Overseer of the Poor

6.   Eliza. Mumpher[300] a poor Child Received into the House on Province Account
℘ Order Samuel Sewall, John Hancock} Esqrs.
Mr. Willm. Whitwell Overseer of the Poor

7th.   Received into the House on province Account Thomas Weller
℘ Order Joseph Jackson, Timo. Newell} Esqrs.
Mr. Willm. Whitwell Overseer &c
Deceasd July 1st. 1768 Funeral Charges 12/

1767. Novr. 11}   Received into the House John Whittemore[301]
℘ Order Mr. William Whitwell Overseer &c

14.   Received into the House Thomas Hubbard[302]
℘ Order Thomas Tyler Esqr. Overseer of the Poor

13.   Discharg'd Mary Woodburn province Charge

16   Received into the House Abigail Cole[303]
℘ Order Captn. Saml. Partridge Overseer &c

18.   Received into the House Eliza. Skinner[304]
℘ Order John Leverett Esqr. Overseer &c

22.   Received into the House on Province Account Ann Hannon[305] & Child
℘ Order Joseph Jackson, Timo. Newell} Esqrs. Selectmen
The Honble. Royall Tyler Esqr. Overseer
went away 30th. Novr.[306]

26   Received into the House on Province Account Edward Tay a poor Lame Man[307]
℘ Order Joseph Jackson, Timo Newell} Esqrs.
The Honble. Royall Tyler Esqr.
went away 21st. Decr. 1767.

26.   Received into the House Edward & Mary Howard Children[308]
℘ Order Willm. White Esqr. Overseer &c

27.   Received into the House Peter Smith a Boy[309]
℘ Order of John Barrett Esqr. Overseer &c

1767. Decemr. 16th.   Received into the House Bethia Miller[310]
℘ Order John Leverett Esqr. Overseer &c

do.   Received into the House Anthony Coffin Province Charge[311]
℘ Order Joseph Jackson, Saml. Sewall} Select Men
Mr. Willm. Greenleaf Overseer of the Poor
went away January 2d. 1768.

23.   Received into the House John Henry Rinninger Prov. Charge[312]
℘ Order Saml. Sewall, Timo. Newell, J. Rowe} Select Men
Thomas Tyler Esqr. Overseer of the Poor

            Ann Bailey a Child bound out Decr. 18th. 1767. prov. Charge

1768. Janua. 9th.   Received into the House Lyson Fabian Province Charge[313]
℘ Order Joseph Jackson, Timo. Newell} Selectmen
Mr. William Greenleaf Overseer of the Poor

do.   Received into the House John Kenney[314]
℘ Order The Honble. Royall Tyler Esqr. Overseer

do.   Received into the House Margtt. Hannah & Mary Cherry
℘ Order Capt. Saml. Partridge Overseer

1768 Janua. 15   Received into the House Sarah Heath a poor Child
℘ Order Willm. White Esqr. Overseer

12th.   Received into the House Chris. Gibson a Lame Man[315]
℘ Order John Gore Esqr. Overseer &c

21.   Susanna Bodge & Child dischargd

30.   Received into the House Thomas Butler[316]
℘ Order the Honble. Royall Tyler Esqr. Overseer &c

Feby. 1.   Received into the House Joseph Langley alias More & his Wife & Three
Children
℘ Order Mr. William Greenleaf Overseer

do.   Received into the House Martha Clough[317]
℘ Order John Barrett Esqr. Overseer of the Poor

5.   Received into the House Mary Ahier[318]
℘ Order Mr. Benja. Dolbeare Overseer &c

9.   Received into the House John Dyer[319]
℘ Order Joseph Jackson, Timo. Newell} Esqrs.
Mr. William Greenleaf Overseer &c

17th.   Received into the House James Martin[320]
℘ Order The Honble. Royall Tyler Esqr. Overseer &c

19.   Received into the House Ann Sample[321] & her Child
℘ Order The Honble. Royall Tyler Esqr. Overseer &c

1768. Februa. 20th. Received into the House Ann Nichles[322]
℘ Order Jonathan Williams Esqr. Overseer &c

March 2.   Received into the House Samuel Macbean[323] a Stranger
℘ Order Joseph Jackson, Saml. Sewall} Selectmen
Mr. Willm. Whitwell overseer of the poor

3.   Received into the House on province Account Dugena Bennaway Wife
& Children[324]
℘ Order The Honble. James Russel, & Honble. Royall Tyler} Esqrs. Two of the Council to
whose Care this Person & Family is committed by Order

3.   Received into the House Eliza. Nathl. & William Corbin poor Childn.
℘ Order John Gore Esqr. Overseer &c

17.   Received into the House Latitia Williams
℘ Order Capt. Saml. Partridge Overseer &c

18.   Received into the House Huldah Waymondersole[325] & her Son
℘ Order John Gore Esqr. Overseer &c

19.   Received into the House Mary Shaw[326]
℘ Order Capt. John Bradford Overseer of the poor

23.   Received into the House Ann Jennings[327]
℘ Order William White Esqr. Overseer of the Poor

1768. March 24th.   Received into the House Mrs[328] Hareblue a sick woman
℘ Order Captn. John Bradford Overseer of the Poor

30.   Received into the House Abigail Nations[329]
℘ Order Mr. William Whitwell Overseer of the Poor

31.   Received into the House Mary Abrahams[330]
℘ Order Mr. William Whitwell Overseer of the Poor

[31]³³¹   Discharg'd Thomas Butler

April 7th.   *<Received into the House on Province Account John Dyer>*
      John Dyer discharg'd (Province Charge) 9th. Lyson Fabian discharg'd
      Province
20   Abigail Branch dischargd (Prov.) (15th.) Eliza. Mumford dischargd
      (Prov)
      John Henry Rinninger dischargd Prov. (17th.)

April 7.   Received into the House 3. Children of Francis Akley
℘ Order John Bradford Overseer of the Poor

do.   Received into the House from Workhouse Sarah Lockland³³²
℘ Order Mr. Benjamin Dolbeare Overseer &c

8.   Received into the House Ann Goster a poor Child³³³
℘ Order Mr. Willm. Whitwell Overseer &c

12th.   Received into the House on Province Accott. Willm. Fling³³⁴
℘ Order Joseph Jackson, Timo. Newell} Esqrs.
And Thomas Tyler Esqr. Overseer &c.

1768. April 20} Received into the House on Province Accott. Eliza. Utinocks³³⁵
℘ Order John Hancock, Timo. Newell} Esqr.
Captn. Saml. Partridge Overseer &c

23.   Received into the House Hannah Duzer³³⁶
℘ Order Mr. Willm. Whitwell Overseer of the Poor

28.   Received into the House Dorcas Ballard³³⁷
℘ Order John Leverett Esqr. Overseer &c

[28]³³⁸   Discharg'd James Martin, Joseph Langley Wife & 3 Children, Christo.
Gibson, Latitia Williams, & Cherrys 2 Children

May 3d.   Received into the House Eliza. & Mary Bennison Children
℘ Order Willm. White Esqr. Overseer of the Poor

4.   Received into the House on Province Account James Butler a poor
Sick Man³³⁹
℘ Order Joseph Jackson, John Hancock} Esqrs. Selectmen
And John Gore Esqr. Overseer of the Poor}
went away June 2d.

10th.   Received into the House on Province Account Willm. Dunlee³⁴⁰
℘ Order Joseph Jackson, Timo. Newell} Esqr. Selectmen And
The Honble. Royall Tyler Esqr. Overseer &c

10th.   Received into the House Latitia Wesson[341]
℘ Order Mr. Joseph Waldo Overseer &c

1768. May 12.}   Received into the House Sarah Dickinson[342] & her Child
℘ Order Captn. John Bradford Overseer

                         James Perrin & Wife went away 8th. May
May 11th.   Discharg'd Saml. McBean——Sarah Seagraves Child
                         Discharg'd Dugena Bennaway Wife & Children (Prov. Charges)
                         Discharg'd Sarah Bright
                         Discharg'd Huldah Waymondosole & Son

May 13.   Received into the House Mary Beale a sick Woman[343]
℘ Order Mr. William Greenleaf Overseer &c

13.   Received into the House on Province Account Katha. Legg[344]
℘ Order Joseph Jackson, Timo. Newell} Esqr. Selectmen
And Mr. William Greenleaf Overseer &c

16.   Received into the House Mary King a poor Woman[345]
℘ Order—William White Esqr. Overseer &c

19.   Received into the House Samuel Roach a poor infirm Man[346]
℘ Order The Honble. Royall Tyler Esqr. Overseer of the Poor &c

23.   Received into the House Thomas Bennet on Province Account[347]
℘ Order Joseph Jackson, John Rowe} Esqr. Selectmen
The Honble. Royall Tyler Esqr. Overseer &c

1768. May 24.   Received into the House Sarah Allen a poor Woman on Province
Accott.[348]
℘ Order Mr. William Whitwell Overseer of the Poor

30.   Received into the House Widow Lorings Child
℘ Order John Gore Esqr. Overseer &c

                         Discharg'd Eliza. Kelly & Child May 23d.

June 5th.   Moses Larkin & Wife went away

14th.   Received into the House Josiah Watts & Mary[349] Watts children of Eliza.
Watts
℘ Order Mr. Joseph Waldo Overseer &c

15th.   Received into the House John Godfrey a poor Child
℘ Order John Gore Esqr. Overseer of the Poor

Dischargd Mary Lintee & Child—Mary Taylor—Hannah Nelson[350]—Ann Moloy[351]—Hannah Dwyer—Ann Nichols[352]—Bethia Miller—Daniel Brackenberry a Child—Susanna Brown—Mary Beale—Ann Sample & 2 Children

18th.   Received into the House from Workhouse Eliza. Wharff
℘ Order Overseers

27.   Received into the House Josiah Stone a young Man sick[353]
℘ Order John Leverett Esqr. Overseer &c

28.[354]   Received into the House on provce. Accott. John Cunningham
℘ Order Joseph Jackson, Saml. Pemberton} Selectmen
And Willm. White Esqr. Overseer

1768. July 2d.   Received into the House on Prov. Account Nicholas Press & Wife
℘ Order Joseph Jackson, Saml. Pemberton} Selectmen
And William White Esqr. Overseer &c

3d.   Received into the House Mary Magrath[355] & Child
℘ Order Mr. Joseph Waldo Overseer &c

4th.   Received into the House John Bernard of Dartmouth in O Engld. on the Province account
℘ Order the Honble. Royall Tyler Esqr.—dated June 19th. 1768.

July 2d.   Received into the House <*on prov*> John Martin
℘ Order Capt. John Bradford Overseer &c

Received into the House June 23d. Sarah Josear a sick Woman[356]
℘ Order Mr. William Greenleaf Overseer &c

12.   Received into the House on Province Account James Hewes[357]
℘ Order Joseph Jackson, Saml. Pemberton} Esqr. Selectmen
The Honble. Royall Tyler Esqr. Overseer &c

14   Received into the House on prov. Accott. John Penrow[358]
℘ Order Joseph Jackson, Saml. Pemberton} Esqr. Selectmen
The Honble. Royall Tyler Esqr. Overseer &c

1768. July 26.   Received into the House Mary Blake subject to Fits
℘ Order The Honble. Royall Tyler Esqr. Overseer &c

29.   Received into the House Sarah Vail a poor Girl
℘ Order Willm. White Esqr. Overseer &c

July 19th.   Dischargd William Fling Province Charge
25th.   <*Ann Kellihorn Ditto*>—Mrs. Hareblue—Issac Herault—John Martin—Thomison Charlton—Dorcas Ballard

July 23d. Received into the House on Province Account Sarah Dunscutt &
Katharine Sullivan
℘ Order Joshua Henshaw, Joseph Jackson} Esqrs. Selectmen
Mr. Willm. Whitwell Overseer &c
went away Octor. 11th. 1769

30. Received into the House Robert Low on Province Account
℘ Order Joshua Henshaw, Joseph Jackson} Esqrs. Selectmen
Captn. Saml. Partridge Overseer &c

Augt. 8th. Received into the House Elizabeth Harris a poor aged Woman[359]
℘ Order William White Esqr. Overseer &c

10. Received into the House Elizabeth Green
℘ Order Thomas Tyler Esqr. Overseer &c

Discharg'd Ann Kellihorn Augt. 10th. 1768.

1768. Augt. 17th. Received into the House on province Account Charles Ryly[360] a Lame
Man
℘ Order Joshua Henshaw, Joseph Jackson} Esqrs. Selectmen
And John Leverett Esqr. Overseer of the Poor &c
discharged 29th. August 1768

19. Received into the House Abigail Waddell Daughter of John Waddell
℘ Order Captn. John Bradford Overseer &c

Discharged Martha Clough—Widow Milward[361]

[do.][362] Received into the House prov. Accott. James Perrin & Wife
℘ Order Joseph Jackson, Saml. Pemberton} Esqrs.
Honble. Royall Tyler Esqr. Overseer

[do.] Received into the House Tabitha Sergant a poor old Sick Woman
℘ Order Willm. White Esqr. Overseer

17.[363] Received into the House Robert & Jas. Vokes Children
℘ Order Thomas Tyler Esqr. Overseer

31. Received into the House Eliza. Flood[364]
℘ Order John Barrett Esqr. Overseer &c

Septr. 15th. <Ann> Jane Bailey & 3. Children went away Prov. Charge

Septr. 14th. Received into the House Sarah Howell an Aged Woman
℘ Order Willm. White Esqr. Overseer &c

1768. Septr. 14.   Received into the House on province Account Richard Swanborough[365]

℘ Order Joseph Jackson, John Ruddock} Esqrs. Selectmen And
Honble. Royall Tyler Esqr. Overseer

21.   Received into the House on province Account Philip Reiley
℘ Order John Hancock, Saml. Pemberton} Esqrs. Selectmen
Mr. Willm. Whitwell Overseer &c
deceased Septr. 28th. 1768. Funeral Charges 12/

27.   Received into the House Elizabeth Smith
℘ Order Thomas Tyler Esqr. Overseer

28.   Received into the House on prov. Account Moses Larkin & Wife[366]
℘ Order Saml. Pemberton, Henderson Inches} Selectmen
Mr. Willm. Whitwell Overseer &c

Octor. 4th.   Mary Clark & 2. Children (prov. Charge) went away

Octo. 1st.   Ann Hynes went away

3d.   Received into the House Benja. <Dav> Varney[367]
℘ Order William White Esqr. Overseer &c

1768. Octo. 4th: Received into the House on province Account John Horden & Edward Row two poor Sick Men
℘ Order Joseph Jackson, Saml. Pemberton} Selectmen
Honble. Royall Tyler Esqr. Overseer &c

Octo. 21.   Discharg'd[368] Edward Row (prov. Charge)

22   Discharg'd Thos. Bennet (prov. Charge)—Sarah Dickinson—Polly[369] Blake

Octo. 6   Received into the House Margtt. Grainger & Child
℘ Order Honble. Royall Tyler Esqr., Willm. Whitwell} Overseers &c

13.   Received into the House Margarett Forbus[370]
℘ Order John Barrett Esqr. Overseer &c

17.   Received into the House a poor destitute Child named S. P—tts[371]
℘ Order Honble. Royall Tyler Esqr. Overseer &c

18.   Received into the House on province Account John Short
℘ Order Joseph Jackson, Saml. Pemberton} Esqrs. Selectmen
Honble. Royall Tyler Esqr. Overseer
Discharg'd Decemr. 10th. 1768

1768 Octo. 18 Received into the House James Birmigham[372]
℘ Order Honble. Royall Tyler Esqr. Overseer &c

20. Received into the House Patrick Hickey
℘ Order Honble. Royall Tyler Esqr.

24. Received into the House on Province Account John Boyd
℘ Order Joseph Jackson, Saml. Pemberton} Esqrs.
Honble. Royall Tyler Esqr. Overseer

Octo.[373] Received into the House Catha. Warwick
℘ Order William White Esqr. Overseer &c

31. Received into the House Sarah Gent
℘ Order John Leverett Esqr. Overseer &c

do. Received into the House a Negro Child Son of Cato a Negro Man of
Governor Bernard[374]
℘ Order Mr. Joseph Waldo Overseer &c.

Novr. 1 Received into the House Fanny Dart a Child
℘ Order Captn. John Bradford Overseer &c

3d. Received into the House Dorcas Ballard & Malcom McCuing a Child
from Wkhouse
℘ Order Captn. John Bradford Overseer &c

1768. Nov. 3d. Received into the House Sarah Varney
℘ Order William White Esqr. Overseer &c

do. Received into the House Thomas Hopper
℘ Order Thomas Tyler Esqr. Overseer &c

12. Received into the House on province Accott. Jacob Smith
℘ Order Joseph Jackson, Saml. Pemberton} Selectmen
Honble. Royall Tyler Esqr. Overseer &c
Deceas'd April 20th. 1769

Discharg'd Margarett Grainger Novr. 5th. 1768

11th. Received into the House Abigl. Branch prov. Charge

19. Received into the House Mary Dumphy
℘ Order Thos. Tyler Esqr. Overseer &c

19th. Discharg'd Richd. Swansbury[375] prov. Charge

24.   Received into the House on prov. Account Saml. Johnson
℘ Order Joseph Jackson, Saml. Pemberton} Esqrs.
Honble. Royall Tyler Esqr. Overseer &c.
deceasd Decemr. 7th. 1768

29.   Received into the House on province Accott. Jerusha Abdelton
℘ Order John Ruddock, Saml. Pemberton} Esqrs.
John Leverett Esqr. Overseer

1768 Nov. 27th.} Discharg'd Robert Low prov. Charge

30   Received into the House Davis Whitman & 3. Children
℘ Order John Leverett Esqr. Overseer &c

Decr. 3d.   Received into the House Mary Gilbert & 2 Children[376]
℘ Order Capt. Saml. Partridge Overseer &c

4   Received into the House John Merryfield
℘ Order John Barrett Esqr. Overseer &c

Novemr. 19th. 1768 Received into the House on prov. Account Jacob Skweller
℘ Order Joseph Jackson, Saml. Pemberton} Esqrs. Selectmen
Thomas Tyler Esqr. Overseer &c

Decr. 16   Received into the House Lewis Merrick & Ruth his Wife
        Also 3. poor Children of Joseph Harleys
℘ Order Willm. White Esqr. Overseer of the poor

17th   Received into the House Lydia Gammons
℘ Order Thomas Tyler Esqr. &c

17th.   Received into the House Eliza. Burges[377] & Child
℘ Order John Gore Esqr. Overseer &c

9th.   Discharg'd Patrick Hickey (10th. Decr.) John Short prov. Charge

27.   Received into the House Eliza. Wharff[378] & Child
℘ Order Mr. Joseph Waldo Overseer &c

Mary Pilsberry[379] came into the House Wednesday May 5 1762 and brought with her Only The Cloaths on her Back, the rest of her things as Household Stuff, Bed & Bedding being in the possession of Benja. Austin Esqr.—Since settled

Mrs. Crawford came into the House February 14th. 1763. and brought with her the following Things or Household Stuff &c.

1. Old pine Table
1. small ditto
1. Bedstead
a Large Trunk contg. Cloathing of sundry sorts, as Sheets Petticoats Coverlids, 3 Gowns old & sundry other Articles
A Small Box full of Rags
a pr. Old Bellows, a Trammell

a pr. Old Tongs, a Feather Bed
A Small Trunk, contg. Shifts Caps & other Wearing Apparell. a pr. Valens, an Old Towell, 3. pr. Stockings, a Muff, a Black Shade, An Old Coat, a Candlestick
An Old Matt & 2 or 3 Old Bottles
Tea Cups &c &c &c

Thomas Eastwick came into the House March 26. 1763. and Brôt with him A Feather Bed, Pillow, Bolster, Two Blankets, And a Chest & Box containing Wearing Apparel. Bedstead left behind at the desire of Mr. Childs who he hired his Room of.

An Account of sundry Goods brought into the Alms House by Mr. George Skinner who came into the House Tuesday April 27th. 1762.

A Feather Bed almost new}
Bolster
2. pillows
2. Blankets
1. Rug
2. pair Sheets
3. pillow Cases
a Sacking Bottom Bedstead
a Close Stool & Pan
a Dutch Looking Glass
a large Quarto Bible & a few other Books
a Silver Pint Porringer
Spoon ditto   a Silver Tea Spoon
a Trunk containing sundry Cloathing vizt. X[380]

A Warming Pan   A Bell Metal Skillet
A Bed Pan   2. pewter plates
A Copper Coffee Pot a Tea Chest (tin)
2. Delph Bowles   & Canisters
A Sugar Canister (Tin)
2. pair Old Shoes—2 Pr. White Gloves
A Curtain (Old) & an Iron Rod—An Old Hand Brush
A small Trunk—An old Wig Box—<*A Walking Cane*>
[…] All Deliverd to […][381] Goldsmith pr. ordr. overseers

a Black back Chair
X A Double Callimanes Night Gown
A Dark Colod. Cloak
A Broad Cloth Do. Light Colour
A Blew Broad Cloth Coat
A Scarlet Serge Jacket
A Black Cloth Jacket
An Old Blew Broad Cloth Coat
A pair Black Velvet Breeches
An old Pair Scarlet Cloth Do.
An old Coat & Jacket
An Old Broad Cloth Great Coat
4. pr. Stockings
a Barcelona Handkerchief
2. Speckled Handkerchiefs
2. Huckabuk Towels   A Tun[…]
4. Shirts   A Tin Lamp
2. Wigs   1 Hatt 2. Cloths Brushes
1. pr. Silver Shoe Buckles
1. pr. Silver Knee Do.
<*1. pr. Gold (odd) Buttons*>   A Worsted Cap
1. Stone Chamber Pot
2. New Caps   A Knife & Fork

Sarah Bailey came into the House Thursday May 6. 1762. and brought the following things—
a Feather Bed
2 Blankets
a Bolster
a pillow
a pair Sheets
2 pillow Cases
a Trunk & Box
contg. sundry Cloathing
2 Chairs
a Joint Stool

1769. Janua. 4th.}[382]   Received into the House on prov. Accott. Patrick Burns
℘ Order John Hancock, Saml. Pemberton} Esqrs. Selectmen
John Leverett Esqr. Overseer &c.

10th.   Received into the House Katerina Baker
℘ Order Capt. Saml. Partridge Overseer &c.

24.   Received into the House Rachel Rule a Child 11. years
℘ Order Capt. Saml. Partridge Overseer &c

25.   Received into the House from Workhouse Sarah Brumett

30   Received into the House on provce. Account Zerviah Smith
℘ Order Joshua Henshaw, Joseph Jackson} Esqrs. Selectmen
Honble. Royall Tyler Esqr. Overseer &c
deceased Octo. 6th. 1769.

Carried to another book

**Register from
12th. Decr. 1768 to 30 Septr. 1788**[383]

1768 Decemr. 12th. Received into the House on Province Account John Dwyer[384]
℘ Order John Hancock, Saml. Pemberton} Selectmen
Consented to by Mr. William Greenleaf Overseer

1769 Jany. 31.   Received into the House on province Account Mary Murray & Child
℘ Order John Hancock, Saml. Pemberton} Selectmen
Consented to by Mr. William Greenleaf Overseer

Feby. 1.   Received into the House John Colson[385]
℘ Order Thomas Tyler Esqr. Overseer

6.   Received into the House on prov. Accott. John Ozard
℘ Order Joseph Jackson, John Hancock} Esqrs. Selectmen
Honble. Royall Tyler Esqr. Overseer &c

16.   Received into the House John Graham a poor Boy
℘ Order Mr. William Whitwell Overseer &c

16.   Received into the House John Lucas a poor Boy
℘ Order John Gore Esqr. Overseer &c

Received into the House Willm. Warner a Boy
℘ Order Mr. Willm. Greenleaf who came with him

18.   Received into the House on prov. Accott. Eliza. Hill
℘ Order Joseph Jackson, John Hancock} Selectmen
Mr. Willm. Whitwell Overseer &c
Discharg'd June 10th. 1769

1769. Mar. 1st.   Received into the House on Prov. Accott. Mary Davison
℘ Order John Hancock, Hendn. Inches} Esqrs. Selectmen
Mr. Wm. Whitwell Overseer &c

1769 Feby. 28.   Received into the House Stephen Stow a poor Boy
℘ Order Honble. Royall Tyler Esqr. Overseer &c

do.   Received into the House Joseph Stanyan
℘ Order Mr. Willm. Whitwell Overseer &c

Mar. 7.   Received into the House Martha Davidson
℘ Order William White Esqr. Overseer

7.   Received into the House Jane Wilson & Child on province Accott.[386]
℘ Order Joseph Jackson, Saml. Pemberton} Esqrs. Selectmen
Honble. Royall Tyler Esqr. Overseer &c

10.   Received into the House Robert McNear[387]
℘ Order Willm. White Esqr. Overseer &c

13.   Received into the House Salome Mann a poor sick Woman
℘ Order Willm. White Esqr. Overseer &c

13.   Received into the House Jesse Tilson[388]
℘ Order Hon Royall Tyler Esqr. Overseer &c

13.   Discharg'd Patrick Burns prov Charge

14.   Received into the House Hannah Harris (Joanna)[389]
℘ Order John Leverett Esqr. Overseer &c

20.   Received into the House Margtt. Grainger
℘ Order Hon. Royall Tyler Esqr. Overseer &c
went away April 1st. followg.

23d.   Received into the House on prov. Accott. James Colley
℘ Order Joseph Jackson   } Selectmen
Hon. Royall Tyler Esqr. Overseer &c
Went away April 3d. 1769.

                       Discharg'd John Horden prov Charge April 1st. 1769.

1769 March 23d.   Received into the House on prov. Accott. John Connell[390]
℘ Order Joseph Jackson   } Selectmen
Honble. Royall Tyler Esqr. Overseer &c

April 9   Received into the House Widow Hunter
℘ Order Mr. Joseph Waldo Overseer &c

17.   Received into the House Ananias Douglass
℘ Order Mr. William Whitwell Overseer &c

19.   Received into the House Ann Middleton
℘ Order Mr. William Whitwell Overseer &c

20   Received into the House Ann More a sick Woman
℘ Order Willm. White Esqr. Overseer &c

24.   Received into the House Margarett Cahart
℘ Order John Barrett Esqr. Overseer &c

                       Discharg'd Thos. Hubbard—Discharg'd Fanny Dart April 19th.
                       Lewis Merrick[391]—Kate Warwick—Eliza. Skinner April 17th.
                       Jacob Sweler[392](Prov. Charge) April 12th.—John Ozard Prov
                       Charge April 24th.
April 25th.   Jesse Tilson went to Board with John Spear of Stoughton at 50/ OT. a week for one
Month agreed to by Honble. Royall Tyler Esqr.

May 1st.   Discharg'd Willm. Dunlee (prov. Charge)
5.   Discharg'd Abigl. Branch (prov. Charge) (6th.) Jas. Hewes & Jon. Conner
13.   Discharg'd John Boyd (prov Charge) (13th.) Mary Murray & Child

15.   Received into the House Mary Clark
℘ Order Mr. Willm. Whitwell Overseer &c

16.   Received into the House Margtt. Galloway[393]
℘ Order John Ruddock, Saml. Pemberton} Esqrs. Selectmen
Mr. Willm. Greenleaf Overseer &c

1769. May 23.   Received into the House Abigail Hale
℘ Order Hon. Royall Tyler Esqr. Overseer

                       Received into the House on province Account March 17th.[394] 1769th.
Oliver Grainger Son of Margtt. Grainger
℘ Order John Ruddock, Saml. Pemberton} Esqrs. Selectmen
Mr. William Greenleaf Overseer &c

June 7.   Received into the House Robert Price an infirm Man
℘ Order Mr. Willm. Whitwell Overseer of the Poor
discharg'd

June 11th.   Discharg'd John Penrow Prov. Charge
                       Discharg'd Ann Middleton, Daniel North, Poll Chadwell
June 24th.   Margtt. Galloway (Prov. Charge)   June 20th. Eliza. Utinocks (Prov)
July 2d.   Jane Wilson (Prov. Charge) & Child

June 29.   Received into the House on Prov. Account Eleanor Stokes
℘ Order Joseph Jackson, Henderson Inches} Selectmen
John Leverett Esqr. Overseer &c
went away Octo. 1st. 1769—& returnd again soon

July 5th.   Received into the House Mary Cherry a Child aged 5 yrs. April 8
1769}[395]
℘ Order Capt. Saml. Partridge Overseer &c

13.   Received into the House Ann Warden & Child
℘ Order John Barrett Esqr. Overseer &c

do.   Received into the House Hannah White a poor Orphan
℘ Order William White Esqr. Overseer &c

17.   Received into the House Mary Hennesey
℘ Order Mr. Benja. Dolbeare Overseer &c

19.   Received into the House Patrick Burk sick[396]
℘ Order Honble. Royall Tyler Esqr. Overseer &c

1769. July 20.   Received into the House on Province Account Katha. Legg
℘ Order John Hancock Esqr., Mr. Jona. Mason} Selectmen
Mr. Willm. Whitwell Overseer of the Poor
<went away Octo. […]>

25.   Received into the House Thomas Hubbard
℘ Order John Barrett Esqr. Overseer &c

1769. July 12th.   Jerusha Abdellor[397] (prov Charge) Jumpt Fence
                       Joanna Dukes & John Bradley jumpt Fence

31.　　　　　　　Received into the House William Denley a sick Man on province
Account
℘ Order Joseph Jackson Esq, Jona. Mason} Selectmen
Mr. Benja. Dolbeare Overseer &c

[do.]³⁹⁸　　　　　Received into the House on Prov. Account Nichos. Altenton
℘ Order Joseph Jackson, Jona. Mason} Slectmen
John Leverett Esqr. Overseer &c　　　Order dated April 29th. 1769
Deceased March 13th. 1770.

August 2d.　　　　Received into the House Sarah Gent³⁹⁹
℘ Order Mr. Willm. Whitwell Overseer &c

3d.　　　　　　　Received into the House on Province Accott. Benja. Price
℘ Order Joseph Jackson, Jona. Mason} Selectmen
Thos. Tyler Esqr. Overseer of the poor &c

4.　　　　　　　Received into the House Jane Stow
℘ Order Capt. Saml. Partridge Overseer &c

1769. August 7th.}　Received into the House Lydia Williams
℘ Order Mr. William Whitwell Overseer &c

11.　　　　　　　Received into the House Tabitha Akley & Child from Workhouse⁴⁰⁰
℘ Order

23.　　　　　　　Received into the House Mary Beal
℘ Order Mr. Willm. Greenleaf Overseer &c

24.　　　　　　　Received into the House Mary Ingersol aged 23 Years June 1769
℘ Order Mr. Benja. Dolbeare Overseer &c

26.　　　　　　　Received into the House Elizabeth a Child of Margtt. Caveneau's⁴⁰¹
℘ Order Mr. Willm. Greenleaf Overseer &c

25th.　　　　　　Received into the House on Province Accott. Eliza. Smith
℘ Order Joseph Jackson Esqr., Mr. Jona. Mason} Selectmen
Mr. Willm. Greenleaf Overseer &c

28.　　　　　　　Received into the House on Province Accott. William Orgah
℘ Order Joseph Jackson, Saml. Pemberton} Esqrs. Selectmen
Thos. Tyler Esqr. Overseer &c
went away Nov. 28th. 1769.

Septr. 2.　　　　Received into the House Mary Wyatt
℘ Order Mr. William Whitwell Overseer &c

[do.][402]   Received into the House James Dawson & Mary his Wife[403]
℘ Order Mr. Willm. Whitwell Overseer &c

7.   Received into the House a poor Child named   Richardson
℘ Order John Gore Esqr. Overseer &c

7th.   Received into the House on province Accott. John Penrow[404]
℘ Order Joseph Jackson, John Hancock} Esqrs. Selectmen
Honble. Royall Tyler Esqr. Overseer &c

       Abigl. Branch Septr. 1st. 1769. from the Country

1769. Septr. 8.   Received into the House Ann Hinds
℘ Order Mr. Willm. Whitwell Overseer &c

14   Received into the House Jeremy[405] Wyatt
℘ Order John Gore Esqr. Overseer &c
Discharg'd & gone to his Master

15.   Received into the House on prov. Accott. John <*Colon*> Colfar
℘ Order   Saml. Pemberton} Selectmen
Consented to Willm. Greenleaf Overseer &c
went away March 2d. 1770.

16.   Received into the House Ann Gutteridge[406] a poor Girl
℘ Order William White Esqr. Overseer &c

       Discharg'd Jonas Webber—Jane Stow—Mary Kinge[407]
Septemr. 18th. Eliza. Smith (Prov. Charge) Ruth Merrick

23.   Received into the House on province Accott. Mary Kinsly & Child
℘ Order Joshua Henshaw, Joseph Jackson} Esqrs. Selectmen
Mr. Benja. Dolbeare Overseer &c
went away Octo. 23d. 1769.

27.   Received into the House Hannah Carter a young Woman
℘ Order John Gore Esqr. Overseer &c

27.   Received into the House on prov. Accott. John Burch
℘ Order Joshua Henshaw, Jona. Mason} Selectmen
Capt. Saml. Partridge Overseer &c
deceased Octor. 6th. 1769.

28.   Received into the House on prov. Accott. Alexr. Thompson[408]
℘ Order Joshua Henshaw, John Ruddock} Esqrs. Selectmen
Mr. Willm. Greenleaf Overseer &c
{went away 13th. Decemr. & returned the 23d. Decemr. 1769 gone 10. days}

1769. Octo. 7th.　　Received into the House a Child of Eliza. Cowleys
℘ Order Thomas Tyler Esqr. Overseer &c

11.　　　　　　Received into the House John　　　　a poor Child
℘ Order John Barrett Esqr. Overseer &c

11.　　　　　　Received into the House James Stevenson
℘ Order Mr. Joseph Waldo Overseer &c

17.　　　　　　Received into the House Jannet Seaward
℘ Order Mr. Benja. Dolbeare Overseer &c

17.　　　　　　Received into the House Mary Crosby[409]
℘ Order Honble. Royall Tyler Esqr. Overseer &c

26. & 27.　　　Received into the House from Workhouse Katha. Darby & John Shaw
℘ Order Mr. William Whitwell Overseer &c

Novr. 1.　　　Received into the House Mary Lasenby[410]
℘ Order Honble. Royall Tyler Esqr. Overseer &c

4.　　　　　　Received into the House Margarett Burnet[411]
℘ Order Mr. Willm. Greenleaf Overseer &c

6.　　　　　　Received into the House Margarett Rhoades[412]
℘ Order Willm. White Esqr. Overseer &c

Discharg'd Eliza. Smallage

10.　　　　　　Received into the House Abigail Hall
℘ Order Mr. Saml. Whitwell Overseer &c

13.　　　　　　Received into the House Jonas Webber
℘ Order Honble. Royall Tyler Esqr. Overseer &c

20.　　　　　　Received into the House Joseph Colburn—(Coburn)
℘ Order Mr. Joseph Waldo Overseer &c

21.　　　　　　Received into the House John Spencer (on province Charge)
℘ Order Mr. Joseph Waldo Overseer &c

22.　　　　　　Dischargd Solomon Harley a Child

1769. Nov. 23d.　　Received into the House on province Account David Hally[413] a poor
sick Man
℘ Order Joseph Jackson, Jona. Mason} Esqr. Selectmen
Honble. Royall Tyler Esqr. Overseer

went away March 9th. 1770.

28.　　　　　　Received into the House Benja. Chubb
℘ Order John Leverett Esqr. Overseer

28.　　　　　　Received into the House on Province Accott. James Brown
℘ Order Jona. Mason, Saml. Pemberton} Selectmen
Mr. Willm. Whitwell Overseer &c
Discharg'd Janua. 15th. 1770.

29.　　　　　　Received into the House on province Account Ann Moree
℘ Order Saml. Pemberton, Jona. Mason} Esqr. Selectmen
Thos. Tyler Esqr. Overseer &c

29.　　　　　　Received into the House on prov. Accott. Elizabeth Smith
℘ Order Saml. Pemberton, Jona. Mason} Selectmen
Mr. Willm. Greenleaf Overseer &c
Discharg'd Janua. 25th.[414] 1770.

30.　　　　　　Received into the House on prov. Accott. Richard Hazard
℘ Order Henderson Inches, Jona. Mason} Selectmen
Mr. Saml. Whitwell Overseer &c

Decr 4.　　　　Received into the House Susanna Downing
℘ Order John Gore Esqr. Overseer &c

4.[415]　　　　Received into the House Mary Chadwell
℘ Order Hon. Royall Tyler Esqr.

1769　　　　　Received into the House Daniel Thompson Novr. 29th.
℘ Order John Leverett Esqr. Overseer &c (Province Charge)
Dyed Decemr. 31st. 1770

Decemr. 13th.　　Received into the House Sarah Mills
℘ Order Mr. Saml. Whitwell Overseer
discharged 15th. day Decem[416]

14.　　　　　　Received into the House on prov. Accott. John Linaker
℘ Order Saml. Pemberton Esqr., Mr. Jona. Mason} Selectmen
Thos. Tyler Esqr. Overseer &c

16.　　　　　　Received into the House Martha Davidson
℘ Order Willm. White Esqr. Overseer &c

19.　　　　　　Received into the House Elizabeth Whitaker[417]
℘ Order Thomas Tyler Esqr. Overseer &c

21.   Received into the House Dorothy Lewis Sick
℘ Order Honble. Royall Tyler Esqr. Overseer &c

21.   Discharg'd Ann Warren

23.   Received into the House on prov. Accott. George Harper
℘ Order Joseph Jackson Esqr., Mr. Jona. Mason} Selectmen
Mr. Saml. Whitwell Overseer &c
Deceas'd Decemr. 28th. 1769.

23.   Received into the House on prov. Accott. Alexr. Thompson
℘ Order Joseph Jackson Esqr., Mr. Jona. Mason} Selectmen
Consented to by Mr. Saml. Whitwell Overseer &c

29.   Received into the House William Kelley
℘ Order Mr. Saml. Whitwell Overseer &c

1769. Decr. 30.   Received into the House 2 Children of James Morris'
℘ Order Mr. Willm. Greenleaf Overseer &c

30.   Received into the House on province Accott. George Peacock
℘ Order Joseph Jackson, John Hancock} Esqrs. Selectmen
Thos. Tyler Esqr. Overseer &c
Discharg'd. Feby. 5th. 1770

1770. Janua. 1.   Received into the House Priscilla Haden
℘ Order Thos. Tyler Esqr. Overseer &c

6.   Received into the House Abigl. Blackman
℘ Order John Leverett Esqr. Overseer &c

do.   Received into the House John Sampson sick
℘ Order Mr. Benja. Dolbeare Overseer &c

                  Received into the House on province Account the followg. persons
James Birmingham[418] Septr. 1st. 1769, Mary Beacham Octo. 3d. 1769, Mary Gorman Octo.
20th. 1769}
℘ Order Saml. Pemberton Esqr., Mr. Jona. Mason} Selectmen
John Leverett Esqr. Overseer &c

Jany. 9.   Received into the House from Workhouse Benja. Stone[419]—Ann
Stone— <*John Malada*>—Susanna Newcomb[420]—Eliza. Raven—Sarah Webb—Mary
Watts—
Phebe Randall—Eliza. Hewey—Sarah Richardson—Mary Gorman (prov. Charge)[421]
℘ Order John Barrett Esqr. in the Name of the Overseers

15th.   Received into the House John Waddel & Wife[422]

℘ Order Mr. Saml. Whitwell Overseer &c

1770. Janua. 17.   Received into the House on province Account Isabella Brown[423]
℘ Order Joseph Jackson, Saml. Pemberton} Esqrs. Selectmen
Mr. Saml. Whhitwell Oversee &c

19th.   Received into the House on province Account John Dolder
℘ Order Joseph Jackson Esqr., Mr. Jona. Mason} Selectmen
Thomas Tyler Esqr. Overseer &c

19.   Received into the House Richard Griffith[424]
℘ Order John Leverett Esqr. Overseer &c

24.   Received into the House Rebecca Pimm[425]
℘ Order Mr. William Whitwell Overseer &c

25.   Received into the House on province Accott. George Carpenter
℘ Order Joshua Henshaw Esqr., Mr. Jona. Mason} Selectmen
Honble. Royall Tyler Esqr. Overseer &c

Feby. 3.   Received into the House Dorcas Osborn & her Child
℘ Order Mr. Benja. Dolbeare Overseer &c

3d.   Received into the House Thomas Butler
℘ Order Mr. Saml. Whitwell Overseer &c

[do.][426]   Received into the House Priscilla Rinnigher[427] on prov. Accott.
℘ Order Joseph Jackson Esqr., Mr. Jona. Mason} Selectmen
Thos. Tyler Esqr. Overseer &c   NB. Order dated Decemr. 25th. 1769

1770 Feby. 7th.   Received into the House Richd. Morgan,[428] Robt. McNear[429]
℘ Order Mr. Willm. Whitwell Overseer &c

10.   Received into the House Thomson[430] Charlton
℘ Order Mr. Willm. Greenleaf Overseer &c

10th.   Received into the House on prov. Accott. Katharine Cuff & Child &
Jane Tolman & Child[431]
℘ Order Joseph Jackson Esqr., Mr. Jona. Mason} Selectmen
Mr. Saml. Whitwell Overseer &c

21.   Received into the House Mary Lintey & Child[432]
℘ Order John Gore Esqr. Overseer &c

Mar. 5.   Received into the House Susanna Jordans Daughter[433]
℘ Order Mr. Joseph Waldo Overseer &c

do.   Received into the House John Whittemore
℘ Order Hon. Royall Tyler Esqr. Overseer &c

8.   Received into the House Polly Dunnis an Infant
℘ Order Mr. Joseph Waldo Overseer &c

do.   Received into the House Ann Stone (from Work house)
℘ Order John Gore Esqr. Overseer &c

10.   Received into the House Sarah Mills sick Woman[434]
℘ Order John Leverett Esqr. Overseer &c

17.   Received into the House Mary Sanders
℘ Order Capt. Saml. Partridge Overseer &c

23.   Received into the House 3 Children of Richd. Fothergill
℘ Order Mr. William Greenleaf Overseer &c

29.   Received into the House on prov. Accott. David Hally (Haley)
℘ Order Joseph Jackson Esqr.   } Selectmen
Hon. Royall Tyler Esqr.

1770. March. Discharg'd Ann Morce[435] (March 19th.) Eleanor Stokes (24th.) Katha.
Cuff & Jane Tolman & 2 Children (24th.)—province Charges.

April 4.   Received into the House Samuel Raymond a Child[436]
℘ Order Capt. Saml. Partridge Overseer &c
to Augt. 4. 1771. 69 weeks 2 days @ 5/

9.   Received into the House Andrew Dunn a Boy
℘ Order Hon. Royall Tyler Esqr. Overseer &c

12.   Received into the House Eliza. Harris
℘ Order Thos. Tyler Esqr. Overseer &c

do.   Received into the House a Child named Eliza. Gray
℘ Order Thos. Tyler Esqr. Overseer &c

18.   Received into the House (from the Work House) Prudence Bennet &
Margarett Davis
℘ Order Mr. Benja. Dolbeare Overseer &c

18th.   Received into the House on province Account Dorothy Williams &
Child
℘ Order Saml. Pemberton Esqr., Mr. Jona. Mason} Selectmen
Mr. Willm. Greenleaf Overseer

19. Received into the House Meheta. Wells—a sick Woman
℘ Order Mr. Saml. Whitwell Overseer &c.

do. Received into the House Jane Coffin
℘ Order John Barrett Esqr. Overseer &c

  Discharg'd (Apl. 17th. 1770) Geo. Carpenter prov. Charge—Apl. 18th.
Do.
18th. David Hally (prov)—Patrick Burk jumpt the Fence
Apl. 25th. Katha. Legg (prov) jumpt the Fence—Joseph Coburn—Mary Gilbert &
Child—Martha Davidson—Dinah Allen

27. Received into the House Martha Clough Sick
℘ Order John Barrett Esqr. Overseer &c

Apl. 30. Discharg'd Richard Hazard (prov Charge)

1770. Apl. 21st. Received into the House Sarah Blewet a poor Sick Woman
℘ Order Mr. Benja. Dolbeare Overseer &c

May 1st. Received into the House Jonathan Silsbury a Boy
℘ Order Mr. Benja. Dolbeare Overseer &c

[do.][437] Received into the House John Williams (prov. Charge)
℘ Order Hon. Royall Tyler Esqr. Overseer &c   order dated April 26. 1770.

2. Received into the House Matthew Hopkins' Wife (sick)
℘ Order Mr. William Greenleaf Overseer &c

2d. Received into the House 2. Boys the Children of Richard & Susan
Smith
℘ Order Joseph Jackson, Saml. Pemberton} Esqrs. Selectmen
Consented to Mr. Willm. Greenleaf Overseer &c

4. Received into the House an Infant Child named
℘ Order Mr. Willm. Greenleaf Overseer &c

6. Received into the House Sarah Hunt Shelden & Child[438]
℘ Order Mr. Benja. Dolbeare Overseer &c

8. Received into the House a Daughter of James McCune
℘ Order Mr. Joseph Waldo Overseer &c

do. Received into the House Eliza. Smallage a widow Woman[439]
℘ Order John Gore Esqr. Overseer &c

9.   Received into the House on province Accott. George Gardner
℘ Order Joshua Henshaw, Joseph Jackson} Esqrs. Selectmen
John Leverett Esqr. Overseer &c

11.   Received into the House from Workhouse Holmes Simpson[440]
℘ Order Mr. Joseph Waldo Overseer &c

16.   Received into the House Mary Rhoads[441] & 2 Children
℘ Order Mr. Saml. Whitwell Overseer &c

1770. May 16.   Received into the House Christopher Atkinson—Lame Man
℘ Order Mr. Saml. Whitwell Overseer &c

                     Discharg'd John Bernard (May 11th. 1770).   John Linaker—Willm.
Dunlee[442]—Alexr. Thompson (Prov Charges May 15th. 1770) John Spencer (prov. May
18th.)   Mary Gorman (Prov 21st. May) <Dorothy Williams> & Mary Beacham (prov.
May 23d.)   Edward Richardson & Wife—polly Watts a Child—Mary Watts jumpt
Fence—Meheta. Wells—Margarett Rhodes—Margarett Burnet & Child—Jannet Seaward—
Malcom McCune[443] a Boy—Dorcas Osborn & Child (May 28th.)

26.   Received into the House on prov. Accott. Mary Joyce <Draps> & Child
℘ Order Joseph Jackson Esqr., Mr. Jona. Mason} Selectmen
John Gore Esqr. Overseer
dischargd July 26th. 1770.

June 2d.   Received into the House Mary Brown distracted Woman sent to
Wkhouse.[444]
℘ Order Capt. Saml. Partridge Overseer &c

5.   Received into the House Mary Davis[445] a poor Blind Woman
℘ Order Mr. Willm. Whitwell Overseer &c

11.   Received into the House Widow Ann Christy[446]
℘ Order Honble. Royall Tyler Esqr. Overseer &c

8.   Received into the House on prov. Account Margarett Jones
℘ Order Joseph Jackson Esqr., Mr. Jona. Mason} Selectmen
Mr. William Greenleaf Overseer &c
Discharged Octor. 4th. 1770

13.   Received into the House on prov. Accott. Elisha Godfrey a sick Man[447]
℘ Order Joseph Jackson Esqr., Mr. Jona. Mason} Selectmen
Mr. Samuel Whitwell Overseer &c

                     <Dischar> Benja. Chubb jumpt Fence 12th. June
[May 1770][448]   Discharg'd Martha Clough

1770. June 15.   Received into the House Lilly Snow Wife of Henry Snow (Lydia)
℘ Order John Gore Esqr. Overseer &c

22.   Received into the House John McDaniel[449]
℘ Order Mr. Joseph Waldo Overseer &c

23.   Received into the House Lydia Rhoads[450]
℘ Order John Leverett Esqr. Overseer &c

23.   Received into the House Gammon Stevens[451]
℘ Order Mr. Benjamin Dolbeare Overseer &c

July 2d.   Received into the House Martha Davidson
℘ Order Honble. Royall Tyler Esqr. Overseer &c

5.   Received into the House Mary Procter sick from Wkhouse[452]
℘ Order Hon. Royall Tyler Esqr. Overseer

do.   Received into the House David Davis a poor Child
℘ Order Willm. White Esqr. Overseer &c

7.   Received into the House Eunice Veacham from Wkhouse[453]
℘ Order Hon. Royall Tyler Esqr.

9.   Received into the House Mary Bowman[454]
℘ Order John Leverett Esqr. Overseer &c

12.   Received into House Sarah Richardson[455]
℘ Order Mr. Joseph Waldo Overseer &c

July 9th.   Discharg'd James Martin (prov. Charge)—July 13th. John Williams prov.
20.   priscilla Rinniger (prov Charge)—Eliza. Wharff & Child
30th.   John Fabreo & Wife (prov)   Nichs. press & Wife 30th. (prov)
                  Hannah Carter, Kata. Darby

July 23d.   Received into the House Mary Webb Aged 18. yrs.[456]
℘ Order Honble. Royall Tyler Esqr. Overseer

1770. July 23d.   Received into the House Priscilla Ransford[457]
℘ Order Hon. Royall Tyler Esqr.   Mr. Waldo not in Town

26.   Received into the House Elizabeth Martin} jumpt Fence Octo. 2d.
1770}
℘ Order Mr. Saml. Whitwell Overseer &c

28.   Received into the House on Province Accott. George Carrell
℘ Order Joseph Jackson Esqr., Jona. Mason} Selectmen
Hon. Royall Tyler Esqr.

Augt. 1.　　　　Received into the House Thomas Lizwell a Boy aged abt. 11 yrs.
℘ Order Saml. Whitwell Overseer &c
went to Mr. Tylers.

　　　　　　　　Received into the House Elias Bowen　　order dated July 30th.
℘ Order Mr. Saml. Abbot Overseer

6.　　　　　　Received into the House on prov. Account Hannah Simpson
℘ Order Joseph Jackson, John Ruddock} Esqrs. Selectmen
Hon. Royall Tyler Esqr. Overseer &c

5.　　　　　　Received into the House on province Account James Batar
℘ Order Joseph Jackson Esqr., Jona. Mason} Selectmen
Mr. Willm. Greenleaf Overseer &c

8.　　　　　　Received into the House on prov. Accott. 2. Childn. Jack & Edwd. Dunn
℘ Order John Hancock, Saml. Pemberton} Esqrs. Selectmen
John Gore Esqr. Overseer &c

8.　　　　　　Received into the House on prov. Accott. Mary McCarthy
℘ Order John Hancock Esqr., Mr. Hendn. Inches} Selectmen
Mr. Willm. Greenleaf Overseer &c

1770. Augt. 1.　　Discharg'd Gammon Stevens, Christo. Atkinson, Mary Rhodes, Susanna
Downing—to the Work house
6.　　　　　　John Dolder (prov Charge)

6.　　　　　　Received into the House on province Account Mary Walker
℘ Order Joseph Jackson, Saml. Pemberton} Esqrs. Selectmen
Mr. Saml. Whitwell Overseer &c　　NB. Order dated July 26. 1770

6.　　　　　　Received into the House Henry Flemings a Boy
℘ Order Mr. Saml. Abbott Overseer &c

21.　　　　　　Received into the House Sarah Curtis
℘ Order John Leverett Esqr. Overseer &c

28.　　　　　　Received into the House Elizabeth Mears & Child
℘ Order John Barrett Esqr. Overseer &c

29.　　　　　　Received into the House Sarah Lewis a Child
℘ Order Mr. William Whitwell Overseer &c

30.　　　　　　Received into the House Willm. Akley a Child
℘ Order Capt. Saml. Partridge Overseer &c

do.   Received into the House John Gilbert a Child
℘ Order Mr. Willm. Greenleaf Overseer &c

Septr. 3.   Received into the House on prov. Accott. John Fabree & Wife[458]
℘ Order Joseph Jackson Esqr., Mr. Jona. Mason} Selectmen
Mr. Joseph Waldo Overseer &c

3.   Received into the House on prov. Accott. a Child named George Parbis[459]
Son to John Parbis a Grenadier in the 14th. Regmt.
℘ Order Saml. Pemberton Esqr., Mr. Jona. Mason} Selectmen
Mr. Willm. Greenleaf Overseer &c

1770. Septr. 5th.   Received into the House on province Account Mary Gorman[460]
℘ Order Saml. Pemberton Esqr., Mr. Jona. Mason} Selectmen
John Leverett Esqr. Overseer &c

9.   Received into the House Ann Moloy
℘ Order Capn. Saml. Partridge Overseer &c

10.   Received into the House on province Account George Carpenter
℘ Order Joseph Jackson Esqr., Mr. Jona. Mason} Selectmen
Mr. Saml. Whitwell Overseer &c

12.   Received into the House Margarett Burnet & her Child
℘ Order Mr. Benja. Dolbeare Overseer &c

17.   Received into the House Robert Williams
℘ Order Mr. Samuel Whitwell Overseer &c

17.   Received into the House Tabitha Akley[461] <& Child>
℘ Order Hon. Royall Tyler Esqr. Overseer &c

22d.   Received into the House Margarett Burton & Hannah[462] Williams 2.
Childn.
℘ Order Mr. William Whitwell Overseer &c

22d.   Received into the House on province Account Francis McDaniel
℘ Order Saml. Pemberton Esqr., Mr. Jona. Mason} Selectmen
Mr. Willm. Greenleaf Overseer &c

24.   Received into the House on province Account Michael Sommers
℘ Order Joseph Jackson, Saml. Pemberton} Esqrs. Selectmen
Hon. Royall Tyler Esqr. Overseer &c

26.   Received into the House from Workhouse Kata. Sullivan (prov Charge)[463]
℘ Order Mr. Willm. Whitwell Overseer &c

22d.   Discharg'd George Gardner (prov)   Mary McCarthy (prov) 26th. Septr.
1770

Elias Bowen

1770. Septr. 28.   Received into the House Benjamin Chubb
℘ Order Mr. Joseph Waldo Overseer &c

Octor. 2d.   Received into the House Josiah Stone
℘ Order John Leverett Esqr. Overseer &c

4th.   Received into the House on province Account Mary Perrin
℘ Order Saml. Pemberton Esqr., Mr. Jona. Mason} Selectmen
John Leverett Esqr. Overseer

5.   Received into the House Jonas Webber
℘ Order John Leverett Esqr. Overseer &c

12.   Received into the House Doctr. Patrick Larey[464] & Eliza. Sloper a Child
℘ Order Mr. William Greenleaf Overseer &c

13.   Received into the House Jannett Sayward
℘ Order John Leverett Esqr. Overseer &c

16.   Received into the House (from Work house) Mary Dunn[465]
℘ Order Mr. William Greenleaf Overseer &c

19.   Received into the House a poor Child from Mr. Emmons in Mr.
Dolbeares Ward
℘ Order Honble. Royall Tyler Esqr. Overseer &c

30.   Discharg'd. Mary Saunders & Child—gone to Jolley Allens
Nov. 2.   Hannah Simpson (prov. Charge) Jumpt Fence

Octo. 31   Received into the House Nathan Shute[466]
℘ Order John Barrett Esqr. Overseer &c

Octo. 1st.   Thoms. Charlton & Eliza. Martin jumpt Fence

31.   Discharg'd Benja. Price province Charge

Novr. 7.   Received into the House on province Accott. John McGee[467]
℘ Order Joseph Jackson, Saml. Pemberton} Esqrs. Selectmen
Mr. Willm. Greenleaf Overseer &c

Novr. 22d.   Discharg'd Josiah Stone

1770. Novr. 8th.   Received into the House on prov. Accott. a Child named Matthews[468]
℘ Order Joseph Jackson, Saml. Pemberton} Esqrs. Selectmen
Mr. Willm. Greenleaf Overseer &c
Deceased Novr. 11th. 1770. Funeral Charges

10th.   Received into the House on province Accott. Benja. Price
℘ Order John Hancock, Saml. Pemberton} Esqrs. Selectmen
Mr. Saml. Whitwell Overseer &c

                     Received into the House on province Accott. Ann King[469]
℘ Order Joseph Jackson Esqr., Mr. Jona. Mason} Selectmen   order dated Octor. 25th.
1770

17.   Received into the House John Ransted & 2 Children
℘ Order Mr. Saml. Whitwell Overseer &c

24.   Received into the House on province Accott. James Constant
℘ Order Joseph Jackson Esqr., Mr. Jona. Mason} Selectmen
Mr. Willm. Greenleaf Overseer &c
discharg'd May 20. 1771

26.   Received into the House Tabitha Akley
℘ Order Mr. Joseph Waldo Overseer &c

27.   Received into the House   Baldridge & her Child from Workho.[470]
℘ Order Mr. Saml. Whitwell Overseer &c

28.   Received into the House on prov. Account Edward Cane[471]
℘ Order John Hancock Esqr., Mr. Jona. Mason} Selectmen
Mr. Willm. Whitwell Overseer &c

30th.   Received into the House Eliza. Woods
℘ Order Mr. Saml. Whitwell Overseer &c

                     Discharg'd Eliza. Harris

1770 Decr.   Received into the House Nicholas Mangent a Boy 11 years Old
℘ Order Mr. Willm. Greenleaf Overseer

Decr. 15.   Discharg'd Sarah Hunt Shelden & Child—(17th.) James Batar (proṽ)—
Eliza. Boston to Wkhouse—priscilla Noden—(25th.) Geo. Carpenter (prov)

22.   Received into the House from Workhouse Christo. Atkinson[472]
℘ Order Mr. Willm. Whitwell Overseer &c

22.   Received into the House Ann Warren from Mr. Tylers[473]
℘ Order Honble. Royall Tyler Esqr. Overseer &c

22.   Received into the House Abigail Clark[474]
℘ Order John Barrett Esqr.

25.   Received into the House on province Accott. James Kilpatrick distracted
℘ Order Joseph Jackson Esqr., Mr. Jona. Mason} Selectmen
Mr. Saml. Whitwell Overseer &c

27.   Received into the House on Provce. Accott. Paul Briant (Hugh)
℘ Order John Hancock, Saml. Pemberton} Esqrs. Selectmen
Mr. Willm. Greenleaf Overseer &c

Decemr. 22d. 1770   Province of the Massa. Bay Dr. To Burying Lawrence
Clemmens   £
℘ Order Joseph Jackson Esqr. one of the Selectmen
Mr. Willm. Greenleaf Overseer

Decr. 31   Received into the House on prov. Accott. David DeArtey
℘ Order Joseph Jackson Esqr., Mr. Jona. Mason} Selectmen
Mr. Willm. Greenleaf Overseer

1771. Janua. 7   Discharg'd Ann Warren
8.   Dorothy Williams & Mary Walker (prov Charges)
9.   George Carell (prov Charge)   (29th.) James Kilpatrick (prov Charge)

1771. Jany. 4. }   Received into the House Dorothy Lewis[475]
℘ Order Hon. Royall Tyler Esqr. Overseer &c

5.   Received into the House Timothy Foster a poor Child 5 years old
Octo. 6. 1770.}
℘ Order Hon. Royall Tyler Esqr. Overseer &c

7.   Received into the House on prov. Account Willm. More & Wife
℘ Order Joseph Jackson Esqr., Mr. Jona. Mason} Selectmen
Mr. Saml. Abbot Overseer &c

10.   Received into the House Lewis Miricks Wife[476]
℘ Order John Gore Esqr. Overseer &c

21.   Received into the House from Workho. Letitia Wesson[477]
℘ Order John Leverett Esqr. Overseer &c

28.   Received into the House from Workho. Mary Brown[478]
℘ Order Capt. Saml. Partridge Overseer &c

29.   Received into the House Esther Burgoin[479]
℘ Order Joseph Jackson Esqr. Selectman
Mr. William Greenleaf Overseer &c

30.   Received into the House on province Accott. Mary Thompson & Child[480]
℘ Order Joseph Jackson, John Hancock} Esqrs. Selectmen
Mr. Willm. Greenleaf Overseer &c

<Feby. 7   *Nicholas Mangent Discharged Bound out*>

Jany. 30   Received into the House on prov. Accott. Robert Patterson
℘ Order John Hancock Esqr., Mr. Jona. Mason} Selectmen
Hon. Royall Tyler Esqr. Overseer

1771. Feby. 9.   Received into the House Margarett Herne a poor Child[481]
℘ Order Mr. Willm. Greenleaf Overseer &c

11.   Received into the House from Wkhouse Christian Isbester
℘ Order Mr. Joseph Waldo Overseer &c

13.   Received into the House Edward Richardson
℘ Order John Gore Esqr. Overseer &c

13.   Received into the House Saml. Prince aged. 5 years.
℘ Order Capt. Saml. Partridge Overseer &c

15.   Received into the House on prov. Charge Alice Osgood[482]
℘ Order Joseph Jackson Esqr., Mr. Jona. Mason} Selectmen
Mr. Willm. Greenleaf Overseer &c

16.   Received into the House Sarah Hunt & Child[483]
℘ Order Mr. Saml. Abbot Overseer &c

7th.   Discharg'd Tabitha Akley to Workhouse—Edwd. Richardson
12.   Discharg'd David DeArty (prov. Charge)   (25th.) Willm. Baldridges
Wife & Child

                      Received into the House Margarett Cunningham[484] Order dated Feby.
7th. 1771
℘ Order John Gore Esqr. Overseer &c

21.   Received into the House Mary Hemingway[485] & 2. Children
℘ Order Mr. Saml. Abbot Overseer &c

22.   Received into the House on prov. Accott. Hector McLean[486]
℘ Order Joseph Jackson Esqr., Mr. Jona. Mason} Selectmen
Mr. Wiliam Greenleaf Overseer &c

1771. Mar 1.   Received into the House   a free Negro
℘ Order Hon. Royall Tyler Esqr. Overseer &c

2.   Received into the House on prov. Accott. Lawrence Dyel[487]
℘ Order Joseph Jackson Esqr., Mr. Jona. Mason} Selectmen
Hon. Royall Tyler Esqr. Overseer &c

5.   Received into the House on prov. Accott. James Hydes[488]
℘ Order John Ruddock, John Hancock} Esqrs. Selectmen
Mr. Willm. Greenleaf Overseer &c

20.   Received into the House from Workhouse Lydia Sloper
℘ Order Capt. Saml. Partridge Overseer &c

22.   Received into the House William Rogers
℘ Order Mr. Saml. Whitwell Overseer &c

26.   Received into the House David Corkrall[489]
℘ Order Mr. Saml. Abbot Overseer

                      Lydia Sloper jumpt Fence—   Burgis & 1. Child

26.   Received into the House on prov. Accott. Mary Connel[490]
℘ Order Saml. Pemberton Esqr., Mr. Jona. Mason} Selectmen
Mr. Saml. Whitwell

30.   Received into the House Susanna Morrice[491]
℘ Order Mr. Daniel Waldo Overseer &c

April 2   Received into the House a Child of Baldridges named Elizabeth Age
11 Mos.
℘ Order Mr. Benja. Dolbeare Overseer &c

1771 April 1[492]   Received into the House on prov Account Lydia Beach
℘ Order Mr. Henderson Inches, Mr. Ebenr. Storer} Selectmen
John Leverett Esqr. Overseer &c

April 4.   Received into the House on prov. Accott. John Trobridge[493]
℘ Order Joseph Jackson, Saml. Pemberton} Esqrs. Selectmen
John Leverett Esqr. Overseer &c

10.   Received into the House on prov. Accott. James Oulis
℘ Order Joseph Jackson, Saml. Pemberton} Esqrs. Selectmen
John Leverett Esqr. Overseer &c

11.   Received into the House Thomas Cloud Reed & Elizã. Liscow Reed
two Children of Thomas Reed
℘ Order Mr. Daniel Waldo Overseer &c

11.   Received into the House Ann Warren[494]
℘ Order John Gore Esqr. Overseer &c

                        Discharged (Edmund Cane Prov Cha. April 13th. 1771) Josiah Stone

24.   Received into the House on prov. Accott. Trance Bryant[495]
℘ Order Joseph Jackson, Saml. Pemberton Esqr.} Selectmen
Hon. Royall Tyler Esqr. Overseer
deceased April 28. 1771.

23d.   Discharg'd Rhodes 2. Children, William Rogers

May 2.   Discharg'd Hugh O'Briant (Prov Charge)—2d. Patrick Larey to Wkho.
                        Eliza. Woods Priscilla Haden & Child (May 8th.) Mary Gorman jumpt
Fence Prov

May 3d.   Received into the House Agnis McAfee a Child on prov. Accott.
℘ Order Mr. Samuel Whitwell Overseer &c
Saml. Pemberton Esqr., Jona. Mason} Selectmen

1771 May 6.   Received into the House on Prov. Accott. Eliza. Hudenox
℘ Order Mr. Jona. Mason, Mr. Ebenr. Storer} Selectmen
Capt. Saml. Partridge Overseer &c

7.   Received into the House Elizabeth Wharffe[496] & her Child
℘ Order Capt. Saml. Partridge Overseer &c

13.   Received into the House on Prov. Accott. Sarah Morgan Trout & Child
℘ Order Joseph Jackson Esqr., Mr. Jona. Mason} Selectmen
Mr. Willm. Greenleaf Overseer &c

10. do.   Received into the House on Prov. Accott. Margarett Burton
℘ Order Mr. Jona. Mason, Mr. Ebenr. Storer} Selectmen
Capt. Saml. Partridge Overseer &c   Order Dated April 1st. 1771.

17th.   Discharged Willm. More Wife & Child[497] (Prov. Charges)
20.   James Constant (Prov)—(27th.) Benja. Price (Prov)—
Rebecca Pimm 26th.

May 22d.   Received into the House on Prov. Accott. Edward Lewis
℘ Order Saml. Pemberton Esqr., Mr. Ebenr. Storer} Selectmen
Mr. Benja. Dolbeare Overseer &c
went away June 13th. return'd again June 22d.

June 4th.   Jumpt Fence Lydia Beach & Margtt. Burton (province Charges)

20th.   Discharg'd Hector McLane (prov) (24th.) Francis McDaniel (Prov
Charge)

Discharg'd John Ranstead & Child, Mrs. Lydia Snow

June 15th.   Received into the House George a Molatto Fellow belong'd to James Barnard}[498]
℘ Order Mr. Saml. Abbot Overseer &c

20.   Received into the House Richard Hennisey a Lame Man
℘ Order Mr. Willm Greenleaf Overseer &c

1771 June 22d.   Received into the House Eleanor McDaniel daugr. of Jno. McDaniel
℘ Order Mr. Daniel Waldo Overseer &c

June 24.   Received into the House John Patten
℘ Order Mr. Saml. Whitwell Overseer &c

July 1   Received into the House Judith Cottrell
℘ Order Mr. Benja. Dolbeare Overseer &c

8.   Received into the House on province Account Francis McDonald
℘ Order Saml. Pemberton Esqr., Mr. Jona. Mason} Selectmen
Mr. Saml. Whitwell Overseer &c

17.   Received into the House on prov. Account Rachel Seymour
℘ Order Saml. Pemberton Esqr., Mr. Jona. Mason} Selectmen
Mr. Saml. Whitwell Overseer &c

18.   Received into the House on Prov. Account Richard Nash
℘ Order Joseph Jackson Esqr., Mr. Jona. Mason} Selectmen
Mr. Daniel Waldo Overseer &c

20.   Received into the House from Work house Mercy Hearn & Eliza. Suckor
℘ Order Mr. Daniel Waldo Overseer &c

22.   Received into the House a Child named Benja. Fitch, Son of Zabdiel Fitch}
℘ Order Mr. Willm. Whitwell Overseer &c

26.   Received into the House on prov. Accott. Michael Foreman
℘ Order Joseph Jackson Esqr., Mr. Jona. Mason} Selectmen
Mr. Benja. Dolbeare Overseer &c
Went away Octor. 16th. 1771

1771 July 26.   Received into the House Lydia Baker a Child
℘ Order Mr. Willm. Whitwell Overseer &c

27. Received into the House Mary Abrahams
℘ Order Mr. Benja. Dolbeare Overseer &c

Augt 2. Received into the House Elizabeth Thomas[499]
℘ Order John Gore Esqr. Overseer &c

3. Received into the House Frances McCorneck & Child[500] (on prov. Accott.)
℘ Order Saml. Pemberton, Joseph Jackson} Esqrs. Selectmen
John Gore Esqr. Overseer &c

5. Received into the House on prov. Accott. Willm. Collins a poor Boy
℘ Order Joseph Jackson Esqr. } Selectmen
Mr. Willm. Greenleaf Overseer &c

Discharg'd. Eleanor McDaniel, Mary Saunders & Child

7. Received into the House Elizabeth Castle[501]
℘ Order of the Board

[do.][502] Received into the House on prov. Accott. Hannah Bennet & Child & Mary Clifford & Child—Order dated August 1st. 1771.
℘ Order Joseph Jackson, Saml. Pemberton} Esqrs. Selectmen
Mr. Willm. Greenleaf Overseer &c

[do.][503] Received into the House on prov. Accott. Winnifred Stone & Child, Ann, Murfey & Mary Hannisey[504]—Order dated Augt. 2d. 1771.
℘ Order Joseph Jackson, Saml. Pemberton} Esqrs. Selectmen
Mr. Willm. Greenleaf Overseer &c

1771. Augt. Received into the House Elizabeth Anderson Daugr. of Susa. Anderson
℘ Order Mr. Willm. Greenleaf Overseer &c

7. Received into the House from the Workhouse Sarah Grainger[505]
℘ Order Mr. Willm. Greenleaf Overseer &c

8. Received into the House Agnis Gordon Widow
℘ Order Mr. Benja. Dolbeare Overseer &c

13. Received into the House Bethia Cotta[506]
℘ Order Mr. Saml. Whitwell Overseer &c

16. Received into the House Robert Bois[507]
℘ Order Mr. John Barrett Esqr. Overseer &c

Discharged Ann Warren, Ann Hynes—Margtt. Cunningham, Christee Isbester jumpt Fence

Augt. 8.　　　　　Received into the House (on province Account) 2. Children of George Whites in Jail[508]
℘ Order Joseph Jackson Esqr., Mr. Jona. Mason} Selectmen
Mr. Willm. Greenleaf Overseer &c

24.　　　　　Received into the House on prov. Accott. Dorothy Williams
℘ Order Joseph Jackson Esqr., Mr. Jona. Mason} Selectmen
Mr. Willm. Greenleaf Overseer &c

24th.　　　　　Received into the House Margarett Holland[509]
℘ Order Mr. William Greenleaf Overseer &c

28.　　　　　Received into the House Sarah Magee[510]
℘ Order Mr. Saml. Whitwell Overseer &c

31.　　　　　Received into the House William Rogers sick
℘ Order Mr. Saml. Whitwell Overseer &c

1771. Septr. 13.　　　Received into the House Sarah Cyer—also her Daugr. Sarah Cyer junr.—on province Account
Saml. Pemberton, Jona. Mason} Selectmen
< ℘ Order> Mr. Daniel Waldo Overseer &c

18.　　　　　Received into the House Bethia Cotta
℘ Order Mr. Benja. Dolbeare Overseer &c

18.　　　　　Received into the House on province Accott. Patrick McLary
℘ Order John Ruddock, John Hancock} Esqrs. Selectmen
Mr. Willm. Greenleaf Overseer &c

20.　　　　　Received into the House Desire Toby a Molatto Woman
℘ Order John Gore Esqr. Overseer &c

24.　　　　　Received into the House 2. Children named Henry & Mary Welch
℘ Order Mr. Willm. Whitwell Overseer &c
　　　　　　Discharged 2. Children of Thos. Reeds—Mary Saunders
　　　　　　Morgan Trout (Prov. Charge) jumpt Fence Septr. 13th. 1771.

27.　　　　　Received into the House Eleanor Murpee on Province Account
℘ Order Joseph Jackson Esqr., Mr. Jona. Mason} Selectmen
Mr. Saml. Whitwell Overseer

Octo. 1.　　　　Received into the House Sarah Magee On Provce. Accott.
℘ Order Joseph Jackson Esqr., Mr. Jona. Mason} Selectmen
Mr. Saml. Whitwell Overseer &c　　　Order dated Septemr. 1st. 1771.

3.	Received into the House from Workhouse Eliza. Man[511] a Child Aged 2. years Novr. 10. 1771.
℘ Order Mr. Willm. Whitwell Overseer &c

1771. Octo. 4	Received into the House on prov. Accott. Jane Wilson & her Son
℘ Order John Hancock Esqr., Mr. Ebenr. Storer} Selectmen
Mr. Willm. Greenleaf Overseer &c
Jumpt Fence with her Son Octor. 12th. 1771.

8.	Received into the House Joseph Pritchard a Sick Man
℘ Order Mr. Willm. Greenleaf Overseer &c

9.	Received into the House Joanna Kenney
℘ Order Capt. Saml. Partridge

[Octo. 9][512]	Discharg'd Lydia Baker a Child—Jane Wilson (Prov. Charge) & Child
	—Hemenway jumpt Fence Octo. 12th. 1771
	Discharg'd Eliza. Thomas & Child—
	Bethia Cotta—P[rovince] Rachel Seymour jumpt Fence <&> P[rovince]
& Elear. Murfee[513] prov Charges Octo. 30th.

Received into the House Margarett Pousley aged 77. years
℘ Order Mr. Benja. Dolbeare Overseer &c   Order dated Octo. 3d. 1771

15.	Received into the House Mary Heancey & Susanna Anderson & Child from the Work House
℘ Order Mr. Saml. Abbot Overseer &c

22d.	Received into the House on prov. Accott. John Macgrey[514] a sick Man
℘ Order Joseph Jackson Esqr., Mr. Jona. Mason} Selectmen
Mr. Daniel Waldo Overseer &c

29.	Received into the House Josiah Stone
℘ Order John Leverett Esqr. Overseer &c

Novr. 1.	Received into the House Nathaniel Shepperd[515] a Child 14 Mos. Old
℘ Order Mr. Daniel Waldo Overseer &c

	Received into the House Dorcas Osborn—Order dated Octo. 17th. 1771.
℘ Order Capt. Saml. Partridge

1771. Novr. 1	Received into the House Patrick Burk
℘ Order Mr. William Greenleaf Overseer &c

4.	Received into the House Mehetable Watting
℘ Order Mr. Saml. Whitwell Overseer &c

6.   Received into the House on province Accott. Peter Kelly
℘ Order John Hancock Esqr., Mr. Jona Mason} Selectmen
Mr. Willm. Greenleaf Overseer &c

8.   Received into the House on prov. Accott. Lucretia Seavi, Margarett
Reed & Nancy Shaye
℘ Order Mr. Henderson Inches, Mr. Ebenr. Storer} Selectmen
Willm. Phillips Esqr. Overseer &c

9.   Received into the House Bethia Cotta aged 22. yrs.
℘ Order Mr. Benja. Dolbeare Overseer &c

13.   Received into the House on prov. Accott. Hugh O'Brian & Wife[516]
℘ Order Mr. Henderson Inches, Mr. Jona. Mason} Selectmen
Mr. Willm. Greenleaf Overseer &c

19.   Received into the House on prov. Accott. William Ronson
℘ Order Saml. Pemberton Esqr., Mr. Jona. Mason} Selectmen
Mr. Benja. Dolbeare Overseer

19.   Received into the House from Workhouse Mary Dickey
℘ Order Mr. Saml. Whitwell Overseer &c

1771. Novr. 20th.   Received into the House on prov. Charge Edward Davis[517]
℘ Order Joseph Jackson Esqr., Mr. Jona. Mason} Selectmen
Mr. Willm. Greenleaf Overseer &c

22d.   Received into the House Ann Wedge[518]
℘ Order William White Esqr. Overseer &c

23.   Received into the House Mary Bartlett[519]
℘ Order Capt. Saml. Partridge Overseer &c

23.   Received into the House on Province Accott. Saml. Prichard[520]
℘ Order Joseph Jackson Esqr., Mr. Jona. Mason} Selectmen
Mr. Willm. Greenleaf Overseer

          Discharg'd Sarah Cyer Prov. Charge Novr. 27th. 1771

Novr. 29.   Received into the House on prov. Accott. James Thompson
℘ Order Saml. Pemberton Esqr., Mr. Jona. Mason} Selectmen
Mr. Saml. Whitwell Overseer &c

Novr. 11   Received into the House on prov. Accott. Patrick Kidney[521]
℘ Order Saml. Pemberton Esqr., Mr. Jona. Mason} Selectmen
Mr. Saml. Whitwell Overseer &c

1771 Decemr. 3d.   Received into the House Robert Wilson & Wife Sick & Lame
℘ Order John Gore Esqr. Overseer &c

3d.   Received into the House Martha Stow sick
℘ Order John Gore Esqr. Overseer &c

5.   Received into the House on Provce. Accott. Sarah Dudings & 2 Children}
℘ Order Joseph Jackson, Saml. Pemberton} Esqrs. Selectmen
Mr. William Greenleaf Overseer &c

7.   Received into the House Joseph Mountfort (Cutler by Trade)[522]
℘ Order Mr. Samuel Abbot Overseer &c

8.   Received into the House Rebecca Whittemore[523]
℘ Order Mr. Saml. Whitwell Overseer &c

11.   Received into the House Jane Wiseaker[524]
℘ Order Mr. Saml. Whitwell Overseer &c

11th.   Received into the House from the Workhouse Mary McLary[525]
℘ Order John Leverett Esqr. Overseer &c

18.   Received into the House Henry Woodward (say Richard) prov. Char[526]
℘ Order Capt. Saml. Partridge Overseer &c
Deceased Janua. 18. 1772

18.   Received into the House Jehodn.[527] Mountfort Wife to Joseph Mountfort
℘ Order Mr. Saml. Abbot Overseer &c

21.   Received into the House on province Accott. Michael Still[528]
℘ Order Joseph Jackson Esqr., Mr. Jona. Mason} Selectmen
Mr. Willm. Greenleaf Overseer &c
Discharg'd March 14. 1772.

1771. Decr. 24}   Received into the House Cornelius Shrowtenbey[529]
℘ Order Mr. Daniel Waldo Overseer &c

27.   Received into the House Thomas Hunter   Black Boy[530]
℘ Order Willm. White Esqr. Overseer &c

1772. Janua. 2d.   Received into the House Daniel North
℘ Order Mr. Willm. Greenleaf Overseer &c

2d.   Received into the House on prov. Accott. Ann More & her Child
℘ Order Joseph Jackson Esqr.
Mr. Saml. Whitwell Overseer &c

3.   Received into the House Tamar Belman
℘ Order Mr. Willm. Whitwell Overseer &c

4.   Received into the House on prov. Account Mary Blake
℘ Order John Hancock Esqr., Mr. Jona. Mason} Selectmen
Mr. Willm. Whitwell Overseer &c

25th.   Received into the House on prov. Accott. Matthias Hanes[531]
℘ Order Joseph Jackson, John Hancock} Esqrs. Selectmen
Mr. Willm. Greenleaf Overseer &c

27.   Received into the House on prov. Account Edward Poor
℘ Order Joseph Jackson Esqr., Mr. Jona. Mason} Selectmen
Mr. Willm. Greenleaf Overseer &c

28.   Received into the House Ann Baldridge from Workhouse[532]
℘ Order Willm. Phillips Esqr. Overseer &c

1772. Janua. 19th.   Received into the House from Workhouse Eliza. Pass
℘ Order Mr. Daniel Waldo Overseer &c

Februa. 6.   Received into the House on province Accott. Sarah Hartshorn & 2. Children}
℘ Order Joseph Jackson, John Ruddock} Esqrs. Selectmen
Mr. Daniel Waldo Overseer &c
1 Child discharged Feby. 7th.

14th.   Received into the House on prov. Accott. David Dolbeare Wife & Child
℘ Order Joseph Jackson Esqr., Mr. Jona. Mason} Selectmen
Mr. Willm. Greenleaf Overseer &c

15.   Received into the House on prov. Accott. George Downing
℘ Order Joseph Jackson Esqr., Mr. Jona. Mason} Selectmen
Mr. Willm. Greenleaf Overseer &c

19.   Received into the House on prov. Accott. James Martin
℘ Order Joseph Jackson Esqr., Mr. Jona. Mason} Selectmen
Mr. Willm. Greenleaf Overseer &c

Februa. 7.   Received into the House Willm., Robert & James Bell Children of James Bell
℘ Order Saml. Whitwell Overseer
Wm. born—May 17. 1766, Robert Augt. 14. 1767, James Janua. 11th. 1769} all Discharged April 8. 1772.

1772. Februa. 10th.   Received into the House Eliza. McCollour a Child
℘ Order John Leverett Esqr. Overseer &c

12.   Received into the House Hepzibah Blackman
℘ Order Mr. Willm. Whitwell Overseer &c

17.   Received into the House a Negro[533] named Boston
℘ Order Mr. Saml. Abbot Overseer &c

22d.   Received into the House Nicholas Brown
℘ Order Mr. Daniel Waldo Overseer &c

                       Discharg'd Eliza. Castle & her Child—March 2d. Matthias Hanes
province Charge

March 2d.   Received into the House Samuel Wheeler & his Wife
℘ Order Mr. Willm. Greenleaf Overseer &c

2d.   Received into the House James McFarland his Wife & Child[534] on the
province Account
℘ Order Joseph Jackson Esqr., Mr. Jona. Mason} Selectmen
Mr. Willm. Greenleaf Overseer &c

10.   Received into the House Elizabeth Murfeye[535]
℘ Order Capt. Saml. Partridge Overseer &c

10.   Received into the House Benja. Williams from the Workhouse
℘ Order Capt. Saml. Partridge Overseer &c

14.   Received into the House on prov. Account William More
℘ Order Mr. John Scollay, Mr. Timo. Newell} Selectmen
Mr. Willm. Greenleaf Overseer &c

1772. March 14th.   Received into the House David & Mary Westly Children of Joseph
Westly[536]
℘ Order Mr. Daniel Waldo Overseer

16.   Received into the House Samuel Legg a sick Man
℘ Order John Gore Esqr. Overseer &c

18.   Received into the House from the Work House Letitia Wesson
℘ Order Capt. Saml. Partridge Overseer &c

22d.   Received Ann Kenney & Child into the House
℘ Order Mr. William Greenleaf Overseer &c

25.   Received into the House Sarah Nesbit & her Sister Mary Cook
℘ Order Capt. Saml. Partridge Overseer &c

                       Discharged Mary Clifford & Child March 5th. prov. Charges

꧁

7th.   Sarah Duding & 2. Children prov. Charges

23d.   <*Ann*> Sarah Keyer[537] (prov.) jumpt Fence (26th.) Wm. Ronson (prov) <*jumpt Fence*> went out of the Gate

28.   Lucretia Seavi (prov) jumpt Fence (28th.) Tamar Bellman jumpt Fence

31.   James Oulis (prov) jumpt Fence (30th.) Joseph Westlys 2. Children

March 31st.   Received into the House John Pattin a Child

℘ Order Mr. Saml. Whitwell Overseer &c

April 3d.   Received into the House on Prov. Account Eliza. Mumfort

℘ Order John Scollay, Timothy Newell} Selectmen

Mr. Daniel Waldo Overseer

1772. April 4. Received into the House Eliza. Castle

℘ Order Mr. Danl. Waldo Overseer &c

6.   Received into the House David a Child of Fortune free Negro

℘ Order Willm. White Esqr. Overseer &c

10.   Received into the House Mehetable Clough

℘ Order Willm. White Esqr. Overseer &c

13.   Received into the House on prov. Accott. Patrick Tobin

℘ Order John Scollay, Saml. Austin} Selectmen

Mr. Saml. Whitwell Overseer &c

17.   Received into the House a Child named Paul White Mothers name Eliza. Castle

℘ Order John Leverett Esqr. Overseer &c

18.   Received into the House Mary Lemoine

℘ Order John Leverett Esqr. Overseer &c

21.   Received into the House Mary White aged 20 years

℘ Order Mr. Benja. Dolbeare Overseer &c

April 8   Discharged 3. Children of James Bell   Winslow to Work house

10th.   Dorothy Williams & Mary Blake[538] (prov Charges) jumpt Fence

13.   Hepzibah Blackman & Child & Eliza. Castle <& Child>

15.   Margtt. O'Briant[539] (prov. Charge) <(20th.) *Wm. More (prov. Charge)*>

22d.   Edwd. Poor (prov Charge)—Joseph Mountfort

27.   Hugh O'Briant[540] & Patrick Tobin (prov. Charges)

do.   Mary Henney[541] jumpt Fence (prov Charge)

29.   Mary Perrin (went away without leave)—Eliza. Mumfort jumpt Fence (prov)

30.   Patrick McLary[542] discharged (prov) May 5th. Poll. Hurley jumpt Fence

1772. April 24   Received into the House on province Accott. Eliza. Smith
℘ Order John Scollay Esqr., Mr. Timo. Newell} Selectmen
Mr. Willm. Greenleaf Overseer &c

May 2d.   Received into the House Margarett Adams
℘ Order Mr. Benja. Dolbeare Overseer &c

4.   Received into the House Lydia Wool a Child of Eliza. Thomas[543]
℘ Order Capt. Saml. Partridge Overseer &c

7.   Received into the House Eliza. Castle
℘ Order John Leverett Esqr. Overseer &c

do.   Received into the House from Workhouse Hannah Anderson a Child
℘ Order Mr. Wm. Whitwell Overseer &c

13.   Received into the House on prov. Accott. James Thompson a Child[544]
℘ Order John Scollay, John Hancock} Esqrs. Selectmen
Mr. Wm. Greenleaf Overseer &c
Discharg'd July 2d. 1772.

13.   Received into the House on prov Accott. James Oulis[545]
℘ Order John Scollay Esqr., Mr. Timo. Newell} Selectmen
Mr. Wm. Greenleaf Overseer

15.   Received into the House   a Child taken up on the Neck[546]
Mr. Daniel Waldo Overseer &c
Deceased soon after[547]

May 7.   Richard Hennsey jumpt Fence <(prov)>   (11th.) dischargd Wm. More
Wife & Child[548] (provce.)
12.   Mcfarlands Child & McCornecks Child (prov)   14th. James Thompson
(prov) jumpt Fence—dischargd Margtt. Holland, Mary Howard & Danl. North
22.   Sarah Magee (prov) & Child—Josiah Stone run away—dischargd Lois
Bleigh
25.   Oliver Grainger (prov) Eliza.[549] Gent run away—Mary Gorman June 1.
1772 (prov)

1772 May 18   Received into the House on prov. Accott. Mary Perrin
℘ Order John Scollay, Thos. Marshall} Esqrs. Selectmen
Capt. Saml. Partridge Overseer

22.   Received into the House on prov. Accott. Dennis Sullivan
℘ Order John Scollay Esqr., Mr. Timo. Newell} Selectmen
Mr. Wm. Greenleaf Overseer

25   Received into the House Lois Bleigh crazy[550]
℘ Order Mr. Wm. Greenleaf Overseer

25.   Received into the House Elizabeth Barbour
℘ Order Mr. Saml. Abbot Overseer

29.   Received into the House Lawrence Collins
℘ Order Mr. Daniel Waldo Overseer &c

[May 1772][551]   Benja. Chubb ran away—Ann Kenney & Eliza. Mears &—ditto [*i.e., ran away*]
June 1   Patrick Kidney[552]prov Charge

3.   Received into the House Elizabeth Mitchell
℘ Order Mr. Saml. Whitwell Overseer &c

3.   Received into the House Hannah Clark a Child between 11 & 12. yrs. Age
℘ Order of the Board Sitting Day

3.   Received into the House Lawrence Collins Wife
℘ Order Mr. Daniel Waldo Overseer &c

6.   Received into the House Thomas Singleton
℘ Order Mr. Benja. Dolbeare Overseer &c

8.   Received into the House Mary McLary from the Workhouse
℘ Order John Leverett Esqr. Overseer &c

                Dischrg'd. Fras. McDaniel (prov) June 4th. 1772—Margtt. Reed (prov.)
June 6th.
22d.   Eliza. Smith (prov) run away—Martha Sorin—prisa. Brisford
25.   George Downing (prov)

1772. June 9th.   Received into the House James Bedsen aged 4. years Decr. 3. 1771 & Samuel Taylor aged 18. Mos. Born Novr. 18. 1770
℘ Order John Leverett Esqr. Overseer &c

10.   Received into the House George Johnson on prov. Account
℘ Order John Scollay Esqr., Thos. Marshall Esqr.} Selectmen
Mr. Wm. Greenleaf Overseer &c

11.   Received into the House Ham Dodge
℘ Order Capt. Saml. Partridge Overseer &c

12.   Received into the House on prov. Accott. James Thompson
℘ Order John Scollay Esqr., Mr. Saml. Austin} Selectmen
Mr. Saml. Abbot Overseer &c

13.   Received into the House on prov. Accott. Lucy Miller & Child
℘ Order John Scollay Esqr., Mr. Saml. Austin} Selectmen
Mr. Wm. Greenleaf Overseer &c

15.   Received into the House from the Workho. Hannah Ross a Child aged
17. Mos. 15th. June
℘ Order Capt. Saml. Partridge Overseer &c

15.   Received into the House on prov. Accott. John Hamilton
℘ Order John Scollay Esqr., Mr. Saml. Austin} Selectmen
Mr. Wm. Greenleaf Overseer &c

15.   Received into the House on prov. Accott. John Douglas
℘ Order John Scollay Esqr., Mr. Saml. Austin} Selectmen
Mr. Wm. Whitwell Overseer &c

1772. June 16   Received into the House Priscilla Brichford from the Workhouse
℘ Order Capt. Saml. Partridge Overseer &c

17.   Received into the House on prov. Accott. Wm. Organ
℘ Order John Scollay Esqr., Mr. Timo. Newell} Selectmen
Mr. Wm. Greenleaf Overseer &c

17.   Received into the House on province Accott. Edmund Cain[553]
℘ Order John Scollay Esqr., Mr. Timo. Newell} Selectmen
Mr. Wm. Whitwell Overseer &c

25.   Received into the House from Workhouse John Davis[554]
℘ Order Mr. Saml. Abbot Overseer &c

July. 2.   James Thompson (prov. Charge) run away—Christo. Atkinson run
away—(2d.) Discharg'd James Thompson a Child (prov Accott.)—Lawrence Collins Wife—
Pat. Burk run away
10.   Discharg'd Dennis Sullivan (prov. Charge)   (11th.) John Ramsay (prov.
Charge)

July 2d.   Received into the House Mercy Miller
℘ Order Mr. Willm. Whitwell Overseer &c

7.   Received into the House on prov. Accott. John Ramsay
℘ Order John Scollay Esqr., Mr. Saml. Austin} Selectmen
Mr. Wm. Greenleaf Overseer &c

11.   Received into the House Lydia Aish a Child[555]
℘ Order John Leverett Esqr. Overseer &c

1772. July 17.   Received into the House on province Accott. John Mairden
℘ Order John Scollay, Timo. Newell} Esqrs. Selectmen
Mr. Willm. Greenleaf Overseer &c
Discharg'd August 8. 1772

18.   Received into the House on prov. Accott. Judith Wright & 4. Childn.
℘ Order John Scollay, Timo. Newell} Esqrs. Selectmen
Capt. Saml. Partridge Overseer &c

24.   Received into the House Hannah Goffe[556]
℘ Order Mr. Wm. Whitwell Overseer &c

29.   Received into the House on prov. Accott. Wm. Haley
℘ Order John Scollay Esqr., Mr. Saml. Austin} Selectmen
Mr. Saml. Abbot Overseer &c

August 8.   Received into the House on prov. Accott. James Buckler
℘ Order Mr. Timo. Newell, Mr. Saml. Austin} Selectmen
Mr. Benja. Dolbeare Overseer &c

11.   Received into the House on province Accott. Margtt. Freetstot
℘ Order Thomas Marshall Esqr., Mr. Oliver Wendell} Selectmen
Mr. Daniel Waldo Overseer &c

11.   Received into the House Thomas Cloud Read a Child
℘ Order John Leverett Esqr. Overseer &c

12.   Received into the House Judith Clark
℘ Order Mr. William Greenleaf Overseer &c

                   Discharg'd Ross' Child—Lawrence Collins—(8th.) John Mairden
(provce.)
19th.   Jno. Hamilton (prov). Mary White—24. Jas. Oulis (prov)   26. Jas.
McFarland (prov)
26.   Jno. Mortal Wife & 2 Childeen

1772. Augt. 21.   Received into the House on prov Accott. John Ryan
℘ Order John Scollay Esqr., Mr. Saml. Austin} Selectmen
Mr. William Greenleaf Overseer &c

21.   Received into the Alms House John Jones
Mr. Saml. Whitwell Overseers
see Below[557]

22d.   Received into the House James Brett
℘ Order John Leverett Esqr. Overseer &c

31.   Received into the House on prov. Accott. Patrick McLaugline
℘ Order John Scollay, Timo. Newell} Selectmen
Mr. Benja. Dolbeare Overseer &c

Septr. 1.   Received into the House on prov. Accott. Eliza. Prince, Abigail Mills[558]
& John Jones[559]
℘ Order John Scollay, Thos. Marshall} Esqrs. Selectmen
Capt. Saml. Partridge Overseer &c

2.   Received into the House from the Workhouse Jos. Greenwood & Eliza.
Taylor
℘ Order John Gore Esqr. Overseer &c

7.   Received into the House Mary Allcock Wife of Jno. Allcock
℘ Order Mr. Saml. Whitwell Overseer &c

9.   Received into the House on Prov. Accott. Peter Grubb
℘ Order John Scollay, Timo. Newell} Selectmen
Capt. Saml. Partridge Overseer &c

10.   Received into the House Mary Slemmond a Child of Sarah Slemmond
℘ Order Mr. Saml. Whitwell Overseer &c

1772. Septr. 10.} Received into the House on Provce. Account Hugh Sloane with a
Broken Leg[560]
℘ Order Timo. Newell, Thoms. Marshall} Selectmen
Mr. Benja. Dolbeare Overseer &c
Deceased Septr. 19th. 1772.

13.   Received into the House on Province Account John Mairn[561]
℘ Order John Scollay, Saml. Austin} Selectmen
Mr. Wm. Greenleaf Overseer &c

15.   Received into the House a Child of Eliza. Oldhams 2 yrs. 1. Mo. Old[562]
℘ Order Mr. Danl. Waldo Overseer &c

16.   Received into the House Francis Akley (Lame)
℘ Order John Leverett Esqr. Overseer &c

19.   Received into the House on Prov. Accott. Thomas Easton
℘ Order John Scollay, Saml. Austin} Selectmen
Mr. Daniel Waldo Overseer &c

    Discharged a Child of Welch's—Cornes. Showdenback,[563] Mary Lintee,
Mary McLary to the Workhouse—Mercy Miller—Slemmons Child
Septr. 3   Peter Kelly (7th.) David Dolbeare Wife & Child & Sarah Magee &
Child Province Charges

9.   John Douglas & Willm. Haley (prov. Charges.)—Peg Adams jumpt Fence

12.   Margtt. Farland prov Charge (19th.) Eliza. Prince Prov. Charge both Jumpt Fence—(21st.) Jas. Buckler prov. Charge run away

Octo. 2.   patrick McLaugline (prov.) (7th.) Mary Frestot (prov. Charge)

13.   George Graves a Child province Charge—(13th.) Mary Thompson & Child (prov)

Septr. 19.   Received into the House Abigail Willis an infirm Woman
℘ Order John Leverett Esqr. Overseer &c

1772. Septr. 23. Received into the House on province Account Nelly Wright Daughter of Judith Wright
℘ Order Mr. Saml. Austin, Mr. Oliver Wendell} Selectmen
Mr. Willm. Greenleaf Overseer &c

24.   Received into the Alms House from the Workho. Gammon Stevens
℘ Order Mr. Willm. Whitwell Overseer &c

25.   Received into the House on prov. Accott. Peter Turner Wife & Child French people
℘ Order John Scollay Esqr., Mr. Saml. Austin} Selectmen
Mr. Willm. Greenleaf Overseer &c

28.   Received into the House on provce. Accott. George Graves a Child[564]
℘ Order John Scollay Esqr., Mr. Timo. Newell} Selectmen
Mr. Willm. Greenleaf Overseer &c

29.   Received into the House Ann Young a Child aged 19. Mos.
℘ Order Mr. Benja. Dolbeare Overseer &c

29.   Received into the House Sarah Gent
℘ Order Capt. Saml. Partridge Overseer &c

30.   Received into the House on prov. Accott. Wm. More Wife & Child
℘ Order John Scollay Esqr., Mr. Timo. Newell} Selectmen
Mr. Wm. Greenleaf Overseer &c

do.   Received into the House John Flowers[565] (Fisherman) Order dated Augt. 29. 1772
℘ Order Mr. Daniel Waldo Overseer &c

Octo. 2.   Received into the House Jeremiah Powell a Child[566]
℘ Order Mr. Wm. Whitwell Overseer &c

1772. Octo. 1.[567] Received into the House from the Workhouse Saml. Goffe (William)
℘ Order Mr. Benja. Dolbeare Overseer &c

∽

[do.][568]   Received into the House Mary Trescot[569]   order dated Septr. 23d.
℘ Order Mr. Daniel Waldo Overseer &c

5.   Received into the House Thomas Lawrence[570] & his Wife
℘ Order John Leverett Esqr. Overseer &c

7.   Received into the House (on province Accott.) Agnis Yaxley & Child
℘ Order Mr. Timo. Newell, Thos. Marshall Esqr. } Selectmen
Mr. Willm. Greenleaf Overseer &c

24.   Discharg'd John Penrow, Lawrence Doyle, Wm. Organ, John Magraw,
Peter Grubb, Kata. Sullivan, Mary Davison Province Charges—(27th.) Lucy Miller & Child
(prov) sent them to Ireland

Octo.   Received into the House Benjamin Bowen distracted (on prov. Accott.)
℘ Order John Scollay Esqr., Mr. Timo. Newell } Selectmen
Mr. Wm. Greenleaf Overseer &c   Order dated July 4. 1772.

                    Received into the House (on prov. Accott.) Hugh O'Brian & Wife
℘ Order John Scollay Esqr., Mr. Saml. Austin } Selectmen
Mr. Willm. Greenleaf Overseer &c   Order dated Septr. 15th. 1772.

16.   Received into the House Mary Newton Sick
℘ Order Mr. Saml. Abbot Overseer &c

do.   Received into the House Eunice Mountfort & 2. Children
℘ Order Mr. Saml. Abbot Overseer &c

1772. Octo. 7.   Received into the House (on prov. Accott.) Patrick McLockland[571]
℘ Order Mr. Saml. Austin   } Selectmen
Mr. Saml. Whitwell Overseer &c

21.   Received into the House (on prov. Accott.) John McIntyne[572]
℘ Order Thos. Marshall Esqr., Mr. Oliver Wendell } Selectmen
Mr. Wm. Greenleaf Overseer &c

22.   Received into the House a Child of Benja. Mountforts aged 2 years
℘ Order Mr. Saml. Abbot Overseer &c

24.   Received into the House from the Workho. Lucy Whittaker
℘ Order Mr. Willm. Greenleaf Overseer &c

29.   Received into the House William Brown[573]
℘ Order Mr. Saml. Abbot Overseer &c

Novr. 2.   Received into the House Isabella Ross
℘ Order Willm. White Esqr. Overseer &c

5.   Dischargd Eunice Mountfort & 1. Child
7.   Judith Wright & 4. Children (prov) Mercy Herne to Workhouse
23.   Wm. More & Wife <& Child> (prov)—Francis Akley—
Willm. Brown 28th.

7.   Received into the House Margarett Holland
℘ Order Mr. Wm. Greenleaf Overseer &c

9.   Received into the House John Peirce[574] his Wife & 3 Children
Mr. Willm. Whitwell, John Leverett Esqr.} Overseers &c

1772. Novr. 10.   Received into the House Ann Stride an old Woman
℘ Order Willm. White Esqr. Overseer &c

12.   Received into the House Eliza. Williams a Girl
℘ Order John Barrett Esqr. Overseer &c

16.   Received into the House on prov. Accott. Margarett Glossup & 2
Childn.
℘ Order John Scollay Esqr., Saml. Austin} Selectmen
Mr. Wm. Greenleaf Overseer &c

16.   Received Miriam Bijah in to the House
℘ Order Mr. Saml. Whitwell Overseer &c

17.   Received into the House on Province Account Eleanor Colter
℘ Order John Scollay Esqr., Mr. Timo. Newell} Selectmen
Mr. Wm. Greenleaf Overseer &c

17.   Received into the House Colin McLarien (on prov. Accott.)[575]
℘ Order John Scollay, Thos. Marshall} Esqrs. selectmen
Mr. Saml. Whitwell Overseer &c
Dyed Novr. 28th. 1772.

17.   Received into the House Jenny[576] a Negrowoman
℘ Order Mr. Danl. Waldo Overseer &c

19.   Received into the House on prov. Accott. Mary Thompson & Child
℘ Order John Scollay Esqr., Mr. Timo. Newell} Selectmen
Mr. Willm. Greenleaf Overseer &c

23.   Received into the House Isabella Sloan a poor Girl
℘ Order Wm. White Esqr. Overseer &c

25.   Received into the House Richard Morgan
℘ Order Capt. Saml. Partridge Overseer &c

1772. Novr. 30.   Received into the House on Prov. Accott. Thomas Jones
℘ Order John Scollay Esqr., Mr. Saml. Austin} Selectmen
Mr. Wm. Greenleaf Overseer &c

Decr. 1.   Received into the House John Gatchell an old Lame Man
℘ Order Wm. White Esqr. Overseer &c

5.   Received into the House Robert Berry
℘ Order John Leverett Esqr. Overseer &c

5.   Received into the House <*Ann*> Winifred Stone & Child (on prov.
Accott.)
℘ Order John Scollay Esqr., Mr. Timo. Newell} Selectmen
Mr. Wm. Whitwell Overseer &c

5.   Received into the House on Prov. Accott. John Fitzgerald[577]
℘ Order John Scollay Esqr., Mr. Timo. Newell} Selectmen
Mr. Wm. Whitwell Overseer &c

7.   Received into the House Bethiah Miller an aged infirm Woman
℘ Order Willm. White Esqr. Overseer &c

8.   Received into the House on Prov. Accott. Willm. Bryan
℘ Order John Scollay, Thos. Marshall} Esqrs. Selectmen
Capt. Saml. Partridge Overseer &c

23.   Discharged Maria a Negro—Gammon Stevens without leave

1773. Jany 5.   John McIntyer prove. Charge

Decr. 16 [*1772*]   Received into the House Willm. Gordon (on Province Accott.)
℘ Order John Scollay Esqr., Mr. Saml. Austin} Selectmen
Mr. Willm. Whitwell Overseer &c

1772. Dec. 16.   Received into the House William Sheppard from Dedham[578]
℘ Order Mr. Willm. Greenleaf Overseer &c

21.   Received into the House on (Provce. Accott.) Peter Anthony
℘ Order Mr. Timo. Newell, Thos. Marshall Esqr.} Selectmen
Mr. Saml. Whitwell Overseer &c

21.   Received into the House from the Workhouse Mary Henshaw
℘ Order Mr. Danl. Waldo Overseer &c

24.   Received into House Richard Holland[579]
℘ Order John Leverett Esqr. Overseer &c

26.   Received into the House (on Prov. Accott.) James Stewart[580]
℘ Order Mr. Timo. Newell, Mr. Saml. Austin} Selectmen
Mr. Danl. Waldo Overseer &c

1773. Jany. 4.   Received into the House (on prov. Accott.) Michael Bryan[581]
℘ Order John Scollay Esqr., Mr. Saml. Austin} Selectmen
Mr. Willm. Whitwell Overseer &c

12.   Received into the House Joseph Boardman Wife[582] & Child
℘ Order John Leverett Esqr. Overseer &c

18.   Received into the House Joseph Mountfort (Cutler)
℘ Order Mr. Willm. Whitwell Overseer &c

20.   Received into the House (on Provce. Account) Henry Reynolds[583]
℘ Order John Scollay Esqr., Mr. Timo. Newell} Selectmen
Mr. Saml. Whitwell Overseer &c

1773. Janua. 20. Received into the House (on Province Account) Margtt. Sabestion[584]
her Husband at Sea
℘ Order John Scollay Esqr., Mr. Saml. Austin} Selectmen
Mr. Willm. Greenleaf Overseer &c

23.   Received into the House Pegg Adams on provce. Accott. a poor Sick
Woman
℘ Order John Gore Esqr. Overseer &c Order dated Septr. 1. 1772

26.   Received into the House Cuff.[585] Negro Man belonged to Mr. Durrin
Blacksmith
℘ Order Capt. Saml. Partridge Overseer &c

[do.][586]   Received into the House (on Provce. Accott.) James West[587] Rope
Maker
℘ Order John Scollay Esqr., Mr. Timo. Newell} Selectmen
Mr. William Greenleaf Overseer &c} NB. Order was Dated Decemr. 30th. 1772.
Deceased Janua. 1773.

       Discharged Jumpt Fence Mary Henshaw

27.   Received into the House Joseph Webb[588]
℘ Order Mr. Willm. Whitwell Overseer &c

29.   Received into the House on prov. Accott. James Griffin
℘ Order John Scollay Esqr., Mr. Timo. Newell} Selectmen
Capt. Saml. Partridge Overseer &c
deceased same day

30.   Received into the House on prov. Accott. Bartho. Curtin[589]
℘ Order John Scollay Esqr., Mr. Timo. Newell} Selectmen
Mr. Saml. Whitwell Overseer &c
his Wife here 3. weeks on prov. Accott.

Feby. 1   Received into the House Robert McNear[590]
℘ Order Capt. Saml. Partridge Overseer &c

1773. Feby. 1st.   Received into the House on province Accott. Thomas Mackay a Child
℘ Order John Scollay Esqr., Mr. <*Mi*[…] > Oliver Wendell} Selectmen
Mr. Wm. Greenleaf Overseer &c
Discharg'd Augt. 20. 1773.

6.   Received into the House on Province Accott. Eliza. Jones & 2 Children
℘ Order John Scollay Esqr., Mr. Timo. Newell} Selectmen
Mr. Saml. Whitwell Overseer &c

14.   Received into the House on province Accott. Willm. Sharp
℘ Order Mr. Timo. Newell, Thos. Marshall Esqr.} Selectmen
Mr. Daniel Waldo Overseer &c—omitted in the last Province Account & to be charg'd in
the next—charg'd since

15th.   Discharg'd Agnis Yaxley (prov. Charge) (23d.) Thos. Jones prov Charge

24.   Received into the House on prov. Accott. Christian Remick[591] his Wife
& 2. Children
℘ Order Mr. Timo. Newell, Mr. Saml. Austin} Selectmen
John Leverett Esqr. Overseer &c   Order Dated Feby. 8th. 1773.

25.   Received into the House Abigail Hairblew
℘ Order Willm. White Esqr. Overseer &c

24.   Received into the House on prov. Accott. Mary Montgomery
℘ Order John Scollay Esqr., Mr. Timo. Newell} Selectmen
Mr. Wm. Greenleaf Overseer &c

March 9th.   Discharg'd William Briant[592] (Provce. Charge)
22.   Michl. Briant (Prov)   22d. Peter Anthony (prov) run away
25.   Pat. McLaughlin (prov)   27th. Rebecca Ingraham Lucy Whittaker
run away
27.   Elear. Colter (prov) run away—April 1. <*Thos. Huston (prov)*> Jos.
Boardman run away—April 6th. Ann More & Child (Prov) run away

1773. Mar. 5.   Received into the House from the Workhouse Dorcas & Rebecca
Ingraham
℘ Order Mr. Saml. Abbot Overseer &c

9.   Received into the House   Coffin[593] Wife of Edwd. Coffin
℘ Order Mr. Saml. Whitwell Overseer &c

9.   Received into the House John Davis
℘ Order Mr. Willm. Whitwell Overseer &c

12.   Received into the House (on Prov. Accott.) Mary Stephens
℘ Order John Scollay Esqr., Mr. Timo. Newell} Selectmen
Wm. Phillips Esqr. Overseer &c

12.   Received into the House 2. Children James & Margarett Bell
℘ Order Mr. Wm. Whitwell Overseer &c

13.   Received into the House from Workhouse Willm. Shepherd
℘ Order Mr. Danl. Waldo Overseer &c

15.   Received into the House Mary Langley with a Broken Arm
℘ Order Willm. White Esqr. Overseer &c

                Received into the House Jane Laha
℘ Order Mr. Saml. Abbot Overseer &c   Order dated March 11. 1773

16.   Received into the House Josiah Hubbard[594] very ill
℘ Order Mr. Saml. Abbot Overseer &c

16.   Received into the House Elizabeth Chamberlain
℘ Order John Barrett Esqr. Overseer &c

17.   Received into the House on prov. Accott. Peter Maloy
℘ Order John Scollay, John Hancock} Esqrs. Selectmen
Mr. Wm. Greenleaf Overseer &c

1773. Mar. 18.   Received into the House on Prov. Accott. Ann Moore
℘ Order John Scollay Esqr., Mr. Timo. Newell} Selectmen
Mr. Saml. Whitwell Overseer &c
Discharg'd April 6. 1773

18.   Received into the House on Prov. Accott. Paris a Negro Man
℘ Order John Scollay Esqr., Mr. Timo. Newell} Selectmen
Mr. Wm. Greenleaf Overseer &c

25.   Received into the House John Pierce a Boy abt. 12 or 13 years
℘ Order John Leverett Esqr. Overseer &c

31.   Received into the House Alice Stevens[595]—dangerously ill
℘ Order Mr. Danl. Waldo Overseer &c
Dyed April 1st. 1773

April 6.　　　　　Received into the House on Prov. Accott. Michael Daily
℘ Order John Scollay Esqr., Mr. Timo. Newell} Selectmen
Mr. Wm. Greenleaf Overseer &c

April 6.　　　　　Discharged Sarah Hartshorn & Child (Prov. Charges)

7.　　　　　Discharged (or run away) Mary Montgomery[596] prov.　(8th.) Hugh
O'Briant (prov) run
9.　　　　　Thos. Huston run away　　(13) Eliza. Jones & 2. Children prov.
Charges—Jos. Webb & Margtt. Holland run away—Abigail Clark run away
May 3.　　　　　Discharged Peter Turner Wife & Child (Prov. Charges) Mary Despe
from Workho. run away—John Pierce Wife & 3. Children
4.　　　　　Michael Daily (prov. Charge) run away

April 10.　　　　　Received into the House from Workhouse Mary Despe
℘ Order Mr. Willm. Whitwell Overseer &c

13.　　　　　Received into the House from Workho. a Child named Katha.
Baldridge
℘ Order Mr. Wm. Whitwell Overseer &c

1773. April 13.　　　Received into the House from the Work House Ruth Evans
℘ Order Mr. Willm. Whitwell Overseer &c

21.　　　　　Received into the House Thomas Stone (an aged Man)
℘ Order John Leverett Esqr. Overseer &c

28.　　　　　Received into the House from Workhouse Matthew Hopkins
℘ Order Capt. Saml. Partridge Overseer &c

May 1.　　　　　Received into the House John Barrett[597] a poor Dumb Child
℘ Order Willm. White Esqr. Overseer &c

6.　　　　　Received into the House on Prov. Accott. Francis McDonald
℘ Order John Scollay, Thos. Marshall} Esqrs. Selectmen
Mr. Wm. Greenleaf Overseer &c

7.　　　　　Received into the House on prov. Accott. Robert Bingham
℘ Order John Scollay Esqr., Mr. Timo. Newell} Selectmen
Mr. Benja. Dolbeare Overseer &c

8.　　　　　Received into the House on prov. Accott. Willm. Ewen a Child 4. yrs.
old Augt. 10. 1773
℘ Order John Scollay Esqr., Mr. Timo. Newell} Selectmen
Capt. Saml. Partridge Overseer &c

May 21st.　　　　　Discharged Francis McDaniel (Prov Charge)

June 1.   Elear. Bennet a Child (prov. Charge) Bound out

May 18   Received into the House on Province Accott. Farris[598] Shirley
℘ Order John Scollay Esqr., Mr. Timo. Newell} Selectmen
Capt. Saml. Partridge Overseer &c

1773. May 18.   Received into the House (on Province Accott.) Edward Butler[599]
℘ Order John Scollay, Thos. Marshall} Esqrs. Selectmen
Mr. Willm. Greenleaf Overseer &c
Deceased the 24th. May 1773

21.   Received into the House (on Prov. Accott.) William Holmes
℘ Order John Scollay Esqr., Mr. Timo. Newell} Selectmen
Capt. Saml. Partridge Overseer &c

June 7.   Received into the House John Hendrick a Child from the Workhouse
aged 4. years 5. Months
℘ Order Mr. Danl. Waldo Overseer &c

8.   Received into the House John & Joanna Laha Children from the
Workhouse province Charges
℘ Order Mr. Danl. Waldo Overseer &c
see their Age in the Order

9.   Received into the House (on Province Accott.) George Mason[600]
(Limner)
℘ Order John Scollay Esqr., Mr. Saml. Austin} Selectmen
John Leverett Esqr. Overseer &c
Deceased June 21st. 1773.

9.   Received into the House (on Province Accott.) George Downing
℘ Order John Scollay Esqr., Mr. Saml. Austin} Selectmen
Mr. Willm. Whitwell Overseer &c

15.   Received into the House (on Province Accott.) 2. Children of Eliza.
Jones's named Willm. & Polly Jones
℘ Order John Scollay Esqr., Mr. Timo. Newell} Selectmen
John Leverett Esqr. Overseer &c

21.   Received into the House from the Workhouse Esther Laha (on provce.
Charge) likewise her Children—from June 8th. 1773.
℘ Order Mr. Benja. Dolbeare Overseer &c

                   Jos. Mountfort run away—Richd. Morgan run away—Discharg'd Robert
Bingham (prov) June 23d.—June 29th. Edwd. Davis (prov)—July 2d. Richd. Nash (prov)
Bartho. Curtin (prov) discharged June 15th. 1773 & his Wife

1773. June 28   Received into the House (on Provce. Accott.) Richard Hennesy[601]—
Infirm
℘ Order John Scollay Esqr., Mr. Saml. Austin} Selectmen
Mr. Willm. Greenleaf Overseer &c

July 1   Received into the House Mary Sharp—Blind
℘ Order Mr. Danl. Waldo Overseer &c

do.   Received into the House Thomas Corndell a Boy—(Condon)
℘ Order Mr. Wm. Greenleaf Overseer &c
Bound to S. Dexter Esqr.

3.   Received into the House on Prov. Accott. Matthew Bright
℘ Order John Hancock Esqr., Mr. Timo. Newell} Selectmen
Mr. Benja. Dolbeare Overseer &c

5.   Received into the House Sarah Kent an infirm Woman[602]
℘ Order Mr. Danl. Waldo Overseer &c

8.   Received into the House on Province Accott. John Downey
℘ Order John Scollay, Thos. Marshall} Esqrs. Selectmen
Mr. Willm. Greenleaf Overseer &c

12.   Received into the House from the Workhouse Willm. Ross & Baxter
Granger
℘ Order Capt. Saml. Partridge Overseer &c
Ross sent back to the Workho.

14.   Received into the House Mary Lovel[603] aged about Eleven years.
℘ Order Capt. Saml. Partridge Overseer &c

14.   Received into the House Judith Clark
℘ Order Mr. Saml. Whitwell Overseer &c

17.   Received into the House Hannah White a poor Child
℘ Order Mr. Willm. Whitwell Overseer &c

1773. July 19.   Received into the House (on the Prov. Accott.) Eliza. Watts[604]
℘ Order Mr. Timo. Newell, Thoms. Marshall Esqr.} Selectmen
Mr. Saml. Whitwell Overseer &c

22.   Received into the House (on Prov. Accott.) Ruth Wakefield
℘ Order John Scollay Esqr., Mr. Timo. Newell} Selectmen
Mr. Saml. Whitwell Overseer &c

23.   Received into the House 2. Children named Willm. & Joseph Barrett
℘ Order Willm. White Esqr. Overseer &c

23.   Received into the House (on Prov. Accott.) Ann Shay & her Child
℘ Order John Scollay Esqr., Mr. Saml. Austin} Selectmen
Mr. Saml. Whitwell Overseer &c

July 26.   Discharg'd Frances McCorneck (prov. Charge) Eliza. Castle

Augt. 12th.   Discharg'd Sarah Remick (Prov. Charge)
August 16th.   Discharg'd Wm. Gordon (prov. Charge)

July 29.   Received into the House (on Prov. Accott.) Michael Cumber
℘ Order John Scollay Esqr., Mr. Saml. Austin} Selectmen
Mr. Danl. Waldo Overseer &c
Dischargd Septr. 25th. 1773

Augt. 25th.   Received into the House (on Prov. Accott.) John Graves[605]
℘ Order John Scollay Esqr., Mr. Timo. Newell} Selectmen
Mr. Wm. Whitwell Overseer &c

26.   Received into the House (on Prov. Accott.) Hannah Yarney a Negro
℘ Order John Scollay Esqr., Mr. Timo. Newell} Selectmen
Capt. Saml. Partridge Overseer &c
Deceased the 28th. Augt. 1773.

1773. August   Received into the House Joseph Ransford[606] Lame
℘ Order John Gore Esqr. Overseer &c   dated August 19th. 1773.

Septr. 3.   Matthew Bright (prov. Charge) run away
Septr. 6th.   Dischargd John Downey (prov. Charge)   21. Wm. Holmes (prov. Charge)
24.   John Ryan (prov. Charge)   (26th.) Ferrers Shirley (prov. Charge) without
leave
25th.   Michl. Cumber (prov. Charge)

Septr. 3d.   Received into the House Ann Dumaresque a poor Child aged abt. 7.
yrs.
℘ Order John Barrett Esqr. Overseer &c

3.   Received into the House Margarett Hill Wife of Robt. Hill Carter
℘ Order John Barrett Esqr. Overseer &c

3d.   Received into the House (on Prov. Account) Peggy & George Erving[607]
Infants
℘ Order John Scollay Esqr., Mr. Timo. Newell} Selectmen
Mr. Danl. Waldo Overseer &c

4th.   Received into the House Jane Doyle a very infirm Woman
℘ Order John Barrett Esqr. Overseer &c

6.   Received into the Alms House a Child of Lydia Slopers abt. 2. yrs. Old named Frederick
℗ Order John Leverett Esqr. Overseer &c

6.   Received into the House (on Prov. Accott.) Eliza. Hodgdon[608]
℗ Order Jno. Scollay Esqr., Mr. Timo. Newell} Selectmen
Willm. White Esqr. Overseer &c

8.   Received into the House (on Prov. Accott.) Judith Keylee & her 3 Childn.
℗ Order Mr. Timo. Newell, Mr. Saml. Austin} Selectmen
Mr. Benja. Dolbeare Overseer &c
1773. Septemr. 8th. Received into the House (on Prov. Accott.) Elizabeth Smith
℗ Order John Scollay Esqr., Mr. John Pitts} Selectmen
Mr. Danl. Waldo Overseer &c

16.   Received into the House from the Workhouse John Taylor & Josiah Fessenden
℗ Order Mr. Willm. Whitwell Overseer &c

17.   Received into the House on Province Accott. Edward Warren
℗ Order John Scollay Esqr., Mr. Saml. Austin} Selectmen
Mr. Wm. Greenleaf Overseer &c
Chaise hire 18/ OT

23d.   Received into the House from the Work house Charles Procter a Sick & Lame young Man belonging to Groton—his Expences to be charg'd to the Selectmen of this Town
℗ Order Mr. Willm. Greenleaf Overseer &c
sent back to the Workhouse 28th. Septr.

23d.   Received into the House (on Prov. Accott.) Hugh Bryann—Sick
℗ Order Mr. Timo. Newell, Thos. Marshall Esqr.} Selectmen
Mr. Danl. Waldo Overseer &c

29.   Received into the House (on Prov. Accott.) James Thompson
℗ Order John Scollay Esqr., Mr. Saml. Austin} Selectmen
John Leverett Esqr. Overseer &c

30.   Received into the House (on Prov Accott.) Peter Hynot
℗ Order John Scollay Esqr., Mr. Saml. Austin} Selectmen
Mr. Willm. Whitwell Overseer &c

Octor. 7th.   Discharg'd Eliza. Smith (prov.)   (12th.) Peggy & Jno. Ervin (Prov)
16.   Ruth Wakefield (prov)—Lawrence Collins—Joseph Rainsford

❧

1773. Octo.　　　　Received into the House (on Prov. Accott.) Martha Ryan & her Child
℘ Order Mr. Timo. Newell, Mr. Saml. Austin} Selectmen
Capt. Saml. Partridge Overseer &c　　NB. Order was dated June 10th. 1773. & is to be charg'd in next prov. Accott. setled
Discharg'd 16th. October 1773.

Octor. 6th.　　　　Received into the House (on Prov. Accott.) John Macgraw
℘ Order John Scollay Esqr., Mr. Timo. Newell} Selectmen
Mr. William Greenleaf Overseer &c

7th.　　　　Received into the House (on Prov. Accott.) John Jackson (wounded)
℘ Order John Scollay Esqr., Mr. Saml. Austin} Selectmen
Mr. Saml. Whitwell Overseer &c

9th.　　　　Received into the House (on Prov. Accott.) Michael Daily got the —
℘ Order John Scollay Esqr., Mr. Saml. Austin} Selectmen
John Barrett Esqr. Overseer &c

11th.　　　　Received into the House (on Prov. Accott.) Francis McDaniel
℘ Order John Scollay Esqr., Mr. Timo. Newell} Selectmen
Mr. Saml. Whitwell Overseer &c

12th.　　　　Received into the House (on Prov. Accott.) Maxwell Gullroy
℘ Order John Scollay Esqr., Mr. Saml. Austin} Selectmen
Mr. Willm. Greenleaf Overseer &c

12th.　　　　Received into the House Lawrence Collins
℘ Order Capt. Saml. Partridge &c

1773. Octor. 15　　Received into the House (on Prov. Accott.) Walter & John Jack two Soldiers Children. Walter Born　　　　John Born Janua. 2d. 1773
℘ Order John Scollay Esqr., Mr. Saml. Austin} Selectmen
Mr. Danl. Waldo Overseer &c

20th.　　　　Received into the House (on Prov. Accott.) Sarah Remick
℘ Order John Scollay Esqr., Mr. Timo. Newell} Selectmen
Mr. Willm. Whitwell Overseer &c

23d.　　　　Received into the House Elizabeth Mallett
℘ Order Mr. Saml. Abbot Overseer &c

[do.][609]　　　　Received into the House Elizabeth Look
℘ Order John Leverett Esqr. Overseer &c　Order dated Octor. 14th. 1773

　　　　Received into the House from the Workhouse Tabitha Akley[610]
℘ Order Mr. Saml. Whitwell Overseer &c

Novr. 3.　　　　　Received into the House by order of the Board Susanna Murkison &
Sarah Brown

6.　　　　　Received into the House Edith Ellerton—from the Workhouse[611]
℘ Order Mr. Saml. Abbot Overseer &c

6.　　　　　Received into the House (on prov Accott.) Alexr. Thompson
℘ Order John Scollay Esqr., Mr. Saml. Austin} Selectmen
Jno. Barrett Esqr. Overseer &c

10th.　　　　　Received into the House on prov. Accott. Patrick Christopher
℘ Order John Scollay Esqr., Mr. Timo. Newell} Selectmen
Mr. Benja. Dolbeare Overseer &c

8th.　　　　　Received into the House Eliza. Addison[612]
℘ Order Jno. Barrett Esqr. Overseer &c

1773. Nov. 18.　　　Received into the House on prov. Accott. Ann Moor & 2 Children
℘ Order John Scollay Esqr., Mr. Timo. Newell} Selectmen
Mr. Saml. Whitwell Overseer &c

19.　　　　　Received into the House on prov. Accott. Sarah Hartshorn & Child
℘ Order John Scollay Esqr., Mr. Timo. Newell} Selectmen
Mr. Benja. Dolbeare Overseer &c

22.　　　　　Received into the House Sarah Thomas—an Aged Woman
℘ Order Mr. Danl. Waldo Overseer &c

24.　　　　　Received into the House on prov. Accott. Thomas Wall
℘ Order John Scollay Esqr., Thos. Marshall Esqr.} Selectmen
John Leverett Esqr. Overseer &c

　　　　　Discharged Mary Langley　(Novr. 8th.) John Jackson & Kata. White
(provce.)
Nov. 26.　　　　　Edward Warren (prov. Charge)　29th. Maxwell Gullroy Prov. Charge

Novr. 15　　　　Received into the House Elizabeth Parker an Aged Woman
℘ Order Mr. Danl. Waldo Overseer &c

27.　　　　　Received into the House Elizabeth Dawson (Daughter of Jas. Dawson)
℘ Order Mr. Willm. Whitwell Overseer &c　　　dated Novemr. 22d. 1773.

26.　　　　　Received into the House Mary Dumphy a Girl
℘ Order Capt. Saml. Partridge Overseer &c

Decr. 1.　　　　　Received into the House on prov. Accott. Francis John Loyd
℘ Order John Scollay Esqr., Mr. Timo. Newell} Selectmen
Mr. Benja. Dolbeare Overseer &c

1773. Decemr. 2d.   Received into the House (on Prov. Accott.) William Farling
℘ Order Thomas Marshall Esqr., Mr. Oliver Wendell} Selectmen
Mr. Danl. Waldo Overseer &c

3d.   Received into the House William Thwing
℘ Order John Leverett Esqr. Overseer &c

6.   Received into the House Increase Simpson
℘ Order Mr. Saml. Whitwell Overseer &c

                    Received into the House John Carter Wife & 4 Children

13th.   Received into the House Benjamin Gold[613]
℘ Order Mr. Saml. Whitwell Overseer &c

15th.   Received into the House George & Katharine[614] Kilcup
℘ Order Mr. Saml. Abbot Overseer &c

15th.   Received into the House Ann Ross & 2. Children
℘ Order John Leverett Esqr. Overseer &c

22d.   Received into the House (on prov Accott.) George Garlick
℘ Order John Scollay Esqr., Mr. Timo. Newell} Selectmen
Mr. Danl. Waldo Overseer &c

22.   Received into the House (on prov Accott.) Patrick Dowdell
℘ Order John Scollay Esqr., Mr. John Pitts} Selectmen
Mr. Saml. Whitwell Overseer &c

27th.   Received into the House (on prov Accott.) Matthew Bright
℘ Order John Scollay Esqr., Mr. Timo. Newell} Selectmen
Mr. Benja. Dolbeare Overseer &c

1774. Janua. 1st.   Received into the House (on prov Accott.) William Smith
℘ Order John Scollay Esqr., Mr. Timo. Newell} Selectmen
Mr. William Whitwell Overseer &c

1773. Decemr. 10th.} Discharg'd Ann More & 1. Child (prov Charges)
11.   Elizabeth Taylor & 2. Children—Mrs. Cotterell jumpt Fence, Mary
Dumphy
25th.   William Sharp prov Charge jumpt Fence—25th. Peter Hynot (prov
Charge) run away

1774. Janua. 12}   Received into the House Sarah Gough[615] came from Weston
℘ Order Capt. Saml. Partridge Overseer &c

13. Received into the House (on prov Accott.) John Wyer
℘ Order John Scollay Esqr., Mr. Saml. Austin} Selectmen
John Barrett Esqr. Overseer &c

14. Received into the House Scipio[616] a Servant to Benja. Gridley Esqr.
℘ Order Mr. William Greenleaf Overseer &c

20. Received into the House Thomas Lewis—Lame
℘ Order Willm. White Esqr. Overseer &c

21. Received into the House Sarah Cahale
℘ Order Mr. Saml. Abbot Overseer &c

25. Received into the House from Workhouse Edward Rumley
℘ Order Mr. Saml. Whitwell Overseer &c

25. Received into the House (on prov Accott.) Bethia Burroughs[617] &
Child
℘ Order John Scollay Esqr., Mr. Timo. Newell} Selectmen
John Leverett Esqr. Overseer &c
came from Weymouth

1774. Jany. 25th.} Received into the House James Tent a Child Born Janua. 31st. 1771 (on
prov. Accott.)
Jno. Scollay, Saml. Austin} Selectmen
℘ Order Mr. Danl. Waldo Overseer &c

29. Received into the House (on prov Accott.) Edward Amos
℘ Order John Scollay Esqr., Mr. Saml. Austin} Selectmen
John Leverett Esqr. Overseer &c

31. Received into the House John Fitzgerald
℘ Order Mr. Saml. Whitwell Overseer &c

Feby. 1st. Discharg'd Patrick Christopher (prov. Charge)
do. John McGraw—Prov

2. Received into the House Hepzibah Darnbrook
℘ Order William White Esqr. Overseer &c

4. Received into the House Elizabeth White[618] wife of Matthew White
℘ Order Capt. Saml. Partridge Overseer &c

11th. Received into the House (on prov. Accott.) Richard Lee
℘ Order John Scollay Esqr., Mr. Jno. Pitts} Selectmen
Mr. Danl. Waldo Overseer &c

15th.   Received into the House (on prov Accott.) Sarah Tate
℘ Order John Scollay Esqr., Mr. Timo. Newell} Selectmen
Mr. Benja. Dolbeare Overseer &c

26.   Received into the House (on prov Accott.) Sarah Dockum
℘ Order Mr. Timo. Newell, Jno. Scollay Esqr} Selectmen
Capt. Saml. Partridge Overseer &c

1774. Feby. 26. Received into the House Thomas Greenough a Child
℘ Order Mr. Willm. Whitwell Overseer &c

Mar. 3d.   Discharged James Thompson (prov Charge) (5th.) Wm. Smith (prov)
Edwd. Rumley to Workhouse—(12th.) Patrick Dowdell (prov)
22d.   Geo. Garlick (prov) (23d.) James Bruce (prov)   (24.) Alexr. Thompson
& Jno. Loyd (prov)
30.   Michl. Daily (prov) (28th.) Judith Keylee & 3. Children (prov)

Mar. 7th.   Received into the House (on prov Accott.) James Bruce
℘ Order Jno. Scollay Esqr., Mr. Timo. Newell} Selectmen
Mr. Benja. Dolbeare Overseer &c
Went away <*in April followg*> the same Month

10.   Received into the House Hannah Allen
℘ Order Mr. Danl. Waldo Overseer &c

11.   Received into the House (on prov Accott.) an Indian Woman belonging
to Natick
℘ Order Jno. Scollay Esqr.   }
Mr. Benja. Dolbeare Overseer &c

12th.   Received into the House (on prov Accott.) an Indian Woman belonging
to Nantucket
℘ Order Jno. Scollay Esqr., Mr. Timo. Newell} Selectmen
Mr. Benja. Dolbeare Overseer &c

14   Received into the House (on prov Accott.) John Russell[619]
℘ Order Jno. Scollay Esqr., Thos. Marshall Esqr.} Selectmen
Mr. Wm. Whitwell Overseer &c

17th.   Received into the House from the Workhouse Andrew Floyd
℘ Order John Gore Esqr. Overseer &c

1774. Mar. 23d. Received into the House on prov Accott. Primus a Negro
℘ Order Jno. Scollay Esqr., Mr. Timo. Newell} Selectmen
Wm. White Esqr. Overseer &c

24   Received into the House from Workho. John Dyman[620]
℘ Order Capt. Saml. Partridge Overseer &c

25th.   Received into the House (on prov Accott.) James Gorman[621]
℘ Order Mr. Timo. Newell, Mr. Saml. Austin} Selectmen
Mr. Wm. Whitwell Overseer &c

April 1st.   Received into the House Elizabeth Sinclair
℘ Order Mr. Saml. Whitwell Overseer &c

4.   Received into the House (on prov Accott.) Cornelius Youngman
℘ Order John Scollay Esqr., Mr. Timo. Newell} Selectmen
Mr. Saml. Whitwell Overseer &c

5.   Received into the House Abigail Flood—distracted
℘ Order Mr. Willm. Whitwell Overseer &c

8th.   Discharged Winifred Stone & Child (prov) John Fitzgerald run away
26.   Francis McDaniel, George Downing & John Stuart[622] (prov. Charges)

April 6   Received into the House on prov. Accott. John Stewart
℘ Order John Scollay Esqr., Mr. Timo. Newell} Selectmen
John Leverett Esqr. Overseer &c

1774 April 9th.   Received into the House (on prov. Accott.) Joseph Cook
℘ Order John Scollay Esqr., Mr. Timo. Newell} Selectmen
Mr. Benja. Dolbeare Overseer &c

13.   Received into the House (on prov. Accott.) Peter Larkin
℘ Order John Scollay Esqr., Mr. Timo. Newell} Selectmen
Mr. Benja. Dolbeare Overseer &c

16.   Received into the House Widow Elizabeth Eustis
℘ Order John Gore Esqr. Overseer &c

19.   Received into the House (on prov. Accott.) Robert Smith
℘ Order John Scollay Esqr., Mr. Timo. Newell} Selectmen
Mr. Benja. Dolbeare Overseer &c

19.   Received into the House (on prov. Accott.) Patrick Hawkins
℘ Order John Scollay, Thos. Marshall} Esqrs. Selectmen
John Leverett Esqr. Overseer &c

23.   Received into the House (on prov Accott.) Bridgewater[623] a Negro
℘ Order John Scollay Esqr., Mr. Timo. Newell} Selectmen
Mr. Benja. Dolbeare Overseer &c

26   Received into the House from the Workhouse Matthew White
℘ Order Mr. Willm. Whitwell Overseer &c

27.   Received into the House William Rogers[624]—a Shoemaker
℘ Order Mr. Willm. Whitwell Overseer &c

1774 May 3d.   Received into the House on prov. Accott. Mary Nichols & Child
℘ Order John Scollay Esqr., Mr. Timo. Newell} Selectmen
Mr. Benja. Dolbeare Overseer &c

May 5.   Discharg'd Peter Larkin (prov) (15th) Robt. Smith (prov) run
Eliza. Williams <*Eliza. Lark*> Thomas Lewis run away
12.   <*Nantuc*> Natick Indian (prov)—(27th.) Joseph Cook (prov)

Received into the House (on Prov. Accott.) John Colman
℘ Order John Scollay Esqr., Mr. Timo. Newell} Selectmen
John Barrett Esqr. Overseer &c Order dated Janua. 28th. 1774
to be put in the next Accott. being omitted.

May 5.   Received into the House Joseph Mountfort
℘ Order Mr. Benja. Dolbeare Overseer &c

9.   Received into House Kezia Stevens—Geo. Augustus Hales Sister
℘ Order John Barrett Esqr. Overseer &c

12.   Received into the House (on prov. Accott.) John Flinge
℘ Order John Scollay Esqr., Mr. Timo. Newell} Selectmen
Mr. Benja. Dolbeare Overseer &c

23.   Received into the House Mary Kellon—Sick
℘ Order Mr. Danl. Waldo Overseer &c

24.   Received into the House a Negro Man named Jack belonging to
Robert Breck
℘ Order Mr. Saml. Abbot Overseer &c

1774 May 26th.} Received into the House Oliver Blanchard a Child of Margarett Thorps
5 yrs. old March 24th. 1774.
℘ Order Mr. Saml. Whitwell Overseer &c

31.   Received into the House Eleazer Newhall an aged Man
℘ Order Willm. White Esqr. Overseer &c

June 1.   Received into the House Hannah Raymar
℘ Order Mr. Saml. Whitwell Overseer &c

do.   Received into the House Francis McDaniel (on prov Accott.)
℘ Order Jno. Scollay Esqr., Mr. Timo. Newell} Selectmen
Mr. Wm. Whitwell Overseer &c

11.   Received into the House (on Prov. Accott.) Michael Dailye
℘ Order John Scollay Esqr., Mr. Timo. Newell} Selectmen
Mr. Willm. Whitwell Overseer &c

16.   Received into the House John Whitty a Boy aged Years
℘ Order Mr. Saml. Whitwell Overseer &c

17.   Received into the House (on prov. Accott.) George Downing
℘ Order John Scollay Esqr., Mr. Timo. Newell} Selectmen
John Gore Esqr. Overseer &c

June 16th.   Discharg'd Nathan Shute (prov) (20th.) Moores Child (prov)
       Jannet Seaward & Eliza. Castle run away

June 10.   Received into the House John Whitty—(very ill)—dyed next day
℘ Order Mr. Saml. Whitwell Overseer &c

1774. June 18. Received into the House (on prov. Accott.) James Whalan
℘ Order John Scollay Esqr., Mr. Timo. Newell} Selectmen
Mr. Willm. Whitwell Overseer &c

22.   Received into the House John Ray—Lame
℘ Order Mr. Danl. Waldo Overseer &c

27.   Received into the House Elizabeth Chamberlain—an Elderly Woman
℘ Order Capt. Saml. Partridge Overseer &c

July 2.   Received into the House Martha Eggleston—sick
℘ Order Mr. Benja. Dolbeare Overseer &c

7.   Received into the House on province Accott. Dennis Cavenaugh
℘ Order John Scollay Esqr., Mr. Timo. Newell} Selectmen
Mr. Wm. Whitwell Overseer &c

13th.   Received into the House Elizabeth Barbour aged 12 or 13. yrs.
℘ Order Mr. Danl. Waldo Overseer &c

15.   Received into the House Benjamin Chubb—Lame
℘ Order John Gore Esqr. Overseer &c

23d.   Received into the House William Brown—a Lame Man
℘ Order Willm. White Esqr. Overseer &c

31.   Received into the House Ebenezer Northy—sick
℘ Order Mr. Daniel Waldo Overseer &c

1774. July 21} Discharged Dennis Cavenaugh, Thos. Wall & Patrick Hawkins (prov.
Charge)

                    Mary Dickey jumpt Fence—(25th.) Matthew Bright (prov)—Mercy Herne & Elizabeth Mallett run away July 31.

1774 Augt. 2.   Received into the House on prov Accott. Thomas Wall
℘ Order John Scollay Esqr., Mr. Saml. Austin} Selectmen
Mr. Wm. Greenleaf Overseer &c

4th.   Received into the House on prov. Accott. William Holmes
℘ Order Oliver Wendell, John Pitts} Selectmen
Mr. Willm. Whitwell Overseer &c

11th.   Received into the House on prov. Accott. Dennis Cavenaugh
℘ Order John Scollay Esqr., Mr. Timo. Newell} Selectmen
John Gore Esqr. Overseer &c

12   Received into the House a Boy named Samuel Greenough
℘ Order Mr. Benja. Dolbeare Overseer &c

22.   Received into the House Priscilla Gill
℘ Order Mr. Willm. Whitwell Overseer &c

1774. Augt. 8th.}   Discharged Richard Lee (prov. Charge)
Octo. 22d.   Discharged Dennis Cavenaugh (prov Charge)

1774. Augt. 15}   Discharg'd James Whalan (prov)
Augt. 26th.   Joanna Laha a Child (prov)   (26th.) Thos. Wall (prov)
28   Margtt. Glossup (prov). Scipio Negro run away
                  Martha Eggleston run away

Augt. 25th.   Received into the House on prov. Accott. Judith Keily & 3. Children
℘ Order John Scollay Esqr., Mr. Timo. Newell} Selectmen
Mr. Willm. Greenleaf Overseer &c

1774. Augt. 29th.} Received into the House Martha Pearse—sick
℘ Order Willm. White Esqr. Overseer &c

30.   Received into the House (on prov. Accott.) William Hayley
℘ Order John Scollay Esqr., Mr. Timo. Newell} Selectmen
John Leverett Esqr. Overseer &c

31.   Received into the House William Dunn a Child of Eliza. Bennets 2 yrs. Old Janua. 1774.
℘ Order John Leverett Esqr. Overseer &c

Septemr. 5.   Received into the House Nancy Crosby a Child
℘ Order Willm. White Esqr. Overseer &c

7th.   Received into the House (on prov. Accott.) <*Peggy*> Joseph Pope & Edward Power 2. Infant Children}
℘ Order John Scollay Esqr., Mr. Timo. Newell} Selectmen
Capt. Saml. Partridge Overseer &c

7th.   Received into the House (on prov. Accott.) Robert Hynes
℘ Order John Scollay Esqr., Mr. John Pitts} Selectmen
Mr. Willm. Whitwell Overseer &c

12.   Received into the House from the Workhouse Mary Hale
℘ Order Mr. Danl. Waldo Overseer &c
Her Husband to pay 3/4 ℘ Week for her Board

1774. Sept. 12th.   Mary Perrin (prov) run away—(25th.) John Ray run away.
27th.   Polly McEwen a Child—Eliza. Taylor to the Workhouse

12th.   Received into the House Fanny Jones a Child (on prov. Accott.)
℘ Order John Leverett Esqr. Overseer &c
Jno. Scollay Esqr., Mr. Timo. Newell} Selectmen

1774. Septr. 13th.   Received into the House Samuel Davis—(White Smith)
℘ Order John Leverett Esqr. Overseer &c

17.   Received into the House Eliza. Ward
℘ Order Mr. Willm. Greenleaf Overseer &c

20.   Received into the House (from the Workhouse) Robert Hill
℘ Order John Barrett Esqr. Overseer &c

24.   Received into the House Elizabeth Taylor & 2. Children
℘ Order John Barrett Esqr. Overseer &c

                    Received into the House (19th. Septr.) Mercy Herne
℘ Verbal Order William Phillips Esqr. Overseer &c

27th.   Received into the House (on prov. Accott.) Catharine McFerron
℘ Order John Scollay Esqr., Mr. Saml. Austin} Selectmen
John Leverett Esqr. Overseer &c

27.   Received into the House Sarah Whittemore (Wife of Edwd. Whittemore)
℘ Order Mr. Saml. Whitwell Overseer &c

28.   Received into the House a Child of Mary Turners
℘ Order Mr. Saml. Whitwell Overseer &c

29.   Received into the House from the Workhouse Mary Henshaw & Child
℘ Order Mr. Willm. Whitwell Overseer &c

Octor. 4th.   Received into the House (on prov. Accott.) Peggy & George Erving
Children
℘ Order Mr. Timo. Newell, Mr. Saml. Austin} Selectmen
Mr. Saml. Abbot Overseer &c
Went away Decemr. 27th. 1774

1774 Octo. 8th.}   Discharg'd Abraham Remick a Child (prov. Charge)
                    Mercy Herne run away. Saml. Davis run away
31   Thomas Barber

1774. Octo. 7th.}   Received into the House Elizabeth Mallet
℘ Order John Leverett Esqr. Overseer &c

11th.   Received into the House (on prov. Accott.) Mary Perrin
℘ Order John Scollay Esqr., Mr. Timo. Newell} Selectmen
Mr. Danl. Waldo Overseer &c

24.   Received into the House Philip Condon a Boy aged about 10 yrs.
℘ Order Mr. Willm. Whitwell Overseer &c

Octo.   Received Thomas Barber into the House—order dated Octo. 18th.
℘ Order John Gore Esqr. Overseer &c

28th.   Received into the House (on prov. Accott.) James Thompson
℘ Order John Scollay, Thoms. Marshall} Esqrs. Selectmen
Mr. Saml. Whitwell Overseer &c

30th.   Received into the House John Wallis a Boy aged 7. yrs. 3d. Octo. 1774
℘ Order Mr. Danl. Waldo Overseer &c

31.   Received into the House Elizabeth Harris & her 3. Sons
℘ Order Mr. Willm. Greenleaf Overseer &c

Novr. 2.   Received into the House Elizabeth Sinclair
℘ Order of the Board Sitting Day

Novr. 16.   William Holmes (prov. Accott.) Run away

1774. Novr. 3}   Received into the House Eleanor Cooley from the Workhouse
℘ Order Mr. Saml. Whitwell Overseer &c

4.   Received into the House Deborah Howard
℘ Order John Gore Esqr. Overseer &c

5.   Received into the House from the Workhouse Jane Collins
℘ Order Mr. Saml. Whitwell Overseer &c

8.   Received into the House (on prov. Accott.) Mary Winchester
℘ Order John Scollay Esqr., Mr. Timo. Newell} Selectmen
Mr. John White Overseer &c

10.   Received into the House Mary Combes—a sick Woman
℘ Order John Gore Esqr. Overseer &c

12.   Received into the House (on prov. Accott.) Sarah Horn
℘ Order Mr. Timo. Newell, Mr. Saml. Austin} Selectmen
Mr. Saml. Whitwell Overseer &c

15.   Received into the House (on prov. Accott.) Mary Tilty a Girl—Soldiers
℘ Order Mr. Timo. Newell, Mr. Saml. Austin} Selectmen
Mr. Benja. Dolbeare Overseer &c

15.   Received into the House from the Workhouse Eliza. Jackson
℘ Order Mr. Benja. Dolbeare Overseer &c

16.   Received into the House (on prov. Accott.) William Sharp
℘ Order John Scollay Esqr., Mr. Timo. Newell} Selectmen
John Barrett Esqr. Overseer &c

22.   Received into the House (on prov Accott.) Anthony Cavilla
℘ Order John Scollay Esqr., Mr. Timo. Newell} Selectmen
Mr. Saml. Abbot Overseer &c

1774. Novr.}   Received into the House Dinah a Negro Woman
℘ Order John Gore Esqr. Overseer &   Dated Septr. 27th.

23.   Received into the House (on prov Accott.) Jonathan Bobbin
℘ Order John Scollay Esqr., Mr. Timo. Newell} Selectmen
Capt. Saml. Partridge Overseer &c
deceased 30th. Novr. 1774.

29.   Received into the House James Bailey a very old Man
℘ Order Capt. Saml. Partridge Overseer &c

30.   Received into the House (on prov Accott.) Robert & Mary Nicholson
Soldiers Children}
℘ Order John Scollay, Thoms. Marshall} Esqrs. Selectmen
John Barrett Esqr. Overseer &c

Decemr. 1.   Received into the House Susanna Munn (a Girl)
℘ Order Mr. Saml. Whitwell Overseer &c

10.   Received into the House (on prov. Accott.) Rebecca Price
℘ Order John Scollay Esqr., Mr. Timo. Newell} Selectmen
Mr. Willm. Whitwell Overseer &c

12.   Received into the House (on prov Accott.) Annis Kempland
℘ Order John Scollay Esqr., Mr. Saml. Austin} Selectmen
Mr. Benja. Dolbeare Overseer &c

17.   Received into the House (on prov Accott.) Eleanor Pue
℘ Order John Scollay, John Hancock} Esqrs. Selectmen
Mr. Willm. Whitwell Overseer &c

17.   Received into the House from the Workhouse Eliza. Taylor
℘ Order Mr. Benja. Dolbeare Overseer &c

Decemr. 27th.   Discharged Peggy & George Ervin Children (on prov. Charge)

1774. Decr. 17.}   Received into the House Abigail Munn
℘ Order Mr. Saml. Whitwell Overseer &c

18.   Received into the House (on prov. Accott.) Margarett Glossup
℘ Order John Scollay, John Hancock} Esqrs. Selectmen
Mr. Benja. Dolbeare Overseer &c

22.   Received into the House James Baker
℘ Order Mr. Danl. Waldo Overseer

26.   Received into the House from Workhouse John Barker & Mary
Lemoine}
℘ Order Mr. Willm. Whitwell Overseer &c

26.   Received into the House Lydia Lacey
℘ Order Mr. Willm. Whitwell Overseer &c

26.   Received into the House Elizabeth Manning—(with Child)
℘ Order Capt. Saml. Partridge Overseer &c

26   Received into the House Michael Condon
℘ Order Mr. Willm. Whitwell Overseer &c

30.   Received into the House Thomas Barber
℘ Order John Gore Esqr. Overseer &c

Notes

1 The first ten pages of Admissions Register 1 are missing. The Register's index, however, includes the names of the individuals that appear on the missing pages. The corresponding index entries are printed here.

2 In the left margin of the first surviving page of Admissions Register 1, every fifth line is numbered to facilitate counting the total number of entries. Next to Rebecca Pimm's name is the notation "80"; Elear. Higgins "5"; Eliza. Jones "90"; Margt. Kitchen "5"; 2 Children "400"; Rebecca Pierce "5"; and John Pilsberry "10." The entry for James Sinclair, 27 Jan. 1759, below, is the final line of the page.

3 "Barbara" in the MS index.

4 "Eleanor" in the MS index.

5 "Marks" in the MS index.

6 "Marks" in the MS index.

7 "Barbary" in the MS index.

8 "Cane" in the MS index.

9 "Lassel" in the MS index.

10 "More" in the MS index.

11 Obscured when the pages were bound.

12 "Alman" in the MS index.

13 Next to the name in the left margin is a "P," i.e. Province.

14 "Howe" in the MS index.

15 "O'Byan" in the MS index.

16 "Griffin" in the MS index.

17 Obscured when the pages were bound.

18 Obscured when the pages were bound.

19 "Mary" in the MS index.

20 Next to the name in the left margin is a "P," i.e. Province.

21 Next to the name in the left margin is a "P," i.e. Province.

22 Next to the name in the left margin is a "P," i.e. Province.

23 Next to the name in the left margin is a "P," i.e. Province.

24 Next to the name in the left margin is a "P," i.e. Province.

25 Next to the name in the left margin is a "P," i.e. Province.

26 "Orn" in the MS index.

27 Next to the name in the left margin is a "P," i.e. Province.

28 "Rebecca Vallicott" in the MS index.

29 "Smith, Anna & Mary" in the MS index.

30 Next to the name in the left margin is a "P," i.e. Province.

31 Next to the name in the left margin is a "P," i.e. Province.

32 Next to the entry in the left margin is a "P," i.e. Province.

33 "Ervin" in the MS index.

34 "Conigen" in the MS index.

35 Next to the name of each Anselm in the left margin is a "P," i.e. Province.

36 Next to the name in the left margin is a "P," i.e. Province.

37 "Lassel" in the MS index. Next to the name in the left margin is a "P," i.e. Province.

38 First entry in Admissions Register 2.

39 "Mrs. Waddle" in Register 1.

40   Supplied from Register 1.

41   The Discharge column in Register 1 includes the notation "gone away" next to both James' and Charles' name.

42   Register 1, Discharge: "Mrs. Bass discharged May 17th. 1764."

43   Register 1, Discharge: "Wkhouse."

44   Register 1, Discharge: "July 1763."

45   Register 1, Age "60"; Death: "Deceased Jany. 23. 1770."

46   "Warwick" in Register 1.

47   Register 1, Age: "55"; Death: "Feby. 22.1772."

48   Register 1, Discharge: "gone to London."

49   Register 1, Discharge: "gone away."

50   Register 1, Discharge: "Patrick discharged April 1765 Wife Dead."

51   Register 1, Discharge: "gone away."

52   Register 1, Discharge: "Bound out."

53   Register 1, Discharge: "gone away."

54   "Sutherland" in Register 1.

55   Register 1, Discharge: "gone away."

56   Register 1: "25."

57   "Addleton" in Register 1.

58   Register 1, Death of Mrs. Campbell: "June 22d. 1764."

59   Register 1, Discharge: "Septr. 1765."

60   Register 1, Age: "30."

61   Register 1, Age: "50."

62   Register 1: "Davidson"; Age: "35."

63   "Wesson" in Register 1.

64   "Michael Cavenaugh" in Register 1.

65   Register 1, Discharge: "April 25."

66   Register 1, Discharge: "[*April*] 23."

67   "Skweler" in Register 1.

68   Register 1, Discharge: "gone away."

69   "Kennaly" in Register 1. Also, Discharge: "gone away."

70   "Simpson" in Register 1.

71   Register 1, Discharge: "gone away."

72   Register 1, Age: "6."

73   Register 1, Age: "70"; Death: "1764 July 24th."

74   "Fullerton" in Register 1.

75   "Cooper" in Register 1.

76   Register 1, Age: "5 yrs."

77   Register 1, Death: "Dead."

78   Register 1, Age: "19 yrs."; Discharge: "gone away."

79   "Mangent" in Register 1. Also, Age: "4 yrs."

80   Register 1, Discharge: "Bound out."

81   Register 1, Age: "23."

82   "Rolston" in Register 1.

83   "John Tincum" in Register 1.

84   Supplied from Register 1.

85   Register 1, Age: "22 yrs."; Discharge: "gone away."

86   Register 1, Discharge: "gone away."

87   "Darrington" in Register 1. Also, Discharge: "June 5th. 1764."

88   "Melvill" in Register 1.

89   Register 1, Burk Discharge: "absent 1765."

90   "Kellam" in Register 1. Also, Age: "19."

91   Supplied from Register 1.

92 "Sender" in Register 1.
93 Register 1, Discharge: "gone away."
94 Register 1, Discharge: "gone away."
95 "Lawrence" in Register 1.
96 Supplied from Register 1.
97 Register 1, Discharge: "gone away."
98 "Do." in Register 1, i.e. 18.
99 "Patrix" in Register 1. Also, Age: "10"; Death: "June 29th. 1764."
100 Register 1 adds, "alias Higgins."
101 Register 1, Age: "14 yrs."
102 "Hicks" in Register 1. Also, Age "70."
103 Register 1, Age: "36."
104 Supplied from Register 1.
105 "Sloper" in Register 1.
106 Register 1, Age: "36."
107 "Cahill" in Register 1. Also, Age: "45."
108 Register 1, Discharge: "gone away & Dead."
109 Register 1, Age: "48."
110 Register 1, Age: "30."
111 Register 1, Age: "35 & 28."
112 Register 1, Age: "77."
113 Register 1, Age: "6."
114 Register 1, Discharge: "Mother gone away"; Death: "Child deceasd May 9. 1765."
115 "Burk" in Register 1. Also, Age: "35."
116 Register 1, Age: "60."
117 Register 1, Age: "30"; Discharge: "Woman gone & 1 Child deceased."
118 Register 1, Age: "25."
119 Delivered or discharged.
120 "Evans" in Register 1.
121 Register 1, Discharge: "Workhouse."
122 Register 1, Age: "64."
123 Register 1, Age: "65."
124 Register 1, Age: "55."
125 Register 1, Age: "53."
126 Register 1, Age: "45, 50}"; Death: "She dyed June 20. 1769."
127 Register 1, Discharge: "all gone."
128 Register 1, Age: "60."
129 Register 1, Death: "Child deceased Octo. 28th. 1764."
130 Register 1 includes the comment "from the Whouse."
131 Register 1, Age: "40, 2, 35," respectively; Mary Discharge: "August 1765"; child Death: "July 15th. 1765."
132 Register 1, newborn Death: "Septr. 1765."
133 Register 1, Age: "20"; Discharge: "gone in the Country."
134 Supplied from Register 1.
135 Register 1, Age: "25"; Discharge: "gone to West Indies."
136 Register 1, Age: "35."
137 Register 1, Age: "60."
138 Register 1, Age: "65"; Discharge: "gone away."
139 Register 1, Age: "35"; Discharge: "gone away."
140 "Darrington" in Register 1.
141 Register 1, Discharge: "Wkhouse."
142 "Ghent" in Register 1. Also, Discharge: "gone away."
143 Register 1, Discharge: "dischargd by Overseers Order."

144 "Wealand" in Register 1.
145 Register 1, Age: "50."
146 Register 1, Age: "35."
147 Register 1, Age: "6."
148 Register 1, Age: "24"; Discharge: "at Service."
149 Register 1, Age: "60."
150 Register 1, Age: "55."
151 Register 1, Age: "12."
152 Supplied from Register 1.
153 Register 1, Age: "65."
154 Register 1, Age: "46."
155 "Leodore" in Register 1. Also, Age: "40."
156 Stanley's name was written in the margin and marked for insertion at this point. Register 1 reads "Stanley." Also in Register 1, Age: "55."
157 Register 1, Age: "30"; Discharge: "Woman gone."
158 Under "By whom sent in" in Register 1, the entry reads: "Overseers at a Meeting."
159 Register 1, Age: "45"; Discharge: "gone away."
160 Register 1, Age: "35"; Discharge: "August 1765."
161 Supplied from Register 1. Also, Age: "22"; Death: "Child dyed April 20. 1765."
162 Register 1, Age: "8"; Discharge: "gone away."
163 Register 1, Age: "70."
164 Register 1, Age: "9."
165 Register 1, Age: "35."
166 "Lintee" in Register 1. Also, Age: "26."
167 Register 1, Age: "40."
168 Register 1, Age: "55."
169 Register 1, Age: "33."
170 Register 1, Age: "60"; Discharge: "Ditto," i.e., 15 Aug. 1765.
171 Register 1, Age: "40."
172 Register 1, Age: "30"; Discharge: "Wkhouse."
173 "Dorrington" in Register 1. Also in Register 1, Age: "25"; Discharge: "Ditto," i.e. Work house.
174 "Murphy" in Register 1.
175 Register 1, Age: "26"; Discharge: "Wkhouse."
176 "Mufford" in Register 1.
177 Register 1, Age: "60."
178 Register 1, Age: "6."
179 Register 1, Age: "50."
180 Register 1, Age: "7."
181 Register 1, Age: "25."
182 Register 1, Age: "50."
183 In Register 1, the date is "14."
184 "Martha" in Register 1.
185 Register 1, Age: "60"; Death: "deced Novr. 18. 1772."
186 Register 1, Discharge: "went to West Indies."
187 Register 1, Discharge: "discharg'd."
188 "Taveneau" in Register 1.
189 "Glen" in Register 1."
190 "McGowen" in Register 1.
191 Register 1, Discharge: "Sepr. 28. 1765."
192 Register 1, Discharge: "Septr. 13th. 1765."
193 Register 1, Discharge: "gone away."
194 Register 1, Age: "2 yrs."
195 Register 1, Age: "22"; Discharge: "gone away."

Notes

~

196 "Grimes" in Register 1.

197 "Nicholson" in Register 1.

198 Register 1 includes the notation: "Woman married Davis Whitman, in the House."

199 "Wealand" in Register 1.

200 Register 1, Discharge: "Woman run away."

201 "Murray" in Register 1.

202 "Dizer" in Register 1.

203 "Riddle" in Register 1.

204 "Palfrey" in Register 1.

205 "Maria" in Register 1.

206 Supplied from Register 1.

207 Register 1, Discharge: "discharg'd."

208 Register 1, Discharge: "do." i.e., discharged.

209 Register 1, Discharge: "do." i.e., discharged.

210 "Lintee" in Register 1. Also, Discharge: "discharg'd."

211 Register 1, Discharge: "run away."

212 Register 1, Age: "40 yrs."; Death: "April."

213 Register 1, Discharge: "put to Nurse."

214 Discharged or delivered.

215 Supplied from Register 1.

216 Register 1, Age: "25."

217 "Owen" in Register 1. Also, Age: "35."

218 Register 1, Age: "70"; Death: "deceas'd Jany. 25. 1772."

219 Register 1, Age: "60"; Discharge: "sent to Scotland."

220 "Seagreave" in Register 1.

221 Register 1, Age: "35."

222 Register 1, Age: "70 & 80."

223 "John" in Register 1. Also, Age: "85."

224 Register 1, Age: "25."

225 Register 1, Age: "80."

226 Register 1, Age: "75."

227 Register 1, Age: "24."

228 Register 1: "19."

229 "Wealand" in Register 1. Also, Age: "35."

230 Register 1: "19."

231 Register 1, Age: "12."

232 Register 1, Age: "60."

233 "Lemoines" in Register 1.

234 "Sherrin" in Register 1. Also, Age: "68."

235 Register 1, Age: "55."

236 Register 1, Age: "50."

237 Register 1, Age: "35."

238 "Sergeant" in Register 1.

239 Register 1, Age: "56."

240 Register 1, Age: "40."

241 Register 1, Age: "24."

242 "Ashur" in Register 1. Also, Age: "55."

243 Register 1, Age: "35"; Discharge: "March 1767."

244 "Kellihorn" in Register 1.

245 "Learned" in Register 1. Also, Age: "30"; Discharge: "discharg'd."

246 "Foreman" in Register 1. Also, Discharge: "Feby. 1767."

247 Register 1, Discharge: "discharg'd."

248 Register 1, Discharge: "Bound out."

249 Register 1, Discharge: "discharg'd."
250 Supplied from Register 1.
251 "Hurley" in Register 1. Also, Discharge: "went away May 5 1772."
252 This word written by the same hand that compiled Register 1.
253 Register 1, Age: "77"; Death: "Man deceas'd Decr. 4 1771."
254 "Burgis'" in Register 1.
255 Register 1, Death: "Dead."
256 "Brackenberry" in Register 1.
257 "Landaroger" in Register 1.
258 Register 1, Discharge: "June 23d. 1768."
259 Register 1, Discharge: "Discharged."
260 Register 1, Death: "Dead."
261 Register 1, Discharge: "gone & married."
262 "Donavan."
263 Register 1, Age: "25.
264 Register 1, Age: "54"; Death: "Mar. 11. 1772."
265 Register 1, Age: "35."
266 Register 1, Age: "40."
267 Register 1, Age: "6."
268 Register 1, Age: "60."
269 Register 1, Age: "26."
270 Register 1, Age: "24."
271 Supplied from Register 1.
272 Register 1, Age: "60."
273 Register 1, Age: "50."
274 Register 1, Age: "55."
275 Register 1 continues, "& Wife." Also, Age: "48."
276 Register 1, Age: "60."
277 Register 1, Age: "50."
278 Register 1, Age: "25."
279 Register 1, Age: "55."
280 Register 1, Age: "30."
281 Register 1, Age: "89 & 80"; wife: "deceasd Jany. 26 1769."
282 Register 1, Age: "55."
283 Register 1, Age: "60"; Death: "deceased Jany. 8. 1772."
284 Register 1, Age: "70."
285 "Bennaway" in Register 1.
286 Register 1, Age: "35."
287 Register 1, Age: "51."
288 Register 1, Age: "60"; Discharge: "in & out sevl. times."
289 Register 1, Age: "55."
290 Register 1, Age: "25"; Discharge: "gone."
291 Register 1, Age: "55"; Death: [*aged*] 63 deceas'd Octo. 17th. 1773."
292 Register 1, Age: "75"; Death: "Septr. 2d. 1772."
293 Register 1, Age: "22"; Discharge: "Woman gone."
294 Register 1, Age: "46"; Discharge: "discharg'd."
295 Register 1, Age: "55."
296 Register 1, Age: "5."
297 Register 1, Age: "40."
298 Register 1, Age: "70."
299 Register 1, Age: "25."
300 "Mumfer" in Register 1. Also, Discharge: "April 15th. 1768."
301 Register 1, Age: "55"; Discharge: "Workhouse."

302   Register 1, Age: "35."
303   Register 1, Age: "56"; Death: "Dead."
304   Register 1, Age: "50."
305   Register 1, Age: "45."
306   Register 1, Discharge: "Novr. 22. 1767."
307   Register 1, Age: "35."
308   Register 1, Age: "7 & 14."
309   Register 1, Age: "8."
310   Register 1, Age: "50."
311   Register 1, Age: "40."
312   Register 1, Age: "55."
313   Register 1, Age: "45."
314   Register 1, Age: "60."
315   Register 1, Age: "56."
316   Register 1, Age: "60."
317   Register 1, Age: "35."
318   Register 1, Age: "55."
319   Register 1, Age: "32"; "P[*rovince*]" written next to the name in the left margin.
320   Register 1, Age: "40."
321   Register 1, Age: "25."
322   "Nichols" in Register 1. Also, Age: "55."
323   "Morbee" in Register 1. Also, Age: "50"; and "P[*rovince*]" written next to the name in the left margin.
324   Register 1: "P[*rovince*]" written next to the name in the left margin; Discharge: "Sent to Quebec."
325   Register 1, Age: "55."
326   Register 1, Age: "40."
327   Register 1, Age: "45."
328   "Mary" in Register 1. Also, Age: "60."
329   Register 1, Age: "55."
330   Register 1, Age: "40."
331   Supplied from Register 1.
332   Register 1, Age: "35."
333   Register 1, Age: "26."
334   Register 1, Age: "28."
335   Register 1, Age: "46"; Death: "Dead."
336   "Dizer" in Register 1. Also, Age: "25."
337   Register 1, Age: "22"; Discharge: "run away."
338   Supplied from Register 1.
339   Register 1, Age: "55"; Discharge: "went to Halifax."
340   Register 1, Age: "40"; Discharge: "dischargd."
341   Register 1, Age: "14"; Discharge: "sent to the Workho."
342   Register 1, Age: "40."
343   Register 1, Age: "45."
344   Register 1, Age: "35"; Discharge: "run away."
345   Register 1, Age: "58."
346   Register 1, Age: "42."
347   Register 1, Age: "45."
348   Register 1, Age: "25"; Discharge: "Septr. 1771."
349   Register 1, Discharge, Mary: "Bound out."
350   Register 1, Discharge: 6 June.
351   Register 1, Discharge: 3 June.
352   Register 1, Discharge: 6 June.
353   Register 1, Discharge: "In & out several times."

354   The admissions records in Register 2 are interrupted at this point by "Record of Children born in the Alms house," 29 Nov. 1763 – 21 April 1767, 3 pages; "Account of People Deceas'd In the Alms house," 25 March 1763 – 10 May 1771, 20 pages; "Account of Children Born in the Alms House," 6 Sept. 1767 – 5 Nov. 1771, 22 Oct. 1771, 4 June 1767, 3 pages; "Account of Deaths in the House Brot forward," 17 May 1771 – 13 Nov. 1771, 1 page.
      These records are included in a combined section in this volume under the heading of "Miscellaneous Almshouse Births and Deaths", see p. 623.

355   Register 1, Discharge: "discharg'd."

356   Register 1, Discharge: "discharg'd."

357   Register 1, Age: "50"; Discharge: "discharg'd May 1769."

358   Register 1, Discharge: "went to Ireland."

359   Register 1, Age: "80."

360   "Ryley" in Register 1.

361   Register 1, Discharge: "Augt. 19. 1768."

362   Supplied from Register 1, here and in the next entry.

363   Register 1: "do.," i.e., 19.

364   Register 1, Death: "Augt."

365   "Swansborow" in Register 1.

366   "Kata." in Register 1.

367   Register 1, Age: "62"; Death: "March 7. 1772."

368   Register 1 records Row's death on this date.

369   "Mary" in Register 1.

370   Register 1, Discharge: "In the Workho."

371   "Pitman (Pitts)" in Register 1.

372   Register 1: "P[*rovince*]" is written next to the name in the left margin; Age: "36"; Death: "Jany. 26. 1771."

373   "Do." in Register 1.

374   Register 1, Name: "Cato a negro Child."

375   "Swansborow" in Register 1.

376   Register 1, Discharge: "Woman Dead & Childn. bound."

377   "Burgis" in Reigster 1. Also, Discharge: "discharg'd."

378   Register 1, Age: "38"; Death: "Woman deced May 10. 1771."

379   The account of possessions brought into the almshouse by Mary Pilsberry and Mrs. Crawford and Thomas Eastwick, below, are written upside down on the reverse of the preceding page of admissions, which begins with the entry of 27 Nov. 1768 discharging Robert Low from the house.

380   Note the corresponding "x" next to the second line of the right column.

381   The bottom edge of the page is worn away, resulting in the loss of two or three words at the beginning and one word in the middle of the line.

382   This and the next four entries are written upside down on the final page of the register.

383   Title page of Admissions Register 3.

384   Register 1, Discharge: "gone away."

385   Register 1, Discharge: "discharg'd in a little time."

386   Register 1, Discharge: "gone."

387   Register 1, Discharge: "Workhouse"; Death: "Dead."

388   Register 1, Discharge: "went into the Country."

389   Register 1, Discharge: "in the Wrokho."

390   "Connel" in Register 1. Also, Discharge: "April–1769."

391   Register 1, Discharge: "April 24. 1769."

392   "Skweller" in Register 1.

393   Register 1: "P[*rovince*]" is written next to the name in the left margin.

394   "[*May*] 23" in Register 1. Also, Discharge: "Bound out 1772."

395   Register 1, Discharge: "Bound."

396   Register 1, Discharge: "gone to Ireland."

397   "Abdelton" in Register 1.

398   Supplied from Register 1.

399   Register 1, Discharge: "run away May 1772."

400   Register 1, Discharge: "gone."

401   "Caveneaughs" in Register 1.

402   Supplied from Register 1.

403   Register 1, Death: "{she dyed June 20th. 1772   He dyed Mar 29. 1773}."

404   Register 1, Discharge: "gone to Ireland."

405   "Jereh." in Register 1.

406   "Gutridge" in Register 1.

407   Register 1, Discharge: "Septr. 16. 1769."

408   Register 1, Discharge: "discharg'd."

409   Register 1, Discharge: "ran away June 1772."

410   Register 1, Discharge: "went to Service."

411   "Burnett" in Register 1.

412   "Rhodes" in Register 1.

413   "Halley" in Register 1.

414   "28" in Register 1.

415   Following the corresponding record in Register 1, is an entry for "Roberts Joseph"; Sent in by: "Mr. Wm. Whitwell"; When Received: "do. [*i.e., Dec. 4*]"; Age: "82"; Death: "Deced Decr. 29th. 1770}."

416   Register 1, Age: "45"; Death: "came in again & dyed Apl. 1 1771}."

417   Register 1, following the surname: "(Mary)"; Age: "48"; Death: "dece'd May 23d. 177[2?]." The final digit of the year was obscured when the pages were bound.

418   Register 1, Age: "36"; Death: "Jany. 26. 1771."

419   Register 1, Age: "68"; Death: "dece'd Decr. 4. 1771."

420   Register 1, Death: "deced Feby. 26 1773."

421   Register 1: "P[*rovince*]" next to Gorman's name only in the left margin.

422   "Abigail Waddel his Wife" in Register 1. Also, Abigail Death: "June 4th. 1772."

423   Register 1, Death: "Decr. 4 1771."

424   "Griffiths" in Register 1. Also, Discharge: "Bound out."

425   Register 1, Discharge: "run away."

426   Supplied from Register 1.

427   "Rinniger" in Register 1.

428   Register 1, Discharge: "run away."

429   Register 1, Age: "35"; Death: "June 25th. 1773."

430   "Thomison" in Register 1.

431   Register 1, Discharge: "gone."

432   Register 1, Discharge: "Warnd out of Town."

433   Register 1, Discharge: "Bound out."

434   Register 1, Death: "April 1. 1771."

435   "Moree" in Register 1.

436   Register 1, Death: "Feby. 3. 1773."

437   Supplied from Register 1.

438   Register 1, Death: "Feby. 27. 1771" does not specify mother or child.

439   Register 1, Age: "72"; Death: "Mar. 27. 1773."

440   Register 1, Discharge: "gone."

441   "Rhodes" in Register 1.

442   "Denley" in Register 1.

443   "McCuing" in Register 1.

444   Register 1, Discharge: "in the Country."

445   Followed by "(Eliza.)" in Register 1. Also, Age: "87"; Death: "Apl. 11 1772."

446 Register 1, Death: "Jany. 13. 1773."
447 Register 1, Age: "26": Death: "Mar. 29. 1771."
448 Supplied from Register 1.
449 Register 1, Death: "April 29th. 1773."
450 "Rhodes" in Register 1.
451 Register 1, Age: "60."
452 Register 1, Age: "50"; Death: "Mar. 17th. 1774."
453 Register 1, Age: "26"; Death: "Mar. 19. 1771."
454 Register 1, Age: "80."
455 Register 1, Discharge: "Workho."
456 Register 1, Discharge: "went to Service."
457 Register 1, Age: "84": Death: "Feby. 10. 1774."
458 "Margtt." in Register 1. Also, Death: "John deceasd Feby. 15. 1771 Wife Do. April 1 1774."
459 "Forbis" in Register 1.
460 Register 1, Discharge: "dischargd."
461 Register 1, Discharge: "Workhouse."
462 "Joanna" in Register 1.
463 Register 1, Discharge: "sent to Ireland."
464 "Lary" in Register 1. Also, "P[*rovince*]" is written next to Lary's name in the left margin.
465 Register 1, Age: "18 yrs."
466 Register 1: "P[*rovince*]" is written next to the name in the left margin.
467 "Magee" in Register 1. Also, Age: "32"; Death: "Mar 28. 1771."
468 The first name is left blank in Register 1.
469 Register 1, Age: "27"; Death: "Mar 31. 1771."
470 Register 1, Discharge: "Workho."
471 Register 1, Discharge: "April 13. 1771."
472 Register 1, Age: "60."
473 Register 1, Discharge: "gone to Service."
474 Register 1, Discharge: "ditto."
475 Register 1, Age: "35"; Discharge: "gone."
476 Register 1, Age: "40"; Death: "Jany. 29. 1771."
477 Register 1, Discharge: "Workho."
478 Register 1, continues "distracted"; Discharge: "sent in the Country."
479 Register 1, adds "a Child."
480 Register 1, Discharge: "Child Bound."
481 Register 1, Discharge: "ditto" i.e., Bound.
482 Register 1, Age: "90 yrs."; Death: "May 9. 1771."
483 Register 1, Age: "24"; Death: "Feby. 27. do. [*i.e., 1771*]."
484 Register 1, Age: "22"; Discharge: "gone to Service."
485 "Hemenway" in Register 1.
486 Register 1, Discharge: "June 20. 1771."
487 "Doyle" in Register 1.
488 Register 1, Age: "35"; Death: "Jany. 20. 1772."
489 "Cockrall" in Register 1.
490 "Connell" in Register 1. Also, Age: "22"; Death: "April 13. 1771."
491 "Morris" in Register 1. Also, Age: "23"; Death: "April 18. do. [*i.e., 1771*]."
492 Register 1: "do."
493 Register 1, Age: "28"; Death: "April 9. 1771."
494 Register 1, Discharge: "went to Service."
495 Register 1, Age: "40."
496 Register 1, Age: "38"; Death: "May 10. 1771."
497 Register 1, Discharge: "May 11. 1772."
498 Register 1, Age: "60": Death: "June 18. 1773."

499   Register 1, Age: "20"; Discharge: "gone to Service."

500   Register 1, Discharge: "Bound out"

501   Register 1, Age: "18"; Discharge: "went to nurse."

502   Supplied from Register 1.

503   Supplied from Register 1.

504   "Hennisey" in Register 1.

505   Register 1: "(Varney)" follows the surname.

506   Register 1, Age: "22"; Death: "May 21. 1772."

507   "Boies" in Register 1.

508   Register 1, Discharge: "Kate Bound."

509   Register 1, Age: "16"; Discharge: "Bound out."

510   Register 1: "P[rovince]" is written next to the name in the left margin.

511   "Mann" in Register 1.

512   Supplied from Register 1.

513   Register 1: "Murpee"; Discharge: "Jumpt Fence Octo. 30. 1771."

514   Register 1: "Magreey"; Discharge: "sent to Ireland."

515   "Sheppard" in Register 1.

516   "Margtt." in Register 1.

517   Register 1, Age: "20."

518   Register 1, Age: "35"; Death: "Decr. 4. 1771."

519   Register 1, Age: "25"; Discharge: "Colo. Hills."

520   Register 1: "(Ideot)" follows the surname; Age: "24."

521   Register 1, Age: "30."

522   Register 1, Age: "60"; Discharge: "any where."

523   Register 1, Age: "55."

524   Register 1: "a Child" follows the surname.

525   Register 1, Age: "16"; Discharge: "Bound."

526   Register 1, Age: "40."

527   "Jehohadn." in Register 1.

528   Register 1, Age: "14."

529   Register 1, Age: "55."

530   Register 1, Age: "5. yrs."; Death: "Janua. 31. 1773."

531   Register 1, Death: "dyed in a Rope Walk."

532   Register 1, Discharge: "Workhouse."

533   Register 1: "of Mrs. Thorntons (paver)"; Death: "Dyed Augt. 28th. 1773."

534   Register 1, Discharge: "Child bound."

535   "Murfey" in Register 1.

536   "Worsley" in Register 1.

537   Register 1: "Cyer" "Daugr."

538   Register 1, Blake Discharge: "May 1772."

539   Register 1: "O'Brian."

540   Register 1: both "O'Brian" and "Briant."

541   Register 1: "Hennisey."

542   Register 1: "Lary."

543   Register 1, Death: "deceasd Feby. 1. 1773."

544   Register 1, Discharge: "In & out at times."

545   Register 1, Discharge: "In & out at times."

546   Register 1: "Boston Neck." The "neck" was the narrow strip of land that attached eighteenth-century Boston, a peninsula, to the mainland at Roxbury.

547   Register 1, Death: "deceasd July 15th. 1772."

548   Separate entries in Register 1 discharge "Willm. More" on "May 11. 1772" and "Ann More & Child" in "May 1772."

549   "Sarah" in Register 1.

550   Register 1, Discharge: "dischargd Bound out."
551   Supplied from Register 1.
552   Register 1: "run away."
553   "Cane" in Register 1.
554   Register 1, Age: "55"; Death: "Augt. 31. 1772."
555   Register 1, Age: "6 yrs."; Death: "Septr. 12 1772."
556   Register 1, Age: "62"; Death: "Novr. 16. 1772."
557   I.e., the entry of 1 Sept. 1772, three entries below.
558   Register 1, Age: "34"; Death: "decẽd Decr. 24. 1772."
559   Register 1, Age: "45"; Death: "decẽd Decr. 3. 1772."
560   Register 1, Age: "40 yrs."
561   Register 1, Death: "Septr. 25. 1772."
562   Register 1, Death: "deced Septr. 28. 1772."
563   "Shrowtenbey" in Register 1.
564   Register 1, Discharge: "Bound out."
565   Register 1, Death: "decẽd Mar. 6. 1773."
566   Register 1, Discharge: "Bound out."
567   Register 1: "do." i.e., 2.
568   I.e., 2, supplied from Register 1.
569   Register 1, Age: "42"; Death: "deced Novr. 5th. 1772."
570   Register 1, Death: "deceas'd June 25. 1773."
571   Register 1: "McLaugline"; Discharge: "gone."
572   Register 1, Discharge: "gone."
573   Register 1, Discharge: "gone."
574   Register 1: "Pierce."
575   Register 1, Age: "55."
576   Register 1: "Jane."
577   Register 1, Age: "21"; Death: "dece'd Jany. 5. 1773."
578   Register 1, Age: "22"; Death: "Jany. 16. 1773."
579   Register 1, Age: "22"; Death: "decẽd Decr. 30th. 1772."
580   Register 1, Age: "55"; Death: "decẽd Februa. 17. 1773."
581   Register 1, Discharge: "dischargd."
582   Register 1: "Eliza."; Death: "deceas'd Mar. 6. 1773."
583   Register 1, Age: "30"; Death: "dece'd Apl. 5. 1773."
584   Register 1: "Sebestian"; Age: "42"; Death: "deceasd June 23. 1773."
585   Register 1, Age: "30"; Death: "deceas'd June 18. 1773."
586   Supplied from Register 1.
587   Register 1, Age: "45."
588   Register 1, Discharge: "discharg'd."
589   Register 1: "& Wife."
590   Register 1, Age: "35"; Death: "Deced June 25th. 1773."
591   Register 1, Age: "40"; Death: "decẽd Mar. 10. 1773."
592   Register 1: "Bryan."
593   Register 1, Age: "47"; Death: "Deceased Mar. 10. 1773."
594   Register 1: "Hobart"; Age: "55"; Death: "Deceasd April 5th. 1773."
595   Register 1, Age: "60."
596   Register 1, Discharge: "April 8. 1773."
597   "Barratt" in Register 1.
598   Register 1: "Ferrers"; Age: "52"; Death: "deceasd Decr. 21. 1773."
599   Register 1, Age: "40."
600   Register 1, Age: "34."
601   "Hennisey" in Register 1.
602   Register 1, Age: "70"; Death: "Decẽd Feby. 26. 1774."

603 Register 1: "Lovell"; Age: "12."

604 Register 1, Age: "35"; Death: "Decẽd Augt. 8. 1773."

605 Register 1: "(George)" follows the surname; Age: "50"; Death: "decẽd Octo. 15. 1773."

606 Register 1: "Rainsford": Discharge: "gone."

607 "Ervin" in Register 1.

608 "Hogsdon" in Register 1.

609 Supplied from Register 1.

610 Register 1, Discharge: "Workhouse."

611 Register 1, Age: "66"; Death: "decẽd Janua. 14th. 1774."

612 Register 1, Age: "55"; Death: "decẽd Jany. 6. 1774."

613 "Gould" in Register 1.

614 Register 1, Age: "36 yrs."; Death: "deced Decr. 18. 1773."

615 "Gouge" in Register 1.

616 Register 1 adds: "a Negro."

617 Register 1, Age: "35"; Death: "decẽd May 1. 1774."

618 Register 1, Age: "49"; Death: "deceasd Feby. 16. 1774."

619 Register 1, Death: "deceas'd Mar. 28. 1774."

620 Register 1, Age: "59"; Death: "decẽd next day."

621 Register 1, Death: "deced May   1774."

622 "Stewart" in Register 1.

623 Register 1, Death: "deceasd April 29. 1774."

624 Register 1: "P[*rovince*]" is written next to the name in the left margin; Age: "50"; Death: "deceasd Apl. 28. 1774."

ALMSHOUSE ADMISSIONS

January 1, 1775 – September 30, 1788

1775 Janua.　　　　Received into the House Margarett Cunningham & her Son Willm.
℘ Order Mr. Willm. Greenleaf Overseer—Dated Decr. 31. 1774

12　　　　　　　Received into the House Ann Larkin
℘ Order Mr. Saml. Whitwell Overseer &c

12.　　　　　　Received into the House Mary Courtney (Big with Child)
℘ Order Capt. Saml. Partridge Overseer &c

17.　　　　　　Received into the House Thomas Lewis a Sick Man
℘ Order John Gore Esqr. Overseer &c

1775. Janua. 19th.}　Received into the House Flora a Negro Woman
℘ Order Mr. John White Overseer &c

20th.　　　　　Received into the House (on prov Accott.) James Dogen
℘ Order John Scollay Esqr., Mr. Saml. Austin} Selectmen
Mr. Danl. Waldo Overseer &c

21.　　　　　　Received into the House Elizabeth Castle (*with Child*)
℘ Order Capt. Saml. Partridge Overseer &c

23.　　　　　　Received into the House (on prov. Accott.) Matthew Bright
℘ Order John Scollay Esqr., Mr. Timo. Newell} Selectmen
Mr. Benja. Dolbeare Overseer &c

25.　　　　　　Received into the House John Cavalleer & his Brother Francis
Children} on the province Account
John Scollay, Saml. Austin} Selectmen
　℘ Order Mr. Benja. Dolbeare Overseer &c

25.　　　　　　Received into the House John Ryan
℘ Order Mr. Wm. Whitwell Overseer &c

26.　　　　　　Received into the House Thomas Lawlor
℘ Order Wm. Phillips Esqr.

28th.　　　　　Received into the House Jacob Nile
℘ Order Mr. Danl. Waldo Overseer &c

Februa. 1.　　　　Received into the House (on prov. Accott.) John Lizard
℘ Order Mr. Timo. Newell, Mr. Saml. Austin} Selectmen
Mr. Saml. Whitwell Overseer &c

2.　　　　　　Received into the House Elizabeth Wheeler & 2 Children
℘ Order John Gore Esqr. Overseer &c

　　　　　　Discharg'd Andrew Flood to the Workhouse

1775. Februa. 6th.}　Received into the House William Hayes
℘ Order John Leverett Esqr. Overseer &c

7.　　　　　　Received into the House Phebe Harris a Molatto
℘ Order John Gore Esqr. Overseer &c

18.   Received into the House Elizabeth Cowley
℘ Order John Leverett Esqr. Overseer &c

March. 6   Discharg'd Eliza. Manning & Child—(7th.) Margtt. Cunningham &
Child
8.   Mary Thompson (prov) run away—(13) Thos. Lawlor
20.   Michl. Dailey (prov) run away—(20th) Thos. Launderkin (prov)
29   Williston, Eliza. Eustis run away

Mar. 8.   Received into the House Mary Fling Sick
℘ Order Jno. Barrett Esqr. Overseer &c

13.   Received into the House Thomas Launderkin (on prov Accott.)
℘ Order Mr. Timo. Newell, Mr. Oliver Wendell} Selectmen
Mr. Wm. Whitwell Overseer &c

14.   Received into the House George Ross a Boy
℘ Order Mr. Wm. Whitwell Overseer &c

20.   Received into the House (on prov Accott.) Thomas Patterson
℘ Order Jno. Scollay Esqr., Mr. Timo. Newell} Selectmen
Mr. Wm. Whitwell Overseer &c

22.   Received into the House John Kelley Wife & Child
℘ Order Mr. Danl. Waldo Overseer &c

30.   Received into the House Ann Carter
℘ Order Mr. Willm. Greenleaf Overseer &c

April 6th.   Discharged Walter Jack (prov)

1775. April 6} Received into the House on (prov. Accott.) John Caten
℘ Order Mr. Timo. Newell   }
Mr. Saml. Whitwell Overseer &c

6.   Received into the House Martha Williston
℘ Order Mr. Edward Procter Overseer &c

6.   Received into the House Elizabeth Colbert
℘ Order Mr. Benja. Dolbeare Overseer &c

10.   Received into the House Hannah Scales (Big with Child) an Inhabitant
of Marblehead
℘ Order Jno. Scollay Esqr., Mr. Timo. Newell} Selectmen
John Leverett Esqr. Overseer &c

10.   Received into the House Thomas Flowers aged 9. years
℘ Order John Leverett Esqr. Overseer &c

15.   Received into the House Mary Crosby—Sick
℘ Order Mr. Benja. Dolbeare Overseer &c

15.   Received into the House John Williams (on prov. Accott.) a Stranger
℘ Order Capt. Saml. Partridge Overseer &c

17.   Received into the House (on prov Accott.) Sarah Christie & Child
℘ Order John Scollay Esqr., Mr. Saml. Austin} Selectmen
Mr. Danl. Waldo Overseer &c

20.   Received into the House (on prov Accott.) John Papkee
℘ Order John Scollay Esqr., Mr. Timo. Newell} Selectmen
Capt. Saml. Partridge Overseer &c

1775. April 22}   Received into the House Elizabeth Cary (an aged Woman)
℘ Order Capt. Saml. Partridge Overseer &c

25.   Received into the House Mary Bartlet from Colo. Hills
℘ Order Capt. Saml. Partridge Overseer &c

26.   Received into the House Eliza. Stevens aged 73. yrs.
℘ Order Mr. Benja. Dolbeare Overseer &c

30.   Received into the House Ann Storey an old Woman
℘ Order Capt. Saml. Partridge Overseer &c

                    Discharged Phebe Harris (April 30th.) Judith Keylee (prov) run away

May 3   Received into the House Peter Cumber—Blind
℘ Order Capt. Edward Procter Overseer &c

4.   Received into the House Mary Turner
℘ Order Capt. Saml. Partridge Overseer &c

4.   Received into the House William Dockum 8 yrs. of Age Feby. 15th. 1775
℘ Order Capt. Saml. Partridge Overseer &c

8.   Received into the House Venus a Negro woman old & infirm
℘ Order Mr. Benja. Dolbeare Overseer &c

9.   Received into the House Mary Davis   Deaf & Dumb
℘ Order Capt. Edward Procter Overseer &c

15.   Received into the House on (prov Accott.) Lucretia Sever
℘ Order John Scollay Esqr., Mr. Timo. Newell} Selectmen
Capt. Saml. Partridge Overseer &c

15.   Received into the House Janny Ricks a Blind Negro
℘ Order Mr. Benja. Dolbeare Overseer &c

May 3d.   George Downing run away (prov)

1775. May 16.}   Received into the House Abigail Munn—Sick
℘ Order John Leverett Esqr.

do.   Received into the House Mary Merrett
℘ Order John Leverett Esqr. Overseer &c

                    Received into the House Mary Larrabee
℘ Order Capt. Edward Procter Overseer (April 21st.)

25.　　　　　　Received into the House Stephen Wire
℘ Order John Leverett Esqr. Overseer &c

25.　　　　　　Received into the House Bethia Bridge
℘ Order Capt. Saml. Partridge Overseer &c

do.　　　　　　Received into the House Sarah Emmons a Girl
℘ Order John Leverett Esqr. Overseer &c

29.　　　　　　Received into the House Mary Howard
℘ Order Mr. John White Overseer &c

31.　　　　　　Received into the House from the Workho. Sarah Dockum
℘ Order John Leverett Esqr. Overseer &c

May 15th.　　　Discharg'd Sarah Dockum (prov)　　(17th.) Baldridge's Child
18.　　　　　　Deborah Howard　　　(June 1st) Ross's Child
May 25　　　　John Keylee, Wife & 2 Children (prov) Agnis Gordon
June 3.　　　　John Caten (prov) run away

June 3d.　　　　Received into the House John William
℘ Order Mr. Saml. Whitwell Overseer &c

June 3d.　　　　Discharged went over the Ferry—James Perrin Wife & Child (prov)
　　　　　　　　Margarett Gooding—Ann Shay & Child (prov) Hugh O'Brian & Wife
(prov)

　　　　　　　　Prudence Bennet—John Banks Wife & Child—Sarah Lawrence
　　　　　　　　Eliza. Campbell—Eliza. Courtney—Mary Crosby—Mary Gray—
　　　　　　　　Mary Briscoe—James Thompson & Matthew Bright (prov)
　　　　　　　　Francis McDaniel (prov) Willm. Goffe—Benja. Chubb—Willm.
　　　　　　　　Farland (prov)—Thos. Lewis—Eliza Mallet—Mary Lemoine
　　　　　　　　Wm. Brown—Michl. Condon　Isabella Ross & Child
　　　　　　　　Eliza. Jackson—Kata. McFerson (prov)

June 5th.　　　　Discharged went over the Neck—Mary Nichols & Child (prov)
　　　　　　　　Eliza. Sinclair—Sarah Curtis & Child—Ruth Evans—Hannah Allen
　　　　　　　　Matthew Hopkins—Cornelius Youngman (prov) Sarah Brown & Child
　　　　　　　　John William—Mary Tilly (prov)

10.　　　　　　Discharged Mary Howard—(26th.) Ann Scales

20.　　　　　　Discharged went over the Neck—Elizabeth Barbour
　　　　　　　　Sarah Emmons—Annis Kempleton (prov) Abigail Hale—Samuel Pitts a
Child

　　　　　　　　Meheta. Clough—Wm. Dockum a Boy　Eliza. Raven
　　　　　　　　Lydia Copp—John Barker—Wm. Hurley Wife & 2. Children (prov)
　　　　　　　　Isaac Fowles—Ann Stone & 1 Child—Richard McClure
　　　　　　　　Joseph Snelling—Benja. Williams—Geo. Cullam a Child
　　　　　　　　Sarah Dockum, Saml. Pritchard (prov) Eleanor Pue (prov)
　　　　　　　　Thomas Flowers a Boy—Andrew Flood—Margtt. Adams (prov)
　　　　　　　　Hannah Kenney—Dinah Negro woman

June 6.　　　　Received into the House (on prov Accott.) Willm. Hurley Wife & 2
Children}
℘ Order John Scollay Esqr., Mr. Timo. Newell} Selectmen
Capt. Saml. Partridge Overseer &c

do.   Received into the House Lawrence Collins
℘ Order Mr. Saml. Whitwell Overseer &c

8.   Received into the House Richard McClure
℘ Order John Leverett Esqr. Overseer &c

12.   Received into the House Jane Cladish
℘ Order Mr. Saml. Whitwell Overseer &c

do.   Received into the House Joshua Hemenway
℘ Order Mr. John White Overseer &c

14.   Received into the House Isaac Fowles
℘ Order Mr. Saml. Whitwell Overseer &c

1775. June 14th.} Received into the House (on prov Accott.) Hannah Bennet
℘ Order John Scollay Esqr., Mr. Saml. Austin} Selectmen
Mr. Saml. Whitwell Overseer &c

15.   Received into the House (on prov Accott.) Mary Smith & Child
℘ Order John Scollay, Thos. Marshall} Esqrs. Selectmen
Mr. Saml. Whitwell Overseer &c

17.   Received into the House John Call
℘ Order Mr. John White Overseer &c

do.   Received into the House from the Workhouse Mary Edgar
℘ Order John Leverett Esqr. Overseer &c

July 4.   Received into the House John Ryan a Stranger
℘ Order Capt. Saml. Partridge Overseer &c

5.   Received into the House (on prov Accott.) Robert Vincent
℘ Order John Scollay, Thoms. Marshall} Esqrs. Selectman
Mr. Saml. Whitwell Overseer &c

12th.   Received into the House Mary Taylor a Stranger
℘ Order Capt. Saml. Partridge Overseer &c

15th.   Received into the House Sarah Richards junr.
℘ Order Capt. Saml. Partridge Overseer &c

17th.   Received into the House John Powell
℘ Order Mr. John White Overseer &c

19.   Received into the House Margarett Thorp
℘ Order Mr. Saml. Whitwell Overseer &c
{Willm. Sharp (Prov) discharged July 12th. 1775

      Discharged Sarah Horn June 15th. (prov) Peter Maloy July 25th. (prov)

1775. July 24th} Received into the House Arabatiah Flagg
℘ Order Mr. John White Overseer &c

25.   Received into the House John Masters
℘ Order Capt. Saml. Partridge Overseer &c

27.   Received into the House John Ranstead
℘ Order Capt. Saml. Partridge Overseer &c

31.   Received into the House Elizabeth Caswall
℘ Order Mr. Saml. Whitwell Overseer &c

August 1st.   Received into the House Violet a Negro belonging to John Hunt
℘ Order Capt. Saml. Partridge Overseer &c

19.   Received into the House by order of the Overseers the following
Persons not as Subjects of the House, but with the Poor of the House —Vizt.

Phillippi & Mary Leblond	Mary Skirling
Andrew Boardman	Margarett Butt
John Masters	Jonah Patterson
Mary Holland	Thomas Sheppard Wife & Child}
Elizabeth Story Widow	Sarah Stevenson & Child
James Langley & Wife	

Received into the Hospital at Salem[1]

27.   Received into the House on the Colony's Accott. Thomas Lewis
℘ Order Isaac Smith Esqr. Overseer &c

Septr. 4.   Received into the House Joseph Mountfort
℘ Order Isaac Smith Esqr. Overseer &c

9.   Received into the House Edward Romley
℘ Order Isaac Smith Esqr. Overseer &c

14.   Received into the House Walter Hogg & his Wife
℘ Order Mr. Wm. Greenleaf Overseer &c

              Received into the House Gammon Stevens—Order dated Augt. 22. 1775
℘ Order Mr. Wm. Greenleaf Overseer &c

1775. Septr. 6th.}   Discharged Henry Snow   6th.) Mary Holland   (7th.) Eliza. Story
Widow   19th.) Eliza. Ward with her Child & Mary Coombes run away   26. Thomas Lewis
run away—Octo. beginning. John Dogan prov. run away

Octor. 3.   Received John Baker & 2. Children into the House
℘ Order Doctr. Ebenezer Putnam Overseer &c

9.   Received into the House George Downing
℘ Order Mr. Willm. Greenleaf Overseer &c

13.   Received into the House Thomas Holt
℘ Order Mr. Gibbins Sharp Overseer &c

Novr. 2.   Discharged Rebecca Whittemore—George Downing run away—
Thomas Holt discharged

30.   Received into the House William Jarvis
℘ Order Isaac Smith Esqr. Overseer &c

Decemr. 4. Received into the House from point Shirley

James Crawford	Mary Drummond & 3. Children
David Poor & Wife	Nathl. Lucas & 1. Child
Abiezer Turner & 2. Children	James Brown & Wife
James Kay	James Westwood
Ebenezer Wallis Wife & 2 Children	
Elizabeth Barnard	

℘ Order Mr. Gibbins Sharp Overseer &c

6. Received into the House Stephen Harris, Wife & 2. Children & Mrs. Mary Western
℘ Order Mr. Gibbins Sharp Overseer &c

Mary Smith & Child & Mary Winchester run away Decemr. 6th. 1775

Received into the House Elizabeth Whittemore
℘ Order Mr. Gibbins Sharp Overseer &c

Discharged James Brown & Wife & Lucas' Child, James Westwood

1775. Decemr. 18th.} Received into the House Richard Morgan, Edward Murphey & Wife
℘ Order Isaac Smith Esqr. Overseer &c

19. Received Wm. Welch, John Richie, & Thomas Demeret into the House
℘ Order Issac Smith Esqr. Overseer &c
discharg'd Decemr. 23d.

1776. Janua. 1 Received into the House Susanna Lewis Wife of Joseph Lewis
℘ Order Isaac Smith Esqr. Overseer &c

2. Received into the House Eliza. Nicholson, Mary King, Sarah Clark & Susanna Barber}
℘ Order Mr. Gibbins Sharp Overseer &c

12. Received into the House Benja. Ross Wife & Child, Adam a Negro & Caesar & his Wife Negroes
℘ Order Isaac Smith Esqr. Overseer &c

Discharged Wm. Welch, John Richie, Thomas Demeret

31. Received into the House Eliza. Cushing, Esther Elsworthy, Eliza. Thornton & Eliza. Ward & Child
℘ Order Mr. Gibbins Sharp Overseer &c

Feby. 13. Received into the House Rebecca Atkins
℘ Order Mr. Gibbins Sharp Overseer &c

20. Received into the House William Farling
℘ Order Isaac Smith Esqr. Overseer &c

Discharged John Masters (Mar 13th.) Richard Morgan run away

22. Received into the House Henry Harris & 3 Children, Willm. Darrington & Lucas a Boy & Mary Powers
℘ Order Doctr. Ebenr. Putnam Overseer &c

March 13th.   Received into the House Mary Scott & 5. Children
℘ Order Isaac Smith Esqr. Overseer &c

18th.   Discharged Abiezer Turner & 2. Children
do.   William Jarvis run away
1776 March 25th.} Received into the House Mary Downe & Daughter, Sarah Plaistead,
Susanna Clear & Mary Ross 2 Children
℘ Order Ebenr. Putnam Overseer &c

Apl. 20.   Received into the House (20th.) John Tarrel
℘ Order Isaac Smith Esqr. Overseer &c

Apl. 21.   Received into the House Priscilla Gardner
℘ Order Doctr. Ebenr. Putnam Overseer &c

                     Discharged Eliza. Murphy—Caesar & his Wife Negroes
                     Susanna Lewis May 1st.   Priscilla Gardner run away
                     Richard Hennisey run away April 29th.
May 9.   Walter Hogg & Wife—William Darrington (28) James Keeve
                          Patterson, Mary Drummond & 3 Childn.—Mrs. Scott & 5
Children —Sarah Gent
28.   Esther Laha

29.   Received into the House   Jackson & her 2. Children
℘ Order Doctr. Ebenezer Putnam Overseer &c.

June 23   Received into the House William Jarvis
℘ order Isaac Smith Esqr. Overseer &c

25th.   Recieved into the House Margret Lane
℘ Order of Isaac Smith Esqr. Overseer &c

July 4th.   Received into the House Mr.   Capen
℘ Order of Isaac Smith Esqr. Overseer &c

                     Discharg'd   Barber

26   Received into the House Elizabeth Fisk & one Child
℘ Order of Isaac Smith Esqr.

August 2   William Jarvis, Mrs. Hale Ran away

Sept. 13   Received into the House Fanny Clark
℘ order Gibbins Sharp Overseer &c

1776   Discharged Mrs. Harris & Son, Elizabeth Fisk & Child, Addam a
Negro,   Poor ran away

Novr. 21   Recievd into the House (on Province Accot.) Deborah Hurley & her
two Children
℘ Order of John Scollay Esqr., Oliver Wendell} Selectmen
Samuel Whitwell Overseer

29th.   Reciev'd into the House Joseph Snelling, Saml. Pritchard, James Perrin
& wife, Elizabeth Raven, Andrew Floyd, Margaret Adams, Anna Stone & Daughter, Sarah
Dockum, Eliner Pew, Polley Tilley, Mehita. Clow, Samuel Pitts, Benja. Williams, Thoms.
Flowers, Elijah Trescot, John Barker
℘ Order of Capt. Samuel Patridge Overseer

29   Reciev'd into the House (on Province Accot.) John White
℘ Order of John Scollay Esqr., John Greenleaf} Selectmen
Jona. Mason Overseer

30th.   Reciev'd into the House Mary Powers
℘ Order Capt. Saml. Partridge Overseer

30   Reciev'd into the House (on Province Accot.) John Lynes & his Wife &
Hugh Bryan & his Wife
℘ Order John Scollay Esqr., John Greenleaf} Selectmen
Saml. Whitwell Overseer

30th.   Reciev'd into the House Jonathan Wheeler
℘ Order Capt. Saml. Partridge Overseer

Decemr: 3d.   Reciev'd into the House Mary Fitzgerell & two Children
℘ Order of Edward Procter Overseer

1776 Decmr. 3d.}   Reciev'd into the House (on Province Accot.) John Wilks an Orphan
Child &c
℘ Order of John Scollay Esqr., Henry Bromfield Esqr.} Selectmen
Capt. Saml. Patridge Overseer

5th.   Reciev'd into the House (on Province Accot.) James Thompson a
Stranger
℘ Order of John Scollay Esqr., John Greenleaf} Selectmen
Jona. Mason Overseer

                           Reciev'd into the House Mary Stride
℘ Order Edward Payne Overseer

6th.   Reciev'd into the House Timothy Call
℘ Order of John White Overseer

6th.   Reciev'd into the House Pegg Holland
℘ Order of John White Overseer

6th.   Reciev'd into the House Margaret Goodwin, Eliza. Campbell & Mary
Brisco
℘ Order of Capt. Saml. Partridge

7th.   Reciev'd into the House Benjamin Taylor & William Taylor
℘ Order John White Overseer

9   Recievd into the House (on Province Accot.) George Downing a
Stranger
℘ Order of Jno. Scollay Esqr., Ebenezer Storer} Selectmen
Samuel Whitwell Overseer

                           Reciev'd into the House Wm. Jarvis
℘ Order Edward Procter Overseer

11th.   Reciev'd into the House Isabella Ross & Isabella Stone
℘ Order of Edward Procter Overseer

1776 Decmr. 13   Recievd into the House Mary Hale
℘ Order of Edward Procter Overseer

14   Reciev'd into the House Abigail Hale
℘ Order of Isaac Smith Esqr. Overseer

       Reciev'd into the House (on Province Accot.) Sarah Hennesy
℘ Order of John Scollay Esqr., John Greenleaf} Selectmen
Major Edwd. Procter Overseer

16th.   Reciev'd into the House (on Accot. Province) Wm. Sharp & his Wife
℘ Order of John Scollay Esqr., Henry Bromfield Esqr.} Selectmen
Isaac Smith Esqr. Overseer &c

17th.   Reciev'd into the House Mary Fullford
℘ Order of Major Edwd. Procter Overseer &c

18th.   Reciev'd into the House John Read
℘ Order of Major Edward Procter Overseer &c

20th.   Reciev'd into the House (on Province Accot.) Mary Jones.
℘ Order of John Scollay Esqr., Samuel Austinm} Selectmen
Saml. Whitwell Overseer &c

24th.   Reciev'd into the House (on Province Accot.) John Kelly and Daughter
℘ Order of John Scollay Esqr., John Greenleaf} Selectmen
Jona. Mason Overseer &c

24   Reciev'd into the House (on Province Accot.) Samuel Osburn his
Order dated Novr. 24th.
℘ Order of John Scollay Esqr., John Greenleaf} Selectmen
John White Overseer &c

31st.   Reciev'd into the House John Bryan Bray a Child
℘ Order of John White Overseer &c

       Dischargd Benjamin Taylor & Wm. Taylor
       James Thompson Run away

1776   Reciev'd into the House Samuel Cox ℘ Order dated 29th. Decmr.
℘ Order Jona. Mason Overseer &c

       Reciev'd into the House (on Province Acco.) James & Barbary Murphy
℘ Order dated 1st. Decmr. 1776
℘ Order John Scollay Esqr., John Greenleaf} Selectmen
Samuel Whitwell Oversr. &c

1777 Januy: 4th. Reciev'd into the House Tabathy Ackley
℘ Order of Isaac Smith Esqr. Overseer &c

6th.   Reciev'd into the House Mary Doake
℘ Order of Samuel Barrett Esqr. Overseer &c

7th.   Reciev'd into the House Ann Pierce
℘ Order William Powell Esqr. Overseer &c

       Reciev'd into the House (on Province Acco.) Henry Brabazon
℘ Order John Scollay Esqr., John Greenleaf} Selectmen
Jona. Mason Overseer

8   Reciev'd into the House Samuel Clarke
℘ Order of Samuel Partridge Overseer &c

11th.   Reciev'd into the House (on Province Accot.) Patrick Tomay
℘ Order John Scollay Esqr., Samuel Austin} Selectmen
Capt. Saml. Partridge Overseer &c
      Reciev'd into the House Simeon Freeman
℘ Order Jonathan Mason Overseer &c

14th.   Reciev'd into the House Ann Fling
℘ Order Major Edwd. Procter Overseer &c

      Discharg'd Margret Holland
      Run away William Thwing

27th.   Reciev'd into the House Mary Whaland
℘ Order of William Powell Esqr. Overseer &c

      Run away John Read

1777 Janu 28th. Reciev'd into the House Elizabeth Procter
℘ Order of Mr. John Sweetser Jur. Overseer &c

Febru. 5th.   Reciev'd into the House (on Province Accot.) James Stewart a Child
℘ Order John Scollay Esqr., Henry Bromfield Esqr.} Selectmn.
Jonathan Mason Overseer &c

7th.   Reciev'd into the House George Mattsen Hanners a Child 9 yrs. Old
August. 1776.
℘ Order Jona. Mason Overseer &c

13th.   Reciev'd into the House Dina Allen a Negro Woman
℘ Order Capt. Samuel Partridge Oversr. &c

19th.   Reciev'd into the House Sarah Cox
℘ Order Edward Procter Esqr. Overseer &c

      Discharg'd Deborah Hurley & 3 Children (on Province Acco. the 15th.
of Feby.)
      John Bryant Bray a Child

21st.   Reciev'd into the House Mary Blackenbury
℘ Order Capt. Samuel Partridge Oversr. &c

22nd.   Reciev'd into the House two Sons of Benj. Scott
℘ Order William Powell Esqr. Oversr. &c

24th.   Reciev'd into the House (on Province Acco.) Matthew Bright & James
Morris
℘ Order of John Scollay Esqr., Saml. Austin} Selectmen
Honbl. Wm. Phillips Esqr. Oversr. &c

Mch 1st.   Reciev'd into the House Betty a Negro Woman (on Provnce. Acco.)
℘ Order of John Scollay Esqr., Ebenezer Storer Esqr.} Selectmen
Jona. Mason Oversr. &c

5th.   Reciev'd into the House (on Provce. Accot.) Benja. Adams
℗ Order John Scollay Esqr., Saml. Austin Esqr.} Selectmen
John White Oversr. &c

6th.   Reciev'd into the House Sarah Ayers
℗ Order of the board of Overseers

1777 March 11th. Reciev'd into the House Ann Hewes
℗ Order Isaac Smith Esqr. Overseer &c

14th.   Reciev'd into the House Elizabeth Barber
℗ Order of Samuel Barrett Esqr. Overseer &c

24th.   Sarah Dockum (Eleanor Pue Provce. Acco.) Ran away
       Sarah Ayers Jump'd the fence
       Tabitha Aickley Discharg'd (George Downing ran away 31st. Pro)

April 3   Reciev'd into the House (on Provnce. Acco.) Sarah Child
℗ Order of Jno. Scollay Esqr., Saml. Austin Esqr.} Selectmen
Mr. Samuel Whitwell Overseer

       Reciev'd into the House (on Prvoince Acco.) Mary Gerrel & Child
℗ Order of John Scollay Esqr., Samuel Austin Esqr.} Selectmen
Edward Procter Esqr. Overseer Order dated 28th. March 1777

5th.   Reciev'd into the House James Flood
℗ Order Honbl. Wm. Phillips Esqr. Overseer &c

Reciev'd into the House Humilles Williams
℗ Order Capt. Saml. Partridge Overseer &c

       Reciev'd into the House John Taylor a Boy of Six years Old
℗ Order Wm. Powell Esqr. Overseer &c

14th.   Reciev'd into the House Elizabeth Griggs
℗ order Mr. John Sweetser jur. Overseer &c

18th.   Reciev'd into the House Eliza. Wardell
℗ Order Capt. Samuel Partridge Overseer &c

19th.   Reciev'd into the House Lucy Nothingbury a Child from Watertown
℗ Order Edward Procter Esqr. Overseer &c

21st.   Reciev'd into the House Robert Clark (on Province Acco.)
℗ Order of John Scollay Esqr., Oliver Wendell} Selectmen
Capt. Saml. Partridge Overseer &c

1777 April 20th. Reciev'd into the House (on Provce. Acco.) John Smith a Child
℗ Order of John Scollay Esqr., Oliver Wendell} Selectmen
Consented to Jona. Mason Overseer &c

1777 Apl. 10th. Discharg'd Henry Brabazon (prov) 15th. Mary Jones (prov)
       Elizabeth Castle ran away

23d.   Reciev'd into the ouse Samuel Taylor a Boy 10 years Old 10th. May
next
℗ Order of Capt. Saml. Partridge Overseer &c

25th.   Reciev'd into the House (on Prov: Acco.) Margt. Adams
℘ Order John Scollay Esqr., Saml. Austin} Selectmen
Consented to Edwd. Payne Overseer &c

29   Reciev'd into the house Martha Williams
℘ Order Isaac Smith Esqr.

30th.   Reciev'd into the ouse (on Prov: Acco.) Mary Vose & her Six Children
three of them at a Birth named Hancock Washington & Lee
℘ Order of John Scollay Esqr., Thos. Greenough} Selectmen
Consented to Wm. Phillips Esqr. Overseer &c

            Reciev'd into the house (on Prov: Accot.) Sarah Hartshorne
℘ Order of John Scollay Esqr., John Greenleaf} Selectmen
Consented to by Capt. Saml. Partridge Overseer &c   the Order dated 29th. Dcemr. 1776

May 12th.   Reciev'd into the House (on Prov: Acco.) Elizabeth Sinclair
℘ Order of John Scollay Esqr., Saml. Austin} Selectmen
Consented to Jona. Mason Overseer &c

            Peg. Glossip run away May 12th

21   Reciev'd into the House Thomas Bonning
℘ Order Mr. Jona. Mason Overseer &c

1777 May 27th.   Reciev'd into the House Saml. Dellarue a Child
℘ Order of Isaac Smith Esqr. Overseer

28th.   Reciev'd into the House Peggy Holland
℘ Order of Mr. Saml. Whitwell Overseer

            Discharg'd Mary Vose & 6 Children the 19th. May (prov)
            & James Morris the 23d. May (prov)

June 4th.   Reciev'd into the house Mary Ross
℘ Order of Wm. Powell Esqr. Overseer &c

5th.   Discharg'd. Benja. Adams (Prov)   11th Mary Grissell (Prov)
9   Benjamin Chubb run away—& Ann Pierce
            Betty Ward & her child run away
17th.   Elizabeth Procter Discharg'd Patrick Tomay & Sara Henesy (Pro)
July 1st.   Sarah Child Discharg'd (prov)

10th.   Reciev'd into the house Thomas Dimond
℘ Order of Edward Procter Esqr. Overseer &c

14th.   Reciev'd into the house Eleanor Daniels
℘ Order of Isaac Smith Esqr. Overseer &c

16th.   Reciev'd into the house John Gottob Tyler (on Pro Acco.)
℘ Order of John Scollay Esqr., Saml. Austin} Selectmen
Mr. Jona. Mason Overseer &c

16   Reciev'd into the house (on Prov. Acco.) Wm. Greene
℘ Order of John Scollay Esqr., Harbottle Dorr} Selectmen
Capt. Saml. Partridge Overseer

     Recived into the House Elizth. Young & Child Order Dated July 1
℘ Order of Isaac Smith Esqr. Overseer

1777 July 26   Received into the House Wm. Saunders a Child (on prov acct.)
℘ Order of John Scolay Esqr., Saml. Austin} Selectmen
Mr. Jona. Mason Oveseer

     Discharged Elizth. Gout Ran away Margt. Adams 16 July (prov)
     Wm. Jarvis Ran away 2 August John Gottob Tyler (prov)

August 6   Recieved into the House Mary Allen a Distrcked woman
℘ Order of Board of Oveseers

     Discharg'd John White run away 11th. (Prov) Mary Smith's Child
Carry'd off (Pro)
     Eliza. Young & child run away Ann Hawes

10th.   Reciev'd into the House Mary McFarling
℘ Order of Edward Procter Esqr. Overseer &c

18th.   Reciev'd into the House Wm. Jarvis
℘ Order of Edward Procter Esqr. Overseer &c

29th.   Reciev'd into the house Mary Rogers
℘ Order of Capt. Samuel Partridge Overseer &c

     Discharg'd Mary McFarling

Septr. 1st.   Reciev'd into the house Abigl. Whetston & Child
℘ Order of Mr. John White Oversr: &c

6th.   Reciev'd into the house Grace Cox
℘ Order of Mr. Edward Payne Overseer

10th.   Reciev'd into the house Patrick Tomay & wife (Prov)
℘ Order of John Scollay Esqr., Saml. Austin} Selectmen
Mr. Jno. White Overseer

     Grace Cox Run away

1777 Octo: 1st.} Reciev'd into the House Rhoda Mountfort a Child
℘ Order of Samuel Barrett Esqr. Overseer &c

6th.   Reciev'd into the House Nancy Handfield alias Freeman a Child
℘ Order of Isaac Smith Esqr. Overseer

     Reciev'd into the House Grace Cox
℘ Order of Edward Payne Overseer

9th.   Reciev'd into the House Thomas Demerry
℘ Order of Edward Procter Esqr. Overseer

11th.   Reciev'd into the House   Bennett
℘ Order of Mr. Edward Payne Overseer

27th.   Reciev'd into the house Thomas Mitchell
℘ Order Capt. Samuel Partridge Overseer &c

29th.   Recieved into the house John Davis
℘ Order of Saml. Barrett Esqr. Overseer

Recieved into the House the Children of   Darcey named Martha,
Mary & Jese Darcey, 9 yrs. 11 mo., 4yrs. 6 mo., & 3 yrs. 6 mo.
℘ Order of Samuel Barrett Esqr. Overseer

30th.   Ran away John Davis

Recieved into the House Polly Hall (Prov:)
℘ Order (dated 9th. Octo) of Jno Scollay Esqr., Saml. Austin} Selectmen
Mr. John White Overseer

Novr. 6th.   Recieved into the House Benja. & Abigl. Hatch
℘ Order of John White Overseer &c

22nd.   Reciev'd into the house Deborah Hurly & two Children
℘ Order of John Scollay Esqr., Saml. Austin} Selectmen
Asented to Mr. Jona. Mason Overseer

25th.   Reciev'd into the house Nancy Lawrence (a deserted Child)
℘ Order of John Scollay Esqr., Saml. Austin} Selectmen
Assented to Capt. Saml. Partridge Overseer

1777 Novr. 27th.   Reciev'd into the House John White (prov. Acct.)
℘ order of John Scollay Esqr., Oliver Wendell} Selectmen
Consented to Jona. Mason Overseer

28th.   Reciev'd into the House Ann Pierce
℘ Order of Samuel Whitwell, Overseer

Discharg'd Dcemr. 1st. Nancy Lawrence (on Prov: Acco.)
Margret Holland Run away

Dcemr. 3   Reciev'd into the House Prince a Negro (Provce. Acct.)
℘ Order of John Scollay Esqr., Oliver Wendell} Selectmen
Consented to ℘ Saml. Whitwell Overseer

3d.   Reciev'd into the House John Black a deserted Child (Prov: Acco.)
℘ Order John Scollay, Gustavus Fellows} Selectmen
Consented to Saml. Whitwell Overseer

4th.   Reciev'd into the House Mary Briscon
℘ order of Capt. Saml. Partridge Overseer

9th.   Reciev'd into the House Betsy Robbins
℘ Order of Wm. Powell Esqr. Overseer

12   Reciev'd into the House Lettice Glazier
℘ Order of The Honbl. Wm. Phillips Esqr. Overseer

12th.   Reciev'd into the House Sarah Partridge on Provce. Acco.
℘ Order Jno. Scollay Esqr., Saml. Austin} Selectmen
℘ Order of Isaac Smith Esqr. Overseer

8th.   Discharg'd   Dawsy & her 3 Children
                 Poll: Doakes

23d.   Reciev'd into the house Mrs. Wilson & Child
℘ Order of John Scollay Esqr., Gust. Fellows} Selectmen
William Powell Overseer

<1777 Decemr. 31st.   Reciev'd into the House Henry Connor
℘ Order of Samuel Whitwell Overseer>

1778 Janu 1st.   Reciev'd into the House Henry Connor (on Prov Acco.)
℘ Order of John Scollay Esqr., Saml. Austin, Gusta. Fellows} Selectmen
Consented to Samuel Whitwell Overseer

                    Reciev'd into the House Robert Hynes his wife & Child (Prov Acco.)
℘ Order of John Scollay Esqr., Saml. Austin, Gusta. Fellows} Selectmen
Consented to Saml. Whitwell Overseer

19th.   Reciev'd into the House James Kelly abot. 7 years Old
℘ Order of Saml. Barrett Overseer

25th.   Reciev'd into the House Sarah Humphreys & Child
℘ Order of Isaac Smith Overseer

29th.   Reciev'd into the House Francis Croizie (Prov: Acco.)
℘ Order of John Scollay Esqr., Saml. Austin} Selectmen
Consented to Saml. Whitwell

Feb. 1st.   Reciev'd into the House John Cole (Prov: Acco.)
℘ Order John Scollay Esqr., Saml. Austin} Selectmen
Consented to Isaac Smith Overseer

                    Recieved into the house a Child named Lucy Katharine
℘ Order of Samuel Whitwell Overseer &c   dated the 7th. January

5th.   Reciev'd into the house Mary Waganor
℘ Order Saml. Partridge Overseer

9th.   Reciev'd into the house Thomas, William, & Saml. Gosling (Prov: Acco.)
℘ Order of John Scollay Esqr., Saml. Austin} Selectmen
Consented to Edwd. Procter Overseer

1778 Feb 11th.   Reciev'd into the house James Poutler (Prov: Acco.)
℘ Order of John Scollay Esqr., Oliver Wendell} Selectmen
Consented to Jona. Mason Overseer

16.   Reciev'd into the house John Hobbs
℘ Order of Samuel Partridge Overseer

Discharg'd Sarah Lochlin Feb: 25th.

Mch 4th. Recieved into the house Eleanor Fowles & her dautr. Hannah
℘ Order of Edward Payne Overseer

11th. Recieved into the house John Tuffts
℘ Order of Capt. Saml. Partridge Overseer

21 Recieved into the house Nancy Holmes
℘ Order of Isaac Smith Esqr. Overseer

28th. Reciev'd into the house Mary Dunstan (Prov: Acco:)
℘ Order of John Scollay Esqr., Oliver Wendell} Selectmen
Consented to Saml. Whitwell Overseer

Discharg'd Betsy Dawson, John Tufts, John Hobbs Hugh O'Bryan
& Jno. Davis Run away William Brown, Grace Cox Run away

Apl. 1st. Reciev'd into the House a negro woman
℘ Order of Wm. Powell Esqr.

8th. Reciev'd into the house two young Children belonging to John Pierce
(Prov Acco.)
℘ Order of John Scollay Esqr., Harbottle Dorr} Selectmen
Consented to Jona. Mason

10th. Reciev'd into the House Mrs. Peters (Prov: Acco.)
℘ Order of John Scollay Esqr., Saml. Austin} Selectmen
Consented to Wm. Powell

1778 Apl. 15th. Reciev'd into the house a Child of Jno. Pierces (Prov: Acco.)
℘ Order of John Scollay Esqr., Saml. Austin} Selectmen
Consented to ℘ Nicholas Bowes Overseer

Recieved into the House Ebenezer Dodge
℘ Order of John White Overseer

Mary Merry Run away,

16th. Recieved into the House Moses Barron & Wife
℘ Order of John White Overseer

22nd. Reciev'd into the House Mary Phillips
℘ order of Saml. Barrett Esqr. Overseer

27 Reciev'd into the house Sarah Butler
℘ Order of Samuel Hewes Overseer

Reciev'd into the House John Gizzell a Boy
℘ Order of Honbl. Wm. Phillips Esqr. Overseer

23d. Run away Margt. OBryant (Provce.) 28th. Sal Wheelen Run away
(Prov)
May 1st. Run away Wm. Sharp & Wife (Prov.)

8th.   Reciev'd into the house Sarah White
℘ Order of John Scollay Esqr., Sam Austin} Selectmen
Consented to Jona. Mason Overseer

13th.   Recieved into the house Edward Richards
℘ Order of Samuel Barrett Overseer

16   Recieved into the house William Jarvis
℘ Order of Edward Procter Overseer

19th.   Reciev'd into the house Mary Doake
℘ Order of Samuel Partridge Overseer

30th.   Reciev'd into the house   a Stranger
℘ Order of Jno. Scollay Esqr., Saml. Austin} Selectmen
Consented to Jona. Mason Overseer

                    Wm. Jarvis—Jno. Fling 25th. May (Prov.) Eleanor Daniels, Margt. Lane
Run away
                    Discharg'd Hepz. Dunbrook—Sal Richards & Child
                    <Dischargd Sarah White>

June 8th.   Reciev'd into the house Thomas Bradford
℘ Order of Isaac Smith Esqr. Overseer

15th.   Reciev'd into the house Mary Ann Campbell (Prov Acco.)
℘ Order of John Scollay Esqr., Nathan Frazier} Selectmen
Consented to Nicho. Bowes Overseer

18th.   Reciev'd into the house Sarah Teague
℘ order of the Board of Overseers,

                    Discharg'd Sarah Wheeler, David Cotrell run away & Thos. Dim[ond],
Mr. Barron

July 22   Receveed into the house Elizabeth Jackson
℘ Order of Mr. John White Overseere

                    Discharged (Sarah Hartshorn July 1 prov) Mary Rogers, Saml. Avery,
Lettis Glazer, William Jarvis Ran away

August 1   Recieved into the House Antony Turrary on (prov Acct)
℘ Order of John Scollay Esqr., Thomas Greenough} Selectmen
Mr. Saml. Whitwell Oveseer

8   Recieved into the House Proodence Cuttin
℘ Order of the Board of Overseers

                    Dischargd. Deborah Hurly & Child (Augt. 11) (prov) Ran away
                    Pol Doaks & (Mary Dunstant 10 august prov)

1778 Augt. 19   Receved into the house (on province Acct.) Elizabeth Burk & Child
℘ Order John Scollay, Gusta. Fellows} Selectmen
Mr. Jona. Mason Overseer

21   Receved into the House Eliza. Dennie a Child
℘ Order Isaac Smith Esqr. Oveseer

25   Recived into the House (Jane Fisher on province Acct.)
℘ Order John Scollay Esqr., Saml. Austin} Selectmen
Willm. Powell Esqr. Oveser

26   Receved into the House (on province Acct.) James Cook a Child
℘ Order John Scollay Esqr., Saml. Austin} Selectmen
Mr. Jona. Mason Overseer
                    Rebeckah Vallacut Ran away (26 augt. Mary Ann Campbell prov) Ran
away

28   Receved into the House William Sharp & Wife (on province Acct.)
℘ Order of John Scollay Esqr., Nathan Frazer} Selectmen
Mr. Nicholas Bowes Oveseer

Sept. 9   Received into the House Mary Doaks
℘ Order of Saml. Barrett Esqr. Overseer

10   Receved into the House Ann Hewes
℘ Order Capt. Saml. Partridge Overseer

1778 Sept. 10   Received into the House (on prov Acct.) Sarah Hartshorn
℘ Order John Scollay Esqr., Saml. Austin} Selectmen
Mr. John Sweetser Overseer

16   Received into the House John Davis
℘ Order of Mr. John White Overseer

17.   Received into the House Mary Thompson (on prov Acct.)
℘ Order John Scollay Esqr., Saml. Austin} Selectmen
Saml. Barrett Esqr. Overseer

18   Received into the House (on prov Acct.) Elizt. Saunders & Child
℘ Order John Scollay Esqr., Saml. Austin} Selectmen
Isaac Smith Esqr. Overseer

21   Received into the House John Read
℘ Order of Mr. John White Overseer

28   Received into the House (on prov Acct.) James Hussey
℘ Order of Mr. Saml. Austin, Ezekiel Price Esqr.} Selectmen
Mr. Saml. Whitwell Overseer

29   Received into the House Elizt. Langley
℘ Order of Isaac Smith Esqr. Overseer

29   Received into the House Sarah Hill
℘ Order of Isaac Smith Esqr. Overseer

29   Receved into the House Elizt. Corben
℘ Order of Edward Procter Esqr. Overseer

                    Discharged (ran away Elizt. Burk and Child Sept. 3 prov) (Sept. 25 Eliz
                    Saunders prov)
                    (James Murphy & wif Sept. 18 prov)

1778 Octr. 14   Received into the House (on prov Acct.) Betsy Florraday a Child
℘ Order John Scollay Esqr., G. Fellows} Selectmen
Mr. Saml. Whitwell Overseer

15   Receved into the House Jane Symonds
℘ Order Mr. Nicholas Bows overseer

17   Receved into the House Thomas Cooper
Wm: Powell Esqr. Overseer

27   Receved into the House (on prov Acct.) Richard Orchand
℘ Order John Scollay Esqr., Saml. Austin} Selectmen
Mr. John White Overseer

                      Mary Phillips Ran away (Disched. Anthony Farrary Octr. 11 prov act.)

27th.   Received into The House Deborah Cornish
℘ Order Nicholas Bowes Overseer of the

Novr. 4   Received into the House On province Account David Harris
℘ Order Samuell Austin, Nathan Frazier} Selectmen
Samuel Whitwell Overseer

Novr. 6th.   Received Thomas Cole into the House
℘ Order John White Overseer

Novr. 6th.   Received into the House Jane Kettle & her Child (On pro. Acct.)
℘ Order John Scollay Esq, Gustavus Fellows, Harbo. Dorr} Selectmen
Samuel Whitwell Overseer

9th.   Received into the House Elezabeth Ward a Child
℘ Order Edward Procter Esqr. Overseer

1778 Novr. 11th.   Received into the House On pro. Accot. John Ferrall and Thomas Hull
℘ Order John Scollay, Samuel Austin} Selectmen
Samuel Whitwell Overseer

13th.   Received into the House Rebecca Williacott
Jonathan Mason Overseer

13th.   Received into the House Fidlia Ward
℘ Order Samuel Whitwell Overseer

15th.   Received into the House Mary Ward
℘ Order Edwd. procter Esq. Overseer

17th.   Received into the House (On Pro. Accot.) Stephen Jones
℘ Order John Scollay, Ezikl. Price} Selectmen
William powell Overseer

18th.   Received into the House Ceaser a Negro man
℘ Order, William powell Overseer

21   Received into the House two Children of Joshua Dutton
℘ Order John Sweetser Overseer

Discharged Elizabeth Harris & her Children
(Thomas Hull Novr. 28th. pro.)
(John Ferral Decr. 1st. Pro.) Hannah Fowle

Dcemr. 3d.   Recieved into the House John How
℘ Order Isaac Smith Esqr. Overseer

Reciev'd into the house John Harris a Boy
℘ Order Wm. Powell Esqr. Oversr.

10th.   Reciev'd into the House (on Prov: Acco.) Willm. Richards
℘ Order Edward Procter Esqr. Oversr.

12   Reciev'd into the House (on Prov: Acco.) John Lewis
℘ Order Jno. Scollay Esqr., Nathan Frazier} Selectmen
Consented to Sam Barrett Esqr. Overseer

14th.   Reciev'd into the House (on Prov: Acco.) Hugh Bryant
℘ Order of Jno. Scollay Esqr., Nathan Frazier} Selectmen
Jona. Mason Overseer

1778 Dcemr. 1st.   Reciev'd … Kelton into the House
℘ Order of Saml. Whitwell Oversr.

19   Reciev'd Rachel Gouge into the house
℘ Order of Edwd. Procter Esqr. Overseer

24th.   Reciev'd Hannah Osborne & one Child into the house
℘ Order of Nicholas Bowes Oversr.

25   Recievd John Hobbs into the House
℘ Order Saml. Partridge Oversr.

31   Recievd Eliza. Burk & Child into the House (Prov)
℘ Order of Jno. Scollay Esqr., Ezek Price} Selectmen
Wm. Phillips Esqr. Overseer

Reciev'd Augustus Hale into the House
℘ Order of Isaac Smith Esqr. Oversr.

1779 Jan 1st.   Reciev'd Elizabeth McGill (Prov) into the house
℘ order of John Scollay Esqr., Nathan Frazier} Selectmen
Edwd. Procter Esqr. Oversr.

Reciev'd Abig. Fowle into the House
℘ order of Jno. Sweetser Oversr.

2nd.   Reciev'd into the House (Prov) David Harris
℘ Order of Jno. Scollay Esqr., Nathan Frazier} Selectmen
Isaac Smith Esqr. Oversr.

Reciev'd into the House Martha Conner & two Children (Prov)
℘ Order of Saml. Austin, Harbottle Dorr} Selectmen
Edwd. Procter Esqr. Oversr.

Discharg'd. Jno. How, Jno. Harris a Boy Run away
Thos. Cooper, David Harris Run away (Prov)

Recievd Fidelia a negro woman into the House
℘ Order of Saml. Whitwell Overseer   the Order dated 22nd. Decmr. 1778

1779 Janu 6th.   Reciev'd into the house Mrs. Barns

℘ Order of the board of Overseers
8th.   Reciev'd into the house Thomas Cooper
℘ Order of Jona. Mason Overseer

              Reciev'd into the house Mary Howard
℘ order of John White Overseer

              Reciev'd into the house Eliza. Procter
℘ Order of Jno. White Overseer

              Reciev'd into the house Richard Morgain
℘ Order of Sam Barrett Esqr. Overseer

              Reciev'd into the House Walter Kirk (Prov Acco.)
℘ order of Samuel Austin, Nathan Frazier} Selectmen
Nicho. Bowes Oversr.

              Reciev'd into the house William Brown
℘ Order Jno. White Overseer

              Reciev'd into the House Nathaniel French
℘ Order of Jno. White Overseer

13th.   Reciev'd into the house Matthew Hopkins
℘ Order of Saml. Whitwell Oversr.

25th.   Reciev'd into the house John Allen (Prov: Acco.)
℘ Order of John Scollay, Ezekl. Price} Selectmen
Nicho. Bowes Overseer

              Reciev'd into the house London a negro (Prov. Acco.)
℘ order of John Scollay, Nathan Frazier} Selectmen
Nicho. Bowes Overseer

              Discharg'd Jane Kettle & Child (Prov 13th Decmr.) Eliza. Corben Run
away

              Reciev'd into the House Elizabeth Linsey (Province)
℘ Order dated 16th Janu: Jno. Scollay, Sam Austin} Selectmen
Sam Whitwell Overseer

              Reciev'd into the house Mary Sinclair (Province)
℘ Order dated 19th. Janu John Scollay, Harb: Dorr} Selectmen
Saml. Partridge Overseer

              Reciev'd into the house Lydia Copp
℘ Order of Mr. Jona. Mason Overseer

Feb 2nd.　　　　　Reciev'd into the house Deborah Hurly & Child (Prov;)
℘ Order of John Scollay Esqr., Samuel Austin} Selectmen
Saml. Whitwell Overseer

　　　　　　　Recived into the House Mary Perry
℘ Order of Samuel Barrett Esqr. Overseer

9　　　　　　Recived into the House Lydia Bell & her Gran Son
℘ Order of Samuel Barrett Esqr. Overseer

15　　　　　Recived into the House Titus a Negro Man
℘ Order of Samuel Barrett Esqr. Overseer

　　　　　　　Recived into the House Eleth. Ivers
℘ Order of Mr. Nicholas Bowes Overseer

20　　　　　Recived into the House Elizth. Castel
℘ Order of Samuel Barrett Esqr. Overseer

　　　　　　　Discharged Willm. Jarvis, Betsy Robins (Sarah Hartshorn Feby. 4 1779
(Prov)

1779 Mar. 25th.　　Received into the House 3 Children Mr. Robt. Fultons
℘ Order Samuel Whitwell Overseer

27th.　　　　　Received into the House a Child Mary Scott
℘ Order Samuel Whitwell Overseer

27th.　　　　　Received into the House Mary Rogers
℘ Order John White Overseer

31st.　　　　　Received into the House Mary Cade
℘ Order Nicholas Bowes Overseer

Apl. 2d.　　　　Received into the House Ezekil Perrigo
℘ Order Edward Procter Esqr. Overseer

　　　　　　　Discharg'd Mathew Hopkins, Walter Kerk, Mar. 22 (prov)
　　　　　　　(Elezabeth Floraday a Child Mar. 2 Prov)
　　　　　　　(John Allen Mar. 4th. Prov) (Mary Sinclear Mar. 13 Prov)
　　　　　　　Elizabeth Burk & Child Mar. 28th. Prov)
　　　　　　　John Davis (Hew Obryant Mar. 23 Prov)

1779 Apl. 8.　　Reciev'd into the House Jane Lemarce
℘ Order of Capt. Saml. Partridge Overseer

10　　　　　Reciev'd into the house Mary Hall a Child (Prov)
℘ Order of Gustavus Fellows, John Scollay Esqr.} Selectmen
Approv'd of by Samuel Barrett Esqr. Overseer

11th.　　　　　Reciev'd into the house Margt. Buckly
℘ Order Capt. Saml. Partridge Overseer

　　　　　　　Recd. into the house Eliza. Bean
℘ Order of Edward Procter Esqr. Oversr.

22nd.   Recd. into the house Elias Robinson
℘ Order of Deacon Jona. Mason Overseer

28th.   Recd. into the house Wm. Jarvis
℘ Order of Edward Procter Esqr. Overseer

1779 Apl. 29   Recd. into the house Hannah Barber
℘ Order of Edward Procter Overseer
              Discharg'd Eliza. Procter, Margt. Buckly, Nathl. Trench
              Run away Eliz Ivers, Bet: Ward & Child, Ebenr. Dodge, R Gouge
              Eliza. Jackson & Child, Grace Cox, Mary Doak

May 7th.   Reciev'd into the house Mary Boydin
℘ Order of Edward Procter Esqr. Overseer

11th.   Recieved into the house <*Eliz*> Sarah Bowen
℘ Order of Edward Procter Esqr. Oversr.

12   Reciev'd Thomas Cooper into the house
℘ Order of Deacon Jona. Mason Oversr.

              Reciev'd Tim Barker A Negro into the house (Prov Acco.)
℘ Order of Jno. Preston, Ezekl. Price} Selectmen
Consented to Saml. Partridge Oversr.

13th.   Reciev'd Eliza. Ives into the house
℘ Order of Deacon Jona. Mason Oversr.

15th.   Reciev'd Allice Collins a Child from Mr. Robt. Fairservice
℘ Order of Willm. Powell Esqr. Oversr.

21st.   Reciev'd Abigail Wallis into the house
℘ Order Capt. Saml. Partridge.

              discharg'd Elizabeth Conner ℘ Order Samuel Austin (Prov)
              Run away Mary Perrin

12th.   Reciev'd into the House Mary Brown
℘ Order of the Board

June 7th.   Reciev'd into the house John Kilby
℘ Order of the board of Overseers

              Discharg'd. Sal: Butler, Run away Eliza. McGill (Provce:)
              Run away Mary Cade, Mrs. Barns, <*Mary Perrin*> (5th. Provce.). Eliza.
Lindsey disch 11th June (prov)
              <*Mary*> Rach Gooch, Mary Bourn, Mary Boyden

1779 June 19th.   Recievd into the house Rachel Hubbert & Rachel Hosah
℘ Order of Edward Procter Overseer

23   Recievd into the house Mrs. Barnes
℘ Order Saml. Barrett Esqr. Oversr.

Recievd into the house Thomas Smith (Provc. Acco.)
℘ Order of Jno. Scollay Esqr., Ezek. Price} Selectmen
Consented to Jona. Mason Oversr.

25th.　　　　　Recievd into the House Nancy Warren
℘ Order Edward Procter Esqr. Oversr.

26　　　　　Recievd into the house Eliza. Gray
℘ Order Will Powell Oversr.

July 2nd.　　　　Reciev'd into the house a Negro Man Nam'd Boston (Prov Acco.)
℘ Order of Jno. Scollay Esqr., Jno. Preston} Selectmen
Consented to Jona. Mason

July 7th.　　　　Reciev'd into the house York a Negro Man
℘ Order of Wm. Powell Oversr.

8th.　　　　　Reciev'd into the house Sarah Bourne
℘ Order of John White Overseer

10th.　　　　　Reciev'd into the house Patience York
℘ Order of Isaac Smith Oversr.

22nd.　　　　　Reciev'd into the house Mary Crosbey
℘ Order of John White Overseer

Discharg'd Mary Brown went to Mr. Henry Plympton July <22> 8th.
Boston a Negro Man (Prov) 23d.

30th.　　　　　Reciev'd into the House Jeremiah Dawsey (Prov Acco.)
℘ Order of John Scollay Esqr., Saml. Austin} Selectmen
Consented to Saml. Whitwell Overseer

Aug: 2nd.　　　　Reciev'd into the House Delight Smith, (Prov Acco.)
℘ Order of John Scollay Esqr.　　　　　　} Selectmen
Willm. Powell Esqr.

1779 Aug: 5th.　　Reciev'd into the house William Jones (Prov: Acco.)
℘ Order of Jona. Williams, Ezekl. Price Esqr.} Selectmen
Consented to Saml. Whitwell Overseer

7th.　　　　　Reciev'd into the house Mary Sinclair (Prov Acco.)
℘ Order of Saml. Austin, Jno. Preston} Selectmen
Consented to ℘ Saml. Partridge Oversr.

Reciev'd into the house Nicholas Benson (Provc: Acco.)
℘ Order of Harbottle Dorr, Jona. Williams} Selectmen
Consented to John White Oversr.

13th.　　　　　Reciev'd into the house Mary Scott
℘ Order of Willm. Powell Esqr. Overseer

16th.　　　　　Reciev'd into the house Margaret Holland & Child (Prov: Acco.)
℘ Order of John Scollay Esqr., Saml. Austin} Selectmen
Consented to Saml. Partridge Oversr.

20th.   Reciev'd into the house Abigail Burke (Provce: Acco.)
℘ Order of John Scollay Esqr., Ezek: Price Esqr.} Selectmen
Consented to Jona. Mason Overseer

                       Discharg'd James Perrin & Timo. Barker (19th. Aug: Provce. Acco.)
                       Mary Fulker (Mary Crosby run away.) (Bet: Castle Returnd.) & Bet.
Ives & Mary Sinclair Run away

30th.   Reciev'd into the house Margaret Adams (Prov Acco.)
℘ Order of John Scollay Esqr., Saml. Austin} Selectmen
Consented to Saml. Partridge Overseer

Sepr. 2nd.   Recd. into the house Ann Kinney
℘ Order of Jona. Mason Overseer

1779 Sepr. 7th.   Reciev'd into the house Eliza. Winbourne
℘ Order of Jona. Mason Overseer

14   Reciev'd into the House John Mahoney (Prov. Acco.)
℘ Order of John Scollay Esqr., Ezekl. Price} Selectmen
Consented to ℘ Saml. Whitwell Overseer

20th.   Reciev'd into the House Thomas Cooper
℘ Order Isaac Smith Esqr.

22   Reciev'd into the House Abigail Burks Child (on Prov Acco.)
℘ Order of Gustavus Fellows, Jona. Williams} Selectmen
Consented to Isaac Smith Overseer

                       Abigail Burk run away the 18th. Inst.

23d.   Reciev'd into the House William Morton (Provc. Acco.)
℘ Order of Harbottle Dorr, Ezekl. Price Esqr.} Selectmen
Consented to Jona. Mason Overseer

29   Reciev'd into the House Joshua Crosby (Provce. Acco.)
℘ Order of John Scollay Esqr., Jona. Williams Esqr.} Selectmen
Consented to Saml. Whitwell Oversr.

Octor. 2nd.   Reciev'd into the House Eliza. Milton & Child (Provce. Acco.)
℘ Order of John Scollay Esqr., Harb. Dorr} Selectmen
Consented to Nicho. Bowes Overseer

                       Discharg'd Eliza: Hewes   (Wm. Morton 29th. Prov Acco.)
                       Run away 24th. Margt. Holland <& Chil> (Provce.)   dischargd Octo.
1st. Wm. Jones (Prov)
                       discharg'd Nicho. Benson (Sepr. 15th. Provce.)   Abigail Wallace (19th.
Sepr.)

                       Reciev'd into the House Ann Currier
℘ Order of Wm Powell Esqr. Overseer

1779 Octo 6th.   Recieved into the House Sarah McDaniel (Prov)
℘ Order of John Scollay Esqr., Ezekl. Price Esqr.} Selectmen
Consented to Edwd. Procter Overseer

11th.   Reciev'd into the House Ann Johnston
℘ Order of Wm. Phillips Esqr. Overseer

13th.   Reciev'd into the House Wm. Robison (Prov Acco.)
℘ Order of John Scollay Esqr., Ezekl. Price Esqr.} Selectmen
Consented to Jonathan Mason Overseer

19th.   Reciev'd into the House Vincent Wymondersold (Prov)
℘ Auot. of John Scollay Esqr., Ezekl. Price Esqr.} Selectmen
Consented to Nicholas Bowes Overseer

21st.   Recieved into the House Francis McDonald (Prov)
℘ Ordr. of John Scollay Esqr., Ezekl. Price Esqr.} Selectmen
Consented to Jona. Mason Overseer

23d.   Recieved into the House Mary Ayers
℘ Order of John White Overseer

27th.   Reciev'd into the House Martha Dorsy (Prov)
℘ Order of John Scollay Esqr., Samuel Austin Esqr.} Selectmen
Consented to Sam. Whitwell Overseer

29   Reciev'd into the House Patk. Culver, Jos: Gould & Saml. Arnold (Prov)
℘ Order of John Scollay Esqr., Ezekl. Price Esqr.} Selectmen
Consented to Sam. Whitwell Overseer

                         Discharg'd a Child of Mrs. Collins Octor. 21st.
                         Run away James Hughes—dischgd Joshua Crosby 28th. Octor.
                         Discharg'd Jos Gould & Sam Arnold (Prov) 3d. Novembr.

1779 Novr: 10th.   Reciev'd into the House Edward Richardson & Wf.
℘ Order of Nicholas Bowes Overseer

11th.   Reciev'd into the House Hugh Bryant & Wife (Prov)
℘ Order of John Scollay Esqr., Ezekl. Price Esqr.} Selectmen
Consented to Willm. Powell Overseer

                         Reciev'd into the House Walter Kirk (Provce. Acco.)
℘ Order of John Scollay Esqr., Samuel Austin Esqr.} Selectmen
Consented to Jona. Mason Overseer

12th.   Reciev'd into the House Cornelius Conneil (Provce.)
℘ Order of John Scollay Esqr., Samuel Austin Esqr} Selectmen
Consented to Nicholas Bowes Overseer

17th.   Reciev'd into the House Andrew Constong (Prov.)
℘ Order of John Scollay Esqr., Ezekiel Price Esqr.} Selectmen
Consented to Saml. Whitwell Overseer

22nd.   Reciev'd into the House Wm. & Thos. Howard & their Mother Provce.
Acco.
℘ Order of John Scollay Esqr., Ezekiel Price Esqr.} Selectmen
Consented Sam Partridge Oversr.

23d.   Reciev'd into the House Hannah Baster & 3 Children
℘ Order of Saml. Whitwell Overseer

25th.   Reciev'd into the House Sarah Hill & her Child
℘ Order of Saml. Barrett Overseer

26th.   Reciev'd into the House Elizabeth Tibbit a young Child   Provce. Acco.
℘ Order of John Scollay Esqr., Ezekl. Price Esqr.} Selectmen
Jona. Mason Overseer

27th.   Reciev'd into the house Lucy Clark (Provce. Acco.)
℘ Order of Wm. Powell Overseer
John Scollay Esqr., Ezekl. Price Esqr.} Selectmen

1779 Novr: 27th.   Reciev'd into the house Robert Garland Cranch (Provce.)
℘ Order of Harbottle Dorr, Nathan Frazier} Selectmen
Consented to Isaac Smith Overseer   NB the Order was dated the 17th.

Reciev'd into the house Mary Lemine
℘ Order of John White Overseer

28th.   Reciev'd into the house John Davis
℘ Order of Capt. Saml. Partridge Oversr.

                    Discharg'd Mrs. Fultons two Children, Sal Hills Child
                    Ran away Hannah Bowman, Sal Hill

Decmr. 5th.   Reciev'd into the House James Perrin & Wife (Prov)
℘ Order of John Scollay Esqr., Jno. Preston} Selectmen
Consented to Jno. White Overseer

7th.   Reciev'd into the House Boston a Negro Servant to Abel Waters of
Danvers (Provce. Acco.)
℘ Order of the Council & House &c
Consented to ℘ Jonathan Mason one of the Overseers

                    Recievd into the House Mary Perkit & her Child (Provce.)
℘ Order of John Scollay Esqr., Nathan Frazier} Selectmen
Consented to Jona. Mason Overseer

11th.   Reciev'd into the House Mary Marshall
℘ Order of Edward Procter Overseer

                    Discharg'd Elizabeth Carey ℘ Order of Capt. Saml. Partridge Oversr.
                    Andrew Constong the 5th.

16th.   Reciev'd into the house Eliza. Strong
℘ Order of Saml. Barrett Overseer

                    Reciev'd into the house Sarah Hier
℘ Order of Wm. Powell Overseer

                    Reciev'd into the house Elizabeth Flood
℘ Order of Saml. Whitwell Oversr.

1779 Decmr. 23d.   Reciev'd into the house Rich'd Morgan
℘ Order of Saml. Hewes Oversr.

28   Reciev'd into the House Sarah Bohannon
℘ order of John White Overseer

1780 Janu 1st.   Reciev'd into the house Thomas & Mary Cross Orphan Children
℘ order of Saml. Barrett, Overseer

8th.   Reciev'd into the house Peter Pecour his wife & Child (Provc.)
℘ Order of Saml. Austin, Ezek. Price Esqr.} Selectmen
Consented to Saml. Partridge Overseer

11th.   Reciev'd into the house Mrs. Acres
℘ Order of Jona. Mason Overseer

12th.   Reciev'd into the house Elizabeth Dutton
℘ Order of Nicho. Bowes Overseer

12th.   Reciev'd into the House <*Eliza.*> Isabella Dawes (Provce.)
℘ Order of Jno. Scollay Esqr., Jno. Preston} Selectmen
Consented to Saml. Whitwell Overseer

12th.   Reciev'd into the house   Mackintosh (Prov)
℘ Order of John Scollay Esqr., John Preston} Selectmen
Consented to Jona. Mason Overseer

17th.   Reciev'd into the house Mr. Wm. Spragues Daughtr.
℘ Order of Jno. Sweetser Overseer

19th.   Reciev'd into the house James Warren
℘ Order of Nicho. Bowes Oversr.

21st.   Reciev'd into the house George Randell
℘ Order of John Scollay Esqr., Jona. Williams Esqr.} Selectmen
Consented to Jno. Sweetser Oversr.

26th.   Receiv'd Elizabeth Quineo into the House
℘ order of Isaac Smith Esqr. Overseer

       Reciev'd into the house Mary Billings
℘ Order of Samuel Patridge Oversr.

Feb. 3   Reciev'd into the house Lydia Newman & Child
℘ Order of Nicholas Bowes Oversr.

1780 Feb: 3d.   Reciev'd into the House Daniel North (Prov)
℘ Order of John Scollay Esqr., John Preston} Selectmen
Consented to Nicholas Bowes Oversr.

5th.   Recd. into the House Sarah Barton (Prov)
℘ Order of Nathan Frazier, Ezekl. Price Esqr.} Selectmen
Consented to Saml. Whitwell Oversr.

7th.   Reciev'd into the House Catharine Croswell (Prov)
℘ Order of John Scollay Esqr., Jona. Williams Esqr.} Selectmen
Consented to John White Oversr.

12th.   Reciev'd into the house Samuel Croswell (Province)
℘ Order of John Scollay Esqr.   } Selectmen
Consented to Jona. Mason Overseer

Feb: 16th.   Run away Robt. G. Cranch (Prov), Mary Lemine, Sarah Barton 12th.
Pro

23d.   Reciev'd into the house Sarah Scot (on Prov Acco.)
℘ Order of John Scollay Esqr.   } Selectmen
Consented to Nicho. Bowes Oversr.

25th.   Reciev'd into the House Ann Sheen & two Childn. Provce.
℘ Order of John Scollay Esqr., Nathan Frazier} Selectmen
Nicho. Bowes Overseer

            Reciev'd into the House on Provce: Acco. Anne Ingraham
℘ Order of John Scollay Esqr., Nathan Frazier} Selectmen
Nicho. Bowes Oversr.

Mch 7th.   Reciev'd into the House Thomas Green (Provce. Acco.)
℘ Order of Gustavus Fellows, Nathan Frazier} Selectmen
Consented to by Nicho. Bowes Oversr.

15th.   Reciev'd into the House Alexander Hamilton (Prov)
℘ Order of Jno. Scollay Esqr., Wm. Mackay} Selectmen
Consented to by Jno. White Overseer

17   Recievd into the House Mary Linty (Prov)
℘ Order of John Scollay Esqr., Wm. Mackay} Selectmen
Consented to Jona. Mason Oversr.

1780 Mch 23d.   Reciev'd into the house Peter Sulkey
℘ Order of Nicholas Bowes Oversr.

            Dischargd on Provce. Acco. Sarah Partridge March 11th.
            on Provce. Acco. Daniel North 15th. Mch
            on Provce. Acco. Peter Pecour & wife & child 18th. March
            on Provce. Acco. Sarah Scott 23d. March
            on Prov: Acco. Alexr. Hamilton 27th. Mch

17th.   Reciev'd into the House Reba. Millen (Prov)
℘ Order of Ezekl. Price Esqr., John Scollay Esqr.} Selectmen
Consented to by John White Overseer

            Discharg'd on Provce. Acco. Catharine Croswell 29th. Mch
            Run away Saml. Croswell (Prov) 24th. Mch Richd. Morgain

Apl. 6th.   Reciev'd into the house Ann Cox & her Daur. Peggy
℘ Order of Saml. Whitwell Oversr.

8th.   Reciev'd into the house Mary Webb
℘ Order of Nicholas Bowes Oversr.

            Run away Mary Haris & Bett Jackson, Pol: Acres
            (& Margt. Bryant 16th April)

May 13th. Elizabeth Milton Ran away (Provce.) Wm. Jarvis R. away
Sarah Bohannan Ran away—Chay. Black R. away
Discharg'd, Lydia Newman

May 17th. Discharg'd Two Children of Goslins (Provce.)

Received into the House Charity Black
℘ Order of Edward Procter Esqr. Overseer} Dated the 6 May
Received into the House, Abigail Lord
℘ Order of John White, Overseer} Dated the 8th. May

May 16 Received into the House, Margarett O:Bryant (Provce.)
℘ Order of Ezel. Price Esqr., Tuttle Hubbard} Selectmen
Consented to by Jona. Mason} Overseer

1780 May 20 Received into the House, Margarett Killgor (Province)
℘ Order of John Scollay Esqr., Nathan Fraizer Esqr.} Selectmen
Consented to by Saml. Whitwell Overseer

May 22nd. Received into the House Elizabeth Gott
℘ Order of Edward Procter Esqr. Overseer

May 22nd. Received into the House Jean Younge
℘ Order of John White Overseer

May 24th. Received into the House Mary Attkins
℘ Order of Harbo. Dorr, Tuttle Hubbert} Selectmen
Consented to by Edward Procter} Overseer

May 28 Received into the House Thomas Gyles
℘ Order of Mr. Saml. Whitwell (Overseer)

June. 2nd. Received into the House Mary Swann
℘ Order of Edward Procter Esqr. Overseer

3rd. Received into the House Mary Ward
℘ Order of Samuel Whitwell

3rd. Received into the House Dorothy Wheeler & Child
℘ Order of Harbl. Dorr, Will. Mackay} Selectmen
Consented to by John White} Overseer.

June 5 Received into the House Mathew Hopkins
℘ Order of Samuel Partridge

5 Ysabellah Dawes (Provce.) Ran away

7 Received into the House William Waldridge
℘ Order of Edward Procter Esqr. (Oversr.)

1780. June 8 Received into the House Joseph Harper
℘ Order of Edward Procter Esqr. (Overseer)

20 Received into the House Four Childn. of Mr. Thos. Eatridge
℘ Order of Nich Bowes (Overseer)

Received into the House, Hipsibah Dunbrook
℘ Order of Wm. Powell Esqr. (Overseer.)

22nd.   Received into the House John Murphy
℘ Order of John Scolley Esqr., Gustavus Fellows} Selectmen
Consented to by Mr. Samuel Whitwell} Overseer

23rd.   Ann Howard (Province) Ran away

Thos. Green & Ann Sheen (Province) Ran away

24th.   Received into the House, Elizabeth Tripe
℘ Order of Samuel Barrett Esqr. (Oversr.)

28th.   Received into the House John Bradley
℘ Order of Harbottle Dorr, Wm. Mackay} Selectmen
Consented to by Mr. John White} Overseer

July 3rd.   Received into the House Sally Harris a Child
℘ Order of Edward Procter Esqr. (Overseer)

Discharg'd Jane Leimerceis

Discharg'd Ann Howard's Child (Province) July 4th.

July 4th.   Received into the House Mary Monk
℘ Order of Joseph Webb Esqr. (Overseer)

7th.   Received into the House Crannah Starr
℘ Order of Edward Procter Esqr., Joseph Webb Esqr.} Overseer

1780 July 7th.   Received into the House Samuel & Anna Laurance
℘ Order of John Scollay Esqr., Gustavus Fellows} Selectmen
Consented to by Capt. Saml. Partridge} Overseer

10th.   Received into the House Elizabeth Laurance
℘ Order of Harbe. Dorr, Nathan Fraizier} Selectmen
Consented to by Edward Procter Esqr.} Overseer

11th.   Received into the House Eleanor Knox & her Child
℘ Order of John Scolley Esqr., Gustavus Fellows} Selectmen
Consented to by Capt. Saml. Partridge} Overseer

11th.   Dischardg Cornelius Corneil (Province)

12th.   John Bradley (Province) Run away

Discharg'd Two Children of Thomas Eatridges

19th.   Discharg'd Saml. & Nancy Laurance (Province)

20th.   Discharg'd Willm. Sharp & Wife (Province)

Sarah Hill & Mary Billings (Run away) (19th. July)

29th.   Received into the House Elizabeth Goff
℘ Order of John Scollay Esqr., Ezekiel Price Esqr.} Selectmen
Consented to by Edward Procter Esqr.}

30th.   Received into the House Sarah Walker
℘ Order of Edward Procter Esqr. (Oveersr.)

Augt. 2nd.   Received into the House John Vintenow
℘ Order of Isaac Smith Esqr. (Oveerseer)

1780 Augt. 4   Received into the House George Sanger
℘ Order of John Scollay Esqr., Ezekeil Price Esqr.} Selectmen
Consented to by Jona. Mason} Oveerseer

8th.   Discharg'd Margtt. O.Bryant (Province)

8th.   Received into the House, Elizabeth Williams
℘ Order of Willm. Phillips Esqr. (Oversr.)

Augt. 4th.   Received into the House John Flanngan
℘ Order of Harble. Dorr, Ezekl. Price} Selectmen
Consented to by Joseph Webb Esqr.} Oveerseer

15th.   Received into the House Elizh. Fethergill
℘ Order of Saml. Whitwell (Oversr.)

17th.   Received into the House John Hill a Child
℘ Order of Gustavus Fellows, Ezekiel Price} Oveerseer [*i.e., Selectmen*]
Consented to by Capt. Saml. Partridge} Oveerseer

24th.   Received into the House John McDonald
℘ Order of Harble. Dorr, Ezekl. Price Esqr.} Selectmen
Consented to by Jona. Mason} Oveerseer

29   Receved into the House Ann Lawrence a Child
℘ Order of Natl. Frazer, Ezekl. Price Esq} Selectmen
Saml. Partridge Oveseer

30   Receved into the House Thomas Mitchel wife and Child
℘ order of John Scollay Esqr., Nathan Frazer} Selectmen
Jona. Mason Oveseer

                         Dischd. Ann Warrin <*Margt. Bryant prov Augt.* [...]>
                         (Dorathy Whealer Sept. 24 Prov) (George Sanger prov Sept. the 4)

1780 Sept. 6   Received into the House Cornelius Corneliuson (Prov. Chard)
℘ Order of John Scolay, Ezekl. Price} Selectmen
Mr. Nickolas Bowes Oveseer

8   Receved into the House Margt. Holland and Child
℘ Order of Edward Procter Esqr. Overseer

12   Receved into the House Elizh. Ivis
℘ Order of Mr. Saml. Whitwell Oveseer

14   Received into the House Wm. Sharp and wife
℘ Order of John Scollay, Ezekl. Price Esqrs.} Selectmen
Capt. Saml. Partridge Oveseer

14   Received into the House Danl. North
℘ Order of John Scollay, Ezekl. Price Esqrs.} Selectmen
Mr. Nicholas Bowes Oveseer

19   Received into the House Patrick Hackett
℘ order of Ezekl. Price Esqr., Tuthill Hubbart} Selectmen
Mr. Saml. Whitwell Overseer

28   Received into the House Dinah a negro woman
℘ Order of John Scollay, Ezekl. Price Esqrs.} Selectmen
Edward Procter Esqr. Overseer

28   Received into the House John Banks & wife
℘ Order of Wm. Powell Esqr. Overseer

28   Recceived into the House Mary Gregory
℘ Order of Harb. Dor, Wm. Mackay} Selectmen
Mr. Jona. Mason Overseer

1780 Sept. 30 Received into the House Mary Ford
℘ Order John Scollay, Ezekl. Price Esqrs.} Selectmen
Jona. Mason Oveseer

   Dischd. Elanor Knox Octr. 3 (Prov)

1780 Sept 14 Receive into the House Naomi Moreland
℘ Order Ezekl. Price, Tuthill Hubbard} Selectmen
Mr. Jonathan Mason, Overseer

   Receive Elizabeth Hopkins into the House her Order Dated. Sept 26.
1780
℘ Order Edward Proctor Esqr., Overseer

1780 Octor. 14th. Received into the House Mary Crosby
℘ Order Mr. John White Overseer

   Dischd. John McDonald Octo 6th. (Prov)
   Dischd. Elanor Knoxs Child (Prov) Octor. 27th.

Octor. 31 Recevid into the House Jane Joice
℘ Order of Saml. Whitwell Overseer

Novr. 3 Receved into the House a Negro woman
℘ Order of Wm. Powell Esq Ovesr.

7   Receved into the House Elizth. Skinner
℘ Order of Mr. John White Overseer

1780 Novr. 8 Recivced into the House Elizth. Pierce State acct.
℘ Order of Ezekl. Price Esqr., Wm. Mackay} Selectmen
Saml. Whitwell Overseer

10   Receveed into House Charls Dix Wallis a Child on State Acct.
℗ Order of John Scollay Esqr., Ezekl. Price Esqr.} Selectmen
Mr. Jona. Mason Overseer

11   Receved into the House Richard Morgain
℗ Order of Mr. John White Overseer

11   Receved into the House Joseph Ranstead
℗ Order Joseph Webb Esqr. Overseer

16   Receved into the House Sarah Bowin
℗ Order of Mr. Saml. Whitnell Overseer

               Receved into the House Hannah Langsford Order Dated Octor. 27th.
℗ Order of Harbt. Dorr, Wm. Mackay} Selectmen
Honl. Wm. Phillips Esqr. Overseer

20   Received into the House Wm. and Junice Hardy Children
℗ Order of John Scolay, Ezekl. Price Esqrs} Selectmen
Mr. Saml. Whitwell Overseer

22   Receved into the House Ann Sampel
< ℗ *Order of John Scolay*>
℗ Order of Ezekl. Price Esqr., Wm. Mackay} Selectmen

28   Receved into the House Elizth. Jackson
℗ Order of Wm. Powell Esqr. Overseer

1780 Novr. 28   Received into the House Elizth. Boone
℗ Order of Mr. John Sweetser Jr. overseer

28   Received into the House Mary Pierce
℗ Order of Capt. Saml. Partridge Oveseer

28   Received into the House Elizth. Corben
℗ Order of Capt. Saml. Partridge Overseer

30th.   Receivd into the House   Parkman
℗ Order Edward Procter Esqr. Overseer

Decr. 4th.   Received into the House Mary Robbins
℗ Order of Mr. John White Overseer

5th.   Received into the house Elezibeth Pumroy
℗ Order of Capt. Saml. Partridge Overseer

               Discharg'd Elezibeth Hopkins & Child

9th.   Received into the house Mary Brown
℗ Order of John Scollay, Nathan Frazier} Selectmen of Boston
Honble. William Phillips Esqr.

1780 Decr. 9th.   Received into the House Luce White
℗ Edward Proctor Esqr. Overseer

11th.   Received into the House   Bennet
℘ Order Samuel Barret Overseer

11th.   Received into the House Mary Steward
℘ Order of Capt. Saml. Partridge Overseer

11th.   Received into the house the Child of Elenor Knoxs
℘ Order of Ezekl. Price Esqr., Tuthell Hubbard} Selectmen
Capt Saml. Partridge Overseer

15th.   Received into the House Ann Burton
℘ Order of John Scollay, Nathan Frazier} Selectmen
Mr. Nicholas Bowes Overseer

15th.   Received into the House Sarah Thompson
℘ Order of Ezekl. Price Esqr., Tuthell Hubbard} Selectmen
William Powell Esqr.

18th.   Received into the house Mary Brown
℘ Order of John Scollay, Ezekl. Price Esqr.} Selectmen
Mr. Nicholas Bowes Overseer

1780 Decr. 20th.   Received into the house Hanery Harris
℘ Order of Gustavus Fellows, Tuthell Hubbard} Selectmen
Capt Samuel Partridge Overseer

26th.   Received into the House Elizibeth Tower
℘ Order of John Scollay Esqr., Nathan Frazier} Selectmen
Mr. Saml. Whitwell Overseer

30th   Ran away Mary Thompson (Provc.)

1781 Jany. 3rd.   Received into the House Mary Crosby, her Order Dated the 27th.
Decr. 1780
℘ Order of Capt. Saml. Partridge (Oveerser)

3rd.   Received in the House Hannah Thompson
℘ Order of Ezekiel Price   } Select
Capt. Saml. Partridge (Oveerr.)

4th.   Received into the House, Margarett Cunningham
℘ Order of Saml. Whitwell (Overseer)

11th.   Received into the House Elizabeth Jeffreis
℘ Order of Ezekiel Price Esqr., Nathan Fraizier} Selectmen
Mr. Nicholas Bowes (Overseer)

1781 Jany. 13   Received into the House Mary Thompson
℘ Order of Ezekiel Price, Wm. Mackay} Selectmen
Consented to by Mr. Jonathan Masson Overseer

14th.   Received into the House Jeny LeMercey
℘ Order of Wm. Powell Esqr. (Oveerseer)

14th.   Received into the House, Charity Leachmore
℘ Order of John White (Oveerser)

16th.   Received into the House Elizabeth Corbin
℘ Order of Joseph Webb Esqr. (Overser)

25th.   Received into the House Bethine Sargant and Son
℘ Order of John White (Overseer)

Feby. 3rd.   Received into the House Elizabeth Hopkins And her Child
℘ Order of Saml. Partridge (Overser)

      Run Away   Pomroy

      Recd. Into the House Mary Higgins her Or[der] dated 31 Jany. 1781
℘ Order of Ezekiel Price Esqr., Tuttle Hubbard} Selectmen
Mr. Nicholas Bowse (Overseer)

Feby. 7   Recd. into House Nancy Gaskin
℘ Order of Ezekiel Price Esqr., Tuttle Hubbard} Selectmen
Mr. Nicholas Bowes (Oveirseer)

9   Recd. into the House Meriah a Negro Woman
℘ Order of Jona. Mason (Oveerseer)

1781 Feby. 14 Elizabeth Ivis (Run away)

19   Discharg'd Ann Burton (Province)

21   Received into the House Silvester Rush a Child
℘ Order of Edward Procter Esqr. (Overseer)

24   Received into the House, John Wood
℘ Order of Ezekiel Price Esqr., Tuttle Hubbard} Selectmen
Consented to by Saml. Whitwell} (Overser)

March 1   Run away Mary Higgins & Nancy Gaskins (Provinc)
      Run away Sarah Bowin

14   Recd. into the House, Stephen Hiter
℘ Order of Harbottle Dorr, Wm. Mackay} Selectmen
Consented to by Edward Procter Esqr.}

19th.   Received into the House Mary Right
℘ Order of Edward Procter Esqr.} Overseer

21   Received into the House Mary Thomas
℘ Order of Nathan Fraizier, Tuttle Hubbard} Selectmen
Consented to by Mr. Nichs. Bowes} Overseer

22   Run away Mary Ford & Child (Province)

27   Recd. into the House, James & Elizh. Smellidge
℘ Order of Mr. Saml. Whitwell} (Overseer)

27   Run away Elizth. Jeffries (Province)

28   Run away John Wood & Elizh. Tower (Province)
      Run away Richard Morgan

1781 Aprill 9   Joseph Gray Lansford (Run away)

10   Recd. into the House York a negro Man
℘ Order of Capt. Saml. Partridge (Overseer)

12th.   Recd. into House Sarah King
℘ Order of Edd. Procter Esqr. (Oversr.)

14th.   Recd. into the House John Lane
℘ Order of Jona. Mason (Overseer)

24th.   Recd. into the House Phillipi Low
℘ Order of Edd. Procter (Overser)

24th.   Recd. into the House Mary Brown
℘ Order of John Scollay Esqr., Tuttle Hubbart} Selectmen
Consented to by Wm. Powell Esqr.} Oveerser

27th.   Recd. into the House Hannah Craft
℘ Order of John Scollay Esqr., Nathn. Fraizier} Selectmen
Consented to by Capt. Saml. Partridge} Oveerser

28th.   Recd. into the House Margtt. Bryant
℘ Order of John Scollay Esqr., Nathn. Fraizier} Selectmen
Consented to by Mr. Jona. Mason} Oveerser

            Dischar'd Stephen Hiter his Order dated Aprill 7 1781

            Dischar'd the Wife & Child of Robertson there Order dated 23 Aprill
1781

            Dischar'd Partrick Hackett his Order dated Aprill 28th. 1781

30th.   Mary Taverner (Run away)

1781 May 5th.   Received into the House Sally Foot
℘ Order of Saml. Barrett Esqr. (Overr.)

15th.   Received into the House, Rose Clough—Margtt. Clough And Two
Children
℘ Order Edwd. Procter Esqr. (Overr.)

19th.   Received into the House, David Fogo
℘ Order of Isaac Smith Esqr. (Overr.)

June 1st.   Received into the House, Richard Simmons
℘ Order of Nathan Fraizier, Ezekiel Price} Selectmen
Consented to by Mr. Saml. Whitwell} Overr.

4th.   Received into the House Nancey Ross
℘ Order of John Scolley Esqr.   } Selectmen
Consented to by Wm. Powell Esqr.} Overr.

            Discharg'd Martha Dausey (Prov) 21st. May

            Dischargd Elizabeth Hopkins & Child

Margarett Holland & Child (Run away)

Lydia Ward Run away

James Smellidge Run away

9th.   Recd. into the House Elenor Boyle
℘ Order Harbottle Dorr, Nathan Fraizer} Selectmen
Consented to by John White} Overr.

12th.   Recd. into the House Joseph Bordman
℘ Order John Sweetser Overseer

1781 June 12th.   Recd. into the House Josiah Boyles
℘ Order Saml. Whitwell Overseer

21th.   Recd. into the House Margret Holland and Saml. Brown her Son
℘ Order Saml. Partridge Overseer

26th.   Recd. into the House Margret Brothers & Child
℘ Order Ezekl. Price Esqr.   } Selectmen
Consented to by Nickolas Bowes} Overseer

28th.   Recd. into the Alms House Mary Perrin
℘ Order John Scollay Esqr., Ezekl. Price Esqr.} Selectmen
Consented to by Nickolas Bowes} Overseer

July 2d.   Recd. into the House Elizabeth Ivers
℘ Order Joseph Webb Esqr. Overr.

Discharg'd Eunice Hardy's two Children (Prove.) June 8th.

Discharg'd Charles Dicks Wallis (Prove.) July 2d. 1781

(Prove. Mary Perrin) & Elizth. Corbin Run away June 13th.

July 12   Recd. into the House Mary Ann Mewes An Infant Child
℘ Order of John Scollay Esqr., Gustavus Fellows} Selectmen
Willm. Powell Esqr. Overseer

20th.   Recd. into the House Mary Cavenough
℘ Order of Saml. Whitwell Overseer

21st.   Recd. into the House Grace A Negro Women
℘ Order Mr. John White Overseer

16th.   Dischargd. Mary Ann Mewes A Child (Provs.)

1781} July 24th.   Recd. into the House Abraham Rhodes
℘ Order of John Scollay Esqr., Ezekl. Price Esqr.} Selectmen
Mr. Nicholas Bowes Overseer

24th.   Recd. into the House Archibald Livingston
℘ Order of Nathan Frazier, Wm. Mackay} Selectmen
Edward Procter Esqr. Overseer

27th.   Recd. into the House William Walten
℘ Order of Mr. Saml. Whitwell} Overseer

Augt. 9   Recd. into the House Willm. Sharp & Wife
℘ Order of John Scolley Esqr., Tuttle Hubberd} Selectmen
Consented to by Saml. Barrett Esqr.} Overseer

11   Recd. into the House Lydia Town
℘ Order of Joseph Webb Esqr. (Oveerser)

14th.   Recd. into the House Hannah Williams's Daughter
℘ Order John Sweetser Junr. (Overr.)

14th.   Received into the House Sarah Dockum & Sarah Jennesson
℘ Order of Capt. Saml. Partridge (Overr.)

25th.   Recd. into the House, Jethro Dodge a Negro
℘ Order Gustavus Fellows, Ezekiel Price} Selectmen
Consented to by Willm. Powell Esqr.} Overseer

                         Run away Mary Perkitt & Child (Prove.) 2nd. Augt.
                         Run away Mary Linty & Child (Prove.) 22d. do.

27th.   Run away Willm. Sharp & Wife (Prove.)
                         Run away Elizh. Williams

1781   Recd. into the House Martha Dausey her Order dated Augt. 2d.
℘ Order John Scollay Esqr., Tuttle Hubbert} Selectmen
Consented to by Mr. John Sweetser Junr.} (Overseer)

Augt. 29   Recd. in the House Elizabeth Harris
℘ Order of Mr. John White (Overser)

30   Received into the House Johannah Decoster
℘ Order of Edwd. Procter Esqr. (Overseer)

Septr. 10th.   Receive'd into the House Eliza. Fooboe
℘ Order of Isaac Smith Esqr. (Overseer)

13.   Recd. into the House Sarah Powell
℘ Order Saml. Barrett Esqr. (Overser)

Octor. 3d.   Recd. into the House Willm. Barron
℘ Order John Scollay, Ezekl. Price} Selectmen
Consented to by Willm. Phillips Esqr.} Overseer

Octor. 3d.   Recd. into the House Susannah Edwards & Child
℘ Order Harbl. Dorr, Willm. Mackay} Selectmen
Consented to by Saml. Barratt Esqr.} Overseer

Octor. 6th.   Reced. into the House Elizebeth Haines
℘ Order Mr. Samuel Whitwell (Overseer)

Octor. 11th.　　　Recd. into the House Mary Richardson & Child
℘ Order Mr. Nicholas Bowes (Overseer)

　　　　　　　Run away Hannah Williams

　　　　　　　Run away　　　　Scott

　　　　　　　Discharged. Jethro Dodge A Negro Octo 10th. 1781 (Provc.)

1781 Octor. 15th.　　Recd. into the House Mary Smith & Hannah Lyddard
℘ Order of Mr. John White (Overseer)

22d.　　　　　　Recd. into the House Rebecca Gouge
℘ Order of Capt Saml. Partridge (Overseer)

26th.　　　　　Recd. into the House Sally Ford A Child
℘ Order Saml. Barrett Esqr.

　　　　　　　Run away Margarett Brethers (Provc.) Octor. 26th.

　　　　　　　Discharged.　　　Caberly　　Novr. 1st.

　　　　　　　Run away Rebecca Gouge

Novr. 9　　　　　Recd. into the House Hepzebeth Atkins
℘ Order of Mr. John White (Overseer)

9th.　　　　　　Recd. into the House Cornelus Youngman (Provs.)
John Scollay, Gustavus Fellows} Selectmen
℘ Order of Capt Saml. Partridge (Overseer)

10th.　　　　　Recd. into the House York A Negro
℘ Order of Capt Saml. Partridge (Overseer)

10th.　　　　　Recd. into the House Margarett Lee
℘ Order Nathan Frazier, Willm. Mackay} Selectmen
Consented to by Edward Proctor Esqr.} Overseer

1781 Novr. 10th.　　Recd. into the House Martha Mullens
℘ Order of Mr. Nicholas Bowes (Overseer)

13th.　　　　　Recd. into the House Betty
℘ Order Gustavus Fellows, Ezekl. Price} Selectmen
Consented to by Capt Saml. Partridge} Overseer

14th.　　　　　Recd. into the House Joseph Gray Ransford
℘ Order of Eward Proctor Esqr. Overseer

14th.　　　　　Recd. into the House Elizebeth Morton
℘ Order of Harbottle Dorr, N. Frazier} Selectmen
Consented to by Edward Proctor Esqr.} Overseer

19th.　　　　　Recd. into the House Mary Ann Pendergrass
℘ Order of Capt Saml. Partridge (Overseer)

20th.   Recd. into the House Elizebeth Cook
℘ Order of Mr. John Sweetser (Overseer)

21st.   Recd. into the House John Davis
℘ Order of Mr. John White (Overseer)

22d.   Recd. into the House Elizh. Williams
℘ Order of the Honble. Willm. Phillips Esqr. Overseer

22d.   Recd. into the House Richard Morgan
℘ Order of Mr. John White (Overseer)

            Run away John Davis   Novr. 2[1st]

1781   Recd. into the House Elizebeth Paster
℘ Order Board of Overseers

Decr. 1.   Recd. into the House Wm. Sharp & Wife
℘ Order of John Scollay Esqr., Tuthell Hubbard} Selectmen
Consented to by Mr. Nicholas Bowes} Overseer

Decr. 7th.   Recd. into the House David Spencer
℘ Order John Scollay Esqr., Nathan Frazier} Selectmen}
Consented to by Mr. John White} Overseer

14th.   Recd. into the House Hannah Burden
℘ Order of Mr. Willm. Mackay, Tuthell Hubbard} Selectmen
Consented to by Edward Procter Esqr.} Overseer

22d.   Recd. into the House James Woods
℘ Order of Mr. Nathan Frazier, John Scollay Esqr.} Selectmen
Consented to by Edward Proctor Esqr.} Overseer

29th.   Recd. into the House Elizabeth Riley & her Child her Order dated.
20th. Novr.
℘ Order John Scollay Esqr., Mr. Wm. Mackay} Selectmen
Consented to by Jonathan Mason} Overseer

            Dischg. Thomas Mitchell   Decr. 19th. 1781

1782 Jany. 7th.   Received into the House Mary Billings & Child
℘ Order of Capt Saml. Partridge (Overseer)

16th.   Received into the House John Miller
℘ Order of John Scllay Esqr., Wm. Mackay} Selectmen}
Consented to by Mr. Jona. Mason} Overseer

1782 Jany. 18th.   Received into the House Mary Burke
℘ Order Mr. Jona. Mason (Overseer)

            Run away Elizibeth Harris   Jany. 7th.

            Received into the House Magat. Brothers (Provs.) Order dated Jany.
4th.}
℘ Order John Scollay Esqr., Nathan Frazier} Select Men
Consented to by Mr. John White} Overseer

30th.   Run away Elizh. Riley & Child (Provs.)

                         Received into the House George Randall & Wife (Provs.) Order dated.
1 Septr. 1781
℘ Order of John Scollay Esqr., Mr. Wm. Mackay} Selectmen
                         Recd. into the House George Randalls Child. (Provs.) Order dated
Octor. 8. 1781
℘ Order John Scollay Esqr., Wm. Mackay} Select men

                         Recd. into the House Tho. Mitchell Child (Provs.) Order dated 26
Octor. 1781
℘ Order John Scollay Esqr., Wm. Mackay} Selectmen}

Feby. 7   Received into the House Mary Tuttell & Child
℘ Order of Mr. John White (Overseer)

7th.   Received into the House Hannah Hammanway
℘ Order of Edward Proctor Esqr. (Overseer)

1782 Feby. 12th.   Received into the House Jno. Morrison
℘ Order Capt Saml. Partridge (Overseer)

                         Received into the House Mary Wright. Feby. 18th.
℘ Order Edward Proctor Esqr. (Overseer)

Feby. 18th.   Received into the House Mary Marro
℘ Order Josh. Webb Esqr. (Overseer)

                         Run away Hepsibeth Atkins (Feby. 13th.)

                         Run away Margarett Holland & Child (22d. Feby.)

                         Run away David Spencer (Provs.) (22d. Feby.)

                         Run away Mary Burke (Feby. 28th.)

                         Received into the House Mary Cumlar (Provs.) Feby. 21st.
℘ Order
Consented to by Mr. John White} Overseer

March 4th.   Recd. into the House Sarah Partridge
℘ Order John Scollay Esqr., Ezekl. Price Esqr.} Selectmen
Consented to by Isaac Smith Esqr.} Overseer

7th.   Recd. into the House Pegg A Negro Woman
℘ Order Honble. Willm. Phillips Esqr. (Overseer)

15th.   Recd. into the House Mary Stephens
℘ Order John Scollay Esqr., Ezekl. Price Esqr.} Selectmen
Consented to by Mr. Nichs. Bowes} Overseer

1782 March 16th.   Recd. into the House Sarah Voux
℘ Order Honble. Wm. Phillips Esqr. (Overseer)

29th.   Recd. into the House Michael Condon
℘ Order Ezekl. Price   } Selectmen
Consented to by Capt Saml. Partridge} Overseer

Discharged. Joseph Gray Ransford

22d.   Run away Margarett Brothers (Provs.)
                       Discharged. John Morrison (April 2d.)

April 3d.   Received into the House A Boy 4 Years old. Mrs. Brown's Child
℘ Order of Samuel Barratt Esqr. (Overseer)

8th.   Received into the House Deliverance Cahill & Maid
℘ Order of Josh. Weebb (Overseer)

26th.   Recd. into the House Jeh[rader] Monfort
℘ Order of Edward Proctor Esqr. (Overseer)

April 3   Run away James Verrin & Wife & Mary Stevens (Provs.)

                       Run away William Sharp (April 27th.)

                       Run away Elizibeth Morton (April 27th.)

May 2d.   Recd. into the House Sarah Whitman
℘ Order of Saml. Whitwell (Overseer)

<4   *Recd. into the House Sarah Partridge*
℘ *Order John Scollay, Ezekl. Price} Selectmen*
Consented to by Isaac Smith Esqr.} Overseer>

1782 May 17th.   Recd. into the House Ann Ruler
℘ Order of Saml. Partridge (Overseer)

4th.   Recd. into the House Martha Smith
℘ Order of Ezekl. Price Esqr   } Selectmen
Consented to by Saml. Partridge} Overseer.

17th.   Recd. into the House a Distracted Women
℘ Order Saml. Barratt Esqr.} Overseer

17th.   Recd. into the House   Ervin & Grandson
℘ Order Jno. Sweetser junr. Esqr.} Overseer

22d.   Recd. into the House Partrick Hacket
℘ Order Ezekl. Price Esqr., Nathan Frazier Esqr.} Selectmen
Consented to by Jona. Mason} Overseer

May 7.   Run away Marthew Hopkins (Provs.)

8.   Dischargd. Mrs. Brown's (Child)

8   Run away Mary Sharp (Provs.)

16th.   Run away Willm. Barron (Provs.)

May 27   Recd. into the House Margaret Brother
℘ Order Ezekl. Price Esqr.   } Selectmen
Consented to by Honbl. Wm. Phillips Esqr.}

June 3d.   Recd. into the House Larry Low
℘ Order of Edward Proctor Esqr.} Overseer

1782 [*June*] 6   Received into the House Mathew Hopkins
℘ order Capt. Saml. Partridge} Overseer

June 6th.   Received into the House Sarah Kettle & Child
℘ Order of Edward proctor Esqr.} Overseer

7th.   Received into the House Mary Kellen
℘ Order of John Scollay Esqr., Ezekl. price Esqr.} Selectmen
Consented to by Jonathan Mason Esqr.} Overseer

11th.   Received into the House Sarah Dawson
℘ Order John Scollay Esqr., Wm. Mackey} Selectmen
Consented to by Edward Proctor Esqr.} Overseer

17th.   Recd. into the House Elizh. Whetsons Child
℘ Order Edward proctor Esqr. (Overseer)

19th.   Recd. into the House Silvester Hitton
℘ Order Harbottle Dorr, Wm. Mackay} Selectmen
Consented to by Isaac Smith Esqr.} Overseer

26th.   Received into the House John Fisher
℘ Order of John Scollay Esqr., Gustavus Fellows} Selectmen
Consented to by Capt Saml. partridge} Overseer

1782 June 19th.   Dischargd. Mary Mullins

                          Run away Elizibeth Williams (June 21st.)

                          Run away Mary Richardson & Child (June 25th.)

                          Run away Larry Low (July 1st.)

July 2d.   Received into the House Sarah Lockland
℘ Order of Nicholas Bowes (Overseer)

4th.   Received into the House patrick A Negro man
℘ Order of Ezekl. price Esqr., Nathl. Frazier} Selectmen
Consented to by Saml. Whitwell} Overseer

6th.   Recd. into the House Lydia Hodgetts & Son
℘ Order of Ezekl. price Esqr., Tuthill Hubbard} Selectmen
Consented to by Jona. Mason} Overseer

6th.   Recd. into the House John Migar a Child
℘ Order of John Scollay Esqr., Tuthill Hubbard} Selectmen
Consented to by John White} Overseer

8th.   Received into the House William Bannon
℘ Order of John Scollay Esqr., Ezekl. Price Esqr.} Selectmen
Consented to by John White} Overseer

1782 July 12th.   Received into the House   Clarke Her Order dated. 12th. May
℘ Order of Nathan Frazier, Ezekl. price Esqr.} Selectmen
Consented to by Saml. Barratt Esqr.} <Overseer>

13th.   Recd. into the House Eleanor Bartlet
℘ Order of Ezekl. price Esqr., Tuthill Hubbard} Selectmen
Consented to by Capt Saml. partridge} Overseer

20th.   Received into the House Elizh. Wyer & Child
℘ Order of John Scollay Esqr., Tuthill Hubbard} Selectmen
Consented to by Willm. powell Esqr.} Overseer

27th.   Received into the House Rachel peterson
℘ Order of Nathn. Frazier, John Scollay Esqr.} Selectmen
Consented to by Jona. Mason} Overseer

Augt. 2d.   Recd into the House June And his Wife Negroe's
℘ Order of John Scollay Esqr., Nathn. Frazier} Selectmen
Consented to by Jona. Mason} Overseer

           Run away Margarett Brothers (provs.) (July 20th.)

           Run away Michael Condon (provs.) July 27th.

4th.   Run away Mary Marrow

8th.   Recd. into the House Mary Ward
℘ Order Mr. Saml. Whitwell (Overseer)

1782 Augt. 12th.   Recd. into the House James Perrin & Wife
℘ Order John Scollay Esqr., Tuthell Hubbard Esqr.} Selectmen
Consented to by Capt Saml. partridge} Overseer

12th.   Received into the House John Oliver
℘ Order Nathan Frazier, Ezekl. price Esqr., Tuthell Hubbard Esqr.} Selectmen
Consented to by Edward proctor Esqr.} Overseer

15th.   Received into the House peggy Holland & Child
℘ Order Honbl. Wm. phillips Esqr. (Overseer)

17th.   Received into the House peter Murphy
℘ Order Mr. Nathn. Frazier, John Scollay Esqr.} Selectmen
Consented to by Edward proctor Esqr.} Overseer

20th.   Received into the House Edward Winslow
℘ Order Mr. Saml. Whitwell (Overseer)
N.B. He is Nine Years Old this month

           Run away Rachael peterson (Provs.) (Augt. 16th.)

22d.   Received into the House the Widow Pattens two Children William
Patten 11 Year Old Feby. 6th., Polly Patten 8 Years Old 27th. Instant
℘ Order John Sweetser Esq} Overseer

1782 Augt. 27th.   Recived into the House on the States Accot. Calvin Hinds
℘ Order Nathan Frazier & Ezekl. Price Esqr.} Select Men
Consented to Edwd. Procter Esqr.} Overseer

Augt. 28th.   Recied into the House On the States Accot. Nancy Wheeler an Infant
Child
℘ Order of John Scolley Esq, Tuttle Hubbard} Select Man
Consented to William Powel Esq} Overseer

28th.   Sarah Damson discharged (prove.)

          Recived in the House on the States Accot. William Murray
℘ Order of Mr. Nathan Frazier, Capt. Willm. Mackey} Select Men
Edwd. Procter Esqr.} Overseer

Septr. 16th.   Received into the House Archd. Livingston
℘ Order Nathan Frazier Esqr., Harbottle Dorr} Selectmen
Consented to by Edward proctor Esqr.} Overseer

23d.   Received into the House Mary Holland
℘ Order Isaac Smith Esqr.} Over Seer

Octo. 3d.   Dischargd. Ann Ruler

19   Received into the house Martha Smith
℘ Order John Sweetser Esqr.} Overseer

20th.   Received into the house Thos. Edwards
℘ Order Honble. Wm. powell Esqr.} Overseer

1782 Octo. 26th.   Received into the house Mary Richardson & Child
℘ Order Honble. Wm. phillips Esqr. (Overseer)

          Dischargd. Erving Ocotr. 9th.

          Dischargd. Jehoedah Mountfort (Octor. 18th.)

          Dischargd. peter Murphy (Provs.) Octor. 7th.)

          Elizth. Wyer Run away (Provs.) (Novr. 3d. 1782)

          Recd. into the House Mary Lewis (Provs.) (Novr. 9th. 1782)
℘ Order John Scollay Esqr., Nathan Frazier Esqr.} Selectmen
Consented to by Nicholas Bowes} Overseer

          Recd. into the House Mary Stephens On the State Acco. her dated.
24th. Octor. 1782
℘ Order John Scollay Esqr., Nathan Frazier Esqr.} Selectmen
Consented to by Nicholas Bowes} Overseer

Novr. 5th.   Recd. into the House Peter Kelly
℘ Order Ezekl. price   } Selectmen
Consented to by Saml. partridge} Overseer

          Received into the house Tamis a Negro Woman her order dated 26th.
Octo.
℘ Order John Scollay Esqr., Nathn. Frazier Esqr.} Selectmen
Consented to by Mr. Saml. Whitwell} Overseer

1782 Novr. 6th.   Received into the house William Maggot
℘ Order Harbottle Dorr Esqr., Ezekl. price Esqr.} Selectmen
Consented to by Nicholas Bowes} Overseer

6th.   Received into the house Saml. Chandler & wife
℘ Order Saml. partridge (Overseer)

13th.   Received into the house Jane Gerrald
℘ Order Honble. Wm. Phillips Esqr. (Overseer)

13th.   Recd. into the House Fanny pitt A Child
℘ Order John Scollay Esqr., Ezekl. price Esqr.} Selectmen
Consented to by John Sweetser junr. Esqr.} Overseer

15th.   Recd. into the house Sarah Toomy
℘ Order John Scollay Esqr., Tuthill hubbard} Selectmen
Consented to by Nicholas Bowes} Overseer

16th.   Recd. into the house Hepzibah Atkins
℘ Order John White (Overseer)

29th.   Recd. into the house Martha Smith
℘ Order Isaac Smith Esqr. (Overseer)

18th.   Martha Smith—Run away
18th.   Mary Stephens—Run away

1782 Novr. 20th.   Received into the house peggy Dampsen
℘ Order Nathan Frazier Esqr., Tuthill Hubbard} Selectmen
Consented to by John White} Overseer

            Dischargd. Margarrett Holland & Child (Novr. 7th. 1782)

Decr. 4th.   Received into the House James Asley
℘ Order John Scollay Esqr., Willm. Mackay} Selectmen
Consented to by Edwd. procter Esqr.} Overseer

14th.   Received into the House Elizebeth Castle
℘ Order Capt Saml. partridge} Overseer

16th.   Received into the House Elizh. Patten a Child
℘ Order John Sweetser Esqr.} Overseer

16th.   Received into the House Susannah Lewis & Child
℘ Order Nathan Frazier Esqr., Harbottle Dorr Esqr.} Selectmen
Consented to by Edwd. procter Esqr.} Overseer

16th.   Received into the House Willm. Sharp & Wife
℘ Order Nathan Frazier Esqr., John Scollay Esqr.} Selectmen
Consented to by Capt Saml. partridge} Overseer

            Kate A Negro Women Dischargd. (Provs.) Decr. 10th. 1782.

1782 Decr. 26th.   Received into the House Judia Thayer
℘ Order John Scollay Esqr.   } Selectmen
Consented to by Mr. John White} Overseer

28th.   Received into the House Elizabeth Lowe
℘ Order John Scollay Esqr.   } Selectmen
Consented to by Mr. Nichs. Bowes} Overseer

28th.   Received into the House Thomas Carlan
℘ Order Edward procter Esqr.} Overseer

30th.   Received into the House Samuel Murphy
℘ Order Mr. Nichs. Bowes} Overseer

<1783 Jany.>   Received into the House Thos. Mitchells Child. Her Order Dated
Octor. 26th. 1781
℘ Order Nathn. Frazier Esqr., Tuthell Hubbard} Selectmen
Consented to by Mr. Nichl. Bowes} Overseer

                    Received into the House Sarah Dawson. Her Order Dated Octor. 5th.
1782
℘ Order Ezekl. price Esqr., Nathn. Frazier Esqr.} Selectmen
Consented to by Capt Saml. partridge} Overseer

1783 Jany. 2d.   Received into the House James Trenholm Child
℘ Order Ezekl. Price Esqr., Tuthell Hubbard} Selectmen
Consented to by Mr. Jona. Mason} Overseer

1783 Jany. 3d.   Received into the House Sarah Rogers
pr. Order Willm. Powell Esqr.} Overseer

15th.   Received into the House Gerald Fitz. Gerrald
pr. Order Ezekl. Price Esqr.
Consented to by Mr. Jona. Mason} Overseer

16th.   Received into the House Sarah Corthen
pr. Order Gustavas Fellows, Ezekl. Price Esqr.} Selectmen
Consented to by Mr. Jona. Mason} Overseer

                    Dischargd. Lydia Hodgetts (Provs.) Jany. 2d. 1783

                    Received into the House Margarett Kennedy. Her Order Dated. Decr.
31st. 1782
℘ Order Nathan Frazier Esqr., John Scollay Esqr.} Selectmen
Consented to by Isaac Smith Esqr.} Overseer

24th.   Received into the House Mary Hog
℘ Order Willm. powell Esqr.} Overseer

30th.   Received into the House Sarah Hoganey
℘ Order Ezekl. price Esqr., John Scollay Esqr} Selectmen
Consented to by Isaac Smith Esqr.} Overseer

1783 Feby. 10th.   Received into the House Eunice Hardy
℘ Order John Scollay Esqr.   } Selectmen
Consented to by Joseph Webb Esqr.} Overseer

20th.   Received into the House James Rogers
℘ Order Capt Saml. partridge} Overseer

24th.   Received into the House Elizibeth Willet & Child
pr. Order Joseph Webb Esqr.} Overseer

24th.   Received into the House John Derrick
℘ Order John Scollay Esqr., Mr. Wm. Mackay} Selectmen
Consented to by Mr. John White} Overseer

24th.   Received into the House Mary Webb
Pr. Isaac Smith Esqr.} Overseer

26th.   Received into the House Mary Edwards two Children
Pr. Order Mr. Isaac Smith Esqr.} Overseer

28th.   Received into the House Hannah Powell
℘ Order Joseph Webb Esqr.} Overseer

March 3d.   Received into the House Francis Hamman
Pr. Order Saml. Barrett Esqr.} Overseer

1783 Feby. 28   Recd. into the House Hannah Thophall
Pr. Order of John Scolly Esqr., Harbottle Dorr Es.} Select Menn
Consented to by Mr. Nichl. Bowes} Overseer

March. 5.   Recd. into the House Michcael Condon
Pr. Order of John Scolly Esqr., Ezekiel Price Esqr.} Select Men
Consented to by Capt. Saml. Partridge} Overser

March. 15th.   Recd. into the House Richard Perrey
Pr. Order of John Scolly Esqr., Tuttle Hubbard} Select Men
Consented to by Mr. John White} Overseer

28th.   Received into the House Willm. Hardy & Infant
℘ Order John Scollay Esqr., [J?] Jeffries Esqr.} Selectmen
Consented to by Edwd. proctor Esqr.} Overseer

24th.   Dischargd. Sarah Kettle & Child

24.   Run away Rhoady Edwards a Child

29th.   Run away Richard perry (Provs.)

31st.   Run away Sarah Cassell

31st.   Run away Mary Ward

1783 April 4th.   Received into the House Anna Banton
℘ Order John Scollay Esqr., Ezekl. Price Esqr.} Selectmen
Consented to by Capt Saml. Partridge} Overseer

26th.   Received into the House Joseph Ransford
℘ Order Joseph Webb Esqr.} Overseer

30th.   Received into the House Mary Crow
℘ Order John Scollay Esqr., Thos. Grenough} Selectmen
Consented to by Capt. Saml. Partridge} Overseer

                        Received into the House Nancy Gilling. Her order dated Septr. 1. 1782
℘ Order John Scollay Esqr., Thos. Greenough} Selectmen
Consented to by Mr. Nichs. Bowes} Overseer

                        Received into the House Mosses McGraugh. His Order Dated. Octo.
1st. 1782
℘ Order John Scollay Esqr., Thos. Greenough} Selectmen
Consented to by Mr. Nichs. Bowes} Overseer

12th.   Run away Hannah Ransford (Provs.) April 12th.

                        Dischargd. Unice Hardy (Provs.) April 28th.

                        Run away Margarett Poor April 28th.

                        Dischargd. John Derrick (Provce.) 21st. Aprill 1783

1783 May 7th.   Received into the House Samuel Wyer a Negro Man
℘ Order of John Scollay Esqr., Ezekl. price Esqr.} Selectmen
Consented to by Willm. Powell Esqr.} Overseer

14th.   Received into the House Christopher Atkins
℘ Order Mr. John White} Overseer

14th.   Received into the House the Following Persons Vizt. Danl. Shaw, John
Stacey, John Smith, George Bartholomew, John Curtis}
℘ Order John Scollay Esqr., Tuthill Hubbard} Selectmen
Consented to by Mr. Jona. Mason} Overseer

19th.   Received into the House James Campbell
℘ Order Harbottle Dorr, Willm. Mackay, Thos. Greenough} Selectmen
Consented to by Mr. Nichs. Bowes} Overseer

20th.   Received into the House Richd. Greenough
℘ Order Edwd. Procter Esqr.} Overseer

21st.   Received into the House Kate a Negro Women
Ezekl. Price Esqr., Tuthill Hubbard } Selectmen
℘ Edwd. Procter Esqr.} Selectmen

21st.   Received into the House Robert Watt & Sister
℘ Order John Scollay Esqr., Willm. Mackay} Selectmen
Consented to by Willm. Powell Esqr.} Overseer

1783 May 29th.   Received into the House Benja. Winsor
℘ Order Ezekl. Price Esqr., Willm. Mackay} Selectmen
Consented to by Mr. Jona. Mason} Overseer

29th.   Received into the House Poll. Duet
℘ Order Capt Saml. Partridge} Overseer

                        Dischargd. Judia Thayer & Child (Provs.) May 12th. 1783

Dischargd. Tho. Mitchell Wife & child (Provs.) 14th. May. 1783

Dischargd. Moses Magrath (Provs:) May 7th. 1783

Dischargd. William Hardy a Child. (Provs.) May 24th. 1783

24th.   Dischargd. Hannah Powell and Child

June 4   Received into the House Judah Clancey
℘ Order Capt Saml. Partridge} Overseer

9th.   Received into the House James McCloyd
℘ Order John Scollay Esqr., Tuthill Hubbard} Selectmen
Consented to by Isaac Smith Esqr.} Overseer

11th.   Received into the House James Lynch
℘ Order Harbottle Dorr, Thos. Greenough} Selectmen
Consented to by Edwd. procter Esqr.} Overseer

12th.   Recived into the House Sarah Dawson & Mary Druvet
℘ Order John White} Overseer

1783 June 17th.   Received into the House David Cocknan
℘ Order Edward procter Esqr.} Overseer

21st.   Received into the House Simean Oslon
℘ Order Capt Saml. partridge} Overseer

23d.   Received into the House Sarah Cowell
℘ Order Mr. Nichs. Bowes   } Selectmen

                        Received into the House William Burke. (His Order Dated. June 5th.)
℘ Order John Scollay Esqr., Willm. Mackay} Selectmen
Consented to by Mr. Saml. Whitwell} Overseer

Dischargd. Silvester Hitton (Provs.) June 9th. 1783

Dischargd. Margaret Dempson (Provs.) June 11th. 1783

Dischargd. Benjamin Winsor (Provs.) June 12th. 1783

Dischargd. James McCloyd (Provs.) June 23d. 1783

Dischargd. Jehoadah Mountford June 14th. 1783

Run away Sarah Dawson & Mary Druvet

Dischargd. James Lynch (Provs.) June 11th. 1783

July 7th.   Received into the House John plumer a Child
℘ Order John Sweetser Esqr.} Overseer

1783 July 8th.   Received into the House Martin Auginsine
℘ Order Ezekl. Price Esqr., Tuthill Hubbard} Selectmen
Consented to by Mr. Jona. Mason} Overseer

12th.   Received into the House Mrs.   Mullins
℘ Order Mr. Nickolas Bowes} Overseer

13th.   Received into the House Susannah Riorden
℘ Order Mr. John White} Overseer

19th.   Received into the House John Elisah
℘ Order Edward procter Esqr.} Overseer

29th.   Received into the House Benja. Chipman
℘ Order John Scollay Esqr., Tuthill Hubbard} Selectmen
Consented to by Honble. Willm. phillips Esqr.} Overseer

Augt. 1st.   Received into the House Elizh. Hopkins & Child
℘ Order John White} Overseer

                  Dischargd. Hannah Tophall, George Bartholomew (Provs.) July 8th.
1783

                  Run away Michael Conden (Provs.) July 18th. 1783

                  Run away Judah Clancey July 28th. 1783

1783   Dischargd. Daniel Shaw (Provs.) July 26th. 1783

                  Dischargd. Peter Kelly (Provs.) July 29th. 1783

                  Dischargd. Willm. Sharp & Wife (Prov) Augt. 4th. 1783

                  Dischargd. Archibald Livingston (Prov) Augt. 4th. 1783

                  Dischargd. Richard Greenough Augt. 4th. 1783

                  Run away Mary Billings Augt. 3d. 1783

Augt. 8th.   Received into the House Timothy Brown
℘ Order William Powell Esqr.} Overseer

9th.   Received into the House Peggy Glifford
℘ Order Honbl. Wm. Phillips Esqr.} Overseer

14th.   Received into the House Easter Brown
℘ Order Ezekiel price Esqr.   } Selectmen
Consented to by Mr. Saml. Whitwell} Overseer

25th.   Received into the House John McKingley
℘ Order John Scollay Esqr., Ezekl. Price Esqr.} Selectmen
Consented to by Capt Saml. Partridge} Overseer

                  <*Received into the House Jno. Ricker*
℘ *Order Edward Procter Esqr.} Overseer*>

1783 Augt. 24th.   Dischargd. Elizibeth Boane

26   Dischargd. John Plumley

Dischargd. Mary Thomas August 19th. 1783 (Provs.)

Sept. 1st.   Received into the House Hannah Duxlory
℘ Order Mr. Jona. Mason} Overseer

Septr. 5th.   Received into the House H Naomi Higgins & Child
℘ Order John Scollay Esqr.   } Selectmen
Consented to by Edwd. Procter Esqr.} Overseer

9th.   Received into the House Mary Law
℘ Order Edward Procter Esqr.} Overseer

10th.   Received into the House John Cumings
℘ Order Mr. Willm. Mackay, Harbottle Doar Esqr.} Selectmen
Consented to by Edward Procter Esqr.} Overseer

19th.   Received into the House John Jones
℘ Order Mr. Willm. Mackay, Thos. Grenough Esqr.} Selectmen
Consented to by Edward procter Esqr.} Overseer

Discharged. John Curtis (Provs.) Dated. Sept 12th. 1783

Run away John Cumings (Provs.) Sept 15th. 1783

Run away Naomi Higgins & Child (Provs.) Septr. 25th. 1783

1783 Sept. 24th.   Received into the House Mary Jenson
℘ Order Ezekl. price Esqr., Thos. Greenough Esqr.} Selectmen
Consented to by Mr. Saml. Whitwell} Overseer

Received into the House Eleanor Richey
℘ Order John Scollay Esqr., Ezekl. price Esqr. } Selectmen
Consented to by Edward procter Esqr.} Overseer

25th.   Received into the House Richard Greenough
℘ Order Edwd. procter Esqr.} Overseer

29th.   Received into the House John & Henry Hilbert—Children. their
Order Augt. 25th. 1783.
℘ Order John Scollay Esqr., David Jeffries Esqr.} Selectmen
Consented to by John White Esqr.} Overseer

29th.   Received into the House Reuben Gorham
℘ Order Ezekl. price Esqr.   } Selectmen
Consented to by Mr. Saml. Whitwell} Overseer

30th.   Received into the House Mrs. Burford
℘ Order Mr. Nichl. Bowes} Overseer

Octor. 3d.   Received into the House Mary Gordard & Child
℘ Order Edward Procter Esqr.} Overseer

4th.   Received into the House Elizh. Jennang
℘ Order John Scollay Esqr., Ezekl. Price Esqr.} Selectmen
Consented to by Joseph Webb Esqr.} Overseer

1783 Octob. 4th.   Received into the House Robert Giffin
℘ Order Ezekl. Price Esqr., David Jeffries} Selectmen
Consented to by Joseph Webb Esqr.} Overseer

7th.   Received into the House Ebenezer Drake
℘ Order Ezekl. Price Esqr., Mr. Thos. Greenough} Selectmen
Consented to by Mr. Jona. Mason} Overseer

11th.   Received into the House Willm. Sharp & Wife
℘ Order John Scollay Esqr., Ezekl. Price Esqr.} Selectmen
Consented to by Capt. Saml. Partridge} Overseer

14th. Received into the House Thomas Hill
℘ Order John Scollay Esqr., Ezekl. Price Esqr.} Selectmen
Consented to by Honble. Willm. Phillips Esqr.} Overseer

17th.   Received into the House. Peter Hunter
℘ Order John Scollay Esqr., Ezekl. Price Esqr.} Selectmen
Consented to by Edward Procter Esqr.} Overseer

24th.   Received into the House Sarah Sweat
℘ Order Captn. Saml. Partridge} Overseer

24th.   Received into the House Mary McCurdy
℘ Order Capt Saml. Partridge} Overseer

                             Discharged. John Jones (Provs.) Octor. 15th. 1783

1783   Discharged. Christopher Atkins (to the Workhouse) Octor. 15th. 1783

                             Discharged. Mrs. Hilberts Child (Provs.) Octor. 15th. 1783

                             Run away Polly Low Octor. 27th. 1783

                             Received into the House Joannah Edy Her dated Octor. 20th. 1783
℘ Order Mr. Jona. Mason} Overseer

Novr. 3d.   Received into the House Lydia Raymond
℘ Order Captr. Samuel Partridge} Overseer

7.   Received into the House Archibald Livingston (Prov)
℘ Order John Scollay Esqr., Ezekl. Price Esqr.} Selectmen
Consented to by Mr. John White Esqr.} Overseer

10th.   Received into the House Abigail Gilbert from the Workhouse
℘ Orderr Captn. Partridge} Overseer

11th.   Received into the House Josiah Jones (Provs.) <(a Child)>
℘ Order John Scollay Esqr., Ezekl. price Esqr.} Selectmen
Consented to by Mr. Jona. Mason} Overseer

12th.   Received into the House Isaac Dawes: a Child
℘ Order Mr. Nichs. Bowes} Overserr

14th.   Received into the House Christopher Atkins from the Workhouse
℘ Order Mr. John White Esqr.} Overseer

1783 Novr. 21st.   Received into the House John Powell a Child of Hannah Powell
℘ Order Honble. Willm. Phillips Esqr.} Overseer
to pay 2/1 ℘ week

25th.   Received into the House James Shaugnesy
℘ Order Mr. Willm. Mackay   } Selectmen
Consented to by Edward Procter Esqr.} Overseer

Run away Mary Bufford Novr. 17th. 1783

Dischargd. Susannah Rioden Decr. 2d. 1783

Decr. 6th.   Received into the House Timothy Howard
℘ Order Ezekl. Price Esqr., Willm. Mackay} Selectmen
Consented to by Mr. Samuel Whitwell} Overseer

Decr. 6th.   Received into the House Grace Cox
℘ Order John Sweetser Esqr.} Overseer

8th.   Received into the House Henry Hilbert a Child
℘ Order John Scollay Esqr., Willm. Mackay} Selectmen
Consented to by Edward Proctor Esqr.} Overseer

12th.   Received into the House John Morris East Indiamen
℘ Order Ezekl. Price Esqr., Willm. Mackay} Selectmen
Consented to by Edward Procter Esqr.}

15th.   Received into the House Elizibeth Cushing
℘ Order John White Esqr.} Overseer

15   Received into the House Nancy Diblin

1783 Decr. 16th.   Received into the House Samuel Dockham
℘ Order Mr. Samuel Whitwell} Overseer

23d.   Received into the House Robert Murchey
℘ Order John Scollay Esqr., Willm. Mackay} Selectmen
Consented to by Isaac Smith Esqr.} Overseer

26th.   Received into the House Job a negroo Man
℘ Order John Scollay Esq., Mr. Willm. Mackay} Overseer [*i.e., Selectmen*]
Consented to by Isaac Smith Esqr.} Overseer

30th.   Received into the House Mary Higgins & Naome Moreland & Child
℘ Order Honbl. Wm. Phillips Esqr.} Overseer

1784 Jany. 1.   Received into the House Mary Standly
℘ Order Captn. Saml. Partridge} Overseer
Consented to by

2d.   Received into the House William Johnson
℘ Order Ezekl. Price Esq., Mr. Willm. Mackay} Selectmen
Consented to by Mr. Jona. Mason} Overseer

Dischargd. John Morris & East Indiamen (Provs.) Jany. 3d. 1784

Run away Mary Higgins Jany. 3d. 1784

3d.   Received into the House Hannah Wyat
℘ Order John Scollay Esqr.   } Selectmen
Consented to by Mr. Jona. Mason} Overseer

1784 Jany. 5th.   Received into the House Mary Wallis & Child
℘ Order Edward Procter Esqr.} Overseer

                      Dischargd. Grace Cox (to the Workhouse)

                      Dischargd. Naomi Moreland & Child (to the Workhouse)

6th.   Received into the House Mrs.   Woods
℘ Order Isaac Smith Esqr.} Overseer

8th.   Received into the House, Mariam Hanford
℘ Order John White Esqr.} Overseer

7th.   Received into the House Lawrence Purdue
℘ Order John Scollay Esqr.   } Selectmen
Consented to by Edward procter Esqr.} Overseer

8th.   Received into the House Ann Waters
℘ Order John White Esqr.} Overseer

15th.   Received into the House Abigail Barratt
℘ Order John White Esqr.} Overseer

17th.   Received into the House William Carlton
℘ Order Ezekl. Price Esqr.   } Selectmen
Consented to by Mr. Jona. Mason} Overseer

24th.   Received into the House. Prudence Bennet from the Workhouse
℘ Order Mr. Samuel Whitwell} Overseer

                      Received into the House Mercy Ellis
℘ Order Isaac Smith Esqr.} Overseer

1784 Jany. 28th.   Received into the House John Bishop
℘ Order Ezekl. Price Esqr.   } Overseer [*i.e., Selectmen*]
Consented to by Mr. Jona. Mason} Overseer

30th.   Received into the House John Wadly
℘ Order Edward Procter Esqr.} Overseer

31t.   Received into the House John Honnewell
℘ Order John Sweetser Esqr.} Overserr

Feby. 8th.   Received into the House Lydia Morse
℘ Order Honer. Wm. Phillips Esqr.} Overseer

10th.   Received into the House Kate Holland & Child Negro
℘ Order John Scollay Esqr., Mr. Tuthill Hubbard} Selectmen
Consented to by Mr. Nicholas Bowes} Overseer

11th.   Received into the House Susannah Franklin
℘ Order John Scollay Esqr., Mr. Tuthill Hubbard} Selectmen
Consented to by Capt Saml. Partridge} Overseer

16th.   Received into the House Phillis A Negro Women
℘ Order John Scollay Esqr., Mr. Tuthill Hubbard} Selectmen
Consented to by Capt Saml. Partridge} Overserr

17th.   Received into the House Jeremiah a Negro Man
℘ Order Ezekl. Price Esqr., Mr. Tuthill Hubbard} Selectmen
Consented to by John Sweetser Esqr.} Overseer

1784 Feby. 19th.   Received into the House Mary Walker
℘ Order
Consented to by Joseph Webb Esqr.} Overseer

28th.   Received into the House John Johnson
℘ Order John Scollay Esqr., Willm. Mackay Esqr.} Selectmen
Consented to by Edward Procter Esqr.} Overseer

March 1st.   Received into the House James Cunningham a Boy Aged. 10 years old
14th. April 1784
℘ Order Honble. Willm. Phillips Esqr.} Overseer

March 5th.   Received into the House Mary Harvey
℘ Order Mr. Samuel Whitwell} Overseer

9th.   Received into the House Davis Cuningham & Nancy Ray from the workhouse
℘ Order Joseph Webb Esqr.} Overseer

21st.   Received into the House Bryan Dandle
℘ Order John Scollay Esqr., Ezekl. price Esqr.} Selectmen
Consented to by Capta. saml. partridge} Overseer

24th.   Received into the House Mary Reid
℘ Order John Scollay Esqr., Mr. Thos. Greenough} Selectmen
Consented to by John White Esqr.} Overseer

Peter Hunter Discharged. (Provs.) March 16th. 1784

Dischargd. Jeremiah a Negro Man March 17th. (provs.)

1784   Dischargd. Robt. Merchie—John McKinzey, John Wales (Provs.)} April
6th. 1784

Dischargd. John Honnewell April 6th. 1784

Received into the House Nancy Gibling / Dated Septr. 1. 1783
℘ Order John Scollay Esqr., Mr. Willm. Mackay} Selectmen
Consented to by

April 7th.   Received into the House Richard Collort
℘ Order Mr. Samuel Whitwell} Overseer

10th.　　　　　　Received into the House Michael Cockran
℘ Order John Scollay Esqr., Mr. Thos. Grenough} Selectmen
Consented to by Edward Proctor Esqr.} Overseer

13th.　　　　　　Received into the House John Honnewell
℘ Order Edward procter Esqr.} Overseer

14th.　　　　　　Received into the House Nelcy Dunnels
℘ Order Edward proctor Esqr.} Overseer

"　　　　　　Received into the House Peter McNeal & Wife (Negro's) Pro
℘ Order Edward proctor Esqr.} Overseer
John Scollay Esqr., Willm. Mackay Es[*qr.*]} Selectmen}

20th.　　　　　　Received into the House Benjamin Sabels
℘ Order John White Esqr.} Overseer

26th.　　　　　　Received into the House Jonathan Edmunds
℘ Order John White Esqr.} Overseer

27th.　　　　　　Received into the House Rose (A Negro Women)
℘ Order John White Esqr.} Overseer

1784　　　　　　Dischargd. Mary Walker (Provs.) April 14th. 1784

　　　　　　　　Dischargd. Simeon Osborn Wife & Child April 21st. 1784

　　　　　　　　Dischargd. Mary Stanley (prov) April 26th. 1784

　　　　　　　　Run away Phillis A Negro (prov) April 12th. 1784

　　　　　　　　Dischargd. Jonah Jones (prov) April 13th. 1784

　　　　　　　　Run away Briant Dandley (prov) April 24th. 1784

April 28th.　　　　Received into the House　Thompson
℘ Order John Scollay Esqr.　　　　　　} Selectmen
Consented to by William Powell Esqr.} Overseer

April 29th.　　　　Received into the House Jehodea Mountfort
℘ Order Edward Proctor Esqr.} Overseer

May 4th.　　　　Recd. into the House Hannah Berre
℘ Order of John White Esqr.} Oversr.

14th.　　　　　　Recd. into the House George Lindor (Provs.)
℘ Order of John Scolly Esqr., Wm. Mackay} Select Men
Consented to by Mr. Samuel Whitwell Ovrr.

17th.　　　　　　Recd. into the House Thos. Gammill a Negro (Provs.) and Dischargd.
him to Bridwell 22 May.

18th.　　　　　　Received Eunice Vose in to the House
℘ order Joseph Webb Esqr.} Oversr.

1784   Dischargd. Richd. Cohvel to the Work House 6th. May

        Dischargd. Susannah Franks 11th. May

        Dischargd. Ann Waters 12th. May

        Martha Smith Run away (Provs.) 10th. May
        James Trenholm do. (do.)   do.

        Dischargd. a Child of Hannah Powells 15th. May

May 25th.   Received into the House Peter Boyer (Provs.)
℘ Order Jonathan Mason Esqr.} Overseer

27th.   Received into the House Michael Melony
℘ Order   } Selectmen
Consented by Mr. J. L. Austin} Overseer

28th.   Received into the House Betsey Woodward a Child
℘ Order John Scollay Esqr., Nathan Frazier Esq.} Selectmen
Consented to by Mr. Samuel Whitwell} overseer

June 5th.   Received into the House Dennis Burns (Provs.)
℘ Order John Scollay Esqr., Ezekl. Price Esqr.} Selectmen
Consented to by Mr. Samuel Whitwell} overseer

6   Received into the House Obidiah Higgins (Prov.)
℘ Order John Scollay, D Jeffries} Esquires / Selectmen
Consented to by Honbe. Willm. Phillips Esqr.} Overseer

11   Received into the House John McKinsey
℘ Order Ezekl. Price Esqr., David Jeffries} Selectmen
Consented to by Capt Saml. Partridge} Overseer

1784 June 14   Received into the House John Hood (Provs.)
℘ Order Ezekl. Price Esqr., David Jeffries} Selectmen
Consented to by Mr. Saml. Whitwell} Overseer

22d.   Received into the House Martan
℘ Order Mr. Jon. L. Austin (Overseer)

July 3d.   Received into the House Polly Ross
℘ Order Mr. Samuel Whitwell (Overseer)

        Dischargd. Betsey Woodward a Child (Prov) June 8th. 1784

        Dischargd. George Landor (Provs.) June 28th. 1784

        Dischargd. John Johnson (Provs.) June 22d. 1784

        Run away Michael Melany (Provs.) June 17th. 1784

        Run away Mary Woods June 21st. 1784

        Run away Timothy Howard (Prov) June 22d. 1784

Run away Ross a Negro Women June 24th. 1784

July 10th.   Received into the House Simeon Osborn, Wife & Child
℘ Order Jono. L. Austin (Overseer)

12th.   Received into the House Susannah Riordiorn
℘ Order John White (Overseer)

      Received into the House Sukey Waterman a Child of Eunice Vose
℘ Order Joseph Webb (Overseer)

16th.   Received into the House Joseph Colesweather
℘ Order Edward Proctor Esqr.} Overseer

1784 July 16   Received into the House John Cooper
℘ Order Ezekl. Price Esqr., David Jeffries} Selectmen
Consented to by Captn. Samuel Partridge} Overseer

16th.   Received into the Almshouse Thomas Johnson
℘ Order Nathan Frazier Esq., David Jeffries} Selectmen
Consented to by Edward Proctor Esq} overseer

17th.   Received into the House Samuel Legg
℘ Order Captn. Samuel Partridge} Overseer

19th.   Receved into the House Mary Killgore (Provs. Accot.)
Willm. Mackay, David Jeffries} Selectmen
℘ Order Edward Proctor Esqr.} overseer

22d.   Received into the House Molly Whitman
℘ Order William Powell Esqr.} Overseer

24th.   Received into the House Elizabeth Henley & Child
℘ Order Mr. Nathan Frazier, Ezekl. Price Esqr.} Selectmen
Consented to by William Powell Esqr.} overseer

24th.   Received into the House Jonathan Harris
℘ Order John White Esqr.} Overseer

      Run away Archibald Livingston (Prov) July 19th. 1784

      Run away Mary Richardson July 19th. 1784

      <Run away John Hood (Prov) July 22d. 1784>

      Dischargd. Nancy Weeler (Provs.) July 15. 1784

      Dischargd. William Sharp & Wife July 26. 1784

1784 July 28.   Received into the House Martha Simons
℘ Order Honble. Willm. Phillips Esqr.} overseer

28   Received into the House Nathl. Dickey. his Order Dated July 12th.
℘ Order Captn. Samuel Partridge} overseer

31   Received into the House Richard Kennedy
℘ Order Ezekl. Price Esqr., David Jeffries} Selectman
Consented to by Mr. Saml. Whitwell} overseer

"   Received into the House Rebeccah Hilbert
℘ Order John Scollay Esqr., David Jeffries Esqr.} Selectmen
Consented to by Mr. Saml. Whitwell

                Run away Martha Simons Augt. 1st. 1784

                Dischargd. to the Workhouse Samuel Legg July 27th.

                Dischargd. to the Workhouse John McKinzey (Provs.) July 27

Augt. 5th.   Received into the House Benjamin Mumford
℘ Order Joseph Webb Esqr. Overseer

5th.   Received into the House Timothy Howard
℘ Order Ezekl. Price Esqr.   } Selectmen
Consented to by Mr. Saml. Whitwell} overseer

5th.   Received into the House John Madan
℘ Order Nathan Frazier Esqr., Ezekl. Price Esqr.} Selectmen
Consented to by Mr. Saml. Whitwell} overseer

18.   Received into the House Rachael Townsend
℘ Order Jon L Austin

20th.   Received into the House Sarah Ayers
℘ Order Nathan Frazier Esqr., John Scollay} Selectmen
Consented to by Edward Proctor Esqr.} Overseer

1784 Augt. 23d.   Received into the House Joseph Lewis
℘ Order John Scollay Esqr., Nathan Frazier Esq} Selectmen
Consented to by Edward Proctor Esqr.

23d.   Received into the House Partrick Falva
℘ Order Nathan Frazier Esqr., Willm. Mackay} Selectmen
Consented to by Edward Proctor Esqr.} Overseer

24th.   Received into the House Ebenr. Goffe & Wife
℘ Order Jona. Webb Esq.} overseer

29th.   Received into the House Sarah Gray
℘ Order of Isaac Smith Esqr.} Overseer

31.   Received into the House Susannah Muns
℘ Order Ezekl. Price Esqr.   } Selectmen
Consented to by Mr. Saml. Whitwell} overseer

                Dischargd. Lydia Morse Augt. 18th. 1784

                Dischargd. Elizabeth Henley & Child (Provs.) Augt. 18th. 1784

                Dischargd. James Hewes. Augt. 18th. 1784

Run away John Madan (Provs.) Augt. 19th. 1784

Run away Richard Kennedy (Provs.) Augt. 21st. 1784

Dischargd. Mary Read (Provs.) Augt. 24th. 1784

Augt. 7 1784   Run away Michael Cocheran (P) Omitted

Septr. 2   Received into the House Silas Holmes
℘ Order Nathan Frazier Esqr., William Mackay} Selectmen
Consented to by Edward Proctor Esqr.} overseer

1784 Septr. 9   Received into the House Mary Moran a Child
℘ Order John Scollay Esqr., Ezekl. Price Esqr.} Selectmen
Consented to by Jona. Mason Esqr.} overseer

13th.   Received into the House Sarah Nowell
℘ Order Edward Proctors Esqr.} overseer

18th.   Received into the House Thomas Johnson
℘ Order Mr. Nathan Frazier   } Selectmen
Consented to by Edward proctor Esqr.} overseer

18th.   Received into the House Daniel Devier
℘ order Mr. Samuel Whitwell} overseer

Run away Sue Holland a Negro Girl (Provs.) Septr. 6th. 1784

Run away Nancy Jibling (Provs.) Septr. 7. 1784

Run away Thomas Johnson (Provs.) Septr. 30th. 1784

Dischargd. John Smith (Provs.) Septr. 1st. 1784

Run away William Johnson (Provs) Septr. 30th. 1784

Dischargd. Margery Clough & Child Septr. 22. 1784

Dischargd. Hannah Berry & Child Sept 23: 1784

24th.   Received into the house Thomas Mannan (Provs.)
℘ Order Thos. Greenough Esqr., John Scollay Esqr.} Selectmen
Consented to by John White Esqr.} Overseer

27th.   Received into the House Sarah Richards
℘ order Capt Saml. Partridge} overseer

"   Received into the House Elizebeth Henley & Child
℘ Order Nathan Frazier Esqr., Willm. Mackay} Selectmen
Consented to by Edward procter Esq} overseer

1784 Septr. 28   Received into the House Daniel Jennings
℘ order Nathan Frazier Esq   } Selectmen
Consented to by Edward Proctor Esq} Overseer

Sept 28th.   Received into the House Elizabeth Farmers two Children
℘ Order Edward Proctor Esq} overseer

Octor. 4th.   Received into the House Thos. Gambutt a Negro Man
℘ Order John Scollay Esqr.   } Selectmen
Consented to by Captn. Sam Partridge} overseer
(Dischargd. to tho Bridewell)

6th.   Received into the House Willm. Sharp & Wife
℘ Order Ezekl. Price Esq   } Selectmen
Consented to by Capt Saml. Partridge} overseer

6th.   Received into the House Thomas a Negro man
℘ Order John Scollay Esqr., Thos. Grenough Esq} Selectmen
Consented to by Capt Saml. Partridge} Overseer

11th.   Received into the House Samuel Vose
℘ order Mr. Saml. Whitwell} Overseer

12   Received into the House Ann Larkin
℘ Order Captn. Saml. Whitwell

15th.   Received into the House Ruth Adams
℘ Order Joseph Webb Esqr.} Overseer

16th.   Received into the House Mary Reed
℘ Order Thos. Greenough Esqr., Mr. Willm. Mackay} Selectmen
Consented to by Edward Procter Esq} overseer

1784 Octor. 16   Received into the House John Hutchinson
℘ Order Edward Proctor Esq} Overseer

                    Run away Kate Holland a Negro Women (Provs.) Octr. 6 1784

                    Dischargd. to the Workhouse Susannah Riodon Octr. 6

                    Dischargd. to the Workhouse Jonathan Harris 6th.

                    Run away Easter Brown (Provs.) 18th.

                    Run away Thomas Johnson (Provs.) 18th.

                    Run away Samuel Wose 23d.

25th.   Received into the House James Cunningham a Boy
℘ Order Capt Samuel Partridge} Overseer

23d.   Received into the House Deborah Howard
℘ order John White Esqr.} overseer

26th.   Received into the House Rebeccah Gauge
℘ order John Scollay Esqr., Thos. Greenough} Selectmen
Consented to by Edward Proctor Esq} overseer

27th.   Received into the House Richard Hubbard
℗ Order John Scollay Esqr., Nathan Frazier Esq} Selectmen
Consented to by Capt Saml. Partridge} overseer

27th.   Received into the House John Majaning
℗ order John Scollay Esqr., Thos. Greenough Esq} Selectmen
Consented to by Capt Saml. Partridge} overseer

29th.   Received into the House Daniel Shaw
℗ Order Ezekl. Price Esqr., John Scollay Esqr.} Selectmen
Consented to by Capt Saml. Partridge} overseer

1784   Received into the House Thomas Johnson his order Dated 11th. Octor.
℗ Order Nathan Frazier Esq., John Scollay Esq.} Selectmen
Consented to by Edward Proctor Esq} overseer

                       Received into the House Ester Brown her order Dated Octor. 25
℗ order Thos. Greenough Esq, Willm. Mackay Esq} Selectmen
Consented to by Mr. Jona. Mason} Overseer

Novr. 1   Received into the House , from the Workhouse Thos. Cross a Boy
℗ order Henry Prentiss} overseer

1.   Received into the House Becky Walliss Child
℗ order Mr. Jona. L. Austin} overseer

2d.   Received into the House Samuel McKan
℗ order Nathan Frazier Esqr., John Scollay Esq} Selectmen
Consented to by Edward Proctor} overserr

                       Run away Daniel Shaw (Provs.) Novr. 2d. 1784

                       Run away James Cunningham a Boy

Novr. 2d.   Received into the House Joseph Simpson
℗ Order Nathan Frazier Esqr., John Scollay Esqr.} Selectmen
Consented to by Edward Proctor Esq} overseer

3d.   Received into the House Philip Bass & Wife
℗ order Edward Proctor Esq} overseer

4th.   Received into the House Elizebeth Mitton
℗ order John Scollay Esqr., Thos. Greenough Esqr.} Selectmen
Consented to by Capt Saml. Partridge} overseer

5th.   Received into the House Edward Collyer & Wife
℗ order Nathan Frazier Esqr., John Scollay Esqr.} Selectmen
Consented to by Edward Procter Esq.}

1784 Novr. 6th.   Received into the House Hannah Powells Child
℗ order Capt Saml. Partridge} overseer

Novr. 8th.   Received into the House Margaret Thomas
℗ order Willm. Mackay Esq, John Scollay Esqr.} Selectmen
Consented to by Mr. Henry Prentiss} overseer

9th.   Received into the House Hannah Berry & Child
℘ order Mr. Jon L Austin} overseer

12th.   Received into the House James Mahaut
℘ order John Scollay Esqr., Nathan Frazier Esqr.} Selectmen
Consented to by Honbl. Wm. Phillips Esq} overseer

12th.   Received into the House Patty Clough a Child
℘ order Mr. Jon L Austin} overseer

15th.   Received into the House <*Edwar*> Fortune a Negro man
℘ order Ezekiel Price Esq, John Scollay Esqr.} Selectmen
Consented to by Jonathan Mason Esq}

17th.   Received into the House Betsey Ryley & Son
℘ order John Scollay Esqr., Ezekl. Price Esq} Selectmen
Consented to by Isaac Smith Esq} overseer

18th.   Received into the House Susanah a Negro women.
℘ order John Scollay Esq, Nathan Frazier Esq} Selectmen
Consented to by Jona. Masson Esq} overseer

20th.   Received into the House Katty Camerin
John Scollay Esqr., Willm. Mackay Esq} Select
℘ order Isaac Smith Esq} Overseer

1784   Discharged. Daniel Jennings (Provs.) Novr. 3d. 1784

                         Dischargd. Edward Collyer & wife (Provs.) Novr. 11.

22d.   Received into the House Mrs. Mary Thomas her order Octor. 8th.
℘ Order John Scollay Esqr., Thos. Grenough Esqr.} Selectman
Consented to by Jona. Mason Esqr.} overseer

23d.   Received into the House John Gill
℘ order Nathan Frazier Esq, John Scollay Esqr.} Selectmen
Consented to by Edward Proctor Esq} Overseer

                         Dischargd. <*into the House*> Rebecca Wallace Novr. 26.

27th.   Received into the House Thomas Johnson
℘ Order Nathan Frazier Esq, John Scollay Esqr.} Selectman
Consented to by Edward Proctor Esq} overseer

Decr. 3d.   Received into the House Nathl. Dickey
℘ Order Captn. Saml. Partridge} overseer

4th.   Received into the House Benjamin Edwards
℘ Mr. Jona. L. Austin} overseer

6th.   Received into the House Mary Pool
℘ Order John Scollay Esqr., Willm. Mackay Esq} Selectmen
Consented to by Mr. Samuel Whitwell} overseer

7th.   Received into the House Elizebeth Fisher & Child
℘ Order Ezekl. Price Esqr., John Scollay Esqr.} Selectmen
Consented to by Joseph Webb Esq} overseer

9th.   Received into the House Peter Hunter
℘ Order Nathan Frazier Esq, John Scollay Esqr.} Selectmen
Consented to by Edward Proctor Esq} overseer

1784 Decr. 10th.   Received into the House John Haney
℘ Order Nathan Frazier Esqr., John Scollay Esqr.} Selectmen
Consented to by Edward Proctor Esqr.} overseer

10th.   Received into the House Daniel Shaw
℘ Order Nathan Frazier Esqr., Willm. Mackay Esqr.} Selectmen
Consented to by Edward Proctor Esq} overseer

10th.   Received into the House Thomas Thorp
℘ order John Scollay Esqr., David Jeffries Esqr.} Selectmen
Consented to by Captn. Saml. Partridge} overseer

11th.   Received into the House Mary Branch & Child
℘ Order John Scollay Esqr., Ezekl. Price Esqr.} Selectmen
Consented to by Isaac Smith Esq} overseer

11th.   Received into the House John Madding
℘ Order Ezekl. Price Esq, John Scollay Esqr.} Selectmen
Consented to by Mr. Saml. Whitwell} overseer

13th.   Received into the House Mosses McGrath
℘ order Ezekl. Price Esqr., John Scollay Esqr.} Selectmen
Consented to by Mr. Saml. Whitwell} overseer

14th.   Received into the House John Berry
℘ Order John Scollay Esqr., Nathan Frazier Esq} Selectmen
Consented to by Jona. Mason Esq} overseer

16th.   Received into the House Mary Richardson
℘ order Mr. Saml. Whitwell} overseer

1784 Decr. 20th.   Received into the House John Chambers
John Scollay Esqr., Thos. Grenough Esq} Selectm.
℘ order Mr. Jona. Mason} overseer

20th.   Received into the House Sarah Richards Child
℘ order Mr. Jona. Mason} overseer

20th.   Received into the House John Richey
℘ Order John Scollay Esqr., David Jeffries Esq.} Selectmen
Consented to by Mr. Saml. Whitwell} overseer

21st.   Received into the House Rachael Wall
℘ Order John Scollay Esq, Thos. Greenough Esqr.} Selectmen
Consented to by Mr. Saml. Whitwell} overseer

23d.   Received into the House Lucy Mellony & Her Child
℘ Order John Scollay Esqr., Willm. Mackay Esq} Selectmen
Consented to by Mr. Saml. Whitwell} overseer

24th.   Received into the House Joseph Renew
℘ Order Willm. Mackay Esq, Thos. Greenough Esq} Selectmen
Consented to by John White Esqr.} overseer

25th.   Received into the House Venard Thomas
℘ Order Willm. Powell Esq.} overseer

28th.   Received into the House Anna Richardson
℘ Order Isaac Smith Esqr.} overseer

29th.   Received into the House Joseph Moy'd
℘ Order Nathn. Frazier Esqr., John Scollay Esqr.} Selectmen
Consented to by Edward proctor Esq} overseer

30th.   Received into the House John Berry
℘ order John Scollay Esqr., David Jeffries Esqr.} Selectmen
Consented to by Jona. Mason Esqr.} overseer

1784 Decr. 30th.   Received into the House Catherine Smith
℘ Order John Scollay Esqr., David Jeffries Esqr.} Selectmen
Consented to by Willm. Powell Esq} overseer

          Discharged. Sarah Eayrs (Provs.) Decr. 4th. 1784

          Dischargd. Unice Vose's Child Decr. 16th. 1784

          Dischargd. Mary Branch & Child (Prov) Decr. 31st. 1784

          Run away John Berry (Provs.) Decr. 25th.

          Dischargd. Sarah Richards & Child Decr. 17th.

1785 Jany. 2d.   Received into the House Thomas Bates
℘ Order Ezekl. Price Esqr., John Scollay Esqr.} Selectmen
Consented to by Willm. Powell Esq} overseer

          Dischargd. John Berry (Provs.) Jany. 3d. 1785

Jany. 5   Received into the house Abigail Howland
℘ Order Capt Saml. Partridge} overseer

10th.   Received into the house James Wainwright
℘ Order Nathan Frazier Esqr., John Scollay Esq} Selectmen
Consented to by Edward Proctor Esq} overseer

12th.   Received into the house John Dougharty
℘ order Willm. Mackay Esqr., John Scollay Esq} Selectmen
Consented to by Edward Proctor Esq} overseer

13th.   Received into the house James Young
℘ order Mr. Saml. Whitwell} overseer

1785 Jany. 13th.   Received into the house Margaret Love & Child
℘ Order Nathan Frazier Esqr., John Scollay Esqr.} Selectmen
Consented to by Edward Proctor Esq} overseer

17th.   Received into the house Margaret Poor
℘ Order John White Esqr.} overseer

18th.   Received into the house Francis Claridge
℘ Order John Scollay Esqr., Nathan Frazier Esq} Selectmen
Consented to by Edward Proctor Esq} overseer

20th.   Received into the house Sarah Goodwin
℘ Order Honbl. Willm. Phillips Esqr.} overseer

24th.   Received into the house Edward Smith
℘ Order Ezekl. Price Esqr., Willm. Mackay Esq} Selectmen
Consented to by Mr. Saml. Whitwell} overseer

> Run away Thomas Bates (Provs.) Jany. 17th. 1785
>
> Run away John Majaning (Provs.) 18th.
>
> Run away Cyrus a negro man (Provs.) 11th.
>
> Discharged. Abigail Howland Jany. 17th. 1785
>
> Discharged. Mrs. Farmers Child 21st.
>
> Discharged. Thomas Thorp (Provs.) 24th.
>
> Dischargd. Edward Dickey 25th.

26   Received into the House Thomas Doyle
℘ Order Nathan Frazier Esqr., Willm. Mackay Esq} Selectmen
Consented to by Edward Proctor Esqr.} overser

1785 Jany. 26th.   Received into the house Alexander Thompson
℘ the order John Scollay Esqr., Willm. Mackay Esq} Selectmen
Consented to by John Sweetser Esqr.} overseer

28th.   Received into the House Nathaniel Dickey
℘ order Capt Saml. Partridge} overseer

> Run away Katherane Smith (Provs.) Jany. 27. 1785
>
> Discharged. Susannah a Negro Women (Provs.) Feby. 11th. 1785
>
> Run away Katherine Camerin (Provs.) Feby. 3d. 1785
>
> Discharged. Frances Claridge (Provs.) Feby. 8th. 1785

Feby. 5   Received into the House Ann Gordon & 2 Children there order Dated
Jany. 25 1785
℘ Order John Scollay Esqr., Nathan Frazier Es[q.]} Selectmen
Consented to by Edward Protor Esq} overseer

8th.   Received into the House Sarah Peirce
℘ Order Ezekl. Price Esqr., Willm. Mackay Esq} Selectmen
Consented to by William Powell Esq} overseer

9th.   Received into the House Sukey Follens
℘ Order Mr. Jona. L Austin} overseer

10   Received into the House John Fisher
℘ Order Nathn. Frazier Esr., Ezek Price Esr. } Selectmen
Consented to by Joseph Webb Esq} overseer

12th.   Received into the House Lydia Lee
℘ Order Willm. Powell Esqr.} overseer

1785 Feby. 15th.   Received into thy House Deborah Harley & 2 Children
℘ order John White Esqr.} overseer

16th.   Received into the House John Willett & Wife
℘ order Edward Proctor Esq} overseer

16th.   Received into the House Dinah Burton Negro
℘ order Mr. Jona. L Austin} overseer

18th.   Received into the House Hannah Johnson & Child Negros
℘ Order John Scollay Esq, David Jeffries Esq} Selectmen
Consented to by Honbl. Willm. Phillips Esq} overseer

18th.   Received into the House Nathl. Thomas
℘ Order Willm. Mackay Esq   } Selectmen
Consented to by Mr. Henry Prentiss} overseer

19th.   Received into the House Elizebeth Ivies (on the state)
℘ Order John Scollay Esqr., Wm. Mackey} Selectmen of Boston
Consented to By

21   Received into the House Lydia Rea & Child
℘ Order Willm. Mackay Esq   } Selectmen
Consented to by Edwd. Proctor Esq} overseer

21.   Received into the House Mary Covan & 4 Children
℘ Order John Scollay Esqr., Willm. Mackay Esq} Selectmen
Consented to by John White Esq} overseer

                Dischargd. Hannah Wyatt (Provs.) Feby. 14. 1785

                Dischargd. Capt Phillip Bass 16th.

                Dischargd. Alexander Thompson (Provs.) 23d.

                Dischargd. Deborah Harley & Child 23d.

<1785   *Run away Catharine Camerin (Provs.) Feby. [22] 1785>*

Feby. 25   Received into the House Sandy a Negro man
℘ Order John Scollay Esqr.   } Selectmen
Consented to by Captn. Saml. Partridge} overseer

28   Received into the House Richard Harris
℘ order Mr. Henry Prentiss} overseer

28   Received into the House Jonathan Harris
℘ order Mr. Henry Prentiss} overseer

28   Received into the House Prudence Cutton
℘ Order Captn. Saml. Partridge} overseer

March 1   Received into the House George King (Provs.)
℘ order Thos. Greenough   } Selectmen
Consented to by John White Esq} overseer

                   Dischargd. John Haney (Provs.) March 1st. 1785

                   Dischargd. Sukey Follens do. 1st. 1785

March 1st.   Received into the House George King
℘ order Willm. Mackay Esqr., John Scollay Esqr.} Selectmen
Consented to by Edward Proctor Esq} overseer

March 5th.   Received into the House Joseph Ross two Sons
℘ Order John Scollay Esqr., Ezekl. Price Esqr.} Selectmen
Consented to by Mr. Samuel Whitwell} overseer

7th.   Received into the House Alexander Thompsons
℘ Order Ezekl. Price Esq   } Selectman
Consented to by Jona. Mason Esq} overseer

1785 March 5th.   Received into the House Elizebeth Sleene her order Dated Feby. 5.
1785
By order of Wm. Mackay Selectman
℘ order Mr. Jona. L Austin} overseer

March 7th.   Received into the House Eleanor Morrison
℘ Order Willm. Mackay Esqr.   } Selectmen
Consented to by Honbl. Willm. Phillips Esq} overseer

                   Dischargd. Polly Ross March 7th.

                   Dischargd. Moses McGrath (Provs.) 7th.

9th.   Received into the House   Snow
℘ order John Scollay Esq   } Selectman
Consented to by Mr. Saml. Whitwell} overseer

March 11th.   Recd into the House Richd. Webber
(Pr. ordor of Jno. Scolley Select men Boston
Admitted by Edwd. Proctor)

                   Dischd. out of the House Jno. Fisher on the State, March 12th. 1785

14th.   Recd. into the house Josh. Hase.
pr. ordor of Saml. Whitwell oversear

March 15　　　　Recd. into the House Louis Mathews a Negero Woman And her Child
Pr. ordor of Jno. Scollay　　　　　} Selectmen of Boston
Consented to by Mr. Saml. Whitwell} oversear of the Poor

16th.　　　　　Recd. into the Hous Jno. Haney on the State accot.
Pr. ordor of Jno. Scollay & Edwd. Tyler} Select men
Consented to by Edwd. Proctor Esqr.}

Dischd Jno. Fitchgerrell March 18th.

March 18th.　　　Recd. into the Hous John McKinsee
Pr. ordor Jno. Scolley　　　　} Select Men
Consented to by Jona. Mason Esqr.} oversear

21　　　　　　Recd. into the Hous Jno. Gray
Pr. ordor Jno. Scolley, Jno. Andres} Select Men of Boston
Consented to by John Swetser} oversear

1785　　　　　Discharged Elizh. Yetton March 22nd. 1785　　　　　(State)

March 19th.　　　Recd. into the House Sarah Ayers
pr. ordor, Jno. Scolley, Jno. Andres} Selectmen of Boston
Consented to by Josh. Webb} one of the oversears

25　　　　　　Recd. into the House Willm. Baldridge a Child Aged 4 years the 15th.
Septr. 1784
Pr. ordor of Mr. Henry Prentiss one of the Oversears of the poor

24th.　　　　　Recd. into the Hous Mary Wainright
Pr. ordor Jno. Scolley, Jno. Andres} Selectmen
Jno. Switser} oversear

Run Away, Snow, (on the State) March 28th. 1785

31th.　　　　　Recd. into the Hous Anna How on the States. Accot.
Pr. ordor of Jno. Scolley　　　} Selectmen of Boston
Consented by Edwd. Proctor Esq} one of the oversears of the poor

Aprl. 2nd.　　　Recd. into the Hous Ruth Peirce
Pr. ordor Mr. Jno. Sweetser; one of the oversears of the poor

9th.　　　　　Dischd. Edwd. Dickey of this town

11　　　　　　Recd. into the House Mary Doake belongg. to this town
By Josh. Webb Esq one of the Oversears

12　　　　　　Recd. into the House Jno. Kelley on the State
Jno. Andrews, Moses Grant} Selectmen
Consented too by Edwd. Proctor One of the Oversears}

12　　　　　　Recd. into the House Rebecca Baldridg
Pr. ordor Mr. Saml. Parkman} oversear

12　　　　　　Recd. into the House George Hammock on the State's Accot.
Pr. Ordor Wm. Mackay　　　　} Select men of Boston
Consented to by Jno. Sweetser on of the oversears

Dischd. out of the Hous Nancy Rea the 7th. aprell 1785

13th.   Recd. into the House Olive Gyles A Negro woman & Child
Pr. Jno. Scolley   } Selectmen of Boston
Consented to by Edwd. Proctor Esq} one of the Oversears of the poor

1785 Marh. 13th. Recd. into the House Jacob Normus (on the State's Accot.)
Pr. ordor of Jno. Scolley, Wm. Mackey} Selectmen of Boston
Consented to by Jona. Mason} one of the overseers of the Poor

March 16   Dischd. Ebenr. Goffe & Wife to the workhouse on the town
       Dischd. Jno. Willett to do.   do.
       Rebecca Baldrage to do.   do.

20th.   Recd. into the Hous Mrs. Goff
Pr. ordor of Henry Prentiss one of the Oversears

Apr. 21   Dischd. Deborah Howard—Belonging to this town

23   Dischd. out of the Hous Thos. A Negero man   (<*Prov*> State)

23th.   Dischd. out of the Hous Mary Dokes   (Town)

25   Recd. into the Hous Robert Osely   on the State
by ordor of Pr. Ordor Ezekl. Price Esqr.} one of the Select men of Boston
Consented to by Jona. Mason} one of the Oversears

25th.   Run Away James Perrin & Wife   (State)

25   dischd. out of the Hous Mary Pool   (State)

27th.   Recd. into the House Saml. Clark a Boy 5 years old feby. 1785
Pr. Ordor Jno. Scolley   } Select men of Boston
Consented to by Edwd. Proctor} one of the overseers of the poor

28th.   Recd. into the Hous Susanna Brown   (on the State Accot.)
Pr. Ordor of Jno. Scollay, Jno. Andress} Selectmen of Boston
Consented to Pr. Jona. Mason} one of the Oversears

28th.   Recd. into the Hous Eunice Hardy   (on the State Accot.)
Pr. ordor of Jno. Scollay Esqr., Jno. Andress} Selectmen of Boston
Consented to by Saml. Whitwell} Oversear

May 2nd.   dischd out of the Hous Jno. Haney �️
     do.   do. Jno. Madden } on the State's Accot.
     do.   do. Sarah Ayers ⎬
     do.   do. Patte Clow
4th.   Mr. Fisher & Child   (on the State)

1785 May 4th. Dischd. Mrs. Fisher & Child

4   Recd. into the House Ruth Adams
Pr. Ordor of Saml. Parkman One of the overseers

5th.   Dischd. out of the Hous Jacob Normus (on the State Acct.)

5   Dischd. out of the Hous Ruth Peirce

May 6th.   Recd. into the Hous Sarah Davis
Pr. Ordor Jno. Sweetser Esqr.

6   Recd. into the Hous Mary Wainwood
Pr. Ordor of Jno. Scollay   } Select men of Boston
Consented to By Wm. Phillips Esqr} one of the Oversears

6   Recd. into the Hous Vinus a Negero Woman   on the State Accot.
Pr. Ordor of Jno. Scollay, Wm. Mackay} Selectmen of Boston
Consented to By Jona. Loring Austen} one of the oversears}

8th.   Discharg'd out of the Hous, Joseph Renew   (on the State)

8   George Hammock Run away   (State)

9   Discharged out of the Hous Debero Harley

10th.   Recd. into the House Elizh. Ewin   (town)
Pr. ordor of Wm. Phillips

11   Recd. into the Almshous Hannah Wiatt   on the States Accot.
Pr. Ordor of Jno. Scollay   } Selectmen of Boston
Approv'd of by Isaac Smith Esqr.} one of the oversears}

12th.   Dischd. out of the Hous Thos. Johnson   (on the State)

13th.   Run Away Thos. Hannan   (on the State)

17th.   Recd. into Aalmshous Jno. Graham   (on the State Accot.)
Pr. Order of Ezekel Price   } Selectmen of Boston
Approv'd of by Isaac Smith Esqr.} one of the Oversears
did Never Come after brot. the ordor

17th.   Received into the Almshous John Wood   (on the State's Accot.)
Pr. Ordor of Ezekl. Price Esq   } Selectmen of Boston
Consented to by Jona. Mason Esqr.} one of the Oversears

19th.   Recd. into the Almshous Sarah Meyers   (on the State Accot.)
Pr. ordor of Ezel. Price Esqr. } Select Men
Consented to by Edwd. Procter Esqr.} one of the oversears

1785 May 20th. Recd. into the Almshous Eliz. Hayter from the work hous
Pr. ordor of Wm. Powell Esqr.
he sais on the State's Accot.

May 23   Recd. into the Almshous Thos. Hanen   (State)
Pr. ordor of Jno. Scollay   } Selectmen of Boston
Consented to by Saml. Whitwell} one of the Oversears

23   Recd. into the Almshous deborah Howard
Pr. ordor of Mr. Saml. Whitwell one of the Overseers of the poor

21th.   Recd. into Elizh. & Benone Harris, Champlen   (on the State)

Wm. Mackey   } Selectmen of Boston
Consented to by Mr. Jno. White} one of the Oversears
Eliz born May 10th. 1779. Benoe. Harris born Aprl. 22d. 1781

27th.   Dischd. out of the Hous Elexr. Thompson   (on the State accot.)

27th.   Dischd. out of the Hous George King   (on Accot. of the state)

28th.   Dischd. out of the Hous Mary Tavenor   (on the state Accot.)

30   Recd. into the Almshous Bengn. Bignall one of the poor of this town
Pr. Ordor of Mr. Jno. White, one of the Oversears

<31th.   *Dischd. out of the Hous Elizh. Champlen* ⎫   *on accot of the state*
                Ditto   do. Benone Harris Champlen ⎬ >

31. should a ben 27} Recd. into the Almshous James Trenholm   on the State Accot.
Pr. Ordor of Edwd. Tyler, Jno. Andress} Selectmen of Boston
Consented to by Edwd. Proctr. One of the Oversears}

May 2nd.   Recd. into the Almshous Joseph Candish
Pr. Ordor of Edwd. Proctor {one of the Oversears

2nd.   Dischd. out of the hous Susanna Brown   (State)

4th.   Dischd. out of the hous Richd. Webber   (on the State)
                Do.   do.   Thos. Doyle   do.

4   Recd. into the hous Hannah Farnum
Pr. ordor of Mr. Jona. Mason One of the Oversears

4   Dischd. out of the Hous Richd. Hubbert   (on the state)
                Ditto   do.   Benjn. Edwards   (on the town)

1785 June 6th.   Recd. into the Almshous Kitty Mory   (State accot.)
Pr. ordor of Ezek. Price   } Selectmen of Boston
Consented to by Wm: Phillips Esqr.}

6th.   Dischd. out of the Almshous Fortain A Negero man   (State)

7   Recd. into the Almshous Catharina a Negero woman   on the state
Pr. ordor of Ezek. Price   } Select men of Boston
Consented to by Saml. Whitwell} one of the Oversears

8th.   Recd. into the Almshous Elizh. Ewen   (of this town)
Pr. ordor of Mr. Jno. White one of the Oversears

10th.   Recd. into the Almshous Deliverance Williams (On Accot. of the town)
Pr. Ordor of Jno. Sweetser, one of the Oversears

May 29th.   Recd. into the Almshous Jno. Cray. (Born the 11th. Feby. last)   State
Pr. Ordor of Jno. Scollay   } Selectmen of Boston
Approved of by Wm. Powell oversear of the ward No. 12}

June 13th.   Recd. into the Almshous Robt. Lilmon   (on the State Accot.)
Pr. Ordor of Moses Grant, Jno. Andres} Selectmen of Boston
Consented to by Edwd. Procter} one of the overseers of the poor

14th.   Recd. into the Almshous Mary Shea & her Blind Child   on the state Accot.
Pr. Ordor of Jno. Andres   } Selectmen of Boston
Approved of By Edwd. Proctor Esqr.} one of the oversears

16th.   Disch out of the Almshous Elizh. Ewin   (on the town)

16   Dischd. out of the Almshous Sussann Lewis a Child   (State)

16   Recd. into the Almshous James Mory   (on the state's accot.)
Pr. ordor of Jno. Scolay & Ezekl. Price} Selectmen of Boston
Consented to by Jona. Mason} one of the Oversears

18th.   Recd. into the Almshous Sarah Ayers   (on accot. State)
Pr. Ordor Jno. Scollay, Ezekl. Price} Selectmen of Boston
Consented to by Isaac Smith Esqr.} one of the oversears}

20th.   Recd. into the Almshous James Ryan a Child   on the State
Pr. ordor of Jno. Scollay   } Selectmen of Boston
Approved. of by Jona. Mason Esqr.} one of the Oversears

1785 June 20   Recd. into the Almshous Thos. Read   (on the State)
Pr. ordor of Ezekl. Price   } Selectmen of Boston
Consented to by Saml. Whitwell} one of the Oversears

<20th.   *Recd. into the Almshous Ann Ryan*   (on the State)
Pr. order of Jno. Scollay   *} Selectmen of Boston*
Approvd. of by
She went out of the hous within 2 howers wh. her Child>

20th.   Dischd. out of the Hous Eliz Patten (a Child)

                Dischd. out of the Hous Mary Richardson

25th.   Recd. into the Almshous Suckey Follens.   of this town
Pr. Ordor of Mr. Jona. L Austen One of the Oversears of the poor

June 27   Recd. into the Almshous Tobias a Negero   on the State
Pr. ordor of Jno. Scolay Esqr.   } Selectmen of Boston
Consented to by Mr. Henry Prentis} one of the oversears

27   Recd. into the Almshous Mary Tucker
Pr. ordor of Josh. Webb Esqr. {one of the oversears of the poor

June 25th.   Recd. into the Almshous William Tepote   (on the State Accot.)
Pr. Ordor of Jno. Scollay Esr.   } Selectmen of Boston
Approd. of by Jno. Sweetser Esq one of the oversears

25   Dischd. out of the Almshous James Tranholm to the workhous
                                                            (on the state)

June 11th.   Recd. into the Almshous Mary Gorden A Child   (on the State Accot.)
Pr. Ordor of Jno. Andrews, Moses Grant} Selectmen of Boston
Consented to by Henry Prentiss} one of the Oversears

July 1   Dischd. Clara. Love a Child   State

5th.   Recd. into the Almshous David Shays   (on the States. Accot.)
Pr. ordor of Ezekl. Price, Jno. Brown} Selectmen of Boston
Consented to by Jona. Mason Esqr.} one of the Oversears

July 8th.　　　　　Recd. Into the Almshous Rbecca Wallis & Child A Negero
Pr. ordor of Ezekl. Price　　　} Selectmen of Boston
Consented to by Mr. Saml. Whitwell} one of the Oversears

July 6th.　　　　　Run away Eliz Hayter & stole 1 Cambt. Riding hod, 1 Shift

1785 July 11th.　　Rece'd into the Almshous Andrew Thompson　　　(on the state Accot.)
Pr. ordor of Jno. Andrews, Moses Grant} Selectmen of Boston
Approved of By Edwd. Proctor Esqr.} one of the Oversears

June 13th.　　　　Dischd. out of the Almshous Thos. Hannen　　　　(on the state)

June 14th.　　　　Dischd. out of the Almshous Jno. Killey　　　　(on the state)

March 1st.　　　　Recd. into the Almshous James Fisher An Infant born in this house
daughter of Eliz Fisher A Strainger. Dischd. with its Mother May the 4th.　　(on the State)
Pr. ordor of Jno. Scolay Esqr., Jno. Brown Esqr.} Selectmen of Boston
Consented to by Jona. L. Austen one of the oversears

March 18th.　　　　Recd. Into the Almshous Jno. Barnard An Infant borne in the hous Son
of Elizh. Sleene. A Strainger &　　　　　　　　　　　　　(on the State)
Pr. ordor of Jno. Scollay Esqr., Jno. Brown Esqr.} Selectmen of Boston
Consented to by By Jona. L Austen} one of the oversears

Aprl. 3d.　　　　　Recd. into Almshous Betsey Coven an Infant daughter of Mary Coven
A Strainger　On the state Accot. born in the hous
Pr. Ordor of Jno. Scolley Esqr., Jno. Brown Esqr.} Selectmen of Boston
Consented to by Jona. L. Austen one of the Oversears

3　　　　　　　　Recd. into the Almshous Nancy Ran An Infant daughter of Elenor
Morrison, A Straniger　　　　　　　　　　　　　　(on the State Accot.)
Pr. ordor of Jno. Scollay Esqr., Jno. Brown Esqr.} Selectmen of Boston
Consented to by Jona. L Austen One of the Oversears

May 4th.　　　　　Recd. into the hous Suckey forster daughter of Eliz Ivers; & Catharine
Hous daughtor of Ann Hous both infants &　　　　　　　　on the States Accot.
Pr. ordor of Jno. Scollay Esqr., Jno Brown Esqr.} Selectmen of Boston
Consented to by Jona. L. Austen

July 3d.　　　　　Recd. into the Almshous Jno. Comede a Negero Child A Strainger
Pr. ordor of Jno. Scollay Esqr., Jno. Brown Esqr.} Selectmen of Boston
Consented to by Jona. L Austen

14th. June　　　　Dischd. out of the Almshous Mary Maccurdey & Mary Fitzgarril (State)

15th.　　　　　　Recd. into the Almshous Elizh. Fleming
Pr. ordor of Edwd. Proctor Esqr.

July 15th.　　　　Recd. into the Almshous Mary Singclear　　　on the state accot.
Pr. ordor of Ezekl. Price Esqr., Jno. Brown Esqr.} Selectmen of Boston
Consent to Pr. Jno. Mason Esqr.} one of the overseers}

16th.　　　　　　Disch'd out of the Hous Suckey Fallens　　　　(town)

18th.　　　　　　Recd. into the Almshous Fanne Clark　　　　town
Pr. ordor of Saml. Whitwell one of the Oversears

〜

<1785 July 18th.   *Recd. into the Almshous Abigal Fossy And Son William undor Neath >*
                                              on the state

July 20   dischd. Susanna Lewis   (on the state Accot.)

20th.   Dischd. Lydia Lee   (town)

<June 27th.   *Recd. into the Almshous Hannah McKinzie*
Pr. ordor of>

July 21   Recd. into the Almshous Joseph Raymeau A Frenchman
Pr. Ordor of Jno. Scollay, Jno. Andress} Selectmen of Boston
Consend. to by Wm. Phillips Esqr. One of the Oversears}

May 6th.   Recd. into the Almshous Anna Hous An Infant, daughter of <*Catharine*>
Anna Hous Born in this hous   (on the state)
Pr. Ordor of Jno. Scollay Esqr., Jno. Brown Esqr.} Selectmen of Boston
Consent to Jona. L Auston, one of the Oversears

July 18th.   Received. into the Almshous Abigail Fossey And William Fossey her son,
together with Hanah McKenzie   (on the state Accot.)
Pr. ordor Jno. Scollay, Jno. Andress} Select men of Boston
Consented to by Henry Prentes one of the oversears}

July 21st.   Run away Hannah Johnson   (on the state)

25th.   Dischd. James Wainwright Wife & Child   (2 on the state)

26th.   Recd. into the Almshous Lucy Duberger A Child on the state 2 years of
age
Pr. ordor of Jno. Scollay Esqr., Jno. Andrews} Selectmen of Boston
Consented to by Edwd. Proctor Esqr. one of the oversears of the poor

Augt. 3d.   Dischd. Thos. Cross a boy   (town)

3d.   Dischd. David Riley a Boy   on the (State)

4   Dischd. Mary Gorden a Garl   (on the State)

5th.   Recd. into the Almshous Thomas Rice his wife & two Children   state
Pr. Ordor of Jno. Scolley   } Select Men of Boston
Consented to Pr. Jno. Mason} one of the Oversears

5th.   Recd. James Gorden a <*boy*> Lad into the Almshous   state
Pr. ordor of Jno. Andrews, Moses Grant} Selectmen of Boston
Consented to by Edwd. proctor Esq. one of the oversears}
the above Namd. James will be 11 years old the 21st. day of this Month Augt.}

1785 Augt. 6th.   Recd. into the Almshous Robt. Forbes his Wife & two Childn. together
With Jos. Forbes a young Man on Accot. of the Commonwelth
Pr. ordor of Jno. Andrews   } Selectmen of Boston
Consented to by Edwd. Proctor Esqr.} one of the Oversears

Augt. 8th.   Dischd. out of the Almshous Daved Shays   (on the state)

9th.   Dischd. Robt. Lilmon   (on the state)

10th.   Dischd. out of the Almshous Abigal Hurley a Child   (on the state)

15th.   Dischd. out of the Hous Eliz Champlen A Child   (State)

16   Recd. into the Almshous Elizh. Hopkins   (on the Town)
Pr. ordor of Edwd. Proctor Esqr.

17   Dischd. out of the Almshous Nathl. Thomas & Margrat his wife   (State)

18th.   Recd. into the Almshous Richd. Crouch   (on the state)
Pr. Ordor of Jno. Browne, Edwd. Tyler} Selectmen of Boston
Consented to by Saml. Whitwell} one of the Oversears of the poor

18   Recd. into the Almshous Joseph Clough   (on the town accot.)
Pr. ordor of Mr. Jno. White one of the overseers of the poor

18th.   Recd. into the hous Abigal Clough a Child 6 years old the 1th. decr.
1785   On the town
Pr. ordor of Jno. White one of the oversr.
In An ordor with Josh. Clough

Augt. 19   Recd. into the Almshous Lydia Whalon & George Whalon Two
Children
Pr. ordor of Jno. Scollay Esqr., Wm. Mackay} Selectmen of Boston
Consented to by Saml. Whitwell One of the oversears

Augt. 22nd.   Recd. into the Almshous Jno. Downey   (on the state)
Pr. ordor of Moses Grant, Jno. Andrews} Selectmen of Boston
Consented to by Edwd. Proctor one of the Oversears}

augt. 24th.   Dischd. out of the Almshous Ellenor Morrison And her Child Nansey
Ran   both on the State

Augt. 24   Recd. into the Almshous Thos. Cross

Augt. 26   dischd. Mary Read out of the Almshous   (on Accot. of State)

Augt. 26   Recd. into the Almshous Ann Watson   On the State's Accot.
Pr. ordor of Jno. Scollay   } Select men of Boston
Consented to by Jno. White one of the Oversears}

1785 Augt. 29th.   Dischd. out of the Almshous James Ryan a Child   (on the state)

Augt. 27th.   Recd. into the Almshous Mary Bright   on the state
Pr. Ordor of Wm. Mackey, Jno. Andrews} Selectmen of Boston
Approved of by Edwd. Proctor one of the Oversears}

Augt. 24   Recd. into the Almshous daved Shay   (on the state)
Pr. ordor of Jno. Scollay Esqr.   } Selectmen of Boston
Approved of by Edwd. Proctor Esqr.} one of the oversears

Augt. 29th.   Recd. into the Almshous James Perrin & wife   (on the state)
Pr. ordor of Jno. Scollay, Jno. Andrews} Selectmen of Boston
Approvd. of by Saml. Whitwell} one of the oversears}

Augt. 30   Recd. into the Almshous Marshel Thaxtor A boy 4 years old Next Novr.
Pr. ordor of Edwd. Proctor one of the oversears

Augt. 27th.   Dischd. John McKinsie   on accot. State

Augt. 30th.   Recd. into the Almshous Polley Russell or Rosherou a Child 10 months
Old   on the States Accot.
Pr. ordor of Mr. Jno. Andrews, Moses Grant} Selectmen of Boston
Approved of by Saml. Whitwell} one of the Oversears of the poor

Septr. 1   Dischd. Lydia Whalon & George Whalon both Childn.   (on the State)

Septr. 1   Dischd. out of the Almshous Anna How & her Child   (state)

Augt. 27th.   Run Mary Harvey   town
                       do. Martha Mullens   do.

Septr. 1   *<dischd. out of the house Elizth. Henly & Child>*   (on accot. state)

Septr. 5   dischd. out of the Almshous Lydia Marten   (on the town)

5th.   Recd. into the Almshous Jno. Thomas & Child   (on the town)
Pr. ordor of Mr. Saml. Whitwell one of the overseers

Augt. 1th.   Recd. into the Almshous Morocco A Negero Woman   on the State
Pr. ordor of John Scolley, John Andrews} Selectmen of Boston
Consented to by Edwd. Proctor Esqr. one of the Oversears}

Augt. 7th.   Recd. into the Almshous Marthor Mullens   on the town Accot.
Pr. ordor of Isaac Smith one of the overseers

1785 Septr. 9th.   Dischd. out of the Almshous Mary Swan   on the town

Augt. 25th.   Recd. into the Almhous Saml. Trescott   (on the State)
pr. ordor of Ezekl. Price, Wm. Mackay} Select men of Boston
Consented to by William Powell Esqr. Oversear

Septr. 10th.   Recd. into the Almshous Susanna Shaw   on the town
Pr. Ordor of Edwd. Proctor Esqr. One of the overseers

Septr. 13   dischd. out of the Hous   Vose & 2 Childn.   town

13th.   *<Recd. into the Almshous Marthor Mullen>*   on the town
13   Recd. into   do. Sarah Richardson   do.

Septr. 15th.   Recd. into the Almshous Fanney the daughtor of the wife Of Richd.
Crouch   (on the State)
Pr. Ordor of Ezekl. Price Esqr., Jno. Browne Esqr.} Select men of Boston
Consented to by Saml. Whitwell} one of the overseers

Septr. 15th.   Recd. into the Almshous Marthor Symons   on the town's Acct.
Pr. ordor of Saml. Whitwell One of the Overseers

Septr. 15th.   Recd. into the Almshous Partrick Shaley   on the State Accot.
Pr. Ordor of Moses Grant} one of the Select men
Consented to by Edwd. Proctor one of the Oversears

Septr. 16th.   Recd. into the Almshous John Clark   (on the State accot.)
Pr. ordor of Wm. Mackey   } Selectmen of Boston
Approved of By Jno. White one of the Oversears

Septr: 21th.   Recd. Mary Colburn into the Almshous   (on the state Accot.)
Pr. ordor of Jno. Andrews, Wm. Brown} Selectmen of Boston
Consented to by Edwd. Proctor Esqr.} one of the Oversears

Septr. 22nd.   Dischd. Eliz. Ivers & Child   (on the state)

24th.   Recd. into the Almshous Jno. McKinzey
Pr. ordor of Ezek Price Esqr., Jno. Brown Esq} Selectmen of Boston
Consented to by Jona. Mason Esqr. one of the oversears

Septr. 26th.   Recd. into Mary Cavenaugh   on the State
Pr. ordor of Jno. Scollay, Jno. Andrews} Selectmen of Boston
Consented to by Edwd. Proctor One of the Oversears

1785 Septr. 27th.   Recd. into the Almshous Mary Backoon   on the Town
Pr. ordor of Josh. Webb Esqr. one of the overss.

Septr. 14   Recd. into the Almshous Christian Machen   (on the state Accot.)
Pr. ordor of Jno. Scallay Esqr., Jno. Andrews} Selectmen of Boston
Consented to by Mr. Saml. Whitwell} one of the oversears

Septr. 27   Recd. into the Almshous Thos. Ferrill   (on the state Accot.)
Pr. Ordor of Moses Grant   } Sellectmen of Boston
Consented to by Edwd. Proctor Esq} one of the oversears

Octr. 3d.   Recd. into the Almhous Charles Austin   (on the state)
Pr. ordor of Jno. Scollay Esq, John Andrews} Selectmen of Boston
Consented to by Saml. Whitwell One of the Oversears}

Octr. 3d.   Dischd. Deborah Howard   (town)

Octr. 3   Recd. into the Almshous Joshua Dutten   (town)

Octr. 6th.   Dischd. out of the Almshous Rebecca Walli & Child Jno. [Cemeral?]
Negero's.   (state)

Octr. 6th.   Dischd. Eliz Hopkins & Child   (town)

<Octr. 6   *dischd. Olive Giles A Negero>*   State

Octr. 6   *<dischd. Jame Mery,>* Dischd. David Shea}   state

Octr. 6th.   Recd. into the Almshous Robt. Lilburn   (on the state Accot.)
Pr. ordor of Jno. Scollay Esqr., Jno. Andrews} Selectmen of Boston
Consented to by Edwd. Proctor one of the Oversears

        Dischd. out of the Almshous Thos. Farmer a boy   (Town)

Octr. 11th.   Dischd. out of the Almshous Marshel Thaxtor a boy   (town)

Septr. 13th.   Dischd. Robt. Forbes }   on the State
do.   ditto   John Forbes}

Octr. 12th.   Dischd. Wm. Tepote   (State)

Octr. 12   dischd. Olive Giles A Negero Womon & Child   (State)

Octr. 17th.	Run Thos. Rice & his wife	(State)

1785 Octr. 20th.   Recd. into the Almshous Jno. Killey   (on Comm. Welth)
Pr. ordor of Jno. Scollay Esqr.   } Selectmen of Boston
Consented to by

Octr. 22nd.   Recd. Into the Almshous Charles Fisher   (on Accot. of the state)
Pr. ordor of Ezekl. Price} one of the Selectmen of Boston
Consented to Pr. Jona. Mason} one of the Oversears

Octr. 24th.	dischd. John Thomas & Child	(town)

Octr. 24th.   Recd. into the Almshous Patty Gerrish   on the State
Pr. ordor of Jno. Scollay Esq   } Selectmen of Boston
Consented to by Saml. Whitwell} one of the oversears

Octr. 25th.	Recd. into the Almshous Wm. Curtis	(town)
Octr. 28th.	Ran away Rice 2 Children	state
Novr. 1th.	Dischd. Thos. Read	(on the state)

Novr. 1   Recd. into the Almshous Deborah Howard   town
Pr. ordor of Mr. Saml. Whitwell

Octr. 14th.   Received into the Almshous George Phillips   (state)
Pr. ordor of Jno. Scallay Esqr., Jno. Brown Esqr.} Selectmen of Boston
Consented to by Isaac Smith Esqr.} one of the oversears

Novr. 3d.   Recd. into the Almshous Priscilla Hoobrok   (town)
pr. ordor of Saml. Whitwell one of the oversears

[*Nov.*] 4   Recd. into the Almshous Mary Jerell   (town)
Pr. ordor of Saml. Whitwell one of the oversears

Novr. 2nd.   dischd. Mary Shea   (state)
Omited in its proper place

Novr. 7th.	dischd. Ann Watson	(on the state)
	dischd. Dennis Burns Octr. 22d.	(State)

Novr. 8th.   Recd. into the Almshous Tabotha Oliver   state
Pr. ordor of Jno. Scollay Esqr.   } Selectmen of Boston
Aproved of By Saml. Whitwell one of the oversear

Novr. 9th.   Recd. into the Almshous Jacob Normus (a Strainger)
Pr. ordor of Jno. Scollay Esqr., Jno. Brown Esqr.} Select men of Boston
Approved of By Mr. Saml. Whitwell} An oversear of the poor

1785 Novr. 10th.   Recd. into the Almshous Ann Jebling   (State)
Pr. ordor of Jno. Scollay   } Selectmen
Approd. of by Edwd. Proctor Esqr. One of the oversears}

Novr. 10th.	Dischd. James Gorden a boy	(state)

10th.   Recd. into the Almshous Daniel Wakefield a Strainger   (State)
Pr. ordor of Jno. Scollay Esqr., Mr. Moses Grant} Selectmen of Boston
Approvd. of by Edwd. Proctor one of the oversears

Novr. 10th.   Sally White A Negero Woman   (on the state)
Pr. ordor of Jno. Scollay Esqr., Jno. Andrews Esqr.} Selectmen of Boston
Approoved of by Mr. Saml. Whitwell one of the Oversears}

Novr. 6th.   Dischd. Robt. Lilman out of the Almshous   (on the state)

12th.   John Allen, Recd. him into the Almshous   (state)
Pr. Ordor of Jno. Scollay Esqr., Mr. Jno. Andrews} Selectmen of Boston
Approved of by Saml. Whitwell one of the overss.

Novr. 3d.   Recd. into the Almshous Love Henley   (on the state)
Pr. ordor of Ezekl. Price   } Selectmen of Boston
Consented to By Jona. Mason Esqr. one of the oversears

Novr. 14th.   Recd. into the Almshous Nichole Lucey   (on the state)
Pr. ordor of Jno. Scollay Esqr., Jno. Andrews} Selectmen
Consented to by Edwd. proctor Esqr. One of the oversears

Novr. 15th.   Recd. Wm. Harris into the Almshous   (town)
Pr. ordor of Jno. White, one of the Oversears

Novr. 16th.   Recd. into the Almshous Jno. Hunnewell & Wife   (town)
Pr. ordor of Edwd. Proctr. Esqr. one of The oversears of the poor

Novr. 16th.   Recd. into the Almshous Mary Shea   (on the state)
Pr. order of John Scollay Esqr., Wm. Mackey} Selectmen of Boston
Apprd. of by Edwd. proctor One of the oversears

17th.   dischd. Charles dix Wallis a boy   (town)

                     Recd. into the Almshous Sucky Follens   (town)
Pr. order of Jona. L Auston one of the oversears

1785 Novr. 17   dischd. Negero Venus   state

Novr. 19th.   Dischd. Jno. Honewell & Wife   town

19th.   Recd. into the Almshous Mary Blake   town
pr. ordor Wm. Powell Esqr.

21   Recd. into the Almshous Elizh. Wood   (town)
Pr. ordor of Wm. Powell Esqr. one of the oversears

23d.   Recd. Into the Almshous Elenor Morrison   on the state
Pr. ordor of Jno. Scollay Esqr., Jno. Brown Esqr.} Selectmen of Boston
Approvd. of By Saml. Whitwell} one of the Oversears

Novr. 21   Recd. into the Almshous Jno. Walnuck   (on the state)
Pr. ordor of Jno. Scollay Esqr., Mr. Jno. Andrews} Selectmen of Boston
Consented to by Edwd. Proctor Esqr. One of the oversears}

Novr. 2nd.   Recd. into the Almshous Eleanor Hayley   (on the state)
Pr. ordor of Jno. Scollay Esqr., Wm. Mackey} Selectmen of Boston
Consented to by John Sweetser Esq One of the Oversears}

Novr. 26   Dischd. Jno. Downey   state

Novr. 24   Dischd. Mary Shea   (state)

Novr. 28th.   Recd. into the Almshous Elizh. Fisher & Child   (state)
Pr. ordor of Jno. Scollay Esq, Edwd. Tyler} Selectmen of Boston
Approved of By Edwd. Proctor Esq one of the oversears}

Novr. 28th.   Recd. into the Almshous Frances Clarage   (state)
Pr. ordor of Jno. Scollay Esqr., Jn Brown Esqr.} Selectmen of Boston
Consented to by Saml. Whitwell one of the oversears}

30   Recd. into the Almshous Negero Catey Hollond   (town)
Pr. ordor of Jona. Mason Esq {one of the oversears

Novr. 23d.   Recd. Into the Almshous Ann Fovell   (on the state)
Pr. ordor Jno. Scollay Esqr. } Selectmen of Boston
Consented to the Jona. Mason Esqr. One of the oversears

decr: 1st.   Recd. into the Almshous Hannah Madden   (state)
Pr. ordor of Jno. Scollay Esqr., Moses Grant} Selectmen of Boston
Consented to by Jona. Mason One of the oversears}

1785 Decr. 7th.   Recd. into the Almshous Luce Russell A Negero
Pr. ordor of Jno. Scalley } Selectmen Boston
Agreed to by Isaac Smith} one of the oversears

Decr. 9   Recd. into the Almshous Sarah Williams   (on the state)
Pr. ordor of Ezek Price   } Selectmen of Boston
Consented to by Jona. Mason} one of the Oversears

Decr. 9   Recd. into the Almshous Jno. Comorell A Molatto boy 2 1/2 years old
                                                                               (State)
9   do.   do.   Olivll Gyles Aged 1 year old Negero   state
Pr. ordor of Jno. Scollay, Jno. Andrews} Selectmen of Boston
Approved of by Saml. Whitwell} one of the oversears

Decr. 9th.   Recd. into the Almshous Robt. Murchie A Strnr. [*i.e., Stranger*]
                                                                               (State Accot.)
Pr. ordor of Jno. Scollay Esqr., Jno. Andrews} Selectmen of Boston
Approvd. by Edwd. proctor Es.} one of the Oversears

decr. 10th.   Dischd. Elenor Morrison out of the hous

Decr. 10th.   Recd. into the Almshous Lydia Marten & her Son Nathl.   (town)
Pr. ordor of Saml. Whitwell One of the Oversears

<13th.   Dischd. Richd Kelley> A Mistake   *<(State)>*

decr. 9th.   Dischd. John Covell A boy bound to Mr. Stephen Salisbury (state)

13th.   Run Sarah Nowell   (town)

13th.   Run Mrs.   Adams   town

Decr. 14   Recd. into the Almshous Sarah freeman And three Children   state
Pr. ordor of Jno. Scollay, Wm. Cunningham} Selectmen
Approvd. of by Edwd. Proctor one of the oversears}

Decr. 14   Recd. into the Almshous Lucy Haden & Child   town
Pr. ordor of John Sweetser} oversear

Decr. 14th.   Recd. into the Almshous Miller Pain A Negero   state
Pr. ordor of Jno. Scoley Esqr., Wm. Cuningham} Selectmen of Boston
Approd. of by Edwd. Procter Esqr. One of the oversears}

Decr. 14th.   Recd. into the Almshous Jno. Morrison a Strainger   (state)
Pr. Ordor of Jno. Scollay, Wm. Cuningham} Selectmen of Boston
Consented to by Saml. Whitwell} one of the Oversears

1785 decr: 17th.   Recd. into the Almshous Mary Garrow And her two Children
Pr. ordor of Moses Grant, Edwd. Tyler} Selectmen
Consented to by Edwd. Proctor one of the Oversears}

decr. 19th.   Recd. into the Almshous Jno. Haney A Strainger   state
Pr. ordor of Jno. Scollay Esqr., Mr. Jno. Andrews} Selectmen
Approved of by Edwd. Proctor Esq} one of the oversears}

decr. 9th.   Recd. into the Almshous Thos. Lawrence   (state)
Pr. ordor of Jno. Scollay Esq., Mr. Jno. Andrews} Selectmen of Boston
Consented to by Edwd. Procter Esqr.} one of the oversears

Decr. 21st.   Recd. into the Almshous Sarah Lovring   (town)
Pr. ordor of Edwd. Proctor Esq One of the oversears

Decr. 21st.   Received into the H[ouse] Jno Hurley   town
Pr. ordor of Edwd. Proctor Esqr. One of the Oversears

Decr. 23rd.   Recd. into the Almshous Flowrah Lewis & Child Negeros   (town)
Pr. ordor Mr. Saml. Whitwell (the oversears)

Decr. 28th.   Recd. into the Almshous Partrick King a Strainger   (state)
Pr. Ordor of Jno. Scollay Esq, Moses Grant} Selectmen
Approvd. of by Edwd. Proctor Esqr.} one of the Oversears

Decr. 28th.   Recd. into the Almshous Katharina Crowley   (state)
Pr. ordor of Jno. Scollay Esq, Jno. Andrews} Selectmen
Approved of by Edwd. Proctor Esq} oversear

Decr. 29th.   Recd. into the Almshous Mary Wyed} Wyed Never Came to the
Almshouse   (state)
Pr. Ordor of Jno. Scollay Esq., Jno. Andrews} Selectmen
Approved of by Edwd. Proctor Esqr.} one of the oversears}

Decr. 30th.   Recd. into the Almshous Wm. Oliver   (on the state)
Pr. ordor of Jno. Scollay Esq, Jno. Andrews} Selectmen
Approvd. of by Saml. Whitwell} one of the oversears

Jany. 2 1786   dischd. Danl. Waikfield   (State)

Jany. 4   Recd. into the Almshous Jno. Lamb   (state)
Pr. ordor of Jno. Scollay Esqr., Edwd. Tyler} Selectmen
Approvd. of by Henry Printes Oversear

Jany 4th.   Recd. into the Almshous Jane Perse   (state)
Pr. ordor of Jno. Scollay Esqr., Edwd. Tyler} Selectmen
Approvd. of by Henry Printiss} one of the oversears

1786   Recd. into the Almshous Mary FitzGerald   town
Mr. Saml Parkman one of The oversears

Jany. 9th.   Recd. into the Almshous Jno. Fullmore from in dublan   (state)
Pr. ordor of Jno. Andrews, Moss. Grant} Selectmen
Appr. of by Edwd. Proctor One of the Overseers}

Jany. 9th.   Recd. into the Almshous Lewis Edwards 3 years old Aprl. Next
Pr. Ordor of Mr. Saml. Whitwell One of the Overseers

10th.   Recd. into the Almshous Jno. Gardner   town
Pr. ordor of Saml. Parkman one of the Oversears of the poor

Jany. 10   Recd. into the Almshous Saml. Roberts, His Son Joseph Agd. 11 years
the 19th. Feby. Next, His daughter Pattey 7 years old the 4 day of June next}   town
Pr. ordor of Saml. Whitwell one of the oversears

Jany. 11th.   Recd. into the Almshous James a Negero Child}   (state)
do.   do.   do.   Clarrisa a Negero do. }
Pr. Ordor of Jno. Scollay, Wm. Mackay} Selectmen of Boston
Apprd. of by Edwd. Procter Esqr. One of the Overseers}

Jany. 12th.   Recd. into the Almshous Richd. Hubbard born in England   (State)
Pr. Ordor of Jno. Scollay Esqr., Wm. Mackay} Selectmen of Boston
Approvd. of by Saml. Whitwell} one of the oversears

Jany. 11th.   Recd. into the Almshous Jno. Randell a Child 4 years old   state
Pr. ordor of Wm. Mackay, Moses Grant} Selectmen of Boston
Consented to by Jona. Mason} Oversear

Jany. 14   Recd. into the Almshous Rossanna A Negero Woman   state
Pr. ordor of Wm. Cunningham   } Selectmen of Boston
Approved of by Isaac Smith an oversear of the poor

Jany. 16th.   Dischd. Rebecca Hilburt   (State)

Decr. 30th.   Recd. into the Almshous Jno. Thompson a Boy 3 years old   (town)
Pr. ordor of Wm. Powell Esq one of the oversears

Jany. 18th.   Recd. into the Almshous Wm. Harpley   (State)
Pr. ordor of Jno. Scollay Esq, Wm. Mackay} Selectmen of Boston
Approd. of By E Proctor An Overseer

1786 Jany. 12th.   Recd. into the Almshous Mary Harvey of Charlston   (on the State)
Pr. ordor of Jno. Andrews   } Selectmen
Approv'd of By Isaac Smith Esqr.} an overseer

Jany. 20th.   Recd. into the Almshous Thomas Thorp   (State)
Pr. Ordor of Edwd. Tyler, Jno. Andrews} Selectmen
Approed of by Edwd. Proctor Esq An Overseer}

Jany. 23d.   Recd. into the Almshous Mary Jones   (town)
Pr. Ordor of Jno. Swetser one of the Overseers

〜

| Jany. 26th. | Discharged William Curtes | (Town) |

| Jany. 22d. | Ran   Richardson | (town) |

Jany. 24th.   Recd. into the Almshous Sarah Ford with her Two Children}   (State)
Pr. Ordor of Jno. Andrews, Moses Grant} Selectmen
Approved of by Jonathon Mason} one of the oversears

Jany. 26th.   Recd. into the Almshous Catharine Cook destetute of a home   State
Pr. ordor of Jno. Scollay Esq   } Selectmen
Consented to by Jno. Sweetser Esq} oversear of ward No. 11

Jany. 28th.   Recd. into the Almshous Marthor Sun the Child of a Strainger
Pr. ordor of Jno. Scollay   } Selectmen
Approved of by Edwd. Proctor Esqr. An oversear

| Feby. 9th. | Dischd. Saml. Roborts | (town) |

| 9 | Run Away Wm. Harris | (town) |

| 10 | Dischd. out of the Almshous Sarah Freeman & 3 Chiln. | State |

11th.   Recd. into the Almshous James Cornish & Elizh. Cornish}   (town)
Pr. ordor of Jno. Sweetser Esqr. one of the oversears

11th.   Dischd. Jno. Comorel a Molatto Child
by ordor of Mr. Jno. Andrews & Moses Grant} select men

12   Recd. into the Almshous Margrat Love a Strainger Sick
Pr. ordor of Jno. Scollay   } Selectmen of Boston
Approd. of by Jno. White An oversear}

Feby. 7th.   Recd. into the Almshous Dinah Sergant a Negero   (state)
Pr. ordor of Jno. Scollay Esqr., Mr. Jno. Andrews} Select men of Boston
Approved of by Mr. H. Prentess an oversear

1786 Feby. 16th.   Recd. into the Almshous Abigal Snow An Indian & Child. Jest deld. of a
Child in A barne   state
Pr. ordor of Jno. Scollay Esqr., Jno. Browne Esqr.} Selectmen
Consented to by Jona. Mason Esqr. one of the Overseers

Feby. 24th.   Recd. into the Almshous Saml. Covell in a distressd. Circums.   State
Pr. ordor of Jno. Scollay   } Select Men of Boston
Consented to by Saml. Whitwell one of the overseers}

Feby. 27th.   Recd. into the Almshous Bantom Phillips a Negero man   town
Pr. ordor of John Browne, Jno. Anrews} Select men
Consented to by Jona. Mason One of the Overseers

Feby. 28th.   Recd. into the Almshous Marthor Egerston   town
Pr. ordor of Edwd. Proctor Esqr. an oversear

March 1th.   Dischd. Jno. Clark a Sailer   state
            Ditto Charles Auston A Ship carpendor   do.

Feby. 28th. Recd. into the Almshous David Dennie   (Ireland a Seman)
Pr. ordor of Jno. Andrews, Moses Grant} Selectmen of Boston
Consented to by Edwd. Proctor Esqr. one of the oversears of the poor

March 3d. Recd. into the Almshous Michael Comly (A German laboror) state
Pr. Ordor of Jno. Scollay Esqr. } Selectmen of Boston
Approvd. of by Edwd. Proctor Esqr. One of the Overseers of the poor}

March the 3d. Recd. into the Almes House William A Negero Child 2 years old (town)
Pr. ordor of Jona. L Austen one of the Overseers

March 4th. Reced. into the Almes House Mary Pool
Pr. Order of John Scollay Esqr. Select Man of Boston
Consent'd to Jona. Mason Esqr. One of the Overseers

March 4th. Run from the Almshous Robt. Lilman   (State)

March 7th. Recd. into the Almshous fanny Clark   (town)
Pr. ordor of Jona. Mason One of the oversears

March 10th. dischd. Rosanna Bennet A Negro   (State)

1786 March 11th. Recd. into the Almshous Jno. Laufour A Frenchman (state)
Pr. ordor of Wm. Cunningham } Selectmen
Consented to by Jno. Sweetser} one of the Overseers

March 11th. Recd. into the Almshous Benjn. Singclear a young man (State)
Pr. Ordor of Jno. Andrews, Jno. Scollay} Selectmen
Approved of by

March 10th. Recd. into the Almshous Nelly Murry *<of this town>* (state)
<Pr. ordor of John Sweetser Esqr. an oversear of the poor>
Wm. Cuningham   } Selectmen
Approved of by Jno. Sweetser Esqr.} an oversear of the poor

March 10th. Recd. into the Almshous James Adams of this town 60 ys. of age
Pr. ordor of Edwd. Proctor Esq One of the Oversears of the poor

March the 11th. Recd. into the Almshous Thos. Murphey A Sailer (on the State)
Pr. ordor of Jno Scollay Esq, Jno. Andrews} Selectmen of Boston
Approved of by Saml. Whitwell} An Overseer

March 11th. Recd. into the Almshous Henry Williams belonging to New york state
Pr. ordor of Moses Grant   } Selectmen
Approd. of by Edwd. Proctor} an oversear

March 13th. Discharged John Chaimbers   (state)
       Run John Lamb do.

14th. Recd. into the Almshous Benjn. Waldo   (this town)
Pr. ordor of Edwd. Proctor Esq} an oversear

March 18th. Recd. into the Abigal Lewis   town
Pr. ordor of Edwd. Proctor. An Oversear

March 20   Recd. into the Almshous Rosanna Bennet A Negero
Pr. ordor of Jno. Scollay Esq, Jno. Andrews} Selectmen
Consented to by Wm. Phillips

March 21   Recd. into the Almshous Wm. King
Pr. ordor of Jno. Scollay, Jno. Andrews} Selectmen
Consented to Wm. Phillips An Oversear

March 21   [Dis]charged Nichs. Lacey   (State)

March 23d.   Dischd. Saml. Trescott   State

March 24   Recd. into the Almshous Cornelos OBryan Ireland   state
Pr. ordor of Jno. Scollay Esqr., Thos. Walley Esq} Select Men
Consented to by Jona. Mason Esq} one of the oversears

1786 March 25th.   Recd. into the Almshous Elizh. Sloan & Child   town
Pr. Ordor of Henry Prentiss one of the Oversears of the poor

March 27th.   Recd. into the Almshous Partrick Kelley   state
Pr. ordor of Moses Grant   } Selectmen
Consented to by Edwd. Proctor Esq} an oversear

March 27th.   Dischd. Partrick Shanley   State

March 27th.   Dischd. Elizh. Sloan & Child   (town)

March 28   Recd. Into the Almshous Wm. Prichard   (town)
Pr. ordor of Edwd. Proctor Esqr. An oversear

Aprl. 4th.   Recd. into the Almshous Polley *<Kelly>* Tilley & Child   State
Pr. Ordor of Jno. Scollay Esq, Jno. Andrews} Selectmen of Boston
Approd. of by Wm. Phillips Esq One of the Oversears of the poor}

Aprl. 5th.   Recd. into the Almshous Ann Wattson   (on the State)
Pr. ordor of Jno. Scolley Esqr., Moses Grant} Selectmen
Approd. of by Edwd. Proctor Esq} an oversear

Aprl. 5th.   Recd. into the Almshous Mary Shee & Child   (on the state)
Pr. Ordor of Jno. Scollay Esq, Moses Grant} Selectmen of Boston
Apprvd. of by Edwd. Proctor An Oversear of the poor

Aprl. 8th.   Recd. into the Almshous Wm. Jones   State
Pr. ordor of Jno. Andrews, Ezekl. Price} Selectmen
Apprvd. of by Jona. Mason Esq One of the Oversears of the poor

Aprl. 10th.   Recd. into the Almshous Jno. Willet a boy   (town)
Pr. ordor of Edwd. proctor Esq An oversear of the poor

Aprl. 6th.   Dischd. Wm. Meloney a boy bound out   state

Aprl. 11   Dischd. *<Mary>* Elizh. Fisher & Child   state

        do. Jno. Killey   do.

13th.   do. John Laufour   do.

Run, Benjn. Singclear

1786 Apr. 11th.　　Recd. into the Almshous Partrick Christia of the Kingdom of Ireland}
Pr. Ordor of Jno. Andews, Moses Grant} Selectmen　　　　　　　　　　　state
Approvd. of By Edwd. Proctor One of the oversears

Aprl. 12　　　　　Dischd. John Hany a German　　　　　　　　　　　　　(state)

Aprl. 12　　　　　Recd. into the Almshous Nancy Howes A Child　　　　　state
Pr. ordor of Jno. Scalley Esqr.　} Selectmen
Approved of by Wm. Phillips Esqr.

Aprl. 12th.　　　　Dischd. Lucey Haden & Child (they belong to Waltham)　　town
　　　　　　　　　Do.　　Mary Pool　　　　　　　　　　　　　　　　　State

Feby. 28th.　　　　Recd. into the Almshous Hayley Borne in this hous Of Elenor Haley
who Came into the hous the Second Novr. 2d. 1786}　　　　　　　　state
Pr. ordor of Jno. Scollay, Jno. Browne} Selectmen
Consented to by Wm. Philips Esqr. An oversear}

Aprl. 12th.　　　　Receved into the Almshous John Breton　　　(Sailer on the state)
Pr. ordor of Jno. Scollay, Jno. Browne} Selectmen
Approved of by Edwd. Proctor Esq An oversear

Aprl. 12　　　　　dischd. Frances Clarrage　　　　　　　　　　　　　state

　　　　　　　　　Saml. Murfey Bound out to Danl. Waldo of Wocestor　　(town)

Aprl. 17　　　　　Dischd. Benjn. Waldo　　　　　　　　　　　　　　town

Aprl. 17th.　　　　Dischd. John Gardenor a Carver by trade　　　　　　(town)

Apr 17th.　　　　Recd. into the Almshous Elizh. Ivies & her Child Caled Elizh. forstor
born in this hous the 4th. May 1785}　　　　　　　　　　　　　　State

Pr. ordor of John Scollay Esq, Jno. Andrews} Selectmen
Consented to by Isaac Smith an oversear

Aprl. 17　　　　　Recd. into the Almshous Thos. Gambel a Negero have ben hear
Eversence the 3d. feby. 1786.　　　　　　　　　　　　on the state a/c
Pr. ordor Jno. Scollay Esq., Ezekell Price Esqr.} Selectmen
Consented to by Jona. Mason One of the oversears

Aprl. 27　　　　　Recd. into the Almshous Hannah Burt　　　　　　　town
Pr. ordor of Edwd. Proctor Esqr., Oversear

1786 Apr. 26　　　Recd. into the Almshous Mary the wife of Saml. Pool And her Three
Children Viz Samuel, Eliz, Polley}
Pr. ordor of Edwd. Proctor Esq An oversear

Aprl. 26th.　　　　Run Mary Whitman　　　　　　　　　　　　　　(town)

28th.　　　　　　Run Ann Gorden & Child　　　　　　　　　　　　(state)

1786 Apr. 29th.　　Recd. into the Almshous Saml. Williams a Englishman　　(state)
Pr. ordor Jno. Scollay Esq, Jno. Andrews} Selectmen
Consented to by Edwd. Proctor Esq, Oversear

Aprl. 29th.   Recd. into the Almshous Catherina Oliver; ten years of Age the 26th.
July 1786   (State)
Pr. order of John Scollay, Jno. Andrews} Select Men
Consented to by Saml. Whitwell One of the Oversears

Aprl. 29th.   Recd. into the Almshous John Hews an Englishman A Sailer   (State)
Pr. ordor of Jno. Scollay Esq, Jno Andrews} Selectmen
Approved of by

May 1th.   Received into the Almshous Thos. Smith a Native of Ireland
Pr. ordor of Jno. Brown   } Selectmen
Consented to Pr. Jona. Mason} one of the overseers

May 2nd.   Recd. into the Almshous Ann Gorden A Child Six years of Age the
Pr. ordor of Jno. Andrews, Moses Grant} Selectmen
Consented to by Edwd. Proctor Esq} an oversear

May 5th.   Recd. into the Almshous Sarah Seagrave   (town)
Pr. Edwd. Proctor Esq An Oversear

          Dischd. James Tranholm Aprl. 10th.

May 8th.   Received into the Almshous Jno. Haney A German   state
Pr. ordor of Jno. Scollay   } Selectmen
Consented to by Edwd. Proctor Esqr. One of the Oversears of the poor

May 12   dischd. Henry Williams   State

May 13   Dischd. John Haney   State
          Ann Watson do.
          <Elenor Morrison & Child>   do.
15   Lewis Edwards a Child   (town)
          Thomas Cross   town

1786 May 19th.   dischd. Bantom Philips   (State)

May 19th.   Reced. into the Almshous Patrick Shandy a Irishman & a Shoe maker
about 35 years old
Pr. ordor of Edwd. Tyler, Jno. Andrews} Selectmen of Boston
Approvd of By Edwd. proctor Esqr. An Oversear

May 20   Recd. into the Almshous Rebecca Baldrage   (town)
Pr. ordor of Mr. Saml. Parkman

May 22nd.   Dischd. out of the Almshous Mary Singclear   (State)
          ditto   ditto   Partrick Christey   do

May 23   Recd. into the Almshous Richd. Harris   (town)
Pr. order of Mr. Edwd. Proctor a oversear

May 30th.   Dischd. Mary Wainwood   (state)

<June 1   *Dischd. Olive a negero Child>* Returnd into the hous}   (state)
do. 3   do. Estor ford, bound out   do.

June 6th.   Recd. into the Almshous Thos. Graves A Sailer
Pr. ordor of Jno. Andrews, Moses Grant} Selectmen
Approved of by Edwd. Proctor Esqr. An oversear}

June 4   Dischd. John Huse

June the 9th.   Dischd. Sarah Myers from the Almshous

June 10th.   Recd. into the Almshous Wm. Curtis A Carpendor Borne In this towne
Pr. Ordor of Edwd. Proctor Esq An Oversear

June 10th.   Run Thos. Graves   (state)

June 12th.   Dischd. Mathew Sun A Child   (state)

June 9th.   Recd. into the Almshous Mary Swan   (town)
Pr. ordor of Jona. L Austen A oversear

June 12   Recd. into the Almshous Eunice Vose And 2 Children
Pr. ordor of Saml. Whitwell An oversear

June 13   Recd. into the Almshous Richd. Poole   (State)
Pr. Ordor of John Scolley Esqr., Mr. Jno. Andrews} Select men of Boston
Approved of by Edwd. Proctor An Oversear of the poor

June 14th.   dischd. Ann Gorden a Child

June 15th.   Recd. into the Almshous Elizh. Colster A Child 27 Months old
Pr. ordor of Edwd. Tyler, Jno. Andrews} Select men
Consented to By Edwd. Proctor one of the oversears

1786 June 19th.   Recd. Olive A Negro woman into the Almshous   state
Pr. Ordor of John Scollay Esqr., Wm. Cuningham} Selectmen of Boston
Approved of by Saml. Parkman An overseer of the poor

June 20th.   Dischd. Thos. Lawrance   state
                  Dischd. John McKinzie   do.

June 20th.   Negero Rosanna's Child   Recd.   state
Pr. ordor of Jno. Scollay, Thos. Walley} Selectmen of Boston
Approved of By Saml. Parkman One of the oversears

June 21st.   Recd. into the Almshous Eliz Colton   (on the state)
Pr. ordor of John Scollay, Thos. Walley} Selectmen of Boston
Consented to by Saml. Parkman one of the oversears

June 21st.   dischd. Jno. & Wm. Ross two Boys   (on the state)

June 23   Mary Covel Bound out to Thos. Child of falmouth County. Cumbd.
[*i.e., Cumberland*]   (state)

June 24th.   Dischd. <*Abigal*> Mrs. Forbes & 2 Children   state

June 25th.   Dischd. Mary Shea Alis Brown with her 2 Children. Sent to Salem by A
Warrant from Josh. Greenleaf Esqr} [hear] Suppd. to be Shea's wife   (on the state)

                  Willm. Curtis Ran A way   (town)

June 27th.   Recd. Into the Almshous Hugh Smith a laborough   State
Pr. ordor of Jno. Andrews, Moses Grant} Selectmen
Approd. of by Edwd. Proctor Esqr. An oversear of the poor

| June 27th. | Dischd. out of the Almshous Flowrah Lewis A Negero | town |

| June 28th. | Dischd. Rebecca Baldrage | town |

June 28th.   Recd. into the Almshous Hannah Wheler   Town
Pr. Ordor of Wm. Phillips an oversear

June 30   Dischd. Wm. Pricherd of this town.

July 1th.   Recd. into the Almshous Ruben Gorham   (state)
Pr. ordor of Jno. Brown Esqr. } Selectmen
Consented to by Wm Powell Esqr.} An oversear

June 30th.   Recd. into the Almshous Mary Wier An inhabent of Charlstown   State
Pr. ordor of Jno. Scollay Esqr., Jno. Andrews} Selectmen
Approd. of By Wm. Powell An oversear

1786 July 3d.   dischd. out of the Almshous James Mory   (state)
     ditto   do.   do.   Elenor Haley & Child   do.

June 15   Recd. into the Almshous Charles De St. Prie two years And three
months old}   state
Pr. ordor of Moses Grant, Mr. Edwd. Tyler} Selectmen
Approvd. of By Edwd. Proctor Esq One of the Oversears of the poor}

July 6th.   Dischd. Joseph Lewis   State
     ditto Sarah Dockum   do.
7th.   Jannah McKinzie & Child   do.

July 8th.   *<Dischd.>* Richd. Hubbard Run   state

July 8th.   *<Dischd.>* Ann Gibling Run   state

July 9th.   Dischd. John Bretton   state

July 10th.   Recd. into the Almshous Coller Castle   (town)
Pr. Ordor of Jona. Mason Esq One of the overseers of the poor

July 10   Dischd. Deborah Hurley   (State)

July 10th.   Recd. into the Almshous Joseph Tragence And Wm. Tragence 2 Boys}
Pr. ordor of Jno. Scolley, Jno. Andrews} Selectmen   state
Approvd. by Edwd. procter An oversear

July 3d.   Recd. into the Almshous Mary Bathaw   State
Pr. ordor of Ezel. Price Esqr. } Selectmen
Consented to by Jona. Mason Esqr.} An oversear

July 13th.   Recd. into the Almshou James Mory   state
Pr. ordor of Jno. Andrews, Moses Grant} Selectmen
Approved of by Edwd. Proctor Esqr. An Oversear}

July 13   Recd. into the Elizh. Damry—with her two Childn.
Pr. Ordor of Jno. Andrews, Moses Grant} Selectmen
Consented to by Edwd. Proctor Esqr. An Oversear}

July 13th.   Dischd. Michal Comley   state

July 15th.	Recd. into the Almshous Elizh. Bright A Child	State
Pr. Ordor of Jno. Scollay Esqr., Jno. Andrews} Selectmen		
Approd. by Edwd. Proctor Esq An Oversear of the poor		

1786 July 15	Recd. into the Almshous James Fitzgerald	State
Pr. order of Jno. Scollay Esq, Jno. Andrews} Selectmen		
Approd. of by Edwd. Proctor Esqr. An oversear}		

July 15th.	Dischd. Mary Garrow & 2 Children	state

July 17th.	Recd. into the Almshous Lucy Haden & Child	(town)
Pr. Ordor of Jnoa. Mason, An oversear		

July 25	Recd. into the Almshous Hipsibath Atkins	town
Pr. ordor of Jona. Mason Esqr. One of the oversears of the poor		

July 26th.	Recd. into the Almshous Michl. Comerly—German	state
Pr. ordor of Jno. Scollay Esqr., Moses Grant} Selectmen		
Consented to by Edwd. Proctor An oversear		

July 30th.	Dischd. Saml. Covel	State
30	George Hurley a boy Bound out	do.
30	dischd. Richard Crouch	do.

July 30th.	dischd. Nelle Murry	State

July 31th.	Recd. into the Almshous James Ferrill a Englishman	State
Pr. Ordor of Jno. Scollay Esqr., Thos. Walley Esqr.} Selectmen		
Consented to by Edwd. Proctor Esqr. One of the oversears of the poor		

July 31th.	Recd. into the Almshous Matthew Sun A Child	(State)
Pr. Ordor of Jno. Andrews, Thos. Walley} Selectmen		
Approd. of by Edwd. proctor Esqr. One of the Oversears}		

Augt. 5th.	Recd. into the Almshous Mary Brown	town
Pr. ordor of Saml. Whitwell (an oversear)		

Augt. 5th.	Recd. into the Almshous Saml. George a Negero	(state)
Pr. ordor of J. Scollay, Jno. Andrews} Selectmen		
Consented to by Edwd. Proctor An oversear}		

Augt. 5th.	Dischd. out of the Almshous Benjn. Bignall	(town)

Augt. 3d.	William Sharp Run	

Augt. 7th.	Dischd. Mary Brown	town

7th.	Dischd. Marthor Symons	do.

	Recd. into the Almshous & dischd. out of it Vizt.	

1786	Recd. into Christopher Foye Augt. 9th.	(State)
Pr. ordor of Jno. Andrews & Jno. Scollay} Selectmen		
Approd. of by Edwd. Proctor Esqr.		

Augt. 5th.	Recd. into the Almshous Betsey daughter of Eliz Colter	(State)
Pr. ordor of Jno. Scollay Esqr., Jno. Andrews} Selectmen		
Consented to by Wm. Powell Esq An oversear of the poor		

Augt. 8th.	Dischd. out of the Almshous Eliz Bright a Child	state
Augt. 10th.	Recd. into the Almshous Susanna Foster a Child, Elizh. Ivers}	State

Pr. Ordor of Moses Grant   } Selectmen
Approved of by Edwd. Proctor Esq An oversear

Augt. 11	Recd. into the Almshous Elizh. Cornish	town

Pr. ordor of Jno. Sweetser One of the Oversears

Augt. 12	Run Hipsibah Atkins	town
Augt. 15th.	Recd. into the Almshous Elizh. Sloan from the Workhous	(town)

Pr. ordor of Wm. Powell an oversear

Augt. 15th.	Recd. into the Almshous Peggy Bowle & Child	(State)

Pr. ordor of Jno. Andrews, Moses Grant} Selectmen
Consented by Wm. Powell Esq An oversear

Augt. 16.	Recd. into the Almshous Margrat Stewart	(State)

Pr. ordor of Ezekl. Price   } Selectmen
Approved of by Saml. Whitwell One of the oversears of the poor}

Augt. 18th.   Recd. into the Almshous Rebecca & Suckey Edes. Rebecca 9 years old,
Suckey 4 do. [*i.e., years old*]
Pr. ordor of Jona. Mason Esqr. An oversear of the poor

Agt. 18th.	Recd. into the Almshous Anna Whitman	town

Pr. ordor of Saml. Parkman An oversear of the poor

Augt. 18th.	Dischd. James Mory to the County Gole	state
Augt. 22	Dischd. Olive a Negero Woman	State
Augt. 29	Dischd. Rebeckah Edes by ordor of Mr. Heny. Prentis	town
Augt. 29th.	Recd. into the Almshous Salley Mason	state

Pr. ordor of Jno. Scollay Esq, Jno. Andrews Esq} Selectmen
Approved of by Edwd. Proctor an oversear

People Recd. into the Almshous & dischd. out of it Viz.

Augt. 25th.	Rosanna Bennet & Child Run Negeros	state
Augt. 29th.	Recd. into the Almshous Thos. Whittle	state

Pr. ordor of Jno. Scollay Esqr., Jno. Andrews} Selectmen
Approd. by Edwd. Pproctor Esq. An oversear

Augt. 31th.	dischd. out of the Almshous Suckey Edes a Child by directions of	
	Jona. Mason Esqr. one of the oversears}	town
Septr. 3d.	Recd. into the Almshous John Driscoll laboror	State

Pr. ordor of Jno. Andrews, Ezekl. Price} Selectmen
Approd. of by Henry Prentis An oversear of the poor

Septr. 4	Dischd. Olive A Negero Child	State
	Dischd. Willm. Oliver	do.

Septr. 5th.	Dischd. Jno. Driscoll	State
Septr. 7th.	Katharina oliver Run	(State)
Septr. 8th.	James White a Negero boy bound out	(town)

Septr. 9   Recd. into the Almshous Charles Johnson of the state Nw. York   State
Pr. Ordor of Jno. Scollay, Jno. Andrews} Selectmen
Appd. of By Edwd. Proctor An oversear of the poor}

Septr. 17th.   Recd. into the Almshous Jno. Willit & Wife   (of Boston)
Pr. ordor of Edwd. Proctor Esq. An oversear

Septr. 27   Dischd. out of the Almshous Jno. Willet   town
           Ditto   Margrat Love   State

Septr. 28   Dischd. David Dennie   (State)

Septr. 28   Recd. into the Almshous Mary Moran
Pr. ordor of Mr. Jno. White an oversear of the poor

Septr. 30th.   Received into the Almshous Fanney Pond   (town)
Pr. ordor of Isaac Smith Esqr. An Oversear

Septr. 30th.   Discharged Wm. Going A Melatto Boy bound to Jeremiah Smith Boice
of Milton   town

Octr. 3   dischd. Thomas Whittle A Seman

Octr. 5   dischd. Fanney Pond   town
           ditto Mary Moran   town
           do. Lucy Haden   do.
           Run Salley Mason   State

1786 Octr. 4   Recd. into the Almshous Joseph Lues & Sarah his wife   State
Pr. ordor of Jno. Scollay & Jno. Andrews Selt.men
Approved of by Saml. Whitwell

Octr. 5th.   Received Mary St. Clear into the Almshous   (State)
Pr. ordor of Jno. Scollay & Jno. Andrews Selectmen
Approd. of by Saml. Whitwell an oversear

Octr. 9th.   <Dischd.> […]²   (state)

Octr. 9th.   Recd. into the Almshous Ann Whitman   town
Pr. ordor of Saml. Whitwell an oversear

Octr. 11th.   Recd. into the Almshous Nancy Sisk   town
Pr. Ordor of Mr. Saml. Whitwell an oversear of the poor

Octr. 12th.   Recd. into the Almshous Polley Roberts & Son   town
Pr. ordor of Saml. Whitwell An oversear of the poor

Octr. 16th   Recd. into the Almshous Leonard Shermon Sailer   (state)
Pr. ordor of Jno. Scolley, Jno. Andrews} Selectmen
Approvd. of by Saml. Whitwell an oversear of the poor

Octr. 16th.   Recd. into the Almshous Mary Whitman   town
Pr. ordor of Jona. L. Auston an oversear

Octr. 16th.   Ann Whitman Run   (town)

Octr. 21   Recd. into the Almshous Wm. Bannister of Ireland   (state)
Pr. ordor of Edwd. Tyler, Jno. Andrews} Select men
Approd. of By Edwd. Proctor An Oversear}

Octr. 21st.   Elizh. Shean Run   (State)

Octr. 20   Recd. into the Almshous Jane Russell   (State)
Pr. ordor of Wm. Cuningham, Jno. Andrews} Selectmen
Approd. of By Mr. Jno. White An oversear of the poor

Octr. 21th.   Recd. into the Almshous Jno. Lynes of Ireland   state
Pr. ordor of Jno. Scollay, Jno. Andrews} Select men
Approvd. of By Edwd. Proctor An Oveesear of the poor

Octr. 23d.   Recd. into the Almshous Thos. Jackson of Ireland   (State)
Pr. ordor of Ezekl. Price   } Selectmen
Approvd. of By Saml. Whitwell An oversear of the poor

Octr. 24th.   Recd. into the Almshous Frances Pond   town
Pr. ordor of Mr. Jno. White an oversear of the poor

1786 Oct 25th.   Recd. into the Almshous Dotson Williams   town
Pr. ordor of Wm. Powell Esqr. An oversear

Octr. 31th.   Recd. into the Almshous Cato Sears a Negero   State
Pr. ordor of Edwd. Tyler, Jno. Andrews} Selectmen
Approd. of by Saml. Whitwell An Oversear

Novr. 1th.   Recd. into the Almshous Timothy Gwire   State
Pr. Ordor of Jno. Andrews, Thomas Walley} Selectmen
Approvd. of By Edwd. Proctor Esq An oversear

Novr. 1   Dischd. Mary Jones & Child   town

Novr. 2.   Recd. into the Almshous Partrick Demey from Ireland   state
Pr. ordor of Jno. Andrews, Moses Grant} Selectmen
Approd. of By Edwd. Proctor An oversear of the poor

Novr. 3   Recd. into the Almshous Rebecca Baldrage   town
Pr. ordor Saml. Parkman An Oversear

Novr. 4   Dischd. Kitte Mory   state

Novr. 7   Recd. into the Almshous Mary Ward   town
Pr. ordor of Jno. White an oversear

Novr. 9th.   Dischd. William Banester   state

Novr. 9   Recd. into the Almshous Thos. Farrell from Ireland   state
Pr. ordor of John Andrews, Moses Grant} Selectmen
Approd. of By Edwd. Proctor Esqr. An oversear}

Novr. 10th.   Recd. into the Almshous Alce Southwick   state
Pr. ordor of Jno. Andrews, Moses Grant} Selectmen
Approd. of by Jno. Sweetser Esqr. An Oversear}

Novr. 10th.   Received into the Almshous Gerret Fitz Gerrald   state
Pr. Ordor of Jno. Scollay, Jno. Andrews} Selectmen
Approd. of by Jno. Sweetser Esqr. An Oversear

Novr. 10   Reced. into the Almshous Jane Dorris of Scotland   State
Pr. ordor of Jno. Andrews, Moses Grant} Selectmen
Approd. of by Jno. Sweetser Esqr. An oversear of the poor

1786 Novr. 17th.   Recd. into the Almshous Wm. Durphy of Ireland   state
Pr. ordor of Ezekl. Price, Jno. Andrews} Selectmen
Consented to by Saml. Whitwell An oversear

Novr. 18th.   Recd. into the Almshous Abraham Savay No Inhabent of Aney town in
the United States
Pr. ordor of Jno. Andrews, Moses Grant} Select Men
Approvd. of by Wm. Powell Esq An oversear

Novr. 20th.   Recd. Dennis Cavenaugh into the Almshous late of Ireland   (state)
Pr. ordor of Jon. Andrews, Jno. Scollay Esqr.} Selectmen
Approd. of by Jona. L. Austen Oversear in ward No. 7

Novr. 23   Recd. Benj. Gold into the Almshous   (town)
Pr. ordor of Jno. Sweetser an Oversear

Novr. 23d.   Recd. into the Almshous Mary Legalley with her four Childn. As
follows Polly, John, Richd. & Bill on the   (State)
Pr. ordor of Ezekl. Price Esqr., Jno. Brown Esqr.} Selectmen
Approd. of by Saml. Whitwell An oversear of the poor}
Note. Both this Woman & her Husband Came from Jersie in 1773.

Novr. 22   Recd. Into the Almshous Michal Cassedy & his Wife Ketherina   (State)
Pr. ordor of Jno. Scollay, Jno. Andrews} Selectmen
Approd. of By Edwd. Proctor Esq An oversear

Novr. 25th.   Recd. into the Almshous Wm. Allenson   (state)
Pr. ordor of Jno. Andrews, Moses grant} Selectmen
Consented to by Edwd. proctor An oversear of the poor

Novr. 25th.   Recd. into the Almshous Mary Lawrance Widow of Thomas Lawrance,
She was Born in Charlstown And Came hear about 12 years agoo As She Saith & her Child
Pr. ordor of Jno. Scollay, Jno. Andrews} Selectmen
Consented to by Jno. White An Oversear

Novr. 25th.   Recd. into the Almshous Jno. Willet   (Town)
Pr. ordor of Edwd. Proctor Esqr. an oversear

Novr. 27   Recd. into the Almshous Pegey Carton   town
Pr. ordor Edwd. Proctor Esqr. an oversear

Novr. 27   dischd. Jno. Willet to the workhous   town

Novr. 27   Recd. into the Almshous

1786 Novr. 27th.   Recd. into the Almshous 2 Childn. Viz. Loveby Cowling five Years old
And Betsey Cowling 3 years old on the   (State)
Pr. ordor of Jno. Andrews, Wm. Cuningham} Selectmen
Approvd. of by Edwd. procter Esqr. An oversear

Novr. 28th.   Recd. into the Almshous Mary Ratford   (State)
Pr. ordor of Edwd. Tyler, Jno. Andrews} Select Men
Approd. of by Jona. L Austen An oversear

Novr. 29   Recd. into the Almshous   Brockhous   (town)
Pr. ordor of Jno. Sweetser Esq An oversear

Novr. 30th.   Recd. into the Almshous Susannna Cowling   (State)
Pr. ordor of John Scollay, Thos. Walley} Selectmen
Approd. of by Edwd. Proctor Esqr. An oversear

decr. 2d.   Dischd. Abigal Snow out of the Almshous   state

decr. 2   Recd. into the Almshous Mary Wakefield & Child   town
Pr. ordor of Saml. Whitwell An oversear of the poor

Decr. 5th.   Dischd. Alce Southwick   state

Decr. 6th.   Dischd. Francis Pond   (town)

Decr. 7th.   Recd. into the Almshous Edwd. Luce A Negero   state
Pr. ordor of Jno. Andrews, Moses Grant} Selectmen
Approved of By Benjn. Eads An oversear

Decr. 8th.   Recd. into the Almshous Jno. Barry   state
Pr. ordor of Jno. Scollay, Jno. Brown} Selectmen
Approd. of by Saml. Whitwell An oversear

Decr. 9   Recd. into the Almshous Rich Crouch   (state)
Pr. ordor of Jno. Scolley, Jno. Andrews} Selectmen
Approd. of by Edwd. proctor an oversear

Decr. 12th.   Recd. into the Almshous Ann Stone   (town)
Pr. ordor of Edwd. Proctor Esqr. an Oversear

Decr. 13th.   Recd. into the Almshous Eve Straines of Jarmony   (state)
Pr. ordor of Ezekl. Price   } Selectmen
Approvd. of by Saml. Whitwell An oversear

1786 Decr. 13th.   Recd. into the Almshous Richd. Hubbard an Englh.man   (state)
Pr. ordor of Jno. Scollay, Jno. Andrews} Selectmen
Approved of by Edwd. Proctor An oversear of the poor

Decr. 16   Recd. into the Almshous Theode. Kingsbury   on the state
Pr. ordor of Jno. Scollay, Jno. Andrews} Selectmen
Approved of by Edwd. Proctor Esqr. an oversear

Decr. 15th.   Recd. into the Almshous Saml. Roberts   (Town)
Pr. ordor of Wm. Powell E[sq.] An oversear of the poor

Decr. 16th.   Recd. into the Almshous Ann Cross   (Town)
Pr. ordor of Jno. White, an oversear

Decr. 18th.   Dischd. Theader Kingsbury   (state)

Decr. 20th.   Dischd. Brockhous   (town)
                     Dischd. Betsey Poole bound out   (do.)

Decr. 20   Recd. into the Almshous Hipsibah Steward   (State)
Pr. ordor of Jno. Scollay Esq, Jno. Andrews} Selectmen
Approd. by Edwd. Proctor An oversear}

Decr. 21th.   Recd. into the Almshous Elizh. Wheler of this town
Pr. ordor of Edwd. Proctor An oversear

Decr. 20   Recd. into the Almshous Vilet Maddison A Negero   state
Pr. ordor of Jno. Scollay Esq, Jno. Andrews} Selectmen
Approd. of By Isaac Smith An oversear

Decr. 21th.   Recd. into the Almshous Richd. demry An Englishman   state
Pr. ordor of Jno. Andrews, Thos. Walley} Selectmen
Approd. of by Edwd. Proctor An oversear

Decr. 22   Recd. into the Almshous A Negero Child about one Month old
Pr. ordor of Saml. Whitwell an oversear

Decr. 23d.   Recd. into the Almshous Nathl. Low of this town
Pr. ordor of Mr. Saml. Whitwell an oversear

Decr. 27   Recd. into the Almshous Margrat Kelley from Ireland   state
Pr. ordor of Jno. Scollay, Ezek Price} Selectmen
Approd. of by Jon. white An oversear}

Decr. 25th.   Mary Ratford Run   (State)

1786 Decr. 26   Recd. into the Almshous Susanna Wallis   (state)
Pr. ordor of Moses Grant, Jno. Andrews} Selectmen
Approvd. of by Edwd. Proctor An Overseer of the poor

Dec. 28   Dischd. Cato Sears a Negero   (state)

Decr. 29th.   Recd. into the Almshous Hannah Raymond a Child Three years of age}
Pr. ordor of Jno. Andrews, Moses Grant} Selectmen   state
Approvd. of by Jno. Sweetser An oversear

Decr. 30th.   Recd. into the Almshous Nathl. Robarts   (town)
Pr. ordor of Mr. Jno. White an Overseer

1787 Jany. 2   Recd. into the Almshous Daniel Pierce   State
Pr. ordor of Ezek. Price   } Selectmen
Consented to by Jona. Mason An oversear

Jany. 5th.   Dischd. Thos. Jackson   (State)

Jany. 6   Recd. into the Almshous Mary Burford   Town
Pr. ordor of Henry Prentes

Jany. 8th.   Recd. into the Almshous Edwd. Winter   Town
Pr. ordor of Saml. Whitwell An oversear

Jany. 8th.   dischd. James Warren bound to Jacob Weld   town

Jany. 12th.   Recd. into the Almshous Neomey McCleas   State
Pr. ordor of Jno. Andrews, Thos. Walley} Selectmen
Approved of by Mr. Jno. White An oversear of the poor

Jany. 13th.   Recd. into the Almshous Katy Simons borne in Ireland   State
Pr. ordor of Ezekl. Price Esqr.   } Selectmen
Approd. of by Saml. Whitwell An Oversear

Jany. 14th.   Recd. into the Almshous A Mallato Child Picked up In Summor Streat,
we have Called it Clarica}   town
Pr. ordor of Edwd. Tyler, Jno. Andrews} Selectmen

Jany. 15th.   Recd. into the Almshous Nancy Lovell of this town
Pr. ordor of Mr. Saml. Whitwell

1787 Jany. 14th.   Recd. into the Almshous Mathew Salter of halifax   State
Pr. ordor of Jno. Scollay Esq, Mr. Edwd. Tyler} Select Men
approd. of by Mr. Saml. Whitwell an oversear of the poor

Jany. 18th.   Dischd. Benoney Harris Champlen A boy bound out   State

Jany. 17   Recd. into the Almshous Elizh. Sun a Garl 7 years old the 10th. day of
apr. Next}   State
Pr. ordor Mr. Edwd. Tiler, Mr. Jno. Andrews} Selectmen
Approd. of by Saml. Parkman An oversear

Jany. 19th.   dischd. out of the Almshous Vilet Madding A Negero woman   state

Jany. 19th.   Recd. into the Almshous Joseph Penate Lagone   state
Pr. ordor of Ezekl. Price, Jno. Brown} Selectmen
Approved of by Saml. Whitwell an oversear

Jany. 19th.   Recd. into the Almshous John Mayhew A frenchman   (state)
Pr. ordor of Moses Grant   } Selectmen
Approvd. of by Edwd. Proctor Esq An oversear of the poor

Jany. 22d.   Recd. into the Almshous Wm. Stevens   State
Pr. ordor of Jno. Scollay Esq, Mr. Jno. Andrews} Selectmen
Approvd. of By Saml. Parkman An oversear of the poor

Jany. 24th. Recd. into the Almshous David Mengomery A Native Of Scotland Came into this
Contry A britis Solder   (on the state)
Pr. ordor of Jno. Scolley Esqr., Edwd. Tyler} Selectmen
Approvd. of by Edwd. Proctor An Oversear of the poor

Jany. 25th. Recd. into the Almshous David Jones A Welch man   (State)
Pr. ordor of Jno. Andrews, Moses Grant} Selectmen
Approd. of by Edwd. Proctor An oversear of the poor

Jany. 27th. Recd. Ruben Snow of the <*Kingm. of Ireland*> Borne at Woborn into the
Almshouse   town
Pr. ordor of Edwd. Proctor An oversear

Jany. 27   Recd. Meriah A Negero Woman into the Almshous
Pr. ordor of J Loring Austen One of the oversears

Jany. 27   Recd. into the Almshous Catherine Moy   (State)
Pr. ordor of Jno. Scollay, Edwd. Tyler} 2 Selectmen
Approvd. of by Edwd. Proctor An overseer

1787 Jany. 29   Recd. into the Almshous Wm. Hall of Ireland a Gardiner   (State)
Pr. ordor of Edwd. Tiler, Wm. Cuningham} Selectmen
Approvd. of by Edwd. Proctor Esqr. An Overseer of the poor

Jany. 30th. Recd. into the Almshous Betsey Tevet Nine years of age The 20th. June 1787
Pr. ordor of Jno. Andrews, Jno. Scollay Esqr.} Selectmen   (State)
Approved of by Edwd. Proctor Esq An overseer of the poor

Feby. 3d.   Dischd. Nancey Sisk & Child   town

Feby. 6th. Dischd. Nathl. Low out of the Almshous   town

Feby. 6   Recd. into the Almshous David Adams   town
Pr. ordor of Edwd. proctor one of the oversears

Feby. 7th   Recd. into the Almshous Adam Roof A German a Stocking wever}   state
Pr. ordor of Jno. Andrews, Moses Grant} Selectmen
Approd. of by Edwd. Proctor Esqr. An overseer

Feby. 7th. Recd. into the Alms Hous Betsy Wier A Mallatto & her 2 Children the oldest is 6
years old Novr. 14th. 1787   (state)
Pr. ordor of Jno. Scollay Esq, Moses Grant} Selectmen
Approd. of by <Henry Prentis> Jona. L. Austen One of the Oversears

Feby. 5th. Recd. into the Almshous Ann Corbet & her two Childn. James   year old, Thos.
years   (town)
Pr. ordor of Mr. Henry Prentess An overseer of the poor

Feby. 9th. Recd. into the Almshous Thomas Buckley of Grate Brittan   (state)
Pr. ordor of Harbo. Dorr, Wm. Cuningham} selectmen
Approd. of by Edwd. Proctor Esq one of the Oversears of the poor}

Augt. 31th.   Recd. into the Almshous Mary Wadle   (state)
Pr. ordor of John Scollay Esqr., Edwd. Tyler} Select Men
Consented to by Saml. Whitwell An overseer
(this Wadley was hear by the Name of Swan for More than on year Not knoing that She was
A Married woman)

Feby. 14th. Recd. into the Almshous one Flora A Negero woman   (State)
Pr. ordor of Edwd. Tyler, Thos. Walley Esq} Select Men
Approd. by Edwd. Proctor Esq An overseer

Feby. 12th.   Dischd. John Lynes   (State)

Feby. 16th.   Recd. into the almshous Samson Brown A Negero
Pr. ordor of Jno. Scollay, Edwd. Tyler} selectmen
Approvd. of by Jno. Sweetser An overseer of the poor

1787 Feby. 21th.   Dischd. Jno. Legalley a boy bound out   (state)

Feby. 21   Recd. into the Almshous Wm. Jackson a Scoth. Sailer   (State)
Pr. ordor of Jno. Andrews   } Selectmen
Approvd. by Edwd. Proctor Esq

<Feby. 22   *Recd. into the Almshous Margrat Gardner*   (town)
Pr. ordor of Jno. Andrews   } Selectmen
approd. of by Edwd. Proctor, An oversear>

Feby. 23   Recd. into the Almshous York Larrabe A Negero   (state)
Pr. ordor of John Scollay, Jno. Andrews} Selectmen
Approd. by Mr. Henry Prentiss one of the Oversears of the poor

Feby. 22d.   Dischd. Margrat Kelley   (state)

Feby. 24   Recd. into the Almshous James Pike   (town)
Pr. ordor of Willm. Powell

Feby. 22   Recd. into the Almshous Margrat Gardiner   town
Pr. ordor of Isaac Smith An oversear of the poor

Feby. 28th.   Recd. into the Almshous Robert Kelley   town
Pr. ordor of Wm. Phillips Esqr. one of the Oversears

March 1st.   Richd. Crouch Run   state

March 3d.   Recd. into the Almshous Becky Capron   town
Pr. ordor of Jona. L Austin One of the overseers of the poor

March 5th.   Recd. into the Almshous Elizh. Wright and her three Children Elizh.,
Salley & John   (state)
Pr. ordor of Jno. Scollay, Edwd. Tyler} Select Men
approd. of by Edwd. Proctor Esq An oversear of the poor

March 6th.   Recd. into the Almshous Margrat Lee of Ireland   state
Pr. ordor of Jno. Scollay Esqr., Jno. Andrews} Select Men
Consented to by Jona. Mason Esqr. One of the oversears}

March 7th.   <Dischd. Wm. Hall> a mistake   (state)
do.   do. Mathew Salter   ditto
9   do. Wm. Atkeson

March 12   Dischd. Michel Casady & wife   (State)

March 13th.   Dischd. John Mayhew a french man

March 1   Recd. into the Almshous Kate Simons Child Caled
Pr. ordor of Jno. Andrews, Jno. Walley} Select Men
Approd. of by

1787 March 15   Dischd. Beckey Capron of Cape Ann   (town)

March 20   Dischd. Richd. Hubbard   State

March 21   Dischd. Nancy Lovell   (town)

March 23d.   Mary Burford Run   (town)

March 26	dischd. Richd. Demry, Eliz Demry & there 2 Childn.	(state)
	Dischd. Catharina Crowley—all went Halifax	state
March 26	Dischd. Thomas Ferrell	(state)

March 27th.   Recd. into the Almshous Henry Williams A Irishman   (state)
Pr. ordor of Jno. Andrews, Edwd. Tyler} Selectmen
Consented to by Edwd. Proctor Esqr. An oversear}

March 20   Recd. into the Almshous Patty Roberts Eight years old The 8th. June
Next}   town
Pr. ordor of Mr. Saml. Whitwell an oversear of the poor

| March 30th. | Discharged Patty Garish | State |

March 30th.   Recd. into the Almshous Ceasar Merrill a Negero   state
Pr. ordor of Jno. Andrews, Edwd. Tyler} Selectmen
Approd. of by Edwd. Proctor Esqr. one of the oversears of the poor

March 31th.	Dischd. Timothy Gwier	State
Aprl. 1th.	Dischd. Margrat Boule & her Child	(State)

Aprl. 2   Recd. into the Almshous Mary Benjn. & her Child   (town)
Pr. Ordor of Mr. Jona. L Austin an oversear of the poor

Aprl. 3d.   Recd. into the Almshous Hannah Phillips a Negero   state
Pr. ordor of Jno. Scollay, Ezekl. Price} Selectmen
Approd. of by Saml. Whitwell An oversear

| Aprl. 4th. | Dischd. Nathl. Marten | Town |
| | Dischd. Mary Richardson | Town |

Aprl. 7th.   Recd. into the Almshous Mary Crafts   Town
Pr. ordor of Henry Hill Esq An oversear of the poor

1787 Aprl. 6th.   Recd. into the Almshous Roger Merithew & wife And Child   (State)
Pr. ordor of Jno. Scollay, Ebenr. Sever} Selectmen
Approd. of by Wm. Powell Esqr. one of the oversears of the poor

Aprl. 7	Margrat Lee Run	state
Aprl. 9th.	Dischd. William Jackson A Scotesh Sayler	(state)
Aprl. 10	Dischd. Wm. Durphey—90 years old as he saith	state
Aprl. 11	Dischd. Eliz Sun A Child pr. ordor Jno. Scollay Esqr.	state
Aprl. 14th.	Dischd. Isaac Corbet bound out	town

Aprl. 16th.   Recd. into the Almshous Jno. Flyn & Eliz his wife   town
Pr. ordor of Jno. Andrews, Ebenr. Sever} Select Men
approd. of by one of the oversears of the poor

Aprl. 14th.   Recd. into the Almshous Gaml. Wallis
Pr. Ordor of Jno. Scollay, Wm. Bordman} Selectmen
Approd. of by Wm. Powell Esqr. An oversear of the poor

Aprl. 16th.   Dischd. David Mongomery   (State)

Aprl. 17th.   Dischd. Eliz Flyn & Thos. Jackson   Town

Aprl. 17th.   Recd. into the Almshous James Phillips
Pr. ordor of Mr. John Codman Junr. One of the Oversears of the poor

Aprl. 20th.   Recd. into the Almshous Elizh. Star & 4 Children   (town)
Pr. ordor of J Lorg. Austin one of the oversears of the poor

April 23d.   Dischd. Leonard Shermon   State

Aprl. 21   Recd. into the Almshous Wm. Matthews his wife & Child   (state)
Pr. ordor of Jno. Andrews, Wm. Bordman} Selectmen
approvd. of by Saml. Parkman An Oversear of the poor

Aprl. 23d.   Recd. into the Almshous Peter Salvetear a Spaniard   state
Pr. ordor of Edwd. Tyler, Jno. Andrews} Selectmen
Approvd. of by Edwd. proctor An oversear of the poor

Aprl. 25th.   Dischd. <*Elizh S[…]*> Mary Crafts   (Town)

Aprl. 24th.   Recd. into The Almshous Nelly Haley   (State)
Pr. ordor of Jno. Andrews, Wm. Bordman} Selectmen
approd. of by Jno. Sweetser an oversear of the poor

1787 Aprl. 28th.   dischd. Deborah Howard   state

Aprl. 30   dischd. Henry Williams   State

May 2d.   Recd. into the Almshous Peter McGwier   State
Pr. ordor of Jno. Andrews, Wm. Bordman} Selectmen
Approd. of by Edwd. Proctor an oversear of the poor

May 2d.   Recd. into the Almshous Deborah Howard   town
Pr. ordor of Mr. Saml. Whitwell One of the oversears of the poor

May 4th.   Recd. into the Almshous Esther Baker   State
Pr. ordor of Ezekl. Price   } Selectmen
Consented to by Jona. Mason one of the oversears

Aprl. 30th.   Dischd. James Ferrell   state

May 5th.   Recd. into the Almshous Edmond Hiffernan of Ireland   State
Pr. ordor of Jno. Andrews, Wm. Bordman} Select Men
Approd. of by Edwd. Proctor Esqr. One of the oversears of the poor

May 5th.   Recd. into the Almshous Huegh McPherson his Wife & Child   (state)
Pr. ordor of Jno. Scollay Esqr., Ezekl. Price Esqr.} Selectmen
Approd. of by   One of the oversears

May 7th.   Dischd. Joseph Penete An Etallion   (state)
                 do.   Cate Simons & Child   (state)

May 7th.   Dischd. Hugh McPherson his Wife & Child   (State)

May 11	Dischd. Peggey Gallison borne at Marbelhed bound Out	town

May 12   Recd. into the Almshous Abigal Blackman   (town)
Pr. ordor of Jno. Codman Junr. one of the oversears of the poor

May 14th.   Recd. Jno. Jacobson into the Almshous
Pr. ordor of Jno. Andrews, Wm. Bordman} Selectmen
approd. by Edwd. Proctor Esqr.}

May 12th.   Dischd. Fanny Clark   (town)

May 15th.   Run Susanna Wallis state

May 16   Recd. into the Almshous Archibald McCowen Ireland   (State)
Pr. ordor of Jno. Andrews   } Selectmen
Approd. of by Edwd. Proctor One of the Oversears of the poor}

                    Dischd. Ruben Snow May 16th.   town

1787 May 17   Dischd. Sarah Lovering   (Town)

May 18th.   Dischd. Joseph Lewis a frenchman   (State)

May 18   Dischd. Wm. Mathews his Wife & Child   (State)
                    ditto Mary Wakefield & Child   (town)

May 19th.   Recd. into the Almshous Thos. Hiett   State
Pr. ordor of Jno. Andrews, Thos. Walley} Selectmen
Consented to by Jona. Mason An overseer of the poor}

May 19th.   Recd. into the Almshous Susanna Riordon   (town)
Pr. Ordor of Mr. Jno. White One of the Oversears of the poor

May 23d.   Dischd. Nelley Haley   state

May 28th.   Run *< Tho Heitt>* Archabel McCowen   state

May 29th.   *<Recd. into the Almshous Jn Pappoon borne of Elenor hale*
Pr. order of Saml. Whittwell one of the overseers of the poor>

May 28   dischd. Ann Fovell on the State}

May 29   Recd. into the Almshous Jno. papoon borne in this hous of Elenor haley
of halifax
Pr. ordor of Jno. Scolley Esq, Mr. Jno. Andrews} Selectmen
Approved of by Saml. Whitwell One of the Overseers

May 29   Recd. into the Almshous Jno. Haney on accot. of the state
Pr. ordor of Edwd. Tyler, Thomas Walley} Selectmen
Approved of by Edwd. Proctor One of the Oversears of the poor

May 31st.   Recd. Peggey Bowles & Child into the Almshous on the Accot. of the
state
Pr. ordor of Jno. Andrews, Wm. Bordman} Selectmen
approvd. of by Edwd. Proctr. Esqr. One of the oversears of the poor

June 2   Recd. into the Almshous Polley Jones & \<*daug*\> Child
Pr. ordor of Mr. Saml. Whitwell One of the oversears of the poor

June 9th.   Dischd. Ruben Gorham ⎫
         do.   Wm. Harpley   ⎬   all on the State
         do.   Jno. Jacobson   ⎭

1787 June 9th.   Recd. into the Almshous Mrs. Ann Payson   Town
Pr. ordor of Henry Hill Esqr. One of the oversears of the poor

June 12th.   Dischd. Joseph Mooyd   State

June 14th.   Dischd. Mary Covell & her two Children   state

June 15th.   Discharged Peggy Castor   Town

June 19th.   Dischd. Mary Pool—the wife of Saml. Poole   Town

June 19th.   Recd. into the Almshous Vilot Gardenor & Child Negero   State
Pr. ordor of Jno. Andrews, Wm. Bordman} Select Men
Approvd. of by Edwd. Proctor Esq One of the Overseers of the Poor

June 20th.   Dischd. Susanna Cowling & her two Children   State

June 21th.   Recd. into the Almshous Deborah Canser from Bridgwater but Belongs
to Marshfeild
Pr. Ordor of Henry Hill Esq One of the oversears of the poor

June 27th.   Dischd. Thomas Smith (1 Eye)   state
                  ditto Thomas Hiatt   do.

June 28th.   Dischd. Peter Salvetear a Spanyard   state

June 29th.   Recd. into the Almshous Eliz Ives & Mehetable Wilds   State
Pr. ordor of Ezek Price & Jno. Scollay Selectmen
Mr. Jno. White an oversear of the Poor

July 2d.   dischd. Polley Roberts and Son   (Town)

July 2d.   dischd. James Pike   town

July 2d.   Recd. into the Almshous Daniel Mors   State
Pr. ordor of Ezekl. Price, one of the Selectmen
approd. by Mr. Saml. Whitwell

July 7th.   Recd. into the Almshous Agnes Should be Nancey And not Agness Dixey
Pr. ordor of Jona. L Austen one of the oversears of the poor   Town

July 9th.   Dischd. Edwd. Smith   (State)

July 11   Elizh. Ives Run   (State)

July 11th.   Recd. into the Almshous Mary Welch   Town
Pr. ordor of Jona. L Austen Esq One of the Oversears of the poor

1787 July 12   Dischd. Betsey Tevet bound out   State

July 12   Recd. into the Almshous Mary Watts   (Town)
Pr. ordor of Edwd. Proctor one of the oversears of the poor

June 15th.   Recd. into the Almshous Richd. Hubbard a Brittan   (state)
Pr. ordor of Jno. Andrewis, Wm. Boardman} Selectmen
Approd. of By Edwd. Proctor Esq One of the Oversears &c

July 12th.   Dischd. Richd. Hubbard   State

July 16th.   Recd. into the Almshous John Chaimbers   State
Pr. ordor of Jno. Scollay, Jno. Andrews} Selectmen
Consented to by Edwd. Proctor One of the oversears of the poor

July 17th.   Dischd. Mehetable Wilds   (State)

March 15th.   Recd. into the Almshous Ann Sample   (State)
Pr. ordor of Jno. Scollay Esqr., Mr. Jno. Andrews} Selectmen
Approd. of by Saml. Whitwell One of the Oversears of the poor

May 7th.   Recd. into the Almshous Mary Fulker   (State)
Pr. ordor of Jno. Scollay Esq, Mr. Jno. Andrews} Selectmen
Approd. of by Saml. Whitwell One of the oversears of the poor

July 18th.   Dischd. Mary Garrell   (town)

July 10th.   Ann Sample Run   (State)
16   Dischd. Ann Fovell   do.

July 19th.   Recd. into the Almshous Ann Black from Nwfoundland   state
Pr. ordor of Jno. Scollay Esq, Mr. Jno. Andrews} Selectmen
Approd. of By Jno. Sweetser One of the oversears of the poor

July 20th.   Dischd. Peter McGwier   (state)

July 23   Recd. into the Almshous James Cuningham 15 years old   (state)
Pr. ordor of Jno. Andrews, Jno. Walley Esqr.} Selectmen
Approved of by Edwd. Edes one of the Oversears of the poor

July 21   Recd. into the Almshous Frances Clarrage   (state)
Pr. ordor of Jno. Scollay Esqr.   } Selectman
Approd. of By Wm. Powell Esq One of the oversears of the poor}

July 25th.   Recd. into the Almshous Lydia Farnum   town
Pr. ordor of Isaac Smith Esqr. one of the oversears of the poor

July 28th.   Recd. into the Almshous Anna Antine   Town
Pr. ordor of Mr. Jno. White One of the oversears of the poor

July 28th.   Frances Clarage Run   State

July 28th.   James Cuningham Run   State

Augt. 2d.   Recd. into the Almshous Mary Phillips   (Town)
Pr. ordor of Mr. Jno. Codman Junr. One of the oversears of the poor

Augt. 2d.   Dischd. James Osborn a boy Bound out   (Town)

Augt. 2d.   Ann Corbet Run

Augt. 4   Dischd. Josh., Elizh. & Lydia Goodrage Mrs. Star's three Childn. Sent to
Beverly—as the laws direct   (Townes Expence)

Augt. 6   Recd. into the Almshous Mathew Riodan, Thos. Carton, Mary
Hanegan, Betsey McGim, & Katharina McMehan
Pr. Ordor of Jno. Scollay Esqr., Mr. Jno. Andrews} Selectmen
Approd. of by Saml. Whitwell One of the Oversears of the poor

Augt. 7th.   Recd. into the Almshous James Calehan A Seman   State
Pr. ordor of Mr. Jno. Andrews, Jno. Scollay Esq.} Selectmen
Consented to by Edwd. Proctor Esqr. One of the Oversears of the poor

Augt. 8th.   Recd. into the Almshous Peggy Higgins from Ireland   (State)
Pr. ordor of Mr. Jno. Andrews, Capt. Edwd. Tyler} Selectmen
Approd. of by Edwd. Proctor Esqr., One of the Oversears of the Poor

Augt. 8th.   Dischd. Thos. Carton   State
          Mathew Rioden, Betsey McGim, Mary Hanegin & Katharina
McMehene   All the States

Augt. 10th.   Dischd. Thos. Corbet a boy   (town)

Augt. 10th.   Recd. into the Almshous Moses McGrath of Ireland   State
Pr. ordor of Jno. Scollay Esqr., Mr. Jno. Andrews} Selectmen
Edwd. Proctor Esqr. One of the Oversears of the poor

Augt. 10th.   Edwd. Hafferon Run   State

1787 Augt. 10th.   Recd. into the Almshous Thomas Branden from Ireland   State
Pr. ordor of Mr. Jno. Andrews, Mr. Wm. Bordman} Selectmen
approd. of by Edwd. Proctor Esqr. one of the overseers of the poor

*<Augt. 11th.   Dischd. Mary Benjman who Came into the Almshous Aprl. 2d. 1787 (She
Returnd the Next Morning the 12th.>*

June 17th.   Recd. into the Almshous Mary McCurdy   State
Pr. ordor of Mr. Jno. Andrews, Mr. Moses Grant} Selectmen
approd. of by Edwd. Proctor One of the Oversears of the poor}

Augt. 16th.   Recd. into the Almshous Henry Croach A German   State
Pr. ordor of Jno. Scollay Esqr., Mr. Ebenr. Seaver} Selectmen
Approvd. of by Mr. Saml. Whitwell One of the oversears of the poor}

Augt. 16th.   Recd. into the Almshous Sarah Gardiner   town
Pr. ordor of Edwd. Proctor Esqr. One of the Oversears of the poor

Augt. 18th.   Recd. into the Almshous Peter Phillips from Canady   (State)
Pr. ordor of Mr. Harbottle Dorr, Capt. Edwd. Tyler} Selectmen
Approd. of by Mr. Jno. White One of the overseers of the poor}

Augt. 20th.   Recd. into the Almshous George Davis 14 Months old   (State)
Pr. ordor of Jno. Scollay Esq, Mr. Jno. Andrews} Selectmen
Approd. of by Mr. Saml. Whitwell One of the overseers of the poor}

Augt. 21st.   Recd. into the Almshous William Preehard   (town)
Pr. ordor of Wm. Powell Esqr. one of the Oversears of the poor

Augt. 2[4]th.   Jane Russell Run   (State)

Augt. 27th.　　　　Recd. into the Almshous Joseph Moeed　　　　(State)
Pr. ordor of Jno. Scolley Esqr., Capt. Edwd. Tyler} Selectmen
Approvd. of by Edwd. Proctor Esqr. One of the oversears of the poor}

Augt. 28th.　　　　Recd. into the Almshous Mary Gerrell　　　　(town)
Pr. ordor of Wm. Powell Esqr. One of the oversears of the poor

July 13th.　　　　Recd. into the Almshous Saml. Duncalf　　　　State
Pr. ordor of Mr. Jno. Andrews, Mr. Willm. Boardman} Selectmen
[Appr]od. by Saml. Whitwell one of the oversears of the poor

<1787 Sept. 3d.　　Recd. Sarah Ears into the Almshous　　　　*(town)*
Pr. ordor of Edwd. Proctr. Esqr. one of the oversears>
See below on the State accot—Sary Smith & Not Ears

Septr. 3d.　　　　Recd. into the Almshous Charles Cathan of Ireland　　　　(state)
Pr. ordor of Ezekl. Price Esqr., Mr. Jno. Andrews} Selectmen
approd. of by Edwd. Proctor Esqr. One of the Oversears of the poor}

Septr. 3d.　　　　Recd. into the Almshous Sarah Jackson　　　　State
Pr. ordor of Jno. Andrews Esq, Wm. Bordman} Selectmen
Approd. by Edwd. Proctor Esqr. One of the oversears of the poor

Septr. 7th.　　　　Recd. into the Almshous Richd. Carney of waterford　　　　State
Pr. ordor of Jno. Scollay Esqr., Mr. Jno. Andrews} Selectmen
Approd. by Edwd. proctor Esqr. An Oversear of the poor

Septr. 8th.　　　　Recd. into the Almshous Allanor ODowling a Irish woman　　　　State
Pr. ordor of Edwd. Tyler, Mr. Jno. Andrews} Select men
Approd. of by Edwd. Proctor Esqr. An oversear of the poor

<Septr. 12th.　　　　Hannah McKinzie And Child Run　　　　*State>*

Septr. 15th.　　　　Dischd. Allinor ODowling An Irish woman　　　　State

Septr. 17th.　　　　Dischd. Ann Antine　　　　town

Septr. 17th.　　　　Recd. into the Almshous Saml. Coes of danvers　　　　town
Pr. Ordor of Edwd. Proctor Esqr. One of the Oversears of the poor

Septr. 18th.　　　　Peggy Higgings Run　　　　(State)

Septr. 19th.　　　　Dischd. Peter Phillips a frenchman　　　　state

Septr. 21th.　　　　Recd. into the Almshous Jack A Negeroman　　　　State
Pr. ordor Mr. Jno. Andrews, Thos. Walley Esqr.} Selectmen
Approvd. of by Wm. Powell An oversear of the poor}

Septr. 14th.　　　　Recd. into the Almshous Sarah Kipping　　　　State
Pr. ordor of Harbottel Dorr, Mr. Jno. Andrews } Selectmen
Approd. by Jno. White One of the Oversears of the poor}

Octr. 3d.　　　　Recd. into the Almshous John McGough of Ireland　　　　state
Pr. ordor of Capt. Edwd. Tyler, Mr. Jno. Andrews} Select Men
Cosented to by Jonathon Mason Esq One of the Oversears of the poor}

Octr. 6th. 1787 Recd. into the Almshous Nathl. Stone   (Town)
Pr. ordor of Edwd. Proctor Esqr. One of the Oversears of the Poor

Octr. 9th.   Recd. into the Almshous Catharina Symons & her Female Child} states
Pr. ordor of John Andrews Eqr., Wm. Bordman Esqr.} Selectmen
Approvd. of by Edwd. Proctor Esqr. One of the Oversears of the poor

Octr. 9th.   Recd. into the Almshous Slone (out of the work hous) (town)
Pr. ordor of Mr. Jno. Sweetser One of the oversears of the poor

Octr. 8th.   Recd. into the Almshous Mary Wakefield   town
Pr. ordor of John Sweetser Esq one of the oversears of the poor

Octr. 13th.   Discharged Roger Merewthew his Wife & Child And kept them one
weak on the books to pay the Cost of the Provetions Provided for there passage home
                    State

Octr. 17   Recd. into the Almshous Timothy Gwier of Ireland (State)
Pr. Ordor of John Scollay Esqr., Mr. Jno. Andrews} Selectmen
Approvd. of by Edwd. Proctor Esq} an overseer

Octr. 17th.   Recd. into the Almshous James Roberts A boy was 6 years old the 30
July 1787   (town)
Pr. ordor of Jona. L Austen an oversear

Septr. 26th.   Recd. into the Almshous Phillis A Negero Woman state
Pr. ordor of Jno. Scolay Esqr., Mr. Jno. Andrews} Selectmen
approvd. of by Mr. Saml. Parkman An oversear of the poor

Octr. 16   Recd. into the Almshous Eliz. Robertson   (town)
Pr. ordor of Mr. Jno. Codman, An oversear of the poor

Octr. 18th.   Recd. into the Almshous Joseph Moffatt   town
Pr. Ordor of Henry Hill Esqr. One of the Oversears of the poor

Octo. 18   Recd. into the Almshous Venus Stanney a Negero woman (State)
Pr. ordor of Ezekel Price Esqr., Mr. Jno. Andrews} Selectmen
Approvd. of by Mr. Jno. White One of the oversears the poor}

Octr. 18th.   Recd. into the Almshous Mary Brown   State
Pr. ordor of Ezel. Price Esqr.   } Selectmen
approvd. of by Jonathan Mason} one of the oversears

Octr. 23d.   Recd. into the Almshous Nabby Lewis   (town)
Pr. ordor of Wm. Powell Esqr. An Oversear

Octr. 23   dischd. Mary Browne   (State)

Octr. 24   Recd. into the Almshous Kate Storer An Negero (State)
Pr. ordor of Mr. Jno. Andrews, Mr. Wm. Bordman} Selectmen
Approvd. of by Saml. Whitwell One of the oversears of the poor}
15 years old the 15th. Aprl. 1787

Octr. 24   Dischd. out of the Almshous Robert Kelley (town)

Octr. 25th.   Recd. into the Almshous Wm. Harpley   (State)
Pr. ordor of Mr. Edwd. Tyler, Mr. Jno. Andrews} Selectmen
Consented to by Mr. Saml. Whitwell One of the oversears of the poor

Octr. 21th.   Recd. into the Almshous Abigal Whittel   State
Pr. ordor of Edwd. Tyler, Mr. Jno. Andrews} Selectmen
Approd. of by Edwd. Proctor Esqr. One of the Oversears of the poor}

Octr. 26   Recd. into the Almshous Kezia Chaffey   (State)
Pr. ordor of Mr. Harbottle Dorr, Capt. Edwd. Tyler} Select men
Consented to by Mr. Jno. White an overseer}

Octr. 28   Sarah Jackson Run   (State)

Octr. 29th.   Recd. into the Almshous Thos. Ratton & wife   (State)
Pr. ordor of Jno. Scollay Esqr., Mr. Jno. Andrews} Selectmen
Approd. of By Saml. Whitwell One of the oversears}

Octr. 31   Received into the Almshous Richd. Colbert   (State)
Pr. ordor of Jno. Scollay Esqr., Mr. Jn Andrews} Selectmen
Approd. of by Saml. Parkman one of the Oversears}

Novr. 1th.   Elizh. Dunker 8 years of age Run   State

Novr. 4   Elizh. Wright Run

Novr. 7th.   Recd. into The Almshous Ann Payson   State
Pr. ordor of Jno. Scollay, Mr. Jno. Andrews} Selectmen
Approvd. of by Jona. Mason Esqr. One of the oversears of the poor

Novr. 4   dischd. Polley Legalley bound out   State

Novr. 8th.   Recd. into the Almshous Jno. Bothesley A frenchman   State
Pr. ordor of Mr. Jno. Andrews, Mr. Jno. Wolley} Selectmen
Approd. by Edwd. Proctor Esqr. An oversears of the poor

Novr. 22th. 1787   <Morrison Run
9   Saml [...] Dischd.   state>
                    Robt. [...] do.

Novr. 10th.   Recd. into the Almshous Mary Pain   State
Pr. ordor of Jno. Scollay Esq, Thos. Walley Esq} Selectmen
Approd. of by Saml. Whitwell One of the oversears of the poor

Novr. 13th.   Recd. into the Almshouse Partrick Drummond   state
Pr. ordor of Mr. Jno. Andrews, Mr. Wm. Pordman} Selectmen
Approd. of by Edwd. Proctor Esqr. One of the oversears}

July 23d.   Recd. into the Almshous Rebecca Turpen   Town
Pr. ordor of Mr. Jno. White An overseer of the poor

Novr. 15th.   Dischd. James Roberts a boy Bound out

Novr. 15th.　　　Recd. into the Almshous Willm. Durphy　　　State
Pr. ordor of Jno. Andrews, Wm. Boardman} Selectmen
approd. of by Mr. Saml. Whitwell One of the oversears of the poor}

Novr. 19th.　　　Dischd. Partrick Drummond　　　State

Novr. 22d.　　　Recd. into the Almshous Lydia Hogetts　　　(State)
Pr. ordor of Edwd. Tyler, Ebenr. Sever} Selectmen
Approd. of by Edwd. Proctor Esq one of the Oversears}

<Novr. 24th.　　　*Dischd. Betsey Wier A Negero Girl bound out*　　　*(state)*>

Novr. 24th.　　　Recd. into the Almshous Marthor Conner　　　dartmouth
Pr. ordor of Edwd. Proctor Esqr. One of the oversears of the poor

Novr. 26th.　　　Reced. into the Almshous Elizh. Smith & William Her Son 2 1/2 years old
Pr. ordor of Jno. Andrews, Wm. Boardman} Selectmen
Approd. by Edwd. Proctor Esqr. one of the oversears

Novr. 26th.　　　Receed. into the Almshous Margrat Leigh　　　state
Pr. ordor of Jno. Anrews, Jno. Scollay Esqr.} Selectmen
Approvd. of by Edwd. Proctor Esqr. one of the oversears of the poor

Novr. 26　　　Recd. into the Almshous Smurdock Campbell　　　(state)
Pr. ordor of Jno. Andrews, Wm. Bordman} Selectmen
Approd. of By Edwd. Proctor Esqr. one of the oversears of the poor}

Novr. 28th.　　　Recd. into the Almshous Mary Burford　　　Town
Pr. ordor of Edwd. Proctor Esqr. One of the Oversears of the poor

Novr. 28th.　　　Recd. into the Almshous Jno. McKinzie　　　(State)
Pr. ordor of Jno. Scollay Esqr., Thos. Walley Esqr.} Selectmen
Consented to by Jno. Mason Esqr. one of the oversears}

Novr. 28th.　　　Recd. into the Almshous James McCormick from Ireland　　　State
Pr. ordor of Jno. Scollay Esqr., Mr. Wm. Bordman} Selectmen
Consented to by Jona. Mason Esq One of the oversears of the poor}

Novr. 28th.　　　Recd. into the Almshous Willm. Sharp & wife　　　state
Pr. ordor of Jno. Scollay Esq., Mr. Wm. Bordman} Select Men}
Consented to by Mr. Jno. Codman One of the oversears of the poor}

Novr. 30　　　Dischd. Molley Watts　　　Town

Decr. 1　　　Recd. into the Almshous Mary Barns　　　(town)
Pr. ordor of Jno. White, an oversear

Decr. 1th.　　　Recd. into the Almshous Eliz Williams
Pr. Ordor of Jno. Scoley Esqr.　　} Selectmen
Approd. of by Saml. Whitwell One of the oversears of the poor}

Novr. 22d.　　　Recd. into the Almshous Jno. Horn　　　State
Pr. ordor of Ezel. Price Esqr.　　} Selectmen
Consented to by Mr. Saml. Whitwell One of the oversears}

Decr. 5th.　　　　Recd. into the Almshous Merian Serle A Negero　　　　(State)
Pr. ordor of Mr. Jno. Andrews, Thos. Walley Esq} Selectmen
Consented to by Jona. Mason Esqr. One of the Oversears of the poor}

Decr. 4th.　　　　Recd. into the Almshous Benjn. Eddy his wife Judath Eddy & Thankfull
Eddy with four Childn. Viz Sibdal 10 years old, Barsalel 7 years old, Luther 6 do.
[*i.e., years old*], Eunice 3 do. [*i.e., years old*]
Pr. ordor of Jno. Scollay, Jno. Andrews} Selectmen
Approd. of by Edwd. Proctor Esqr. Oversear of the poor

Decr. 6th.　　　　Dischd. 2 of Mrs. Wrights Children　　　　State

1787 Decr. 6th.　　　Recd. into the Almshous Susanna Wallace　　　　State
Pr. ordor of Jno. Scollay Esq, Mr. Willm. Bordman} Selectmen
Approd. By Edwd. Proctor Esqr. One of the oversears of the poor}

Decr. 6th.　　　　Recd. into the Almshous Jane Russell　　　　State
Pr. ordor of Mr. Jno. Andrews, Jno. Scollay Esq} Selectmen
Approd. of by Edwd. Proctor Esqr. Oversear of the poor}

Decr. 8　　　　Recd. into the Almshous Sarah Walnock　　　　State
Pr. ordor of Mr. Jno. Andrews　　　} Selectmen
Approd. of by Edwd. Proctor Esq An oversear of the poor}

December 10th.　　　Recd. into the Almshous Henry Kendell & Ruth his Wife
Pr. ordor of Ezek Price Esqr.　　　} Selectmen
Approd. of by Saml. Whitwell One of the oversears of the poor}

Decr. 3d.　　　　Recd. into the Almshous Mary the wife of Willm. Pryer　　　　(State)
Pr. ordor of Jno. Andrews, Thos. Walley Esqr.} Selectmen
Approd. By Edwd. Proctor Esqr. One of the oversears}

Decr. 12　　　　Recd. into the Almshous Eliz Berry　　　　State
Pr. ordor of Jno. Andrews Esq, Mr. Ebenr. Sever} Selectmen
Approd. by Jno. Sweetser Esq One of the Oversears of the poor}

Decr. 3d.　　　　Recd. into the Almshous Thos. Milliken　　　　(Town)
Pr. ordor of Edwd. Proctor} oversear

Decr. 12th.　　　　Recd. into the Almshous Thos. More　　　　(State)
Pr. ordor of Mr. Jno. Andrews, Mr. Ebenr. Sever} Selectmen
Approvd. of by Mr. Jona. L. Auston one of the oversears of the poor

<Decr. 13th.　　　*Run Judath Eddy 17 years of age*　　　　*state*
Returnd. the Next [...]>

Decr. 14th.　　　　Recd. into the Almshous Alice Stoddar　　　　(Town)
Pr. ordor of Mr. Jno. White (oversear)

Decr. 15th.　　　　Recd. into the Almshous Ann Delaney & her Child　　　　state
Pr. ordor of Ezekl. Price, Mr. Wm. Bordman} selectmen
Approd. of by Jona. Mason Esqr. One of the Oversears of the poor}

Decr. 19th.　　　　Recd. into the Almshous Jno. Legalley
Pr. ordor of Thos. Walley Esqr., Mr. Ebenr. Seaver} Selectmen
Approd. of by Edwd. Proctor Esqr. one of the oversears of the poor}

1787 Decr. 20th.   Recd. into the Almshous Thos. Loring of this   (town)
Pr. ordor of Jona. Mason Esqr. One of the oversears of the poor

Decr. 20th.   Recd. into the Almshous Sarah Leachman   state
Pr. ordor of Mr. Edwd. Tyler, Mr. Jno. Andrews} Selectmen
Approd. of by Edwd. Proctor Esq One of the oversears of the poor}

Decr. 20th.   Recd. into the Almshous John durphy of Ireland   (State)
Pr. ordor of Mr. Jno. Andrews, Capt. Edwd. Tyler} Selectmen
approd. of by Edwd. Proctor Esqr. One of the Oversears of the poor}

Decr. 20th.   Recd. into the Almshous Hipzibah Atkins   (town)
Pr. ordor of Jno. White} oversear

Decr, 21   Recd. into The Almshous Jno. Williams he must be Taken Care of where
he is until he Can be Movd.   (State)
Pr. ordor of Jno. Scollay Esqr., Mr. Jno. Andrews} Selectmen
Consented to by Edwd. Proctor Esqr. One of the Oversears of the poor}

Decr. 18th.   <Ann [Ryan] Run>   state

Decr. 20th.   Recd. into the Almshous Timothy Brown a Clargeman   state
Pr. Ordor of Mr. Jno. Andrews, Thos. Walley Esqr.} select Men
approd. by Mr. Saml. Whitwell One of the Oversears of the poor}

Decr. 19th.   Recd. into the Almshous Susanna Franks & 2 Children whose husband
Was in the British Armey, A German}   state
Pr. ordor of Jno. Andrews Esqr., Mr. Ebenr. Sever} Selectmen
Approd. of by Edwd. Proctor Esq One of the Oversears of the poor

Decr. 20th.   Recd. into the Almshous on the State Accot. Hannah Waples   state
Pr. ordor of Mr. Harbottle Dorr, Mr. Edwd. Tyler} Selectmen
Approd. of by Mr. Jno. White Oversear}

Decr. 19th.   Ann Black Run   (State)

Decr. 26   Recd. into the Almshous Marthor Greer   State
Pr. ordor of Jno. Scollay Esqr., Mr. Jno. Andrews} Selectmen
approd. by Mr. Saml. Whitwell One of the oversears of the poor}

Decr. 26   Recd. into the Almshous Margrat Conerlly 15 years old   State
Mr. Jno. Andrews, Mr. Ebenr. Seaver} Selectmen
Consented to by Edwd. Proctor One of the Oversears}

1787 decr. 27th.   Recd. into the Almshous Richd. Crouch   (state)
Pr. ordor of Jno. Andrews Esqr., Mr. Ebenr. Seaver} Selectmen
Approd. of by Edwd. Proctor Esq one of the oversears}

Decr. 28th.   Recd. into the Almshous William Sprag   (town)
Pr. ordor of Mr. Jno. Codman Junr. oversear

Decr. 31th.   Recd. into the Almshous Barney Oliver   (state)
Pr. ordor of Jno. Scollay Esqr., Mr. Jno. Andrews} Selectmen
Approd. of by Edwd. Proctor Esq Oversear}

Decr. 31th.   Dischd. Margrat Conerley 15 years old by ordor of   (state)
Mr. Jno. Andrews, Mr. Ebenr. Sever} Selectmen
Edwd. proctor Esqr.

1788 Jany. 1th.   Recd. into the Almshous Betey Bruer   State
Pr. ordor of Jno. Scolley Esqr., Thos. Walley Esqr.} Selectmen
Approd. of by Edward Proctor Esqr. one of the oversears of the poor}
Jany. 12th. her Child

Jany. 4th.   Recd. into the Almshous Jno. Fitzgerrell   State
Pr. ordor of Jno. Andrews, Mr. Wm. Bordman} Selectmen
Approd. by Edwd. Proctor Esqr. One of the oversears of the poor}

Jany. 5th.   Recd. into the Almshous Mary Tuttle   (Town)
Pr. ordor of Henry Hill Esqr. One of the oversears of the poor

Jany. 4th.   Dischd. Thos. Milliken   (Town)

Jany. 9th.   Dischd. Patty Roberts bound out   (Town)

Jany. 9th.   Recd. into the Almshous Mary Sanders   (State)
Pr. ordor of Edwd. Tyler, Mr. Jno. Andrews} Selectmen
Approd. of by Edwd. Proctor Esqr. An Oversear of the poor}

Jany. 9th.   Recd. into the Almshous Elizh. Woodbridg Belonging to Marbelhed As
She Saith}   town
Pr. ordor of Jona. Mason Esqr. One of the oversears of the poor

Jany. 10th.   Dischd. Thos. Wallis a boy bound out   Town
                    Dischd. Nathaniel Stone   do.

Jany. 10th.   Recd. into the Almshous Nathl. & Betsey Pierce   town
Pr. ordor of Jno. White Esqr. (Oversear)

Jany. 11   Recd. into the Almshous Frans. Clarrage & his wife Mary
Pr. ordor of Jno. Scollay Esqr., Jno. Andrews Esq} Selectmen
approd. by Saml. Whitwell & Saml. Parkman 2 oversears}

1788 Jany. 12th.   Recd. into the Almshous Fredrck Ayers   (Town)
Pr. ordor of Henry Hill Esqr. (oversear)

Jany. 9th   Recd. into the Almshous Daniel Benjman   state
Pr. ordor of Jno. Brown Esqr.   } Selectmen
Approd. of by Jno. Sweetser Esqr. One of the Oversears of the poor}

Jany. 12th.   Dischd. Barney Oliver   State

Jany. 13th.   Dischd. Fredrick Ayers   Town

Jany. 14th.   Recd. into the Almshous Mary Harper   state
Pr. ordor of Jno. Scollay Esqr., Jno. Andrews Esqr.} Selectmen
Apprd. of Jno. Sweetser Esqr. An oversear of the poor}

Jany. 17th.   Dischd. Wm. Baldrage bound out   (Town)

Jany. 21.   Recd. into the Almshous Lucia Willes   (Town)
Pr. ordor of Edwd. Proctor Esq oversear

Jany. 22d.   Recd. into the Almshous Grace Trott a Negero   (State)
Pr. ordor of Ezek. Price, Mr. Wm. Bordman} Selectmen
Opprod. of by Jona. Mason Esq One of the oversears of the poor}

Jany. 3d.   Recd. into the Almshous   Lishman's Child   State
Pr. ordor of Ezekl. Price Esqr., Mr. Ebenr. Seaver} Selectmen
Approd. By Jona. Mason Esq One of the oversears of the poor

Jany. 10tl .   Recd. into the Almshous Jno. Wintor—A Molatto   State
Pr. ordor of Ezekl. Price Esq, Mr. Ebenr. Seaver} Selectmen
Approd. by Jona. Mason Esq One of the oversears of the poor

Jany. 12th.   Recd. into the Almshous   Brewer's Child Born in the hous   State
Pr. ordor of Ezekl. Price Esqr., Mr. Ebenr. Seaver} Selectmen
Approd. of by Jona. Mason Esqr. One of the oversears of the poor}

Jany. 14th.   Recd. into the Almshous   Downing A Child Born in the hous
Pr. ordor of Ezekl. Price Esq, Mr. Ebenr. Seaver} Selectmen
Approd. of by Jno. Mason Esq One of the oversears of the poor}

Jany. 26   Recd. into the Almshous Elizh. Lewis   State
Pr. ordor of Jno. Scolay Esqr., Ezekl. Price Esq} Selectmen
Consented Pr. Jona. Mason Esq one of the oversears of the poor}

1788 Jany. 30th.   Recd. into the Almshous Morris McLocklen from Ireland   (state)
Pr. ordor of Jno. Scollay Esq, Mr. Ebenr. Sever} Selectmen
Approd. of by Edwd. Proctor Esq Overseear}

<Feby. 1th.   Recd into the Almshous   A Child about 9 Months old left in Mr. Burts
Entery
Mr. Jno. White one of the oversears of the poor}>

Jany. 14th.   <Dischd. Eliz [Berry?]>   State

Jany. 22d.   Recd. into the Almshous James Gardner 7 years old the Middle of feby.
1788}   State
Pr. ordor of Capt. Edwd. Tyler, Jn Andrews Esqr.} Selectmen
Consented to pr. Jona. Mason Esqr. One of the Oversears}

Feby. 2d.   Recd. into the Almshous Mary Lisanby   (town)
Pr. ordor of Mr. Jno. White An overseear of the poor

Feby. 1   Recd. into the Almshous Wm. Stevens A Child   State
Pr. ordor of Mr. Harbottle Dorr, Capt. Edwd. Tyler} Selectmen
Consented to by Mr. Jno. White One of the Oversears of the poor}

Feby. 6th.   Recd. into the Almshous Negero Adam   State
Pr. ordor of Jno. Scollay Esqr., Capt. Edwd. Tyler} Selectmen
approd. of by Edwd. Proctor Esq One of the Oversears of the poor}

Feby. 7th.   Recd. into the Almshous Wm. Jones
Pr. ordor of Mr. Harbottle dorr, Captn. Edwd. Tyler} Selectmen
approd. of By Edwd. Proctor Esqr. One of the oversears of the poor}

Feby. 7th. Recd. into the Almshous Ann Mayhew with Henry Mahew And An
Infant Child} State
Pr. ordor of Mr. Harbottle Dorr, Capt. Edwd. Tyler} Selectmen
Consented to by Mr. Jno. White one of the oversears of the poor

Feby. 9th. Recd. into the Almshous Catherina Cook state
Pr. ordor of Jno. Scollay Esq, Mr. Wm. Bordman} Selectmen
Approd. of by Edwd. Edds one of the oversears of the poor}

Feby. 11 Recd. into the Almshous John Mansfield State
Pr. ordor of Jno. Scollay Esqr., Ezekl. Price Esqr.} Selectmen
Approd. by Jona. Mason Esqr. one of the oversears of the poor}

1788 Feby. 1 Recd. into the Almshous Nancy Challandor a Child 9 Months old
Pr. ordor of Thos. Walley Esqr., Jno. Scollay Esqr.} Selectmen State
Approd. of by Mr. Jno. White One of the oversears of the poor}

Feby. 9th. Recd. into the Almshous Polley Greenleaf Davis (State)
Pr. ordor of Ezekl. Price Esqr., Mr. Wm. Bordman} Selectmen
approd. of by Jona. Mason Esq one of the oversears of the poor}

Feby. 12th. dischd. Elizh. Woodbrig belonging to Marbelhead

Feby. 13th. Recd. into the Almshous James McQwin Scotland (State)
Pr. ordor of Jno. Scollay Esq, Thos. Walley Esq} Selectmen
Consented to by Edwd. Proctor Esq One of the oversears of the poor}

Feby. 13th. Recd. into the Almshous Elizh. Dawson (Town)
Pr. ordor of Jona. Mason One of the oversears of the poor

<Feby. 13 *Dischd. Judah Eddy* (State)>

Feby. 15th. Recd. into the Almshous Jno. Peirce State
Pr. ordor of Jno. Scollay } Selectmen
approd. of by Edwd. Proctor Esqr. One of the oversears of the poor}

Feby. 15th. Recd. into the Almshous Rachel Drew, Charls drew years old &
Catharina drew
Pr. ordor of Harbottle Dorr, Capt. Edwd. Tylor} Selectmen
Approd. of by Mr. Jno. White One of the oversears}

Feby. 18 Recd. into the Almshous Mary Essenger Town
Pr. ordor of Henry Hill Esqr. one of the oversears of the poor

Feby. 21th. Dischd. Mary Sanders State

Feby. 20 Recd. into the Almshous Barnibus Oliver state
Pr. ordor of Jno. Scollay Esq, Mr. Ebenr. Seaver} Selectmen
Approd. of by Edwd. Proctor Esqr. An oversear of the poor}

Feby. 23d. Recd. into the Michel Rennals of Ireland State
Pr. ordor of Jno. Scollay Esqr., Mr. Wm. bordman} Selectmen
Approd. of by Edwd. Proctor Esqr. One of the oversears of the poor}

1788 Feby. 23 Recd. into the Almshous A Child Called Sarah Mann 3 years old the 3d.
of feby. 1788 State
Pr. ordor of Ezekl. Price Esq } Selectmen
Consented to pr. Jona. Mason Esqr. One of the Overseers of the poor}

Feby. 26	Recd. into the Almshous Jno. Mayhew A frenchman	State

Pr. ordor of Jno. Scollay Esq, Ezek Price Esqr.} Selectmen
Consented To by Jona. Mason Esq One of the oversears of the poor}

Feby. 28th.	Recd. into the Almshous Mary Black	(state)

Pr. ordor of Jno. Scollay Esq, Mr. Ebenr. Seaver} Selectmen
approvd. of by Edwd. Proctor Esqr. one of the oversears of the poor}

Feby. 27	Recd. into the Almshous A Molatto Child borne of Polly Greenleaf Davis who is Called }	state

Jno. Scollay Esqr., Thos. Walley Esqr.} Selectmen
Approd. of by Edwd. Proctor Esq One of the oversears of the poor}

Feby. 27th.	Dischd. Barnebus Oliver A portgea	state
	Dischd. Betsey Tevet 9 years old bound out	do.
	Dischd. Nathl. Peirce 9 year old Bound out	Town

March 3d.	Dischd. Jno. Durphey	State

March 3	Recd. into the Almshous Mary Webb from the work hous	Town

Pr. ordor of Wm. Powell Esqr. An oversear of the poor

March 4th.	Recd. into the Almshous Thos. Hancock	State

Pr. ordor of Jno. Scollay Esqr., Mr. Wm. Bordman} Selectmen
Approd. of by Edwd. Proctor Esqr. An oversear of the poor}

Marh. 5th.	Recd. into the Almshous Jno. Connor for 2 weaks	state

Pr. ordor of Jno. Scoley, Capt. Edwd. Tyler} Selectmen
Consented to by Jona. Mason Esq one of the oversears of the poor}

March 5th.	Recd. into the Almshous Beckey Thomes, born in Nw. york	state
	ditto a Child Called Matthew	state

Pr. ordor of Jno. Scollay Esqr., Mr. Wm. Boardman} Selectmen
Approd. by Jona. Mason Esq one of the oversears of the poor

March 5th.	Recd. into the Almshous a blind Child Called Polley Amory	state

Pr. ordor of Jno. Scollay Esqr., Mr. Ebenr. Seaver} Selectmen
approd. of by Jno. Sweetser Esqr. an oversear of the poor}

1788 March 7th.	Recd. into the Almshous Abigal Hubbard	town

Pr. ordor of Jno. Codman Juner One of the oversears of the poor}

March 5th.	Recd. into the Almshous Abigal Hurley a garl	State

Pr. ordor of Jno. Scollay Esq, Jno. Andrews Esq} Select Men
Apprvd. of by   one of the oversears of the poor

March 10th.	Abigal Hubbard Run	Town

March 15th.	Jno. McGoff Run	State

March 15th.	Dischd. James Calehon	State

March 17	Dischd. Jno. Botherley	State

March 15	dischd. Thos. Hancock	State

March 18th.	Dischd. Cala Drew bound out	State

March 18	Dischd. Henry Kendel & Ruth his wife	State
March 18th.	Dischd. Meriah Serl a Negero	state
March 18th.	Dischd. Sarah Lishman & Child	state
March 21st.	Recd. into the Aalmshous James Henly A Child born in the Hous this	
day		state

Pr. ordor of Jno. Scollay Esqr., Jno. Andrews Esqr. } Selectmen
Approd. of by Edwd. Proctor Esqr. oversear

March 20	Dischd. Abigal Hurley a garl bound out	State
March 24th.	Reeceive James Cornish into the Almshous	Town

Pr. ordor of Jona. Mason Esq One of the oversears of the poor

March 24th.	Dischd. out of the Almshous Morris McLocklin	State

Returnd by An ordor of Mr. Jno. Scollay & Edwd. Proctors (within three howers)

March 25	Recd. into the Almshous Ruth Adams	Town

Pr. ordor of Edwd. Proctor Esqr. One of the oversears of the poor

March 29th.	Dischd. Mary Garrell	Town
	<Run Jno. Mayhew a frenchman	State
	Run Wm. […]	do.>
1788 March 31th.	Hipsabah Atkins Run	Town
	Elizh. Peirce do.	do.
	Benjman Eddy Run	State
Aprl. 1th.	Recd. into the Almshous Mary Payne	State

Pr. ordor of Jno. Andrews Esqr., Mr. Wm. Bordman} Selectmen
Consented to by Edwd. Proctor Esqr. One of the oversears of the poor}

Aprl. 1th.	Dischd. Jno. Fitz Gerrell	State
Aprl. 2	Recd. into the Almshous Mary Sanders	State

Pr. ordor of Jno. Andrews   } Selectmen
Approd. of by Edwd. Proctor one of the oversears of the poor

Aprl. 2d.	Dischd. Wm. Sprage out of the hous	Town
do.	Dischd. Eliz Williams do.	State
Aprl. 2d.	Recd. into the Almshous Edwd. Murrey	State

Pr. ordor of Edwd. Tylor, Mr. Ebenr. Sever} Selectmen
Apprd. of by Mr. Saml. Whitwell One of the oversears}

Aprl. 3d.	Dischd. Jno. Connor	State
Aprl. 5th.	Dischd. Richd. Crouch	State
Aprl. 5	Dischd. Thos. Brandon	(State)
Aprl. 5th.	Recd. into the Almshous Anna Cox	state

Pr. ordor of Jno. Scollay Esqr., Jno. Andrews Esqr.} Selectmen
approd. of By Edwd. Proctor Esqr. One of the oversears of the poor}

Aprl. 8th.	*<Dischd.>* Eliz Robertson Run	Town
	<Dichd. John [Chambers?]	*State>*
Aprl. 8th.	Michl. Rennals Run	State
Aprl. 8th.	Dischd. Mary Ratton	(State)
Aprl. 10th.	Dischd. Suckey Riadon	(Town)

Aprl. 2d. Recd. into the Almshous Polley—A bastard Child of Cate Symons born in the hous
Pr. ordor of Jno. Scollay Esqr., Jno. Andews Esqr.} Selectmen
Approd. of By Edwd. Proctor Esq Oversear}

Aprl. 2d. Recd. into the Almshous Betsey A bastard Child of Mary Sanders
Pr. ordor of Jno. Scollay Esq, Jno. Andrews Esq} Selectmen
Approd. of by Edwd. Proctor Esqr. one of the oversears of the poor}

1788 Aprl. 11 Recd. into the Almshous Susanna Serallie on the State Acct.
Pr. ordor of Jno. Scollay Esq, Thos. Walley Esq} Select Men
Pr. ordor of Edwd. Proctor Esqr. One of the oversears of the poor}

<Aprl. 11th. *Run Thomas Loring* *Town>*

Aprl. 11th. dischd. Eliz Star So. Cald. wh. her 2 Childn. Sent to Beverly town

Aprl. 10th. Recd. into the Almshous Rebecca Downs A Garl will be A 11 years old the 5th. Septr. 1788 State
Pr. ordor of Ezekl. Price Esqr. } Selectmen
Approd. of by Mr. Saml. Whitwell One of the oversears of the poor}

Aprl. 12 Recd. into the Almshous Ann Crumwell a Molatto Garl Eight years old in March last State
Pr. ordor of Ezl. Price Esq } Selectmen
approd. of by Edwd. Proctor Esqr. One of the oversears of the poor}

Aprl. 6th. Abigal Lewis Run Town

Aprl. 14th. Recd. into the Almshous Salley Dunken Six years old & Thos. Wright born in June 1786} State
Pr. ordor of Ezl. Price Esq, Jno. Andrews Esq} Selectmen
Consented to by Jona. Mason Esqr. One of the oversears of the poor}

Aprl. 14 Dischd. Hannah Waples State

Aprl. 14 Recd. into the Almshous Abigal Howland Town
Pr. ordor of Edwd. Proctor Esq oversear

Aprl. 13th. Dischd. John Chaimbers State

Aprl. 16th. Dischd. Ann Payson State

Aprl. 15 Recd. into the Almshous Franks A Child born In the Almshous
A Garl} State
Pr. Ordor of Jno. Scollay Esq, Thos. Walley Esq} Selectmen
Approd. of by Edwd. Proctor Esq An oversear of the poor}

Aprl. 16th. Recd. into the Almshous Jack Freeman A Negero (State)
Pr. ordor of Ezekl. Price Esqr., Mr. Ebenr. Sever} Selectmen
Approd. of by Edwd. Proctor Esqr. One of the oversears of the poor}

Aprl. 5th. dischd. John Wilkins (State)
aprl. 17 do. Mary Paindo.

1788 Aprl. 18th. Recd. into the Almshous Betsey McGwier A bastard Child of Dorcas
Hinds State
Pr. ordor of Jno. Scollay Esqr., Jno. Andrews Esqr.} Selectmen
Consented to by Mr. Saml. Whitwell One of the Oversears of the poor}

Aprl. 18th. Recd. into the Almshous Elizh. Lee State
Pr. ordor of Jno. Andrews Esqr., Mr. Wm. Bordman} Selectmen
Approd. of by Edwd. Proctor Esqr. One of the oversears of the poor}

Aprl. 18th. Richd. Corbert Run State
Moses Mcgrathh do. do.

Aprl. 19th. Dischd. Mary Lisemby Town

Aprl. 21 <*Dischd. Wm. Jones*> State

Aprl. 22d. Recd. into the Almshous Mary Ayers State
Pr. ordor of Mr. Wm. Bordman, Mr. Ebenr. Seaver} Selectmen
Approd. of by Saml. Whitwell One of the oversears of the poor}

Aprl. 23d. Ann Cox Run State

Aprl. 24th. Dischd. Jno. McKinzie State

Aprl. 25th. Recd. into the Almshous John Tyrrel State
Pr. ordor of Ezekl. Price Esqr. } Selectmen
Consented to by Jona. Mason Esqr. One of the oversears of the poor}

Aprl. 26th. Recd. into Almshous Jno. Murphey from Ireland State
Pr. ordor of Jno. Andrews Esqr., Mr. Wm. Bordman} Selectmen
Approd. of by Edwd. Proctor Esq One of the oversears of the poor}

Aprl. 26th. Recd. into the Almshous Susanna Riedon (town)
Pr. ord of Jno. White Esqr. One of the oversears of the poor

Aprl. 26 Dischd. Mary Sanders (State)

Aprl. 26 Dischd. Samson Brown A Negero state

Aprl. 28th. Dischd. Susanna Wallis State

Aprl. 29th. Recd. into the Almshous Dorr A Child Town
Pr. ordor of Mr. Jno. Codman Junr. one of the oversears of the poor}

Aprl. 29th. Recd. into the Almshous Wm. Jones State
Pr. ordor of Jno. Andrews Esqr., Mr. Wm. Bordman} Selectmen
apprd. of by Edwd. Proctor Esqr. one of the oversears}

1788 Aprl. 29th. Dischd. James McConnick State
Dischd. Wm. Jones State

⤚

Aprl. 30   Recd. into the Almshous Dorothy Hall   State
Pr. ordor of Edwd. Tyler, Mr. Wm. Bordman} Selectmen
Approd. of by Jona. Mason Esqr. One of the oversears of the poor

May 2d.   Recd. into the Almshous Jona. Adams   Town
Pr. ordor of Edwd. Proctor Esqr. One of the oversears of the poor

May 2d.   Recd. under my Care to be Supported At the Charge of the Common
Welth Joseph Jaines
Pr. ordor of Jno. Andrews Esqr., Jno. Scolley Esqr.} Selectmen
Approd. of by Jona. L. Austin One of the oversears of the poor}

May 2d.   Recd. into The Almshous Hannah Burk   State
Pr. ordor of Mr. Harbottle Dorr, Capt. Edwd. Tyler} Select Men
Approd. of by Jno. White Esqr. One of the oversears of the poor}

May 3d.   dischd. Peggy Bowles & Child   State

May 3d.   Recd. into the Almshous Jno. Connor of Ireland   State
Pr. ordor of Jno. Scollay Esq, Jno. Andrews Esq} 2 Selectmen
Consented to by Saml. Whitwell One of the oversears of the poor}

May 3d.   Recd. into the Almshous Peggy Fitz Gerreld of Ireland   state
Pr. ordor of Jno. Scolley Esqr., Jno. Andrews Esq} Selectmen
Approd. of by Edwd. Proctor Esqr. One of the oversears of the poor}

May 5th.   Mary Sharp, Jane Russell, Rebecka Thompson} Run   State

May 6th.   Dischd. Eliz Lewis   State

May 10th.   Dischd. Jno. Mansfield   State

May 14th.   Dischd. Daniel Benjaman   State

May 14   Recd. into the Almshous Thos. Brandon   State
Pr. ordor of Jno. Andrews Esqr., Mr. Ebenr. Seaver} Selectmen
Consented to by Edwd. Proctor One of the oversears of the poor}

May 15th.   Dischd. Mary Burford   Town

May 15   Recd. into the Almshous Eliz Clough   Town
Pr. ordor of Mr. Saml. Parkman one of the overseers
NB the bed that Mrs. Clough brott into the Almshous belongs to her daughtor}

May 10   Dischd. Edwd. Murry   State

1788 May 16th.   Dischd. Mary Webb to the workhous   Town

May 21d.   Dischd. Thos. Brandon   State

May 21d.   Recd. into the Almshous Eliz Sirk   State
Pr. ordor of Ezekl. Price Esqr., Mr. Wm. Boardman} Selectmen
Approd. of by Saml. Whitwell One of the oversears

May 24th.	Recd. into the Almshous Nathl. Berry	State
Pr. ordor of Jno. Andrews Esqr., Jno. Scollay Esqr.} Selectmen		
Consented to pr. Jona. Mason Esqr. One of the oversears of the poor}		

May 22d.	Thomas Loring Run	Town

May 26th. Proctor	Dischd. Lucey Willis, But the Next day with an ordor from Capt	Town

May 26th.	Dischd. James McQuim	State

May 26th.	Dischd. Susanna Franks & Child	State

May 27	Dischd. Abigal Howland	Town

May 27	Dischd. Jno. Connor	State
	Dischd. Jno. Murphey	State

May 27	Recd. into the Almshous Lucey Willis	Town
Edwd. Proctor Esqr. oversear		

May 24th.	Judah Eddy Run {Recd. into the hous by the Request of the Request	
of the Select men on the same ordor		State

May 29th.	Dischd. Eliz Brewer	State

May 30th.	Recd. into the Almshous Cate Lloyd a Negero	State
Pr. ordor of harbo. Dorr, Mr. Wm. Bordman} Selectmen		
Approd. of by Jno. White Esqr. One of the oversears of the poor		

May 31	Recd. into the Almshous Thos. Brangden A Convick from Ireland	
Pr. ordor of Jno. Scollay Esqr., Jno. Andrews Esqr.} Selectmen		
Approd. of by Edwd. Proctor an oversear of the poor}		

May 31	Dischd. Cate Symons & Child	State

June 3d.	Recd. into the Almshous Sarah Armstrong	State
Pr. ordor of Jno. Scollay Esqr., Ezekl. Price Esqr.		
Approd. of by Mr. Wm. Smith one of the oversears of the poor}		

June 3d.	dischd. Jack Freeman	State

1788 June 2d.	Thos. Brandon Run	State

May 28	Recd. into the Almshous Frances Carns his Wife Mehitabel there Child	
Polley 4 years old the 4th. Novr. 1788}		State
Pr. ordor of Ezekl. price Esqr., Mr. Wm. Bordman} Selectmen		
Saml. Whitwell, oversear}		

June 4th.	Recd. into the Almshous Ann Cox	State
Pr. ordor of Jno. Scollay Esq, Jno. Andrews Esq} Selectmen		
Approd. of by Edwd. Proctor Esq One of the oversears of the poor}		

May 29th.	Susanna Servalley Run	State

June 6th.	Dischd. Wm. Jones	State
June 6th.	<*Dischd.*> Eliz Berry Run	State
June 9th.	Dischd. Peggy Fitz Gerrell	State
May 27th.	Run Nathl. Berry—belonging to Roadisland	State

June 10th.   Recd. into the Almshous Phillis Brown A Negero And her Child} State
Pr. ordor of Jno. Scollay Esqr., Thos. Walley Esqr.} Selectmen
Apprd. of by Saml. Whitwell overseer

June 10th.   Recd. into the Almshous Elizh. Mayter   State
Pr. ordor of Jno. Scollay Esqr., Jno. Andrews Esqr.} Selectmen
Approd. of by Saml. Whitwell one of the oversears of the poor}

| June 5th. | Dischd. Negero Florow & Child | State |

June 11th.   Recd. into the Almshous Peggy FitzGerrell   state
Pr. ordor of Jno. Scollay Esqr., Jno. Andrews Esqr.} Select Men
Approvd. of by Jno. Mason Esq One of the oversears of the poor}

June 7th.	Dischd. Ann delaney & her 2 Chilren	state
June 16th.	Dischd. Wm. Harpley	State
June 16th.	Dischd. Ann Mayhew & her two Childn.	State
June 17th.	Dischd. Frances Clarrage & Wife	State

June 17th.   Recd. into the Almshous Margrat Hurley   Town
Pr. ordor of Edwd. Proctor oversear

June 18th.   Recd. into the Almshous Katy Townsend of Ireland   State
Pr. ordor of Jno. Andrews, Mr. Ebenr. Sever} Selectmen
Approd. of by Edwd. Proctor Esq one of the oversears of the poor}

| June 19th. | Dischd. Saml. Gosling bound out | Town |
| June 20 | dischd. Partrick Shanley | State |

1788 June 21th.   Recd. into the Almshous Hannah Blunt   Town
Pr. ordor of Jona. L. Austin An overseer

| June 24th. | Dischd. Elizh. Smith & her Child | state |

June 27th.   Recd. into the Almshous Sarah Rice & Child belonging to Portland or
falmouth   (Town)
Pr. ordor of Edwd. Proctor Esq oversear

June 28th.	Dischd. George Randol a boy Bound out	State
	Dischd. Rebecca Downe a garl do.	State
June 28	Dischd. Jno. Pierce	(State)

June 30   Recd. into the Almshous Catharina Mills   Town
Pr. ordor of Edwd. Proctor Esqr. Oversear

July 1th. Recd. into the Almshous Sarah Mack State
Pr. ordor of Jno. Andrews Esqr., Jno. Scollay Esqr.} Selectmen
Approd. of by Edwd. Proctor E[*sq*.] One of the oversears of the poor}

July 2d. Recd. into the Almshous Mary Sharp State
Pr. ordor of Jno. Scollay Esqr., Thos. Walley Esqr.} Selectmen
Approd. of by Edwd. Proctor Esqr. One of the oversears of the poor}

July 3d. Dischd. Charles Drew (a boy bound out) State

July 5th. Dischd. Sarah Rice & Child belong to Portland in the County of
Cumberlan

July 5th. Dischd. Rebecca Boldrage & Child Town

July 2d. Recd. into the Almshous Ann Black, from Nw. foundland state
Pr. ordor of Jno. Scolley Esqr., Thos. Walley Esqr.} Selectmen
Approd. of by Edwd. Proctor Esqr. One of the Oversears of the poor}

July 8th. Recd. into the Almshous Sarah Coney & Child State
Pr. ordor of Edwd. Tyler, Mr. Wm. Bordman} Selectmen
Approd. of by Jno. White Esqr. One of the oversears of the poor}

July 9th. dischd. Lucey Willis (Town)

July 9 Dischd. Catharina Mills Town

July 10th. Run Cate Townsand State

1788 July 11th. Recd. into the Almshous Jno. Hunnewell on the Accot. of the State
Pr. ordor of Jno. Scollay Esqr., Jno. Andrews Esqr.} Selectmen
Approd. of by Edwd. Proctor Esqr. One of the oversears of the poor

July 4th. Recd. an ordor to Supply Josh. Jaine's wife As if She was in The hous}
Pr. ordor of Jno. Andrews } selectmen state
Approd. of by Edwd. Proctor one of the overs of the poor

July 10th. Recd. into the hous Susanna Jones (big with A bastard Child) (Town)
Pr. ordor of Ezl. Price Esqr., Jno. Andrews Esq} Selectmen
Approd. of by Edwd. Proctor Esqr. One of the Oversears of the poor}

July 12th. Recd. into the Almshous Elizh. [Plummer?] wh. A Veneral disorder
(State)
Pr. ordor of Capt. Edwd. Tyler, Jno. Andrews} Selectmen
Approd. of by Edwd. Proctor Esqr. One of the oversears of the poor

July 14th. Recd. into the Almshous Sarah Leachman & Child State
Pr. ordor of Edwd. Tylor, Jno. Andrews Esqr.} Selectmen
Approd. of by Edwd. proctor Esq One of the oversears of the poor}

July 14th. Peggy Fitz Garrell Run State

July 16th. Rachal Drew Run State

July 17th. Recd. into the Almshous Jno. Fowler State
Pr. ordor of Jno. Andrews } Selectmen
Approd. of by Edwd. Proctor Esqr. One of the oversears of the poor

July 18th.   Dischd. Abigal Clow a Garl bound out   (Town)

July 18   Recd. into the Almshous Mary McIntier & 2 Children   state
Pr. ordor of Mr. Wm. Bordman   } Selectmen
Approd. of by Edwd. Proctor Esqr. One of the oversears of the poor}

July 18th.   Recd. into the Almshous Hannah Boston   State
Pr. ordor of Mr. Ebenr. Sever, Mr. Wm. Bordman} Selectmen
Approd. of by Edwd. proctor Esqr. one of the oversears of the poor}

July 19th.   Recd. into the Almshous Jane Russell
Pr. ordor of Jno. Scollay Esqr.   } Selectmen
Edwd. Proctor Esqr. Oversear

July 21th.   Dischd. John Fowler   State

July 21st.   Sarah Armstrong Run   State
                  Dischd. Mary Mcintier & 2 Children   do.

1788 July 23d.   Dischd. Mehitable Carnes & Child   State

July 24th.   Dischd. James Gardiner bound out   State

July 24th.   Dischd. Fanney Crouch A Child   State

July 25th.   Dischd. Barzalel Eddy a boy bound out}   State
                  Dischd. Sibble Eddy a Garl   do. }

July 25th.   Recd. into the Almshous Nancy Milligan 2 years old   State
Pr. ordor of Jno. Scollay, Jno. Andrews} Selectmen
Approd. of by Edwd. Proctor Esq One of the oversears of the poor}

July 26th.   Recd. into the Almshous Mary Dailey of Ireland   State
Pr. ordor of Jno. Scollay Esqr.   } Selectmen
Approd. of By Edwd. Proctor Esq One of the oversears of the poor}

July 28th.   Dischd. out of the Almshous Kitte Mory   State

July 29th.   Recd. into the almshous Mary Killey   State
Pr. ordor of Edwd. Tyler, Thos. Walley Esqr.} Selectmen
Approd. of By Edwd. Proctor Esqr. one of the oversears of the poor}

July 30th.   Recd. into the Almshous Partrick Shanly of Ireland   State
Pr. ordor of Jno. Andrews, Ezl. Price} Selectmen
Approd. of by Edwd. Proctor Esqr. One of the oversears of the poor

July 30   Recd. into the Almshous Michal McClocklen of Ireland   State
Pr. ordor of Jno. Scollay Esqr., Thos. Walley Esqr.} Selectmen
Approd. of by Edwd. Proctor Esqr. One of the oversears of the poor}

July 24th.   Dischd. Jona. Adams out of the Almshous   Town

Augt. 1th.   Recd. into the Eliz Smith & her Child a boy   (State)
Jno. Scollay & Jno. Andrews Esq} Selectmen
Mr. Saml. Whitwell oversear}

Augt. 4th.	Dischd. Eliz <Smith> Wheler & Child	Town
Augt. 4th.	Dischd. Matthew Sun a Child	State
Augt. 4th.	Dischd. Hannah Berry & Child	Town
Augt. 6th.	Dischd. Eliz Plumley	State
Augt. 4th.	Jno. Hunnewell Run	State
	Timothy dwier do.	do.

Augt. 8   Recd. into the Almshous James Comberford   State
Pr. ordor of Jno. Scoley Esq, Mr. Wm. Bordman} Selectmen
Approd. of by Edwd. Proctor Esq one of the oversears of the poor}

1788 Augt. 12th.	Dischd. Elizh. Smith & Child	State

Augt. 12th.   Recd. into the Almshous Rebecca Kerley from the work hous & her
Bastard Child
Pr. ordor of Jno. Scollay Esq, Captn. Edwd. Tyler} Selectmen
Approd. of by Edwd. Proctor Esqr. One of the oversears of the poor}

Augt. 13th.   Recd. into the Almshous Robert Hoey—the Son of Anna Hoey 3 years
old the 26th. Sept. 1788
Pr. ordor of Jno. Andrews   } Selectmen
Approd. of By Edwd. Proctor Esqr. One of the Oversears of the poor}

Augt. 18th.   Recd. into the Almshous Jane Sigourney A Molatto Garl About 11 years
old And No Covenant Servant As She sais}   State
Pr. ordor of Jno. Andrews Esqr.   } Selectmen
Approd. of By Edwd. Proctor Esqr. One of the oversears of the poor}

Augt. 19d.	Dischd. Ann Crumwell a Molatto Bound out	State

Augt. 19th.   Recd. into the Almshous Lowes Plummer & 2 Children}   State
Pr. ordor of Capt. Edwd. Tyler, Jno. Andrews Esqr.} Selectmen
Approd. of by Saml. Whitwell one of the Oversears of the poor}

Augt. 22d.   Recd. into the Almshous Jno. Gillion Of Ireland   State
Pr. ordor of Captn. Edwd. Tyler, Jno. Andrews Esqr.} Selectmen
Approd. of by Edwd. Proctor Esqr. One of the oversears of the poor}

Augt. 22d.	dischd. Mary Dailey	State

Augt. 27   Recd. into the Almshous Margrat Carton   Town
Pr. ordor of Jona. L Austin One of the oversears of the poor

Augt. 29th   Recd. into the Almshous Peggy Fitzgerreld   State
Pr. ordor of Wm. Bordman, Capt. E Tyler} Selectmen
Approd. of by Edwd. Proctor One of the Oversears of the poor}

Sept. 1th.	Dischd. Negero Phillis Brown & Child	State

Septr. 1   Recd. into the Almshous James McQuim   State
Pr. ordor of Ezekl. Price Esqr., Mr. Wm. Bordman} Selectmen
Approd. of by Edwd. Proctor Esqr. one of the oversears of the poor}

Septr. 1th.	Dischd. Richd. Legalley bound out	State

1788 Septr. 3d.   Recd. into the Almshous Joanna Spoonor A Child
Pr. ordor of Jno. Andrews Esqr., Mr. Wm. Bordman} Selectmen
Approd. of By Edwd. Proctor One of the oversears of the poor}

Septr. 3d.	Recd. into the Almshous Wm. Holmes	State

Pr. ordor of Jno. Andrews Esqr., Mr. Wm. Bordman} Selectmen
Approd. of By Edwd. Proctor Esqr. One of the oversears of the poor}

Septr. 4th.	Recd. into the Almshous Josh. Johnston & Wife	Town

Pr. ordor of Mr. Jno. Codman Junr. One of the oversears of the poor

Septr. 6.	dischd. Daniel Morse	state

Septr. 9th.	Wm. Hemes Run	State
	Juah Eddy Run	do.

Septr. 8th.	Recd. into the Almshous Rachel Drue	State

Pr. ordor of Mr. Harbo. Dorr, Capt. Edwd. Tyler} Selectmen
Approd. of by Mr. Jno. White [one][3] of the Oversears of the poor}
did not stay not one day}

Septr. 8th.	Recd. into the Almshous Jno. Gandol about 15 years old	Town

{Pr. ordor of Edwd. Proctor Esqr. One of the oversears of the poor

Septr. 13d.	dischd. Morris McClockling An *Irishman*	State

Augt. 14th. 1788	Recd. into the Almshous Mary Brown	State

Pr. Ordor of Jno. Scollay Esq, Mr. Wm. Bordman} Selectmen
Approd. of by Edwd. Proctor One of the oversears}

Septr. 6th.	Dischd. Mary Brown Sent to Gole	state

Sepr. 13d.	Dischd. Rebecca Hurley	Town

Septr. 18	Recd. into the Almshous Ann Cox	Town

Pr. ordor of Jno. White Esqr. One of the oversears of the poor

Septr. 20	Recd. into the Almshous <*Polly & Elizh.*> Mary Garrow with Polley	

Crain & Betsey Garrow her tw[o] Children}   State
Pr. ordor of Jno. Andrews Esq, Ezekl. Price Esqr.} Selectmen
Approd. of By Edwd. Proctor Esqr. one of the oversears of the poor}

Septr. 24d.	Recd. into the Almshous Mary Jackson	Town

Pr. Ordor of Edwd. proctor Esq One of the oversears of the poor

1788 Septr. 24th.	Dischd. Jno. Fla[nn]	State
	Sent Rebecca Kirley to the workhous	do.

Septr. 26th.	Recd. into the Almshous Peter Swan A britanor	State

Pr. ordor of John Scolley Esq, Ezekl. Price Esqr.} Selectmen
Approd. of by Edwd. Proctor Esqr. One of the oversears of the poor}

<*Septr. 27th.*>	Pegg Fitz Gerrell Run} Returnd the Second day}	State

Septr. 29th.   Mary Kelley Run   State

Septr. 30th.   Recd. into the Almshous George McCan   State
Pr. ordor of Jno. Scolley Esqr., Capt. Edwd. Tyler} Selectmen
approd. of by Edwd. Proctr. Esqr. One of the oversears of the poor}

Septr. 30th.   Sarah Gardiner Run   Town

Notes

1   This line was written along the right margin of the entry.
2   The name has been erased.
3   The edge of the manuscript is torn, resulting in the loss of one word.

ALMSHOUSE ADMISSIONS
October 1, 1788 – August 30, 1795

The line entry format gives way to column entries on February 7, 1791.

Persons Recd. into the Almshous & discharged out Viz
Admissions Register 4 begins.

1788

| Octr. 1th. | Recd. into the Almshous John Crage | State |

Approd. by Edwd. Proctor Esqr. one of the oversears of the poor}
Pr. ordor of Edwd. Tyler, Jno. Andrews Esqr.} Select men

Octr. 1th.   Recd. into the Almshous Adam Roop   State
Approd. of by Edwd. proctor Esq one of the oversears of the poor}
Pr. ordor of Jno. Andrews Esqr., Ezekl. Price Esqr.} Selectmen

Octr. 1   Recd. into the Almshous Jno. Frederick Scofskuske   State
Approd. of by Edwd. Proctor Esq One of the oversears of the poor}
Pr. ordor of Jno. Scollay Esq, Mr. Ebenr. Seiver} Select men

Octr. 2d.   Recd. An ordor to Suply Wm. Scollay his two Children And Nurs with
Such provisions and Sunderys As the people Are Supplyd. with in this hous
Approd. of by Edwd. Proctor Esqr. One of the Oversears of the poor}
Pr. order of Jno. Scolley Esq, Jno. Andrews Esqr.} Selectmen

Octr. 4th.   Recd. into the Almshous Agnes Richards of <Nw. york?> Rhoad I   (State)
Consented to by Mr. <Saml. Whitwell> Jno. White One of the oversears of the poor}
Pr. ordor of Mr. Harbt. Dorr, Captn. Edwd. Tyler} Selectmen

Octr. 4th.   Recd. into the Almshous Jno. Kingston a Child   State
Consented to by Saml. Whitwell One of the oversears of the poor}
Pr. ordor of Jno. Scollay Esqr., Mr. Wm. Bordman

Octr. 4th.   Pegg Carter Run

Octr. 4d.   Recd. into the Almshous Anna Athridge   Town
Pr. ordor of Jno. White Esqr. One of the oversears of the poor

Octr. 6th.   Recd. into the Almshous Thos. Barry of Ireland   State
Apprd. of By Edwd. Proctor Esqr. One of the oversears of the poor}
Pr. ordor of Jno. Scollay Esqr., Captn. Edwd. Tyler} Selectmen

Octr. 6th.   Recive Jno. Hunnewell into the almshous   Town
Pr. ordor of Henry Hill Esqr.

Octr. 6th.   Recd. into the Almshous Margrat Conorley and James Lewis a boy} State
Approd. of by Edwd. Proctor Esqr. one of the oversears of the poor}
Pr. ordor of Jno. Scollay Esqr., Jno. Andrews do.} Selectmen

Octr. 6th.   Dischd. James Lewis a boy bound out   State

Octr. 7th.   Recd. into the Almshous Timothy McGwier   State
Approd. of by Edwd. Proctor Esqr. One of the oversears of the poor}
Pr. ordor of Captn. Edwd. Tyler, Jno. Walley Esqr.} Selectmen

Octr. 8th.   Recd. into the Almshous Robt. Smith
Approd. of by Edwd. Proctor Esqr. One of the oversears of the poor
Pr. ordor of Jno. Andrews Esqr., Mr. Wm. Boardman} Select men

Octr. 9th.   Recd. into the Almshous Cloe[1] A Negero Woman   State
Approd. of by Mr. Saml. Parkman One of the oversears of the poor}
Pr. ordor of Thos. Walley Esqr., Jno. Scolley Esq} Selectmen

Octr. 7th.   Recd. into the Almshous <*Luisa*> Levice A Negero Woman
Approd. of by Edwd. Proctor Esqr. One of the oversears of the poor}
Pr. ordor of Capt. Edwd. Tyler, Jno. Scollay Esqr.} Selectmen

Octr. 9   Recd. into the Almshous Wm. Furgus a Strainger
Approd. of by Edwd. Proctor Esqr. One of the oversears of the poor}
Pr. ordor of Thos. Walley Esqr., Mr. Wm. Bordman} Selectmen

Octr. 10th.   Margrat Conarley Run   State

Octr. 9th.   Recd. into the Almshous Jno. & Polley Frank   State
Approd. of by Saml. Whitwell One of the oversears of the poor}
Pr. ordor of Jno. Scollay Esq, Ezekl. Price do. [Esq]} Selectmen

Octr. 10th.   Dischd. Jno. Fredrick Scofskuske a duchman   State

Octr. 7th.   Recd. into the Almshous Luse Patten[2]   Town
Pr. ordor of Edwd. Proctor One of the oversears of the poor

Octr. 13th.   Recd. into the Almshous Jabez Samson   Town
Pr. ordor of Jno. Sweetser Esqr. One of the oversears of the poor

Octr. 13th.   Recd. into the Almshous Michal Harris A Sweed   on the State
Approd. of by Jno. White Esqr. One of the oversears of the poor}
Pr. ordor of Mr. Harbt. Dorr, Capt. Edwd. Tyler} Selectmen

Octr. 14th.   Recd. into the Almshous Abigal & Susanna Price   Town
Pr. ordor of Jno. Sweetser Esqr. onne of the oversears of the poor

Octr. 14th.   Dischd. Sarah Leachman & Child   State

Octr. 14th.   Recd. into the Almshous John Gandol   Town
Pr. Henry Hill Esqr. one of the oversears of the poor

Octr. 15th.   Dischd. Thos. Berry   State

1788
Octr. 15th.   Recd. into the Almshous Elizh. Williams   State
Approd. of by Saml. Parkman one of the oversears of the poor}
Pr. ordor of Jno. Andrews Esq, Mr. W Wm. Bordman} Selectmen

Octr. 15th.   Recd. into the Almshous James Adams   Town
Pr. ordor of Edwd. Proctor Esqr. one of the oversears of the poor}

Octr. 17th.   Recd. into the Almshous Matthew Landerkin   State
Consented to by Jona. Mason Esqr. One of the oversears of the poor}
Pr. ordor of Ezekl. Price Esq, Capt. Edwd. Tyler} Selectmen

Octr. 17th.   Dischd. Luse Cuningham bound out   Town

Octr. 17th.　　　Recd. into the Almshous Mary Read　　　　　　State
Consented to by Edwd. Proctor Esqr. One of the oversears of the poor}
Pr. ordor of Mr. Harbt. Dorr, Capt. Edwd. Tyler} 2 Selectmen

Octr. 22d.　　　Recd. into the Almshous Jane Bates who belongs to Waymouth
Consented to by Edwd. Proctor Esqr. One of the oversears of the poor}
Jno. Scollay Esqr., Ezekl. Price Esqr.} Selectmen

Octr. 23d.　　　Susanna Jones Run　　　　　　　　　　　　State

Octr. 22d.　　　Recd. into the Almshous Morris McLocklen Irishman　　State
Consented to by Edwd. Proctor Esq One of the oversears of the poor}
Pr. ordor of Jno. Scollay Esqr., Mr. Wm. Bordman} Selectmen

Octr. 20th.　　　Recd. into the Almshous Ann Chalendor[3]　　　State
Consentd. to by Jno. White Esqr. One of the oversears of the poor}
Pr. ordor of Harbt. Dorr, Capt. Edwd. Tyler}Selectmen

Octr. 24th.　　　Recd. into the Almshous Jno. Moran of Dublon　　State
Consented to by Edwd. Proctor Esqr. One of the oversears of the poor}
Pr. ordor of Mr. Wm. Bordman, Capt. Edwd. Tyler} Selectmen

Octr. 24d.　　　Dischd. Susanna Riadon　　　　　　　　　Town

Octr. 28th.　　　Dischd. Hannah Burk　　　　　　　　　State

Octr. 28th.　　　Recd. into the Almshous Sophia Mendez　　　State
Approd. of By Edwd. Proctor Esq One of the oversears of the poor}
Pr. ordor of Jno. Andrews Esq, Mr. Wm. Bordman} Selectmen

Octr 21st.　　　Recd. into the Almshous Mary Mumfort　　　State
Approd. of by Saml. Whitwell One of the oversears of the poor}
Pr. ordor of Jno. Scolley Esqr., Ezekl. Price Esqr.} Selectmen

Octr. 30th.　　　Recd. into the Almshous Jno. McGoff an Irishman　　State
Consenteed to by Mr. Saml. Whitwell One of the oversears of the poor}
Pr. ordor of Jno. Andrews Esqr., Mr. Wm. Bordman} Selectmen

Octr. 30th. 1788　Recd. into the Almshous Jno. McKinzie　　　State
Apprd. of by Saml. Whitwell Esq One of the oversears of the poor}
Pr. ordor of Jno. Andrews Esqr., Mr. Wm. Bordman} Select men

Octr. 30　　　Dischd. Michal McLocklin　　　　　　　　State

<Octr.> Septr. 1th. Recd. Alice Stoddard Aelis　　　into the Almshous　State
Consented to by Edwd. Proctor Esqr. One of the oversears of the poor}
Pr. ordor of Jno. Walley Esq, Jno. Scollay Esq} Selectmen

Octr. 22d.　　　Recd. into the Almshous Paletiah Hunt　　　(Town
Pr. ordor of Mr. Jno. Codman One of the oversears of the poor}

Novr. 1th.　　　Recd. into the Almshous Rose Capen a Negero　　State
Approd. of by Edward Proctor Esqr. One of the oversears of the poor}
Pr. ordor of Jno. Scollay Esqr., Mr. Wm. Bordman} Selectmen

Novr. 1th.   Recd. into the Almshous Mary Kepon[4]   State
Approd. of by Edwd. Proctor Esqr. One of the oversears of the poor}
Pr. ordor of Jno. Andrews Esqr.   } Selectmen

Novr. 3d.   Recd. into the Almshous Elizh. Powers   State
Approd. of by Edwd. Proctor Esqr. One of the oversears of the poor}
Pr. ordor of Wm. Bordman Esq, Jno. Andrews Esq} Selectmen

Octr. 22d.   Mary Garrow Run from the workhous   State

Octr. 28th.   Recd. into the Almshous Robt. Lilburn   State
Approd. of by Jno. White Esqr. One of the oversears of the poor}
Pr. ordor of Jno. Andrews, Capt. Edwd. Tyler} Selectmen

Novr. 5th.   Recd. into the Almshous Saml. North   State
Approd. of by Edwd. Proctor Esqr. One of the oversears of the poor}
Pr. ordor of Mr. Ebenr. Seaver, Mr. Wm. Bordman} Selectmen

Novr. 10   Dischd. Matthew Landerkin   State

Novr. 10   Dischd. Jno. Crage   State

Novr. 11   Recd. into the Almshous Sarah Galley and Her three Children   Town
Pr. ordor of Edwd. Proctor Esqr. One of the oversears of the poor

Novr. 9   Recd. into the Almshous An Infant Child Caled   A bastord born of
Mary Mumfort}   State
Approd. of by   one of the oversears of the poor
Pr. ordor of Capt. Edwd. Tyler Esqr., Mr. Ebenr. Sever} Selectmen

1788
Novr. 12th.   dischd. Jane Sigourney a molatto Garl bound out   State

Novr. 11   Recd. into the Almshous Thos. Ethredge[5] Ann Ethredge Polley And Wm.
There two Children   Town
Pr. ordor of Jno. White—one of the oversears of the poor

Novr. 13th.   Recd. into the Almshous Jeremiah Mahaney or Supply him out of the
Almshous   State
Approd. of by Edwd. Proctor Esqr. One of the oversears of the poor}
Pr. ordor of Jno. Andrews, Mr. Wm. Bordman} Selectmen

Novr. 14th.   Recd. into the Almshous Mary Webb from the workhous
Pr. order of Edwd. Proctor Esqr. One of the oversears of the poor

Novr. 20th.   Recd. into the Almshous Elizh. Stevens   State
Consented to by Edwd. Proctor Esq one of the oversears of the poor}
Pr. ordor of Mr. Wm. Bordman, Jno. Andrews Esq} Selectmen

Novr. 19th.   Recd. into the Almshous Bethiah Fowle   Town
Pr. ordor of Jno. Sweetser Esq One of the oversears of the poor

Novr. 16th.   Dischd. Mary Tilty Run   State

Novr. 22d.   Dischd. Ann Ethredge a garl bound out   Town

Novr. 22	Recd. into the Almshous Saml. Sargant[6]	Town
Pr. Edwd. Proctor oversear		
Novr. 29th.	Dischd. Saml. Alias George McCann[7]	State
Novr. 25th.	Recd. into the Almshous Joseph Coburn	Town
Pr. ordor of Jno. Codman Junr. Oversear of warde 10}		
Novr. 25	Recd. into the Almshous Jno. Mayhew a frenchman	State
Consented to Mr. Saml. Whitwell one of the oversears of the poor}		
Pr. ordor of Jno. Scollay Esqr. } Selectmen		
Novr. 26th.	Dischd. Levice Lisha of Stoughton	
Novr. 26th.	Dischd. Adam Ropes	
Novr. 25th.	Recd. into the Almshous Thos. Smith one Eye	State
Approd. of by Edwd. Proctor Esqr. one of the oversears of the poor}		
Pr. ordor of Jno. Andrews Esqr., Jno. Scollay Esqr.} Selectmen		
Novr. 29th.		State[8]
Decr. 1th. 1788	Recd. into the Almshous Elizh. Wier of Germany	Town
Pr. ordor of Mr. Jno. Codman Junr.		
Novr. 26th.	Recd. into the Almshous Judah Eddy	State
Consentd. to By Edwd. Proctor Esqr. One of the oversears of the poor}		
Pr. ordor of Mr. Wm. Bordman, Jno. Andrews Esqr.} Selectmen		
Novr. 29th.	Recd. into the Almshous Ann Sample	State
Approvd. of by Edwd. Proctor Esqr. One of the oversears of the poor}		
Pr. ordor of Jno. Andrews Esq, Jno. Scollay Esqr.} Selectmen		
Decr. 2d.	Recd. into the Almshous Mary Wakefeild and son	Town
Pr. ordor of Edwd. Proctor Esqr. One of the oversears of the poor		
Decr. 2	Recd. into the Almshous Willm. Curtis	Town
Pr. ordor of Edwd. Proctor Esqr. One of the oversears of the poor		
Novr. 13th.	Recd. into the Almshous Nancy Farror[9] Aged 6 years old the 4 feby. 1789	
George Farror 4 years old the 13th. July 1789}		State
Approd. of by Mr. Saml. Parkman One of the oversears of the poor}		
Pr. ordor of [Mr.] Jno. Scolley Esqr., Mr. Ebenr. Seaver} Selectmen		
Novr. 15th.	Recd. into the Almshous Mary Garrow	
Approvd. of by Edwd. Proctor Esqr. One of the oversears of the poor}		
Pr. ordor of Ezekl. Price Esqr., Jno. Scollay Esqr.} Selectmen		
Decr. 3d.	Mary Webb Sent to the workhous	Town
	Jno. Hunnewell Sent to the workhous	do.
	Wm. Curtis Sent to do.	do.
	Mary Garrow Sent to do.	State
decr. 6th.	Dischd. Saml. Sargent	Town

decr. 9th.   Recd. into the Almshous James Brown
Approd. of by Edwd. Proctor Esqr. one of the oversears of the poor}
Pr. ordor of Jno. Scollay Esqr., Mr. Ebenr. Sever} Selectmen

decr. 10th.   Dischd. Elizh. Wier   town

Decr. 10th.   Recd. into the Almshous Richd. Deane of Harford   State
Approd. of by Edwd. Proctor Esq One of the oversears of the poor}
Pr. ordor of Jno. Scolley Esq, Jno. Andrews Esq} Selectmen

1788
Boston, decr. 11th. Recd. into the Almshous Ann Delaney[10] And her 2 Children} State
Consented to by Jona. Mason Esq One of the oversears of the poor}
Pr. ordor of Jno. Scollay Esqr., Ezekl. Price Esqr.} Selectmen

Decr. 12th. 1788 Recd. into the Almshous Polley Cartor[11]   State
Approd. of by Edwd. Proctor Esqr. One of the Oversears of the poor}
Pr. ordor of Jno. Andrews Esq, Mr. Wm. Bordman} Selectmen

Decr. 13th.   Dischd. James Brown   State

Decr. 13th.   Recd. into the Almshous Anna Richardson   Town
Jona. L Austin overseer

Decr. 15th.   Dischd. Jno. McGoff   State

Decr. 15th.   Recd. into the Almshous Jno. Chaimbers[12] A Jarsey man (State
Approd. of by Edwd. Proctor Esqr. One of the Oversears of the poor}
Pr. ordor of Jno. Andrews Esq, Mr. Willm. Bordman} Selectmen

Decr. 15th.   Recd. into the [*Almshouse*] Thos. Brandon of Ireland   State
Approvd. of by Edwd. Proctor Esq One of the oversears of the poor}
Pr. ordor of Jno. Scollay Esqr., Jno. Andrews Esqr.} Selectmen

decr. 17th.   Recd. into the Almshous Rachel Wall   State
Approd. of by Edwd. Proctor Esqr. One of the oversears of the poor}
Pr. ordor of Mr. Wm. Bordman, Jno. Andrews Esqr.} Selectmen

Decr. 17th.   Recd. into the Almshous Elizh. Matthews[13] (grate Britton) State
Consented to by Edwd. Proctor Esqr. One of the oversears of the poor}
Pr. ordor of Jno. Scolley Esqr., Mr. Harbt. dorr} Select men

decr. 18th.   Recd. into the Almshous Elams Gifford   State
Approd. of by Edwd. Proctor Esqr. One of the oversears of the poor}
Pr. ordor of Capn. Edwd. Tyler, Mr. Wm. Bordman} Selectmen

Decr. 16th.   Recd. into the Almshous Lydia Gullies A Child 2 1/2 years old State
Approd. by Edwd. Proctor Esq One of the oversears of the poor}
Pr. ordor of Capt. Edwd. Tyler   } Selectmen

Decr. 19th.   Recd. into the Almshous Michal McClochlen[14] Irish   State
Approd. of by Edwd. Proctor Esqr. One of the oversears of the poor}
Pr. ordor of Mr. Wm. Bordman, Jno. Andrews Esqr.} Selectmen

Decr. 19th.   Recd. into the Almshous Thos. Bell   Town
Pr. ordor of Mr. Saml. Parkman One of the oversears of the poor

Decr. 20th. 1788   Recd. into the Almshous George Peters   State
Approd. of by Jno. Sweetser Esqr. one of the oversears of the poor}
Pr. ordor of Jno. Scollay Esq, Mr. Wm. B[o]rdman} Selectmen

Decr. 20th.   Recd. into the Almshous Mary Telty[15] a solders drap[16]   State
Pr. ordor of Ezekl. Price Esq
Approd. of by Jon. Mason Esqr. One of the oversears of the poor}

Decr. 22d.   Dischd. Mary Mumford & Child   State

Decr. 22d.   Recd. into the Almshous Ann Whitman Belonging to Waymouth}
                                        on accot. of the Town Boston
Pr. ordor of Mr. Saml. Parkman One of the oversears of the poor

Decr. 23d.   Recd. into the Almshous Eliz Eliot   Town
Pr. ordor of Henry Hill One of the oversears of the poor}

Decr. 23d.   Recd. into the Almshous Jonathan Webb   Town
Pr. ordor of Jno White Esqr.

decr. 24th.   Recd. into the Almshous Mary Ralford[17]   State
Approd. of by Edwd. Proctor Esqr. One of the oversears of the poor}
Pr. ordor of Mr. Wm. Bordman   } Select men

Decr. 25   Recd. into the Almshous Michal Cr[o]wley   Town
Pr. ordor of Edward Proctor One of the oversears of the poor

Decr. 25   Recd. into the Almshous 2 Children Caled Sophia Camble And Hariot
Camble
Pr. ordor of Mr. Saml. Whitwell

decr. 26th.   Dischd. Elizh. Powers   State

Decr. 26th.   Recd. into the Almshous Jno. Brown   State
Consented to by Edwd. Proctor Esqr. One of the oversears of the poor}
Pr. ordor of Mr. Wm. Bordman   } Select men

Decr. 29th.   Recd. into the Almshous Nathl. Bourn   Town
Edwd. Proctor Esqr. Oversear

Decr. 30th.   Recd. into the Almshous Ephram Bailey   State
Approd. of by Edwd. Proctor Esqr. One of the oversears of the poor}
Pr. ordor of Jno. Anderson Esqr., Mr. Wm. Boardman} Selectmen

Decr. 31th.   Recd. into the Almshous Susanna Wallis   State
Approd. of by Edwd. Proctor Esqr. One of the oversears of the poor}
Pr. ordor of Jno. Andrews Esqr., Mr. Wm. Bordman} Selectmen

1788
decr. 31th.   Recd. into the Almshous david Dennie   State
Approd. of by Edwd. Proctor Esq One of the oversears of the poor}
Pr. ordor of Jno. Scoley Esqr., Capt. Edwd. Tyler} Selectmen

decr. 31   Recd. into the Almshous Elenor Dukes of Ireland   State
Approd. of by E Proctor Esqr. one of the oversears of the poor}
Pr. ordor of Jno. Andrews Esqr., Mr. Wm. Bordman} Selectmen

1789
Jany. 1th.   Recd. into the Almshous Pattey Walker   State
Approd. of by Edwd. Proctor Esqr. One of the oversears of the poor}
Pr. ordor of Jno. Andrews Esqr.   } Selectmen

Jany. 1th.   Recd. into the Almshous Mary Purkit[18] and Betsey three years old   State
Approd. of by Saml. Whitwell One of the oversears of the poor}
Pr. ordor of Thos. Walley Esqr., Jno. Andrews Esqr.} Selectmen

Jany. 5th.   Recd. into the Almshous Jno. Willet   Town
Pr. ordor of Edwd. Proctor one of the Oversears of the poor

Jany. 6th.   Recd. into the Almshous Elizh. Wakefield   Town
Pr. ordor of Mr. Saml. Parkman Oversear

1788
Decr. 31th.   Recd. into the Almshous Jno. Wilkinson And his Daughter Elizh.—five
years old
Approd. of by Edwd. Proctor Esq One of the oversears of the poor}
Pr. ordor of Jno. Andrews Esq, Captn. Edwd. Tyler} Selectmen

[1789]
Jany. 5th.   R[un]   Mary Ratford   State

Jany. 7th.   Recd. into the Almshous Sarah Rice   State
Consented to by Henry hill Esqr. One of the oversears of the poor}
Pr. ordor of Thos. Walley Esqr., Ezekl. Price Esqr} Selectmen

Jany. 8th.   dischd. Jno. Willit   Town

Jany. 8th.   Recd. into the Almshous Jno. Willis of Verganey   State
Approd. of by Edwd. Proctor Esq one of the oversears of the poor}
Pr. ordor of Jno. Andrews Esq, Thos. Walley Esq} Selectmen

Jany. 8th.   Recd. into the Almshous Mary Payne borne at Charlstown   (State
Approd. of by Jno. Sweetser Esqr. one of the oversears of the poor}
Pr. ordor of Jno. Scollay Esq

Jany. 9th.   Recd. into the Almshous Bryant O'donell Ireland   State
Approd. of by Edwd. Proctor Esq One of the oversears of the poor}
Pr. ordor of Jno. Scollay Esq, Capt Edwd. Tyler} Selectmen

1789 Jany. 12   Recd. into the Almshous Mary Woodlet   State
Consented to by Mr. Saml Parkman One of the oversears of the poor}
Pr. ordor of Jno. Andrews Esqr., Mr. Wm. Bordman} Selectmen

Jany. 16th.   Recd. into the Almshous Polley Wakefield   Town
Pr. ordor of Edwd. Proctor Esqr. one of The oversears of the poor

Jany. 16th.   Recd. into the Almshous Mary Burford   Town
Pr. ordor of Edwd. Proctor Esqr. one of the oversears of the poor

Jany. 17th.   Recd. into the Almshous Robt. Giffin of Ireland
Approd. of by Edwd. Proctor Esqr. One of the oversears of the poor}
Pr. ordor of Jno. Scollay Esqr., Jno. Andrews Esqr.} Selectmen

Jany. 17   Recd. into the Almshous Wm. Jones   State
Approd. of by Mr. Saml. Parkman One of the oversears of the poor}
Pr. ordor of Ezekl. Price   } Selectmen
Jany. 19th.   Dischd. Thos. Bell   Town

Jany. 20th.   Recd. into the Almshous Ruben Knight a Child 4 Months old   State
Approd. of by Edwd. Proctor Esqr. one of the oversears of the poor
Pr. ordor of Jno. Scolley Esqr., Mr. Wm. Bordman} Selectmen

Jany. 21th.   Recd. into the Almshous Negero Dinah Freeman And Her Child 19
Months old   State
Approd. of by Edwd. Proctor Esqr. One of the oversears of the poor}
Pr. ordor of Jno. Andrews Esqr., Thos. Walley Esqr.} Selectmen

Jany. 21th.   Dischd. George Peters   State

Jany. 22d.   Recd. into the Almshous Nancey Sherley   State
Consented to by Edwd. Proctor Esq One of the oversears of the poor}
Pr. ordor of Thos. Walley Esqr., Mr. Ebenr. Seaveer} Selectmen

Jany. 21th.   Recd. into the Almshous Nathl. Aushton   State
Approd. of by Edwd. Proctor Esq One of the oversears of the poor}
Pr. ordor of Jno. Scollay Esqr., Mr. Ebenr. Sever} Select men

Jany. 24   Recd. into the Almshous Sarah Allen and Her three Melotto Children}
Approd. of by Edwd. Proctor One of the oversears of the poor   State
Pr. ordor of Thos. Walley Esqr., Mr. Ebenr. Seaver} Selectmen

Jany. 27th.   Recd. into the Almshous Sarah Segrave[19]   Town
<*Approd. of by Edwd. Proctor Esq One of the oversears of the poor}*>
Pr. ordor of Wm. Phillips Juner One of the oversears of the poor

1789
Jany. 28   Recd. into the Almshous Anna Hoey And her Child Named Polley (State)
Approvd. of by Edwd. Proctor Esq one of the oversears of the poor}
Pr. ordor of Capt. Edwd. Tyler, Mr. Ebenr. Seaver} Selectmen

Decr. 7   Recd. Harriot LeGalley a Child borne in this hous on this day   (State)
Approd. of by Edwd. Proctor Esq One of the oversears of the poor
Thos. Walley Esq, Mr. Ebenr. Seaver} Selectmen

Feby. 3d.   Dischd. Nathl. Ashton   State

Feby. 3   Recd. into the Almshous Sarah Johnson   State
Approd. of by Jno. Sweetser Esq One of the oversears of the poor}
Pr. ordor of Jno. Scollay Esq, Ezekl. Price Esqr.} Selectmen

Feby. 5th.   Recd. into the Almshous Richd. Peirce his wife And three Children
Pr. ordor of Henry Hill Esq One of the oversears of the poor}   Town

Feby. 5th.   Dischd. Robt. Gofford   State

Feby. 6th.   Dischd. Wm. LeGalley a boy bound out   State

Feby. 6th.   Dischd. Mary Sharp R[un]   State

Feby. 9th.	dischd. Sarah Rice R[*un*]	State
Feby. 9th.	Recd. into the Almshous Marthor James & Child Pr. ordor of Edwd. Proctor Esqr. one of the oversears of the poor}	Town
Feby. 5th.	Dischd. Thomas Brandon	State
Feby. 11th.	Recd. into the Almshous Cate Simons & Child Polley Manro—12 Months old the 1 of March 1789} Approd. of by Edwd. Proctor Esqr. One of the oversears of the poor} Pr. ordor of Jno. Andrews Esqr., Mr. Wm. Bordman} Select men}	State
Feby. 11th.	Dischd. Polley Crane alies <*Marion?*> Garrow Bound out}	State
Jany. 12th. omited in place	Recd. into the Almshous Wm. Spooner And Mary His wife} Approd. of by Edwd. Proctor Esqr. One of the oversears of the poor} Pr. ordor of Jno Scollay Esq, Mr. Wm. Bordman} Selectmen	
Feby. 13th.	Recd. Anna[20] Ethredge into the Amshous A Inhabtt. of this town Pr. ordor of Mr. Saml. Whitwell one of the oversears of the poor}	
Feby. 13th. Dischd. 14th.	Recd. into the Almshous Thos. Dollover[21] of Nw. Hamshier Pr. order of [22]	State
1789 Feby. 18th.	Recd. into the Almshous Saml. Mongomery of Ireland Approd. of by Edwd. Proctor Esqr. One of the Oversears of the poor} Pr. ordor of Jno. Scolley Esqr., Thos. Walley Esqr.} Selectmen	State
Feby. 18th.	Recd. into the Almshous Ebenr. Cox Pr. ordor of Edwd. Proctor One of the oversears of the poor	Town
Feby. 18th.	Recd. into the Almshous Solamon Nash Pr. ordor of Mr. Saml. Parkman One of the oversears of the poor	Town
Feby. 21th.	Dischd. Polley Wakefield Dischd. Kate Symons	Town State
Feby. 18th.	Recd. into the Almshous Elizh. Berry Approd. of by Edwd. Proctor Esq One of the oversears} Pr. ordor of Mr. Edwd. Tyler, Thos. Walley Esqr.} Selectmen	State
Feby. 20th. 20th.	Rachel Wall Run} <*feby. 24th. Recd.*> Eliz Mathews Run}	State do.
Feby. 25	Recd. into the Almshous Thomas Burk Approd. of by Edwd. Proctor one of the oversears of the poor Pr. ordr Jno. Scolley Esq, Capt. Edwd. Tyler} Selectmen	State
Feby. 25th.	Recd. into the Almshous James Brown Approvd. of by Edwd. Proctor Esqr. One of the oversears of the poor} Pr. ordor of Harbl. Dorr Esq, Mr. Ebenr. Sever} Selectmen	State
Feby. 26th.	Recd. into the Almshous Hannah Armstrong Approd. of by Edwd. Proctor Esq One of the overs of the poor Pr. ordor of Mr. Harbol. Dorr, Mr. Edwd. Tyler} Selectmen	State

Feby. 26th. Recd. into the Almshous Partrick Bennet		State

Feby. 26th.   Recd. into the Almshous Partrick Bennet   State
Approvd. of by [23] one of the oversears of the poor
Pr. ordor of Jno. Scollay Esq, Jno. Andrews do. [*i.e., esq.*]} Selectmen

Feby. 27th.   Recd. into the Almshous Benjman Eddy   State
Approd. of by Jona. Mason Esq One of the oversears of the poor}
Pr. ordor of Jno. Andrews Esqr., Mr. Wm. Bordman} Selectmen

March [3d.]   Dischd. James Brown   State

March 4th.   Dischd. Nathl. Boarn   Town
      Dischd. John Wilkins   State

March 6th.   Discharged Benjn. Eddy   State
      Ditto   John Mathews a Child   do.

      Ditto   Eliz Wilkinson a Child   State

Feb 24th.   Recd. back into the Almshous Thos. Brandon   State
Omited by being Sent to the Workhous

March 10th.   Dischd. Ann Ethredge   Town

March 10th.   Recd. into the Almshous Mary Sanders   Town
Pr. ordor of Mr. Jno. Codman Junr. One of the oversears of the poor

March 12th.   Recd. into the Almshous Jno. Devan   State
Approd. of by Edwd. Proctor Esq One of the oversears of the poor}
Pr. ordor of Jno. Andrews Esq, Thos. Walley Esq} Selectmen

March 12th.   Recd. into the Almshous Edwd. Smith An Englishman   State
Consented to by Jona. Mason one of the oversears of the poor}
Pr. ordor of Ezekl. Price Esq   } Selectmen

March 10th.   Dischd. Wm. Spooner & wife   State

March 14th.   Recd. into the Almshous Jack hill a Negero
Approd. of by Edwd. Proctor Esq an oversear of the poor
Pr. ordor of Wm. Borardman   } Selectmen
Sent out by ordor of Mr. Bordman and the ordor Returnd to him

March 14th.   Recd. into the Almshous Benjn. Kneeland   Town
Pr. ordor of Mr. Saml. Whitwell one of The oversears of the poor

March 16th.   Dischd. Sarah Coney & Child   State

March 17th.   dischd. Partrick Shanley I think the most troublisom Man that Ever has ben in the hous sence I have ben hear a drunken Quarrelson fiteinging decriped Rech As I know of}   State

March 17th.   Dischd. Partrick Bennet an Irishman   State

March 18th.   Recd. into the Almshous George Reynolds   State
Pr. ordor of Edwd. Proctor Esq One of the oversears of the poor}
Pr. ordor of Jno. Andrews Esq, Capt. Edwd. Tyler} Selectmen

March 19th.   Recd. into the Almshous Thos. Green—of Road Island   State
Consentd to By Jona. Mason Esq one of the oversears of the poor}
Pr. ordor of Jno. Andrews Esq, Mr. Wm. Bordman} Selectmen

Feby. 14th.   Recd. into the Almshous Margrat Davis   State
Approd. of by Mr. Wm. Smith one of the oversears of the poor}
Pr. ordor of Jno. Scollay Esq, Mr. Ebenr. Seaver} Selectmen
This order was kep in the workhous Accasioned it out of ordor

March 18th.   Dischd. Margrat Davis

March 18th.   Dischd. Richd. Doan   State

March 18th.   Dischd. Wm. Fergos   State
do.   18   do.   Mary Garrow

March 26th.   Recd. into the Almshous Benjn. Eddy   State
Approd. of by Jona. Mason Esq One of the oversears of the poor}
Pr. ordor of Jno. Andews Esqr., Thos. Walley Esq} Selectmen

March 24th.   Recd. into the Almshous Edwd. Beacham of London   State
Consented to by Saml. Whitwell one of the oversears of the poor}
Pr. ordor of Capt. Edwd. Tyler, Mr. Ebenr. Seaver} Selectmen

March 28th.   dischd. Ebenr. Cox   Town

March 31th.   Recd. into the Almshous Jno. Murphey of Ireland   State
Approd. of by Edwd. Proctor One of the oversears of the poor}
Pr. ordor of Wm. Bordman   } Selectmen

March 23d.   dischd. Thos. Brandon out of the workhous   State

Aprl. 2d.   dischd. John Moran   State

Aprl. 2d.   Recd. into the Almshous Eliz Wakefield   Town
Pr. ordor of Edwd. Proctor Esq an oversear of the poor}

Aprl. 2d.   dischd. Susanna Wallis   State

Aprl. 3d.   Dischd. Jno. Brown   State

Aprl. 4   Dischd. Michal McLochlen   State

Aprl. 4   Mary Whitman Run   Town

Aprl. 4th.   Elenor Dukes Run   State

March 3d.   Recd. into the Almshous a Infent Child of Polly Cartor[24] Cald. hannah
Approd. of by Jona. Mason Esq one of the oversears of the poor}   State
Pr. ordor of Jno. Andrews Esq, Mr. Wm. Bordman} Selectmen

March 23d.   Recd. or borne in the Almshous Nance Sherley's Child a boy   State
Approd. of by Edwd. Proctor Esq overseer}
Pr. ordor of Mr. Edwd. Tyler, Mr. Wm. Boardman} Selectmen

1789

Feby. 26th.   Recd. into the Almshous Joseph Purket an Infent born in the Almshous of Mary Purket
Consented to by Jona. Mason Esq One of the oversears of the poor
Pr. ordor of Jno. Andrews Esq, Thos. Walley Esq} Selectmen

Aprl. 7th.   Recd. Wm. Tayler into the Almshous born in England   State
Consented to by Jona. Mason Esq One of the oversears of the poor}
Pr. ordor Jno. Scollay Esq, Ezekl. Price Esq} Selectmen

Aprl. 9th.   Recd. George Blackman into the Almshous   State
Consented to by Edwd. Proctor Esq one of the oversears of the poor}
Pr. ordor of Jno. Andrews Es[q], Capt. Edwd. Tyler} Selectmen

Aprl. 14th.   Dischd. Charls De. St. Pree a boy bound out   State
               Ditto   Hannah Armstrong   do.

Aprl. 14   Dischd. An Richardson   Town

Aprl. 15   Dischd. Saml. Mongomery   State

Aprl. 15   Dischd. Benjn. Eddy   State

Aprl. 15th.   Mary Lawrance[25] Run & Child   State

Aprl. 17th.   Recd. into the Almshous Sarah Coney & her Child   State
Apprd. by E Proctor Esq oversear}
E Tyler & Wm. Bordman} Selectmen

Aprl. 22d.   Dischd. Mary Woodlet   State

Aprl. 21th.   Recd. into the Almshous Betsey Crage   State
Approd. by Edwd. Proctor one of the oversear of the poor}
Pr. ordor of Jno. Scoley Esq, Ezekl. Price Esq} Selectmen

Aprl. 22d.   Dischd. Marthor James & Child   Town

Aprl. 18th.   Dischd. <*John Wills omited*>

Aprl. 23d.   dischd. James Cumberford   State

Aprl. 23   Dischd. Odanial Bryant   State

Aprl. 28th.   Recd. into the Almshous Andre Corrente but am Directed that he Shall be Supplyd. At his lodgings}   State
Approd. of by Edwd. Proctor Esqr. one of the oversears of the poor}
Pr. ordor of Jno. Andrews Esqr., Mr. Wm. Bordman} Selectmen

Aprl. 28th.   Dischd. Ann Delaney & her two Children   State

Aprl. 28th.   Dischd. Eliz Wakefield   Town

May 1th.   Dischd. Morris McLochlen   State

May 1th.   Reced. into the Almshous Saml. Marsh belong. to Conitticut}   state
Approd. of by Edwd. Proctor Esq One of the Overseers of the poor}
Pr. ordor of Jno. Andrews Esq, Mr. Ebenr. Seaver} Selectmen

May 1th.	Recd. into the Almshous Wm. Brown & wife & 2 Children	town

Pr. ordor of Edwd. Proctor one of the oversers

May 9d.	Dischd. Wm. Scolley his Nurs & two Children	State

May 4th.	Recd. into the Almshous Edwd. Harper	State

Approd. of by Edwd. Proctor Esqr. One of the oversears of the poor}
Pr. order of Jno. Andrews Esq, Mr. Wm. Boardman} Selectmen

May 5th.	Dischd. Jno. Chaimbers	State

May 6th.	Dischd. Mary Read R[un]	State

May 9th.	Dischd. Jonathon Webb	Town

May 11th.	Dischd. Sarah Allen & her three Molatto Children}	State

May 13th.	Recd. into the Almshous Richd. LeGalley a boy	State

Consented to by Edwd. Proctor Esqr. One of the oversears of the poor
Pr. ordor of Jno. Andrews Esq, Thos. Walley Esq} Selectmen

May 14th.	Recd. into the Almshous Wm. Peake	Town

Pr. ordor of Mr. Saml. Parkman one of the oversears of the poor

May 14th.	Recd. into the Almshous Sarah Richards a Child	State

Approd. of by Jno. White Esq One of the oversears of the poor}
Pr. ordor of Mr. Harbl. Dorr, Capt. Edwd. Tyler} Selectmen

May 18th.	Dischd. out of the hous Wm. Tayler	State

May 18th.	Recd. into the Almshous Thos. Ethridge a boy Eight years old the 15th.	
Augt. 1789		Town

Pr. ordor of Saml. Whitwell one of the oversears of the poor

May 19th.	Recd. into the Almshous Polley Sherman Child Borne Septr. 8th. 1787	
	Consented to by Jno. White Esqr. (oversear)	State

Pr. ordor of Harbl. Dorr, Capt. Ebenr. Tyler} Selectmen

May 15th.	Dischd. Peter Swan	State

May 15th.	Discharged Edwd. harper	State

May 20th.	Dischd. Willm. Jones State	

1789		
May 20th.	Recd. into the Almshous Phillip Hilt & Elizh. his wife	State

Approd. of by Jno. Sweetser Esq One of the oversears of the poor
Pr. ordor of Jno. Andrews Esqr., Thos. Walley Esq} Selectmen

May 22d.	Dischd. Jno. Gillard	State
	Dischd. James McQuinn	do.

May 23d.	Recd. into the Almshous Frances[26] Clark	Town

Pr. ordor of Jno. Sweetser Esq One of the oversears of the poor

May 26	Dischd. Nancy Shirley & Child	State

May 27th.	Dischd. Robert Lilman	State
May 28th.	Mary Benjiman Run—lef her Child	Town
May[27]		State
June 3d.	Dischd. Jno. Murphey	State
June 3d.[28]		State
June 5th.	Dischd. Mathew Wakefield a boy bound out	Town
June 6	dischd. Ann Haye & her daughtor	State
June 5th.	Recd. into the Almshous Sarah Finn & 3 Children Consented to by Edwd. Proctor Esqr. One of the oversears of the poor Pr. ordor of Mr. Harbl. Dorr, Capt. Edwd. Tyler} Selectmen	State
June 7th.	Recd. into the Almshous Mary Sharpe Approd. of by Edwd. proctor Esq one of the oversears of the poor} Pr. ordor of Jno. Scoley Esqr., Mr. Wm Bordman} Selectmen	State
June 10th.	Recd. into the Almshous Richd. McCluer Pr. ordor of Jona. Mason, one of the oversears of the poor	Town
June 10th.	Recd. into the Almshous Saml. Mongomery Approd. of by Jno. White Esq one of the oversears of the poor} Pr. ordor of Jno. Andrews Esqr., Mr. Wm. Bordman} Selectmen	State
June 12th.	Recd. into the Almshous Holms Simpson Pr. order of Jona. L. Austin one of the oversears of the poor	Town
June 12th.	Recd. into the Almshous Nancy Watts Approd. of by Saml. Whitwell One of the oversears of the poor} Pr. ordor of Ezekl. Price } Selectmen	State
June 13th.	dischd. Joseph Jaines & wife	State
June 11th.	Recd. into the Almshous Elizh. Robinson approd. of by Edwd. Proctor Esqr. one of the oversears of the poor} Pr. ordor of Jno. Andrews Esqr., Mr. Wm. Bordman} Selectmen	State
June 12th.	Recd. into the Almshous Andrew Gardner Approd. of by Edwd. Proctor Esq One of the oversears of the poor} Pr. ordor of Jno Andrews Esqr., Mr. Wm. Boardman} Selectmen	State
June 15th.	Dischd. Thomas Burk	State
June 15th.	Dischd. Mary Johnson & Child	Town
June 15th.	Recd. into the Almshous Rebecca Putton and child} Pr. ordor of Mr. Saml. Parkman on[e] of the overseers	Town
June 17th.	dischd. Salley Dunken bound out	State

June 17th.   Recd. into the Almshous Richd. Walker   State
Consented to by Mr. Saml. Parkman One of the oversears of the poor}
Pr. ordor of Jno. Scollay Esqr., Ezekl. Price Esqr.} Selectmen

June 18th.   Dischd. Sarah Finn & two Children to the pesthous   State
                  Sarah Finn Returnd

June 17th.   Recd. into the Almshous Wm. Finley of the Ile of Man   (State)
approd. of by Mr. Saml. Parkman of the oversears of the poor}
Pr. ordor of Jno. Andrews Esqr., Mr. Wm. Bordman} Select men

June 18th.   Recd. into the Almshous Henry Mayhew 5 years old   State
Approd. of by Edwd. Proctor Esqr. one of the oversears of the poor}
Pr. ordor of Jno. Andrews Esq, Thos. Walley Esq} Selectmen

June 20th.   Received Ann Hill & Child into the Almshous   State
Consented to by Edwd. Proctor One of the oversears of the poor}
Pr. ordor of Wm. Bordman, Ezekl. Price Esq} Selectmen

June 20th.   Recd. into the Almshous Wm. Langford   Town
Pr. ordor of Jno. White Esqr. One of the oversears of the poor}

June 18th.   Recd. into the Almshous Abigal Chubb   Town
Pr. ordor of Jno. Sweetser one of the oversears of the poor}

June 22d.   dischd. George Renals   State

June 23d.   Dischd. Saml. Mongomery   State

<*June 16*> May 27   Recd. into the Almshous Sarah Joseph   State
Approd. of by Saml. Whitwell one of the oversears of the poor}
Pr. ordor of Jno. Andrews Esqr., Mr. Wm. Bordman} Selectmen

June 16th.   Recd. into the Almshous Elizh. <*Valentine*> Lewis   State
Approd. of by Mr. Saml. Whitwell one of the oversears of the poor}
Pr. ordor of Jno. Andrews Esq, Mr. Wm. Bordman} Selectmen

1789
June 30th.   Dischd. Sarah Coney & Child   State

June 30th.   Recd. into the Almshous Partrick Quin   State
Consented to by Jno. Mason Esq One of the oversears of the poor}
Pr. ordor of Ezekl. Price Esq, Jno. Scollay Esqr.} Selectmen

July 2d.   Dischd. Richd. Walker & Patte his wife   State
                  Dischd. Willm. Finley   State

July 2d.   Recd. into the Almshous Joseph Brazer   State
Approd. of by Jona. Mason Esqr. One of the oversears of the poor}
Pr. ordor of Ezekl. Price Esqr.   } Selectmen

July 2d.   Dischd. Ann Whitman   Town

June 18th.   Dischd. out of the workhous Saml. Duncalf   State

July 9th.	dischd. Holms Simpson	Town
July 10th.	Dischd. Jane Galley bound out	Town
July 11th.	Recd. into the Almshous Mary Scott Pr. ordor of Jno. White Esqr. one of the Oversears of the poor	Town
July 11th.	Dischd. Thos. Smith one Eye	State
July 15th.	Recd. into the Almshous Thos. Cross Pr. ordor of Jno. White Esqr. Oversear	Town
July 16th.	Recd. into the Almshous Eliz dalman Pr. ordor of Jona. Mason Esq One of the overseers of the poor	Town
July 17th.	Recd. into the Almshous Cockren[29] John Approd. of by Mr. Saml. Parkman One of the overseers of the poor} Pr. ordor of Capt. Edwd. Tyler, Mr. Wm. Bordman} Selectmen	State
July 18th.	Disd. Mary Wakefield	Town
July 18	dischd. Nathl. Adams	Town
July 18	Recd. Into the Almshous Edmon Jones a Welchman Pr. ordor of Jno. Scolley Esq, Capt. Edwd. Tyler} Selectmen Approd. of by Edwd. Proctor Esqr. One of the overseers of the poor}	State
July 20th.	Dischd. Elizh. Jennen	State
July 21th.	Dischd. Polley Goddard bound out	Town
1789 May 28th.	Recd. Wm. Spoonor into the Almshous Consented to by Edwd. Proctor Esq one of the overseers of the poor} Pr. ordor of Jno. Scolley Esq, Capt. Edwd. Tyler} Selectmen	State
June 13th.	Dischd. Wm. Spooror	State
July 22d.	<*Rec into Almshous Wm. Spooner 3 day then turn*[30]	*Town>*
July 22d.	Recd. Ebenr: Cocks[31] into the Almshous Pr. ordor of Edwd. Proctor Esqr. oversear	Town
July 22d.	Recd. Hannah Fayerweather into the Almshous Consented to by Jona. Mason Esq One of the overseers of the poor} Pr. ordor of Jno. Scollay Esq, Mr. Ebenr. Sever} Selectmen	State
July 23d.	Recd. into the Almshous Thos. Armstrong, Irishman Approd. by Edwd. Proctor Esq one of the overseers of the poor} Pr. ordor of Mr. Benjn. Bordman } Selectmen	State
July 24th.	Dischd. Jane Bates who belonges to hingam	Town
	Dischd. Ann Hill & Child—Run	Town

July 25th.	Disch'd. R[un] Edmon Jones a Welchman	State

<July 25th.> dischd. Joseph Brazer Contineud on the book tel Augt. 2d. furnished him with provision to go to phalidelpha

State

July 27th.	Dischd. Jno. Cockren	State
July 25th.	dischd. Run Agnes Richards	State
July 27th.	Dischd. Nancey Watts	State

July 27th. Recd. Benjn. Eddy into the Almshous
Pr. ordor of Jno. Andrews Esq   } Select men

July 27th. Henry Mayhew a boy Run   on the state

July 27th. Recd. into the Almshous Ketty Steward & her 2 Children State
Consented to by Edwd. Proctor Esqr. One of the oversear of the poor}
Pr. ordor of Mr. Harbl. Dorr, Mr. Edwd. Tyler} Selectmen

July 28	dischd. Sophey Manders	State

Augt. 1th. Recd. into the Almshous John Hogan of Ireland State
Approd. of by Edwd. Proctor Esqr. one of the oversears of the poor}
Pr. ordor of Jno. Andrews Esq, Mr. Wm. Boardman} Selectmen

Augt. 1th.	Mary Scott dischd.	Town

July 27th. Recd. into the Almshous Jno. Mitchell State
Pr. ordor of Jno. Andrews Esq, Mr. Wm. Bordman} Selectmen
Approd. of by Edwd. Proctor Esqr. One of the oversears of the poor}

July 30 Recd. into the Almshous Christian Mahoan State
Approd. of by Mr. Saml. Whitwell One of the oversears of the poor}
Pr. ordor of Jno. Andrews Esq, Capt. Edwd. Tyler} Selectmen

1789
Augt. 3d.	dischd. John Devall	State

Augt. 4th. Recd. into the Almshous Elizh. Denne Town
Pr. ordor Jno. White Esqr. one of the oversears of the poor

Augt. 10th.	Dischd. Thos. Armstrong	State

Augt. 10th. Recd. into the Almshous Jacob Wendol[32] Town
Pr. ordor of Jona. L Austen overseer

Augt. 13th. Recd. into the Almshous Frank Allen a Child 15 Months old State
Approd. of by Edwd. Proctor Esqr. One of the oversears of the poor}
Pr. ordor of Jno. Scolley Esqr., Jno. Andrews Esqr.} Selectmen

Augt. 10th. Recd. Ann[33] Hoey & Child into the Almshous
Approd. of by Saml. Parkman one of the oversears of the poor}
Pr. ordor of Jno. Andrews Esqr., Mr. Wm. Boardman} Selectmen

Augt. 13d.   Recd. into the Almshous Mary Burns & Nancy Murphey
Pr. ordor of Jona. Mason Esq one of the oversears of the poor

Augt. 12th.   Recd. into the Almshous Mary McLachlin[34]   State
Approd. of by Mr. Saml. Parkman One of the oversears of the poor}
Pr. ordor of Jno. Andrews Esqr., Capt. Edwd. Tyler} Selectmen

Augt. 17th.   Recd. into the Almshous three Children Polley, Esther & Mercy Henly
Polley Henly borne May 13th. 1782
Esther   do.   Septr. 15th. 1784
Marcy   do.   decr. 26th. 1786
Pr. ordor of Saml. Parkman one of the oversears of the poor

<Augt. 17th.   Dischd. F   C   >[35]   State

Augt. 24th.   Dischd. Abigal Whitte   State

Augt. 24th.   Dischd. Kitty Stewart & her 2 Children   State

Augt. 26th.   Recd. into the Almshouse the widow   Fowell[36]   Town

Augt. 26th.   Recd. into the Almshous George Hampton a German   State
Approd. of by Edwd. Proctor Esqr. one of the oversears of the poor
Pr. ordor of Jno. Scollay Esq, Capt. Edwd. Tyler} Selectmen

Augt. 28th.   Recd. into the Almshous Richd. Crouch   (State)
Consentd. to by Edwd. proctor Esq one of the oversears of the poor}
Pr. ordor of Capt. Edwd. Tyler, Jno. Andrews Esqr.} Selectmen

Augt. 28th.   dischd. Jno. Mitchel R[un]   State

1789 Augt. 26th. Recd. into the Almshous Jno. Parkett a boy   State
Approd. of by Mr. Saml. Whitwell One of the oversears of the poor}
Pr. ordor of Jno. Andrews Esq, Jabz Hatch Esqr.} Selectmen

Augt. 31th.   Recd. into the Almshou[se] A Bastard Child of Mary Johnson's Cald.
Joseph Russel}   Town
Pr. ordor of Mr. Jno. Codman one of the oversears of the poor

Augt. 31th   dischd. Eliz Crage   State

Augt. 2d.   Sarah Sharp A Child   State
Pr. ordor of Thos. Walley Esq, Mr. Ebenr. Sevear} Select men

Septr. 3d.   Recd. into the Almshous Jno. Gillard of Ireland   State
Approd. of by Jona. Mason Esqr. one of the oversears of the poor}
Pr. ordor of Jno. Scollay Esqr., Mr. Wm. Boardman} Selectmen

Septr. 3d.   Recd. into the Almshous Thos. Tyrrell   State
Consented to by Jona. Mason Esqr. one of the oversears of poor}
Pr. ordor of Jno. Scollay Esqr., Mr. Wm. Boardman} Selectmen

Septr. 8th.   Dischd. R[un] Mary Sharp   State

Septr. 14th.   Recd. into the Almshous Amme[37] Russel   State
Pr. ordor of Mr. Harbl. dorr, Capt. Edwd. Tyler} Selectmen
Consented to by Jno. White Esq one of the oversears of the poor}

Septr. 16   Recd. into the Almshous Mary Fletcher   (State)
Approvd. of by Saml. Parkman one of the oversears of the poor}
Pr. ordor of Ezekl. Price Esqr., Jno. Andrews Esqr.} Selectmen

Septr. 11th.   Recd. into the Almshous Mary Cowell & Child   Town
Pr. ordor of Jona. L Austin Esqr. oversear

Septr. 19th.   Recd. into the Almshous Eliz Floyd   Town
Pr. ordor of Jona. L Austin oversear

Septr. 20th.   Dischd. Jno. Parkhart a boy bound out   State

Septr. 20th.   Sarah Finn Runn   State

Septr. 20th.   Rebecca Puttom & Child Run   Town

Septr. 22d.   dischd. Wm. Langford   Town

Septr. 23d.   Recd. into the Almshous Marten McLoehlen[38]   State
Approd. by Edwd. Procter Esqr. one of the oversears of the poor}
Pr. ordor of Mr. Wm. Boardman, Mr. Ebenr. Seaver} Select men

Septr. 23d.   Recd. Saml. Mongomery into the Almshous   State
Approd. of by Edwd. Proctr. one of oversears of poor}
Pr. order of Jno. Andrews Esq, Mr. Ebenr. Sever} Selectmen

1789
Septr. 24th.   <Dischd. Rebecca Puttom & Child>   State

Septr. 25th.   Dischd. George Hampton   State

Septr. 28th.   Recd. into the Almshous Mary Richardson   Town
Pr. ordor Jno. Sweetser oversear; ward 11

Sept. 28th.   Recd. into the Almshous Edwd. Thompson   State
Consented to by Edwd. Procter Esq One of the oversears of the poor
Pr. ordor of Mr. Edwd. Tyler, Jno. Andrews Esqr.} Selectmen

Septr. 28th.   Elizh. Barry Run   State

Octr. 1th.   Recd. into the Almshous Ebenr. Redock   Town
Pr. ordor of Edwd. Proctor Esqr. One of the oversears of the poor

Septr. 28th.   Recd. into the Almshous Abigail Brown & her 3 Children   State
Approd. of by Jona. Mason Esq One of the Oversears of the poor}
Pr. ordor of Capt. Edwd. Tyler, Jno. Andrews Esqr.} Selectmen

Octr. 2d.   Dischd. Benjn. Kneeland   Town

Octr. 3d.   Dischd. John Hogen   State

Octr. 6th.   Dischd. Mary Burford   Town

Octr. 6th.	Dischd. Thomas Tyrrell	State
Octr. 7th.	Recd. into the Almshous Wm. Langford	Town
Pr. ordor of Jno. White Esqr.		
Octr. 9th.	Dischd. Sarah Johnson	State
Septr. 28	dischd. Mary Ratford, Dischd. Elizh. Lewis, Dischd. Sarah Joseph}from	
the workhous		State
Septr. 7	dischd. Thos. Mitchel from the workhous	State
Octr. 10th.	Dischd. Thos. Ethredge a boy bound out	Town
Octr. 10th.	Recd. Jno. Willit into the almshous	Town
Pr. ordor of Edwd. Proctr. Esq One of the oversears of the poor		
Octr. 8th.	Recd. into the Almshous Charles Burnes a Child 3 weaks old	State
Approd. of by Mr. Saml. Parkman One of the oversears of the poor		
Pr. ordr Jno. Scollay Esqr., Jno. Andrews Esqr.} Selectmen		

1789

Octr. 12	Recd. into the Almshous Ebenr. Cooks	Town
Pr. ordor of Edwd. Proctor Esqr., oversear		
Octr. 12th.	dischd. John Finn A boy	State
Octr. 13th.	Dischd. Marten McLochlen	State
Octr. 13th.	Recd. into the Almshous Eliz Wood	Town
Pr. ordor of Henry Hill Esqr. One of the oversears of the poor		
Octr. 13d.	Recd. into the Almshous Judeth Lowe born in Ireland	State
Approd. of by Edwd. Proctor Esq One of the oversears of the poor}		
Pr. ordor of Jno. Andrews } Selectmen		
Septr. 25	Recd. into the Almshous Peter Russell a Child Belonging Ammy Russell	
approd. of by Mr. Saml. Parkman one of the oversears of the poor}		
Pr. ordor of Thos. Walley Esq, Mr. Ebenr. Seaver} Selectmen		
Octr. 12th.	Recd. into the almshous Wm. McKinzie a Child	
approd. of by Mr. Saml. Parkman one of the oversears}		
Pr. ordor of Thos. Walley Esq, Mr. Ebenr. Seaver} Selectmen		
Octr. 16th.	Dischd. Jno. Willet to the workhous	Town
Octr. 17th.	Dischd. Mary Cartor & Child R[un]	State
Octr. 17	dischd. Judath Eddy Run	State
	d[o.] Murphy Run a garle 10 years old	
Octr. 19th.	Recd. into the Almshous Mary Peters She borne at Ipswich Married A	
frenchman} her husband now in town		State
Approd. of by Edwd. Proctr. One of the oversears of the poor}		
Pr. ordor of Jno. Scoley Esqr., Capt. Edwd. Tyler} Selectmen		

Octr. 14th. Recd. into the Almshous Elizh. Berry born in Ireland State
Approd. of by Edwd. Proctor Esqr. One of the oversears of the poor}
Pr. ordor of Jno. Andrews Esqr., Mr. Ebenr. Seaver} Selectmen

Octr. 19th. Recd. into the Almshous Mary Dowrick Town
Pr. ordor of Mr. Jno. Codman Juner One of the Oversears of the poor

Octr. 22d. Recd. into the Almshous James frost Town
Pr. ordor of Mr. Saml. Parkman one of the oversears of the poor

Octr. 24th. Recd. into the Almshous Mary Pool Town
Pr. ordor of Jona. L Austin one of the oversears of the poor

1789
Octr. 21th. Recd. into the Almshous Mary Sharp State
Aprod. of by Edwd. Proctor Esqr. one of the oversears of the poor}
Pr. ordor of Jno. Andrews Esq } Selectmen

Octr. 28th. Recd. into the Almshous Ruth Kendall England State
Approd. of by Saml. Parkman one of the oversears of the poor}
Pr. ordor of Thos. Walley Esqr., Jno. Scollay Esq.} Selectmen

Octr. 29th. Recd. into the Almshous Henry Kendol[39] An Englishman State
Pr. ordor of Saml. Parkman One of the oversears of the poor}
Pr. ordor of Jno. Scollay Esqr., Mr. Harbl. dorr} Selectmen

Octr. 30th. Recd. into the Almshous James Pike his wife & Child Town
Pr. ordor of Mr. Saml. Parkman one of the oversears of the poor

Occtr. 30th. Recd. into the Almshous Thos. Cross Town
Pr. ordor of Mr. Saml. Parkman one of the oversears of the poor

Octr. 22d. Dischd. Edwd. Thomas R[*un*] State

Novr. 4th. Rec'd. into the Almshous Fredrk. Eyrs[40] Town <*State*>
Pr. ordor of Henry Hill Esqr. (oversear)

<*Novr. 7th.* *dischd. Jeremh. Malone* *State*>

Novr. 9th. <*Dischd. Brown Run*> Town

Novr. 12th. Recd. into the Almshous Nathl. Adams Town
Pr. ordor of Jno. Codman Junr. (oversear)

Novr. 7th. Recd. into the Almshous Eliz Ivers
Approd. of by Edwd. Proctor Esqr. one of the oversears of the poor}
Pr. ordor of Jno. Andrews Esq, Mr. Ebenr. Seaver} Selectmen

Novr. 16th. Recd. into the Almshous Barnabus Maxwell A Welchman State
Consented to by Jno. White Esqr. One of the Oversears of the Town}
Pr. ordor of Edwd. Tyler, Mr. Harb Dorr} Selectmen

Novr. 16th. Recd. into the Almshous Ann Ethredge Town
Pr. ordor of Jno. White one of the oversears of the poor

~

Novr. 16th.	Dischd. Mary McLachlen	State

Novr. 16th.　　　Recd. into the Almshous Mary Johnson　　　Town
Pr. ordor of Jno. White Esqr. one of the Oversears of the poor

Novr. 16　　　Recd. Mary Burford into the Almshous　　　Town
Pr. ordor of Edwd. Proctor Esqr. one of The oversears of the poor

Novr. 16th.　　　Recd. into the hous Diana Cotton Nurs to James Morwood　　　State
Apprd. of by Edwd. Proctor Esqr. one of the oversears of the poor}
Pr. ordor of Jno. Andrews Esqr., Capt. Edwd. Tyler} Selectmen

Novr. 16　　　Recd. into the Almshous James Morewood　　　State
Consented to by [Edward Proctor?] One of the oversears of the poor}
Pr. ordor of Harbl. Dorr Esq., Capt. Edwd. Tyler} Selectmen

Novr. 19th.　　　Dischd. Jno. Richards A boy bound out　　　Town

Novr. 19th.　　　Recd. into Sarah Jackson　　　State
Approd. of by Saml. Whitwell Esq One of the oversears of the poor}
Pr. ordor of Edwd. Tyler, Jno. Andrews Esq} Selectmen

Novr. 18　　　Recd. into the Almshous Sarah Johnson
Pr. ordor of Jona. L. Austen Esq one of the oversears of the poor}

Novr. 19th.　　　Dischd. Mary Pool　　　Town

Novr. 20th.　　　Recd. Ephrom Fenno into the Almshous　　　Town
Pr. ordor of Mr. Saml. Whitwell one of the oversears of the poor

Novr. 21th.　　　Recd. into the Almshous Betsey Vinteno　　　Town
Pr. ordor of Henry Hill Esqr. one of the oversears of the poor

Novr. 25th.　　　Recd. into the Almshous Henry Luckis　　　Town
Pr. ordor of <Mr.> Jno. White Esqr. one of the oversears of the poor

Novr. 25　　　Recd. into the Almshous Sarah Coney & Child　　　State
Approd. of by Edwd. Proctor Esq One of the oversears of the poor}
Pr. ordor of Jno. Andrews Esq, Jno. Walley Esq} Selectmen

Novr. 28　　　Recd. into the Almshous Thos. Brandgon[41] Irishman　　　State
Approd. of by Edwd. Proctor Esqr. One of the oversears of the poor}
Pr. ordor of Mr. Edwd. Tyler, Mr. Ebenr. Seaver} Selectmen

Novr. 28th.　　　<Dischd. James Pike>　　　Town

Decr. 1th.　　　Recd. into the Almshous Benjn. Burdet　　　Town
by ordor of Henry Hill oversear

Decr. 1th.　　　Recd. into the Almshous Elizh. Craige wife of Jno. Crage　　　State
Consented to by Mr. Saml. Whitwell one of the oversears of the poor}
Pr. ordor of Mr. Ebenr. Seaver, Thos. Walley Esq} Selectmen

decr. 2d. Recd. into the Almshous Mary Everton Pr. ordor of Jona. Mason Esqr. one of the oversears of the poor		Town
decr. 7th. Recd. into the Almshous Thos. Loring Pr. ordor of Edwd. Proctor Esqr. one of the oversears of the poor		Town
<Decr. 6th. Recd. into the Almshous Mary Hinds from the Workhous *Pr. ordor of Henry hill Esqr. one of The oversears of the poor>*		*Town*
Decr. 8th. Dischd. James Frost		Town
Decr. 7th. Recd. into the Almshous Mary Hinds Consentd. to by Edwd. Proctor Esq one of the oversears of the poor} Pr. ordor of Jno. Andrews Esq, Ezekl. Price Esqr.} [*Selectmen*]		State
Decemr. 8th. Dischd. Eliz Craige Run		State
Decr. 10 Recd. into the Almshous Michl. Condon & Wife Approd. of by Jno. Sweetser Esq One of the oversears of the poor} Pr. ordor of Jabez Hatch Esqr., Ezekl. Price Esqr.} Selectmen		State
Decr. 11th. Recd. into the Almshous Polley Wintor[42] A Child Consented to by Mr. Saml. Whitwell One of the oversears of the poor} Pr. ordor of Mr. Ebenr. Seaver, Ezekl. Price Esqr.} Selectmen		State
Decr. 12 Recd. into the Almshous Hugh Kemple of Ireland Approd. of by Mr. Saml. Whitwell One of the oversears of the poor Pr. ordor of Capt. Edwd. Tyler, Jno. Andrews Esq.} Selectmen		State
Decr. 15th. Recd. into the Almshous Margt. Kilgore[43] Consentd. to by Edwd. Proctor Esqr. One of the oversears of the poor} Pr. order of Edwd. Tyler Esq, Mr. Ebenr. Seaver} Selectmen		State
Decr. 19th. Recd. into the Almshous Nicholas Dulash a Child 2 years old Consented to by Edwd. Proctor Esq One of the oversears of the poor} Pr. ordor of Jno. Andrews Esqr., Thos. Walley Esqr.} Selectmen		State
Decr. 19th. Recd. into the Almshous Pompy[44] Soyer a negero Consented to by Mr. Saml. Whitwell One of the oversears of the poor} Pr. ordor of Harbl. Dorr Esq, Capt. Edwd. Tyler} Selectmen		State
decr. 23 Dischd. Ann Hoey And her daughtor		State
decr. 23d. dischd. Cowell Run		Town
Decr. 23d. Recd. into the Almshous Saml. Sergant Pr. ordor of Mr. Saml. Whitwell one of the oversears of the poor		Town
Decr. 18th. Recd. into the Almshous Catharina[45] McPherson Consented to by Edwd. Proctor Esqr. One of the oversears of the poor} Pr. ordor of Edwd. Tyler Esq, Mr. Ebenr. Seaver} Selectmen		State
Decr. 21th. Recd. into the Almshous Cornelius drisky for a fortnite born in Ireland Pr. ordor of Jno. Scoley Esq, Mr. Wm. Bordman} Selectmen Apprd. of by Edwd. Proctor Esq one of the oversears of the poor		State

1789

Decr. 23d.   Recd. into the Almshous Jno. Bothree a Frenchman   State
Consented to by Edwd. Proctor Esq One of the oversears of the poor}
Pr. ordor of Jno. Scolay Esqr., Mr. Ebenr. Seaver} Selectmen

Decr. 23d.   Recd. into the Almshous Jno. McQueen a Scotchman   State
Consented to by Edwd. Proctor Esq One of the oversears of the poor}
Pr. ordor of Jno. Scolley Esq, Capt. Edwd. Tyler} Selectmen

Decr. 23d.   Recd. into the Almshous Lucy Willis   Town
Pr. ordor of Mr. Saml. Whitwell one of the oversears of the poor

Decr. 26th.   Recd. into the Almshous Thos. Cross   Town
Pr. ordor of Edward Proctor Esqr. One of the oversears of the poor

Decr. 31th.   Recd. into the Almshous Nancy Madesen[46] of providance   State
Consented to by Saml. Whitwell Esq One of the oversears of the poor}
Pr. ordor of Ezekl. Price   } Selectmen

Decr. 31th.   Recd. into the Almshous Jno. Karr An Irishman   State
Consented to by Edwd. Proctor Esq One of the oversears of the poor}
Pr. ordor of Jno. Andrews Esq, Mr. Wm. Bordman} Selectmen

[*1790*]
Jany. 2d.   dischd. Sarah Jackson R[*un*]   State

1790
Jany. 6th.   Recd. into the Almshous Wm. Donnet A Child 2 years old   State
Consented to by Jno. Mason Esq One of the oversears of the poor}
Pr. ordor of Jno. Scollay Esq, Jno. Andrews Esqr.} Selectmen

Jany. 6 1790   Recd. into the Almshous Andw. Robenson[47] & wife   State
Consented to by Jona. Mason Esqr. One of the oversears of the poor}
Pr. ordor of Eber. Seavor, Jabez Hatch Esq} Select men

Jany. 7th. 1790 Recd. into the Almshous Ann Whitman   Town
Pr. ordor of Edwd. Proctor Esqr. one of the oversears of the poor}

Jany. 8th.   Recd. into the Almshous Hannah Harres[48]   Town
Pr. ordor of Edwd. Proctor Esq One of the oversears of the poor

<*Jany. 8th.   dischd Dorothy Horne R[un], do.* [i.e., dischd.] *Saml North R[un]} both
Returnd acknologing the falts*>   State

Jany. 15th.   Recd. into the Almshous Rebecca Carr with her two Childn. Named
Consented to by Edwd. Proctor Esq One of the oversears of the poor}   State
Pr. ordor of Jno. Andrews Esqr.   } Selectmen

Jany. 15th.   Recd. into the Almshous Jno. Flyn of   State
Consented to by Mr. Saml. Whitwell One of the oversears of the poor
Pr. ordor of Jno. Scollay Esq, Thos. Walley Esq} Selectmen

1790
Jany. 14th.   Recd. An ordor to Supply Andrew Currente a frenchman With Every
Ration of wood and provetions As if he ware In the Almshous   (State)
Consentd to by Jona. Mason Esqr. One of the oversears of the poor}
Pr. ordor of Jno. Andrews Esqr., Capt. Edwd. Tyler} Selectmen

Jany. 11th.   Recd. into the Almshous Hebron Matterson A boy Consentd. to by Edwd.
Proctor Esq One of the oversears of the poor}   State
Pr. ordor of Jno. Andrews Esq, Capt. Edwd. Tyler} Selectmen

Jany. 16th.   Recd. into the Almshous Dennis Hogen[49] of Limbrick   State
Consented to by Edwd. Proctor Esq One of the oversears of the poor}
Pr. ordor of Jno. Andrews Esqr., Mr. Wm. Boardman} Selectmen

Jany. 16th.   Recd. into the Almshous Mehitable Levingston[50]   State
Consented to by Jno. Sweetser Esq one of the oversears of the poor}
Pr. ordor of Jno. Scollay Esqr., Mr. Ebenr. Sever} Selectmen

Jany. 21th.   Recd. into the Almshous James Frost   Town
Pr. ordor of Mr. Saml. Parkman One of the oversears of the poor

Jany. 22d.   Recd. into the Almshous Catharina Walker   State
Approd. of by Edwd. Proctor Esqr. One of the oversears of the poor}
Pr. ordor of Jno. Scolley Esqr., Mr. Wm. Bordman} Selectmen

Jany. 22d.   Recd. into the Almshous Wm. Kennady[51]   Town
Pr. Verbol ordor of Jona. L Austen one of the oversears of the poor

Jany. 24   Recd. into the Almshous Jno. Mitchell of Ireland   State
Consented to by Edwd. Proctor Esq One of the oversears of the poor}
Pr. ordor of Jno. Scollay Esqr., Mr. Wm. Bordman} Selectmen

Jany. 25th.   Recd. into the Almshous Ruth Bergan   Town
Pr. ordor of Jona. L Austen Esq. One of the Oversears of the poor

Jany. 25   Dischd. Eliz Vinlanough R[*un*]   Town

Jany. 23d.   Dischd. Cornelos Driskey R[*un*]   State

Jany. 25th.   Recd. into the Almshous Nabby Green A Negro Child 9 Months old
Approd. of by Mr. Saml. Whitwell One of the oversears of the poor}   State
Pr. ordor of Ezekl. Price Esq   } Selectmen

Jany. 27th.   Recd. into the Almshous Cornelius O Bryan[52] A Irishman   State
Consented to by Edwd. Proctor Esqr. one of the oversears of the poor}
Pr. ordor of Jno. Andrews Esqr., Mr. Ebenr. Seaver} Selectmen

1790
Jany. 27th.   Recd. into the Almshous Deborah Townsand[53] of Abington   <*State*>
Consented to by Jno. White Esq One of the oversears of the poor}
Pr. ordor of Jno. Scollay, Captn. Edwd. Tyler} Selectmen

Jany. 29th.   Dischd. Hebron Materson A boy bound out   State

Jany. 29th.   Dischd. Ann Crumwell[54]   Town

Jany. 27   Recd. into the Almshous Marthor[55] Tuck of andover   State
Approd. of by Wm. Philips Esq Junr. One of the oversears of the poor}
Pr. ordor of Jno. Scollay Esqr., Mr. Ebenr. Seaver} Selectmen

Jany. 29   Recd. into the Almshous one Amos Round of Swansey
Consented to by Jno. White Esq One of the oversears of the poor}
Pr. ordor of Harbottle Dorr, Capt Edwd. Tyler} Selectmen

Jany. 30th.	Dischd. Adam Ayers	Town
Feby. 1st.	dischd Nancy Materson	State
Feby. 1st. Pr. ordor of Jona. L Austin Esqr. One of the oversears of the poor	Recd. into the Almshous Holms Simpson	Town
Feby. 1	dischd. Jno. Mitchell R[*un*]	State
Feby. 2d. Consented to by Jno. Sweetser Esq One of the oversears of the poor} Pr. ordor of Mr. Wm. Bordman, Jno. Andrews Esqr.} Selectmen	Recd. into the Almshous Thos. Kennedy of Ireland	State
Decr. 3d. Omited in Place the Mastor of the workhous haveing the ordor Consented to by Mr. Saml. Parkman One of the oversears} Pr. ordor of Jno. Andrews Esqr., Mr. Wm. Bordman} Selectmen	Recd. Cate Townsand[56] into the Almshous	State
Feby. 3d. Approd. of by Mr. Saml. Parkman One of the oversears} Pr. ordor of Jno. Scolley Esq, Mr. Ebenr. Seaver} Selectmen	Recd. Celia Ervin[57] into the Almshous	State
Feby. 3d.	dischd. Susanna Waterman bound out	Town
Feby. 4th. Apprd. of by Saml. Whitwell One of the oversears of the poor} Pr. ordor of Ezekl. Price Esq } Selectmen	Recd. into the Almshous Robert Watson of Ireland	State
Feby. 6th. approd. of by Edwd. Proctr. Esq One of the oversears of the poor} Pr. ordor of Jno. Scollay Esqr. } Selectmen	Recd. into the Almshous Edwd. harper of Ireland	State
1790 Feby. 10th. Apprd. of by Edwd. Proctor Esq One of the oversears of the poor} Pr. ordor of Jno. Andrews Esqr., Mr. Wm. Bordman} Selectmen	Recd. into the Almshous Rodolph Pellinger A German	State
Feby. 8th. Consented to by Saml. Whitwell One of the oversears of the poor} Pr. ordor of Ezekel Price Esqr., Mr. Wm. Bordman} Selectmen	Recd. into the Almshous Sarah Finn & Child	State
Feby. 9th.	Dischd. Sarah Richardson R[*un*]	Town
Feby. 11th. Consented to by Mr. Saml. Parkman One of the oversears of the poor} Pr. ordor of Captn. Edwd. Tyler, Mr. Wm. Bordman} Selectmen	Recd. into the Almshous William Burns of Philadelphia	State
feby. 12th.	Dischd. Edwd. harper	State
Feby. 16th. Pr. ordor of Saml. Whitwell Esqr. one of the oversears of the poor	Recd. into the Almshous Jno. Cole	Town
Feby. 18th.	Dischd. Johanna Spoonor[58] bound out	State
Feby. 18th.	Dischd. Thos. Cross Run	Town

Feby. 19   Recd. into the Almshous Susanna Gyer[59] a Child 3 years of Age   Town
Pr. ordor of Mr. Saml. Parkman one of the oversears of the poor

Feby. 22   Recd. into the Almshous Timothy donnavin[60]   State
Consented to by Wm. Smith one of the Oversears of the poor
Pr. ordor of Ezekl. Price Esq, Capt. Edwd. Tyler} Selectmen

Feby. 26th.   Dischd. Mary Peters R[un]   State
                 Dischd. Eliz Ives R[un]   State

Feby. 27th.   Recd. into the Almshous Olive White   State
Consented to by Edwd. Proctor Esqr. One of the oversears of the Poor
Pr. ordor of Mr. Harbtl. dorr, Capt. Edwd. Tyler} Selectmen

Feby. 28th.   Recd. into the Almshous Nathl. Boarn   Town
Pr. ordor of Edwd. Proctor Esqr. One of the Oversears of the poor

Mar: 1   Recd. into the Almshous Elizabeth Hayden   Town
℘ order Mr. John Codman jr: One of the Overseers of the poor

1790
March 3d: Recd: into the Almshouse Olive Whitney & a Child nam'd James   State
Consented to by Edwd. Procter One of the Overseers of the Poor}
℘ ordr: Thos. Walley, Eben: Seaver} Select Men

March 3d.   Discharg'd Polly Moran, a Child   State

March 3d.   Discharg'd John Cole & James Frost} Sent to the Workhouse}   Town

Marc[h] 7th.   Recd. into the Almshouse Reb:[61] Edmonds   Town
℘ Order Jno. Codman jr: one of the Oversears of the poor

March 10th.   Recd. into the Almshouse Eliza. Ivers   Town
                 Discharg'd S: Montgomery
℘ order Colo: Procter one of the Overseers of the Poor

March 12th.   Recd: into the Almshouse Polly Willis aged 3 years Daughter to Lucy
Willis   Town
by Verbal Order of Mr. John White, one of the Overseers of the Poor

March 12th.   Nancy Fitzgerald, Entd.   Town
by Verbal order of Mr. John Sweetser, one of the Overseers of the Poor

March 17th.   James Brown, Entd.   State
Consented to by Colo. Proctor, One of the Overseers of the Poor
by order of Messrs. Thomas Walley & Thos. Edwards—Selectmen

17th.   Discharg'd Ann Chaloner   State
                 Eliza. Condon   Do.

18th.   Discharg'd Michael Crowley   Town

22d.   Recd. into the Almshouse Nancy Challender   State
Consented to by Colo. Proctor One of the Overseers}
℘ Ordr. Wm. Boardman one of the Select Men

1790 Mar: 22d.} Recd. into the Almshouse Michael Crowley By ordr. John White Esqr. One of the Overseers		Town
25th. Discharg'd Reb: Edmonds		Town
26th. Recd. into the Almshouse Prince Knight a Negro Consented to by Colo. Procter, One of the Overseers of the poor} By order Jno. Scollay Esqr. & Wm. Boardman, Selectmen		State
28th. Recd. into the Almshouse Joshua Hubbard & Wife By Order Jno. Codman jr. One of the Overseers of Poor		Town
27th. Discharg'd Abigail Brown & her son		State
29th. Discharg'd Henry Kendall & his Wife		State
30th. Discharg'd Andrew Robertson & his Wife		State
31st. Wm. Procter, rec'd. into the Alms house by order John White Esqr. one of the Overseers		Town
31st. Recd. into the Almshouse Eliz: Jenney Consented to by Colo. Procter by order Thos. Walley & Thos. Crafts, Selectmen		State
Apl. 5th. Discharg'd Mary Sharpe R[un]		State
5th. Nancy Fitzgerald—discharg'd		Town
6th. Polly Cowell—a Child—discharg'd		Town
6th. Wm. Burns—discharg'd		State
8th. Polly[62] Benjamin entered by Order J: L: Austin Esqr. one of the Overseers		Town
8th. Discharg'd John McKenzie		State
1790 Apl. 12th.} Recd: into the Almshouse Mary Tarbel ℘ Ordr. John Codman jr: Overseer		Town
14th. Recd. Ichabod Willaston[63] into the Almshouse ℘ ordr. Edwd. Edes one of the Overseers		Town
14th. Dischargd. John Bothree		State
14th. Recd. into the Almshouse Mary Bulkley & her daughter Polly Consented to by Colo. Procter ℘ Order Thos. Walley & Thos. Crafts} Selectmen		State
14th. Discharg'd Eben: Ruddock		Town
15th. Discharg'd Timo. Donevan		State

15th.   Recd. into the Almshouse Pat: Shanly & Daughter   State
Consented to by Colo. Procter
℘ Order Wm. Boardman Select Man
Discharg'd same day

18th.   Discharg'd James McQuin   State

19   Recd. into the almshouse Elizabeth Ryon[64] & her Child Thos   State
Consented to by Edward Procter Esqr.
Pr. Order John Scollay & Wm. Bordman} Selet. men

19   Recd. into the almshouse Rebecca Cornett   Town
Pr. Order of Mr. Edward Edes one of the overseers of the Poore

20   Dischargd. Cornelus Obrion   State

20   Recd. John Reed into the almshouse   State
Consented to Pr. Jona. Mason overseer of the Poor
Pr. Order of John Scollay Selectman

1790 Apl. 21}   Recd. into the Almshouse Roger Bardy   State
Consented to by Edward Procter Esqr.
Pr. Order of John Scollay & Harb Dorr Selet. men

          Discharg'd John Willet—bound out   Town

21st.   Recd. Geo: & Charles Jolly—sons of Wm. Jolly   State
Consented to by Henry Hill Esqr.
℘ Order Thos. Crafts & Thos. Edwards Select Men
Geo: 10 ys. old July 4th. Charles 8 the 5 Novr. 1790

22d.   Recd. into the almshouse Nancy DCosta[65] & Daughter ailes [*alias?*]
House Mar[*rie*]d a Londner   State
℘ order Saml. Parkman one of the Overseers

24   Recd. into the Almshouse Mary Sharp Wife to Wm. Sharp Consented to
Edward Procter Esqr.   State
Pr. Order John Scollay   } Selt. men

26   Dischargd. Thos. Brandgon   State

26   Discharg'd Betsy Dennie & her child   Town

26   Recd. into the Almshouse Dina Minot   State
Consented to Edward Proctr Esqr.
Pr. Order of John Scollay & Thos. Crafts} Selet. men

26   Horn Dorothy Dischargd.   State

26   Recd. into the Almshouse Alexander Whright[66]   State
Consented to Edward Procter Esqr.
Pr. Order of John Scollay & Thos. Crafts Esqrs.

27   Dischargd. Robt. Watson   State

27   Dischargd. Edward Beacham   State

28	Recd. into the almshouse Wm. Curtis	Town

Pr. Order of Edward Procter Esqr. one of the Overseers of the Poor
Run

30	Recd. into the Almshouse Pegey Hurly	Town

Pr. Order of Edward Procter Esqr one of the overseers of the Poor

1790 May

1	Recd. into the alms House Elizh. Goodwin	Town

Pr. Order of John Sweetcher Esqr. Overseer of the Poor

1	Recd. into the Almshouse Mary Pool	Town

Pr. Order of Jona. Mason Esqr. one of the overseers of the Poor

1	Recd. into the almshouse Pegg Symmes	State

Consented to Edward Procter Esqr.
Wm. Bordman, Thos. Edwards} Selectmen

Recd. into the Almshouse Wm. Ryan, son to Eliza. Ryan born in the
house the 22d. Ulto. (Omitted)   State

4	Recd. into the Almshouse Sophie Manders[67]	

Consented to Jona. Mason
John Scollay & Thos. Crafts Esqrs.} Seletmen

8	Dischargd Pomp a Negro Man	State
10	Dischargd. Patrick Quin	State
10	Dischargd. John Carns	State
10	Dischargd. Charles jolley Bound out	State
10	Dischargd. Sarah Seegreaves	Town
11	Dischargd John Gillard	State
11	Dischargd. Jane Rusell	State
12	Recd. into the Almshouse Thos. Lawson	State

Consent to Edward Procter Esqr. overseer of the Poore
Pr. Order of Wm. Bordman & Ebenr. Seaver} Selectmen

12	Dischargd. Elizh. Rion & two Children	State

	Recd. into the Almshouse William Thurston	State

Consented to Edward Procter Esqr
Pr. order of John Scollay, Harbl. Dorr} Select Men

1790

May 13	Recd. Edward Irland[68] & his Wife	Town

Pr. Order of Edwd. Procter Esqr. one of the Overseers of the Poor

13	Reced. John Brown a Child Son to John Brown 4 years old May 23	State

Consented to Jona. L Austin
Pr. order of Ebenr. Sever & Wm. Bordman} Select men

13	Recd. into the Almshouse Saml. Covel & His Son Saml. aged 6 years the 4th. of Janury Last the Father Born at Cape Cod	State

Pr. order of Mr. Saml. Parkman one of the overseers of the Poor

15	Recd. into the almshouse Hartford Robert a disordd. Negrom[an]	State

Pr. order of John Scollay, Thos. Crafts} Select Men
Consented to Pr. Edwd. Procter
sent to work House

15	Recd. Mary Watts in to the alms house	

Pr. order of Edward Procter one of the overseers of the Poore

15	Recd. into the almshouse James Downe an Irish man	State

Consented to Edward Procter Esqr. one of the Overseers of the Poor
Pr. Order of Wm. Bordman one of the Select men

17	Dischargd. Holems Simson	Town

20	Recd. into the almshouse Lucy Malony[69]	State

Pr. order of Thos. Crafts, Thos. Edwards} Select men
Consented to Edward Procter Esqr. one of the overseers of the Poor

20	Recd. Nathl. Corben into the almshouse	Town

Pr. order of Mr. Saml. Parkman one of the overseers of the Poor

21	Dischargd. James Downe	State
	Dischargd. Mary Tuttle	Town
	Dischargd. Mary Pool	Town
22	Dischd. Pegey Symmes	State
22	Dischd. Wm. Curtis Run	Town
22	Dischd. James Brown Run	State

1790
May 22

	Recd. into the Alms house Saml. Trescot	State

Pr. order of Harbo. Dorr Select man
Consent to Edward Procter Esqr. overseer of the Poor

22	Recd. into the almes House Ruth Mathur and 2 Children	State

Pr. Wm. Bordman Select man
Consented to Jon Lorin Austin Overseer of the Poor

22	Recd. into the almshouse Phillis Eustis a Black woman	State

Pr. order Wm. Bordman Selectman
Consented to Wm. Smith one of the overseers of the Poor

22	Dischd. Richard Crouch	State
24	Dischd. Roger Bardy State	
24	Dischard Poll Benjman & Child	State

| 24 | Dischd. Denis Hogen State | |
| 25 | Dischd. Joshua Hubbard | Town |

26   Recd. into the almshouse Peter Essenger   Town
Pr. Order of Mr. Saml. Parkman one of the overseers of the Poor

| 26 | Recd. Polle[70] Benjman & Child into the almshouse | State |

28   Recd. Daniel Benjman into the almshouse
Pr. order of Edward Procter Esqr.

June 1st.	Discharg'd Rodolph Pelliger	State
	<Discharg'd Mary Tuttle> Enter'd the 21st.	Town
1	Dischargd. Fillis Eustis	State

1   Recd. Richard Langley[71]   State
Consented to Edwd. Procter Esqr.
Pr. Order of John Scollay, Wm. Boardman

2   Recd. Mary Grainger & her Child into the Alms house   Town
Pr. Order of Edward Procter Esqr

2   Recd. Mary Hinds in to the almshouse   State
Pr. order John White overseer

| 2 | Dischargd Wintrop Gray (Alias Carr) | State |

1790
June 2   Recd. into the Alms House John Kelley   State
Consented to Edward Procter Esqr. overseer of the Poor
Pr. order Harbottle Dorr, Thos. Walley Selectmen

2   Recd. into the alms House John Gillard   State
Consented to Edward Procter Esqr.
Pr. order of John Scollay, Wm. Bordman} Select men

2	Dischd. ame Rusell & her Son Peter Jeffers	State
8	Dischd Saml. Tr[e]scot & Betty Wier the 7th.	both State
<8	*John Reed aged about 35 years>*	

9   Recd. into the alms house Benjman Sinclear[72] Born in Vermont   State
Consented to Edward Procter
Pr. order of John Scollay, Thos. Walley} Esqr. Selecct Men

9	Dischargd Saml. Sargent	Town
11	Dischagd. Mary Buckley & her Daughter Mary	State
11	Dischargd. Elizth. Haden	Town
21	Dischargd. Judea Low	State

22	Receved into the Alms house Sarah Goodwin of Peknopsket	
Pr. order of Wm. Smith overseer		

23	Recd. in to the almshouse ann Milton	Town
Pr. Order of Jona. Mason Esqr. one of the overseers of the poor		

26	Recd. into the almshouse Polle[73] Webb from the Workhouse at the Requst	
of the Doctr		Town

28	Recd. into the alms house Thos. Braggadon	State
Consented to Jona. Mason Esqr. one of the Oversers of the Poor		
Pr. order of Thos. Crafts & Harbottle Dorr Esqrs.} Select Men		

Recd. William Pomroy into the Almshouse — State
Consented to John White one of the overseers of the Poor
Pr. order of John Scollay & Wm. Bordman} Select Men

1790 June 30	Dischargd. David Denia	State

June 30	Recd. into the alms House Michael Taylor an Irish Pedler	State
Consented to Edward Procter one of the Overseers of the Poor		
Pr. order of Ebenr. Sever & Thos. Crafts Esqr.} Select Men		

July 3	Recd. into the almshouse Benjn. Edey	State
Consented to Edward Procter overseer		
Pr. Wm. Bordman—Select Man		

July 3d.	Recd. into the Almshouse—Judath Low[74]	State
Consented to Saml. Parkman		
Pr. order of Wm. Boardman Selectman		

1790		
July 7	Recd. Thos. Murfey[75] into the alms House	State
Jona. Mason overseer		
pr. order Mr. Scolay & Bordman		

Dischargd Jno. Morrison — State

July 7	Recd. into the almshouse Mary Nottage a Child of about 7 years old	State
Consented to John Sweetsur overseer of the Poor		
Pr. order of Thos. Walley & Wm. Bordman—Selectmen		

July 10	Dischargd John Keley	State

July 10	Dischargd. Sarah Coney but Left her Child Nancey aged 4 years}	State

July 15	Recd. into the almshouse Henry Williams	State
Consent to Edward Procter overseer of the Poor		
Pr. order of John Scollay Select man		

Recd. into the almshouse Mary Dawes <& her Child> — Town
Pr. order of Mr. Saml. Parkman

22	Dischargd. Elizh. Brown and her 2 Children	Town

| 23 | Recd. into the Almshouse Patrick Shandy | State |
| | Pr. order of Mr. Henery Hill overseer of the Poor | |

24	Recd. into the almshouse Marian Mathewson	State
	Consented to Pr. Edward Procter	
	Pr. order of John Scolay & Jabez Hatch Select men	

| 1790 July 26 | Judea Low Run | State |

| 27 | Dischargd. Thos. Braggadon | State |

| 29 | Recd. into the alms House John Griggs & his Wife} | Town |
| | Pr. order of Wm. Smith overseer | |

| 29 | Dischargd. Nancey Howes | State |

| 31 | Dischargd Michel Taylor | State |

31	Recd. into the almshouse George Lee	State
	Consented to Jona. Mason Esqr. overseer of the Poor	
	Pr. order of Thos. Crafts Esqr. Select Man	

| | Discharg'd Jeremiah Carr the 14th. instant bd: out & his Mother Ann: alias Gray the 28th. | State |

| 31 | Dischargd. Wm. Procter | Town |

| Augt. 4 | Dischargd Sarah Goodwin | State |

4	Recd. into the almshouse Freedrick Dominique	State
	Jona. Mason overseer of the Poor	
	Pr. order of Thos. Walley & Thos. Crafts} Select men	

| 4 | Dischargd James Matthews Bound out | State |

7	Recd. into the almshouse Judith Kelly & her two Infant Children	State
	Consented to Jona. Mason of the overseers of the Poor	
	Pr. order of John Scollay & Thos. Crafts Selectmen	
	Jane 7 1/2 & Margret 4 years of age	

| 9 | Recd. into the alms House Anna Richardson | Town |
| | Pr. Order of Mr. Jona. L Austin one of the over Seers of the Por | |

| 9 | Recd. into the almshouse Thos. Cross | Town |
| | Pr. order of Mr. John White one of the overseers of the Poor | |

9	Recd. into the almshouse John Fleming	State
	Consented to Saml. Parkman one of the overseers of the poor	
	Pr. order of John Scollay one of the Select men	

1790 Augt. 9th.	Recd. into the almshouse Mary Sharp	State
	Consented to Edward Procter one of the overseers of the Poor	
	Pr. order of Harbottle Dorr & Wm. Bordman Select men	

| 12 | Recd. into the almshouse Thos. Loring | Town |
| | Pr. order of Edward Procter one of the overseers of the poor | |

12	Dischargd Hugh Kemple	State
12	Recd. Elizebath Farrier & two Children into the Almshouse	State

Consent to Jona. Mason one of the Overseers of the Poor
Pr. order of Thos. Crafts, Wm. Bordman} select men

12	Recd. into the Almshouse Mary Garrar[76]	State

Consented to Jona. Mason one of the overseers of the Poor
Pr. order of John Scollay & Ezekl. Price} Select men

14	Dischargd. Mary Singclare[77]	State
14	Recd. into the Almshouse John Hews[78]	State

Consented to Jona. Mason Esqr. one of the overseers of the Poor
Pr. order of John Scollay & Thos. Crafts Esqr. Select men

14	Recd. into the almshouse Joseph Colesworthy	Town

Pr. order of John Codman one of the overseers of the Poor

14	Dischargd. Henry Luckus	Town
21	Recd. into the almshouse Henry Luckis	Town

Pr. order of John White one of the overseers of the poor

Polly Davis Married to Rd. Harris the 8th. instant

1790 Augt. 23	Dischargd. Timothey Gyear[79]	State
30	John Fling Dischargd	State
Sept. 1	James Brown discharg'd	State
3	Discharged Ann Whitman	Town
3	Dischargd. John Hewes	State
3	Recd Nancy Moter into the almshouse a Child about 5 years of age	Town

Pr. Order of Edwd. Edes one of the overseers of the poor

<4	*Dischd. Ruth Mathers to the Workhouse*	*State*

Pr. order of Jona. Mason one of the Overseers of the Poor>

4	Recd. into the alms hous Patty Dorsey	State

Consent to Pr. Jona. Mason one of the overseers of the Poor
Pr. order of John Scollay & Wm. Bordam Selectmen

4	Recd. into the almshouse Nancy Garrel	Town

Pr. order of the Board of overseers on Sitting Day

6	Recd. into the Alms house John Kelly	State

Consented to Pr. Jona: Mason one of the overseers of the Poor
Pr. order of Ezekel Price one of the Select Men

6	Dischd. Henry Lockos	Town

6	Dischd. Merian Mathewson	State
6	Discd. James Pike	Town
10	Discd. Michael Comley	State
10	Discd. Hugh Smith	State

< 10   *Discd. Mary Mathewson*   *State>*

10	Discd. Hannah McKenzie[80]	State
10	Discd. Ruth Matthews	State
10	Discd. Richard Langley	State
10	Discrd. amos Rownds	State
10	Discd. Elizh. Berrey	State

1790
Septr. 10th.   Dischargd John Hanny   State

< 10   *Discd. John Howes*   *State>*

| 13 | Discd. John Kelley | State |
| 13 | Discd. Ann Cox | Town |

15   Recd. in to the Almshouse Robert Woodson A black Man   State
Consented to Saml. Parkman overseer of the poor
Pr. order of John Scollay, Ezekl. Price Select men

16   Recd. into the almshouse Thos. Brannagaw   State
Consented to Edward Procter overseer of the Poor
Pr. order of Jabz Hatch, & Thos. Crafts} Select men

17   Dischd. Michel Crawley[81]   Town

18   Discd. Polley Webb into the Workhous   Town
Pr. Verble order Jona. Mason ovseer

18   Recd. into the Almshouse Mary Sharp   State
Consented to Henry Hill one of the overseers of the Poor
Pr. order of John Scollay & Thos. Crafts} Select men

18   Discd. Mary Dawes (& Ann Chaloner, State)   Town

22   Recd. into the Almshouse Margret Fitzgerel[82]   State
Pr. order of Harbl. Dorr & Eben Sever} Select men
Consented to Edward Procter one of the Overseers of the Poor

22   Recd. John Keily into the almshouse   State
Consented to Edward Edes
Pr. order of Thos. Walley & Wm. Bordman} Select men

22	Recd. Ann Fovel & Mary Hogg into the almshouse	State

Consented to Edward Edes one of the overseers of the Poor
Pr. Order of Thos. Walley & Ebenr. Seavers} Select men

22	Recd. into the almshouse Hugh Smith	State

Consented to Saml. Parkman one of the overseers of the poor
Pr. order of Thos. Walley & Wm. Boardman} Select men

1790
Septr. 25th.   Dischargd Robert Woodson a Black man   State

25   Discd. Cathrne Cook   State

27   Discd. Nathaniel Corborn   Town

29   Recd. into the Almshouse Boston a Negro man   State
Consented John Sweetser one of the overseers of the Poor
Pr. Order of Ebenr. Seaver & Thos. Crafts} Select men

29   Dischargd Fradrick Domineque   State

29   Recd. into the almshouse Timothy Guire
Consented to John Sweetser one of the Overseers of the Poor
Pr. order of John Scollay & Wm. Bordman} Select men

30   Discd. John Fliming   State

30   Recd. into the almshouse Hannah Leahea   State
Consented to Jona. Mason one of the overseers of the Poor
Pr. order of Thos. Walley, Wm. Boardman} Select men

Octr.
4   Recd. Mary Pool into the almshouse   Town
Pr. order of Edward Procter one of the overseers of the Poor

4   Disd. Henry Williams   State
          & Polly Paine

5   Recd. Mary Cowell a Child 5 years old   Town
Pr. order John Codman one of the overseers of the Poor

6   Recd. into the Almshouse Budd Robenson   Town
Pr. order of Edwd. Procter one of the over Seers of the Poor

8   Recd. into the almshouse Johua Hunnewill[83]   Town
Pr. order of Wm. Smith one of the overseers of the Poor

8   Recd. into the almshouse Luce Newell a Black woman on the States acct.
Consented to Jona. Loring austin   State
Ezekl. Price, Thos. Craft Selectmen

1790
Octr. 8   Disd. Luce Maloney   State

12   Disd. Ann Frobile   State

| 12 | Recd. into the almshouse Cathrine Towsand[84] | State |

Consent to Edward Procter one of the ovseers of the Poor
Pr. Order of Thos. Crafts & Thos. Edwards} Select men

| 12 | Recd. into the almshouse Henry Lucas | Town |

Pr. order of Saml. Parkman one of the ovseers of the Poor

| 12 | Dischargd. Budd Roberson to the Workhouse a Distracted Man | Town |

Pr. order of Mr Jona. Mason one of the overseers of the Poor

| 12 | Recd. into the Almshouse Elizh. Sheene & her Son Robert Carr | Town |

Pr. order of Mr. J L Austin one of the overseers of the Poor

| 16 | Recd. into the almshouse Ann Whitman | Town |

Pr. order of Mr. John White one of the oversers of the Poor

| 18 | Recd. into the almshouse Robt. Dunlap | State |

Consent to Jona. Mason one of the oversers of the Poor
Pr. order of John Scollay & Thos. Crafts Selectmen

| 19 | Recd. into the almshouse Ebenzr. Ruduck | Town |

Pr. order Edward Procter one of the overseers of the Poor

| 21 | Dischargd. Elizh. Sheene | Town |

| 21 | Recd. James Meadows[85] into the almshouse on the States account | State |

Pr. order of Mr. Stephen Gorham one of the overseers of the Poor

| 22 | Recd. into the almshouse Fradrick Eairs[86] | Town |

Pr. order of Edward Procter one of the overseers of the poor

1790
| October 27 | Dischargd. Elizh. Farrer & her three Children | State |

| 28 | Recd. into the almshouse George Fisher | State |

Consented to Wm. Phillips one of the overseers of the Poor
Pr. order of Thos. Walley Select man

| 28 | Recd. into the almshouse Robert Wooson[87] a Black man | State |

Consented to Saml. Parkman overseer}
Pr. order of Thos. Walley, Jabez Hatch} Selectmen

| 28 | Recd. into the Almshouse John Murphey[88] | State |

Pr. order of John Scollay & Ezekel Price Selectmen
Consented to Wm. Phillips overseer

| 29 | Cathrine Townsand Run | State |

| 29 | Recd. into the almshouse Ruben Goreham[89] | Town |

Pr. order of Jona. L Austin

| 29 | Recd. into the almeshous John Gillard | State |

Consented to Jona. Mason ovseer
Pr. Order of John Scollay, Harbottle Dorr} Select men

Novr. 1	Recd. into the almshouse Sarah Perre	Town

Pr. Order of Mr. John White one of the overseers of the poor

2	Recd. Mary Webb into the Almshouse from the Workhouse	State

Pr. order of Mr. Jona. Mason

4	Recd. into the almshouse Judeth Low[90]	State

Consented to Edwd. Procter one of the overseers of the poor
Pr. order of John Scollay, Ezekl. Price} Select men

	Discd. Ruben Goreham	Town

4	Recd. into the almshouse Edward Beacham	State

Consented to Saml. Parkman ovseer
Pr. order of Harbottle Dorr & Ebenr. Seaver Selectmen

5	Recd. into the almshouse James Pike	Town

Pr. order Mr. Jona. Mason one of the overseers of the Poor

1790 Novr.

5	Recd. into the Almshouse Sarah Adams	Town

Pr. order of Mr. Edward Edes overseer

5	Recd. into the Alms house Mary Richardson	Town

Pr. order of Mr. Saml. Parkman one of the overseers of the Poor

5	Recd. into the almshouse Philles How a Black woman	State

Consented to Pr. Edward Procter one of the ovseers of the Poor
Pr. order of Harbottle Dorr & Wm. Boardman Select Men

12	Dischd. Thos. Cross to the Workhouse	Town

Pr. order of John White one of the oversers of the Poor

12	Recd. into the almshouse Mary Pirce[91]	Town

Pr. order of Edward Procter Esqr. one of the overseers of the Poor

14	Recd. into the almshouse Daniel Loring	Town

Pr. Order of Mr. Saml. Parkman

	Recd. into the Almshouse Sarah Seagreaves[92]	Town

Pr. order of Mr. John Codman one of the over Seers of the Poor

18	Recd. into the almshouse John Woods on account of the State	State

Consented to Edward Procter overseer
Pr. order of Ezekle Price Selectman

18	Recd. into the alms Jenny Doane a black woman	State

Pr. order of John L. Austin

18	Recd. into the Almshouse Polly[93] Tilty	State

Consent to Jona. Mason one of the overseers of the Poor
Pr. order of Thos. Walley one of the Select Men

19	Recd. Lidia Rider into the almshouse	State

Consent to Jona. Mason one of the overseers of the Poor
Pr. order of Wm. Boardman Selectman

1790

Novr. 21	Recd. into the Almshouse Wm. McMoran	State

Consented to Jona. Mason one of the overseers of the Poor
Pr. order of Thos. Crafts & Thos Walley Select men

21	Dischargd James Meadows	State

24	Recd. into the almshouse John Bryant	State

Consented to Saml. Parkman one of the overseers of the Poor
Pr. order of Ebenr. Sever & Wm. Boardman Select men

26	Recd. Wm. Kennedy into the Almshouse	Town

Pr. order of Saml. Parkman one of the Overseers of the Poor

26	Recd. into the Almshouse Michael Comley	State

Consented to Jona. Mason one of the Overseers of the Poor
Pr. order of Ezekl. Price one of the Selectmen

27	Recd. into the almshouse Ann Vallier a Distracted woman	State

Pr. order of Jona. Mason one of the overseers of the Poor / Sent Ditto the workhouse
orderd. to the almshouse by Thos Edwards one of the Selectmen
Sent to the wokhouse the Same Day
(sent to the Work house)

27	Recd. into the almshouse Wm. Spooner & Wife	State

Pr. order of Mr. John Codman one of the overseers of the poor

27	Recd. into the almshouse Cathrine Freeman a Black woman on the State	State

account
Pr. order of Henry Hill one of the overseers of the poor

27	Recd. Harriot Brown into the almshouse 2 1/2 years old	State

Consented to Jona. Mason overseer of the Poor
Pr. order of Harbl. Dorr, Wm. Bordman Select men

30th.	Recd. Sharp Wm. into the almshouse	State

Consented to Saml. Parkman overseer of the poor
Pr. order of Ezek Price and Thos. Crafts Select men

	Recd. into the Almshouse Juba a blk boy (the 10th. instt.)

Consented to by S: Parkman
by ordr. Thos. Walley, Jabez Hatch} Select Men
(sent to Workhouse)

1790 Novr. 30	Recd. Cole John	Town

Pr. order of Edward Procter one of the overseers of the Poor

<Decr. 2d.	*Dischargd. Wm. Spoorer & his Wife*	*State>*

2	Recd. into the almshouse Salley Conday	State

Consented to Jona. Mason one of the overseers of the poor
Pr. order of Harbotle Dorr, Ebenr. Seaver} Select men

2	Recd. into the almshouse Sarah Eddey	Town

Pr. order of Mr. Henry Hill one of the overseers of the Poor

3 Recd. John Cobourn[94] into the almshouse Pr. order of Saml. Parkman	Town

3   Recd. John Cobourn[94] into the almshouse — Town
Pr. order of Saml. Parkman

6   Recd. into the almshouse Titus Freeman a Black man — State
Consented to John Sweetser one of the overseers of the Poor
Pr. Order of Ebenr. Seaver Select man

9   Recd. into the Almshouse Frances[95] Moren — State
Consented to Edward Procter overseer of the Poor
Pr. order of Thos Crafts & Ezekl. Price} Select men

9   Recd. into the Alms house Frank Hutson[96] — State
Consented to John L Austin one of the overseers of the poor
Pr. order Wm. Boardman one of the Select men

9   Recd. into the Almshouse Hannah Wapples — State
Consented to Edward Procter overseer of the Poor
Pr. order of Harbottle Dorr & Wm. Boardman} Select men

9   Recd. Sarah Lovering into the Almshouse — Town
Pr. order of Saml. Parkman one of the overseers of the Poor

1790
Decr. 9   Recd. Susannah Frank into the almshouse — State
Consented to Edward Procter one of the overseers of the Poor
Pr. order of Wm. Boardman one of the Select men

9   Recd. Hannah McKinzey[97] into the almshouse — State
Consented to Edward Procter one of the Overseers of the Poor
Pr. order of Ezekl. Price & Wm. Bordman Selectmen}

9   Recd. into the Almshouse Mary Wayod a Stranger — State
Consented to Edwd. Procter one of the Overseers of the Poor
Pr. order of Thos. Crafts, Ebenr. Seaver} Select men

9   Recd. Mary Fling into the almshouse — Town
Pr. order of Edward Procter one of the overseers of the Poor

9   Recd. John Healey into the Almshouse — State
Consented to Edward Procter one of the overseers of the Poor
Pr. order of Thos. Crafts & Ezl. Price Select men

9   Recd. James McQuin into the Almshouse — State
Consented to Edward Procter one of the overseers of the Poor
Pr. order of Wm. Boardman Select man

11   Recd. a Femail Black Child about 7 or 8 months old[98] found in Mr. — State
Lucas's yard
Consented to John Sweetser one of the overseers of the Poor
Pr. order of Mr. Ebenzr. Seaver one of the Selectmen
dischd: the 27th. Jany. [17]91

11   Recd. Catharine English into the almshouse — State
Consented to Edward Procter one of the Overseers of the Poor
Pr. order of Ezekel Price one of the Selectmen

1790
Decr. 14d.   Recd. Mordicai Johnson into the almshouse   State
Pr. order of Ezekl. Price & Thos. Crafts Selectmen}
Consented to Edward procter one of the overseers of the Poor

14   Recd. Lidea Marstin into the almshouse   Town
Pr. Order of Edward Procter one of the Overseers of the Poor

16   Recd. Saml. North into the almshouse   State
Consented to Edward Procter one of the Overseers of the poor
Pr. order of Ezekl. Price one of the Selectmen

17   Recd. Benjn. Fowler into the almshouse   State
Consented to John Sweetser one of the overseers of the Poor
Pr. Order of Ebenr. Seaver one of the Selectmen

17   Recd. John Berry into the almshouse   State
Consented to Edward Procter one of the overseers of the poor
Pr. order of Ebenr. Seaver Select man
(Discharg'd the 19th.)

21   Dischagd. William Fossey Bund out   State

21   Recd. ann Chaloner into the almshouse   State
Consented to Jona. Mason overseer
Pr. order of Ezekl. Price Select Man

21   Dischd. Elice Stoddar   Town

22   Recd. John Hartley into the Almshouse Born in Old England   State
Consented to Edwd. Procter overseer of the Poor
Pr. order of Jabez Hatch & Thos Crats Select men

22   Recd. into the almshouse John Parrick and his wife Jane with their Son
John Negros   State
Pr. order of Thos. Walley & Ebenr. Seaver Select men
Consented to John Sweetser overseer Junr.} Black

1790
Decr. 28   Recd. Michel Crowley into the almshouse   Town
Pr. order of Edward Procter one of the overseers of the Poor

29   Recd. into the almshouse William Procter   State
Consented to Edward Procter overseer of the Poor
Pr. order of Wm. Boardman one of the Select men

29   Recd. Philip Fling into the almshouse   State
Consented to Saml. Parkman one of the overseers of the Poor
Pr. order of Ebenr. Seaver & Jabez Hatch Select men

29   Recd. Phillip Delanty into the almshouse   State
Consented to Jona. Mason one of the overseers of the Poor
Pr. Order of Ezekl. Price & Wm. Boardman} Select men

29	Recd. Ann Payson into the almshouse Consented to Jona. Mason one of the Overseers of the Poor Pr. order of Wm. Boardman & Ebenr. Seaver Select men	State
31	Recd. Jack Pemberton a Black man Consented to John White one of the overseers of the Poor Pr. order of Harbo. Dorr, Wm. Boardman} Select men	State
	January 1791 Recd. into the almshouse Patrick Burns from New York Consented to Edward Procter one of the overseers of the Poor Pr. order of Wm. Boardman one of the Selectmen	State
3	Recd. Alexander Thomson from Scotland Consented to Stephen Gorham overseer of the Poor Pr. order of Thos Walley one of the Select men	State
3	Dischargd. Saml. North to the Workhouse	State
3	Anna Callahan admitted into the almshouse Consented to Jona. Mason one of the overseers of the Poor Pr. order of Wm. Boardman & Ezekl. Price} Select men	State
1791 January 6	Dischargd. John Brown Bound out	Town
6	Dischd. Robt. Carr Bound out	Town
6	Recd. Mathew Son a Child to Mathew Son a Boy allmost Six years of age into the almshouse Consented to Jona. Mason one of the overseers of the Poor Pr. order of Thos. Walley & Ebenezr. Seaver} Select men	State
7	Recd. John Flinn[99] into the almshous Consented to Jona. Mason one of the overseers of the poor Pr. order of Thos. Edwards Select Man	State
7	Discd. Sarah Seagreeves	Town
	Recd. Daniel Loring into the almshouse Pr. order of Edward Procter one of the Overseers of the Poor	Town
10	Recd. Sarah Pray into the Alms house Consented to Jona. Mason one of the overseers of the Poor Pr. order of Wm. Boardman & Thos. Crafts Select men	State
10	Elizebeth Berrey Run	State
10	Ann Cox Run	Town
10	Recd. John Anderson into the almshouse Consented to Jona. Mason overseer of the Poor Pr. order of Wm. Boardman & Thos. Edwards Select men	State
13	Dischargd. John Briant	State

13	Recd. Nancy Willard	State

Consented to Edward Procter one of the overseers of the Poor
Pr. order of Tos. Walley, Wm. Boardman} Select men

13	Recd. Saml. Jenkens into the almshouse	Town

Pr. order of Mr. John White one of the overseers of the Poor}

1791
Janur. 13	Recd. Mary McClockin[100] into the almsho[use]	State

Consented to Edward Procter overseer of the Poor
Pr. order of Thos. Walley & Thos. Crafts} Select men

13	Recd. Hannah Hartley[101] & her two Children Polly Tennaney & Nancy	

Hartley}   State
Consented to John Codman jur. overseer of the poor
Pr. order of Thos. Walley & Wm. Boardman} Select men

13	Recd. Peter Bray into the almshouse	State

Consented to John White one of the overseers of the Poor
Pr. order of Harbotle Dorr one of the Select men

13	Recd. into the almshouse John Palfrey & his two Children Thos. & John	

Pr. order of Mr. Saml. Parkman one of the overseers of the Poor   Town

15	Recd. into the Almshouse Robert Hill	State

Consented to John White one of the overseers of the Poor
Pr. order of Harbotle Dorr & Wm. Boardman one of the Select Men

15	Recd. Ebenr. Cox & his Wife ann into the almshous	Town

Pr. order of Mr. Henry Hill one of the overseers of the Poor

	Dischargd. John Palfrey Jur.	Town

	Recd. Michall Cassaday & his Wife Kathrine	State

Consented to Saml. Parkman one of the Overseers of the Poor
Pr. order of Thos. Crafts & Thos Edwards} Select men

1791
Jany. 19th.	Discharg'd Robt. Hill	State

19th.	Recd. Lucy Bradford into the Almshouse	Town

by Order Colo. Procter

19	Recd. Saml. North into the almshouse	State

Consented to by E: Procter
Pr. order of Ez Price, Wm. Boardman

22	Recd. Catharine Cook into the almshouse	State

Consented to John White one of the overseers of the Poor
Pr. Order of Harbl. Dorr, Ezekl. Price Select Men

26	Discd. Micheal Cassady & his Wife Cathrine	State

28   Recd. John Mellhorn & his Wife Jane into the alms House State
Consented to Edward Procter one of the overseers of the Poor
Pr. order of Wm. Boardman, Ezekl. Prich Select men}

31st.   Recd. Nabby Barry aged 10 yrs. (alias Cox) into the Almshouse State
Consented to by Colo: Procter
℘ ord Wm. Boardman Select Man

Feby. 1st.   Recd. Wm. Hartly into the Almshouse
Consented to by S: Parkman One of the Overseers
℘ order Wm. Boardman, Thos. Crafts} Select Men

2d.   Recd. Sarah Burnia[102] into the Almshouse
Consented to by Jona: Mason Overseer
℘ ord. Eb: Seaver, J. Hatch} Select Men
(S: Burnham)

3d.   Recd. Sarah Rouslow into the almshouse a Child 7 years of age Last
novemr.   State
Consented to John White overseer
Pr. order of Harbl. Dorr} Select Man

Names	Time of Admission & Discharge	Town or State	By what Overseer	By what Selectman
Patrick Burns	1791 dischd: feby. 7th.	State		
Robt. Hoiate	Dischd. feby. 8th	State	dld. to his Father	
Sarah Williamson	Admited feby. 10	State	S Parkman	{ Wm. Boardman Thos. Walley
Alaxander Tomson	Disd. febr. 14	State		
John Woods	Dischd. feby. 15	State		
George Fisher	Dischd. feby. 15	State		
Nabby Barry alias Cox	Dischd. 17th Feby.	State	bound out	
Polly Pool	Dischd: 17th. Feby.	Town	bound out	
Lambeth Murphy	Admitd. feby. 15th.	State	Edwd. Procter	{ Harb: Dorr Thos. Edwards
Mary Brown a Child	Admitd: feby. 17	Ditto	Do.	Wm. Boardman
Thos. Wier	Admitd: feby. 17	State	Do.	Harb: Dorr
Henry Blackbour[103]	admitd. feby. 19	State	Edwd. Proctr.	Harbl. Dorr
Luce Newel & her son John Newel	Dischd. feby. 21	State		
Luther Eddy	dischd: feby. 9th.	State & returnd Marh. 16th. brot. here By the Court		
Mrs: Hollis[104] & 4 childn:	admitd: feby: 21	Town	Hy: Hill	
Luce Meloney[105]	Admitd. feby. 22	State	Edwd. Procter	Thos. Walley Jabz Hatch
Henry Blackbourn	dischd. feby. 23d.	State		
John Coburn	dischd: feby: 24th.	Town		
Thos: Wier	dischd: feby: 24	State		
James Welch	Admitd. feby: 24	State	Ed: Procter	Wm. Boardman
Cath: Townsend	Admitd: Feby. 23d.	State	Colo: Procter	Wm. Boardman
Mark McLauchlin	Admitd: Feby. 26th.	Do.	Do.	{ Ez: Price Thos. Crafts

Names	Time of Admission & Discharge	Town or State	By what Overseer	By what Selectman
Benja: Fowler	dischd. Mar: 2d.	Do.		
Mary Wayod	Dischd. Marh. 3d.	Do.		
John Melidge	Admitd.—5th.	Do.	Edwd. Eades	
Minor Freeman (a Black)	admitd. 5	State	Edwd. Eades	Wm. Boardman Thos. Walley
Thos. Branagan	Dischd. Mar: 7th.	State		
Robert Dunlap	Dischd. Marh. 9	State		
John Mitchell	Admitd. Mar 10th.	State	Saml. Parkman	Wm. Bordman Thos. Crafts
George Ray	admitd. marh. 10	Town	Edwd. Procter	
Wm. McMoran	Dischd. marh. 12	State		
Olive White	Admitd. mar. 12	State	Edwd. Procter	Wm. Boardman
Mordica Johnson	Dischd. marh. 12	State		
Wm. Buckley	admitd. mar 12	State	Edwd. Procter	Wm. Boardman Thos. Crafts
Daniel Benjman[106]	Dischd. mar 14	Town		
Eliza: Stevens	Admitd: Mar 16th.	State	Ed: Procter	{ Wm. Boardman { Thos. Edwards
Peter Michal[107] a blk	Admitted Mar: 16th.	Do:	Edd. Procter	Wm. Boardman
Luther Eddy	Admited mar. 16	State		
John Anderson	Dischd. mah. 16	State		
Patrick Shanley	Dischd. marh. 16	State		
Saml. Covel	Dischd. marh. 16	State		
Jams. Welch	Dischd. mar. 16	State		
Saml. Jenkins	Dischd. Marh. 16	Town		
Timothey Carrel[108]	Admitd. marh. 18	State	Edd. Procter	Wm. Boardman
Edwd. Beacham	Dischd. marh. 21	State		
James McQuin	Dischd. marh. 21	State		

Almshouse Admissions, 1788–1795

Names	Time of Admission & Discharge	Town or State	By what Overseer	By what Selectman
John Cole	Run marh. 21	Town		
Mary Webb & Child	Run marh. 21	Town	Returnd in two Days	
Mary Sharp	Ditto Ditto	State		
Sarah Williamson	Ditto Ditto	State		
John Gillard	Dischd. marh. 21	State		
Filip Delance	Dischd. marh. 22	State		
Wm. Ryan	Admitd. mar 24	State	Edd. Procter	Wm. Boardman
Bridget Cox from Jail	Admitd. mar 28	State	Edwd. Procter	Ebenr. Seaver Thos. Edwards
<*Anna Lewis and Sarah Lewis her children*>	Nance English admit march 28 a Child	State	Jona. Mason	Wm. Boardman
Eleanor Ritchie	Dischd. aprl. 1st.	State		
Sarah Griffith	admitd. aprl. 4th.	Town	Henry. Hill	
Margrett Harrison	admited. aprl. 6	State	Edwd. Procter	Wm. Boardman
Saml. Covel	Bound out aprl. 7th. to Jeremh. Whitemore of Spencer State			
Sarah Man	Bound to Ditto aprl. 7th.	State		
Sarah Condon	Dischd. apr. 7	State	to Jona. Wild Walpole	
Edward & Luce[109] Franks	admitd. aprl. 8	State	Jona. Mason	Wm. Boardman
Joshu Hubbard & Abigal his Wife	Dischd. aprl. 8	Town		
James Peas	Admitd. 8	Wilbraham	Stepm. Gorham	
Richard Corbett	Admitd. 9	State	Jona. Mason	Ezek Price
adam Dogget	admited 10	State	John Codman	Charles Bulfinch
anna Etheridge[110]	admitd. 12	Town	John Lorg. Austin	
John Murfey[111]	Dischd. 12	State		
James Downe	Admitd. 13	State	Edwd. Procter	Thos. Edwards Charls Bulfinch

Names	Time of Admission & Discharge	Town or State	By what Overseer	By what Selectman
John Kuhn	admitd. 14	State	John Sweetser	Ebenr. Seaver
Mary Webb	Discd. to workhouse 14	Town		
John Kiley his Wife Judea[112] & Child	Dischd. 14	State		
Sarah Finn	dischd. 19th.	State		
Sarah Burnal	Run 19	State		
Nancy Rawson a Black	Admitd. 23	State	Edwd. Procter	Ezekl. Price
Wm. Rian[113]	Discd. 25	State		
Elizth. Warner & Child	admitd. 25	State	Jona. Mason	Thos. Crafts Wm. Bordman
York Cox a Blak	Admitd. 25	State	Stepn. Gorham	Ebenr. Seaver
Mary Sharp	Admitd. 25	State	Ed Procter	Wm. Boardman
John Murfee	Admitd. 26	State	Edd. Procter	Wm. Boardman Thos Crafts
Timoy. Carrel	Dischd. 27	State		
<*Thos.*> Lambeth Murfe[114]	Dischd. Marh. 28	State		
Ebenr. Rudock[115]	Dischd. aprl. 27	Town		
Danel Loring	Dischd. aprl. 27	Town		

omited two Children of Lidea Marstens. Born in the House april 19 1791 named Wm. Eustis & Polle Dunn admited[116]

Names	Time of Admission & Discharge	Town or State	By what Overseer	By what Selectman
Elizh. Robertson	Dischd. May 1st.	State		
James Downe	Dischd. 2d.	State		
Wm. } Twins of Polly } Lyda: Marston[117]	Admitd. 19th. Apl: Admitted 19th. Apl:	Town Town		
John Coon	Dischd. May 3	State		
Nancy Rawson a blk.	dischd: May 4th.	State		
Jeremiah Mahany[118]	admitd. May 4	State	Wm. Smith	Wm. Bordman Saml. Cabot

Names	Time of Admission & Discharge	Town or State	By what Overseer	By what Selectman
Patrick Shandly[119]	admd. May 7	State	Wm. Smith	Thos. Edwards Wm. Little
judea Low	Dischd. May 10	State		
Wm. Clare Hannah his Wife & Joseph Their Son	admitd. 16	State	Edwd. Procter	Wm. Boardman Thos. Edwards
Pheebe Gee a Black	admitd. 16	State	Edwd. Procter	Wm. Boardman Thos. Edwards
Elam Gifford	Dischd. 16 to Workhouse	State		
James Pike Wife & Child	Dischd. 16	Town		
John ayers his wife & Child	Admitd. 20	State	Loring Austin	
Wm. Buckley	Dischad. 23	State		
<John> Wm. Hartley	Dischd. 23	State		
Wm. Procter	Dischd. 23	State		
Henry Luckos	Dischd. 23	Town		
Aandrow George Hardk	admitd. 23	State	Edwd. Procter	Ezek Price
Olive White	Dischd. 23	State		
<George Jolley>				
Cathn: English & Child	dischd: 27th. May	State		
Peter Bray a blk	dischd: 27th. May	State		
Wm. Ryon[120] } dischd. next day	Admitd. 27	State	Edd. Procter	Wm. Boardman Tons. Edwards
John Brian	admitd. 28	State	Jona. Mason	Chars. Bulfinch
Jane Polard[121] and her Son John Blacks[122]	dschd. 30	State		
Hannah Hollis & 4 Children	dschd. 30	Town		
Reb: Baldrige	Admitted the 29th.	Town	<(died same day)>	
<John Brian	Run 31>			

Almshouse Admissions, 1788–1795

Names	Time of Admission & Discharge	Town or State	By what Overseer	By what Selectman
Geo: Jolly (bd. out)	dischd. 28th May	State		
Thos Branagan	admitd. June 1	State	S Parkman	Thos Walley Thos. Crafts
Luther Eddy	run June 1st.	State		
Frank Hodson	do: June 4th.	Do.		
Jerẽ: Mehaney[123]	to the Workho: 4th.	Do.		
John Bryan	dischd: 6th. June	Do.		
Thos. Branagan	dischd. 5 June	Do.		
Jack Pollard a Black	Discd. 9	Do.		
Sarah Lovring	Dischd. 9	Town		
Elizabeth Warner	Dischd. 10	State	Returnd. the 15th.	
John Briant[124]	admitd. June 11th.	State	Jona. Mason	Wm. Boardman
Thos. Branagan	admitd. 13	State	Jona. Mason	Thos. Crafts
Mary Brown a molato Child	Dischargd. 14	State		
Mary Roleston[125]	admitd. 16	Town	Jona. Mason Verbl order	
Erick Osterman	admitd. 17	State	Edwd. Procter	Wm. Bordman Ebenr. Seaver
Mary McCollom	admitd. 22	State	S Parkman	S Cobot
Luce Willis	Dischargd. 22	Town		
Erick Osterman	Dischd. 27	State		
Juba West a Black man	admitd. 27	State	John Sweetser	Ebenr. Seaver Thos. Crafts
James Downey	admitd. July 1	State	Jona. Mason	Thos. Walley Wm. Litle
Mary Sharp	Dischd. 2d.	State	To the work house	
Wm: Procter	admitd. 2	State	Edwd. Procter	Wm. Boardman Thos. Edwards
Ann Murphey[126]	Bound out 4th.	State		

Names	Time of Admission & Discharge	Town or State	By what Overseer	By what Selectman
Mary Hartley	Bound out 6	State	Returnd	
Henry Eaton Mayhew	Bound out 7	State	from the Work house	
Ann Murphey	Bound out 4th.	State		
Denis Cavnough	Dischd. 8	State		
Mary Tilton an Infant	Admitd. July 2d.	State	Edwd. Procter	Wm. Bordman Thos. Edwards
Mark McLaucklin[127]	Dischd. 2	State		
Sarah Lanford[128]	Dischd. 12	Town		
Mark McClocklin[129]	admitd. 12	State	Saml. Parkman	Wm. Boardman
Hannah Lahea[130] & Child	admited. 12	Town	Edwd. Procter	
Fradrick Aires	Dischd. 13	Town		
Mary McCollom	Dischd. 14	State		
John Briant	Dischd. 14	State		
Dennis Cavenaugh[131]	Admtd. 16	State	Jona. Mason	Thos. Crafts Thos. Edwards
Anna Etheridge	Dischd. 18	Town		
Thos. Bragedon	Dischd. 18	State		
Hannah Waples	Dischd. 19	State		
Ann Jarrel	Dischd. 19	Town		
Hannah Perkins	admitd. 20	State	Edd. Procter	Ezekl. Price
James Frost	admitd. 21	Town	Edwd. Procter	
James Comerford	admitd. 21	State	Edwd. Procter	Ezekl. Price Wm. Boardman
Wm. Lanford	Run	Town		
Cathre. English & Child	admited July 21	State	Edwd. Procter	Thos. Crafts
Thos. Bragedon[132]	admitd. 22	State	Edd. Procter	Thos. Crafts
Elizth. Burkhurt	Bound out To Wm. Chafe of Freeport July 22	State		Wm. Boardman

Names	Time of Admission & Discharge	Town or State	By what Overseer	By what Selectman
John Fretchman	admitd. 23	State	Wm. Smith	Thos. Crafts Thos. Walley
Hannah Perkins a Child	admit 23	State	Edwd. Procter	Thos Crafts
John McKinsey[133]	admitd. 25	State	Edwd. Procter	Wm. Boardman
John Gillard	admitd. 25	State	Edwd. Procter	Wm. Boardman
Fradrick aires	admitd. 25	Town	Edwd. Procter	
John Palfrey	Dischd. 26	Town		
androw George Hardk[134] a Sweed.	Dischd. 26	State		
Lidea Marting[135]	Dischd. 26	Town		
Thos. Furrs aged 16 Months	admit 28	State	Ed. Procter	Wm. Boardman Thos. Edwards
John Flinn	Dischd. Augt. 1	State		
Mark McClockline	Dischd. 2	State		
Hannah Clare	Dischd. 2	State		
Patte Dorsey	Dischd. 6	State		
Margreat Harrason	Dischd. 8	State		
James Jones & Elizh. his Wife also Their Son Wm.	admited augt. 8	State	Edwd. Procter	Ezekl. Price
Sarah Pray	dischd. the 5th.			
Abigail Lord	Admitd. 12	State	Edwd. Procter	Wm. Boardman
Sofriah Manders	Discd. 12	State		
James Comerford	Dischd. 12	State		
Luce Willis	admitd. 13	Town	Edwd. Procter	
Hannah Lahay	Run the 8 Return'd the 12th.			
John Morar	Admitd. 16	State	Ed. Proctor	Ezl. Price
Ebenr. Ruddock[136] 21st. Sent to the work hous	Admitd. 18	Town	Edwd. Procter	

Almshouse Admissions, 1788–1795

Names	Time of Admission & Discharge	Town or State	By what Overseer	By what Selectman
Abigail Lord	Dischd. 18	State		
James Barrey	admitd. 21	State	Edwd. Procter	Wm. Boardman Ezekl. Price
Robert Wylie	admitd. 21	State	Edwd. Procter	Wm. Boardman Ezekl. Price
Mark McClocklin[137]	admitd. 22	State	Edwd. Procter	Thos. Crafts
Luther Edey[138]	Returnd 22d.	Pr. order of Col. Procter		
Ebenezr. Cox	Dischd. 29	Town		
Abigal Lord	admited 31	State	Edwd. Procter	Wm. Boardman
Susanah Coplin	admitd. augt. 31	State	Edwd. Procter	Wm. Boardman Thos. Crafts
James Frost	Dismist 31	Town		
Hannah Duxbury & her Child Hannah	Dismist Septr. 1	Town		
John Willet	admitd. 1	Town	John White	
Nelly Dukes	admitd. 3	State	Edwd. Procter	Wm. Boardman
Nance Garrel	Dischd. 3d.	Town		
John Flory & Wife & 2 Children	admitd. 8	State	Edwd. Procter	Ezekl. Price Wm. Little
Catrine[139] Vose	Dischd. 10	Town	Bund out	
Betsey Perce[140]	Dischd. 10	Town	Bound out	
Betsy Hardwick	admitd: 12th.	State	Joña. Mason	Ezek Price Wm. Boardman
Wm. <Persons> Perch	admited 14	State	Wm. Smith	Wm. Boardman
John Mellidge	Dischd. 14	State		
Isaac Wendell & Wife	admitd. 14	Town	Willm. Smith	
Anne Lewis & Wm. Lewis & Salle Lewis the Children of John Lewis a Strangr.	admitd. 16	State	Jona. Mason	Thos. Crafts Thos. Edwards

Almshouse Admissions, 1788–1795

Names	Time of Admission & Discharge	Town or State	By what Overseer	By what Selectman
Mary Cowell a Child to go to water Town	Dischd. 20	Town	Edwd. Procter	
Joseph Whitemore Jur. aged 9 years the 10th. of Octr. next	admitd. 20	Town	Ed Procter	
John Willet	Dischd. 21 Sept.	Town		
John Snow	admitd. 21	State	S Parkman	Thos. Walley
Hannah Lahay	Dischd. 21	Town		
Salle Ipson 6 ys. old last June	admitd. 23	Town	Stepn. Goraham	
Polle Do. 4 ys. old Janr. Last				
John Brian	admitd. 23	State	Edwd. Procter	Wm. Boardman
Cuffee ames	admitd. 23	State	S. Parkman	Wm. Boardman S Cabot
Magnus Tellot[141] & Wife Polle McClannen a Child	admitd. 23 admited 30	State Town	Edwd. Procter Stepn. Gorham	Wm. Boardman
Saml. Whitmore[142] will be 5 years octobr. 10th.	admtd. 30	Town	Ed Procter	
Thos Brown	admitd. 30	State	Ed. Prorcter	Wm. Boardman Ebenr. Seaver
Betsey Bennt[143] & Saml. Bennit one 7 years the other 3 years of age	admitd. 30	State	Wm. Smith	Chars. Bulfinch
Hannah Fuller	admitd. Octor. 1	Town	S Parkman	
Patty Dorsey	admitd. 1	State	John White	Wm. Boardman Chars. Bulfinch
Dannel Loring	admitd. 1	Town	Edwd. Procter	
Thos. alexander	admitd. 1	State	Edd. Procter	Wm. Boardman Chars. Bulfinch
Luther Edey	Dismist. sept: 15th.	State		
Robt: Phillips	Admitd: 4th. Octo.	State	Edwd: Procter	E: Price C: Bulfinch
Eliz: Hardwick	dchd: 2	Do.		

Names	Time of Admission & Discharge	Town or State	By what Overseer	By what Selectman
Polly Ballard	admitd. Octo. 4	Town	E: Edes	
Luther Edey[144]	admitd. Sent 6th. to the Workhouse	State		Eze. Price
John Morroson[145]	admitd. 7	State	Jona. Mason	Thos. Edwards
Eliz Farriar[146] George Nancy & Betsey her Children	admit 7 Octr.	State	John Sweetser	E Seaver Thos. Crafts
Thos. Alaxander	Dischd. 11th.	State		
Wm. Perch	Dischd. 11	State		
John allen	admitd. 19	State	Ed. Procter	Wm. Boardman Thos. Crafts
Danl. Rimick	admitd. 15	Town	Henry Hill	
John Snow	Dischd. 19	State		
Sarah Garfilt	admit 19	Town	Step Gorham	
Sarah Warner	admit 20	State	Jona. Mason	Ez Price Wm. Boardman
Saml. Larebea[147]	admitd. 20	Town	Jona Mason	
Robert Wylie	Dischd. 20	State		
Saml. Hicks	admitd. 20	State	Stepn. Gorham	Ez Price Wm. Little
Elsey Stoddard	admited 22	Town	Stepn. Goram	
Luce Willis	Run the 12th.	Town		
Thos. Hines	Bound out	State		
Salle Cades Rusel[148]	Bound out	Town		
Dennis Hogan	admited 26	State	Edwd. Procter	Ez Price Wm. Boardman
<*John Battis a Molato*	*Dismist. 26*	*State*>		
Thos. Brown	Dismist 26	State		
Saml. North	Dischd. 27	State		
Julia Anna Scherve a child 4 years	admited 29	State	Ed. Procter	Ezek Price Wm. Boardman

Names	Time of Admission & Discharge	Town or State	By what Overseer	By what Selectman
Thos. Brown	admitd. 1st. Nov:		Dischd. pr. order of the oveersers	Colo. Crafts
Marey Garrow	Run Octr. 31			
<Mary Brown & her 3 Childn. admited Novr. 2		*Town*	*Ed. Procter>*	
Abigarl Luden of Brantre	admitd. Novr. 3d.		Jona.Mason	
James Williams	admitd. 7	State	Jona. Mason	Ezek Price Saml. Cabot
Saml. North	admitd. 8	State	Ed. Procter	Thos Edwards Charls Bulfin[ch]
Luce Willis	admitd. 10	Town	Ed. Procter	
Abigail Hubbard	Admitd. 10	Town	S Parkman	
Mary Garreau	admited 10	Town	Henery Hill	
Peter Williston W Hous	Admitd. Octor. 29th.	State	Ed. Procter	Wm. Boardman Thos. Walley
John Ingersol a Black	admitd. Novr. 10	State	S. Parkman	Ez Price Wm. Litle
David Chamberlin[149]	admitd. 12	State	Jona. Mason	Ez Price Thos. Edwards
Joseph Langley	admitd. 15	Town	Henry Hill	
Daniel Peirce	admitd. 19	Town	Jona. Mason	
Daniel Remick	Dismist 21	Town		
<Wm. Cleare	*Dismist 21*	*State>*		
Antoney Evens[150]	admitd 21	State	Ed Procter	Wm. Boardman Ezek Price
Wm. Perry	admited 22	Town	Ed Procter	
Mary Pike	admited 23	Town	John White	
Mary Viall[151]	admited 23	Town	John White	
Abigal Luden	Dismist 25	of Brantre		
Daniel Benjn.[152] & 1 Child	admited 26	Town	Jona. Loring Austen	

Almshouse Admissions, 1788–1795

Names	Time of Admission & Discharge	Town or State	By what Overseer	By what Selectman
a Grand Child of Benjns. Named ann Cooley	admited 26	State	Jona. Mason	Wm. Boardman Ez Price
James Williams	Dischard Novr. 29	State		
James Barrey	Dischargd. 29	State		
Wm. Perrey	Dischargd. 30	Town		
Hannah Tuxbury[153]	Bound out 30	Town		
Mark McClocklin	Dischargd. Decr. 1	State		
Abigal Simpson	admid. 2	Town	Wm. Smith	
Thomas Davis	Admited 3	State	John White	Wm. Boardman
James Kelley	Admited 5	State	Henry Hill	Thos. Crafts
<Mary Reed omited	*Novr. 14 admitd.*	*State>* Wm. Smith		Wm. Boardman Thos. Edwards
Wm. Parsons	Admitd. 6	State	S: Parkman	Thos. Edwards Thos. Crafts
Salle & Polle⎫ Gepson ⎭	Dischd. Novr. 6	Town		
Marey Reed[154]	admitd. Novr. 14	State	Wm. Smith	Wm. Boardman Thos. Edwards
<Thos. Davis	*admited Decr. 6*	*State>* John White		Wm. Boardman Thos Edwards
Francis Hudson	admited [*Dec.*] 7	State	John Sweetser	Ebr. Sever Thos. Crafts
John Clerke[155]	admitd. 8	State	Wm. Smith	Wm. Boardman Thos. Crafts
Partrick Hufron	admitd. 8	State	Ed Procter	Thos Crafts Wm. Boardman
James Comerford	Admited 9	State	Jona. Mason	Ebenr. Seaver John Edwards
Mary Bufford	Admit 9	Town	Ed Procter	
John Holbrook	admited 9	State	Ed. Procter	Wm. Boardman Thos. Crafts

Almshouse Admissions, 1788–1795

Names	Time of Admission & Discharge	Town or State	By what Overseer	By what Selectman
Edwd. Beacham	admit 10	State	Jona. Mason	Wm. Boardman Thos. Crafts
ann Warren	admit 10	Town	Edwd. Procter	
James Pike	admited Decr. 14	Town	John White	
antoney Evens	Dischard. 15	State		
John Griffith	admit 15	Town	John White	
Wm. Lanford[156]	admited 15	Town	Stephn. Gorham	
Elizth. Warner	Dischargd 15	State		
Saml. Legg	admitd. from workhous 15	Town	Wm. Phillips	
Eunice Danee a black	admit 15	State	Jona. L austian	Ez Price Charls Bulfinch
James Comerford	Dismist 17	State		
Sarah Stone	admited 17	Town	Edwd. Edes	
Dainel Peirce	Dischargd. 20	Do:		
Josep Langley	admited 20	Town	Henry Hill	
Patt Kelly	admited 20	State	S Parkman	Wm. Boardman Eben Sever
Elizth. Hartwick[157] from Workhouse	admitd. 12	Town	Ed. Procter	
John Collier	Admited 21	Town	Stepn. Gorham	
Violet Madderson	Admited 21	State	Jona. Mason	Ebenr. Sever Thos. Crafts
John Griggery[158]	Admitd. 22	Town	Wm. Smith	
Sally Harris from Biddeford	admit 23	Town	Edd. Procter	
Dl. Peirce	Admitd. 27th. Decr.	Town		
Benjn. Churchill	Admit Decr. 29	State	John White	Thos. Edward Wm. Little
Sarah Lovring[159]	Admit 29	Town	Saml. Parkman	
Eliza. Berrey	Admitd. 29	Town	Stepn. Gorham	

Almshouse Admissions, 1788–1795

Names	Time of Admission & Discharge	Town or State	By what Overseer	By what Selectman
John Collier	Dischd. 30	Town		
Velis Akely	Admit 30	State	Edd. Procter	Ebenr. Seaver Wm. Little
Janury 5 [1792] Thos. Davis	Dischd. Janry. 5	State		
Mary Keef James & Timothey Keef her Children	Admited 5	State	Edwd. Procter	Wm. Little Charls. Bullfinch
Danl. Peirce	Dischd. 6	Town		
Ruth Mathers[160]	Admit 6	Town	John White	
Sarah Freeman & her 2 Children Sina & Hanna Indens[161]	Admited 7	Town	John White	
Danil Peirce	Dischd. 10	do:		
Venefred[162] Stone	Admitd. 10	State	John White	Wm. Boardman Thos. Edwards
anne Etheredg[163]	admit 10	Town	L austin	
Elizth. Flurrey	Discharged 10	State		
Abigal Simons	Dischd. 13	State		
James Kirk	admited 15	State	Stepn. Gorham	Wm. Bordman Thos. Crafts
Olive White a Black	omited Novr. the 20th 1791	State	Edwd. Procter	Ezek Price Tos. Edwards
Nancy Arbour a Black	admited Janur. 15 [1792]	State	John White	Wm. Boardman
Mary Pain[164]	admited 15	State	Stepn. Gorham	Wm. Boardman Thos. Crafts
Robrt Miller	admited 20	State	John White	Wm. Litle Wm. Bordman
<Nancy arbour	admitd. 20	State	John White	Wm. Boardman Ezek Price>
Rose Badger & 3 Children	admitd. 23	State	John White	Wm. Little Ez Price

Names	Time of Admission & Discharge	Town or State	By what Overseer	By what Selectman
Edwd. Harper	admited 23	State	Jon L Austin	Ez Price Thos. Walley
Michael Rellings	admited 24	State	Wm. Smith	Eben Sever Thos. Walley
alexd. Loyd[165]	admit 25	State	Wm. Smith	Cs. Bulfinch Thos. Walley
John Taylor	Admit 25	State	Ed. Procter	E Seavor Thos. Crafts
Betsey Battst[166] a Black	admit 25	State	Jona. Mason	C Bulfinch Wm. Boardman
Thos. Alexander	Admited 29	State	Edd. Procter	Wm. Little Ebenr. Seaver
Jos. Brick	admited 30	Town	Edd. Procter	
Daniel Peirce	Admit 30	Town	Saml. Parkman	
John Beapteste a Child	admitd. Febry. 1st.	State	Jona. L Austin	Thos. Crafts Thos. Edwards
Wm. White	admited 2	State	S Parkman	Wm. Boardman Thos. Crafts
Wm. Stevens[167]	Bound out	State		
John Finn	Run a boy 2	State		
abigail Whillet	Admited 4	Town	S Gorham	

<Estor [Foard?] Returnd & Recd. in to the house pr. Verble order of the overseers State>

John Fitsgarel[168]	Admited Febr. 6	Town	Henry Hill	
Joseph Townsand[169]	Admit a Black 8	State	Edd. Procter	Thos. Edwards Wm. Little
Lidea Moss	admited 8	Town	Jona. Mason	
John Gillard	Dischargd. 9	State	Returnd the Next Day	
Jos. Bragadon	Dischargd. 9	State	Returnd the next Day	
Michel Renolas[170]	Dischd. 9	State		
Vilett Matterson	Dischd. 10	State		

Almshouse Admissions, 1788–1795

Names	Time of Admission & Discharge	Town or State	By what Overseer	By what Selectman
James Downey	admited 10	State	S Parkman	Wm. Little T Crafts
Thos. Branagan John Gill & Thos. Alaxander	Sent to work hous 13	State	Henr. Hill	
John Webb & Ballak His Wife	Admited 14	State	Jona. L austin	Ezk Price Thos. Walley
Thos. Brick	Dischargd 14	Town		
Saml. Whitemore	Bound out 14	Town		
James Brown	Bound out 17	State		
Elizth. Dannie	Admited 19	Town		
ann Farrier[171]	Bound out Febr. 23d.	State		
Elizabeth Condon	Admited 23	State	John Sweetser	Wm. Boardman Ebenr. Seaver
James Frost	Admited 24	Town	S Parkman	
Elizebth. Woodman	admited 23	State	Jon. White}	Wm. Little
Henry & Charles Woodman Her Children	admited 25	State	John White}	Wm. Little Wm. Bordman
Danl. Peirce	Dismist 27	Town		
Jack Tuckerman	admit Omited Janr. 20	State	Stepn. Gorham	Wm. Bordman Thos. Crafts
Mary wainwood	Admited Feb 29	State	S Parkman	Wm. Boardman C Bulfinch
Joseph Langle	Dischd. Febr. 23d.	Town		
Saml. Soudon	admited 29	State	Saml. Parkman	Wm. Boardman Thos. Craftes
Jane Clark	admitd. Marh. 2	State	Edd. Edes	Wm. Boardman Thos. Crafts
Cathrine English	Dismist 5	State		
Thos. Whitworth a Black	admitd. 2d.	State	Ed. Edes	Ezekl. Price Thos Crafts

Almshouse Admissions, 1788–1795

Names	Time of Admission & Discharge	Town or State	By what Overseer	By what Selectman
Easter[172] Ford Returnd	admited 2	State	Steph. Gorham	Wm. Bordman Thos. Crafts
Mary Gordon Returnd	admited 2	State	Steph. Gorham	Wm. Bordman Thos. Crafts
Mary Dawes	admitd. 10	Town	Saml. Parkman	
Nance Cox	admited 10	Town	John White	
Patt. Kelle	Dismist 13	State		
Velis Akely	Dismist 14	State		
Patrick Huffrin	Dismist 14	State		
Jane Prescut[173] a Black	admited 14	State	Jona. Mason	Ezek Price Thos. Crafts
Wm. Person	Dismist 14	State		
John Hany[174]	admited 14	State	S Parkman	S Cabot Thos. Crafts
James Kerk	Dismist 14	State		
Susanah Foster[175]	Bound out 17	State		
James Downey	Dismist 19	State		
<Jack Tuckerman	Dismist March 17	State	Steph. Gorham>	
Peter Warner & his Wife Eliz	Admited March 19	State	Jona. Mason	Ezl Price Wm. Boardman
Edward Beacham	Dismist 19	State		
Edward Furlong	Admited 21	State	Wm. Smith	Ebenr. Sever Chars. Bulfinch
<George Farrier	admited>			
Wm. Lanford	Dismist 22	Town		
<Edwd. Beacham	Dismist 22	State> entd. above		
Mary Downey	admited 22	State	Ed. Procter	Wm. Little Wm. Boardman
Hannah Adams	Dismist 31	Town		

❧

Names	Time of Admission & Discharge	Town or State	By what Overseer	By what Selectman
Sarah Freeman & her 2 Children Sine & Hanah	} Dismist 31	Town		
Wm. Dockim[176] & his Wife Meriam	admited 31	Town	Henry Hill	
John Griggs	Dismist april 2	Town		
John Griffis	Dismist 3	Town		
James Frost	Dismist 4	Town		
Ann Burd[177] Born in Charstown	admited 4		John Codman	
Luther Edey	Dismist 6			
George Farrier <admited>	Omited March 29th.	State	Jona. Mason	Ezekl. Price Thos. Edwards
Thos. Smith	Admitted 6	State	Edwd. Procter	Wm. Boardman Thos. Crafts
Benjn. Churchell	Dismist 9	State		
Ruth Mathews	Dismist 9	Town		
James Reed	admited April 9	State	S Parkman	Wm. Little Wm. Boardman
Elizh. Eskrine	admited 9	Town	John Sweetser	
John Fits Gerell	Dischargd 10	Town		
Mary Perkit	Dischargd. 11	State	& her Child Jon. Brown	
Daniel Collins	admited 11	State	Jona. Mason	C Bulfinch Wm. Scollay
Mary Butler & her 2 Childn. Nelle & Polley	} admited 12	State	Jona. Mason	E Seaver Wm. Boardman
Easter Ford[178]	Bound out 12	Town		
Henry Woodman	Bound out 12	Town		
Marther[179] Dorsey	Dischargd 12	State		
Mary Keef	Dischargd 12	State		

~

Names	Time of Admission & Discharge	Town or State	By what Overseer	By what Selectman
John Taylor	Dischargd 16	State		
abigil Willet	Dischd. 16	Town		
James Pike	Dischd. 16	Town		
Wm. Bovey Penne	a Child Dischd. 16	Town		
Jack Tuckerman	Dischargd 17	State		
Androw[180] Gardner	Dischd. 18	<State> Town		
<Wm. Bovey Penne	Discharged aprl. 18	Town>		
Mary Hines	Dischd. 18	State		
Sally Hunt	admited 18	Town	W Parkman	
John Greigs[181]	admited to Lodge in the house till Seting Day			S. Gorham
<Jack Huston	Dischargd. 20	State> see below		
Daniel Collins	Dischargd. 20	State		
Frank Hutson	Dischargd 20	State		
Patrick Monagin	admitd. 21	State	Henry Hill	Ezekl. Price Thos. Crafts
Lucy Clark a Child	admited 21	Town	Wm. Phillips	
Elizebth Hardwick	Dischd. 21	Town		
Anne Lewis & her Son Wm.	Dischargd. 21	State		
<Mary Keef	Dischargd 21	State> Entd. before		
Wm. Sharp	Dischargd. 30	State		
Dinis Hogain	Dischargd 30	State		
Peter Hunnawell[182] a child	Admited 30	Town	Jona. Mason	
Susanna Hunnawell[183] a child	admd. 30	Town	Jona. Mason	
Ann Payson	Dischargd 30	State		
Timothey Keeth a Child	Dischargd. May 1	State		

Names	Time of Admission & Discharge	Town or State	By what Overseer	By what Selectman
James Keeth a Child	Dischargd. 1	State		
Saml. Souden	Dischargd. 1	State		
William White	Dischargd 2	State		
Sarah Stone	Dischargd 4	Town		
John Wilson	admited 4	State	Ed. Procter	Wm. Boardman Thos. Edwards
James Osborn	admited 5	Town	pr. order of the Board	
Mary Dawes	Dismist 5	Town		
William Procter	Dischargd. 5	State		
Ebenezr. Carlile	admitd. 5	State	Jona. Mason	Wm. Boardman Ez Price
Charlestown Flucker	admited 7	State	Henry Hill	Ezekl. Price Ebenr. Seaver
Pheabe Flucker	admited 7	State	Henry Hill	Ezekl. Price Ebn. Seaver
Hannah Powell	admited 8	State	Jona. Mason	Thos. Crafts Wm. Scollay
Mary Downey	Dischargd 9	State		
Salle Harris	Dischargd 9	Town		
Rose Badger & her 3 Childn.	Dischargd 9	State		
John Lee Galley	Dischargd 9	State		
James Jones Elizh. His wife & their Son Wm.	Dischargd 9	State		
<Elezth. Condon	Dischargd May 10	State>	Returnd. the 11	
Nicholas Dulash	bound out 16	State		
Frances Crispin a Black Boy	admited May16	State	John Codman	C Bulfince Wm. Scollay
Nancey Fisher a Child 13 months old	admited 16	Town	John White	

Names	Time of Admission & Discharge	Town or State	By what Overseer	By what Selectman
Hannah McKinzey[184]	bound Out 16	State		
Joseph Sheehay	admited 19	State	Jona. Mason	Thos. Crafts Thos. Edwards
Prince Hitchbourn[185] a Black admited 19		State	Heny. Hill	Ebn. Seaver Thos. Crafts
Ann Trainhorn Retd. from Charlestown	admid. pr. order of the overseers 22	State		
John Franks[186]	Bound out 22	State		
Mary Wanewood	Dischargd 23	State		
Patrick Shanley	Dischargd 23	State		
Eliz Woodman	Dischargd 23	State		
Peter Hunnewell	bound out	Town		
Mary Ennis	admited 24	State	Wm. Smith	Thos. Walley Wm. Scollay
William Procter	Admited 24	State	Ed. Procter	E Price Wm. Scollay
Jack Webb a Black	Dischargd 29	State		
Edward Furlong	Dischargd June 1	State		
Mary Rose	admited 1	Town	Stephen Gorham	
Ebenezr. Carlile	Dischargd	State		
John Willson	Dischargd June 4	State		
Joshua P K Dehagat ales [alias] Hancock	admited 4	State	John Sweetser	Ezl. Price T Crafts
Mary Buffit	Dischargd. 5	Town		
Mary McLucklin	Dischargd. 5	State		
Hanah Cartright	admited 5	Town	Ed Procter	
[Jane][187] Prescots. Child [born in?] the house [Named R]obt. Brown	admited 7	State	Edwd. Procter	Wm. Boardman Ezekl. Price

Names	Time of Admission & Discharge	Town or State	By what Overseer	By what Selectman
Vilet Matterson[188] a Black	admid. 7	State	Edward Edes	Thos. Crafts Wm. Scollay
Charlstown Flucker	Dischargd 11	State		
Androw Gardner	admited 11	State say Town	} Ed. Edes	Thos. Crafts Wm. Scollay
Sarah Edey	admited 11	Town from Work hous pr. Verble order Mr. White		
Wm. Etridge	Bond out 13	Town		
Mary Delay	Bound out 13th.			
Thos. Branagan	admited 13	State	Edwd. Edes	Thos. Walley Thos. Crats
<Peter Hunnewell Dischargd the Same day>	*admited 14*	*Town*	*Jona. Mason*	
Elizh. Robertson	admited 14	Town	Wm. Smith	
James Pike	admited 14	Town		
Nero Davis a Black	admited 14	State	Jon. Sweetser	Eben Seaver Thos. Crafts
Mehitable Carnes	Admitd 15	State	Jona. Mason	Ezekl. Price Ebenr. Seaver
Marthey Darsey[189]	admited 18	State	Edward Procter	
Ann Foble	admited 18	Town	John Sweetser	
Hannah Perkins & her Child Margret	Dismist 18	State		
Rachael Mungerl	admited 18	State	Sent to work hous Jona. Mason	Thos. Crafts Wm. Scollay
Joseph Sheehay	Dismist 19	State		
Salle Hunt	Dischargd 19	Town		
John Mozar omited	Dischard Decr. 1 1791			
Elizabeth Cowen	admited 21 [*June 1792*]	State	S Parkman	Wm. Boardman Ezek Price
Charles Doll	admited 23	State	Jona. Mason	Ezek Price Thos. Crafts

Names	Time of Admission & Discharge	Town or State	By what Overseer	By what Selectman
Eliz. Williams	Dischargd 24 to the Hospital on acct. of having the Small pox			State
Polle Sherman	Discd. 24 a Child to the Hospitabl for Sml. Pox			
Wm. Counts	admited 25	Town	Ed. Edes	
Alexander Thomas	Admited 26	State	Jona. Mason	Wm. Boardman Wm. Scollay
Mary Pike & her Son Wm.	Dischd. to the Hospital	Town		
John Schrider	admited 26	State	John Sweetser	Ez Price Thos. Crafts
Mary Gordon	Bound out 26	State		
Jane Prescut a Black	Dischd. 28	State		
Robt. Brown Jane Priscuts. Child		State	Dischargd 28	
Sarah Gray	admited 28	Town	John Codman	
Thos Colley	admited June 29	State	Ed. Procter	Wm. Boardman Thos. Edwards
John Schrider	Dismist July 2d.	State		
Timothey Howard	Run 2nd.	State		
Mary McConnock	Run 2d.	State say Town		
Elizth. Condon Dinah a Black say Providence	Dismist 2d. Amited 2nd.	State State	Jona. Mason	Ebenr. Seaver Thos. Crafts
Patrick Monagin	Run 2nd.	State		
Alaxander Loyed	Dismist July 3	State		
Hannah Powel	Dismist 5	Town		
Wm. Peek	Dismist 5	Town		
aged 25 Hannah Deagles	admited 5	State	Jona. Mason	Thos. Crafts Wm. Scollay
Josh. Deagles aged 17	Admited 5	State	Jona. Mason	Thos. Crafts Wm. Scollay

Almshouse Admissions, 1788–1795

Names	Time of Admission & Discharge	Town or State	By what Overseer	By what Selectman
Alaxander Tomson	Dismist 9	State		
Mary Burfert	Admited 9	Town	Ed. Procter	
Timothy Howard	Admited 9	State	S Parkman	Ezekl. Price Thos. Crafts
Mary Ross	Dismist 12	Town		
Mary Ayres a Child	admited 14	State	Edwd. Procter	Wm. Boardman Ezekl. Price
Michel Crowley	Dismist 16	Town		
Marthey Dorsey[190]	admited 16	State	Edwd. Edes	Wm. Bordman Wm. Scollay
Meriam Handfeild[191]	Dischargd 18	Town		
Joshua Hubbard	Dischargd 18	Town		
abigal Hubbard his Wife	Dischargd 18	Town		
<Meriam Handfeild	Run 18>	see above		
Luce Willis	Run 18	Town		
axam Richards	admited 24	State	S Parkman	Wm. Boardman Wm. Little
Thos. Colley	Dismist 26	State		
James Reed	Dischargd 26	do.		
Wm. Dockim	Dischargd 26	Town		
Stephen Jones a Molato	admid. 28	State	Jona. Mason	Thos. Crafts
Elizth. Dennes. Child	Born in the House			Wm. Scollay
John McGoff	admited 28	State	Jona. Mason	Wm. Boardman Thos. Crafts
George Appelton[192] an Enfant a molato	admd. 28	State	Jona. Mason	Thos. Crafts Wm. Scollay
Bengn. Pool	admited 30	Town	Ed Procter	
Elizh. Cowen	Dischargd Augt. 1	State		
Vilet Maderson	Run 1	State		

Almshouse Admissions, 1788–1795

Names	Time of Admission & Discharge	Town or State	By what Overseer	By what Selectman
Mary Burfret	Dischargd 1	Town		
Ann Cox	Dismisst Augst. 2	Town		
James Butler[193] a Child	admited 2	State	Jona. Mason	Thos. Crafts Wm. Scollay
William Dockum	admited 3	Town	Henery Hill	
Mary Selvester[194]	admitd. 3 Born in plymoth	State	Ed. Edes	
Mary Fling[195]	amited 4	State	S Parkman	Ezekl. Price Thos. Edwards
Stephen Jones a molato Child	Dischrgd 4	State		
John McGoff	Dischargd 6	State		
Daved Greegs[196] a Child	admited 6 Mary Selvesters Child			
Joseph Whitemore	Bound out 6			
Isaac Downes	admited 7	Town	Stepn. Gorham	
Peter Warner & his wife Eliz	Dischargd 7	State		
Frances Crispin	Dischargd 7	State	a Black Lost his Legs	
Mary Sharp	admited 7 say returnd	State	Wm. Smith	Thos. Crafts Wm. Scollay
Delight Smith	Dismist 8	Town	Returnd the 9th.	
Peter Hunnewell	admited 8	Town	Jona. Mason	
Wm. Sharp	admited 9	State	Jona. Mason	Ebr. Seaver Thos. Crafts
Isaac Wendal & Wife Dismist	Dismist augst 13	Town		
Wm. Procter	admited 13 say returnd	State	Ed Procter	Wm. Boardman Thos. Edwards
Benjn. Pool	Dismist 13	Town		
Peter Murfey[197]	admited 14	State	Wm. Phillips	Wm. Bordman Thos. Crafts

Almshouse Admissions, 1788–1795

Names	Time of Admission & Discharge	Town or State	By what Overseer	By what Selectman
Mary Keef	admitted 15	State	Jona. Mason	Wm. Boardman Thos. Crafts
Marthey Dorsey	Dismist 16	State		
Felix Holbrook	admitted 16 a Blak	State	Jona. Mason	Ebenr. Sever Wm. Scollay
Sarah Ston[198]	admitted 17	Town	John White	
Jane Clarke	Dismist 18	State		
Polle Sherman a Child	admitted 19 from the Hospitl.	State		
Becky[199] Spear an orphan	admd. 19	Town	S Parkman	
Mary McLaucklan[200]	admd. 24	State	Jona. Mason	Thos. Crafts Wm. Scollay
Cathrine Hunnewell	admited 25	Town	S Parkman	
Ann Pason[201]	admited 25	State say town	Jona. Mason	Ez Price Thos. Crafts
John McKenzie	Run 28	State		
James Timothey Keef	admited 29	State	Ed Procter	
Benjn. Tyler	admited augst 30	State	Wm. Phillips	Wm. Litle Ez Price
Elizh. Selvester[202] & 3 Children	admited 31	Town	Edd. Procter	
Sarah Waid[203] an Inden	admited 31	Town	Jona. Mason	
Roseanah[204] Dawson a child	admited 31	State	J Mason	Wm. Bordman Tho Edwards
Eliz Coville[205]	admited 31	Town	Jona. L Austin	Disc nex morg. pr. Mr. Austins. order
<Hannah> Eliza. Berrey	Dismist 31	Town		
John Dawson & Magret Dawson	admited Septr 1	State	J Mason	Wm. Bordman Thom. Edwards
Sarah Tuckerman a Child	admited 1	Town	S Gorham	

Names	Time of Admission & Discharge	Town or State	By what Overseer	By what Selectman
Toll[206] Tuckerman a Child admitted 1		Town	S Gorham	
Alexandr. Fisher	admited 1	State	Jona. Mason	Thos. Crafts Ezl. Price
Peter Swan	Admited 2	State	Jona. Mason	Thos. Edwards Wm. Boardman
James Downey	Admited 3	State	Wm. Phillips	Wm. Little Thos. Crafts
Mary Owen & her daughr. Mary Admid. 3		State	Jona. Mason	Chals. Bulflinch Ez Price
Eleoner Peirce & her 2 Children Eleoner & Hannah	} Admitted 4th.	State	Jona. Mason	Thos. Crafts Wm. Bordman
Wm. White	admited 5	State	Wm. Phillips	Wm. Boardman Thos. Crafts
Nancy Morris a child	admited 8	State	Edwd. Procter	Thos. Walley
Francis Rosemary & His Child Lewis	admited 8	State	Jona. Mason	Er. Seaver Wm. Boardman
<Nancy Morris a child	*admited 8*	*State*	*Ed. Procter>*	Thos. Walley Wm. Bordman
Fredrick Webster	admited 8	State	Jona. Mason	Wm. Boardman Thos. Crafts
Catrin[207] Ramsdal	admited Born in the House }	Town	Sepr. 3d.	
Eliz Cornish Eliz Moore Eliz Shehane	admited 8 from Workhouse	Town		
Saml. Hicks	Dismist Septr. 2 to Ransford Island			State } omited
Mary Everton	Dismist Septr. 2 to Ransford Island & Died the 13th.			Town }
Elizh. Coburn	Admited 10	Town	Jona. Mason	
Elizh. Barker	admited [10]	Town	Henry Hill	
Mary McGlocklin Meriam Dockum	Run 10	State Town		

Almshouse Admissions, 1788–1795

❧

Names	Time of Admission & Discharge	Town or State	By what Overseer	By what Selectman
Elizth. Moore Elizth. Danne Sarah Gaffet Eliz Burn[208]	Run} 10	State Town Town		
Provedenc Green	admited 15 a Black	State	John. L Austin	Thos. Crafts Wm. Scollay
Ebenezer Ruddock[209]	admited 15	Town	Henry. Hill	
Cathrin Hunnewell	Run Septr 16	Town		
Fradrick Webster	Run 16	State		
Mary Ross	admited 18	Town	Stevn. Gorham	
Barney Mathews[210]	admited 19	State	Heny. Hill	Thos. Crafts Thos. Edwards
Jedediah Chester	admited 20	State	Jona. Mason	Wm. Bordman Ezek Price
Susanah Mayo A Child	admited 22 5 months old	Town	Wm. Smith	
Charity Brinton	admited 24	Town	S Gorham	
James Barns	admited 24	State	John. Codman	Wm. Bordman Thos. Crafts
Soloman Slokham	admited 26	State	S parkman	Wm. Little Wm. Boardman
Mary Voux	admited 28	Town	Wm. Smith	
Elizh. Farrer a Child	Bound out augt. 22	State		
Axom Richards	Dismist. Octr. 1 Returnd the next Day	State}		
Mary Cole	admited 1	State	H Hill	T Crafts Wm. Scollay
Saml. Parks	admited 2	State	Jona. Mason	Ezekl. Price Thos. Crafts
Susanah Mayo	Dismist 3	Town		
an Infant Boy fund at Mr. Thathers. Dore namd. Thos. Jones	admited 3	Town		

Names	Time of Admission & Discharge	Town or State	By what Overseer	By what Selectman
Charity Brinton	Dismist 4	Town		
Mary Butler & her) 2 Children ∫	Dismist Octr 4	State		
Luce Roberts 4	admited S Pox 4	State	Jona. Mason	Ezekl. Price Ebenr. Seaver
<Mary Cole S Pox	*admited 4>*	See under the first		
Joseph austin of Dracut	admitd. 4	Town	S Gorham	
Sewall Harrington 4	admited 4	Town	Mr. austin	
Peter Swan	Dischargd. to the Work H 4	State		
Sarah Benjamin	admited 4 Small P	Town	Jona. L. Austin	
Cesar Gray,[211] Black	admited 4	State	Jona. Mason	Wm. Boardman Thos Edwards
Frances Rosemary	Dischargd 5	State		
Lewis Rosemary	Dischargd 5 Child	State		
Scipio Jacob a Blak.	admited 6	State	Jona. Mason	Ebenr. Seaver Thos. Crafts
Charity Brinton	admited 8	Town	Sten. Gorham	
Eliz Selvester & one Child	Dismist 8	Town		
<Nan[cy] Morris a Child	*dismist 10)* *to the alms∫>*	*State*		
Wm. Procter	Dismist 10	State		
Mary Downey	admited 10	State	Saml. Parkman	Wm. Little Wm. Boardman
George Rammor	admited 11	Town	Ed. Procter	
Jacob Apstros[212]	admited 11	State	Jona. Mason	Ez Price Wm. Boardman
Mary Ross	Dismist 12	Town	Small Pox	
Hannah Cooper	admited 12	State	Wm. Phillips	C Bulfinch Wm. Scollay

~

Names	Time of Admission & Discharge	Town or State	By what Overseer	By what Selectman
Wm. armstrong	admited 15	State	S Parkman	Ezek Price Wm. Little
Mary Owen & Daughter Mary	Dischd. 15	State		
Marther Dorcy[213]	admited 15	State	Wm. Phillips	C Bulfinch Wm. Scollay
Elizh. Coburn	Dismist 17	Town		
Rose Morris from Jal	admited 18	State	Wm. Smith	Ezl. Price Thos. Crafts
Prince Goinge[214] a Black	admited 18	State	S Gorham	Ezl. Price T Crafts
Saml. Parks	Dismist 22	State		
abraham Frost	admitd. to house Small Pox	Town	Ed. Procter	
Thankfull Edmonds	admited from the work house 22	<State>	Lorg. L austin	
Thankful Edwardss. Child namd. Elizth. Roion	Admited 22	State	Born in the House	
William Armstrong	Dismist 24	State		
Catrine Tillet	admited 1792 Octer 26	Town	Ed Procter	
Axam Richards	Dischd. 30	State		
Henry Luckis	admited 30	Town	S Gorham	
Thos. Bragdon	30th. admid.	State[215]		
Dinah Roberts & her 3 Children Rhoda Henry & Mary	admited 30	State	B Wm. Phipleps	C Bulfinch Wm. Scollay
Jack Fox	admited 31	State	Wm. Phillips	C Bulfinch Wm. Scollay
Cathrine Molloy[216]	admited 31	State		
Cathrine Molloy	Dismist Novr. 3	State		
Peter Underwood	admited 3 Dischd. nex Day	State	Ed. Procter	Wm. Boardman Thos. Crafts
Dennis Hogan	Admited 3	State	Jona. Mason	Wm. Little

Names	Time of Admission & Discharge	Town or State	By what Overseer	By what Selectman
Elenor Richie returnd	admitted 7	State	Wm. Smith	Er. Seaver Wm. Scollay
Jacob Aptros	Dischargd. 10	State		
Edwd. Gorman[217]	admitted 8	State	John White	Wm. Little
Sarah Benjmin	Dismist 10	Town		
Isaac Wendal[218]	admitted 10	Town	Ed. Procter	
Mary Cole	Dischargd 14			
Sophia Truant the Daughter of Gillam Truant a French man	admitted 14	State	S Parkman	Wm. Little Ezl. Price
Mary Truant	admitted 14	State	S Parkman	Wm. Little
Hannah Mullin	admitted 1792 November 15	Town	Jona. L Austin	
Luce Roberts	Dismist 15	State	S Pox	
Henry Kendall & Luce his Wife	admitted 15	State	Wm. Smith	Ezek Price Thos. Crafts
Elizabeth Fullam	admitted 15	State	John Sweetser	Ebr. Seaver Wm. Scollay
Mary Selvester[219] & her Child	admitted 17	State	Ed. Procter	Wm. Boardman Thos. Crafts
Elizabeth Lewis	Admitted Novr. 19	State	S Gorham	Wm. Little
Charlestown Flucker	Admitted Novr. 21	State	Jona. Mason	Ezekl. Price
Edward Kneeland	Admitted 19	Town	S Gorham	
Abraham Frost	Dismist 22	Town	S Pox	
Androw Morris	admitted [22]	State	Wm. Smith	Ez Price
Patrick Kelley	admitted 22	State	S Parkman	Wm. Boardman
Androw Morris	admitted 22	State	Wm. Smith	
Thos. Alaxander	Admited 24	State	Jona. Mason	Thos. Walley
Wm. Brown	admitted 24	Town	S Parkman	Town
Wm. Lewis a Child	admitted 24	State	John Sweetser	Ebr. Seaver Wm. Boardman

꩜

Names	Time of Admission & Discharge	Town or State	By what Overseer	By what Selectman
Velis Akley[220]	admited 24 Sent to work house	State	Saml. Parkman	Wm. Little
John Gillard	admited 26	State	S Gorham	Wm. Scollay
Elizh. Fenno	admited 1792 Novr. 27	Town	Wm. White	Deschargd.
an Infant Child found on the Mill Bridge Name [Saml.?] Mill Bridg[221]	admited 27	Town	Ed. Procter	
Sarah Burnet	admited 27	Town	Ed. Procter	
Mrs. Cowel ⎱ Mary Dowrick ⎰	Returnd 27			
Jedediah Chester	Runn 30th.			
Marcy (Say Mary)[222] Garrow	Returnd. 30	State	Jona. Mason	T Carafts Wm. Scollay
Wm. Spooner Mary His wife	admited 30	State	S Goraham	Wm. Boardman Thos. Crafts
John Morton B[lack]	admited Decr. 1	State	H Hill	E Price Thos. Crafts
Ann Chaloner	Run 1	State		
Elizabeth Dracey	admited 1	State	John Sweetser	Ebr. Seaver
Thos. Curtis	admited 3	State	Jona. Mason	Wm. Boardman Thos. Crafts
Mary Buckley	admited 3	State	John White	Wm. Boardman
Saml. Hicks Returnd from Ransfords. Island	Decr. 3	State		
Meriame Dockim[223]	admited 4	Town	H Hill	
Daniel Benjmin[224] ⎫ Saml. Leage ⎪ Mary Webb ⎬ Mary Procter ⎪ Ayles Fulker[225] ⎭	admited from Workhouse		Ed. Proct[er]	
<Wm. Spooner & Wife	Dischargd 6	State>		
John Sanders from Delewar State	admited 7	State	Saml. Parkman	Wm. Boardman Thos. Crafts

Names	Time of Admission & Discharge	Town or State	By what Overseer	By what Selectman
Wm. Cocks[226]	admited 6	State	H Hill	Thos. Walley
Rosannah Dorsey	Bound out Decr 1792 6	State		
Marther Dorcy[227]	Dischargd 6	State		
Wm. Langford	admited 6	Town	S Gorham	
Aron Emmons	admited 6	Town	S Gorham	
Catey[228] Hunnewell	admited 8	State	Wm. Smith	Wm. Bordman Thos. Crafts
<Oliver Giles a Black	*add. 9 Disc. the nex day>*	*State*		*Wm. Little*
<Thos. Alexander	*admited 12 Sent to the workhous the next Day>*	*State*	*Ed. Procter*	*Wm. Scollay*
Wineford Stone	admited 12	State	Jona. Mason	Thos. Crafts T Edwards
John Milladge[229]	admited 12	State	S Parkman	
John Richey	admited 12	State	Wm. Smith	Wm. Boardman Wm. Scollay
Mary Pike & Child	admited 13	Town	Jona. L Austin	
Elizebth Fullam	Dischargd 15	State		
Wm. Procter	Admited 17	State	H Hill Ed. Procter	T Crafts Wm. Scollay
John Anderson	Admited 17	State	John Sweetser	Ebn. Seaver
Elizh. Woodman	Admited 17	State	Lorin Austin	Thos. Edwards Wm. Little
Mary McLaugklan[230]	admited 18	State	H Hill	Wm. Boardman E Price
James Willson[231]	admited 18	State	John Codman	Wm. Boardman T Edwards
Eliz Cornish	Dismt. to Work House 21	Town	Loring Austin	
John Bradbury & his Wife ann	admited 21	State	S Gorham	Wm. Boardman Thos Crafts

Almshouse Admissions, 1788–1795

Names	Time of Admission & Discharge	Town or State	By what Overseer	By what Selectman
Elizth. Berrey	admited 21 Decr. 1792	State	H Hill J Codman	T Crafts Wm. Scollay
Wm. Copps	admited 24	State	Jona. Mason	Wm. Boardman Ezek Price
John Smith	admited 25	State	H Hill	Thos. Walley
Sarah Aires	Run 25	Town		
Elizth. Woodman	Dischargd 27	State		
John Sanders	Dischargd 27	State		
Richard Crout	admited 28	State	Ed. Procter	Wm. Little
John Davidson	admited 28	State	Jona. Mason	Thos. Crafts Wm. Scollay
John Greeggs[232]	admited 29	Town	Wm. Smith	
Fednant[233] Wiseman	admited 29	State	John Seetser	E Sever
John Dawson, Magret Dawson & John ther Son a Boy	Dismist 29	State		
Patrick Shanley	admited 29	State	Ed. Procter	Wm. Bordman T Edwards
January 1st. 1793 William Spooner	Dischargd 1st	State	Runaway	
Sarah Dracey a Child	Admd. 1	State	H Hill	Thos. Crafts Wm. Scollay
Wm. Peake	admited 2	Town	Ed. Procter	
Elizabeth Duggel	admited 3d.	State	Jona. Mason	E. Price Thos. Crafts
Peter Swan	admited 4 from Work Hs.	State	E. Edes	
Nancy Stone	4th. admited from Work house	Town	E Edes	
Wm. Procter	Run Janr. 4	State		
Mary Buckley	Bound out 9th.	State		

Names	Time of Admission & Discharge	Town or State	By what Overseer	By what Selectman
Nance Morres	Bound out 9	State		
Mary Wanewood[234]	admited 12	State	Jona. Mason	T Crafts T Edwards
Ed. McGlockling	Admited 14	State	S Parkman	Wm. Boardman Wm. Little
Sarah Pray	admited 18	State	Jona. L Austin	E Price Wm. Boardman
John Stiles	admited 21	State	Jona. L Austin	Wm. Boardman E Price
Wineford Stone	Run 24	State		
John Stiles	Run 24	State		
Edward Beacham	Admited 24	State	Jona. Mason	E Price Wm. Scollay
Cate. Tillett[235]	Admited 25	Town	John White	
Luther Edey Chd.[236]	admited 25	State	S Gorham	Wm. Boardman Wm. Scollay
Thos. Curtis	Dismist 25	State		
Elizth. Fullam	Admited 29	State	S Parkman	Ezek Price Thos. Crafts
John Marton	Dismist 31	State		
Stephen Marshall Died in Bringin to the House	Janry. 31	State	S Gorham	
Wm. Spooner & Wife	Admited 31	State	S Gorham	Wm. Scollay Wm. Little
Wm. Spooner & Wife Mary	Dist. Febr. 7	State		
Hannah Perkins & her Daughter Margt.	admited 7	State	Ed. Edes	Ez. Price
Elizt. Fenno	admited 7	Town	H Hill	
Wineford Stone	admited 7th.	State	W Phillips	Ezek Price
Mary Anderson	admited 11	State	John White	Ez Price Thos. Crafts

❧

Names	Time of Admission & Discharge	Town or State	By what Overseer	By what Selectman
John Lewis	admited 11	State	Ed. Edes	Thos Crafts Wm. Scollay
<Mary Anderson Entered above	admited 11	State	John White>	Ez Price Tos. Crafts
David Hulbert	admited 14	State	Wm. Smith	Wm. Little Wm. Boardman
Jane Clark	admited 14	State	Ed. Edes	Thos. Crafts Wm. Scollay
Amelie Caine a Black	admited 16	State	John Codman	Eb Seaver
Edward McGlocklin	dismiss'd 16	State		
George Jolley a child	admited 21	State	By the Hol. Board of overseers	Tos. Crafts Wm. Scollay
Susanah Bentley	admeted 21	Town	Ed. Procter	
John Bradbury & his Wife ann	Dismist 22	State		
William Cox	Dismist Febr. 23	State		
Poly, Saly & Michiel[237] Allen Children of Speedwell allen Negro	admited 26	State	Jona. Mason	E. Price Thos. Crafte
Thomas Alexander	discharged 25	State		
Elizh. Fullam	Dischargd 26	State		
Alaxander Fisher	Dischargd 26	State		
Morrice[238] OQuill	admited 26	State	S Parkman	Wm. Little Wm. Bordman
Caterine Tilott	Dismist 28	Town		
Richard Crouch	Dismist 28	State		
John McKinezey[239] an infant Born in the House Feby. 26	admited 28	State	Ed. Procter	Wm. Bordman
Wm. Brown	Dismist 28	Town		
Hannah Hollis & her 3 Children Polle John & Thos	admited 28	Town	Henry Hill	

Names	Time of Admission & Discharge	Town or State	By what Overseer	By what Selectman
Alexander Fisher	admited March 1	State	Wm. Phillips	Tos. Wallay Wm. Scollay
Nance Tomson[240] & her 2 Children John & <Joseph> Wm.	admited 1	Town	Henry Hill	
Holemes Simpson	admited 2	Town	Jona. L Austin	
Nancy Munroe & her 2 Children Nancy & Betsey inhabentance of Lexenton	admited March 6	Town	Henry Hill	
Cate Hunnewill	Dismist 6	State	& Returnd at Night	
Patrick Kelley	Dismist 7	State		
Sarah Johnson	Dismist 7	Town		
Elizh. Lewis	Dismist 7	State		
Mrs. Bagger from Reding pr. or[der] of the Hol Bord [Delevrs?]	admited 7	Town		
Edward McLoglen[241]	admited 7	State	Born in Iarland S Gorham	T Walley T Crafts
Mathew Walker, Distracted	admtd. 10	State	Mr. Parkman	Wm. Bordman Wm. Scollay
Nance Munrow & her 2 Children	Dismist 12	Belong to Lexentown		
Charlstown Flucker	Dischargd. 13	State		
Sarah Jonson[242]	admited	Town	Jona. Loring austin	
Timy. Richardson & wife Shadinah & 3 Children Timy. 6 yers Levaney[243] 4 yers Ebenezer—2 years	admited 15	Town	Ed. Procter	
Edward Powers	admited 17	State	S Parkman	Wm. Bordman Wm. Scollay
John Lewis	Dismist 18	State		

Almshouse Admissions, 1788–1795

Names	Time of Admission & Discharge	Town or State	By what Overseer	By what Selectman
Henry Kendal & Luce his Wife	Dismist 18	State		
Edward McGlockling	Disd. 19	State		
Mary Anderson	Run 19			
Robrt Allerson	admited 19	State Run next Day	Jona. Mason	E Price Thos. Crafte
Pattey Dorcy[244]	admited 20	Town	John Sweetser	
Cathrine English	admited 20 from Goal	State	S Parkman	T Walley Wm. Scollay
Mary King	admited 20	Town	S Gorham	Brot to Bed with a Boy namd. John Greenlef Whiple March 21st.
David Hulbert	Dischargd 22	State		
John & William Kirk	admited 22	Town	John White	
Ebenezer Selvester[245]	Bound out 22	State		
Alaxander Fisher	Run 25	State		
Daphney a Blak born in afrck	admited 26	State	Jona. Mason	E Price Thos Edwards
Nancy Hunter Stevens a Negro Child	admited 26	State	Jona. L Austin	Thos. Crafts Wm. Scollay
Salley Stone	Dismist 26	Town		
Charles Doll	Dismist 28	State		
John Smith	Dismist 28	State		
Peter Swan	Dismist 28	State		
Daniel Benjman	Dischad. 29	Town		
Luther Edey	Run March 29	State		
Salle and Michael Allen Black children	Dismist. 29	State		

Almshouse Admissions, 1788–1795

Names	Time of Admission & Discharge	Town or State	By what Overseer	By what Selectman
Morrice OQuill	Dischargd. 31	State		
Patrick Shanley	Dischargd. April 1	State		
Holms Simpson	Dischargd 1	Town		
Elizabeth Fenno	Dischargd 1	Town		
Cathrine English	Run	State		
Merriam Dockum	Dismist 1	Town		
Hannah Perkins & Margrit her Daughter	Dismist 2	State		
John Box	Admitted April 2d.	Town	J L Austin	
Mary Selvester	Dischargd 8	State		
Wineford Stone	Dismist 9	State		
John Johnson	admited 9	State	Saml. Parkman	Thos. Crafts Wm. Little
Thos. Holden a Child	admited 10	State	Henry Hill	Charls Bulflinch Wm. Scollay
Matthew Sun	admited 14	State	Jona. Mason	Ezek Price Thos. Crafts
Wm. Copps	Dischargd. 15	State		
John Wright[246] Bound out march 27th.	Dischargd April 17	State		
Wm. Thomson[247]	admited 17	State	John White	C. Bulflinch Wm. Scollay
Edward Beacham	Dismist 20	State		
Isaac Wendal	Dismissd. 22	Town		
Mary Sharp	Run 22	State	Returnd. the 25th.	
Prince Newman	admited 22	State	Jona. Mason	El. Price Wm. Scollay
Wm. Dockham	Dischargd 22	Town		
James Willson	Dischargd 22	State		

Names	Time of Admission & Discharge	Town or State	By what Overseer	By what Selectman
Mary Downey	Dischargd 24	State		
Mary King & her Child	Dischargd 25	Town		
Sarah Tuckerman	Bound out	Town		
Nancey Lovrign[248] a Child	admited 25	State	Ed. Procter	Wm. Little
Sophia Truant	Bound out 29	State		
Nancy Rea	Admited 27	Town		
Wm. Langford	Dischargd 30	Town		
Polly Foster	Admited	Town		
Luce Willis	admited 30	Town	Died the Same Night	
Dorothy Walch	admited May 2d. 1793	Town	John White	
John Millitt	Dischargd 6	State		
John Mitchal[249]	admited 3d.	State	Jona. Mason	Wm. Boardman Ebr. Seaver
James Kief[250]	Bound out 2d.	State		
Sarah Adams	admited 6	Town	Ed. Edes	
Timy. Richardson & his wife and Two Children	Dismist 8	Town		
Mathew Walker	Discharged 8	State		
Alice Baker	admited 8	Town	John Codman	
Isaac Downs	Dismist 9	Town		
James Downey	Dischargd 9	State		
Wm. Sharp	Dischargd. 12	State		
Charlotte Williams[251]	Bound out 14	*<State>* say Town		
Bartholum Tuckerman	Bound out 14	Town		
Sarah Cleverly[252]	Bound out 14	*<State>* Say Town		
Julla Aann Serieves[253]	Bound out 14			
Mary Foster	Dischargd. 14	Town		

Names	Time of Admission & Discharge	Town or State	By what Overseer	By what Selectman
Elenor Peirce & her Child Hannah her Child Eloner Remains in the House	Dismist 14	State State		
Aron Emmorson	Dischargd May 14	Town		
John McFarlin	admited 14	State	S Parkman	Thos. Crafts
Denis Cavanaugh	Dismist 16	State		
John Gillard	Dischargd 16	State		
Elizth. Leach	Admited 16	Town	John White	
John Greggs	Dischargd 18	Town		
Mary Franks[254] a Child	Bound out 20	State		
John Ritchie	Dischargd 21			
Mary Pike	Dischagd. 21	Town	now mared. to Edmd. Gorman State	
Mary Gorman[255]	admited 21	State	S Parkman	Thos. Walley Ebenr. Seaver
George Goley	Bound out 22	State		
John McKinzee	admited 22	State	S Parkman	T Edwards Wm. Scollay
Merriam Dockum	admited 22	Town	H Hill	
John McMarhon	admited 24	State		Wm. Bordman Thos. Edwards
John Davedson	Dismist 24	State		
Nance Moulton[256]	Bound out 24	Town		
<John McMarhon> Entd. before	<admited 24	State	S Parkman	Wm. Bordman Thos. Edwards>
Lamberth Murphy	admited 24	State	Jona. Mason	T Edwards Wm. Scollay
Susanah Riden	admited 25	Town	Ed. Procter	
Salam Poor A B[lack][257]	admited 25	State	Jona. Mason	Thos. Crafts Thos. Edwards
Hannah Cooper	Dismist 25	State		

∽

Names	Time of Admission & Discharge	Town or State	By what Overseer	By what Selectman
Hehabie Rice	admitted 27	Town	S Gorham	
Thankful Edmans	Dischargd 28	Town	*<& her Child>*	
Elizebth Drace	Dischargd 28	State		
John Johnson	Dischd. 28	State		
William Thomson	Dischd. Child. 28th.	State		
John McMarhon	Dismist 30	State		
Michel[258] Renolds	admitted 30	State	Wm. Phillips	Wm. Little Wm. Bordman
Wm. Kirk a Child	Dischargd June 1	Town		
Michel Renolds	Dischargd 5	State		
Elizth. Condon	admitted 5	State	S. Parkman	E Price T Walley
Nance Rea[259]	Bound out June 6	Town		
Charlote Dawes	admitted a child 6	Town	Saml. Parkman	
Charlote Selvester[260]	Bound out 8	State		
Harriet Brown	Discharged 8	State		
Salam Poor a Black	Dismist 10	State		
Nancey Willis	admitted 10	Town	Edwd. Edes	
Dinah Roberts & her Child Mary	Dismist 11	State	a Black	
Ebenezer Richardson	Dischargd 12	Town		
Susanah Franks	Dismist 13	State		
Denis Hogon	Dismist 13	State		
Patience Hunt alies Feno[261] & Child	admitted 14 Black	State	John Sweetser	Ezek Price
James Downey	admitted 14	State	Ed. Edes	Wm. Little
Jude[262] White a Black	admitted 15	State	S Gorham	Wm. Little Wm. Scollay

Names	Time of Admission & Discharge	Town or State	By what Overseer	By what Selectman
Velias Akely	discharged 15	State		
David Chambeland	Dismist [18]	State		
Mary Sharp	Run 20	State		
Timothey Dwere[263]	Sent to the Work house 20			
Timothy Howard	Run 22	State		
Elizth. Woodroof	admited 22	Marblehead	Mr. Codman	
Henry Luckus	Run 22	Town		
William Lewis	Dischargd. a Child	State		
Merriam Dockum	Dischargd 24	Town		
Sall White a Black alias Sarah Humphries	Dischargd 24	Town		
Wm. Anderson	Admited 26 Dismist the next Day	State	Jona. Mason	Ezek Price Thos. Crafts
Charlotte Daws	Bound out	Town		
Eleaner Perce & Hanah her Child	admited 27	State	Jona. Mason	Thos Walley Wm. Little
Mrs. Collines'[264] Child	admited 28	Town	H Hill	
Salle Stone	admited 28	Town	John Sweetser	
Nancy Thomson	Dischargd. 28	Town		
Mary Wanewood	Dischargd July 1	State		
Scipio Brailey a black	admd. 4	State	Wm. Smith	C Bulflinch Wm. Scollay
Polly Ballard	Disch. 4	Town		
The Child of James Jones	admited 4	State	S Parkman	Wm. Little Wm. Bordman
Lambert Murphy	Dischd. 4	State		
Quomino Frizier B[*lack*][265]	admited 4	State	S Parkman	C Bulflince Wm. Scollay

Names	Time of Admission & Discharge	Town or State	By what Overseer	By what Selectman
Prince Kingsman	admd. 4	State	Ed. Edes	Wm. Scollay Wm. Bordman
Wm. Fenno	admited 4	Town	H Hille	
Charles Woodman	Discharged 4	State		
Elizh. Colton & her Child Eliz Colton	Dischargd. 9	Town		
Mary Truant	Dischargd. 9	State		
Patience Hunt alias Fenno	Dischd. 10	State		
Thos. Holden a Child	Bound out 9	State		
Charity Brinton	Run 9	Town		
Elizabeth Woodroof	Run 9	marblhead		
Saml. Laten	admited 10	State	Jon. Sweetser	Ebenr. Seaver
Lydia Marston	Dischargd 11	Town		
Ketay[266] Hunnewell	admited 14	State	S Gorham	Wm. Boardman Wm. Little
Wm. Peake	Dischargd 14	Town		
Morrice[267] OQuill	admited 18	State	Jona. Mason	El. Price Thos. Crafts
Elizth. Sheild alias Sheen	admited 19	Little Cambridge	J L Austin	
Sarah Dunkin[268]	admited 23			
George Black alias Hall	admited 24	State	H Hill Esqr.	Thos. Walley
Mary McLuchlin	Dismist 24	State		
Ebenezr. Cox	admited 27	Town	Edwd. Procter	
Hannah Hollis, Polly John & Thomas her Children	Dismist 27	Weymouth		
Thos Davenport	admited 29	Dorchester	Jona. Mason	
Mary Sharp	admited & Sent to work House 29	State	Ed. Procter	

Almshouse Admissions, 1788–1795

❧

Names	Time of Admission & Discharge	Town or State	By what Overseer	By what Selectman
Timothey Howard	admited 29	State	S Parkman	Thos. Crafts Wm. Scollay
Edward Powers	Dischargd 31	State		
Dinah Gibbs	admited august 1	State	John White	Wm. Little
Scipio Braley	discharged 1st.	State		
Judea White, B[lack]	Dischargd 3	State		
Saml. <Eason> say Laton,[269] B[lack] Dischargd 3 State				
Mary[270] Foster	admited 3	Town	S Gorham	
Patty Dorcy	dischd. 6th.	Town		
John Gandel Jur.	dischd. 6th.	Town		
Polly Peirce	Bound out 6	Town		
David Chamberland[271]	admited 7	State	Jona. Mason	El. Price Thos. Crafts
Judith Gane[272] & 3 Children Saml., Betty & John	admited 7	State	Wm. Smith	Ez Price Thos. Crafts
Wm. Sprage[273]	admited 12	Town	Ed. Edes	
Prince Kingsman	Disd. 12	State		
John Gillard	admited 15	State	S Gorham	Thos. Walley
Abigal Peirce	Dischargd 15	Town		
Joshua P K Dehacket alis Patrick Hancock	Dischargd 15	State		
Daved Chamberland	Dist. to Workhouse 15 State			
Cain Clough a Black	admid. 15 Sent to the workhouse	State	Jona. L Austin	Wm. Little
A Child of Mary King named John Whipple	Admitd 16	Town	S Gorham	
Wm. Curtis	admited 17	Town	Wm. Smith	
Phillys Watson B[lack][274]	admited 17	State	John White	Wm. Little

Names	Time of Admission & Discharge	Town or State	By what Overseer	By what Selectman
Mary Ross	admited 17	Town	S Gorham	
Judith Gane & 3 Children Saml., Bettey & John	Dischargd 19	State		
Susannah Kean & her Child the wife of Tubal Kean of Pembrook	admd. 19	Town	S Gorham	
Eunice Edey[275]	Bound out 19	State		
John Bothren a French man	Admd. 21	State	S Parkman	Wm. Bordman Wm. Little
Nathl. Fowle His Wife Lidia & 4 Children Thankful 12 years Nathl. 9 Helener[276] 5 Isaac 2	admited 22 Dischargd. 23	Town	Jona. L Austin	
Michael Conner[277]	admited augt. 22	State	S Gorham	Ezek Price Thos. Crafts
Aron Emmons	admited 22	Town	S Gorham	
John Gleason	admited 23	State	S Parkman	C Bulfinch Wm. Scollay
Elizth. Mahoney	admited 24	State	Ed. Edes	Wm. Bordman Wm. Scollay
John Gillard	Run 24	State		
Charety Brenton[278]	admited 24	Town	S Gorham	
Elizth. Woodman	admited 26	State	S Parkman	Wm. Boardman Wm. Scollay
Michiel Conner	Dischargd 27	State		
Natl. Fowles & 4 Children Thankl., Natl., Elener. Isaac	admited 30	Town	S Parkman	
Nancey Lovering	Dischargd. Septr 1	State		
Wm. Curtis	Dischargd 3	Town		

Names	Time of Admission & Discharge	Town or State	By what Overseer	By what Selectman
Charety Brinton	Dischargd 4	Town		
Isaac Davis agd 8 yers Septr 9. 1793	admited September 5	Town	H Hill	
John Kuter and his Wife Hannah alies Coon	admited 5	State	Wm. Smith	Wm. Little C Bulflinch
Saml. Leighton B[lack][279]	admited 5	State	Jona. Mason	E Price Thos. Crafts
Susanah Ridon	admited 7	Town	Ed. Procter	
Mary Garrow	Aadmited 10	State	from W House H Hill	
Ann Thomson[280]	admited 10	Town	J Codman	
Isaac Davis	Bound out 12	Town		
Hannah Hollis Wife of Semmeon Hollis	Admited 13		of Waymouth H Hill	
Phillis Watson	Dischargd 14	State	A B[lack][281] Returnd at Night	
Sarah Kamp	admited 14	Town	S Gorham	
John Tompson[282]	admited out of W House 14	Town	H Hill	
Mary Willson & Child Jane	admitd. 14	State	Jona. Mason	T Crafts Wm. Scollay
Elizh. Woodman	Dischargd 14	State		
Anna Jasper	admited 15	State	S Parkman	Wm. Little Wm. Bordman
John Morris a B[lack][283] Child	admitd. 15	State	Jona. Mason	Wm. Bordman Thos. Edwards
Wm. Sprague	Dismist 17	Town		
Saml. Eston <auls [alias?] Gleson> a B[lack][284]	Discd. 16	State		
John Gleason	Dischargd 18	State		
Kian Clow	admitd. from W House 18	State	John Codman	
Elizabeth Lewis	admited 19	State	Jona. Mason	Wm. Little Thos. Walley

Names	Time of Admission & Discharge	Town or State	By what Overseer	By what Selectman
Wm. Peake	admitted 19	Town	H Hill	
Judah Ganes[285] & four Children John [4?] yers, Eliz 5, Saml. 7 & 3 weeks	admited Sept. 19	State	Ed. Procter Luchick [*Lucretia*]	Wm. Little Wm. Bordman
Thankl. Edmeinds[286] & Child	admtd. from W H 20	Town	H Hill	
A man by the Name of Wm. Fenno Recd. 20 From W H		Town	John Codman	
Nelly Murry[287]	admited 20	Town	Ed. Procter	
Elizebth Sheen alis Sheild from Cambridge	Dismist 24	*<Town>*		
Mary Willson	Dischargd 25	State		
Francias Loring a B[*lack*][288]	admitd. 26	State	S Gorham	Wm. Little Thos. Crafts
Thos. Davis	admited 27	State	Wm. Smith	Wm. Bordman Wm. Little
James Downey	admited 27	State	Ed. Procter	Wm. Little
Hannah Jones	admited 27	Town	Ed. Edes	
Sophia Smith	admited 27	State	Wm. Phillips	Ezekl. Price Thos. Crafts
Elenor Peirce	Dischargd 29	State		
Lambert Murphy	admitd. [*October*][289] 2	State	Jona. Mason	Wm. Bordman Wm. Scollay
Timothey Blackman [or][290] Blackburn	admited Octr. 3	Town	H Hill	
Anna Warren	admitted 3d.	Town	J L Austin	
Dennis Cavenough[291]	Admitted 5	State	J Mason	E Price Wm. Little
Joseph Hart	Admitted October 7	State	J Mason	Wm. Little Thos. Edwards
Frank a Black	admited 7	State	Jona. Mason	Thos. Crafts Wm. Scollay
Wm. Peake	Dischargd 9	Town		

Names	Time of Admission & Discharge	Town or State	By what Overseer	By what Selectman
Thomas Branigan[292]	admitted [9] Work house	State	Edwd. Edes	Thomas Wally Wm. Scollay
Wm. Cusett	admitted 9	State	Ed. Procter	Wm. Bordman
George Black	Dismis'd 9th.	Do.		
Harry a Black	admitted 10	State	John Sweetser	Ebenr. Seaver
John Kutter alus [alias] Coon	Run 10	State		
Wm. Curtis	admitted 10	Town	Wm. Smith	
Jack Roby & his mother Hannah Roby	admitted 10	State	L Austin	Chars. Bulflinch
Violet Hudson	admitted 11	State	L Austin	C Bulflinch
James Johns	admitted 11	State	S Parkman	Wm. Bordman T Crafts
George Son of George Holley[293] a B[lack][294]	admitted 14	State	Wm. Smith	E Price Wm. Little
Ceazar Gray	Dismist 16	State		
Elizth. Stebbens	Admited 16	Town	John White	
The Wife of Mark McLocklin	admitted 16	State	S Gorham	Wm. Little Thos Crafts
Edward Beacham	admitted 16	State	L Austin	Wm. Little
George Hall a B[lack]	Dischargd. 17	State		
John Gillard	admitted 17	State	S Parkman	Er. Seaver Wm. Little
Fortune Harris a B[lack][295]	Dischargd 17	State		
Wm. Perch	admitted 17	Town	Wm. Smith	
Patrick Kelley[296]	admitted 17	State	Jona. Mason	Wm. Little Thos Crafts
John Gardner	admitted 17	State	Jona. Mason	Thos. Crafts Wm. Little
Cesar Gray[297] a Black	admitted 18	State	John Seetser	Ebn Seaver (Died 20th. Augt. 1795)

Almshouse Admissions, 1788–1795

Names	Time of Admission & Discharge	Town or State	By what Overseer	By what Selectman
Ledia Gulgahs & 2 Childn. Polley & Hannah	admited 18	State	Jona. Mason	Wm. Boardman Wm. Scollay
Zephs. Bates & 2 Childn.	admited 18	Town	L Austin	
John Gillard	Sent to Work H 22	State	Jon. White	
Morris OQuill	Dischargd 23	State		
Joseph Tart	Dismist 25	State		
The Child of Joseph Paverit	admd. 26	State	Jona. Mason	Wm. Little Wm. Scollay
Wm. Lewis a Child	admited 28	State	Jona. Mason	Ezek Price Thos. Edwards
Elizebth Stebbens	Dischargd 30	Town		
Marther Charles & her 3 Children	admited 30	State	Wm. Phillips	Ezek Price Thos. Crafts
Patrick Heverner[298]	admited 30	State	S Gorham	Ezek Price Thos. Crafts
Cesar Eleas a B[lack][299]	admited 30	State	L austin	C Bulfinch
Saml. North	Dismist to Work House 31	State	Ed. Procter	
John Gillard	Recd from Work House 31	State	Ed. Procter	
Mary Benjamen[300]	admited Novmr. 1	Town	John White	
Quomino Frazier	Dismist 2	State		
Molly a Black	admitted 5	State	J Mason	Thomas Crafts
Charles Woodman a child of Charles Woodman & His Wife Eliz	admited 6	State	H Hill Jona. Mason	Wm. Little
Margrett & Sables Mary	admited 9	Town	H Hill	
Elizabeth Bennet	Bound out 9th.	State		
James Johns	Dismist 12	State		
George Black				
Hannah Riordn[301]	admited 12	State	Jona. L austin	Wm. Bordman Thos. Edwards

❧

Names	Time of Admission & Discharge	Town or State	By what Overseer	By what Selectman
Elizth. Sprauge[302]	admitted 13	Town	Ed. Procter	
Mary Downy	admitted 13	State	Wm. Phillips	Wm. Little Thos. Edwards
James Doughty } alus [*alias*] Doley }	admitted 14	State	Jona. Mason	Thos. Crafts Wm. Little
Moses Stevenson	admitted 15	State	Jona. L Austin	Ezl. Price T. Crafts
Marther Charles	Dismist 15	State		
Polly Webb	Recd. from Work house 15			
<*Elizabeth Spraug*	*admitted 13*	*Town*	*Ed. Procter*>	
Sarah Whitcomb	admitted 20	Town	S Gorham	
James Frost	Admited 20th.	Town		
Eliz Garro[303]	Dischd. to mr austin	State	a Child	
Mary Jones	Disch. to Mr. Calandor a Child	Town		
Elizth. Charles	Dismist 21	State		
Thos. Rowlinson	Admited 21	State	Jona. Mason	Ezekl. Price Thos. Edwards
Rebacha Kirilly	admitted 22	Town	John White	
Rebacha Stacey & son	admitted 25	State	Jona. Mason	Wm. Bordman
Polley Gulgah	Bound out 26	State	Jona. Mason	Wm. Scollay
Sarah Burnick	Admitted 27	Town	John White	
Polly Burrnes[304]	Admitted 27	Town	John White	
Thos. Perkins	{ admited 27 } { & Discharged }	State	Jona. Mason	Thos. Walley Wm. Scollay
Wm. Sharp	admitted 28	State	Jona. Mason	Ezek Price Thos. Crafts
Nathl. Fowle his } Wife & 4 Children }	admitd. 28	Town	Ed. Edes	

this Family came to the House see 22d. augt. went away and have this day returned.

Names	Time of Admission & Discharge	Town or State	By what Overseer	By what Selectman
Elizth. More[305] Wife of John More	Admitted 28	State	Ed. Procter	Wm. Little Thos. Crafts
Harry {a Black}	Dischd.	30		
Androw Richardson	admitd. Decemr. 1	State	John White	Wm. Little
Susanh Ridan[306]	admited 2	Town	Ed. Procter	
Charity Brinton	Run 2	Do.		
Pattey Dorsay[307]	admited 3	Town	Jona. Mason	
Sarah Duncan	Discharged	Do.		
Samuel Leighton	Discharged	State		
Charles Woodman	admited Decr. 4	State	Jona. Mason	Wm. Boardman Ezekl. price
Mary Folker	admited 4	Town	Wm. Smith	From Work house
Thos. Alaxander[308]	admited 4	State	Jona. Mason	Thos. Walley C Bulflinch
Sarah Rowen & her Daughter Susanah	admited 5	State	Jona. Mason	Wm. Boardn. Ezek Price
Androw Robenson[309] & Wife	admited 6	State	Jona. Mason	Wm. Little Wm. Bordman
Thankful Fowle	Bound out 7	Town		
Daved Chamberland[310]	admtd. 7 from work H	State	H Hill	
Wm. Perch	Dismist 7	State		
Hannah Cooper	admited 9th.	Town	Mr. White	
John Richie[311]	admited 9	State	Jona. Mason	Wm. Scollay Wm. Bordman
Sarah Moore & Daughter Harroit & son Paskel	admited 9	Town	Ed. Procter	
Nathl. Fowles	Run 10	Town		
Isaac Downs[312]	admited 14	Town	John White	
Patty & Charles abbigall	Dischargd. 14	State		

Almshouse Admissions, 1788–1795

Names	Time of Admission & Discharge	Town or State	By what Overseer	By what Selectman
Rebeca Kent	Dismist 14	Town		
Wm. Langford	admited 14	Town	S Gorham	
Merian Handfeild[313]	admited 17	Town	Ed. Procter	
Polly White	admited 17	State	John White	Wm. Little
Moses Stevenson	dismist 19	State		
Harroit Brown alias Harriot Moore	Dismist 19	Town		
Archbald McDannel[314]	admited 21	State	Wm. White	Wm. Bordman Wm. Scollay
Sarah Rowen & her daughter Susanah	admited 21	State	Jona. Mason	Wm. Scollay Wm. Bordman
Decr. 23 Elenor Richie, Mary Downey & Eliz Lewis sent to the work House[315]				
Thos. Davis	Dismist 26	State		
Julins Eckley	admited 27	State	S Parkman	Ezekl. Price E Seaver
Olive a Black	admited 27	State	Wm. Phillips	Ezekl. Price Thos. Crafts
<John Gardner	Dismist 1794 Janury 10 State>			
Nancy Lovebridg[316]	admited Decr. 28	State	S Parkman	T Edwards Wm. Little
Thos. Rice	admited 28	State	Jona. Mason	Wm. Little Wm. Bordman
Eunice Vose	admited 28	Town	Jona. L Austin	
George Graff	admited 31	State	Wm. Phillips	Ezel. Price Thos. Crafts
Joseph Bangs	admited Janur. 1 1794	State	Wm. Phillips	Thos. Edwards Wm. Little
Nelly Peirce	admited 1	State	John. Sweetser	Thos. Walley Ebenr. Seaver
John Clark	admited 1	State	Jona. mason	Thos. Walley Wm. Sollay

Almshouse Admissions, 1788–1795

Names	Time of Admission & Discharge	Town or State	By what Overseer	By what Selectman
Alaxander Thompson & his Daughter Btsey[317]	admited 2	State	Jona. Mason	Ezl. Price Thos. Crafts
Peggy Symmes	admited 5	Town	Saml. Parkman	
Wm. & Thos. Dungar	admited 5 Born in the House	State		
George Clark	admited 5	Town	Ed. Procter	
Elenor Loines from W House 7				
Thomas Perkins	admited 7	State	Jona. Mason	Thos. Walley Wm. Scollay
John Flynn & Wife Elizabeth	admited 7	State	Jona. Mason	Thos. Crafts Thos. Edwards
John Gardner	Dismist 10	State		
Elcy Stodard	Dismist 10	Town		
John Nicklos[318]	admited 14	State	Jona. Mason	Ezekl. Price Thos. Crafts
Elenor Richie	admited 15	State	From the Work house	
Elizebth Duggel	Dischargd 17	State		
Elmira Duggel a child	Dismist 17	State		
york Cox a Black	Dischargd 17	State	to Work house	
Feebe Gee	Dischagd 17	State	to work house	
Elizth. Moore	admitd. from W H 17	State		
John Ayers[319]	Bound out 18	State		
Thos. Alexander	Dismist 22	State		
Rebeckah Curley	Dismist 22	Town		
Alaxander Thomson	Dischargd 24	State & Returnd the <sa> [i.e., same day]		
Alexander Lord from Mareyland	admited 25	State	S Gorham	Wm. Bordham Thos. Crafts
Susanah Rowen	Dismt. 27	State		
Jack French	admited 27	State	Wm. Phillips	Ezl. Price Thos. Crafts

Names	Time of Admission & Discharge	Town or State	By what Overseer	By what Selectman
Peter Brown	admited 29	State	S Gorham	Ezl. Price Thos. Crafts
Alaxander Thomas	Dischargd 31	State		
Kathrine Bryant	admited 31	State	Jona. Mason	Ez Price Ebenr. Sever
George Powel[320]	admited Febry. 1	State	John White	Wm. Little Wm. Bordman
Mary Shirbun[321]	admited 3	State	John White	Wm. Little
Mary Murrey[322] & Polly her Daughter a Child	admited 3	State	S Gorham	Ez Price Wm. Little
Daniel Dorran	admited 8	State	Jona. Mason	Wm. Scollay Thos. Crafts
<Edward Gorman	*admitd. 8*	*State>*		
Lucy Whitman	admited 9 A B[lack]	State from Situate	Henry. Hill	Ebenr. Seavor Wm. Little
Jeremiah Murphey[323]	admited 10	State	S Parkman	Thos Crafts
Peggy Symmes A B[lack]	Dismist 12	State		
Sarah Kemp	admited 12	Town	John White	
ann Hartley	Bound out 14	Town	a Child	
Mary Ross	admited 18	Town	S Gorham	
John Gillard	Dismist 20	State		
Ebenezer Cox	admited 20 from work H	Town	Ed. Edes	
Lidia Gulgar	Dismist 24	State		
<Mary Croffe & Child	*admited 26*	*State*	*Henry Hill*	*E. Seaver>*
Henry Trussett	admited 26 from W H	State	Heny. Hill	
Mary Graff & her Son Gorge	admited 26	State	H Hill	Ebenr. Seavor Wm. Scollay
Henry Trussell	admited 27 from Amsbury from work House		H Hill	Dismist the same Day
Mary Murrey & Child	Dismist 28	State		

Names	Time of Admission & Discharge	Town or State	By what Overseer	By what Selectman
Julins Eckley	Dismist 28	State		
Nancy Thomson *<& her son Wm.>*	Dismist 28	Town	Returnd the same Day	
Daved Dannee	admited 28	State	Jona. Mason	Thos. Crafts Wm. Boardman
Quommono Frazer	admited 28	State	Jona. Mason	Ez Price Wm. Little
Wm. Lewis	Bund out March 1	State		
Jack French	Dismist 5	State		
John Brown	Admited 6	Town	John White	
Sarah Moore	Dismist 7	Town		
Nancey Shepard	admited 8	State	John White	Wm. Little
<Thomas Rice	*Dischargd. 11*	*State>*		
alaxandor Minot	admited 11	State	S Gorham	Wm. Little Ezl. Price
Wm. Valloon	admited 11	State	Ed. Procter	Wm. Scollay
Polley White	Dismist 12	State		
Olive White	Dismist 12	State		
Thos Rice	Dismist 13	State		
Polley McClaron	Returnd. 13 from her Servis with Dr. Cotton			Town
<Wm. Vallon	*admited 11*	*State*	*Edwd. Proctor*	*Wm. Scollary>*
Wm. Curtis	Dischargd 17	Town		
Cyrus Kent	admitted 17th.	State	Jno. Sweetser Jr.	
Cato Smith	admited 17	State	Jona. Mason	Thos. Edwards Wm. Scollay
Rebeckah Kirrely[324]	admited 17	Town	John White	Dischargd. same Day
Andow & Mary Robertson Dischd. 18		State		
Thomas Perkins	Dismist 18	State		

Almshouse Admissions, 1788–1795

Names	Time of Admission & Discharge	Town or State	By what Overseer	By what Selectman
Sarah Gardner	admitted 19	Town	John White	
Wm. Fulloon	admitted 20	State	Wm. Phillips	
Patrick Haveren	Dismist 21	State		
John Nickols	Dismist 24	State		
Joseph Bangs	Dismist 24	State		
Eliza. Flyn	Dismist 24	State		
Benjn. Pool	admitted 24	Town	Jona. Mason	
Wm. Langford	Dismist 25	Town		
Isaac Fowles	Dismist 25	Town		
Nelley Fowles[325]	Dismist 25	Town		
Daniel Doran	Dismist 26	State		
Hannah Riordian	Dismst. 27	State		
Edward Gorman	Dischargd. 27	State		
Mary Gorman	Dismist 27	State		
Wm. Pike	Dismist 27	Town	a Child	
Elizth. Pallisear	admitted 27	Town	Henry Hill	
Benjn. Gould	admitted 27	Town	Henry Hill	
Jeremiah Murphey	Dismist 28	State		
Betsey Person	admitted 28	State	Jona. Mason	
Elizth. Woodman	Dismist april 1	State		
Wm. <Ph> Valloon	Dismist 1	State		
Susanah Harty	admitted 1	State	H Hill	
Mary Sherburne	Dismist 2			
<George Washington	Bound out 3	Town>		
Eliz Garrow	Returnd 3	State		
Rachal Gaffit	admitted 4	Town	S Gorham	

Almshouse Admissions, 1788–1795

Names	Time of Admission & Discharge	Town or State	By what Overseer	By what Selectman
John Gillard found Ded in a Barn & Bured from the alms House on the State acct.				
	april 5		Jona. Mason	
Daved Chamberlin	Dismist 7	State		
Benjn. Gould	Dismist 7	Town		
Patrick Kelly	Dismist 8	State		
Hannah Reedey[326]	admited 11	State	Jona. Mason	
Henry Erving	admited 12	Town	Jona. Mason	10 ys. old next augst.
Wm. Kerkam[327] Run the same Day	admited } 12	State	Jona. Mason	Liverpool old England
Peter Brown	Run 14	State		
Hanah Reedey	Run 14	State		
Betsey Vintino[328]	admited [14]	Town	S Gorham	
Thos. Rowlinson	Dismist 14	State		
George Washington	Dischargd 15	State	Bound out	
Eliz Ryan, Thankful Edmons Child	Dischargd. 16	Town	pr. order of mr Hill	
Dennis Cavanaugh	Dischd. 16	State		
Jack Roby	Dischargd 18	State	Returnd next Day	
Hannah Roby	Dischargd 18	State		
Betsey McPearson	Dischargd 19	State		
John Hammanway[329]	admited 19	Town	Ed. Procter	
Edward Beacham	Dischargd 21	State		
Sarah Whitcomb	Dischargd 21	Town		
Sarah Rowen	Dischargd 21	State		
Michal Soren	admited 22	State	Jona. Mason	a Native of Nantz
Peter Brown	admited 22	State	John Sweetser	from Iarland
Isabella a Black Woman	admitd. 24	State	Henry Hill	

Names	Time of Admission & Discharge	Town or State	By what Overseer	By what Selectman
Hannah Cooper	Dischargd 26	Town		
Androw Gardner	Dischargd 29	Town		
Mary Ross	Dismt. May 1st. [*1794*]	Town		
Elizth. Vinetow	Dismt. 1	Town		
Hannah Waples[330]	admitd. 1	Town	S Parkman	
Polley McClaron	Bound out 1	Town	Returnd the Same Day	
<*John Mil[kan?] & Wife*	*Dischd.*	*State>*		
Ester Henly	Dismist 2	Town	Returnd same Day	
Saml. Duncalf	admtd. 3	Town	Henry Hill	
Polly Hammon[331]	admd. 5	Town	Wm. Phillips	
Mary Clark wife of Wm. Clark forenor }	admtd. 5	State	S Gorham	
Ann Thomson	Dischargd 6	Town		
Nancy Ettrage[332]	admited 6	Town	Ed. Edes	
Hannah Riordia Edey[333]	admitd. from W. H 8	State	S Parkman	En[tere]d. Next page[334].
Mary Buffit	8	Town ⎫	from Work House	
Mary Hynds[335]	8	State		
Grace Cox	8	Town		
Elizth. Castle	8	State		
Elizth. Cornish	8	State ⎬		
Mary Sharp	8	State		
<*Philys Coks*>	8	State		
Fanny Swift	8	State ⎭		
	pr. order of the overseers			
George Seal	admited 8	Town	John Sweetser	
Alexander Minot	Dismist 9	State		
John Allen	Dismist 9	State	Returnd the Same Day	
Charles Woodman	Dismist 9	State		
Hannah Riordia[336] <*Edey*>	admited 8	State	Saml. Parkman	
Henry Erving	Bound out 10	Town		

Almshouse Admissions, 1788–1795

Names	Time of Admission & Discharge	Town or State	By what Overseer	By what Selectman
Jules Ackley	admited 10	State	Ed. Procter	Run Same Day

May 8th the Following Person Sent to
the Workhouse pr. order of the Overseers

Names	Time of Admission & Discharge	Town or State	By what Overseer	By what Selectman
Isaac Downs		Town		
David Dana		State		
Qumino Frazier		State		
John Healy		State		
Timy. Howard		Do.		
Cyrus Kent		Do.		
John McKinzey		Do.		
John McFarland		Do.		
Alxdr. Minot		Do.		
George Powell		Do.		
Cato Smith		Do.		
John Clark		Do.		
Alaxdr. Lord		Do.		
Richard Langley[337]	admited	State	S. Gorham	
John Ritchee	Dischargd 15	State		
Mary Buffit	Dismist 15	Town		
John Dawson	admited 15	State	H Hill	
John Millhorne	Dischargd May 15	State		
George Graff	Dischd. 15	State		
Mary Graff & their Son	Dischd. 15	State		
Hannah Riordia <*Edey*>	Dischargd 15	State		
Elenor Peirce & heir Child Elenor }	Dismist 16	State		
Robt. Polly & his Wife alus [*alias*] [Quse?]	admited 16	State	John Sweetser	
Wm. Davedson[338]	admited 17	State	Wm. Smith	
Sarah Rowin[339] & Child	admited 17	State	Ed. Procter	
Pattey Dorcey	Dischargd 19	State		
Mary Benjman	Dischargd [19]	Town		
Thomas Price	admitd. 19	State an Irishman		J Codman

Names	Time of Admission & Discharge	Town or State	By what Overseer	By what Selectman
Judith Gains & her Daughter Lucressey[340]	Dischd. 19	State		
Qumino Frazier[341]	Returnd from W H 23 pr. order Mr. Hill		State	
Cato Smith	Retd. from W H 23 pr. order Mr. Hill		State	
John Hely[342]	Retd. from W H 20 pr. order of Mr. Hill		State	
Susannah Ridan	Dismist 26	Town		
John Clarke[343]	admited 26 27 Sent to work House	State	Saml. Parkman	
John McKenzey[344]	admtd. 29 from Work Hs.	State	J. Codman	
Thos. Haden[345] Irish man	admit May 29 Dischd. the Next Day	State	Saml. Parkman	
Polle Hammon	Dischd. 31	Town		
Susanah Barber	admited 31	Town	Ed. Procter	
Jack Roby	Dischargd 31	State		
Pattey Dorsay	Dischargd 31	Town		
Grace Cox	Run 31	Town	Returnd	
Eliz moore	Run 31	State	& her Child Returnd	
Polley McClaron	Dischd. June 5	Town	Bound out	
John McFarland[346]	admited from W House			
Hannah Waples	Dismist 7	Town		
John Loranbon	admited 10	State	Wm. Smith	a french man Salor
Susannah Keen & Child	Dismt. 12 of Pembrock	Wife of Tubal Kean St. Gorham		
Nathl. Fowle	admited 16	Town	Wm. Smith	
Elizth. Condon	Dismist 17	State		

Recd. a Child that was found in Mr. Whitmore's yard a Boy about 4 months old Named Peter Pender

| Hannah Waples[347] | admited 20 | Town | Sam Parkman | |

Almshouse Admissions, 1788–1795

❧

Names	Time of Admission & Discharge	Town or State	By what Overseer	By what Selectman
Jack & Phillis Bulflinch[348]	admited June 21	State	Stephen Gorham	
Merriam Hanfield	Dischargd			
Phebe Gee from Work house	admited 23	State	John White	
Mary Clark & her Child	Dismist 24	State		
Wm. Spooner & Wife	admited 24	Town	Ed. Procter	Run
Mather Dorcy[349]	admited 24	Town	Ed. Edes	
John Millhorn[350]	admited 24	State	Wm. Smith	
Wm. Donnot[351]	Bound out	State		
Elizth. Garrow	Bound out	State		
Joseph Rusell[352]	Bound out	Town		
Elizth. Moore	Dischargd 25	State		
Ruth Brewer	admited 27	State	Wm. Smith	
Betsey Moore	admited 27	State	Wm. Phillips	
Betsey allen	admited 27	Town	John White	
Grace Cox	Dischargd 27	Town		
Sally Kemp	admited July 3d.	Town	Stephen Gorham	
John Morris a Black	Bound out	State		
Cathrine Maley	admt. 5	State	Jona L. Asting	
Elizh. Castle	admited 5	Town	Wm. Smith	
John Holden	admited 6	State	John White	
Sarah Kemp	admited 8	Town	Stepn. Gorham	
maryann[353] The Wife of Boston Jarvis	admited 8	State a Black	H Hill	
Mary Hinds	Dismist 10	Town		
Susannah Keen[354]	admited 10	Town	Saml. Parkman	Pembrok
Michael Sorren	Dischargd 14	State		

Almshouse Admissions, 1788–1795

Names	Time of Admission & Discharge	Town or State	By what Overseer	By what Selectman
John Loranbon	Dischargd 14	State		
Wm. Davedson	Dischargd 14	State		
Mary Ross	admited 14	Town	Stepn. Gorham	
Catarine Barbadoes	admitd. 15	State	John Seetser	from W H
Sall Harris	admited from Work house			
Sarah Adams	Run 15	Town		
Mary Buffett	Dischargd 21	Town	[Juner?][355]	
Eunice Edde[356]	admited 21	State	Jona. Mason	
James Henley	Bound out 21	State		
Susanah Ridan	admited 21	Town		
Patty Egeleston	admited 22	Town	Wm. Smith	
Rebeca Cornish	admited 22	Town	Ed. Procter	
Pegey Marton[357]	admited 22 W. H	State	Jona. L Auston	
Mary Burn[358]	admited 24	State	Jona. Mason	
Elizth. Pallisor	Dischargd	Town		
Sarah Eddy Poley Lewis } Marbl Saley Stevens } Head Meriam Dockum	admited 28 admited from the Workhous [admitted]	Town Town	Wm. Smith Saml. Parkman	
Lidia Dungar	Augt. 2 admid.	State	Lorin Austen	
John Kemp	admited augt. 2	Town	Stephen Goram	
Mary McLucklin	Discd. 4	State		
Jane Brown	admited 4	Town	Ed. Edes	
Susanah Rewen	Dischargd 4	State		
Pattey Egelston	Dismist 5	Town		
Sally Crafts[359]	admited 5 from W H born in Westford		Jon. White	
John Johnston (a Scotch)	Admitted 5	State	S Parkman	

Almshouse Admissions, 1788–1795

~

Names	Time of Admission & Discharge	Town or State	By what Overseer	By what Selectman
Wm. Perch	admited Augst. 6	State	Wm. Smith	Born in the Wt. of England
Susanah Ridan	Run 6	Town		
Mary Burns	Run 6	State		
Mary Sharp	admited 6	State	Jona. L austen	
Androw Gardner	admited 7	Town	Ed. Procter	
Mr Hune	admited 8	State	Saml. Parkman	Died the next Day
Mary Hinds[360]	admited 9	Town	Wm. Smith	
Elizth. Lewis	Dischargd 11	Marblhead	pr. order of Mr. Hill	
Mary Buffitt	Dischargd Augst. 12	Town		
Backus Connant[361]	admited 12	State	John Sweetcher	
John Avis	admited 12	Town	Stephen Gorham	
Sarah Adams	admite 12	Town	Ed. Edes	
Hannah Reed	admited 12	State	Henry Hill	
James Millino[362]	admited 13	State	Steph Gorham	
Rose Brewer	Dischargd 15	State	a Black	
Cathrine Mallay[363]	admited 15	State from Iarland	Wm. Smith	
Mary Scott	admited 16	Town	Jona. L Austin	
Katy Holly	admited 16	State	Jona. L Austen	
Timothey Hayden	admited 18	State	S Gorham	
Nancey Cross	Dischargd 18	Town		
Polly Cowell	admited 19	Town	St. Gorham	
Elizth. Oakwel & her son Cornelus alius Sheen	admited 19	State	John Codman	W H
Cathrine Mallay	Run 20	State		
Nancy Thomson[364]	admited 20	Town	Ed. Procter	
John Flyn[365]	Dischargd 22	State		

Names	Time of Admission & Discharge	Town or State	By what Overseer	By what Selectman
Cathrine Mallay	Dischargd 25	State	see above	Run 20th.
Meriam Handfeild[366]	Dischargd Augt. 25	Town		
<Thos Haden	*Run 26*	*State>*		
John Johnson	Run 26	State		
Mary Webb	Run 26	Town		
Cathrine Holland	Run 26	State		
James Millino	Dischargd 27	State		
Wm. Hall	admited 27	State	Edwd. Procter	
Wm. Hall	Dischargd Sept 2	State		
Wm. Perch	Dischargd	State		
Elizth. Lee	admited	Town	Ed. Procter	
Levene[367] Richardson a Child / Ebenezr. Richardson a Child / Noble Spencer a Child	admited 2d. a Verble order from the Board of overseers	State		
Saml. Hicks	Dischargd 4	State	Marred Nance Etherige the 5 of augst	
Hannah Reed	Dischargd 4	State		
<Susanah Ridan	*Dischargd 4*	*Town>*		
Jane Galley[368]	Bound out [5]	Town		
Backus Connant	Dischargd 5	State		
Elizth. Denney	admited 5	Town	John White	
Elizth. Bovey	admited 5	Town	Wm. Smith	
Sukey Kain	admited 5	State	Jona. Mason	Run
Nath Fowle	Receved. Septr 6	Town	Wm. Smith	
Nathl. Fowle	Dischargd 8	Town		
Wm. Ryan[369]	Bound out 12	State		
Luce Dodge a: B[*lack*][370]	ad[m]ited 12	State	John Codman	
Mehitabel atkins a: B[*lack*][371]	admited 12	State	Wm. Smith	

~

Names	Time of Admission & Discharge	Town or State	By what Overseer	By what Selectman
Nance Warren	admited 13	Town	Ed. Procter	
Sallay Dunkin[372]	admited 16	Town	Jona. Mason	
Sarah Kemp	Dischargd 16	Town	Junr.	
John Millhorn[373]	admited 17	State	Wm. Smith	
Mark McClocklin[374] & his Wife mary	admited 18	State	John Sweetser	
Juliuns ackly	admited 18	State	Saml. Parkman	
Jancey Dirck [a] Du[t]chman	admited 20	State	Wm. Smith	
Levene Richardson	Bound out	State		
Henry Kendall & Wife Ruth	admited 20	State	Jona. Mason	
Peter Williston a Dutch man	admited 20	State	Saml. Parkman	
Mary Vial	admited 22	Town	Jona. L Austian	
William Langford	admited 22	Town	Stephen Gorham	
Catrine Barbados[375]	Dismist 23	State		
Wm. Curtis	admited 25	Town	S Gorham	
Hannah Cathright	Dismist 26	Town		
John Johnston	admited 26 a scotsman	State	S Parkman	
Mary Sponer	admited 26 from W H	State	John White	Run
Elizebth Dennie	Dischargd. 27	Town		
Susannah Rowen	Bound out 29	State		
Cetias a Black woman	admited 27	State	Loring Austin	
John Hoar of Redding	admitd. 27	Dischd.	Henry Hill	
Hannah Cowper	admited 27	Town	John White	
Juleuns ackly	Dischargd 30	State		
Peter Williston a Du[t]ch man	Disd. 30	State		
Nathl. Fowle	admited Octr. 1	Town	Ed. Procter	} Dischargd to work House

Names	Time of Admission & Discharge	Town or State	By what Overseer	By what Selectman
Mary Sharp	admited 2	State	Ed. Procter	
Mary Swan	Dismist 2	Town	Returnd in a Week	
Betey Denney	admited 2	Town	L Austin	
Christane[376] Bentick a Dane	admd. 3	State	S Gorham	
Wm. Stanford a native of G Briton	admitd. 3	State	S Gorham	
Joseph Ackley (German)	Admitted 6	State	Edwd. Procter	
Alex Manous a Frenchman	Admitted 6	State	S Gorham	
Polly Gorden & her 3 Children, Wm. 7 years old the furst of Last June, James 5 years the 23d. of next Decr., <Polley> Salle 2 years the 14 of Last aprl.	a[d]mited Octr 6	Town	Wm. Phillips	
<Eliz> Betsey Dennie	Dischargd 8	Town		
Enock Chace	admitd. 9 of [france?]	State	John Codman	
Mary Benjn. & her Daughter	admit 10	Town	L Austin	
Sophia Ackley	admited 10	Town	Jona. Mason	
Thomas Bull	admited 10 From Ierland	State	S Gorham	
Peggy Winslow a Black	admtd.	State	Wm. Smith	
Timo. Hayden	admited 13	State	Wm. Smith	
Betsey Pierce	admited 14	Town	Jona. Mason	Exchd. in [Dentrs?][377]
Polly Foster	admited 14	Town	S Gorham	
Ann Thomson	Dischargd 14	Town		
Martha Pausand	admited 15	State	S Gorham	she being the widow of a Forenor
Mary Bukley[378]	admited 15	State	S Gorham	
Betse Pierce	Dischargd 21	Town		
Daniel Benjamin	admtd. 18	Town	S Gorham	
Susannah Lewis	admited 21	Town	S Parkman	

Names	Time of Admission & Discharge	Town or State	By what Overseer	By what Selectman
Dennis Cavnagh[379]	admitd. 21	State	S Gorham	
Richard Allen	admited 21	State	a Black Jona. Mason	
<*William Stanford*	*admited 23*	*State*	*S Gorham>*	
Hannah Chamberland[380]	ad[m]ited 23	Town	Ed. Procter	
Edward Beacham	admid. 25	State	S Gorham	
Ebinezr. Rudock[381]	admited 27	Town	Ed. Procter	
Mary Webb	Run 27	Town		
Sally Badger	Dismist 27	Town		
Gulan Akly	admited 27	State	Ed. Procter	
Nickelos French	admited 27	Town	S Gorham	
Richard Rowen	admited 28	State	Ed. Procter	
Hannah Reed	admited 31	State	Jona. Mason	
Thankl. Edmons Child Name Betsey Rion[382]	admd. Novr. 4	Town	Henry Hill	
Charls Town Flucker	admd. 4	State	Henry Hill	
Timothey Howard	admited from the Work Hous 15	State	Wm. Smith	
Eliz Cornish	Dischargd. 5	Town		
Sarah Cowell	Dischagd 5	Town		
John Easterbrok[383] his wife Peggy & 2 Children Lurance & John	admitd.	State	L Austin	
Joseph Bangs a German	admited 10	State	S Parkman	
Edward Beacham	admited 13	State	S Gorham	
Jna. Landgill	admited 13	State	Henry Hill	from Iarl[an]d
Enock Chace	Dischargd 14	State		
John Penn	admited 15	State	Stepn. Gorham	
Mary Scott	Dismist 17	Town		
Mary Dawes	admited 17	Town	a Child S. Parkman	

Names	Time of Admission & Discharge	Town or State	By what Overseer	By what Selectman
Morris OQuell[384]	admited 17	State	Saml. Parkman	
Ebenzr. Cox	admit. 17 for 8 Days	Town	Ed. Procter	
James Dokerty	admit 17	State	John Codman	
Joseph Brick	admited 21	Town	John White	
Mary Burn[385]	admited 22	Town	St. Gorham	Came in by the name of Green
Eulis Eckly	admited 22	State	Willm. Phillips	
James Stevens	admited 22	State	Jon. Sweetser	
Sukey Parsons a Malato	admd. 22	State	Jona. L Austin	
Hannah Shimmin a Black	admd. 24	State	St. Gorham	
James Dorkerty	Dischargd 26			
James John[386]	admited 26	State	Saml. Parkman	
Timothey Keef	Bound out 26	State	a Child	
James Stevens	Dischargd Decr. 2	State		
Sarah Whitcomb	admd. 2	Town	Jona. Mason	
Alexr. Manous	Dischargd 4	State		
Hannah Fowl	admited 4	Town	John Sweetser	
Marther Christa[387]	admited 6	State	John White	
Mary Jones	admited 6	Town	Returnd from Mr. Calender	
Elizh. Denney	admited 7	Town	Ed Procter	
John Penn	Run 10	State		
Sarah Harris	Run 10	Town		
3 Children of Wm. Higgons,[388] Danel, Hanah & Joseph	Receved 11	State	Henry Hill	
George Dormant	Receved 11	State	Wm. Smith	

∾

Names	Time of Admission & Discharge	Town or State	By what Overseer	By what Selectman
Joseph Bangs	Dischargd 15	State		
James John	Dischargd 16	State		
Thankful Rutherford alies [alias] Edmons[389]	admited 16	State		

To the Board of Edward Powers from Octr. 27th. 1793 to Decr. 1st. Five weeks at [390]
To Ditto from July 28 to Octr. 27th 1794. 13 weeks at
the above person was put into the almshouse by Order of the Supreem Court as a States. poor

Names	Time of Admission & Discharge	Town or State	By what Overseer	By what Selectman
Elizth. Higgens[391] from W H & her Child Wm.	admd. 16	State	Ed. Procter	
Mary Miller & 4 Children Polle 7 years, Nance 5, Jane 3, Thomas 1 year old	admd. 16	State	S Gorham	
Maryann Stwart[392]	admid. 17	State	Henry Hill	
Wm. Sprage[393]	adimted 17	Town	Ed. Procter	
Ebenzr. Rudock	Dischd.	Town		
Abigail Hubbard	admitd. 26	Brooklin	L. Austin	
Dugal Wiskie	admited 26	Scotland State	Jona. Mason	
Cesar Gardner	admited 26	State a Black	Saml. Parkman	
Morris OQuill	Dischargd 27	State		
Nancy Thomson[394]	admited 27	Town	Ed. Procter	
Lucy Haden[395]	admited 27	Town	Henry Hill	She is from Walltham
Joseph Pulfut A B[lack][396]	admitd. 27	State	Ed. Procter	
Ed. McLucklin	Dischargd. 28	State		
<John Penn	Runn 28>	State	see 10th Decemr.	
James Dorty	admited 31	State	Jona Mason	
Wm. Gordian	Bound out 1795 Janr. 1	Town		
Edwd. Beacham	admited 2	State	S Gorham	
Thos. Bull	Dischargd 5	State		

Almshouse Admissions, 1788–1795

Names	Time of Admission & Discharge	Town or State	By what Overseer	By what Selectman
Robert Burn a Child	admd. 6	Town	Ed. Procter	the Child was 5 years old aprl. 21 1794
John Flynn & Wife	admitd. 6	State	Jona. Mason	
Elizh. Sanders	admited 6	State	Stn. Gorham	
Mary Webb	admitd. 6	Town	Henry Hill	
Alexr. Minor a French man	admited 9	State	Saml. Parkman	
Wm. Croston	admited 9	State	Jona. Mason	
George Dorman	Discd. 15	State		
Eliz Woodman	admitd. 20	State	S Parkman	
Cloe Holland	admited 20	State	Wm. Smith	
Susannah Cain the Wife of Tubal Cain	admitd. 21	Pembrock	Henry Hill	from Work House
Joseph Bangs	admited 22	State	S Parkman	
Nance Hartley	Bound out 23 a Child	State		
Hannah Cooper	Dischargd 22	Town	Returnd 30 John White order	
Mary Jones	Bound out 22	Town		
Robt. Brown	admited 22	State	Jona. Mason	
Ebenezr. Richardson	Discd. 23 a Child	State		
Joseph Pulfut a B[lack]	Dischagd 26	State		
Noble Spencer mollato	Dismt. 27	State	Bound out	
Christian Bennedic	Discd. 29	State		
James Hill a Native of Ierla[n]d	admitd. Febry. 2	State	S Gorham	
Mary Lewis	admited 2	State	John	
Mary Galey a French woman	admited 3	State	Henry Hill	
Peggy Esterbrokes & her Child Larance	Dischd. 4	State		

Almshouse Admissions, 1788–1795

〜

Names	Time of Admission & Discharge	Town or State	By what Overseer	By what Selectman
Eliz Farrier a Child	admited 5	State	Returnd By order of the Board	
Nance Brimmer, Child	admitd. 5	Town	Wm. Smith	Returd.
Michel[397] Leonard	admited 6	State	Saml. Parkman	
Nichalos French	admited 6	Town	Wm. Smith	
an Infent Child Namd. John Sincler Allen Born in the House the Father an Irish Man				
an Infent Born the House namd. Wm. Leather the Father Scotsman				
Elizth. Hinks	admited 9	Town	John Sweetser	
Jacob Emmons & 2 Sisters Hannah & woodcock	admid. 9	Town	Jona. L Astin	
Nichalos French	Dismist 9	Town		
Saml. Jones an English Man	admited 12	State	Saml. Parkman	
Elizth. Sheen & Child	Dismt. 14	Town		
Sarah Coombs	admited 14	Town	Ed. Procter	
Wm. Bass	admited	Town	Ed. Procter	
Nance Brimer	Dischd. 23	Town		
Hannah Shimmins	Discd. 26	State	a black Returnd the next Day	
Cyras Eustis a Black	admited 27	State	Henry Hill	
Katy Tillot[398]	admited 27	Town	Ed. Procter	
Elizth. Woodman	Dischargd. 27	State		
Benjn. Ross	admited 28	Town	S Gorham	
Richard Anderson a yalow man[399] admited & Chargd. to the Town of Northampton Wm. Smith[400]	March 4			
James Hill	Dischargd 6	State		
Sophy Kilby	admt. a B[lack][401] 7	State	Henry Hill	
Dugal Whiskey	Dischargd 9	State		

Almshouse Admissions, 1788–1795

Names	Time of Admission & Discharge	Town or State	By what Overseer	By what Selectman
Hannah Hartley alus Berry	Dischargd 9	Town		
Thos. Aubany	admited 11	State	Wm. Smith	
Nance Thomson	Dischargd 12	Town		
Turquil McNeal	admited 16	State	Ed. Procter	
Mardicki Worren[402] a B[lack]	admit 16	State	S Gorham	
Susanah Ingraham & Child	admited 17	Town	St Gorham	
Edward Beacham	admitd. 19	State	St. Gorham	
Henry Kendall	Dischargd 19	State		
Ruth Kendall his wife	Do. 19	State		
Alexander Minot A B[lack]	Dischd. 20	State		
Scipio Franklin	admited 21	State	St. Gorham	
Jack Fugin	admited 21	State	Ed. Procter	
Timothey Hyden	Dischargd 23	State		
Susanah Ingraham & Child	Discd. 23	Town		
Elizh. Hinks	Dischargd 24	Town		
Abigall Hubbard	Dischargd 26	Town		
Katy Tillot	Dischargd 26			
James Docketty	Dischargd 31	State		
Dennis Welsh	admited 30	State	Henry Hill	
Polly Cowell	Dischargd 31	Town		
Frederick Milstruz	admited aprl 1	State	St. Gorham Died 20th. augt. 1795	
Elisha Davis	admited 1	Town	Ed. Procter	
James Dockety[403]	admited 2	State	John Sweetser	
Manuel Dysanttos[404]	admited 3	State	St. Gorham a Native of Portagal Died the Same night	

Names	Time of Admission & Discharge	Town or State	By what Overseer	By what Selectman
Mary Bass	admited 3	Town	Ed. Procte	
Elizabeth Blakston	admitd. 3	from Portland	Jon L Austin	
Susana Barber	admited 4	Town	Ed. Procter	
Wm. Pike a Child	admited 4	Town	St. Gorham	
Joseph Breck	Dischargd 11	Town		
James Jones	admited 11	State	St. Gorham	
Wm. Higgins A Child	Dischargd 13	Town		
John Flynn & his wife Elizth. His wife in Lynn	Dischagd 13	State Town	Born in Ireland	
Susanah Kean	Dismist 16	Town	Pembrook	
Wm. Cronston	Dismist 17	State	Born in Ireland	
James Dockerty	Dismist 18	State	Irish Man	
Michael Leonard	Dischard. 20	State	Irishman	
Wm. Curtis	Dischd. 20	Town		
Thankful Edmonds & 2 Children 20		Town		Betsey Ryon & Wm. Retheford
Robert Brown	Dischargd 22	State	an Iirish man	
Sukey Parsons	Dischd. 22	State	a molato	
Jesse Harding	admited 23	Cape Cod	Redford Webster Dischargd 25	
Nancy Thomson	admt. 25	Town	Ed. Procter	
Hannah Waples	Dischargd 25	Town		
Susannah Ridan	Dischargd 27	Town		
Polly Wendal[405]	admited 27	State	a Black Wm. Smith	
Elizabeth Rion a Child[406] a Child of Thankful Edmuns	admitd. 27	Town	from Workhouse	
Denis Wish	Dischargd 28	State		

Names	Time of Admission & Discharge	Town or State	By what Overseer	By what Selectman
Thos. More his Wife & Child	admited 28	Town	Wm. Smith	
Sarah or Sukey Rowen	Dismist 30	Town	Born in Roxbury	
Joseph Waters	admited May 1	State	Great Britn.	S Gorham
Elizth. Higgins & 4 Children Discharged		Town		
Dennis Daly[407] his Wife & Child}	admitd. 1	State	St. Gorham Hannah & Elijah her Son	Irisman
Elizth. Farrier	Bound out 1	State		
Patty Gerrill	admited 2	Town	Wm. Smith	
Thos. Rice	Dischargd 5	State		
<Robert Brown	*Dischd. 6*	*State>*	Error	
Michael Lenord	admitd. 1	State	Wm. Phillips	
Benjn. Spooner	admited 6	State	J L Auston	
Mary Lewis	Dischd. 8	State		
Thos Fosset a Sick Child	admd. 8	Town	by order of the Board	
Sukey Keen[408]	admited 8	Town	John Codman Pombrook	
Alaxander Minot	admitd. 8	State	St. Gorham	
Timothy Hayden	admitd. 8	State		
Mary Miller & her 4 Children	Dischargd May 9	State	for Halifax	
The State Dr. to Cash for the above persons Pasige £9				
Androw Moran	admited 10	State	Ed. Procter	
Thos. Rice	admited 11	State	St. Gorham	
James John	Dischrgd 12	State		
Elizh. Sanders	Dismist 12	State	Say Town	
Elizh. Rion a Child	Dischd. 12	Town		
Mary Galley	Dischd. 12	State		
Ceser Gardner	Dismist 12	State		

Almshouse Admissions, 1788–1795

Names	Time of Admission & Discharge	Town or State	By what Overseer	By what Selectman
Catherine Hunnell	admited 14	State	from Ireland	Wm. Smith
Ebenr. Ruddock	admited 18	Town	St. Goraham	
Betsey Allen a chd.	Dischargd 19	Town		
Maurice[409] OQuill	admited 20	State	a Native of Ireland St. Gorham	
James Robberson[410]	admited 20	State	Ed. Edes	
Sally Harris	admited from Work House	State	Oliver Brewster	
James Gones	admited 23	State	Wm. Smith	
Mary Hynds	Dischargd 25	Town	Returnd the Next Day	
Timothy Hayden	Dismist 25	State		
Susannah Kean	Dismist 25	Town	Pembrook	
Micheal Lenord	admited 25	State	Wm. Smith	
Peter Whitcomb a Black	admd. 26	State	Redford Webster	
Cezar Gray	admited 27	State	John Codman	
Wm. Kimball belongin to Norton	admited 28		Wm. Smith	
Lucy Brown	admitd. June 1	Newton	Ed. Procter	
Saml. Brown	admited 2 a B[lack]	State	Henry Hill dismised next day	
Easter White	admited 4	Town	Ed. Procter	
Thos. Walker	admited 4	Town	Ed. Procter	
Mary Pown	admitd. 4	Town	R Webster	
Eliz Brewer	admited 5	Town	St. Gorham	
John Hemminway	Run 5	Town		
Ceser Kent	Dischd. 5	State		
Luce Brown	Dismist 9	Newton		
Peggy Roberts	admited 9	Town	S Gorham	Dat'd. aprl. 1
George Powel	Dismist 10	State	from the Wt. Indes 2 year ago	

Names	Time of Admission & Discharge	Town or State	By what Overseer	By what Selectman
Alme Davis	admited 11	Town	R Wibster	
Benjn. Roos	Admited 13	Town	Ed. Edes	
Richard Anderson	Dischargd 16	*<State>* Negro	Northampton	
Charles DeVoll he Died the Same Night	admited 22	State	St. Gorham	Geurnsey man
Robt. Brown	admited 23	State	Ed. Procter	
Benjn. Spooner	Dismist 23	State		
Polley Webb	Run 23	Town		
Wm. Sharp	Run 23	State		
Thos. Rice	Dischargd 23	State	*<admited the Same day by an order from Mr. Hill>*	
Cabub[411] Greenvile	admited 24	State	R Webster	
Richd. Langley	Dischargd 27	State		
Wm. Davidson	admited 27	State	Wm. Smith	
James Roberson	Dismist 29	State		
Henry Luacus[412]	admited 30	Town	John Sweetser	
Mary McCurday	Dismist July 7	Town		
Wm. Sharp	admited 7	State	Wm. Smith	
Turquill McNeil	Dischd. 8	State		

Names	Time of Admission & Discharge	Town or State	By what Overseer	When Discharged
Rachal Langley	admited 11	State	a Native of Grate Briton St. Gorham	
Martha Dorcy	Dischd. 11	Town		
Thos. Aubany	Dischd. 12	State		
Elizth. Warner	admited 19	State	Henry Hill	
John Devan	admited 12	State	a Native of Connectut Wm. Phillips	
Mary Buckley	Dischd. 13	Town		
Saml. Jones	Dischd. 14	State		
[413] Harper	admited 14	State	Run at Night	
an Infant Molato Child found in the Bural Ground Namd. [414]	admited 14	Town	Ed. Edes	Died 31st. augt. 1795
Nance Gair & her two Children	admited 18	Town	A Welles	
Thos. Walker	Dischd. 20	Town		
Elizth. Denny & Child	Run 20	Town		
John Goffe[415] Born in Iarland a Salor	admitd. 20[416]	State	H Hill	18th. Augt. 1795
Nancy Parks	admited 21	Springfield	Wm. Smith	(Run away 7th. Septr. Do.[417])
Mahitabl Atkins	Dischargd 23	a Negro woman		
Elizebeth Smith	admitd. 23	Town	Wm. Smith	
Grace Cox	admited 26	Town	Wm. Phillips	
James Willson	admited 27	State	Ed. Procter	
Wm. Warner his Wife & Child	admited 30	Town	J L Austin	
Saml. Hicks	omited	State		Discharged Augt. 3d.
Wm. Davidson	Dischargd Augst 1	State		
John[418] Dobbies's Wife and 2 Children	admited 1	State	J L Austin	
Fanny Dickerson	admited 1		Henry Hill	

〜

Names	Time of Admission & Discharge	Town or State	By what Overseer	When Discharged
Wm. Curtis	admited 1	Town	S Gorham	
Richard Adams A B[*lack*][419]	admited 3	Scituate	Wm. Smith	
William Warner	Discharg 4	Town		
John Dobbie's Wife & Children	Dis. 4	State		
Timothey Dwire	admited 5	State	Wm. Smith	
Poll Edmuns[420] A Child	admitd. 5	Town	Wm. Smith	
Ame Davis	Dischargd 7	Town		
Thomas <*Daly*> Haily[421]	admited 10	State	Ed. Procter	19th. augt. 1795
<*Timothey Dwire*	*admited 10 Work house*	*State*>		
James Orsburn[422]	admited 10	Work House		
Thankfull Edmons	admited 10	Work house		
Wm. & Elizh. Lovridge John & Thos. thier Children	admited 10	State	S Gorham	
Calab Greenman	Dischd. 10	State		
Cathrine Hunnewell	Dischd. 10	Town		
Thomas Greenough	Augt. 14th. 1795	State Foreigner	Stepn. Gorham	
Alexander Minot	Do.	State	Do.	Augt. 26th 1795
Eliza Brown	Do. 15th. Do.	Town	Oliver Brewster	
William Gillahen	Do. 17th. Do.	State	William Smith	Do. 28th. Do.
Miss Mary Buckley	Do. 18th. Do.	Town	Henry Hill	
Hannah Berry	Do.	Do.	Stephen Gorham	
Charlotte Greely (Black child)	19th. Do.	State	Do.	
Ceasar Gray B[*lack*][423] man (Omitted)	April 7th. 1795	Do.	from the Work house	Died 20th. Augt. 1795
Edward Beacham	augt. 20th. Do.	Do.	Stephen Gorham	

Names	Time of Admission & Discharge	Town or State	By what Overseer	When Discharged
William Curtis	Do. 22d.	Town	Redford Webster	
John Blake & his Wife	Do. 24th.	Town	Henry Hill	
Quneno Frazier Black man	Do. 25th.	State	William Smith	
John Shone	Do. 26th.	Do.	Do.	
Jacob Blackburn	Do. 27th.	Do.	Edward Proctor	
Jacob Blackburn's Wife	Do.	Do.	Do.	
Jacob Blackburn's Child	Do.	Do.	Do.	
Wm. Rutherford[424] a child born of Thankfull Rutherford (Alias) Edmonds	Febry. 5th. 1795 Do.			Died 31st. augt. 1795
Betsey Mason of Newbury-Port	Augt. 31st. Do.		William Smith	
John Brown	Do. 25	Town	Redford Webster	Died 5th. Septr. Do.

Notes

1	"Chloe" in MS index.
2	"Luce Potter" in MS index.
3	"Chalender" in MS index.
4	"Kepson" in MS index.
5	"Etheredge" in MS index.
6	"Sargent" in MS index.
7	Entered as George McCann in the MS index.
8	The main text of the entry was erased.
9	"Farrow" in the MS index.
10	"Delany" in the MS index.
11	"Carter" in the MS index.
12	"Chambers" in the MS index.
13	"Matthew" in MS index.
14	"McLocklin" in MS index.
15	"Tilty" in MS index.
16	Perhaps "drab," i.e. prostitute.
17	"Ratford" in MS index.
18	"Purket" in MS index.
19	"Segrove" in MS index.
20	"Ann" in MS index.
21	"Dolliver" in MS index.
22	Blank in MS.
23	Blank in MS.
24	"Carter" in the MS index.
25	"Lawrence" in MS index.
26	"Francis" in MS index.
27	The text of the entry has been erased.
28	The text of the entry has been erased.
29	"Cockran" in MS index.
30	The end of the word or the next word is illegible.
31	"Cox" in MS index.
32	"Wendall" in MS index.
33	"Anna" in MS index.
34	"McLochlin" in MS index.
35	The name, other than the initials is illegible.
36	The first name is blank in the ms.
37	"Ann" in MS index.
38	"Martin McLochlen" in MS index.
39	"Kendall" in MS index.
40	"Eayrs" in MS index.
41	"Brandon" in MS index.
42	"Winter" in MS index.
43	"Killgore" in MS index.
44	"Pompey" in MS index.

45   "Catherine" in MS index.
46   "Matteson" in MS index.
47   "Robinson" in MS index.
48   "Harris" in MS index.
49   "Hogan" in MS index.
50   "Mahetable Livingston" in MS index.
51   "Kennedy" in MS index.
52   "O'Brien" in MS index.
53   "Townsend" in MS index.
54   "Cromwell" in MS index.
55   "Matthew" in MS index.
56   "Townsend" in MS index.
57   "Erving" in MS index.
58   "Joanna Spooner" in MS index.
59   "Geyer" in MS index.
60   "Donnovan" in MS index.
61   "Robert" in MS index.
62   "Mary" in MS index.
63   "Williston" in MS index.
64   "Ryan" in MS index.
65   "Decosta" in MS index.
66   "Wright" in MS index.
67   "Sophia Mendez" in MS index.
68   "Ireland' in MS index.
69   "Maloney" in MS index.
70   "Mary" in MS index.
71   "Longley" in MS index.
72   "Sinclair" in MS index.
73   "Mary" in MS index.
74   "Judith Lowe" in MS index.
75   "Murphey" in MS index.
76   "Garrow" in MS index.
77   "Sinclair" in MS index.
78   "Hewes" in MS index.
79   "Geyer" in MS index.
80   "McKinzie" in MS index.
81   "Crowley" in MS index.
82   "Fitzgerald" in MS index.
83   "Hunnewell" in MS index.
84   "Townsend" in MS index.
85   "Medows" in MS index.
86   "Eayrs" in MS index.
87   "Woodson" in MS index.
88   "Murphy" in MS index.
89   "Gorham" in MS index.
90   "Lowe" in MS index.
91   "Peirce" in MS index.
92   "Seegreaves" in MS index.
93   "Mary" in MS index.
94   "Coburn" in MS index.
95   "Francis" in MS index.
96   "Hatson" in MS index.
97   "McKinzie" in MS index.

98   Squeezed into the top right hand corner of the entry are the words "nam'd Katy Brown."
99   "Finn" in MS index.
100   "McLochlin" in MS index.
101   Interlined in the MS index is "alias Berry." See also the entry for 9 March 1795, below.
102   "Burnham" in MS index. See final line of this entry.
103   "Blackbourn" in the MS index.
104   "Hanh. Hollis" in the MS index.
105   "Maloney" in MS index.
106   "Benjamin" in MS index.
107   "Michael" in MS index.
108   "Carrol" in MS index.
109   "Lucy" in MS index.
110   "Etheredge" in MS index.
111   "Murphy" in MS index.
112   "Judith Keily" in MS index.
113   "Ryan" in MS index.
114   "Murphy" in MS index.
115   "Ruduck" in MS index.
116   This entry was written at the bottom right-hand corner of the MS page. The children are indexed under the names of Eustis and Dunn. See also the entry for 19 April, three lines below.
117   The children are indexed under the name of Marston.
118   "Mahoney" in MS index.
119   "Shanley" in MS index.
120   "Ryan" in MS index.
121   "Pollard" in MS index.
122   In the MS index the son is entered with the surname of "Black." I.e., "Blacks" does not denote race in this instance.
123   "Jeremiah Mahoney" in MS index.
124   "Bryant" in MS index.
125   "Roulstone" in MS index.
126   "Murphy" in MS index.
127   "McLauchlin" in MS index. (See note 129 below).
128   "Langford" in MS index.
129   "McLauchlin" in MS index.
130   "Leahea" in MS index.
131   "Cavnough" in MS index.
132   "Braggadon" in MS index.
133   "McKinzie" in MS index.
134   "Andrew Hardk" in MS index.
135   "Martin" in MS index.
136   "Ruduck" in MS index.
137   "McLauchlin" in MS index.
138   "Eddy" in MS index.
139   "Catherine" in MS index.
140   "Pierce" in MS index.
141   "Tillor" in MS index.
142   "Whitemore" in MS index.
143   "Bennett" in MS index.
144   "Eddy" in MS index.
145   "Morrison" in MS index.
146   "Farrier" in MS index.
147   "Larabee" in MS index.
148   "Russell" in MS index.

149 "Chamberlain" in MS index.
150 "Evans" in MS index.
151 "Vial" in MS index.
152 "Benjamin" in MS index.
153 Identified as a child in the MS index.
154 "Read" in MS index.
155 "Clerk" in MS index.
156 "Langford" in MS index.
157 "Betsey Hardwick" in MS index.
158 "Gregory" in MS index.
159 "Lovering" in MS index.
160 "Mathur" in MS index.
161 Indexed as Sina Indens and Hannah Indens.
162 "Winefred" in MS index.
163 "Ann Etheredge" in MS index.
164 "Paine" in MS index.
165 "Lloyd" in MS index.
166 "Battest" in MS index.
167 Identified as a child in the MS index.
168 "Fitzgerald" in MS index.
169 "Townsend" in MS index.
170 "Michael Renolds" in MS index.
171 Identified as a child in the MS index.
172 "Esther" in MS index.
173 "Prescot" in MS index.
174 "Hanny" in MS index.
175 Identified as a child in the MS index.
176 "Dockum" in the MS index.
177 "Bird" in MS index. Identified there as a child.
178 Identified as a child in the MS index.
179 The MS index reads "Patty say Martha."
180 Written below "Androw" is "James."
181 "Griggs" in MS index.
182 "Hunnewell" in MS index.
183 "Hunnewell" in MS index.
184 "McKinzie" in MS index; indentified as a child therein.
185 "Hitchborn" in MS index.
186 Identified as a child in the MS index.
187 The entry is obscured by an ink blot. Text is supplied from the entries of 28 June, below.
188 "Madderson" in the MS index.
189 Identified in the MS index as Patty, "say Martha" Dorsey.
190 Identified in the MS index as Patty, "say Martha" Dorsey.
191 "Handfield" in the MS index.
192 "Appleton" in MS index.
193 "Butters" in MS index.
194 "Silvester" in MS index.
195 "Flin" in MS index.
196 "Griggs" in MS index.
197 "Murphy" in MS index.
198 "Stone" in MS index.
199 "Rebecca" in MS index.
200 "McLochlin" in MS index.
201 "Parson" in MS index.

202 "Silvester" in MS index.

203 "Wade" in MS index.

204 "Rosana" in MS index.

205 "Coille" in MS index.

206 "Barthw." in MS index.

207 "Cathne." in MS index.

208 "Burns" in MS index.

209 "Ruduck" in MS index.

210 "Matthews" in MS index.

211 Punctucation supplied. Identified as "colored" in the MS index.

212 "Apstrof" in MS index.

213 The MS index reads "Patty say Martha Dorsey."

214 "Going" in MS index.

215 This entry was interlined.

216 "Molly" in MS index.

217 "German" in MS index.

218 "Wendell" in MS index.

219 "Silvester" in MS index.

220 "Akely" in MS index.

221 The entry in the MS index does not include a first name and is entered under "M" as "Mill Bridge."

222 Parentheses supplied; the previous two words were interlined by the clerk.

223 "Dockum" in MS index.

224 "Benjamin" in MS index.

225 "Alice Fucker" in MS index.

226 "Cox" in MS index.

227 "Dorsey" in MS index.

228 "Cathne. in MS index.

229 "Melidge" in MS index.

230 "McLochlin" in MS index.

231 "Wilson" in MS index.

232 "Griggs" in MS index.

233 "Ferdinand" in MS index.

234 "Wainwood" in MS index.

235 "Cathne. Tillet" in MS index.

236 The surname is spelled "Eddy" in the MS index. "Chd." is inserted above the line.

237 "Mitchell" in MS index.

238 "Morris" in MS index.

239 "McKinzie" in MS index.

240 "Thompson" in MS index.

241 "McGlockling" in MS index.

242 "Johnson" in MS index.

243 "Sevaney" in MS index.

244 "Martha Dorsey" in MS index.

245 Identified as a child in the MS index.

246 Identified as a child in the MS index.

247 "Thompson" in MS index.

248 "Lovering" in MS index.

249 "Mitchell" in MS index.

250 Identified as a child in the MS index, where the name is "John Keef.

251 Identified as a child in the MS index.

252 Identified as a child in the MS index.

253 Identified as a child in the MS index, where the name is "Tulla Ann."

254 "Polly Frank" in MS index.
255 "German" in MS index.
256 Identified as a child in the MS index.
257 Identified as "colored" in the MS index, where the first name is spelled "Selem."
258 "Michael" in MS index.
259 Identified as a child in the MS index.
260 Identified as a child in the MS index, where the name is spelled "Silvester."
261 "Fenno" in MS index.
262 "Judith" in MS index.
263 "Dwire" in MS index.
264 Punctuation supplied. "Collins" in MS index.
265 Identified as "colored" in the MS index.
266 "Cathne" in MS index.
267 "Morris" in MS index.
268 "Sally Dunken" in MS index.
269 "Laten" in MS index.
270 "Polly" in MS index.
271 "Chamberlain" in MS index.
272 "Gains" in MS index.
273 "Sprague" in MS index.
274 Identified as "colored" in the MS index.
275 Identified as a child in the MS index, where the name is spelled "Eddy."
276 "Elenr." in MS index.
277 "Connor" in MS index.
278 "Brinton" in MS index.
279 Identified as "colored" in the MS index.
280 "Thompson" in MS index.
281 See entry of 17 Aug. 1793, above.
282 "Thompson" in MS index.
283 Identified as colored in the MS index.
284 Identified as colored in the MS index.
285 "Judith Gains" in MS index.
286 "Edmonds" in MS index.
287 "Murray" in MS index.
288 Identified as "colored" in the MS index.
289 Interlined above Murphy's date of admission is *<October Sept 30 November>*.
290 Supplied from the MS index.
291 "Cavnough" in MS index.
292 "Branagan" in MS index.
293 "Holly" in MS index.
294 Identified as colored in the MS index.
295 Identified as colored in the MS index.
296 "Kelly" in MS index.
297 This is how the name is entered in the MS index. In the admission entry "Gray" is interlined above the line and "Richards" is interlined below the line.
298 "Hevernor" in MS index.
299 Identified as "colored" in the MS index.
300 "Benjamin" in MS index.
301 "Riorden" in MS index.
302 "Sprague" in MS index.
303 "Garrow" in MS index.
304 "Burns" in MS index.
305 "Moore" in MS index.

306 "Riden" in MS index.
307 "Martha Dorsey" in MS index.
308 "Alexander" in MS index.
309 "Robinson" in MS index.
310 "Chamberlain" in MS index.
311 "Richey" in MS index.
312 "Downes" in MS index.
313 "Hanfield" in MS index.
314 "McDonnel" in MS index.
315 This entry obviously was omitted and later written in free space to the right of the entries for 19 Dec., above.
316 "Lovebridge" in MS index.
317 The father's surname is written "Thomson" in the MS index; the daughter's "Thompson."
318 "Nickols" in MS index.
319 Identified as a child in the MS index.
320 "Powell" in MS index.
321 "Sherburn" in MS index.
322 "Murray" in MS index.
323 "Murphy" in MS index.
324 "Kirilly" in MS index.
325 "Fowle" in MS index.
326 "Reedy" in MS index.
327 "Kerkham" in MS index.
328 "Vinteno" in MS index.
329 "Hemmenway" in MS index.
330 "Wapples" in MS index.
331 "Hammond" in MS index.
332 "Etheridge" in MS index.
333 The MS index reads "Hannah Riorden."
334 See the duplicate entry for Hannah thirteen lines below.
335 "Hines" in MS index.
336 "Riorden" in MS index.
337 "Longley" in MS index.
338 "Davidson" in MS index.
339 "Rowen" in MS index.
340 "Lucretia" in MS index.
341 "Frazer" in MS index.
342 "Healey" in MS index.
343 "Clark" in MS index.
344 "McKinzie" in MS index.
345 "Hayden" in MS index.
346 "McFarlin" in MS index.
347 "Wapples" in MS index.
348 "Bulfinch" in MS index.
349 "Patty Dorsey" in MS index.
350 "Mellhorn" in MS index.
351 Identified as a child in the MS index.
352 "Russell" in MS index.
353 The first name was interlined above the entry.
354 "Kean" in MS index.
355 Perhaps "Junior"; i.e., either John Codman Jr. or William Phillips Jr.
356 "Eddy" in MS index.
357 "Martin" in MS index.

358 "Burns" in MS index.
359 "Craft" in MS index.
360 "Hines" in MS index.
361 "Conant" in MS index.
362 "Milleno" in MS index.
363 "Maley" in MS index.
364 "Thompson" in MS index.
365 "Flynn" in MS index.
366 "Hanfield" in MS index.
367 "Sevaney" in MS index.
368 Identified as a child in the MS index.
369 Identified as a child in the MS index.
370 Identified as colored in the MS index.
371 Identified as colored in the MS index.
372 "Dunken" in MS index.
373 "Mellhorn" in MS index.
374 Separate entries in the MS index read "Mark McLauchlin" and Mary McLochlin."
375 "Barbadoes" in MS index.
376 "Christian" in MS index.
377 Possibly "indentures."
378 "Buckley" in MS index.
379 "Cavnough" in MS index.
380 "Chamberlain" in MS index.
381 "Ruduck" in MS index.
382 "Ryan" in MS index.
383 "Easterbrooks" in MS index.
384 "O'Quill" in MS index.
385 "Burns" in MS index.
386 "Johns" in MS index.
387 "Christie" in MS index.
388 "Higgins" in MS index.
389 "Edmonds" in MS index.
390 Blank in the MS, here and in the line immediately following.
391 "Higgins" in MS index.
392 "Stewart" in MS index.
393 "Sprague" in MS index.
394 "Thompson" in MS index.
395 "Hayden" in MS index.
396 Identified as "colored" in the MS index.
397 "Michael" in MS index.
398 "Tillet" in MS index.
399 Identified as "colored" in the MS index.
400 Overseer William Smith's written order dated 3 March and addressed to "Mr. Whitwell" is interleaved in the register between pages 189 and 190. The order is annotated "June 16th. Dischargd" by the same hand that kept the register.
401 Identified as "colored" in the MS index.
402 "Warren" in MS index. Also identified there as "colored."
403 "Dokerty" in MS index.
404 "Dysanthos" in MS index.
405 "Wendall" in MS index.
406 "Ryan" in MS index.
407 "Daley" in MS index.
408 "Kean" in MS index.

409 "Morris" in MS index.
410 "Roberson" in MS index.
411 "Caleb" in MS index.
412 "Lucas" in MS index.
413 Blank in MS.
414 Blank in MS.
415 "Goff" in MS index.
416 "July 19th. 1795" is interlined above this date.
417 I.e., 1795.
418 "Jas." in MS index.
419 Identified as "colored" in the MS index.
420 "Edmunds" in MS index.
421 "Hailey" in MS index.
422 "Osborn" in MS index.
423 Identified as "colored" in the MS index.
424 "Retheford" in MS index.

ALMSHOUSE ADMISSIONS
September 8, 1795 – December 31, 1800

Here the entries become alphabetical.

Names	Time of Admission	State	Town	Towns they belong to¹	By what Overseer	When dischd., Died, Bound out, Run away.	Time they have been here in this State
Avis <Samuel> John	1795 Sept. 8th.		Do. 1		John Sweetser		Dischd. 6th. Septr. 1796
Adams Richard²	Octor. 8th.	Do. 1		Black man	Stephen Gorham	Dischd. 16th. Novr. 1795	5 Weeks. 4 Days
Adams John	Do. 10		1		Arnold Welles junr.	Dischd. 24th. Augt. 1797	
Adams Richard	Novr. 16	1		West Indias	Wm. Smith Stephn. Gorham}	Run away 10th. March 1797	
Andrews John	Decr. 29		Do.			Sent to the Work house	
Allen Peter	1796 Febry. 29	1		France	Jonathan L. Austin	Run away about 3d. May 1796	
Armstrong Thos.	March [1?]st.		1	Child	John Codman	Died 2d. Octor. Do.	
Atkins Mahitable	Do. 17		1		Stephen Gorham	Dischd. 19th. June 1797	
A Child Dead Born	April 12			of Hannah Allen		Buryed 13th. April 1796	
Allen Betsey Child	Augt. 3d.		1		Whole board	Bound out Mr. Thacher of Cambreage	
Adams Sarah	Octor. 10th.		1	with Child by John Green }	Arnold Welles	Dischd. 9th. April 1799	
Anderson Thos.	Do. 19	<1>	1	Ireland	Wm. Philips junr.	Died 30th. Janry. 1798	40 years
Avis <Saml.> John	Do. 22		1		Jona. L. Austin	Died 18 May 18[29?]	
Anderson Sukey	Do. 28		1	Marblehead	Redford Webster	sent to the W. house 4th. Novr. 1796	
Armstrong James	Novr. 12		1		William Smith	Dischd. 24th. Augt. 1797 to Work house	

¹ On some of the MS pages this column is titled "Where born."
² Marked for entry at this point is the interlineation "Absent a few days Remitted."

Names	Time of Admission	State	Town	Towns they belong to[1]	By what Overseer	When dischd., Died, Bound out, Run away.	Time they have been here in this State
Anderson James	Do. 29	1		African	Redford Webster	Dischd. 30th. Septr. Do.	
Anderson Josph. Child	Decr. 22	<1>	1	Ireland	Jona. L. Austin	Bound Out 27th. Octor. Do.	not alowed to [....][3]
Do. Sally Child	Do.	<1>	1	Do.	Do.	Bound Out 28th. Octor. 1801	State Do.
Allen James	1797 Febry. 13	1		Philada.	Edward Proctor	Dischd. 12th. April 1797	
Adams Richd.	March 11	1		West Indias	Redford Webster	Dischd. 1st. June Do.	
Adams Richd.	Octor. 27	1		Do.	William Smith	Died 29th. Octor. Do.	
Adams John	Do. 28		1	Boston	Do.	Died 7th. Janry. 1801	
Armstrong James	Do.		1	Do.	Do.	Dischd. 9th. May 1798	
Anderson Wm.	1798 Janry. 4th.	1		Ireland	Henry Hill	Dischd. 10th. Janry. 1798	14 years
Do.	May 4th.	1		Do.	Do.	Dischd. 21st. May Do.	Do.
Allin John	Octor. 22	1		Do.	Edward Procter	Died 6th. Janry. 1799	25 years
Adams Mary	Decr. 18		1	Boston	John Sweetser	Died 15th. Novr. 1800	age 64 years
Armstrong James	1799 May 31st.		1	Do.	Arnold Welles junr.	Dischd. 26th. July 1799	
Amnett Jacob	June 14	1		New York	Wm. Smith	Dischd. 18th. April 1800	4 years
Adams Daniel	Do. 24		1	Boston	Do.	Dischd. 6th. Novr. 1799	
Ayre Sophia	July 1st.	1		Wellfleet	Jona. L. Austin	Dischd. 4th. Augt. 1799	[Eary?]
Adams Hugh	Do. 17	1		Ireland	John Vinall	Dischd. 19th. July 1799	5 years
Anderson Wm.	Augt. 26	1		Do.	Henry Hill	Dischd. 18th. Novr. Do.	15 years

[3] The edge of the page is torn away.

Names	Time of Admission	State	Town	Towns they belong to[1]	By what Overseer	When dischd., Died, Bound out, Run away.	Time they have been here in this State
Allen Sarah	Septr. 4		1	Marblehead	Jona. L. Austin	Dischd. 11th. Octor. 1799	10 weeks
A[ubur]y Thos. & Mary his Wife	1800 Janry. 3d.	1		Virginia	Stephen Gorham	Dischd. 18th. June 1800	7 years
	Do.	1		Do. <*Marble Head*>	Do.	Dischd. Do. Do.	Do.
Adams Scipio Negro	Feby. 3d.		1	Boston	Jona. L. Austin	Dischd. 7th. Feby. 1800	
[D]o.[4] Amy Child	Do.		1	Do.	Do.	Do.	
[D]o. James Do.	Do.		1	Do.	Do.	Do.	
Cornelus Ary	March 12th.	1		England	Henry Hill	Dischd. 31st. March 1800	7 Days
Ammell Jacob	April 30	1		New York	Redford Webser	Dischd. 5th. May Do.	4 years
Adams Scipio, Negro	May 12		1	Boston	Jona. L. Austin	Dischd. 10th. June Do.	
Airey Betsy, (Child)	July 7th.		1	Do.	Do.	Dischd. 19th. July Do.	age 7 years
Armstrong William	Do. 24th.	1		Ireland	Henry Hill	Dischd. 23d. Augt. Do.	one year
Abraham Thomas	Do.	1		England	Redford Webster	Dischd. Do. Do.	8 Days
Allen Jenny	augt. 5	1		Philada.	Shearja. Bourne	R. away 12th. augt. Do.	1 year
Allen Polly	Do.		1	<*Salem*> Portsmouth	Do.	Do. Do.	
Allen Polly	Do. 22d.		1	Do.	Do.	R. away 31st. Augt. Do.	1year
Adams Daniel	Novr. 14		1	Boston	John Sweetser	Died 15 July 1802	
Anderson William	Do. 13	1		Ireland	Henry Hill	Dischd. 29th. April 1801	16 years
Allen Polly	Decr. 30		1	<*Salem*> Portsmouth	Shearja. Bourne	Dischd. 10th. Janry. 1801	1 year
Burns Robert (child)			Do.			Dischd: 14th. Augt. 1795	
Blackston Eliza				Portland		Run away 31st. Do.	21 Weeks 3 Days

[4] In this and the following entry the edge of the manuscript is torn.

Names	Time of Admission	State	Town	Towns they belong to[1]	By what Overseer	When dischd., Died, Bound out, Run away.	Time they have been here in this State
Brown Eliza	1795 Augt. 15th.		Do. 1		Oliver Brewster	Run away 20th. Novr. Do.	
Buckley Mary	Do. 18th.		Do. 1		Henry Hill	Died Sept 23d. 1807	
Berry Hannah	Do.		Do. 1		Stephen Gorham	Dischd. 30th. June 1796	
Beacham Edward	Do. 19th.	1		England	Do.	Dischd. 16th. Octor. 1795	age 80 years
Blake John & Wife Ann	Do. 24th.		Do. 2		Henry Hill	he Died 9th. March 1800 she Dischd. 28th. April Do.	
Blackburn Jacob	Do. 27th.	Do. 1		England	Edward Proctor	Died 23d. Octor. 1796	8 Weeks, 1 Day
Do. Wife & Son	Do.	Do. 2		Nova Scotia	Do.	Dischd. 24th. March 1797	
Brown John	Do. 25th.		Do. 1	Boston	Redford Webster	Died 5th. Septr. Do. 1795[5]	5 Days
Blackston Eliza	Septr. 5th.			Portland	Edward Proctor	Dischd. 10th. Do.	
Ballard Mary			Do.			Bound Out 6th. Augt. Do.	
Bell Hannah		Do.		Ireland		Died 26th. Septr. Do.	16 Weeks. 6 Days
Benjamin Daniel			Do.			Died 6th. Octor. Do.	
Barns Lucy	Octor. 8			from the Work house Born in Lynn		Run away 12th. Do.	4 Days
Brison Abraham	Do. 14		1		Stephen Gorham	Dischd. 22d. Do.	
Beacham Edward	Do. 17	1		England	Do.	Dischd. 5th. July 1796	
Bartlet Else	Do. 20	1		Scotland	Redford Webster	Died 27th. Decr. 1795	5 Do. [weeks] 6 Do. [days]
Bangs Joseph	Do. 31	1		Holland	Wm. Smith	Dischd. 7th. March 1796	
Brown Mary	Novr. 4th.		1		Whole Board	Died 23d. Septr. Do.	

[5] The year was interlined above "Do."

Names	Time of Admission	State	Town	Towns they belong to[1]	By what Overseer	When dischd., Died, Bound out, Run away.	Time they have been here in this State
Brown Robert	Do. 14	1		Ierland	Edward Procter	Died 30th. Janry. 1796	
Batts Rachel	Decr. 1st.	1		Fort cumberland	Do.	Dischd. 28th. July 1797	
Bass William			D			Dischd. 10th. Decr. 1795	
Brown John	Do. 22d.	1		England	Stephen Gorham	Dischd. 24th. March 1796	
Bass William	Do. 31	1		Boston	Ed. Procter	Sent to the Workhouse 24th. Augt. 1797	
Baker Mary	1796 March 11	1		Do.	John Codman	Dischd. 14th. Septr. Do.	
Bullian John	Do. 21	1		Ireland	Edward Proctor	Died 21st. April 1796	
Baker Rebecca	Do. 11	1		(child)	Stephen Gorham	Dischd. 14th. Septr. Do.	
Baker Charles	April 9	1		(child)	Jona. L. Austin	Dischd. 14th. Do. Do.	
Baily Polly	Do. 21	1		Isleshoals	Redford Webster	Run away 1st. May Do.	
Billings Joseph	March 15		1		Stephen Gorham	Died 10th. June Do.	
Bradlee Nabby	June 7	1		Rhode Island	Jona. L. Austin	Died 11th. March 1818	one Week
Bradlee Betsey a Child	Do.	1		Do.		Bound Out 26 June 1799	Do.
Bass Mary	June 29		1		Edward Proctor	Died 10th. Decr. Do.	
Bates Gamaliel	July 9		1	born of Hannah Holland		Dischd. 27th. Augt. Do.	
Bradlee John (child)	Do. 13	1		born of Nabby Bradlee		Died 21st. Augt. 1797	
Bager Dublin	July 25	1		Negro	Redford Webster	Died 27th. July 1796	
Dos. Wife	Do.	1		Do.	Do.	Discharged & 2 Children	
Do. Children	Do.	4		Do.	Do.	Boy Dublin bound out Augt. 12th. 1796 Rose bound out 7th. Septr. Do.	

Names	Time of Admission	State	Town	Towns they belong to[1]	By what Overseer	When dischd., Died, Bound out, Run away.	Time they have been here in this State
Bank Joseph	Augt. 14th.	1		German	Redford Webster	Dischd. 29th. Augt. 1796	
Bates Gamaliel a Child	Do. 27		1	(born of Hannah Holland)		Died 12th. Septr. Do.	
Beacham Edward	Septr. 18	1		England		Died 12th. Febry. 1797	
Bury or Bovey Elizabeth	Do. 24		1		Edward Proctor	Dischd. 12th. Septr. Do.	
Bradford Edward	Octor. 2d.	1		Virginia	John Sweetser	Died 3d. Octor. 1796	
Badcock Nancy B[lack] Woman	Do. 22		1		Jona. L. Austin	Died 6th. Novr. Do.	
Berry Elizabeth	Novr. 2d.	1		Quebec	Whole board	Dischd. Febry. 7th. 1797	
Barker Caleb	Do. 7		1	Haverill	Stephen Goram	Dischd. (Do. Do.)	
Bowen Jane	Do. 14		1		Henry Hill	R. away 10th. May Do.	
Buffett Mary	Do. 15		1		Stephn. Gorham	Dischd. 18th. April 1797	
Bullman Sarah	Do. 19		1		Edward Proctor	Dischd. 7th. July 1798	
Brimal Eliza	Do. 18		1	Plymouth	Do.	Dischd. 24th. Novr. Do.	
Burni Sarah Wife of Wm. Burnix	Do. 27 }	1	1	Ireland	Stephen Gorham	Run away in May Do.	
Battle Dinah Negro Do. Child	Decr. 3d. Do.	1 / 1		West India	{Wm. Smith	Dischd. 30th. Novr. 1797	
Black Man	Do.	1		China	Stephen Gorham	Dischd. 1st. Janry. 1797	
Ball Peter a Child	Do. 11th.		1	Born of Elcy Holden, His Father gone to Petersburgh with Captn. Fairchild		Dischd. 13th Febry. 1797	
Bell Mrs. Sarah & her 2 Children	17 Decr. Do.	1} 2}		Plymouth	Oliver Brewster	Dischd. 26th. June 1798 & Daugr. & Frances her Child Boy Dischd. 28th. April Do.	

Names	Time of Admission	State	Town	Towns they belong to[1]	By what Overseer	When dischd., Died, Bound out, Run away.	Time they have been here in this State
Brown John	Do. 22d.	1		Ireland	Do.	Dischd. 30th. Decr. 1796	
Bean Cotton	Do. 24		1		Wm. Smith	Dischd. 3d. Janry. 1797	
Bell William	Do. 25	1		England	Do.	Dischd. 18th. Augt. Do.	
Brown Sarah	Do. 24		1	Marblehead	Edward Proctor	Died 29th. July 1799.	{age 86 years {45 years
Blackstone Betsey	1797 Janry. 2d.		1	Portland	Oliver Brewster	Dischd. 2d. Febry. 1797	
Bayley Mary	Do. 4	1		Isle Shoals	Thos. Perkins	Dischd. 10th. June Do.	R. away
Bass William	Do.		1		Do.	Dischd. 24 Augt. Do.	to W: house
Brown Sarah	14		1	B[*lack*] Woman	Wm. Phillips jr.	Dischd. 24 Novr. Do.	
Brimal Eliza	Febry. 13		1	Plymouth	Wm. Smith	Dischd. 20th. Febry. Do.	
Bowman or Bowen Jacob	March 29	1		England	Stephen Gorham	Dischd. 2d. Novr. Do.	14 years
Blackstone Eliza	April 12th.		1	Portland	Wm. Smith	Dischd. 21st. April Do.	
Brick Joseph	Do. 13		1	Boston	Edward Proctor	Dischd. 25th. Do.	
Brown Samuel	Do. 17		1	Do.	Do.	Dischd. 24th. Augt. 1797	Sent W House
Beverly William	Do. 24	1		London	Redford Webster	Dischd. 22d. May 1797	1 day
Batts Susanna, a child	May 4		1	Boston	Edward Proctor	Dischd. 8th. June Do.	
Brick Joseph	Do. 12		1	Do.	Oliver Brewster	Dischd. 12th. Do. Do.	
Brown Sarah	June 1st.	1		New Hamshire	Do.	Dischd. 6th. June 1797	
Brown Sarah Born of Do.	Do.	1				Died 4th. June 1797	
Brison Anne	Do. 8	1		West Indias	Henry Hill	Dischd. 28th. Do. Do.	

Names	Time of Admission	State	Town	Towns they belong to[1]	By what Overseer	When dischd., Died, Bound out, Run away.	Time they have been here in this State
Baily Mary	June 12	1		Isle Shoals	Redford Webster	Dischd. 24 Augt. Do.	sent W. H—
Boylston Jenny, Neg[r]o	Do. 17		1	Boston	Wm. Smith	Dischd. 22d. Novr. 1799	
Blackman John Child	June 24		1	Boston	Henry Hill	Dischd. June 1798	
Bolton Elizabeth	July 6		1	Do.	John Sweetser	Dischd. 4th. Septr. 1798	
Burrill David	Do. 10		1	Do.	Stephen Gorham	Dischd. 19 July 1797	
Briseau Ama	Do. 11	1		West India	John Sweetser	Dischd. 31 July Do.	
Blackstone Elizth. alias Lucy Day	Do. 18		1	Portland or Freeport	Wm. Smith	Dischd. 29th. Augt. Do. Freeport	Lucy Day of
Bates Rachel	Augt. 7	1	<1> 0	<Boston> Fort Cumberland	Henry Hill	Died 22d. Augt. 1798	22 years
Breedy a Child Born of Esther Cordis. Negro	8	1		West Indias	William Smith	Dischd. 21st. Augt. 1797	
Brown Lucy	Do. 15	<1> 0	1	Brookline or New Town	Do.	Dischd. 9th. Octor. Do.	Run away
Burrill David	Septr. 9		1	Lynn	Edward Proctor	Dischd. 19th. Septr. 1797	35 years in Bosn.
Brown Robert	Do. 14		1	Ireland	Thos. Perkins	Dischd. 30th. March 1798	about 4 years
Buckley Elizth.	Do. 23		1	Boston	Henry Hill	Died 20th. Septr. 1802	age 62 year
Do. Saml. a Child	Do.		1	Hallowell	Do.	Run away 20 Octor. 1797	
Banks James	Do. 25		1	Penobscot	Jona. L Austin	Dischd. 18th. Octor. 1797	
Buffett Mrs. Mary	Octor. 3d.		1	Boston	Stephen Gorham	Dischd. 2d. Decr. Do.	
Benall Thos. a Child	Do. 20		1	his mother born in Liverpool	Oliver Brewster	Bound out 22d. June 1799	3 years his father 4 years
Brick Joseph	Do. 26		1	Boston	Wm. Smith	Dischd. 27th. Octor. 1797	

Names	Time of Admission	State	Town	Towns they belong to[1]	By what Overseer	When dischd., Died, Bound out, Run away.	Time they have been here in this State
Bass William	Do. 27		1	Do.	Edward Proctor	Died 10th. July 1800	
Brown Samuel	Do. 28		1	Do.	William Smith	Discharged 6th. Mar 1807	
Baily Mary	Do.	1		Isle Shoals	Do.	Died 7th. June 1801	<14> 17 years
Borse Michael	Novr. 15	1		Malta	Oliver Brewster	Run away 1st. Febry. 1798	3 Days in Italy
Breland John	Do. 16	1		Holland	Stephen Gorham	Dischd. 12 Do.	4 months
Butler Andrew a deaf & Dumb men	Do. 20		1	Martha's Vineyard	Arnold Welles	Dischd. 9th. April Do.	
[..]6							
Blackburn John a Child	28 <1> 0		1	Boston	Oliver Brewster	Dischd. 8th. Febry. 1798	
Brick Joseph	Decr. 18		1	Boston	Edward Procter	Dischd. 12th. July 1799	
Brown Ann & her Child	Do. 19 Do.	1 1		Boston Do.	Do. Do.	Dischd. 9th. March 1798 Do.	
Brewer Daniel, born Novr. 23d. of Nancy Cross					his father	Bound Out 9th. March 1803	Daniel Brewer
Ballard John	Decr. 30		1	Boston	Edward Procter	Dischd. 24th. July 1798	
Barnes Lucy	1798 Janry. 23d.	1		at Sea	Wm. Phillips jur.	her father born in Scotland, mother in England died 23d. May 1798	
Brown John	Febry. 1st.		1	Boston	Stephen Gorham	Dischd. 13 Febry. 1798	been in this State 4 years age 24
Bolton Betsey child		1		Do.	(Dischd. 4th. Septr. 98)	Born 24th. Janry. 1798 of Betsey Bolton	
Brown John	Febry. 15	1		Do.	Arnold Welles	Dischd. 13th. March Do.	
Ball Peter a Child	March 17th.	1		Do.	Stephen Gorham	Died 17th. Augt. 1798	
Brown John	Do. 24	1		Do.	Redford Webster	Dischd. 28th. March 1798	

6 An entire entry has been effaced.

Names	Time of Admission	State	Town	Towns they belong to[1]	By what Overseer	When dischd., Died, Bound out, Run away.	Time they have been here in this State
Burns Mary	28	1		Ireland	Edward Edes	Sent to the W. house 30th. Do.	1 year
Brackett Arthur	April 27	1		Africa	Thos. Perkins	Died 16th. May 1798	25 years
Baptiste Paul	May 21st.	1		Havanah	Do.	Dischd. 4th. June Do.	3 Weeks
Breedy Elanor	June 20	1		Ireland	Oliver Brewster	Dischd. 27th. Do.	one year
Blake Rosenna a Negro	July 4th.		1	Hingham	Thomas Perkins	Died 6th. July 1798	
Blanch John	Augt. 6	1		England	Redford Webster	Dischd. 31st. July 1799	2 Months
Bolton Elizabeth	Septr. 4		1	<Boston> Bridgwater		Dischd. 7th. Septr. Do.	
Bolton Betsey her Child	Do.		1	Do.		Dischd. Do.	
Benjamin Mary jur.	Do.		1	Do.	Whole board	Died 13d. Augt. 1802	
Berry John Sailor	Octor. 4th.	1		New York	Stephen Gorham	Died 11th. Octor. 1798	5 years
Brown James	Do. 10	1		Ireland	Oliver Brewster	Dischd. 30th. May 1799	21 years
Brown John	Do. 31	1		England	William Smith	Dischd. 6th. April 1799	7 years
Buckley Horace	Do.	1		Connecticut	Do.	Dischd. 5th. Novr. 1798	2 Weeks
Blair Daniel	Novr. 3	1		England	Oliver Brewster	Dischd. 15 Decr. Do.	2 years
Brown Thos. Filley a Child	Novr. 1		1	Boston	Thos. Perkins	Bound out 8th. Do. Do.	10 Weeks
Boodh Godlip John	Do. 9	1		Germany	Jona. L. Austin	Dischd. 22d. June 1799	10 Weeks
Ballard John	Do. 20		1	Boston	Edward Edes	Dischd. 2d. July 1799	
Baubeun Francis	Do. 29	1		Germany	Do.	Dischd. 31st. Decr. 1798	6 Weeks
Brooks Elizabeth	Decr. 1st.	1		New York	Henry Hill	Dischd. 6th. Novr. 1799	2 Months
<Barswell Marther	Do. 6	1		Andover	Edward Edes>	Rong Enter'd[7]	

[7] Above the surname the clerk interlined and then canceled the name "Carswell."

Names	Time of Admission	State	Town	Towns they belong to[1]	By what Overseer	When dischd., Died, Bound out, Run away.	Time they have been here in this State
Brown John	Do. 11		1	Boston	Oliver Brewster	Dischd. 12th. Decr. 1798	
Bill Nathl. and his Wife & 2 Children	1799 Janry. 3d. Do.		1 / 3	Dedham Do.	Edward Proctor Do.	Dischd. 15th. Janry. 1799 Do.	
Boyer Abraham	Febry. 5		1	Boston	William Smith	Dischd. 22d. July Do.	
Barret John	Do. 4		1	Do.	whole board	Died 12th. Augt. 1800	
<Bennison Betsey>	Do.		1	Do.	Do.	Error her Name is Warden	
Buffott Mary	Do. 18		1	Do.	Wm. Smith	Dischd. 9th. May 99	
Benjamin Nancy	March 16	1		England	Arnold Welles jur.	Dischd. 23d. March 1799	R. Prentice 4 months
Hannah Bodge	April 3		1	Quincy	Henry Hill	Dischd. 6th. May Do.	
Baker Quarco, Negro	March 30		1	Boston	Jona. L. Austin	Died 16th. April 1799	age 36 years
Bowen William	April 16	1		New York	Stephen Gorham	Dischd. 23d. April Do.	2 Days
Bugby Susanna	May 6		1	Boston	William Phillips jur.	Dischd. 5th. Decr. Do.	
Benjamin Nancy	Do. 7	1		England	Redford Webster	Dischd. 3d. Septr. 1799	R. Prentice 4 months
Bridge Charity	Do. 30		1	Boston	Do.	Dischd. 9th. augt. 99	
Brown John	June 11		1	Do.	William Phillips jur.	Died 9th. Octor. Do.	
Brison Amy	July 3d.	1		Gaudeloup	Edward Edes	Dischd. 29th. July 1799	4 years
Benjamin Joseph Chl[il]d	Augt. 6	1		England	born of Nancy Benjn.	Dischd. 3d. Septr. Do.	
Bufford Mary	Do. 24		1	Boston	Edward Procter	Dischd. 12th. June 1800	
Burns Mary	Septr. 1		1	Do.	Arnold Welles jur.	R. away 28th. Do. Do.	

Names	Time of Admission	State	Town	Towns they belong to[1]	By what Overseer	When dischd., Died, Bound out, Run away.	Time they have been here in this State
Belknap Mary child	Do. 7		1	Boston	Jona. L. Austin	Bound out 26th. April 1800	{Her mother {born in Salem
Borge Hannah	Do. 24		1	Quincy	Henry Hill	Dischd. 14th. Octor. 99	<2 months>
<Bener> Bean John	Do. 25	1		Germany	Redford Webster	Dischd. 14th. Octor. 99	two Weeks
7 Black men Lascars	Octor. 15	7		East Indies	Edward Procter	3 Dischd. 25 Decr. Do.	2 months
Brown John	Do. 22	1		England	Do.	Died 10th. Janry. 1800	8 years
Brimhall Elizth.	Novr. 7		1	Plymouth	Redford Webster	12th. Decr. Dischd. 1799	2 months
Bouditch Nathl.	Do. 12	1		Connecticut	Jona. L. Austin	Died 20th. Novr. 1799	3 months
[Bu]ckley[8] William	Do. 14	1		Ireland	Henry Hill	Dischd. 7th. April 1800	one Day
[. . .] Brown	Do. 18	1		Cambridge	Redford Webster	Dischd. 19th. Novr. 1799	
Ballard John	Decr. 4	1		Boston	Stephen Gorham	Dischd. 23d. May 1804	
Brick Joseph	Do. 26	1		Do.	Redford Webster	Run away about 10th. Janry. 1800	
<Smith Betsey	1800 Janry. 7th.	1		Do.	Edward Procter>	Rong Entered	
Breck Joseph	Do. 29	1		Do.	Edward Edes	Run 27th. Feby. 1800 away	
Banks Lillister	Febry. 9	1		North Carolina	William Smith	Dischd. 12th. March Do.	4 years—age 17 years
Brimhall Elizath.	Do. 13th.		1	Plymouth	Redford Webster	Dischd. 3d. March 1800	
Brimmer Nancy	Do. 14	1		Boston	William Smith	Dischd. 27th. Febry. Do.	
Bean Joseph	Do. 16	1		New Hampshire	Stephen Gorham	Died 18th. Do. Do.	one day
Black David	March 6	1		Scotland	Oliver Brewster	Dischd. 17th. Octor. Do.	
Brick Sally child	Do. 24		1	born of Elcy Holden		Born 24th. March Do. her father Edwd. Brick Dischd. 30th. July 1800	

8 The bottom left corner of the page is torn, resulting in the loss of several letters in this and the following entry.

Names	Time of Admission	State	Town	Towns they belong to[1]	By what Overseer	When dischd., Died, Bound out, Run away.	Time they have been here in this State
Edward Beison	April 20	1		England	Jona. L. Austin	Died 3d. July 1800	two years
Briseau Amy	May 19	1		West Indies	Stephen Gorham	Dischd. 29th. May Do.	6 years
Butler Henry	June 17	1		Baltimore	Do.	Dischd. 15th. July Do.	two days
Bufford Mary	July 2d.		1	Boston	William Smith	Dischd. 24th. Do.	
Brown Sukey	Augt. 5th.		1	Glocester	Shearja. Bourne	Dischd. 20th. Augt. Do.	
Briseau Amy	Do. 17	1		West Indies	William Phillips jur.	Dischd. 17th. Octor. Do.	4 years
Barnes Peggy	Do. 23d.		1	Roxbury	Shearja. Bourne	R. away 31st. augt. Do.	
Barber James	Do. 25		1	Boston	Henry Hill	Died 31st. Augt. 1800	
Blackburn Mary	Sepr. 6	1		England	Shearja. Bourne	R. away 27 Sepr. Do.	
Beverly William	Do. 9th.	1		Delaware	Oliver Brewster	Dischd. 16th. Septr. Do.	one Week
Bird Mary	Do.		1	Dorchester	Henry Hill	Bound out 27th. Do.	
Barker Caleb	Octor. 2d.	1		England	Jona. L. Austin	Dischd. 27th. Octor. Do.	2 Months
Battes John, negro	Do. 8	1		West Indies	Edward Edes	R. away 14th. Octor. Do.	1 1/2 Do.
Do.	17	1		Do.	Do.	Dischd. 2d. Novr. Do.	
Brewer Betsey	Do. 23		1	Boston	Henry Hill	Dischd. 17th. Febry. 1801	
Buckley William	Novr. 1st.	1		Ireland	Edward Edes	Died 26 Decr. Do.	one year 1800
Bess Rose Negor	Do. 4		1	Boston	Jona. L. Austin	Died 18th. Janry. 1801	age 60 years
Barnes Peggy	Do. 17		1	Roxbury	Shearja. Bourne	Dischd. 3d. Decr. 1800 by order S. Bourne	
Brick Joseph	Decr. 20 1795		1	Boston	Redford Webster	Dischd. 28th. Febry.	Run away 1801

Names	Time of Admission	State	Town	Towns they belong to[1]	By what Overseer	When dischd., Died, Bound out, Run away.	Time they have been here in this State
	1975						
Curtis William	Augt. 22d.		Do. 1		Redford Webster	Run away 20th. Septr. 1795	
Cowell Sarah	Septr. 4th.		Do. 1		John Sweetser	Died 17 Sepr. 1805	
<Chandlner> Chaloner Nancy	Do. 10th.		Do. 1		Edward Proctor	Died 14th. Octor. 1795	
Curtis William	Do. 24		1		William Smith	Died 20th. Decr. "	
Connor John	Do. 28	1		Ireland	Stephen Gorham	Dischd. 13th. Octor. "	2 Weeks 1 Day
Cox Ebenezer	Do. 29		1	Boston	Do.	Dischd. 2d: Octor. "	
Counts William	Octor. 17		1		Edward Edes	Died 23d. Do. "	
Curtis Charles	Do. 24	1			John Sweetser	Run away 7th. Novr. "	2 Weeks
Crage Elizabeth	Novr. 17	1		Holland	Edward Proctor	Dischd. 21st Decr. "	3 Do.
Crowley Michell	Do. 23		1		Do.	Died 24th. June 1794	
Chase Catharine	Do. 26		1		Henry Hill	Dischd. 20 July 1797	
	1796						
Clough Martha	May 21		1		Edward Proctor	Died 10th. Octor. 1796	
Cushing Hannah	June 28		1		Do.	Died 19th. Novr. 1797	
Circomle Ceasor	July 4	1		His mother a Sqaw	Stephen Gorham	Died 18th. July 1796	
Crafts Rachel	Do. 7	<1>	1	Connecticut	Redford Webster	Died 21st. Augt. 1797	lived in this State 10 years
Kelley Patrick	Augt. 8	1		Ireland	Stephen Gorham	Run away 22d. Augt. 1796	
Cox Ebenezer	Septr. 10		1	Boston	Wm. Philips junr.	Dischd. 20th. June 1797	
Corbin Nathl.	Do. 28		1		Edward Proctor	Died 21st. Febry. 1803	

Names	Time of Admission	State	Town	Towns they belong to[1]	By what Overseer	When dischd., Died, Bound out, Run away.	Time they have been here in this State
Cale Jacob	Octor. 12	1		N. Carolina	Edward Edes	Bound out 10th. April 1797	4 months
Crosby Anna	Novr. 3		1		Wm. Smith	Dischd. 8th. Novr. Do.	
Cook Betty	Do. 15	1		Newhampshire	Do.	Dischd. 20th. Octor. 1798	
Collins Mary	Do. 21		1		Redford Webster	Died 6th. Decr. 1797	
Combe Hannah	1797 Janry. 11	1		Foreigner	Stephen Gorham	Run away in May Do.	
Curtis Charlotte	Febry. 21st.	child			Jona. L. Austin	Bound Out Mar 19th. 1804	5 months old
Carter George	27	1		England	Do.	Dischd. 11th. March 1797	
Covell Saml.	April 11	1		Chatham	Edward Proctor	Discharged 2d. July 1807	
Elizabeth Do. Wife	Do.		1	Boston	Do.	Do. 2d. July 1807	
Clark Henry Peterson a Child	Do.	1		Do.	Do.	Bound out 18th. April 1797	
Chace Nabby	Do. 15	1		Newport	Wm. Smith	Dischd. 22d. April Do.	
Cunningham Peggy	Do. 18	1		Boston	Jona. L Austin	Dischd. 24 Augt. Do.	Sent Workhouse
Curlin Peter	June 7		1	Ireland	Stephen Gorham	Dischd. 20th. April 1798	one month Sailor
Cain Sukey	Do. 14	1		Salem	Redford Webster	Run away 20th. June 1797	
Conner John	July 4		1	Ireland	William Smith	Dischd. 18th. July 1797	one year
Conden Peggy	Do. 12	1		Nantucket	Henry Hill	Run away 15 Septr. Do.	
Cunington Wm.	Do. 30		1	London	Stephen Gorham	Dischd. 5th. Octor. Do.	
Combs Mary	Augt. 9th.	1		London	Edward Proctor	Dischd. 12 Febry. 1798	9 months
Cross Nancy	12		1	Boston	Thomas Perkins	Dischd. 12th. April 1803	
Church John Negro	22	1		Do.	Oliver Brewster	Died 18th. Decr. 1797	

Names	Time of Admission	State	Town	Towns they belong to[1]	By what Overseer	When dischd., Died, Bound out, Run away.	Time they have been here in this State
Corn Elizabeth	Septr. 6	1		Ireland	Redford Webster	Dischd. 20th. April 1798	2 years
Cowell Joseph	Septr. 7		1	Boston	Arnold Welles	Dischd. 19th. Septr. 1797	
Chipman Charles a Child	Octor. 4		1	Do.	Stephen Gorham	Bound out May 5th. 1802	
Croswell Nathaniel	Do. 7		1	Do.	Redford Webster	Dischd. 30th. March 1798	
Cooper John (Sailor)	Do. 14	1		Virginia	J L Austin	Dischd. 3d. Febry. 1798 (R[un])	8 years
Cunningham Peggy & Child	Do. 28		2	Boston	William Smth	Bound Out 6th Decr. Do. Peggy C Died 1 June 1811	child bound to Jno: McKenzie
Cox Ebenezer	Novr. 16		1	Do.	Stephen Gorham	Dischd. 6th. April 1798	
Courrier Abigail	Do. 20	1		New Hampshire	Arnold Welles jur.	Dischd. 1st Febry. 1798	3 months
Jona. Chapman	Decr. 7		1	Boston	Stephen Gorham	Dischd. 18th. June Do.	
Crane Ruth	1798 Janry. 2d.	1		Dorchester or Quincy	Henry Hill	Dischd. 9th. Febry. 1798	
Crawley John	Do. 6th.	1		England	Edward Edes	Dischd. 8th. Febry. 1798	18 months
Courrier Abigail	Febry. 2	1		N Hampshire	Thos. Perkins	Dischd. 12 Do.	3 months
Crossan Nancy	Do. 18	1		Connecticut	Stephen Gorham	Dischd. 5th. March Do.	one Week
Sarah Covell	March 20		1	Boston	born of Elizath. Covell	Died 5th. Febry. 1801	
Collins Judith	Do. 28	1		Ireland	Arnold Welles jur.	Dischd. 18th. Octor. 98	9 month
Coaster James	April 2d.	1		Germany	Do.	Dischd. 17th. Octor. 1798	3 Weeks
Croswell Nathl.	Do. 6		1	Boston	Redford Webster	Dischd. 28th. June 1798	
Cowen Elizabeth	Do. 19	1		Philada.	Wm. Phillips jur.	Bound Out 28th. May 1798	6 years
Collins Mary Born	Do. 29	1		of Judith Collins		Died 7th. Octor. 1798	

Names	Time of Admission	State	Town	Towns they belong to[1]	By what Overseer	When dischd., Died, Bound out, Run away.	Time they have been here in this State
Cunningham Johanna	March 15		1	Boston	Redford Webster	Dischd. 19th. May 98	
Cooper John (Sailor)	May 7	1		Virginia	Do.	Died 7th. Augt. Do.	10 Weeks, age 24 years
Cox Ebenezer	July 25		1	Boston	Oliver Brewster	Dischd. 6th. Do. Do.	
Crosswell Nathl.	Augt. 2d.		1	Do.	Redford Webster	Died 5th. Augt. 1798	
Cunningham Johannah	Octor. 19		1	Do.	Edward Procter	Died 28th. May 1799	
James Coaster	Do. 26	1		Germany	Oliver Brewster	Dischd. 6th. April 1799	3 Weeks
Curtis Charles	Novr. 24	1		Ireland	Edward Procter	Died 5th. March 1799	3 years
Corn Elizabeth	Decr. 13	1		Do.	Stephen Gorham	Dischd. 22d. April R[un] W[ay] Do.	2 years
Champlain Thomas	1799 Janry. 1st.	1		England	Oliver Brewster	Dischd. 2d. April 1799	3 months
Cowell Polly	Do. 2d.		1	Boston	Stephen Gorham	Dischd. 24th. Do. Do.	
Cornwall Robert & Sarah his Wife	Do. 4 Do.	1 1		Do. Hull	Henry Hill Do.	Dischd. 16th. April 1799 Dischd. Do.	
Nancy their Daughter	Do.		1	Boston	Do.	Dischd. 22d. Febry. 1799	
Deliverance Do.	Do.	1		Do.	Do.	Dischd. 16th. April Do.	
Robt. their Son	Do.	1		Do.	Do.	Dischd. Do.	
David Do.	Do.	1		Do.	Do.	Dischd. Do.	
Carswell Margaret	Decr. 7	1		Andover	Edward Edes	Died 19th. Janry. 1801	
Castle Betsey	Febry. 4	1		Boston	Whole Board	R away 10th. Septr. Do.	
Cane Sukey	Do.	1		Do.	Do.	R. away 28th. March 1799	
Cross Thomas	Do.	1		Do.	Do.	Died 26th. Octor. 1807	

Names	Time of Admission	State	Town	Towns they belong to[1]	By what Overseer	When dischd., Died, Bound out, Run away.	Time they have been here in this State
Cleverly Samuel	Do.		1	Do.	Do.	Died 2d. July 1799	
Cox Ebenezer	Do.		1	Do.	Do.	Dischd. 28th. May Do.	
Cox Grace	Do.		1	Do.	Do.	Run away 28th. May Do.	
Courrier Abigail	Do.	1	<1> 0	N Hampshire	Do.	Dischd. 16th. Febry. 1799	Run away
Crossan Nancy Indian	Do.	1		Connecticut	Do.	Do.	Do.
Coocks Thomas	March 15		1	Belfast	Thomas Perkins	Died 7th. April 1799	County of Hancock
Chapman Jona.	April 20		1	Boston	Stephen Gorham	Died 29 Sept 1812	
Cornish Elizath.	May 4th.		1	Do.	Oliver Brewster	Dischd. 12th. May 1801	
Cox Grace	July 5		1	Do.	Arnold Welles	Dischd. Octor. 13th. 1802	
Condon Jenny Negro	Do. 8	1		Rhode Island	John Vinall	Dischd. 2d. Novr. 1799	11 years
Cheeseman Elizath.	Do. 12		1	Lynn	Edward Procter	Run away 15th. July 99	
Cox Ebenezer	Augt. 7		1	Boston	Whole board	Died 25th. Augt. Do.	by a fall
Clark John	Do. 13	1	<D>	England	Edward Edes	Died 10th. Janry. 1800	16 years
Corn Elizabeth	Do. 26	1		Ireland	Oliver Brewster	Died 13th. Septr. 1799	2 years
Condon Janny Negr.	Novr. 5	1		Rhode Island	John Vinall	Out Feb. 8, 1822	11 years, aged 52 yrs in 1820
Cowell Polly	Do. 7		1	Boston	Oliver Brewster	Dischd. 27th. Novr. 1799	
Cook Sophia, Negro	Do. 22d.		1	Boston	William Smith	Dischd. 3d. Janry. 1800	
Carter George	Do. 30	1	<1> 0	England	Henry Hill	Dischd. 21st. April Do.	
Conant Flora Negro	Decr. 4	1		Africa	John Sweetser	Died 23d. July Do.	37 years

Names	Time of Admission	State	Town	Towns they belong to[1]	By what Overseer	When dischd., Died, Bound out, Run away.	Time they have been here in this State
Capen Mary	Do. 13	1		Ireland	Redford Webster	Disch 15th. Decr. 1799	3 years
Chase Catharine	1800 Janry. 10		1	Germany	Henry Hill	Died 31st. March 1802	51 years
Cheeseman Elizath.	Febry. 24		1	Boston	Edward Procter	Died 25th. Septr. 1803	
Clemens Willm.	March 12	1		Philadelphia	Henry Hill	Dischd. 29th. March 1800	one day
Cumston Henry	April 17		1	Boston	William Smith	Died 12th. May Do.	
Cox mary	Do. 23		1	Do.		Run away 12th. Augt. Do.	
Crage James	June 10th.	1		New York		Dischd. 31st. July 1800	8 years
Covell Betsey	July 6th.		1	Boston	born of Elizath. Covell	Died 8th. Decr. 1801	
Crane Eliz	Do. 28	1		Philadelphia	Wm. Smith	Dischd. 29th. Augt. 1800	6 years
Case Katherine Negro	Augt. 5	1		Rhode Island	Shearja. Bourne	R. away 12th. Augt. Do.	4 years
Carlton Lydia & Child Betsey	Do. Do.		2	Stoneham	Jona. L. Austin	R away Do.	{4 years, her Husband born in Ireland
Callahan John	Septr. 9th.	1		Ireland	William Smith	Dischd. 10th. Decr. 1800	17 years
Coleby Sally	Do. 25	1		Providence	Shearja. Bourne	Dischd. 27th. Septr. 1800	one year
Clark Fanny	Do. 29		1	Boston	Henry Hill	Dischd. 25 Novr. 1802	
Coleby Sally	Octor. 6th.	1		Providence	Shearja. Bourne	R. away 14th. Octor: 1800	one year
Cain Sukey	Octor. 17		1	Salem	Stephen Gorham	R. away 31st. Do. Do.	
Chevalier Mary	Novr. 5		1	Boston	Whole board	Dischd. 20th. April 1801	
Crane Elizath.	Do. 7	1		Philadelphia	Stephen Gorham	R. away 20th. Febry. 1801	6 years
Cornelus George	Do. 8	1		New Jersey	Do.	Run away about 1st. Decr. 1800	7 years

Names	Time of Admission	State	Town	Towns they belong to[1]	By what Overseer	When dischd., Died, Bound out, Run away.	Time they have been here in this State
Cain Sukey	Do. 25		1	Salem	Willm. Smith	Dischd. 10th. Janry. 1801	
Collins Michael	Do. Do.	1		Ireland	Redford Webster	Dischd. 7th. April Do.	6 years
Dwire Timothy	1795 Augt. 5th.	Do. 1		Ireland	William Smith	Dischd. 8th. Septr. 1796	
Davis Anne	<Do. 7th.>		Do.	Cape Ann		Dischd. 7th. Augt. 1795	
Dennis Martha	Octor. 12	1		Boston	Arnold Welles	Dischd. 14th. Novr. 1797	
Dyke Mary	Do.	1		Do.	Henry Hill	Died 25th. Janry. 1806	
Dawson Margarett	Do. 16	1		Ireland	Edward Proctor	Dischd. 2d. Decr. 1796	
Dockum Mariam	Decr. 7		1	Boston	Henry Hill	Dischd. May 1st. Do.	
Dailey Hannah	Do. 14		1	Do	Stephen Gorham	Dischd. Do.	
Dennis David	1796 Janry. 19th.	1		Ireland	Stephen Gorham	Dischd. 26th. April 1796	
Duffee James	Do. 28	1		Do.	Do.	Dischd. 23d. March Do.	
Davis Jonathan	Do. 31	1		England	Do.	Dischd. Do. Do.	
Davan John	April 11th.	1		Connecticut	Edward Proctor	Dischd. 16th. May Do.	
Dockum <Mary> Mirraim	May 26	1		Boston	Henry Hill	Run away 25th. Augt. Do.	
Dennis David	June 23	1		Ireland	William Smith	Dischd. 1st. Octor. Do.	
Davis Polly	July 11	1		England	Oliver Brewster	Dischd. 1 Decr. Do.	4 years
Dumet Lewis	Do. 29	1		France	William Smith	Dischd. 1st. March 1797	
Dana Elizabeth	Septr. 6		1	Boston	Edward Proctor	Dischd. 29th. March 1797	
Osgood Ebenezer a Child	Do.	1		born of E. Dana	Do.	Do.	

Names	Time of Admission	State	Town	Towns they belong to[1]	By what Overseer	When dischd., Died, Bound out, Run away.	Time they have been here in this State
Dwire Timothy	Do. 22	1		Ireland	Do.	Died 1st. February 1806	
Dorcy Martha	Octor: 3d.		1	Boston	Arnold Welles junr.	Dischd. 8th. Octor. Do.	
Dawson Margarett	Do. 17	1		Ireland	William Smith	Dischd. 22d. Augt. 1797	
Dilmore Daniel	Novr. 15	1		Ireland	Do.	Dischd. 3d. Decr. Do.	
Dulgars Lucy	Decr. 2		1	Boston	Wm. Philips jr.	Dischd. 10th. April Do.	
Dunn Jacob	Do. 5		1		Thos. Perkins	Died 7th. Do. Do.	
Dunnavan Jno.	6		1	Ireland	Stephen Gorham	Dischd. 30th. Septr. Do.	been in this State 3 Weeks
Done Jacob	Do. 21	1		New York	Edward Edes	Dischd. 27th. July 1797	
Dobbie Rachel	Febry. 7th. 1797	1		<*Old York*> Penobscot	Jona. L. Austin	Dischd. 14th. Febry. 1797	Wife of John Dobbie of Scotland
Do. Rachel a Child	Do.	1		Do.	Do.	Do.	
Do. Naomi Do.	Do.	1		Do.	Do.	Do.	
Dobbie Rachel	Do. 15	1		Penobscot	Do.	Dischd. 7th. Augt.	
Do Rachel a Child	Do.	1		Do.	Do.	Do.	
Do. Naomi Do.	Do.	1		Do.	Do.	Do.	
Davan John	April 19	1		Connecticut	Do.	Dischd. 12th. June 1797	
Davis Liffe Bl[*ack*] Woman	Do. 22		1	Lancaster	Henry Hill	Died 14th. May 1797	
Driscol Dennis	May 31	1		Ireland	Stephen Gorham	Died 31st. Augt. Do.	
Davis Sarah	June 17		1	Boston	Wm. Smith	Died 24th. July 1798	
Dulgah Lidia	Augt. 2d.		1	Do.	Jona. L. Austin	Dischd. 12th. Febry. 1798	

Names	Time of Admission	State	Town	Towns they belong to[1]	By what Overseer	When dischd., Died, Bound out, Run away.	Time they have been here in this State
Dorcey Patty	Septr. 12		1	Do.	Edward Proctor	Dischd. 15th. Septr. 1797	Sent to the W: house
Dowzen Hendrick	Do. 23	1		Holland	Do.	Died 30th. Do. Do.	
Dunnevan John	Octor. 16	1		Ireland	Henry Hill	Died 20th. Novr. Do.	
Dawson Margaret	Novr. 6	1		Do.	Thos. Perkins	Died 19th. Novr. 1798	20 years
Dunn, Michael	Novr: 14	1		Ireland	Oliver Brewster	Dischd. 10th. April 1798	12 Months
Dennis Martha	Do. Do.		1	Boston	Do.	Dischd. 1st. July 1814	
Drazia Elizabeth	Do. 20	1		Bristol	John Sweetser	Dischd. 9th. April 1798	22 years
Dailey Eliza, Born	Do. 23		1	of Nancy Revere, Lawrence Dailey		Dischd. 30th. April Do.	her Father
Dobbei Rachel & her two Children	Do. 27 / Do. Do.	1	2	Penobscot say Castine / Do.	Jona. L. Austin / Do.	Dischd. 20th. Decr. 1797 / Do.	
Dagells Michael	Decr. 5	1		Novascotia	Thomas Perkins	R. away 8th. July 1801	13 years
<Two Negro men>	Do. Do.	2		*Isle France*	*Do.>*	Entered wrong Page.	
Davan John	1798 / Janry. 10	1		Connecticut	William Smith	Run away 14th. June 99	20 years
Dugan Elizabeth & Sarah her child	Febry. 6 / Do.	1 / 1		Philada. / Do. }	Oliver Brewster	Dischd. 24th. April 1798	6 years
Dunham mary	Do. 19	1		Rhode Island	Henry Hill	Dischd. 16 May Do.	2 years
Dexter Peggy	Do. 28	1		Scotland	Thomas Perkins	Dischd. 14th. March 1798	13 months
Dinnison Jack a Child Born	Do.	<1> 0	1	Boston	of Peggy, a Negro	Dischd. 15 Do. Do.	
Davidson William	March 24	1		England	Jona. L Austin	Dischd. 9th. April Do.	5 years
Dennis John	April 6	1		New York	Arnold Welles jur.	Dischd. 9th. May Do.	22 years

Names	Time of Admission	State	Town	Towns they belong to[1]	By what Overseer	When dischd., Died, Bound out, Run away.	Time they have been here in this State
Drazia Elizabeth	Octor. 8	1		England	John Sweetser	Dischd. 22d. Febry. 1799	22 years
Dolbee Thomas	1799 Febry. 4th.		1	Boston	Whole board	R. away 22d. April Do.	
Dorrel Hepha. say Hitty	Do.		1	Do.	Do.	Died 25 April 1814	
Dawsy Patty	Do. 18		1	Do.	John Sweetser	R. away 28th. March 1799	
Dockum Mirraim	March 21		1	Do.	Redford Webster	Dischd. 26th. March 1799	
Dawsy Patty	June 28		1	Do.		Run away 15th. Novr. Do.	
Doane Wm. (child)	Do. 30		1	Do. born of Elizath. Ewen		Dischd. 31st. July 1800	{His Father {Wm. Done
Dockum Mirraim	Septr. 11		1	Do.	Henry Hill	Dischd. 8th. March 1800	
Ducas James & Elizabeth his Wife	Octor. 16 Do.	1 1		London Ireland	Redford Webster Do.	Dischd. 10th. May Do. Dischd. 21st. Novr. 1799	9 years Do.
Doane Crowell	Novr. 4th.		1	Boston	Stephen Gorham	Dischd. 22d. Janry. 1800	
Delahunty Katherine	Do. 9th.	1		Ireland	Henry Hill	Dischd. 21st. Novr. 1799	2 years
Dean Jeremiah	Do. 29	1		Exeter	William Phillips jur.	Died 7th. Decr: Do.	1 month
Drasy Elizabeth	Do.	1		England	John Sweetser	R. away 3d. July 1800	22 years
Daniels Joseph	Decr. 11		1	Milton	Henry Hill	Dischd. 9th. June 1800	37 years
Dawsy Patty	1800 Janry. 23d.		1	Boston	from Salem	R. away 20th. May 1800	
<Dean> or Bean <William	*Feby. 16*	*1*		*Dartmouth*	*Stephen Gorham*	*Died 18th. Feby. 1800>*	
Denny David	April 16	1		Ireland	Redford Webster	R. away 3d. July Do.	15 years
Day Lucy	June 19		1	Freeport	William Smith	R. away 31st. July Do.	

Names	Time of Admission	State	Town	Towns they belong to[1]	By what Overseer	When dischd., Died, Bound out, Run away.	Time they have been here in this State
Dockum Mirraim	July 5		1	Boston	Henry Hill	R. away 8th. July 1801	
Drazia Elizabeth	July 10	1		England	Jona. L. Austin	Died 10th. Janry. Do.	22 years
Daniel Dickenson's Child} Antha	Do. 31		1	Boston	Do.	Dischd. 31st. July 1800	
Day Lucy	Augt. 4th.		1	Freeport	Shearja. Bourne	R. away 12th. Augt. 1800	
Davis Polly	Do.	1		England	Do.	Do. Do. Do.	7 years
Davan John	August 11th.	1		Connecticut	Redford Webster	Died 10th. Octor. 1800	
Day Lucy	Do. 23d.		1	Freeport	Shearja. Bourne	R. away 31st. Augt. 1800	
Dyer John	Septr. 6		1	Boston	Edward Proctor	Dischd. 15th. Octor. Do.	
Dutton Betsey	Augt. 26		1	Do.	Oliver Brewster	Died 30th. Decr. Do.	
Donnison Andrew	Septr. 27	1		London	John Sweetser	Died 26th. July 1801	one year
Done Wm. Child	Octor. 9th.		1	Boston	Edward Edes	Bound out 4th. Janry. 1804	
Dearing Ruth	Do.		1	Do.	Redford Webster	Run away 14th. Novr. 1800	
Dolbeare Thomas	Do. 17		1	Do.	Jona. L. Austin	Run away 1st. May 1806	
Dunn Michael	Decr. 3d.	1		Ireland	Thomas Perkins	Dischd. 8th. April 1801	3 years
Decoster Ezekiel	Do. 6		1	Boston	Do.	Dischd. 27th. Janry. 1801	
Day Lucy	Do. 18		1	Freeport	Shearja. Bourne	Run away 2d. July Do.	
Downes John	Do. 22		1	Boston	William Phillips jur.	Died 20th. June 1801	
Dodge Patience Negro	Do.		1	Lumenburgh	Henry Hill	Dischd. 7th. Augt. Do.	
Edmonds Polly	1795 Augt. 5th.		Do. 1		William Smith	Dischd. 5th. Septr. 1795	

Names	Time of Admission	State	Town	Towns they belong to[1]	By what Overseer	When dischd., Died, Bound out, Run away.	Time they have been here in this State
Edmonds Thankfull		Do.	Do.			{Sent to the Work house Augt. 10th. 1795	15 Weeks. 2 days
Eddy Eunice		Do.				Run away 15th. Septr. Do.	
Enquitain John	Septr. 21	1		St. Malos	J. L. Austin	Dischd. 31st. March 1796	
Edwards ned	1796 Janry. 11th.	1	1	Ireland	Stephen Gorham	Dischd. 14th. March 1796	
Ewen Eliza	June 2d.		1		Edward Proctor	Run away. 16 June Do.	
Edward Ned	Do. 6	1		Ireland	Wm. Smith	Dischd. 11th. July Do.	
Etheridge Mary	July 13	1	1		whole board	Dischd. in Novr. Do.	
Ewen Eliza	Augt. 19	1	1		Edward Proctor	Dischd. 4th. March 1797	
Ewen Polly Born	Novr. 18	1	1	her Father's Name John Bean		Do.	
Edmonds Thankfull alais Rutherford	1797 Janry. 6	1			Redford Webster	Run away 7 Febry. 1797	
Eddey Bathsheba	Febry. 21	1	1	Indian	Wm. Phillips Jr.	Dischd. 10 March Do.	
Ewen Elizath. & child	April 3d.		2	Boston	Edward Proctor	Dischd. 8th. June Do.	
Eddey Bathsheba	May 27	1	1	Indian	Oliver Brewster	Run away 3d. June 1797	
Ewen Elizabeth & Polly her child	June 28		1 / 1	Boston / Do.	Edward Proctor / Do.	Run away with her Child / Do.	
Ewen Elizabeth	July 7		1	Do.	Do.	Do.	
Ewen Polly a child	Do.		1	Do.	Do.	Do.	
Ewen Elizabeth	aug 26	1	1	Do.	Oliver Brewster	Dischd. 31 Augt. 1797	

Names	Time of Admission	State	Town	Towns they belong to[1]	By what Overseer	When dischd., Died, Bound out, Run away.	Time they have been here in this State
Ewen Polly a child	Do.			Do.	Do.	Do.	
East William	Octor. 10	1		Germany	Stephen Gorham	Dischd. 23d. April 1798	15 years
Eddy Bathsheba	Novr. 14	1		Indian	Oliver Brewster	Dischd. 12th. Decr. 1797	
Eddy Eunice	Do. 17	1		Do.	Henry Hill	Dischd. 13th. Do.	
Eddy Eunice	1798 July 24	1		Do.	Stephen Gorham	Run away. 8th. Augt. 98	6 years
Eddy Ziby	Augt. 6	1		Indian	Redford Webster	Dischd. 14th. Septr. Do.	6 years
Ewen Elizabeth	Novr. 17		1	Boston	Oliver Brewster	Dischd. 6th. Decr. Do.	
English John	Do. 22	1		Germany	Edward Edes	Died 23d. Octor. 1801	15 years
Ewen Elizabeth	Decr. 17		1	Boston	William Smith	Dischd. 22d. Decr. 1798	
Do.	1799 Janry. 11	1		Do.	Redford Webster	Dischd. 23d. Janry. 1799	Run away
Ewen Elizabeth	March 30		1	Do.	Stephen Gorham	Dischd. 31st. July 1800	
Eddy Eunice	April 1st.	1		Indian	William Smith	Run away 16th. April 99	6 years
Eddy Eunice	Do. 27	1		Do.	Edward Procter	Do. 30th. May Do.	Do.
Eddy Bathsheba	June 15	1		Do.	Wm. Phillips jur.	Dischd. 26th. Septr. Do.	6 years
Male child born of Do.	July 23d.	1		Do.		Died 24th. July 1799	
Edes Betsey	Septr. 27		1	Boston	Jona. L. Austin	Run away Septr. 28th. Do.	
Ewing William	1800 Janry. 3d.	1		New York	Stephen Gorham	Dischd. 27th. May 1800	one day
Edy Zib, Indian	Augt. 5	1		Mountreal	Shearja. Bourne	R. away 12th. Augt. Do.	8 years
Ewings Abner	Do. 16	1		N. Carolina	Stephen Gorham	Died 1st. Octor. Do.	one month

Names	Time of Admission	State	Town	Towns they belong to[1]	By what Overseer	When dischd., Died, Bound out, Run away.	Time they have been here in this State
Ewing William	Novr. 4	1		New York	Shearja. Bourne	Dischd. 29th. Augt. 1801	10 months
Elizabeth Edes	Decr. 9th.		1	Boston	Jona. L. Austin	Dischd. 3d. Janry. 1801	
Evans Mary	Do. 30		1	Do.	Shearja. Bourne	R. away 28 April Do.	
Frazier Qunenc alias Quomino	1795 Augt. 25th.	Do. 1		Negro	William Smith	Run away 14th. May 1797	
Fosdick Thos. born of Esther White	Septr. 5th.		Do. 1			Dischd. 17th. Septr. 1795	
Furrs Thomas child			Do.			Bound Out 24th. Octor. Do.	
French Nicholas	<Novr.> Octor. 30th.	1		Came in 9 Novr.	Stephen Gorham	Dischd. 20th. May 1796	
Ford Sarah	Novr. 23	1		Virginia	Edwd. Proctor	Dischd. 8th. May 1796	
Flynn John	Decr. 4	1		Ireland	Jona. L. Austin	Dischd. 6th. April Do.	
Flynn Elizabeth	Do.		1	Lynn	Do.	Do. Do.	
Foot Jonathan	Do. 5		1	Salem	William Smith	Died 15th. Augt. 1797	
Ford James. Alias Rich	1796 Febry. 17	1		born of Sally Ford		Dischd. 8th. May Do.	{ His father Name Gairus Rich, of Western
Follins George	Do. 19		1		Henry Hill	Died 25th. Novr. Do.	
Follins Georges Wife	Do.		1		Do.	Died 23d. Decr. Do.	
Fosdick Thomas	June 21st.		1	a child of E. W.	Thos. Perkins	Died 4th. July Do.	
Flyn Sarah	July 5		1		John Sweetser	Died 20 Decr. Do.	

Names	Time of Admission	State	Town	Towns they belong to[1]	By what Overseer	When dischd., Died, Bound out, Run away.	Time they have been here in this State
Fowles Bethiah	Augt. 15		1			Dischd. 5 June 1797	
Foot Malachi	Septr. 21		1		Edward Proctor	Dischd. 10th. April 1797	
Foster Mary	Octor. 28		1	Marble Head	Redford Webster	sent to the W. house 4th. Novr. 1796	
Flynn John	Decr. 29	1		Ireland	Edward Proctor	Dischd. 6th. April 1797	
Flynn Elizabeth	Do.	1		Do.	Do.	Do. Do.	
Ford Sarah	1797 Janry. 7th.		1		Wm. Smith	Dischd. 5 June Do.	
Ford James Alias Rich (Child)[9]	Do.		1		Do.	Dishd. 7th. Febry. 1797	
Foulke Martin Jno.	Febry. 15	1		Germany	Do.	Dischd. 9th. Do. 1798	18 years
Foster Jack a Child	Do. 16		1	Black Child	Redford Webster	Died 22d. Febry. 1797	
French Nicholas	26	1			Do.	Dischd. 3d. April Do.	
Ford Sarah child	27		1			Dead Born Do.	
James Ford a Child	May 17		1		Wm. Phillips Jur.	Dischd. 5 June Do.	
Fowles Bethiah	June 6		1		Edwd. Proctor	Dischd: 24 Augt. Do.	Sent Work house
Fowles Bethiah	Augt. 28		1	Boston	Arnold Welles	Died 22d. Sept 1815	
Franklin John	Octor. 21	1		So. Caroline	Henry Hill	Died 12th. May 1798	6 months
Fish William	Do.		1	Sandwich	Thos. Perkins	Dischd. 30th. Octor. 1797	Now lives in Littlebury Kennebuk
Fowles Hannah	Do. 28		1	Boston	Oliver Brewster	Died 21st. March 1801	
Flynn John	Decr. 4th.	1		Ireland	Thoms. Perkins	Dischd. 25th. Novr. 1802	14 years
Flynn Elizabeth	Do.	1		Do.	Do.	Died 4th. Janry. 1798	Do.

[9] Closing parentheses supplied.

Names	Time of Admission	State	Town	Towns they belong to[1]	By what Overseer	When dischd., Died, Bound out, Run away.	Time they have been here in this State
Fortune Negro man	Do. 2d.	1		Isle France	Do.	Dischd. 8th: July Do.	one month
Fairservice Robt.	Do. 16		1	Boston	Wm. Smith	Dischd. 11th. April 1798	
Wm. Fredrick Negro	1798 Janry. 30th.	1		West Indies	Do.	Dischd. July 3d. Do.	2 months
Frazier Quamino	May 7	1		Do. Negro	Do.	Died 9th. May 1798	10 years
Foundling Negro male Child	26	1		Left at the door		Died 15th. Octor. Do.	named Charles
Field Thomas	May 28	1		Ireland	Edward Procter	Dischd. 10 Novr. Do.	8 years
Ferer Francis Sailor	June 27	1		Italy	Stephen Gorham	Dischd. 2d. Augt. 1798	3 Days
Furlong Edward	1798 Augt. 29th.	1		Ireland	John Sweetser	Dischd. 24th. Septr. 1798	30 years
Frazier Elizabeth	Septr. 17		1	Boston	Edward Edes	Died 26th. Janry. 1799	
Fredrick William Negro	Octor. 6	1		West Indies	William Phillips jur.	Dischd. 17th. Octor. 98	one year
Forbes Cyrus Negro	Novr. 1st.		1	Boston	Thos. Perkins	Dischd. 12th. June 99	
Fredrick William Negro	Do. 7	1		West Indies	Whole board	R. away 28th. March 99	one year
Field Thomas	Decr. 8	1		Ireland	Edward Procter	Dischd. 26th. Janry. 1799	8 years
Furlong Edward	1799 Janry. 2d.	1		Do.	Wm. Phillips jur.	Dischd. 6th. May Do.	30 years
Fowler Robert	Do. 12	1		Do.	Stephen Gorham	Dischd. 18th. Janry. Do.	24 Do.
Furness Joseph	Do. 16	1		Do.	Redford Webster	Dischd. 30th. May 1799	2 year
Furrs Thomas Child	May 9		1	Boston	Edward Procter	Bound Out Do. Do.	
Finley Thomas	Do. 18	1		England	John Sweetser	Dischd. 30th. May Do.	1 Week
Furlong Edwd.	Do. 20	1		Ireland	Edwd. Edes	Dischd. 12th. June Do.	30 years

Names	Time of Admission	State	Town	Towns they belong to¹	By what Overseer	When dischd., Died, Bound out, Run away.	Time they have been here in this State
Ferrett Nathaniel	Do. 18		1	Boston	Jona. L. Austin	Bound out 3d. June	age 9 years
Foltz Herman	Do. 27		1	Do.	Do.	Dischd. 30th. May 1799	
Finley Thomas	June 16	1		England		Dischd. 20th. June Do.	1 Week
Fovell Hannah child	Do. 25		1	Lynn	William Smith	Dischd. 6th. Augt. Do.	
Fenough Betsey	July 3d.		1	Marblehead	Arnold Welles jur.	Dischd. 5th. July 99	
Farris Abigail Negro and her Child	augt. 27 Do.		1 / 1		Jona. L. Austin	Dischd. 3d. Janry. 1800 Dischd. Do.	
Farras Lewis a Child	Octor. 6		1	Boston	Born 6th. Octor. 99	Dischd. 3d. Janry. 1800	
Fowles Sally	Do. 21		1	Do.	Henry Hill	Dischd. 31st. Do.	
Do.	Novr. 12		1	Do.	Do.	Dischd. 13th. Janry. 1800	
Christopher Francis	Decr. 2d.	1		Virginia	Thos. Perkins	Died 3d. Decr. 1799	
Ferriter Jane	1800 Janry. 15		1	Boston	Oliver Brewster	R. away 30th. Janry. 1800	
Foalke Richd. child	April 10	1		<Germany> Boston	Jona. L. Austin	Dischd. 10th. Octor. Do.	age 4 years
Fitgerrald Nancy	May 9		1	Boston	Stephen Gorham	Dischd. 23d. May 1800	
Field Thomas	June 11	1		Ireland	Redford Webster	Dischd. 5th. Febry. 1801	10 years
Fitzgerald Edward	Do. 12	1		Do.	Do.	Died 27th. July 1800	20 years
Fowles Sally	Augt. 5		1	Boston	William Phillips jur.	Died 21st. June 1801	
Fitch Rebecca	Do. 8	1			Shearjashub Bourne	Dischd. 9th. augt. 1800	
Fadrix Padack Susanna	Do. 23d.	1		Charleston	Do.	R, away 31st. augt. Do.	
Do.	Septr. 6		1	Do.	Do.	Dischd. 9th. Septr. Do.	

Names	Time of Admission	State	Town	Towns they belong to[1]	By what Overseer	When dischd., Died, Bound out, Run away.	Time they have been here in this State
Fitgerrald Nancy	Do. 16		1	Boston	Edward Procter	R. away 10th. Augt. Do.	
Foster William	Novr. 5th.	1		England	Stephen Gorham	Dischd. 28th. Janry. 1801	one day
Furlong Edward	Do. 17	1		Ireland	Henry Hill	Dischd. 3d. March Do.	30 years
Gray Ceaser B[lack] M[an]		Do.		Negro		Died 20th. Augt. 1795	11 Weeks 4 Day
Greenough Thomas	1795 Augt. 14th.	Do.	1		Stephen Gorham	Dischd: in 1796	
Gillahen William	Do. 17th.	Do.	1		William Smith	Dischd. 28th. augt. Do.	11 Days
Greely Charlotte (B[lack] Child)	Do. 19th.	Do.	1		Stephen Gorham	Died 8th. Septr. Do.	2 Weeks 6 Days
Goff John	Septr. 4th.	Do.	1	Ireland	Do.	Died 16th. Octor: 1797	6 Weeks
Greenvile Caleb		Do.				Dischd. 10th. Augt. Do.	6 Weeks 5 Days
Gordan Saml. (child)	Do. 5th.		Do. 1		Edward Proctor	Bound out 17th. March 1796	To Elisha Snow junr. of Truro Farmer
Greegs John	Do. 16th.		Do. 1		Do.	Died 26th. Augt. Do.	
Gardner Ceaser	Do. 23	1		Negro	Redford Webster	Died 20th. Octor. Do.	3 Weeks 6 Days
Gould Peggy & Child	24	2		Do.	Stephen Gorham	Child Died 14th. Octor. Do.	2 Do. 6 Do.
Gordon James (Child)			Do.			Bound Out 25th. Augt. Do.	
Gellard Ann			Do.			Dischd. 2d. Octor. Do.	
Gair Patty & child	Omitted July 18			1	Arnold Welles	Dischd. 7 Decr. Do.	
Gair Nancy Child	Do.		1		Do.	Bound Out 3d. June 1799	
Gair James	Novr. 6		1		Do.	Dischd. 8th. Febry. 1796	

Almshouse Admissions, 1795–1800

Names	Time of Admission	State	Town	Towns they belong to[1]	By what Overseer	When dischd., Died, Bound out, Run away.	Time they have been here in this State
Gould Peggy		Do.				Dischd. 10th. Novr. 1795	6 Weeks 5 days
Greenman Caleb	1796 Janry. 29	1		Rhode Isalnd	William Smith	Dischd. 4th. May 1796	
Gair James	Febry. 13th.		1		Do.	Run away 15th. April Do.	
Gair Patty	March 10		1		Do.	Dischd. 6th. April Do.	
Gair Patty (Child)	20		1		Stephen Gorham	Run away Do.	
Green David	April 5th.	1		{Rhode Island {Molato man	John Sweetser	Dischd. 9th. Do.	
Gordon Charlotte	Do. 22		1	Westford	Henry Hill	Dischd. 18th. April 1797	
Gerald Ann	Do. 27		1		Thomas Perkins	Dischd. 20th. June	
[Gardner] Andrew, Son	(June 18.)		1	of Andrew & Mary Gardner, born	Thomas Perkins	Bound out 18th. July 1801	
Gorham Benjn.	July 5		1	Portland	Thomas Perkins	Dischd. 22d. Augt.	
Giles Abigail	Septr. 26		1		Redford Webster	Died 9th. Febry. 1798	
Greenough Saml.	Decr. 21		1		Thos. Perkins	Died 9th. Febry. 1797	
Greeman Caleb	Do. 27	1		Rhode Island	Stepn. Gorham	Dischd. 12th. June Do.	
Green Betsey	Janry. 13th. 1797		1	Born of Sarah Adams		Died 8th. June 1798	F[ather] John green
Gunner Robt.	Do. 22d.		1	Born of Sarah Brown		Dischd. 24th. Novr. 1797	
Gair James	June 10		1	Boston	Edward Proctor	Dischd. 10th. July 1797	
Garnet William	July 2d.	1		England	Stephen Gorham	Dischd. 27 Do.	
Gould Abraham	Do. 17		1		Do.	Died 7 Septr. Do.	
Graham John	augt. 16	1		Scotland	Do.	Dischd. 14th. Novr. Do.	5 Weeks

Names	Time of Admission	State	Town	Towns they belong to[1]	By what Overseer	When dischd., Died, Bound out, Run away.	Time they have been here in this State
Robt. Gladstone	Septr. 18	1		England	Do.	Died 26th. Septr. 1797	
Gordon Charlotte	Do. 19		1	Westford		Dischd. 25 Do. Do.	
Gerald Ann	Novr. 11		1		Do.	Dischd. 25 April 1798	
Gridley Judy	Do. 20		1	Boston	Arnold Welles jur.	Died 2d. Decr. 1797	
Goodwin John	Do. 21	1		England	Jona. L. Austin	Dischd. 9th. March 1798	14 years
Graver Daniel	Decr. 3	1		Germany	Henry Hill	Dischd. 15th. Febry. Do.	12 years
Graham John	1798 Janry. 12	1		Scotland	Thomas Perkins	Died 19th. Janry. 1801	10 Weeks
Gordon Ann	March 1st.	1		Philadelphia	Thomas Perkins	Died 9th. June 1798	20 years
Greneau Joseph	April 3d.	1		West Indias	William Smith	Dischd. 25th. May 1798	one day
Green Samuel	Do. 21		1	Boston	Redford Webster	Dischd. 21st. May 1798	
Graver Daniel	Do. 25	1		Germany	Stephen Gorham	Dischd. 7th. June Do.	1 year
Gandell John jur.	May 18		1	Boston	Thos. Perkins	Dischd. 22d. Do.	
Game William	Do. 26	1		England	William Smith	Dischd. 4th. Octor. Do.	3 years
Gair James	Do. 28		1	Boston	Edward Procter	Dischd. 8th. June 1798	
Hannah Gardner, born	June 2d.		1	Daughter of Andrew & Mary Gardner	Whole board	Bound out 26th. Novr. 1802	
Gully Sarah	Augt. 3d.		1	Boston		Dischd. 21st. augt. 98	
Goodwin Elizabeth	Octor. 4	1		England	Edward Edes	Dischd. 10th. Octor. Do.	14 years
Gordon Lydia	Do. 9th.		1	Newbury Port	Henry Hill	Dischd. 21st. May 1799	
Goodwin John	Do. 31	1		England	Thos. Perkins	Dischd. 25th. March 1799	14 years

Names	Time of Admission	State	Town	Towns they belong to[1]	By what Overseer	When dischd., Died, Bound out, Run away.	Time they have been here in this State
Game William	Novr. 2d.	1		Do.	Do.	Dischd. 28th. Janry. 1799	3 years
Green Cato Negro	Do.		1	Africa	Henry Hill	Died 25th. Febry. Do.	35 years
Green Samuel	Novr. 8		1	Boston	Redford Webster	Dischd. 28th. Janry. 1799	
Gerald Molly	Do. 23d.		1	Do.	Jona. L. Austin	Dischd. 23d. Febry. Do.	
Gray Sally	Decr. 21		1	Boston	Sent in from the Work house her leg Broke	Died 28th. Septr. 1805	
Gerrald Ann	1799 Febry. 4th.		1	Do.	Whole board	Dischd. 28th. Septr. 1799	
Greene Lydia	March 13th.	1		Providence	William Smith	Died 4th. April 1799	9 months
Gray Sally Born	April 15		1	Boston	(of Sally Gray)	Died 1st. March 1801	
Glover John	May 27		1	Newbury Port	Jona. L. Austin	Dischd. 30th. May 1799	
Green Samuel	Do. 28		1	Boston	Henry Hill	Died 28th. June 1799	
Gardner <William> James	June 8	1		Novascotia	Redford Webster	Died 18th: July Do.	5 years
Gains Samuel	July 12		1	Boston	John Sweetser	Dischd. 7th. Augt. Do.	
Gavet Charles	Septr. 9	1		New York	Stephen Gorham	Died 10th. Septr. Do.	8 years
Gordon Charlotte	Do. 18		1	Boston	Oliver Brewster	Dischd. 15 Novr. Do.	
Gulley Sarah	Do. 20		1	Do.		Dischd. 26th. Septr. Do.	
Green Rhoda	Octor. 5	1		Hampton falls	Redford Webster	Died 5th. Novr. Do.	6 years
Griggs Nathaniel	Novr. 13		1	Boston	John Sweetser	Dischd. 15th. Do. Do.	
Goodwin John	Decr. 2d.	1		England	Redford Webster	Dischd. 17th. March 1800	14 years
Garfield Edward	Do. 26 1800		1	Waltham	Do.	Died 10th. Janry. 1800	

Names	Time of Admission	State	Town	Towns they belong to[1]	By what Overseer	When dischd., Died, Bound out, Run away.	Time they have been here in this State
Gillfilen Robert	Janry. 13th.	1		Scotland	John Sweetser	Dischd. 2d. March Do.	4 years
Gair James	27		1	Boston	Stephen Gorham	Dischd. 29th. Do. Do.	
Gafford Sally	Feby. 1st.		1	Do.	Jona. L. Austin	Dischd. 14th. April Do.	
Green Barilla Indian	Janry. 31		1	Old Town Martha's Vineyard	Wm. Smith	Dischd. 18th. Febry. 1800	7 years
Grant Elizath. & Child	Febry. 12	2		England	Jona. L. Austin	Dischd. 12th. March Do.	5 years
Gilles John & his Wife Jenny	Do. 24 Do.	1	1	Scotland Do.	Thos. Perkins Do.	Run, away, 23d. May 1800 Dischd. 4th. July Do.	16 years 45 years
Graves Thomas	Do.	1		Baltimore	Arnold Welles jur.	Dischd. 7th. April 1800	6 Weeks
Green Barilla Indian	May 12th.	1		{old Town, on {Martha's Vineyard	Jona. L Austin	Dischd. 4th. July Do.	6 years
Gillis John	June 13	1		Scotland	Do.	4th. July Dischd. 1800	16 years
Gordon Lydia	Do. 24		1	Newbury port	Edward Procter	Died 13th. Augt. Do.	
Grant Elizabeth	July 11	1		England	Oliver Brewster	Dischd. 31st. Do. Do.	5 years
Green Barrilla	Augt. 2d.		1	Old Town	Willm. Phillips jur.	Dischd. 14th. Augt. 1800	
Gardner Olive	Do. 4		1	Hingham	Shearja. Bourne	Dischd. 13th. Augt. 1800	
Gaffit Sally	Do. 5		1	<Charlestown> Boston Do.	Do.	Run away 12th. Do. Do.	
Gillis John	Septr. 12	1		Scotland	Redford Webster	Dischd. 28 Novr. Do.	16 years
Gair James	Octor. 17		1	Boston	Stephen Gorham	Dischd. 3d. March 1801	
Green Isaac	Do. 28	1		Philada.	A Welles	Dischd. 9th. July 1803	one month
Gray Jane	Novr. 17		1		Shearja. Bourne	R. away 10th. Janry. 1801	
Gardner Eunice	Do. 28	1		Rhode Island	Do.	Dischd. 13th. April Do.	1 year

Almshouse Admissions, 1795–1800

Names	Time of Admission	State	Town	Towns they belong to[1]	By what Overseer	When dischd., Died, Bound out, Run away.	Time they have been here in this State
Gillis John	Decr. 2d.	1		Scotland	Redford Webster	Dischd. 21st. May Do.	16 years
Gaffit Sally	Do. 30		1	<Charleston> Boston	Shearja. Bourne	R. away 23d. Do. Do.	
Healy John		Ireland[10]					
Hunnewell Cathare.	1795 Augt. 10th.	Do.		Ireland		Dischd. 10th. Augt. 1795	5 Weeks 5 Days
Hailey Thomas		Do.	1		Edward Proctor	Dischd. 19th. Do.	1 Week 2 Days
Henshaw Dinah	Septr. 10th.		1	Boston	Henry Hill	Died 12th. Janry. 1796	
Henshaw Jack	Octor. 5th.		1		Do.	Died 10th. Octor. 1795	
Harding Sears	Do: 12th.		1		Stephen Gorham	Died 13th. Do.	
Hammanway John	Do. 31		1		Edward Proctor	Died 21st. May 1796	
Howard Benjn.	Novr. 20		1		Do.	Dischd. 20th. Octor. Do., Omitted	
Howard Mary	Do. 25		1		John Sweetser Junr.	Dischd. Do. Do.	
Holland Mary	Do. 27	1		Ireland	Stephen Gorham	Dischd. 3d. Janry. 1796	
John Do: Child	Do.		1		Do.	Do.	
Mrs. Ann Hill	Decr. 29		1	Marble Head	William Smith	Dischd. 21st. June Do.	
Homer Saml. Child	1796 Janry. 6		1	Born of Sally Kittle		Bound out 11th. March 1803	
Hassoch Rachel			Do.	Boston		Died 22d. Janry. 1796	
Hubbard Abigail	Decr. 28th: 1795		1	Do.	Stephen Gorham	Dischd. 3d. May Do.	
Hines Jane	1796 March 3d.	1		New York	Edward Proctor	Dischd. 12th. March 1796	

[10] This entry written in pencil and by another hand than the rest of the register.

Names	Time of Admission	State	Town	Towns they belong to[1]	By what Overseer	When dischd., Died, Bound out, Run away.	Time they have been here in this State
Hovey Mary	Do. 30th.		1		Jona. L. Austin	Died 28 April 1797	about 80 years old
Hardwick Elizth.	April 23	1		Dutch woman	Edward Proctor	Dischd. 28th. April Do.	
Do.	May 10	1		Do.	Do.	Dischd. 1st. July Do.	
Holland Hannah	Do. 13		1	Boston	Oliver Brewster	Dischd. 27th. Augt. Do.	
Hubbard Abigail	July 30		1		Jona. L. Austin	Died 22d. Septr. Do.	
Hunniwell Katy	Augt. 25		1		Stephen Gorham	Died 16th. Septr. Do.	
Hardwick Elizabeth	Septr. 5	1		Du[t]ch woman	William Philips jr.	sent to the W. house 4th. Novr. 1796	
Hewes James	Do. 8th.	1		from Boston the W. house	Do.	Died 30th. Augt. 1803	
Holland Hannah	Augt. 27th.	1		Boston		Dischd. Octor. 12th. Do.	
Hollis Hannah	Octobr. 29th.	1			Stephen Gorham	Dischd. Janry. 14. 1797	
Pratt Thomas her[11] A Child	Do.		1		Do.	Do.	
Nancy Hicks	Novr. 18	<1>	1	Born of Nancy Hicks her Father	Henry Hill	Dischd. 8th. May 1798	English man
Harwell George	Do. 28	1		Black man	Arnold Welles junr.	Died 4th. Decr. <Do.> 1796	
Hillman Nancy	Decr. 1st:		1		Edward Proctor	Died 19th. Do. Do.	
Holden Elcy	Do. 11		1	Boston	Do.	Dischd. 13th. Febry. 1797	
Holmans Jane Child	20		1	Born of Jane Rowen / her Father		Dischd. 10th. Janry. Do.	Saml. Holmans
	1797						
Hamilton Tabitha	Janry. 10	1		New Jersey	Henry Hill	Dischd. 17th. June […][12]	10 years
Do. William child	Do.	1		Do.	Do.	Do.	
Do. John Do.	Do.		1	Do.	Do.	Do.	

[11] This word is interlined. I.e., the child of Hannah Hollis.
[12] A stain obscures the year.

Names	Time of Admission	State	Town	Towns they belong to[1]	By what Overseer	When dischd., Died, Bound out, Run away.	Time they have been here in this State
Do. Owen Do.	Do.	1		Do.	Do.	Do.	
Ham Mary	Do. 31	1		Indian	Stephen Gorham	Dischd. 1st. June Do.	
Hinds Rebecca	Febry. 21		1	Boston	Redford Webster	Dischd. 24th. Febry. 1797	
Mrs. Huffins	25		1		Jona. L. Austin	Died 20th. April Do.	
Hardwick Elizabeth	27	1		Du[t]ch woman	Thos: Perkins	Dischd. 10th. April 1797	
Holland Hannah	March 11		1	Dorchester	Edward Edes	Dischd. 10th. April 1797	
Asa Hamilton born of Tabitha Hamilton		1		Boston	Dischd. 17th. June 1797	Born 6th. April 1797	His mother born in New Jersey
Henley Elizabeth	7th. April 1797	1		1	Danvas	Redford Webster	Dischd. 6th. June Do.
Hart Catharine	25th. Do.		1	Boston	Thomas Perkins	Dischd. 22d. May 1797	
Howard Timothy	18 June Do.	1		Ireland	Edward Proctor	Dischd. 23d. Augt. Do.	Run away
Hayden Timothy	Augt. 2d.	1		Do.	Stephen Gorham	R. away. 23d. Decr. 1797	2 years
Holly George Negor	Do. 10	1		Affica	Redford Webster	Died 10th. Augt. 1797	
Haynds Mary	Septr. 7		1	Boston	Do.	Dischd. 12th. Decr. Do.	
Howard Timothy	Do. 8	1		Ireland	Do.	Died 2d. Sept 18[0]9	
Harris Francies	Do. 9	1		New London	Edward Proctor	Dischd. 3d. Novr. 1797	
Horn Van	Do. 14	1		New York	Redford Webster	Died 7th. Decr. Do.	3 Weeks
Hovey Amos	Do. 30		1	Boston	Do.	Died 22d. Octor. 1801	
Hope Wm's. Child	Octor. 5		1	(Molato)	Jona. L. Austin	Died 24 Octor. 1797	
Hackett Hugh	Do. 10	1		Ireland	Redford Webster	Dischd. 7th. Novr. Do.	{been in this State 7 years

Names	Time of Admission	State	Town	Towns they belong to[1]	By what Overseer	When dischd., Died, Bound out, Run away.	Time they have been here in this State
Hillman Matthew	Novr. 20		1	Martha's Vineyard	Arnold Welles jur.	Dischd. 16th. May 1798	
Hutchenson Julia Negro	Do. 28	1		Affrica	Jona. L. Austin	Dischd. 13th. Septr. Do. / Came from Rhode Island 26 years ago	
Hamilton Tabitha	Decr. 19th.	1		New Jersey	Do.	Dischd. 8th. May 1798	10 years
Do. William a Child	Do.	1		Do.	Do.	Do.	
Do. John Do.	Do.	1		Do.	Do.	Do.	
Do. Owen Do.	Do.	1		Do.	Do.	Do.	
Do. Asa Do.	Do.	1		Do.	Do.	Do.	
Henson Jack Negro	Do. 28	1		Denmark	Do.	Died 24th. March 1798	10 years
Hohn John	1798 Febry. 2d.	1		Germany	Edward Procter	Dischd. 9th. April 1799	44 years
Hollis Hannah & John her Child	Do. 16 / Do.	1 / 1		Boston / Do.	Henry Hill / Do.	Dischd. 9th. April 1798 / Do.	John Hollis
Hinds Mary	Do. 21	1		Do.	Redford Webster	Dischd. 5th. March 1798	
Henley Elizabeth	Do. 25	1		Do.	Do.	Dischd. 19 May Do.	
Hamilton William	March 5th.	1		New Jersey	Edward Proctor	Dischd. 16th. April 1798	10 years
Holden Elcy	Do. 17		1	Boston	Stephen Gorham	Dischd. 17th. March Do.	
Hillman Cornelus Child	April 11	1		Do.	Edward Procter	Bound Out 5th. July Do.	
Hollis Hannah & her Child John	Do. 18 / Do.	1 / 1		Do. / Do.	William Phillips jur. / Do.	Dischd. 7th. Octor. 1799 / Bound Out 23d. Apl. 1803	
Hadley Elizabeth	May 2d.	1		England	Edward Edes	Dischd. 7th. Febry. 1799	1 year
Hadley Wm. a Child	Do. 12	1		Do.	Redford Webster	Dischd. 31st. May Do.	Do.

Names	Time of Admission	State	Town	Towns they belong to[1]	By what Overseer	When dischd., Died, Bound out, Run away.	Time they have been here in this State
Handrick Polly	June 17		1	Boston	Jona. L. Austin	Dischd. 16th. Octor. 1798	
Hagarty William	Do. 26	1		Ireland	Redford Webster	Dischd. 2d. Augt. 1798	1 Week
Hendley Ann	Do. 29		1	Boston	Henry Hill	Died 26th. March 1799	age 97 years
Hall James	July 23	1		England	Oliver Brewster	Dischd. 17th. Septr. 1798	5 years
Hogard Eilza.	Do. 27	1		Do.	Henry Hill	Discd. 31st. July 1798	one month
Hall John (Sailor)	Augt. 6	1		Do.	Redford Webster	Died 29th. Decr. Do.	2 year
[...][13] Sarah	Novr. 10		1	Boston	Edward Procter	Dischd. 23d. March 1799	
[...]lh Stephen	Decr. 11	1		New York	William Smith	Dischd. 9th. April Do.	1 year
Howard Benjn. & his Daughter Mary	17th. Decr. 1798 Do.	1 1		Boston Do.	Edward Procter Do.	Died 6th. Febry. 1799 Bound out 3d. April Do.	
Hodson John	Do. 26	1		England	Arnold Welles	Dischd. 2d. April 1799	one Day
Hubbard Sylvanus	1799 Janry. 2d.		1	Boston	William Smith	Died 11th. Octor. 1801	
Hamblin Hannah	Do. 11		1	Barnstable	Redford Webster	Dischd. 8th. April 1799	
Holland Peter Negro	D 14		1	Hull	William Smith	Dischd. 22d. Septr. Do.	
Handrick Polly	Do. 29		1	Boston	Edward Procter	Dischd. 6th. Augt. Do.	
Harper Lucy Negro	Febry. 4	1		West Indies	Whole board	Died 27th. Febry. 1802	
Hynds Mary	Do.		1	Boston	Do.	Dischd. 12th. June 1800	
Howard Mary	Do.		1	Do.	Do.	bound out 30th. April 1799	
Hohn John	April 16		1	Germany	Redford Webster	Dischd. 15th. Octor. 1800	44 years

13 The bottom left corner of the page is both torn and effaced, resulting in the loss of the surname for this and the following entry.

Names	Time of Admission	State	Town	Towns they belong to[1]	By what Overseer	When dischd., Died, Bound out, Run away.	Time they have been here in this State
Hamblin Hannah	May 1		1	Barnstable	Stephen Gorham	Died 3d. May 1799	
Holderphole John	Do. 7	1		Germany	Oliver Brewster	Dischd. 30th. May Do.	2 years
<Roch Robert>	Do. 15	1		Ireland	William Smith>	(wrong Entered)	<5 years>
Hogan John	June 6th.		1	Boston	Arnold Welles jur.	Dischd. 19 June Do.	
Haynes John	Septr. 9th.	1		Germany	Stephen Gorham	Dischd. 17th. March 1800	15 years
Hergin Bart	Octor. 30	1		Ireland	Do.	Dischd. 3d. Decr. Do.	one year
Holden Elcy	Decr. 2d.		1	Boston	Edward Procter	Dischd. 30th. July Do.	{with Child by {Edward Brick
Asa Wallis Hill	Do. 4	1		Virginia	William Smith	Dischd. 10th. April 1800	4 months
Handrick Polly	Do. 5	1		Boston	Oliver Brewster	R., away 5th. May Do.	
Hollis Hannah	Do. 10	1		Do.	Do.	Dischd. 18th. Janry. 1800	
Herrick Stephen	Do. 13	1		New York	Do.	Dischd. 25 July Do.	2 years
Hearsey Patty Born of		1		England	Mary Kemp	Decr. 22d. 1799 Dischd. 25th. March 1800	
Hoare Elizath.	1800 Febry. 24	1		England	Arnold Welles jur.	Died 3d. March 1800	9 months
Harvey Saml.	29th. March	1		New York	Thos. Perkins	Dischd. 28th. April Do.	one Day
Haney John	April 6	1		Germany	Wm. Phillips jur.	Run away. 17th. Octor. Do.	15 years
Hazard Mary Ann	Do. 14	1		Ireland	John Sweetser	R. away 21st. April Do	one Day
Wibert Polly	May 26		1	Boston	Jona. L Austin	R. away 25th. July Do.	
Higgins, William Peggy, & Maria Children	June 8 Do.	1 2		Do. Do.	Do. Do.	Dischd. 12th. June 1800} Do. Do.	by order of Jona. L Austin

Names	Time of Admission	State	Town	Towns they belong to[1]	By what Overseer	When dischd., Died, Bound out, Run away.	Time they have been here in this State
Henderson John	Do. 7	1		New York	Arnold Welles jur.	Dischd. 20th. June Do.	3 Days
Haskell John	Do. 24	1		Do.	Edward Procter	Dischd. 6th. Septr. Do.	two Days
Hubbard Sear	July 1st	1		Connecticut	Redford Webster	Run away 7th. July 1800	one month
Hinds Mary	Augt. 4		1	Boston	Shearja. Bourne	Dischd. 17th. Febry. 1801	
Hohn John	Octor. 22		1	Germany	William Smith	Dischd. 9th. April 1802	45 years
Handrick Polly	Novr. 5		1	Boston	Jona. L Austin	Dischd. 3d. April	
Howard Mary	Do. 17	1	<1> 0	England	Shearja. Bourne	Run away 30th. Decr. 1800	7 years
Hickey John	Decr. 10		1	England	Redford Webster	Dischd. 7th. May 1801	35 years
Hows Sukey (Molato)	Do. 30	1		Portsmouth	Henry Hill	Dischd. 24th. Janry. 1801	2 months
Jennins Elizabeth			Do.			Died 10th. Septr. 1795	
Johnson Richard		Do.		Holland		Dischd. 13th. Novr. Do.	23 Weeks. 5 days
Johnson Sam	1796 Janry. 4th.	1		A Negro } New York	Henry Hill	Dischd. 6th. April 1796	
Joe Black man	Do.	1		West Indias	Stephen Gorham	Dischd. 10th. Septr. Do.	
Jones Peter Born	May 21st.		1	Son of Peter Jones, & Mary Baker	Stephen Gorham	Dischd. 14th. Septr. Do	The father now at Sea
Jones William	June 15	1		London	Stephen Gorham	Run away 16th. June Do.	
Johnson Saml. Black man	Novr. 7	1		New York	Do.	Dischd. 5th. May 1797	
Johnson Collin	Decr. 3	1		Affrica Last from Canady	Redford Webster	Died 6th. Febry. 1797	(2 Days) came from Canada
Jones James	Do. 17 1797	1		England	Stephen Gorham	Dischd. 5th. April Do.	

Names	Time of Admission	State	Town	Towns they belong to[1]	By what Overseer	When dischd., Died, Bound out, Run away.	Time they have been here in this State
Johnson Saml. Negro	Octor. 27	1		New York	Wm. Smith	Died 8th. Febry. 1798	6 years
Johnson Matthew	Novr. 7	1		England	Stephen Gorham	Died 19th. Novr. 1797	8 Weeks
<John John> James Jones	Decr. 12	1		Do.	Jona. L. Austin	Dischd. 30th. April 1798	about 10 years
	1798						
Jacob Herbert	Janry. 6th.	1		Do.	Henry Hill	Dischd. 5th. March 1798	6 months
Jemorson John	June 2d.	1		Scotland	Edward Procter	Dischd. 23d. June Do.	2 months
Jones Eliza.	Novr. 2d.		1	Boston	Thos. Perkins	Dischd. 22d. Novr. 1799	
Jones James	Decr. 6	1		England	Henry Hill	Dischd. 30th. May 1799	about 10 years
Jones William	Do. 10	1		Do.	William Smith	Dischd. 22d. Febry. 1799	one Week
	1799						
Jemmison John	Febry. 4	1		Scotland	Whole board (R[un])	Dischd. 30th. May Do.	
Jenkins Nathl.	July 8		1	Boston	Redford Webster	Dischd. 8th. Febry. 1800	Run away
Johnson Wm.	Octor. 19	1		Ireland	Stephen Gorham	Dischd. 22d. Novr. 1799	8 years (Thief)
Jones James	Decr. 8	1		England	Redford Webster	Dischd. 17th. March 1800	10 years
	1800						
Jones James	March 22	1		Do.	Do.	R. away 25th. July Do.	
Johnson Eunice	April 5	1		Do.	Wm. Phillips jur.	Dischd. 31st. Augt. Do.	15 years
Jenkins Nathl.	May 7th.		1	Boston	Whole Board	R. away 10th. Octor. Do.	
Jones Will[iam][14]	Septr. 12	1		England	Thos. Perkins	Dischd. 18th. March 1801	2 years
Jones J[ames]	Octor. 1st.	1		Do.	Redford Webster	Died 10th. Octor. 1800	10 years
Jenkins Nathl.	Do. 12		1	Boston	Edward Procter	Died 18 Decr. 1800	age 50 years

[1] The MS is stained, obscuring a portion of this and the following entry.

14 The MS is stained, obscuring a portion of this and the following entry.

Names	Time of Admission	State	Town	Towns they belong to[1]	By what Overseer	When dischd., Died, Bound out, Run away.	Time they have been here in this State
Jones William jur.	Decr. 5	1		Ireland	William Smith	Dischd. 20th. Febry. 1801	one Day
Jones Edmund	Do. 27		1	Newbury port	Redford Webster	Dischd. 2d. Janry. 1801	
	1795						
King John	Septr. 25	1		New York	William Smith	Dischd. 1st. Decr. 1795	
Kittle Sally	Octor. 19th.		1	Boston	John Sweetser Junr.	Run away with her Son Saml. Homer May [...] 1796	
Kimball Asa	Decr. 27	1		Connecticut	Henry Hill	Run away Same Day	
	1796						
King Mary	Febry. 4th.		1	Boston	Edward Proctor	Dischd. 11th. Octor. 1796	
Kittle Sally & Son	June 1st.		2	Do.	John Sweetser	Dischd. 29th. March 1797	
Kelley Patrick	Septr. 5th.	1		Ireland	Do.	Died 10th. Septr: 1796	7 years
Kimball Wm.	Decr. 8th.		1	Norton	William Smith	Dischd. 14th. Janry. 1797	
	1797						
King Polly	March 18		1	Boston	Henry Hill	Dischd. 30th. Augt. Do.	
Kittle Sally & Son	April 1st.		2	Boston	Thos. Perkins	Dischd. 6 June 1797 Sally Kittle only	
Kimball Wm.	Do. 4		1	Norton	William Smith	Dischd. 10 May 1797	Sent to the Work hous
Kimball Wm.	March 5th.		1	Do.	Stephen Gorham	Dischd. 2d. April 1798	
	1798						
King Charles	June 8th.	1		England	Edward Procter	Run 30th. May 1799	15 years
Kidder Joseph a Child	Augt. 2d.		1	His mother Amey Davis born in Cape Ann } Henry Hill		Dischd. 23d. Septr. 1802	
Kimball Wm.	Do. 15		1	Norton	Stephen Gorham	Died 17th. augt. 1798	
Kittle Sally &	Septr. 25		1	Boston	Edward Edes	Dischd. 2d. April 1799	John Tileston } Englishman
Tileston Sally her Child	Do.		1	Do.	Do. her father	(Died 2d. Octor. 1798)	

Names	Time of Admission	State	Town	Towns they belong to[1]	By what Overseer	When dischd., Died, Bound out, Run away.	Time they have been here in this State
Kennedy David	Novr. 26	1		Scotland	William Smith	Dischd. 14th. Decr. Do.	4 Days
Kittle Sally	1799 May 30th.		1	Boston	John Sweetser	Dischd. 13th. April 1803	
King William	June 11		1	Ireland	William Phillips jur.	Died 9th. Novr. 1800	33 years
Kemp Mary	Septr. 18	1		England	Redford Webster	Dischd. 25th. March 1800	22 years
King Charles	Do. 24	1		England	William Smith	Dischd. 6th. June Do.	15 years
King Charles	1800 July 2d.	1		England	justice Bourne	R. away 20th. May 1801	16 years
Kemp Sarah or Mary	Augt. 4	1		England	Shearja. Bourne	R. away 17th. Octor. 1800	22 years
King Sally	Novr. 17		1	Boston	Do.	R. away 7th. April 1801	
King Mary	Do. 25		1	Boston	Jona. L. Austin	Dischd. 7th. July 1803	
Lovebridge Wm. Eliza. his Wife John & Thos. their Children	1795 Augt. 10th. Do.,	1	3	England Boston	Wm. Lovebridge Wife & Son Thos. Stephen Gorham	Dischd. 23d. March 1798 Dischd. 9th. April Do. John Died 24th. Septr. 1795	6 Weeks. 3 Days
Langford William	Octor. 26		1	Boston	Do.	Dischd. 11th. April 1797	
Lenoard Pero	Decr. 1st.	1		Negro	John Sweetser Junr.	Dischd. 11th. Febry. 1796	
Lee Elizabeth	Do. 3		1		Oliver Webster	Dischd. 24th. March Do.	
Lembert Henry	1796 Febry. 12th.	1		New York	William Smith	Dischd. 4th. Do. 1796	
Lockhart Charls.	March 10	1		Virginia	Do.	Died 23d. March Do.	
Lewis Abigail	July 2d.		1	Boston	Stephen Gorham	Died 29th. March 1804	

Names	Time of Admission	State	Town	Towns they belong to[1]	By what Overseer	When dischd., Died, Bound out, Run away.	Time they have been here in this State
Langford Sally	Augt. 7th.		1	Boston	Arnold Welles jr.	Died 27th. March 1800	
Linch Dennis	Do. 15	1		Ireland	Henry Hill	Run away 22d. Augt. 96	been in this State 2 months
Loyns James	Sept. 28	1		Do.	Edward Proctor	Dischd. 5th. Octor. Do.	
Leatherby Patty	Octor. 16		1	Westford	Thomas Perkins	Dischd. 30 Novr. Do.	
Langford Wm.	Novr. 25		1	Boston	Stephen Gorham	Died 29th. March 1798	
Michael Leanard	1797 March 7th.	1		Ireland	William Smith	Dischd. 5th. April 1797	
Lane Peter a Molato	Do. 20	1		Savannah in Georgia}	Jona. L Austin	Dischd. 1st. Novr. Do.	
Leanard Michael	April 18	1		Ireland	Do.	Dischd. 10th. May 97	
Lock James a Child	Augt. 6		1	Nantucket	Born of Peggy Conden	Died 18th. Augt. Do.	
Leonard Michael	Septr. 7	1		Ireland	Redford Webster	Dischd. 20th. Octor. 1797	14 years
Long Edward	Do. 12	1		Do.	Jona. L Austin	Dischd. 5th. Octor. 97	
Leonard Michael	Octor. 20	1		Ireland	Henry Hill	Dischd. 10th. April 1798	14 years
Lenox John	Do. 29	1		Germany	Redford Webster	Dischd. 31st. May Do.	2 1/2 years
Leonard Mary	1798 March 21	1		Scotland	Jona. L Austin	Dischd. 9th. April 1798	22 years
Lovebridge Wm.	April 4	1		England	Whole board	Dischd. Do.	
Lawley John	June 1st.	1		Ireland	Thos. Perkins	Dischd. 6th. June Do.	15 years
Lewis Susanna	Do. 15		1	Boston	Jona. L. Austin	Dischd. 21st. July Do.	
Loring Benjn.	augt. 4		1	Do.	Wm. Smith	Died 4th. augt. Do.	

Names	Time of Admission	State	Town	Towns they belong to[1]	By what Overseer	When dischd., Died, Bound out, Run away.	Time they have been here in this State
Leonard Michael	Octor. 20	1		Ireland	Arnold Welles jur.	Dischd. 1st. April 1799	15 years
Lewis Thomas	Novr. 3		1	Boston	Edward Procter	Dischd. 4th. Decr. 1798	
Lovebrige Wm.	Novr. 1	1		England	Thos. Perkins	Dischd. 2d. April 1799	
Lovell Joseph	Decr. 5		1	Sharon	Redford Webster	Dischd. 15th. May Do.	
Loughton Wm.	1799 Janry. 17		1	Boston	Edward Proctor	Dischd. 12th. July Do.	
Latherbee Patty	Do. 24		1	<Portland> say Westford	Thos. Perkins	Run away 19th. March 99	
Leonard Michael	June 8	1		Ireland	Stephen Gorham	Dischd. 28th. June 1799	15 years
Lenox Polly a child	Sept. 9		1	Newburyport	Do.	Dischd. 22 Septr. Do.	
Lovell Joseph	Do. 20		1	Sharon	Redford Webster	Died 16th. Octor. Do.	
Leander Hugh	Do. 23d.	1		England	Arnold Welles jur.	Dischd. 21st. Novr. Do.	one Week
Leonard Michael	Octor. 3d.	1		Ireland	Wm. Smith	Dischd. 16th. Novr. Do.	15 years
Leatherby Patty	Do. 4th.		1	Westford	John Sweetser	Run away 22d. Janry. 1800	
Lawley John	Do. 21		1	Ireland	Thos. Perkins	Dischd. 7th. Novr. 1799	15 years
Leonard Micheal	Novr. 30		1	Do.	Redford Webster	Dischd. 25th. Augt. 1800	15 years
Lascur	Decr. 15th.	1		Isle France	Edward Procter	Dischd. 25th. Decr. 1799	2 months
Lascur	Do. 24		1	Do.	Do.	Do.	Do.
Lewis Rhoda (Molato)	Do. 27		1	Natick	Redford Webster	Died 4th. Janry. 1800	2 years
Leatherbee Patty	1800 Janry. 24		1	Westford	Jona. L. Austin	R. away, 5th. May Do.	
Levingston Elizabeth	March 12		1	Boston	Wm. Smith	Died 2d. Jany. 1808	

Names	Time of Admission	State	Town	Towns they belong to[1]	By what Overseer	When dischd., Died, Bound out, Run away.	Time they have been here in this State
Lincoln Peter	April 2d.	1		Swedland	Edward Procter	Dischd. 16th. april 1800	5 years
Two Lascurs	Do. 15	2		Isle France	Jona. L. Austin	Dischd. 24 Do. Do.	2 Months
Leonard Micheal	Septr. 3d.	1		Ireland	Redford Webster	R. away 21st. May 1801	15 years
<Loveritt> Lovebridge Elizabeth	Novr. 15		1	Marblehead	Edward Procter	Died 2d. Janry. 1801	
Laisinby Mary	Do. 11		1	Boston	John Sweetser	Died, 19th. Sept. 1803	
<Leward> Sophia (Seward)	Do. 17		1		Shearja. Bourne	Died 30th. Novr. 1801	
Leatherbee Patty	Do. 25		1	Westford	William Smith	Dischd. 30th. Decr. 1800	
Lewis Thomas	Decr. 25th.		1	Boston	Edward Procter	Dischd. 29th. Decr. 1800	
Milstreaz Fredrick	1795	Do.		Prusia		Died 20th. Augt. 1795	11 Weeks 4 Day
Minot Alexr.	Augt. 14th.	Do.	1	Black man	Stephen Gorham	Dischd. 26th. Do.	1 Week 5 Days
Molato Child	Do. 31st.	Do.		Found on Corps Hill		Died 31st. Do.	6 Weeks 6 Days
Mason Betsey	Do. 31st.			Newbury Port	William Smith	Dischd. 9th. Septr. Do.	1 Week 2 Days
Molato Child	Septr. 8th.	Do.	1	Found at the door		Died 14th. Do.	6 Days
McLauchlin Mary		<Do.>	1	Disallowed by the commitee		Dischd. 15th. Do. came back}	15 Week 2 days
McLaucklin Mark & his Wife Mary	Octor. 6th. Do.	<1>	1	Ireland	Edward Proctor Do.	Dischd. 13th. June 1797 / Died 10th. Janry. 1797	Disallowed by the Commitee
McKenzie Alan	Do. 10	1		Scotland	Jona. L. Austin	Dischd: 13th. Octor. 1796	3 days
Moor Elizabeth	Do. 13	1		Ireland	Edward Proctor	Sent to the W. house 1st Decr. Do.	
Millage John	Do. 16	1		England	Redford Webster	Dischd. 19th. April 1796	
Martin Peggy	Do. 28	1		Ireland	Oliver Brewster	Run 29th. Octor. 1795	1 Day

Names	Time of Admission	State	Town	Towns they belong to[1]	By what Overseer	When dischd., Died, Bound out, Run away.	Time they have been here in this State
Murray Rebeca	Novr. 24	<1>	1	<Scotland>	Redford Webster	Dischd. 24 Augt. 1797} sent to the Work house	
Murray James (child)	Do.	<1>	1		Do.	Do.	
Murphy John	Decr. 9th.	1		Ireland	Oliver Brewster	Run away 1st. March 1796	
Molato Child Boy	Do. 16	1		found in the Shed	Henry Hill	Died 28th. March Do.	
Molato Child Girl	1796 Janry. 26	1		found in the Street	Arnold Welles junr.	Died 7th. Octor. Do.	
McIntire Mahatible	March 1		1	Salem	Stephen Gorham	Dischd. 4th. April Do.	
Melhorn Jane	April 16		1	Marblehead	Arnold Welles	Dischd. 28th. Do. Do.	
McKenzie Thos.	Do. 30	1		Black boy	Stephen Gorham	Bound out 30th. Do. Do.	
Melhorn Jane	May 13		1	Marblehead	William Smith	Dischd. 10th. July Do.	
McChurly Saml.	July 18	<1>		Ireland	Edward Proctor	Died 20th. Novr. 1797	not alowed
Melhorn Jane	Augt. 3d.		1	Marblehead	Whole board	Sent to the Work house	
Chance Molato Child a boy	Do. 21st.	1		found in the Street	Wm. Smith	Died 26th. Septr. 1796	
Makin Willm.	Do. 22	1		England	Do.	Dischd. 20th. Octor. Do.	ten years
Mackay John	Septr. 13	1		Ireland	Jona. L. Austin} Wm. Smith	Dischd. 30th. Janry. 1797	5. years
Macken Christian	Do. Do.	1		Scotland	Oliver Brewster	Dischd. 30th. Novr. Do.	27 years
Maden John	Augst. 30	1		Ireland	Edward Proctor	Dischd. 19th. April 1797	13 years
Maden Abigal	Septr. 22	<1>		Do.	Do.	Dischd. 5th. Novr. 1796	not alowed
Maden Peggy a Child	Do.	<1>		Do.	Do.	Dischd. 19th. April 1797	Do.
Morarty Polly Do.	Do.	1			Wm. Smith	Dischd. 25th. Augt. Do.}	not alowed by the
Catharine Do. a Child	Do.	1			Do.	Dischd. 8th. May 1799}	Commite of accot.

Names	Time of Admission	State	Town	Towns they belong to[1]	By what Overseer	When dischd., Died, Bound out, Run away.	Time they have been here in this State
Moore Partrick	Octor. 17	1		Ireland	Edward Proctor	Dischd. 20 April 1797	20 years
Magdelene B[lack] Woman	Do. 28	1		Hispaniola	Do.	Run away 14th. May 1797	
Morgan John	Novr. 25	1		Londondary	Arnold Welles	Dischd. 3d. Decr. 1796	9 months
Morgan Esther	1797 Janry: 4		1		Edwd. Proctor	Dischd. 7th. March 1797	
Mellin Robt.	Do	1		Ireland	Thos. Perkins	Died 13th. Janry. 1797	
Morse Mary	7th.		1	Boston	Henry Hill	Dischd. 7th. March	not alow[ed] by the Com[mitte][15]
Milladge John	March 10	1	1	England	Redford Webster	Died 8th. Octor. 1801	age 75 y[ears]
Morse mary	June 13	1		<Boston> Portland	Redford Webster	Dischd. 5th. Octor. 1799	
Matha Martin	1797 Febry. 12th.		1	Boston	Henry Hill	Dischd. 9th. Febry. 1798	
Matha Do. a Child	Do.		1	Do.	Do.	<Bou> Dischd. Do.	
Catherine Do. Do.	Do.		1	Do.	Do.	Bound Out 4th. Octor. 1797	
John Do. Do.	Do.		1	Do.	Do.	Bound Out 15th. April Do.	
Charlote Do. Do.	Do.		1	Do.	Do.	Dischd. 9 Febry. 1798	
Richd. Do. Do.	Do.		1	Do.	Do.	Dischd. Do.	
Melhorn Jane	March 7		1	Marblehead	Do.	Dischd. 6th. June 1797	R away
Moor Sarah	Do. 21	<1>	1	Boston	Wm. Phillips jur.	Dischd. 6th. May 1797	
Murry John, Negro	Do. 22	1		Do.	Redford Webster	Dischd. 22d. June Do.	
McCurttey Michael	Do. 29	1		Ierland	Edward Proctor	Run away 6th: April 1797	

[15] The bottom right corner of the page is torn off, resulting in the loss of text here and in the next entry.

Names	Time of Admission	State	Town	Towns they belong to[1]	By what Overseer	When dischd., Died, Bound out, Run away.	Time they have been here in this State
Melhorn John	Do.	1		Holland	John Sweetser	Dischd. 12th. June 1797	R. away
Morse Martha & two Children vizt.	May 13	1		London	Henry Hill	Dischd. 29 May 1797	
Morse, James Harrison a Child	Do.	1		Do.	(Died 28th. Septr 1797)	Do.	
Morse Amelia (Molato) a Child	Do.	1		New York	her Father Abraham Borchius, Negro		
Melledge John & Mary his Wife	Do. 20	1			Do.	Dischd. 16th. June 1797	
	Do.	1			Do.	Dischd. 16 June 1797	
Martella John	Do. 23	1		a Spaniard	Jona. L. Austin	Dischd. 1st. Janry. 1798	3 months
Mayfield Edward	June 8	1		England	Henry Hill	Died 9 Decr. 1810	18 years
Morison John	July 27		1	Scotland	Wm. Phillips jur.	Died 5th. Augt. 1803	45 years
McCarthey Charles	Do. 21	1		Ireland	Oliver Brewster	Died 23d. Augt. 1797	29 years
McCarthey Mary	Do.		1	Boston	Do.	Died 6th. Octor. Do.	
Mowet Francis	Augt. 6	1		Ireland	Stephen Gorham	Died 22d. Augt. 1797	6 months
Marston Lydia	Do. 10		1	Boston	Do. & Arnold Welles	Dischd. 14th. Septr. Do.	
Martin Patty	Septr. 9		1	Do.	Redford Webster	Dischd. 30th. Do. Do.	
Magloclin Mark	Do. 8		1	Ireland	Do.	Dischd. 21st. March 1798	
Miller, George Jacob	Do. 11	1		Germany	Henry Hill	Died 18th. Decr. 1797	
Miller Hannah (Wife)	Do.		1	Marblehead	Do.	Dischd. 7th. Octor. 97	
Miller Simeon Howlen (son)	Do.		1	Boston	Do.	Dischd. Do.	
Martin John born	Octor. 4th.	1		of Mary Combe		Died 4th. Octor. 1797	
Mears Patrick	Do. 17	1		Ireland	Do.	Dischd. 9th. April 1798	
Murry Rebecca & Child James	Do. 28	2		Boston	William Smith	Dischd. 21st. July 1800 bound out 20th. Febry. 1799	

Names	Time of Admission	State	Town	Towns they belong to[1]	By what Overseer	When dischd., Died, Bound out, Run away.	Time they have been here in this State
<Dawson Margaret	*Novr. 6*	*1*		*Ireland*	*Thos. Perkins>*		
Morarthy Mary child	Novr. 4	<1> 0	1	Ireland	Wm. Smith	Dischd. 19th. July 1798	
Martin Edward	Do. 18	1		Philada.	Stephen Gorham	Dischd. 30th. Janry. 1798	1 month
Magdeline Negro	Do. 28	1		Hispaniola	William Smith	Run away 2d. Decr. 1797	1 year
Melhorn John	1798 Janry. 12	1		Holland	William Phillips jr.	Dischd. 19th. Janry. 1798	
Martin Edward	Febry. 3d.	1		Philada.	Stephen Gorham	Dischd. 12 Febry. Do.	3 months
John Melledge	Do. 13		1	Boston	Henry Hill	Dischd. 4th. April Do.	
Mary Melledge	Do.	1	1	England	Do.	Dischd. 24th. Janry. 1800	19 Years
Murry George	Do. 24		1	Boston	Edward Procter	Dischd. 6th. April 1798	
[Mo]rse[16] Jethaniel	May 7	1		England	Arnold Welles jur.	Died 26 May Do.	one Week
[Ma]son Peggy	Do. 16		1	Boston	Edward Procter	Dischd. 28th. July Do.	
[McLauc]klin Mark	Do. 30		1	Ireland	Stephen Gorham	Died 2d. augt. Do.	
Miller Katy	June 17th.	1		Ireland	Jona. L. Austin	Run away 30th. June 98	2 years
Mayo Mary Ann	July 2d.		1	Boston	Wm. Smith	Died 11th. Septr. 1800	
Morris Edward	Do. 5	1		Ireland	Redford Webster	Died 8th. July 1798	33 years
Morton Kath:	Do. 6		1	Philada.	Henry Hill	Died 25th. augt. Do.	4 years
Mason Margaret	augt. 10	1		Boston	Edward Procter	Dischd. 20th. Febry. 1799	
Maden John	Do. 22	1		Ireland	Do.	Died 6th. Septr. 1798	14 years
Mays Lettice	Octor. 9	1		Do.	Oliver Brewster	Dischd. 21st. Decr. Do.	50 years

16 The bottom left corner of the page is torn, resulting in the loss of text in this and the next two entries.

Names	Time of Admission	State	Town	Towns they belong to[1]	By what Overseer	When dischd., Died, Bound out, Run away.	Time they have been here in this State
McDonal Daniel	Do. 21	1		Scotland	Arnold Welles jur.	Dischd. 4th. Febry. 1799	3 years
Morse Uriah & his Daughter	Novr. 22 Do.	1	1	Walpole Do.	Wm. Smith Do.	Dischd. 30th. April Do. Dischd. 22d. June Do.	
Mongo Rachel & her Child (Elias)	Do. 23d. Do.	1 1	1	England Do.	Do. Do.	Died 23d. Augt: 1816 Bound Out 22d. April 1802	two Days 4 years Do. 2 years[17]
Moore Sarah	Decr. 10	1		Boston	Edward Procter	Died 23d. Janry. 1799	
Mitchel Richd.	Do. 8th.	1		England	Oliver Brewster	Dischd. 7th. Febry. Do.	3 year
Melledge John	1799 Janry. 9th.	1		Boston	Edward Procter	Dischd. 31st. March Do.	
Murry John	Do. 31	1		France	Redford Webster	Dischd. 10th. Febry. 1799	one year
Moore Elizath.	Febry. 4	1		Ireland	Whole board	Dischd. 8th. April Do.	
Martin Peggy	Do.	1		Do.	Do.	R. away 28th. March 1799	4 years
Mason Peggy	April 14	1		Boston	Edward Procter	R. Do. 8th. Augt. Do.	
Mackenny Jona.	Do. 24	1		Pownalborough	Redford Webster	Run away 30th. april Do.	
McElroy William	Do. 26	1		Boston	Edward Procter	Dischd. 15 May Do.	
Hannah Morse	July 18	1		Do.	Arnold Welles	Dischd. 25th. Augt. 1800	
Millhorn John	Octor. 12	1		Holland	Thos. Perkins	R. away 5th. May 1800	16 years
McElroy William	Novr. 7	1		Boston	Edward Procter	Died Decr. Do.	
McMannis Henry	Do. 22	1		Ireland	William Smith	Dischd. 17th. April 1800	One Week
Mongo John a Child	March 4th.	1		Born of Rachel Mongo		Died 8th. Octor. Do.	
Mason Margaret	Decr. 17	1		Boston	Wm. Smith	Dischd. 12th. June 1800	
McLane Isabella	Do. 9	1		Pownalboro	Do.	Dischd. 1st. May 1800	50 years

17 These two words are entered in a column titled "age."

Names	Time of Admission	State	Town	Towns they belong to[1]	By what Overseer	When dischd., Died, Bound out, Run away.	Time they have been here in this State
	1800						
Molato Male Child	Janry. 16	1		left within the Door about 8 o'clock PM		Died 14th. Septr. Do.	
Matthews Nancy Negro	Do. 24	1		Rhode Island	Jona. L. Austin	Dischd. 27th. Feby. 1800	10 years
McCarty Sarah	Febry. 1	1		Cape Britton	Edward Procter	Dischd. 21st. July Do.	27 years
Marley Partrick child	April 5	1		England, Born of Eunice Johnson 5th. April		Dischd. 31st. Augt.	1 Day
Moran Mary & her child Harriot	May 15th. Do.	1 1		Boston Do.	William Phillips jur. Do. (her Father)	Dischd. 22d. May 1800 Dischd. Do. Do.	Paul Hitchborn
Morrison Andrew	Do. 31	1		Canada	Arnold Welles jur.	Dischd. 3d. Augt. Do.	4 Days
Martin Lydia & her Daughter	July 6 Do.	1 1		Boston Do.	Jona. L. Austin Do.	Dischd. 26th. Do. Do. Dischd. 6th. Augt. Do	Charlotte Foalke
Martin Peggy	Augt. 4th.	1		Ireland	Sheraj. Bourne	R. away 17th. Octor. Do.	6 years
Monk Betsey & George her son Francis her son	Do. 5		3	Waldoborough Waldoborough Do.	Jona. L. Austin	Dischd. 30th. June 1801 Bound out 16th. Octor. 1800 Dischd. 30th. June 1801	5 years
Mahony Thos.	Do. 11	1		Ireland	Thos. Perkins	Dischd. 25th. Septr. 1800	2 months
Mead Abigail	Do. 23d.	1		Portsmouth	Shearja. Bourne	R. away 31st. Augt. 1800	2 year
Marstin Betsey	Do.		1	Lynn	Do.	R, away Do. Do.	
Mayo Elisha	Septr. 24		1	Eastham	Wm. Smith	Dischd. 8th. Octor. Do.	
Man who has lost part of his Tongue}	Octor. 6th.	1		a foreigner	Edward Edes	R. away 15th. Novr. 1800	one month
Elizabeth Moore & her child} Henry (son of John Murffey)}	Do.	2		Ireland	Do.	Dischd. 6th. April 1802	6 years
Millhorn Jane	Do. 19		1	Marblehead	Henry Hill	Dischd. 25th. Octor. 1800	

Names	Time of Admission	State	Town	Towns they belong to[1]	By what Overseer	When dischd., Died, Bound out, Run away.	Time they have been here in this State
James McClure	Do. 27	1		Newyork	Jona. L. Austin	Dischd. 12th. April 1802	12 years
Malem Edward	Do. 29		1	Boston	Do.	Died 24 Sept 1807	
McCordy Hariot	Do. 27	1		Canada	Stephen Gorham	Dischd. 8th.Augt. 1801	12 years
Mead Abigail	Novr. 17	1	<1> 0	Portsmouth	Shearja. Bourne	R away 9th. Febry. 1801	2 years
Marstin Betsey	Do.		1	<Lynn> Boston	Do.	Do. 28th. April Do.	
Monk Abigail	Do. 15		1	Boston	Edward Edes	Dischd. 5th. Septr. Do.	<2 years>
Mays Lettice	Do. 18		1	Ireland	Do.	Died 4th. March 1801	40 years
Mahony Thos.	Do. 24	1		Do.	Redford Webster	Dischd. 7th. April 1801	5 months
Milhorn John	Decr. 4	1		Holland	Thomas Perkins	Died 10th. June Do.	
Millen John	Do. 10	1		<England> Germany	Edward Procter	Dischd. 5th. March 1801	3 years
Mackin Hugh	Do. 9	1		Ireland	Wm. Phillips jur.	Dischd. 11th. May Do.	2 years
Melvill Elizabeth Mrs.	Do. 1	1		Boston	Jona. L. Austin	Dischd. 5th. Janry. 1805	
McLane Arabella	Do. 8		1	Wiscassett	Wm. Smith	Dischd. 15th. April 1801	
Morse Hannah	Do. 26		1	Boston	Henry Hill	Did not return 28th. Septr. 1809	
Nexon Dickerson Susanna	1795 Sept. 17th.		1		Stephen Gorham	Dischd. 15th. Octor. 1795	
Natreves Andrew	Octor. 5th.	1		Sweden	William Smith	Dischd. 20 Octor. 1795	2 Weeks. 1 Day
Norris James	1797 Janry. 7th.	1		Ireland	Stephen Gorham	Dischd. 11th. April 1797	
Nugent Rachel	Febry. 23		1	Boston	Henry Hill	Dischd. 3d. April 1797	Delivered of a Dead child Febry. 28th. 1797

Names	Time of Admission	State	Town	Towns they belong to[1]	By what Overseer	When dischd., Died, Bound out, Run away.	Time they have been here in this State
North Samuel	Octor. 27	1		Ireland	Edward Proctor	Dischd. 13th. Novr. Do.	
Nolen Richard	1798 Janry. 16	1		Do.	Do.	Dischd. 12 Febry. 1798	2 Weeks
Newell Cato Nego.	April 23	1		Africa	Jona. L. Austin	Died 7th. Novr. Do.	40 years
Nooney John	Septr. 19	1		Ireland	Stephen Gorham	Dischd. 19th. Decr. Do.	5 years
Nash James	Octor. 8	1		Boston	Do.	Died, 17th. Octor. 1798	
Nooney John	1799 April 27	1		Ireland	Thomas Perkins	Dischd. 20 Septr. 1799	6 years
Newell Sally (child)	July 18		1	Boston	Arnold Welles	Dischd. 25 Augt. 1800	
Newell Cato Nego.	Novr. 4th.	1		Africa	Edward Edes	Dischd. 28th. May 1800	16 years
Newman Mary	1800 June 16	1		Connecticut	Thomas Perkins	Died 26th. Octor. 1803	9 years
Newell Polly	Decr. 15		1	Lynn	Redford Webster	Dischd. 10th. Janry. 1801	
Neward Dinah} Negro alias Howard }	Do. 30	1		Rhode Island	Jona. L. Austin	Dischd. 23d. Febry. Do.	2 years
Osburne James	1795		Do.			Sent to the Work house 10th. Augt. 1795	
Osburne James	Septr. 3d.		Do.		Stephen Gorham	Dischd. 1st. Augt. 1796	
OQuill Maurice	Decr. 12	1		Ireland	Do.	Dischd. 23d. Janry. 1796	
OQuill Maurice (child)	1796 March 13		1	Born of Betsey Shean		Died 16th. Octor. 1798	
Betsey Do. Child	Do.		1	Do.		Died 25th. Septr. 1798	
Orrill Henry	Octor. 21		1		Do.	Died 8th. Augt. 1798	

Names	Time of Admission	State	Town	Towns they belong to[1]	By what Overseer	When dischd., Died, Bound out, Run away.	Time they have been here in this State
Olive B[lack] Woman	[1797] April 3d. 1797		1	Born in Affrica}	Redford Webster	Dischd. 31 May 1797	
Osgood, David Sawer	May 15th. Do.		1	Boston	Wm. Phillips jur.	Died 19th. augt. Do.	a Child
Osborn John	Augt. 1t.		1	England	Wm. Smith	Dischd. 23d. Do. Do.	1 year Sailor
Ogier Abraham	Novr. 7		1	London	Stephen Gorham	Died 25 July 1798	24 years
Mary his wife	Do.		1	Do.	Do.	Dischd. 4th. Septr. Do.	Do.
Owens Mary	1798 Janry. 13th.		1	Marblehead	Wm. Smith	Died 11th. Febry. 1798	
Olive a negro woman	Augt. 16		1	West India	Redford Webster	Died 21st. Augt. Do.	about 25 years
Ormond Hannah	1799 May 18		1	Africa	Henry Hill	Dischd. 10th. Octor. 1799	five years
Oliver Quickly	June 11		1	Do.	Wm. Phillips jur.	Died 10th. Decr. Do.	43 years
Ormond Charlotte	July 14		1	Born of Hannah Ormond		Dischd. 10 Octor. –99 Her Father James Ormond	
Obrin John	Octor. 15		1	Ireland	Edward Proctor	Dischd. 30th. Novr. 1799	15 years
Oliver Adam	1800 April 12		1	Boston	Henry Hill	Died 10th. May 1800	
Osgood John	June 2		1	Do.	Edward Edes	Dischd. 19th. June Do.	
Parks Nancy	1795 July 21st.		1	Springfield	William Smith	Run away 7th. Septr. 1795	6 Weeks. 6 Days
Poor Salem	Septr. 21		1		Stephen Gorham	Dischd. 26th. Do	5 Days
Peters <James> Say Jonas	Octor. 7th.		1	Amsterdam	Edward Proctor	Dischd. 18th. Janry. 1796	
Pilsbury Isaac	Do. 20		1		Jna. L. Austin	Dischd. 10 July Do.	

Names	Time of Admission	State	Town	Towns they belong to[1]	By what Overseer	When dischd., Died, Bound out, Run away.	Time they have been here in this State
Parsons Sukey	Do. 31	1		New York	William Smith	Dischd. 11th: May Do.	
Poley Bart	Novr. 25	1		Ireland	Redford Webster	Dischd. 21st. Decr. 1795	
Payson Ann			Do.			Dischd. 2d. Decr. 1795	
Perkins Thomas	Decr. 18	1		England	Stephn. Gorham	Dischd. 29 Do.	
Priezing Abm.	Do. 28		1		Henry Hill	Dischd. 24th. March 1796	
Patten Mary	Janry. 1st. 1796			1	Arnold Welles Junr.	Dischd. 12th. Febry. 1796	
Preston Rebecca	Do. 2		1		Edward Proctor	Dischd. 6th. Janry. 1796	
Perkins Thomas	Do. 7	1		England	Stephen Gorham	Dischd. 6th. April Do.	
Polydor B[lack] man	Do. 19	1		Negro	William Smith	Died 14th. Febry. Do.	
Pearce Mrs. Nabby	Febry. 3d.		1	Plymouth	Henry Hill	Dischd. 7th. April Do.	
Peirce Simon	Do. 4d.	1		England	Do.	Died 24th. Febry. Do.	
Peirce Rebecca	Do. 17	1		Connecticut	Do.	Dischd. 13th. April Do.	
P[ierce] Eliza Dos. Child	Do.	1			Do.	Do. Do. Do.	
Putam Rebacca	March 10		1		Edward Proctor	Dischd. 5th. April Do.	
Patterson John	Do. 23	1		Ireland	William Smith	Dischd. 7th. Octor. Do.	
Paine Bella	May 14	<1>	1	Black Woman	Redford Webster	Dischd. 4th. July Do.	
Posey Edmond	Do. 20	1		Black Child	Henry Hill	Died 4th. June Do.	
Preston Rebecca	June 6		1		Stephen Gorham	Died 15th. Do. Do.	
Patterson Sally	Septr. 7	1	<1> 0		Wm. Smith	Died 18 Decr. Do.	
Phaeman Patrick	Do. 28	1		Ireland	Stephen Gorham	Dischd. 7th. April 1801	about 12 years

Names	Time of Admission	State	Town	Towns they belong to[1]	By what Overseer	When dischd., Died, Bound out, Run away.	Time they have been here in this State
							Sells Lemon
Peirce Nabby	Novr. 4		1	Plymouth	John Sweetser	Died 7th. March 1797	
Perkins Thos.	Do. 17	1		England	Stepn. Gorham	Died 29th. Novr. 1796	
Isaac Pilsbury	1797 Janry. 4th.		1	Boston	Thos. Perkins	Dischd. 24th. Augt. 1797	Sent W. house
Panot Rebacca	March 31		1	Boston	Do.	Died 5th. July 1797	age 43 years
Patten Mary	June 13		1	Do.	Redford Webster	Died 15th. April 1801	
Puttam Rebacca	augt. 26		1	Do.	Thos. Perkins	Dischd. 1st. Febry. 1798	
Peters John His Wife, & 2 Children	Octor. 11 Do.	1	3	France Boston	Arnold Welles Do.	Dischd. 18th. May Do. Dischd. 23d. Janry. 1798	20 years Children Dischd. his Wife run away 16 May
Powell John	Do. 24	1		New York	Edward Proctor	Dischd. 28 April 1798	4 weeks
Parker John	Do. 26	1		Do.	Do.	Dischd: 23d. March 1798	4 Days
Pilsbury Isaac	Do. 28		1	Boston	Willm. Smith	Dischd. 7th. July Do.	Run away
Peirrier Lewis Negro	Decr. 2d.	1		Isle France	Thos. Perkins	Dischd. 8th. July Do.	one month
Poley Mary	Do. 26		1	Boston	Edward Procter	Dischd. 18th. Janry. 1798	
Peggy a Negro	1798 Febry. 15		1	Do.	Arnold Welles jur.	Dischd. 15 March Do.	{ With Child by { Jack Dinnis
Puttman Rebecca	1798 March 9		1	Boston	Edward Procter	Dischd. 10 April 1798	
Parkman Elias	April 12		1	Do.	Do.	Dischd. April 12, 1825	supd. 18 yrs old
Peires John black man	May 2d.	1		West Indias	Arnold Welles	Died 4th. May 1799	5 year

600

Names	Time of Admission	State	Town	Towns they belong to[1]	By what Overseer	When dischd., Died, Bound out, Run away.	Time they have been here in this State
Peirce Benjamin	Do. 30		1	Boston	Henry Hill	Dischd. 25th. July 1798	
Puttman Rebecca	June 18		1	Do.	Edward Edes	Dischd. 24th. July 1798	
Powers Edward	Do. 8th.	1		Ireland	Edward Procter	Dischd. 8th. Septr. Do.	15 years
Panot Sukey	July 21	1		England	Oliver Brewster	Bound out 4th. augt. 1798	1 years
Perch William	Augt. 7		1	Do.	Jona. L. Austin	Dischd. 15th. Octor. Do.	33 years
Pirce Margaret	6		1	Boston	Edward Procter	Run away 20th. 98	
Puttman Rebecca	Do. 18		1	Do.	Do.	Dischd. 19th. March 1799	
Pirce Margaret	Septr. 18		1	Do.	Do.	Died 11th. Janry. 1799	
Powers Edward	Do. 9	1		Ireland	Do.	Run away 1 Oct. 1807	15 years
Pilsbury Isaac	Novr. 21		1	Boston	Jona. L. Austin	R. away 4th. June 1803	
Pike Mary (or Peeke)	Decr. 22		1	Do.	Wm. Smith	Died 18 Janry. 1812	
Pettman Sarah	1799 Janry. 15th.		1	Salem	Redford Webster	Died 16th. Janry. 1799	
Parker Josiah	Febry. 4		1	Boston	Whole board	Dischd. 26th. March Do.	
Perry Jesse	March 5th.		1	Do.	Henry Hill	Do. Do. Do.	
Poole Mary	Do. 19		1	Weston	Edward Procter	Dischd. 19th. June Do.	
Prat Hannah	May 23		1	Boston	Edward Edes	Dischd. 2d. Septr. Do	
Puttman Rebecca	June 3d.		1	Do.	William Smith	Dischd. 5th. May 1800	
Pilsbury Samuel	July 9th.		1	Do.	Edward Edes	Dischd. 3d. Janry. 1800	
Phillips <William> say James	Augt. 22d.	1		Philadelphia	Henry Hill	Dischd. 15th. Novr. 1799	R. away one year

Names	Time of Admission	State	Town	Towns they belong to[1]	By what Overseer	When dischd., Died, Bound out, Run away.	Time they have been here in this State
P[...][18] Samuel	Septr. 20		1	Kittery	Arnold Welles jur.	Dischd. 30th. Septr. Do.	
[P]ishpay Polly	Do. 24		1	Medford	Stephen Gorham	Dischd. 11th. Janry. 1800	
Prat Hannah	Do. 25		1	Do.	Arnold Welles jur.	R. away 28th. Sepr. 99	
Pearce Lettice Mrs.	Octor. 31		1	Dorchester	William Smith	Dischd. 5th. Novr. Do.	
Perry Alexr.	Novr. 9	1		England	Arnold Welles jur.	Dischd. 18th. Janry. 1800	3 months
Prat Hannah	Do. 14		1	Lancaster	Jona. L. Austin	Dischd. 7th. Do.	
Prat Hannah	1800 Janry. 10th.		1	Chelsea	Edward Procter	Dischd. 25th. March Do.	
Paine Sarah	March 22d.		1	Boston	Edward Edes	Dischd. 2d. April Do.	
Do.	June 8		1	Do.	Arnold Welles jur.	Dischd. 12th. June Do.	
Parker Josiah	May 15		1	Do.	Wm. Donnison	Dischd. 29th. Do. 1801	
Potter David Negro	Augt. 21	1		Virginia	Shearja. Bourne	Dischd. 1st. Septr. 1800	16 years
Pilsbury Saml.	Septr. 1st.		1	Boston	Redford Webster	Died 23d. Octor. Do.	
Pendegrass Elenor	Octor. 1st.	1		Ireland	Do.	Died 27th. Decr. Do.	6 years
Perry William	Do. 2d.		1	Boston	Jona. L. Austin	Dischd. 23d. Febry. 1801	
Prat Hannah	Novr. 17		1	Lancaster	Shearja. Bourne	R. away 28th. April Do.	
Paddock Sukey	Do.		1	Charlestown	Do.	Dischd. 19th. Janry. 1801	
Paine Sally	Do. 24		1	Boston	Redford Webster	Dischd. 27th. Decr. 1800	
Plaisted Elisha	Do. 29	1		Portsmouth	Do.	Dischd. 3d. April 1801	18 months
Peters John	Decr. 23d.	1		France	Jona. L. Austin	Dischd. 10th. March 1801	18 years
Hannah his Wife	Do.	<1> 0 1		Boston	Do.	Do.	

[18] The edge of the page is worn, resulting in the loss of some text in this entry as well as the next.

Names	Time of Admission	State	Town	Towns they belong to[1]	By what Overseer	When dischd., Died, Bound out, Run away.	Time they have been here in this State
John & Mary their Children	Do.	<2>	2	Do.	Do.	Do.	Do.
Quinlar Jane	1798 Dec. 17th.	1		Halifax	William Smith	Dischd. 2d. May 1799	5 years
Quinlar Daniel	1799 Febry. 13	1		Ireland	John Sweetser	Dischd. 2d. April 1799	Do.
Quinlar Jane	May 29	1		Halifax	Henry Hill	Dischd. 24th. Augt. Do.	5 years
Wm. Rutherford Born of Thankfull Rutherford (alias Edmonds)	1795 Febry. 5th.	Do.				Died 31st. Augt. 1795	13 Weeks 1 Days
Ross Benjamin	Septr. 22	1		Boston	J L.Austin	Died 21 Nov 1810	
Ritchie John	Octor. 10	<1>	1	Ireland	Stephen Gorham	Dischd. 10th. June 1796	Disallowed by the Commitee
Rice Thomas	Novr. 1st.	1		Do.	Henry Hill	Died 27th. Febry. 1796	
Robertson James	Do. 9	1		Scottland	Redford Webster	Dischd. 30th. May Do.	
Reed Katy B[lack] W[oman]	Do. 13	1		So. Carolina	Wm. Smith	Dischd. 8th. April Do.	
Raymond Jona.	1796 Janry. 11th.	1			Do.	Died 20th. Janry. 1796.	
Rutherford John	March 14	1		Scotland	Do.	Dischd. 4th. April Do.	2 years
Raymond Elanor	May 14	1			John Sweetser	Dischd. 24 Augt. 1797	Sent to the Work house
Robertson Andrew	Do. 18	1		Ireland	Edward Proctor	Dischd. 23d. May 1796	
Robertson Mary	Do.	1		Do.	Do.	Dischd. Do. Do.	

Names	Time of Admission	State	Town	Towns they belong to[1]	By what Overseer	When dischd., Died, Bound out, Run away.	Time they have been here in this State
Russell Robert	Do. 30	1		Scotland	William Smith	Run away 22d. June Do.	
Robertson Nancy	June 10		1	Bolton	Edward Proctor	Dischd. 19th. Janry. 1798	
Rice Hepha.	July 2d.		1		Stephen Gorham	Dischd. 24th. Augt. 1797	Sent to the Work House
Rice Thos. Wm.	7	1		Ireland	A. Welles junr.	Dischd. 17th. Augt. 1797	
Ruddock Ebenr.	Septr. 23d.		1		Edward Proctor	Dischd. 10th. April 1797	
Rutherford John	Novbr. 4th.	1		Scotland	William Smith	Run away 7th. Febry. 1797	1 year
Rogers William a Child	Do.		1		Redford Webster	Dischd. 4th. Novr. 1796	
Rogers Wm. a Child	Do. 5		1		Edward Edes	Dischd. 22d. Augt. 1797	
Ryan William	Do. 26	1		Ireland	Wm. Smith	Dischd. 11th. April 1797	
Rice Thomas	Decr. 10	1		Philada.	Thomas Perkins	Dischd. 6 June Do.	2 years
Jane Rowen	Do.		1		Edward Proctor	Dischd. 10th. Janry. 1797	
Reed Mary	1797 Janry. 4th.		1		Henry Hill	Dischd. 27th. April 1797	
Rutherford John	March 29	1		Scotland	Wm. Smith	Dischd. 2d. May Do.	
Ryon William	April 13th.	1		Ireland	John Sweetser	Dischd. 18th. augt. Do.	
Remmick Daniel	May 18th.		1		Edward Proctor	Dischd. 23d. May 1797	
Ruddock Ebenr.	Do. 23		1	Boston	Redford Webster	Dischd. 10 June Do.	Run away
Robinson Thos.	June 19	1		Ireland	William Smith	Died 11 Decr. Do.	
Robertson James	Do. 20	1		Scotland	Redford Webster	Died 23d. June 1797	
Roberts Thos.	July 10		1	Boston	Edwards Proctor	Dischd. 27th. July Do.	
Rutherford John	26	1		Scotland	Henry Hill	Dischd. 7th. Septr. Do.	Run away

Names	Time of Admission	State	Town	Towns they belong to[1]	By what Overseer	When dischd., Died, Bound out, Run away.	Time they have been here in this State
Ride Edward	Septr. 13	1		Ireland	Thos. Perkins	Dischd. 21st. Do. Do.	one month
Richey John	Octor. 9	<1> 0	1	Do.	Edward Edes	Died 14th. April 1799	age 77 years
Revere Nancy	Do. 18		1	Boston	William Smith	Dischd. 30th. April 1798	
Raymond Elanor	Do. 28		1	Do.	Do.	Died 18th. Septr. 1805	
Rice Hepha.	Octor. 28		1	Boston	William Smith	Died 28th. Novr: 1809	
Richia alias Pew Elanor	Do.		1	Do.	Do.	Died 12th. Octor. 1800	18 years
Rutherford John	Novr. 8	1		Scotland	Stephen Gorham	Dischd. 20th. June 1798	
Roberson Thomas	17	1		Ireland	Henry Hill	Dischd. 30th. Decr. 1799	one Year
Rogers William a Child	Do. 20		1	Medford	Do.	Bound Out 9th. May 99	
Sarah Rogers Do.	Do.		1	Do.	Do.	Dischd. 4th. Febry. 1801	
Reed John	Do. 21	1		Philadelphia	Redford Webster	Run away 6th. April 1798	17 years
James Roberts	Decr. 11	1		Georgia	Edward Proctor	Dischd. 26th. July 1799	5 months
Ravin Elizabeth	1798 April 28	1		Boston	Edwd. Procter	Dischd. 14th. May 1798	
Reed John	Augt. 17	1		Philadelphia	Stephen Gorham	Died 23d. Augt. Do.	17 years
Rutherford John	Octor. 5	1		Scotland	Oliver Brewster	Dischd. 2d. April 1799	4 years
Roderigee Frederick Negro	Decr. 5	1		Portugae	Redford Webster	Died 12th. Decr. 1798	2 months
Ryan William	1799 Febry. 4th.	1		Ireland	Whole board	R, away 5th. May 1800	
Ridan Sukey	Do.		1	Boston	Do.	Died 19th. Septr. 1801	
Ramsdale Silas Child	Do. 12	1	1	Bound out 20th. }	October 1801 Thomas Perkins	Silas Dischd. 16th. Decr 1800 Bound out 1st. April 99	F Lynn & M Sharon
Ramsdale Joseph Do.	Do.	1	1				

Names	Time of Admission	State	Town	Towns they belong to[1]	By what Overseer	When dischd., Died, Bound out, Run away.	Time they have been here in this State
Robinson William, &	March 21	1		Maryland	William Smith	Dischd. 7th. June 1799	8 years
Nancy his Wife	Do. 28	1		Do.	Oliver Brewster	Dischd. Do. Do.	
Rutherford John	April 4th.	1		Scotland	Do.	R. away 22d. April Do.	4 years
Read Sarah	May 13		1	Boston	William Smith	Dischd. 30th. May Do.	
Roch Robert	Do. 15	1		Ireland	Do.	Dischd. 30th. Augt. Do.	5 years
Ramsdell Nabby	July 18		1	Boston	Arnold Welles	Dischd. 30th. July Do.	
Raynders John	Octor. 14	1		Holland	Henry Hill	Died 22d. Octor. 99	3 Weeks
Rutherford John	Decr. 2d.	1		Scotland	Stephen Gorham	Dischd. 17th. March 1800	4 years
Rowen Susanna &	Do. 12		1	Boston	Henry Hill	Dischd. 29 Janry. 1800	{J. Stanton his Father
John Stanton her Child	Do.		1	Do.	Do.	Died 27th. Janry. 1800	
Ramsdale Nabby	1800 Janry. 18		1	Do.	Redford Webster	Died 29 Octr. 1809	
[Reyn]old[19] Michael & Child	April 12	2		Ireland	John Sweetser	Dischd. 14th. April 1800	7 years
Mary Ratford	Do. 21		1	Boston	Stephen Gorham	R: away 23d. Do.	
Reynold Michael & / Nancy his child	Do. 26 / Put to board with Mrs. Patience watts of Medford @ 4/ pr. Week	2		Ireland	Edward Edes	He Dischd. 8th. May 1800 / 26th. Do. Do.	7 years
Ryan John	Do. 30		1	Do.		Dischd. 15th. July Do.	6 Weeks
Richardson James	June 20th.		1	Virginia	Jona. L. Austin	R, away 17th. Octor. Do.	9 years
Richardson Lydia	Do. 24		1	Boston	Edward Procter	Died 1st. Decr. Do.	
Ryan William	Do. 26	1		Ireland	Henry Hill	Died 12th. Oct 1811	
Rind Wm. (Seaman)	Augt. 6		1	Do.	Redford Webster	Dischd. 5th. Septr. 1800	2 Years

19 The edge of the page is worn away resulting in the loss of text at the beginning of the entry.

Names	Time of Admission	State	Town	Towns they belong to[1]	By what Overseer	When dischd., Died, Bound out, Run away.	Time they have been here in this State
Rind or Ryan James	Do. 25	1		Do.	Do.	Dischd. Do. Do.	1 year
Rinner John	Septr. 15		1	Boston	Do.	Dischd. 14th. Octor. Do.	
Rutherford John	Octor. 20	1		Scotland	Wm. Smith	Died 21st. Janry. 1801	4 years
Mrs. Sarah Reed	Novr. 14		1	Boston	Do.	Died 25th. Septr. Do.	
<Russel John> Roch Ralph	Novr. 30	1		Italy	Redford Webster	Dischd. 9th. Febry. 1801	3 Days / [Pa?]
Rammon John	Decr. 9	1		England	Edward Procter	Dischd. 14th. Janry. 1801	2 years
Robinson Joseph child	Decr. 27th. 1800		1	Boston	Henry Hill	Dischd. 20th. Octor. 1801	
Do. Elias	Do.		1	Do.	Do.	Dischd. 17th. Septr. 1801	
Do. John	Do.		1	Do.	Do.	Dischd. 12th. May 1803	taken out by his Aunt Mary Ingalls of North Hampton
Rumrill James	Do. 26		1	Do.	Stephen Gorham	Dischd. 7th. Febry. 1801	
Stone John	1795 augt. 26th.	Do. 1			William Smith	Dischd: 21st. Septr. 1795	26 Days
Shepherd Ann	Septr. 7th.		Do. 1		Edward Proctor	Died 19th. May 1797	
Simpson Josiah	Do. 18th.	1			Redford Webster	Dischd. 7th. March 1796	
Sharp Charles	Do. 19	1		England	Edward Edes	Dischd. 9th. Septr. Do.	one year Negro
Hannah Shimmin		Do.		Negro Woman		Run away 20 Septr. 1795	16 Weeks
Sadler William	Do. 25	1		England }	Jon L. Austin	Died 20th. Feb. 1818 <Disallowed by the Commitee>	
Sadler's <William> Mary[20] Wife	Do. 25	1		Do.		Died 17th. Dec 1817 alowed by the Committee	
Stone Neley	Octor. 20		1	Marblehead 1	Edward Proctor	Dischd. 28th. Novr. Do.	5 Weeks 4 Day

20 Mrs. Sadler's given name is interlined above the canceled text.

Names	Time of Admission	State	Town	Towns they belong to[1]	By what Overseer	When dischd., Died, Bound out, Run away.	Time they have been here in this State
Spencer Charlotte molato Child	Do. 25	1		Her Mother born in N. Caroline	Henry Hill	Died 19th. April 1796	
Stebbens Elizth.			Do.			Died 30th. Octor. 1795	
Shining Hannah	Novr. 30	1		Negro	John Sweetser Junr.	Run away 28th. April 1796	
Smith George	Decr. 8	1		Ireland	William Smith	Dischd. 12th. March 1796	
Stewart, Mary Ann	1796 Janry. 18	Do.		Do.		Died 10th. Decr. 1795	
Simmonds John			1		Edward Proctor	Dischd. 9th. Febry. 1796	
Scott Mary	Do. 23d.		1		Do.	Dischd. 2d. July Do.	
Smith Edward			Do.	England		Died 2d. Febry. 1796	
Polly Shores & her 2 Children	Febry. 11	1			William Smith	Dischd. 12th. Do. Do.	
	Do.	2			Do.	Dischd. Do. Do.	
Sharp Jane / child Born of	20		1	Dorcas Sharp		Bound out 26 Decr. 1801	
Smith Samuel	March 3th.		1	Boston	Edward Proctor	Dischd. 10th. Febry. 1801	
Smith George	Do. 20	1		Ireland	William Smith	Run away 20th. April 1800	
Stone Mary	April 7		1		Edward Proctor	Run away 20 July Do.	
Sloane Isabella	Do. 11		1		Arnold Welles junr.	Dischd. 20th. April Do.	
Sullivan Phillip	Do. 15	1		Ireland	Stephen Gorham	Dischd. 10th. June Do.	
Springfield Mrs. Mary	Do. 29	1		France at Sea[21] [alias?]	Henry Hill	Died 25th. Septr. 1799	
Shepherd Mary	Decr. 2d. 1795		1	Omitted	Whole board	Dischd. 2d. Febry. 1797	
Kenney Hannah child		1		Born of Mary Shepherd	Do.	Died 16th. Janry. 1797	
Springfied John a child	1796 April 29	1		Born of Mary Springfield	Springfield	Bound Out 21st. July 1802	about 3 months

21 The previous two words are interlined and marked for insertion at this point

Names	Time of Admission	State	Town	Towns they belong to[1]	By what Overseer	When dischd., Died, Bound out, Run away.	Time they have been here in this State
Sharp Mary	July 1st.		1		Oliver Brewster	Dischd. 27th. July 1796	
Stevens Charles	Do. 11	1		England	Stephen Gorham	Dischd. 26th. Janry. 1797	
Stone Polly	Augt. 4th.		1		Edward Proctor	Died 3d. Septr. Do.	
Smith Rebecca Negro	Septr. 21st.	1		New York	Henry Hill	Dischd. 9th. April 1798	9 years
Smith Mary a Child	Do.	1				Dischd. Do.	
Smith Lewis Do.	Do.	1				Dischd. Do.	
Stone Winifeed	Do. 22d.		1	England	Thos. Perkins	Dischd. 20th. Octor. 1796	Run away
Scollay Rebecca & four Children	Octor. 20	<4>	1 / 4	<Ireland> Boston / Do.	Wm. Smith	Dischd. & one Child June 6th. 1797 / 3 of the Children Dischd. 26th. April 1797	15 years
Scoct Mary	Octor. 25	1		Ireland	Edward Proctor	Died 28th. Octor. 1796	
Smith Charles	Novr. 5	1		Ireland	Do.	Died 7th. Novr. Do.	
Smith Rachel	Do. 21		1	Boston	Henry Hill	Dischd. 24 Do. Do.	
Sanders Edward a Child	Do. 22		1	Do.	Edward Proctor	Dischd. 3d. April 1797	
Sanders Nathniel Do.	Do.	1		Do.	Do.	Do.	
Sanders Richard Do.	Do.		1	Do.	Do.	Do.	
Stone Winfred	Decr. 10	1		England	Do.	Dischd. 10th. March Do.	
Steward William	Do. 23d.	1		London	Do.	Dischd. 28th. April Do.	
Savage Richard	1797 Janry. 8th.	1		New York	Redford Webster	Dischd. 21st. June Do.	
Shimmin Hannah	Febry. 4	1		Negro	Thos. Perkins	Dischd. 14 May 1798	
Scott Sam. Black man	March 7	1		New York	Do.	Dischd. 22 June 1797	3 months

Names	Time of Admission	State	Town	Towns they belong to[1]	By what Overseer	When dischd., Died, Bound out, Run away.	Time they have been here in this State
Stone Nancy	Do. 10		1	Do.	Oliver Brewster	Dischd. 24 Augt. Do.	W[ork] H[ouse]
Stone Winfred	Do. 20		1	England	Wm. Phillips jur.	Dischd. 22d. Augt. 1797	
Smith Jno.	June 15	1		Garmany	Henry Hill	Dischd. 30th. Novr. Do.	20 years
Solomon Abraham	Do. 24	1		Poland	Edward Proctor	Dischd. 6th. July 1797	one Week
Sevenhousen Conelis	July 8	1		Amsterdam	Do.	Died 31th. Do.	7 Weeks
Rebecca Stackpole Alias Puttum	Do. 14		1	Boston	Thomas Perkins	Dischd. 25 July 1797	
Smith Phebe Negro	May 15	1		New York	Whole board	Dischd. 14th. Augt. Do.	5 years
Smith Charles a Child Born July 26		1		of Phebe Smith		Do.	
Smith James Do. Born Do.		1		of Do.		Do.	
Shelton Benjamin	Augt. 9		1	Salem	William Smith	Dischd. 24th. augt. 1797	sent W house
Stevenson Suley a Child Born of Lydia Marston	Do. 14		1	Boston, her father's Name John Stevenson		Died 25th. augt. 1797	
Sprague William	Septr. 6		1	Do.	Redford Webster	Died 23d. Septr. Do.	
Smith <George> say John	Do. 12	1		Philada.	Wm. Smith	Dischd. 5th. Octor. Do.	
Simpson Josiah	Octor. 17		1	Boston	Henry Hill	Dischd. 10th. Novr. Do.	
Shelton Benjamin	Do. 28		1	Salem	Wm. Smith	Dischd. 6th. Decr. Do.	
Stone Sally	Do.		1	Do.	Do.	Died 9th. Septr. 1799	
[Sto]ne[22] Nancy	Do.		1	Do.	Do.	Died 13th. Do. 1800	
[...]ens Elizabeth	Novr. 3d.		1	Charles Town	Jona. L. Austin	Died 5th. April 1799	
Swain Sarah	Do. 9		1	Boston	Stephen Gorham	Dischd. 31st. May 1798	

22

1   The edge of the page is worn away, resulting in the loss of text in this and the following entry

Names	Time of Admission	State	Town	Towns they belong to[1]	By what Overseer	When dischd., Died, Bound out, Run away.	Time they have been here in this State
Selleck Edward	Decr. 14	1		Standford	Edward Proctor	Dischd. 15th. Janry. 1798	2 Week
Spires James	Do. 17	1		Virginia	William Smith	Dischd. 12 Febry. Do.	3 Weeks
Stone Edward	Do. 25		1	Boston	Redford Webster	Dischd. 25th. April, 1798	
Sellecks Edward	1798 Febry. 3d.	1		Standford	Redford Webster	Died 25th. March 1798	2 months
Sinnot Lois	Do. 28	1		Connecticut	Do.	Dischd. 30th. March Do.	3 Days
Sinnot Betsy Child	Do.	1		Do.	Do.	Dischd. Do.	Do.
Smith James Negro Child	Do. 26	1		New York	Thos. Perkins	Dischd. 11th. April 1798	5 years
Sehreon Mary	March 5th.	1		Ireland	Edward Procter	Dischd. 12th. March 1798	1 year
Sinnot Thomas	Do. 17	1		Do.	Do.	Dischd. 23d. Do. Do.	3 Weeks
Southward Mary	Do. 22d.		1	Ashburnham	Henry Hill	Dischd. 26th. May Do.	
Nancy Stevens	March 23d.	1		Portsmouth	Jona. L. Austin	Dischd. 16th. Octor. 1798	7 years
Spooner Rachel	May 21	1		Hingham	Thomas Perkins	Dischd. 31st. May 1798	
Sharp Rosenna Negro	June 1	1		Rhode Island	Stephen Gorham	Died 16th. July Do.	5 years
Swain Sarah	Do. 15		1	Boston	Jona. L. Austin	Dischd. 6th. July Do.	
Smith Rebecca Negro	Do. 19	1		New York	Edward Edes	Dischd. 2d. Septr. 1799	7 years
Mary her Child	Do.	1			Do.	Bound out 13th. April 1799	
Lewis her Child	Do.	1			Do.	Dischd. 2d. Septr. Do.	
Spear Joseph	July 10th.		1	Boston	Edward Procter	Died 16th. Junly[23] 1798	
Stevens Liffee	June 29	1		New Hampshire	Henry Hill	Dischd. 30th. April 1799	7 Weeks

[23] Thus in MS.

Names	Time of Admission	State	Town	Towns they belong to[1]	By what Overseer	When dischd., Died, Bound out, Run away.	Time they have been here in this State
Southward Polly	Augt. 4th.		1	Ashburnham	Do.	Dischd. 14th. Septr. 1798	
Stone Edward	Do. 11		1	Do.	Redford Webster	Dischd. 20th. augt. 98	
Stevens Liffee a child	Do. 26	1		born of Liffee Stevens of N. Hampshire		Died 3d. Decr. Do.	John Holton of Salem her father, who Died 4th. March last
Stone Winfred	Octor. 13	1		England	Oliver Brewster	Dischd. 5th. Novr. 98	
Southworth Mary	Do. 15		1	Ashburnham	Do.	Dischd. 22d. Decr. Do.	
Smith Elizabeth	Do. Do.		1	Do.	Arnold Welles	Dischd. 18th. Decr. 1798	
Smith Betsey	Do.		1	Do.	Do.	Dischd. 4th. Decr. 1798	
Stone Winfred	novr. 5th.	1		England	Oliver Brewster	Run away 4th. July 1800	
Shimmin Hannah	Do. 10	1			Edward Procter	Dischd. 1st. Decr. 1798	
Shepherd Mary	Do. 16		1	Boston	Willm. Smith	Dischd. 16th. April 1799	
Sears Joshua	Decr. 13	1		Connecticut	William Phillips Jur.	Dischd. 26 Decr. 1798	one month
Sandey or Sarndis Elizth.	Do. 24		1	Marblehead	Stephen Gorham	Discd. 9th.April 99	been Boston 37 years
Silvester Elizabth.	Do. 31		1	Lynn	Redford Webster	Dischd. 22d. April 1800 her Husband in Plymouth	
Stone Edward	1799 Janry. 8		1	Boston	Do.	Dischd. 13th. March 1799	
Stevens Nancy	Febry. 4th.	1		Portsmouth	Whole board	R away 22d. April Do.	7 years
Swift <Sally> or Fanny	Do.		1	Boston	Do.	Died 12th. Feb. 1820	aged 75 Feb. 1820
Simson Homes	Do.		1	Do.	Do.	Dischd. 22d. April 1799	Run away
Sharp Mary	Do.		1	Do.	Do.	<Dischd. 6th. June 1803> Died 11th. Novr. 1803	
Screen James	Do. 8		1	Ireland	Stephen Gorham	Dischd. 23d. April 1799	fifteen years

Names	Time of Admission	State	Town	Towns they belong to[1]	By what Overseer	When dischd., Died, Bound out, Run away.	Time they have been here in this State
Simpson Ebenr.	Do. 15		1	Boston	Redford Webster	Died 24th. Febry. 1799	
Smith Elizabeth	April 13		1	Do.	Arnold Welles	Dischd. 30th. Janry. 1800	
Smith Betsey	Do.		1	Do.	Do.	Dischd. 2d. Septr. Do.	
<*Sloan Wm.*> Child	June 14	1		Do.	born of Rachel Mongo	Died 8th. Octor. Do. (John Mongo)	
Sharp William	Do. 16	1		England	Edward Edes	Dischd. 31st. Octor. 1801	
Sheppard Mary	Augt. 6		1	Boston	Jona. L. Austin	Dischd. 20th. Augt. 99	
Sawer Mary	Septr. 3		1	Do.	Wm. Phillips jur.	Died 12th. Novr. Do.	
Stevens Nancy	Do. 25	1		Portsmouth	Henry Hill	R away 12th. Novr. 1800	7 years
Southworth Mary	Octor. 11		1	Boston	Jona. L Austin	Dischd. 12th. June 1800	
Swinson Andrew	Do. 26	1		Norway	Stephen Gorham	Dischd. 16th. Novr. 99	3 Weeks
Smith Betsey	1800 Janry. 7th.		1	Boston	Edward Procter	Dischd. 30th. Janry. 1800	
Spooner Benjn.	March 3d.	1		So. Carolina	William Smith	Died 8th. March Do.	20 years
Sears Joshua	May 27	1		Connecticut	Oliver Brewster	Dischd. 9th. July Do.	2 years
Elizabeth Smith	May 31st.		1	Boston	Oliver Brewster	R. away 6th. Decr. 1803	
Sambo / French Negro	June 30	1		West Indies	Jona. L. Austin	Died 7th. July 1800	3 years
Smith Betsey	<*Augt.*> 4		1	Boston	Shearja. Bourne	R away Decr. 2d. Do.	
Simmons Catharine	Do. 22	1		Rhode Island	Do.	R away 31st. augt. 1800	9 weeks
Simpson Josiah	Octor. 7		1	Boston	Redford Webster	Dischd. 3d. Novr. Do.	
Searl Jonathan	Do. 13	1		Connecticut	Henry Hill	Run away about 1st. Decr.	5 years
Seward Jerusha alais Simmons	Novr. 17				Shearja. Bourne	Dischd: 21st. Novr. 1800	

Names	Time of Admission	State	Town	Towns they belong to[1]	By what Overseer	When dischd., Died, Bound out, Run away.	Time they have been here in this State
<Do.> [*i.e., Seward*] Sophia	Do.			Boston	Do.	Run away 7th. April 1801	
Smith Theodore, child	Do. 18	1		Boston	Edward Procter	Bound Out 14th. Janry. 1801	5 years old 26th. April last
Saunders Sally	Do. 22	1			Shearja. Bourne	R. away 10th. Janry. Do.	
Talloon William	1795 Septr. 8th.	1		Ireland	John Sweetser	Dischd. 12th. May 1796	
Tinsley Priscilla	Do. 29			Marblehead	Henry Hill	Dischd. 13th. Octor. 1795	2 Weeks
Tillet Caty	Octor. 9		1		Edward Proctor	Dischd. 30th. March 1796	
Thompson Betsey			1	Melato child		Bound out & Dischd. the House 17th. Octor. 1795	19 Weeks. 6 Days 17th. Octor. 1795
Tuckerman Jack	Novr. 5	1		West Indias	Arnold Welles	Run away 10 Novr. 1795	5 Do.
Thomson Alexr.	Decr. 3	1		Scotland	Willm. Smith	Dischd. 8 Decr. Do.	
Tuttle Mary	Do. 26		1		John Sweetser	Dischd. 27th. Janry. 1796	
Tuckerman Jack	Do. 30	1		West Indias	Stephen Gorham	Dischd. 6th. April Do.	
Tynsberry Mary	[1796] May 14	1			Redford Webster	Dischd. 17th. May Do.	
Theophilus, Alexandr.	Novr. 7th.	1		England	Wm. Smith	Dischd. 13th. Febry. 1797	9 year
Tellit Caty	Decr. 5		1		Edward Proctor	Dischd. 7th. Febry. 1797	
Taylor Peggy	1797 Janry. 24	1			Redford Webster	Dischd. 24 Augt. Do.	Sent to the Work house
Tuckerman Jack	Febry. 3d.	1		West Indians	Wm. Smith	Dischd. 16 March 1797	
Trodia Laurence	March 10	1		France	Oliver Brewster	Died 12th. March 1797	from the Work house

Names	Time of Admission	State	Town	Towns they belong to[1]	By what Overseer	When dischd., Died, Bound out, Run away.	Time they have been here in this State
Tuckerman Jack	Do. 17	1		West Indias	William Smith	Dischd. 12th. May Do.	
Tellit Caty	June 12		1	Boston	Edward Proctor	Dischd. 5th. Septr. Do.	Run away
Thomson Anne	Do. 14		1	Do.	Oliver Brewster	Died 10th. Novr. 1797	
Toby Stephen	July 28		1	Sandwich	Redford Webster	Died 5th Augt. 1797	Paid for by the Town
Taylor Peggy	Octor. 28		1	Boston	William Smith	Dischd. 6th: Septr. 1798	
Thompson Alexr.	Novr. 7	1		Scotland	Edward Proctor	Dischd. 9th. Decr. 1797	16 years
Theophilus Alexd.	Decr. 29.	1		England	William Smith	Dischd. 24th. april 1798	9 years
Tom a Black man	1798 March 21	1		an Old Negro	Jona. L Austin	Died 9th. May Do.	
Mary Tuttle	Do. 23		1	Boston	Thomas Perkins	Dischd. 24th. May Do.	
Theophilus Alexr.	July 19th.	1		England	Arnold Welles jur.	Dischd. 24th. Octor. Do.	9 years
Tillick Katty	Novr. 2d.		1	Boston	Thos. Perkins	Dischd. 2d. April 1799	
Thorndike Nancy	Do. 18		1		John Sweetser	Died 19th. Novr. 1798	
Thompson Alexr.	Do. 22	1		Scotland	Stepen Gorham	Dischd. 31st. Decr. Do.	16 years
Thomson Nancy	Decr. 6		1	Boston	Do.	Dischd. 11th. May 1799	
Turner Nancy alias Betsey Hoselton }	Do. 18	1		Philadelphia	Redford Webster	Died 25th. Decr. 1798	
Theophilus Alexr.	1799 Janry. 9	1		England	Arnold Welles jur:	Dischd. 15th. April 1799	9 years
Thomas Mary Negro	Febry. 18		1	west Indies	Stephen Gorham	Dischd. 20th. March 1799	3 years
Thomas Joseph Child Born	27	1		of Mary Thomas Negro		Dischd. Do.	
Tillick Katty	April 6th.		1	Boston	Edward Procter	R. awy 28th. May 1799	

615

Names	Time of Admission	State	Town	Towns they belong to[1]	By what Overseer	When dischd., Died, Bound out, Run away.	Time they have been here in this State
Thompson, James	Augt. 3d.		1	Woburn Precinct	Edward Edes & Redford Webster	Dischd. 31st. Augt. Do.	Or Burlington
Taylor William	Do. 23d.	1		England	Henry Hill	Dischd. 2d. Septr. Do.	18 months
Trayhorn, Ann	Do. 31		1	Boston	Whole board	Dischd. 16th. Do. Do.	
Tillet Caty	Septr. 12		1	Do.	Edward Procter	Died 4th. Novr. 1799	
Tolman Nathal.	Decr. 8		1	Needham	William Smith	Dischd. 11th. Decr: Do.	57 years
James Thompson	Decr. 10th.		1	Woburn		Dischd. 13th. Decr. 1799	
James Thompson	Do. 25		1	Do.	John Sweetser	Dischd. 15th. March 1800	
Thompson Nancy	1800 March 10th.		1	Boston	Edward Procter	Dischd. 26th. April Do.	
Tuttle mary	Do. 31st.		1	Do.	Do.	Dischd. 20th. July 1801	
Trayhorn Ann	April 5		1	Do.	Jona. L. Austin	Dischd. 7th. april 1800	
Theophilus Alexander	May 5	1		England	Stephen Gorham	Dischd. 6th. Octor. Do.	10 years
Taylor Margaret	Augt. 4	<1> 0	1	Boston	Shearja. Bourne	R. away 31st. Augt. 1800	
Trueman Barny	Septr. 3d.	1		England	Redford Webster	Died 5th. Septr. Do.	3 years
Tubb Ephraim	Decr. 17		1	Pembroke	Edward Procter	Dischd. 22d. Decr. Do.	
Thomson John	Do. 27	1		England	Edward Edes	Died 16 Janry. 1801	20 years
Theophilus Alexander	Do. 28	1		Do.	Arnold Welles	Dischd. 18th. March Do.	10 years
Vuson Domminic	1796 May 10th.	1		Burdo in France	Edward Proctor	Dischd. 24th. June 1796	

Names	Time of Admission	State	Town	Towns they belong to[1]	By what Overseer	When dischd., Died, Bound out, Run away.	Time they have been here in this State
Vose Eunice	1797 Novr. 25th.	1		born in Groton	Arnold Welles	Died 10th. Novr. 1817	liv'd in Boston 26 years
Vranchx Jacob	1800 June 4th.	1		Germany	Arnold Welles jur.	Dischd. 17th. Augt. 1800	16 years
Vickery <Eliza.> Rebecca	July 3d.		1	Boston	Henry Hill	Dischd. 29th. July 1800	
Vose Sylvia Negro	Octor.		1	Milton	Shearja. Bourne	R. away 14th. Octor. Do.	
White Esther	1795 June 4th.		Town		Edward Proctor	Dischd. 17th. Septr. 1795	
Ward's James Servant	Octor. 5th.	1		Docr. Warren to pay His board & Charges	William Smith	Do. 24th. Octor. Do.	2 Weeks 5 Days Paid for
Whitemore Joseph (Boy)	Do. 26	1			Edward Edes	Do. 29th. Decr. Sent to the Work house	
Willis Hugh	Novr. 4th.	1		England	John Sweetser Junr.	Died 10th. Novr. 1796	
Williams Ruth	Do. 14		1		Arnold Welles	Dischd. 20 Janry. 1796	
Williams Ruth Junr.	Do.		1		Do.	Do. 20 Febry. Do.	
Wendell Nuton (B[*lack*] child)	Do.	Do.				Died 16 Nov. 1795	24 Weeks 1 day
Wendell Polly	Do.	Do.				Dischd: 24th. Do.	25 Do. 2 Do.
Waterman Eliza	Do. 26		1		Henry Hill	Dischd. 20th. May 1796	
Welch Thomas	Decr. 3		1	Conecticut	Oliver Brewster	Dischd. 4th. Decr. 1796	1 Day
Williams Moses	Do. 16		1	Born of Ruth Williams Junr.		Died 28th. Janry. 1796	
Weeks Lewis born of Katy Reed	Do. 17		1	of So. Carolina		Died 23d. Febry. Do.	9 Weeks 1 Day

Names	Time of Admission	State	Town	Towns they belong to[1]	By what Overseer	When dischd., Died, Bound out, Run away.	Time they have been here in this State
Wilkinson Peter & his Wife Alias Mary Lewis	1796 Janry. 19th. Do.	1 1		Holland Do.	Stephen Gorham Do.	Died 20th: Janry. 1796 Dischd. 28th. Octor. Do.	
Waples Hannah	April 15		1		Edward Proctor	Disd. 20th. June 1797	
Webster Ebenr.	May 19	1		Conecticut	Henry Hill	Dischd. 23d. May Do.	
Wheaton Betsy	July 21		1		Do.	Dischd. 27 Augt. Do.	
Waterman Lucy	Do. 22		1	Born of Betsy Wheaton		Dischd. Do. Do.	Simeon Waterman her father
Webb Polly	Augt. 6		1		John Sweetser	Died 21st. Febry. 1797	
Wormly Philip	Do. 29	1		Bengall	Edward Proctor	Died 31st. Augt. 1796	two years
Winslow Magant	Novr. 30		1	B[lack] Woman	Stephen Gorham	Died 7 Decr. Do.	
Wait Polly Wm. her son a Child	Decr. 13 Do.	1 1		B[lack] Woman	Do. Do.	Run away with her Child 5th. Decr. 1797	
Walker Ezekiel	1797 Janry. 2d.		1		Edward Proctor	Died 9th. March 1797	
Williston Mary	Do. 4		1		Thos. Perkins	Died 20 May Do.	
Walker Thos.	Febry. 10		1		Oliver Brewster	Dischd. 24th. Augt. 1797	Sent to the Work house
White Mary	Do. 23		1	Boston	Edward Proctor	Died 18th. May 1801	73[24]
Williams Robt.	March 3d.		1	Do.	Do.	Died 10th. Sept. 1818	
Williams Adam & his Wife, Negros	April 22 Do.	1 1		West Indias Do.	Henry Hill Do.	Died 15th. May 1799 Died 23d. Janry. 1798	He Cannot tell
Wainwood Mary	Do. 25	1		Rhode Island	Edward Edes	Died 23d. May 1797	
Ward William	July 8	1		Connecticut	William Smith	Dischd. 23d. Augt. Do.	Sailor

24 Entered in a column titled "age."

Names	Time of Admission	State	Town	Towns they belong to[1]	By what Overseer	When dischd., Died, Bound out, Run away.	Time they have been here in this State
Williams Evan	Do. 21	1		England	Stephen Gorham	Dischd. 24 Do. Do.	Sent to the Work house 6 d[...][25]
Wilkinson Mary Alias Lewis	May 23		1	Marblehead		Died 23d. Septr. Do.	from the [...][26]
Walker John	Octor. 5		1	Boston	Jona. L. Austin	Dischd. 17th. Octor. Do.	
Wheeler John	Do. 7	1		Germany	Oliver Brewster	Died 14th. Janry. 1798	14 years
Wheeler Mary his wife	Do.		1	Weymouth	Do.	Dischd. 22d. Do. Do.	
Williams Evan	Do. 28	1	<1> 0	<Boston> England	William Smith	Dischd. 30th. April Do.	one Week
Walker Thomas	Do.		1	Boston	Do.	Dischd. 15th. May 1799	
Woodman Eliza.	Novr. 1st.		1	Do.	Redford Webster	Dischd. 30th. March 1798	
Woodman Charles	Do. 28	1		Halifax	Stephen Gorham	Dicshd. 23 March 1798	25 years
John Wilson a Child	Novr. 29th.	1		Father born in Scotland mother in England	Redford Webster	Died 22d. Janry. 1800	
Woldram Jacob	Do. Do.	1		New York	Do.	Dischd. 13 Febry. 1798	2 Weeks
White Boston, Black Man	Decr. 2	1		affrica	William Smith	Dischd. 10th. March Do.	10 Years
Wheeler Ephraim	Do.		1		Henry Hill	died 24th. Decr. 1797	
Warren James	1798 Janry. 13th.		1	Boston	Whole board	Died 12th. May 1800	In a fit
Warner William's Son child	Do. 16	1		Do.	Stephen Gorham	Dischd. 11th. Octor. 1798	
Warner Martha	Do. 24		1	Do.	Wm. Phillips jur.	Dischd. 25th. Augt. 1798	
Woldram Jacob	Febry. 15	1		New York	Arnold Welles	Dischd. 20th. Febry. 1798	2 Weeks
Woldram Jacob	Do. 21st.	1		New York	Redford Webster	Dischd. 17th. March Do.	2 Do.

25 Entered in a column titled "age." The edge of the page is worn away.
26 The remainder of the entry is covered by a strip of paper pasted to the MS to repair a tear.

Names	Time of Admission	State	Town	Towns they belong to[1]	By what Overseer	When dischd., Died, Bound out, Run away.	Time they have been here in this State
Warner Nathaniel & Hannah his Wife	March 2d. / Do.		1 / 1	Boston / Do.	Edward Procter / Do.	Dischd. 23d. June 1808 / Died 31 Mar. 1808	
Warren Nancy Born	Do. 17	1		Rhode Island	of Mary Dunham	Dischd. 16th. May 1798	
Woodman Charles	April 3d.	1		Halifax	Redford Webster	Discd. 21st. June Do.	25 years
Woodman Elizabeth	Do. 7		1	Boston	Henry Hill	Dischd. 30th. April 98	
Woodman Elizabeth	May 14		1	Do.	Redford Webster	Dischd. 30th. June Do.	
Woodman Elizabeth	July 7		1	Do.	Wm. Smith	Dischd. 7th. Octor. 1799	
White William, Negro	Do. 12	1		London	Redford Webster	Died 16th. July 1798	5 years
Woodman Charles	augt. 4	1		Halifax		Dischd. 18th. augt. Do.	
Williams Sarah	Do. 1	1		Ireland	Oliver Brewster	Dischd. 13th. Septr. Do.	1 month
White Elizth. and Anthony her Son a Child	Octor. 29 / Do.	1 / 1		Do. / Do.	Stephen Gorham / Do.	Dischd. 9th. Novr. Do. / Do. Do.	2 years / Do.
Woodward Isaac	Novr. 22d.	1		at Sea	Edward Procter	Dischd. 24th. Decr. Do.	7 years
Wiesen Christain	Decr. 4	1		Germany	Henry Hill	Dischd. 3d. May 1799	3 years
Webb Thomas	Do. 7	1		Philada.	Arnold Welles jur.	Dischd. 24th. Decr. 1798	2 Weeks
Williams Mary, Negro	1799 Janry. 5	1		West Indies	Redford Webster	Dischd. 2d. April 1799	22 years
Waterman Susanna	Do. [22]		1	Boston	Do.	Discharged 13 Mar 1799	
Williams Evan	Do. 28	1		England	Henry Hill	Dischd. 15th. Febry 1799	1 year
Whitemore Joseph	Febry. 4		1	Boston	Whole board	R. away 20th. May 1803	
Willet John & his Wife, Dorcas	Do. / Do.		1 / 1	Do. / Do.	Do. / Do.	Dischd. 11th. May 1799 / Dischd. 9th. April 1799	

Names	Time of Admission	State	Town	Towns they belong to[1]	By what Overseer	When dischd., Died, Bound out, Run away.	Time they have been here in this State
Woodward Isaac	Do.	1		at Sea	Do.	R. away 28th. March 1799	7 year
Wyatt Polly	Do. 9		1	Boston	Redford Webster	R. away 22d. April Do.	
Woodman Charles	Do. 22d.	1		Halifax	Oliver Brewster	Dischd. 12th. July Do.	26 Years
[Wa]rden[27] Elizabeth	Do. 4		1	Boston	from the Work House	Died 21st. April 1807	Omitted
[Wi]lliams Evans	March 28	1		England	Stephen Gorham	Dischd. 30th. May 1799	1 year
[Wi]llet Dorcas	April 16		1	Boston	Redford Webster	Dischd. 22d. July Do.	
Lavina Wickum	June 7		1	Do.	John vinall	Dischd. 20th. Octor. Do.	
Walter Fanney	Do. 17	1		Portsmouth	Jna. L. Austin	Dischd. 7th. Octor. 1799	1 year
Williams Mary. Negro	Do. 19	1		West Indies	John Vinall	Dischd. 2d. Septr. 1799	22 years
Willoughby Margaret	Do. 22d.	1		Virginia	Do.	Dischd. 2d. Novr. 1799	3 years
White Moses	Do. 29		1	Boston	Stephen Gorham	R. away 21st. Augt. 99	
West Hannah Nego.	July 2d.	1		New York	John Vinall	Dischd. 19th. July 1799	5 years
Wood Debby	Do. 18		1	Boston	Arnold Welles	Died 27th. Octor. 1800	
White Betsy Negro	Do. 24	1		West Indies	John vinall	Dischd. 24th: July 1799	4 or 5 years 6 hou[...][28]
Willet Dorcas	July 30		1	Boston	John Sweetser	R. away 12th. June 1800	
Willet John	Augt. 12		1	Do.	Edward Edes	R. away 5th. May 1800	
Woodward Isaac	Septr. 24	1		on the Seas	Stephen Gorham	Run away 15th. Novr. 99	7 years
Warner Wm. Child	Do. 25		1	Boston	Arnold Welles jur.	Dischd. 7th. July 1800	
Weston Susanna	Octor. 9		1	Do.	Stephen Gorham	Died 31st. Janry. 1800	

27 The edge of the page is worn away, resulting in the loss of several letters in this and the next two entries.
28 Entered in a column titled "age."

Names	Time of Admission	State	Town	Towns they belong to[1]	By what Overseer	When dischd., Died, Bound out, Run away.	Time they have been here in this State
Whitecomb Richd.	Do. 12		1	Do.	Do.	Dischd. 26th. June Do.	
Wilds Katy	Novr. 16		1	Do.	Jona. L. Austin	Died 18th. Novr. 1799	
Williams Prince Negro	Do. 18	1		Africa	<John Sweetser,> say Henry Hill	Dischd. 22d. April 1800	16 years
Warner Martha	Do. 21st.		1	Braintree	William Smith	Dischd. 7th. July Do.	
Williams Evan	1800 Janry. 31	1		England	Redford Webster	Dischd. 6th. March 1800	1 year
Walter Fanney	Febry. 14	1		Portsmouth	Willm: Phillips jur.	R. away 31st. July Do.	1 1/2 year
Willims Evan	April 10	1		England	John Sweetser	Dischd. 20th. May 1800	1 year
Williams Elizath.	Do. 28		1	Boston	Edward Edes	Dischd. 6th. Augt. Do.	
Witet Abigail	June 5		1	Do.	Stephen Gorham	Dischd. 17th. July Do.	
Wales Hannah	July 29		1	Qunicy	Edward Procter	Dischd. 1st. Septr. Do.	
Wibird Polly	Do. 30		1	Boston	Jona. L. Austin	R. away 12th. Augt. 1800	
Walter Fanney	Augt. 4th.	1		Portsmouth	Shearja. Bourne	Dischd. 26th. May 1801	2 years
Williams Mary Negro	Do. 5	1		West Indies	Do.	Run away 31st. Augt. 1800	22 years
White Polly Negro	Do.		1	Malden	Do.	R. away 12th. Augt. Do.	
Whittemore Joseph Senior	Septr. 1st.		1	Boston	William Smith	Died 10th. May Do.	
Wybert Polly	Do. 6		1	Do.	Shearja. Bourne	R. away 27th. Sept. 1800	
Wybert Susannah	Do.		1	Do.	Do.	Do.	
Willard: A: Cabel	Do. 13		1	Do.	Edward Edes	Dischd. 30th. Septr. Do.	
Wybart Patty	Octor. 6	1		France	Shearja. Bourne	Dischd. 7th. Octor. Do.	4 years
Williams Ruth	Do. 4th.		1	Boston	Do.	Run away 14th. Do.	

Names	Time of Admission	State	Town	Towns they belong to[1]	By what Overseer	When dischd., Died, Bound out, Run away.	Time they have been here in this State
White James	Do. 28	1		New York	William Phillips jr.	Dischd. 23d. March 1801	1 month
Welsh John	Novr. 4	1		Ireland	Stephen Gorham	Dischd. 7th. April Do.	3 Weeks
Waterhouse Richd.	Do. 10		1	Boston	Do.	Died 24th. Septr. Do.	
Wybert Patty or Polly	Do. 17	1		<France> Salem	Shearja. Bourne	Dischd. 10th. Janry. 1801	4 years 8[29]
Walsh Edward	Do. 18	1		Ireland	Stephen Gorham	Dischd. 18th. Decr. 1800	3 years
Weiser Christien	Decr. 1st.			Germany	Jona. L. Austin	Dischd. 23d. April 1801	5 years
Whitecomb Richd.	Novr. 25		1	Boston	Do.	Died 5th. Novr. 1804	74 years[30]
Wild Benjn. Child	Decr. 3		1	Do.	Henry Hill	Bound Out 27th. March 1802	
Williams Prince Negro	Do. 12	1		Africa	John Sweetser	Dischd. 22d. Janry. 1802	17 years / not allowd.
White Diana Negro	Do. 14		1	Roxbury	Stephen Gorham	Dischd. 15th. Janry. 1801	
Diana her Child	Do.		1	Do.	Do.	Do.	
Warner Martha & her Child <Wm.>	Do. 27 Do.		1 1	Braintree	Henry Hill Do.	Dischd. 11th. May Do. Bound Out 12th. Septr. Do.	Say Augustin
Wybart Patty or Polly	Do. 30		1	Salem	Shearja. Bourne	Dischd. 10th. Janry. 1801	
Young Ebenr.	1799 Febry. 4		1	Boston	Whole board	Died 4th. Augt. 1799	
yeaton Elizath.	June 14		1	Marblehead	Henry Hill	Dischd. 10th. July 1799	been in this Town 20 years
yeaton Elizath.	1800 Do. 5th.		1	Do.	Edward Procter	Dischd. 18th. June 1800	

[29] Entered in a column titled "age."
[30] Entered in a column titled "age."

MISCELLANEOUS ALMSHOUSE
BIRTHS AND DEATHS
1756 – 1771

These are the only systematically organized lists of Almshouse births and deaths in the eighteenth-century records. The extensive lists of admissions and discharges do note occasional births and deaths in the Almshouse but cannot be used to calculate full statistical frequencies. The best that can be done is to assume that the births recorded in these lists for a single year might indicate a rough estimate of annual births in a steady almshouse population and turnover. The same holds true for the list of deaths. These kinds of data are much more systematically recorded and organized, with much more detail by the second and third decades of the nineteenth-century. These lists are found in Box 9, Registers 1 and 2 of the manuscript records. Please see Notes 2 and 3 below.

Account of Children Born in the Alms House from the Year 1756.[1]

	[Child's Name]	[Birth Date]			Mothers Name	
	Nathl. Phillips	August	17th.	1756	Mary Waterman	
	Susanna McGown	Janua.	27	1757	Mary McGown	
	Joffs a Mulatto	April	27	1757	Eliza. Davis	
	William Harris	May	26	1757	Alice Harris	
	Richard Bill	Janu	16th.	1758	Mary Dorothy	Dead
	Saml. Eddy	Feby	1	1758	Joanna Eddy	Dead
	Kata. Devereux	Apl.	11	1758	Kata. Devereux	
	Rachel Rawson	Apl.	22	1758	Rachel Rawson	
	John Marrow	May	16	1758	Ann Marrow	
	Peter Salter	June	8	1758	Susa. Salter	
Camp Women	Sarah Saunders	Septr.	22	1758	Mary Bodge	
	John Bensy		30	1758	Abigl. Bensy	
	John McDonald	Octo.	6	1758	Margt. McDonald	
	Ann Guy		12	1758	Bridget Guy	
	William Gault		29	1758	Mary Gott	
	Eliza. Barger	Novr.	28	1758	Eliza. Barger	
	Mary Young	Decr.	8	1758	Mary Young	
	Katha. Stevens	Janua.	21	1759	Katha. Stevens	
	Mary McGown	Februa.	1	1759	Mary McGown	
Captives from Canaa.	Barbara Jordan	Mar.	17	1759	Barbara Jordan	
	Margt. Thompson		28	1759	Margt. Thompson	
	Susanna Cain	May	5	1759	Susanna Cain	
	Rufus Winkley	July	10	1759	Sarah Winkley	
	Mary Bill	Mar.	9	1760	Mary Bill	
	John Manson	July	2	1760	Sarah Manson	Dead
	Mary Davis	Novr.	25	1760	Mary Davis	

John Watson		30	1760	Eliza. Lambert	
Eliza. Blanch	Apl.	7	1761	Mary Blanch	
Edward McGown	May	5	1761	Mary McGown	
Meheta. Lewis	July	21	1761	Meheta. Lewis	
Jacob Tuckerman	Augt.	7th	1761	Sarah Freeman	deced. Octo. 10th. 1763. Æt. 2 yrs.
Barto. Meloney	Decm.	12	1761	Mary York	
Ann Lintee		20	1761	Mary Lintee	
Eliza. Mullins		31	1761	Mary Mullins	
Hannah Barry	Feby.	10	1762	Mary Young	
Sarah Lassley	Mar.	20	1762	Ann Lassley	
Sarah Elson	Apl.	24	1762	Abigl. Elson	
Ann Tyrrell	Augt.	29	1762	Ann Tyrrell	
Sarah Perry	Mar.	24	1763	Eliza. Marshall	
Willm. Booze	Apl.	15	1763	Eleonar Booze	Deceased Septr. 9. 1763.
Eliza. Hammond	May	9	1763	Mary Hammond	
Hannah Winship	Augt.	31	1763	Hannah Burrell	Dead
Eliza. Pimm	Novr.	15	1763	Rebecca Pimm[2]	

Miscellaneous Almshouse Births and Deaths, 1756-1771

Record of Children born in the Alms house[3]

1763 Novr. 29 Margaret Forbush brot. to bed with a Son Nam'd [Thomas][4]

1764 Janr. 19th. Margaret Lawrance with a Daughter[5] the Father She Sayes his Name is Josiah Parker

1764 June 10 Margarett Cavernex[6] with A Son Nam'd George Herrin as the Mother Sayeth

June 24 Sarah Seergraves With A Girl Nam'd Sarah the Father of the Child, his name is Thomas Johnson[7] as She Sayes

Sepr. 9th. Hannah Bomfort of A Son Nam'd Robert

Octor. 22d. Mehettable Lewis of A Daughter Named Susanna

Octor. 30th. Alce Mollogen[8] of A Daughter Nam'd Margaret

1765 Janr. 6th. Mary Turner of a Son Named James Rogers

Janr. 21st. Christian Isbuster of A Daughter

Janr. 28 Elizabeth Clough alias Mortall of a Son[9] and Daughter

June 13 Jane Price of a Daughter named Susanna Thomas

July 29 Rebeckah Bradley of a Son named Thomas

1765. Augst. 2d. Mary Tuttle brot. to bed with a Daughter Mollatto

Decmr. 31 Mary Watt[10] brot. to bed with a Daughter Hannah[11]

Ditto 31 Eliza. Nickolson brot. to bed with a Daughter[12] Still born

1766 Janr. 3d. Lydia Richardson brot. to bed with a Son[13]

Janr. 7 Thomison Charleton brot. to bed With a Son Named George Sandiman[14]

Janr. 20 Dorothy Lewis brot. to bed With a Daughter[15]

March 1st. Margarett Johnson brot. to bed With a Son Willm. Fitzpatrick

March 28 Mary Waterman brot. to bed With 3 Children 2 boys & 1 Girl

April 1 Eliza. Clough brot. to bed with a Son[16]

April 24 Christian Isbuster brot. to bed with a Daughter

May 12 Anna Lenox brot. to bed with a Boy

May 21st. Judith Simmons[17] brot. to bed With a Girl

1766 June 5th. Mary Linte[18] brot. to bed With a Boy

June 27 Mary March brot. to bed With a Daughter the Father of the Child She Says his Name is Henry Miller[19]

628

Miscellaneous Almshouse Births and Deaths, 1756-1771

Septr. 3d.   Susanna Sloper Brôt to bed with a Daughter The Father of the Child

Do. 4th.   Dorcas Ballard Brôt to Bed with a Son The Father of the Child

Do. 14   Mary Turner Brôt to Bed With a Negrow female Child

Do. 24   Abigail Glover alias Elson Brot. to Bed With a Girl Named Abigail Negrow the Last presented to the Grand Jury

Octor. 10   Nancy Storey brôt to bed with a Negrow Male Child Novr. 4th Went Away from the house

Febr. 10 1767   Eliza. Kelley Alias Hase brot. to bed With a Male Child

April 5   Mary Clark brot. to bed With a Male Child

April 12   Mary Haynes brot. to bed with a Male Child

Ditto 13   Margaret Grainger brot. to bed With a Male Child

Ditto 21   Mary McGraw brot. to bed With a Daughter

Account of Children Born in the Alms House

Septr. 6. 1767.   Christian Isbester Brot. to Bed with a Girl

Octo. 25th.   Goodwin[20] Brot to Bed with a Boy

Novr. 27.   Eliza. Skinner Brot to Bed with a Boy

Decr. 3.   Susanna Bodge alias Jarden Brot to Bed with a Girl

Februa. 8 1768.   Martha Clough Brot to Bed with a Girl

17   Mary Tuttle Brot to Bed with a Boy

20th.   Sarah Brown Brot to Bed with a Boy

May 1st.   Rebecca Bradley Brot to Bed with a Boy

June 12th.   Ann Sample Brot to Bed with a Boy

18th.   Wharff Brot to Bed with a Girl

Decr. 29.   Eliza. Burges Brot to Bed with a Girl

Janua. 6 1769.   Sarah Dunseutt Brot to Bed with a Girl

24.   Sarah Varney   a Boy

25.   Katha. Sullivan   a Girl

Feby. 12th.   Zerviah Smith   a Boy

April 30th.	Mary Banks	a Girl	
Novr. 23d.	Eliza. Burnet	a Girl	
29.	Ann Hynes	a Boy	
	Priscilla Haden Brot to Bed of a Boy Janua. 9th. 1770.		
May 12. 1770.	Thomison Charlton	a Boy	
23.	Mary Saunders	a Girl	
June 6.	Eliza. Harris	a Boy	
July 31.	Margarett Jones	a Girl	
Augt.	Mary McCarthy	a Girl	
Augt. 20th.	Mary Gooding	a Girl	
Nov 13	Mary Walker	a Boy	Molatto
Decr. 11th.	Mary Whitman	a Boy	
April 13. 1771.	Christian Isbester	a Girl	
May 27.	Margarett Cunningham	a Boy	
June 24.	Abigail Clark	a Girl	
July 16	Ann Warren	a Boy	
Augt. 2.	Eliza. Thomas	a Girl	
Octo. 5.	Mary Banks	a Girl	
14th.	Sarah Magee (Prov)	a Boy	
Novr. 5.	Dorcas Osborn	a Girl	
	Eliza. Castle Octo. 22d.	a Boy	
June 4. 1767.	Mary <Waterman> Banks	Twins 1. Boy 1. Girl	

Account of People Deceas'd In the Alms house[21]

1763

Rebeckah Hall Ætat 45 Years Obit March the 25th. 1763

Jeremiah Rhoads Ætat 83 Yeares Obit April 5th.

Mary Croxford Ætat 70 Years Obit April 26 abt. 2 clock in morñg

Miscellaneous Almshouse Births and Deaths, 1756-1771

Mary Pilsberry Ætat 62 Years Obit May 8th.

Ann Pool Ætat 65th. Years Obit May 19th.

Joseph Milton Ætat 4 Years Obit June the 1st.

Arthur Keeves Ætat abt. 9 Years Obit June 8th.

Sarah Child Ætat 74 Years Obit June 13th.

Ann Droron[22] A Child 2 Years & 7 months old Obit June 25th.

Hannah Collis Ætat 45 Years Obit July 30th.

Rose A Negrow Woman Ætat Abt. 50 Yeares Obit Augst. 3d.

Mary Procter Ætat 68 Yeares Obit Augst. 10th.

Robert Ingolls Ætat 50 Years Obit Ditto 12th.

Mary Champny A mollatto Child 17 months old Obit Augst. 22d.

Elenor Bowe Ætat 29 Years Obit Augst. 25th. 1763

Mary Patterson Ætat 72 Years Obit September the 3d.

William Bowe A Child Abt. 5 months Old Obit Septemr. 9th.

Edward McGown Ætat 54 Years Obit Septemr. 11th.

Eliza. Scinner Ætat 60 Years Obit Sepr. 27th.

Christopher Procter Ætat 82 Years Obit Sepr. 28th.

Jacob Tuckerman A Child Abt. 2 Years Old Son of Sarah Freeman Obit October the 10th.

Jane Champion Ætat 82 Years Obit Octor. 18th.

Sarah Bumsted Ætat 56 Years Obit Octor. 28th.

William Waters Ætat 64 Years Obit November 4th.

Susannah Knott Ætat 75 Years Obit Novr. the 5th.

Mercy Street Ætat 52 Years Obit November the 26th.

George Skinner Ætat 90 Years Obit November 27th.

Michel Cavenu Ætat 50 Years Obit Decemr. 15th. left at his Dec'd £400 in Cash

Rachel Scrivener Ætat 63 Yeares Obit Decemr. 18th.

John Lukas Ætat 73 Years Obit Decemr. 20th. 1763

Hannah Winship a Child abt. 6 Months Old (Daughter of Hannah Burrell) Deceas'd December 30th. 1763

Miscellaneous Almshouse Births and Deaths, 1756-1771

Michel Butler Ætat 50 Years Obit January the 3d. 1764

John Bennet Ætat 80 Years Obit Janr. 10th. 1764 morning

Sarah Ryan Ætat 55 Years Obit Janr. 10th. at night

James Bassett a negrow man Alias Burnal Ætat 75 Yeares Obit Janr. 18th.

Elizabeth Fadre Ætat 40 Years Obit Janr. the 24th.

Wm. Woods A Child Abt. 7 months old Obit Febr. 18th. the mothers Name Abigail Farrier

Samuel Burnal Ætat 83 Years Obit Febr. the 26th.

John Warrick Ætat 45 Yeares Obit Febr. 26th.

Sarah Moor Ætat 83 Years Obit Febr. 28th.

A Child Abt. 6 weeks old Daughter of Margaret Lawrence Obit March the 1st.

Hannah Bass A Child Abt. 2 Yeares Old Obit March the 5th.

Susannah Florance Ætat 75 Yeares Obit March 6th. 1764

Abigail Waddle Ætat 65 Yeares Obit March the 8th.

Sarah Bailey Ætat 84 Yeares Obit Ditto the 8th.

Mary Ozmont Ætat 38 Years Obit April 4th. of the Small pox Inoculated[23]

Eliza. Hammon A Child Abt. 11 Months Old Obit April 5th. of Small Pox Inoculated

Tincom Ætat 70 Yeares Obit April 7th.

Mary Bill a Child 4 Years Old Obit April 13th of the Small pox Inoculated 15th. Day of March / had no Effect / had in Natural Way

Ralph Curtis Ætat 28 Years Obit April 17th.

Saml. Linty abt. 4 years old Obit April 21 of Small pox in the Natural way In the work house Decd. thear

Mehitable Lewis abt. 3 years Old Obit April 26th. of Small pox In the work house, Not Inoculated

Johannah Marshall Ætat 75 Years Obit April 26th.

Mary Fleet Ætat 84 Years Obit Ditto 28th.

Ann Street Ætat 40 Years Obit April 30th. alias Desain a blind woman / with Small pox in the Natural Way

Judith Cox Ætat 60 Yeares Obit April 30th.

Sarah Fessingdon Ætat Abt. 50 Yeares, Obit May 5th. with Small pox In the Natural Way

Eliza. Ruddock Ætat 22 Yeares Obit May 9th. 1764 Dec'd In the work house—with Small pox Enoculated

Miscellaneous Almshouse Births and Deaths, 1756-1771

Mary Evens Ætat 66 Yeares Obit May 9th.

Freelove Bass 4 Yeares Old Obit May 9th.

Margarett Lawrance Ætat 30 Yeares Obit May 10th: With the Small pox In the Natural Way

William Briant Ætat 13 Yeares Obit May 19th. of Small Pox in the Natural Way

Hannah Snelling Ætat 37 Yeares Obit May 28th. of Small Pox in the Natural Way

Cornelius Campbell Ætat 69 Yeares Obit May 30th.

Hannah Rust Ætat 53 Yeares Obit May 31st. of Small Pox in the Natural Way

Mary Long Ætat 60 Yeares Obit May 31

Dorcas Campbell Ætat 97 Years Obit June 22d. 1764

Thomas Eastwick Ætat 68 Years Obit June 25th.

Josiah Sneeling Ætat 58 Years Obit June 29th.

Frances Salter Ætat 45 Years Obit June 29th.

Hannah Roberts Ætat 53 Years Obit July 1st.

Josiah Scudder a Child abt. 3 Years Old Obit July 3d.

Hercules Brailsford Ætat 81 Years Obit July 15th.

David Tweed Ætat 65 Years Obit July the 25th.

Cuber A Negrow Woman Ætat 65 Years Obit Augst. 2d.

George Herrin A Child Abt. 7 Weeks Old Obit Augst. 3d. the mother of the Child's Name is Margarett Cavernex

Issac Peirce Ætat 78 Years Obit Augst. 4th.

James Millins Ætat 73 Years Obit Augst. 6th.

Jonathan Edmund Ætat 73 Years Obit Augst. 24th.

Sarah Elson A Child 2 Years Old Obit September the 1st. 1764

John Belsworthy Ætat 36 Years Obit Sepr. the 3d.

Mary Croutch Ætat: 63 Years Obit Septr. the 18th.

Francis Utinock A Child 5 months Old Obit Septr. 21st.

John Presberry Ætat 60 Years Obit Septr. 22d.

Elizabeth Morgan Ætat 64 Years Obit Septr. 28th.

Mehettible Hicks Ætat 82 Years Obit Octobr. 2d.

William Bradley A Child Ætat abt. 13 months Obit Octr. 28th.

Sarah Beetle Ætat 63 Years Obit November 12th.

Thomas Milton a Child abt. 2 years Old Obit Novemr. 15th.

Alexander Martin Ætat 73 Years Obit Novr. 20th.

Sarah Freeman Ætat 60 Years Obit Janr. 9th. 1765

Hannah Hoar Ætat 59 Years Obit Janr. 14th.

William Davison Ætat 30 Years Obit Febr. 14th.[24]

An Infant male Child abt. 3 Weekes Old of Eliza. Clough's Alias Mortals Obit Febr. 16th. 1765

Thomas Slooper A Child Abt. 9 months Old Obit Febr. 27th. the Mother's Name is Olive Slooper

John Hewit Ætat 64 Years Obit March 11th.[25]

Edward Turpin A Child Abt. 2 Years Old Obit March 20th.

Margarett Hasell Ætat 49 Years Obit March 23d.

Hannah Thornton Ætat 70 Years Obit April the 7th.

Mathew Wheeland Ætat 26 Years Obit April 14th.

Pelatiah Martin A Mollatto Child Abt. 3 Years Old Obit Aprl: 17th.

Robert Boyd A Child Abt. 6 months old Son of Sarah Haden Obit April 21st.

Eliza Addelton Ætat 40 Years Obit May the 6th.

Thos. Wharf A Child Abt. 2 Years Old Obit May 9th.

Joseph Simson Ætat Abt. 12 Years Obit May 10th. 1765

Mrs. Joanna Delotte Ætat 65 Obit May 16th. 1765

George Follin A Child Abt. 3 Years Old Obit June 3d.

Thomas Manson a Child about 4 1/2 years old Obit June 4th. A.M.

Hannah Chadwick Ætat. 75. Obit June 5th. 1765.

James Rogers a Child 4 months old Obit June 6th. his mother Name is Mary Turner

Susanna Fullerton Ætat 27 Years Obit June 14th.

Charles Brooks Abt. 5 Years old Obit June 17th.

Nathaniel Bird Ætat 45 Years Obit June 21st.

John Gray Ætat 28 Years Obit June 26th.

A Child abt. 8 month's Old Daughter of Mrs. Lewis Obit July 6th.

Thankfull Spear Ætat 70 Years Obit July 9th. AM

Mary Berry Ætat 32 Years Obit July 12th. P.M.

Eliza. Taylor A Child Abt. 2 Years Old Obit July 15th. AM

Thomas Forbus Abt. 20 Months Old Obit Augst. 8th. 1765

Miles Henley Ætat 35 Years Obit Augst. 20th. A poor Strainger from the Granades Dec'd abt. 24 hours after brot. to the house

Mary Shaw Alias Freeman Ætat 55 Years Obit Augst. 21st.

Mary Tuttle A Molatta Child 3 Weeks Old Daughter of Mary Tuttle Obit September 24th.

Samuel Young Abt. 5 Years Old Obit Octor. 5th.

John Higgins a Child abt. 18 Months old Obit Octr. 9th.

Lawrence Cooper Ætat 25 Years Obit Octor. 21st.

John Cowley A Child Abt. 19 Months Obit Octr. 31

Deliverance Bailey Ætat 70 . . . Years Obit Novr. 4th.

John Wheeland Ætat 43 Years . . . Obit Novr. 26th.

An Infant of Eliza. Nickolson Still born Decemr. 31st.

Edward Lack Ætat 63 Years Obit Janr. 3d. 1766

Elizabeth Sutherland Ætat 90 Years Obit January 9th.

Susannah Austin Ætat 60 Years Obit Janr. the 9th. 1766

Judith Novman Ætat 65 Years Obit Janr. 16th.

Ann Goffe Ætat 56 Years Obit January the 25th.

Margarett Ridle Ætat 31 Years Obit Janr. 28th.

Katharain Crane Ætat 67 Years Obit Febr 11th.

John Domineca Ætat 28 Years Obit Ditto 18th.

Robert Lenox Ætat 70 Years Obit Ditto 22d. p[o]x

David McLane Ætat 52 Years Obit Ditto 23d.

Silvester Smith Ætat 56 Years Obit March the 1st.

Thomas Martin Ætat 40 Years Obit March the 12th.

Miscellaneous Almshouse Births and Deaths, 1756-1771

Rebekah Choat Ætat 64 Years Obit Ditto 13th.

Sarah Lish Ætat 47 Years Obit Ditto 15th.

Susannah Smith wife of Sylvester Smith Ætat 55 Years Obit Ditto 20th.

John Jarvis Ætat 70 Years Obit Ditto 21st.

Katharain MacDaniel A Child Abt. 4 Years Old Obit March 22d. 1766

2 Infant Children abt. 10 Days old & 1 Child 13 Days old Dec'd April 7th. & April 10th. The Mother of them Mary Waterman Alias Banks

Elizabeth Brewer Abt. 8 years Old Obit April 16th

Penelope George Ætat 84 Years Obit April the 19th.

Deborah Lambert Ætat 70 Years Obit May 29

John Rice Ætat 82 Years Obit June 16th.

A Young Child abt. 4 Months Old A Daughter of Christian Isbuster Obit Augst. 6th.

Jane McLoud Ætat 45 Years Obit Augst. 26

Jane Carter Ætat 42 Years Obit Augst. 30th.

Joseph Boucher Ætat: 60 Years Obit Septemr. 1st.

Grace Isles Ætat: 72 Years Obit Septemr. 4th.

John Brew Ætat 74 years Obit Septemr. 8th.

Docter Gasper York Ætat 65 Years Obit Septr. the 19th. 1766

An Infant Male Child of Dorcas Ballards fourteen Days Old Deceas'd September 19th. 1766

Mary Poor / Wife of David Poor / Ætat 62 Years Obit Sepr. 26

Briget Nevel Ætat 28 Years Obit Octor. the 8th. Daughter of Mary Poor

Elizabeth Davis Ætat 60 Years Obit Octobr. 31st.

Roger Slegg Ætat 30 Years Obit Nov. 16th.

Ephraim Coneway A Negrow Man Ætat 45 Years Obit Novr. 22d.

Mehitable Lewis Ætat 41 Years Obit Novr. 29th.

John Child Ætat 78 Years Obit Decemr. the 4th.

Rebeckah Wesson[26] Ætat 76 Years Obit Ditto the 4th.

Ann Brazier Ætat 65 Years Obit Ditto the 5th.

A Molatah Male Child Abt. 2 Month's Old Obit Ditto the 5th.

❧

Mary Weeb Ætat 56 Years Obit Decemr. the 7th.

Ann Johns Ætat 45 Years Obit Decemr. the 13th.

Peter A Negrow Man Ætat 50 Years Obit Decmr. 18th.

Elizabeth Gray Ætat 95 Years Obit Decemr. 30th.

George Glinn[27] Ætat 78 Years Obit Janr. 2d. 1767

Benjamin Phillips Ætat 50 Years Obit Janr. 3d.

Benjamin Bodg Ætat 65 Years Obit Febr. 7th.

Jane Young Ætat 76 Years Obit Febr. the 16th.

William Lee Ætat 70 Years Obit March the 29th.

Lawrance Bride Alias Briant Ætat 30 years Obit April 15th.

Jean Fifield a negro Woman[28] Ætat 75 Years Obit Ditto 22d.

James Clark Ætat 24 Years Obit May 5th. 1767

Sarah Pibbit Ætat 84 Years Obit May 8th.

Jo Bill a Negrow Man Ætat 70 Years Obit May 22d. 1767

Mary Chubb[29] deceas'd June 3d. 1767. Ætat 57. years.

Mary Phips deceas'd June 11th. 1767. Ætat 60. years.

A Child of John Banks ætat 3 weeks. deceas'd July 2d. 1767.

Elizabeth Garrick deceasd July 24. 1767. Ætat 77 yr.

Isaac Doubt Ætat 79 years 8 mos. Obit August 1st. 1767.

a Child of Ann Lenox aged 15 Mos. deceasd August 22d. 1767.

a Child of Mary Turner aged   deceasd Septemr. 10th. 1767.

a Child of Christian Isbester aged 7 days deceasd Septr. 13th. 1767

a Child of Judith Symonds aged   deceasd Septr.

John Miers Ætat 45 yrs. deceased October 14. 1767.

James Miller Æt. 22. yrs. deceased Novemr. 9th. 1767

Sarah Brown Æt. 50 yrs. deceasd Novr. 26. 1767.

Richard Barrett Æt. 35. yrs. deceasd Janua. 7th. 1768

Miscellaneous Almshouse Births and Deaths, 1756-1771

Eliza. Glover Æt. 47. yrs. deceasd Janua. 10th. 1768

Mary Brown Æt. 55. yrs. deceasd Janua. 21. 1768

Amey Coleworthy Ætat 78. yrs. deceas'd Februa. 6th. 1768

A Child of Stokes Daughter deceas'd Feby. 15th. 1768.

A Child of Margarett Johnsons deceas'd Februa. 18th. 1768

Mary Ahier deceased March 9th. 1768. Ætat 60. years.

Sarah Clark deceased March 20th. 1768. Ætat 55. years.

Ann Hobbs deceased March 31st. 1768. Ætat 40. years.

Elizabth. George deceased April 18th. 1768 Ætat 70. years.

Elizabeth Frothingham deceased June 14th. 1768. Ætat 88. years.

Thomas Weller deceased July 1st. 1768 Ætat 35. years.

Saml. Roach deceased July 27th. 1768 Ætat 30. years

A Child of Abigl. Glovers. Augt. 12th. 1768.

Mary Colman (Prov. Charge) deceased Septemr. 17th. 1768. Ætat 53 yrs.

Philip Reiley (Prov. Charge) deceased Septr. 28th. 1768. Ætat 22. yrs.

a Child of Christee Isbusters deceased Octo. 29th. 1768. Ætat 3. yrs.

Thomas Hopper deceased Novr. 14th. 1768. Ætat 21. Years

A Negro Child of Cato's Servant to Govr. Bernard[30]

Saml. Johnson deceas'd Decemr. 7th. 1768. Ætat 30 years.

Peter Brown deceas'd Janua. 5th. 1769 Ætat 82. years. (prov. Charge)

Sarah Heath deceas'd Janua. 8th. 1769. Ætat 4. years

Katerina Baker deceas'd Janua. 20. 1769. Ætat 40. years

John Lovless[31] deceas'd Janua. 24. 1769. Ætat 9. years

Margarett Webber deceasd Janua. 26. 1769. Ætat 84. years.

Moses Larkin (prov. Charge) deceas'd Februa. 27th. 1769. Ætat 60 yrs.

Rachel Negro Woman deceased March 17th. 1769. Ætat 70. yrs.

Widow[32] Simpson deceased April 8th. 1769. Ætat 60. yrs.

Widow Hunter deceas'd April 11th. 1769. Ætat 40 yrs.

Miscellaneous Almshouse Births and Deaths, 1756-1771

Jacob Smith (Prov. Charge) deceas'd April 20th. 1769. 36. yrs.

Joseph Stanyan deceased June 1st. 1769. Ætat 60. years.

Alice Brew deceased June 5th. 1769. Ætat 70 years

Meheta. North deceased June 20th. 1769. Ætat 64. years

Mary McLane deceas'd June 23d. 1769. Ætat 75. years.

Mary Hennesey deceas'd July 19th. 1769 Ætat 55. years.

Luke Ryan deceas'd July 28. 1769. Ætat 54. years

Thomas Marston (Prov Charge) deceas'd Augt. 5th. 1769. Æt. 75 yrs.

Sarah Howell deceased August 14th. 1769. Ætat 92 years

Mary Beal deceased August 24. 1769. Ætat 51. years.

William Grigg deceased Augt. 31. 1769. Ætat 69. years

Mary Wyatt deceased Septr. 3d. 1769. Ætat 50. years.

Eliza. a Child of Caveneaughs decd. Septr. 14. 1769. Ætat

Mary Ingersoll deceased Septr. 18. 1769 Ætat 23. years

Lydia Williams deceased Septr. 19th. 1769. Ætat 18 years

A Child of Lydia Richardsons deceased Septr. 26 1769

Margarett Cahart deceased Octor. 5th. 1769. Ætat 60. yrs.

John Burch (prov) deceased Octo. 6. 1769. Ætat 50. yrs.

Zerviah Smith (prov.) deceased Octor. 6th. 1769. Ætat 37. yrs.

Ruth Treboo deceased Octor. 9th. 1769. Ætat 45. yrs.

Ann Warden deceased Octo. 10. 1769. Ætat 55 yrs.

A Child of Mary Kinsleys Octo. 11th. 1769. Ætat 2. yrs.

A Child of Zerviah Smiths Octo. 13. 1769. Ætat 7 Mos.

Tabitha Sergeant deceased Octo. 19. 1769. Ætat 63. yrs.

Salome Mann deceased Octo. 19th. 1769. Ætat 60. yrs.

Margarett Rogers deceased Octor. 31st. 1769. Ætat 50. yrs.

Ann Hynes Child deceased Decr. 3. 1769.

Stephen Rollo deceased Decr. 4th. 1769. Ætat 63.

Miscellaneous Almshouse Births and Deaths, 1756-1771

Josiah Watts a Child deceased Decr. 23. 1769. Ætat 2 1/2 yrs.

A Child of John Banks deceased Decr. 24. 1769. Ætat 8 Mos.

George Harper (prov. Charge) deceasd Decr. 28th. 1769. Ætat 25 yrs.

A Child of Mrs. McGraths deceas'd Janua. 3d. 1770. Æt. 3. yrs.

John Sampson deceased Janua. 10th. 1770. Ætat 36. years

Hannah Burk deceased Janua. 23d. 1770. Ætat 60. yrs.

Nichos Altenton (prov. Charge) deceas'd March 13. 1770. Ætat 25. yrs.

John Whittemore deceased March 31st. 1770. Ætat 60. years

John Sergeant deceased April 30th. 1770. Ætat 73. years

Sarah Blewett deceased May 8th. 1770 Ætat 64. years

Mary Greenough deceas'd June 4. 1770 Ætat 70. years

William Daniels deceased June 25. 1770. Ætat 60. years

Eliza. Harris deceased July 14. 1770. Ætat 75. years.

John Smith's Child deceas'd July 16. 1770. Ætat 2. years.

Margarett Davis deceased July 23. 1770. Ætat 34. yrs.

Ruth Lee deceased July 23d. 1770. Ætat 74. yrs.

Edward Dunn a Child (on prov. Accott.) August 28th. 1770. Ætat

a Child of Charlton Tomisons deceasd August 31. 1770. Ætat

a Child named Matthews deceas'd Novemr. 11. 1770. prov.

a Child of Eliza. Harriss. deceased Decemr. 2d. 1770.

a Child of Mary Walkers (a Molatto) deceasd Decr. 23d. 1770

Joseph Roberts deceasd Decemr. 29th. 1770. Ætat 82. yrs.

Daniel Thompson (prov. Charge) deceas'd Decr. 31st. 1770. Ætat 26. yrs.

Margarett Ware deceased 12th. Decr. 1770. Ætat 95.

1771 Jan. 8.   Hannah Perraway deceased Ætat 55. years.

[Jan.][33] 11   Michael Sommers (Prov Charge) deceased Ætat 22 years

a Child of Mores (prov. Charge) deceased Jany. 20th.

Jany. 26. 1771.   James Birmingham deceased (Prov. Charge) Janua. 26th. 1771. Æt. 36. yrs.

Miscellaneous Almshouse Births and Deaths, 1756-1771

29.	Lewis Miricks wife deceased January 29th. 1771. Ætat 40	
Feby. 15	John Fabree prov. Charge deceasd Feby. 15th. 1771. Ætat 50 yrs.	
27.	Sarah Hunt	Ætat. 24 years.
March 19	Eunice Feacham	Ætat. 26 years
28.	John McGee province Charge	Ætat 32. years
29.	Elisha Godfrey prov	Ætat 26. years
31	Ann King prov	Ætat. 27. years
April 1	Sarah Mills	Ætat 45 years
7.	Elizabeth Smith (alias Cole)	Ætat 73
8.	Susanna Morris	Ætat 23.
9	John Trowbridge (Prov Charge)	Ætat 28. years
11.	John Kenney	Ætat 76.
13.	Mary Connel (Prov. Charge)	Ætat 22.
28	Trance Bryant (Prov. Charge)	Ætat 40. yrs.
May 6.	Eliza. Carnes	Ætat 55 yrs.
do.	Susanna Dix	Ætat 70. yrs.
8.	a Child of Davis Whitman's	
9.	Alice Osgood (Prov)	Ætat 90. yrs.
10	Eliza. Wharrfe	Ætat 38. yrs.
May 17. 1771.	Robert Williams deceased	Æt. 63. yrs.
18.	A Child brot out of Emmon's Entry	
June 8.	Ann Gorge deceased	Ætat 75 yrs.
July 22.	a Child of Mary Hemenways	
Augt. 1	Hannah Anselman (prov. Charge) deceased	Ætat 51. yrs.
28	a Child of Christian Isbesters	
31	Robert Boies deceased	Ætat 70. yrs.
Septr. 3.	Violet a Negrowoman	
23.	Desire Toby a Molatto Woman	

26.	a Child named Agnis McAfee on prov. Account	
	William Rogers (6th. Septr.) Aged 60 years	
Sept. 30th.	a Child of Richard Goodings	
Octo. 8.	a Child	
Octo. 11th.	Eliza. Utinocks[34] Prov. Charge	Ætat 35. years
[P][35] 17.	Morgan Trouts Child	
27.	Mary Odlin	Ætat 95. years
29th.	Abigl. Hall	Ætat 52. years
Novr. 1.	Jonas Webber	Ætat 93. years
	Isaac Orr deceas'd Octo. 22d. aged 70 years	
13.	John Dunn deceased a Child	

Notes

1   Entered in Admissions Register 1.

2   Register 1, "Account of Children Born … from … 1756" continues through 1 May 1768, but the entries duplicate the "Record of Children born in the Alms house" entered in Admissions Register 2. Because Register 2 apparently predates Register 1 the latter's "Account" is not printed in its entirety. Additions and differences are recorded in notes to the "Record of Children born … ," below.

3   Entered in Admissions Register 2 on three pages following the record of 28 June 1768 admitting John Cunningham to the almshouse and carried twenty pages forward to continue for another three pages.

4   Supplied from Register 1, "Account of Children Born … from … 1756."

5   "Lucretia Lawrence"; "deceased" in Register 1, "Account of Children Born … from … 1756."

6   "Cavenex" in Register 1, "Account of Children Born … from … 1756."

7   Register 1, "Account of Children Born … from … 1756" records the child's name as "Thomas Johnson."

8   "Mulliken" in Register 1, "Account of Children Born … from … 1756."

9   "John Mortall"; "Boy deces. Feby. 16. 1765" in Register 1, "Account of Children Born … from …1756."

10   "Watts" in Register 1, "Account of Children Born … from … 1756."

11   Register 1, "Account of Children Born … from … 1756" gives the surname of "Ethridge."

12   Register 1, "Account of Children Born … from … 1756" gives the child's name also as "Eliza. Nicholson."

13   "John Johnson" in Register 1, "Account of Children Born … from … 1756."

14   "Sandeman" in Register 1, "Account of Children Born … from … 1756."

15   "Sarah Lewis" in Register 1, "Account of Children Born … from … 1756."

16   "John Mortall" in Register 1, "Account of Children Born … from … 1756."

17   "Symmonds" in Register 1, "Account of Children Born … from … 1756."

18   "Lintee" in Register 1, "Account of Children Born … from … 1756."

19   Register 1, "Account of Children Born … from … 1756" contains the note: "The reputed Father one Henry *Mylerd* at Halifax. NB. As *℘* Ltres sent to her it seems likely *Mylerd* is his proper Sir name & not *Miller*."

20   "Gooding" in Register 1, "Account of Children Born … from … 1756."

21   Entered in Admissions Register 2.

22   Register 1, "Anna Paine."

23   Register 1, Death: "dyed of Small pox April 4 1764 Natl. way}."

24   Following this entry, in the right bottom corner of the page is the notation "59 in the yeare."

25   Register 1, Death: "March 10th. 1765."

26   "Weston" in Register 1.

27   "Glen" in Register 1.

28   Register 1, in an undated entry following that of 2 Dec. 1766: "Jane a Negro of Mrs. Fyfields."

29   "Stanley" in Register 1.

30   The entry in Register 1 reads "Cato a negro Child"; Death: "Nov. 1768."

31   "Lovelace" in Register 1.

32   "Dorcas" in Register 1.

33   Supplied from Register 1.
34   "Hudenox" in Register 1.
35   I.e., "Province."

CHILDREN BOUND OUT
1756 – 1790

This list of children who were indentured as apprentices and/or servants is transcribed from a manuscript that was included in Admissions Register 1 (Overseers, box 9, folder 1). These children were wards of the Overseers under various legislative acts (the complete documentation of this aspect of the Overseers' mandate is contained in Towner). The list below runs from April 1756 to February 1790, while Towner's list is from 1734 to 1805. (The dates refer to the date when the child was "bound out", that is, the start of the term of service.) Towner worked from the original indenture records in the possession of the City of Boston. Because Towner worked from the full indenture manuscripts, he was able to note the occupational terms of the service and the location of the master, in all cases. Here, most of the clerks provide locations, but not all do, and none of the clerks identify the nature of the service or the trade of the apprenticeship. Most of the names below can be found in Towner's list, but some are not, which suggests that some indenture forms did not survive. Thus, Towner's numbers are slightly lower than the eventual total for child indentures. The eleven hundred original printed indenture forms cited, abstracted and listed by Towner were found in the Boston City Clerk's office in six volumes and subsequently microfilmed for the Institute of Early American History and Culture, Williamsburg, Va. See Towner, 417, n. 1, and 434. The originals are now in the Boston Public Library, Rare Books and Manuscripts.

Children Bound Out, 1756-1790

Childrens Names	when Bound	to Whom	when Free
Anthony Frazier	April 21st. 1756	Jacob Yeaton	Septemr. 3d. 1770
William Thomas	May 11th. 1756	Joseph Johnston	Octo. 6. 1776.
Isaiah Thomas	June 4th. 1756	Zechariah Fowle	Janua. 8. 1769
James Gordon	June 18th. 1756	Robert McClure	April 25 1767
Eliza. Manning	June 18th. 1756	John Tilson	Novemr. 15. 1768
Richard Griffis	June 29th. 1756	Samuel Bates	July 20. 1771.
James Perraway	July 3. 1756	Israel Ashley	June 2. 1766
Mary Miller	August 5 1756	Revd. Gad Hitchcock	March 16. 1768.
William Brackett	August 6 1756	William Lombard	Augt. 6. 1772.
Mary Courtney	August 6 1756	William Lombard	Augt. 6 1769.
James Negro Boy	August 26 1756	Alexr. Chamberlain	Septr. 12 1767.
Thomas Negro Boy	August 26. 1756	Alexr. Chamberlain	Novr. 20 1765.
Narius Townson	August 28. 1756	Joseph Boardman	Septr. 15. 1764.
William Townsend	Septemr. 1. 1756	John Brintnall	Septr. 17. 1767
Robert Humphrys	Octor. 6. 1756	Joseph Dyer	Septr. 16. 1771
Thomas Field	Novr 3. 1756	Paul Knowles	Decemr. 17. 1770
Bartholomew Lynch	Decemr. 1. 1756	Joseph Roundey	April 24. 1771
John Stone	Decemr. 1. 1756	John Skillins	March 11. 1761.
Mary Noell[1]	Janua. 5. 1757	Andrew Belcher Esqr.	May 13. 1765
Francis Cummont	Februa. 2. 1757	Ph. Godfrid Cast	Janua. 1. 1766.
Thomas Sharp	Februa. 4. 1757	John Glover	March 16. 1770
Robert Merchie	Februa. 17. 1757	Barnabas Howard	March 5 1767.
Abigail Craige	March 2. 1757	Ebenr. Fisher junr.	Janua. 16 1769.
Thomas Pilsberry	March 12 1757	Isaac Phillips	Septr. 12. 1766.
John Casker	April 6. 1757	Matthew Hayward	Septr. 16. 1771
Ruth Negro Girl	May 4. 1757	Alexr. Chamberlain	March 1 1769.
Thomas Bantom	June 22. 1757	Saml. Mower junr.	April 15 1761.

Children Bound Out, 1756-1790

Childrens Names	when Bound	to Whom	when Free
Elizabeth Noel	July 6. 1757	William Hudson	August 13 1768
Elizabeth Moody	July 7. 1757	John Phillips	Decemr. – 1767.
Jeremiah Wyatt	July 30. 1757	Seth Ross	June 28. 1774.
Penelope Curtain	August 4. 1757	Saml. Bartlett	Augt. 4. 1767.
Robert Clark	Septr. 13. 1757	Matthew Kingman	March 15. 1772.
John Fisk	Septr. 15. 1757	Thos. Bently	Feby. 12 1762.
John Boyd	Octor. 27. 1757	Joseph Billings	Novr. 15. 1760
Stephen Grover	Novemr. 10. 1757	William Blair	Novr. 10. 1768
Hill Green	Decemr. 8. 1757	John Phillips	April 30. 1764.
Joseph Miller	Decemr. 31. 1757	Ebenr. Fletcher	Januar. 1. 1773.
Thomas Peak	Janua. 23. 1758	Benja. Cutler	March 22. 1771.
Phillip Peak	Janua. 23. 1758	Jonas Stone	April 18. 1773.
Samuel Allen	Feby. 1. 1758	Saml. Ridgaway junr.	Decr. 20. 1764
Robert Layman	March 24. 1758	James Packard	Octo. 15. 1771.
Mary Little	May 1. 1758	Joseph Jackson	May 10. 1761.
Mary Devereux	May 1. 1758	Nathl. Warner	Novr. 15 1764.
Margt. Blake	June 20. 1758	William Penniman jur.	July 9. 1770
Peter Salter	June 27th. 1758	Isaac Harrington jur.	June 9th. 1779
Katha.[2] Miller	July 22 1758	Saml. Sellon	March 19th. 1764
Mary Peck	Augt. 2 1758	James Smith	May 5. 1767.
Joseph Ervin	Augt. 2 1758	Gideon Lyman	Augt. 22. 1773.
Joseph Fessenden	Septr. 6 1758	Michael Wormsted	April 22 1774
Sarah Whaley	Septr. 6 1758	Mary Chipman	Septr. 6. 1765
Abigail Cox	Septr. 6 1758	William Warland	May 15. 1762
Parker Fessenden	Septr. 6 1758	Michael Wormsted	March 2. 1772.
John Perraway	Octo. 2 1758	William Crowel	Augt. 15. 1775.
Richard Bowers	Octo. 2 1758	Richard Jutt	Septr. 26. 1774

Children Bound Out, 1756-1790

Childrens Names	when Bound	to Whom	when Free
Katharine Stanton	Octo. 4 1758	Thomas Hitchborn jur.	Feby. 14. 1770
John Nichols	Decemr. 7 1758	Edward Langdon	June 4. 1769
William Gray	Janua. 3 1759	Samuel Barnard	July 15. 1765.
Mary Craige	Februa. 7 1759	Saml. Ridgaway junr.	Augt. 10. 1765
Bound since} Daniel Hanglin	Februa. 7 1759	James Thwing	Februa. 13. 1764
James Thompson	Februa. 7 1759	Daniel Graves	June 11. 1774.
Charles Taylor	Februa. 7 1759	William Bourn Esqr.	Novemr. 16. 1767
Martha Holmes	Februa. 7 1759	Jeremiah Smith	March 9. 1770
Bound since} Margt. Hendly	March 7 1759	Nathl. Ridgaway	Novemr. 1. 1769
Mary Martin	March 7 1759	Alexr. Sampson	Decemr. 10. 1769.
John Taylor	May 2 1759	Saml. Ridgaway junr.	Octor. 22. 1771.
Daniel Conwill	June 6 1759	John Moody	Februa. 7. 1769
Margarett Waters	June 6 1759	Ezekl. Tilston	June 15. 1763.
Susanna Perraway	June 6 1759	Robt. Haward junr.	Janua. 20. 1771.
Robert Kilby	Mar 1. 1758	Cadwallador Ford	Septr. 15. 1772
Eliza. Ruddocks	Decemr. 6 1758	Saml. Denney	June 2. 1761.
Ann Ingersoll	May 2. 1759	Phineas Lyman	June 20. 1770
Susanna Brown	June 18. 1759	Margt. Ashley	March 6. 1768
John Banks	Octo. 3. 1759	Andrew Adams	Augt. 16. 1766
Mary Davis	Octo. 3. 1759	Daniel Henshaw	Septr. 12. 1771
Agnus Lillie	Feby 6. 1760	Ichabod Jones	Novr. 10 1767.
William Gaskin	Feby 6. 1760	Abraham Mullett	Augt. 22. 1770
Mark Noble	Feby 14. 1760	Moses Marsh	July 6. 1774
John Fairservice	Feby 15. 1760	Valentine Tidd	Janua. 6. 1775.
Rebecca Taylor	Feby 28. 1760	Saml. Holbrook	Janua. 15. 1768
William Tuckerman	Feby 28. 1760	Thomas Rice	Augt. 22. 1765
Margt. Hendly	March 4. 1760	James Cocks	Novr. 1. 1769

Children Bound Out, 1756-1790

Childrens Names	when Bound	to Whom	when Free
Mary Rogers	May 7. 1760	Robert Thompson	May 21. 1763
William Thwings[3]	May 7. 1760	Seth Ross	Octo. 17 1766
Susanna Holmes	June 4 1760	Paul Mandell	May 28. 1773
Arthur Keeve	June 4. 1760	Paul Mandell	April 19. 1776
William Shirley	April 4. 1760	Joseph Striker	June 6. 1772
Mary Dumphy	June 4. 1760	Thomas Thompson	Augt 10. 1763
Sarah Hoar	May 7. 1760	David Willmerth	April 24. 1762
John Shirley	May 10 1760	John Fraser	Jany 1. 1776
Stephen Harris	July 2. 1760	Joshua Kimball	Jany 5. 1775
Eliza. Simpson[4]	Octo. 3. 1759	Moses Bass	Novr. 12 1769
Thomas Lillie	July 2 1760	Joseph Selman	Feby 23d. 1776
James Dumphy	July 2 1760	Charles Hoar	Novr. 7. 1774
Sarah Whitney	July 7 1760	Saml. Waterman	April 6. 1772
George Walker	Augt. 6 1760	Isaac Wendell	March 10. 1765
Eliza. Lillie	Augt. 6 1760	Saml. Dexter	Augt. 1. 1769
Abraham Fobey	Octo. 3 1759	Willm. Morre	Septr. 10. 1771
Robert Stokey	Octo. 3 1759	Fras. Wyman junr.	Apl. 6. 1774
Thos. Craigie	June 14 1759	Saml. Bridge	Feby 12. 1775
Kata. Stanton	Augt. 1 1759	Wm. Simpkins	Feby 14. 1768
John Davis	May 2 1759	Oliver Smith	June 26. 1775
Lydia Gray	June 6 1759	John Jones	Jany 10. 1764
Willm. Curtain	June 6 1759	John Jones	Augt. 24. 1774
Henry Peak	Septr. 5 1759	John Anthoine	Octo. 15. 1770
mistake ⎰ Agnus Lillie	Feby. 6 1760	Ichabod Jones	Novr. 10. 1767
⎱ Wm. Gaskins	Feby. 6 1760	Abraham Mullett	Augt. 22. 1770
bound since⎬ Jona. Johnson	Octo. 1 1760	David Gardner	Octo. 1. 1767
Eliza. Clough	Octo. 1 1760	Herk. Blanchard	July 24. 1772

649

Children Bound Out, 1756-1790

Childrens Names	when Bound	to Whom	when Free
James Melvin	Octo. 1 1760	John Stirling	April 1. 1774
Willm. Burk	Octo. 1 1760	Francis Ingraham	June 9 1766
Daniel Hanglin	Novr. 17 1760	Nathl. Loring	Feby 13. 1764
Eliza. Caroll	Novr. 5 1760	Hugh Vans	Novr. 1. 1767
Sarah Kenney	Novr. 5 1760	Thos. Barrons	June 1. 1767
John Burk	Novr. 5 1760	Thos. Bell	June 4 1773
Mary Kenney	Decr. 3 1760	Saml. Wyman	Novr. 15. 1769
John Briant	Decr. 3 1760	Oliver Farrar	May 1. 1774
Jona. Johnson	Jany 7 1761	Hugh McDaniel	Octo. 1. 1767
Willm. Pierce	Mar. 4 1761	John Adams junr.	Feby 24. 1771
Thomas Caryll	April 1 1761	Benja. Stow	Feby 27. 1775.
Willm. Sheppard	May 6 1761	Saml. Dexter	Octo. 12. 1771.
John Dollison	June 3 1761	Joshua Townsend jur.	Octo. 19. 1777
Mary Russell	April 1 1761	James Orr	Mar. 15. 1770
Wm. Calder	April 1 1761	Gad Lyman	Novr. 4. 1774.
<John Banks	*Octo. 2 1759*	*Andw. Adams*	*Augt. 16. 1766.>*
Mary Nichols	Augt. 6 1760	Perez Marsh	Decemr. 5. 1772.
Jonathan Johnson	Janua. 7 1761	Hugh McDaniel	Octo. 1. 1767.
William Pierce	Feby. 6 1761	John Adams	Feby 24. 1771.
Thomas Caryl	Feby 6 1761	Benja. Stow	Feby 27. 1775.
Mary Russell	April 1 1761	James Orr	March 15. 1770.
William Sheppard	May 6 1761	Saml. Dexter	Octor. 12. 1771.
John Dollison	June 3 1761	Joshua Townsend	Octor. 19. 1777.
Thomas Banks	July 1 1761	Wm. Williams	Octor. 20. 1773.
Paul Ewen	July 1 1761	Paul Spear	Augt. 15. 1772.
Edward Deane	July 1 1761	Benja. Burt	July 18. 1771.
Benja. Wright	July 2 1761	Edward Foster	July 3. 1763.

Children Bound Out, 1756-1790

Childrens Names	To Whome Bound	of what Town	When Bound	When Free
Eliza. Kenney	James Reed	Cambridge	July 8. 1761.	May 12th. 1771.
Mary Pimm	Thomas Gardner	Boston	Septr. 2. 1761	Septr. 20. 1771.
Martha Townsend	John Cunningham	Boston	Septr. 2. 1761	June 15 1768
Ann Wise	Elipha. Leonard junr.	Easton	Octo. 6. 1761.	Novr. 22. 1772.
John Legg	George Dodge	Northampton	Septr. 26. 1761.	Septr. 1. 1776
Saml. Harris	Samuel Harris	Boston	Octo. 7. 1761.	Decr. 12. 1766.
Jane Butler	Saml. Preston	Littleton	Nov. 26. 1761.	Feby 12. 1773.
George Lish	Daniel Diman	Plymouth	Decr. 2. 1761.	Feby 19. 1774.
Hannah Prest	John Hancock	Charlestown	Decr. 2. 1761	Decr. 22. 1772
Eliza. Obison	John Winslow	Boston	Decr. 2. 1761	June 6. 1772
James Sucker	Willm. Warland	Boston	Decr. 9. 1761	Feby 15. 1767.
Mary Treboo	James Falkner	Medford	Feby 3. 1762.	Novr. 10. 1773
Mary Barrett	Josiah Searl	South hampton	Mar 3. 1762.	Novr. 25. 1772
Josiah Snelling	Ezekiel Dodge	Abington	April 7. 1762.	Jany. 2. 1778
William Loveless	John Freeto	Mblehead	April 7. 1762.	June 11. 1778
Joseph Osborn	Ephraim Deane	Eastham	June 16. 1762.	Octo. 2. 1774
Enoch Jarvis	Hugh McDaniel	Boston	June 2. 1762.	May 13. 1772.
John Burk	James Lemont	George Town	June 9. 1762.	June 4. 1773.
Sarah Allen	William Gridley	Roxbury	July 7. 1763	July 15. 1774.
Susanna Brown	Margarett Ashley	Westfield	June 18. 1759	Mar. 6. 1768
Sarah Richards	Zechh. Pool junr.	Medford	July 7. 1762.	Jany. 9. 1772.
Sarah Whitney	Saml. Waterman	Halifax (NE)	July 17. 1762.	April 6. 1772.
Ebenr. Bowman	John Martin	Brunswic	Augt. 16. 1762.	Feby 29. 1774.
William Williams	Jabez Harlow	Plymouth	Septr. 1. 1762.	Augt. 3. 1768
Eliza. Jones	Alexr. Mayors	Boston	Septr. 6. 1762.	March 17. 1771
Sarah Gouge	Zecha. Mayhew	Kilmark	Septr. 18. 1762.	Novr. 27. 1769.
Thomas Cox	Zecha. Mayhew	Kilmark	Septr. 18. 1762.	Feby 11. 1775.
Eliza. Gregory	Jason Haven	Dedham	Octo. 6. 1762.	Septr. 14. 1771.

Children Bound Out, 1756-1790

Childrens Names	To Whome Bound	of what Town	When Bound	When Free
Margt. Cunningham	Hezekh. Welch	Boston	Octo. 6. 1762.	Augt. 15. 1767
John Shootesmith	Thomas Smith	Boston	Octo. 6. 1762.	Augt. 16. 1769
Joseph Akley	Timothy Winship	Boston	Octo. 14. 1762.	June 10. 1773.
Danforth Champney	Hudson Vickery	Eastham	Octo. 18. 1762.	Septr. 2d. 1776
Susanna McGown	Jonas Buckingham	Rutland	Nov. 10. 1762.	Jany. 27. 1775.
Gershom Ewen	David Spear	Boston	Decr. 1. 1762.	Decr. 20. 1773.
Mary Barber	Nicholas Hopping	Charlestown	Decr. 2. 1762.	Feby 22. 1768
John Griffin	Saml. Thomson	Holden	Decr. 15. 1762.	May 16. 1778
Ann Killeron	William Sheppard	Boston	Jany. 5. 1763.	Decr. 16. 1775.
Francis Woods	Daniel Waldo	Boston	Jany. 5. 1763.	Augt. 17. 1767
Eliza. Carroll[5]	Andrew Eliot	Boston	Feby 2. 1763.	Novr. 1. 1767
Sarah Burk	Saml. Gray	Boston	Mar 2. 1763.	Apl. 2. 1768.
George Walker	Thomas Palfrey	Boston	Mar. 7. 1763.	Mar. 15. 1765
Kata. Thwing	William Sutton	Boston	Mar. 12. 1763.	Octo. 15. 1771.
Mary Burk	Ann Pain	Boston	Apl. 6. 1763.	Apl. 10. 1766
Mary Baner	Bartho. Sutton	Boston	Apl. 6. 1763.	May 15. 1771
Oliver Merrick	Richard Boynton	Boston	Apl. 6. 1763	Janua. 5. 1764
Lydia Gregory	Joseph Badger	Boston	Apl. 6. 1763	Novr. 15. 1773.
Francis Akley	Edward Houghton	Lancaster	May 4. 1763.	Mar. 16. 1772.
Peter Hammond	John Mosely	Westfield	May 24. 1763.	Februa. 14 1775.
Mary Green	Thos. Smith	Boston	July 6. 1763.	Mar. 10. 1774.
Addison Jacobs	John Brewer	Boston	July 6. 1763.	Jany. 6. 1770
Mary Snelling	Israel Loring	Boston	July 6. 1763.	Septr. 26. 1767.
Abigail Buckley	James Graham	Boston	Augt. 3. 1763.	June 3d. 1775.
Thomas Peak	Willm. Dickman	Boston	Septr. 1. 1763	Mar. 22d. 1771
Sarah Burk	John Flowers	Boston	Septr. 7th. 1763.	April 2d. 1768
Lettuce Boston	Benja. Emmons	Boston	Sepr. 7. 1763	Septr. 1. 1775

Children Bound Out, 1756-1790

Childrens Names	To Whome Bound	of what Town	When Bound	When Free
Elias Cox	Thomas Holbrook	Barnstable	Octo. 3. 1763.	Mar. 25. 1779.
William Everton	Joseph Ashley	Westfield	June 3. 1763.	April 23. 1776.
Mary Turner	Joseph Patterson	District Ware	Novr. 5. 1763.	Novr. 1. 1765.
Saml. Hardiman	Joshua Beales	Boston	Novr. 18. 1763.	Septr. 1. 1769.
Andw. Croge	Silas Fowler	Westfield	Decr. 31. 1763.	May 15. 1778
James Dumphy	Bildad Fowler	Ditto	Jany. 4. 1764.	Septr. 17. 1774.
Ignatius Lyndes[6]	Daniel Bagg	ditto	Jany. 2. 1764.	April 25. 1775.
Eliza. Thwing	Palfrey Collins	Boston	Jan. 4. 1764.	June 4. 1769
Mary Smith	Elijah Warner	Hardwick	Jan. 4. 1764.	Mar. 14. 1777.
Saml. Myrick	Elijah Doane	District Welfleet	Jan. 20. 1764.	Jany 11. 1766.
Rebecca Ryan	Willm. Thompson	Billerica	Feby 1. 1764.	Novr. 8. 1774.
Hannah Meney	Saml. Badger	Boston	June [6] 1764	Jany. 20. 1773
George Richardson	Willm. McKinstry	Taunton	June 11. 1764.	Augt. 30. 1778.
Joseph Prince	John Hawkes	Lynn	Septr. 14. 1764.	March 1. 1777.
Willm. Bright	Saml. Marshall	Salem	17. 1764	Augt. 7. 1773.
Sarah Snelling	John Longley	Boston	Sepr. 5. 1764.	Mar. 1. 1774
Lucretia Melvin	John Greenwood	Ditto	5. 1764.	May 25. 1775
Ann Bleigh	Christo. Ranks	Ditto	June 6. 1764	Augt. 19. 1768
Mary Scudder	Lemuel Cox	Ditto	ditto	Augt. 25 1771
Ebenr. Blancher	Edwd. Langdon	Ditto	ditto	Februa. 1. 1777
Benja. Champney	Thomas Emmons	Ditto	ditto	Septr. 3. 1770
George Richardson	Willm. McKinstry	Taunton	June 11th. 1764.	Augt. 30. 1778
Mary Higgins	Edwd. Winter	Boston	July 4. 1764.	July. 1st. 1772.
Patrick Welch	Saml. Emmons	Ditto	ditto	Decemr. 25. 1774
Joseph Prince	John Hawkes	Lynn	Septr. 14. 1764.	March [1] 1777
Willm. Bright	Saml. Marshall	Salem	17. 1764.	Augt. 7. 1773
Eliza. Jones	Hezediah Coley	Boston	Octo. 3. 1764.	March 17. 1771

653

Children Bound Out, 1756-1790

Childrens Names	To Whome Bound	of what Town	When Bound	When Free
Thomas Akley	Jason Haven	Dedham	3. 1764.	Octo. 3d. 1777
John Akley	Saml. Williams	Springfield	11. 1764.	April 1st. 1779.
Sarah Forbus	Saml. Williams	Ditto	ditto	Octor. 27. 1775.
<Christo. Lynch	*Francis Shaw*	*Boston>*		
Mary Inglish	Hezekiah Gay	Stoughton	Novr. 1. 1764.	Decr. 8. 1776
Willm. Sheppard	Samuel Dexter	Dedham	7th. 1764.	Octo. 12. 1771
John Plant	Joseph Wheeler	Harvard	14. 1764.	Sepr. 28. 1775
Susanna Brown	Charles Pynchon	Springfield	17. 1764.	Mar. 6. 1768
Jeremy[7] Wyatt	Saml. Edwards	Concord	Feby. 6. 1765.	June 28 1774
Jane Taylor	Thomas Wendell	Boston	6. 1765.	July 1. 1775
John Brown	John Mason	Dedham	Feby. 8. 1765.	Decr. 15. 1779.
Mary Clough	David Brewer	Worcester	12. 1765.	Octo. 2. 1776
Hannah Melvin	Jona. Ferre	Brimfield	20. 1765.	Mar. 15. 1777
Thomas Ryan	Saml. Draper	Boston	Mar. 6. 1765.	May 13. 1771
Susanna Follings	Thomas Russel	Ditto	6. 1765.	Jany 7. 1772
Christo. Lynch	Francis Shaw	ditto	6. 1765.	29. 1772
Thomas More	James Flagg	Pownalborô	Apl. 26. 1765.	Octo. 1. 1779
Mary McGee	Willm. Dickman	Boston	Apl. 5. 1765.	Apl. 15. 1770
Jannet Ware	Jonathan Wyman	Woburn	Apl. 3. 1765.	Novr. 15. 1775
Sarah Follings	Ebenr. Blake junr.	Wrentham	Apl. [5] 1765.	Novr. 29. 1775
Willm. Thwing	Saml. Emmons	Boston	Apl. 4. 1765.	Octo. 17. 1776
Margtt. Forbus	Joshua Bently	Boston	May 1. 1765.	Mar. 27. 1777
Lydia Curtis	Joshua Blanchard	Ditto	1. 1765.	Decr. 28. 1774
Willm. Smith	Lewis Thomas	Bristol	4. 1765.	June 21. 1778
Joseph Fothergill	Nathl. Dickinson	Deerfield	June 15. 1765.	Apl. 10. 1778
Mary Barber	Seth Catlin	Ditto	15. 1765.	June 15. 1768
Matthew Hopkins	John Ruddock	Boston	July 20. 1765.	Decr. 27. 1774

Children Bound Out, 1756-1790

❧

Childrens Names	To Whome Bound	of what Town	When Bound	When Free
Mary McGowen	Saml. Minot	Ditto	Augt. 7. 1765.	Feby. 1. 1777
Willm. Warner	Thomas Emmons	Ditto	7. 1765	June 7. 1778
John Burgis	Thomas Bacon	Bedford	7. 1765.	Septr. 13. 1779
John Rogers	Willm. McAlpin	Boston	Septr. 11. 1765	Augt. 27. 1771
Eliza. Kellam	Moses Dorr	Roxbury	Octo. 30. 1765.	Septr. 10. 1776
Margtt. McCloud	Saml. A Otis	Boston	Mar. 5. 1766	June 15. 1773
Sarah Richards	Saml. Marshall	Boston	April 2. 1766	Janua. 9. 1771
Sarah Burk	John Lovering	Ditto	<April> Mar. 5. 1766	April 2. 1768
Richard Warren	Saml. Hatch	Well Fleet	May 7. 1766	Decr. 20. 1781
Saml. Smith	Edward Smith	Ditto	May. 24. 1766	Decr. 27. 1778
Joseph Maxfield	Abraha. Burbank	Springfield	May 29. 1766.	Decr. 15. 1778
Edward Taveneaug's[8]	James Brown	Well Fleet	June 4. 1766.	Augt. 23. 1780
Willm. Palfrey	Willm. James	Georges	July 1. 1766	Decr. 18. 1781.
Eliza. Bradshaw	Danl. Kellogg	Amherst	July 2. 1766	Octo. 18. 1778
Stephen Burgis	Saml. Basset	Well Fleet	July 2. 1766	May 5. 1781
Mary McGowen[9]	Joshua Spooner	Brookfield	July 3. 1766	Feby. 1. 1777
Francis Dizer	John Martin	Brunswick	July 6. 1766	April 4. 1780
Katha. Murphy	Robert Loyd	Blandford	July 7. 1766	Janua. 1. 1771
Rehanus Lewis	Josiah Brewer junr.	Worcester	July 17. 1766	Novr. 9. 1778
Willm. Smith	Josse Holbrook	George Town	Augt. 22. 1766	June 21. 1779
John Forbus	Joshua Combs junr.	Ditto	Augt. 22. 1766	Janua. 20. 1781
Joseph Osborn	Edward Bacon junr.	Barnstable	Augt. 23. 1766	Octo. 2d. 1774
Eliza. Lyniard	Joseph Calef	Boston	Octo. 1. 1766	Mar 15. 1770
Ann Cromartie	Willm. Wheat	Ditto	Octo. 1. 1766	Feb. 25. 1774
John Jackson	John Gray	Ditto	Octo. 22 1766	Mar 10 1773
Barto. Meloney	Benja. Pritchard	Mblehead	Octo. 24. 1766	Decr. 12. 1782
Benja. Lemoine[10]	Robert Stutson	Well Fleet	Novr. 6. 1766	Jany. 10. 1781

Children Bound Out, 1756-1790

Childrens Names	To Whome Bound	of what Town	When Bound	When Free
Sarah Sprague	Edward Jackson	Boston	Novr. 14. 1766	Augt. 16. 1770
Ann Ingolls	James Nolton	Ditto	Decr. 3. 1766	July 10. 1774
Jane Taylor	Saml. Adams	Booth Bay	Decr. 5. 1766	July 31. 1774
James Goffe	John Clark	Eastham	Jany. 5. 1767	Mar. 17. 1781.
Saunders Chambers	James Anthony	Nantucket	Jany. 7. 1767	Decr. 25. 1771
Robt. Wharff	Samuel Snow	Mblehead	Jany 14. 1767	July 7. 1782
John Williams	Philip Lecraw	Ditto	Jany. 27. 1767	June 1. 1780
Mary Hicks	John Turner junr.	Pembooke	Feby. 18 1767	Septr. 1. 1777
John Lemoine	Thomas Arey	Edgartown	Mar 27. 1767	July 26. 1780
Tamar Allen	Mark Clark	Harwich	April 18. 1767	July 4. 1776
Jeremiah Wyatt	Zacheus Green	Concord	April 29. 1767	June 28 1774
Matthew Hopkins	Elijah Doubleday	Boston	May 6. 1767.	Decemr. 27 1774
John Plant	David Loring	Ditto	May 7. 1767	March 29. 1779
Saml. Bradley	Peter Pease	Edgartown	Mar. 27. 1767	Janua. 1. 1782
Eliza. Jones	Nathan Stone	Yarmo.	May 13. 1767	Mar. 17. 1771
Henry Iverd	Aaron Welds	Sturbridge	June 2. 1767	Jany. 1. 1779
Lydia Gregory	Benja. Austin Esqr.	Boston	June 3. 1767	Novr. 15. 1773
Nichs. Mangent	Wm. Crawford Esqr.	Pownalbo.	June 3. 1767	<May> Jany. 1. 1781
Richd. McGrath	Isaiah Holbrook	Wellfleet	July 1. 1767	May 6. 1784
Eliza. McGrath	Joseph Brightman	Falmo.	July 7. 1767	Mar. 1. 1779
Richard Griffiths	Joseph Blake	Hardwick	July 29. 1767	July 20. 1771
Lettuce Boston	Joseph Blake	ditto	do.	Septr. 1. 1775
Henry Carrigan	Jacob Yeaton	Marblehead	Augt. 5. 1767	Augt. 1. 1780
Eliza. Williams	Nehemiah Webb	Sandwich	Aug. 25. 1767	Augt. 1. 1777
Eliza. Utinocks	Saml. Gregg	Derry N.H	Septr. 2. 1767	Jany 1. 1777
Jacob Winslow	Saml. Morton	Athol	Septr. 24. 1767	Mar. 10. 1779
Mary Goggins[11]	Timo. Ruggles junr.	Hardwick	do. do.	Decr. 1. 1779

Children Bound Out, 1756-1790

Childrens Names	To Whome Bound	of what Town	When Bound	When Free
Wm. Warren	Timo. Ruggles junr.	do.	do. do.	Augt. 15. 1783
Ann Evans	Dr. Edward Durant	Holliston	Sept. 30. do.	Septr. 17. 1776
Thomas Warren	Anthony Combs	Harpswell	Octo. 20 1767	Mar. 15. 1784
Benja. Ballard	Thos. Bentley	Boston	23. 1767	Nov. 9. 1770
John Watson	Joshua Atwood	Well fleet	29 1767	Novr. 7. 1781
Francis Woods	John Greenleaf	Boston	Novr. 12 1767.	Augt. 17. 1774
Elear. Berry	Thos. Rogers	ditto	18 do.	July 10. 1777
Ebenr. Dumaresque	Nathl. Martyn	Harvard	19 do.	Novr. 25. 1781
Abigl. Coles	John Shaw	Raynham	26 do.	Feby. 20. 1778
Edward Howard	John Abbe	Hopkington	28 do.	Octo. 15. 1775
Agnes Bayley	Jeremiah Bumstead	Boston	Decr. 8 do.	Feby. 18. 1773
Geo. Richardson	Geo. Leonard 3d.	Norton	9 do.	Augt. 30. 1778
Edwd. McGown	Elijah Butler	Edgartown	Jany. 1 1768	May 5. 1782
Saml. Cherry	Jas. Lindsey	Easton	7 do.	May 15. 1777
Thos. Ryan	Abra. Tuckerman	Boston	15 do.	May 15. 1771
Peter Smith	John Sinnet	Blanford	20. do.	June 24. 1781
Thos. Osborn	Zadok Chapin	Springfield	Feby. 3 do.	May 15. 1780
Mary Webb	Wm. Spry Esqr.	Roxbury	Mar 1 do.	[blank in MS]
Mary McGee[12]	Saml. Emms	Boston	9 do.	Apr. 15. 1770
Michl. Sheppard	John Hayden	Hopkington	10 do.	Octo. 15. 1779
Wm. Smith	Jerh. Hawes	Wellfleet	11 do.	Mar. 4. 1777.
Richard Caten	Daniel Bliss Esqr.	Rutland	16 do.	Augt. 15. 1782
Joseph Gray	Joseph Higgins	Wellfleet	17 do.	April 15. 1784
Corne[13] Kellihorn	James Thompson	Petersham	17. do.	Apl. 15. 1785
James Raven	Andw. Adams	Milton	17 do.	Jany 1. 1778
Nathl. Corbett[14]	David Howse	Wellfleet	19 do.	May 25. 1782
Margtt. Cherry	Hugh McLane	Milton	19 do.	May 15. 1772

Children Bound Out, 1756-1790

Childrens Names	To Whome Bound	of what Town	When Bound	When Free
Mary Shaw	Wm. Biggs	Truro	24. do.	July 15. 1771
Edward Kelly	Edwd. Selfridge	Rutland	Apl. 6. do.	May 1. 1784
Eliza. Corbin	Jas. Dyar	Weymo.	12. do.	June 5. 1775
Tamar Bellman	Jabez Tupper	Sandwich	16 do.	July 15. 1771
Robert Smith	Theodore Dohone	Boston	20 do.	Apl. 16. 1780
Ph. Wybird Kennedy[15]	Isaac Wibird	do.	22. do.	Apl. 8. 1769
Sarah Akley	Joshua Clap	Scituate	May 9 do.	Mar 1. 1777
Mary Turner	Charles Phelps Esqr.	Hadley	21. do.	May 1772
Katha.[16] Fitzgerald	Nathl. Page	Hardwick	26 do.	Augt. 15. 1780
Eliza. Williams	Timo. Paine Esqr.	Worcester	June 9 1768	Octo. 20. 1774
John Bradley	Timo. Biglio	do.	16. do.	Feby. 12. 1781
Thos. Burns	Chas. Callahan	Pownalboro.	28 do.	July 29. 1781
Wm. Delahunt	Jno. Worthington Esqr.	Springfield	30 do.	Octo. 20. 1779
Mary Bennison	Saml. Clap	Scituate	July 19 do.	April 1. 1775
Saml. Akley	John Merrill	Topsham	23. do.	June 17. 1785
Eliza. Bennison	Thomas Stevenson	Hingham	Augt. 4 do.	July 26. 1772
Sarah Dunn	Daniel Watson	Cambridge	13. do.	Septr. 22. 1775
Ann Gostere[17]	Benja. Prentice	Watertown	15. do.	Augt. 15. 1780
Willm. Milton	Chas. Cushing Esqr.	Pownalboro	31. do.	Nov. 7. 1776
Robt. Vokes	Danl. Oliver Esqr.	Hardwick	Septr. 2 do.	May 27. 1782
Mary Akley	Dr. Edwd. Russell	N. Yarmo.	6 do.	Decr. 20. 1780
Eliza. Lemoine	Thos. Patten	Watertown	Octo. 1. do.	Augt. 1. 1780
Margt. Forbus	John Hancock	Eastward	[blank in MS]	Mar. 27. 1777
Wm. Corbett	Cornes. Mansis	Haverhill	12 do.	Apl. 26. 1784
Peter Bouts	Shubael Downs	Harwich	15. do.	May 15. 1776
Robt. Humphrys	John Smith	Boston	Novr. 1. do.	Septr. 16. 1771
Jas. Vokes	Shubael Lovell	Barnsta.	16 do.	Nov. 23. 1783

Children Bound Out, 1756-1790

Childrens Names	To Whome Bound	of what Town	When Bound	When Free
Mary Dumphy	Henry Folger	Sherburn	24. do.	Septr. 1. 1774
Saml. Hartley	Daniel Parks	Boston	25 do.	Jany. 15. 1783
Sarah Lassley	Elijah Leonard	Springfield	25. do.	Feby 15. 1780
Susanna Smith	Jona. Crosby	Boston	Decr. 10 do.	Septr. 11. 1779
Matthew Hopkins	Alexr. Landale	Boston	do. do.	Decr. 27. 1774
Abigl. Waddle	Joseph Clift	Marshfield	14 do.	June 23. 1777
Geo. Coffin	Willm. Dodge	Lincoln	31. do.	Feby. 13. 1782
Geo. Harley	Andw. Dennis	Marblehead	Janua. 9. 1769.	May 2. 1779
John Lucas	Nehemiah Hinds	Greenwich	Feby. 22 do.	April 10. 1779
Benja. Harley	Josiah Brewer junr	Worcester	Mar. 13 do.	April 9. 1781
William Warner	Saml. Foster	Harwich	21 do.	June 7. 1778
Mary Barrett	Lemuel Pomroy	Southampton	1. do.	Septr. 25. 1772
Rachel Rules	Capt. Saml. Foster	Harwich	21 do.	Augt. 15. 1775
Stephen Stow	Edward Winter	Boston	April 5. do.	Feby. 15. 1776
Davis Whitman	Wm. Wesson junr.	Hopkington	do. do.	May 25. 1783
Ann Forrest	Jona. Dwight	Springfield	12 do.	Mar. 14 1779
Nathl. Procter	Richard Clark	Milton	May 9. 1769	Augt. 12. 1780
Ann Cromartie	Ruth Decosta	Boston	June 7. do.	Feby. 25. 1774
Mary Brooks	Thos. Matthew	Plymo.	17 do.	June 1775
Ann Davis	Sylvanus Higgins	Connecticut	July 3 do.	July 13. 1772
Eliza. Pimm	James Barter	Mblehead	Augt. 21. do.	Decr. 15. 1781
Eliza. Mullins	Robert Rand	Boston	Septr. 6. do.	Decr. 31 1779
Nathl. Rhodes	Abram. Hammatt	Nantucket	8. do.	Apl. 10 1779
Francis Appleton	Mr. Thos. Walker	Boston	Octo. 4 do.	Septr. 27. 1776
Ann Guthridge[18]	James Frost	Cambridge	21. do.	May 10. 1776
John Godfrey	Matthew Knight	Lancaster	26 do.	May 15. 1785
Hannah Barry	Hannah Oulton	Falmo.	Novr. 4 do.	Feby. 10. 1780

Children Bound Out, 1756-1790

Childrens Names	To Whome Bound	of what Town	When Bound	When Free
Sarah Dunscutt	John McClenche	Amherst	24 do.	Jany. 6. 1787
Hannah White	Palfrey Collins	Boston	Decr. 6 do.	Jany. 20. 1777
Ann Cromartie	Bossenger Foster	Boston	Jany. 4 1770.	Mar. 10. 1773
James Morris	Ezekl. Holbrook	Well Fleet	Mar 28 do.	Mar. 6 1778
Lydia Green	Chas. Baxter	Braintree	1. do.	Jany 1. 1781
Richard Fothergill	Elkanah Hopkins	Harwich	Apl. 10 do.	Apl. 10. 1781
Mary Morris	Sarah Dawes	Boston	May 4. do.	Novr. 23. 1778
Sarah Fothergill	Cornes. Fellows	Gloucester	17. do.	Septr. 5. 1775
Hannah Barjer	James Burton	Boston	18. do.	Octo. 30. 1779
Mary Fothergill	Jurashaddai Dotey	Hardwick	23. do.	Mar 20. 1781
Katha. Twing	John Lowder junr.	Roxbury	June 6. do.	Octo. 15. 1771
Jona. Silsberry	John Ingersoll	Westfield	6 do.	May 22. 1783
Andrew Dunn	James Campbell	Westfield	6 do.	Mar 8. 1780
Richard Smith	Seth Loomis	Westfield	6. do.	May 22 1783
Nathl. Bristow	Abner Fowler	Westfield	21 do.	Jany. 1. 1784
Robert McNeir	Stephen Huzzey	Nantucket	26 do.	Jany. 8. 1779
Wm. Ross	Adner Sackett	Westfield	30 do.	Jany 13. 1782
Sarah Pattin	Aaron Hunt	Hardwick	July 6 do.	May 25. 1782
Lydia Rhodes	Geo. Pynchon	Springfield	19. do.	June 17. 1773
Thos. Liswell	Abner Fowler	Westfield	Augt. 28. do.	July 15. 1781
Michl. Stewart	John Bound	Boston	Septr. 5. do.	July 10. 1779
Susanna Whitman	Saml. Emmes	Boston	7 do.	Aug. 10. 1778
Robert Burgoin	Edward How	Boston	7. do.	Septr. 7. 1778
Margtt. Burton	Jona. Warner	Hardwick	Novr. 1. 1770	July 20. 1780
Willm. Newhall	David Munro	Charlestown	7. do.	May 18. 1775
John Plant[19]	Paul Mandell	Hardwick	17 do.	Mar 29. 1779
James Melvin	Richd. Carpenter	Boston	Decr. 12 do.	Apl. 1. 1774

Children Bound Out, 1756-1790

Childrens Names	To Whome Bound	of what Town	When Bound	When Free
John Gilbert	Elnathan Sampson	Dartmo.	17 do.	Decr. 17. 1785
Josiah Burk	John How	Boston	Jany. 2 1771	Augt. 5. 1778
Ebenr. Blancher	Abraham Hammatt	Plimouth	24 do.	Feby. 1 1777
Thos. Akley	Jason Haven	Dedham	Feby. 6 do.	Octo. 3. 1777
Nichs. Mangent	Peter Chapin	New Malboro.	7 do.	Jany. 1. 1781
Henry Flemings	Isaac Hunter	New Braintree	14 do.	Augt. 17. 1783
Timothy Foster	David Baldwin jur.	Spencer	14 do.	Augt. 22 1786
James Ranstead	Joseph Johnson	New Braintree	19. do.	May 16. 1785
Sarah Lewis	Paul Mandell	Hardwick	26. do.	Jany. 20. 1784
Ann Allen	Paul Mandell	do.	26 do.	Septr. 8. 1780
James Bailey	Benja. Ruggles	do.	27 do.	Feby. 18. 1784
Enoch Jarvis	Hugh Tarbett	Boston	March 6 do.	May 13. 1772
Willm. Ranstead	Edward Maylem	do.	6 do.	April 10 1783
Joseph Lillie	Richard Billings	do.	April 11 do.	June 18. 1779
Esther Burgean	David Durfy	Dartmouth	May 7. do.	Septr. 15. 1781
Hannah Powell	Nathan Stone	Yarmouth	30. do.	April 14. 1780
Neal Peacock	Edward Russell	No. Yarmouth	June 12. do.	Augt. 28. 1781
James McLary	Andrew Gillespie	Boston	June 5 do.	July 15. 1781
Anthony Haswell	Isaiah Thomas	do.	July 23 do.	April 6. 1777
Ann Wilkinson	Saml. Gray	do.	Septr. 3. do.	Decr. 25. 1787
Wm. Collins	Rd. Neck	Marblehead	4 do.	May 15. 1782
Margtt. Bright	Silas Stone	Brookfield	25 do.	July 15. 1784
Richard Butler	Wm. Androws	Boston	23. do.	Feby. 28. 1777
James Fling	Nathl. Downs	Harwich	23. do.	Novr. 4. 1778
Eliza. Gray	Dr. Saml. Gardner	Milton	Octor. 21. do.	April 2. 1783
Henrietta Jeans	William Billings	Sunderland	25 do.	Septr. 3. 1784
Thos. Akley	Jason Haven	Dedham	Novr. 6 do.	Octo. 3. 1777

Children Bound Out, 1756-1790

Childrens Names	To Whome Bound	of what Town	When Bound	When Free
Wm. McFarland	Mr. Saml. Ridgaway jur.	Boston	6 do.	Augt. 28 1784
Mary McLary	Ezra Weston	Duxborough	Decr. 7. do.	July 12 1774
Jane Wiseaker	Elisha Gray		26. do.	Mar. 18. 1781
Willm. Fullerton	John Moseley	Westfield	Janua. 7. 1772	May 27. 1776
Samuel Prince	John Field	Amherst	12	Feby. 13. 1787
Susanna Jordan	Asa Waite	New Braintree	22	Mar. 26. 1779
Mary Liswell	Benja Ingersoll	Boston	Feby. 5	May 29. 1781
Geo. Forbis[20]	Paul Mandell	Hardwick	6	Octo. 15. 1788
Henry Welch	Reuben Newcomb	Wellfleet	April 7	Augt. 9. 1785
Martin McFarland[21]	Elisha Allis	Hatfield	27	Septr. 23. 1787
Mary Liscow	Elisha Allis	Do.	do.	April 21. 1783
Oliver Standards[22]	Elisha Ingraham	Amherst	May 22.	April 18 1783
Eliza. Wharff	Martin Smith	Do.	do.	July 18 1786
Joanna Williams	Noah Colman	Hatfield	June 15	Octo. 6. 1782
Thomas Bradley	James Bacon	Barnstable	Augt. 1	July 28. 1786
Napthali Newhall	Saml. Ridgaway jur.	Boston	5	June 25. 1788
Michael Stewart	Willm. Haynes	Do.	6.	July 10. 1779
Benja. Fitch	James Holmes	New Braintree	6	Augt. 15. 1787
Eliza. Barbour	Jona. Balch	Boston	28.	Feby. 3. 1781
Margtt. Freestot[23]	Moses Bagg	Springfield	24	May 8. 1781
Nathl. Rust	James Provence	Boston	Octo. 14	July 27 1779
Joseph Stringer	Job Wheelwright	Do.	14	April 15. 1780
Hannah White	Jacob Edes	Do.	15.	Jany. 20 1779
Thomas Cloud Reed	Barnabas Atwood	Wellfleet	17.	June 4 1785
Jane Leadbetter	Benja. Bass	Boston	Decr. 9	Octor. 19. 1777
Benja. Buffard	John Boyes	Rutland	do.	Decr. 6. 1787
Robert McNear	Stephen Hussey	Nantucket	Mar. 4. 1773	Jany. 8 1779

Children Bound Out, 1756-1790

Childrens Names	To Whome Bound	of what Town	When Bound	When Free
Wm. Boardman	Henry Mellen	Hopkington	16	Jany 30. 1780
John Remick[24]	Nathl. Cook	Boston	26	Septr. 30. 1788
Edward Jones[25]	Wm. Gregg	Londonderry	April 2	Augt. 31. 1779
Thomas[26] Codd	Samuel Benjamin	Watertown	7	Sept. 16. 1785
Benja. Harley	Willm. Dickman	Boston	May 14.	Apl. 9. 1781
Elear. Bennet[27]	Mary Gorham	Charlestown	31.	Mar. 15. 1785
John Plant[28]	Timo. Ruggles jur.	Hardwick	June 4	Mar. 29 1779
Willm. Warren	Paul Mandell	Do.	4	Augt. 15. 1783
Cornes. Laha[29]	Thomas Gerry jur.	Marblehead	June 11. 1773	July 6. 1785
Eliza. McColloch	Israel Williams jur.	Hatfield	22.	July 25. 1783
Margtt.[30] Richardson	Benja. Howland	Eastward	25	June 15. 1779
Thomas Condon	Saml. Dexter Esqr.	Dedham	July 6	Mar. 15. 1783
Eliza. White[31]	Saml. Coney junr.	Easton	7	July 14. 1785
Michl. Shephard[32]	John Hayden	Hopkington	8.	Octo. 15. 1779
Mary Lovell	Charles Cushing Esqr.	Pownalboro.	19.	Jany. 25. 1780
Hannah White	James Fullerton	Boothbay	20	Jany 20. 1779
Benja. Hunt	John Hicks	Boston	Augt. 4	May 26. 1779
Sarah Pattin	Thos. Robinson	Hardwick	Septr. 1	May 25. 1782
Thomas Burdeway	Edwd. Compton How	Boston	do.	Decr. 25. 1778
John Wallis Laha[33]	Joseph Stacey	Mblehead	3	Octo. 6. 1786
Ann Dumaresque	Elisha Parks	Westfield	Octor. 12	Sept. 1. 1784
Katha. White[34]	Doctr. Nathl. Coffin	Falmouth	22	May 15. 1785
Davis Whitman	John Wilson Esqr.	Hopkington	Novr. 1	May 25. 1783
Benja. Harley	John Brewer	Boston	3	April 9. 1781

Children Bound Out, 1756-1790

	Childrens Names	To whom Bound	town	when Bound	when free
State	Nancy Rea	Wm. Stimpson	Charlston	Apr. 2 1785	febry. 1st. 1796
State	Eliz Champlen	Nath Paine	Boston	Augt. 12th. 1785	May 10th. 1797
State	Susanna Lewis	Abram. Jackson	Newbury Port	June 14 1785	July 14th 1796
State	Mary Gorden	Daniel McCarty	Roxbury	Aug 4 1785	Sept. 4th. 1795
State	James Gorden	Justus Forward	Belchertown	Novr. 10th. 1785	Augt. 21st. 1795
town	Temothy Brown[35]	Saml. Fowler	Westfield	June 15 1785	Sept. 15 1798
do.	Benjman Scott	Wm. Chandler	Salam	Augt. 16th. 1785	Novr. 15 1789
do.	Marthor Clough	Eliz Perkens	Boston	June 16th. 1785	Aug 18th. 1793
do.	Eliz. Patten	Elezer Weld	Roxbury	June 25 1785	Novr. 16th. 1795
do.	Thos. Farmer	Ezra Ripley	Conkord	Augt. 19 1785	Jany. 13th. 1799
do.	Charles Dix Wallis	Calab Wilder	Ashburn	Octr. 31 1785	Jany. 1th. 1800
State	Abigall Hurley	Elezer Portor	Hadley	Augt. 10 1785	Novr. 20th. 1796
do.	John Covell	Sephen Salisbury	Worcester	Decr. 5th. 1785	April. 18th. 1793
do.	David Riley	Danl. McCarty	Roxbury	Augt. 3d. 1785	Decr. 31th. 1799
Town	Sarah Harris	Joshua Bullard	Holliston	feby. 1th. 1786	Feby. 12th. 1789
ditto	Joshua Roberts	Wm. Mock	Boston	Feby. 2 1786	feby. 19th. 1796
State	Wm. Meloney	Wm. Crofford	Bath	Apr. 5th. 1786	July 9th. 1801
Town	Estor Ford	Marthor Penchen	Salam	June 7 1786	Septr. 18th. 1794
State	Hurley George	Aron Stratton	Littleton	July 28th. 1786	decr. 3d. 1797
Town	Connor Henry	Abram. Adams	Boston	Sept. 11th. 1786	May 1th. 1791
Town	William Going	Jerh. Smith Boice	Milton	Octr. 30th. 1786	April. 3. 1801
Town	Saml. Murphey	Danl. Waldo	Wocester	April. 11th. 1786	Septr. 3d. 1797
Town	Saml. Pool	George Partridge	duxborough	May 1 1786	Sepr. 26 1796
State	Mary Covell	Thos. Child	Falmouth	June 21 1786	Jany. 6th. 1792
Town	Betsey Pool	Stephen Child	Roxbury	Novr. 24 1786	Augt. 2d. 1797
Town	James White A Negero indenter Exchd.	Stephen Fales	Tanton	Septr. 8th. 1786.	April. 3d. 1799
State	Ben Harris Champlen	Aron Long	Shelborn	Jany. 18th. 1787	April. 22d. 1802

664

Children Bound Out, 1756-1790

	Childrens Names	To whom Bound	town	when Bound	when free
Town	James Warren	Jacob Wilds	Roxbury	Jany. 8th. 1787	Jany. 10th. 1799
Town	Stephen Ingals	David Burrell	Boston	March 7th. 1787	June 1th. 1793
State	Jno. Legalley	Waltor Bell	Colerain	Marh. 7th. 1787	May 3d. 1799
Town	John Corbot	Nathl. Bradley	Boston	Aprl. 5th. 1787	July 12th. 1795
Town	Isaac Corbet	Elezer Crafts	Manchester	Aprl. 5th . 1787	Marh. 10 1797
Marhead	Peggey Gallison	Joseph McClintick	Mendom	May 4th. 1787	decr. 10 1793
State	<Elizebeth Tovet	John Wait	Marblehead	July 10th. 1787	June 10th. 1796>
Town	James Osborn	Stacey Read	Cambridg	Augt. 2 1787	Aug 14th. 1799
State	Nancy Hinds	Jona. Warner Esqr.	Hardwick	Novr. 1 1787	Aprl. 23th. 1797
[bavarly?]	Ann Goodrage	Danl. Bilings	Hardwick	Novr. 1 1787	Jany. 15 1795
Boston	James Roberts	Josh. Washburn	Lacestor	Novr. 15 1787	July 30 1802
do.	Wm. Baldrage	Timy. Bigelow	Wocestor	decr. 15th. 1787	Septr. 15 1801
Town	Thomas Wallis	Isaac Stone	Oakham	decr. 14th. 1787	Novr. 20 1798
do.	James Taunt	Elijah Bacon	Bedford	Feby. 6th. 1788	Feby. 4 [17]92
do.	Patty Roberts	Josh. Stratton	Holden	Jany. 9th. 1788	June 8 1797
do.	Nathl. Peirce[36]	Jona. White	Wst. Springfield	Feby. 29 do.	June 14 1800
State	Elizh. Tevett	Timothy Burbanks	do.	do.	June 20 1796
State	Catharina Drew	Saml. Nicholson	Charlstown	March 18 1788	decr. 26 1796
do.	Abigal Hurley	Joseph Bent	Milton	do. 20 1788	decr. 9 1797
do.	Charles Drew[37]	Seth Padelford	Taunton	June 3d. 1788	Aprl. 26th. 1803
State	Saml. Goslen	Tedder Valentine	Marbelhead	June 19. 1788	May 24 1797
State	Rebecca Down[38]	Jno. Langdon	Powanborough	do. 23d. 1788	Augt. 17 1794
do.	George Randol	ditto	do.	do 23d. 1788	Octr. 8th. 1802
Town	Abigal Clough	Henry Skinner	Woolwich	July 2d. 1788	Novr. 2d. 1796
State	James Gardener	Jno. Langdon	Pownalboro	July 4 1788	Feby. 15. 1802
do.	Barzall. Eddy	Thos. Hopkins	Portland	July 24 1788	feby. 10th. 1801
do.	Sibbel Eddy	do.	do.	do. do.	May 13th. 1794

❧

	Childrens Names	To whom Bound	town	when Bound	when free
do.	*<James Gardener*	*John Langdon*	*Pownalborou*	*Jul>*	
State	Ann Crumwell	Josh. Bacheldor	Chelsee	Augt. 19th. 1788	March 3 1797
do.	Richd. LeGalley	Abrm. Beman	Portland	July 26 do.	Novr. 27 1800
do.	James Lewis	Neheh. May	Goshen in hamsr.[39]	Octr. 6 1788	March 23d. 1801
Town	Luce Cunningham	Saml. Cutter	North yarmth.	Octr. 2d. 1788	Feby. 1th. 1799
State	Jane Sigourney a Mullatto	Joseph Williams	Springfeld	Octr. 16th. 1788	Augt. 1th. 1795
Town	Ann Ethredge	William Coffen	Glocestor	Octr. 29 1788	decr 25 1794
do.	James White a Negero	Benja. Bussey	Dedham	Jany 8th. 1789	Aprl. 3 1799
State	Willm. LeGalley	Thos. Ives	Grate Barringn.	do. 29th. 1789.	decr. 9th. 1802
State	Mary Crane	Thos. Baker	ditto	Feby. 10th 1784	octr. 15th. 1796
Town	James Taunt	John Bacon Exchd. Indentr.	Bellecria	Marh. 1 1789	Feby. 4 1792
State	Charles De St. Pree	Ezekl. Allen	Manchestor	Aprl. 11th. 1789	June 24 1804
Town	Mathew Waikfeild	Saml. Fowler	Pittsfeild	June 4th. 1789	decr. 31 1801
State	Sarah Dunken	Jona. Rawson	Brantree	June 17th. 1789	June 15th. 1799
Town	Jane Galley	Thos. Smith	Sandwich	July 10th. 1789	Octr. 22 1797
do.	Polley Godard	Abrm. Williams	Sandwich	July 16th. 1789	Augt. 13th. 1799
State	Jno. Burkhart[40]	Volentine Tedoer	Marbelhed	Septr. 17th. 1789	octr. 5th. 1798
<Town	*Mary Godordf*	*Abraham Williams*	*Sandwich>*		
town	John Richards	Jno. Sprage Esqr.	Lancestor	Novr. 14th. 1789	May 29th. 1802
do.	Rohdy Negeros	Saml. Joye.	Goldsbury	Octr. 15th. 1789	Octr. 15th. 1792
State	Hebron Materson	Richd. Hunewel	Penobscot	Jany. 15 1790	Novr. 15 1804
State	Ann Crumwell	ditto	do.	Jany. 20 1790	Marh. 3d. 1797
Town	Sueky Waterman	Benjn. Beale	dochestor	feby. 2d. 179[?]	free 20th. feby. 1800

Notes

1   "Noel" in MS index.
2   "Catha." in MS index.
3   "Thwing" in MS index.
4   "Simson" in MS index.
5   "Caroll" in MS index.
6   "Lynes" in MS index.
7   "Jeremiah" in MS index.
8   "Taveneau" in MS index.
9   "McGown" in MS index.
10 The MS index reads "Lemoine <*John*> (Benja.)." See also entry of 27 March 1767, below.
11 "Goggin" in MS index.
12 Next to the name in the left margin is a "p," i.e. province.
13 "Corns." in MS index.
14 "Corbet" in MS index.
15 "Wibird Kennedy" in MS index.
16 "Kate" in MS index.
17 "Goster" in MS index.
18 "Guttridge" in MS index.
19 Next to the name in the left margin is a "p," i.e. province.
20 Next to the name in the left margin is a "p," i.e. province.
21 Next to the name in the left margin is a "p," i.e. province.
22 "Standard" in MS index.
23 Next to the name in the left margin is a "p," i.e. province.
24 Next to the name in the left margin is a "p," i.e. province.
25 Next to the name in the left margin is a "p," i.e. province.
26 "Edward" in MS index.
27 Next to the name in the left margin is a "p," i.e. province.
28 Next to the name in the left margin is a "p," i.e. province.
29 Next to the name in the left margin is a "p," i.e. province.
30 "Peg" in MS index.
31 Next to the name in the left margin is a "p," i.e. province.
32 "Sheppard" in MS index.
33 Next to the name in the left margin is a "p," i.e. province.
34 Next to the name in the left margin is a "p," i.e. province.
35 In this and the next 32 entries, the child's last name was written before their first name.
36 In this and the next entry, the child's last name was written before their first name.
37   The child's last name was written before the first name.
38 In this and the next 19 entries, the child's last name was written before their first name.
39 I.e., New Hampshire.
40 In this and the next five entries, the child's last name was written before their first name.

THE OVERSEERS' FINANCES
1738 – 1769

The manuscript financial records of the Overseers exist in what appear to be complete sequence for the period from 1738 to 1769 (Financial Register, Overseers, box 1, folder 2). The file has been tabulated in aggregate form in the introduction to this volume (see footnote 100 in the introduction). There are only a few scattered manuscript pages of mostly incomplete accounts for the Workhouse (box 13, folder 1) ranging from the 1740s to the 1770s, and these have been summarized along with the Almshouse figures in footnote 100. No comparable run of financial records appears in the eighteenth-century manuscripts after 1770.

The mid-century records are quite detailed in places and include specifics on all types of accounts, including salaries for Almshouse keepers, charges to townspeople for in-home care for poor and often mentally ill wards of the Overseers, and the costs of provisioning and maintaining the Almshouse. Otherwise, the records show clearly the annual budgets for the Overseers as a branch or office or department (in the modern sense) of civic government and administration. Also, the records show the practice of outdoor relief, in which individual Overseers would fund the poor in the latter's homes out of their own pockets and be recompensed later.

The Financial Register, quite simple in its design and maintenance, is organized by monthly financial statements that summarize debits and bill the Town of Boston for funds to cover those debited expenditures. Individual recipients as well as creditors are identified. In addition to a running monthly record, the financial statements are expressed in annual summaries and in decennial reviews. The final few pages in the Register are part of this financial record, but refer to some random and separate data that do not fall into the sequence of monthly accounts.

The values shown here are in pounds, shillings and pence, the British imperial system based on the unit of the pound sterling which is preceded by the £ symbol. This was the standard currency system in colonial America but was eliminated during the Revolution and replaced by the dollar and its decimal subdivision. The Imperial (or Sterling) system of pounds, shillings and pence remained in use in the United Kingdom, and in parts of the British Empire and Commonwealth, until 1971. The pound was subdivided by 20 shillings, each shilling consisting of 12 pence. Thus the pound consisted of 240 pence. Pence were subdivided further by half-pence and quarter-pence ("farthings"), and the 1/2 and 1/4 included below reflect those subdivisions as they were cited. The designation for shillings was the "s," or more commonly "/-," and when pence were given alone, they were identified with a "d." In the entries below, the first figure refers to pounds, the second to shillings, and the third to pence.

~

Boston April 4th: 1738.

Granted by the Overseers of the Poor vizt.

To William Ross 20/ Joseph Davis 20/	£2.		
Sarah Marrable 10/ Mercy Rayner 10/	1.		
Hannah Tapper 10/ Tabitha Walter 15/	1. 5.		
Mary Wire 10/ Sarah Willis 10/	1.		
Widow Dantry 15/ Widow Holland 10/	1. 5.		
Widow Ingolsby for Lynde	10.		
Hannah Haden 15/ Nurse Kenny 20/	1. 15.		
Esther Egian	10.	9. 5.	
To Henry Dyre in full of His Disburstments		69. 6. 11	
		£78. 11. 11	

Boston May 2d. 1738.

Granted by the Overseers of the Poor vizt.

To William Ross 20/ Joseph Davis 20/	2.		
Sarah Marrable 10/ Mercy Rayner 10/	1.		
Hannah Tapper 10/ Tabitha Walter 15/	1. 5.		
Mary Wire 10/ Sarah Willis 10/	1.		
Widow Dantry 15/*<Widow Holland 10/>*	0. 15.		
Widow Ingolsby for Lynde	10.		
Hannah Haden 15/ Nurse Kenny 20/	1. 15.	8. 5.	
<Esther Egian>	*<10.>*		
To John Hunt Esqr in full of his Accot.	104.		
Henry Dyre in full of his disburstmts.	111. 5. 10	215. 5. 10	
Dr: Edwd. Ellis one quarter Salary		12. 10.	
		£236. 10	

Boston June 6. 1738

Granted by the Overseers of the Poor vizt.

To William Ross 20/ Jos: Davis 20/ Sarah Marrable 10/	2. 10.
Mercy Rayner 10/ Han: Tapper 10/ Tabitha Walter 15/	1. 15.
Mary Wire 10/ Sarah Willis 10/ Widow Dantry 15/	1. 15.

Widow Ingolsby for Lynde 10/ Hannah Haden 15/	1. 5.	
Nurse Kenny 20/ Esther Egian 10/	1. 10.	8. 15.
To Edwd. Bromfield in full of his Accott.	90. 1. 4	
Henry Dyre in full of his Disburstmts.	86. 4	
Thos. Hancock in full of his Accot.	27. 10. 3	203. 11. 11
		£212. 6. 11

Boston July 4th: 1738.

Granted by the Overseers of the Poor Vizt.

To Willm. Ross 20/ Joseph Davis 20/ Sarah Marrable 10/	2. 10.	
Mercy Rayner 10/ Han: Tapper 10/ Tabi: Walters 15/	1. 15.	
Mary Wire 10/ Sarah Willis 10/ Wido Dantry 15/	1. 15.	
Widow Ingolsby for Lynde 10/ Hannah Haden 15/	1. 5.	
Nurse Kenny 20/ Esther Egian 10/	1. 10.	8. 15.
To Capt. Joshua Cheever in full of his Accot.	5. 10.	
To Ditto for Intrest of 300£ for 3 mo.	4. 10.	
To Capt. Danl. Henchman in full of his Accott.	63.	
To Henry Dyre in full of his Disburstmts.	89. 4. 5	162. 4. 5
		£170. 19. 5
To Dr: William Davis in full of his Accot. for the Province		66. 15.
To Dr. Edw: Ellis........ in full of his Accot. for Ditto		113. 3. 6
		£350. 17. 11

Boston August. 1. 1738

Granted by the Overseers of the Poor Vizt.

To Willm. Ross 20/ Jos: Davis 20/ Sarah Marrable 10/	£2. 10.	
Mercy Rayner 10/ Hannah Tapper 10/ Tab: Walters 15/	1. 15.	
Mary Wyre 10/ Sarah Willis 10/ Wido. Dantry 15/	1. 15.	
Wido. Ingolsby for Lynde 10/ Hannah Haden 15/	1. 5.	
Nurse Kenny. 20/ Easter Egian 10/	1. 10.	£8. 15.
To Doctr. Edward Ellis for his Qrs. Sallery		12. 10.
To Mr. James Allen in ful of his Nt. for 100 Bush: Rye		52. 10.
To Thomas Moulin in full of his accot.		9.
To William Knox for 50 Cord of wood		100.
To Francis Warden in full of his Note for Coffins		20. 17. 4

To John Ruck Esqr in full of his accot. ... 90. 8.
To Saml. Greenwood Esqr.   Do. ... 9. 17. 6
To Dan Henchman   Do. ... 10. 16.
To Henry Dyre in full of his Disburstments ... 89. 13. 2
To Ditto for Half Yrs. Sallary from 10th. Janry. to 10th. July ... 70.

£474. 7.

Boston Septr. 5. 1738.

Granted by the Overseers of the Poor Vizt.

To William Ross 20/   Jos: Davis 20/   Sar: Marrable 10/   £2. 10.
   Mercy Ranger 10/   Han: Tapper 10/   Tab: Walters 15/   1. 15.
   Mary Wyre 10/   Sarah Willis 10/   Wido. Dantry 15/   1. 15.
   Wid Ingolsby for Lynde 10/   Hannah Hayden 15/   1. 5.
   Nurse Kenny 20/   Easter Egian 10/   1. 10.   £8. 15.
To Jacob Wendell Esqr for 2 Hogshds. Molasses   47. 5.
To Daniel Henchman in ful of his acct.   23. 13.
To Mr. Charles Henly his accot. of Shoes   41. 4. 8
To Mr. Joshua Dodge his accot. of Shoes   13. 2. 3
To Henry Dyre in full of his Disbursments   100. 11. 11

£234. 11. 10

Boston Octor: 3d: 1738.

Granted by the Overseers of the Poor Vizt.

To William Ross 20/   Joseph Davis 20/   2.
   Sarah Marrable 10/   Mercy Ranger 10/   1.
   Tabi: Walter 15/   Hannah Tapper 10/   1. 5.
   Mary Wyre 10/   Sarah Willis 10/   1.
   Widow Dantry 15/   Widow Ingolsby for Lynde 10/   1. 5.
   Hañah Hayden 15/   Nurse Kenny 20/   1. 15.
   Esther Egian   10.   8. 15.
To Henry Dyre in full of his Disburstmts.   70. 11. 3
To Thomas Hubbard in full of his Accott.   107. 13. 9
To Edwd. Bromfield.................Ditto   30. 3. 5
To John Ruck Esqr....................Do.   31. 3.   239. 11. 5

£248. 6. 5

Boston Novr. 7th. 1738

Granted by the Overseers of the Poor

To William Ross 20/ Joseph Davis 20/	£2.	
Sarah Marrable 10/ Mercy Rayner 10/	1.	
Tab: Walter 15/ Hannah Tupper 10/	1. 5.	
Mary Wyre 10/ Sarah Willis 10/	1.	
wido. Dantry 15/ Wido. Ingolsby for Lynde 10/	1. 5.	
Hannah Hayden 15/ Nurse Kenney 20/	1. 15.	
Easter Eagian 10/ Samul Smith for wife 15/	1. 5.	£9. 10.
To William Knox in ful of his Acct: for wood	£111.	
To Doctr. Edwd. Ellis in full of his Qtr. Sallery	12. 10.	
To Henry Dyre in ful of his Disbursments	76. 16. 1	£200. 6. 1
		£209. 16. 1

Boston Decr. 5th. 1738

Granted by the Overseers of the Poor

To William Ross 20/ Joseph Davis 20/	£2.	
Sarah Marrable 10/ Mercy Rayner 10/	1.	
Tabitha Walter 15/ Hannah Tupper 10/	1. 5.	
Mary Wire 10/ Sarah Willis 10/	1.	
Wido. Dantry 15/ Wido. Ingolsby for Lynde 10/	1. 5.	
Hannah Hayden 15/ Nurse Kenny 20/	1. 5.	
Easther Eagian 10/ Saml. Smith for wife 15/	1. 5.	£9. 10.
To Henry Dyre in full of his Disbursments	90. 1. 1	
To Fran[c]is Warden in full of his Accot.	30. 10	120. 1. 11
		£129. 11. 11

Boston Janua 2d. 1738/9.

Granted by the Overseers of the Poor

To William Ross 20/ Joseph Davis 20/	2.
Sarah Marrable 10/ Mercy Raynor 10/	1.
Tabitha Walter 15/ Hannah Tapper 10/	1. 5.
dead.) Mary Wire Dead[1] Sarah Willis 10/	10.

Widow Dantry 15/ Widow Ingolsby for Lynde 10/	1. 5.	
Hannah Haden 15/ Nurse Kenny 20/	1. 15.	
Easther Egian 10/ Saml. Smith for wife 15/	1. 5.	9. 00.[2]
To Capt. Henry Dering in full of his Accot.	43.	
Edw Bromfield Do.	106. 2.	
Henry Dyre in full of his disburstmts.	145. 12. 7	294. 12. 9
		£303. 12. 9

Boston Febry. 6 1738

Granted by the Overseers of the Poor

To Willm. Ross 20/ Joseph Davis 20/	£2. 0. 0	
Mercy Rayner 10/ Tabitha Walter 15/	1. 5.	
Hannah Tapper 10/ Sarah Willis 10/	1.	
Wido. Dantry 15/ Wido. Ingolsby for Lynde 15/	1. 10.	
Hannah Hayden 15/ Nurse Kenney 20/	1. 15.	
Easther Egian 10/ Saml. Smith for wife 15/	1. 5.	£8. 15.
To Thomas Hubbard Esqr in full of his Accot.	£28. 13. 5	
Israel Hearsy for wood ℘ Capt. Greenwoods order	21. 12.	
William Cunningham Glasior in ful of his Bill	8. 3. 6	
Henry Dyre in full of his Disbursments	91. 7. 2	
Doctr. Edwd. Ellis in full of his Qt. Sallary	12. 10.	£162. 6. 1
		£171. 1. 1

Boston March 2d. 1738.

Granted by the Overs[ee]rs[3] of the Poor

To Willm. Ross 20/ Joseph Davis 20/	2.	
Mercy Rayner 10/ Tabitha Walter 15/	1. 5.	
Hannah Tapper 10/ Sarah Willis 10/	1.	
Widow Dantry 15/ Wid. Ingolsby for Lynde 15/	1. 10.	
Hannah Haden 15/ Nurse Kenney 20/	1. 15.	
Esther Egian 10/ Saml. Smith 15/	1. 5.	8. 15.
To John Ruck Esqr in full of his Accot.	£23. 16. 6	
Capt. Jeff: Bedgood … Do.	8. 10. 9	
Joshua Cheever Esqr	28. 2. 6	

Danl. Henchman	20.	18.	7			
Majr. John Hill	96.	9.	5			
William Speakman for Bran	10.	3.	6			
Edward Bromfield	26.	1.	6			
Francis Warden for Coffins &c	10.	8.	3			
William Tyler Esqr	27.	11.				
William Downe	39.	1.	9			
John Hunt Esqr	2.					
Thomas Moulin	10.	6.				
Edward Ellis in ful of his Bill	240.					
Henry Dyre in full of his Sallary & Months Bill of Expenses	96.	18.	2	£640.	7.	11
				£649.	2.	11

Boston April 3d. 1739.

Granted by the Overseers of the Poor

To William Ross 20/ Joseph Davis 20/	£2.					
Mercy Rainer 10/ Tabitha Walter 15/	1.	05.				
Hannah Tapper 10/ Sarah Willis 10/	1.					
Wido. Dantry 15/ Wido. Ingolsby for Lynde 15/	1.	10.				
Hannah Hayden 15/ Nurse Kenny 20/	1.	15.				
Easther Egian 10/ Saml. Smith 15/	1.	5.		£8.	15.	
To John Hill in full of his Accot.	16.	3.				
To Henry Dyre in full of his Disbursments	73.	10.	7	89.	13.	7
				£98.	8.	7

Boston May 1. 1739.

Granted by the O[verseers][4] of the Poor

To William Ross 20/ Joseph [Davis 20/]	2.		
Mercy Rainer 10/ Tabi[tha Wal]ter 15/	1.	5.	
Hannah T[a]pper 10/ Sarah William 10/	1.		
Widow Dantry 15/ Widow Ingolsby for Lynde 15/	1.	10.	
Hannah Hayden 15/ Nurse Kenny 20/	1.	15.	
Easther Egian 10/ Saml. Smith 15/	1.	5.	£8. 15.
To John Hill in full of his Accott.	113.	9.	3

Joseph Shed Ditto	10. 18. 4	
Dr. Edward Ellis in full for his Salary for one quartr.	12. 10.	
Henry Dyre in full of his Accott. Disburstmts.	64. 6. 2	£201. 3. 9
		£209. 18. 9

Boston June 5. 1739.

Granted by the Overseers of the Poor

To Joseph Davis 20/ Mercy Rayner 10/	£1. 10.	
Tabitha Walter 15/ Hannah Tapper 10/	1. 5.	
Sarah Willis 10/ Wido. Dantry 15/	1. 5.	
Wido. Ingolsby for Lynde 15/ Hannah Hayden 15/	1. 10.	
Nurse Kenney 20/ Eas[t]her Egian 10/	1. 10.	
Samuel Smith 15/ Mary Lax 10/	1. 5.	£8. 05.
To Joshua Dodge in full of his accot.	5. 7.⁵	
Henry Dyre in full of his Disbursments	122. 15. 6	£128. 2. 6
		£136. 7. 6

Boston. July 3. 1739.

Granted by the overseers of the Poor

To Joseph Davis 20/ Mercy Rayner 10/	£1. 10.	
Tabitha Walter 15/ Hannah Tapper 10/	1. 5.	
Sarah Willis 10/ Wido. Dantry 15/	1. 5.	
Wido. Ingolsby for Lynde 15/ Hannah Hayden 15/	1. 10.	
Nurse Kenny 20/ Eas[t]her Egian 10/	1. 10.	
Saml. Smith 15/ Mary Lax 10/	1. 5.	£8. 5.
To Wm. Tyler Esqr for 100 Bush Rye	35.	
To Thos. Hubbard Esqr in full of his Accot.	95. 17. 4	
To Henry Dyre in full of his Disbursments	86. 1. 5	216. 18. 9
		£225. 3. 9

Boston 7th. Augt. 1739.

Granted by the Overseers of the Poor

To Joseph Davis 20/ Mercy Rayner 10/	£1. 10.	

Tabitha Walter 15/ Hañah Tapper 10/	1. 5.		
Sarah Willis 10/ Wido. Dantry 15/	1. 5.		
Wido. Ingolsby for Lynde 15/ Ha. Hayden 15/	1. 10.		
Nurse Kenny 20/ Esther Egian 10/	1. 10.		
Saml. Smith 15/ Mary Lax 10/	1. 5.	£8. 5.	
To Jacob Wendell Esq in full of his accot.	166. 16. 9		
To John Hill ....ditto	97. 15. 9		
To Edwd. Bromfield............ ditto	163. 9. 6		
To Danl. Henchman Esq ditto	95. 18.		
To Henry Dyre in full of his disbursts. £166. 10. 2			
To Ditto .... 1/2 years Salary 70.	236. 10. 2	£760. 10. 4	
		£768. 15. 4	
To Docr. Edwd. Ellis in full for one Qrs. Salary	12. 10.		
To Ditto. in full of his Province Account to the 1 May last	144. 17.	157. 7.	
		£926. 2. 4	

Boston Septemr. 4th: 1739.

Granted by the Overseers of the Poor

To Joseph Davis 20/ Mercy Rayner 10/	1. 10.		
Tabitha Walter 15/ Hannah Tapper 10/	1. 5.		
Sarah Willis 10/ Widow Dantry 15/	1. 5.		
Widow Ingolsby for Lynde 15/ Hanr Haden 15/	1. 10.		
Nurse Kenny 20/ Esther Egian 10/	1. 10.		
Saml. Smith 15/ Mary Lax. 10/	1. 5.		
Dorothy Torry 20/ Lidia Torry 20/	2.	10. 5.	
To Charles Henley in full of his Accot. for Shoes	18. 12. 6		
Thos: Moulin & Compa: Ditto for Funerals	9. 5.		
Fras. Warden in full of his Accot.	13. 16. 6		
Hugh Kennedy Ditto (for the Province)	8. 10.		
Henry Dyre in full of his Accot.	270. 11. 1	320. 15. 1	
		£331. 1	

Boston Octobr. 2d. 1739.

Granted by the Overseers of the Poor &ca.

To Joseph Davis 20/ Mercy Rayner 10/	1. 10.				
Tabitha Walter 15/ Hannah Tapper 10/	1. 5.				
Sarah Willis 10/ Widow Dantry 15/	1. 5.				
Widow Ingolsby for Lynde 15/ Hanr Haden 15/	1. 10.				
Nurse Kenny 20/ Esther Egian 10/	1. 10.				
Saml. Smith 15/ Mary Lax 10/	1. 5.				
Dorothy Torry 20/ Lidia Torry 20/	2.		10. 5.		
To Henry Dyre in full of his Accot. Disburstmts.			77. 10. 3		
			£87. 15. 3		

Boston Novr. 7 1739

Granted by the Overseers of the Poor

To Joseph Davis 20/ Mercy Rayner 10/	£1. 10.			
Tabitha Walter 15/ Hannah Tapper 10/	1. 5.			
Sarah Willis 10/ Wido. Ingolsby for Lynde 15/	1. 5.			
Hanh: Haiden 15/ Nurse Kenny 20/ Easthr. Egian 10/	2. 5.			
Samuel Smith 15/ Mary Lax 10/	1. 5.			
Dorothy Torry 20/ Lidia Torry 20/	2.		£9. 10.	
To Thomas Hubbard in full of his accot.	29. 2			
Samuel Hunt .... Do.	7. 13.			
Hugh Kennedy .... Do.	3.			
Dr. Ellis his Qtr. Sallary	12. 10.			
Henry Dyre in full of His Accot.	143. 3. 2		195. 6. 4	
			204. 16. 4	

Boston 5 Decemr. 1739.

Granted by the Overseers of the Poor

To Joseph Davis 20/ Mercy Rayner 10/	£1. 10.			
Tabitha Walter 15/ Hañah Tapper 10/	1. 5.			
Sarah Willis 10/ Wido. Ingolsby for Eliza. Lynde 15/	1. 5.			
Anna Hayden 15/ Nurse Kenny 20/	1. 15.			
Esther Egian 10/ Mary Lax 10/	1.			
Dorothy Torry 20/ Lydia Torry 20/	2.		8. 15.	
To Henry Dyre in full of his accot.			102. 12. 2	
			£111. 7. 2	

꙳

Boston 2d. Janry. 1739.

Granted by the Overseers of the Poor

To Joseph Davis 20/ Mercy Rayner 10/	£1. 10.		
Tabitha Walter 15/ Hannah Tapper 10/	1. 5.		
Sarah Willis 10/ Wido. Ingolsby for Eliza. Lynde 15/	1. 5.		
Anna Hayden 15/ Nurse Kenny 20/	1. 15.		
Easther Egian 10/ Mary Lax 10/	1.		
Dorothy Torry 20/ Lidia Torry 20/	2.	8. 15.	
To Edward Bromfield in full of his Accot.	£44. 2. 11		

Province Charge { William Cunningham Glasior · Edward Drinker in full of his Disbursments on Michael Carter a Sailor who fel from a mast Head—and Dy'd at his House }

William Cunningham Glasior	5. 16.
Edward Drinker in full of his Disbursments on Michael Carter a Sailor who fel from a mast Head—and Dy'd at his House	11.
To Henry Dyre in full of his Accot. of Disbursments	146. 14. 6

£207. 13. 5

£216. 8. 5

Boston Februa 6. 1739/40.

Granted by the Overseers of the Poor &ca.

To Joseph Davis 20/ Mercy Rayner 10/	1. 10.		
Tabitha Walter 15/ Hannah Tapper 10/	1. 5.		
Sarah Willis 10/ Widow Ingolsby for Lynde 15/	1. 5.		
Hañah Haden 15/ Nurse Kenny 20/	1. 15.		
Esther Egian 10/ Mary Lax 10/	1.		
Dorothy Torry 20/ Lidia Torry 20/	2.	8. 15.	
To Dr: Ellis his Quars. Salary	12. 10.		
Henry Dyre in full of his Accott.	118. 9. 4	130. 19. 4	

£139. 14. 4

Boston Febru 27th. 1739/40

Granted by the Overseers of the Poor Vizt.

To Joseph Davis 20/ Mercy Rayner 10/	1. 10.
Tabitha Walter 15/ Hannah Tapper 10/	1. 5.
Sarah Willis 10/ Widow Ingolsby for Lynde 15/	1. 5.

679

Hannah Haden 15/ Nurse Kenny 20/	1. 15.		
Mary Lax 10/ Dorothy Torry 20/	1. 10.		
Lidia Torry 20/	1.	8. 5.	
To Francis Warden in full of his Accott.	17. 6. 11		
Francis Richie for wood	24. 10.		
Samuel Greenwood Esq in full of his Accot.	8. 2.		
Andrew Oliver Esq .... Ditto	5. 16. 6		
Thomas Hubbard Esq .... Do.	18. 6.		
William Downe .... Do.	11. 18.		
William Tyler Esq .... Do.	18. 16.		
Jeffry Bedgood .... Do.	9. 16. 6		
Edwd. Bromfield .... Do.	9. 12. 6		
William Spikeman .... Do.	5. 8. 6		
Jacob Wendell Esq .... Do.	29. 11.		
Thomas Hancock .... Do.	19. 4.		
Samuel Hunt .... Do.	4. 7.		
Danl. Henchman Esq	19. 2. 6		
Majr. Jno. Hill	25. 12.		
Joseph Shed	19. 3. 4		
Charles Henley	8. 2.	254. 14. 9	
Carried Over		£262. 19. 9	
Brôt Over		£262. 19. 9	
Thomas Mullens in full of his Accott.	9. 8.		
To Joshua Cheever Esq Ditto	54. 12. 6		
To Henry Dyre in full of his Accott., including his			
Salary for half a Year	89. 16. 7	153. 17. 1	
		£416. 16. 10	

Boston April 2d: 1740.

Granted by the Overseers

To Joseph Davis 20/ Mercy Rayner 10/	1. 10.
Tabitha Walter 15/ Hannah Tapper 10/	1. 5.
Sarah Willis 10/ Widow Ingolsby for Lynde 15/	1. 5.
Hannah Haden 15/ Nurse Kenny 20/	1. 15.
Mary Lax 10/ Dorothy Torry 20/	1. 10.

Lidia Torry	<u>1.</u>	8. 5.
To Edward Bromfield in ful of his accot.	35. 6. 9	
John Hill Do.	38. 4. 3	
Willm. Speakman	10. 12. 6	
Henry Dyre in full of his accot.	<u>87. 18. 10</u> £172. 2. 4	
	£180. 7. 4	

Boston May 7th: 1740.

Granted by the Overseers of the Poor Vizt.

To Joseph Davis 20/ Mercy Rayner 10/	1. 10.	
Tabitha Walter 15/ Hannah Tapper 10/	1. 5.	
Sarah Willis 10/ Widow Ingolsby for Lynde 15/	1. 5.	
Hannah Haden 15/ Nurse Kenny 20/	1. 15.	
Mary Lax 10/ Dorothy Torry 20/	1. 10.	
Lidia Torry 20/	<u>1.</u>	8. 5.
To Henry Dyre in full of his Disburstments		<u>210. 2</u>
		£218. 5. 2
To Edward Ellis		<u>200.</u>
		£418. 5. 2

Boston 4 June 1740

Granted by the Overseers of the Poor

To Joseph Davis 20/ Mercy Reyner 10/	£1. 10.	
Tabitha Walter 15/ Hañah Tapper 10/	1. 5.	
Sarah Willis 10/ Wido. Ingolsby for Lynd 15/	1. 5.	
Anna Hayden 15/ Nurse Kenny 20/	1. 15.	
Mary Lax 10/ Dorothy Torry 20/	1. 10.	
Lydia Torry	<u>1.</u>	8. 5.
To John Hill in full of his accot. for Wood) Molossos & Rum)	71. 13. 9	
To Henry Dyre in full of his disbursments	<u>128. 18. 3</u> <u>200. 12.</u>	
	£208. 17.	

Boston July 2d. 1740

Granted by the Overseers of the Poor

To Joseph Davis 20/ Mercy Rayner 10/	£1. 10.	
Hannah Tapper 10/ Sarah Willys 10/	1.	
Wido. Ingolsby for Lynde 15/ Anna Hayden 15/	1. 10.	
Nurse Kenny 20/ Mary Lax 10/	1. 10.	
Dorothy Torry 20/ Lydia Torry 20/	2.	7. 10.
To Thomas Moulin in full of his accot.	9. 10.	
To Henry Dyre in full of his Disbursments	88. 5. 5	
To James Boutinea for the Passage of Eliza		
Dudley to Jersey ⅌ Capt. Gersey	10.	£107. 15. 5
		£115. 5. 5

Boston 6. Augt. 1740

Granted by the Overseers of the Poor.

To Joseph Davis 20/ Mercy Rayner 10/	£1. 10.	
Hañah Tapper 10/ Sarah Willis 10/	1.	
Wido. Ingolsby for Lynde 15/ Anna Hayden 15/	1. 10.	
Nurse Kenny 20/ Mary Lax 10/	1. 10.	
Dorothy Torry 20/ Lydia Torry 20/	2.	7. 10.
To Thomas Hubbard		99. 8. 3
To Andrew Oliver		6. 17. 6
To Henry Dyre in full of his disbursments		76. 1. 9
		£189. 17. 6

Boston 3d. Sept. 1740

Granted by the Overseers of the Poor.

To Joseph Davis 20/ Mercy Reyner 10/	£1. 10.	
Hañah Tapper 10/ Sarah Willis 10/	1.	
Wido. Ingolsby for Lynde 15/ Anna Hayden 15/	1. 10.	
Nurse Kenny 20/ Mary Lax 10/	1. 10.	
Dorothy Torry 20/ Lydia Torry 20/	2.	7. 10.
To Charles Henly in full of his bill		10. 10.
Henry Dyre in full of his disbursments		79. 3. 4
John Hill ....in full of his disbursmts.		34. 3.
		£131. 14. 4

Boston October 1st: 1740.

Granted by the Overseers of the Poor.

To Joseph Davis 20/ Mercy Rayner 10/	1. 10.	
Tabitha Walter 15/ Hannah Tapper 10/	1. 5.	
Sarah Willis 10/ Widow Ingolsby for Lynde 15/	1. 5.	
Anna Hayden 15/ Nurse Kenny 20/	1. 15.	
Mary Lax 10/ Dorothy Torry 20/	1. 10.	
Lidia Torry	1.	
Philip Marlow	15.	9.
To Dr: Edw: Ellis 1/4 salery to May last	12. 10.	
Ditto in full of his Accot.	104. 17. 6	
Fra: Warden Do.	18. 18.	
Henry Dyre Do.	72. 7. 5	208. 12. 11
		£217. 12. 11

Boston Novr. 5th. 1740

Granted by the Overseers of the Poor

To Joseph Davis 20/ Mercy Rayner 10/	1. 10.	
Hannah Tapper 10/	10.	
Sarah Willis 10/ Wido. Inglesby for Lynde 15/	1. 5. 0	
Anna Hayden 15/ Nurse Kenney 20/	1. 15.	
Mary Lax 10/ Dorothy Torry 20/	1. 10.	
Lydia Torry 20/ Philip Marlow 15/	1. 15.	8. 5.
To Majr. John Hill in full of his disbursements	35. 2. 9	
Edward Bromfield in full of his disbursements	190. 18. 5	
Henry Dyre, in full of his disbursements	93. 18. 8	319. 19. 10
		£328. 4. 10

Boston 3. Decr. 1740

Granted by the Overseers of the Poor

To Joseph Davis 20/ Mercy Reyner 10/	£1. 10.
Hañah Tapper 10/ Sarah Willis 10/	1.
Widow Ingolsby for Lynde	15.
Anna Hayden 15/ Nurse Kenny 20/	1. 15.

Mary Lax 10/ Dorothy Torry 20/	1. 10.	
Lydia Torry 20/ Philip Marlow 15/	1. 15.	8. 5.
To Thos. Cushing .... 378 bushls. corn . 7/9	£146. 9. 6	
To Jacob Wendell Esq ...... in full of his disbursmts.	30. 18. 11	
To Willm. Tyler Esq .... ditto	7. 17.	
To Saml. Hunt .... ditto	15. 7.	
To Henry Dyre .... ditto	79. 1. 11	279. 14. 11
		£287. 19. 4

Boston Janry. 7 1740

Granted by the Overseers

To Joseph Davis 20/ Mercy Rayner 10/	£1. 10.	
Hannah Tapper 10/ Sarah Willis 10/	1.	
Wido. Ingolsby for Lynde	15.	
Ann Hayden 15/ Nurse Kenny 20/	1. 15.	
Mary Lax 10/ Dorothy Torry 20/	1. 10.	
Lidia Torry 20/ Phillip Marlow 15/	1. 15.	8. 5.
To Jeffry Bedgood in full of his accot.	10. 5.	
To Henry Dyre in full for his Disbursments	96. 17. 10	
To Thomas Hubbard Esqr in full of His accot.	49. 4. 6	£156. 7. 4
		£164. 12. 4

Boston 4 Febr. 1740

Granted by the Overseers of the Poor

To Joseph Davis 20/ Mercy Reyner 10/	£1. 10.	
Hañah Tapper 10/ Sarah Willis 10/	1.	
Widow Ingolsby for Lynde	15.	
Anna Hayden 15/ Nurse Kenny 20/	1. 15.	
Mary Lax 10/ Dorothy Torry 20/	1. 10.	
Lydia Torry 20/ Philip Marlow 15/	1. 15.	£8. 5.
To Henry Dyre in full of his disbursments		97. 8. 11
To Docr. William Clark . 3 Qrs. Salary		37. 10.
		£143. 3. 11
To Edward Bromfield in full of his disbursments		162. 7.
		£305. 10. 11

The Overseers' Finances 1738-1769

Granted by the Overseers of the Poor, Vizt.

To Joseph Davis 20/ Mercy Rayner 10/		1.	10.	0	
Hannah Tapper 10/ Sarah Willis 10/		1.	0.	0	
Wido. Inglesby for Lynde		0.	15.	0	
Hanna Hayden 15/ Nurse Kenny 20/		1.	15.		
Mary Lax 10/ Dorothy Torrey 20/		1.	10.		
Lydia Torrey 20/ Philip Marlow 15/		1.	15.		
		8.	5.		
To William Tyler Esqr. in full of his disbursements		22.	6.	3	
Capt Jeffrey Bedgood....................Do.		4.	15.		
Andrew Oliver Esqr........................Do.		7.	14.		
Joshua Cheever Esqr.......................Do.		133.	18.	8	
Capt William Downe.....................Do.		50.	4.		
Daniel Henchman Esqr..................Do.		29.	5.		
Isaac White ....Do.		24.	3.	4	
		£280.	11.	3	

Brought Over	£280.	11.	3		
To Thomas Moulin & Co. in full of his Bill		17.	1		
Thomas Ethdridge.........................Do.		23.	0.	6	
Francis Warden ....Do.		24.	3	6	
William Speakman.........................Do.		10.	3.	3	
Timothy Barrons ....Do.		13.	3		
Thomas Hubbard ....Do,		17.	1.		
Thomas Crafts ....Do.		5.	0.	0	
Edward Bromfield ....Do.		45.	9.	4	
Samuel Hunt ....Do.		11.	18.		
Majr. John Hill...............................Do.		77.	17.	3	
Jacob Wendell Esqr.........................Do.		1.	8.	1	
Henry Dyre, 3/4 years Salary 10th. Janry. past 105.					
in full of his disbursments	113.14. 9	218.	14.	9	
Edward Ellis, Physitian, in full of his Bill		59.	19.	6	
William Clarke,.... Ditto............ditto	135. 17. 9				941. 8. 2

Granted by the Overseers of the Poor

To Joseph Davis 20/ Mercy Rayner 10/	£1. 10.	
Johanna Spilier 10/ Hannah Tapper 20/	1. 10.	
Sarah Willis 10/ Wido. Ingolsby for Lynde 15/	1. 5.	
Hannah Hayden 15/ Nurse Kenny 20/	1. 15.	
Mary Lax 10/ Dorothy Torrey 20/	1. 10.	
Lydia Torry 20/ Phillip Marlow 15/	1. 15.	£9. 05.
To Maj. John Hill in full of his accot.	£21. 16.	
Wm. Cunningham Glazier in ful of his acct.	4. 8. 9	
Henry Dyre in full of His accot.	125. 19. 1	£152. 3. 10
		£161. 8. 10

Boston 6 May 1741

Granted by the Overseers of the Poor

To Joseph Davis 20/ Mercy Reyner 10/	£1. 10.	
Joanna Spillier 10/ Hannah Tapper 20/	1. 10.	
Sarah Willis 10/ Wido. Ingolsby for Lynde 15/	1. 5.	
Anna Hayden 15/ Nurse Kenny 20/	1. 15.	
Mary Lax 10/ Dorothy Torry 20/	1. 10.	
Lydia Torry 20/ Philip Marlow 15/	1. 15.	£9. 5.
To Docr. Willm. Clark ....1 Qrs. Salary	£12. 10.	
To Edwd. Bromfield ....in full of his disbursmts.	131. 11. 6	
To John Hill . 1 hhd. Molosos	34. 13. 9	
To Henry Dyre .... in full of his Accot.	124. 10. 3	
To Ditto .... 1 Qrs. salary	35.	338. 5. 6
		£347. 10. 6

Boston June 3. 1741.

Granted by the Overseers of the Poor

To Joseph Davis 20/ Mercy Rayner 10/	1. 10.
Hannah Tapper 20/ Sarah Willis 10/	1. 10.
Widow Ingolsby for Lynde	15.
Ann Hayden 15/ Nurse Kenny 20/	1. 15.
Mary Lax 10/ Dorothy Torry 20/	1. 10.
Lidia Torry 20/ Philip Marlow 15/	1. 15.

Joanna Spillier		10.		£9.	5.
To Henry Dyre …in full of his disbursmts.	£68.	11.	2		
To Thos. Hubbard Esq. ditto	53.	10.		122.	1.	2
				£131.	6.	2

Boston 30. June 1741

Granted by the Overseers of the Poor.

To Joseph Davis 20/ Mercy Reyner 10/	£1.	10.			
Hannah Tapper 20/ Sarah Willis 10/	1.	10.			
Widow Ingolsby for Lynde		15.			
Anna Hayden 15/ Nurse Kenny 20/	1.	15.			
Mary Lax 10/ Dorothy Torry 20/	1.	10.			
Lydia Torry 20/ Philip Marlow 15/	1.	15.			
Joanna Spillier		10.		£9.	5.
To Majr. John Hill ....in full of his disbursts.	63.	15.	4		
Edward Bromfield ....ditto	69.	5.	3		
Robert Saco	8.	17.		141.	17.	7
To Henry Dyre .... ditto				335.	16.	6
				£486.	19.	1

Boston Augst. 5 1741.

Granted by the Overseers of the Poor

To Joseph Davis 20/ Mercy Rayner 10/	£1.	10.			
Hannah Tapper 20/ Sarah Willis 10/	1.	10.			
Wido. Ingolsby for Lynde		15.			
Anna Hayden 15/ Nurse Kenny 20/	1.	15.			
Mary Lax 10/ Dorothy Torry 20/	1.	10.			
Lidia Torry 20/ Phillip Marlow 15/	1.	15.			
Joann Spiller		10.		£9.	05.
To Doctr. William Clarks Qrs. Sallary	£12.	10.			
To Henry Dyre his Qrs. Sallary	35.				
To Ditto in full of his accot. of Disbursment	94.	5.	3		
To Doctr. William Clarke in full of his accot.					
for medicins & attendance of Sundry persons on acct.					
of the Province from May 10th. 1739 to 21 Feb 1740	40.	11.	3	£182.	6.	6
				£191.	11.	6

Granted by the Overseers of the Poor

To Joseph Davis 20/ Mercy Rayner 10/	1. 10.
Hannah Tapper 20/ Sarah Willis 10/	1. 10.
Widow Ingolsby for Lynde	15.
Ann Hayden 15/ Nurse Kenny 20/	1. 15.
Mary Lax 10/ Dorothy Torry 20/	1. 10.
Lidia Torry 20/ Philip Marlow 15/	1. 15.
Joanna Spillier	10. 9. 5.
To Timothy Banon in full of his bill	16. 11.
Nathl. Holmes ditto	40. 2. 6
Charles Henly do.	26. 1.
Thos. Moulin & Co. do.	15. 15.
Andrew Oliver Esq do.	10. 10.
Thomas Hubbard Esq do.	90.
Henry Dyre in full of his accot.	98. 8. 4 297. 7. 10
	£306. 12. 10

Granted by the Overseers of the Poor

To Joseph Davis 20/ Mercy Reyner 10/	£1. 10.
Hannah Tapper 20/ Sarah Willis 10/	1. 10.
Widow Ingolsby for Lynde	15.
Anna Hayden 15/ Nurse Kenny 20/	1. 15.
Mary Lax 10/ Dorothy Torry 20/	1. 10.
Lydia Torry 20/ Philip Marlow 15/	1. 15.
Joanna Spillier 10/ Hañah Henderson 15/	1. 5. £10.
To Francis Warden ......in full of his bill	£31. 19.
To Colo. John Hill ......ditto	35. 15. 1
To Edwd. Bromfield ......ditto	150. 1. 4
To Henry Dyre .... ditto	109. 5. 327. 1. 3
	£337. 1. 3

The Overseers' Finances 1738-1769

❧

Boston Novemr: 4. 1741.

Granted by the Overseers of the Poor

To Joseph Davis 20/ Mercy Rayner 10/	1. 10.		
Hannah Tapper 20/ Sarah Willis 10/	1. 10.		
Widow Ingolsby for Lynde	15.		
Ann Hayden 15/ Nurse Kenny 20/	1. 15.		
Mary Lax 10/ Dorothy Torry 20/	1. 10.		
Lidia Torry 20/ Philip Marlow 15/	1. 15.		
Joanna Spillier	10.		
Hannah Henderson	15.	10.	
To Henry Dyre in full of his disburstmts.	122. 6. 5		
To William Clark . Qrs. Salary	12. 10.		
To Henry Dyre . Qrs. Salary	35.		
To Shanon	20.		
To Samuel Hunt	15. 10.		
To Daniel Henchman Esq	20. 8. 9	225. 15. 2	
		£235. 15. 2	

Boston 2d. December 1741

Granted by the Overseers of the Poor

To Joseph Davis 20/ Mercy Rayner 10/	1. 10.		
Hannah Tapper 20/ Sarah Willis 10/	1. 10.		
Widow Ingolsby for Lynde	15.		
Anna Hayden 15/ Nurse Kinney 20/	1. 15.		
Mary Lax 10/ Dorothy Torry 20/	1. 10.		
Lydia Torry 20/ Philip Marlow 15/	1. 15.		
Johanna Spillier 10/ Hannah Henderson 15/	1. 5.	10.	
To Capt William Downe in full of his Bill		89. 1. 3	
To Charles Hendly, in full of his Accompt		20.	
To Joseph Busch in full for 1 hhd. Molasses		24. 10. 4	
To Henry Dyre, in full of his disbursements		87. 4. 6	
		£230. 16. 1	

Boston 6. Janr. 1741

Granted by the Overseers of the Poor.

To Joseph Davis 20/ Mercy Reyner 10/	£1. 10.		
Hannah Tapper 20/ Sarah Willis 10/	1. 10.		
Widow Ingolsby for Lynde	15.		
Anna Hayden 15/ Nurse Kenny 20/	1. 15.		
Mary Lax 10/ Dorothy Torry 20/	1. 10.		
Lydia Torry 20/ Philip Marlow 15/	1. 15.		
Joanna Spillier 10/ Haῆah Henderson 15/	1. 5.	£10.	
To Colo. John Hill ....in full for his disbursments	£33. 9.		
To Henry Dyre...................ditto	170. 3. 2		
To Joseph Holbrook............ ditto	5. 17.	209. 9. 2	
		£219. 9. 2	

Boston 3d. Febr. 1741

Granted by the Overseers of the Poor.

To Joseph Davis 20/ Mercy Reyner 10/	£1. 10.		
Haῆah Tapper 20/ Sarah Willis 10/	1. 10.		
Widow Ingolsby for Lynde	15.		
Anna Hayden 15/ Nurse Kenny 20/	1. 15.		
Mary Lax 10/ Dorothy Torry 20/	1. 10.		
Lydia Torry 20/ Philip Marlow 15/	1. 15.		
Joanna Spillier 10/ Hana. Henderson 15/	1. 5.	10.	
To Jacob Wendell Esq.............in full of his disbursmts.	51. 6. 11		
ditto ....3 Boxes Glass	69.		
To Dan. Henchman Esq. in full of disbursmts.	57. 17. 10		
To ⁶ Kenton............... in pt. for slating	10.		
To Joseph Russell................... in pt. for repairing} the Almshouse	50.		
To Henry Dyre......................in full his disbursmts.	124. 11	362. 5. 8	
To Docr. Jno. Delhond..........for Medicines for one Glover		10.	
		£382. 5. 8	

☙

Boston Februa   1741.

Granted by the Overseers of the Poor

To Joseph Davis 20/ Mercy Rayner 10/	1. 10.	
Hannah Tapper 20/ Sarah Willis 10/	1. 10.	
Wido. Ingolsby for Lynde	15.	
Ann Hayden 15/ Nurse Kenny 20/	1. 15.	
Mary Lax 10/ Dorothy Torry 20/	1. 10.	
Lidia Torry 20/ Philip Marlo 15/	1. 15.	
Joannah Spilier	10.	
Hannah Henderson	15.	£10.
To Jeffry Bedgood in full of his Disburstmts.	12. 15.	
To Wm. Tyler Esq ditto	9. 9.	
To Danl. Henchman Esq ...Do.	9. 13.	
To Thos. Hubbard Esq .....Do.	172. 13. 4	
To Joshua Cheever Esq ....Do.	75. 10.	
To Samuel Hunt ....Do.	23. 10.	
To Isaac White ....Do.	11. 16.	
To And. Oliver ....Do.	19. 12.	
To Edw: Bromfield ....Do.	265. 18.	
To Tho: Moulin ....Do.	10. 18.	
To Fra: Warden ....Do.	15. 10. 10	
To Willm. Speakman ....Do.	10. 13. 6	
To Tho: Pain ....Do.	65. 7. 6	

To Wm. Clarke ....Do.	210. 17.		
a 1/4 years Salary	12. 10.	223. 7.	
To Jacob Wendell Esq		51. 1.	
To Henry Dire	133. 9. 3		
a Qrs: Salary	35.	168. 9. 3	1146. 4. 1
			£1156. 4. 1

The Overseers' Finances 1738-1769

Boston 7. Apr. 1742

Granted by the Overseers of the Poor

To Joseph Davis 20/ Mercy Reyner 10/	£1. 10.	
Hañah Tapper 20/ Sarah Willis 10/	1. 10.	
Widow Ingolsby for Lynde	15.	
Anna Hayden 15/ Nurse Kenny 20/	1. 15.	
Mary Lax 10/ Dorothy Torry 20/	1. 10.	
Lydia Torry 20/ Philip Marlow 15/	1. 15.	
Joanna Spillier 10/ Hañah Henderson 15/	1. 5.	£10.
To John Hill Esq ....in full his disbursments	£196. 4. 7	
To Joseph Shedd ....ditto for carting	35. 16. 6	
To Willm. Wheeler junr.......bill for brick & stone	5. 9. 6	
To James Fosdick ....ditto for 1 m⁷ Slates	4.	
To Danl. Greenleaf ....ditto for Medicines	2. 11.	
To Henry Dyre ....in full of his disbursmts.	131. 5.	
To Nathl. Barber ....30 bushls. beans	27.	402. 6. 7
		£412. 6. 7

Boston 5 May 1742.

Granted by the Overseers of the Poor.

To Joseph Davis 20/ Mercy Reyner 10/	£1. 10.	
Hannah Tapper 20/ Sarah Willis 10/	1. 10.	
Widow Ingolsby for Lynde	15.	
Anna Hayden 15/ Nurse Kenny 20/	1. 15.	
Mary Lax 10/ Dorothy Torry 20/	1. 10.	
Lydia Torry 20/ Philip Marlow 15/	1. 15.	
Joanna Spillier 10/ Haña. Henderson 15/	1. 5.	£10.
To Daniel Henchman Esq. in full of his dis- bursments for Corn &c	42. 14.	
To Jacob Hurd ....for 50 bushls. corn	35.	
To Docr. William Clark ....a Qrs. Salary	12. 10.	
To Henry Dyre ....in full his disbursmts.	106. 14. 4	196. 18. 4
		£206. 18. 4

692

The Overseers' Finances 1738-1769

~

Boston June 2d. 1742

Granted by the Overseers of the Poor

To Joseph Davis 20/ Mercy Rayner 10/	£1. 10.		
Hannah Tapper 20/ Sarah Willis 10/	1. 10.		
Wido. Ingolsby for Lynde	15.		
Hannah Hayden 15/ Nurse Kenny 20/	1. 15.		
Mary Lax 10/ Dorothy Torry 20/	1. 10.		
Lidia Torry 20/ Phillip Marlow 15/	1. 15.		
Joanna Spiller 10/ Hannh. Henderson 15/	1. 5.	£10.8	
To Andrew Oliver Esqr in ful for Timber &c for Alms Hs.	77. 2. 6		
To Edwd. Winter in full for Iron work at Alms House	32. 14. 6		
To Thos. Hubbard Esqr in ful of his Bills for the building } & Supplying the Poor	200. 3. 9		
To Mr. Edw: Bromfield ful for Provisions & wood &c	304. 18. 8		
To Messrs. Calder & Torrey in ful for Beer for the workmen	5. 5.		
To Robert Kenton in full Balla. of his accot.	26. 2.		
To the Brick layers in full of their accotts. for work & stuff at			
House Vizt.—Jacob Parker	470. 10.		
Joshua Blanchard	505. 10.		
William Fairfield	473.		
To Francis Warden in full for work & Stuff at A: House	87. 9. 6		
To Henry Dyre in full of his disbursments	146. 13. 7		
To Nathl. Barbour Short draft last time	3.		
To Joseph Russell in full of his accot:	345. 3		
Benja Russell in full of his accot.	141. 6. 4		
William Bower in full of his accot. <for Boards>	16.		
Hopestill Foster in full for Boards	96. 4. 3		
Willis & Fitch in full of their accot.	40. 12. 4		
Onesiphorus Tilestone in full of his accot.	222. 11. 6		
Thomas Gouge Painter in full of his accot.	79. 5. 4		
George Bickmore in full of his accot. for Carting	3. 3.	£3276. 12. 6	
		£3286. 12. 6	

Boston July 14th: 1742.

Granted by the Overseers of the Poor.

To Joseph Davis 20/ Mercy Rayner 10/	1. 10.	
Hannah Tapper 20/ Sarah Willis 10/	1. 10.	
Widow Ingolby for Lynde	15.	
Hannah Hayden 15/ Nurse Kenny 20/	1. 15.	
Mary Lax 10/ Dorothy Torry 20/	1. 10.	
Lidia Torry 20/ Philip Marlow 15/	1. 15.	
Joanna Spiller 10/ Hannah Henderson 15/	1. 5.	£10.
To Daniel Henchman in full of his acct. for Rye &c	45. 1.	
To Henry Dyre in full of his Acct. of Disbursmts.	193. 8. 11	
To Ditto for half years Sallary	70.	£308. 9. 11
		£318. 9. 11

Boston 4o. Augst: 1742

Granted by the Overseers of the Poor

To Jos: Davis 20/ Mercy Rayner 10/	1. 10.	
Wido. Ingolsby for Lynde	15.	
Hannah Hayden 15/ Nurse Kenny 20/	1. 15.	
Mary Lax 10/ Philip Marlow 15/	1. 5.	
Dorothy Torry 20/ Lidia Torry 20/	2.	
Joanna Spiller 10/ Hañah Henderson 15/	1. 5.	8. 10.
To. Danll: Henchman Esq in full of his Accot.	45. 1.	
To. Francs: Warden—in full of his Accot.	33. 12. 4	
To. Ellis Wilson—in full of his 9	5. 4.	
To Henry Dyre in full of his disbursmts.	82. 9. 5	
To Henry Atkins for carying Jane Dean & Anñ Nyles to Newfoundland	13.	179. 6. 9
		£187. 16. 9

The Overseers' Finances 1738-1769

❧

Granted by the Overseers of the Poor

To Joseph Davis 20/ Mercy Rayner 10/	£1. 10.	
Hannah Hayden 15/ Nurse Kenny 20/	1. 15.	
Mary Lax 10/ Phillip Marlow 15/	1. 5.	
Dorothy Torrey 20/ Lidia Torrey 20/	2.	
Joanna Spiller 10/ Hannah Herderson 15/	1. 5.	
Wido. Ingolsby for Lynde	15.	£8. 10.
To Mr. Edward Bromfield in ful of His Acctt. for wood	£102. 10.	
To Doctr. Edward Ellis in full of his *Province* Acct.	82. 18.	
To Doctr. Wm. Clark in full of his *Province* Act.	102. 5.	
To Mrs. Hannah Dyre Admx: to Her Husbd: H Dyres Est in full of Disbursments for the House	117. 12. 7	
To Mrs Hannah Dyre for the Support of the House	140.	
To Wilfrett Fisher in full of his Accot.	26. 17.	584. 12. 7
		593. 2. 7
To Wm. Cunningham in full of his Accot.		21. 2
		£614. 2. 9

Granted by the Overseers of the Poor

To Joseph Davis 20/ Mercy Rayner 10/	1. 10.	
Hannah Hayden 15/ Nurse Kenny 20/	1. 15.	
Mary Lax 10./ Philip Marlow 15/	1. 5.	
Dorothy Tory 20/ Lidia Tory 20/	2.	
Joanna Spiller 10/ Hannah Henderson 15/	1. 5.	
Wido. Ingolsby . for Lynde	15.	£8. 10.
To Thomas Hubbard Esqr. in full of his Accot	£80. 7. 3	
To Mr. Wm. Blair Townsend his acct. for 50 Bush: Wheat	45.	
To Thomas Moulin in full of his accot.	16. 3.	
To Mr. Edward Bromfield in part of his accot.	100.	
To Mr. Samuel Hunt in full of his accot.	12. 15.	
To Mrs. Hannah Dyre in full of her acct. of Expences	290. 15. 2	£545. 5
		£553. 10. 5

The Overseers' Finances 1738-1769

~

Granted by the Overseers of the Poor

To Joseph Davis 20/ Mercy Rayner 10/	£1. 10.	
Hannah Hayden 15/ Nurse Kenny 20/	1. 15.	
Mary Lax 10/ Phillip Marlow 20/	1. 10.	
Dorothy Torrey 20/ Lidia Torrey 20/	2.	
Johanna Spiller 10/ Hannah Henderson 15/	1. 5.	
Wido. Ingolsby for Lynde 15/	15.	£8. 15.
To Mr. Edward Bromfield in full of his Accot.	114. 14. 4	
To Danl. Henchman in full of his Accot.	8. 17.	
To Mr. Edward Jackson	78. 8. 8	
To Mrs. Hannah Dyre in full for Expences	110. 8	£312. 8
		320. 15. 8

Boston 1st. December. 1742

Granted by the Overseers of the Poor.

To Joseph Davis 20/ Mercy Rayner 10/	1. 10.	
Hannah Hayden 15/ Nurse Kenny 20/	1. 15.	
Mary Lax 10/ Philip Marlow 20/	1. 10.	
Dorothy Torrey 20/ Lydia Torrey 20/	2.	
Johanna Spiller 10/ Hannah Henderson 15/	1. 5.	
Wido. Ingolsby for Lynde	15.	8. 15.
To Thomas Ethdridge, in full of his Accompt	22. 17.	
To John Hill .... ditto	237. 10. 10	
To Hannah Dyre, in full of her disbursements	181. 15. 7	442. 3. 5
		£450. 18. 5

Boston 5th. January. 1742

Granted by the Overseers of the Poor, Vizt.

To Joseph Davis 20/ Mercy Reynor 10/	1. 10.
Hannah Hayden 15/ Nurse Kenny 20/	1. 15.
Mary Lax 10/ Philip Marlow 20/	1. 10.
Dorothy Torrey 20/ Lydia Torrey 20/	2.
Joanna Spiller 10/ Hannah Henderson 15/	1. 5.

Widow Ingolsby for Lynde	15.	8. 15.	
To Hannah Dyre, in full of her disbursements	230. 7. 7		
Jones & Griffen in full of their Bill	20.		
William Tyler Esqr. for 50 bushs. Wheat	49. 10.		
Joshua Cheever Esqr. for 50 .... ditto	49. 10.		
Edward Winter, in full of his Accompt	9. 12. 9	359. 4	
		£367. 15. 4	

Boston Febry. 2d. 1742.

Granted by the Overseers of the Poor

To Joseph Davis 20/ Mercy Reyner 10/	1. 10.	
Hannah Haden 15/ Nurse Kenny 20/	1. 15.	
Mary Lax 10/ Philip Marlow 20/	1. 10.	
Dorothy Torry 20/ Lidia Torry 20/	2.	
Joanna Spiller 10/ Hannah Henderson 15/	1. 5.	
Widow Ingolby for Lynde	15.	8. 15.
To Hannah Dyre in full of her disbursments		119. 6.
		£128. 1.

Boston March 2. 1742.

Granted by the Overseers of the Poor

To Joseph Davis 20/ Mercy Reyner 10/	1. 10.	
Hannah Haden 15/ Nurse Kenny 20/	1. 15.	
Mary Lax 10/ Philip Marlow 20/	1. 10.	
Dorothy Torry 20/ Lidia Torry 20/	2.	
Joanna Spiller 10/ Hannah Henderson 15/	1. 5.	
Widow Ingolby for Lynde	15.	8. 15.
To Hannah Dyre in full of her disbursements	193. 5. 8	
Edward Bromfield in full of his Acctt.	241. 15. 2	
Daniel Henchman Esqr.............ditto	22. 5.	
William Tyler........ Esqr.............ditto	40. 8.	
William Downe.... Esqr.............ditto	88. 3. 10	
Andrew Oliver ..... Esqr.............ditto	19. 5. 9	

Joshua Cheever..... Esqr............ditto		81. 14. 6			
Thomas Hubbard .... ditto		90. 9. 6			
John Hill Esqr......................... ditto		96. 17. 8			
Jacob Wendell Esqr.................. ditto		71. 10. 1			
John Phillips .... ditto		146. 11. 8			
Samuel Hunt .... ditto		27. 11. 6			
Isaac White .... ditto		1. 8.			
John Kneeland....................... ditto		49. 19.			
Samuel & Robert Campbell .... ditto		24. 13. 6			
Francis Warden .... ditto		51. 18. 3			
Thos. Moulen......................... ditto		4. 15.			
Samuel Duncan .... ditto		5. 2.			
Charles Hendley .... ditto		29. 4.		1286. 18. 1	
				£1295. 13. 1	

Brought over			£1295. 13. 1	
To Bryant Parrott in full of his Acctt.		29. 16.		
Doctr. William Clarke in full of his Acctt.	189. 15. 6			
for half years Salary	25.	214. 15. 6		
To Mrs. Hannah Dyre, Administx. to Mr. Henry Dyre decd. 1/2 Mo. Salary from 10th. July to 23d. Augt. last, when he dyed		16. 15. 6		
Her half years Salary ending 23d. Feby. past	60.	76. 15. 6		
To Thomas Hubbard Esqr. allowed him for his Advance of sundry large Summ's for the use of the poor of the Town, during 18 last months past, there being now more than One Thousand pounds remaining due to him on that account		50.	371. 7.	
			£1667. 1	

Boston April 6th. 1743

Granted by the Overseers of the Poor

To Joseph Davis 20/ Mercy Rayner 10/	£1. 10.	
Hannah Hayden 15/ Nurse Kenny 20/	1. 15.	
Mary Lax 10/ Phillip Marlow 20/	1. 10.	
Dorothy Torrey 20/ Lydia Torrey 20/	2.	
Johanna Spiller 10/ Hanh: Henderson 15/	1. 5.	
Wido. Ingolsby for Lynde 15/	15.	£8. 15.
To Hannah Dyre in full of her Disbursments	139. 9. 6	
To Colo. Wm. Downe for 20 Cord wood	50.	£189. 9. 6
		£198. 4. 6

Boston 11o. May 1743

Granted by the Overseers of the Poor

To Joseph Davis 20/ Mercy Rayner 10/	1. 10.	
Hanãh Hayden 15/ Nurse Kenny 20/	1. 15.	
Mary Lax 10/ Phillip Marlow 20/	1. 10.	
Dorothy Torrey 20/ Lidia Torrey 20/	2.	
Johaña Spiller 10/ Hañ: Henderson 15/	1. 5.	
Wido. Ingolsby for Lynde 15/	15.	8. 15.
To Willis & Fitch in full of their Accot.	45. 11. 4	
Danll: Henchman Esq in full of his accot.	40.	
Hañ: Dyre in full of her disbursments	234. 10. 7	
Jere: Bumstead for 1/2 Years Sallery		
due 21o. April	17. 10.	
Docr. Willm. Clark . a Quarters salary	12. 10.	350. 1. 11
		358. 16. 11

Boston 1st. June 1743

Granted by the Overseer's of the Poor

To Joseph Davis 20/ Mercy Reyner 10/	1. 10.	
Hannah Hayden 20/ Nurse Kenny 20/	2.	
Mary Lax 10/ Philip Marlow 20/	1. 10.	
Dorothy Torrey 20/ Lydia Torrey 20/	2.	

Johanna Spiller 10/ Hannah Henderson 15/	1. 5.	
Widow Ingolsby for Lynde	15.	9.
To Doctr. William Clarke in full of his accot.	100. 12. 6	
of medicines out of Hs.		
To Thomas Hubbard, in full of his Acctt.	79. 15. 6	
To Hannah Dyre in full of her monthly disburesments	149. 2. 8	329. 10. 8
		£338. 10. 8

Boston 29th. June 1743

Granted by the Overseers of the Poor

To Joseph Davis 20/ Mercy Reynor 10/	1. 10.	
Hannah Hayden 20/ Nurse Kenny 20/	2.	
Mary Lax 10/ Philip Marlow 20/	1. 10.	
Dorothy Torrey 20/ Lydia Torrey 20/	2.	
Johanna Spiller 10/ Hannah Henderson 15/	1. 5.	
Wido. Ingolsby for Lynde	15.	9.
To Hannah Dyre, in full of her monthly disbursements	162. 15. 7	
To John Hill Esqr. his Accot.	239. 10. 6	
To William Downe Esqr. his Accot.	55.	457. 6. 1
		£466. 6. 1

Boston 3d. August 1743.

Granted by the Overseers of the Poor.

To Joseph Davis 20/ Mercy Reyner 10/	£1. 10.	
Hañah Hayden 20/ Nurse Kenny 20/	2.	
Mary Lax 10/ Phillip Marlow 20/	1. 10.	
Dorothy Torry 20/ Lydia Torry 20/	2.	
Joanna Spillier 10/ Hanna. Henderson 15/	1. 5.	
Wido. Ingolsby for Lynde	15.	9.
To Edward Bromfield.................... in pt. of his accot.	£200.	
To John Phillips ....in full of ditto	65. 10.	
To Andrew Oliver ....in full of ditto	52. 15.	
To Hannah Dyer ....in full of ditto	187. 4.	
To Docr. John Loring ....in full of ditto	93. 2.	598. 11.
		607. 11.

The Overseers' Finances 1738-1769

~

Granted by the Overseers of the Poor

To Joseph Davis 20/ Mercy Reyner 10/	£1. 10.				
Haña. Hayden 20/ Nurse Kenny 20/	2.				
Mary Lax 10/ Philip Marlow 20/	1. 10.				
Dorothy Torry 20/ Lydia Torry 20/	2.				
Joanna Spillier 10/ Haña. Henderson 15/	1. 5.				
Wido. Ingolsby for Lynde	15.	9.			
To Docr. John Loring.....a Quarter's salary to 11th. Augt.		12. 10.			
To Mrs. Hañah Dyre.........half a years salary} to 23d. Augt.	57. 10.				
to make up the last half years salary} as ℘ agreement	5.				
in full of her disbursments	176. 11. 1	239. 1. 1			
To Charles Henley...... in full of his accot. for Shoes		31. 19.			
To Saml. Hunt .... in full of his disbursments		10. 12.			
		£303. 2. 1			

Granted by the Overseers of the Poor.

To Joseph Davis 20/ Mercy Reyner 10/	£1. 10.				
Hañah Hayden 20/ Nurse Kenny 20/	2.				
Mary Lax 10/ Philip Marlow 20/	1. 10.				
Dorothy Torry 20/ Lydia Torry 20/	2.				
Joanna Spillier 10/ Haña. Henderson 15/	1. 5.				
Widow Ingolsby for Lynde	15.	9.			
To Mrs. Hannah Dyre. in full of her disbursments		183. 6. 9			
		£192 6 9			

Boston Novr. 2d. 1743

Granted by the Overseers of the Poor

To Joseph Davis 20/ Mercy Reyner 10/	£1. 10.	
Hannah Hayden 20/ Nurse Kenny 20/	2.	
Mary Lax 10/ Phillip Marlow 20/	1. 10.	
Dorothy Torry 20/ Lidia Torry 20/	2.	
Joanna Spillier 10/ Han: Henderson 15/	1. 5.	
Wido. Ingolsby for Lynde	15.	£9.
To Mrs. Hannah Dyre in ful of her disbursmts.	£136. 4. 11	
To Jer Bumsteed for 1/2 year Sallary	17. 10.	
To John Hill in full of his accot.	41. 13. 6	
To Edward Bromfield in full of his accot.	34. 3. 8	
To Isaac Walker in full of his accot.	28. 19. 6	
To Daniel Henchman in ful for Wheat	80.	
To Francis Warden in full of his accot.	32. 2. 9	
To Thomas Moulin in full of his accot.	15. 3.	
To Doctr. John Loring in full . including his Sallary	89. 1. 6	£474. 18. 10
		£483. 18. 10

Boston Decr. 7th. 1743

Granted by the Overseers of the Poor

To Joseph Davis 20/ Mercy Rayner 10/	£1. 10.	
Hannah Hayden 20/ Nurse Kenny 20/	2.	
Mary Lax 10/ Phillip Marlow 20/	1. 10.	
Dorothy Torrey 20/ Lidia Torrey 20/	2.	
Johann Spiller 10/ Hannah Henderson 15/	1. 5.	
Thompson	1.	9. 5.
To Mrs. Hannah Dyre in full of Her Disbursmts.	£220. 19. 11	
To Mr. George Rogers in ful of his Accot.	60. 18. 1	
To Mr. John Phillips in full of his Accot.	54. 1. 9	
To Thos. Hubbard Esqr. in ful of his accot.	56. 17. 3	392. 17.
		402. 2.

The Overseers' Finances 1738-1769

Granted by the Overseers of the Poor

To Joseph Davis 20/ Mercy Rayner 10/	£1. 10.	
Hannah Hayden 20/ Nurse Kenny 20/	2.	
Mary Lax 10/ Phillip Marlow 20/	1. 10.	
Dorothy Torrey 20/ Lydia Torrey 20/	2.	
Johann Spiller 10/ Hannah Henderson 15/	1. 5.	
Thompson 20/	1.	9. 5.
To Mrs. Hannah Dyre in pt. of Her Disburstmts.	160.	
To Ditto ....in full of her accot.	130. 15. 11	
To Charles Henly.................in full of his accot.	14. 4. 6	
To John and Jona. Simpson..... in full of their accot.	126.	431. 5
		£440. 5. 5

Granted by the Overseers of the Poor,

To Joseph Davis 20/ Mercy Rayner 10/	1. 10.	
Hannah Hayden 20/ Nurse Kenny 20/	2.	
Mary Lax 10/ Philip Marlow 20/	1. 10.	
Dorothy Torry 20/ Lidia Torry 20/	2.	
Johanna Spiller 10/ Hannah Henderson 15/	1. 5.	
Thompson	1.	9. 5.
To Hannah Dyre in full of her Disburstmts.	97.	
To Doctr. John Loring for a Qrs. Sallery 12. 10.		
To Ditto...in full of his Bill 88. 14. 6	£101. 4. 6	198. 4. 6
		£207. 9. 6

Granted by the Overseers of the Poor

To Joseph Davis 20/ Mercy Rayner 10/	£1. 10.
Hannah Hayden 20/ Nurse Kenny 20/	2.
Mary Lax 10/ Phillip Marlow 20/	1. 10.
Dorothy Torry 20/ Lydia Torry 20/	2.

Johann Spiller 10/ Hannah Henderson 15/	1.	5.				
Thompson 20/	1.			9.	5.	
To Hannah Dyre in full of her Disburstments						
143. 7. 5 deduct for picking oacum 17£	126.	7.	5			
To Jacob Wendell Esqr.........in full of his Accot.	63.	7.	6			
To John Hill Esqr...............in part	30.					
To Ditto ....in full of his Accot.	51.	10.	4			
To William Tyler Esqr. in full his Accot.	62.	16.				
To William Downe Esqr. in full his Accot.	49.	17.	5			
To Thomas Hubbard Esqr. in full of his Accot.	170.	19.	5			
To Edward Bromfield in full of his Accot.	57.	7.				
To Daniel Henchman Esqr. in full of his Accot.	13.	19.				
To Andrew Oliver Esq ...... in full of his Accot.	98.	5.				
To John Phillips .... in full of his Accot.	11.	9.				
To Samuel Hunt .... in full of his Accot.	18.					
To Isaac Walker .... in full of his Accot.	35.	3.	1			
To Geo: Rogers .... in full of his Accot.	7.	8.	6			
To Sarah Smith .... in full of her Accot. Wood	140.	7.	6			
To Francis Warden .... in full of his Accot.	23.	14.				
To Hannah Dyre for Half Years salery Endg. 23d. Inst.	70.					
To Doct. John Loring for Extraordinary Expence of						
medicine &c. in the Year Past	20.			1050.	11.	2
				£1059.	16.	2

Boston April 4th. 1744

Granted by the Overseers of the Poor

To Joseph Davis 20/ Mercy Rayner 20/	£2.				
Hannah Hayden 20/ Phillip Marlo 20/	2.				
Nurse Kenny 20/ Mary Lax 10/	1.	10.			
Dorothy Torry 20/ Lydia Torry 20/	2.				
Johanna Spiller 10/ Hannah Henderson 15/	1.	5.			
Thomson	1.			£9.	15.
To Hannah Dyre in full of Her Disbursments				218.	4.	1
				[£227.	19.	1]

Boston May 2d. 1744

Granted by the Overseers of the Poor,

To Joseph Davis 20/ Mercy Rayner 20/	2.
Hannah Hayden 20/ Philip Marlo 20/	2.
Nurse Kenny 20/ Mary Lax 10/	1. 10.
Dorothy Torry 20/ Lidia Torry 20/	2.
Johanna Spiller 10/ Hannah Henderson 15/	1. 5.
Thomson dead	0. £8. 15.
To Messrs. Willis & Fitch in ful of their accot.	8. 3. 5
To James Cunningham Glazier in ful of his Act.	4. 4.
To Eliza. Loring Admx. to Estate of Doctr. Jno. Loring⎫	
in full of her Accot. ⎭	76. 7. 5
To Ditto in full on the Province Accot.	1.
To Doctr. Wm. Clarke in full of his Accot.	50. 17. 6 £140. 12. 4
To Hannah Dyre in full of Her disbursments	114.
	£263. 7. 4

Boston June 6th. 1744

Granted by the Overseers of the Poor

To Joseph Davis 20/ Mercy Rayner 20/	2.
Anna Hayden 20/ Phillip Marlow 20/	2.
Nurse Kenny 20/ Mary Lax 10/	1. 10.
Dorothy Torry 20/ Lidia Torry 20/	2.
Joanna Spiller 10/ Hannah Henderson 15/	1. 5. 8. 15.
To Hannah Dyre......... in part of her Disburstments	100.
To Ditto .... in full of Ditto	144. 1.
To John Hill Esqr. .... in full of his Accot.	126. 15. 6
To Charles Henly........ in full of his Accot.	12. 9. 383. 5. 6
	£392. 6

At a Meeting of the Overseers of the Poor of the Town of Boston 4th. Decr. 1745 [10]

Present   William Tyler Esqr.

              John Hill Esqr.

                                    Thos. Hubbard

              Daniel Henchman Esqr.

              Mr. Edward Bromfield

              William Downe Esqr.

              Andrew Oliver Esqr.

              Capt John Phillips

              Mr. Isaac Walker

              George Rogers Esqr.

              Ebenez Storer

The aforesaid Overseers takeing into consideration the great Numbers they have of late been obliged to send into the Almshouse for relief, as also the grievous Visitation by sickness, whereby great Care & Labour has been devolved on the Mistress of said House, Voted

That the sum of Thirty pounds (Old Tenor) be allowed & paid to Mrs. Hannah Dyre (the parsenl Mistress of sd. House) for her [late?] Extraordinary services, & that a draft be made therefor accordingly

Also, Voted,

That Fourty pounds (Old Tenor) be added to her Annual Salary to commence from this Time, so as to make up the Sum of one hundred & Eighty pounds, ℘ Annum.

1746 May 7.   Docr. Hugh Kennedy was unanimously chosen Physician for the Almshouse & for the Poor of the Town. Who refusd ser[vice][11]

20th.   Doctr. Wm. Rand was unanimously chosen Physician for the almshouse & for the Poor of the Town. On the following Terms

Five shillings Old Tenor ℘ day for visiting the Poor of the Alms house & Work house.

Five shillings for the first visit of the Poor out of the House 2/6 fo[r] after visits.

Medicine to be chargd at the Apothecarys price

for amputations & Salivations Ten pounds Old Tenor

1749. July 8   Doctr. Gillam Tayler was unanimously chosen Physician for the alm[sh]ouse & for the Poor of the Town on the Same Terms as Docr. Wm. Rand above mentioned which was read to him to wch. he agreed.

1747/8

March 3.   Supplyd Widow Bule on The Province and ℘ Tho. Hubbard Esqr.

              1/2 Cord Wood 65/   money 20/   4.   5.

May 4.   Agreed to allow Francis Wardan 50/ for Coffins for Grown ℘rsons: Children in Proportion

Gentlemen,   Boston 7th. Sept. 1748

      Whereas I have had the Care of a poor Child, named Joseph Rooker who hath been with me severall years, but am apprehensive it will be for the Advantage of sd. Child to be put out apprentice to some proper Calling, I am desirous of resigning him & accordingly now do the Same to you desireing the favour of you to take the like care of him, as of other poor Children belonging to the Town & to bind him out to some Trade as to you shall seem best.

                                             Roger Hardcastle

To the Gentlemen, Overseers
of the Poor of Boston

1748 Novr. 2.   Memo. agreed with mr. Simon Eliot Sawyer to Allow 20/ ℘ week O.T. to pay for the Nursing of a Poor Child named Hannah Hide being now about 14 months—until further orders.

1752 May 6.   Agreed to allow Mr. Bands & assistants 1/4 Each Lawful money for burying the Dead during the Small Pox & fevers raging

1753
May 15.   Voted to chose a Doctr. for the Alms House on the first Wednesday in May annually.

                At a Meeting of Eleven Overseers Voted for a Doctr. on Sorting the same it appeared that Doctr. Joseph Adams was chose Physition & Chirurgeon for the Year Ensuing

1753
Novr. 7.   At a Meeting of the Overseers Voted that 3/4 ℘ Week Lawful Money be allowed for the support of Hannah Goffe a ℘rson disorder'd in mind the same to be paid to   Simms of Wobourn so long as She keeps wth. him or untill further Orders.

1754
May 1.   At a Meeting of the Overseers it was agreed to come upon the choice of a Doctor; and the Votes being collected it appeared that Docr. Joseph Adams was unanimously chosen.

1755
5 May   at a meeting of the Overseers Docter Adams was Again Chosen Docter for the present year

1756

May 5   At a Meeting of the Overseers it was Agreed To Come Upon the Choice of a Doctor, and the Votes Being Collected it appeared that Doctor James Pecker was Chosen

Boston July 3 1744

Granted by the Overseers of the Poor

To Joseph Davis 20/ Mercy Rayner 20/	2.		
Hannah Hayden 20/ Phillip Marlo 20/	2.		
Nurse Kenny 20/ Mary Lax 10/	1. 10.		
Dorothy Torrey 20/ Lydia Torry 20/	2.		
Johanna Spiller 10/ Hannah Henderson 15/	1. 5.	8. 15.	
To Hannah Dyre in full of her Accot.	140. 8. 7		
To Thomas Hubbard Esqr. in part	70.		
To Ditto ....in full of his Accot.	91. 7. 6		
To Ebenr. Storer in part of his Accot.	118. 14. 8		
To John Phillips in full of his Accot.	55.		
To Thomas Moulin ....in full of his Accot.	7. 12.		
To Francis Warden in full	20. 2	503. 2. 11	
		£511. 17. 11	

Boston August 1st. 1744.

Granted by the Overseers of the Poor

To Joseph Davis 20/ Mercy Rayner 20/	2.		
Hannah Hayden 20/ Phillip Marlo 20/	2.		
Nurse Kenny 20/ Mary Lax 10/	1. 10.		
Dorothy Torry 20/ Lydia Torry 20/	2.		
Johanna Spiller 10/ Hannah Henderson 15/	1. 5.	8. 15.	
To Hannah Dyre....... in part of her Acct. Disburstmts.	120.		
To Ditto ....in full of Ditto	151. 9. 6		
To Willm. Downe Esqr.....in full of his Accot.	66. 14.		
To Andrew Oliver Esqr. in full of his Accot.	32.		
To John Ruddock in full of his Accot. for wood	32. 11.		
To Edward Bromfield in part of his Accot.	120.		
To Daniel Henchman Esqr. in full of his Accot.	93. 17. 2	616. 11. 8	
		£625. 6. 8	

Boston 6 Sepr. 1744

Granted by the Overseers of the Poor

To Jos. Davis 20/ Mercy Rayner 20/	2.	
Anna Hayden 20/ Phillip Marlow 20/	2.	
Nurse Kenny 20/ Mary Lax 10/	1. 10.	
Dorrothy Torry 20/ Lidia Torry 20/	2.	
Johanna Spiller 10/ Hannah Henderson 15/	1. 5.	8. 15.
To Hannah Dyre in full of her Disburstments	170. 3. 5	
To Ditto .... half Years Sallery Ending 23d. Augt.	70.	
To Edward Bromfield in full of his Accot.	84. 1.	
To Thomas Hubbard in full of his Accot. Error		
To Edward Winter in full of his Accot.	10. 17. 6	
To Thomas Hubbard in part of his Accot.	40.	
To Ditto ....in part	40.	
To Ditto ....in full of his Accot.	48. 5. 6	463. 7. 5
		£472. 2. 5

Boston 3d. October 1744.

Granted by the Overseers of the Poor

To Joseph Davis 20/ Mercy Rayner 20/	2.	
Anna Hayden 20/ Phillip Marlow 20/	2.	
Nurse Kenny 00/[12] Mary Lax 10/	10.	
Dorothy Torry 20/ Lydia Torry 20/	2.	
Johonna Spiller 10/ Hannah Henderson 15/	1. 5.	7. 15.
To Hannah Dyre in full of her Disburstmts.	144. 5. 3	
To John Hill Esqr. in full of his Accot.	41.	
To Isaac Walker in full of his Accot.	125. 4. 7	
To Silvester Gardner in full of his Accot.	7. 7. 9	
To Charles Henly.............in full of his Accot.	19. 2. 6	
To Thomas Ethridge in full of his Accot.	14. 9.	
To Thoms. Moulin...........in full of his Accot.	11. 6.	362. 15. 1
		£370. 10. 1

~

Boston 7th. Novr. 1744

Granted by the Overseers of the Poor

To Joseph Davis 20/ Mercy Reyner 20/	2.	
Anna Hayden 20/ Philip Marlow 20/	2.	
Dorothy Torrey 20/ Lydia Torrey 20/	2.	
Mary Lax 10/ Hannah Henderson 15/	1. 5.	
Joanna Spiller	10.	7. 15.
To Hannah Dyre in full of her disbursements	218. 2. 6	
Ebenezer Storer in full of his Accompt	94. 13. 10	312. 16. 4
		£320. 11. 4

Boston 5th. December 1744

Granted by the Overseers of the Poor

To Joseph Davis 20/ Mercy Rayner 20/	2.	
Anna Hayden 20/ Phillip Marrow 20/	2.	
Dorothy Torrey 20/ Lydia Torrey 20/	2.	
Mary Lax 10/ Hannah Henderson 15/	1. 5.	
Joanna Spiller 10/	10.	7. 15.
To Hannah Dyre in full of her Disburstments	144. 10. 2	
To John Savel in full of his Accot.	12.	156. 10. 2
		£164. 5. 2

Boston 2d. Janry. 1744

Granted by the Overseers of the Poor

To Joseph Davis 20/ Mercy Rayner 20/	£2.	
Anna Hayden 20/ Phillip Marlow 20/	2.	
Dorothy Torrey 20/ Lydia Torrey 20/	2.	
Mary Lax 10/ Hannah Henderson 15/	1. 5.	
Joanna Spiller 10/	10.	7. 15.
To Hannah Dyre in full of her Disburstmt.	115. 8. 5	
To Edward Bromfield in full of his Accot.	34. 5. 6	149. 13. 11
		£157. 8. 11

The Overseers' Finances 1738-1769

Boston 6th. Feby. 1744.

Granted by the Overseers of the Poor

To Jos. Davis 20/ Mercy Rayner 20/	2.	
Anna Hayden 20/ Phillip Marlow 20/	2.	
Dorothy Torrey 20/ Lydia Torrey 20/	2.	
Mary Lax 10/ Hannah Henderson 15/	1. 5.	
Joanna Spiller 10/	10.	7. 15.
To Hannah Dyre in full of her Disburstments		146. 11
		153. 15. 11

Boston 6th. March 1744

Granted by the Overseers of the Poor

To Jos. Davis 20/ Mercy Rayner 20/	2.	
Anna Hayden 20/ Phillip Marlow 20/	2.	
Dorothy Torrey 20/ Lydia Torrey 20/	2.	
Mary Lax 10/ Hannah Henderson 15/	1. 5.	
Joanna Spiller 10/	10.	7. 15.
To Hannah Dyre in full of her Disburstmts.	227. 12. 7	
To Ditto half years Sallery Ending 23d. Feby.	70.	
To William Tyler Esqr .... in full of his Accot.	37. 4. 8	
To John Hill Esqr. .... in full of his Accot.	63. 8. 6	
To Thoms. Hubbard Esqr. in full of his Accot.	17. 1. 3	
To Edward Bromfield <Jr> Esq full of his Accot.	49. 12.	
To John Phillips in full of his Accot.	44. 4.	
To Isaac Walker in full of his Accot.	69. 14. 6	
To Geo: Rogers Esqr. in full of his Accot.	46. 2. 2	
To Ebenr. Storer in full of his Accot.	95. 10.	
To Thomas Moulin & Compa. in full of his Accot.	5. 7.	
To Francis Warden .... in full of his Accot.	30. 13. 2	
To Charles Henly.................... in full of his Accot.	13. 4. 6	
To Daniel Henchman Esqr. in full of his Accot.	44. 5. 6	
To John Savel in full of his Accot.	6.	
To John Ruddock in full of his Accot.	19. 10.	839. 9. 10
		847. 4. 10
To Jacob Wendell Esqr..........in full of his Accot.	109. 17.	
To Wm. Downe Esqr............in full of his Accot.	11. 9.	121. 6.
		£968. 10. 10

Boston 3d. April 1745

Granted by the Overseers of the Poor

To Joseph Davis 20/ Mercy Rayner 20/	2.	
Anna Hayden 20/ Phillip Marlow 20/	2.	
Dorothy Torrey 20/ Lydia Torrey 20/	2.	
Mary Lax 10/ Hannah Henderson 15/	1. 5.	
Joanna Spiller 10/	10.	7. 15.
To Hannah Dyre in full of her Disburstments		149. 13. 3
		£157. 8. 3

Boston 1st. May 1745

Granted by the Overseers of the Poor

To Joseph Davis 20/ Mercy Rayner 20/	2.	
Anna Hayden 20/ Phillip Marlow 20/	2.	
Dorothy Torrey 20/ Lydia Torrey 20/	2.	
Mary Lax 10/ Hannah Henderson 15/	1. 5.	
Joanna Spiller 10/	10.	7. 15.
To Hannah Dyre in full of her Accot. Disburstmts.	367. 2. 3	
To William Salter in full for Wood ℗ Accot.	51. 12.	
To Edward Ellis in part	150.	568. 14. 3
		576. 9. 3

Boston 5th. June 1745

Granted by the Overseers of the Poor

To Joseph Davis 20/ Mercy Rayner 20/	2.	
Anna Hayden 20/ Phillip Marlow 20/	2.	
Dorothy Torrey 20/ Lydia Torrey 20/	2.	
Mary Lax 10/ Hannah Henderson 15/	1. 5.	
Joanna Spiller 10/	10.	7. 15.
To Hannah Dyre in part of her Disburstments	150.	
To Ditto .... in full of her Disburstments	169. 18. 8	
To Ebenr. Storer in full of his Accot.	118. 16. 6	
To Green & Walker in full	88. 9.	
To Thoms. Hubbard Esqr. in full	152. 9	679. 4. 11
Carrd. Over		686. 19. 11

The Overseers' Finances 1738-1769

Boston June 5th. 1745

Granted by the Overseers of the Poor

Sum brot. over	£686. 19. 11
To John Hill Esqr. in full of his Accot.	82. 7. 6
	£769. 7. 5

Boston 2d. July 1745

Granted by the Overseers of the Poor

To Joseph Davis 20/ Mercy Rayner 20/	2.	
Anna Hayden 20/ Phillip Marlow 20/	2.	
Dorothy Torrey 20/ Lydia Torrey 20/	2.	
Mary Lax 10/ Hannah Henderson 15/	1. 5.	
Joanna Spiller 10/	10.	7. 15.
To William Downe Esqr......... in full of his Accot.	80.	
To Edward Bromfield............ in full of his Accot.	90. 8.	
To John Phillips in full of his Accot.	72.	
To Hannah Dyre in part of her Disburstmts.	160.	
To Ditto .... in full of Ditto	160. 4. 8	562. 12. 8
		£570. 7. 8

Boston Augst. 7th. 1745

Granted by the Overseers of the Poor

To Joseph Davis 20/ To Mercey Rayner 20/		2.	
Anna Hayden 20/ Philip Marrow 20/		2.	
Dorothy Torey 20/ Lydia Torey 20/		2.	
Mary Lax 10/ Hannah Henderson 15/		1. 5.	
Joana Spiller		10.	7. 15.
To Hannah Dyer in full of	her Act.	300. 6. 11	
Thos: Hubbard Esqr.	Ditto	71. 12.	
Andr. Oliver Esqr.	Do.	144. 18.	
Charles Henley	Do. for Shoos	38. 6. 6	
Francis Warden	Do. his Act.	58. 10. 3	613. 13. 8
			621. 8. 8

The Overseers' Finances 1738-1769

Boston 4th. Septemr. 1745.

Granted by the Overseers of the Poor

To Joseph Davis 20/ Mercy Rayner 20/	£2.	
Anna Hayden 20/ Phillip Marlow 20/	2.	
Dorothy Torrey 20/ Lydia Torrey 20/	2.	
Mary Lax 10/ Hannah Henderson 15/	1. 5.	
Joanna Spiller	10.	7. 15.
To Hannah Dyre in part of her accot.	144. 10. 3	
To Hannah Dyer in full of her Disburst.	71. 6. 1	
To Ditto halfe years Sallary	70.	
To Thomas Moulin in full of his accot.	7. 19.	
To John Hill Esqr. in part	15.	
To ditto in full of his accot.	30. 12. 10	
To Eleazar Darby in full of his accot.	62.	401. 8. 2
for 20 Cord Wood		409. 3. 2

Boston 2d. October 1745

Granted by the Overseers of the Poor

To Joseph Davis 20/ Mercy Rayner 20/	2.	
Anna Hayden 20/ Phillip Marlow 20/	2.	
Dorothy Torrey 20/ Lydia Torrey 20/	2.	
Mary Lax <10/> 00/ Hannah Henderson 15/	15.	
Joanna Spiller 10/	10.	7. 5.
To Hannah Dyre in part of her acct.	100.	
To Ditto .... in full of her disburstmts.	143. 8. 2	243. 8. 2
		£250. 13. 2

Boston 6th. November 1745

Granted by the Overseers of the Poor

To Jos. Davis 20/ Mercy Rayner 20/ Anna Hayden 20/	£3.	
Phillip Marlow 20/ Dorothy Torrey 20/ Lyda. Torrey 20/	3.	
Hannah Henderson 15/ Joanna Spiller 10/	1. 5.	7. 5.
To Hannah Dyre in part £100. To Do. in full		
of her Disburstmts.	115. 17. 82	215. 17. 8
To Andrew Oliver Esqr. in full of his Accot.		30. 3. 6

714

To John Savel for Benja. Phillips Board	12.	
To Charles Henly in full of his Accot.	18. 2. 6	
To Nath. Band in full of his Accot.	6. 14.	
	290. 7. 8	

Boston 4th. Decemr. 1745

Granted by the Overseers of the Poor

To Joseph Davis 20/ Mercy Rayner 20/	2.	
Phillip Marlow 20/ Dorothy Torrey 20/	2.	
Lydia Torrey 20/ Hannah Henderson 15/	1. 15.	
Joanna Spiller 10/	10.	6. 5.
To Hannah Dyre for her Extraordy. Service the Year past		30.
To Hannah Dyre in full of her Disburstmts.	145. 14. 5	
To Daniel Henchman Esqr: in full of his Accot.	33. 11.	179. 5. 5
		£215. 10. 5

Boston 1 Jany. 1745/6

Granted by the Overseers of the Poor

To Jos. Davis 20/ Mercy Rayner 20/	2.	
Phillip Marlow 20/ Dorothy Torrey 20/	2.	
Lydia Torrey 20/ Hanh. Henderson 15/	1. 15.	
Joanna Spiller 10/	10.	6. 5.
To Hannah Dyre in full of her Disburstmts.	96. 11.	
To John Savel.........in full of his Accot.	12. 10.	109. 1.
		£115. 6.

Boston 5th. February 1745/6

Granted by the Overseers of the Poor

To Joseph Davis 20/ Mercy Rayner 20/	2.	
Phillip Marlow 20/ Dorothy Torrey 20/	2.	
Lydia Torrey 20/ Hannah Henderson 15/	1. 15.	
Joanna Spiller 10/	10.	6. 5.
To Hannah Dyre in full of her Disburstmts.	112. 8. 7	
To Edward Winter in full of his Accots.	10. 11. 3	122. 19. 10
		£129. 4. 10

The Overseers' Finances 1738-1769

Boston 26 Feby. 1745/6

Granted by the Overseers of the Poor

To Jos Davis 20/ Mercy Rayner 20/		£2.	
Phillip Marlow 20/ Doroy. Torrey 20/		2.	
Lydia Torrey 20/ Hannah Henderson 15/		1. 15.	
Joanna Spiller 10/		10.	£6. 5.
To Hannah Dyre in full of her Disburstmts.		317. 14. 2	
To Ditto for One Qr. Salary to Decr. 4	£35.		
for One Qr. Ditto to 4 March. @ 180	45.	80.	
To John Hill Esqr.... in pt. of his Disburstmts.	15.		
To Ditto ....in full	236. 4. 6	251. 4. 6	
To Thoms. Hubbard Esqr. in pt. of his Disbursts.	40.		
To Ditto ....More	40.		
To Ditto ....in full	38.11. 3	118. 11. 3	
To Daniel Henchman Esqr. in full		25. 17.	
To Edward Bromfield .... in full		30. 2. 10	
To Andrew Oliver Esqr. ..... in full		19. 3.	
To John Phillips .... in full		57. 14. 6	
To Isaac Walker .... in full		61. 13. 4	
To Geo. Rogers Esqr. .... in full		111. 10. 6	
To Ebenr. Storer .... in full		139. 4. 6	
To Edward Ellis .... in pt. of his Accot.		90. 13. 9	
To Francis Warden .... in full		42. 3. 4	
To Green & Walker .... in full		41. 17. 6	
To John Blower .... in full		176. 4.	
To Wm. Tyler Esqr. .... in full		77. 7. 1	
To Isaiah Barrett .... in full for Wood		15. 12.	
To Nath. Band ....in full for Funerals		11. 19.	
To Silvester Gardner ....in full for Medicine		144. 19. 9	1813. 12.
			1819. 17.

Boston 2d. April 1746

Granted by the Overseers of the Poor

To Jos: Davis 20/ Mercy Rayner 20/	2.	
Phillip Marlow 20/ Dorothy Torrey 20/	2.	
Lydia Torrey 20/ Hannah Henderson 15/	1. 15.	
Joanna Spiller	10.	6. 5.
To Hannah Dyre in full of her Disburstments		186. 12.
		£192. 17.

The Overseers' Finances 1738-1769

Boston 7th: May 1746.

Granted by the Overseers of the Poor.

To Jos: Davis 20/ Mercy Reyner 20/	£2.	
Philip Marlow 20/ Dorothy Torry 20/	2.	
Lydia Torrey 20/ Haňah Henderson 15/	1. 15.	
Joanna Spiller	10.	6. 5.
To Hannah Dyre.............. in part disbursmts.	£100.	
To Ditto .... in full . ditto	106. 4. 10	
To Charles Hendly........... in full for Shoes	12. 14. 6	
To Thacher & Bioise........ in full for Wood	49. 9. 6	
To Nathl. Band .... his bill for Funerals	11. 10.	279. 18. 10
		286. 3. 10

Boston 6 June 1746

Granted by the Overseers of the Poor

To Jos. Davis 20/ Mercy Rayner 20/	2.	
Phillip Marlow 20/ Dorothy Torry 20/	2.	
Lydia Torrey 20/ Hannah Henderson 15/	1. 15.	
Joanna Spiller 10/	10.	6. 5.
To Hannah Dyre in full of her Disburstmts.	117. 12. 5	
To Daniel Henchman in full of his Accot.	98. 18.	
To John Phillips in full of his Accot.	86. 7.	
To Green & Walker in full of his Accot.	161. 13.	
To Eleazer Dorby in full for 40 Cord Wood	150.	614. 10. 5
		£620. 15. 5

Boston July 1st. 1746.

Granted by the Overseers of the Poor

To Joseph Davis 20/ Mercy Rayner 20/	2.	
Philip Marlow 20/ Dorothy Torry 20/	2.	
Lidia Torry 20/ Hannah Henderson 15/	1. 15.	
Joanna Spillier	10.	6. 5.
To Hannah Dyer in full of her Disburstmts.	180. 6	
To Willis & Fitch in full of their Accott.	24. 15. 8	
To Ebenezer Storer in full of his Accott.	147. 11. 3	352. 7. 5
		£358. 12. 5

717

Boston 6 August 1746.

Granted by the Overseers of the Poor

To Joseph Davis 20/ Mercy Rayner 20/	2.		
Phillip Marlow 20/ Dorothy Torrey 20/	2.		
Lydia Torrey 20/ Hannah Henderson 15/	1. 15.		
Joanna Spiller	10.	6. 5.	
To Hannah Dyre in full of her Disburstmts.	273. 5. 8	273. 5. 8	
		279. 10. 8	

Boston 3d. Sepr. 1746.

Granted by the Overseers of the Poor

To Joseph Davis 20/ Mercy Rayner 20/	2.		
Phillip Marlow 20/ Dorothy Torrey 20/	2.		
Lydia Torrey 20/ Hannah Henderson 15/	1. 15.		
Joanna Spiller 10/	10.	6. 5.	
To Hannah Dyre in full of her Disburstmts.	127. 4. 6		
To Wm. Downe Esqr. in full of his Accot.	68. 8. 6		
To Edward Bromfield in full his Accot.	77. 1. 2		
To John Savel in full of his Accot.	25.	297. 14. 2	
		£303. 19. 2	

Boston 1 October 1746

Granted by the Overseers of the Poor

John Davis 20/ Mercy Rayner 20/	2.		
Phillip Marlow 20/ Dorothy Torrey 20/	2.		
Lydia Torrey 20/ Hannah Henderson 15/	1. 15.		
Joanna Spiller 10/	10.	6. 5.	
To Hannah Dyre in full of her Disburstments	150. 1. 4		
To Ditto for half Years Sallery Ending 4 Sepr. last	90.		
To John Hill Esqr. in full of his Accot.	82. 2. 6	322. 3. 10	
To George Rogers Esqr. in full of his Accot.		76. 12. 2	
		£405. 1.	

Boston 5. Novr. 1746

Granted by the Overseers of the Poor

To John Davis 20/ Mercy Rayner 20/	2.		
Phillip Marlow 20/ Dorothy Torrey 20/	2.		
Lydia Torrey 20/ Hannah Henderson 15/	1. 15.		
Joanna Spiller 10/	10.	6. 5.	
To Hannah Dyre in full of her Disburstmts.	217. 6. 10		
To Andrew Oliver Esqr. . . . in full	92. 13.		
To Charles Henly in full for Shoes	14. 6	324. 4	
To William Rand in part for Medicine & Attendance		200.	
		£530. 5. 4	

Boston 3d. December 1746

Granted by the Overseers of the Poor

To John Davis 20/ Mercy Rayner 20/ Phill Marlow 20/	3		
Doro: Torrey 20/ Lyda. Torrey 20/ Hanh. Henderson 15/	2. 15.		
Joanna Spiller	10.	6. 5.	
To Hannah Dyre in full of her Disburstmts.	280. 18. 2		
To John Sprague Physitian in full	20.		
To Francis Wardan in full	25. 16. 3	326. 14. 5	
		£332. 19. 5	

Boston 7th. Jany. 1746./7

Granted by the Overseers of the Poor

<John> Joseph Davis 20/ Mercy Rayner 20/	2.		
Phillip Marlow 20/ Dorothy Torrey 20/	2.		
Lydia Torrey 20/ Hannah Henderson 15/	1. 15.		
Joanna Spiller 10/	10.	6. 5.	
To Hannah Dyre in full of her Disburstmts.	234. 5. 5		
To Thomas Hubbard Esqr. in full of his Accot.	70. 8.		
To Daniel Henchman Esqr. in full of his Accot.	37. 16.	342. 9. 5	
		348. 14. 5	

❧

Boston 4 Feby. 1746/7

Granted by the Overseers of the Poor

Joseph Davis 20/ Mercy Rayner 20/	2.	
Phillip Marlow 20/ Dorothy Torrey 20/	2.	
Lydia Torrey 20/ Hannah Henderson 15/	1. 15.	
Joanna Spiller 10/	10.	6. 5.
To Hannah Dyre in full of her Disburstmts.	203. 13. 1	
To Edward Bromfield in full of his Accot.	66. 7.	
To John Phillips Esqr. in full of his Accot.	49. 5.	
To Ebenr. Storer in full of his Accots.	357. 4. 6	
To John Blower in full	31. 9.	
To Nathaniel Band in full	13. 3.	721. 1. 7
		727. 6. 7
To Wm. Rand in Part		200.
		£927. 6. 7

Boston 25 Feby. 1746/7

Granted by the Overseers of the Poor

To John Davis 20/ Mercy Rayner 20/	2.	
Phillip Marlow 20/ Dorothy Torrey 20/	2.	
Lydia Torrey 20/ Hannah Henderson 15/	1. 15.	
Joana Spiller 10/	10.	6. 5.
To Hannah Dyre in full of her Disburstmts.	167. 7.	
for half years Sallery due 4th. March	90.	
To Wm. Tyler Esqr. in full of his Accot.	65. 7	
To John Hill Esqr. in full	161. 4.	
To Thomas Hubbard Esq. in full	38. 3. 9	
To Edward Bromfield in full	29. 13.	
To Wm. Downe Esq. in full	11. 14.	
To Andrew Oliver Esq. in full	28. 16.	
To Isaac Walker .... in full	101. 5. 2	
To Geo. Rogers Esqr. .... in full	115. 17.	
To Ebenr. Storer........... in full	27. 14.	
To Josiah Waters Junr. .... in full	2. 12. 6	
To Francis Wardan........ in full	26. 11.	
To Samuel Grant.......... in full	8.	

To Wm. Rand in full of his Accot. for the Town⎫
   to this day   ⎭   54. 19.

To Daniel Henchman Esqr. in full   31.   959. 17.

                                                966. 2.

Boston the 1st: April 1747

Granted by the Overseers of the Poor

To John Davis 20/   Mercy Rayner 20/   P. Marlow 20/   3.

    Dorothy Torrey 20/   Lydia Torrey 20/   2.

    Hannah Henderson 15/   Joanna Spiller 10/   1. 5.   6. 5.

To Hannah Dyre in part of her Disburstmts.   200.

To Ditto .... in full of her Disburstmts.   199. 3.

To Edward Winter, in full..........of his Accot.   22. 13.   421. 16.

                                           £428. 1.

Boston 6 May 1747

Granted by the Overseers of the Poor

To John Davis 20/   Mercy Rayner 20/   £2.

    Phillip Marlow 20/   Dorothy Torrey 20/   2.

    Lydia Torrey 20/   Hannah Henderson 15/   1. 15.

    Joanna Spiller 10/   10.   6. 5.

To Hannah Dyre in part of her Disburstmts.   200.

To Ditto in full   214. 12. 5

To Robert McClure & Co. in full for Labour in⎫
    Opening & Closing the Drain   ⎭   21.

To Edward Bromfield in part   50.

To Wm. Rand in part   100.   585. 12. 5

                                         591. 17. 5

Boston 3d. June 1747

Granted by the Overseers of the Poor

To John Davis 20/ Mercy Rayner 20/	2.	
Phillip Marlow 20/ Dorothy Torrey 20/	2.	
Lydia Torrey 20/ Hannah Henderson 15/	1. 15.	
Joanna Spiller 10/	10.	6. 5.
To Hannah Dyre in full for her Disburstmts.	274. 12. 6	
To John Hill Esqr. in pt. . . of his Accots.	15.	
To Ditto . . . in full	174. 18.	
To John Phillips Esqr: in full of his Accot.	141. 12.	
To Andrew Oliver Esqr. for 100 Bus. Corne 150 Rye	250.	
To Green & Walker in full of their Accot.	225.	1081. 2. 6
To Charles Henly in full		9. 15.
		£1097. 2. 6

Boston 7 July 1747

Granted by the Overseers of the Poor

To John Davis 20/ Mercy Rayner 20/	2.	
Phillip Marlow 20/ Dorrothy Torrey 20/	2.	
Lydia Torrey 20/ Hannah Henderson 15/	1. 15.	
Joanna Spiller	10.	6. 5.
To Hannah Dyre in part of her Disburstmts.	£282. 7. 8	
To Ditto ....in full of her Disburstmts.	51. 8. 5	
To Green & Walker in full of their Accot.	156. 5. 4	
To Isaac Walker in part of his Accot.	25.	
To William Tyl[er E]sqr.[13] ...for Wood 20 Cord	120.	
To William Downe Esqr. in full	214.	
To Nathaniel Band his Accot. Burying	7. 11.	
To Daniel Henchman Esqr. for Wood 20 Cord	120.	976. 12. 5
		£982. 17. 5

The Overseers' Finances 1738-1769

Granted by the Overseers of the Poor

To John Davis 20/ Mercy Rayner 20/	2.	
Phillip Marlow 20/ Dorothy Torrey 20/	2.	
Lydia Torrey 20/ Hannah Henderson 15/	1. 15.	
Joanna Spiller 10/	10.	6. 5.
To Hannah Dyre in full of her Disburstmts.	245. 6. 5	
To William Tyler Esqr for Corne	50.	
To Andrew Oliver Esqr for Disburstmts. ℘ Accots.	39. 15. 6	
To Ebenr. Storer in full of his Accots.	213. 10.	
To Francis Wardan in full of his Accot.	30. 19. 9	579. 11. 8
		£585. 16. 8

Boston 3d. September 1747

Granted by the Overseers of the Poor

To John Davis 20/ Mercy Rayner 20/	2.	
Phillip Marlow 20/ Dorothy Torrey 20/	2.	
Lydia Torrey 20/ Hannah Henderson 15/	1. 15.	
Joanna Spiller 10/	10.	6. 5.
To Hannah Dyre in full of her Disburstments	183. 6. 10	
To Ditto for half years sallery Ending 4th. Inst.	90.	
To John Hill Esqr. in full of his Accot.	107. 16.	
To Wm. Rand in part	300.	
To Geo. Rogers Esqr. in full of his Accot.	92. 2. 6	773. 5. 4
		£779. 10. 4

Boston 7th. October 1747.

Granted by the Overseers of the Poor.

To John Davis 20/ Mercy Rayner 20/	2.	
Phillip Marlow 20/ Dorothy Torrey 20/	2.	
Lydia Torrey 20/ Hannah Henderson 15/	1. 15.	
Joanna Spiller 10/	10.	6. 5.
To Hannah Dyre in full of her Disburstmts.	385. 8. 8	
To Wm. Rand in part	300.	685. 8. 8
		£691. 13. 8

❧

Boston 10 Novemr. 1747.

Granted by the Overseers of the Poor

To John Davis 20/ Mercy Reyner 20/	£2.	
Phillip Marlow 20/ Dorothy Torrey 20/	2.	
Lydia Torrey 20/ Hannah Henderson 15/	1. 15.	
Joanna Spiller 10/	10.	6. 5.
To Hannah Dyre in full of her Disburstmts.	282. 3. 3	282. 3. 3
		£286. 8. 3

Boston 3d. December 1747

Granted by the Overseers of the Poor

To John Davis 20/ Mercy Rayner 20/	2.	
Phillip Marlow 20/ Dorothy Torrey 20/	2.	
Lydia Torrey 20/ Hannah Henderson 15/	1. 15.	
Joanna Spiller 10/	10.	6. 5.
To Hannah Dyre in part of her Disburstmts.	300.	
To Ditto ....in full of ditto	316. 12. 10	
To Nath. Band in full of his Accot.	18. 1.	634. 13. 10
		£640. 18. 10

Boston 7th. January 1747

Granted by the Overseers of the Poor

To John Davis 20/ Mercy Rayner 20/	2.	
Phillip Marlow 20/ Dorrothy Torrey 20/	2.	
Lydia Torrey 20/ Hannah Henderson 15/	1. 15.	
Joanna Spiller 10/	10.	6. 5.
To Hannah Dyre in full of her Disburstmts.	344. 16.	
To Daniel Henchman Esqr. in full of his Accot.	134. 19. 1	
To John Phillips Esqr.....Ditto	18. 2.	
To Ditto as Exer. to B. Clarks Estate being so much } Advand. for Wood }	390.	
To Thatcher & Boice for Wood in full	70. 13.	
To Robt. Mcclure in full of his Accot.	6. 10.	
To Nathl. Band in full of his Accot.	12. 17.	977. 17. 1
		£984. 2. 1

The Overseers' Finances 1738-1769

Boston 3d. ffeby. 1747/8

Granted by the Overseers of the Poor.

To John Davis 20/ Mercy Rayner 20/	2.		
Phillip Marlow 20/ Dorothy Torrey 20/	2.		
Lydia Torrey 20/ Hannah Henderson 15/	1. 15.		
Joanna Spiller 10/	10.	6. 5.	
To Hannah Dyre in full for Disburstmts.	182. 13. 5		
To Charles Henly in full for shoes	24. 12.		
To Wm. Rand in part of his accot.	200.	407. 5. 5	
		£413. 10. 5	

Boston 3 March 1747/8

Granted by the Overseers of the Poor

To John Davis 20/ Mercy Rayner 20/		2.	
Phillip Marlow 20/ Dorothy Torrey 20/		2.	
Lydia Torrey 20/ Hannah Henderson 15/		1. 15.	
Joanna Spiller 10/		10.	6. 5.
To Hannah Dyre in full for Disburstmts.		344. 15. 2	
To Ditto for half Year Sallery Ending 4 Inst.		90.	
To Jacob Wendell Esqr. in full of his Accot.		114. 8. 6	
To Wm: Tyler Esq. Ditto		84. 16. 4	
To John Hill Esqr Ditto in part	66.		
To Do.......... in full	224. 2. 10	290. 2. 10	
To Thomas Hubbard Esqr. in part	116.		
To Do............................. in full	61. 4. 1	177. 4. 1	
To Daniel Henchman Esq. in full		64. 17. 6	
To Edwd. Bromfield his Accot. 187. 3. deduct 50£ drawn in part. May last		137. 3.	
To Wm. Downe Esq. in full		40. 8. 6	
To Andw. Oliver Esq in full		64. 11.	
To John Phillips Esq. Do.		34. 9.	
To Isaac Walker his Accot. 139. 7. deduct £25 July		114. 7.	
To Ebenr. Storer in full of his accot.		420. 18. 1	1978. 1.
Carried forward			£1984. 6.

The Overseers' Finances 1738-1769

~

Granted by the Overseers of the Poor

	Sum brought Over		£1984.	6.
To Green & Walker in full of their accots.	£95. 19. 9			
To Francis Warden in full Do.	49. 3. 4			
To Nathl. Band ..... in full	3. 12.			
To John Blower in full of his Accot.	15.			
To Doctr. Thomas Boylston in full of his Accot.	261. 19. 6			
To Doctr Wm. Rand in full of his Accot.	279. 14. 10			
To Doctr. Edward Ellis in part	160.	865. 9. 5		
		£2849. 15. 5		

Boston Apll. 6th. 1748

Granted by the Overseers of the Poor

To John Davis 20/ Mary Rayner 20/	2.		
Philip Marlow 20/ Dorothy Torey 20/	2.		
Lydia Torey 20/ Hannah Henderson 15/	1. 15.		
Joanna Spiller	10.	6. 5.	
Hannah Dyer in full of her Act. Disbursmts.		538. 2. 5	
		544. 7. 5	

Boston May <3d.> 4 1748

Granted by the Overseers of the Poor

To John Davis 20/ Mercy Rayner 20/	2.		
Phillip Marlow 20/ Dorothy Torrey 20/	2.		
Lydia Torrey 20/ Hannah Henderson 15/	1. 15.		
Joanna Spiller 10/	10.	6. 5.	
To Hannah Dyre in full of her Disburstments		551. 6. 1	
To Ebenr. storrer in full of his Accot.		106. 11. 10	
		£664. 2. 11	

Boston 1 June 1748

Granted by the Overseers of the Poor

To John Davis 20/ Mercy Rayner 20/ Phillip Marlow 20/	3.			
Dorothy Torrey 20/ Lydia Torrey 20/	2.			
Hannah Henderson 15/ Joanna Spiller 10/	1. 5.		6. 5.	
To Hannah Dyre in full for her Disburstmts.	322. 1. 5			
To John Hill Esq. in part of his Accot. £31.				
To Ditto .... more	35.			
To Ditto .... in full	186. 7.	252. 7.		
To William Downe Esqr. for Wood ℘ Accot.	181. 5.			
To Andrew Oliver Esqr. in full of his Accot.	33. 8. 6			
To John Phillips Esqr. in full for Wood &c.	182. 3.			
To Green & Walker in part of their Accot. 120.				
To Ditto in full of their Accot.	149. 19. 4	269. 19. 4		
To Ebenr. Storer for Wood ℘ accot.	131. 5.			
To John Barrett money he paid Hannah Dyre				
to purchase Corne	300.	1722. 9. 3		
		[1728. 14. 3][14]		

Boston 5 July 1748

Granted by the Overseers of the Poor

To John Davis 20/ Mercy Rayner 20/ Phillip Marlow 20/	3.		
Dorrothy Torrey 20/ Lydia Torrey 20/	2.		
Hannah Henderson 15/ Joanna Spiller 10/	1. 5.	6. 5.	
To Hannah Dyre in part of her Disburstmts. 200.			
To Ditto .... in full of her Disburstmts. 231. 5. 3	431. 5. 3		
To William Tyler Esqr. for Rye ℘ Accot.	78.		
To Doctr. William Rand in part of his Accot.	300.		
To Francis Warden .... in full of his Accot.	34. 17. 6		
To Nathl. Band in full	1. 15.	855. 17. 9	
	Exa.	£862. 2. 9	
To John Blower in full of his Accot.		33. 3. 4	
		£895. 6. 1	

Boston 3. August 1748

Granted by the Overseers of the Poor

John Davis 20/ Mercy Rayner 20/	2.	
Phillip Marlow 20/ Dorrothy Torrey 20/	2.	
Lydia Torrey 20/ Hannah Henderson 15/	1. 15.	
Joanna Spiller 10/	10.	6. 5.
To Hannah Dyre in part of her Disburstments	204. 15. 4	
To Ditto .... in full of her Disburstments	57. 14. 3	262. 9. 7
		£268. 14. 7

Boston 7 Sepr. 1748

Granted by the Overseers of the Poor

To John Davis 20/ Mercy Rayner 20/	2.	
Phillip Marlow 20/ Dorrothy Torrey 20/	2.	
Lydia Torrey 20/ Hannah Henderson 15/	1. 15.	
Joanna Spiller	10.	6. 5.
To Hannah Dyre in full of her Disburstmts.	285. 8.	
To Nathl. Band in full of his Accot.	10. 10.	
To Francis Warden in full of his Accot.	24. 9.	320. 7.
		£326. 12.

Boston 6th. October 1748

Granted by the Overseers of the Poor

To John Davis 20/ Mercy Rayner 20/	2.	
Phillip Marlow 20/ Dorothy Torrey 20/	2.	
Lydia Torrey 20/ Hannah Henderson 15/	1. 15.	
Joanna Spiller 10/	10.	6. 5.
To Hannah Dyre in pt. of her Disburstmts.	200.	
To Ditto .... in full..........of ditto	203. 8.	403. 8.
		409. 13.
To Doctr. Edward Ellis in full for sallery & all accots. to this day		70.
		479. 13.

Boston 2 November 1748

Granted by the Overseers of the Poor

To John Davis 20/   Mercy Rayner 20/   £2.

 Phillip Marlow 20/   Dorrothy Torrey 20/   2.

 Lydia Torrey 20/   Hannah Henderson 15/   1. 15.

 Joanna Spiller 10/   10.   6. 5.

To Hannah Dyre in full of her Disburstments   270. 4. 2

          £276. 9. 2

Boston Decr. 7th. 1748

Granted by the Overseers of the Poor

To John Davis 20/   Mercy Reynor 20/   2.

 Philip Marlow 20/   Dorothy Torrey 20/   2.

 Lydia Torrey 20/   Hannah Henderson 15/   1. 15.

 Joanna Spiller 10/   10.   6. 5.

To Hannah Dyre in full of her Disbursements.   633. 3. 8

          £639. 8. 8

Boston 4 January 1748/9

Granted by the Overseers of the Poor

To John Davis 20/   Mercy Rayner 20/   2.

 Phillip Marlow 20/   Dorothy Torrey 20/   2.

 Lydia Torrey 20/   Hannah Henderson 15/   1. 15.

 Joanna Spiller 10/   10.   6. 5.

To Hannah Dyre in full of her Disburstmts.   295. 1.

To Docr. Wm. Rand in part of his Accot.   300.

To Charles Henly in full of his Accot.   44. 1.   639. 2.

          £645. 7.

The Overseers' Finances 1738-1769

Granted by the Overseers of the Poor

To Jos. Davis 20/ Mercy Rayner 20/	2.	
Phillip Marlow 20/ Dorrothy Torrey 20/	2.	
Lydia Torrey 20/ Hannah Henderson 15/	1. 15.	
Joanna Spiller 10/	10.	6. 5.
To Hannah Dyre in full of her Disburstmts.	330. 12. 2	

To Benjamin Hayward for taking a poor Infant⎤
Child ℘ Agreement ⎦ 50.

To Nathanl. Band in full of his Accot.	15. 8.	396. 2
		402. 5. 2

To <Hanna> Joseph Davis 20/ Mercy Rayner 20/	£2.	
Phillip Marlow 20/ Dorrothy Torrey 20/	2.	
Lydia Torrey 20/ Hannah Henderson 15/	1. 15.	
Joanna Spiller 10/	10.	6. 5.

To Hannah Dyre in part of her Disburstmts. £89. 4. 4
To Ditto in full   of do.   73. 13. 2

To Ditto <half> One Years Sallery Ending

4th. Inst.	180.	342. 17. 6
To The Honble. Jacob Wendell Esqr. his Accot. in full	246. 1.	
To Wm. Tyler Esqr. .... his Accot. Do.	61. 7. 4	
To John Hill Esqr. .... his Accot. Do.	399. 10.	

To Thomas Hubbard Esqr. his Accot. in pt.   £55.
To Do. .... more   72.

To Do. .... more in full	142. 12.	269. 12.
To Daniel Henchman Esqr..his Accot. in full	320. 15. 6	
To Edward Bromfield..........in full of his Accot.	650. 18. 9	
To Wm. Downe Esqr. ....in full of his Accot.	22. 13. 9	
To Andw. Oliver Esqr. ....in full of his Accot.	312. 8. 10	
To John Phillips Esqr. ....in full of his Accot.	68. 9.	2694. 13. 8
Sum Carrd. Over		2700. 18. 8

The Overseers' Finances 1738-1769

March 1. 1748.

Granted by the Overseers of the Poor

Sum brought forward		£2700. 18. 8	
To Isaac Walker in full of his Accot.	£92. 12. 10		
To Ebenr. Storrer in full of his Accot.	635. 3.		
To John Barrett in full of his Accot.	314. 19.		
To Francis Warden in full of his Accot.	82. 14.		
To Docr. Wm. Rand in full of his Accot.	206. 8. 6	1331. 17. 4	
		4032. 16.	

Boston 5th. April 1749

Granted by the Overseers of the Poor

To Jos. Davis 20/ Mercy Rayner 20/	2.	
Phillip Marlow 20/ Dorrothy Torrey 20/	2.	
Lydia Torrey 20/ Hannah Henderson 15/	1. 15.	
Joanna Spiller 10/	10.	6. 5.
To Hannah Dyre in full of her Disburstmts.	401. 8. 4	
To Daniel Henchman Esqr. 300 Bushell Corn	300.	
To John Phillips Esqr. in full of his Accot.	25. 5. 9	
To George Ray's in full of his Accot.	13. 19.	740. 13. 1
		746. 18. 1

Boston May 3d. 1749

Granted by the Overseers of the Poor

To Jos: Davis 20/ Mary Rayner 20/	2.	
Phillip Marrow 20/ Dorothy Torrey 20/	2.	
Lydia Torrey 20/ Hannah Henderson 15/	1. 15.	
Joanna Spiller	10.	6. 5.
Hannah Dyer in part of her Disbustmts.	204. 5. 4	
Ditto in full of her Disburstmts	218. 17. 8	
Green & Walker in full of their Act.	149. 16.	
Isaac Walker in full of his Act.	12. 11. 6	585. 10. 6
		591. 15. 6

꩜

June 7 1749

Granted by the Overseers of the Poor

To Jos. Davis 20/ Mercy Rayner 20/	2.	
Phillip Marlow 20/ Dorrothy Torrey 20/	2.	
Lydia Torrey 20/ Hannah Henderson 15/	1. 15.	
Joanna Spiller 10/	10.	6. 5.
To Hannah Dyre in full of her Disburstments		306. 11. 1
To Nathanl. Band in full of his Accot.		33. 9.
		£346. 5. 1

Boston 5 July 1749

Granted by the Overseers of the Poor

To Mr. Miller 20/ Mercy Rayner 20/	2.	
Phillip Marlow 20/ Dorrothy Torrey 20/	2.	
Lydia Torrey 20/ Hannah Henderson 15/	1. 15.	
Joanna Spiller 10/	10.	6. 5.
To Hannah Dyre in full of her Disburstmts.		295. 3.
To John Greenleaf for nursing & Doctg. Peter Harrod		50.
		351. 8.

Boston 2 August 1749.

Granted by the Overseers of the Poor

To [15] Miller 20/ Mercy Rayner 20/	2.	
Phillip Marlow 20/ Dorrothy Torrey 20/	2.	
Lydia Torrey 20/ Hannah Henderson 15/	1. 15.	
Joanna Spiller 10/	10.	6. 5.
To Hannah Dyre in full of her Disburstmts.		387. 17. 1
To John Hill Esqr. in part of his Accot.	£300.	
To Ditto .... more	15.	
To Ditto .... ditto	52. 10.	
To Ditto .... in full	70. 13. 6	438. 3. 6
To John Phillips Esqr. in full of his Accot.		64. 6.
To Hopestill Foster in full of his Accot.		21. 5.
To Wm. Rand…in pt.		297. 9. 9

[*Sum Carried Over*] 1215. 6. 4

The Overseers' Finances 1738-1769

August 2. 1749

Granted by the Overseers of the Poor

Sum brought Over	1215. 6. 4
To Simon Eliot for Nursing Hide's Child to 4th. July last	35.
To Andrew Oliver Esqr. in full of his Accot.	54. 8.
To Wm. Rand in full of his Accot. to the 8 June	50.
To John Heyler for Boarding Doctr. Rand's Negro being deducted out Sd. Rands Accot.	57.
	1411. 14. 4

Sepr. 6. 1749

Granted by the Overseers of the Poor

To Miller 20/ Mercy Rayner 20/ P. Marlow 20/	3.		
Dorrothy Torrey 20/ Lydia Torrey 20/	2.		
Hannah Henderson 15/ Joanna Spiller 10/	1. 5.	6. 5.	
To Hannah Dyre in pt. of her Disburstmts. 96. 9			
To Ditto .... in full of her Disburstmts. 103. 7.		199. 7. 9	
To John Barrett somuch he supplyd H Dyre for the House		200.	
To John Hill Esqr. his Accot. in full		126. 8.	
To Charles Henly in full of his Accot.		15. 6.	
		£547. 6. 9	

October 4. 1749

Granted by the Overseers of the Poor

To Miller 20/ Mercy Rayner 20/ Phillip Marlow 20/	3.		
To Dorrothy Torrey 20/ Lydia Torrey 20/	2.		
To Hannah Henderson 15/ Joanna Spiller 10/	1. 5.	6. 5.	
To Hannah Dyre in full of her Disburstments	298. 15. 5		
To Francis Warden in full of his Accot.	86. 1.		
To Nathanl. Band in full of his Accot.	29. 4.	414. 5	
		420. 5. 5	

Boston 1 November 1749

Granted by the Overseers of the Poor

To	Miller 20/ Mercy Rayner 20/	2.		
	Phillip Marlow 20/ Dorrothy Torrey 20/	2.		
	Lydia Torrey 20/ Hannah Henderson 15/	1. 15.		
	Joanna Spiller 10/	10.	6. 5.	
To Hannah Dyre in full of her Disburstments			331. 1. 1	
			£337. 6. 1	
To Wm. Downe Esqr. in full of his Accos.			64. 3. 5[16]	
			£401. 9. 6	

Boston 6 December 1749

Granted by the Overseers of the Poor

To	Miller 20/ Mercy Rayner 20/	2.		
	Phillip Marlow 20/ Dorrothy Torrey 20/	2.		
	Lydia Torrey 20/ Hannah Henderson 15/	1. 15.		
	Joanna Spiller 10/	10.	6. 5.	
To Hannah Dyre in full of her Disburstments	£		398. 18. 2	
To Ebenezer Storer in part of his Accot.	500.			
To John Hill Esqr. in full of his Accot.	647. 4.		1147. 4.	
			1552. 7. 2	

Boston 3d. Jany. 1749.

Granted by the Overseers of the Poor

To	Miller 20/ Mercy Rayner 20/	£2.		
	Phillip Marlow 20/ Dorrothy Torrey 20/	2.		
	Lydia Torrey 20/ Hannah Henderson 15/	1. 15.		
	Joanna Spiller 10/	10.	6. 5.	
To Hannah Dyre in full of her Disburstmts.			352. 16. 9	
To Edward Bromfield in part of his Accot.			300.	
To Wm. Downe Esqr. in full of his Accot.			31. 10.	
To John Phillips Esqr. in full			32.	
To Isaac Walker in full of his Accot.			69. 14.	
carried Over			792. 5. 9	

Brot. Over	£792. 5. 9	
To Ebenezer Storer in full of his Accot.	271. 8.	
To John Barrett in full of his Accot.	159. 9. 6	
To Doctr. Gillam Tailor in full to 1 Jany.	278. 10. 9	
	1501. 14.	

Boston 7 Feby. 1749/50

Granted by the Overseers of the Poor

To Miller 20/ Mercy Rayner 20/	2.	
Phillip Marlow 20/ Dorrothy Torrey 20/	2.	
Lydia Torrey 20/ Hannah Henderson 15/	1. 15.	
Joanna Spiller 10/	10.	6. 5.
To Hannah Dyre in part of her Disburstmts.	328. 18. 11	
To Ditto ....in full of do.	250. 16. 3	579. 15. 2
To Daniel Henchman Esqr. in full	53. 9. 6	
To Andrew Oliver Esqr........Do.	278. 6	
To Green & Walker.............Ditto	217. 12. 4	
To Charles Henly................Ditto	18. 12.	567. 14. 4
		1153. 14. 6

Boston 7 March 1749/50

Granted by the Overseers of the Poor

To Miller 20/ Mercy Rayner 20/	2.	
Phillip Marlow 20/ Dorothy Torrey 20/	2.	
Lydia Torrey 20/ Hannah Henderson 15/	1. 15.	
Joanna Spiller 10/	10.	6. 5.
To Hannah Dyre in full of her Disburstmts.	452. 11. 8	
To Ditto for 1 Years Sallery Ending the 4th. day	180.	632. 11. 8
To Jacob Wendell Esqr. in full of his Accot.	£117. 18. 10	
To Wm. Tyler Esqr. Do.	54. 5. 6	
To John Hill Esqr. Ditto	194. 5. 6	
To Thomas Hubbard Esqr.	147. 13. 6	514. 3. 4
carried Over		1153.

The Overseers' Finances 1738-1769

∾

Granted by the Overseers of the Poor

Sum brought from Otherside		£1153.
To Wm. Downe Esqr. in full of his Accot.	£34. 14. 6	
To Edward Bromfield in full of his Accot.	40. 13. 6	
To Daniel Henchman Esqr. in full of his Accot.	18.	
To Andrew Oliver Esqr. in full of his Accot.	16. 6.	
To Isaac Walker in full of his Accot.	40. 16.	
To John Barrett in full of his Accot.	150. 12. 6	
To Francis Warden in full of his Accot.	45. 10.	
To Robert Willson in full of do.	75.	
To Nathanl. Band in full of do.	33. 10.	
To Saml. Dix........in full of do.	38. 10.	493. 12. 6
		1646. 12. 6

Boston 4th: April 1750

Granted by the Overseers of the Poor

To Miller 4/ Mercy Rayner 4/	8.	
To Phillip Marlow 4/ Dorrothy Torrey 4/	8.	
Lydia Torrey 4/ Hannah Henderson 4/	8.	
Joanna Spiller 3/	3.	1. 7.
To Hannah Dyre in full of her Disburstmts.	40. 8. 1	
To John Hill Esqr. in full of his Accot.	13. 3. 2	
To John Blower in full of his Accot.	15. 16.	69. 7. 3
Lawful money		£70. 14. 3
To Mr. David Jeffries		

Boston 2 May 1750

Granted by the Overseers of the Poor.

To Miller 4/ Mercy Rayner 4/	8.	
To Phillip Marlow 4/ Dorrothy Torrey 13/4	17. 4	
Lydia Torrey 13/4 Hannah Henderson 4/	17. 4	
Joanna Spiller 3/	3.	2. 5. 8
To Hannah Dyre in full of her Disburstmts.	43. 7. 8	
To Green & Walker Corne & Rye ℘ accot.	29. 14. 8	

To Charles Henly in full of his Accot.   19. 4   74. 1. 8

                      Lawful   £76. 7. 4

To John Loyd in full for Nursing John Finlys Child   5. 4.

                            £81. 11. 4

Boston 6th. June 1750.

Granted by the Overseers of the Poor

To   Miller 4/   Mercy Rayner 4/   £   8.

   Phillip Marlow 4/   [17] Torrey 13/4   17. 4

   Hannah Henderson 4/ Joanna Spiller 3/   7.   1. 12. 4

To Hannah Dyre in full of her disburstmts.   50. 14. 5

To Green & Walker in full for Grain ⅌ Accot.   44.

To Hopestill Foster in full for Wood ⅌ Accot.   1. 12.

To Nathanl. Band in full of his Accot.   1. 19. 4

To Samuel Dix for taking care of Sarah Teague⎫

   13 Weeks Ending 1 Inst....@ 4/   ⎭   2. 12.   100. 17. 9

                Lawful Money   £102. 10. 1

To Henry Spring for taking Wakefields Child   4.

                            106. 10. 1

Boston 3d. July 1750

Granted by the Overseers of the Poor.

To   Miller 4/   Mercy Rayner 4/   8.

   Phillip Marlow 4/   Torrey 13/4   17. 4.

   Hannah Henderson 4/ Joanna Spiller 3/   7.   1. 12. 4

To Hannah Dyre in full of her Disburstmts.   21. 13. 4

To John Hill Esqr. in full of his Accot.   137. 10. 4

To Doctr. Gillam Tailer in full of his Accot.   36. 6. 5 1/2 195. 10. 1 1/2

                    Lawful   £197. 2. 5 1/2

The Overseers' Finances 1738-1769

〜

Granted by the Overseers of the Poor

To Miller 4/ Mercy Rayner 4/	8.	
Phillip Marlow 4/ Torrey 13/4	17. 4	
Hannah Henderson 4/ Joanna Spiller 3/	7.	1. 12. 4
To Hannah Dyre in full of her Disburstmts.		62. 10. 2
To Samuel Dix for keeping Sarah Teague from the last day of February to 31 July being 22 Weeks @ 4/		4. 8.
		68. 10. 6
To John Helyer in part of his Accot. for the Maintainance Sundry Persons in the Work House Subjects of the Alms House, distracted &c.		50.
To Wm. Tyler Esqr. in full of his Accot.		3. 1.
		£121. 11. 6

Granted by the Overseers of the Poor

To Miller 4/ Mercy Rayner 4/	8.	
Phillip Marlow 4/ Torrey 13/4	17. 4	
Hannah Henderson 4/ Joanna Spiller 3/	7.	1. 12. 4
To Hannah Dyre in full of her Disburstmts.		62. 5
		63. 12. 9

Granted by the Overseers of the Poor

To Miller 4/ Mercy Rayner 4/	8.	
Phillip Marlow 4/ Torrey 13/4	17. 4	
Hannah Henderson 4/ Joanna Spiller 3/	7.	1. 12. 4
To Hannah Dyre in full of her Disburstmts.	48. 14. 4	
To John Hill Esqr. in full of his Accot.	23. 15. 2	72. 9. 6
		£74. 1. 10

The Overseers' Finances 1738-1769

Granted by the Overseers of the Poor

To Miller 4/ Mercy Rayner 4/	8.		
Phillip Marlow 4/ Torrey 13/4	17. 4		
Hannah Henderson 4/ Joanna Spiller 3/	7.	1. 12. 4	
To Hannah Dyre in full of her Disburstmts.	70. 13. 3		
To Green & Walker in full of their Accot.	17. 6. 8		
To Francis Warden in full of his Accot.	9. 12. 6	97. 12. 5	
		99. 4. 9	

Granted by the Overseers of the Poor

To Miller 4/ Mercy Rayner 4/	8.	
Phillip Marlow 4/ Torrey 13/4	17. 4	
Hannah Henderson 4/ Joanna Spiller 3/	7.	1. 12. 4
To Hannah Dyre in full of her Disburstmts.		35. 8. 2
To Ebenr. Storer in part of his Accot.		4.
To John Helyer in part of his Accot. for the support of Sundry ℘sons in the Workhouse subjects of the Alms House distracted &c.		40.
To Nathaniel Band in full of his Accot.		5. 2.
		86. 2. 6

Granted by the Overseers of the Poor

To Miller 4/ Mercy Rayner 4/	8.	
Phillip Marlow 4/ Torrey 13/4	17. 4.	
Hannah Henderson 4/ Joanna Spiller 3/	7.	1. 12. 4
To Hannah Dyre in full of her Disburstmts.		42. 6. 6
To Green & Walker in full of their Accot.		5. 14. 8
To Isaac Walker in full of his Accot.		7. 18. 9 1/2
To John Phillips Esqr. in full of his Accot.		2.
To Doctr. Gillam Tailer in full of his Accot.		59. 13. 2
To Thomas March in full of his Accot.		19. 19. 11 1/2
To John Orr in full of his Accot.		2. 8.
To Charles Henly in full of his Accot.		9. 9 1/2
		£142. 3. 2 1/2

Boston Febry. 6th. 1750

Granted by the Overseers of the Poor

To Miller 4/ Mercy Rayner 4/		8.					
Phillip Marlow 4/ Torrey 13/4d		17.	4.				
Hannah Henderson 4/ Joana Spiller 3/		7.		1.	12.	4	
To Hannah Dyer in full of her Disbustments	30.	14.	5				
To John Barrett in full of his Act.	52.	17.	8 1/4	83.	12.	1 1/4	
				85.	4.	5 1/4	

Boston 6 March 1750

Granted by the Overseers of the Poor

To Miller 4/ Mercy Reyner 4/	£	8.				
To Philip Marlow 4/ Torrey 13/4		17.	4.			
To Hana. Henderson 4/ Joanna Spillier 3/		7.		1.	12.	4
To Hannah Dyer…in full her disbursmts.	36.	13.	11			
one year's Salary to the 4 Inst.	24.					
one year's Interest of £200	12.			72.	13.	11
To Willm. Tyler Esqr….in full of his Accot.				3.	3.	2
To Jno. Hill Esqr................... ditto				42.	17.	11 1/4
To Tho Hubbard Esqr............ Ditto				17.	7.	5
To Danl. Henchman Esqr. ditto				8.	1.	10 1/2
To Edwd. Bromfield Esqr. ...... in part of his Accot.				20.		
To Willm. Downe Esqr.......... in full				2.	15.	6 1/2
To Andr. Oliver Esqr.............. in part				50.		
To Ditto .... in full				31.	17.	
To Ebenzr. Storer .... in part				66.	16.	1/2
To Ditto .... in full				22.	16.	5
Carried over				£340.	1.	7 3/4

6 March 1750

Brought over	£340.	1.	7 3/4	
To Nathl. Band ....Accot. for burials	3.	1.		
To Saml. Dix.....keepg. Sarah Teague 31 weeks fr. 31 Janry. at 4/	6.	4.		
To Francis Warden ....Accot. for Coffins &c.	5.	19.	8	
	£355.	6.	3 3/4	

Boston 3 April 1751

Granted by the Overseers of the Poor

To Millar 4/ Mercy Rayner 4/	£	8.			
To Phillip Marlow 4/ Torrey 13/4		17.	4		
To Hannah Henderson 4/ Joanna Spiller 3/		7.		£1. 12.	4
To Hannah Dyre in full of her Disbursments	33. 14.	5			
To John Leverett in full of his Accot.	4.			£37. 14.	5
				£39. 6.	9

Boston 1 May 1751

Granted by the Overseers of the Poor

To Miller 4/ To Mercy Reyner 4/	£	8.			
To Philip Marlow 4/ To Torrey 13/4		17.	4		
To Haña. Henderson 4/ To Joanna Spillier 3/		7.		1. 12.	4
To Hannah Dyer..........in full of her disbursments				31. 9.	4
				£33. 1.	8

Boston June 5th. 1751

Granted by the Overseers of the Poor

To Miller 4/ To Mercy Reyner 4/	£	8.			
To Phillip Marlow 4/ To Torrey 13/4d.		17.	4		
To Hannah Henderson 4/ To Joana Spiller 3/		7.		1. 12.	4
To Hannah Dyer in full of her Disbursments				44. 10.	9
				£46. 3.	1

Boston July 2: 1751

Granted by The Overseers of the Poor

To Miller 4/ To Mercy Reyner 4/	£	8.			
To Phillip Marlow 4/ To Torrey 13/4		17.	4.		
To Hannah Henderson 4/ Joana Spiller 3/		7.		1. 12.	4
To Hannah Dyer in full of her disbusts.	26. 14.	4			
To John Phillips Esqr.	6. 11.	2 1/2			
To Francis Warden in full for his Acct.	4. 13.	4			
To Samll. Bacon of Needham for Takeing Joseph Frizell a Poor Ricketey Child of two Years Old	6. 13.	4			
To Gillam Tayler in full of his Acct.	39.	7		83. 12.	9 1/2
				£85. 5.	1 1/2

Granted by the Overseers of the Poor

To Miller 4/ To Mercy Reymer 4/		8.	
To Phillip Marlo 4/ To Hanh. Henderson 4/		8.	
To Joana Spiller 3/		3.	19.
To Hannah Dyer in full of her Disburstments			31. 4.
To Nathl. Band in full of his Acct.			4. 5. 8
			£36. 8. 8

Granted by the Overseers of the Poor

To Miller 4/ Mercy Rayner 4/	£	8.	
To Phillip Marlo 4/ To Hanh. Henderson 4/		8.	
To Johanna Spiller		3.	19.
To Hannah Dyre in full of Her Disbursments			23. 1. 6
To John Hill Esqr in full of his accot.			145. 11. 2
To Mr. Edwd. Bromfield in full of his Accot.			22. 10. 9 1/2
To Samuel Dix of Reading for keeping Sarah Teague } 26 weeks at 4/ ⅌ from Mar: 1. 1750 to Sepr. 4. 1751 }			5. 4.
			£197. 6. 5 1/2

Granted by the Overseers of the Poor

To Miller 4/ Mercy Rayner 4/		8.	
To Phillip Marlow 4/		4.	
To Hannah Henderson		4.	
To Joanna Spiller		3.	19.
To Hannah Dyre in full of her Disbur.	27. 11. 11		27. 11. 11
			£28. 10. 11

The Overseers' Finances 1738-1769

Boston Novemr. 8th: 1751.

Granted by the Overseers of the Poor

To Miller 4/ Mercy Rayner 4/	8.		
Phillip Marlow 4/ Han: Henderson 4/	8.		
Joannah Spiller	3.	19.	
To Hannah Dyer in full		65. 10. 5	
To John Phillips Esq		8. 14. 11 1/4	
To Francis Warden		3. 19. 7	
		£79. 3. 11 1/4	

Boston 4th. Decr. 1751

Granted by the Overseers of the Poor	s	£	s	d
To Miller 4/ Mercy Rayner 4/	8.			
To Phillip Marlow 4/ Han: Henderson 4/	8.			
To Joannah Spiller 3/	3.		19.	
To Hannah Dyer in full for Disbursments			36. 15. 10	
To Mr. Ebenezr. Storer			65. 8. 11 1/2	
To Andrew Oliver Esqr.			41. 19. 3	
To Isaac Walker			2. 6. 11	
			147. 9. 11 1/2	

Boston 1st. Januy. 1752

Granted by the Overseers of the Poor		s		
To Miller 4/ To Mercy Raymer 4/	£	8.		
To Phillip Marlow 4/ Han: Henderson 4/		8.		
To Joanah Spiller 3/		3.	19.	
To Mrs. Hannah Dyer in full of her Disbursments			45. 9. 3	
To a former Acct. given in of Natl. Bands	1. 18. 8			
To sd. Bands in full to this Day	1. 17. 6		3. 16. 2	
To the Honl. Jacob Wendell Esqr. in part			14. 2. 6	
			£64. 6. 11	

The Overseers' Finances 1738-1769

Boston Febry. 5 1752

Granted by the Overseers of the Poor

To Millar 4/ Mercy Rayner 4/	£	8.		
To Phillip Marlow 4/ Han: Henderson 4/		8.		
Joanna Spiller		3.	£	19.
To Hannah Dyer in ful of Her disbursments	£32. 12. 5			
Mr. John Barrett in full of his accot.	52. 15. 6 1/2			
Daniel Henchman in full of his accot.	35. 3 1/2			
Mr. John Franklin in full of his accot.	8. 9. 5			
To Colo. William Downe in full of his accot.	2. 12.			
To Joseph Lasenby in full of his account for maintaining the Distracted & Sick that are propper Subjects of the alms house	142. 17. 10			
To Joseph Sherborne in full of his accot.	30. 1	£304. 7. 7		
		£305. 6. 7		

Boston 4th. March 1752

Granted by the Overseers of the Poor

	£	s	£	s	d
To Miller 4/ To Mercy Raymer 4/	8.	0			
To Phillip Marlo 4/ To Henderson 4/	8.				
To Joanna Spiller...........................3/	3		19.		
To Hannah Dyre in part of her Disbursments			13.	6.	8
To The Honl. Jacob Wendell Esqr. his acct. in full			8.	5.	8
To John Hill Esqr. his acct. ....Do.			87.	4.	5 3/4
To Thos. Hubbart Esqr. his acct..............Do.			16.	17.	8 1/4
To Danl. Hinchman Esqr. his acct..........Do.				13.	4
To Andw. Oliver Esqr. his acct. ....Do.			8.	19.	7
To John Phillips Esqr. his acct................Do.			4.	4.	11 1/4
To Capt. Ebenr. Storrer his acct.............Do.			25.	19.	6 1/4
To Francis Wardens acct.........................Do.			9.	12.	6
To Jabez Tuttles acct. ....Do.			3.	2.	8
To John Blower's acct............................Do.				22.	4.
To Nathl. Band's acct............................Do.			3.	19.	2
To Joseph Leasenbys acct. for mentaining the Distracted & Sick that are proper Subjects of the Almshouse	£		17.	4.	
To Ms. Hana. Dyres acct. in part	3. 12.				
To Ditto in full of her Acct.	21. 6. 2		24. 18. 2		
			247. 11. 4 1/2		

744

The Overseers' Finances 1738-1769

Granted by the Overseers of the Poor

To Millar 4/ To Mercy Rayner 4/		£ 8.		
To Phillip Marlo 4/ To Herderson 4/		8.		
To Johanna Spiller		3.	£ 19.	
To Hannah Dyre			11. 11. 1	
To Joseph Lasenby's account for maintaing the Distracted & Sick that are propper Subjects of the Alms House			12. 2. 4	
To Hannah Dyre in full for one years Sallary ending 4th. March			24.	
To Doctr. Gillam Taylor in part of his account			40.	
			£88. 12. 5	

Granted by the Overseers of the Poor.

To Miller 4/ Mercy Rayner 4/ P. Marlow 4/	12.		
To Joanna Spiller 3/ Hannah Henderson 4/	7.	19.	
To Hannah Dyre in full of her Disburstments	35. 17. 9		
To Edward Bromfield in part of his Accot.	18.		
To Green & Walker in full of their Accot.	14. 2.	67. 19. 9	
		£68. 18. 9	
To Joseph Lasenby for maintanance of Distracted sick &c. subjects of the Almshouse		11.	
		£79. 18. 9	

.

Granted by the Overseers of the Poor.

To Miller 4/ Mercy Rayner 4/ P. Marlow 4/	12.		
To Joanna Spiller 3/ Hañah Henderson 4/	7.	19.	
To Hannah Dyre in full of her Disburstmts.	33. 13. 9		
To Gillam Taylor in part	30.		
To Joseph Lasenby's accot. for maintaining the Distracted & Sick &c. Subjects of the Almshouse	8. 16.		
To Francis Warden's accot. in full	16. 12. 4	89. 2. 1	
		90. 1. 1	

To David Lenox in full of his accot.   3.   9.   4
To John Williston in full . Do.   1. 17.   4   5.   6.   8
                                                                                       £95. 7.   9

Boston 1 July 1752.

Granted by the Overseers of the Poor vizt.
To   Miller 4/   Mercy Rayner 4/   P. Marlow 4/   12.
To Joanna Spiller 3/   H. Henderson 4/   7.   19.
To Hannah Dyre for her Disburstments   36. 19.   4
To Jos. Lasenby's Accot. for maintg. the Poor & distracted}
    in the Workhouse to July 1   9. 16.
To David Lenox in full of his Accot.   5. 8.   4
To John Williston in full of his Accot.   1.   8
To Docr. Jos Adams in full of his Accot.   11. 11. 10   64. 16.   2
                                                                                     65. 15.   2
To Nath. Band in full of his Accot.   20. 11.   6
                                                                                    £86. 6.   8

Boston 5 Augt. 1752

Granted by the Overseers of the Poor
To   Miller 4/   Mercy Rayner 4/   8.
To Phillip Marlow 4/   To Hannah Henderson 4/   8.
To Joanna Spiller 3/   3.   19.
To Hannah Dyre in full of her Disburstmts.   41. 18. 10
To Green & Walker in full of their Accot.   38.   11
To Isaac Walker Junr. ...... in full   2. 5.
To Francis Warden .... in full   9. 17.   3
To Charles Henly.......... in full   5. 10.   5
To Joseph Lasinby for support of the Distracted &}
    Sick in Workhouse subjects of the Almshouse }   12. 12.   110.   4.   5
                                                                                  £111.   3.   5
To Oliver & Phillips in full of their Accot.   12.   1.   8
                                                                                  £123.   5.   1

The Overseers' Finances 1738-1769

Granted by the Overseers of the Poor

To Miller 4/ Mercy Rayner 4/ Phillip Marlow 4/	12.	
To Hannah Henderson 4/ Joanna Spiller 3/	7.	19.
To Hannah Dyre in full of her Disburstments	24. 12. 7	
To Samuel Dix of Reading for keeping Sarah Teague		
a distracted Ꝑrson from 4th. Sepr. 1751. to 2 sepr.		
1752. is 51 Weeks 5. dayes @ 4/	10. 6. 10	
To Joseph Lasinby for the Support of Distracted &		
Sick Ꝑrsons in the Workhouse Subjects of the Almshouse	13. 18.	
To Doctr. Gillam Taylor in part of his Accot.	50.	
To Doctr. Miles Whitworth in part of his Accot.	30.	128. 17. 5
		129. 16. 5

Boston October 4 1752

Granted by the Overseers of the Poor

To Miller 4/ Mercy Rayner 4/ Phillip Marlow 4/	£ 12.	
To Hanh: Henderson 4/ Joanna Spiller 3/	7.	
To Hannah Dyre in full of her Disbursments	23. 16. 6	
To Joseph Lasenby for the Support of Distracted		
& Sick persons in the work House Subjects of		
the alms House	10. 9. 4	
To Nathaniel Band in full of his account	5. 6. 4	£40. 11. 2

Boston 1st. Novr. 1752

Granted by the Overseers of the Poor

To Miller 4/ Mercy Rayner 4/ Phillip Marlow 4/	12.	
To Hannah Henderson 4/	4.	16.
To Hannah Dyre in full of her Disbursms.	41. 3. 9	
To Joseph Laseninby for the Support of Distracd.		
and Sick persons in the Workhouse, Subjects		
of the Almshouse	11. 8.	
To John Roulston in full of his Acct.	9. 4	
To Thos. Williston in full of his Acct.	15. 8	
To Godfrid Kast in full of his Acct.	6.	59. 16. 9
		60. 12. 9

Boston 6 December 1752.

Granted by the Overseers of the Poor

To   Miller 4/   Mercy Rayner 4/

    Phillip Marlow 4/   Hannah Henderson 4/   16.

To Hannah Dyre in full of her Disburstmts.   55. 5. 2

To Joseph Lasinby for Support of the Distracted

    & Sick ℘rsons in Workhouse Subjects of Alms House   <u>14.</u>   70. 1. 2

Boston 3d. Jany. 1753.

Granted by the Overseers of the Poor.

To   Miller 4/   Mercy Rayner 4/

    Phillip Marlow 4/   Hannah Henderson 4/   16.

To Hannah Dyre in full of her Disburstments   40. 16. 2

To Francis Warden in full of his Accot.   8. 1. 2 1/2

To Joseph Lasinby in full for Support of the distracted

    & sick ℘rsons in Workhouse subjects of the Alms House   <u>13. 12.</u>   63. 5. 4 1/2

Feby. 8th. 1753

Granted by the Overseers of the Poor.

To Miller 4/   Mercy Rayner 4/   P. Marlow 4/

    Hannah Henderson 4/   16.

To Hannah Dyre in full of her Disburstments   33. 1. 1

To John Phillips Esqr. his Accot.   16. 7. 7

To Charles Henly in full   7. 1.

To Jos. Lasinby for Support Poor & distracted this Month   16. 14.

To Gillam Taylor in part   75.

To Docr. Miles Whitworth in full   <u>28. 18. 8</u>   175. 18. 4

Boston 28th. Feby. 1753

Granted by the Overseers of the Poor

To   Miller 4/   Mercy Rayner 4/   8.

To Phillip Marlow 4/   H. Henderson 4/   8.

To Joanna Spiller   <u>3.</u>   19.

To Hannah Dyre in full of her Disburstmts.   41. 3. 1 1/4

    deduct 100 Dollars paid by A Oliver Esqr.   <u>30.</u>   11. 3. 1 1/4

The Overseers' Finances 1738-1769

~

To John Hill Esqr. in full of his Acco 204. 4. 10 3/4

To Ebenr. Storrer & Son in full for Wood 53. 5. 10

To John Barrett Sundrys ℘ Accot. 15. 18. 2 3/4

To John Tudor in full of his Accot. to March last 16. 2. 1 3/4

To Thoms. Hubbard Esqr. disburstmts. 1. 12. 2

To Daniel Henchman Esqr. for disburstmts. 35. 10.

To Gillam Tailer in full of his accots. to 31 Jany. last 2. 7. 3 1/2

To Nathl. Band in full 2. 12.

To The heirs Execrs. or adminrs. of Saml. Dix of Reading
    for Support of Sarah Teague a Distracted ℘rson
    24 Weeks Ending this day… @ 4/ ℘ Week 4. 16.

£348. 10. 8

NB. the Above 100 Dollars advancd by A. Oliver Esqr.
    was part of the money recd. from the Country Towns, wch. is towards her Expence
    for the poor vissited wth. the small Pox

                          Boston   April 1753.

Granted by the Overseers of the Poor

To   Miller 4/ Mercy Rayner 4/ 8.

To Phillip Marlow 4/ H. Henderson 4/ 8.   16.

To Hannah Dyre in full of her disburstments 41. 2. 11

To Joseph Lasinby for Support of distracted & sick ℘rsons
    in the Workhouse subjects of the Alms House 27. 8.

To William Downe Esqr. full of his Accots. 2. 12.

To Hannah Dyre in full for One Years Sallery Endg. the
    4th. March last 24.

£95. 18. 11

                        Boston 2d. May 1753.

Granted by the Overseers of the Poor.

To   Miller 4/ Mercy Rayner 4/ 8.

To Phillip Marlow 4/ H. Henderson 4/ 8.   16.

To Hannah Dyre in full of her disburstments 24. 6. 6

To Green & Walker in full of their Accot. 27.

To Doctr. Gillam Tailor in full to this day 24. 10. 3

To Joseph Lasinby for Support of Distracted & sick ℘rsons
    in the Work House Subjects of the Alms House 11. 4.

£87. 16. 9

Boston 7th. June 1753

Granted by the Overseers of the Poor

To Miller 4/ Mercy Rayner 4/ Phillip Marlow 4/ H Henderson 4/	16.
To Hannah Dyar in full of her Disburstments	39. 11. 9
To Green & Walker in full of their Accot.	35. 13.
To Nathanl. Band in full of his Accot.	2. 2.
To Jos. Lasinby for Support of Distracted & sick ℘rsons in the Workhouse Subjects of the Alms House	15. 2.
	£93. 4. 9

Boston 4 July 1753.

Granted by the Overseers of the Poor.

To Miller 4/ Mercy Rayner 4/ Phillip Marlow 4/ H Henderson 4/	16.
To Hannah Dyre in full of her Disburstmts.	40. 15. 3
To Green & Walker in full of their Accot.	11. 3. 7 1/2
To Joseph Lasinby for Support of Distracted & sick ℘rsons in the Work House Subjects of the Alms House	15. 12.
	£63. 6. 10 1/2

Boston 2 Augt. 1753.

Granted by the Overseers of the Poor.

To Miller 4/ Mercy Rayner 4/	8.	
To Phillip Marlow 4/ H. Henderson 4/	8.	
To Joanna Spiller	3	19.
To Hannah Dyre in full of her Disburstments		74. 11. 10
To Francis Warden in full of his Accot.		6. 7. 1
To Docr. Jonathan Davis Roxbury in full his Accot.		17. 6

To The Widow of Samuel Dix of Reading for the
     Support of Sarah Teague a Distracted ℘rson
     23 Weeks @ 4/ ℘ Ending 31st. last Month
		4. 12.

To Joseph Lasinby for Support of distracted & sick
     ℘rsons in the Work house Subjects of the Alms
     House
		13. 18.

To Hannah Dyre for Interest of money She advanced for Support of the Alms house		12. 10.
To Edward Winter in full of his Accot.		16. 3 1/2
		£114. 11. 8 1/2

The Overseers' Finances 1738-1769

Boston 5th. Sepr. 1753

Granted by the Overseers of the Poor

	£	s	d
To Miller 4/ Mercy Rayner 4/ }		16.	
To Phillip Marlow 4/ H Henderson 4/ }			
To Hannah Dyre in full of her disburstments		27. 11.	
To Green & Walker in full of their Accot.		4. 12.	
To Joseph Lasinby for Support of distracted & Sick }			
𝄞rsons in the Work House Subjects of the Alms }			
House		17. 5. 4
	£50.	4.	4

Boston 3d. Octor. 1753

Granted by the Overseers of the Poor

	£	s	d
To Miller 4/ Mercy Rayner 4/		8.	
To Phillip Marlow 4/ H. Henderson 4/		8.	
To Hannah Dyre in full of her Disbursments		43. 15. 6
To Joseph Lasinby for Support of distracted and }			
Sick Persons in the Work house, Subjects of }			
the Alms house }		11. 16.
To Francis Warden in full of his acct.		2. 12. 4
To David Lenox in full of his acct.		12.
		59. 11. 10

Boston 7 Novr. 1753.

Granted by the Overseers of the Poor.

		£	s	d
To Miller 4/ Mercy Rayner 4/	8.		
To Phillip Marlow 4/ H. Henderson 4/	8.	16.	
To Hannah Dyre in full of her disburstmts.		39. 18. 10
To Green & Walker in full of their Accot.		24. 2. 8 3/4
To Doctr. Joseph Addams in full of his Accot.		48. 8. 5
To John Franklin in full of his Accot.		1. 8. 10
To Charles Henly in full of his Accot.		4. 8. 4
To Joseph Lasinby for Support of distracted & sick }			
𝄞rsons in the Work House Subjects of the Alms House }		11. 4.
	£130.	7.	6 3/4

The Overseers' Finances 1738-1769

Granted by the Overseers of the Poor.

To	Miller 4/ Mercy Rayner 4/	8.	
To Phillip Marlow 4/ H. Henderson 4/		8.	16.
To Hannah Dyre in full of her Disburstmts.			26. 7. 7
To Nath. Band in full of his Accot.			2. 8. 10
To Joseph Lasinby for Support of distracted & Sick Ꝑrsons in the Work house Subjects of the Alms House			11. 12.
			41. 4. 5
To John Blower in full of his Accot.			11. 10.
			£52. 14. 5

Granted by the Overseers of the Poor.

To	Miller 4/ Mercy Rayner 4/		
To Phillip Marlow 4/ H Henderson 4/		16.	
To Joanna Spiller Error			
To Hannah Dyre in full of her Disburstmts.		37. 5. 11	
To Doctr. Gillam Tailer in full		1. 13. 9	
To Joseph Lasinby for Support of distracted & sick Ꝑrsons in the Workhouse Subjects of the Alms House		11. 14.	51. 9. 8

Granted by the Overseers of the Poor

To	Miller 4/ Mercy Rayner 4/		
To Phillip Marlow 4/ H Henderson 4/		16.	16.
To Hannah Dyre in full of her Disburstmts.		58. 2.	
deduct money recd. of Isa. Winslow for Maintence. of German[s?] Sent here	£ 5. 10.		
deduct money Collo. Wendell supplyd. her out of what he recd. from the Country being for Expence of poor visited wth. the smallpox in this House pd. in [6th?] Feby: last	26. 13. 4	32. 3. 4	25. 18. 8

To Joseph Lasinby for Support of Distracted &
   Sick ℘rsons in the Work house Subjects of
   the Alms House

                                         11. 14.

                                         38. 8. 8

Boston 27th. Feby. 1754

Granted by the Overseers of the Poor

To Mercy Rayner 4/   Phillip Marlow 4/
   Hannah Henderson 4/   12.

To Hannah Dyar in full of her Expences   38. 12. 2

To John Hill Esqr. in full of his Accot.   132. 14. 9

To Thomas Hubbard Esqr. in full of do.   33. 12. 3

To Edward Bromfield ......in full Do.   33. 15. 7

To Andrew Oliver Esqr. ....in full Do.   18.   4

To Ebenr. Storer in full ....Do.   63. 12. 11

To Joseph Lasinby for Support of distracd.
   & Sick ℘rsons. Subjects of Alms House   11. 19.   332. 19.

Boston 3d. April 1754

Granted by the Overseers of th[e] Poor

To Mercy Rayner 4/   Phillip Marlow 4/
   Hannah Henderson 4/   12.

To Hannah Dyre in full of her Disburstmts.   48. 9. 11

To Francis Warden in full   12. 2. 11 3/4

To Charles Henly in full   3. 17. 4

To Nathl. Band in full   2. 6. 8

To Michael Burn in full   2. 14. 4

To James Bucklie in full   5. 3. 4

To The Widow of Saml. Dix of Reading
   for the Support of Sarah Teague a Distractd.
   ℘rson 35 Weeks Ending 2d. Inst. @ 4/ ℘ Week   7.

To Joseph Lasinby Support of Distracted
   & sick ℘rsons in the Work House subjects
   of the Alms House   9.   91. 6. 6 3/4

The Overseers' Finances 1738-1769

Granted by the Overseers of the Poor

To Mercy Rayner 4/ Phillip Marlow 4/ H Henderson 4/	12.		
To Hannah Dyar in full of her disburstmts	44.	6	
To Joseph Lasinby for Support of distracted & sick ⎫			
℘rsons in the Work house Subjects of the Alms Ho. ⎭	9.	4	
	£53. 12. 10		
To Aaron Clinton for keeping Joseph Clifford a poor ⎫			
child aged 15 Months to be free at 21 years, as ℘ ⎬			
Indenture ⎭	8.		
	61. 12. 10		

Granted by the Overseers of the Poor

To Mercy Rayner 4/ Phillip Marlow 4/ H Henderson 4/	12.		
To Hannah Dyar in full of her Disburstmts.	35. 18.	3	
To Edward Bromfield 50. Bushell Rye @ 2/8	6. 13.	4	
To Green & Walker in full of their Accot.	28. 5.	1 1/2	
To Joseph Lasinby for Support of distracted & ⎫			
Sick ℘rsons in the Work house Subjects of the ⎬			
Alms. house ⎭	13. 13.	4	
To Hannah Dyar One Years Sallery Ending the ⎫			
4th. March last ⎭	24.		
To Doctr. Joseph Adams in part of his Accot.	50.		
	£159. 2.	1/2	

Granted by the Overseers of the Poor

To Mercy Rayner 4/ P. Marlow 4/ H Henderson 4/	12.		
To Hannah Dyar in full of her Disburstmts.	46. 17.	2	
To Green & Walker in full of their Accot.	23. 17.	7	
To Jos. Adams in full of his Accot.	15. 18.		
To Jos. Lasinby for support of distracted & sick Prsons ⎫			
in the Work House Subjects of the Alms House ⎭	11. 17.	4	
	£99. 2.		

～∾

Granted by the Overseers of the Poor.

To Mercy Rayner 4/ P. Marlow 4/ H. Henderson 4/	12.		
To Hannah Dyar in full of her disburstmts.	45.	16.	1
To Nathl. Church for 50 Cord Wood @ 12/8	31.	13.	4
To Benja. Pollard Esqr. for Support of Nath. Smith 30 Weeks Ending 27th. July Inst. at 2/8	4.		
To Jos. Lasinby for Support of distracted & Sick ℘rsons in the Workhouse Subjects of the Alms house	11.	9.	
	£93.	10.	5

Granted by the Overseers of the Poor.

To Mercy Rayner 4/ P. Marlow 4/ H Henderson 4/	12.		
To Hannah Dyre in full of her disburstmts.	29.	8.	5
To Joseph Lasinby for support of distracted & Sick ℘rsons in the Work house Subjects of the Alms house	9.		
	£39.		5

Granted by the Overseers of the Poor

To Mercy Rayner 4/ P. Marlow 4/ H Henderson 4/	12.		
To Hannah Dyre in full of Disburstments	43.	6.	4
To Joseph Lasinby for Support of distracted & Sick ℘rsons In the work house Subjects of the Alms house.	8.	17.	4
To Francis Warden in full	6.		2
	£58.	15.	10

Granted by the Overseers of the Poor

To Mercy Rayner 4/ Phillip Marlow 4/ H Henderson 4/	12.		
To Hannah Dyar in full of her Disburstmts.	42.	2.	7
To Nath. Band in full of his Accot.	4.	13.	4
To Joseph Lasinby for Support of distracted & sick ℘rsons in the Work House Subjects of the Alms House	12.	14.	8
	£60.	2.	7

Boston 4th. Decr. 1754

Granted by the Overseers of the Poor

To Mercy Rayner 4/ Philip Marlow 4/ H Henderson 4/	12.		
To Hannah Dyar in full of her Disburstmts.	34.	19.	2
To Joseph Lasinby for Support of distracted & Sick Ørsons in the Workhouse Subjects of the Alms house	11.	7.	8
To Docr. Joseph Adams in part of his Accot.	25.		
To David Lenox in full		6.	8
	£72.	5.	6

Boston 1 Jany. 1755

Granted by the Overseers of the Poor vizt.

To Mercy Rayner 4/ P. Marlow 4/ H Henderson 4/	12.		
To Hannah Dyar in full of her Disburstmts.	41.	16.	
To Joseph Lasinby for support of distracted &c. in the Work house Subjects of the Alms House	13.	9.	4
To Francis Warden in full of his Accot.	3.	6.	8
	£59.	4.	

Boston 4 Feby. 1755

Granted by the Overseers of the Poor.

To Mercy Rayner 4/ P. Marlow 4/ H Henderson 4/	12.		
To Hannah Dyar in full of her Disburstmts.	46.	14.	3
To Edward Bromfield 20 Bus. Rye @ 2/8	2.	13.	4
To Andrew Oliver Esqr. in full	40.	13.	8 1/2
To The Widow of Samuel Dix of Reading for the Suppport of Sarah Teague a Distracted Ørson 43 Weeks Ending 30 Jany. last @ 4/	8.	12.	
To Benja. Pollard Esqr. for Support Nath. Smith 22 Weeks Ending 25 Decr. Last ....@ 2/8	2.	18.	8
To Danl. Henchman Esqr. 2 Barrells Pork…@ 3£	6.		
To Jacob Wendell Esqr. & son in full	21.	19.	7
To Jos. Lasinby for Support of distracted & sick Ørsons in the work house Subjects of the alms House	17.	16.	8
To Ebenr. Storer & son in part of their Accot.	120.		
	£268.		2 1/2

The Overseers' Finances 1738-1769

∾

Granted by the Overseers of the Poor

To Mercy Rayner 4/ P. Marlow 4/ H Henderson 4/		12.	
To Hannah Dyre in full of her Disburstmts.	34. 16. 9		
To Ditto 1 year Sallery Endg. 4th. Inst.	24.	58. 16. 9	
To John Hill Esqr. his Accot. in full		83. 16. 10	
To Ebenr. storer & son in full		33. 7. 8 1/2	
To John Barrett in full		49. 6. 10 1/2	
To Thos. Greene Esqr. in full for Wood		40.	
To Estate of B Clark Int. money		6. 4. 9 1/2	
To Jos. Lasinby for support of distracted &c.		13. 8. 8	
To Charles Henly in full		1. 8.	
To Docr. Joseph Adams in full		55. 2. 1	
		£342. 3. 8 1/2	
To Thos. Hubbard Esqr. in full		4. 10. 7	
		346. 14. 3 1/2	

Granted by the Overseers of the Poor vizt.

Mercy Rayner 4/ P. Marlow 4/ H Henderson 4/	12.	
To Hannah Dyar her Disburstments	37. 15. 5	
To Joseph Sherburne in full his Accot.	15. 11. 10	
To Joseph Lasinby for Support of Distracted & sick		
℘rsons in the Workhouse Subjects of the alms house	13. 8.	
	£67. 7. 3	

Granted by the Overseers of the Poor

To Mercy Rayner 4/ P. Marlow 4/ H Henderson 4/}	12.	
To Hannah Dyar her Disburstments	42. 6. 10	
To Green & Walker their Accot. in full	25. 19. 11	
To David Jeffries 100 Bushell Corn	12.	
To Francis Warden in full	6. 17. 4	
To Charles Henly Ditto	2. 11. 8	
To David Lenox Ditto	1. 2. 8	
To Joseph Lasinby for Support of Distracted &c.	16. 4.	
	107. 14. 5	

Granted by the Overseers of the Poor

To Mercy Rayner 4/ P. Marlow 4/ H Henderson 4/	12.		
To Hannah Dyar in full of her Disburstmts.	27.	10.	5
To Nathl. Band in full of his Accot.	5.	16.	8
To Docr. Joseph Adams in part of his Accot.	20.		
To Jos. Lasinby for Support of Distracted &c.	14.	10.	8
	68.	9.	9

Granted by the Overseers of the Poor

To Mercy Rayner 4/ P. Marlow 4/ H Henderson 4/	12.		
To Hannah Dyar in full of her disburstmts.	39.	9.	5
To The Widow of Saml. Dix of Reading for the Support of Sarah Teague a distracted ℘rson 21 Weeks 4 dayes Ending 30th. June last @ 4/	4.	6.	2
To Joseph Lasinby for Support of Distracted & sick ℘rsons in the Workhouse Subjects of the Alms House	14.	16.	
	£59.	3.	7

Granted by the Overseers of the Poor

To Mercy Rayner 4/ P. Marlow 4/ H Henderson 4/	12.		
To Hannah Dyar in full for Disburstmts.	47.	5.	8
To Docr. Silvester Gardner for curing Haslett the 1/2 pt. of his Accot: the Other paid by Collo. Henshman	1.	6.	8
To Edward Bromfield for 100 bus. Rye [is?] Corn	12.		
To Jabez Hatch Wood ℘ Accot.	8.	16.	
To Docr. Joseph Adams in full of his Accot. to 1 June…last	9.	19.	7
To Ditto in full of his Accot. to 4th. Inst.	19.	1.	4
To Francis Warden in full of his Accot.	4.	7.	4
To Joseph Lasinby for Support of Distracted & Sick ℘rsons in the Workhouse Subjects of the Alms House	18.	14.	8
	£122.	3.	3

The Overseers' Finances 1738-1769

Granted by the Overseers of the Poor

To Mercy Rayner 4/ P. Marlow 4/ H Henderson 4/		12.	
To Hannah Dyar in full of her Disburstmts.	38.	3.	7
To Benja: Pollard Esqr. in full of his Accot. for the Support of Nath. Smith	4.	12.	2
To Joseph Lasinby for Support of distracted & Sick persons in the Work House Subjects of the Alms House	15.	4.	
	£58.	11.	9

Granted by the Overseers of the Poor

To Mercy Rayner 4/ P. Marlow 4/ H Henderson 4/		12.	
To Hannah Dyar in full of her Disburstmts.	27.	2.	5
To Joseph Lasinby for Support of Distracted & sick persons in the Work House Subjects of the Alms House	13.	17.	4
	£41.	11.	9

Granted by the Overseers of the Poor

To Mercy Rayner 4/ P Marlow 4/ H. Henderson 4/		12.	
To Hannah Dyar in full of her Disburstmts.	47.	3.	7
To James Bois for 10 Cord Wood	6.	13.	4
To Nath. Band in full of his Accot.	2.	15.	6
To Francis Warden in full of his Accot.	4.	11.	8
To Joseph Lasenby for Support of Distracted & sick persons in the Work House Subjects of the Alms House	17.	18.	8
To Docr. Jos. Adams in pt. of his Accot.	25.		
	£104.	14.	9

The Overseers' Finances 1738-1769

Boston 3 Decr. 1755.

Granted by the Overseers

To Mercy Rayner 4/ P. Marlow 4/ H Henderson 4/	12.
To Hannah Dyar in full her Disburstmts.	31. 1. 7
To saml. Delucena for 6 Mo. Support of Roger Stainer Ending 2d. Inst.	2.
To Jos. Lasinby for Support of Distracted & Sick persons in the Workhouse Subjects of the Alms House	14. 8.
	£48. 1. 7

Boston 7 Jany. 1756.

Granted by the Overseers of the Poor.

To Hannah Dyre . in full of her Disburstmts.	55. 6.
To Mercy Rayner 4/ P. Marlow 4/ H Henderson 4/	12.
To Jos. Lasinby for support of Distracted & sick ℔rsons in the Work house Subjects of the Alms House	19. 12.
	£75. 10.
To Daniel Henchman Esqr. in full of his Accot.	34. 18. 4 1/4
To Ebenr. storer & son in full of their Accot.	180. 5. 7 1/2
	£290. 13. 11 3/4

Boston 4th. Feby. 1756

Granted by the Overseers of the Poor

To Mercy Rayner 4/ P. Marlow 4/ H Henderson 4/	12.
To Hannah Dyar in full of her Disburstmts.	24. 4. 7
To The Widow of Saml. Dix of Reading for the Support of Sarah Teague a distracted ℔rson 31 Weeks Ending 2d. Inst. @ 4/	6. 4.
To Docr. Jos. Adams in pt. of his Accot.	35.
To Jos. Lasinby for Support of Distracted & sick ℔rsons in the Work House Subjects of the Alms Ho.	14. 8.
Carried Over	£80. 8. 7

Granted by the Overseers of the Poor

Sum brought Over	80.	8.	7
To Francis Warden in full his Accot.	10.	18.	7 3/4
To John Blower in full his Accot.	6.	19.	8
To Edward Winter in full his Accot.		7.	9 1/2
To Abiah Holbrook............. Ditto	1.	13.	
To Roger McKnight........... Ditto	2.	13.	4
To James Clark .... Ditto		10.	2
	£103.	11.	2 1/4

Boston March 3: 1756

Granted by the Overseers of the Poor

To Mercy Reyner 4/ P Marlow 4/		8.	
To H Henderson 4/		4.	
To Hannah Dyer in full of her Disburtments	29.	16.	4
To Joseph Lasinby for Support of Distracted & Sick persons in the work house Subjects of the Almshouse	13.	6.	
To Francis Warden in full his Acct.	0.	0.	0
To Thomas Hubbard Esqr.	15.	5.	7
To Daniel Henchman Esqr. his balle.	4.	1.	5 1/2
To John Hill Esqr. .... his Acct.	77.	15.	9
To Jabez Hatch .... his Do. for bale.	30.		
To Joseph Sherburne........... his Do. for bale.	14.	2.	8
To Charles Hendley .... his Do. for Do.	3.		8
To James Fosdeck Junr......... his Do.	5.	4.	4
To Royal Tyler .... his Do.	57.	7.	4 1/4
To Andrew Oliver Esqr........ his Do.	24.	14.	3
To Nathel. Band .... his Do.	3.	16.	4
To Jacob Wendell Esqr......... his Do.	33.	11.	8 1/4
	£312.	14.	5

The Overseers' Finances 1738-1769

Boston 7 April 1756

Granted by the Overseers   the Poor

Mercy Rayner 4/ P. Marlow 4/	8.	
Hannah Henderson	4.	
To Hannah Dyar in full of her Disburstments	41. 5.	
To Ebenr. Storer & son in full their Acco.	44. 5. 6 1/2	
To Green & Walker in full Ditto	31. 3. 5	
To Isaac Walker in full..........Ditto	13. 9. 7	
To Nathl. Greenwood Ditto	21. 1. 10	
To Daniel Henchman Esqr. in full	2. 3. 1	
To The Estate Benja. Clark Interest	2. 6. 9 1/2	
To Doctr. Joseph Adams in Part	20.	
To Hannah Dyar 1 years Sallery Ending 4th. March last	24.	
To Abia Holbrook in full	12.	
To Joseph Lasinby for Support of Distracted & sick ℘rsons in the Work House Subjects of the Alms House	17. 18. 8	
To James Ellis for keeping Mary Allen a Poor distracted Woman to 26 Feby. last 52 Weeks @ 4/	10. 8.	
To saml. Biggelow for keeping Mary Smith 52 Weeks Endg. the 14th. Feby. last .. 1/4	3. 9. 4	232. 15. 3

Boston May 5th. 1756

Granted by the Overseers of the Poor

Mercy Rayner 4/ P. Marlow 4/	8.	
Hannah Henderson	4.	
Hannah Dyer in full her disburstts.	29. 14.	
John Phillips Esqr. for Cash he paid Mrs. Dyer in part of her Last Months Accot. which is deducted out	13. 6. 8	
Mr. Royall Tyler Ditto	13. 6. 8	
Mr. Isaac Smith	8. 12. 8	
Joseph Lizenby	16. 1. 4	81. 13. 4

The Overseers' Finances 1738-1769

Boston June 2d: 1756

Granted by the Overseers of the Poor to

Mercy Rayner 4/ P. Marlow 4/	8.	
Hannah Henderson	4.	
Hannah Dyer in full of her Disbursents	12. 17. 11	
Saml. Delucena for 6 Months support of Roger Strainer ending 2d: Inst	2.	
Francis Warden in full of his Accot:	8. 18. 7	
Nathaniel Band ditto	2. 13. 8	
Joseph Lazenby for the support of the Sick & Distracd: in the Workhouse Subjects of the Almshouse	13. 10. 8	
Dr: Joseph Adams in full to this day	50. 14. 8	
David Lenox in full of his Acct:	1. 16.	
John Williston .... ditto	1. 4.	
Thomas Williston .... ditto	17. 7	95. 5. 1

Boston July 7th: 1756

Granted by the Overseers of the Poor

To Mercy Rayner 4/ P: Marlow 4/	8.	
Hannah Henderson	4.	
Hannah Dyer in full of her Disbursents	33. 16. 9	
Jacob Wendell Esqr: in part of his Accot:	14.	
Thomas Flucker so much supplyd Mrs: Dyer	20.	
Phillips & Apthorp in full	31. 10.	
John Willston .... ditto	2. 9. 2 1/2	
Thomas Williston ..... ditto	1. 16.	
Joseph Lazinby for the support of the Sick & Distracted in the Workhouse Subjects of the Almshouse	14. 12.	
		118. 15. 11 1/2

Boston 5 Augst: 1756

Granted by the Overseers of the Poor

To Mercy Rayner	£ 4.	
Philip Marlow	4.	
Hannah Henderson	4.	
Hannah Dyer in full of her Disbursents	32. 16. 2	

David Lenox		0.	0		
Nathl: Band		3. 16.	2		
David Lenox		1. 2.	8		
Joseph Lazenby for support of the Sick & Distracd: in the Workhouse Subjects of the Almshouse		11. 14.	8		
Jonathen Sympson			9. 4		
Thomas Ethridge		1. 9.	4		
Joseph Pynchon Esqr: in full for Medicines & Attendance of Chapman		10.			
Francis Warden		9. 15.	6	71. 15. 10	

Boston 1 Sepr: 1756

Granted by the Overseers of the Poor

To Mercy Rayner	£	4.		
Philip Marlow		4.		
Hannah Henderson		4.		
Hannah Dyer in full of her Disburstmts: £28. 11				
1/2 Years Salary ending the 4th: Inst: 12.		40. 11		
Phillips & Apthorp 200 bus: Corn		26. 13. 4		
Joseph Lazenby for support of the Sick & Distracd: in the Workhouse Subjects of the Almshouse		12. 6. 8		
Charles Henley		1. 5.		
Edward Winter		12. 6		
John Roulston		12.		
Thomas Williston		3. 4.	85. 6. 5	

Boston Octor: 6. 1756

Granted by the Overseers of the Poor

To Mercy Rayner	£ 0.	4.		
Philip Marlow		4.		
Hannah Henderson		4.		
Samuel Procter in full of his Disburstments		40. 9. 10		
Joseph Lazenby for support of the Sick & Distracd: in the Workhouse Subjects of the Almshouse		16. 7. 4		
Jacob Wendell Esqr: & Son in full of his accot.		14.		
John Williston		12.		
Nathaniel Band		3. 8. 6	75. 9. 8	

❧

Boston 3d. Novr. 1756

Granted by the Overse[e]rs of the Poor

To Mercy Rayner 4/   P. Marlow 4/ ⎱

To Hannah Henderson 4/   ⎰   12.

To Saml. Procter in full of his Accot.   38. 19. 8

To Jos. Lasinby for Support of the ⎫

   Sick & distracted in the Work ⎬

   house Subjects of the Alms House ⎭   10. 18. 8

To Doctr. James Pecker in full to ⎱

   10th. August last Deductg. Medicines ⎰   21. ———   71. 10. 4

Boston 1 Decr: 1756

Granted by the Overseers of the Poor

To Mercy Rayner…Dead   0.[61]

   Philip Marlow   4.

   Hannah Henderson   4.

   Samuel Procter in full of his Accot: 52. 11. 2 1/2

   David Lenox…ditto   0.   0.   0

   John Phillips Esqr: ditto   2.   3. 2 1/2

   The Estate of Benja: Clark Interest   2.   2. 10

   Joseph Lasinby for Support of the Sick ⎫

   & Distracted in the Work house Subjects ⎬

   of the Almshouse   ⎭   11. 4. 8   68. 10.

Boston 5th: Janry: 1757

Granted by the Overseers of the Poor

To Philip Marlow   4.

   Hannah Henderson   4.

   Samuel Procter in full of his Accot: 27. 8. 10 3/4

   Joseph Lasenby for Support of the Sick & ⎫

   Distracted in the Work house Subjects of ⎬

   the Almshouse   ⎭   15. 13. 4

   John Clark Esqr: in full of his Accot: 33. 9.

   William Sutton . . ditto   1. 6. 10

   Samuel Dulucena for 6 Months support of ⎱

   Roger Stayner ending the 7th: Decr: ⎰   2. ———   80. 6.   3/4

The Overseers' Finances 1738-1769

Granted by the Overseers of the Poor

To Philip Marlow	4.		
To Hannah Henderson	4.		
To Samuel Procter in full of his accot:	17.	10.	10
To Joseph Lasenby for the Support of the Sick & Distracted in the Work house Subjects of the Almshouse	12.	6.	8
To Green & Walker in full of their accot:	79.	13.	1
To Phillips & Apthorp 35 Hogs 4530[ee?]: @ 2d: 10/15	50.	6.	8
To John Phillips in full of his accot:	1.	4.	4
To Jacob Wendell Esqr:........... ditto	26.	8.	7
To Francis Warden	12.	8.	8
To the Widow of Saml: Dix of Reading for the Support of Sarah Teague a Distracted Person from 2d: Febry: 1756 to this day is 52 Weeks................ @ 4/	10.	8.	
To David Lenox in full of his accot:	1.	10.	8

212. 5. 6

Granted by the Overseers of the Poor

To Philip Marlow 4/ To Hannah Henderson 4/	8.		
To Samuel Procter in full of his Disbursments £7. 12. 1 3/4			
Interest allowed for his Advance 4.			
1/2 Years Salary ending the 1st: Inst: 12.	23.	12.	1 3/4
To Joseph Lazenby for the Support of the Sick & Distracted in the Workhouse Subjects of the Almshouse	12.	10.	8
To John Hill Esqr:...........................his accot:	8.	8.	6
To Isaac Walker ....ditto	12.	5.	
To John Barrot..................................ditto	42.	1.	10 1/2
To Royall Tyler ....ditto	72.	16.	2 1/2
To William Phillips............................ditto	21.		7
To Andrew Oliver Esqr:.....................ditto	39.		
To Nathaniel Greenwood ....ditto	23.	5.	7 1/2
To Thomas Fluker Esqr:....................ditto	35.	5.	3
To John Tudor ....ditto	23.	13.	5
To Ebenezer Storer Esqr: & Son........ditto	187.	10.	1 1/2

To Samuel Downe ....ditto	24.	13.	1			
To Nathaniel Band...........................ditto	4.	8.	2			
To Edward Winter ....ditto	4.	13.	3			
To Peter Cooledge for Mary Allen a disordered Woman	5.	1.	7			
To Jabez Hatch　　　　　　　his accot:	35.			575.	13.	5 3/4

Boston 6th: Apr: 1757

Granted by the Overseers of the Poor

To Philip Marlow	4.					
To Hannah Henderson	4.					
To Andrew Oliver Esqr: for Cash he paid Mr: Procter in part of the last Months accot: which is deducted out	20.					
To Samuel Procter in full of his Disburstments	6.	8.	8 3/4			
To Nathl: Greenwood in full of his accot:	2.		1			
To Joseph Lasenbey for the Support of the Sick & Distracted in the Workhouse Subjects of the Almshouse	13.	13.	4			
To Samuel Bigelow for keeping Mary Smith from 14th: Febry: 1756 to the 4th: Inst: is 59 Weeks　　　　@ 1/4	3.	18.	8	46.	8.	9 3/4

Boston May. the 4o. 1757

Granted by the Overseers of the Poor

To Philip Marlow	0.	4.	0			
To Hannah Henderson	4.					
To Samuell Proctor	7.	2.	10			
To John Phillips Esqr. for Cash. he paid Mr. Proctor in part. of the last Mo. Acct. deducted	20.					
To Ebenezer Storer Esqr. for Ditto...as above	20.					
To Mr. Isaac Walker for Ditto as ℘ Do.	20.					
To Joseph Lasenby for the Support of the sick & Distracted in the Work House Subjects of the Almshouse	10.	18.	8			
To James Boies...for his Acct. for Wood	31.	13.	4			
To Edes & Gill...for Paper & Warrants	1.	5.	4	111.	8.	2

The Overseers' Finances 1738-1769

Boston June the 1st. 1757.

Granted by the Overseers of the Poor

To Philip Marlow	0. 4. 0	
To Hannah Henderson	0. 4. 0	

To Joseph Lasenby . for his Acct: for the Support
of the Sick & Distracted in the Work
House Subjects of the Almshouse   13. 8. 8   13. 16. 8

Carrd. Over

Brought Forward   £13. 16. 8

To Samuel Delucene…for boarding Roger
Stayner…from the 7o. Jany. 1757. to the 7o. Inst.   2.

To John Tudor…for Cash he paid Mr. Proctor
in part of the last Mo: Acct. Deducted   20.

To Samuell Robinson…for Acct. for boarding
& Nursing Samuell Williams
a Distracted person   10. 5. 8

To Francis Warden his Acct. for Work for the
Almshouse   21. 13. 2 1/2

To Robert Fulton…his Acct. for Diging a Drean: 3. 15. 0   71. 10. 6 1/2

Boston July the 5th. 1757.

Granted by the Overseers of the Poor viz

To Philip Marlow	0. 4. 0	
To Hannah Henderson	0. 4. 0	

To Joseph Lazenby…for the Support of the
sick & Distracted in the Work House subjects
of the Almshouse   13. 13. 4

To Mr. William Phillips…for Cash he paid Mr.
Proctor in part of the last Month's Acct. deducted   20.

To Mr. Royall Tyler…for…Ditto   20.

To Mr. John Barrett…for…Ditto   39. 6. 3

To Samuell Proctor…for his acct. in the Month: of May[21]   9. 19. 6 1/2

To Ebenezer Storer Esqr. & son   64. 11. 0

To James Ellis…Acct. for keeping Mary Allen
from the 4o. March 1756 to 22d. Sepr. following
28 Weeks @ 4/ 1 ⍺ shoes 4/4 1/2   5. 19. 4 1/2

To Samuel Proctor…for his Acct. in June	5. 14. 6	
To Thomas Flucker Esqr. for Cash pd. Benja.⎫ Phillips…for 100 Cord ⎬	56. 13. 4	

To Peter Coollidge…for his Acct. for keeping ⎫
   Mary Allen…from the 2d. March to the 6 July…with ⎬
   shoes &c as ℘ Acct. ⎭
	4. 18. 7	

To Cornelius Sweasey…for Nursing Margartt ⎫ McCunnelhey ⎬	2. 2. 8	243. 6. 7

Boston August the 4o. 1757

LM

Granted by the Overseers of the Poor		
To Phillip Marlow	0. 4. 0	
To Hannah Henderson	0. 4. 0	
To Joseph Lasinby	11. 9. 4	
To Samuell Proctor…for his ballance	3. 17. 6 1/4	
To John Blowers…in full…for his Acct.	36. 11. 7	
To James Pitts Esqr. for Cash Advancd. Mr. Proctor	55. 14. 8	
To Mr. William Phillips…for Ditto	20.	
To James Pecker…for One Years Salary. ⎫ Ending the 10o. Instant ⎬	100.	228. 1. 1 1/4

Boston September the 7th. 1757

LM

Granted by the Overseers of the Poor		
To Phillip Marlow	0. 4. 0	
To Hannah Henderson	0. 4. 0	
To Joseph Lasinby…for his Acct.	16. 4. 0	
To Samuell Proctor…in full for his Acct. Last Mo.	11. 19. 6	
To Mr. Benjamin Dolebeare for Cash Advand.	20.	
To Isaac Smith ………………… for Ditto	20.	
To Nathaniel Band………for his Acct. for burying	4. 1. 4	
To James Pitts Esqr. for Cash pd. for 50 bus. Corne	6.	
To Samuell Proctor…for…halfe a Years Salary ⎫ Ending the first Instant £12. 0. 0 ⎬	12.	90. 12. 10

The Overseers' Finances 1738-1769

Granted by the Overseers
 of the Poor—vizt.

To Philip Marlow 4/   4.

To Royal Tyler for support of   }
 John Presman before he
 came into the Alms House   }   2. 1. 10 1/2

To Joseph Lasinby support of
 the Idle & Indigent distracted
 &c. in the Work House Subjects of
 the Alms House as ℘ Accot.   }   12.

To Samuell Proctor…for the ballo. of his Acct.   7. 3. 7

To Andrew Oliver Esqr…for Cash . Advancd.   20.

To David Lenox . for his bill for Burying }
 of Severall Persons   0. 12. 10   42. 2. 3 1/2

Granted by the Overseers of the Poor

Phillip Marlow   0. 4. 0

John Tudor…for Cash pd. for 260 bushs. Corn }
 the 4 Augs. last   31. 4. 0

John Phillips Esqr. for Cash . Advance   20.

Isaac Smith . for Cash pd. for 40 Cord Wood @ 11/4 }
 the 5 July   22. 13. 4

Samuell Proctor . for the ballo. of his Acct. last Mo.   37. 5. 7

Joseph Lasenby for his Acct. . to this day   11. 9. 4

John Raulstone for his bill for burying }
 James Croxford   0. 10. 8   123. 6. 11

Boston December the 7o. 1757

Granted by the Overseers of the Poor

Phillip Marlow   0.   4.   0

Joseph Lasinby . . for the Support of *<the Idle*

    & Indigent> the Distracted Subjects of the Almhouse}   15.   8.   0

Carrd. Over   £15. 12.   0

Brought Over   £15. 12.   0

John Larrabee . . for making a Coffin   0.   6.   8

To Samuell Proctor . . for the ballance of his}

    Acct. last Month   39.   3.   2 3/4

To Royal Tyler . . for Cash Advancd.   20.

To John Tudor . . for Cash Advancd.   20.

To Peter Coollidge . . for Nursing Mary Allen a

    Distracted Woman from the 6o. July last to the

    <7o. July> to this Day is 22 Weeks @ 4/ & for

    a Petticoat is 10/8}   4. 18.   8

To Francis Warden . for his Acct. to this day   16.   9.   6

To Edward Winter . . for . . . Ditto   3.   1. 10

To Samuell Delucene . . for Board of Roger}

    Stayner . from the 7o. June to this day is 6 mo.}   2._____ 121. 11. 10 3/4

Boston January the 4th. 1758

Granted by the Overseers of the Poor

Phillip Marlow   0   4.   0

Joseph Lasenby . for his bill . . for . the Support}

    of the *<Idle &>* Distracted & sick Subjects of}

    the Almshouse   11.   1.   8

To Royal Tyler . . for Cash Advancd.   20.

To John Phillips Esqr. for his Acct. for Money}

    Advancd. as ℘ Accompt to Saml. Parsons}   3. 17.   4

To Samuell Proctor . . for the ballance of his}

    Acct. last Month   45. 17.   8

£81.   0.   8   81.   0.   8

The Overseers' Finances 1738-1769

Granted by the Overseers of the Poor

Phillip Marlow	0.	4.	0
Joseph Lasinby for his bill for the Support)			
of the sick & Distracted)	12.		
William Phillips … for Cash Advancd.	20.		
Carrd. Over	£32.	4.	0

Brought Over	£32.	4.	0
Isaac Smith for Cash Advancd.	20.		
Benjamin Dolebear....................Ditto	20.		
John Barrett..............................Ditto	21.	3.	6
To Samuell Bigelo …for keeping Mary Smith			
from the 4o. Aprill 1757… to the 6o. . . Inst. is			
44 Weeks @ 20d.}	3.	13.	4
Isaac Walker ....for his Accompt… to this day	7.	10.	10
Hone. Jacob Wendell Esqr. & sons.......... Ditto	35.	9.	4
Hono. Andrew Oliver Esqr.................... Ditto	12.	0.	7
Benjamin Dolbeare .... Ditto	18.	3.	2
To the Widow of Saml. Dix . of Reading for the			
Support of Sarah Teague a Distracted Person from			
the 2d. Feb of 1757…to the 2d. Inst. is			
52 Weeks @ 4/ 10. 8. 0	10.	8.	0

180. 12. 9

Granted by the Overseers of the Poor. viz

Phillip Marlow	0.	4.	0
Joseph Lasinby . . for his bill for the Support of the)			
sick & Distracted)	12.	18.	4
Nathaniel Band . . for his bill for Buryalls	2.	2.	2
William Phillips .....in full ..... of his Accot. to this day	13.	0.	7
Isaac Smith ....in full......of .... Ditto	26.	16.	10 1/2
Benjamin Dolebeare in full ...of .... Ditto	3.	13.	0
Isaac Walker ....in full......of .... Ditto	1.	8.	1
John Tudor.............in full......of .... Ditto	16.	0.	6 3/4

∾

Ebenezer Storer Esqr. & son in full of .... Ditto	16.	13.	6 3/4
Thomas Flucker Esqr. in full of .... Ditto	21.	6.	3 1/2
John Barrett...........in full.....of .... Ditto	10.	13.	0
Royall Tyler ....in full ....of .... Ditto	21.	16.	8
Obediah Law .....for his Acct. for makeing a Cistern &c.	15.	9.	0
John Ronsted ....for his Acct. for Burying Sundy. persons	0.	12.	0
James Pitts Esqr. ... in full...of Ditto	20.	4.	5 1/4
Samuell Proctor ...for the ballance of last Month Acct.	25.	0.	0 1/2
Ditto...Proctor... for Interest of Money Advd. of Town	7.	6.	10 3/4
Hono. ... Andrew Oliver...in full...of his Acct.	2.	8.	9
Carrd. Over	£217	11	3[22]

Boston Aprill the 5th. 1758

Granted by the Overseers of the Poor viz				
To Roger McKnight ... his Acct. for Diging a [Unit?]	20.	5.	0	
To Joseph Lasenby for his Acct. for keeping the Distracted & sick Subjects of the Almshouse	15.	3.	4	
To Phillip Marlow		4.		
To Samuell Proctor...for his Acct. last Month	44.	9.	8 1/4	£80. 2. 0 1/4

Boston May 3 1758

Granted by the overseers of the Poor vizt.				
To Joseph Lasinby for his accot. for keeping the Distracted & Sick Subjects of the alms House	11.	9.	4	
To Samuel Proctor for his accot. Last month		7.	1 1/4	
To James Gardner Truckage		14.	8	12. 11. 1 1/4
To Phillip Marlow				4.
				£12. 15. 1 1/4

Boston June 7th. 1758.

Granted by the Overseers of the Poor—Vizt.

To Benja: Dolbeare for Service done in the house	8.		
To John Phillips Esqr. Cash advanced	10.		
To Melatiah Bourn Do. advand. Last month	10.		
To Isaac Smith Do. Lent this month	10.		
To Thomas Flucker Do.	10.		
To Joseph Lasinbey his accot. for Keeping the Disstracted & Sick, Subjects of the almshouse	15.		
To Samuel DeLucene in full for Boarding Roger Stayner to the first Instant	2.		
To Francis Warden for his accot. for Coffins &c. to this time	5. 4		
To Peter Coollidge for his accot. for Keeping the Widdow Mary Allen &c. to this time	6. 5	68. 8. 9	
To Samuel Procter for Ballance his account last month		11. 7 1/4	
		£79. 9. 4 1/4	

Town of Boston   Dr:

Sum Brought Forward	£70. 8 1/2	1374. 15. 1	
Royall Tyler ....Ward No. 1	21. 16. 8		
Thomas Flucker Esqr. 11	21. 6. 3 1/2		
William Phillips 10	13. 7		
James Pitts Esqr. 7	20. 4. 5 1/4		
Benjamin Dolbear 5	21. 16. 2		
Isaac Smith 12	26. 16. 10 1/2	195. 1. 8 3/4	
		£1569. 16. 9 3/4	

Supra   Cr:

By Province Accot. for Board of Sundry Persons
    in the Almshouse from 1 March 1757 to 1st.
    September   63. 15. 3

By Ditto from 1st. Sept: to 1 March 1758   92. 8. 5 1/4   156. 3. 8 1/4

By Sundrys drawn for this year which was
   Expended last year viz:

James Boies for Wood	£31. 13. 4
Francis Warden, Repairs	21. 13. 2 1/2
John Blowers ditto	36. 11. 7
Jacob Wendell Sugar & Wood	9. 2. 8
Saml. Bigelow keepg. Mary Smith	3. 18. 8
Saml. Robinson do. Saml. Williams	10. 5. 8
James Ellis do. Mary Allen	5. 19. 4 1/2 119. 4. 6
	£275. 8. 2 1/4

Ballance of the Above Accot: which is the Town Expence⎫
    for the Poor this year   ⎭   1294.   8.   7 1/2

£1569. 16. 9 3/4

old Tenor

Expended in	1738	£3298. 17. 6	Expended in 1750 Law: Money	£1483. 5. 5	
	1739	3103. 19. 2	1751	1310. 1. 5 1/4	
	1740	3489. 15. 3	1752 Small Pox	1362. 6. 6 1/2	
	1741	4187. 4	1753	1175. 14. 3/4	
Built New End	1742	8514. 8. 8	1754	1408. 16. 9 1/2	
	1743	5058. 9. 11	1755 1384. 17. 8	1636. 14. 6 1/2	
	1744	4627. 16. 2	1756 1769. 6. 11	1636. 14. 6 1/2	
	1745	5925. 3. 6	drawn for in 1757 ⎫		
	1746	5516. 7. 3	which was Expended ⎬		
	1747	10333. 14. 0	in 1756 ⎭ 119. 4. 6		
	1748	10897. 11. 3	3273. 9. 1		
	1749	10671. 10. 10			

Old Tenor   £75,624. 13. 10

Began & Ended by Mr. Wm. Phillips
this Memo: is made by the Unanimous
Order of the Overseers June 1758

NB These two years are put
together as great part of
the Expence of 1755 was drawn
for in 1756

Expended 1757 £1569. 16. 9 3/4

deduct Expenses⎫
in 1756   ⎭ 119. 4. 6   1450. 12. 3 3/4

£11,464. 5. 7 1/2

The Overseers' Finances 1738-1769

Boston July 5th. 1758

Granted by the Overseers of the Poor—Vizt:

To Joseph Lasinby for His accot. for keeping the subjects of the Alms House	12.	1.	4
To Phillip Marlow for two months	8.		
To Ebenezer Storor Esqr. & son	31.	14.	5
To Phillips & Apthrop	7.	17.	1
To Ebenezer Storor Esqr. . Money Advd.	10.		
To Mr. John Barret...................... do.	10.		
To Mr. John Tuder .... do.	10.		
To John Phillips Esqr.	8.	3.	1

90.   3.   11

Boston August 2d. 1758.

Granted by the Overseers of the Poor .... Vizt:

To Joseph Lasinby for his accot. for keeping the subjects of the alms house	14.	10.	8			
To Royal Tyler Esqr. …Money Advd.	10.					
To Mr. William Phillips .... do.	10.					
To James Pitts Esqr................ do.	10.					
To Samuel Procter	13.	6.	8 1/2	57.	17.	4 1/2

Boston September 6th. 1758.

Granted by the Overseers of the Poor .... Vizt.

To Phillip Marlow for two Months	8.					
To Joseph Lasenby for his accot: for keeping the Distracted & Sick Subjects of the Alms House	20.	5.	4			
To Nathaniel Band for Alms House Funerals	4.	12.	10			
To Isaac Walker … for Money Advanced	10.					
To Benjamin Dolbeare..............do.	10.					
To Samuel Procter for half years Salary due 1st. Int:	12.					
To Samuel Procter for Ballance Last mo. acct.	4.	13.	11			
To Edward Winter	1.	19.	7	63.	19.	8

776

The Overseers' Finances 1738-1769

❧

Boston October 4th. 1758.

Granted by the Overseers of the Poor ....Viztt.

To Phillip Marlow	4.	
To Joseph Lasinby for his accot. for keeping the Disstracted & Sick Subjects of the alms House	13. 17. 4	
To Samuel Deluceney for Boarding Roger Staner to 1st. Instant 4 mo.	1. 6. 8	
To Samuel Procter . his Ballance	18. 1	33. 8. 1

Boston Novemr. 1t. 1758

Granted by the Overseers of the Poor .... Vizt:

To Phillip Marlow	4.	
To Joseph Lasinby for his accot. for keeping the Disstracted & Sick Subjects alms house	13. 12.	
To Nathl. Band	2. 1. 8	
To William Sutton	1.	
To James Pitts Esqr.	15. 3. 6	
To Mess Phillips & Apthorp	7. 17. 1 this drawn for 5th. July	
To Melatiah Bourn	5. 6. 9 1/2	
To Samuel Procter his Ballance	29. 1. 9 1/2	
To the Widow of Sam Dix of Reding for the Support of Sarah Teague a Disstracted Person from 2d: February to 2 Augt. Last is 26 weeks…@ 4/ ⅌ week	5. 4.	
To Samuel Mansfield his acct. for Shoes the Ballance at this day	11.	90. 10. 10

Decemr. 6: 1758

Granted by the Overseers of the Poor .... Vizt.

To Phillip Marlow	4.	
To Joseph Lasinby for his accot. for keeping the Disstracted, & sick subjects Alms house	15. 18.	
To John Mills Carpenter Coffins &c	9. 7. 2	
To Samuel Procter for his account	117. 8. 8	142. 17. 10

The Overseers' Finances 1738–1769

❧

Boston Januy. 3d. 1759.

Granted by the Overseers of the Poor .... Vizt.

To Phillip Marlow   4.

To Joseph Lasinby for his account for keeping
 the Disstracted & sick subjects of the
 Alms House   11. 9. 4

To Peter Coollidge for Keeping the Widow
 Mary Allen from the 7th. day of June
 Last to this day 30 Weeks @ 4/ 6.

To James Pecker for 3/4 years Salery from
 10th. augt. 1757…to 10th. May 1758 £75.

To Ditto for half a year from 10th.
 May 1758 to 10th. Novemr. 30. 105.

To Samuel Procter for the Ball. his accot. 51. 6. 6 3/4

To John Mills for his accot. to this time 8. 11. 6 182. 11. 4 3/4

Boston February 7th. 1759.

Granted by the Overseers of the Poor .... Vizt:

To Phillip Marlow   0. 4.

To Joseph Lasinby for his accot. for Keeping
 the Disstracted, & Sick subjects of the
 Alms House   16. 6. 8

To Ebenezer Storor Esqr. & son their accot. for
 Supplyes to alms House   20. 9. 7 1/4

To James Pitts Esqr. Ditto   6. 7. 11 1/2

To The Widow of Samuel Dix of Reading
 for the Support of Sarah Teague a Disstracted
 Person from 2d. augt. Last to the 2d. Instt. 5. 4.

To Samuel Bigelo for Keeping Mary Smith
 from 6th. February 1758 to 6th. Instant
 52 Weeks—@ 20d.   4. 6. 8

To Samuel Procter for the Ballance of his
 accot.   41. 12. 11 1/4 94. 11. 10

The Overseers' Finances 1738-1769

Boston March 7 1759.

Granted by the Overseers of the Poor .... Viztt.

To Phillip Marlow				0. 4.
To Joseph Lasinbey his accot. for Keeping the Sick, & disstracted, Subjects of alms House				11. 18.
To Nathanael Band accot. to this time				5. 1.
To Samuel Procter for half years Salery due [1]st. instant		12.		
To Ditto for Interest of money advanced} the Town		8.	20.	
To Thomas Dawse his accot.			12. 1.	9
To Royal Tyler Esqr.	no. 1. in full		31. 14.	6 1/2
To Mr. John Tudor	2. Ditto		19. 2.	7
To Ebenezr. Storor Esqr. & son	3. Ditto		34. 10.	
To Mr. John Barrett	4. Ditto		11. 19.	
To Mr. Benja: Dolbeare	5. Ditto		27.	6
To Mr: Isaac Walker	6. Ditto		12. 3.	
To James Pitts Esqr.	7. Ditto		39. 8.	9
To John Phillips Esq	8. Ditto		1. 16.	
To Mr. William Phillips	9. Ditto		15. 19.	
To Melatiah Bourn	10. Ditto		42. 12.	3
To Thomas Flucker Esqr.	11. Ditto		56. 6.	6
To Mr. Isaac Smith	12. Ditto		38. 17.	6 1/4
To Samuel Procter Ballance his accot.			9. 18.	9

390. 13. 1 3/4

Memo. the whole Expence of the year[23]

An Account of Expences…for the Almshouse & the Poor out of
the House from March 1758 …to March 1759

Expense..........in Aprill	£80. 2.	0 1/4
Ditto ....in May	12. 15.	1 1/4
.....................in June	79. 9.	4 1/4
.....................in July	90. 3.	11
.....................in August	57. 17.	4 1/2
.....................in September	63. 19.	8
.....................in October	33. 8.	1
.....................in November	90. 10.	10

.... in December	142. 17. 10	
.... in January	182. 11. 4 3/4	
.... in February	94. 11. 10	
.... in March	390. 13. 1 3/4	1318. 19. 8 3/4

Sundry Draughts . drawn on the Town Treasurer⎫
for Wood Grain &c ⎬ 277. 12. 3
                                                            £1596. 11. 11 3/4

Deduct . for Sundry Draughts on		
the Province Treasurer viz	139. 8. 8 1/4	
	116. 6. 3	
	160. 0. 0	415. 14. 11 1/4
		£1180. 17. 1/2

Boston April 4th. 1759.

Granted by the Overseers of the Poor .... Viztt.

To Phillip Marlow	0. 4.	
To Joseph Lasinby for his accot. for keeping⎫		
the Sick & Disstracted Subjects of almshouse⎭	11. 0. 0	
To Samuel Procter his accot.	45. 18. 4 1/4	57. 2. 4 1/4
To Abiel Holbrook	12.	
		£57. 14. 4 1/4

Boston May 2d. 1759.

Granted by the overseers of the Poor.. Viztt.

To Phillip Marlow	0. 4.	
To Joseph Lasenby his accot. for Keeping⎫		
the Sick & Disstracted subjects		
of the Alms House ⎭	12. 0.	
To Samuel Procter for the Ballance⎫		
of his account ⎭	64. 13. 4 1/2	
To John Mills Carpenter for his⎫		
accot. up to this time ⎭	27. 17. 4	104. 14. 8 1/2

The Overseers' Finances 1738-1769

~

Boston June 6th. 1759.

Granted by the overseers of the Poor... Viztt.

To Phillip Marlow	4.	
To Joseph Lasenby his accot. for Keeping the Sick & Disstracted Subjects of the Alms House	15. 0. 0	
To Samuel Procter for the ballance his accot.	<u>73. 0. 0 3/4</u>	<u>88. 4. 0 3/4</u>

Boston July 4th. 1759.

Granted by the Overseers of the Poor .... Viz

To Phillip Marlow	0. 4.	
To Joseph Lasinby his accot. for keeping the Sick & Disstracted, Subjects of the Alms House	15. 4.	
To Samuel Procter for the Ballance of his account	51. 13. 11 3/4	
To Samuel Mansfield for his accot. for Shoes to this day	<u>31. 10.</u>	<u>98. 11. 11 3/4</u>

Boston 1st. August 1759

Granted by the Oversers of the Poor .... Vizt.

To Philip Marlow	£0. 4.	
To Joseph Lasenby his Accot. for keeping the Sick & Distracted Subjects of the Alms-House	13. 16.	
To Peter Coolidge for Keeping Mary Allen 26 Weeks &c .. ℘ Accot.	6. 4.	
To Samuel Procter for the Balla. of his Accot.	58. 17. 10 1/2	
To John Mills his Accot. for Carpenters Work	<u>30. 9. 10</u>	<u>109. 11. 8 1/2</u>

The Overseers' Finances 1738-1769

Granted by the Oversers of the Poor Viztt.

To Phillip Marlow	4.					
To Joseph Lasenby his accot. for keeping the Sick & Distracted Subjects of the Alms House	15.	0.	0			
To Nathanael Band for Alms House Funerals &c	4.	10.	4			
To Samuel Procter half a Years Salary due first Instant	12.					
To Samuel Procter for the Ballance of his account	36.	2.	11	67.	17.	3

Granted by the Overseers of the Poor .... Vizt.

To Phillip Marlow	4.					
To Joseph Lasenby for his accot. for Keeping the Disstracted & Sick subjects of Alms House	13.	1.	4			
To Edward Winter his Bills for repairs	2.	3.	7			
To Doctr. James Pecker for half a years Salery from 10th. novr. 1758 to 10th. May 1759 in full	30.					
To Samuel Procter for the Ballance of his accot.	28.	19.	10	74.	8.	9

Granted by the Overseers of the Poor .... Viztt.

To Phillip Marlow	4.					
To Joseph Lasenby for his accot. for keeping Distracted & Sick Subjects of the Alms House	14.	6.	8			
To Samuel Procter for the Ballance of his accot.	71.	9.	1/2	85.	19.	8 1/2

The Overseers' Finances 1738-1769

Boston Decembr. 5 1759

Granted by the Overseers of the Poor .... Viztt.

To Phillip Marlow	0.	4.	
To Joseph Lasenby for his accot. for Keeping the Sick, & Disstracted subjects of the Alms House	10.	8.	0
To Samuel Procter for the Ballance of his accounts	50.	3.	1 3/4 60. 15. 1 3/4

Boston Januy. 2d. 1760.

Granted by the Overseers of the Poor .... Vizt.

To Phillip Marlow	0.	4.	
To Joseph Lasenby for his account for Keeping the Sick & Distracted subjects of the Alms House	10.	8.	
To John Mills Carpentor for his accot. to this day	21.	12.	11 1/2
To Samuel Bigelo for Supporting Mary Smith from 6th. February 1759 to 26 Decembr. following is 46 weeks—@ 20d:	3.	16.	8
To John Phillips Esqr. for Cash advd. Mr. Procter	26.	13.	4
To Samuel Procter for the Ballance of his accot.	43.	18.	6 1/2 106. 13. 6

Boston February 6th: 1760.

Granted by the Overseers of the Poor .... Viztt.

To Phillip Marlow	0.	4.	
To Joseph Lasenby his accot. for Keeping the Subjects of the alms House	15.	3.	4
To Mr. William Phillips Cash lent	20.		
To Mr. John Tudor .... Ditto	6.	13.	4

To Peter Cooledge for Keeping the Widow
   Mary Allen from 4th. July 1759 to 2d. Jany.
   26 weeks @ 4/ ℘ week   5. 4. 0
   Clothing for Ditto   <u>1. 8. 4</u>   <u>6. 12. 4</u>
                                             48. 13. 0

The Grant Continued   48. 13. 0

To The Widow of Samuel Dix of Reding
   for the support of Sarah Teague a Disstr-
   acted Person from the 2d. Feby. 1759.
   to 2d. Instant 52 Weeks @ 4/   10. 8.
To James Pitts Esqr. Cash lent   20.
To Samuel Procter for the Ballance
   of His accot.   <u>21. 15. 0 3/4</u> <u>52. 3. 3/4</u>
                                        <u>100. 16. 0 3/4</u>

Boston February 27. 1760.

Granted by the Overseers of the Poor .... Viztt.
To Phillip Marlow   0. 4.
To Joseph Lasenby his accot. for Keeping the
   Sick & Disstracted Subjects of Alms House   29. 10. 0
To Samuel Procter for half years Salery due
   1st. March   12. 0. 0
   Ditto for Interest of Money advanced   <u>8. 0. 0</u>   20. 0. 0
To Royal Tyler Esqr. for Cash Lent as ℘ Rect.   6. 13. 4
To John Mills   4. 11. 5 1/4
To Royal Tyler Esqr. in full of his accot. No. 1–3   34. 7. 4
To John Tuder …Ditto   2   14. 5. 2
To Ebenezr. Storor Esqr. Ditto   3   15. 14. 4
To Mr. John Barret Ditto   4   14. 13. 7
To Mr. Benja. Dolbeare Ditto   5   26. 13. 4
To Mr. Isaac Walker Ditto   6   12. 13. 4
To James Pitts Esqr. Ditto   7   36. 14. 1 1/2
To Mr. William Phillips Ditto   9   18. 16. 11
To Melatiah Bourn Ditto   10   52. 13. 10
To Thomas Flucker Esqr. Ditto   11   26. 17. 10
To Mr. Isaac Smith   Ditto   12   34. 1. 2 1/2

To Docr. Miles Whitworth for 3/4 of years
Salery @ £60–₱ annum due 2d. Instant }   45. 0. 0

To Samuel Procter for the Ballance of his accot.   17. 10.   3/4

To Joseph Bradford junr. Glazier   9. 10. 11 1/4

To Joseph Low Carpenter for Coffins &c to this
day }   8. 16.

To Thomas Dawes mason in full   <u>5. 7. 2</u>   <u>434. 13. 11</u>

An Account of Expences for the Alms House and for the
Poor out of the House from March 1759. to March 1760

Expence in	April	57. 14.	4 1/2
	May	104. 14.	8 1/2
	June	88. 4.	0 3/4
	July	98. 11.	11 3/4
	August	109. 11.	8 1/2
	Septemr.	67. 17.	3
	October	74. 8.	9
	November	85. 19.	8 1/2
	December	60. 15.	1 3/4
	January	106. 13.	6
	Februa. 6th.	100. 16.	0 3/4
	Ditto—27th.	434. 13.	11

Sundry Drafts for Grain Wood and
Pork }   <u>329. 1. 5</u>   <u>1,719. 2. 7</u>

Deduct received of the Province Treasurer
for Support of the Province Poor
From 1st. March 1759. to 1st. Septemr.   145. 16. 9

1st. Septr. to 1st. March 1760   <u>161. 17. 4 3/4</u>   <u>307. 14. 1 3/4</u>

                                                    <u>1,411. 8. 5 1/4</u>

︵◠︶

Boston April *<2d.>* 3 1760.

Granted by the Overseers of the Poor .... Vizt.

To Phillip Marlow	4.		
To Joseph Lasenby his accot. for keeping the Sick & Distracted, Subjects of the Alms House	16.	14.	
To Josiah Waters his accot. for Pa[i]nting	22.	7.	10
To Samuel Mansfield Do. for Shoes	23.	8.	
To Nathaniel Band	3.	1.	8
To Robert Hill Carter	7.	4.	1 1/2
To Samuel Procter for the Ballance of His account	58.	7.	8 3/4
	131.	7.	4 1/4

Boston May 7 1760

Granted by the Overseers of the Poor .... Vizt.

To Phillip Marlow	4.		
To Joseph Lasenby his Accot. for keeping the Sick & Distractd;	15.	14.	
To Henry Bromfeild for James Fosdick Junr. Accot. indorsed. over to him it being for work done at the Alms house by sd. Fosdick	2.	16.	8
To John Phillips Esqr. for Cash Lent	15.		
To Mr. Isaac Walker do.	15.		
To Mr. John Tudor do.	15.		
To Royall Tyler Esqr.	15.		
To Mr. Wm: Phillips	21.	12.	
To Mr. Bn Doalbear	15.		
To Mr. Isaac Smith	15.		
To Melatiah Bourne Esqr.	15.		
To Thos. Flucker Esqr.	15.		
To Mr. Saml. Dexter	15.		
To Mr. Jona. Mason	15.		
To Mr. Jno. Barrett	15.		
To Saml. Procter for the Ball of his Accot.	14. 12. 7 3/4	£219. 19.	3 3/4

The Overseers' Finances 1738-1769

〜

Granted by the Overseers of the Poor

To Phillip Marlow	£	4.	
To Joseph Lasinby for keeping the sick & Distracktd;	12.	10.	8
To Benj Dolbeare his accot. for [Post se?] for the work house	3.	12.	4
To John Phillips Esqr. Cash Advanced.	3.		
To Isaac Walker do.	3.		
To John Barrett do.	3.		
To John Tudor do.	3.		
To Royall Tyler Esqr. do.	3.		
To Thos: Flucker Esqr. do.	3.		
To Benja. Dolbear do.	3.		
To Isaac Smith do. & Sugar	7.	5.	0
To Melath. Bourne Esqr. do.	3.		
To Saml. Dexter do.	3.		
To Jona. Mason do.	3.		
To Saml. Procter for the Ballance of his Accot.	42.	5.	7 3/4

£95. 17. 7 3/4

Granted by the Overseers of the Poor

To Phillip Marlow	£	4.	
To Joseph Lasinby for keeping the Sick & Distractd;	13.	1.	4
To Nathanl. Bands Accot.	3.	19.	4
To Samuel Procter for the Ballce. of his Accot.	51.	1.	6

£68. 6. 2

The Overseers' Finances 1738-1769

⌒

Granted by the Overseers of the Poor

To Philip Marlow	£ 0. 4.	
To Joseph Lasinby for keeping the) Sick and Distracted	16. 13. 4	
To John Phillips Esqr. for Cash lent	6.	
To Saml. Procter for the Balance) of his Accot.	45. 4. 10	68. 2. 2

Granted by the Overseers of the Poor

To Phillip Marlow	£ 4.	
To Joseph Lasinby for keeping the) sick & Distractd;	12. 10. 8	
To John Roulstone for Burying	1. 5.	
To Peter Coollidges Accot. for keepng) Mary Allen at Medfeild	7. 17.	
To John Mills Accot. for Makg. Coffins & Work done for Alms house	13. 18. 2	
To Samuel Procter for the ballance) of his Accot.	62. 7. 3 3/4	£98. 2. 1 3/4

Granted by the Overseers of the Poor

To Philip Marlow	£ 4.
To Joseph Lasinby Accot. for keeping the Sick & Distractd.	29. 8.
To Samuel Procter for the) Ballance of his Accot.	51. 13. 0 1/4
To ditto for half years Sallary) due the 1st. Last Month	12.
	£93. 5. 0 1/4

Granted by the Overseers of the Poor

To Phillip Marlow	4.
To Joseph Lasinby for keeping the) Sick & Distractd.	25. 10.
John Mills for Makg. Coffins &c. for) the Almshouse	11. 4. 2
To Nathl. Band for Burying	3. 6. 6
To Hannah Dix for the Board of Sarah Teague a Distractd. Person from Feb: 2 1760 to the 2 of this Instant is 9 months at 4/ ℘ week	7. 16.
To Thomas Tyler Esqr. for monies Subscribed. for Supplyg. the Almshouse	10.
To Saml. Procter for the Ballance of) his Accot.	<u>114. 17. 8 3/4</u> £172. 18. 4 3/4

Granted by the Overseers of the Poor

To Phillip Marlow	£ 4.
To Joseph Lasinby for keeping the) Sick & Distractd;	20. 8.
To John Phillips Esqr. for Cash Advanced. for the use of Almshouse	16.
To John Tudors ditto	24.
To Samuel Procter for the) Ballance of his Accot.	<u>36. 18. 8</u> £97. 10. 8

Granted by the Overseers of the Poor

To Phillip Marlow	£ 4.
To Joseph Lasinby Accot. for keeping) the Sick & Distractd.	27. 4.
To Edward Winters Accot. for Black) smiths work for the house	4. 3. 10 1/2

❧

To Samuel Mansfeild Accot.⎱
  for Shoes for the house ⎰   <u> 3. 16. </u>

                                        £35. 7. 10 1/2

                                      Boston February 4th. 1761

Granted by the Overseers of the Poor

To Phillip Marlow   £   4.

To Joseph Lasinby Accot. for keeping⎱
  the Sick & Distractd.   ⎰   22. 6.

To Samuel Procter for the Ballce.⎱
  of his Accot.   ⎰   <u>31. 1. 0 1/4</u>

                                 £53. 11.   1/4

An Account of Expences for the Alms House & for
the Poor of the House & repairs from March 1760 to March 1761

Aprill Expended in	Aprill	131.	7.	4 1/4		
	May	219.	19.	3 3/4		
	June	95.	17.	7 3/4		
	July	68.	6.	2		
	August	68.	2.	2		
	Sepr.	98.	2.	1 3/4		
	October	93.	5.	1		
	Novr.	172.	18.	4 3/4		
	Decer.	97.	10.	8		
	Jany.	35.	7.	10 3/4		
	Febry.	53.	11.	0 1/4		
	March	<u>581.</u>	<u>13.</u>	<u>2</u>	1,716.	1.	0 1/4
	Wood Grain &c.				<u>390.</u>	

                                  £2,106. 1. 0[24]

Deduct recd. Out of the ⎱
Province Treasury for the ⎰
Province Poor   <u>331. 4. 8</u>

                               £1,774. 17. 4 [25]

The Overseers' Finances 1738-1769

❦

Boston March 4th. 1761

Granted by the Overseers of the Poor

To Phillip Marlow	£	4.	
To Joseph Lasinby for keeping) the Sick & Distractd.	26.	2.	
Nath Band for Burying	2.	8.	8
Robert Hills Accot. for Carting	9.	13.	2 1/4
Josiah Smith for Shoes	24.	18.	4
John Mills for Coffins &c.	6.	5.	10 1/2
Royall Tyler Esqr. in full for his Accot. No. 1	45.	10.	10 1/4
Saml. Dexter ward No. 2	40.	16.	2 1/2
John Tudor 3	11.	7.	4
John Barritt 4	15.	17.	4
Benja. Dolebeare 5	21.	2.	9
Isaac Walker 6	7.	11.	3
Jona. Mason 7	52.	5.	10 1/4
John Phillips Esqr. 8	2.	3.	1
Wm. Phillips 9	22.	2.	11 1/2
Meletiah Bourne Esqr 10	30.	14.	6
Thomas Flucker Esqr. 11	38.	5.	
Isaac Smith 12	93.	18.	8
To Samuel Procter for the) Ballance of his Accot.	106.	5.	3 3/4
To Saml. Procter for half a years Salery due the 1st. of this Instt.	12.		
To ditto for one years Interists upon Two hundred pounds in Mr. D. Jeffries hands	12.		
	£581.	13.	2

The Overseers' Finances 1738-1769

Granted by the Overseers of Poor

To Phillip Marlow	£	4.	
To Jos: Lasinby for keeping the⎫ Sick & Distractd: ⎭	24.		
To John Tudor for wood Omittd.⎫ in his Accot. ⎭	1. 11.	8	

To Captn. Ebenr. Thayer Junr. for
    keeping two French Neutrals
    that ware Sick at Brantree Twenty
    Six weeks—@ 8/
	10. 8.		

To Saml. Procter for the Ballce.⎫ of his Accot. ⎭	70. 0. 9 1/4		
	£106. 4. 5 1/4		

Granted by the Overseers of the Poor

To Phillip Marlow	£ 4.	
To Joseph Lasinby for keeping⎫ the Sick & Distractd, ⎭	28. 4.	
To Saml. Procter for the ballce.⎫ of his Accot. ⎭	44. 13. 5 3/4	£73. 1. 5 3/4

Granted by the Overseers of Poor

To Phillip Marlow	£ 4.
To Joseph Lasinby for keeping the⎫ Sick & Distractd. ⎭	21. 12.
To John Mills his a/c for Makg. Coffins &c.	6. 2. 6 1/4
To Thomas Gray for 1 ℔s. Stript Duffells	9. 1. 4
To John Roulston his Bill <for Burying>	19. 4.
To Joseph Bradford his Bill	2. 9. 8 1/2
To Samuel Procter for the Ballce. his⎫ Accott. ⎭	40. 1. 3
	80. 10. 1 3/4

To Miles Whitworth for Fifteen
   Months Saly. @ 60£ to 2d. Last   75. 0. 0   155. 10. 1 3/4
   Month

Boston 1st. July 1761.

Granted by the Overseers of the Poor
To Philip Marlow   £ 0. 4.
To Joseph Lasinby for keeping
   sundry sick & distracted persons   21. 12.
To Hannah Dix for boarding
   Sarah Teague a distracted person
   from Novr. 2d. 1760. to Jany. 1st. 1761.   1. 16.
To John Dix for boarding Sarah
   Teague a distracted person from
   Jany. 1st. to July 1st. 1761.
   6 Months @ 4/. ℘ Week   5. 4.
                    Carried over £28. 16.

             Sum brought over   28. 16.
To Samuel Procter for the Balance
   of his Accot.   111. 17. 2 3/4 140. 13. 2 3/4

Boston 5th. Augt. 1761

Granted by The Overseers of the Poor
To Philip Marlow   £   4. 0
To Joseph Lasinby for keeping
   Sundry Sick & Distracted Persons   22. 0. 0
To Samuel Procter for the Ballce.
   of his Accott.   49. 15. 0
To John Phillips Esqr for Cash
   Lent for the Use of the Alms
   House   20.
To John Bemus for Nursg. Willm.
   Wifes Chilld: Taken out the Alms
   House & Cash paid Doct. Russell   4. 0. 0   £95. 19. 0

The Overseers' Finances 1738-1769

Boston 2d. Sept. 1761.

Granted by the Overseers of the Poor

To Philip Marlow		£ 4.	
To Joseph Lasenby for keeping sundy. sick & distracted Persons		17. 12.	
To Simon Plymton for keeping Mary Allen a distracted Person from Sept. 3d. 1760. to this day		12. 7. 3	
To Henry Bromfield for Cash lent for the Use of the Almshouse		18.	
To Samuel Procter for Balls: of his Accot.	29. 18. 4 1/4		
To Ditto for half a Years Salary ending 1st. inst.	12.	41. 18. 4 1/4	£90. 1. 7 1/4

Boston 8th. October 1761

Granted by the Overseers of the Poor

To Philip Marlow	4. 0.	
To Joseph Lasenby for keeping Sundy. sick & distracted Persons	13. 10.	
To Shippie Townsend his Bill for makeg. the pump &c.	2. 13. 9	
To Samuel Procter for Ballance his Accott.	99. 1. 7	115. 9. 4

Boston Novembr. 4th. 1761

Granted by the Overseers of the Poor

To Phillip Marlow	£ 4	
To Joseph Lasinby Acco For keepg. Sundry Sick & distractd. Persons	10.	
To Hopestill Fosters accot. For [Staff] to repair the Almshouse	6. 11.	
To Sam Procter For the ballce. of his Accot.	110. 2. 2 3/4	
	£126. 17. 2 3/4	

The Overseers' Finances 1738-1769

Boston 9th. December 1761

Granted by the Overseers of the Poor

To Josiah Smith his a/c for Shoes	17.	5.	4
To Joseph Lasinby Accott. for Keepg.⎫ 　Sundry Sick & distracted persons ⎭	9.	4.	0
To Phillip Marlow	4.	0	
To Samuel Procter for the Ballce.⎫ 　of his Accott.　　　　　　　⎭	92.	2.	10 3/4　118. 16. 2 3/4

Boston 6th. Jany. 1762

Granted by the Overseers of the Poor ⎫
To John Phillips Esqr for Cash lent ⎭

for the Use of the Alms House	10.	0.	0
To Joseph Lasinby Accott. for Keeping⎫ 　Sundry Sick & distracted persons ⎭	12.	8.	0
To Obadiah Curtis for a Hand Cart	3.	9.	4
To Robert Hill for Carting Corn	7.	12.	2 1/4
To John Mills his Accott. for Carpenters Work⎫ 　for the Alms House　　　　　　　　　⎭	24.	0.	0.　57. 9. 6 1/4

⎭

£ "　"　26

Boston 3th. Feby. 1762

Granted by the Overseers of the Poor

To Joseph Lasinby Accott. for Keepg.⎫ 　Sundry Sick & distracted Persons ⎭	13.	12.	0
To Edward Winter his a/c for Smiths Work	3.	4.	10　16. 16. 10
To Thomas Dawes his Accott. for Masons work			13. 10. 8
			£30. 7. 6

The Overseers' Finances 1738-1769

Granted by the Overseers of the Poor

To Royall Tyler Esqr for his a/c Ward N	1		33. 8. 0 1/2
To Samuel Dexter Esqr for Do. N	2		26. 17. 3 3/4
To Joseph Gardnier Esqr for Do.	3		9. 18. 8 1/4
To John Barrett Esqr ....for Do.	4		12. 19. 10
To Benjm. Dolbears ....for Do.	5		26. 1. 10
To Isaac Walker ....for Do.	6		13. 2. 0
To Jonathan Mason...............for Do.	7		42. 13. 9 1/2
To John Phillips Esqr ....for Do.	8		0. 19. 0
To Willm. Phillips Esqr..........for Do.	9		8. 14. 2 3/4
To Melatiah Bourne Esqr......for Do.	10		41. 6. 11 1/2
To Henry Bromfield ....for Do.	11		38. 18. 8
To Isaac Smith ....for Do.	12		54. 7. 5 1/2

To Ebenezer Thayer for his a/c Keepg. two
French Neutrals ⎱   7. 12. 0

To Nathl. Band for his a/c   6. 5. 0

To John Mills his a/c for Carpenters Work   1. 5. 4

To Joseph Lasinby Accott. for Keeping Sundy.
Sick & Distracted Persons ⎱   15. 14. 0

To Miles Whitworth for 10 Months
Salrey from May 2d. to this day @
60£ ℔ annum ⎱ 50. 0. 0

Do. for Extra Services in Medins. and
Attendance to a Number of French
People assigned to the Town by the
Genl: Cort after the Agreement made
with Said Whitworth ⎱ 10. 0. 0   60. 0. 0   400. 4. 1 3/4

Sum Brought Over   £400. 4. 1 3/4

To Samuel Procter for The
Ballce. his Accott. ⎱ 57. 3. 10

Ditto for 6 Monthes Salery
to 1st. Instant ⎱ 12. 0. 0   63. 3. 10

     463. 7. 11 3/4

The Overseers' Finances 1738-1769

An Account of Expences for the Almshouse & for
the poor of the House & repair &c from March 1761. to March 1762

Expended in	April	£106.	4.	5 1/4			
	May	73.	1.	5 3/4			
	June	155.	10.	1 3/4			
	July	140.	13.	2 3/4			
	Augst.	95.	19.	0			
	Sept.	90.	1.	7 1/4			
	Octbr.	115.	9.	4			
	Novr.	126.	17.	2 3/4			
	Decer.	118.	16.	2 3/4			
	Jany.	57.	9.	6 1/4			
	Feby.	30.	7.	6			
	March	463.	7.	11 3/4	1,573.	17.	8 1/4
Wood Grain &c.					391.	16.	11
					£1,965.	14.	7

Deduct. Recd. of the Province }
Treasurer for the province poor} 310.

£1,655. 14. 7

Boston Aprill 7th 1762

Granted by the Overseers of the Poor

To Joseph Lasinby his accot. for keeking [*keeping*] the
Sick & Distracted £12.

To Josiah Smith his a/c for Shoes 10. 18. 8

To Simon Plymtons a/c for keeping }
Mary Allen from September 3th. }
1761 to March 3 1762 } 6. 14. 8

To Samuel Procter for the Ballc. }
of his Accot. } 28. 18. 3 1/2

£58. 11. 7 1/2

∽

Boston 5th. May 1762

Granted by the Overseers of the Poor

To Joseph Lasinby his Accott. for Keepg.

the Sick & Distracted .... £ 8. 16. 0

To Samuel Procter for the Ballce.

of his Accott. £114. 12. 9

To Ditto Allowd for Intrest ⎫

on his Accott. for the last year ⎭ ___18. 0. 0___ ___32. 12. 9___

£141. 8. 9

Boston June 2d. 1762.

Granted by the Overseers of the Poor

To Joseph Lasinby for keeping sundry ⎫

sick and distracted Persons ℘ his Acco. ⎭ 11. 4. 0

To Robert Hill for Carting Grain 5. 6. 1 1/2

To Benja. Clarke for Rent of a House ⎫

for the Use of the French People ⎬

2 Years, ending May 7th. 1762. ⎭ 32.

To John Ruggles for Work & Sundries ⎫

for the Almshouse ⎭ 14. 0. 11

To Samuel Procter for the Balance ⎫

of his Accot. ⎭ ___74. 1. 1 3/4___

£136. 12. 2 1/4

Boston July 7th. 1762.

Granted by the Overseers of the Poor.

To Joseph Lasinby for Keeping ⎫

sick & distracted Persons ⎬

℘ his Accot. ⎭ 14.

The Overseers' Finances 1738-1769

Granted by the Overseers of the Poor

To Joseph Lasinby for Keeping

    sick & distracted Persons ⅌

    his Accot.   12. 8.

To Samuel Procter for the Balla.

    of his Accot.   21. 5. 3 1/2

                             33. 13. 3 1/2

Boston 1th. Septr. 1762

Granted by the Overseers of the Poor

To Joseph Lasinby for Keeping the

    sick & distracted Persons ⅌ a/c   12. 8. 0

To Abraham Puttman for Paving

    ⅌ his a/c   19. 11. 0

To Roger Mc.Knight his Accott.   12. 9. 0

To Nathaniel Band his Accott.   5. 11. 2

To James [Eyres?] his a/c for Paving stones   3. 10. 8

To Simon Plymton a/c for Keeping

    Mary Allen from March 3d. to

    3 September 1762   5. 4. 0

To Samuel Procter for the Ballance

    of his Accott.   74. 4. 7 1/2

                    £132. 18. 5 1/2

To Samuel Procter for Half

    years Saly. to this day   12. 0. 0

                    £144. 18. 5 1/2

Boston Octob 13th. 1762

Granted by the Overseers of the Poor

To Joseph Lasenby for keeping sundry sick & distracted

    persons ⅌ a/c   £17. 4.

To Robert Hill for Carting Grain   3. 1. 4

To Wells & Swain their a/c for Stones

    Gravel & carting dirt   14. 2.

To Samuel Procter for the Ballance

    of his Accot.   83. 15. 5 1/2 £118. 2. 9 1/2

The Overseers' Finances 1738-1769

Boston 4th. November 1762

Granted by the Overseers of the Poor

To Joseph Lasinby for Keeping
    sundy. Sick & distracted   8.   2.   0
To Nathanil Band his Accott.   2. 13. 10
To Samuel Procter for Ballce.
    his Accott.   __25.   2.   8 3/4__
                                              £35. 18.   6 3/4

Boston 1th. December 1762

Granted by the Overseers of the Poor

To Joseph Lasinby for Keeping
    sundry Sick & Distracted   11.   4.   0
To Shippie Townsend his a/c for
    a pump &c. for the use the Alms House   8. 17.   4
To Samuel Procter for the Ballce.
    his Accott.   __132.   6.   0 1/4__
                                              £152.   7.   4 1/4

Boston 5th. Jany. 1763

Granted by the Overseers of the Poor

To Joseph Lasinby his a/c for
    Keeping the Sick & Distracted   12. 10.   0
To Samuel Brown for his a/c
    for 51 Load Clay for the Use the Alms
    House   11. 18.   0
To Samuel Procter for the Ballc.
    his Accott.   __59. 12.   7 1/4__
                                             £84.   0.   7 1/4

To Cochran & Cambell for their
    a/c Wharfage & Carting 33 Cord
    wood   __7. 14.   0__
                                             £91. 14.   7 1/4

The Overseers' Finances 1738-1769

∾

Boston 2th. Feby. 1763

Granted by the Overseers of the Poor

To Joseph Lasinby for Keeping
   sundry Sick & Distracted   12. 16. 0

To Josiah Smith his Accott. for
   Shoes Supply'd the Alms House   26. 18. 8

To John Rogers, his Bill for Wharfg.
   Cording & Carting 6 1/2 Cord Wood   1. 3. 10

To Martin Gay his a/c for a Copper
   qt. 400 Kettle for the Use Alms House 24. 12. 0

To John Champany his Accott. for
   Slating the Alms House   1. 12. 8

To John Phillips Esqr his Accott.
   for 61 1/2 yards Tow Cloth ...1/4   4. 2. 0

To Joseph Goldthwait his Bill
   for 6. 1/3 Cord Wood   1. 10. 5

To John Ruggles his Bill for
   Carpenters Work   33. 8. 8

To Samuel Procter for the Ballce.
   His Accott.   56. 6. 4

                      £162. 10. 7

To John Dix. his a/c for Keepg.
   Sarah Teague a Distractd
   Person—30 Weeks @ 4/   6. 0. 0

To Jonathan Dix for Keepg.
   Sarah Teague a Distracted
   Person—52 Weeks @ 4/8   12. 2. 8

                      £180. 13. 3

The Overseers' Finances 1738-1769

Boston 2th. March 1763

Granted by The Overseers of the Poor

To Joseph Lasenby for Keeping Sundy. Sick & Distracted	30.	0.	0
To Josiah Waters his Accott. for Paintg.	3.	5.	6
To Nathl. Gardner for his 1/3 of 9 Cord wood [Seizd.?] & for the Use the Alms House	1.	16.	0
To Timothy Atkins. his Accott.	2.	12.	10
To Simon Plymton his Accott. for Board Mary Allen 26 Weeks &c.	6.	2.	8
To Nathl. Band his Accott. for Burying	5.	3.	8
To Royal Tyler Esqr his Accott. Ward N 1	36.	15.	0
To Royal Tyler Esqr his Accott. for Ward N 2	14.	1.	8
To Samuel Dexter for Ward N 2	11.	19.	5 1/4
To Joseph Gardner Esqr his Accott. for Ward N 3	25.	16.	9 3/4
To John Barrett Esqr his a/c Ward N 4	19.	11.	9
To Benjm. Dolbear his a/c Ward N 5	39.	16.	4 1/2
To Isaac Smith Esqr do. for Ward 6	23.	19.	4
To Jonathan Mason his a/c for Ward N 7	53.	1.	4
To William Phillips Esqr Ward N 9	6.	18.	2
To Melatiah Bourn Esqr. Ward 10	44.	1.	0
To Henry Bromfield for . . . N 11	47.	3.	2
To William Whitwell for . . . 12	46.	12.	10
To Edward Winter. /Smith/ his a/c	5.	5.	5
To Thomas Dawes /Mason/ his a/c	11.	7.	4
To Samuel Procter for the Ballance his Accott.	56.	12.	2 1/4
To Ditto for Half Years Salery due 1th. Instant	12.	0.	0

504. 2. 5 3/4

The Overseers' Finances 1738-1769

❧

An Account of Expences for the Alms House, and
for the poor, Out of the House, from March 1762 .. to March 1763.

and repairs of the house

Expence's in

Aprill	58.	11.	7 1/2
May	141.	8.	9
June	136.	12.	2 1/2
July	14.		
August	33.	13.	3 1/2
September	144.	18.	5 1/2
October	118.	2.	9 1/2
November	35.	18.	6 3/4
December	152.	7.	4 1/4
January	91.	14.	7 1/4
February	180.	13.	3
March	504.	2.	5 3/4
	£1,612.	3.	4 1/2

Sundry draughts on the Town⎫
Treasurer for Wood grain &c. ⎭   498. 9. 9   2,110. 13. 1 1/2

Deduct receivd., Out of⎫
the Province Treasury for the province Poor⎭   491. 3. 1

£1,619 10. 0 1/4

Boston March 16th. 1763

Granted by The Overseers of The Poor
To John Barrett Esqr. for 50 bus. Corn @ 3/8d.
    for the Almshouse   9. 3. 4

Boston April 6th. 1763

Granted by The Overseers of The Poor
To Joseph Lazenby for keeping⎫
    sundry distracted persons ⎭   £14. 6. 0

Samuel Proctor, for the Balle.⎫
    of his acct.   ⎭   57. 9. 10 1/2 £71. 15. 10 1/2

The Overseers' Finances 1738-1769

Boston May 4th. 1763

Granted by The Overseers of The Poor

To Joseph Lazenby for keeping sundry distracted Persons	12.	8.	0		
Samuel Proctor for Balle. of his acct.	60.	6.	3 1/4		
Ditto in full for Interest on Sundries advanc'd to the 2d. March last	15.	2.	9		
Dr. Jonathan Davis of Roxbury in full of his acct. attending sundry Neutrals sick belonging to Town	4.	9.	8	£92. 6. 8 1/4	

Boston June 1st. 1763

Granted by The Overseers of The Poor

To Joseph Lazenby for keeping sundry poor distracted Persons	20.	16.	0
To Samuel Proctor for Ballce. of his acct.	63.	8.	10 3/4
To Jonathan Day, in full of Dr. Nathaniel Ames's acct.	2.	7.	0
	86.	11.10 3/4	

Boston June 10th. 1763

Granted by The Overseers of The Poor

To John Barrett Esqr. 50 bus. Rye @ 4/8	11.	13.	4
To Benja. & Edward Davis, 50 bus. Rye @ 4/	10.		
	£21.	13.	4

Boston July 6th. 1763

Granted by The Overseers of The Poor

To Joseph Lazenby for keeping sundry distracted persons	19.		
To Samuel Proctor Balle. of his acct.	69.	8.	1 1/4
To Dr. Nyott Doubt for 14 months Salary from March 8th. 1762. to May 8th. last at 60£. ℘ annum	70.		

             ❧

To Benjamin Clarke for one year's
   Rent of a House for the French Neutrals ⎫
   ending the 7th. May last ⎭   16.

To John Ruggles for his acct. for Work ⎫
   done at the Almshouse ⎭   10. 15. 2 1/2

To Henderson Inches for 26. bus. Rye ⎫
   @ 38/. 0 [ld]. T[eno]r. in May last ⎭   6. 11. 8 3/4

To Joseph Bradford Junr. for his acct. ⎫
   for Work done at the Almshouse ⎭   <u>2. 14. 10 1/2</u> £194. 9. 11

Boston Augst. 3d. 1763

Granted by The Overseers of the Poor
To Samuel Proctor, the Ballance of his acct.   78. 2. 3
To Joseph Lazenby keeping distracted persons   <u>16.</u>
                                          £94. 2. 3

Boston Septr. 7th. 1763

Granted by The Overseers
To Samuel Proctor for the Ballance of acct.   93. 16. 0
   Joseph Lazenby, keeping distracted persons   19. 10. 0
   Nathaniel Band, acct. for Funerals   4. 5. 10
   Robert Hill, acct. for Carting   12.
   Samuel Proctor, half year's Salary, due the 1st. Inst. <u>12.</u>
                                      £141. 11. 10

Granted Septemr. 23d.
To Eliakim Raymond for 100 bus. Rye @ 3/   £<u>15.</u>

The Overseers' Finances 1738-1769

Boston October. 5th. 1763

Granted by The Overseers

To Samuel Proctor for the Ballance of acct.	80.	7.	0 3/4
Joseph Lazenby, keeping distracted persons	14.	16.	0
Andrew Hall, for 45 pr. Shoes	11.	14.	0
Jonathan Davis, for his acct.	6.	9.	0
£113.	6.	0 3/4

Boston Novr. 3d. 1763

Granted by The Overseers

To Samuel Proctor, for the Balla. of acct.	54.	17.	0 1/2
Joseph Lazenby, keeping distracted persons	12.	4.	0
John Shute of Malden for boarding two			
Children of Mary Jennings 20 weeks @ 2/8d.	2.	13.	4
69.	14.	4 1/2

Boston December 3d. 1763

Granted by The Overseers

To William Knowles for 100 bus. Corn, &
90 bus. Rye   £28. 8. 0

Decr. 9th.

Granted by The Overseers

To Samuel Proctor for the Balla. of his acct.	119.	16.	8
Joseph Lazenby, keeping distracted persons	12.	18.	0
John Ruggles, acct. for Work & Materials	34.	14.	6
167.	9.	2

Boston January 4th. 1764.

Granted by The Overseers

To Joseph Lazenby, keeping distracted persons	14.	16.	0
Nathaniel Band. his acct. for Funerals	3.	16.	0
	18.	12.	0

Boston February 2d. 1764

Granted by the Overseers

To Joseph Lazenby, keeping distracted persons	14.	16.	0
Robert Hill, for his acct. for Carting	4.	18.	0
	19.	14.	0

Boston March 7th. 1764

Granted by The Overseers

To Joseph Lazenby, keeping distracted persons	22.	2.	0
Andrew Hall for his acct. for Shoes	23.	5.	4
Edward Winter (Smith) his acct.	14.	6.	9
Nathaniel Band's acct. for Funerals	1.	19.	6
Carrd. Over	61.	13.	7

1764.

March 7th.

Brot. Over	£61.	13.	7
To Thomas Dawes. for his acct.	95.	16.	1
Samuel Delucena his acct. for Roger Stayner's Board. from June 7th. 1758. 5 mo. @ £4. ℘ ann.	1.	13.	4
To Benja. Hammett. his acct. for Ward N. 1	26.	11.	0
William Whitwell ......Do................. 2	50.	8.	10
Joseph Gardner Esqr...Do................. 3	23.	13.	0
John Barrett Esqr........Do................. 4	15.	16.7	1/2
Benjamin Dolbeare....Do................. 5	29.	4.	2
Isaac Smith Esqr.........Do................. 6	15.	19.	7
Ebenezer Storer ....Do................. 7	37.	9.	8
Royal Tyler Esqr.........Do................. 8	1.	4.	0
Melatiah Bourn Esqr..Do................. 9	10.	17.	1

Jonathan Mason.........Do............... 10	42. 19.	9
Henry Bromfield ....Do............... 11	41. 9.	6
Henderson Inches......Do............... 12	30. 4.	3
To Josiah Water's Acct. for painting	4. 0.	8
Samuel Proctor, for the Balla. of his acct.	74. 14.	3 1/2
Ditto, for half a year's Salary, due the 1st. Inst.	12.	
	575. 15.	5

An Account of Expences for the Alms House from
March 1763 to March 1764 & For the Poor out of the
House & Repairs for the House

April 6	£71. 15.	10 1/2	
May 4	92. 6.	8 1/4	
June 1	86. 11.	10 3/4	
July 6	194. 9.	11	
August 3	94. 2.	3	
Septembr. 7	141. 11.	10	
October 5	113. 6.	0 3/4	
Novembr. 3	69. 14.	4 1/2	
December 9	167. 9.	2	
January 4	18. 12.		
February 2	19. 14.		
March 7	575. 15.	5	
	£1,645. 9.	5 3/4	

To Sundry Draughts on		
the Town Treasurer for		
wood & Graine &c.	1,019. 10.	6 3/4
	2,665.	1/2
Deduct receivd. out of the		
Province Treasurery for the		
Province Poor	546. 16.	2
	£2,100. 3.	10 1/2

Boston 4th. April 1764

Granted by the Overseers of the Poor

To Joseph Lazinbys a/c for keeping the sick

 & Distracted as ℘ his Accot.   £22. 14.

To Willm. Pell for the Board his

 Mother from

 Octobr. 5 to April 5th. is 26 weeks @ 3/4   4. 6. 8

To Samuel Procter for the

 Ballce. his Accott.   1. 12. 8

To Samuel Procter for Allowance

 for Interist for Money Advand.

 by him for the Town from

 March 1st. 1763 to March 1 1764   20.‾‾‾‾   £48. 13. 4

April 20th. Granted by The Overseers

To Isaac Smith for 448 bus. Corn @ 17/. O[ld] T[eno]r. is   50. 15. 6

Boston May 2d. 1764

Granted by The Overseers

To Benjamin Hammett for his acct. Ward No. 1.

 William Whitwell .... Do. 2

 Joseph Gardner Esqr......... Do. 3

 John Barrett Esqr.............. Do. 4

 Benjamin Dolbeare.......... Do. 5

 Isaac Smith Esqr............... Do. 6

 Ebenezer Storer .... Do. 7   18. 5. 6

 Royal Tyler Esqr............... Do. 8

 Melatiah Bourn Esqr........ Do. 9

 Jonathan Mason .... Do. 10   ‾‾‾‾‾‾‾‾‾

Carrd. Over

~

May 2d. [*1764*]

Brought Over   £

To Henry Bromfeild, his acct. Ward .. N. 11

     Henderson Inches...........Do. 12

<*Joseph Lazenby, keeping sick & distracted*⟩

     persons—as ℘ acct.   ⟩   20.>

Meml. The above are enter'd in the Book of acct. for

     Small Pox Expences

Boston May 2d. 1764

Granted by The Overseers

To Joseph Lazenby keeping distracted persons   20.

     Samuel Proctor for Balla. of his acct.   71. 10. 6

     John Ruggles for his acct.   <u>13. 15. 7</u>

           105. 6. 1

Boston June 6th. 1764

Granted by The Overseers

To Joseph Lazenby keeping distracted persons   24.

     Samuel Proctor for Balla. of his acct.   <u>87. 10. 11</u>

           111. 10. 11

Boston July 4th. 1764

Granted by The Overseers

To Joseph Lazenby, keeping distracted persons   18. 4. 0

     Samuel Proctor, Balla. of his acct.   41. 16. 1

     Nathaniel Band's, acct.   4. 18. 10

     Edward Winter in part of his acct.   13.

     William Pell, boarding his mother from⟩

     April 5th. 13 weeks @ 3/4d.   ⟩   2. 3. 4

        John Shute, boarding two Children of Mary Jennings⟩

     34 weeks—@ 4/ to the 1st. Inst.   ⟩   <u>6. 16. 0</u>

           <u>86. 18. 3</u>

The Overseers' Finances 1738-1769

Boston August 1st. 1764

Granted by The Overseers

To Samuel Proctor Ballance of his acct. £59. 19. 1
  Joseph Lazenby, keeping distracted persons   19. 4. 0
                                              £79. 3. 1

Boston September 5th. 1764

Granted by The Overseers

To Samuel Proctor, for the Ballance of his acct.   84. 7. 5 3/4
  Ditto for half years Salary, due the 1st. Inst.   12.
  Joseph Lazenby, keeping distracted persons   21. 6. 0
  William Pell, for boarding his mother)
  from July 4th. 9 Weeks . . . @ 3/4d.   )   1. 10. 0
  Nathaniel Band's acct. for Funerals   1. 16. 0
                                                  £120. 19. 5 3/4

Boston October 3d. 1764

Granted by The Overseers

To Samuel Proctor, for the Balla. of his acct.   80. 12. 1 1/4
  Joseph Lazenby, keeping distracted persons   18. 19. 0
  Andrew Hall, his acct. for Shoes   22. 8. 8
  Jonathan Dix, his acct. keepg. Sarah Teague)
  a distracted person 87 Weeks @ 4/8   }
  to this day   )   20. 6. 0
                                                  £142. 5. 9 1/4

Boston 7th. November 1764

Granted by The Overseers

To Samuel Proctor, for the Ballce. of his Accot. 104. 15. 9 1/4
To John Ruggles for his Accott. . Error
To Benja. Dolbeare . . Do.   14. 19. 4
To Joseph Lazinby, Keeping distracted persons   20. 12. 0
                                                  £140. 7. 1 1/4

Boston Decr. 5th. 1764

Granted by The Overseers

To Samuel Proctor, Balla. of his acct.	117.	7.	4 3/4
Joseph Lazenby, keeping distracted persons	16.	14.	0
Royal Tyler Esqr. . acct. Ward N. 8	13.	13.	11 1/2
John Ruggles's acct. for Work	23.	11.	6
Nyot Doubt his Salary from May 8th. 1763. to June 8th. 1764. 13 mo. @ £60 ℗ annum	65.		
	£249.	15.	6 1/4

Boston January 2d. 1765

Granted by The Overseers

To Samuel Proctor, for the Balla. of his acct.	49.	17.	2
Joseph Lazenby, acct. keeping distracted persons	26.	2.	0
	£75.	19.	2

Boston February 6th. 1765

Granted by The Overseers

To Samuel Proctor, Ballance of his acct.	54.	10.	0 1/2
Joseph Lazenby, keeping distracted persons	35.	2.	0
Henry Rhoades, acct. 4 pr. Bucketts	3.	14.	8
Joseph Bradford, two accts. for Glazing	5.	18.	7
Simon Plimpton, boarding Mary Allen from March 7th. to Septr. 7th. 1763. 26 weeks @ 4/	5.	4.	0
Ezekiel Adams, boarding Do. from Septr. 7th. 1763. to Septr. 7th. 1764. &c—two accts.	11.	16.	1
John Shute's acct. boardg. Wm. Chadwell to *<Jany. 26>* this day	0.	19.	1
	£117.	4.	5 1/2

The Overseers' Finances 1738-1769

Boston March 6th. 1765.

Granted by The Overseers

To Benjamin Hammett, his acct. for Ward N. 1.	£39. 18.	6 1/2
William Whitwell ....Do.................... 2.	55. 17.	4
Joseph Gardner Esqr.......Do.................... 3.	26. 1.	4
John Barrett Esqr...........Do.................... 4.	28. 7.	9
Benjamin Dolbeare........Do.................... 5.	16. 2.	6
Isaac Smith Esqr.............Do.................... 6.	8. 13.	9
Ebenezer Storer ....Do.................... 7.	45. 17.	8
Royal Tyler Esqr.............Do.................... 8.	13. 8.	7
Melatiah Bourn Esqr......Do.................... 9.	12. 2.	5
Jonathan Mason.............Do................. 10.	35. 10.	1 1/2
<Henry Bromfield .... Do................ 11.>	0. 0.	0
Henderson Inches..........Do................. 12.	43. 5.	5
To Samuel Proctor, Ballance of his acct.	43. 18.	8
Ditto, for half a year's Salary, due the 1th. Inst.	12.	
Joseph Lazenby, keeping distracted persons	32. 16.	0
William Pell for boarding his mother)		
from Septr. 5th. 26 Weeks . @ 3/4d. ∫	4. 6.	8
Edward Winter, for his acct.	3. 1.	4
Robert Hill, his acct. for Carting	17. 7.	2
Thomas Dawes, for his acct. for Work	11. 8.	9
Nathaniel Band's . acct.	6. 2.	4
Hezzediah Coley's acct. 5 pr. Bucketts	4. 13.	4
William Whitwell . for 50 bus. Rye @ 4/	10.	
	£470. 19.	8

[*March*] the 7th. [*1765*]

Granted by The Overseers

To Henry Bromfield his acct. Ward N. 11   £29. 18.   0

[*March 1765*]

whole drafts of this year is	3,505. 16.	8
drafts on province Treasurer	532. 11.	5
Expended for the Town	£2,973. 5.	3

813

Boston April 3 1765

Granted by the Overseers of the Poor

To Joseph Lazinby for his Accot. for keeping
    distracted persons   £27. 18.

To Royall Tyler Esq. for his Accot. for Cash⎫
    Advanced for the poor   ⎭   15. 6. 8

To Ezekiel Adams Accot. for keeping Mary
    Allen a distracted from Septembr. 7 1764 to
    March 7th. 1765 . 26 Weeks @ 4/   5. 4.

To Andrew Hall for his Accot. for Shoes to⎫
    the 4th. of last month   ⎭   33. 16. 8

To Shippie Townsend for Mendg. the pump   1. 1. 2

To John Shute for the Board of Mrs. Jennings.
    2 Children forty weeks at 4/ & Making
    Cloaths for Do. to the 9th. Instant   8. 5. 4

To Samuel Proctor for Allowance for Interest
    of money advanc'd by him for the Town
    from March 1st. 1764. to March 1st. 1765   <u>22. 10. 0</u>

£<u>114. 1. 10</u>

Boston May 1st. 1765

Granted by the Overseers of The Poor

To Sam Procter for the Ballce. of his Accot. due⎫
    the 3d. April Omittd.   ⎭   £54. 8. 1

    for Ballce. of his Accot. this day   82. 0. 6

To Joseph Lazenby for his Accot.   28.

To Michael Prisbury for mendg. Windows⎫
    at the Sugar House   ⎭   <u>4. 5.</u>

£<u>168. 13. 7</u>

The Overseers' Finances 1738-1769

∽

Granted by the Overseers

To Saml. Procter Ballance his Accot.	£96.	19.	9 3/4
Joseph Lazenby, for keeping Poor Persons	32.	2.	
Benjamin Church Junr. for his Accot. for Medicines &cc. to the 1st. May last	30.		
Benja. Clark for Rent of a House to the 7th. May 2 years—a £16	32.		
Isaac Cazneau for Rent of a House to the 1st. Inst. 5 Months a £8 ℘ Annum	3.	6.	8
	£194.	8.	5 3/4

Boston July 3d. 1765

Granted by The Overseers

To Samuel Proctor, Ballance of his acct.	£70.	2.	0
Joseph Lazenby, keeping poor persons	24.	2.	0
Nathaniel Band, his acct. for Funerals	5.	3.	10
John Ruggles, his acct. for Work	19.	11.	6
Simon Plimpton, for short Charge on a former Draft, for Board of Mary Allen 23 Weeks—@ 8d.	0.	15.	4
William Pell, for boarding his Mother from March 6th. 17 Weeks—@ 3/4d.	2.	16.	8
	£122.	11.	4

Boston August 7th. 1765

Granted by The Overseers

To Samuel Proctor, Balla. of his acct.	£60.	15.	5 3/4
Joseph Lazenby, keeping poor & distracted persons	30.	18.	0
	£91.	13.	5 3/4

The Overseers' Finances 1738-1769

Boston September 4th. 1765.

Granted by The Overseers

To Samuel Proctor, for Ballance of his acct.	£64.		
Ditto, half a years Salary due the 1st. Inst.	12.		
Joseph Lazinby, keeping poor & distracted persons	20.	12	0
Jonathan Davis, his acct. for French Neutrals	6.	13.	8
	£103.	5.	8

Boston October 2d. 1765.

Granted by The Overseers

To Samuel Proctor for Balla. of his acct.	£64.	6.	3
Joseph Lazinby, keeping poor distracted persons	18.		
Isaac Cazneau for one quarter's rent of a house due the 1st. Inst.	2.		
Royal Tyler Esqr. his acct. for Daniel Bass &c.	17.	4.	9
Andrew Hall, for his acct. for Shoes	22.	7.	5 1/2
	£123.	18.	5 1/2

Boston October 2d. 1765

Granted by The Overseers

To Ebenezer Storer 180 bus. Rye @ 2/10d.	£25.	10.	0

Boston November 6th. 1765

Granted by The Overseers

To Samuel Proctor, Ballance of his acct.	138.	0.	9
Joseph Lazenby, keeping distracted persons	24.	10.	0
Nathaniel Band, his acct. for Funerals	4.	5.	10
William Pell for boarding his Mother from July 3. 18 Weeks . . @ 3/4d.	3.		
Carrd. Over	£169.	16.	7
Brot. Over	£169.	16.	7
To Edward Winter, his acct. for Work	2.	18.	5 1/2
	£172.	15.	0 1/2

The Overseers' Finances 1738-1769

Granted by The Overseers

To Samuel Proctor, Ballance of his acct.	£96.	17.	0
Joseph Lasinby, keepg. distracted persons	30.	6.	0
Dr. Isaac Rand, his acct. for Medicine & attendance for Sullivan's Daughters	20.	10.	2
Ezekiel Adams acct. keepg. Mary Allen a distracted person from March 7th. to Septr. 7th. last. 26 Weeks—@ 4/	5.	4.	0
Samuel Grant Esqr. towards the Board of John Roberts from Augst. 7th. 18 weeks @ 2/	1.	16.	0
	£154.	13.	2

Granted by the Overseers . . . viz.

To Samuell Procter the ballance of his Acct.	73.	16.	9
Joseph Lasenby keeping sick and distracted people	25.	4.	0
	£99.	0.	9

Granted by The Overseers

To Samuel Proctor, Ballance of his acct.	£84.	5.	11 3/4
Joseph Lazinby, keepg. distracted persons	26.	10.	0
William Pell for his Mother's Board from the 6th. Novr. 13 Weeks @ 3/4d.	2.	3.	4
	£112.	19.	3 3/4

Brought Over	£112.	19.	3 3/4
To Royal Tyler Esq. Ballance of his acct.	10.	13.	5
William Bell . acct. for Work	3.	6.	4
Jonathan Dix, his acct. keepg. Sarah Teague a distracted person. from October 3d. 1764. 70 Weeks . . . . @ 4/8	16.	6.	8
Isaac Cazneau for Rent of a house 4 months to the 1st. <Janr.>	2.	13.	4
	£145.	19.	0 3/4

❦

Boston March 5th. 1766

Granted by The Overseers

To Benja. Hammatt his acct. for Ward N. 1	£55.	15. 4 1/2
William Whitwell ......Do....................2	64.	3. 11
Joseph Gardner Esqr....Do....................3	27.	0. 1 1/4
John Barrett Esqr.........Do....................4	35.	2. 5
Benjamin Dolbeare.....Do....................5	30.	10. 9
Isaac Smith Esqr..........Do....................6	13.	7. 7
Ebenezer Storer ....Do....................7	60.	14. 6 1/2
Royal Tyler Esqr..........Do....................8	5.	17. 0
Melatiah Bourn Esqr...Do....................9	33.	
Jonathan Mason ....Do....................10	30.	15. 6
Henderson Inches.......Do..................11	27.	11. 0
John Avery Esqr. ....Do..................12	53.	13. 0
Samuel Proctor, Ballance of his acct.	44.	7. 3
Ditto for half a year's Salary due the 1st. Inst.	12.	
Joseph Lasinby, keepg. distracted persons	23.	12. 0
Samuel Grant Esqr. towards the Board of		
John Roberts fm Decr. 11th. 1765. 12 Weeks @ 2/.	1.	4. 0
Carrd. Over	£518.	14. 5 1/4

Brot. Over	£518.	14. 5 1/4
To Samuel Ruggles, Balla. of his acct.	68.	9. 5
Andrew Hall . acct. for Shoes	28.	15. 6
Robert Hill . . . Do. for Carting	15.	19. 11
Josiah Waters . . Do. for painting	5.	3. 2
Nathaniel Band, acct. for Funerals	4.	6. 4
Dr. Paul Landrie . . his acct.	3.	
	£644.	8. 9 1/4

the drafts for this year amount to	£2658. 17. 7 1/2
drafts on province Treasurer	585. 9. 2 1/2
Expended for the Town	£2073. 8. 5

The Overseers' Finances 1738-1769

Boston April 2d. 1766

Granted by The Overseers

To Samuel Proctor, Ballance of his acct.	£39.	4.	5 1/2
Joseph Lasinby keepg. distracted persons	18.	16.	0
John Avery Esqr. his acct. for Ward N. 12	4.	11.	3
	£62.	11.	8 1/2

Boston May 7th. 1766

Granted by The Overseers

To Samuel Procter, Balla. of his acct.	£99.	18.	10 1/4
Joseph Lazinsby, keepg. distracted persons	21.	10.	0
Nathaniel Band's acct. for Funerals	2.	9.	6
William Pell, his acct. for his mother's Board from Feby. 5th. 13 Weeks @ 3/4d.	2.	3.	4
Ezekiel Adams, keepg. Mary Allen a Distracted person from Septr. 7th. 26 weeks @ 4/	5.	4.	0
Isaac Cazneau, Rent of a House one quarter due the 1st. April	2.		
William Greenleafe for 50 bus. Rye @ 24/ O[ld] T[eno]r. is	8.		
	£141.	5.	8 1/4

Boston June 4th. 1766

Granted by the Overseers

To Samuel Procter Ballce. of his Accot. for Allowance for Interest of Money Advanc'd by him for the Town from	75.	6.	9 1/2	
March 1 1765 to March 1 1766	24.		99.	6.	9 1/2
To Joseph Lasinbey keepg. Sick & Distracted persons			15.	12.	
			£114.	18.	9 1/2

The Overseers' Finances 1738-1769

Boston July 2nd. 1766

Granted by the Overseers

To Samuel Procter Ballce. of his Accot.	68.	11	
To Wm. Greenleaf for Grain &c.	32. 14.	11	
To John Leveret Esqr. for Grain	16.		
To Isaac Cazneau a quarters Rent	2.		
To Joseph Lazenby keepg. distracted persons	16. 16.		
To Elisha Savel <*Bill for Ammon Browr*>	3. 14.		
To Wm. Pell for his mothers Board from May 7th. 8 weeks @ 3/4	1. 6. 8		
To John Ruggles Carpenters. Accot.	32. 19. 4	£173. 11. 10	

Boston August 6th. 1766

Granted by the Overseers

To Samuel Procter Ballce. of Accot.	189. 2. 11	
To Edwd. Winter for his Accot.	4. 16. 1	
To Andrew Hall for Shoes	19. 16. 9 1/2	
To Edwd. Carnes for Rent	4. 14.	
To Wm. Greenleaf for provisions	23. 6.	
To Samuel Marshall for his Accot. for medicine & attendance from May 1st. 1765 to June 5th. 1766	32. 10.	
To Joseph Lazenby keepg. distracted persons	26.	£300. 5. 9 1/2

Boston Sepr. 3rd. 1766

Granted by the Overseers

To Samuel Procter Ballce. of Accot.	88. 4	
Joseph Lazenby keepg. Distracteds	22.	
Thomas Newell note of Carting	5. 16. 8	
Shippey Townsend for his Note	17. 11.	
John Means for his Note	8.	
Isaac Smith for supplys to Nutrals	17. 13. 6	
ditto for Digging Vault	6.	
Joseph Dean for keepg. a Child of Meriam Fife	3.	
Samuel Procter for 1/2 years Salery due the first Inst.	12.	£163. 8. 5

The Overseers' Finances 1738-1769

Granted by the Overseers

To Samuel Procter Ballce. of his Account	68.	5.	8
To Isaac Cazneau for a Months Rent & repairs	1.	8.	4
To Joseph Lazenby keepg. distracted people	29.	10.	
To Thoms. Newall his Accot. of Cartg. dirt	5.	16.	8
To Nathl. Band for his Accot. of Funerels	4.	4.	8
To Ebenr. Storer for Boards & for digg. a Vault	10.	12.	8
To Henderson Inches his Accot. for ditto	10.		
To Jonathan Mason his Accot. for ditto	3.		
To Joseph Gardner Esqr. his Accot. for ditto	4.		
To Daniel French his Accot. for Medicine & Attendance	1.	10.	
	£138.	8.	

Granted by the Overseers

To Samuel Procter Ballce. of his Account	112.	15.	6 1/2
To Wm. Pell for his mothers board from July 2nd. to Novr. 5 is 18 Weeks @ 3/4	3.		
To Alexander Young for keepg. Margaret Johnson	3.	17.	8
To Roger McKnight for Accot. of Labour	2.	14.	
To Joseph Lazenby keeping distracted people	22.	14.	
To Benjamin Clark for Rent to Sepr. 1	9.	6.	8
To Ezekiel Adams keepg. Mary Allen	5.	9.	
To Joseph Bradford Glaziers Accot.	3.	7.	5 1/2
	£163.	4.	4
To Mary Langford keepg. Ann Langford	4.	4.	
	£167.	8.	4

The Overseers' Finances 1738-1769

Boston Decr. 3d. 1766

Granted by The Overseers

To Samuel Procter Balla. of his acct.	£91. 5. 2 1/2
Joseph Lasinby keepg. distracted persons	24. 16. 0
William Whitwell for Cash pd. for Wheat in Augst.	26. 16. 0
Samuel Grant Esqr. towards the Board of John ⎫ Roberts from March 5th. 39 Weeks @ 2/ ⎭	3. 18. 0
John Means, for Work at the Almshouse	7. 2. 8
Jabez Nichols for Mary Mirick's Board ⎫ 18 Weeks 1/2 @ 2/. Funeral Charges 6/ ⎭	2. 3. 0
	£156. 0. 10 1/2

Boston January 15th. 1767

Granted by The Overseers

To Samuel Procter, Ballance of his acct.	£81. 12. 1 1/2
Joseph Lasinby, keepg. distracted persons	37. 10. 0
William Whitwell, for Cash pd. for Corn	19. 1. 3
Jonathan Davis, for his acct.	4. 3. 8
Andrew Hall for his acct. for Shoes	15. 17. 2 1/2
Joseph Shed, Balla. of his acct.	6. 7. 8
John Ruggles, acct. for Repairs	145. 18. 4
	£310. 10. 3

Boston Febry. 11th. 1767

Granted by the Overseers

To Samuel Procter Ballce. of his Account	82. 8. 9
Wm. Pell for his mothers board from Novr. 5th. to Febry. 11 is 15 weeks @ 3/4	2. 10.
Edward Winter Blacksmiths Accot.	8. 5. 2
Joseph Lasinby keepg. distracted persons	35. 12.
Thomas Dawse his Account	19. 9. 7 1/2
	£148. 5. 6 1/2

Boston March 4th. 1767

Granted by the Overseers

To Benja. Hammett for his Accot. for Ward.... No. 1	9.	5.	1
To William Whitwell Do. part of No. 1 .... & No. 2	125.	4.	1
Joseph Gardner Esqr. Do. part of No. 1 ..... & 3	48.	2.	2
John Barrett Esqr......... do............................ 4	34.	7.	9 1/2
Benjamin Dolbear ...... do............................ 5	40.	16.	7
Isaac Smith Esqr.......... do............................ 6	21.	10.	8
Ebenezer Storer .... do............................ 7	94.	7.	6 1/2
Royal Tyler Esqr.......... do............................ 8	21.	11.	1
Melatiah Bourn Esqr... do............................ 9	27.	19.	6
Jonathan Mason .... do............................ 10	47.	19.	1 1/4
Henderson Inches....... do............................ 11	36.	3.	1
Wm. Greenleaf .... do............................ 12	95.	14.	
Samuel Procter Ballce. of his Accot.	79.	14.	3
Ditto for half a years Salary due the 1st. Inst.	12.		
Joseph Lazenby keepg. distracted persons	30.	6.	
Carr'd Over	£725.	0.	11 1/4

Brought Over	£725.	0.	11 1/4
To Robert Hill for Carting	14.	15.	6
Wm. Greenleaf for his Accot. Meal &c	10.	17.	5
Jos: Waters for his Account	6.	13.	10
Nathl. Band for Accot. of Funerals	5.	6.	8
John Barret Esqr. for Accot. Grain	55.	15.	10
Joseph Bradford for his Accot.	7.	17.	1
Cochran & Campbel Accot. Wood for Ward			
No. 1 to Sepr. 10th.	11.	15.	8
	£838.	2.	11 1/4

whole Drafts of this year amount to	£3057. 18.	1
Drafts on province Treasurer	566. 2.	
Expended for the Town	£2491. 16.	1

The Overseers' Finances 1738-1769

〜

Boston April 1st. 1767

Granted by the Overseers of the Poor

To William Greenleaf his accot: for Corn & Meal	34. 13. 5
To Joseph Lasinby his Accot: for distracted people	31. 4.
To Samuel Procter Ballce. of his Accot.	67. 17. 4 1/4

To Jonathan Dix for keeping Sarah Teague
   a Distracted Woman from Febr. 5th. 1766 is
   60 Weeks @ 4/8
	14.

To Samuel Procter for Interest of his Accot. from March 1 1766 to March 1st. 1767	24.
	£171. 14. 9 1/4

Boston May 7th. 1767

Granted by the Overseers of the Poor

To Samuel Procter for the Ballance of his Accot:	63. 10. 10 1/2
To Joseph Lasinby his Accot: for keeping distracted people	40. 10.
To Andrew Hall his Accot: for Shoes	12. 7. 2
To Ezekiel Adams for keeping Mary Allen a distracted Woman	5. 4.
To William Pell for his mothers board from the 11th. Feby. to 7th. May is 12 Weeks at 3/4	2.
To Elisha Savil his accot: for Medicines & attendance to Ammon Breaux	11. 4.
To Ebenezer Storer his accot: disburstments for ward No. 7	6. 5. 11 1/2
To William Whitwell his accot: disburstments for sundry wards were no overseers was affixed	9.
	£139. 9. 4

The Overseers' Finances 1738-1769

❧

Granted by the Overseers of the Poor .... Vizt:

To Samuel Procter for the Ballance of his Accot:	71. 10. 10	
To Joseph Lasinby his Accot: for keeping distracted people	32. 8.	
To John Shute for keeping William Chadwell from		
the 15th. Feby: 1765 to the 20th. April 1767 is 113 Weeks at 2/	11. 6.	
To William Whitwell for 50 Bushells Rye at 3/	7. 10.	
	£122. 14. 10	

Mr: Procters accot: Expences	59. 10. 10	these sums makes
1 Quarters Salary to the 1st. Inst:	6.	out Mr: Procters Balla:
Intrest on £400 for 3 months	6.	
	71. 10. 10	

Granted by the Overseers of the Poor .... Vizt:

To Paul Farmer for the Ballance of his Accot:	72. 10. 10
To Joseph Lasinby his accot: for keeping distracted people	27. 12.
To Jonathan Mason for supplys to the poor in ward No: 10	1. 16. 2
To John Gore Esqr: his accot: for supplys to the French neutrals & Samuel Roach a distracted person	19. 7. 10
To Doctor Joseph Gardner for 1 years Salary ending the 1st. June last	30.
To John Whetcomb Esqr: for the Selectmen of Bolton's Expens: in taking care of Joshua Rand in his Sickness, & for his funeral charges, the draft is drawn in favr: Mr: Whetcomb ℘ desire of the Selectmen ℘ order on file	3. 17. 4
To Andrew Hall his accot: for making & mendg: Shoes	7. 13. 10 1/2
To Thomas Craft for 39 Weeks board of Abigail Young from 31st. October last to the 1st. July 1767 at 2/ ℘ Week	3. 18.
To James Otis Esqr: for what he paid John Otis for Nursing boarding Cloathing & the Doctors Bill for Nicholas Mangitt ℘ Accot: on file	11. 5.
To Benjamin Clarke for what he supply'd Dina Allen a Negro Woman with	2. 1. 4
	£180. 2. 4 1/2

The Overseers' Finances 1738-1769

Granted by the Overseers..Vizt:

To Paul Farmer for the Ballance of his Accot:	70.	6.	8 1/2
To Joseph Lasinby his accot: for keepg: distracted People	38.	2.	
To Messrs: Whitwell Williams & Tyler for 400 Bushells Wheat	96.	13.	4
To William Whitwell for 110 Bushells Corn the 24th. April last at 2/6	13.	15.	
To William Whitwell for 141 Bushells Corn the 16 June last at 2/8	18.	16.	
To John Leverett for Mollasses Sugar & Hogs fatt	41.	9.	7
To Timothy Newell for Nails	2.	9.	8
To Benja: Phillips for 190 Cord Wood	133.		
To Nathll. Band his accot: for burial of Sundry People	4.	1.	2
To Philemon Chandler for Doctor Daniel Hows accot: for board & attendance of Samll. Roach	6.	18.	3
To Edward Winter his accot: for Iron Work	1.	13.	10
To Joseph How for 11 Weeks board of his Brõ: John How a distracted person from the 15th. May to the 5th. Augt: at 2/8	1.	9.	4
To The Treasurer of the Town of Malden for the time being for the board Julia Perkins & Eliza: King from the 1st. Jany. last to the 30th. July last is 30 Weeks at 2/8	4.		
	£432.	14.	10 1/2

Granted by the Overseers of the Poor ....Vizt:

To Paul Farmer for the Ballance of his Accot:	56.	10.	7
To Joseph Lasinby his accot: for keepg: distracted people	31.	4.	
To Joseph Shed his accot: for Carting	3.	2.	6
To Joseph & Daniel Waldo's accot: for Pork & Beans	23.	6.	
To John Leverett's Accot: for Pork	7.	2.	4
To Robert Hill's Accot: for Carting Grain	11.	19.	6
	£133.	4.	11

The Overseers' Finances 1738-1769

❧

Boston Octor: 7th. 1767

Granted by the Overseers of the Poor .... Vizt.

To Paul Farmer for the Ballance of his Accot.	65.	8.	5
To Joseph Lisanby his accot: for keeping distracted people &c	36.		
To John Ruggles his accot: for Repairing the Almshouse & Work House	127.	4.	
To Mary Hatch & Son accot: for 190 1/4 Cord Wood for the almshouse & Work House	133.	3.	6
To Hugh McDaniel for 17 Weeks board of Mary Brown a distracted person at Tolmans at 6/	5.	2.	
To Ezekiel Adams for 22 Weeks board of Mary Allen a distracted person at 4/	4.	8.	
To Jonathan Dix for 27 Weeks board of Sarah Teague a distracted person at 4/8	6.	6.	
To William Pell for 22 Weeks board of his mother at 3/4	3.	13.	4
To Joseph How for 31 Weeks board of Mary Davis from the 4th. March to this day at 2/	3.	2.	
	£384.	7.	3

Boston Novemr. 4 1767

Granted by the Overseers of the Poor   Vizt.

To Thomas Newell Cartg. Stones to Alms House	2.	18.	
To Nathaniel Band for Burying sundry persons	2.	13.	8
To Joseph Lasinby's Accot: for keeping distracted people &c	33.	18.	
To Adam Knox's Accot: for Paving Stones	3.	2.	9
To Thomas Hodson's Accot: for Gravel	4.	8.	
To Edward Winter's Accot: for Iron Work	2.	2.	11
To James Fosdicks Accot: for Paving	13.	12.	
To Paul Farmer for the Ballance of his Accot:	64.	19.	3 1/2
To Philemon Chandler for 13 Weeks board of Samll. Roach at 4/8	4.	6.	8
To Philemon Chandler for Daniel Hows Bill for Medicines & attendance on Samuel Roach a distracted person	2.	19.	3
	£135.	0.	6 1/2

The Overseers' Finances 1738-1769

❧

Granted by the Overseers of the Poor .... Vizt:

To Paul Farmer for the Ballance of his accot:	137.	9.	2 1/2
To Joseph Lasinby his accot: for keepg: distracted people &c	37.	10.	
To The Treasurer of the Town of Malden for 18 Weeks board of Julia Perkins & Eliza: King from the 1st. Augt. last to the 3d. Instant at 2/8	2.	8.	
To John Dyer for work done at the almshouse and workhouse	4.	1.	
To Hopestill Foster for Timber [Joice?] &c ℘ Accot:	5.	5.	8
To Joseph Payson for 25 Loads Gravell ℘ Accot:		16.	8
To The Honble. Royall Tyler Esqr: 3 Bls: Pork at 60/	9.		
	£196.	10.	6 1/2

Granted by the Overseers of the Poor .... Vizt:

To Paul Farmer for the Ballance of his Accot:	81.	11.	3 1/2
To Joseph Lasinby his accot: for keeping distracted people &	32.	5.	
To Shippie Townsend his accot: for mendg: Pumps &c	1.	10.	11
To John Ruggles his accot: for work done at the Alms house & Work House	28.	5.	
	£143.	12.	2 1/2

Granted by the Overseers of the Poor .... Vizt:

To Paul Farmer for the Ballance of his accot:	70.	15.	10 1/2
To Joseph Lasinby his accot: for keeping distracted people &c	31.	4.	
To Thomas Dawes Esqr: Accot: for masons work	25.	9.	6
To Onesiphorus Tilestone Esqr: his accot: for boards	5.	16.	2
To Robert Pierpont his accot: for Oak Timber for the Alms house	1.	17.	5 1/2
To John Means accot: for work & Clay for the Almshouse	1.	18.	4
To William Pell for 17 Weeks board of his mother from the 7th. Octor: to this day at 3/4	2.	16.	8
	£13918.		

The Overseers' Finances 1738-1769

Granted by the Overseers of the Poor to the following Person[s][27]

To Paul Farmer for the Ballance of his Accot.			61. 19. 9
To Joseph Lasinby his accot: for keeping distracted people &c			31. 4.
To Samll: Grant Esqr: for 69 Weeks board of Jno: Roberts from 3d. Decemr: 1766 to 2d. March 1768 at 2/			6. 18.
To Philemon Chandler for 17 Weeks board of Samll: Roach from 4 Novr: last to this day at 8/ 1 pr: Shoes at 7/			7. 3.
To Edward Winter's Accot: for Iron Work			2. 18. 1
To Joseph How for 21 Weeks board of Mary Davis from the 7th. Octor: last to the 6th. Inst: . . . at 2/			2. 2.
To Paul Farmer for three quarters of a years Salary ending the 1st. Inst.			18.
To Thomas Crafts Junr: accot: for Painting the Work house Fence &c			12. 9. 8
To Ezekiel Adams for 26 Weeks board of Mary Allen 16 Weeks at 4/8 10 Weeks at 4/			5. 14. [ ]
To William White Esqr: Accot: for Ward No: 1			77. 10. 3
To Jonathan Williams Esqr: ditto for do:....... 2			65. 4. [ ]
To John Leverett's .... ditto for do........ 3	31. 10.		
Cash paid Benidick Webber for 24 Weeks board of his mother Rebecca Webber from the 6th. July last to the 14th: Decemr: last at 2/6 ℗ Week	3.		34. 10.
To John Barrett Esqr: Accot: for Ward No:..... 4			20. 16. [ ]
To Mr: Benjamin Dolbear's ditto.................5			62. 10. [1]
To Mr. William Whitwell's ditto....................6 [1/4]			22. 13. 5
To John Gore Esqr: ditto ....7 11 [1/2]			80. 16.
To Honble. Royall Tyler Esqr: ditto 8	11. 13. 6 3/4		
his Supplys for the house ℗ Accot	14. 0. 5 1/4		25. 14.
To Mr: William Greenleafs Accot: for Ward....9			18. 1. 1
To Mr: Joseph Waldo's Accot. for Ward.........10			55. 15. 10
To Capt. Samll. Partridge's ditto .....ditto .....11 3 [1/2]			34. 19.
To Thomas Tyler Esqr: ditto............ditto 12			40. 1. 8 [1/4]
			£687. 2. [6]

The Overseers' Finances 1738-1769

~

Granted by the Overseers of the Poor to the followg. Persons

To Paul Farmer for the Ballance of his Acco.	73.	10.	9
To Joseph Lassinby for taking care of Sick and distracted people	37.	10.	
To John Hill Esqr. his Acco. for Sundry warrants &c. for the Alms house & Work house	1.	10.	
To Natha. Band Acco. for Burying People	3.	8.	10
To Jona. Williams Esqr. Acco. for Supply toward No. 2	2.	16.	11
To John Ruggles Acco. for work done at Alms house	13.	5.	1
To Nicholas Butler for Cloathg. to Micha. Sheppard	1.	19.	7
To Joseph How for 34 Weeks board of his broth. John from 5th. Augst. last to 6th. April 1768 at 2/8	4.	10.	8
To Joseph Bradfords Acco. for Glazing	6.	0.	7
	£144.	12.	5

Boston 17th. May 1768

Granted by the Overseers of the Poor to the followg. Persons … Vizt.

To Paul Farmer for the Ballance of his Acco.	79.	1.	10
To Joseph Lisenby's Acco. for taking care of Sick and distracted people	41.	10.	
To John Leverett Esqr. for wheat & Rye ℘ Accot.	136.	15.	
To John Scollay Esqr. for 805 Bushells Corn 2/	80.	10.	
To John Scollay Esqr. for 415 Bushs. ditto 2/	41.	10.	
	£379.	6.	10

Boston June 1st. 1768

Granted by the Overseers of the Poor to the following Persons—Vizt:

To Paul Farmer for the Ballance of his Accot:	32.	11.	8
To Joseph Lasinby's Accot: for keeping Sick & distracted People	14.	8.	
To Doctor Joseph Gardner for 1 years Salary's ending the 4th. Inst.	30.		
To William Greenleaf for 7 Bls: Rye Flour 12. 0. 8 at 10/	6.	0.	8 1/2
To John Leverett for Butter Flour &c ℘ Accot:	15.	9.	4

To William Pell for 17 Weeks board of his mothers board   }
    from the 3d. February last to this day   }
        2. 16. 8

£101. 6. 4 1/2

To Jonathan Dix for 34 Weeks board to this day of Sarah Teague }
    a distracted person . . . at 4/8   }
        7. 18. 8

£109. 5. 0 1/2

Boston July 6th. 1768

Granted by the Overseers of the Poor to the follg. Persons…Vizt:

To Paul Farmer for the Ballance of his Accot.   62. 9. 4 1/2

To Joseph Lasinby's Accot: for keeping Sick & distracted peope: 39. 18.

To William Greenleaf for Pork & Beans   17. 14.

To Benjamin Phillips for 173 Cord Wood……….. 13/4   115. 6. 8

To John Gore Esqr: for 3 Bls. Pork ………………… 60/   9.

To Robert Robins for 40 Cord Wood……………. 13/4   26. 13. 4

To The Treasurer of the Town of Malden in full for the }
    board of Julia Perkins & Eliza. King to the 1st. Inst: }   4.

To Paul Farmer for one years Intrest of £80 he lent the }
    Town for the use of the almshouse to the 1st. June last }   4. 16.

279. 17. 4 1/2

Boston August 3rd. 1768

Granted by the Overseers of the Poor to the followg. perso[ns][28]

To Joseph Lasinby for his Acco. keepg. }
    distracted persons   }   34. 4.

To Edward Winter for Smiths work   1. 17. 9

To Joseph Butler for 6 days Labour   1. 4.

To Nathl. Band for Burials   3. 6. 2

To Mary Hatch & Son for 65 Cord wood 13/4   43. 6. 8

To Paul Farmer his Ballance   71. 7. 11

£155. 6. 6

~

Granted by the Overseers of the Poor to the follg: Persons—Vizt:

To Paul Farmer for the Ballance of his Accot:	74.	13.	3
To Joseph Lasinby's Accot: for keepg: distracted & Sick people	36.		
To John Leverett for Rye Flour &c ℔ Accot:	32.	7.	8
To Eze: Adams for keeping Mary Allen a distracted person	5.	16.	
To Ward Noyes Bill for Visitts & Medicines to Samll. Roach	18.		
	149.	14.	11

Boston Octor: 5th. 1768

Granted by the Overseers of the Poor to the follg. Persons …Vizt:

To Paul Farmer for the Balla: of his Accot.	98.	9.	8
To Joseph Lasinby his Accot: for keeping Sick and distracted people	28.	16.	
To [29] Tolman for the board of Mary Brown from 15th. June to Octor: 5th. 1768 is 16 Weeks at 6/	4.	16.	
	£132.	1.	8

Boston Novr. 2nd. 1768

Granted by the Overseers of the Poor to the followg. Persons

To Paul Farmer for the Balla. of his Accot.	52.	11.	8
To Joseph Lazenby keepg. Distracted people	28.	16.	
To John Gore Esqr. pd. Passage of Widdow Hawk	5.	12.	
To John Ruggles Accot: for work done at the Almshouse & workhouse	34.	1.	6
To Samuel Shute for 9 Weeks Nursing of Thos: Knight to the 29th. Ulto: at 2/8	1.	4.	
To Abigail Hairblue for 16 Weeks at 1/4 to the 28th. ulto: being what the Overseers allowed her out of the house	1.	1.	4
	£123.	6.	6

The Overseers' Finances 1738-1769

Granted by the Overseers of the Poor to the follg: Persons . . Vizt:

To Paul Farmer for the Balla: of his Accot:	96. 14. 1
To Joseph Lasinby for keepg: Sick & distracted people	33.
To William Pell for 27 Weeks board of his mother) to this day . . . at 3/4	4. 10.
To The Treasurer of The Town Malden for 22 Weeks) board Julia Perkins & Eliza: King to the 2 Inst: at 2/8)	2. 18. 8
To Samuel Grant Esqr: for 40 Weeks board of Jno.) Roberts to this day at 2/)	4.
	£141. 2. 9

Boston Jany: 4th. 1769

Granted by the Overseers of the Poor to the follg: Persons

To Paul Farmer for the Ballance of his Accot.	40. 11. 11
To Joseph Lasinby's Accot: for keeping Sick & distracted) People	25. 16.
To Nathl. Band's Accot: for burying People	5. 15. 10
To ³⁰Tolman for 13 Weeks board Mary Brown) from 5th. Octor: 1768 to 4 Jany. 4th. 1769 at 6/)	3. 18.
To Bennedick Webber for 13 Weeks board of his mothr:) from 25th. Sepr: last to the 25th. Decr: last at 2/6)	1. 12. 6
To Paul Farmer's Accot: for Leather	14. 13. 8
	£92. 7. 11

Boston Febry: 1st. 1769

Granted by the Overseers of the Poor to the following Persons

To Paul Farmer for the Ballance of his Accot:	99. 15. 11
To Joseph Lasinby for keeping Sick & distracted people	28. 16.
To Shippie Townsend for mending the Pumps	1. 7.
To John Scollay Esqr: for Intrest on Corn bot: of him	2.
To Abigail Hairblue for 13 Weeks allowance to this) day at 1/4	17. 4.
To Samuel Shute for 13 Weeks Nursing Thos: Knights) to the 28th. ulto: at 2/8)	1. 14. 8
To Joseph & Daniel Waldo's Accot: for Pork & Hogs fatt	8. 16. 8
	£143. 7. 7

The Overseers' Finances 1738-1769

~

Granted by the Overseers of the poor to the
following Persons.. Vizt.

To Paul Farmer for Balla. of his Ac/c				67.	18.	7
To Joseph Lasinby for keepg. Sick & distracd.				27.	12.	
To Paul Farmer for 1 Years Salary to this day				24.		
To Eziekel Adams for 25 weeks Board} of Mary Allen to this day at 4/				5.		
To Edward Winter for Iron work				2.	12.	5
To John Hill Esqr. Acco. for Commitments				3.	3.	
To Robert Hill for Carting Grain				9.	4.	6
To Thos. Crafts Junr. Acco. for Painting				7.	9.	6
To Wm. Pell for 12 week board of his mother 3/4				2.		
To The Honble. Royal Tyler for pork & fish				11.	2.	8
To John Bradford for Sugar & Molasss.				36.	19.	5
To Natha. Bands Acco. for Burying people				3.	1.	10
To Capt. Saml. Patridge for Sundrys for} the Almshouse				31.	12.	1
To Joseph How for 23 weeks Board of} Jno. Hows wife 2/8				3.	1.	4
52 weeks Board Mary Davis to} the 6 Instant . . 2/				5.	4.	
To Tho. Dawes Esqr. Acco. for Masons work				6.	8.	2
To Joseph Butler for work done at Almsehouse				1.	6.	

To William White Esqr: for Supplys to Ward......... No: 1}	102.	0.	8			
To Capt: John Bradford .... for ditto 2	55.	14.	4			
To John Leverett .... for ditto 3	60.	5.	1 3/4			
To Mr. Wm: Whitwell .... for ditto 4	39.	3.	9			
To Mr. Benja. Dolbeare .... for ditto 5	27.	12.				
To John Barrett Esqr: .... for ditto 6	12.	8.	7			
To John Gore Esqr: .... for ditto 7	80.	19.				
To Honble: Royall Tyler Esqr: for ditto 8	11.	19.	9			
To Mr. Wm. Greenleaf ......for ditto...............9	13.	8.	4			
To Mr. Joseph Waldo ....for ditto.............. 10	55.	18.				
To Capt. Sam Partridge ....for ditto............... 11	33.	2.	11			
To Thos: Tyler Esqr. ....for ditto.............. 12	<u>49.	2.	8</u>	541.	5.1 3/4	
To Mr. Benja. Dolbeare for Supplys to the Almshouse				<u>12.	15.	2</u>
				£801.	15.	9 3/4

[…][31] Several persons above Mention'd the sums […] [a]ffix'd to their Names Amounting together to […]   Lawful Money

    [D]avid Jeffries   J. W.

[Treasu]rer of the Town of Bosn.   <u>J. H. &c.</u>

Boston Decr.   175–

Whareas Mr. A, B, of C, has received into his House D. E. a poore Wooman belonging to the Town of Boston, We the Subscribers Overseers of the poor of sd. Town hereby oblige oure Selves & Successers at all Times to save Harmless the sd. Town of Wobourn from any Charge that may Arise by sd. D. Es. being their, and will receive her again at aney Time when desired by sd. A. B.

We the subscribers of the Town of   do hereby recommend Mr.   of said Town as a person of sober life & Conversation & in good Circumstances & further Certify that both he & his wife are suitable persons to be Intrusted with the education of any Child which may be bound to them as an apprentice

This Indenture m[ad]e[32] The   day of   Witnesseth that AB of Boston &c i[n C]onsideration of the value of ____ Pounds Lawfull Money of NE part whereof has been received and part whereof remains to be received of ____ has put herself a Servant to David Jeffries & his Assigns, & with them to live after the manner of & Servant in doing all manner of Household work for the Term of Four Years, The said David or his Assigns to find her sufficient Meat Drink Lodging and Apparell during said Term and the said AB. doth hereby Covenant with the said David for him and his Assigns to Live with him or them during said Term as a Servant and obey all their Lawfull Commands. And the said David doth hereby Covenant with the said AB to find her as is above expressed during said Term.

    In Witness whereof the Parties above named have herewith Interchangeably set their Hands & Seals the day and Year first above written.

Signed sealed &c ⎫
In presence of Us ⎬

May 7: 1746.

Memo. Agreed to allow Nathl. Band Twenty shillgs. […][33] Funerals within the House & twenty five […] untill the House shall be furnished with […] then to deduct Four shillings on that accou[nt.]

1752

Account of mony recd. by the Overseers of the Poor from severall Towns in this Province for the Support of those poor of the Town of Boston who have had the small pox.   Vizt.

Jacob Wendell Esqr: old Tenr.

from the Revd. Mr. Appleton of Cambridge	114. 14. 2	
Revd. Mr. Barnard of M: head	166. 1. 1 1/2	
Mr. Broadstreet of do.	85. 1.	
Mr. Parsons of Newbury	78. 8.	
from the Episcopal Church do.	24. 1. 8	
Doctr. Miller of Braintree	10. 4. 4	
Mr. Bryant of Do.	40. 10.	
Mr. Stevens of Kittery	37. 1.	556. 1. 3 1/2

John Hill Esqr.

from the Church at Stow	2. 2. 6	
Ditto Hannover	7. 10.	
Ditto Menotomy	8. 7. 6	
Ditto Wrentham	6. 6.	
Ditto Pembrook	7. 9. 4 1/2	31. 15. 4 1/2

Thomas Hubbard Esqr.

from the Revd. Mr. Green of Barnstable	40. 14.
Mr. Williams of Sandwich	45.
Mr. Smith of Yarmouth North Precint	8. 13.
Mr. Dennis Do. South Precint	9.
Episcopal Church in Salem	40. 1. 6
Mr. Turrell of Medford	47. 13. 10
Mr. Loring [of] Sudbury	6. 12.
Mr. Collen of Newtown	18.
Mr. Rogers of Kittery	12. 12. 7 1/2
Mr. Gay of Hingham	23. 3. 9
Mr. Tucker of Newbury 1st. Church	42. 10.

Mr. Bourn of Situate North Parrish	33. 7. 7 1/2	
Mr. Wales of Marshfeild	9. 11.	
Mr. Mayhew of Chilmark	17. 14. 6	
Mr. Emmerson of Malden	16. 9. 10	
Mr. Weld of Attlebourgh	9. 14. 9	
from Plymtown	1. 7.	
Eastham	11. 17. 2	
Mr. Walter of Roxbury	23. 18. 8	418. 1. 3

Daniel Henchman Esqr.

from the Revd. Mr. Brown	6. 18. 10	
Mr. Bliss of Concord	10. 17. 5	
from Marshfeild	15. 3. 7	
Mr. Bowman of Dorchester	32. 12.	
Mr. Leonard of Plymouth	34. 11.	
Mr. Thacher of Wareham	13. 0. 1	
Mr. Ruggles of Rochester	10. 19.	124. 1. 11

Carryd. Over		£1129. 19. 10

Summ Brought Over		1129 19 10

Mr. Edward Bromfield

From the Revd. Mr. Hooey of Rochester	19. 6. 3	
Mr. Brett of Freetown	3. 8. 1 1/2	13. 4. 4

Andrew Oliver Esq

From the Revd. Mr. Robins of Milton	35.

Jno. Phillips Esqr.

From the Revd. Mr. Barnard of Andover North Parish	50.
Mr. Barnard of Haverill	33. 6. 3
Mr. Prescott of Danvers So: Parish	13.
Mr. Parsons of Bradford	13. 13. 9
Mr. Balch of Ditto	3. 15.
Mr. Chandler of Rowley	7. 2. 6
Mr. Russell of Barnstable	22. 11. 3
Mr. Phillips of Andover So. Parish	7. 8. 9

Mr. Cushing of Salisbury	8. 5. 7	
Mr. Rogers of Ipswich	16.	
Mr. Potter of Chebacco	15. 11. 3	
Mr. Wigglesworth	3. 12. 4	194. 6. 8

Mr. Isaac Walker

From the Revd. Mr. Webster of Salisbury	28. 12. 3	
Mr. Wise of Berwick	27. 6. 4	55. 18. 7

Mr. Ebenezer Storrer

From the Revd. Mr. Townsend of Medfeild	16. 0. 10	
Mr. Balch of Glochester	3. 11. 6	
Mr. Jacques	22. 5. 8	
Mr. Rogers	16. 8.	
Mr. White of Glochester	61. 18. 6	
Mr. Jewett	10. 14. 6	130. 19.

John Barrett

From the Revd. Mr. Lowell of Newbury	110. 14. 8	
Mr. Hales of Do.	21. 5. 2 1/2	
Mr. Johnson of Do.	13. 0. 7	
Mr Parsons of Byfeild parish	15. 12. 2	
Mr. Dexter of Dedham	21. 12. 10	
Mr. Tyler of Do.	8. 9. 3	
Mr. Wingeit of Almesbury	6. 14. 4	
Mr. Chevers of Eastham	19. 15.	
Mr. Crocker of Do.	15. 2. 11	
Mr. Lyman of York 1st. Church	60.	292. 6.

11 1/2

Mr. Joseph Sherburne

From the Revd. Mr. Sparhawk of Salem	50.	
Mr. Levitt of Do.	6. 12. 2	56. 12. 2

꙳

Mr. John Tudor

From the Revd. Mr. Roby of Lynn	8. 11. 13	
Chatham	5. 1. 3	
1th. Church In Falmouth	48. 9. 7	
Manchester	4. 10.	66. 12. 1
	Old Tenor	1975. 9. 8
	Makes Lawfull money	263. 7. 11

Extract from the will of the Hone. James Bowdoin Esqr.

I give the poor of the Town of Boston Thirty pounds old tenour ℘ Annum to be paid for their use to the Overseers of the poor of said Town yearly for ten years after my decease
The Above was distributed by the Overseers

Extract from the will of Mr. John Dennie of Boston Mercht.

I give & bequeath to the poor of the Town of Boston Twenty pounds Lawfull mony of this Province
The Above was distributed by the Overseers

Extract from the will of Mr. Thomas Palmer of Boston Mercht.

I give to the poor of the Town of Boston to be paid into the hands of their Overseers Thirty Pounds Lawfull mony of Great Brittain
the Above was distributed by the Overseers

Extract from the Will of Mrs. Blackadore of Boston

Item, I give and bequeath to the Poor of the Town of Boston the Sum of Twenty Six pounds thirteen Shillings & four pence Lawful Money to be paid to the Overseers of the Poor of the same Town.

Transferrd. into another book

Account of Person's in Alms house, on the Province Acctt.

Old Mrs: Bayley at the North end
old Mrs: Judivin New Boston
Mrs: Black'dos old Maid Ann
Brought from scotland with her
Fourty five years, ago; a Widdow
very Poor, & Objects of Charity[34]

Nov. 18.   Anthony De[nnie?] from Newfoundland ℘ Capt.   both feet froze

                 Catharine Bowen's child, a boy of 2 1/2 years old in the house from 1st. May
                 past
Sept. 3.   John Lucas, Mariner, hurt by a Gun—went away 17th. Novr.
Apr. 15.   Jamima Smith & child with child, layd in, Went away with 1 child 15th Jany.
Oct 27.   Thos. Gibson Mariner, ℘ Ordr. of T. Hancock went away 19th. Novr.
Dec. 21.   Eliza. Young from Albany, lay in 4th. Jany.
Jany. 14.   Cash Pd. ℘ A Oliver Esq for John Crocker Mariner Sick 10/
Nov. 2.   pd. T. Warden for 2 Coffins for 2 Strangs.   40/
                 pd. T. Moulen for burying Do.   30/

Notes

1   "Dead" was written over "10/." The subtotal for the line was also changed from £1. to 10 shillings.

2   The clerk corrected the entry from £9. 10.

3   Two letters have been supplied where there is a hole in the MS.

4   Text has been supplied here and in the next three lines where the MS is torn.

5   An entry following this was canceled and is now unreadable.

6   Blank in MS.

7   Ten shillings was entered mistakingly in the subtotal.

8   Blank in MS.

9   The following minutes and notations from meetings of the *Overseers* fill 3 MS pages in the Financial Register at this point. The monthly account format resumes on page XXX, below.

10   The edge of the MS is torn, resulting in the loss of text here and in two dated entries immediately below.

11   Amount changed from 20 shillings.

12   There is a small hole in the MS.

13   Total left blank in MS.

14   Blank in MS, here and in succeeding entries.

15   This amount was written over "63. −19. −11".

16   Blank in MS, here and in succeeding entries.

17   This amount was written over another figure, possibly 23. 16. 1, and written again in the column to the left.

18   The amount was changed from 4. to 0.

19   Several words in this entry have been canceled and/or interlined. This is the editor's best reading for the entry.

20   End of entry not found.

21   This line is in a different hand than the main entry.

22   This subtotal should read £2,106. 1. 0 1/4.

23   The correct total is £1,774. 16. 4 1/4.

24   Thus in ms.

25   The edge of the MS is ragged, the last letter no doubt torn off. Likewise, the final column of numbers in the entries below are often missing.

26   The edge of the page is torn.

27   Blank in MS.

28   Thus in MS.

29   The corner of the MS is torn, resulting in the loss of text here and below.

30   A hole in the MS has resulted in the loss of several letters here and below.

31   The corner of the MS is torn, resulting in the loss of text here and below.

32   The preceding six lines are written on a slip of paper pinned to the MS at this point.

MISCELLANEOUS
FINANCIAL DOCUMENTS
1795 – 1800

There are two separate Overseers files contained in this section. The documents refer to charges issued to the State or to individual towns for the care of non-residents of Boston who came under the administration of the Overseers.

The first is identified as the Boston Asylum Ledger and is contained in Box 15, Folder 1 of the Overseers Records (see "Guide," p. 19). The numbers in brackets at the left margin are the page numbers from the manuscript. The term "Asylum" was used increasingly to refer to Almshouse functions after 1800.

The second file is a list of Notifications from Admissions Register 5 in Box 11, folder 1 of the Overseers Records (see "Guide," p. 15).

Richard Harris		Dr.	Dollars	Cents		Contra		Cr.	Dollars	Cents
[1] 1795						1795				
Octor. 1st.	To 1/2 of his Pension for 6 months		12.			Novr. 13th.	By Cash		12.	
1796						1796				
Janry. 1st.	To 1/2 of his Do.	for 3 months	6.			Janry. 13th.	By Cash		6.	
July 1st.	To 1/2 of his Do.	for 6 Do.	12.			July 5th.	By Cash		12.	
Octor. 1st.	To 1/2 of his Do.	for 3 Do.	6.			Octor. 7th.	By Cash		6.	
1797						1797				
July 1st.	To 1/2 of his Do.	for 6 Do.	12.			July 10th.	By Cash		12.	
Octor. 1st.	To 1/2 of his Do.	for 3 Do.	6.			Octor. 26	By Cash		6.	
1798						1798				
July 1st.	To 1/2 of his Do.	for 6 Do.	12.			July 31st.	By Cash		12.	
Octor. 1st.	To 1/2 of his Do.	for 3 Do.	6.			Octor. 24	By Cash		6.	
1799						1799				
Janry. 1st.	To 1/2 of his Do.	for 3 Do.	6.			Febry. 28	By Cash		6.	
April 1st.	To 1/2 of his Do.	for 3 Do.	6.			May 9	By Cash		6.	
			$84.						$84.	
1804	The Town of Raynham	Dr.				1816	Contra	Cr.		

Date	Debit (Dr.)			Date	Credit (Cr.)	
June 6th.	To the burial of Samuel Chamberlain		$7.	Feby. 5	By P L of the Board	$7.
[2] 1795	James Ward	Dr.	Dollars Cents	1795	Contra — Cr.	
Novr. 10th.	To your board for 2 Weeks & 5 Days @ s12/ 5.		42	Novr. 10th.	By Cash of Daniel Sargent jur.	5. 42
1796	Hugh Willis deceas'd	Dr.		1796	Contra — Cr.	
Janry. 26th.	To his board & funeral Charges		6. 79	Janry. 26	By Cash of Capt. Jackson	6. 79
1796	Lewis John, a Negro	Dr.		1796	Contra — Cr.	
July 31	To a Coffin for a Molato man		1. 75	July 31st.	By Cash	1. 75
[3] 1796	John Bean	Dr.	Dollars	1796	Contra — Cr.	
Decr. 24th.	To your note of hand for		40.	Decr. 24th.	By Cash	40.
1804	The Town of Wilmington	Dr.			Contra — Cr.	
April 12th.	To the burial of Mary Seely, of your Town		$7.		Wrong	$7.
[4] 1797	James Scott	Dr.	Dollars	1797	Contra — Cr. Dollars Cents	
Janry. 3d.	To boardg; Your black-man		3. 75	Janry. 3d.	By Cash	3. 75

Town of Wilbraham   Dr.

1803

To the board of Aa'ron Elwell from 19th. to 25th. Novr. 1 week @ 12/	2.
To Doctr.s attendence & Medicines for Do.	1.
To funeral Charges for Do.	7.
	10.

Contra   Cr.

1804

Febry. 18. By a letter recd. 2d. April, from Wilbraham; Certifies, that the said Aa'ron Elwell did not belong to, Said Town, I believe that he Gain'd An Inhabitancy in Boston C F Rong Charg'd $10.

---

[5] 1797   **James Smith Negro**   Dr.

To the board of your Wife & 2 Children	$38.

Contra   Cr.

1797

By Cash	16.	20
Smith is Dead Balance Bad Debt	21.	80
	$38.	

1797   **Nantucket Town**   Dr.

Septr. 15th. To, Board of Peggy Conden 9 Weeks & 3 day @ 12/ from 12th. July To 15th. Septr.	$18.	85
1804 To the board of Reuben Allen from the 17th. April, To 2d. May; is 2 W & 1 day @ 12/ }	4.	29
To the Docter's attendance & Medicines	2.	14
April 18 To Shoes 7/6 Hose 3/9 ...11/3	1.	88
	$8.	31
May 8th. To add 6 Days more @ s12/ pr. Week	1.	71
	$10.	02

Contra   Cr.

1803 March 15th. By Error, Nantucket, did not own her	$18.	85
1804 May 8 By Cash in full	10.	2

		Dr. Dollars				Cr. Dollars Cents
1805				**1805**		
July 3d.	To the board of Mary Elliot from 13th. April To 3d. July is 11 Weeks & 4 Days @ ...12/	23.	14	July 3d.	By Cash in full	34. 71
	To the Doctor's attendance & medicines	11.	57			
		$34.	71			

[6] 1797 Freeport Town   Dr. Dollars   Contra   Cr.

		Dr. Dollars				Cr. Dollars Cents
Augt. 29th.	To board of Lucy Day &c.	68.		**1799**		
				Febry. 28	By Cash	68.
1800	To the board of Lucy Day in the Alms House from the 18th. June To the 30th. July 6 Weeks @ 2$	12.		**1802**		
	To the Doctr. Attendance & Medicines	6.		Febry. 8.	By Cash	148. 27
July 2d.	To a Shift 6/3	1.	4			
	Sent the above Accot. the 2d. Augt. last	$19.	4			
	To Lucy Day's board from 4th. to the 12th. Augt. is 1 week & 1 day @ 2$ per Week	2.	29			
	To Do. Board from 23d. Augt. to 31st. Augt. is 1 week & 1 day @ 2$	2.	29			
	To Do. Board from 18th. Decr. 1800 to 12th. Febry. 1801 is 8 weeks @ 2$	16.				
Febry. 11th.	To a shift 6/3	1.	4			
	To the Doctor's attendance & Medicines 8 Weeks	8.				
1801	sent the above accot. the 12th. Febry. last	48.	66			

	To Lucy Day's board from 11th. Febry. to the 8th. June, is 16 weeks & 5 Days @ 3$ }	50.14	
March 19	To a Shift 6/3	1. 4	
	To the Doctor's attendence & Medicines	16.71	67.89
June 8th.	sent the above accot. 8th. June 1801		$116.55
	To Lucy Day's board, from 8th. June to the 2d. July 1801 is 3 Weeks & 3 days @ 3$	10.29	
	To the Doctor's attendence & Medicines	3.43	13.72
	To asa Miller's board, from 25th. May to the 6th. July 1801: is 6 weeks @ 2$	12.0	
	To the Doctor's attendence & Medicines	6.0	18. $148.27

[7] 1797	Sandwich Town	Dr.	Dollars
Augt. 5th.	To board &c for Stephen Toby		13.30
Mar 25th. 1802	To bringg. Elizath. James To the Alms-House		25
	To Do. board from 23d. to 28th. March 1802, is 5 Days @ 2$ per week }		1.43
	To funeral charges for Do.		7.
Do Do.	To a shift for Do. 6/3		1. 4
	To the Doctor's Attendence & Medicines		1.
	(The selectmen say that she did not belong to Sandwich)$10.72		

Contra	Cr.
By Cash	13. 30
By Error, as the Town of Sandwich do not own the said Elizabeth James }	10. 72

1797 Octor. 4

Dr.				Cr.		
1803 Janry. 1st.	To funeral charges for Mary Cowhat	7.	1803 March 22d.	By Cash	7.	
		$17.72			$17.72	
1804	Denied					
May 17th.	To the burial of Elizabeth Harris an Indian; Inhabitant of Sandwich, as she said}	7.	1817 Feby. 5	By PL of the Board	7.	
		$24.72			$24.72	

[8] 1797 Salem Town		Dr.	Dollars	Contra		Cr.
Decr. 6th.	To board &c of Benjn. Shelton	36.12	1800 Janry. 23	By the Town of Salem accot. for Supporting in their Alms House Sundry persons belonging to the Town of Boston / alowed by the Overseers	$62. 67	
1799 Janry. 21st.	To board &c of Sarah Pettman	9. 7				
March 5th.	To the Overseers Draft on the Town Treasurer for the balance}	17.48				
		$62.67				

1800	To Polly Allen's board in Our Alms House from the 5th. To 12th. Augt. 1800—1 week @$2	2.	1801 June 3d.	By an over Charge for Polly Allen and Sukey Cain}	21.	71
	To Do. from 22d. Do. To 31st. Do. 1 Do. & 2 days	2.57		By the Town of Salem's accot. against the Town of Boston}	9.	33
	To Do. from 30th. Decr. To 10th. Janry. 1801 1 W. 4 D @ Do	7.71		By Cash for Balance	19.	45
		3.14				

NB. Polly Allen born in Portsmouth

To Patty (alias Polly) Wybert Board in Do. from 17th. Novr. 1800 To 10th. Janry. 1801— 7 W. 5 day @ Do.} 15. 43

To Sukey Cain's board in Do. from 25 Novr. 1800 to 10th. Janry. 1801—7 Weeks @ Do. } 14.
37. 14

1801

Febry. 5th. To Esther White's board, from 23d. Janry. to 5th. Febry. 1801 is 1 W. 6 D. @ s12/ } 3.71

To the Docter's attendance & Medicines 2.0 5. 71

To Christopher Crowell's board from 5th. to the 23d. Febry. 1801, is 2 Weeks & 4 days @ 2$ 5. 14

To the Docter's Attendance & Medicines 2. 50
$50. 49

To Sally Hortan's board from 31st. Augt. To 22d. Septr. 1801—3 Weeks & 1 Day @ 2$ 6.29

To the Doctor's attendance & Medicines 3. 9. 29

Paid Doctr. W. H To Doctr. Willm. Hunt's accot. &c for
Octor. 13th. Lydia Smith belonging to Salem} 26. 92 1/2

To Polly Wybert's board from 21st. To 24th. Decr. 1801 is 3 Days @ 2$ pr. Week 0.86

Decr. 22d. To a shift 6/3 1.4

25 To funeral charges 7.0
8. 90
$45. 11 1/2

1802

Febry. 2d. By Cash in full to this day

$50. 49

$45. 11 1/2

[9] 1797

		Dr.	Dollars				Cr.	Dollars
Novr. 19th.	Mathew Johnson, deceas'd				1797 Novr. 30th.	Contra		
	To board &c and funeral Charges		11. 50			By Cash		11.50

		Dr.					Cr.	
1797 Novr. 30th.	Andrew & Samuel Homer				1797	Contra		
	To their note of hand for		150.			Novr. 30 By Sundry goods to the amount of		150.

		Dr.					Cr.	
1805 Janry. 26th.	The Town of Dighton				1805	Contra		
	To the Burial of Christiana Talbut		7.		June 4th.	By Cash in full		$7.

[10] 1798

		Dr.					Cr.	
Janry. 2d.	Daniel Brewer				1798	Contra		
	To your Note of hand for		$150.		March 31st.	By Cash		60.
					1804 april 6th.	By balance (Bad Debt)		90.
								$150.

		Dr.					Cr.	
1798 April 9th.	Martha's Vineyard				1804	Contra		
	To board &c of Andrew Butler (Dumb man)		41. 25		april 6th.	By Balance, bad Debt, being out Law		$93. 42
May 16th.	To board of Matthew Hillman		52. 17					
			$93. 42					

[11] 1798

New York City	Dr.			1798	Contra	Cr.	
March 31	To burying a boy belonging to your city		6.	March 31	By Cash		6.

1803

The Town of Kingston	Dr.			1803	Contra	Cr.	
	To the board of Eunice Gardner. Mullatto. from 10th. May To 27 July is 11 W. 1 day @ 12	22.	29	July 27	By Cash		$23.
May 11th. 33	To a shift 6/3	1.	4				
		$23.	33				

[12] 1798

Castine Town	Dr.			1798	Contra	Cr.	
July 31st.	To the board &c of James Banks	$13.	57	July 31st.	By Cash		$13. 57

1798

Adam Babcock	Dr.			1798	Contra	Cr.	
Novr. 10th.	To the board &c of 2 black-men	$143.	69	Novr. 10th.	By Cash		$143. 69

[13] 1798

Cash	Dr.			1798	Contra	Cr.	
March 31st.	To Cash left by Mary Owen Deceas'd	$2.	77	March 31	By the Town of Boston paid it, as pr. Journal (Page 34)		2. 77
Octor. 31st.	To Do. left by Catharine Morton deceas'd	39.	84	Novr. 30	By Do.Do. Page (43)		39. 84
Novr. 30	To Do. for the board of Thos. Feild for 3 Weeks	1.	50	Do.	By Do. Do. (43)		1. 50
July 5th. 1799	To Do. for the board &c of Betsey Farrow	1.	7	1799 July 31	By Do. Do. (52)		1. 7
		$45.	18				

1801

March 10th. To Benjamin Hammatt Senr. Recd. of him Which he recd. of Edward Procter Esqr. to pay Lucy Harper's passage to the West Indies (but did not pay it) } 8.

			$45.	18

1801

March 31st. By the Town of Boston, paid it as per Journal Page 74 } 8.

---

[14] 1798   Thomas C. Amory   Dr.

Novr. 16th. To a Sailor's board for 5 Weeks & 1 Day @ 12/ $10. 29

1798   Contra   Cr.

Novr. 16th. By Cash $10. 29

1798   John Stoughton consul from Spain   Dr.

Janry. 1st. To the board of John Martella a Spanard 31 W. 5 d. @ s12/   63. 43

To a pare Shoes s9/   1. 50

$64. 93

1798   Contra   Cr.

Novr. 24th. By Cash on accot.   30.

By Balance charge this State which was paid $34. 93

$64. 93

---

[15] 1799   Dedham Town   Dr.

Janry. 16th. To the board of Nathl. Bill, Wife & 2 Children 2 Weeks $12.

1799   Contra   Cr.

Febry. 28 By Cash $12.

1803

Sept. 29th. To board of Ichabod Farrington from 29th. Sepr. to 11th. Octor. 1803 is 1 Week 5 days @ 2$ } 3. 43

To Docter's attendance & Medicines 12/   2.

To Board of John Tyler from Octor. 6th. to Do. 28th. 1803 is 3 Weeks & 1 Day @ 2$ 6.29

1803

Decr. 15th. By Cash on accot.   16. 43

Dr.					Contra	Cr.
Doctrs. attendance & Medicines	3.14					
Funeral Charges for Tyler	7.0	16. 43				
		$21. 86				
To the Board of Eliphalet Dean from 20th. to 25th. augt is 5 Days @ 12/ per week	1.43					
To funeral charge for Do.	7.0	8. 43		1805		
To the board of Mary Freeborn Negro, from the 6th. to 11th. Novr. 5 days @ s12/ per week	}1.43					
To the Docter's attendance & Medicines, Nursg. &c for Do.	3.0					
To funeral Charges for Do.	7.0	11. 43		May 11	By Cash	$19. 86
		$19. 86				

Weymouth Town Dr.			1799	Contra	Cr.
1804			March 2d.	By Cash	31. 57
To the board &c of Mary Wheeler	31. 57				
To the board of Ruth Turner from the 16th. July To 3d. augt. 2 W & 4 days @ 12/	5. 14		1804		
Augt. 3d. To shoes 6/	1.		Augt. 3d.	By Cash	$6. 14
To Cash paid for bring her to the Alms-House—75 Cent	$6. 14	75		By Do. recd. for bringg. her to the AA House	72
	6. 89				$6. 86
	$6. 86				
To board of Hannah Hollis from 14th. Novr. to 5th. Decr. 1804 is 3 Weeks @ 12/	}6.		Decr. 5th.	By Cash in Full	$9.

Dr.

1805

To the Docter's attendance & medicines   3.
   9.

To the board of Elizath. Gay from 5th. Augt.}
to 7th. Octor. is 9 weeks @ 12/   18.

To the Docter's attendence & Medicines for Do. 9.
   $27.

---

[16] 1799

July 10th.   Marblehead Town   **Dr.**
Octor. 11   To board &c of Elizabeth Yeaten $8.
   To board &c of Sarah Allen   11. 93
   $19. 93

To the board of Mary Widger from the 12th. March
To the 18th. June 1800 is 14 Weeks @   2$ 28.

To the board of Elizath. Yeaten from the 5th. To
the 18th. June 1800 2 Weeks @ 2$ 4.
To the Docrs. Attendance & Medicines 2   6.
To Do.   Do.   Do. for Mary Widge   3.
   $37.

May 7   To Cash pd. Mr. Redford Webster for the funeral
Charges of Mrs. Worden, including   7. 8
18/ advanced during her last sickness
She was the wife of Thos. Worden, who lived
with Lemont.   Carrd. to Folio (38)
   $44. 8

1805
Octor. 7th.   By Cash in full $27.

Cr.

1799   Contra
July 10th.   By Cash $8.
Octor. 4   By Do.   11. 93
   $19. 93

1800
June 18th.   By Do. in full   37.
Augt. 30th.   By Do. in full   7. 8
   $44. 8

Medford Town	Dr.				1800	Contra	Cr.	
1799	To the board &c of Polly Pushpay from the 24th. Septr. to the 11th. Janry 1800. 15 W. 4 D. @ 2$ 31. 14				Septr. 8	By Cash (per the hands of Redford Webster)	38.	14
	To the Docr. attendance & Medicines	7.			May 26	By Cash (per the hands of Redford Webster)	6.	
		$38. 14					$44. 14	
June 18th. 1800	To the burial of Joshua Reed, Hatter of your Town, (by order of Redford Webster)	6.						
		$44. 14						
	To the board of Martha Cristie from 24 June to 8th. July 1801—2 weeks @ 2$	4.0						
	To the Doctors Attendance & Medicinea	2.0	6.					
	To the board of Martha Cristia from Novr. 1st. 1802 To 8th. Febry. 1803 is 14 weeks 1 day @ 2$	28.29						
1803	To the Doctor's attendence & medicines	14.14	42.43					
			$48.43					
March 25	To add 6 Weeks & three days for Do. Dischd. her this day (and sent the accot. amounting to $67.71) carried to Folio (98)	19. 28						
			$67. 71					

[17] Cape Ann, Town of Gloucester	Dr.		1800	Contra	Cr.
	To the board of Sukey Brown 2 Weeks from the 5th. to the 20th. Augt. 1800 @ 2$	4.	Augt. 20th.	By Cash	$4.

Octor. 29th. 1801 To the burial of Betsey Ingersol, the Wife of James Ingersol, both born in Cape Ann, The Town of Gloucester } 6.

Nov. 13 To the burial of Ann Grimes of Gloucester 6.

Novr. 3 & 11th. To Shoes 6/ Shift 6/3 for Do. 2. 4

To the board of Hannah Curry from the 1st. Octor. To 22d. Decr. 1801. is 11 W. 5 ds. @ 2$23. 43

To the board of Safford & her 2 children from the 4th. Novr. (Gloucester, Disowns her, and her children)

To the board of John Atkins from 25th. Janry. to 1st. Febry. 1802 is 1 week} 2.

carried to Folio (64) $39. 47

1799

Newbury-Port   Dr.

Septr. 22d. To the board of Polly Lenox a child 2 weeks @ 12/ 4.

Sepr. 3d. 1800 To the Overseers Draft on the T. Treasurer for 80.

1801
Febry. 25th. To the burial of Lydia Marston's Child Widow of — Marston, both of Newbury Port, (they have been in Boston only a few months) 4. 50

1802 To Nancy Townsend's board from the 5th. Janry. to 17th. March 1802, is 10 weeks & 1 Day @ 2$ 20. 29

Contra   Cr.

By board of Susannah Lewis from Decr. 25th. 1798 to 15th. Octor. 1799 —42 Weeks @ 2$ 84.

1802
May 26 By Cash 28. 29

By balance due 4. 50

$32. 79

Dr.

Febry. 18th.	To the Doctor's attendence & medicines	7.
	To a pair of Shoes 6/	1.
		$32. 79

[18] 1799   Plymouth Town   Dr.

	To the Board of Elizath. Brimhall from the 7th. Novr. to the 12th. Decr. 1799. 5 Weeks @ 2 $	10.
	To the Doctor's attendence & Medicines	5.
		$15.
1800	To the board of Elizath. Brimhall from the 12th. Febry. to the 3d. March 2 Weeks & 5 days @ 2$	5. 43
	To Doctor's accot. for Salivating her	5.
		10. 43
1803	To the board of Dilley White from the 14th Decr. 1802 To 8th. April 1803 is 16 W. 3 ds. @ 2$ }	32. 86
Decr. 17	To B. gown s9/ Petticoat 18/ Shoes 6/ Shift 6/	36. 54
1803 March 18	To Soocks 2/ Shift 6/3 8/3	1. 37
		$40. 77
Novr. 2d.	To the burial of, Eunice Gardner, Mulatto belonging to Plymouth	7.
	Carried to Folio (115)	$47. 77

Cr.

1800   Contra   Cr.

Janry. 27th.	By Cash	$15.
April 15	By Cash in full	10. 43
1803		
May 30th.	By your accot., for the board, nursing and funeral Charges for Mary LeBaron }	19. 43
	Carried over, to Folio—(115)	

1797	Town of Penobscot	Dr.		1804	Contra	Cr.
	To the board of Rachel Dobbie & her two Children from the 7th. of Febry. 1797 To 20th. Decr. Do. 45 Weeks each @ 4$ pr. Week $180.			April 6	By balance, bad Debt, being Out Law	182.
Decr. 14 & 19	To a pair Shoes s6/ Shift 7/6 Child a shift 4/ 2. 92	$182. 92				
[19] 1798	Quincy Town	Dr.		1798	Contra	Cr.
Febry. 9th.	To the board of Ruth Crane, 5 Weeks & 3 D. @ 12/	$10. 86			By Ruth Crane. Town of Quincy, Disown her	10. 86
1804 Janry. 20th.	To the Board of Mary Spencer & her child from the third to 20th. Janry. 2 Week @ 3$ } 6.	$16. 86		1817 Feby. 5	By PL of the Board	6. $16. 86
	Ashburnham Town, say Boston,	Dr.		1799	Contra	Cr.
	To the board &c of Mary Southward from the 22d. March To the 26th. May 1798 / 9 W. 2 D. @ 2 $18. 57				By Mary Southward Dr. Ashburnham Disown her	$49. 71
	To the board of Do. from 4th. augt. To 14th. Septr. 1798—5 Weeks & 6 Day @ 2$ pr. Week } 11. 71					
	To the board of Do. from 15th. Octor. To the 22d. Decr. Do.—9 Weeks & 5 Days @ 2$} } 19. 43	$49. 71				
	To the board of Do. from 11th. Octor. to the Decr. 1799					

[20] Davis Colemore Curtis, of Georgetown. Dr.

To the board &c of your Daughter Charlotte from the 21st. Febry. 1797 to

Contra Cr.

1799 Westford Town. Dr.

Novr. 22d. To the board &c of Patty Leatherbee (alias Crafts) From 6th. Augt. to 22d. Novr. Includg. 15$ for the Doctr. Attende. & Medicines } 45. 62

To the board of Do. from 22d. Novr. To 22d. Decr. 4 Weeks & 2 Days @ 2$ } 8. 57

To the Doctor's Attendence & Medicines 4.

To the board of Do. from 21st. Decr. 1799 to the 22d. Janry. 1800: 4 Weeks & 3 Days @ 2$ } 8. 86

$67. 05

1800 Contra Cr.

By Patty Leatherbee, Westford, disown her $67. 5

---

[21] 1799 Portland Town. Dr.

Octor. 5th. To the board &c of Mary Morse $152. 64

1803 To the board of John Hall from the 3d. Janry 1803 to 14th. April 1804 is 66 weeks & 6 days @ 12/ } 133. 71

Janry. 3d. To 2 Shirts for Do. 12/6 July 9th. Trousers 6/ 3. 8

Octor. 31st. To Hose 3/9 Novr. 29th. Shirt 6/3 Shoes 7/6–17/6 2. 92

1803 Contra Cr.

May 9th. By Cash Recd. by the hands of Stephen Codman 152. 64

	Dr.				Cr.
1804					
Febry. 23	To cloth Trousers 15/ Shirt 6/3 21/3	3. 54		By Amt. Transfer'd to fol 52	213. 10
	To the Docter's attendance & Medicines	66. 85			
April 14	To Cash Paid his Passage to Portland	3.			
	To the board of John Hall from 14th. Augt. 1804 to	$213. 10			

	Belfast Town	Dr.		Contra	Cr.
1799			1800		
May 18th.	To the board &c of Thomas Coocks	17. 7	April 24	By Cash in full	17. 7
1803			1803		
July	To Charles Ruthleaf Board from 7th. July to 27th. Do. is 3 weeks @ 12/ 6.0		July 26	By Cash in full	10. 29
	To shir 6/3 Trousers 6/ shoes 7/6 3.29				
	To Cash for bringg. Him to the A: H. 1.	10. 29			

	Weston Town	Dr.		Contra	Cr.
[22] 1799			1800		
June 19th.	To the board of Mary Poole 13 Weeks @ 12/ $26.		March 5th.	By (Error) Mary Poole by law is an Inhabitant of the Town of Boston }	$26.
1802			1802		
Febry. 12th.	To the board of Catharine Middlesex & her two Children from 12th. Febry. To the 12th. March 1802 is 4 weeks @ 4$ the three } 16.		March 13th.	By Cash in full	16.

	Medfield Town	Dr.		Contra	Cr.
1799			1800		

June 22d.	To the board of Uriah & Lucretia Morse	$114.	57

	Janry. 10th.	By Cash		$26.	50
	22d.	By Mr. Artemas Woodward Note payable			
	Febry. 28th.	in all the month of March next for		37.	39
	(Recd. payt.)				
		By an over charge 25 Weeks & 1 Day		50.	28
				$114.	57

---

[23] 1799   <u>Barnstable Town</u>   Dr.

May 4th.	To the board of Hannah Hamblin, 13 Week @ s12/26.			s12/26.
	To funeral charges	6.0		
	To Doctor's attendence & Medicines 13.0		19.	
			$45.	
1801				
May 12th.	To Sundries for Sarah Loring, alowed by the Selectmen of Barnstable as per their Letter of the 8th. Instant		36.	
Mar. 18 1802	To burial of Rhody Miles an Indian		7.	
			$43.	
	To the board of Saml. Cary from the 22d. June To 25th. July 1802. is 4 weeks & 5 days @ 2$		9.	43
	To the Doctors attendence & Medicines		5.	
			$14.	43

sent the accot. and wrote the 29 July Do.

1800   <u>Contra</u>   Cr.

July 14th.	By Cash	37.	
	By abatement in the Docrs. accot.	8.	45.
1802			
July 27th.	By Cash		36.
	By Rhody Miles do not own (Error)	7.	
			43.
Augt. 16	By Cash	$14.	43

1799	Wellfleet Town	Dr.		1799	Contra		Cr.
Augt. 4th.	To the board of Sophia Arey 5 Weeks @ 2$		10.	Novr. 19	By Cash		20.
	Doctor's attendance & Medicines		10.	1803			
	To the board of Ann Fowler from the 6th. Decr. last to the 21st. March 1803. is 15 weeks @ 2$ }30.			April 8th.	By Cash in full		$99. 43
	To the Doctor's attendance & Medicines		15.	Augt. 30th.	By Cash in full		$29. 75
	To the board of Betsey Fowler. Alias Pitchard from 20th. Decr. last to the 21st. March 1803 is 13 W. @ Do. }26.						
	To the Docter's attendance & Medicines		13.				
			84.				
	To add 18 days more each	10.29					
	To the Doctors attendence & medicines	5.14	15.43				
			$99.43				
	To the board of Sarah Buntin from the 14th. July to the 30th. augt. 1803. is 6 W: 5 D		13.43				
	To the board of John her son 13:4 [...] @ 1$		13.57				
	To Shoes 3/ Gown & Petticoat 9/ Gown 4/6		2.75				
			$29.75				

[24] 1799	Town of Lynn	Dr.			1800	Contra	Cr.		
augt. 6th	To the board of Hannah Fovell, a Child. 6 Weeks @ 6/		6.		March 5th.	By (Error) Hannah Fovell (a child) by Law is an Inhabitant of the Town of Boston		$6.	
	To Polly Newell's board from 15th. Decr. 1800 to 10th. Janry. 1801 is 3 Weeks 3 days @ 12/		6.	86					
1802	To the board of Margaret Hudson from the 10th. May last, To the 23d. July 1802 is 10 weeks & 4 Days @ 2$ per week		21.	14	1802				
June 4th.	To a shift 6/3		1.	4	Augst. 9th.	By Cash		25.	32
	To Thos. her child from 8th. To 23d. July is 2 weeks & 1 days @ 1$ per week		2.	14					
	To the Doctor's attendance & medicines		1.						
			$25.	32					
1803									
Janry. 11	To the burial of James Parsons	$7.0							
octor. 13th. 1802	To Sally Tinkham's board &c	15.18							
octor. 10th. 1803	To Cash pd. Henry Edes, Cost in the Case with Lynn	11.64							
Do. 11th. Novr.	To the burial of Catharine Gager	7.0		40. 82					
	Carried over To Folio (111)								
	Sheffield Town	Dr.				Contra	Cr.		

[25] 1799   Town of Woburn   Dr.

Date	Description		1799	Contra Cr.	
Augt. 31	To the board of James Thompson 4 W & 1 D. @ s12/	8. 28	Decr. 14	By Cash	$12 . 46
	To a shirt 6/3 To carrying to Woburn s12/	3. 4	1800		
Decr. 13	To the board of James Thompson 4 days @ Do.	1. 14	Octor. 2d.	By Do.	24. 18
		$18. 46	1801		
	To the board of James Thompson from the 24th. Decr. 1799 To the 15th. March 1800 11 Weeks & 4 Days @ 2$ per Week	23. 14	July 1st.	By Cash on accot.	2.64
1800			1804		
Janry. 24th.	To a shirt 6/3	1. 4	Augt. 7th.	By Cash in full	8.4 10. 68
		$24. 18			
1801 June 19	To bringing James Thompson to the Alms-House not paid <0.50>				
	To his board from 19th. June to 1st. July 1 week & 4 Days @ 2$ 3.14	3. 64			
augt. 7th. 1804	To Board of Lois Convis 3 W. 1 d. @ 12/ & 75 cents	7. 04			
	for bringg. her to the Alms-House	7. 04			
		$10. 68			

1799   Town of Bridgewater   Dr.

Date	Description		1800	Contra Cr.	
Septr. 7th.	To the board &c of Elizab. Bolton & child	53. 28	Febry. 24th.	By Cash	$53. 28
1802				Do not own Hannah Bess (Loss)	7.
Janry. 13	To burial of Hannah Bess	7.			$60. 28
		$60. 28	1804		

1804
To the board of Silas Stutafunt from the 23d. June To the 17th. July is 3 Weeks and 3 days @ 2$ per week } 6. 86
To the Docter's attendance & Medicines 3. 43
$10. 29

July 24th. By Cash in full 10. 28

---

[26] 1799   Town of Sharon   Dr.

Octor. 16th. To the board of Joseph Lovell 4 weeks @ s12/ 8.
To funeral charges 6.
To the Doctor's attendence & Medicines 4.
$18.

Contra   Cr.
1800
Janry. 2   By Cash $18.

1799   Town of Dorchester   Dr.

Novr. 6th. To the board of Lettice Pearce 2 Week @ 12/ 2.0
Doctor for attendance & Medicines 3. $5.

To the board of Supply Clap from the 21st. March, To 14th. April 1801. 3 W. 3 day @ 2$ 6. 86

1801
Octor. to 16th. To the board of Mary Bird a child, from 4th. Novr. 4 weeks & 5 days @ 6/ } 4. 71

Octor. 15 To a Baize Gown & Petticoat 9/   Shift 3/3 2. 4
6. 75

To the board, of John Burk a child, of Elizath. Bird from the 14th. Novr. to the 24 Do. 1801 is 1 Week & 3 Days @ 6/ pr. Week } 1. 43

Contra   Cr.
1800
March 4th. By Cash in full $5.
By Cash in full—deducted from their Accot. against the Town 6. 86
Novr. 16 By Cash 6. 75
Do. 24 By Cash 2.

Dr.

1802		
Novr. 18	To a pair Shoes	57 / 2. 0
	To board of Joseph Goff from 5th. May to 5th. June 1802—is 4 W.3 days @ 2$	8. 86

[27] 1799   Captn. Jacob Lewis   Dr.

	To 7 Lascurs's board from the 15th. Octor. to the 15th. Decr. 8 Weeks & 5 Days Each @ 2$		122.
Decr. 10th.	To 7 pair Shoes for Do.	@7/ £2. 9. 0	
	To 7 pair Hose for Do.	@ 3/ 1. 1. 0	
	To 7 pair Mitts for Do.	@ 1/6 0.10. 6	
	To 7 Baize Shirts for Do.	@ 9/ 3. 3. 0	
	To 7 pair Trousers	@ 15/ 5. 5. 0	
12	To 7 Woolen Jackets	@ 18/ 6. 6. 0	
		£18.14. 6	62. 41
25	To the board of 3 Lascurs from the 15th. Decr. to the 25th. Do. 1 Week & 3 Days each. 4W & 2 Days @ 2$		8. 57
	To the board of 1 Lascur from the 15th. Decr. to the 25th. Do. 1 Week & 3 Days (Who came from Salem) @ 2$ pr. Week		2. 86
	To the board of Lascur from Do. 1 Day		29
	To Do. a boy from the 15th. Decr. to the 2d. Janry. 1800 2 Weeks & 4 Days @ 2$		5. 14
	To the Board of 3 Do. from 15th. Decr. to the 10th. Janry. 1800—3 Weeks & 4 Days Each @ Do.		21.42

Cr.

1802		
June 9th.	By Cash	$8. 86

Contra   Cr.

1800		
Septr. 24	By Cash Carried To the Town of Boston's Credit (see large Ledger Folio 4)	213. 83
	By Do. Carried to the Credit of Const. Freeman, being 12 per Cent on $160.28	13. 36
		$227. 19

1800
Janry. 10th. To Doctr. Fleet for medicines for 3 Lascurs   4. 50
     $227. 19

[28] 1799	Town of Needham Dr.		1804 Contra Cr.

Decr. 11th. To the board of Nathl. Tolman 4 Days @ 12/   1. 14   Augt. 25   By Cash on accot.   31.0
8th. To a Shirt 6/3   1. 4   By note for Balance   5.4
    $2. 18

1804   To the board of Mary Cook from the 7th. June To 25 Augt. is 11 W. & 2 days @ 12/   22. 57   1805 March 21   By Cash recd. for the above note   36. 4
To the Docter's attendance for Do.   11. 29
    $36. 04

1805   To the board of Sarah Howe from 11th. Febry. to 21st. March is 5 Weeks & 3 ds. @ 12/10.86 }
To the board of Wm. her child from 18th. Febry. to 21st. March is 4 w & 3 day @ 6/   4.43 }

1805 March 21   By Ebenr. McIntosh & Amos Fuller's Note of hand Payable on Demand for twenty one Dollars 86 Cents }   21. 86

To the board of Mary her child from 13th. to 21st. March is 1 week & 1 day   1.14 }
To the Doctor's attendance & medicines for Mrs: H   5.43 $21. 86

May 11th.   Recd. pay in full for the above note CF)

1804	Town of wrentham Dr. say Boston	1804 Contra Cr.

Janry. 17   To the burial of Job Blake $7.   By Job Blake Balance Boston   9.

To Supportg, him & family P. S. Snelling

2.
9.

---

[29] 1799   William Pratt   Dr.   Contra   Cr.

To the board of your Wife Hannah in our Alms–House, from the 23d. May To the 2d. Septr. 14 Weeks & 4 Days @ 2$ 29. 14

To the board of Do. from 25th. Septr. To 28 Do. 3 Days   86

To the board of Do. from the 14th. Novr. To the 24th. Decr. 5 Weeks, & 5 Days @ 2$ }   11. 43

$41. 43

1800
Janry. 1st.
By the Town of Boston, Wm. Pratt being poor, and not able to pay any part of the accot. the Overseers forgave the Debt $41. 43

Jeremiah Leonard   Dr.   Contra   Cr.

[30] 1800   Town of Natick   Dr.   Contra   Cr.

Janry. 4th.
To the board of Rhoda Lewis 1. Week & 1 D @ 2$ 2. 29

To funeral Charges   6.

To, the Doctor's attendence & Medicines   2.

$10. 29

By Natick Do not own Rhoda Lewis $10. 29

John Houstin   Dr.   Contra   Cr.

To the board of your Negro Woman Peggy

1802
Octor. 31
By Cash $4. 29

NB. due to C Freeman she being state poor (24 Cents)

from 17th. To 27th. July 1802. 1 W. 3 ds. @ 12/   2. 86

To the Docrs. attendance & medicines   1. 43

$4. 29

---

[31]

Town of Waltham	Dr.		Contra		Cr.
To the board of Edward Garfield from the 26th. Decr. 1799. To the 10th. Janry. 1800 2 Weeks @ 2$	4.		1800		
To funeral Charges for Do.	6.		Febry. 21 By Cash		$13. 4
To the Doctor's attendence & Medicines	2.				
1800					
Janry. 7th. To a Shirt 6/3	1. 4				
	$13. 4				

[32] 1800

Town of Hingham	Dr.		Contra		Cr.
Augt. 13th. To board of Oliver Gardner from the 4th. to the 13th. Augt. 1 Week & 2 Days	2. 57		1800		
To board of Fanny, or Tryeny, Sprague from 29th. June To 11th. augt. 1802, is 6 Weeks & 1 Day @ 2$ pr. Week	12. 29		augt. 13 By Cash in full		2. 57
To the Doctor's attendence & Medicines	2.		1802		
	$14. 29		Augt. 11th. By Cash		$14. 29

[33] 1800   Anthony Crane   Dr.

To the board of your Wife Elizabeth in the Alms–House from the 28th. July to the 29th. Augt. 4 Weeks & 4 Days @ 2$	9. 14
To the Doctor attendence Medicines	3. 50
	$12. 64

1800   Contra   Cr.

augt. 29   By Cash in full $12. 64

1804   Town of Hanover   Dr.

To the board of Snow House from the 15th. March To 20 June 13 W. 5 ds. @ 2$ }	27. 43
To 2 shirts 12/6 Shoes 7/6 Hose 3/9 23/9	3. 96
	$31. 39

1804   Contra   Cr.

June 20th.   By Cash in full   31. 39

---

[34]   James Ryan   Dr.

To his board in the Alms–House from the 25th. Augt. to the 5th. Septr. 1800. 1 W. 5 D. @ 2	$3. 43
To the board of his Wife in Do. 1 W. 3 Ds. @ Do. 2.	85
To the Doctor's Attendance & Medicines	2.
	$8. 28

1800   Contra   Cr.

Septr. 5th.   By Cash in full $8. 28

---

[35]   Town of Charlestown   Dr.

To the board of Susanna Paddock from

1801   Contra   Cr.

June 13th.   By Case $33. 18

	the 23d. Augt. to the 31st. 1800. 1 Week 1. Day @ 2$	2.	28
	To the board of Do. from 6th. to 9th. Septr. 3 Days @ Do.		86
	To Sukey Paddock's board from 17th. Novr. 1800 to 19th. Janry. 1801. is 9 Weeks @ 12/		18.
	To a Shift 6/3	1.	4
	To the Doctor's attendance & Medicines	9.	
		$31.	18
	To the board of Sukey Paddock from 2 May to 9th. Do. 1 week	2.	
		$33.	18
1801			
Augt. 10th.	To Cash in full	34.	7
		$67.	25
1802			
June 14	To Susannah Pease, Alias Paddock's board from 14th. June to 16 Do. 1802 2 Days @ 2$ per week		57
	To Sukey Parddock's board from 7th. July to		
	To John Edes, his Wife, & Child's board from 10th. To 23d. July 1802 is 5 W. 4 ds. @ [...] }	$9.	27
	To the Doctors attendance & Medicines, for Curing them of the Itch &c }	6.	

augt. 10th.	By the Town of Charleston accot. for Sundries	34.	7
		$67.	25
1802			
June 16th.	By Cash recd. of her Husband Mr. Pease		57
1803			
Febry. 22d.	By Cash in full to this day	16.	84
March 18th.	By Cash in full to this Day	2.	

	Dr.			Contra	Cr.
To Sukey Edes, board from 20th. To 22d. July. 2 Days—@2$ per Week } To bring her to the Alms-House }	1. 57				
	$16. 84				
To the board of Sukey Edes from the 12th to the 18th. March 1803, is 1 week }	2.				

[36] 1800

The Town of Stow	Dr.			Contra	Cr.
Octor. 4th. To burying of Olive Warner	$6.			By Stow, Do not own Oliver Warner	$6.

The Town of Newbury Port	Dr.			Contra	Cr.
			1801		
To the board of Catharine Hayden, from 6th. Octor: 1802 To 6th. augt. 1804 is 43 Weeks & 4 Days @ 12/ }	87. 14		Febry. 25	By the balance brought from Folio (17) Error the said Marston did not belong to Newburyport }	4. 50
To the Docter's attendance & medicines for Do.	43. 57		1805		
	$130. 71		March 14th.	By Cash recd. for Mehitable Kulm Pike	15. 71
To balance from Folio (17)	4.50				$20. 21
To the board of Mehitable Kulm Pike from 4th. Febry. to 8th. March 4 W. 4 ds. @ 12/ }	9.14		1806		
To the Docter's attendance & Medicines 4.57 for Do.			Janry. 8th.	By Cash on accot.	3. 88
To a Straw bed for ditto	2.0			By Amt. transferd to Ledger 2 fol	130. 71
	20. 21				154. 80

1805

May. 30th. *<To the funeral charges for John short* 7.>

1806

Janry. 8

To James Hayes board 1 week	2.0		
To Shirt 7/6 Hose 3/9 11/3	1. 88	3. 88	
		$154. 80	

[37]

The Town of Eastham   Dr.

To the board of Elisha Mayo from the 24th.
Sept. To the 8th. of Octor. 1800. 2 W: @ 2$ 4.
To the Doctor's attendance & Medicines   2.
                                              $6.

1801

June 3d.   To Cash paid for Seth Done, in fits   2.

Do.   To Do. paid John Clark for Board &
           Nursing Mrs. Thankfull Haggerman
           from 1st. March 13 Weeks @ 18/   39.

Septr. 2d. To Cash paid John Clark for board &
           Nursing of Mrs. Thankfull Haggerman
           from 1st. June 13 Weeks @ 3$ 39.

Novr. 5th. To Cash paid John Clark for the board
           and nursing of Thankfull Haggerman
           from the 1st. Septr. To the 1st. Novr. 1801.
           is 8 Weeks 5 days @ s18/   25
                                               26. 14
                                             $106. 14

To Willard Doane's board from the 14th. To the
21st. Janry. 1802. 1 week}   2.

1800

Octor. 8th.   Contra   Cr.
              By Cash $6.

1802

Janry. 22   By Cash in full to this day $109. 18

              By Cash in full to this day   86
                                            $110. 4

1802				
Janry. 14th.	To a Shirt for Do.	6/4	1. 4	
			$109. 18	
	To Willard Doane's board from the 21st. To the 24th. Janry. 1802 is 3 Days . . . @ 2$ pr. Week		86.	
			110. 4	
1803				
	To the board of Crowell Doane from the 6th. Decr. 1802 To the 6th Janry. 1803 is 4 weeks & 3 days @ s12/	8.86		
Decr. 6 & 30	To 2 Shirts @ 6/3...12/6	2.8		
	To Doctors' attendance & medicins. &c	4.6		
	To funeral Charges	7.0		
	Wrote & Sent the accot. Janry: 8th. 1803		22.	

1803			
March 5th.	By Cash	22.	

[38] Town of Marblehead   Dr.

	To Jane Millhorn's board from the 18th. to 25th. Octor. 1800—1 Week s12/	$2.	
	To Sarah Perry's board from 2d. to the 16th. Janry. 1801 is 2 Weeks 1 Day @ 12/	4. 29	
	To the Doctr. attendance & Medicines	2.	
	To Sarah Perry's board from 16th. To 28th. Janry. 1801	2.	
		8. 27	
1801			
	To Deborah Simmonds Alias Hammond board from 11th. to 27th. Febry. 2 W. 2 days @ 2$	4. 57	

Contra   Cr.

1800			
Octor. 25th	By Cash	$2.	
1801			

To the Doctor's Attendance & Medicines	2. 30		Janry. 23d.	By Cash	$8. 29
To funeral Charges	6. 50		Septr. 15th.	By Cash	$22. 80
	$13. 37				
To Rebecca Gee's alias Candish, Board from 29th. June to 7th. July 1801 is 1 W. 1 d.	2.29		1802		
To the Doctrs. attendance & Medicines	1.14		Janry. 2d.	By Cash	21. 72
To funeral charges	6.	9. 43	Novr. 16	By Cash	20. 57
		$22. 80			
To Sally Norris's board from the 11th. July to 24th. Sept. 1801. is 6 W. 2 days @ 2$	12. 57				
To the Doctr. Attendance & Medicines @ 1$	6. 29				
To Sally Norris's board 1 week 3 Days @ 2$	2. 86				
		$21. 72			
1802					
March 22d. To burial of Polly New's child, 9 months old born in the poor House in Marblehead Where her mother, said Polly belongs	4. 50				
June 22d. To Sarah Perry, her maiden name Goodwin board from 22d. June to 25th. Do. 3 Days @ 2$}	86				
To cash pd. for bringg. her to the W. H	50				
To Elizabeth Yeaton's board from 15th. Octor. to 16 Novr. 1802 is 4 weeks & 4 Days @ 12/}	9. 14				
Bringg. her/ 75					

To Shoes 6/ Docr. attendence &c. 4.57   5. 57

Carried to Folio (89) $20. 57

	Contra	Cr.		
1801				
Janry. 28th.	By Cash Carried to Town of Boston's Credit	15.	46
	By Do. Carried CF Credit / Roch being State poor	1.	40
Febry. 9	By Do. Carried to Town of Boston's Credit	3.	14

[39] Ralph Roch (of Italy)   Dr.

To your board from 30th. Novr. 1800 to 28th. Janry. 1801. is 8 Weeks 3 Days @ 12/ }   16.   86

To the Doctors attendance & Medicines 6 Weeks 6.

To your Board from 28th. Janry. To 9th. Febry. 1801. 1 Week & 4 Days @ 12/ }   3.   14

26.   0

NB. I am not sure that Captn. Norton paid me 6 Dollars for the Doctor's bill (which I alowed Roch for) CF

	Contra	Cr.
1801		
Febry. 14	By Cash recd. of your Father in full	$1. 14

[40] Eli Lane (of Cohasset)   Dr.

To your Board from 10th. to 14th. Febry. 1801 4 days @ 2$ per Week $1.   14

	Contra	Cr.		
	By Diana White & Child an Error	18.	21
1801				
Novr. 28th.	By Cash	$15.	51
Decr. 23d.	By Cash		57
		$16.	8

[41] Town of Roxbury   Dr.

To Diana White, Negro, & Diana her child's board from 14th. Decr. 1800, To 15th. Janry. 1801. is 4 Weeks 4 days @ 3$ pr. Week   13.   71

The Doctor's attendance & Medicines   4.   50

$18.   21

To Peggy Barnes's board from 23d. Augt. To

	31st. Do. 1800 1 Week & 1 Day @ 2$	2. 29
	To Do. board from 17th. Novr. To 3d. Decr. 1800. 2 Weeks & 2 Days @ 2$	4. 57
1800		
Novr. 21st.	To a Shift 6/3	1. 4
	To Peggy Barnes's board, from 6th. Febry. to the 20th. Do. 2 Weeks @ 2$	4.
1801		
Febry. 12	To a shift 6/3	1. 4
	To Do. board, from 1st. May To 10th. Do. } 1 Week & 2 Days @ Do.	2. 57
		$15. 51
Decr. 23d.	To Peggy Barnes's board 2 Days @ 2$ pr. Week	57
		$16. 8
	To Prince William Negro, Board from 12th. Decr. 1800 To 22d. Janry. 1802, is 58 Weeks @ 2$	116.
1801 April 29	To Shoes 7/6	1.25
June 16	To Duck Trouses 7/6	1.25
Octor. 3	To 2 Shirt @ 6/3	2.8
Novr. 16	To Shoes 7/6 Hose 3/9 11/3	1.88
	To Cloth Trousers	2.50
		8. 96
		124. 96

1802		
Septr. 17	By Cash in full for Peggy Barnes	6.
"	By balance Due to the Town of Boston } Carried to Folio (85)	124. 96

1802 May 10th.   To Peggy Barnes's board, from the 10th. to
          the 13 May 1802 is 3 days @ 2$ per. Week   86

          To Peggy Barnes's board from 7th. To 23d. July ⎫ 4. 57
          is 2 weeks & 2 Days @ 2$ ⎭

Septr. 16 & 17   To Do. for two Days   57
                                                                   ─────
                                                               $6. 00

Notifications

Names	When Notified	Towns, belong to	When admitted		Price[1]
1797					
Peggy Conden	Aug. 2d.	Nantucket	from 12th. July		at 2 Dols.
Lucy Day	2d.	Freeport	2 Jany.	Recd. 68$ in full 1st. March 1799	2 Dol.
Stephen Toby	2d.	Sandwich	28 July	in full paid $13.30	2 Dol.
Jacob Cook	12	Foxboro	31 July		2 Dls.
<John Wheeler> Error	*<Nov 1*	*Weymouth*	*7 Octr.*		*2 Dls>*
Benj: Shelton	1	Salem	9 Aug		2 Dls
Andrew Butler } Mathew Hillman }	Edgar Decr. 6	Martha's vineyard	20 Novr.		2 Dols.
Wm. & Sarah Rogers	Dec. 6	Medford	20 Nov.		1 Dol. each
Enice Vose	Dec. 6	Groton	25 Nov.		2 Dol
Sukey Robins	Decr. 11th.	Cape Ann	1 Decr.		2 Dols
Clarissa Rogers	Decr. 11	Newbury Port	23d. Novr.		2 Dols
Delia Atkins	Decr. 11	Plymouth	2d. Novr.		2 Dols
Rachel Dobbie & 2 childen	Decr. 15	Bagadowze on Penobscot River}	27 Novr.	(say Castine)	4 Dollars
Mary Wheeler	Decr. 18th.	Weymouth	7th. Octor.	Recd. $31.57 in full 2d. March 99	2 Dollars
Ruth Crane	Dec 20th.	Quincy	10th. Novr.		2 Dollars

1   Heading supplied from the final MS page of Notifications.

Miscellaneous Financial Documents, 1795–1800

Names	When Notified	Towns, belong to	When admitted	Price[1]
Mary Owins	1798. Feby: 7	Marblehead	13 Jany.	2 Dollr.
Mary Southward	April 1st. 1798	Ashburnham	22 March 1798	2 Dols.
Charlotte Curtes	July 5th.	Georgetown	21 Feb. 1797 — notifd. her father	1 Dol.
Captn. Adam Babcock for his two Blackmen	Do. 6th.	Boston	2d. Decr. 1797 to 8th. July 1798	2 Dollars
Lydia Gordon	Oct. 9	Newbury port	9 Oct. 1798	2 Dol
Uriah Morse & daught:	Decr. 5 1798	Walpole	from 22d. Nov. 1798	at 4 Dol. ℘ wk
Nathl. Bill, his Wife, & two Children	Janry. 4th. 1799	Dedham	from 3d. Janry. 1799 — Recd. in full $12.0 26th. Febry. 99	at $2 Dollr. p Week
Elizabeth Silvester	Do. 5th.	her Husband born in Plymouth	from Decr. 31st. 1798	@ Do.
Patty Letherbee	<Feb 6> March 7	<Portland> Westford	from 24 Jany.	@ 2 Dollr.
Peter Holland Negro	March 20th.	Hingham	from 13th: Janry. 1799	@ 2 Dollars
Mary Morse	Do.	Portland	from 12th. June 1797	@ 2 Dollars
Thos. Cox	Apl. 3	Belfast	from 23d. March 1799	@ 2 Dol
Mary Poole	Apl. 3	Weston	from 20 Do.	@ 2 Dol
Uriah Morse & Daughter	May 2d.	Medfield	from 22d. Novr. 1798	@ 2 Dollrs. Each
Hannah Hamblin	Do.	Barnstable	from 11th. Janry. 1799	@ 2 Dollrs.
Sophia Arey	July 3	Wellfleet	from 1 July 1799 — Recd. in full $20.0 19 Novr. 99	@ 2 Dollr.
Eliz Yeaton	Do.	Marblehead	from 14 June — (Recd. $8 in full)	@ 2 Dol
Mary Pool	Do.	Weston	from 19 June — (Born in Boston)	@ 2 Dol

Names	When Notified	Towns, belong to	When admitted	Price[1]
Hannah Fovell	3 July 1799	Lynn	from 25 June to	@ 2 Dol. pr Week
Hannah West	3 July	Sheffield	2 July	@ 2 Dol.
Betsey Farrow	3 July	Marblehead	3 July	(Recd. $1.7 in full) @ 2 Dol
James Thompson	6 Augt.	Woburn	3 Augt.	@ 4 Dollr.
Elizath. Bolton & Child	22d. Do.	Bridgwater	from 22d. May	@ 3 Dollrs. pr. Week
Polly Lenox a child	9 Septr.	Newbury port	7th. Septr.	@ 2 Dollars
Sarah Allen	2 Octr.	Marblehead	from 4 Sepr.	(Recd. $11.93 in full) @ 2 Dollrs.
Joseph Lovell	2 Oct	Sharon	20 Sepr.	2 Dol
Polly Pushpay	2 Octr.	Medford	20 Sepr	2 dol
Polly Leatherby	6 Nov	Westford	4 Octr.	2 dol
Elizabeth Brimhall	26 Novr.	Plymouth	from 7 Novr.	@ 2 Dollars
James Thompson	10th. Decr.	Woburn	from 10 Decr.	
Nathl. Tolman	11th. Decr.	Needham	from 8th. Do.	
James Thompson	26th. Decr.	Woburn	from 25th. Do.	@ 2 Dollars
Charlotte Curtis	26th. Decr.	Georgetown	from 21st. Febry. 1797	@ 1 Dollar
Edward Garfield	27 Do.	Waltham	from 26 Decr. 1799	@ 2 Dollars
Rhoda Lewis	28 Do.	Natick	from 27 Do.	@ 2 Do.
James Thompson	30th. Janry. 1800	Woburn	from 25th. Decr. last	@ 2 Dollars
Barilla Green	5 Feb	Woburn	from 31 Janr.	@ 2 Dol
Martha Larrabee	6 Do.	Woburn	from 6th. Novr. 1799	@ 2 Dollars
Martha Larrabee	21 Do.	Burlington	from 21st. Do. Do.	@ 2 Dols.

Names	When Notified	Towns, belong to	When admitted		Price[1]
Mary Widger alias Aubiny	1800 June 12th.	Marblehead	from 12th. March 1800	Do.	@ 2 Do.
Elizath. Yeaton	Do.	Do.	from 5th. June	Do.	@ 2 Do.
Lucy Day	June 21 1800	Freeport	from 18 Do.	Do.	@ 2 Do.
Sally Gaffit	Augt. 6	Charleston	from 4th. augt.	Do.	@ 2 Do.
Polly White Nego.	Do.	Malden	from Do.	Do.	@ 2 Do.
Sukey Brown	Do.	Glocester	from Do.	Do.	@ 2 Do.
Olive Gardner	Do.	Hingham	from Do.	Do.	@ 2 Do.
Polly Allen	Do.	Salem	from Do.	Do.	@ 2 Do.
Hannah Wales	Do.	Quincy	from Do.	Do.	@ 2 Do.
Lucy Day	Do.	Freeport	from Do.	Do.	@ 2 Do.
Elisha Mayo	Septr. 28th. Do.	Eastham	from 24th. Septr.	Do.	@ 2 Do.
Ephraim Tubb	Decr. 19th. Do.	Pembroke	from 17th. Decr.	Do.	@ 2 Do.
Lucy Day	1801 Janry. 5	Freeport	from 18th. Decr. 1800	Do.	@ 2 Do.
Arabella McLane	Do.	Wiscassett	from 8th. Do.	Do.	@ 2 Do.
Diana White Negro & Child	Do.	Roxbury	from 14th. Do.	Do.	@ 3 Do. (for both)
Polly Newell	Do.	Lynn	from 15th. Do.	Do.	@ 2 Do.
Martha Warner & Son	Do.	Braintree	from 27th. Do.	Do.	@ 2 Do.
Polly Allen	Do.	Salem	from 30th. Do.	Do.	@ 2 Do.
Sally Gaffit	Do.	Charlestown	from Do. Do.	Do.	@ 2 Do.

Sent the Accot. for the burial of Joshua Reed to the Town of Medford 10th. Septr. 1800.[2]

Names	When Notified	Towns, belong to	When admitted	Price[1]
Patience Dodge Negro	25th. Decr. 1800	Lunenburgh	from 22d. Decr. 1800	@ 2 Dollars
Patty Wybert	5th. Janry. 1801	Salem	from 17th. Novr. Do.	@ 2 Do.
Sukey Cain	Do. Do.	Do.	from 25 Do. Do.	@ 2 Do.
Sarah Parry	Do. Do.	Marblehead	from 2d. Janry. 1801	@ 2 Do.
Elizabeth Silvester	6th. Do. Do.	Lynn	from 4th. Do. Do.	@ 2 Do.
Thomas Delano	8th. Do. Do.	Bath	from 5th. Do. Do.	@ 2 Do.
Sukey Paddock	17th. Janry. Do.	Charlestown	from 17th. Novr. 1800	@ 2 Do.
Patience Dodge Negro Woman	24 Do. Do.	Ipswich, or Hamilton	from 22d. Decr. Do.	@ 2 Do.
Easther White	26th. Do.	Salem	from 23d. Janry. 1801	@ 2 Do.
Patience Dodge	9 Feby 1801	Wenham	from 22 Decr. 1801	@ 2 Do.
Eli Lane	14th. Do.	Cohasset	from 10th. Feby. 1801	@ 2 Do.
Elizabeth Monk & Son	14 Do.	Waldoboro	from 5th. Augt. 1800	@ 2 Do. (for both)
Deborah Simmonds Her maiden Name Hammond	16 Do.	Marblehead	from 11th. Feby. 1801	@ 2 Do.
Christopher Crowell	17th. Do.	Salem	from 5th. Febry. Do.	@ 2 Do.
Pegg Barnes	Do.	Roxbury	from 6th. Do.	@ 2 Do.
Supply Clap	1st. April	Dorchester	from 21st. March	@ 2 Do.
Mary Kelley & her child Mary Do.		Old York	from 11th. Do.	@ 3 Do. (for both)
James Cutler	Do.	Waltham	from 24th. Do.	@ 2 Do.

2 Written along the left margin of the MS.

Names	When Notified	Towns, belong to	When admitted		Price[1]
Susanna Keene Wife of Zubal Keene	Do.	Pembrook	from 23d. Febry.		@ 2 Do.
Nancy Wendell & her Son	Do.	Cambridge	from 13d. March	for both	@ 3 Do.
Eunice Gardner, (Molato)	13th. Do.	Plymouth	from 28th. March		@ 2 Do.
<Mary Killey & her child Mary	17th. Do.	Old-York	from 11th.>		
Mary Smith	6th. May 1801	Hallowell	from 20 April 1801		@ 2 Do.
Peggy Barnes	6th. Do.	Roxbury	from 1st. May		@ 2 Do.
Sukey Ralfe	6th. Do.	Portland	from Do.		@ 2 Do.
Patty Sabins	6th. Do.	Brookfield	from 2d. Do.		@ 2 Do.
Polly Allen	6th. Do.	Salem	from 29th. April		@ 2 Do.
Janny Wade	6th. Do.	Salem	from Do.	(her Father Peter Francis)	@ 2 Do.
Hannah Wood	6th. Do.	Walpole	from 2d. May		@ 2 Do.
Lucy Paddock	6th. Do.	Charlestown	from 2d. Do.		2 Do.
Mrs. Haggerman formerly Rich	3d. June Do.	Eastham	from 1st. March Do.		@ 3 Do.
Betsey Pillow, or Pillar	4 June Do.	Kittery	from 17th. May Do.		@ 2 Do.
Elisha P. Warfield	Do.	Heath	from 19th. Do.		@ 2 Do.
Peter Lane Negro	Do.	Bedford	from 21st. Do.		@ 2 Do.
Prince William Negro	17th. June Do.	Roxbury	from 12th. Decr. 1800		@ 2 Do.
Lydia Amsden & 3 Children	20th. Do. Do.	Framingham	from 18th. May 1801		@ 5 Do.
James Tompson	20th. Do. Do.	Woburn	from 19th. June Do.		@ 2 Do.
Mary Ball	6th. July Do.	Concord	from 5th. July Do.		@ 2 Do.

Names	When Notified	Towns, belong to	When admitted		Price[1]
Elizabeth Loynes	7 Do.　Do.	Randolph	from 30 Do.　Do.	for the Whole	@ 5 Do.
Nathl. Miles & Peter Lines	6th. Augt.　Do.	Randolph	from 4 Augt.　Do.	for both	@ 2 Do.
[S]ally[3] Morris, alias Norris	18th. Septr. Do.	Marble–head	from 11th. July Do.		@ 2 Do.
[Ol]ive Varrell	Octor. 2	york	from 1st. Octor. Do.		@ 2 Do.
Ebenr. Chandler	15 Oct. 1801	Andover	June 5 1801		12/
Susanna Severy	16 Do.	Sutton	Augt. 30th. Do.		Do.
Lydia Smith	13 Do.	Salem		Sundry accot. for her $26.92 1/2	
Elizabeth Pillar	6 Novr.	Kittery	Octor. 30		@ 2$ per week
Mary Bird, a child	13th. Do.	Dorchester	Do. 14		@ 1$ Do.
Polly Wybert	22d. Decr.	Salem	Decr. 21st.		@ 2$ Do.
Peggy Barnes	22d. Do.	Roxbury	Do. 21st.		@ Do. Do.
Sally Safford, & her	22d. Do.	York	4th. Novr.		@ Do. Do.
Childn. John & Jeremiah	22d. Do.	Do.	4th. Do.		@ Do. for both
Sarah Norris	24th. Do.	Marblehead	23d. Decr.		@ Do. per Week

Ebenr. Chandler,[4] Rigger aged 60 Son of Benj. Chandler of Andover, who probably was warned out of Newbury, being a native of Andover. Ebenr. his son does not know where he was born, but lived in Newbury very young & lived & married & had two children in Newbury from whence he moved to Boston in 1775.

Served his time with Capn. Gideon Woodwell, a ship Carpenter & afterwards worked as a Journeyman carpenter.

1. Heading supplied from the final MS page of notifications.
2. Written along the left margin of the MS.
3. The corner of the MS is worn away, resulting in the loss of text in this line and the next.
4. This entry written on a slip of paper interleaved at this point in the volume.

SAMUEL WHITWELL'S ACCOUNTS
1769 – 1792

Samuel Whitwell served as an Overseer for twenty-one years, a remarkable length of service and even more remarkable for the fact that he served most of that time in Ward 10. We can be sure that he knew the circumstances of most of the 200 or so households and the transient workers who were in Ward 10 at any time, and after years as an Overseer, his relationships with needy residents were personal and constant. The document is not part of the Overseers Manuscript Collection but is a separate and private document in the MHS collection. It is, nevertheless, a vital surviving evidence of the Overseers' routine duties and management outside the institutional framework. Whitwell's accounts show his regular personal disbursements to the poor in his ward, from his own resources and his claims to the town treasurer for reimbursement. What gives the document special value is that it is the only known surviving ledger of its kind, and while we assume that every Overseer kept some account of his "out of doors" contributions, it is disappointing that more account books cannot be found. So it is that Whitwell's book takes on a special significance and can be seen speculatively as an example of every Overseer's private relationships with the poor who did not end up in the Almshouse. It can be seen also in relation to the individual claims that appear in the Overseers Financial Records transcribed in this volume.

The numbers in brackets at the left margin are the page numbers noted in the manuscript.

Samuel Whitwell's Accounts, 1769–1792

◠

Samuel Whitwell's
Book—April 1769

INDEX

[1]　　　　The Town of Boston for Sundry Disburs ⎫
　　　　　　　　tments for the poor in Ward No. 2　⎭　　Dr.

1769

April　　4　　To 2 foot wood to Mehitable Orange　　　　　5.　4

　　　　　　　To Cash to ditto (sister Sick)　　　　　　　　　2.

	8	To ditto Eliza. Nichson	1.	6
		To 2 foot wood to Thomas Bennitt	5.	4
	10	To 4 ditto to Robert Way	9.	4
	17	To Cash to Priscilla Gill	6.	
		To ditto to Sarah White @ 6/ ℘ Mo.	6.	
		To 4 foot wood to John McLarrey	9.	4
		To Cash to Thomas Bennitt	1.	6
	20	To 2 foot wood to Mehile. Orange	5.	4
	22	To Cash to Sarah Blewitt	1.	6
	26	To ditto to Thomas Bennitt	1.	6
		To ditto paid John Cades for Abigl. Oranges funerall	10.	
	29	To ditto to Thomas Bonnett	1.	6
May	2	To ditto to Jemima Wheaton	2.	
	3	To ditto to Sarah White	3.	
	5	To ditto to Eliz Nichson	1.	6
		To ditto paid Mary Snelling for Schooling	17.	4
	6	To ditto to Thomas Bennitt	1.	6
		To ditto to Margrett Butler	1.	6
	8	To ditto to Sarah Blewitt	1.	6
	12	To 2 foot wood to Thom Bennitt	5.	
	16	To Cash to priscilla Gill	6.	
		To ditto to Sarah White	3.	
	26	To ditto to Jema. Wheaton	2.	
	27	To ditto to Sarah Blewitt	1.	6
June	7	To ditto to Thom. Bennitt	3.	
	15	To ditto to Prisa. Gill	6.	
		To ditto to Sarah White	6.	

		To ditto to Rebeca. Knowlton		3.	4
		Sum Carrid Over	£6.	10.	4
[2] 1769		Ward No. 2. Sum Brought Over	6.	10.	4
June	16	To Cash to Hanah Story		2.	
	17	To ditto to Eliza. Nichson		2.	
		To ditto to Jemima Wheaton		2.	
		To ditto to Thom Bennitt		2.	
	20	To ditto to Chrisr. Atkinson		2.	4 3/4
	23	To ditto to Sarah Blewitt		2.	
	26	To ditto to Hah. Story		2.	
July	3	To ditto to ditto		2.	
	4	To ditto to Chrr. Atkinson		1.	2 1/2
		To ditto to Thomas Bennitt		2.	
	10	To ditto to Hannah Story		2.	
	11	To ditto to Thom Bennett		2.	
	12	To ditto to Eliza. Nichson		2.	
	13	To ditto to Chrisr. Atkinson		1.	2 [1/4]
	14	To ditto to Sarah White		6.	
		To ditto to Jemima Wheaten		2.	
	17	To ditto to Hah. Story		2.	
	20	To ditto to Thomas Bennitt		2.	
	22	To ditto to Sarah Blewitt		2.	
	24	To ditto to Hanh. Story		8.	
	26	To ditto to Thom Bennitt		2.	
Augt.	2	To ditto paid Mary Snelling for Schooling		14.	5
	3	To ditto to Thom Bennitt		2.	
	5	To ditto to Hanh. story		4.	

		To ditto to Jemima Wheaton		2.	
	10	To ditto to Thom Bennitt		2.	
	12	To ditto to Eliza. Nichson		2.	
		To ditto to Hannah story		2.	
	14	To ditto to Chrisr. Atkinson		1.	6
	15	To ditto to Sarah White		6.	
		To ditto to Thomas Bennitt		2.	
	21	To ditto to Hanh. Story		2.	
	25	To ditto to Thomas Bennitt		2.	
	26	To ditto to Sarah Blewitt		2.	
		Sum Carrid Up	£11.	5.	0 1/2
[3] 1769		Ward No. 2 sum Brought Up	11.	5.	0 1/2
Augt.	28	To Cash to Hannah Story		2.	
Sept.	3	To ditto to Edith Ellerton		1.	4
	5	To ditto to Hanah Story (Sister Sick)		2.	
		To ditto to Jemima Wheaton		2.	
		To ditto to Thomas Bennitt		2.	1/2
	9	To ditto to Chrisr. Atkinson		2.	4 3/4
	11	To ditto to Hanah Story		2.	
	18	To ditto to Sarah White		6.	
	23	To ditto to Christopher Atkinson		2.	4
	25	To ditto to Hannah Story		4.	
		To ditto to Eliza. Nichson		2.	
	26	To ditto to Sarah Blewitt		2.	
		To 4 foot wood to Tabatha Nunk		9.	4
	27	To Cash to Thomas Bennitt		2.	
		To Ditto to Marcy Hern		1.	6
Octor.	2d.	To ditto to Christopher Atkinson		1.	2 1/2

	To ditto to Sarah White	3.		
	To ditto to Hannah Story	2.		
	To ditto to Thom Bennitt	2.		
	To ditto paid John Cades for Mr. Flemmings funerall	10.		
5	To ditto to Rebeka Knowlton	3.	4	
6	To ditto to Thomas Bennitt	2.		
9	To ditto to Hanh. story	2.		
11	To ditto to Chrisr. Atkinson	1.	2 1/2	
	To ditto to John Hemmingways wife	3.	4	
	To 2 foot wood to ditto	5.		
12	To Cash to Thomas Bennitt	2.		
14	To 4 foot wood to Joseph Mumford	7.	4	
	To Cash to Sarah White	2.		
	To ditto to Jemima Wheaton	2.		
16	To ditto to Christopher Atkinson	1.	2 1/2	
	To 2 foot wood to ditto	5.		
	Sum Carried Over	£16.	3.	6 3/4

[4] 1769	Ward No. 2. Sum brought Over	16.	3.	6 3/4
Octobr. 16	To Cash to Hannah Story	2.		
	To 2 foot wood to Mary Blackenbury	5.		
18	To Cash to Thomas Bennitt	2.		
20	To 2 foot wood to James West	5.		
	To Cash to Marcy Hern	1.	4	
23	To ditto to Chrisr. Atkinson	1.	2 1/4	
24	To ditto to Hannah Story	2.		
25	To ditto to Thomas Bennitt	2.		
	To 2 foot wood to ditto	5.		

	26	To Cash to Eliza. Nichson		2.	
	29	To ditto to Christopher Atkinson		1.	9 1/2
	30	To ditto to Hannah Story		2.	
Novr.	1	To ditto to Mary Davis		6.	
		To ditto to Jemima Wheaton		2.	
	2	To ditto to Thomas Bennitt		2.	
	4	To ditto to Christopher Atkinson		1.	2 1/2
		To ditto to Jerh. Roades		1.	4
		To 2 foot wood to ditto		5.	
		To Cash paid John Cades for Blackenbury Childs funerall		6.	
		To 2 foot wood to James West		5.	
	6	To Cash to Hannah Story		2.	
		To 2 foot wood to Christoph. Atkinson		5.	
	10	To Cash to Thomas Bennitt		2.	
	14	To ditto to Hannah Story		8.	
		To ditto to Jeremiah Roads		1.	2 1/2
		To 2 foot wood to Thomas Bennitt		5.	
	17	To [2] ditto to Sarah Carter		5.	
		To 2 ditto to Eliza. Carter		5.	
		To 2 ditto to Elizabeth Nichson		5.	
		To Cash to ditto			8
		Sum Carried Over	£21.	2.	3 1/2
[5] 1769		Ward No. 2 Sum Brought Up	£21.	2.	3 1/2
Novr.	18	To 2 foot wood to Joseph Mountfort		5.	
		To Cash to Sarah White		6.	
	21	To 2 foot wood to Christopher		5.	
	23	To 4 Ditto to Sarah Brown		7.	8

893

❧

		To Cash paid Mary Snelling for Schooling		13.	10 1/2
		To ditto to Jerh. Roads		1.	4
		To ditto paid John Cades for Hammar Pea-rsons Funerall		10.	
		To ditto to Chrisr. Atkinson		1.	2 1/2
		To ditto to ditto		1.	6
		To ditto to Jeremh. Roads		1.	6
		To 4 foot wood to Hugh Taylor		7.	8
		To 4 foot ditto to Jeremh. Roads		7.	8
	24	To Cash to Ralph Carter		1.	4
		To 4 foot wood to Rebeka Knowlton		8.	
		To 4 Ditto to patience Munday		7.	8
	28	To 4 ditto to Wm. Leich, wife		8.	
		To Cash to Mary Roads		1.	4
		To 2 foot wood to Sarah Curtis		5.	
		To 4 Ditto to Thomas Bennitt		8.	
		To Cash to ditto		2.	8
		To 4 foot wood to Mehittable Orange		8.	
		To Cash to ditto		1.	6
Decr.	2	To 2 foot wood to Jemima Wheaton		5.	
		To Cash to ditto		1.	6
		To ditto to Hannah Story		8.	
	5	To ditto paid Jno. Cades for Mrs. Atkinsons funerall Mrs. West & Mr. Roads	1.	10	
		To Cash to Mary Davis		6.	
	6	To Ditto to Mrs. White to Bury her Mother		6.	
		Sum Carried Over	£29.	18.	8 1/2
[6] 1769		Ward No. 2, Sum brought Over	£29.	18.	8 1/2
Decr.	8	To 2 foot wood to Sarah Cahale		5.	

11	To 4 foot ditto to Margratt Butler	8.	8
	To Cash to Christopher Atkinson	1.	4
	To ditto to Mary Roads	1.	4
12	To 2 foot wood to Margt. Decost	5.	
13	To 2 Ditto to Sarah Cutler	5.	
14	To Cash to Margrt. Decost (Sick)	2.	
	To 2 foot wood to Sarah Blakenburry	5.	
	To Cash to Thom Bennitt	2.	
	To 2 foot wood to Robt. McCurdy	5.	
16	To Cash to Elizabeth Nichson	2.	
	To 2 foot wood to John Waddle	5.	
18	To Cash to Margret Decost	2.	
	To ditto to John Waddle	1.	4
	To do. paid Jno. Cades for Mrs. Butler's Funerall	10.	
20	To 4 foot wood to Webb Pearson	8.	
	To Cash to Thomas Bennitt	2.	
	To 4 foot wood to Mary Cox	8.	8
21	To 2 foot ditto to Margt. Decost	5.	
	To Cash to ditto	1.	6
22	To Ditto to Robt. McCurdey	1.	4
	To ditto to Christopher Atkinson	1.	4
	To 2 foot wood to ditto	5.	4
23	To 2 ditto to Thomas Burns	5.	
	To 4 ditto to Elener French	9.	4
26	To 4 ditto to Mehital. Orange	9.	4
	To Cash to Ditto	1.	4
28	To ditto to Robt. McCurdy	1.	6

	To ditto to John Hemmingway's wife		1.	4
29	To 2 foot wood to Robt. McCurdey		5.	4
	To Cash to Thomas Bennett		2.	
	To ditto paid Jude Greenleaf Schooling		6.	11 1/4
	To 2 foot wood to Margret Decost		5.	4
	Sum Carried Up	£36.	19.	11 3/4
[7] 1770	Ward No. 2. Sum brought Up	36.	19.	11 3/4
Januy. 1	To 2 foot wood to Eliza. Nichson		5.	4
	To Cash to ditto		1.	
3	To ditto to Mary Davis		6.	
	To 4 foot wood to Ralph Carter		9.	4
	To Cash to Hugh Taylor		2.	8
	To Cash paid for Diging Well at Workhouse	2.		
	To ditto to Widow Roads		1.	6
5	To 2 foot wood to Sarah Cahale		5.	4
	To Cash to Thomas Bennitt		2.	
6	To ditto to Chrisr. Atkinson		1.	6
	To ditto to Rebeka Knowlton		1.	4
9	To 2 foot wood to Jemima Wheaton		5.	4
10	To 2 ditto to Sarah Brown		5.	4
11	To 4 ditto to John McLarre		9.	4
	To Cash to Sarah Curtis (sick)		1.	6
	To 2 foot wood to ditto	0	5.	4
12	To Cash to Thom Bennitt		2.	
15	To ditto to John Waddles wife		1.	
	To ditto to Christopher Atkinson		1.	6
17	To ditto to Mary Blackenbery		1.	6
	To ditto to Hannah Story		6.	

	To 2 foot wood to Silas Ivory		5.	4
	To 2 ditto to Christor. Atkinson		5.	4
18	To 2 ditto to Mehit. Orange		5.	4
	To Cash to ditto		2.	
	To 2 foot wood to Rebecka Knowlton		5.	4
20	To 4 foot ditto to Webb Pearson		9.	4
	To Cash to Jemima Wheaton		1.	6
	To ditto to Sarah Curtis		1.	6
22	To ditto to Margret Decost		1.	6
24	To ditto to Rebecka Knowlton		15.	
	To 2 foot wood to Joseph Andrews		5.	4
	To 2 Ditto to Margret Butler		5.	4
	Sum Carried Over	£45.	17.	7 3/4
[8] 1770	Ward No. 2 sum Brought Over	45.	17.	7 3/4
Jany. 25	To Cash to Rob McCurdey		1.	4
25	To 2 foot wood to ditto		5.	4
	To Cash to George Killcup		1.	4
	To 2 foot wood to ditto		5.	4
26	To Cash to Mary Roads		2.	
	To 2 foot wood to Jona. Harris		5.	4
	To Cash to ditto		3.	0
	To ditto to Ralph Carter		2.	8
	To ditto to Chris Atkinson		1.	6
	To ditto paid Mary Snelling for Schooling Sundry poor Children		13.	10 1/2
27	To Cash to Thom Bennitt		2.	
	To 2 foot wood Mehita. Orange		5.	4
	To Cash to ditto		1.	4

Feby.	1	To 2 foot wood to Mary Stride	5.	
		To 2 ditto to Eliza. Nichson	5.	
		To 2 ditto to Mary Roads	5.	
	2	To Cash to Thomas Bennitt	2.	
		To 2 foot wood to Chrisr. Atkinson	5.	4
		To 2 ditto to Wm. Leech	5.	
	3	To 2 ditto to Josa. Hemmingway Junr.	5.	
		To 2 ditto to Ellener Trench	5.	
		To Cash to Jemima Wheaton	2.	
		To 4 foot wood to Wm. Farmer	9.	4
	5	To Cash to Hannah Story	2.	
		To ditto to Margt. Decost	1.	
		To ditto to Christor. Atkinson	1.	6
		To ditto to Mary Davis	6.	
	8	To 2 foot wood to John Kippen	5.	
	9	To Cash to Thomas Bennitt	2.	
	10	To ditto to Ralph Carter	2.	
		To ditto to Rebecka Knowlton	2.	
		Sum Carried Up	£51. 18.	2 1/4
[8][1] 1770		Ward No. 2 brought Up	£51. 18.	2 1/4
Feby.	10	To Cash to George Killcup	1.	4
		To 2 foot wood to ditto	5.	
		To 4 ditto to Webb Pearson	9.	4
		To 2 ditto to Thomas Bennitt	5.	
		To Cash to Mary Roads	1.	4
	12	To ditto to Chrisr. Attkinson	1.	4
		To ditto to Hannah Story	2.	

1   Thus in MS.

	To 2 foot wood to Elizh. Burns		5.		
14	To 2 ditto to Sarah Cahale		5.		
17	To 2 ditto to Rebeka Knowlton		5.		
	To Cash to Rob McCurdy		1.	4	
	To 2 foot wood to ditto		5.		
	To Cash to Chrisr. Atkinson		1.	4	
	To 2 foot wood to Marg Butler		5.		
	To 2 ditto to Joseph Andrews		5.		
	To 2 ditto to Jemima Wheaton		5.		
	To Cash to ditto		1.	6	
	To ditto to Thom Bennitt		2.		
19	To ditto to Mehittable Orange		1.	4	
	To 2 foot wood to ditto		5.		
	To Cash to Hanh. Story		2.		
	To 4 foot wood to John McLarry		9.	4	
20	To 2 ditto to Ralph Carter		5.		
	To Cash to ditto		1.	6	
21	To 2 foot wood to Hanh. Story		5.		
22	To 2 ditto to James Bells wife		5.		
23	To 2 ditto to Mary Cox		5.		
24	To Cash to Thomas Bennitt		2.		
	To ditto to Margt. Decost		1.		
	To ditto to Chrisr. Attkinson		1.	4	
	Sum Carried Over	£57.	8.	2 1/4	
[9] 1770	Ward No. 2 Sum brot. Over	57.	8.	2 1/4	
Feby. 24	To Cash to Mary Roads		1.	4	
	To ditto to Jno. Giles		3.		

		To ditto to John Kippen	1.	4
		To ditto to Geo Killcup	1.	4
	26	To 2 foot wood to Joseph True	5.	
		To 2 ditto to Jeah Carter	5.	
		To 2 ditto to Hugh Taylor	5.	
		To 2 ditto to Mary Roads	5.	
		To Cash to Hanh. Story	2.	
	27	To 2 foot wood to Jona. Harris	5.	
		To Cash to ditto	1.	6
		To 2 foot wood to Jno. Kippen	5.	
		To 2 ditto to Geor Killcup	5.	
		To 4 ditto to Hannah Moulton	9.	4
	28	To 2 ditto to Christopher Atkinson	5.	
March	2	To 4 ditto to Margrett Lee	9.	4
		To 4 ditto to Wm. Farmer	9.	4
		To Cash to Thom. Bennitt	2.	
		To 4 foot wood to Webb Pearson	9.	4
	3	To Cash to Jemima Wheaton	2.	
		To 2 foot wood to Margrt. Butler	5.	
		To 2 do. to Sarah Hunt	5.	
		To 4 do. to Thom Bennitt	9.	4
	5	To 2 ditto to Sarah Brown	5.	
		To 2 ditto to Patiance Munday	5.	
		To 2 ditto to Elizabeth Burns	5.	
		To 4 ditto to Elias Bowin	9.	4
		To 2 ditto to Th Scott	5.	
		To Cash to Hanh. Story	2.	
		To ditto to Thom Bennitt	2.	

Samuel Whitwell's Accounts, 1769–1792

〜

				£64.	12.	8 1/4
1770		Supra	Cr.			
March	7	By the Overseers draught on [Mr.] Jeffreys⟩ Town Treasurer ⟩ for	£64.	12.	8 1/4
[12]² 1770		Ward No. 2. Sum brought Up		10.	11.	10 1/4
April	14	To 2 foot Wood to Ralph Carter			4.	8
	16	To Cash to Hanh. Story			2.	
	17	To 2 foot wood to Jno. McLarry			4.	8
	18	To Cash to Jemima Wheaton			2.	
	19	To 2 foot wood to Mehittable Orange			4.	8
	20	To Cash to Tho. Bennett			2.	
	21	To ditto to Christor. Atkinson			1.	6
	23	To ditto to Mary Roads			1.	6
		To ditto to Hanh. Story			2.	
	24	To ditto paid Abrm. Rogers for Coffin for T Bennitt			8.	
	30	To ditto to Hanh. Story			2.	
		To ditto to Christopher Atkinson			1.	6
May	1	To ditto to Jemima Wheaton			2.	
		To 2 foot wood to Jno. Kippen			4.	8
		To Cash paid Mary Snelling for Schooling⟩ 4 poor Children 3 mo. @ 2/ ℘ week ⟩			13.	10 1/2
		To ditto to Mary Davis			6.	
		To ditto paid Jno. Cades for T Bennitts⟩ Funerall ⟩			10.	
	7	To ditto to Hannah Story			2.	
		To ditto to Annas Jack			1.	6
	8	To ditto to Christopher Atkinson			1.	6
		To ditto to Mary Roades			1.	6

2   Pages 10 and 11 of the MS are missing.

	11	To ditto to Jno. Gyles	3.		
	12	To 2 foot wood to Eliz Nickson	4.	8	
	14	To Cash to Hannah story	2.		
	16	To ditto to Christopher Atkinson		4	
	18	To ditto to Ralph Carter	8.		
		To ditto to Rebecka Knowlton		1.	1
		Sum Carried Over	£15.	10.	11 1/4

[13] 1770		Ward No. 2. Sum brought Over	15.	10.	11 1/4
May	21	To Cash to Hannah Story	2.		
	26	To ditto to Annas Jack	1.	6	
	30	To ditto to Hanh. story	2.		
June	1	To ditto to George Kilcup	2.	4 3/4	
	2	To ditto to Ralph Carter	2.		
	4	To ditto to John McLarry	3.		
		To ditto to Mary Davis	6.		
		To ditto to Hanh. story	2.		
	5	To 2 foot wood to Ralph Carter	4.	8	
		To 2 ditto to Jno. McLarry	4.	8	
	7	To 2 ditto to Hanh. story	4.	8	
	9	To Cash paid Mr. Greenleaf for schooling	6.	11 1/4	
	11	To ditto to Hannah Story	2.		
		Sum Carried to foot of accot.	£17.	14.	9 1/4

for ward No. 12 folio 21

[14]		The Town of Boston for disburstmnts. in Ward No. 12	Dr.	
1770				
May	11	To Cash to Nat. Richardson	3.	

	29	To ditto to ditto	1.	6
June	7	To ditto to Christopher Power	1.	4
		To ditto paid Katherine Delanee for her Childrens board from Marh. 3d. to 6th. June 1770 13 & 1/2 wks. @ 1/ }	13.	6
	11	To Cash to Rob Williams	1.	
		To 4 foot wood to ditto	8.	
	15	To 2 ditto to Ebenezr. Young	4.	8
	18	To Cash to Jno. Barker	4.	
		To ditto to Christophr. Power	1.	4
	23	To ditto to Nathanl. Richardson	3.	
	30	To ditto to Jno. Barker	3.	
		To ditto to Christor. Power	2.	
July	11	To ditto to Heny. Air	2.	8
	14	To ditto to Robert Williams	1.	4
	23	To ditto to Nat Richardson	4.	1 1/2
		To ditto to Jno. Basker	1.	6
	25	To ditto to Heny. Air	1.	6
	28	To ditto to Robt. Williams	1.	6
		To ditto paid Mr. Fisher for keeping a bastard Child from Mah. 2d. to July 27th. 21 Weeks @ 16d. [...] }	1.	8.
Augt.	1	To ditto to Danl. McKane	2.	
		To 4 foot wood to Ditto	8.	
	8	To Cash to Nath Richardson	3.	
	9	To ditto to Christopher Powers	2.	8
		To ditto to Ebenezer Young	6.	
	11	To ditto Anna Pindergrass for Schooling	3.	
		To ditto to Mary Soper to the 3d. Int. at 6/ ℘ Month ℘ Vote of the Overseers }	6.	
		To ditto to Robt. Williams	1.	6

	25	To ditto to Ditto		1.	6
		Sum Carried Over	£6.	0.	7 1/2
[15] 1770		Ward No. 12. Sum brought Over	6.	0.	7 1/2
Augt.	27	To Cash to Nathl. Richardson		6.	
Septr.	1	To ditto to widow Powers		1.	6
	6	To ditto to Robt. Williams		1.	2 1/2
		To ditto to Geo. Buckhart		3.	
	10	To ditto to Mary Nutby		1.	6
		To 4 primmers for poor children at Mrs. Pendergrasses School		1.	4
	11	To Cash to Nat Richardson		3.	
	12	To ditto to Mary powers		1.	6
		To ditto to Mary Soper to 3 Inst.		6.	
		To ditto to Geo. Buckhart		1.	4
		To ditto to Geo Buckheart		3.	
	15	To ditto to Thom Welch		3.	4
		To ditto to John Ranstead		2.	8
	20	To ditto to Danl. McKane		3.	
	22	To ditto to Robert Williams		1.	
	26	To ditto to Thomas Reeds wife		1.	6
	28	To ditto to Geo Buckhart		2.	
Octor.	1	To ditto to Thomas Welch		1.	4
		To ditto to Mary powers		2.	5
		To ditto to Mary Soaper		6.	
	3	To ditto to Mrs. Mather for schooling Jno. Welchs 2 Children 9 weeks @ 2/ 0 Tenr.		4.	9 1/2
	5	To ditto to Nathl. Richardson		2.	8
		To ditto to John Barker		6.	

6	To ditto to Sarah Paine ℘ Vote 1/ ℘ Week		4.	
	To ditto to Mrs. Pendergrass		2.	4
10	To 4 foot wood to Danl. McKane		8.	8
12	To 2 foot ditto to James steward		4.	8
	To Cash to Ditto		1.	4
15	To ditto paid Anna pendergrass for schoo-ling 4 Children 53 Weeks to Octo 1st.		8.	8 3/4
16	To ditto to Mary Nutby		1.	6
	To ditto to Mary Powers		2.	
	Sum Carried Up	£10.	19.	11 1/4
[16] 1770	Ward No. 12 Sum brought Up	10.	19.	11 1/4
Octobr. 16	To Cash to Tho Welch		2.	4 3/4
17	To 4 ft. wood Mary Nutby		8.	8
	To 4 foot ditto to Mary Powers		8.	8
	To 4 ditto to Eliz Goodwin (in frog lane)		8.	8
24	To Cash to Thom Welch		2.	8
27	To ditto to Nathl. Richardson		2.	8
	To ditto to Tho. Welch		3.	4
	To 6 foot wood to ditto		14.	
	To 4 foot ditto to Nathl. Richardson		9.	4
	To 4 foot ditto to Wido Fisher		9.	4
30	To 2 yds. Baze & 1 Yd. Ozenbrigs to Tho Welch		5.	5 1/2
31	To 4 foot wood to Jane McClure		9.	4
	To 4 Ditto do. to Joanna Stone		9.	4
Novr. 3	To Cash to Nat Richardson		2.	
	To ditto to Mary Soper		6.	
	To ditto to Sarah Peirce		4.	
9	To ditto to Nathl. Richardson		2.	

	To ditto to Mary Powers		3.	3/4
	To 4 ft. wood to Widow Hunnewell (next house to Coll. Hill)	9.	4	
	To Cash to Jno. Barker		6.	
	To 4 ft. wood to Mrs. Mather		9.	4
	To Cash to Tho Welch		4.	
19	To ditto to ditto		4.	
23	To ditto to Mrs. Fisher for a pr. Shoes for bastard Child	1.	6	
24	To ditto to Widow McClure		1.	4
	To ditto to Widdow Hunnewell		1.	4
	To ditto to Nathl. Richardson		4.	
27	To ditto to Tho Welch		2.	4
29	To 6 foot wood to ditto		14.	
	Sum Carried Over	£19.	8.	0 3/4

[17] 1770		Ward No. 12 Sum brought Over	19.	8.	0 3/4
Novr.	29	To 4 foot wood to Widow Peters		9.	4
Decr.	1	To 4 foot Ditto to Ebenez Young		9.	4
		To 4 ditto to John Loring (in white hors yard)		9.	4
	3	To 4 ditto to Heny. Air		9.	4
		To 4 ditto to Margt. Roades		9.	4
		To Cash to Thom Welch		3.	4
		To Ditto to Nathl. Richardson		2.	
		To Ditto to Widow McClure		2.	
		To 4 foot wood to Widow Obriant (opost. the Lamb)	9.	4	
		To 4 do. to <*widow*> Mary Blake (Jehots. [Corest])	9.	4	
	10	To Cash to Ebener. Youngs wife		3.	
		To 2 foot wood to Josh. steels wife		5.	
		To Cash to Mary powers		3.	
		To do. to Tho Welch for 2 yds. Baze & 1 yd. ozenbrigs	6.	0	

		To ditto to ditto		3.	4
		To Ditto to John Barker		1.	6
		To ditto to Nathl. Richardson		4.	
	12	To ditto to Sarah Peirce		6.	
	17	To 4 foot wood to Widow stone		9.	4
		To Cash paid Anna prendergrass Schooling 4 Children 11 weeks from 1st. Octo to this day		11.	8 1/2
	18	To 12 y wool deld. Mrs. Farmer @ 1/4		16.	
	21	To 2 foot wood to Thoms. Reedes wife		5.	
		To Cash to Tho Welch		4.	
	24	To ditto to Widow McClure		2.	4 3/4
		To 6 foot wood to ditto		14.	
		To 4 foot Do. to George Buckhart		9.	4
		To 6 foot do. to Thom Welch		14.	
		To 4 foot ditto to Eliza. Goodwin		9.	4
		To Cash to ditto		1.	4
	26	To Cash paid Mrs. Mather for Schooling 2 Children 12 Children 12 weeks @ 2/ ea		6.	4 1/4
		To Cash Eliza. Shephard in Mr. Bakers house		2.	8
	29	To ditto to Nathl. Richardson		4.	
		Sum Carrid Over	£30.	2.	0 1/4
[18] 1770		Ward No. 12 Sum Brot. Up	30.	2.	0 1/4
Decr.	29	To Cash to David Scudder		2.	4 3/4
		To ditto to Ebenez. Younges wife		1.	6
	31	To 2 ft. wood to Josh. steeles wife		5.	
1771		To Cash to Mary powers		3.	
Jany.	1	To Ditto to Heny. Air		2.	
	3	To Ditto to Thomas Welch		3.	4

	To Ditto to Jno. Barker		3.	4	
	To 4 foot wood to David Scudder		9.	4	
	To Cash to Ditto		2.	8	
	To Ditto to Thomas Reedes wife		2.	4 3/4	
5	To ditto to Nathanl. Richardson		2.		
7	To ditto to Widow McClure		2.		
	To ditto to Eliza. Shepphard		2.	8	
	To ditto to Widow Nutby		2.	4 3/4	
9	To ditto to Nicholas Foster		2.	4 3/4	
	To ditto to Thom Reeds wife		2.		
12	To ditto to Sarah Peirce		4.		
	To ditto to Nath Richardson		2.		
15	To 4 ft. wood to Mrs. Nutby		9.	4	
17	To Cash to Jno. Barker		2.	8	
	To ditto to Mary Powers		3.		
	To ditto to Larance Collins		2.	8	
	To 4 foot wood to ditto		9.	4	
	To Cash paid Anna perdergrass for Schooling 4 poor children to 21 Jany.—5 weeks @ 2/ each }		5.	4	
19	To Cash paid Mrs. Fisher for keeping a bastard child 25 weeks frm. 27 July to 20 Jany. at 16d. }	1.	13.	4	
	To Cash to Eliz Shephard		2.	8	
	To ditto to Nathl. Richardson		2.		
	To 4 foot wood to Jane Fisher		9.	4	
	To Cash to ditto		2.	8	
	To ditto to Mary Soaper to 1st. Inst.		12.		
	Sum Carried Over	£37.	10.	9 1/4	
[19] 1771	Ward No. 12. Sum brought Over	37.	10.	9 1/4	
Jany. 23	To 6 foot wood to Thom Welch		14.		

		To Cash to ditto	3.	4
		To Ditto Nicholas Foster	2.	
		To ditto to Wm. Atkins (near Dr. Byles meeting)	2.	8
		To 4 foot wood to ditto	9.	4
		To Cash to Larrance Collings	1.	6
		To ditto to James McClure	3.	
		To ditto to Thom Reeds wife	2.	
		To ditto to John Barker	1.	6
	26	To 4 foot wood to Ebenr. Young	9.	4
		To Cash to Nathl. Richardson	2.	
	28	To 4 foot wood to Mary Obriant	9.	4
		To 4 ditto to Widow Stone	9.	4
		To 4 ditto to Heny. Air	9.	4
	30	To 4 ditto to Mary A[nw.?] opost. the Lamb	9.	4
	31	To 2 ditto to Josh. steeles wife	5.	
Feby.	2	To Cash to Daniel McCane	3.	4
		To ditto to Nath Richardson	2.	
	4	To ditto to Mary powers	3.	
	6	To ditto to Nicholas Foster	2.	8
		To 4 foot wood to Mathw. steward	9.	4
		To Cash to ditto	1.	6
	7	To ditto to David Scudder	3.	
		To 4 foot wood to Ditto	9.	4
		To Cash to Jane McClure	2.	8
		To ditto to John Basker	2.	
		To 4 foot wood to Widow Hunnywell	9.	4
		To Cash to Nathl. Richardson	2.	

	11	To 3 foot wood to Mary Roades		7.	
		To 6 Ditto to Tho Welch		14.	
		To 4 ditto to Josh. Hatter		9.	4
	16	To Cash to Nat Richardson		2.	8
		Sum Carried Up	£46.	7.	11 1/4
[20] 1771		Ward No. 12. Sum brought Up	46.	7.	11 1/4
Feby.	16	To Cash to Mary Obriant		2.	
		To 4 foot wood to James Butler		9.	4
		To 4 ditto to Jno. pendergrass		9.	4
		To Cash paid Anna Pendergrass for Schooling 4 poor children 4 weeks		4.	3 1/2
		To ditto to Thom Reed		1.	6
	18	To 4 foot wood to Eliza. Goodwin		9.	4
		To 4 Ditto to Willm. Atkins		9.	4
		To Cash to Nicholas Foster		2.	8
		To ditto to Wm. Atkins		1.	6
		To ditto to John Barker		3.	
	22	To ditto to Jane McClure for wood		7.	4
		To ditto to Josh. steels wife		3.	4
		To ditto to George Buckhart		1.	4
	23	To ditto to Natl. Richardson		1.	4
Marh.	1	To 4 foot wood for Widow stone		9.	4
	2	To 2 Ditto to Mary powers		5.	
		To Cash to Ditto		1.	4
		To 4 foot wood to Daniel McCane		9.	4
		To 2 foot wood to Josh. steels wife		5.	
		To Cash to Sarah Peirce		7.	
		To 4 foot wood to Thom Welch		9.	4

To 2 foot wood to Jno. Loring				5.	
To Cash paid Mrs. Fisher for keeping a bastard Child from Jany. 20 to 6 Mah.—is 6 & 1/2 week @ 16d.				8.	8
To Cash paid Mrs. Mather for Schooling 2 Children 10 weeks @ 2/ each ℘ week				5.	4
	Sum Carried Over		£52.	18.	10 3/4
[21] 1771	Ward No. 12	Sum brought Over	£52.	18.	10 3/4
March 4	To Cash paid Anna Pendergrass for Schooling 4 poor children 2 weeks @ 2/ each ℘ week			2.	1 3/4
	To Cash to Nathanl. Richardson			2.	
5	To ditto to Nicholas Foster			1.	6
	To 2 foot wood to Heny. Aire			5.	
	To Cash to John Barker			1.	6
	To 2 foot wood to Widow Peters			5.	
			£53.	16.	0 1/2
	Deduct for an Abatemment made me by the Wharfinger for overcharge on wood between June & Jany. Last			1. 13.	
			£52.	3.	0 1/2
	Ward No. 2 Sum brot. forward from folio 13			17. 14.	9 1/4
			£69.	17.	9 1/4
	Supra	Cr.			
1771					
March 6	By an Error in Casting			1.	
	By the Overseers Draught on Dr. Jeffrys Town Treasurer			69. 16.	9 1/4
			£69.	17.	9 1/4

~

[22]   The Town of Boston, for disburstmts. Ward No. 12   Dr.

1771

Marh.	8	To Cash to David Scudder		8
		To Ditto William Atkins	3.	
		To Ditto Widow Winbourn	1.	4
		<To 2 foot wood to Ebenzr. Young […]>		
	9	*<To 4 ditto to Nat Richardson […]>*		
		To Cash to Ditto	2.	
		To ditto to Nicholas Foster	1.	6
		To ditto to Widow Fisher deld. her daughter Russell	1.	6
		<To 4 foot wood to James steward […]>		
		To Cash to ditto	1.	2 1/2
		To ditto to Wm. Baldridge	1.	6
	19	To ditto to Nathl. Richardson	2.	
		To ditto to Wm. Atkins	2.	
		To ditto to John Barker	3.	
		Sum Carried to ward No. 10 £	19.	8 1/2

[23]   The Town of Boston for Disburstmts. Ward No. 10   Dr.

		Sum fm. Ward No. 12		19.	8 1/2

1771

March	19	To Cash to Partrick Daley		4.	10 1/2
		To Ditto to Eliza. Hall for boarding Joseph Lillie from Decr. 8th. 1770 to Marh. 20 1771 is 14 1/2 Weeks @ 20/ ℘ week	1	18.	8
		NB he is a boy wth. one Legg			
		To Cash to Eliza. Butt		6.	
	25	To Ditto to Anna Eaglestone for Schooling Melah. Foot, Poly & Mary Watts from 17th. Decr. to 25 March 14 weeks @ 2/ ℘ week each		11.	2 1/2
May	6	To Ditto to Ditto for Schooling ditto 6 weeks to the day		4.	9 1/2

	10	To Ditto to Isaac Cherry	1.	4
	11	To Ditto to Lewis Cooney	3.	
		To Ditto to Eliza. Butt	6.	
	18	To Ditto to Isaac Cherry	1.	6
		To Ditto paid Mr. Procter for Books & pens for Josh. Lillie	6.	
	27	To Ditto to Patrick Larry	2.	
		To 4 foot wood to Rebecka Butler in Mh. Last	8.	
		To Cash omd. in Mah. to Rachel McGee	6.	
		To Ditto to Rachel McGee	6.	
June	1	To Ditto to Sarah Peirce	13.	
	5	To Ditto to Eliz Hale for boardg. of Josh. Lillie from 20 March to 11 Aprl. last 3 weeks @ 2/8d.	8.	
		To Ditto to Eliza. Butt	6.	
	20	To Ditto to Rachel McGee	5.	4
July	13	To Ditto to Lewis Croney	3.	4
	25	To Ditto to Anna Eagleston for Schooling	6.	8
Augt.	1	To ditto to Rachel McGee	6.	
	2	To ditto to Eliza. Butt	6.	
	27	To ditto to William Rogers Corn Lane	1.	4
	28	To ditto to Eliza. Hales, Blowers's house long lane	2.	
		Sum Carried Up	£9. 2.	8 1/2
[24] 1771		Ward No. 10. Sum brot. Up	9. 2.	8 1/2
Sept.	2	To Cash to Rachel McGee	6.	
	7	To ditto to Robt. Gleen	3.	
	9	To ditto to Mary Dixon for Schoog. 3 Childn. 13 weeks	10.	4 3/4
	16	To ditto to Greenleaf a Constable for comitting Ebenr. Cobourn to workhouse	1.	4
	21	To ditto to Jane Dunlap	3.	

Octor.	1	To ditto to Rachel McGee	6.		
		To ditto to Mary Peirce at bottom Decosters Alley	3.		
	20	To ditto to Sarah for her child 20 weeks @ 1/	1.		
		To 6 foot wood to Doritha Mirriam (Decosters Alley)	12.		
	24	To Cash to Mrs. Larkin in Milk street	4.		
	30	To Ditto to Rachel McGee	6.		
		To 6 foot wood to Ditto	12.		
		To 6 ditto to John Bulfinch	12.		
Novr.	1	To Cash to Elizabeth Hailes	3.		
		To 6 foot wood to ditto	12.		
	9	To 6 ditto to Eunic Cook	12.		
	12	To Cash to Mariah Bijah free Negro	2.		
	13	To ditto to Elizabeth Parker Milk Street	6.		
	14	To ditto paid Anna Eagleston for Schooling 3 poor Children 17 Weeks	13.	4	
	20	To Cash Eliz Sinclair Green's lane	1.	4	
		To 7 Cord wood to Hanh. Allen (Blowers's house)	9.	4	
		To 6 foot ditto to Mary Hawke (long lane)	12.		
		To 6 ditto to Rebecka Clarke (fishers ally)	12.		
Decr	2	To Cash to Rachel McGee	6.		
		To 6 foot wood to Eliza. Lee (Greens lane)	12.		
		To 4 ditto to John Hobbs (Greens barricks)	8.		
		To 6 ditto to prudence Delaplace (Milk street)	13.		
		To Cash to Ditto	1.	6	
	4	To 6 foot wood to Dorathy Maning in the old three horse Shoes	13.		
			£20.	17.	11 1/4
[25] 1771		Ward No. 10, Sum brot. Over	£20.	17.	11 1/4

Decr.	4	To 6 foot wood to James Westwood (Long lane)	13.	
	6	To Cash to Mariah Bijah	2.	
	10	To ditto to Elizabeth Packer	6.	
		To 6 foot wood to Elizabt. Hartley (Wiswalls house)	13.	
	17	To Cash to Elizabeth Sinclair	1.	4
	18	To 4 foot wood to Elizabith Goodwin (Long lane)	8.	8
		To Cash to ditto	1.	6
	23	To ditto paid Mary Dixon Schooling 3 Children 12 Weeks	9.	7 1/4
	24	To ditto to Widow Cooke	1.	4
	25	To 6 foot wood to Joshua Cornish (Long lane)	14.	
	26	To 4 foot ditto to Hanah Missick	9.	4
1772	31	To Cash to ditto	3.	4
Jany.	1	To Ditto to Rachel McGee	6.	
	3	To ditto to Samuel Chandler	1.	6
		To 6 foot wood to ditto Greens lane	14.	
		To 4 ditto to Eunice Cooke	9.	4
	6	To 2 ditto to Mariah Byjah 5/ Cash 1/4d.	6.	4
	7	To 4 ditto to Elizabeth Sinclair	10.	
	10	To Cash to Elizabeth Packer	6.	
	11	To 4 foot wood to John Hobbs	9.	4
		To Cash to ditto	1.	9
		To ditto to Rebecka Wainwright	2.	8
	13	To ditto to Hanah Allen	6.	
	18	To ditto to Joshua Cornish	1.	6
	22	To 6 foot wood to Hannah Kent	15.	
	25	To 4 ditto to Joshua Cornish	10.	
	27	To 4 ditto to Mary Peirce	10.	

	29	To Cash to Rebecka Wainwright		3.	8
		To ditto to Elizabith Hales		2.	8
		To ditto to Widow Hartley		2.	2
		To ditto to Hannah Missick		3.	8
		Carried up	£31.	2.	7 1/2
[26] 1772		Ward No. 10 Sum brot. Up	31.	2.	7 1/2
Jany.	29	To Cash to John Hobbs		2.	
		To 4 foot wood to Eliz Goodwin		10.	
Feby.	3	To Cash to Rachel McGee		6.	
	5	To ditto to Hannah Kent		2.	
	6	To ditto to Eliza. Packer		6.	
	7	To ditto to James Bell's wife		3.	4
	8	To 4 foot wood to Mrs. Coredry oppt. Dr. Gardner's		10.	
	12	To 4 ditto to Sam Chandler		10.	
		To 4 ditto to James Westwood		10.	
	18	To 4 ditto to Dory. Maning		10.	
		To 4 ditto to Elizabeth Hartley		10.	
	25	To 4 ditto to John Whitty in Jehonets Shop		10.	
	27	To 4 ditto to Sarah Nicholson in do.		10.	
		To 4 ditto to Prudence Delaplace 24 day 10/ Cash 1/4d.		11.	4
		To 4 ditto to Hugh Smith Blowers' house		10.	
March	2	To Cash paid Anna Eagleston Schooling 3 poor Children 12 Weeks		9.	7
		To ditto to Hannah Missick		3.	
	3	To 4 foot wood to Eliza. Lee		10.	
		To Cash to Mariah Bijah		2.	8
		To Cash to Rachel McGee		6.	
		To ditto paid Miss Sarh. Rogers Schooling a Child 14 weeks		3.	8 1/4

		To 4 foot wood to Thompson 30th. Jany. last	10.		
			£39.	8.	3 1/4
1772		Supra	Cr.		
Mah.	4	By the Overseers draught on Mr. Davd. Jeffreys Town Treasurer	£39.	8.	3 1/4

[27]		The Town of Boston for disbursment in Ward No. 10	Dr.		
1772					
March	5	To 4 foot wood to John Hobbs	10.		
		To 4 ditto to Elizabeth Hales	10.		
		To 2 ditto to Eunic Cook	5.		
	6	To Cash to Elizabeth Parker	6.		
	7	To 4 foot wood to Hanah Missick	10.		
		To 4 ditto to Rebecka Clarke	10.		
	9	To 4 ditto to Joshua Cornish	10.		
	10	To 4 ditto to Susanna Thomas Grenes Lane	10.		
	12	To 4 ditto to Mary Cowdry	10.		
	13	To 4 ditto to Jno. Bulfinch	10.		
	14	To 4 ditto to Dorithy Merriam	10.		
		To Cash to ditto	3.		
	16	To 4 foot wood to Eliza. Goodwin	10.		
		To 4 foot ditto to John Whitty sick & wife	10.		
		To Cash to Hannah Allen	1.	6	
	17	To 6 foot wood to Dean. James Mayes	15.		
	18	To Cash to Eliza. Sinclair	2.		
		To 4 foot wood to Rachel McGee	10.		
	21	To 2 ditto to John Tucker's wife	5.		
		To 4 ditto to Thomas Price head long lane	10.		

	24	To Cash to John Hunt		6.	
	27	To ditto to Thomas Price sick		6.	
		To ditto to Eliza. Parker		6.	
April	4	To ditto to Rachel McGee		6.	
		To ditto to Hannah Missick		5.	5
		To ditto to Mary Peirce		3.	
	13	To 2 foot wood to John Hobbs		5.	
	18	To Cash to Elizabeth Hales		2.	8
	21	To 4 foot wood John Whitty		9.	4
		To Cash to Thomas Rice		6.	
	30	To Cash to Widow Parker		6.	
		Sum Carried Up	£11.	8.	11
[30][3] 1772		Ward No. 10.　　Sum brot. Up	£27.	1.	6 3/4
Decr.	1	To Cash to Rachel McGee		6.	
		To ditto to Eliza. Parker		6.	
	4	To 4 foot wood to Mary Hawkes		10.	
	7	To 4 ditto to Widow Larking		10.	
	8	To 4 ditto to Eunic Cook		10.	
		To Cash to ditto		2.	
	9	To 6 foot wood to Doritha Maning		15.	
	11	To 4 ditto to Eliza Egen		10.	
		To Cash to ditto		1.	4
	13	To ditto to Anna Eagleston for Schoolg. 2 of Watts's & 1 of Foots childn. fm. 12 July		15.	11 1/4
	14	To ditto pd. Mary Dixson Schooling 3 of peirces childn. 12 weeks		9.	7 1/2
	19	To 4 foot wood to John Hobbs		10.	
		To 4 ditto to Sarah Tuckerman sick		10.	

3　Pages 28 and 29 of the MS are missing.

		To Cash to ditto	1.	6
		To ditto to Jno. Bulfinch	3.	
1773)	24	To ditto to Rebeka Smellage	2.	8
Januy.	1	To ditto to Rachel McGee	6.	
		To ditto to Eliza. Parker	6.	
		To ditto to ditto to buy Coat	6.	
	5	To ditto Merriam Bijah	1.	6
		To 4 foot wood to Eliza. Hales	10.	
		To Cash to ditto	1.	6
	6	To ditto to John Bullfinch	3.	
	9	To ditto to Daniel Langleys wife	6.	
		To 4 foot wood to do. she & her mother) being burnt out	10.	
		To Cash to John Whitty	3.	
		To ditto to James Mayes	6.	
		Sum Carried Over	£36. 3.	7 1/2
[31] 1773		Ward No. 10. Sum brot. Over	£36. 3.	7 1/2
Jany.	9	To Cash to John Hobbs	2.	4
		To ditto to Sarah Tuckerman	2.	
	13	To 4 foot wood to Joshua Cornish	10.	
		To 4 ditto to Rebecka Wainwright	10.	
		To Cash to Dorithy Merriam	6.	
		To ditto to prudence Deplace sick	6.	
		To 4 foot wood to ditto	10.	
	14	To 4 foot ditto to Thomas Rice sick	10.	
		To 4 ditto to Saml. Chandler	10.	
	15	To 4 ditto to Bethene Sargent	10.	
	16	To Cash to John Hobbs	2.	

	20	To 4 foot wood to Sarah Mills	10.	
	22	To 4 foot ditto to Edward peirce	10.	
	23	To 4 foot ditto to Eliza. Goodwin	10.	
Feby.	1	To Cash to Eliza. Parker	6.	
		To 2 foot wood to James Westwood	5.	
		To Cash to Rachel McGee	6.	
		To ditto to Sarah Tuckerman sick	3.	
		To 4 foot wood to Ditto	10.	
	2	To 4 ditto to John Hobbs	10.	
		To 2 ditto to John Gault	5.	
		To Cash to ditto	1.	6
	4	To 4 foot wood to Mrs. Smellage	10.	
		To 4 ditto to John Morrison	10.	
	5	To Cash to Thomas Rice	3.	4
	6	To ditto to Dean. Mayes Childrn. Sick	9.	4
		To 4 foot wood to John Whitty	10.	
	12	To Cash to John Bullfinch	2.	8
		Sum Carried Up	£46. 3.	9 1/2

[32] 1773		Ward No. 10, Sum brot. up	£46. 3.	9 1/2
Feby.	13	To 6 foot wood to Mrs. Peirce	15.	
	15	To 4 foot ditto to Thomas Price	10.	
		To Cash to ditto	2.	
	16	To 4 foot wood to John Bullfinch	10.	
		To 4 ditto to Joshua Cornish	10.	
	22	To 4 ditto to Edward Peirce	10.	
		To Cash to Eliza. Parker	6.	
	23	To 4 foot wood to Eunic Cook	10.	

		To Cash to ditto	2.	8
		To 4 foot wood to Samuel Chandler	10.	
	24	To 4 foot ditto to James Westwood	10.	
		To 4 ditto to prudence Deplace sick	10.	
		To Cash to ditto	1.	6
	27	To ditto to Thomas Price	4.	6
Mah.	2	To ditto to Sarah Mills	2.	8
			£51. 18.	1 1/2

1773		Supra	Cr.	
Mah.	3d.	By the Overseers draught on } Mr. David Jeffreys Town Treasur.}	£51. 18.	1 1/2

[33]		The Town of Boston for disbursments Ward No. 10:	Dr.	
1773				
March	5	To 4 foot wood to John Hobbs	10.	
		To Cash to Rachel Magee	6.	
		To 4 foot wood to Sarah Mills	10.	
	6	To Cash to sarah Tuckerman	2.	
		To 4 foot wood to John Whittey	10.	
	10	To Cash to Wm. Cox (sick & lost one leg)	3.	
		To 4 foot wood to Eliza. Goodwin	10.	
		To Cash to ditto	1.	4
	11	To 4 foot wood to Dorathy Manning	10.	
	12	To 4 ditto to Eliza. Hales	10.	
		To Cash to ditto	1.	6
		To 4 foot wood to Mary Hawkes	10.	
	16	To 4 foot ditto to Thomas Rice	10.	
		To Cash to Rachel Magee	1.	4

	18	To ditto to Jno. Bulfinch		2.	4
	19	To 4 foot wood to Wm. Cox sick		10.	
	22	To Cash to widow Parker		4.	6
		To ditto to widow Smellage		3.	4
		To 8 foot wood to Joshua Cornish	1.		
	30	To Cash to Thomas Rice		2.	
April	3	To ditto to Sarah Tuckerman		2.	8
	5	To ditto to Rachel Magee		6.	
	10	To ditto to widow Smellage		1.	6
	13	To 2 foot wood to John Hobbs		4.	4
	16	To Cash to William Cox sk		3.	4
	17	To ditto to Thomas Rice		2.	
	19	To ditto to Widow parker		6.	
		To 1/2 Cord wood to John Whittey		8.	
		Carried Up	£8.	10.	2
[34] 1773		Ward No. 10, Sum brought Up	£8.	10.	2
April	24	To Cash paid Anna Eagleston for schooling 2 Children of Mary Watts & 1 of Mehittable Foots to 25th. Instant in full		11.	2 1/2
	29	To Cash to Elizabeth Sinclair		2.	
May	1	To Ditto to Martha Ryan wife of John Ryan}		1.	4
	3	To Cash to widow parker		3.	
	8	To ditto to Tho Rice		2.	
		To ditto to Rachel Magee		6.	
	10	To ditto to Widow Parker		1.	6
	15	To ditto to Sarah Tuckerman		2.	4 3/4
	17	To ditto to Widow Parker		1.	6
	24	To ditto to Widow Parker		3.	

	25	To ditto to Widow Smellage	2.	8
June	1	To ditto to Widow Hales	2.	
		To ditto to Widow Magee	6.	
	7	To ditto to Widow parker	4.	6
	28	To ditto to Ditto	6.	
		To ditto to Mary Caides sick	3.	
	30	To ditto to widow Smellage	3.	
July	2	To ditto to Anna Larkin	1.	6
	12	To ditto to widow parker to the 18	1.	6
	15	To ditto to Elizabeth Watson	1.	4
	17	To ditto to Widow Smellage	1.	6
		To ditto to Mary Caides	3.	
		To ditto to Rachel Magee	6.	
		Carried Over	£12. 6.	1 1/4
[35] 1773		Ward No. 10 sum brot. Over	£12. 6.	1 1/4
July	27	To Cash to Anna Larkin	3.	4
August	2	To ditto to Rachel Magee	6.	
	9	To ditto to widow parker to 16 Int.	6.	
	10	To ditto to widow Smellage	2.	
		To ditto to James Mayes	6.	
	12	To ditto to Mary Cades	3.	
	30	To ditto to Miriam Byjah	1.	2
		To ditto to Anna Eagleston for schoolg. 2 children from April 25th. to this day	9.	7
Septemr.	2	To Cash to Rachel Magee	6.	
	6	To ditto Widow parker to 13th.	6.	
	11	To 6 foot wood to James Mayes	12.	
	20	To Cash to Anna Larkin	1.	6

	26	To ditto to widow parker		3.	
	29	To ditto to widow Hales		1.	6
		To ditto to Mary Cades		3.	
Octor.	1	To ditto to Rachel Magee		6.	
	4	To ditto to Widow Smellage		1.	9 1/2
	7	To 4 foot wood to Eunice Cook		8.	
		To Cash to Dorithy Merrium		1.	6
	10	To ditto to Eliza. Parker		6.	
	16	To 6 foot wood widow Manning		12.	
	25	To Cash to Eliza. parker		1.	6
		To ditto to Mary Cades		3.	
		To ditto to Deacon Mayes		5.	4
	28	To 6 foot wood to Jno. Hunt		12.	
		Sum carried Up	£18.	13.	3 3/4
[36] 1773		Ward. No. 10. sum brot. Up	£18.	13.	3 3/4
Octor.	30	To Cash paid Anna Eaglestone for schooling 2 poor children to this day }		3.	8 3/4
		To Cash to Mariah Byjah		1.	4
Novr.	4	To 6 foot wood to Jno. Bulfinch		12.	
		To Cash to Rachel Magee		6.	
	8	To ditto to Elizabeth parker		1.	6
		To 6 foot wood to John Hobbs		12.	
	9	To 6 foot ditto to Rachel Magee		12.	
	11	To 4 foot ditto to John Whittey		8.	
	16	To 6 foot ditto to prudence Delaplaice		12.	
		To Cash to ditto		1.	6
		To 4 foot wood to Elizabeth Hales		8.	
		To Cash to ditto		2.	

	17	To ditto to Anna Larkin		1.	6
		To ditto to Mary Cades		3.	
	24	To 4 foot wood to Samuel Chandler		8.	
		To Cash to John Rice for Boarding} Increase Simpson		1.	6
		To 4 foot wood to Elizabeth Goodwin		8.	
	29	To Cash to Tho Rice for boarding Increas} Simpson to this day		2.	6
Decr.	1	To 6 foot wood to Mary Hawkes		12.	
		To Cash to Rachel Magee		6.	
		To ditto to James Mayes		6.	
	8	To 4 foot wood to James Westwood		8.	
		To Cash to Jno. Rice boarding Incs. Simpson		1.	6
		Sum Carried Over	£25.	11.	4 1/2
[37] 1773		Ward No. 10 sum brot. Over	25.	11.	4 1/2
Decr.	14	To 4 foot wood to Jno. Whittey		8.	
		To Cash to Mary Cades		3.	
		To 4 foot wood to Joshua Cornish		8.	
	18	To Cash to Anna Larkin		1.	6
	20	To 6 foot wood to John Hobbs		12.	
	22	To 2 foot wood to Mary Flyng		4.	
	25	To Cash to Mary Fling		1.	6
	29	To 4 foot wood to Mary Cowdry		8.	
		To 4 foot ditto to Elizabth. Sinclair		8.	
	31	To 4 foot ditto widow Smellage		8.	
1774)		To Cash to ditto		1.	6
Jany.	1	To ditto to Anna Larkin		1.	6
	3	To ditto to James Mayes		6.	
		To ditto to Rachel Magee		6.	

5	To 4 foot wood to Mary Fling sick		8.	8
	To Cash to ditto		1.	6
7	To ditto to James Flood		1.	6
10	To Ditto to Elizabeth Sinclair		1.	6
11	To 6 foot wood to John Bulfinch		13.	
12	To 4 foot ditto to James Flood		8.	8
14	To 4 foot ditto to Samuel Chandler		8.	8
	To Cash to Mary Cades		5.	
20	To ditto pd. Mrs. Thayer for Nursing Mary Fling		2.	8
	To Cash to Elizabeth Hales		2.	8
21	To ditto to Elizabeth Sinclair		1.	6
	Sum Carried up	£32.	3.	8 1/2
[38] 1774	Ward No. 10. sum brot. Up	32.	3.	8 1/2
Jany 22	To 1/2 Cord wood to John Whittey		8.	8
	To 1/2 ditto do. to Joshua Cornish		8.	8
24	To 4 foot ditto to Widow Smellage		8.	8
	To Cash to ditto		1.	6
	To 6 foot wood to John Hobbs		13.	
25	To Cash to Elizabeth Haslett		3.	
26	To ditto to John Hunt		2.	
28	To 6 foot wood to widow Manning		13.	
	To Cash to ditto sick		1.	6
	To 6 foot wood to Elizabeth Haslett		13.	
29	To 4 foot wood to Tho Rice		8.	8
	To Cash to Samuel Chandler		2.	
	To ditto to John Hobbs		2.	
	To ditto to Mary Hawkes		2.	1

		To ditto to Anna Larkin	1.	6	
		To ditto to Prudence Delaplace	3.		
		To ditto to Mary Cowdry	2.		
		To ditto to James Mayes	2.	8	
		To ditto to James Flood	2.	8	
Feby.	1	To 4 foot wood to Jona. Maker	8.	8	
		To Cash to Jno. Hobbs	1.	6	
	9	To 6 foot wood to Mary Coudry sick	13.		
	10	To 4 foot ditto to widow Steward	8.	8	
	11	To Cash to Rachel Magee	6.		
		To ditto to Widow Hales	2.	4 3/4	
		To ditto to Mary Cades	4.		
		Sum carried Over	£39.	7.	6 1/4
[39] 1774		Ward No. 10. sum brot. Over	39.	7.	6 1/4
Feby.	12	To Cash to John Hobbs	1.	6	
	14	To 4 foot wood to Saml. Chandler	8.	8	
	15	To Cash to widow Manning	2.		
		To ditto to prudence Delaplace	1.	4	
		To 4 foot wood to Ditto	8.	8	
	17	To 4 do. do. to Eliza. Hales	8.	8	
		To Cash to Ditto	1.	4	
		To ditto pd. Mrs. Sarah Rogers schooling} Eliza. Bryants child	4.		
	19	To Cash to widow Larkin	2.		
		To ditto to James Mayes	1.	4	
	21	To ditto to John Whittey	1.	4	
		To 4 foot wood to ditto	8.	8	
	22	To Cash to John Hobbs	2.	4 3/4	

	23	To 4 foot wood to widow Peirce			8.	8
	24	To Cash to Eliza. Haslett			3.	
		To ditto to Mariah Byjah			1.	
	26	To Ditto to John Bulfinch			3.	
		To 4 foot wood to ditto			8.	8
		To Cash to Jona. Maker			1.	6
March	1	To ditto to Rachel Magee			6.	
		To ditto to John Hobbs			1.	6
				£43.	12.	9

1774		Supra	Cr.		
March	2d.	By the overseers draught on Mr. David Jeffries Town Treasurer }	£43.	12.	9

[40] The Town of Boston for Disbursments in Ward No. 10 Dr.

1774

March	4	To Cash	to Widow Smellage	0.	1.	4
		To 4 foot wood	to ditto		8.	8
	5	To Cash	to John Hobbs		1.	6
		To Ditto	to Jona. Maker		2.	
		To Do.	to widow Larkin		2.	
	7	To Do.	to Dorithy Manning		2.	
	10	To 4 foot wood	to John Hobbs		8.	8
		To 4 foot ditto Jehonnots shop	to Eliz. Whittemore in }		8.	8
	12	To 6 foot ditto	to James Mayes		13.	
		To Cash	to Jona. Maker		1.	6
	14	To ditto	to John Hobbs		1.	4
		To 4 foot wood	to Joshua Cornish		8.	8

15	To 6 ditto	to Eliza. Haslett		13.	
17	To Cash	to widow Cowdry		2.	
	To ditto	to John Bullfinch		2.	8
	To ditto pd. Anna Eagleston Schooling			1.	8
18	To ditto	to Jonathan Maker		1.	8
19	To ditto	to widow Larkin		2.	1
26	To 4 foot wood	to John Whittey		8.	8
	To Cash	to John Hobbs		2.	
28	To 4 foot wood	to Jona. Maker		8.	8
29	To Cash	to widow Manning		2.	8
April 2	To ditto	to widow Larkin		1.	8
4	To ditto	to Elizabeth Haslett		3.	4
	To ditto	to John Bullfinch		3.	4
7	To ditto	to Rachell Magee		6.	
	To 4 foot wood	to Ditto		8.	8
		Sum Carried Over	£6.	7.	5

[41] 1774   Ward No. 10. Sum brot. Over   £6.   7.   5

April 9	To Cash	to Jona. Maker		1.	6
11	To 4 foot wood	to Samuel Chandler		8.	8
12	To 4 ditto	to widow Goodwin		8.	
	To Cash	to ditto		1.	6
13	To ditto	to Eliza. Whittemore		1.	6
	To ditto	to John Hobbs		3.	3
16	To ditto	to widow Maning		1.	6
	To ditto	to Anna Larkin		1.	6
23	To ditto	to widow Steward		3.	4
25	To ditto	To John Hobbs		2.	8
30	To ditto	to widow Larkin		2.	

				£	s.	d.
		To ditto	to John Bullfinch		3.	4
May	2	To ditto	to Rachel Magee		6.	
	6	To ditto	to Elizabeth Haslett		4.	4
	9	To ditto	to John Hobbs		2.	4 3/4
		To 2 foot wood	to ditto		4.	
		To Cash	to Sarah Whittemore		2.	
	14	To ditto	to John Hobbs		2.	
		To ditto	to Sarah Whittemore		2.	4 3/4
	18	To ditto	to widow Smellage		2.	8
		To ditto	to Dorithy Maning		3.	
	21	To ditto	to John Hobbs		1.	6
	24	To 4 foot wood	to widow Smellage		8.	
	28	To Cash	to John Hobbs		2.	4 3/4
		To ditto	to widow Larkin		1.	6
	30	To ditto	to widow Hales		2.	4 3/4
June	2	To ditto	to Nurse Manning		2.	
		Sum Carried Up		£10.	12.	9
[42] 1774		Ward No. 10 Sum brot. Up		£10.	12.	9
June	2	To Cash	to Rachel Magee		6.	
	4	To ditto	to John Hobbs		2.	
	7	To ditto	to James Mayes		3.	
		To 6 foot wood	to ditto		12.	
	11	To Cash	to John Hobbs		2.	8
		To Sundries	to John Whitteys wife sick		1.	6
		To Cash pd. Lettice Williams for nurs-}ing John Whitteys wife}			4.	9 1/2
	17	To Cash to Elizabeth Haslett			3.	4
	18	To ditto	to John Hobbs		2.	1

	21	To ditto	to Hugh Smith		1.	6
	22	To ditto	to Jona. Makers wife		1.	4
		To ditto	to Dorithy Maning		3.	
	25	To ditto	to John Hobbs		2.	4 3/4
		To ditto	to Hugh Smith		2.	8
		To ditto	to Jona. Maker		1.	4
July	1	To ditto	to Anna Ruler		3.	
		To ditto	to Anna Larkin		2.	
	2	To ditto	to John Hobbs		2.	
		To ditto	to Jona. Maker		1.	4
		To ditto	to Hugh Smith		1.	4
		To ditto	to Rachel Magee		6.	
	5	To ditto	to Sarah Whittemore		2.	
	7	To ditto	to John Hobbs		1.	4
		To ditto	to Saml. Chandler		2.	
		To ditto	to John Bullfinch		3.	
	9	To do.	to Jona. Maker		1.	4
		To ditto	to Hugh Smith		2.	8
	11	To ditto	to Anna Ruler		3.	4
		To ditto	to John Hunt		3.	4
	16	To ditto	to Jno. Hobbs		2.	
		To ditto	to Jona. Maker		1.	4
		To ditto	to widow Larkin		2.	
			Sum Carried Over	£15.	2.	4 1/4
[43] 1774			Ward No. 10 Sum brot. Over	£15.	2.	4 1/4
July	16	To Cash	to Hugh Smith		2.	
	18	To ditto	to Dorithy Manning		3.	

22	To ditto	to Anna Ruler	3.	
23	To ditto	to John Hobbs	2.	1
	To ditto	to Hugh Smith	2.	8
	To ditto	to Jona. Maker	2.	
28	To ditto	to widow Coudey	2.	4 3/4
30	To ditto	to John Hobbs	2.	
	To ditto	to Jona. Maker	1.	9 1/2
	To ditto	to Hugh Smith	2.	
	To ditto	to Anna Larkin	1.	6
	To ditto	to John Bullfinch	3.	
Augt. 2	To ditto	to Eliza. Haslett	3.	
3	To ditto	to Hugh Smith	1.	4
	To ditto	to Widow Magee	6.	
	To ditto	to Sarah Whittemore	2.	4 3/4
6	To ditto	to John Hobbs	1.	9 1/2
	To ditto	to Jona. Maker	1.	6 1/2
	To ditto	to James Mayes	3.	4 3/4
9	To ditto	to Abiel wood Greens lane	2.	
	To ditto	to widow Manning	3.	
13	To ditto	to John Hobbs	2.	1
	To ditto	to Jona. Maker	1.	4
	To ditto	to Anna Larkin	2.	
	To ditto	to Abiel Wood sick	6.	
	To ditto	to Hugh Smith	2.	
	To ditto towards Abiel Woods} funeral}		6.	
	To ditto	to Elizabeth Haslett	3.	7 1/4
20	To ditto	to Jona. Maker	1.	6

				£	s	d
		To ditto	to Hugh Smith		2.	1
	22	To ditto	to John Hobbs		2.	
		Sum Carried up		£19.	2.	10 1/4
[44]	1774	Ward No. 10 Sum brt. up		19.	2.	10 1/4
Augt.	23	To Cash	to widow Smellage		3.	5
		To ditto	to Anna Ruler		3.	
	25	To ditto	to Sarah Whittemore		2.	
	27	To ditto	to John Hobbs		2.	1
		To ditto	to Jona. Maker		2.	
	29	To ditto	to Widow Manning		1.	6
Septer.	1	To ditto	to Rachel Magee		6.	
	3	To ditto	to John Hobbs		2.	4 3/4
		To ditto	to Jona. Maker		2.	4
	5	To ditto	to John Riddle		1.	2 3/4
		To ditto to Mrs. Stuard to buy a Sping. wheel			8.	
	10	To ditto	to John Hobbs		2.	
		To ditto	to Jno. Bullfinch		3.	4
		To ditto	to Jona. Maker		1.	6
		To ditto	to Anna Larkin		2.	4 3/4
	14	To ditto	to widow Smellage		3.	4
		To ditto	to Eliza. Haslett		3.	7 1/4
	16	To ditto	to Anna Ruler		1.	6
		To ditto	to Dorithy Manning		3.	4
	17	To ditto	to Jno. Hobbs		2.	4 3/4
		To ditto	to Jona. Maker		1.	9 3/4
	20	To ditto	to Sarah Whittemore		2.	4 3/4
	21	To 6 foot wood	to Jno. Bullfinch		13.	
	25	To Cash	to Jno. Hobbs		2.	4 3/4

		To ditto	to Jona. Maker		2.	
		To ditto	to Anna Larkin		2.	
		To ditto	to Saml. Chandler		1.	4
	28	To 6 foot wood	to ditto		13.	
		To Cash	to widow Smellage		3.	7 1/4
Octor.	1	To ditto	to John Hobbs		2.	
		To ditto	to Jona. Maker		2.	
	3	To ditto	to Rachel Magee		6.	
		To 6 foot wood	to John Hunt		13.	
		To Cash	to James Mayes		6.	
			Sum carried Over	£25.	10.	9
[45] 1774			Ward No. 10, Sum brot. over	25.	10.	9
Octor.	5	To Cash	to Dorithy Manning		1.	
	6	To ditto	to Jno. Hobbs		2.	
		To 6 foot wood	to Rachel Magee		14.	
	8	To Cash	to Jona. Maker		2.	2
		To ditto	to Anna Larkin		2.	
	14	To ditto	to Eliza. Haslett		3.	
	15	To ditto	to John Hobbs		2.	1 1/4
		To ditto	to Jona. Maker		1.	7
		To ditto	to Dorithy Maning		1.	4
	22	To ditto	to John Hobbs		2.	
		To ditto	to Jona. Maker		1.	6 1/2
		To ditto	to Ann Larkin		2.	
		To ditto	to Ann Ruler		3.	
	28	To ditto	to Jno. Hobbs		2.	4 3/4
		To ditto	to Jona. Maker		2.	4 3/4

		To 2 foot wood	to Jno. Hobbs		4.	8
Novr.	3	To Cash	to Rachel Magee		6.	
	5	To ditto	to Anna Larkin		2.	
		To ditto	to Jona. Maker		2.	
		To ditto	to Jno. Hobbs		2.	
	7	To ditto	to Eliza. Haslett		3.	
	8	To ditto	to Widow Smellage		3.	0 3/4
		To ditto	to James Mayes		6.	
	12	To ditto	to John Hobbs		2.	4 3/4
		To ditto	to Jona. Maker		2.	
	16	To ditto	to widow Merrium at the head of Long lane		2.	
		To 4 foot wood	to ditto		9.	4
	19	To Cash	to Jno. Bullfinch		6.	
		To ditto	to Mary Watt		2.	8
		To 4 foot wood	to ditto		9.	4.
		Sum carried up		£30.	15.	8 3/4
[46] 1774		Ward No. 10, sum brot. up		30.	15.	8 3/4
Novemr.	19	To Cash to Jona. Maker			1.	9 1/2
		To 4 foot wood	to Joshua Cornish		9.	4
	21	To 4 ditto	to Jno. Hobbs		9.	4
		To Cash	to ditto		2.	
		To ditto	to Ann Larkin		2.	4
		To ditto	to Eliza. Haslett		2.	8
	23	To ditto	to widow Smellage		3.	
	24	To ditto	to Eliz Hail		2.	8
		To 6 foot wood	to ditto		14.	
	25	To Cash	to Hugh Smith		1.	4

	26	To ditto	to Jona. Maker		3.	10 1/2
		To 4 foot wood	to ditto		9.	4
		To Cash	to Jno. Hobbs		2.	
		To 6 foot wood	to Saml. Chandler		14.	
	29	To 6 ditto	to widow Smellage		14.	
		To 6 ditto	to Mary Hawks		14.	
Decr.	2	To Cash	to Rachel Magee		6.	
		To ditto	to Jo. Hemmingway wife) DeCostas alley		1.	6
		To 6 foot wood	to prudence Delaplace		14.	
		To Cash	to ditto		1.	6
	3	To Ditto	to Jona. Maker		1.	4
		To 6 foot wood	to Eliz Haslett		14.	
		To Cash	to ditto		2.	8
		To ditto	to John Hobbs		2.	4 3/4
		To ditto	to Ann Larkin		2.	6
	6	To ditto	to Abigal Munn in) Long lane		1.	4
		To ditto	to Mary Watt		2.	8 1/2
	10	To ditto	to Jona. Maker		2.	
		To ditto	to John Hobbs		2	.8 1/2
	12	To 6 foot wood	to Nurse Stuard		14.	
			Sum Carried over	£39.	10.	0 1/2
[47] 1774			Ward No. 10 Sum brot. over	39.	10.	0 1/2
Decr.	12	To Cash	to James Mayes		6.	
		To ditto	to Deboh. Welch		1.	9
		To 6 foot wood	to ditto at Mrs. Allen's) near So: battery		14.	
		To Cash	to Abigail Mun			7

13	To ditto	to Jas. Brown Jehonots shop	1.	4	
	To 4 foot wood	to ditto	9.	4	
	To 6 foot ditto	to widow Goodwin	14.		
	To Cash	to ditto	3.	4	
14	To ditto	to Samuel Chandler	2.	4	
	To 6 foot wood	to Dolley Dickey at } Mr. Tabb's the taylors }	14.		
	To Cash	to Rachell Magee	4.		
	To 2 foot wood	to Lettice Williams in } Jehonnots Shop }	5.		
	To 4 foot ditto	to Mary pledger in Mr. } Walcots house }	9.	4	
17	To 4 foot ditto	to Jno. Hobbs	9.	4	
	To Cash	to ditto	2.	4	
	To ditto	to Jona. Maker	2.		
	To ditto	to Ann Larkin	2.		
20	To ditto	to Ann Ruler	3.	4	
	To ditto	to John Hemmingway	1.	6	
	To 4 foot wood	to ditto	9.	4	
21	To Cash	to Deacon Bullfinch	6.		
23	To ditto	to Cuff Lewis free negro	1.	6	
24	To ditto	to Jno. Hobbs	2.		
	To ditto	to Jona. Maker	2.		
	To ditto	to Elizabith Haslett	3.		
	To ditto	to John Hobbs	2.	4	
		Sum carried up	£46.	1.	8 1/2
[48] 1774		Ward No. 10. sum brot. up	46.	1.	8 1/2
Decr. 31	To Cash	to Ann Larkin	2.		
	To ditto	to Jona. Maker	2.		

1775 Jany. 5	To 4 foot wood	to Mary Watt sick		10.	
	To 4 foot ditto	to Jno. Hobbs		10.	
	To Cash	to ditto		2.	
	To ditto	to Jona. Maker		2.	
9	To ditto	to Widow Smellage		2.	
	To 6 foot wood	to ditto		15.	
	To 4 foot ditto	to Richd. Cattern		10.	
	To Cash	to Rachel Magee		6.	
10	To 4 foot wood	to Josa. Cornish		10.	
13	To Cash	to Eliza. Haslett		3.	4
	To 4 foot wood	to Saml. Chandler		10.	
14	To Cash	to John Hobbs		2.	
	To 4 foot wood	to Elizabith Agen		10.	
	To Cash	to Jona. Maker	1.	4
17	To 4 foot wood to widow Merrium in Mr. Wollcots house head log. lane			10.	
20	To 4 foot wood	to Anna Ruler		10.	8
	To Cash	to Ditto	1.	6
21	To Ditto	to John Hobbs	1.	9 1/2
	To Ditto	to Jona. Maker		2.	
27	To Ditto	to Elizabeth Hail		3.	
	To Ditto	to James Mayes		6.	
	Sum Carried over		£52.	14.	4
[49] 1775	Ward No. 10. sum brt. over		52.	14.	4
Januy. 27	To Cash	to Elizabeth Haslett		2.	
28	To 4 foot wood	to John Hunt		10.	8
	To 2 ditto	to Mary Pledgett		5.	4
	To Cash	to John Hobbs		2.	

		To ditto	to Jona. Maker		1.	6
	30	To 4 foot wood	to Mary penniman⎞			
		in Greenleafs hous Long lane	⎟		10.	8
		To 2 foot ditto	to Lettice Williams		5.	4
Feby.	1	To 4 foot ditto	to John Bullfinch		10.	8
	4	To Cash	to Jona. Maker		1.	6
		To Ditto	to John Hobbs		2.	
	6	To Ditto	to Rachel Magee		6.	
	9	To Ditto	to James Mayes		6.	
	10	To Ditto	to John Hobbs		2.	
	11	To Ditto	to Jona. Maker		1.	6
	13	To 4 foot wood	to Josa. Barrett (horne lane)		10.	8
	14	To Cash	to Eliza. Haslett		2.	8
	15	To 4 foot wood	to widow Smellage		10.	8
		To Cash	to ditto		1.	4
		To 4 foot wood	to prudence Delaplace		10.	8
		To Cash	to ditto		1.	4
	16	To ditto	to Joshua Barret sick		1.	6
	17	To 4 foot wood	to Mary Watt		10.	8
	18	To Cash	to John Hobbs		1.	9 1/2
		To Ditto	to widow Maker		1.	9 1/2
	23	To Ditto	to Elizabeth Haile		1.	4
		To 4 foot wood	to Ditto		10.	8
			Sum carried up	£59.	6.	7
[50] 1775			Ward No. 10 sum brot. up	59.	6.	7
Februy.	25	To Cash	to Widow Maker		1.	4
		To Ditto	to John Hobbs		2.	
		To 4 foot wood	to Thoms. Greenleaf⎞			
			omitted Jany. 3 last⎰ ⎟		10.	

	To 2 foot wood	to Henry Horne	5.	4
28	To Cash	to Eliza. Haslett	2.	8
			£60.	7. 11

1775		Supra	Cr.	
March	1	By the overseers of the poors ⎫ Draught on Mr. David Jeffries ⎬ Town Treasurer for ⎭	£60.	7. 11

[51]		The Town of Boston, Disbursments Ward No. 10	Dr.	
1775				
March		To 6 White wool & 3 1/2 black for the use ⎫ of the work house omitted in former a/c ⎭	11.	10 1/2
	4	To Cash to John Hobbs	2.	
		To ditto to Widow Maker	1.	4
	8	To 4 foot wood to John Bulfinch	10.	
	9	To 4 ditto to widow Welch	9.	4
		To Cash to ditto	1.	4
		To pd. Lydia Harris, boarding 3 Child- ⎫ ren 1 week @ 2/ each ⎭	6.	
	11	To ditto to Rachell Magee	6.	
		To ditto to John Hobbs	2.	
		To ditto to widow Maker	1.	9 1/2
	14	To ditto to Sarah Ghent	1.	6
		To 4 foot wood to Anna Ruler	10.	
	15	To Cash to Eliza. Haslett	1.	6
	18	To ditto to John Hobbs	1.	8
		To ditto to Widow Maker	1.	9 1/2
	20	To 4 foot wood to Eliza. Boon	13.	
	25	To Cash to John Hobbs	2.	

					£	s	d
		To ditto	to Widow Maker			2.	
	28	To ditto	to Elizabeth Haslett			2.	
Apl.	1	To ditto	to widow Maker			1.	6
		To ditto	to John Hobbs			1.	8
	3	To 6 foot wood	to Rachl. Magee			6.	
	5	To 4 ditto	to widow penniman			8.	8
		To Cash	to Rachell Magee			6.	
			Sum Carried forward		£5.	14.	11 1/2
[52] 1776			Ward No. 10, sum brought up		£5.	14.	11 1/2
April.	9	To Cash to John Hobbs				1.	8
		To do. to Widow Maker				1.	8
	12	To ditto to John Hobbs				2.	
		To 4 foot wood to ditto				8.	8
	15	To 4 ditto	to Eliz Haslett			8.	8
		To Cash to Nurse Steward				1.	9 1/2
		To ditto to widow Maker				1.	6
	22	To ditto	John Hobbs			1.	6
		To ditto	widow Maker			1.	6
July	15	To ditto	Eliza. Hail			1.	2 1/2
Augt.	2	To ditto	John Hobbs			1.	
1776							
June	10	To ditto	widow Maker			4.	
		To ditto	John Hobbs			4.	
	12	To ditto for 5 yds Tow Cloth @ 2/				10.	
		To do. for makg. frock & Trousers for Benj. Cox				2.	6
Augt.	17	To do. for Medicines for John Banks				2.	
	20	To ditto	to John Kelly			1.	8

	6	To ditto	ditto		2.	6
Sept.	9	To ditto	ditto		1.	6
Octor.	12	To ditto pd. Benja. Burdick for boarding Mr. Ingerson Sick 6 weeks @ 6/		1.	16.	
Novr.	12	To ditto	Widow Winburne		1.	
	14	To ditto	Widow Wailing			10
		To ditto	Sarah Brown		3.	
		To ditto	Sarah Curtis		3.	
	21	To 4 foot wood	Sarah Adams		14.	
		To Cash	Esther Glover		4.	
		Sum Carried forward		£11.	16.	1 1/2
[53] 1776		Ward No. 10, Sum brot. forw'd		£11.	16.	1 1/2
Novr.	26	To 1 shirt to John Goffs			10.	
Decr.	7	To 4 foot wood	John Bulfinch		16.	
	11	To 4 do.	Sarah Carter		16.	
	13	To 2 do.	Mary Adams		8.	
	17	To 4 do.	Nurse steward		16.	
	23	To Cash	Mariah Bijah		1.	9
	25	To 4 foot wood	Sarah Warner		18.	
1777						
Jany.	7	To 4 foot Do.	Prude. Delaplace		18.	
	8	To 4 do. do.	Mary Adams		18.	
	10	To 2 do. do.	Mariah Bijah		9.	
	20	To Cash	ditto		3.	
	29	To ditto	Richd. Whitcomb		2.	4
	31	To 4 foot wood	Sarah Carter		18.	
Feby.	1	To 4 foot do.	Anna Ruler		18.	
	6	To 4 foot do.	Anna Tyler		18.	

	To Cash	Mary Butler			3.	6
March	1	To ditto	Anna Tyler		4.	
	3	To 4 foot wood	prude. Delaplace		18.	
	4	To Cash	Anna Ruler		3.	
				£22.	14.	8 1/2

1777		Supra	Cr.		
March		By the Overseers draft on Mr. Davd. Jeffries Town Treasurer }	22.	14.	8 1/2

[54]   The Town of Boston, disbursment Ward No. 10.   Dr.

1777

March	13	To Cash to Mary Adams		10.	
	18	To 1/2 Cord wood to Jesse Cox		14.	
April	7	To 1/2 Cord ditto to ditto		16.	
		To Cash to Widow Laha		1.	8
	18	To 1/2 Cord wood to Anna Tyler		16.	
May	3	To Cash to widow Anna Cox		5.	
July	28	To ditto to George Hogney french mans wife		6.	
Aug	8	To ditto to Mary Stone sick		6.	
Sept.	3	To ditto to Anna Tyler		12.	
	13	To ditto to Peter Barbour's wife		5.	4
Octor.	6	To ditto to Anna Tyler		12.	
	27	To ditto to Joshua Lane's wife		6.	
Novr.	8	To 2 foot wood to Sarah Carter	1.	4.	
	10	To 2 foot ditto to Prudence Delaplace	1.	4.	
	17	To Cash to Rachel Magee		12.	
	27	To ditto to Mary Adams		6.	
	30	To ditto to Mariah Byjah		6.	

Decr.	2	To ditto to John Lane		6.
	9	To ditto to George Hogney's wife		6.
	16	To 2 foot wood to Mrs. Butler	1.	4.
		To 2 ditto to Mrs. Hogney	1.	4.
	17	To 2 ditto to Eliza. Bulfinch	1.	4.
		To 2 ditto to John Lane & Cash 3/	1.	7.
		To 2 ditto to Sarah Carter	1.	4.
		Amount Caried Over	£15.	17.
[55] 1777		Ward No. 10. Amo. brot. Over	15.	17.
Decr.	22d.	To 2 foot wood to Hanah Bijah	1.	10.
		To 4 foot wood to Rachl. Magee	3.	
	24	To 2 foot ditto to prude. Delaplace	1.	10.
	31	To Cash to Eliza. Cromartee		12.
1778 Jany.	1	To ditto to Anna Cox		6.
	5	To ditto to John Lane		6. 4
	7	To ditto to Eliza. Haslett		6.
	13	To ditto to Mary Adams		6.
	14	To ditto to John Lane		4.
		To ditto to Anna Cox		5.
	16	To 2 foot wood to John Lane	1.	10.
		To Cash to Hanah Bijah		6.
	24	To ditto to Barsheba [Heskg]		6.
	26	To ditto to Mary Butler		6.
	28	To 2 foot wood to Mary Adams	1.	10.
	30	To 2 ditto to Sarah Carter	1.	10.
	31	To 2 ditto to John Lane	1.	10.
Feby.	4	To 2 ditto to Anna Cox	1.	13.
	6	To Cash to Mariah Bijah		6.

	10	To ditto to Mary Butler		8.	
	16	To 2 foot wood to Mary Adams		1.	13.
	17	To 2 ditto to Anna Cox		1.	13.
		To 2 Ditto to Eliza. Fulton		1.	13.
		Amount Carried Up	£38.	6.	4
[56] 1778		Ward No. 10 Amo. brot. Up	38.	6.	4
Feby.	17	To 2 foot wood to Rachl. Magee		1.	13.
	19	To 2 foot ditto to John Lane		1.	13.
	20	To 2 ditto to prudence Delaplace		1.	13.
	25	To Cash to Mary Butler			6.
	28	To ditto to Eliza. Fulton			6.
		To 2 foot wood to prudence Delaplace} omitted 19 March last }			14.
			£44.	11.	4

	Supra	Cr.

1778					
Mah.	5	By the Overseers draft on } David Jeffries Esqr. Town Treasur. }	£44.	11.	4

[57]		The Town of Boston disbursmts. Ward No. 10	Dr.

1778					
March	7	To Cash to John Lane			6.
		To ditto to Eliz Fulton			6.
	10	To ditto to Mary Butler			6.
		To 2 foot wood to Thom Goshins wife		1.	13.
	11	To 2 ditto to Anna Cox		1.	13.
	16	To 2 ditto to Eliza. Fulton		1.	13.

	17	To 2 ditto	to John Lane	1.	13.	
		To 2 ditto	to Sarah Carter	1.	13.	
		To 2 ditto	to Silence Davis	1.	13.	
	20	To 2 ditto	to Widow Holman	1.	13.	
	21	To 2 ditto	to Samuel Davis	1.	13.	
	26	To Cash	to Mariah Bijah		6.	
	27	To ditto	to Robt. Fultons wife		12.	
April	1	To ditto	to John Hayden		12.	
		To ditto	to widow Delaplace		6.	
	6	To 2 foot wood to widow Holman		1.	13.	
		To 2 ditto to R. Fultons wife		1.	13.	
	7	To Cash to Fidella a Negro woman			6.	
	9	To 2 foot wood to Jno. Lane		1.	10.	
		To 2 ditto to Widow Magee		1.	10.	
		To Cash to Robt. Fultons wife			12.	
	30	To ditto to Robt. Davis			12.	
May	1	To 2 foot wood to ditto		1.	4.	
		Carried Up		£24.	18.	
[58] 1778		Ward No. 10. sum brt. Up		24.	18.	
May	3	To Cash to Widow Davis			5.	
	7	To 2 foot wood to John Lane		1.	4.	
	19	To Cash to widow Delaplace			6.	
	20	To ditto to Robt. Fultons wife			6.	
	25	To ditto to Meriam Bijah			6.	
June	11	To ditto to widow Magee			8.	4
	12	To ditto to widow Davis			8.	4
August	20	To ditto to George Hogney			12.	
	27	To ditto to widow Gween			12.	

Septem	5	To ditto to George Hogney		6.	
		To ditto to Susana Davis		4.	
Novr.	5	To ditto to Widow Delaplace		12.	
	14	To ditto to Eliz Fulton		12.	
	17	To ditto to Silance Davis		12.	
	18	To ditto to James Brown sick		10.	
		To 2 foot wood to widow Davis	2.	2.	
		To Cash to James Brown sick		12.	
	28	To ditto to Robt. Fultons wife		12.	
		To 2 foot wood to widow Botterell	2.	2.	
		To 2 ditto to James Browne	2.	2.	
		To 2 ditto to widow Davis	2.	2.	
		To 2 ditto to widow Delaplace	2.	2.	
		To Cash to ditto		6.	
		Sum Carried forward	£44.	1.	8
[59] 1778		Ward No. 10. brot. forward	44.	1.	8
Decr.	3	To Cash to James Brown		12.	
	7	To ditto to Robert Fulton		6.	
	10	To ditto to James Brown		6.	
		To 2 foot wood to widow Davis	2.	2.	
	11	To Cash to Mary Butler		12.	
	13	To ditto Mariah Bijah		6.	
	15	To 2 foot wood to Anna Cox	2.	2.	
		To 2 ditto to Robt. Fultons wife	2.	2.	
	23	To 2 ditto to Widow Brown	2.	2.	
	28	To 2 ditto to Silance Davis	2.	8.	
	29	To 2 ditto to Mariah Bijah	2.	14.	

		To Cash to Mrs. Fullerton		12.	
1779	31	To 2 foot wood to widow Carney	2.	14.	
Januy.	1	To Cash to Anna Ruler		12.	
	2	To 2 foot wood to Widow Adams	2.	14.	
		To 2 ditto to Mariah (Negro)	2.	14.	
	4	To 2 ditto to Anna Cox	2.	14.	
		To 2 ditto to widow Carter Novr. last	2.	14.	
	8	To 2 ditto to ditto	2.	14.	
	12	To Cash to widow Cromartee		12.	
	13	To 2 foot wood to Chrisr. Mackher	2.	14.	
	20	To Cash to Mary Butler		12.	
	25	To 2 foot wood to Widow Cox	2.	14.	
	26	To Cash to widow Delaplace		18.	
		Carried forward	£84.	11.	8
[60] 1779		Ward No. 10. brot. forward	84.	11.	8
January	27	To 2 foot wood to Ann Ruler	2.	14.	
Februy.	4	To Cash to Mrs. Fulton		18.	
	6	To ditto to Mary Butler		9.	
		To ditto to Meriam Bijah		9.	
	13	To ditto to widow Cox		12.	
		To 2 foot wood to ditto	2.	14.	
		To Cash Meriam Bijah		12.	
	16	To 2 foot wood to widow Adams	2.	14.	
	23	To 2 ditto to Chrisr. Mackher	2.	14.	
March	2	To Cash to Mary Butler		18.	
			£99.	5.	8

Supra	Cr.	

1779					
March	2d.	By the Overseers Draught on ⎫ David Jeffries Esq Town Treasurer ⎭	99.	5.	8

[61]　　　　The Town of Boston Disbursments Ward No. 10　　Dr.

1779

March	22	To Cash to Miriam Bijah		12.
		To ditto to Mary Butler		12.
	27	To ditto to Mariah Negro woman		12.
May	10	To ditto to Meriam Bijah		12.
Novr.	18	To ditto to ditto	1.	4.
Decr.	15	To ditto to widow Cox	2.	8.
	17	To ditto to widow Procter	1.	16.
	20	To ditto to Miriam Bijah	1.	10.
	30	To ditto to ditto	1.	16.

1780

Jany.	7	To ditto to widow Procter	2.	8.
	8	To ditto to widow cox	1.	16.
	15	To ditto to Widow Procter	3.	
	19	To ditto to Meriam Bijah	1.	16.
		To ditto to Lydia Raymer	3.	12.
	25	To ditto to widow Procter	3.	12.
	31	To ditto to Susanna Barber	3.	12.
Februy.	1	To ditto to widow Cox	3.	12.
	5	To ditto to widow Procter	3.	
	7	To ditto to Mariah (Negro)	3.	
	21	To ditto to widow Procter	3.	
	24	To ditto to Susannah Barber	3.	

£46. 10.

1780		Supra	Cr.	
March	1st.	By the Overseers Draught on ⎰ David Jeffries Esqr. town Treasur. ⎱	£46. 10.	

[62] The Town of Boston disbursmts. Ward No. 10   Dr.

1780

March	6	To Cash to Widow Procter	3.	
	8	To ditto to widow Cromartee	1.	4.
		To ditto to widow Cox	3.	
	14	To ditto to widow Procter	2.	8.
	31	To ditto to widow Cox	3.	
		To ditto to Mariah Negro woman	3.	
April	22	To ditto to Elizabeth Egen	4.	16.
Decr.	23	To ditto to widow D Welsh	9.	
			£29.	8.

1781   Supra   Cr.

March	8	By the Overseers draught on David Jeffreys Esq Town Treasurer	29.	8.

[63] The Town of Boston Disbursts. Ward No. 10   Drs.

1781

March	16	To Cash to Josh. Peirce	6. .		
	17	To ditto to Josa. Barrett	9. .		
	28	To ditto to Mr. Blake	12. .		
		Paper Curcy.	27. .	7.	3.
Decr.	27	To ditto to John Riddles wife		1.	6.
	29	To ditto to Eliza. Haslett		1.	6.
1782					
Feby.	2	To ditto to Jno. Riddles wife		2.	5.
	4	To ditto to Michl. Malonys wife		2.	5.
	6	To ditto to Elias Cox		2.	5.

ᕫ

March	4	To ditto to ditto	3.	.	
			£1.	0.	6
		To allowance for depretiation on former draughts}	12.	15.	6
			13.	16.	

1782		Supra	Cr.		
March	6	By the Overseers Draught on David Jeffreys Esqr. for the ballance	£1.	0.	6
		By ditto for Depressiasion alowed for former Draughts on the Treasurer	12.	15.	6
			£13.	16.	0

[64]   The Town of Boston disbursts. Ward No. 10   Dr.

1782

March	19	To Cash to Mrs. Malony	1.	6
		To ditto to Elizabeth Cox	2.	
April	2	To ditto to ditto	3.	
	16	To ditto to Mrs. Dollar	3.	
June 7		To ditto paid Tuffts the Constable for Comitting Nancy Jones to the Work House	1.	6
Augt.	20	To Cash to Ebenezer Youngs wife	6.	
Novr.	2	To ditto to ditto	3.	
	12	To ditto to Richard Sisk	3.	
		To ditto to Mrs. Malony	3.	
	29	To ditto to Richard Sisk	2.	8
Decr.	5	To ditto to Mrs. Dollar	3.	

(1783)	23	To ditto to ditto		2.	8
Jany.	11	To ditto to Rich: Sisk		3.	4
	29	To ditto to Widow Sisk		2.	8
Feby.	1	To ditto to widow Browne		2.	8
	3	To ditto to Mrs. Malony		1.	4
	10	To ditto to Mrs. Young		3.	4
		To ditto to Widow Dollar		3.	
	26	To ditto to Hugh Smith		2.	8
				£2. 13.	4

1783		Supra	Cr.		
March	5	By The Overseers draught on ⎫ Peter Boyer Esqr. Town Treasurer⎰ for		£2. 13.	4

Recd. the above and all other of thes accounts in full ℘ Saml. Whitwell

[65] The Town of Boston Disbursements

Ward No. 10 Dr.

1783.

March 11th.	Hugh Smith	Cash		2.	5
	Mrs. Mahoney	Do.		2.	5
12	Widow Cox			1.	6
22	Hugh Smith			2.	
25	Eliza. Calder			2.	5
	Mrs. Maloney			1.	2 1/2
May 6	Widow Cavaneu			1.	6
June 9	Widow Brown			2.	5
June 22	Widow Dollar			3.	4
29	Widow Brown			2.	
Augt. 16	Cash paid Ware for crying that the Workhouse Windows were broke			3.	

꩜

Sept.	30	Widow Dollar Cash	6.	
Novr.	7	Widow Jackson	1.	2 1/2

1784

Jany.	9	Sarah Nickerson (Long lane)	3.	4
		Mrs. Dollar	3.	
	14	Widow Adams	3.	4
	27	To Jno. Palfrey's Wife [ak?] Mrs. Wise	3.	4
	30	Mrs. Adams	3.	4.
Febry.	14	Mrs. Dollar	6.	
	16	Ebenr. Youngs Wife	6.	
March		Widow Dollar	6.	
			£3. 5.	7

Received the above in full to this Day.

Sam Whitwell

[66]   The Town of Boston Disbursements

Ward No. 10   Dr.

1784

April	1	To Widow Dollar Cash	6.	
July	3	To Widow Dollar	5.	
	5	To Mrs. Dixon for Schooling 2 ⎫ of Mrs. Dollars' Grand-Children ⎬	13.	
Sept	11	To Widow Dollar	6.	
Oct	5	Paid Mrs. Dixon for Schooling 2 of Mrs. Dollars Grand-Children 13 Weeks	13.	
Nov	17	Elizh. Woods (Widow)	3.	
Decr.	4	Lydia Smith	3.	4
	11	Widow Hannah Stevens	4.	

	29	Widow Dollar		6.	
	30	To Mrs. Dixon for Schooling 2 } of Mrs. Dollars Grand-Children }		13.	
1785					
Jany.	26	To Cash to Joshua Barrett		6.	
	27	To Widow Elizh. Wood		6.	
Feby.	1	To Edward Brazer		3.	7 1/2
	8	Ann Egleston		3.	
	12	Widow Dollar		6.	
		Christian Makher		4.	
	28	To Joshua Barrett		3.	4
Marh.	2	Receiv'd the above in full to this Day	£5.	4.	3 1/2

pr Sam Whitwell

[67] The Town of Boston Disbursements

Ward No. 10   Dr.

1785						
March	3d.	To Cash Gave Elizath. Wood		£	2.	
	14	To	Abigail Hiller		2.	8
	18	To	Mary Adams		3.	4
	22	To	Ann Egelston		3.	0
	23	To	Widow Dollar		6.	8
April	8	To	Joshua Barrett		6.	
		To 1 lb Thread dld Mrs. Farmer			3.	6
	9	To Eliza Haslip			6.	8
May	3	To Ditto			4.	6
	13	To Widow Dollar			6.	

June	3	To Elizath. Haslip	6.	8
July	7	To Widow Dollar	6.	
	11	To Eliza Haslip	6.	
Aug.	27	To Ditto	6.	8
Sep	3	To Widow Dollar	6.	8
	6	To Widow Eliza Woods	3.	
	28	To Hannah Dimon	6.	8
Oct	27	To Elizabeth Robertson	1.	11
Nov	7	To Widow Dollar	6.	8
	21	To Hannah Dimon	6.	0
	26	To Lidia Martin	1.	6
Dec	5	To Widow Dollar	6.	4
	31	To Joshua Barrett	3.	4
		Sum Carried Over	£5. 11.	9

[68] The Town of Boston Disbursements

Ward N. 10 £

1786

Jan	2	Sum Brought Over	5. 11.	9
		To Cash Gave Wm. Lewis	6.	
		To Hugh Smith	1.	4
		To George Seal	3.	4
	7	To Hannah Dimon	3.	4
	11	To Mrs. Dollar	6.	
	16	To Edward Brazeir	4.	6
Feb	1	To Mrs. Dollar	6.	
	2	To Joshua Barrett	3.	
	14	To Edward Brazeir	4.	6
	16	To Mrs. Dollar by one Load of Wood	10.	

25	To Joshua Barrett			3.	
27	To Mrs. Dollar			6.	
		Supr.	Cr.	£8. 8.	9

By the Overseers Draught on Peter Boyer Esqr. Town Treasurer
for the Ballance

July	10	Receved the above in full

[69] The Town of Boston for disbursments in Ward No. 10 Dr.

1786

March	17	To Cash to Grace Brown in Long lane		4.	6
April	14	To ditto to Hannah Dimon		3.	
	15	To ditto	to Grace Browne	1.	6
Novr.	28	To ditto	to Elizabeth Glover		9
	29	To ditto	to Brockus	1.	
Decr.	8	To ditto	to Abigail Ray	3.	

1787

Jany.	22	To ditto	to Edward Braizier	3.	
Feby.	5	To ditto	to Marcy Barnes	3.	
	9	To ditto	to Christopher Avery	3.	4
March	3	To ditto	to Marcy Barnes	3.	
	"	To ditto	to Edward Braizier	3.	
	5	To ditto	to Jona. Raymond	1.	6
	6	To ditto	to Widow Dollar	3.	
				£1. 13.	7

	Supra Cr.

1787

March	By the Overseers draft on Peter Boyer Esq Town Treasurer }	£1. 13. 7

[70] The Town of Boston for disbursments Ward No. 10 Dr.

1787

March	28	To Cash to Abigail Blackman (long lane)		4.	6
June	10	To ditto to Mary Wheaton at Mrs. Walcuts		3.	
	11	To ditto to Widow Thorp (Brack Reeds House)		3.	
	25	To ditto paid Mrs. Walcutt schooling⎫ Mrs. Wheatons child 8 weeks a 8d. ⎭		5.	4
July	11	To ditto to Marcy Barnes		3.	
	18	To ditto to Widow Dollar		6.	
	28	To ditto to widow Thorp		1.	6
Sept.	8	To ditto to Elizabeth Welsh		2.	3
	"	To ditto to M: Barnes		1.	6
Octobr.	13	To ditto paid M. Vintenon for schooling⎫ Mrs. Baxters son 33 weeks a 8d. ⎭	1.	2.	
Novr.	10	To ditto to Mrs. Dollar		3.	
Decr.	15	To ditto to Wm. White's wife		3.	
	"	To ditto to John Walker		3.	
	20	To ditto to Elizabeth Welsh		1.	6
	28	To ditto to Mary Fletcher		1.	6
1788	"	To ditto Advanced Capt. Partridge		6.	
Jany.	16	To ditto to Widow Dollar		3.	
	18	To ditto to Mary Fletcher		3.	
Feby.	8	To ditto do.		1.	6
	15	To ditto to Samuel Lane		3.	
		To ditto to Widow Brown		3.	
	19	To ditto to Lemuel Stutson		3.	
	23	To ditto to Mary Fletcher		1.	6
			£4.	8.	1

⌒

				Supra	Cr.		
		By draft on Town Treasurer in full			£4.	8.	1

[71]		The Town of Boston disbursments Ward No. 10.		Dr.		

1788

Month	Day				£	s	d
March	7	To Cash	to Elizabeth Welsh			1.	6
	8	To ditto	to Edwd. Braizier			3.	
April	10	To ditto	to Mrs. Dollar			3.	
	16	To ditto	to Lemuel Stutson			6.	
	28	To ditto	to Samuel Lane			3.	
May	14	To ditto	to Lemuel Stutson			3.	
	28	To ditto	to	ditto		2.	8
June	13	To ditto	to	ditto		3.	
	26	To ditto	to	ditto		2.	8
July	5	To ditto	to	ditto		1.	6
	12	To ditto	to	ditto		1.	6
	19	To ditto	to	ditto		2.	
	26	To ditto	to	ditto		1.	6
Augt.	2	To ditto	to	ditto		2.	1
Sept.	5	To ditto	to Mary Edwards			3.	
Octor.	7	To ditto paid Mary Brown schooling Hannah Durant 13 weeks @ 6d.				6.	6
	30	To ditto to Mary Edwards				6.	
Novr.	25	to ditto to ditto				4.	6
	28	To ditto to Widow Thorp				3.	3
Decr.	1	To ditto to Anna Powell				2.	9
		To ditto pd. Mrs. Brown schooling Hannah Durant 3 weeks				1.	6
	10	To Cash to Edward Braizeir				6.	

	18	To ditto to Abigail Ray		3.	4
		Amount carried up	3.	13.	3

[72] Ward No. 10—continued

1788		To Amount brought forward	3.	13.	3
Decr.	26	To Cash to Mary Edwards		4.	6
	"	To ditto to Anna Powell		2.	1
1789					
Jany.	16	To ditto to ditto		1.	6
	24	To ditto to Elizabeth Welsh		2.	5
	"	To ditto to Edward Braizier		3.	
	"	To ditto to Mary Edwards		3.	
	26	To ditto to Susanna Brown		1.	1
Feby.	4	To ditto to Anna Powell		1.	6
	5	To ditto to widow Dollar		6.	
	25	To ditto to Anna Powell		1.	6
	28	To ditto to Mary Edwards		3.	
		To ditto to Mrs. Edwards omitted posting 27 Septemr:		3.	
			£5.	5.	10

Supra   Cr.

1789					
March		By the Overseers draght. on Peter Boyer Esqr. Town Treasurer	5.	3.	9
		Balance short drawn for carried to new accot.		2.	1
			£5.	5.	10

[73]   The Town of Boston disbursments for Poor in Ward No. 10   Dr.

1789

March	4	To Balance short drawn for in last years account		2.	1
	16	To Cash to Eliza. Welsh		1.	6
	21	To ditto to Anna Powell		3.	
	27	To ditto paid Mary Brown for schoolg. Hannah Durant 3 weeks		1.	6
	28	To ditto to Mary Edwards		3.	
April	8	To ditto to Elizabeth Welsh		1.	6
	29	To ditto to Mary Edwards		3.	
May	22	To ditto to Mrs. Dollar		3.	6
	30	To ditto to Elizabeth Welsh		2.	3
June	19	To ditto to Mary Edwards		1.	6
Augt.	7	To ditto to Mrs. Dollar		6.	
Septr.	23	To do. paid Mary Nicols for schooling Mrs. Chandlers two children 3 weeks		3.	
Novr.	3	To Cash to Mrs. Edwards		1.	6
Decemr.	5	To ditto to Mrs. Dollar		3.	
	16	To ditto paid Sally Rand for schooling Mrs. Chandlers two children 12 Weeks @ 6d. each		12.	
	19	To Cash to Mary Wheaton		3.	
		Amount carried forward	£2.	11.	4

[74][4]   Ward No. 10 continued

1790		To Amount brought forward	2.	11.	4
Jany.	8	To Cash to Ebenezer Torrey		1.	6
Feby.	9	To ditto to the Widow Ray		4.	
	15	To ditto to widow Leverett		3.	

---

4   This is the last page numbered in the MS.

〰

	17	To ditto to Margrett Yates		3.
March	3	To ditto to Widow Taylor		3.
	"	To ditto paid Mrs. Rand for schooling } two children of Mrs. Chandlers 12 Weeks }		12.

£3. 17. 10

1790   Supra   Cr.

March   By the Overseers draught on }
Peter Boyer Esqr town Treasurer }   3. 17. 10

Memorandums

1790

June		Drawn	1 bl Rum of Jos: Hal gals.	
			1 Do. Vinegar of Mr. Langley gals.	
	21st.	Drawn	1 Do. Rum 33 gals. of Wm. Porter on Deacon Bailey's Accot.	
		Drawn	30 bushls. Corn of Js. Thompson the 14th. dld Mr. Welch	
<July	1>	Entd.	*<Recd. 22. 10. 0 from Deacon Phillips* } *for which I gave my Recept* } *on account of his Tax>* }	
		Drawn	Recd. 1 Hogsd. of Molases } from Thos. Perkins } 108 Gals. @ 1/9 Trucking 1/	9. 10.
	17	Drawn	Recd. 6 pr. womans Shoes from David Lewis @ 4/6	
	17	Drawn	Recd. of Messrs. Crockers 147 yds. of Tow Cloth at 1/	7. 7.
			<Bot of Wm. Dawes 12 [ll. peas?] 8/ Paid> Enter'd	
Augt.	2d.		1 bl. Vinegar gals. of Mr. Langley 6	
Octr.	1		1 bl. Vinegar.	

༃

1790

Sept.	11	David Lewis Cr. by 6 pr. Mens Shous at 6 36/ & 4 pr. womans @ 4/6	2.	14.	
	6	Recd. of Henry Hill 49 Galls.⎱ of Wine at 4/3 ⎰	£10.	5.	3
	11	1 bb. of Rice from Joseph Perce⎱ 1. 3. 8 Neet at 20/ ⎰	1.	16.	5 1/2
	18	David Lewis Cr.			
		By 6 pr. mens Shous @ 6/	1.	16.	
		By 6 pr. Womans @ 4/6	1.	7.	
		<6 pr. womans Shous from⎱ Mr. Brown omited at 4/6 ⎰	*1.*	*7.>*	
	25	David Lewis Cr. by 9 pr.⎱ womans Shous—@ 4/6 ⎰	2.	0.	6
Octr	2	David Lewis Cr. by 7 pr. mens⎱ Shous @ 6/ ⎰	2.	2.	
	6	Davd. Lewis Cr. by 1 pr. Boys 3/8 To 4 pr. Mens @ 6/	1.	7.	8

Octr 6th. David Lewis
paid by a Draft on the Town
Treasurer

1791				£	
May	16	Paid Mrs. Strater		1.	6
	23	1/6 the 30 1/6 June 6th 1/6		4.	6
June	13	1/6 the 27th. 1/6 July 4th. 1/6		4.	6
July	18	1/6		1.	6
Augst.	1	To Cash 1/6 the 8th. 1/6		3.	
	16	To Do. 1/6 the 22d. to Do. 1/6 the 29th. 1/6		4.	6
Septr.	5	To Do. 1/6 the 12 to Do. 1/6 the 19th. 1/6		4.	6
	26	To Ditto 1/6 Octr. 3d. 1/6		3.	
Octr.	10	To Do. 1/6 the 17 1/6		3.	
		Omitted Charg in 2 weeks		3.	
	24	To Cash 1/6 31st. To Cash 1/6		3.	
				£1. 16.	
Novr.	18	To Cash 1/6 <28th. 1/6> Decr. 5th. 1/6		3.	
Decr.	12	To Cash 1/6 the 19th. 1/6		3.	
	26	To Cash 1/6		1.	6
Janr	2	To Cash 1/6 the 9th. 1/6		3.	
	16	To 1/6 the 23d. 1/6 the 30th. 1/6		4.	6
Febr	6	To 1/6 the 13 1/6 the 20th. 1/6		4.	6
	27	To Do. 1/6		1.	6
March	22	To Mrs. Keeth 1/6 to Mrs. Chandler 1/6		3.	
				£1. 4.	

1791				
May	16	Receved of Mr. John Amorey to give Mrs. Strater 1/6 pr. week		6.
June	18	Recd. of Mr. Amory to give to Mrs. Strater 1/6 pr. week		£1. 10.
				1. 16. 0
Novr.	18	Recd. from Ditto for Ditto		1. 4.

Capt: Benjamin Hammatt

Dr.

6. 15.

Cr.

1790	Contra	Vizt.		
	By an allowance of 6d. ⅌ Week for the following Persons in the Workhous (being State Boarders)			
	Eleanor Lyndes from the 6th Apl. to the 1st. Septr. is 21 Wks 1 day @ 6		10.	7
	Mary Faulkner 21 Wks 1 day		10.	7
	Reb: Kinsley 21 Wks. 1 day		10.	7
	Saml. North from 17th June to 1st. Septr: is 11 Wks. @ 6d.		5.	6
			£1. 17.	3

Saml. Brown of Concord

Dr.

1790			
1791			
Janur.	5	To a Draft on the Town Tresure	6. 15.

Cr.   £

1790				
Novr.	4	By 4 pr. Womans Shous @ 4/6		18.
	24	By 4 pr. Womens Shous @ 4/6		18.
		By 5 pr. mens Do. @ 6/	1.	10.
Decr.	11	By 1 pr. mens & pr. Womans Shous		10. 6
Janur.	4	By 9 pr. Womens Shous @ 4/6	2.	0. 6
		By 3 Ditto mens @ 6/		18.
			6. 15.	0

Peter Boyer Town Treasr.

Dr.

1790			£	s	d
May 5th.	To Overseers Dft. for		£22.	13.	10
June 2d.	To do.	for	84.	18.	1
			£107.	11.	11

Contra   **Cr.**

1790			£	s	d
Apl.	15	By Cash	£22.	11.	4
	30	By do.	30.		
			£52.	11.	4
		Balance due Carried to the debit of Jos: Russells Accot. below	55.	0.	7
			£107.	11.	11

Joseph Russell Town Treasr:

Dr.

1790			£	s	d
Augt.	To balance of the above Accot.		£35.	0.	7
4th.	To Overseer's Dft.	for	68.	13.	2
Sept: 1	To Do.	for	37.	6.	10
Octo. 6	To Do.	for	50.	0.	11
Nov. 3	To Do.	for	77.	16.	1
Decr. 1	To Do.	for	57.	16.	3
1791					
Jany. 5	To Do.	for	68.	18.	10
Feby. 2d.	To Do.	for	23.		
Mch. 2	To Do.	for	36.	14.	4
			£469.	7.	

Contra   **Cr.**

1790			£	s	d
Augt.	By Cash	this Month	£109.	6.	
Sept	By Do.	this Mth	117.	10.	8 1/2
Octr.	By Do.	this Mth	12.	9.	2 1/2
Novr	By Do.	this Mth	41.	8.	8
Decr.	By Do.	this Mth	57.		
1791 } Jany. }	By Do.	this Mth	28.		
Feby.	By Do.	this Mth	32.	15.	8
Mar 2d.	By Do.	this Mth	20.	16.	8
			£419.	7.	
	By bala. due Card: to his Debit—next page }		50.		
			£469.	7.	

Joseph Russell Town Treasr. Dr.

1791				£	s	d
Mar:	3d	To bala: of Accot: ꝑ Adjustt.		£50.		
Apl. 6		To Overseer's Order for		45.	2.	2
May 4		To ditto for		236.	7.	8
				£331.	9.	10

Contra Cr.

1791				£	s	d
Mar	8	By Cash of Js:Thompson		£30.		
	16	By Do. of Do.		30.		
Apl:	14	By Cash		75.		
	16	By ditto		35.	2.	2
	21	By ditto £100 (27th.) £40		140.		
May 20th.		By ditto		21.	7.	8
				£331.	9.	10

Joseph Russell Town Treasr. Dr.

1791			£	s	d
June 1st.	To Overseers dft. for		£75.	2.	2 1/2
July 6	To. Do. for		27.	0.	9
			£102.	2.	11 1/2
	Balc. due to the Treasr.		35.	17.	1/2
			£138.	0.	0
Augt. 3d.	To Overseers dft. for		31.	13.	4
Sept. 7	To do. for		20.	4.	10
			£59.	18.	2
	Bala. carried to his		9.	18.	10 1/2
	At. next page		£69.	17.	0 1/2

Contra Cr.

1791			£	s	d
June 4th.	By Cash		18.		
	25	By do.	90.		
July 6	By do.		30.		
			£138.		
	By bala.		£35.	17.	1/2
Augt. 3	By Cash		34.		
			£69.	17.	0 1/2

Dr.   Joseph Russell Town Treasr:

1791				
Octo. 5	To Overseers dft.	for	£19.	2. 8
Novr: 2	To do:	for	45.	0. 4
Decr.	To do.	for	78.	12. 10
1792				
Jany. 4	To do.	for	40.	2.
Feby. 1	To do.	for	26.	16. 1
			£209.	13. 11

<March 7   To Overseers Draft for   47.   7.>

APPENDICES

Appendices

Appendix 1

The Massachusetts Township Act, 1692

The following is a selection from the 1692 Act establishing the office of Overseers of the Poor.

From *The Acts and Resolves, Public and Private, of the Province of Massachusetts*, 21 vols. (Boston, 1869–1922), 1:64-68. Province Laws, 2d session, 1692–93, chapter 28, "An Act for Regulating of Townships, Choice of Town Officers and Setting Forth their Power."

[Sect. 4.] That the freeholders and other inhabitants of each town, ratable at twenty pounds estate, … shall choose three, five, seven or nine persons, able and discreet, of good conversation, inhabiting within [said] town, to be selectmen or townsmen and overseers of the poor, where other persons shall not be particularly chosen to that office (which any town may do as they shall find it necessary and convenient)….

[Sect. 7.] That the Selectmen or overseers of the poor of each town (where there are such chosen and specially appointed for that service) are hereby impowered and ordered to take effectual care that all children, youth, and other persons of able body living within the same town or precincts thereof (not having estates otherwise to maintain themselves) do not live idly or mispend their time in loitering, but that they be brought up in some honest calling, which may be profitable unto themselves and the publick. And if any person or persons fit and able to work shall refuse so to do, but loiter [or] mispend his or her time, wander from place to place, or otherwise misorder themselves, and thereof be convicted… such person or persons shall… be sent to the house of correction and at their entrance be whipped on the naked back, by the master of such house or other such as he shall procure, not exceeding ten lashes; and be there kept to hard labour until he or she be discharged by such justice or justices or quarter sessions of the peace for the same county. And it shall and may be lawful for the overseers of the poor or selectmen in each town where there are no other persons specially chosen and appointed to be overseers of the poor, [that] they are hereby ordered with the assent of two justices of the peace, to bind any poor children belonging to such town to be apprentices where they shall see convenient, a manchild until he shall come to the age of twenty-one years, and a woman-child to the age of eighteen years, or time of marriage; which shall be as effectual to all intents and purposes as if any such child were of full age and by indenture of covenant had bound him or her self.

[Sect. 9.] [Persons entertained in any town by the space of three months and not warned out to be reputed inhabitants]… and the proper charge of the same in case through sickness, lameness, or otherwise they come to stand in need of relief, to be born by such town, unless the relations of such poor impotent person in the line or degree of father or grandfather, mother or grandmother, children or grandchildren be of sufficient ability; then such relations respectively shall relieve such poor persons in such manner as the justices of the peace in that county where such sufficient persons dwell shall assess.

Appendix 2

The Massachusetts Poor Relief Act, 1794

This is a very small portion of the act of the General Court of what was by then the Commonwealth of Massachusetts that effectively confirmed the primary role of the Overseers of the Poor in the public administration of poor relief. The powers granted to the Overseers by this act were as comprehensive as any in their past and would remain in force until after 1822, when the City of Boston received its first charter and the Overseers' authority began to be modified.

The Act was passed in February 1794 and was intended to be used in relation to the Settlement Act of 1793. Together, the acts expand the criteria for lawful settlement in towns, and expand the Overseers' means of restricting settlement by warning out. The Act is reprinted in full in The Overseer's Guide; or, A History of the Laws of Massachusetts, Respecting the Settlement, Support, Employment, and Removal of Paupers: With Notes and References to Adjudged Cases *(Brookfield, Mass., 1815). The following selection identifies the Act's intent.*

"An Act providing for the relief and support, employment and removal of the poor, and for repealing all former laws made for those purposes."

[Sect. 1] Be it enacted… that every town and district within this Commonwealth shall be holden to relieve and support all poor and indigent persons, lawfully settled therein, whenever they shall stand in need thereof, and may vote and raise monies therefor, and for their employment, in the same way that monies for other town… charges are voted and raised. And may also, [annually] choose any number [up to twelve] to be Overseers of the Poor, and where such are not specially chosen, the Selectmen shall be Overseers… *ex officio*."

[Sect. 2] Be it further enacted, that said Overseers shall have care and oversight of all such poor and indigent persons… and shall see that they are suitably relieved, supported and employed either in the Workhouse, or other tenements belonging to such towns or districts, or in such other way and manner as they, at any legal meeting, shall direct, or otherwise at the discretion of said Overseers, at the cost of such town or district.

The act then proceeds to specify five further areas of Overseer authority in the maintenance of their mandate.

The act makes it easier for the Overseers to:

1. Recover the costs of poor relief from the families of recipients.

2. Warn out all who cannot satisfy the "settlement" requirements.

3. Charge the state directly for costs incurred in providing for nonresidents.

4. Remove and apprentice (indenture) children of the poor.

5. Assign to the Workhouse any of the poor who frequent bawdy houses, gamble, or otherwise indulge in "lewd behaviour."

Appendix 3

The Boston Workhouse Act, 1735

The Overseers of the Poor attempted to amass a full transcription of the provincial legislation and Town Meeting instructions regarding the official status of the Workhouse and so replicated by hand the pertinent material. This file, taken from the Overseers' manuscript records, box 13, folder 1, is 40 pages long. It is not clear when it was compiled by the Overseers, but it ranges from 1735 to 1803 and is the work of several hands. The following selection identifies the main features of the Act. The Act itself is published in Acts and Resolves, *2:757ff.*

"An Act for employing and providing for the Poor of the Town of Boston Passed 28th May 1735. See Province Law Book Page 302."

Whereas the Town of Boston is grown considerably populous, and the Idle and Poor much increased among them, and the Laws now in force relating to them, not so suitable to the Circumstances of the said Town, which are different from those of the other Towns in the Province. Therefore,… Be it enacted by the…General Court … that [annually in March] the Town of Boston are… impowered to chuse twelve Overseers of the Poor…for twelve several Wards Respectively, into which [Boston] shall be divided each Overseer to have the more especial care of his particular Ward,… which [they] shall visit…whensover they may judge there is Occasion, at least once in every Month; and shall also…every Month assemble together to consider and determine the most proper Methods for the Discharge of their Office.

And whereas the Poor…upon the decay of Trade become still more numerous and want Means to employ and set themselves to Work…or by ill Habits become idle and slothfull and very burthensome to the Town…in such case or whenever the…Town of Boston shall…judge it necessary or convenient to erect, provide or endow an House for the Reception and Employment of the Idle and Poor [it] shall be authorized and impowered so to do; which house shall be under the Regulation of the Overseers of the Poor… [The Town is] hereby authorized to make purchases and receive Donations for endowing the said Work House, to the Value of Three Thousand Pounds per Annum; and to sue and be sued, in all Affairs of said House; the several Donations always applied according to the Will of the Donors.

And…the Overseers…shall have the Inspection, Ordering, and Government of the…House, with Power of appointing a Master or Masters, and… Assistants….

And…each one of the Overseers…shall have Power to send any idle and indigent Person… to the…House for Entertainment and Employment, for the the Space of twenty-four Hours; and any two of the said Overseers shall have Power to continue to send to said House such… Persons till discharged by the major Part of said Overseers at a monthly Meeting… .

And whereas there are sometimes Persons rated to the publick Taxes, who are notwithstanding unable or negligent to provide Necessaries for the Sustenance and Support of their Children: Be it enacted That the Overseers shall have the same Power of binding out into good Families the Children of such, as where the parents are rated nothing; provided such Persons are not rated for their personal Estate or Faculty.

And for as much as there is great Negligence in sundry Persons as to the instructing and educating their Children, to the great Scandal of the Christian Name and of dangerous Consequence to the rising Generation[:] Be it further enacted, That where Persons bring up their Children in such gross Ignorance, that they do not know, or are not able to distinguish the Alphabet or twenty-four Letters at the Age of six Years, … the Overseers … are hereby impowered and directed to put or bind out into good Families, such Children, for a decent and Christian Education, as when Parents are indigent and rated nothing to the public Taxes; unless the Children are judged uncapable, through some inevitable infirmity.

[The] Assignation of each Ward to the… immediate Care of a particular Overseer will give the …Overseers Opportunity of a more exact Knowledge of the Town, and all Intruders into it… the aforesaid Overseers… are impowered to warn any and all… who are not Inhabitants, to depart the Town.

Appendix 4

The Boston Workhouse Rules of Management, 1739

The following are the regulations that were drawn up by the Overseers of the Poor under the authority of the 1735 Workhouse Act. These were presented to a committee of the Town Meeting and amended and passed by the Town Meeting of October 12, 1739. The text is in manuscript in Overseers, *box 13, folder 1, and in published form in the* Boston Records *12:234–40. According to Wiberley, 90, these are the only surviving "detailed workhouse regulations from the colonial period." While details of the Workhouse population do not exist, as they do for the Almshouse, the Workhouse rules offer a rare glimpse into the behavioral standards and the operational regimen of an eighteenth-century American workhouse that was intended to employ gainfully the chronically unemployed or unemployable, and to correct and rehabilitate the idle poor. It is not known how much, if any, of the corporal punishment noted here was ever carried out. This is a slightly abridged copy of the* Rules and Orders:

Rules and Orders for the Management of Workhouse lately Erected in the Town of Boston; for Employing and Maintaining the Idle and Poor, belonging to said Town.
Labor improbus omnia vincit

The General Method [Contents] …

❧

Rules and Orders for the Management of the Work House in Boston

I *Rules relating to the Overseers of the Poor who, by Law have the Direction of the said House.*

1.   That there shall be a General Meeting of the Overseers at the House, the third Tuesday of every Month, at three O'Clock in the Afternoon, to inspect all Accounts, and examin [sic] into the Behaviour of the People committed to the House, and their own Officers and Servants, and to redress all Difficulties that occur to the Master, and to consider all Complaints Made by the Poor, and to consult and advise about such further Rules and Methods as may be for the advantage of said House.

2.   That a Committee of the Overseers, consisting of Three (Two of which are impowered to act) take the more immediate Inspection of the House for one month by turns … .
II *Rules relating to the Master and Mistress of the House.*

1.   That the Master and Mistress be Persons of approv'd Integrity and Ability, Who shall be chosen annually …[T]he Overseers … shall have Power to Agree with [them] for their Yearly Salaries: But if the … Master and Mistress be found guilty of immoral or irregular behaviour, the Overseers [can] dismiss them, and place others in their room.
2.   That the Master keep a Register of the Names, Ages, Occupations and Places of Nativity, and of their last abode, of all Persons… Admitted into the House, as well as an Account of the Time of their Entry and of their Deaths or Dismission from the House.
3.   That the Master keep the Gates, at all times, well Secured… And if any be desirous to see, or speak with any Persons committed to the House, the Doorkeeper is not to call them, Without leave: And if any Person be suspected of bringing in any strong Liquors, or carrying out any thing, belonging to the House, or any Person therein, the Doorkeeper is to stop them, and give notice to the Master, that so due Enquiry and Search may be made forthwith, and the Guilty punished: But yet all such, as in an orderly way, would see the House, shall be treated with proper Respect and Civility, by the Master, and in his absence by the next officer of the House.
4.   That Master at the Hours appointed for going to Bed, which in the Summer … shall be at Ten O'Clock, and in the Winter… at Nine O'Clock shall see all fires and Lights extinguished, Excepting what shall be absolutely necessary, and that these be left under proper care.
5.   That the Mistress take care that the Victuals be well and reasonably Dress'd, the Bread and Beer prepared according to the Direction of the Overseers; that the Rooms be Swept, and Beds made every Day; that the Windows be frequently Opened for Airing the House; that the House shall be Washed, as often as shall be judg'd

necessary; that the Table-Linnen, Dishes &c, be clean; that the People be kept clean and neat in their Apparel, and have clean Linnen to Shift Once every Week, and the Beds Shifted Once a Month in the Summer Season ....

6. That the Master buy the Provisions, and Materials for Work, and other Necessaries; and dispose of what is Manufactured, to the best advantage, according to the Advice and Directions of the Overseers... .

7. That the Master keep Books of Accounts of all Expences, and Profits of the House, to be Pass'd upon, and allowed by the Overseers... to be Open to the Inspection of the Town, whenever they shall see cause to appoint a Committee ... .

That the first Book contain An Inventory of all Furniture, Linnen and Woolen Cloathing bought, and of the necessary Utensils belonging to said House, with an Account how they are disposed of.

That the next Book Contain An Account of all the Provisions &c bought; as also the Quantities of each Sort Expended every Day, and of the Number of Persons provided for, each Day.

And that the last Book contain An Account of all the Stock, and Materials for Carrying on the Work of the House, which has been purchased, or sent to be manufactored, as also the Names of the Persons by whom sent; with an Account how such Goods are disposed of, and the Profits arising on the same.

8. That the Master and Mistress be Obliged to Observe such further Rules . . . made by the Overseers . . . Agreeable to the Law of the Province.

III. *Rules relating to the Persons that shall be Admitted into the House.*

1. That None shall be Admitted without a written Order, under the Hand of One or more of the Overseers.

2. That upon their Admission, they be Examin'd, Whether they are free from Lice and foul Distemper; And such as shall not be found clean, shall be put into some particular Room, 'till they be perfectly cleans'd: And that they be Obliged to take Care to keep themselves Wash'd and Comb'd, and their Cloathes neat and whole, and to Change their Linnen Once a Week.

3. That they Several Persons in the House constantly Repair at the stated Hours to their proper Apartments: where they shall work orderly at such Business, and so many Hours as the Overseers shall direct.

4. That they constantly attend the Worship of God, in the House and observe the Rules prescribed for their Meals.

5. That when any Children shall be Received into the House, there shall be some suitable Women appointed to attend them; Who are to take Care that they are Wash'd, Comb'd and Dressed every Morning, and be Taught to Read, and Instructed in the Holy Scriptures and Assemblies Catechism,...And that the rest of their Time be employ'd in such Work as shall be Assigned them; And when they arrive to a sutable [sic] Age They shall be Bound out into good Families, as the Law directs.

6. That when any Persons are taken Sick, they shall be removed into the Alms-House,

if it be done with Safety, and be put under the Care of said House 'till further Order: But if a removal shall be judg'd dangerous, then they shall have a Nurse and the Town's Physician to attend them, where they are.

IV. *Rules relating to the Work and Employment of the People in the House.*

1. That the Bell shall be rung every Morning to call the Family up; and such Persons as are able, shall repair to the several Places appointed for them to do their work in, and shall be kept diligently at work from Such Hours in the Morning, to such Hours in the Evening, as the Overseers shall from time to time direct; Excepting so much time as shall be allow'd for Meals, and Religious Worship.

2. That the common Work of the House be Picking of Oakum, Unless for such Trades–Men, whose Business may be well accomodated [sic] in the House, and it shall be judged more profitable to employ them in their proper Trades; Such as Taylors, Shoemakers, Mopmakers, Nailers &c. And that such of the Women as are capable, be employ'd in Carding, and Spinning Wooll, Flax, Yarn for Mops, and Cotton Yarn for Candlewick, Knitting, Sewing &c. But that these things be determined and regulated by the Overseers, or their Committee.

3. That Whereas the Poverty and Ruin of many Families is often Owing to the Idleness and Viscious Courses of one of the Heads of it, more particularly of the Masters, Who may have been bred to some good Trade, that by Industry would comfortably support them, the rest of the Family being Industrious, and in a capacity of Earning something considerable towards their own Support, so that it might be judg'd proper to order said Persons up to the House and Employ them there; In that case, An Account shall be kept of their Earnings, and after a reasonable deduction for their Maintenance in the House, the Overplus shall be applied to the Support of their Family in such Ways and Methods, as the Overseers or their Committee shall direct.

V. *Rules relating to the Diet and Victualling of the House, and the proper Seasons thereof.*

1. That the Overseers shall… as often as they … judge necessary… Agree upon the Diet of the House, to be continued 'till further Order… to the Master for his direction.

2. That the Hour of Dining be Twelve a Clock, at which time the People of the House shall all be called together, and Dine in one room (if it will contain them) having their Tables cover'd with sutable Cloths, Dishes Trenchers &c. and the Commons for the Day, as directed by the Overseers: That None be allowed to Dine in their separate rooms, unless in case of indisposition: But that as to their Breakfast and Supper, it may be dilivered to them out of the Kitchen, between the Hours of Eight to Nine in the Morning, and of Six and Seven in the Evening.

3. That they be allowed from the Hour of Twelve to One for the time of Dining: and that from Eight to Nine in the Morning, and from Six to Seven in the Evening, be allowed for the other Meal times, and for Attendance on Divine Worship.

VI. *Rules relating to the Religious Worship of the House.*

1. That the Master every Morning . . . and every Evening . . . Call the People together, and Read a sutable portion of the Holy Scriptures to them, and Pray with them; And as often as they Eat togethe, Ask a Blessing, and return Thanks.
2. That he take especial Care, that the Sabbath be duly Observed; And besides the Morning and Evening Service, he shall be Obliged (until other provision be made) to call the whole Family together, at least One part of the Day, and spend a sutable portion of Time in Praying, Singing of Psalms and Reading some practical discourses of Divinity, that shall be Appointed by the Overseers.

VII. *Rules relating to the Government of the House, both with and respect to Rewards and Punishments.*

1. That all Immoralities and Disobedience to the Government of the House, and other Misbehaviour, be by the Master noted in a Book, and laid before the Overseers, or their Committee; that by their Authority and Admonition, such Rudeness and Immorality may be restrained, and Peace and good Order maintained, and all obstinate, perverse and unruly Persons punished, according to their Crimes.
2. That such as shall duly Observe the fore-going Order, and faithfully Perform their several Tasks shall be Intitled to One penny out of every Shilling they Earn, to be disposed of by the Overseers for their [inmates'] greater Comfort.
3. That Whereas some slothful Persons may pretend Sickness or Lameness, to excuse themselves from Labour: It is Ordered, That such Persons shall pass a proper Examination by the Physician; And if it should Appear upon his Report and other concurring Circumstances that those Persons made false Excuses they shall be punished by such an Addition of Labour To their daily Stint or some other way, as the Overseers . . . shall determine.
4. That no Person presume to Smoke Tobacco in their Beds, On penalty of being denied Smoking for One week; And that if convicted a Second Time, He or She shall be punished as for other Misdemeanours.
5. That no Person presume to Beg Money, or any other thing, directly or indirectly, from any Person, that shall come to Visit the House, on penalty of being denied their next Meal.
6. That no Person presume to go out of the House without Liberty; And that every One who Obtains leave, shall return in good Order, at the time appointed, On penalty of being denied going out for One Month for the first Offence, and for Three Months for every Offence afterwards.
7. That no Person shall Neglect to repair to their proper places for Work; Or being there, shall refuse to work, loiter or be idle; Or shall not well perform the Task of work set them; Or shall waste or spoil any of the Materials, or Tooles of the several Manufactures; Or shall deface the Walls, or break the Windows, Or shall distirb the House by Clamour, Quarelling or Fighting or abusive Language; Or shall bring any

strong Liquors into the House without Leave; Or shall be Absent from Divine Service without reasonable Excuse; Or prophane the Sabbath; Or carry it disrespectfully to their Governours; Or shall be Guilty of Lying, or wanton and lascivious Behaviour; Or shall Drink to Excess, Steal or prophanely Curse and Swear; Or in any Other respect Act immorally or irregularly, they shall be Punished, either by denying them a Meal, or Whole days allowance, or by Gaging, or causing them to wear a Collar round about their Necks with a wooden Clog to it, or by Obliging them to stand on a Stool in a publick Place, with a Paper fix'd on their Breast, denoting their Crime in Capitals, for the space of One Hour, Or by Ordering them into a Dungeon to be kept with Bread and Water, not exceeding Forty Eight Hours, Or by an Addition of Labour to their daily Task, according to the nature and circumstance of the Crime; and in Case of frequent repetition and Obstinancy in their Crimes, they shall be Punished by Order of One or more Justices of the Peace, by removal into Bridewell, or otherwise as the Law directs.

8. That the Committee of Overseers, at their Weekly Meeting, have Power to punish all breaches of the foregoing Orders, Excepting those that are referred to the Cognizance of a Justice of Peace: And in all such Cases a Majority of the Overseers shall be called together.

9. That the Master of the House have Power, in the intervals between the Meetings of the Committee of the Overseers, to punish the breaches of the foregoing Orders, according to the Instructions he shall receive in writing from the Overseers or Directors of the House from time to time; And that in the Cases of Difficulty Arising, which may need a more speedy Consideration, he shall call the Committee together for their Advice and Assistance.

10. That if any Person in the House shall discover any other Person who shall be Guilty of any of the foregoing Offences, Such Person shall receive some such Reward or Incouragement as shall be Ordered by the Overseers or their Committee: And, if any Person shall know of any of the Offences aforesaid, and doth not discover the same, Such Person shall be Punished according to the discretion of the Overseers.

11. That the foregoing Rules and Orders of the House be publickly Read, every Monday Morning, that none may plead or pretend Ignorance of them.

THE END

Appendices

❧

The Diet of the House for the first Quarter.

	Breakfast	Dinner	Supper
Lords Day			
Monday			
Tuesday			
Wednesday			
Thursday			
Fryday			
Saturday			

N.B. Small Beer to be given as there may be Occasion.[a]

[a]This dietary chart was left blank in the manuscript and in the Town Meeting minutes.

In addition to the very comprehensive rules in the 1739 regulations, the Town Meeting periodically adjusted the conditions of behaviour and management. One such amendment survives in manuscript form in Overseers *box 13, folder 1, and is attached to the manuscript containing the 1739 codes.*

The Overseers finding it necessary, for the better Governing the House, to make some further Rules for the Conduct of the Master; Have accordingly on this fith day of April 1758 it being their monthly meeting past [passed] these which follow:

1st That he do not release any person from the House untill he has obtained the consent of the major part of the Overseers under their hands, at some general meeting, and that he permit no person to go out on any other occasion without the consent of the ruling Overseer.

2 That so often as he shall be directed by four of the Overseers; (the Chairman allways to be one) to warn a generall Meeting, he do it immediately; and if the occasion of the meeting be for the release of any person from the House, He also notify for whom the application is made taking especial care to warn those gentlemen who signed their Commitment.

3 That he take care none be admitted to speak with any person committed to the House when he is absent, and that he himself admit none, unless he can attend them to the Room be within hearing of all that may pass and see that they are out of the yard before he leave them.

4 That he so contrive his out door business as to be allways at home between the hours of Eight and Ten in the morning to wait on the ruling Overseer, and to attend such as may in an orderly manner desire to speak with their Friends.

5 That at every monthly meeting he lay before the Overseers the commitment as well as the release of every person received into or discharged from the House the month past.

The Boston Overseers Incorporation Act, 1772

The following selection is from an act of the Massachusetts General Court on April 23–25, 1772, following a petition to the legislature in which the Overseers of the Poor sought to control the receipt and distribution of all private funds intended for poor relief. The Overseers had long been solely responsible for the public care and control of the dependent poor within their jurisdiction. But the legal designation of the Overseers, by act of "incorporation," as the authorized agency for the management of private funds in addition to public monies established the Overseers as a genuine monopoly in the fiscal support and management of the poor. The preamble of the act (the first paragraph below) is, in fact, drawn from the Overseers petition which is in Massachusetts Archives (Boston), 118, "Towns, 1763–1774;" 572. The act is in Acts and Resolves *5:177–78, and in manuscript form in* Overseers, *box 13, folder 1.*

An Act for incorporating the Overseers of the Poor of the Town of Boston

Whereas many charitably disposed persons have given & bequeathed considerable sums of money and other interest and estate to the Poor of the Town of Boston & their use, & many other persons are well inclined to make charitable donations to the same good purpose, but the Overseers of the Poor of the same Town not being incorporated, the good intentions of those who have made & those who incline to make such charitable donations, have been wholly frustrated or not carried into full effect.

Be it therefore enacted by the Governor, Council and House of Representatives, that the Overseers for the time being of the Poor of the Town of Boston… be created, made, erected and incorporated into a body politic by the name of the Overseers of the Poor of the Town of Boston in the Province of the Massachusetts Bay in New England, and that they and their successors...have perpetual succession by such name.

…That all and singular sum and sums of money, interest and estate, real or personal, of what name or nature soever heretofore given, or at any time hereafter to be given, granted, bequeathed or devised by any way or means whatsoever to the Poor of the Town or to their use, not exceeding the sums & value in this Act aforementioned, be & the same hereby is & shall be to all intents & purposes vested in the same Overseers & their successors in their said corporate capacity and they are hereby enabled in the same capacity to receive, manage, lease, let & dispose the same according to best discretion to & for the use & benefit of the Poor of the said town.

Provided always, & be it hereby enacted, that the said Overseers shall not be able to receive or be capable of having or holding any monies or personal estate of any kind or nature whatsoever at any time above and beyond the sum and amount of Sixty Thousand Pounds lawful money of this Province, accounting and reckoning the whole monies and value of all the personal estate, personal securities, and choses in action, which they shall own or be vested withal in their corporate capacity together, & that all Gifts & Bequests of money or personal estate of any kind made to the said Corporation, or which by the tenor of this act they might take or be vested with shall be utterly void at all times hereafter when their whole Stock … together amount to … sixty thousand pounds.

…That the …. Overseers & their successors … have a perpetual succession … to sue or be impleaded by its said corporate name to purchase lands & hold them not exceeding the sum of five hundred pounds… by the year, & to manage, lease, bargain & sell or otherwise dispose of all or any part thereof & do all acts as natural persons may, as from time to time the said Corporation shall judge best for the benefit, advantage & use of said poor.

…That the said Corporation shall have a common seal & power, &… is hereby authorized to make by-laws & private statutes & ordinances not repugnant to the laws of the land, for the better government of the said Corporation & its finances, to choose a treasure[r], clerk, & other subordinate officers as from time to time shall be found necessary, & all or any of them again at pleasure to displace.

Be it further enacted, that all instruments which said corporation shall lawfully make by the name aforesaid and sealed with their common seal, and all acts done or matters passed upon, by the consent of a major part of the said Overseers for the time being, shall bind said Corporation and be valid in law.

Act passed 23d [to] 25th April 1772

Within the range of the 1772 act was the ability of the Overseers to administer individual trusts—in effect, to establish a "corporation within a corporation." For example, in 1803, the Commonwealth of Massachusetts passed a law establishing a trusteeship for the specific purpose of administering private funds for the use of older paupers, orphans and abandoned children. The 1803 act is attached to Overseers, *box 13, folder 1, and reads in part, as follows:*

"An Act to incorporate Oliver Wendell and others together with the Overseers of the poor… by the name and title of The Trustees of John Boylston's charitable donations for the benefit and support of aged poor persons and of orphans and deserted children." The act names Wendell, William Cooper, Ebenezer Stour, William Smith, and John Pitts as trustees of Boylston's will, but after their "decease" the Overseers "shall have perpetual succession" as trustees.

Appendix 6

The Lists of Elected Overseers, 1690/91–1800.

The earliest recorded appearance of the Boston Overseers of the Poor as an official branch of the town administration is in the Boston Town Records, *7:206, for March 9, 1690/91. This was the first election of Overseers by the Town Meeting and included a petition to the General Court that led to the formal legislation that actually created the office. That legislation of 1692 was not specific to Boston but Boston was the only town for nearly a century to use Overseers as a separate town office. In all the other Massachusetts towns the local Selectmen administered poor relief (see Appendix 1). The election of Overseers was recorded annually in the town records along with all the civic administration lists. Before 1707 the Overseers appear to have been chosen by the Selectmen, but thereafter it seems that the Town Meeting did the appointing indicating a separate if collaborative status for the Overseers and the Selectmen. The earliest extant citation from the Overseers' own records is 1742. The list that follows is drawn from* Boston Town Records, *volumes 7, 8, and 12, and from Robert F. Seybolt's invaluable* The Town Officials of Colonial Boston, 1630–1775 *(Cambridge, Mass., 1939) for the years before 1742 and thereafter from the Overseers' records themselves. Seybolt's compilation is exhaustive, and while it is derived mostly from the published* Boston Town Records *and the manuscript volumes of the Boston Town papers (at the Boston Public Library), it does use a very broad range of contemporaneous sources including newspapers. Seybolt is especially useful in cross reference and in establishing consistent spellings for the Overseers' names, and in the use of titles such as "Esquire," "Captain," "Honorable," "Mister," and so on. Seybolt is also useful for comparing the Town Papers with the transcriptions in the* Boston Records, *and in clarifying the idiosyncracies and omissions of the various recording and transcriptions clerks. Town officials were chosen annually at the March Town Meeting, usually held during the first half of the month. Until 1752 the official Anglo-American year ended on March 25. Thus the use of 1690/91, and 1691/92 and so on, in the records. The Overseers' own lists from 1742 to 1752 do not use the split year form but refer to March 8, 1741/42, for example, as March 8, 1742. This list does not include the few men who were appointed and "refused" the appointment and did not serve for even one year as Overseers.*

Overseer	Title	First Appointment	Years of Service
Abbott, Samuel	Mr.	1771	4
Alford, John	Colonel	1719/20	1
Allen, Jeremiah	Mr.	1712/13	2
Austin, Jonathon	Mr. (Esquire in 1789)	1784	18
Avery, John	Esquire	1765	1
Ballantine, John Jr.	Captain	1709/10	1
Banister, Thomas	Mr.	1706/07	1
Barrett, John	Mr. (Esquire in 1761)	1748	26
Barrett, Samuel	Mr. (Esquire in 1782)	1776	8
Bedgood, Jeffery [Jeffry]	Mr. (Captain in 1732)	1725/26	16
Bliss, A.	?	1704/05	1
Bolt [Boult], John	Mr.	1706/07	3
Borland, John	Mr.	1703/04	3
Bourn, Nathaniel	Esquire	1758	9
Bowes, Nicholas	Mr	1778	6
Bradford, John	Captain	1768	1
Brattle, Thomas	Esquire	1703/04	2
Brewster, Oliver	Mr. (Esquire in 1797)	1796	8
Bromfield [Brumfield], Edward	Esquire	1701/02	4
Bromfield, Edward Bromfield, Henry	Mr. Mr.	1734/35 1761	21 3
Brown, Edward	Mr.	1691/92	1
Byfield, Nathaniel	Esquire (Captain in 1701)	1700/01	2
Calef, Robert Chauncy, Charles	Mr. Mr.	1701/02 1709/10	2 3
Checkley [Chickley], Samuel[l]	Lieutenant (Captain in 1701)	1691/92	3
Cheever, Joshua	Captain	1734/35	8
Clark, Francis	?	1704/05	2
Clark, Timothy	Captain (Esquire in 1717/18)	1714/15	16
Clark, William	Mr.	1703/04	3
Codman, John Jr.	Mr.	1787	9
Coleman, William	Mr.	1690/91	1
Davis, Benjamin	Captain	1700/01	1
Deering [Dereing;Dering],Henry	Mr.	1697/98	5
Deering, Henry	Captain (Esquire in 1731/32)	1721/22	8
Dexter,Samuel	Mr.	1760	3
Dolbeare, Benjamin	Mr.	1757	20
Down [Downe;Donne], William	Captain	1736/37	14
Draper, Richard	?	1697/98	1
Drummer, Jeremiah	Esquire	1701/02	2

Edes, Edward	Mister	1786	18
Eyre, John	Esquire	1700	1
Flucker, Thomas	Mr.	1756	5
Franklin, John	Mr.	1751	1
Frizzell, John	Mr.	1711/12	3
Gardner, Joseph	Esquire	1761	6
Gooch [Gouch], James	Mr.	1714/15	14
Gore, John	Esquire	1767	8
Gorham, Stephen	Esquire	1790	13
Greenleaf, William	Mr.	1766	10
Greenwood, Samuel	Mr. (Captain, 1732; Esquire, 1735)	1724/25	14
Greenwood, Nathaniel	Captain	1755	2
Hammett, Benjamin	Captain	1763	4
Harris, William	No title given.	1706/07	1
Heath, Eliza	Mr.	1703/04	1
Henchman, Daniel	Captain (Esquire in 1738)	1734/35	21
Hews, Samuel	Mr.	1777	4
Hill, John	Mr. (Captain, 1734; Major, 1738)	1731/32	25
Hill [Hull], Henry	Mr.	1787	24
Hirst, Grove	Mr.	1707/08	7
Holyoke, Elizur	1702/03	1702/03	3
Hubbard, Thomas	Mr. (Esquire in 1737/38)	1733/34	22
Hunt, John	Mr. (Esquire in 1734/35)	1730/31	6
Hunt, Samuel	Mr.	1738/39	5
Hutchinson, Elisha	Esquire (Colonel in 1701)	1700/01	2
Hutchinson, William	Mr. (Colonel; Esquire)	1714/15	5
Inches, Henderson	Mr.	1763	4
Jackson, Jonathan	Mr.	1725/26	8
Keeling [Keeler], Samuel	Captain	1706/07	2
Legg, John	Mr.	1714/15	8
Leverett, John	Esquire	1767	9
Lewis [Lewise] Ezekiel	Mr.	1706/7	2
Lindall, Timothy	Mr.	1711/12	2
Lynde [Lind; Lynd], Samuel	Mr. (Esquire in 1702/3)	1691/2	8
Marshall, J.	No title given.	1704/05	1
Martin [Martyn], Edward	Captain	1714/15	1
Mason, Jonathan	Mr.	1760	28
Minot, Stephen	Mr.	1703/04	2
Oliver, Andrew	Esquire	1739/40	19

Oliver, Daniel	Mr. (Esquire in 1717/18)	1714/15	16
Oliver, Nathaniel	No title given.	1700/01	1
Pain, Edward	Mr.	1776	3
Palmer, Thomas	Esquire	1703/04	8
Parkman, Samuel	Mr. (Esquire in 1791)	1785	11
Partridge, Samuel	Captain	1767	18
Pemberton, Benjamin	Mr.	1706/07	2
Perkins, Thomas	Esquire	1796	26
Phillips, John	Deacon (Captain, 1743; Esquire,1748)	1742	21
Phillips, William	Mr. (Esquire,1772; Honorable, 1785)	1756	22
Phillips, William, Jr	Mr. (Esquire, 1797; Honorable, 1817)	1788	34
Pitts, James	Captain	1713/14	1
Pitts, James	Esquire	1757	3
Pitts, John	Mr.	1705/06	2
Powell, William	Esquire	1776	12
Prentice [Prentis; Prentiss], Henry	Mr.	1784	3
Proctor [Procter], Edward	Mr. (Major,1776; Colonel,1778; Esquire,1787)	1775	35
Prout, Timothy	Mr.	1718/19	6
Robie [Robe], William	Mr.	1691/92	1
Rogers, George	Mr.	1743	5
Ruck, John	Mr. (Esquire, 1722/23)	1706/07	28
Savage, Ephraim	Captain	1704/05	1
Savage, Habijah	Captain	1709/10	5
Sewall [Sewell], Samuel	Esquire	1700/01	3
Sheepreeve, William	No title given.	1704/05	1
Sherburne, Joseph	Mr.	1751	5
Smith, Isaac	Mr. (Esquire in 1776)	1757	21
Smith, John	No title given.	1704/05	1
Smith, Thomas	Mr. (Captain in 1713/14)	1712/13	6
Smith, William,	Mr.	1788	29
Stoddard, Anthony	Mr.	1710/11	1
Stoddard, Simeon [Symeon;Simion]	Mr.	1690/91	6
Storer, Ebeneezer	Mr. (Esquire in 1755)	1744	21
Sweetser, John	Mr. (Esquire in 1785)	1776	26
Thatcher, Oxenbridge	Mr.	1724/25	1
Thrasher, Francis	Mr.	1701/02	2
Townsend, Penn	Colonel	1713/14	1
Tudor, John	Mr.	1751	9

Tyler, Royall	Mr. (Esquire, 1760; Honorable, 1765)	1755	17
Tyler, Thomas	Esquire	1768	4
Tyler, William	Esquire	1732/33	18
Wadsworth, Joseph	Captain	1719/20	1
Waldo, Daniel	Mr.	1771	5
Waldo [Woldo], Jonathan	Mr.	1720/21	3
Waldo, Joseph	Mr.	1767	4
Walker, Benjamin	Mr.	1690/91	3
Walker, Isaac	No title given	1742	20
Walker, Thomas	Mr.	1700/01	1
Webb, Joseph	Mr.	1781	5
Webster, Redford	Mr. (Esquire, 1797)	1796	28
Welles, Arnold, Jr.	Mr. (Esquire, 1797)	1796	6
Welsteed [Wellsteed], William	Mr.	1703/04	9
Wendell, [Wendall], Jacob	Esquire (Honorable, 1735/36)	1728/29	26
White, Isaac	Mr.	1738/39	3
White, John	Mr.	1714/15	1
White, William	Esquire	1767	8
Whitwell, Samuel	Mr.	1769	21
Whitwell, William	Mr.	1762	14
Williams, Jonathan	Mr.	1722/23	3
Williams, Jonathan	Esquire	1767	1
Williams, Nathaniel	Mr.	1690/91	1
Winslow, Edward	Mr.	1708/09	3

INDEX

Index

≈

Note: Variant spellings of personal names abound in the text. Although small, obvious errors can safely be corrected, more radical corrections would make the reader's task of tracking down a name harder rather than easier. Therefore, many of the variants have been left as separate entries in the index. Readers may want to scan adjacent entries and similar-sounding names.

Index

Index

Index

Index

Index

Index

Index

Index

Index

Flood, Andrew, 130, 272, 275
Flood, Elizabeth, 299
Flood, James, 283, 926–27
Flood, Joanna, 131
Flora (negro), 272, 373
Floraday, Elezabeth, 294
Florance, Susannah, 632
Florence, Susanna, 123
Florow, and child (negroes), 396
Florraday, Betsy, 291
Flory, John, and wife and children, 458
Flowers, John, 232, 268n.564
Flowers, Thomas, 273, 275, 279
Floyd, Andrew, 248, 279
Floyd, Elizabeth, 423
Flucker, Charlstown, 487, 518
Flucker, Pheabe, 470
Flucker, Thomas (or Fluker), 763, 766, 769, 773–74, 779, 784, 786–87, 791, 985
Flurrey, Elizabeth, 464
Flyn, Elizabeth, 507
Flyn, John (or Flynn), 428, 514, 538n.365
Flyn, John and Elizabeth, 375–76
Flyn, Sarah, 568
Flyng, Mary, 925
Flyng, Sarah, 115
Flynn, Elizabeth, 568–69
Flynn, John, 568–69
Flynn, John, and wife, 521
Flynn, John and Elizabeth, 504, 524
Foalke, Richard, 571
Foard, Estor, 465
Fobey, Abraham, 649
Foble, Ann, 472
Fogo, David, 309
Folker, Mary, 502
Follens, Suckey, 347
Follens, Sucky, 354
Follens, Sukey, 341–42
Follin, George, 634
Follings, Sarah, 654
Follings, Susanna, 654
Follins, George, and daughter, 155, 259n.119
Follins, George, and wife, 568
Follins, Mary, Sarah, and John, 154, 259n.108
Foltz, Herman, 571
Fooboe, Elizabeth, 311
Foot, Jonathan, 568
Foot, Malachi, 569
Foot, Sally, 309
Forbes, Abigail, and children, 363
Forbes, Cyrus, 570
Forbes, John, 352
Forbes, Joseph, 349
Forbes, Margaret, 166
Forbes, Mr. and Mrs., and children, 349
Forbes, Robert, 352

Forbes, Sarah, 157
Forbetty, John, 143
Forbis, George, 662
Forbus, John, 140, 172, 655
Forbus, Margaret, 654, 658
Forbus, Sarah, 654
Forbus, Thomas, 635
Forbush, Margaret, 628
Forbush, Margarett, and children (or Forbus), 148, 162, 258n.59
Ford, Easter (Esther), 467–68, 534n.172, 534n.178
Ford, Estor, 362, 664
Ford, James (alias Rich), 568–69
Ford, Mary, 305
Ford, Mary, and child, 308
Ford, Sally, 312
Ford, Sarah, 568–69
Ford, Sarah (child), 569
Ford, Sarah, and children, 358
Foreman, Michael, 218
Forrest, Ann, 659
Forrest, Margery, and child, 143
Forstor, Elizabeth, 361
Fortain (negro), 346
Fortune (negro), 337, 570
Fosdeck, James Jr., 761
Fosdick, Ann, 151, 258n.85
Fosdick, James, 692, 827
Fosdick, John, 123
Fosdick, Margaret, 123
Fosdick, Thomas, 568
Fosset, Thomas, 525
Fossy, Abigail, and son William, 349
Fost, Mary, 123
Foster, Hopestill, 693, 732, 737, 794, 828
Foster, Jack, 569
Foster, Mary, 490, 569
Foster, Mary (Polly), 495, 536n.270
Foster, Nicholas, 908–12
Foster, Polly, 490, 517
Foster, Susanah, 467, 534n.175
Foster, Susanna, 366
Foster, Timothy, 214, 661
Foster, William, 572
Fothergill, Joseph, 162, 654
Fothergill, Mary, 660
Fothergill, Richard, 660
Fothergill, Sarah, 660
Foulke, Martin John, 569
Fovel, Ann, 441
Fovell, Ann, 355, 377, 379
Fovell, Hannah, 571, 864, 882
Fowell, Widow, 422
Fowl, Hannah, 519
Fowle, Abigail, 292
Fowle, Bethiah, 407
Fowle, Hannah, 292
Fowle, Nathaniel, 511, 515–16
Fowle, Nathaniel, and wife and children, 501
Fowle, Nathaniel and Lidia, and

children Thankful, Nathaniel, Helener (Elener) and Isaac, 496, 536n.276
Fowle, Thankful, 502
Fowle, Zachariah, 51
Fowler, Ann, 863
Fowler, Benjamin, 446, 451
Fowler, Betsey (alias Pitchard), 863
Fowler, John, 397–98
Fowler, Robert, 570
Fowles, Bethiah, 569
Fowles, Eleanor, and daughter Hannah, 288
Fowles, Hannah, 569
Fowles, Isaac, 275–76, 507
Fowles, Nathaniel, 57, 502
Fowles, Nathaniel, and children Thankful, Nathaniel, Elener, and Isaac, 496
Fowles, Nelley (or Fowle), 507, 537n.325
Fowles, Sally, 571
Fox, Jack, 480
Foye, Christopher, 365
Francis, Christopher, 571
Frank (negro), 498
Frank, John and Polley, 405
Frank, Susannah, 445
Franklin, Benjamin, 32
Franklin, John, 569, 744, 985
Franklin, Scipio, 523
Franklin, Susannah, 329
Franks (child), 392
Franks, Edward and Luce (Lucy), 452, 533n.109
Franks, John, 471
Franks, Mary (Polly Frank), 491, 536n.254
Franks, Susanah, 492
Franks, Susanna, and children, 386, 395
Franks, Susannah, 331
Frazer, Quommono, 506
Frazier, Anthony, 646
Frazier, Elizabeth, 570
Frazier, Qumino, 510
Frazier, Qumino (or Frazer), 511, 537n.341
Frazier, Qunenc (alias Quomino), 568, 570
Frazier, Quneno, 530
Frazier, Quomino, 500
Frazier, Thomas, 117, 123
Fredrick, William, 570
Freeborn, Mary, 854
Freeman, Cathrine, 444
Freeman, Dinah, and child, 412
Freeman, Jack, 393
Freeman, Minor, 451
Freeman, Sarah, 137, 155, 627, 634
Freeman, Sarah, and children, 356, 358
Freeman, Sarah, and children

Index

Sina and Hanna Indens, 464, 534n.161
Freeman, Simeon, 282
Freeman, Titus, 445
freemen vs. servants, 25
Freeport Town, 847–48
Freestot, Margaret, 662
Freeto, Elizabeth, 158, 160, 260n.148
Freetoo, Elizabeth, 154
Freetstot, Margarett, 230
French, Daniel, 821
French, Elener, 895
French, Jack, 504, 506
French, Nathaniel, 293
French, Nicholas, 522, 568–69
French, Nickelos, 518
Frestot, Mary, 232
Fretchman, John, 457
Fretoo, Elizabeth, 151
Frith, Elizabeth, 123
Frizell, Joseph, 741
Frizier, Quomino, 493
Frizzell, John, 985
Frobile, Ann, 441
Frost, Abraham, 480–81
Frost, James, 425, 427, 429, 431, 456, 458, 466, 468, 501
Frothingham, Elizabeth, 638
Fugin, Jack, 523
Fulker, Ayles (Alice Fucker), 482, 535n.225
Fulker, Mary, 155, 259n.121, 297, 379
Fullam, Elizabeth (Elizabeth), 481, 483, 485–86
Fuller, Amos, 868
Fuller, Hannah, 459
Fuller, Rebecca, 123
Fullerton, Mrs., 948
Fullerton, Susanna, 123, 138, 142, 634
Fullerton, Susannah, 146, 159
Fullerton, William, 662
Fullford, Mary, 281
Fullinton, Susannah (or Fullerton), 150, 258n.74
Fullmore, John, 357
Fulloon, William, 507
Fulton, Elizabeth, 945, 947
Fulton, Mrs., 948
Fulton, Robert, 768, 947
Fulton, Robert, children of, 294
Fulton, Robert, wife of, 946–47
Fulton children, 299
Furgus, William, 405
Furlong, Edward, 467, 471, 570, 572
Furness, Joseph, 570
Furrs, Thomas, 457, 568, 570

Gaffet, Sarah, 478
Gaffit, Rachal, 507

Gaffit, Sally, 576–77, 883
Gafford, Sally, 576
Gager, Catharine, 864
Gains, Judith, and daughter Lucressey (Lucretia), 511, 537n.340
Gains, Samuel, 575
Gair, James, 572–74, 576
Gair, Nancy, 572
Gair, Nancy, and children, 528
Gair, Patty (child), 573
Gair, Patty, and child, 572–73
Galey, Mary, 521
Galley, Jane, 420, 515, 666
Galley, John Lee, 470
Galley, Mary, 123, 525
Galley, Sarah, and children, 407
Gallison, Peggey, 377, 665
Gallop, Sarah, 123
Galt, Mary, 123
Gambel, Thomas, 361
Gambutt, Thomas, 335
Game, William, 574–75
Gammill, Thomas, 330
Gandel, John, 495
Gandell, John, Jr., 574
Gandol, John, 400, 405
Gane, Judith, and children Samuel, Betty, and John (or Gains), 495–96, 536n.272
Ganes, Judah (Judith Gains), and children John, Elizabeth, Samuel, and Luchick (Lucretia), 491, 498, 536n.285
Gardener, James, 665–66
Gardenor, John, 361
Gardenor, Vilot, and child, 378
Gardiner, James, 398
Gardiner, Margrat, 374
Gardiner, Sarah, 380, 401
Gardner, Andrew, 418, 573
Gardner, Androw, 472, 509, 514
Gardner, Andrew (James), 469, 534n.180
Gardner, Cesar, 520
Gardner, Ceser, 525
Gardner, Eunice, 576, 852, 858
Gardner, George, 208, 212
Gardner, Hannah, 574
Gardner, James, 388, 773
Gardner, John, 357, 499, 503–4
Gardner, Joseph, 92n.82, 802, 807, 809, 813, 818, 821, 823, 825, 830, 985
Gardner, Margrat, 374
Gardner, Mary, 171
Gardner, Nathaniel, 802
Gardner, Olive, 576, 883
Gardner, Oliver, 870
Gardner, Priscilla, 279
Gardner, Sarah, 507
Gardner, Silvester, 709, 716, 758
Gardner, William James, 575

Gardner, Winnes, 123
Gardnier, Joseph, 796
Garfield, Edward, 575, 870, 882
Garfilt, Sarah, 460
Garish, Patty, 375
Garlick, George, 246, 248
Garnes, Elizabeth, 116
Garnet, William, 573
Garns, Mrs., 115
Garrar, Mary (or Garrow), 439, 532n.76
Garreau, Mary, 461
Garrel, Nance, 458
Garrel, Nancy, 439
Garrell, Mary, 379, 391
Garrick, Elizabeth, 129, 150, 258n.73, 637
Garro, Elizabeth (or Garrow), 501, 536n.303
Garrow, Betsey, and children, 400
Garrow, Elizabeth, 507, 512
Garrow, Marcy, 482
Garrow, Marey, 461
Garrow, Mary, 400, 407–8, 415, 497
Garrow, Mary, and children, 356, 365
Gaskin, Nancy (or Gaskins), 308
Gaskin, William, 130, 648
Gaskins, William, 649
Gasper, Docter, 636
Gatchell, John, 235
Gauge, Rebeccah, 335
Gault, John, 920
Gault, William, 626
Gavet, Charles, 575
Gay, Elizabeth, 855
Gay, Martin, 801
Gay, Mr., 836
Gee, Feebe, 504
Gee, Phebe, 512
Gee, Pheebe, 454
Gee, Rebecca (alias Candish), 876
Gellard, Ann, 572
General Court: authority granted the Overseers, 23, 71, 972; creation of the Overseers, 13, 19–20; definition of the poor, 13, 25; funding from, 26; incorporation of the Overseers, 13, 22, 30, 87n.40, 981–82; Poor Relief Act (1794), 20, 972; sovereignty of, 92n.78
Gent, Sarah (Elizabeth; or Ghent), 158, 227, 232, 259n.142, 267n.548, 279
George (mulatto), 218
George, Elizabeth, 638
George, Elizabeth, and grandson, 170
George, Hurley, 664
George, Penelope, 114, 123, 636
George, Samuel, 365
Gepson, Polle, 462

Index

Index

Index

Index

⌘

Index

Index

Index

Index

Index

Index

Index

⌒

Index

Index

∾

Index

Index

Index

COLOPHON

This book is set in Bembo, a font which originated in Venice, an important typographic center in 15th and 16th century Europe. The original design, cut by Francesco Griffo circa 1499, was lighter and more harmonious in weight than earlier roman faces and the text was more inviting and easier to read. The font was revived in the early part of the twentieth century by the English Monotype Company. In the 1980s, Monotype produced a faithful digital rendition of the original metal revival. The display type is Bell, a font designed by Richard Austin in 1788.

Book design by Jeanne Abboud
Index by Roberts Indexing Services
Printed and bound by David B. Livesey